INSIDE AutoCAD®

The Complete AutoCAD Guide

Special Edition by Rusty Gesner

With Assistance From Jim Boyce

Original Authors D. Raker and H. Rice

New Riders Publishing, Gresham, Oregon

INSIDE AutoCAD®

The Complete AutoCAD Guide

Special Edition by Rusty Gesner With Assistance From Jim Boyce
Original Authors Daniel Raker and Harbert Rice

Published by:
New Riders Publishing
1025 E. Powell, #202
Gresham, OR 97030 USA

Library of Congress Cataloging-in-Publication Data

Gesner, Rusty. INSIDE AutoCAD: The Complete AutoCAD Guide —
Special ed. / by Rusty Gesner with assistance from Jim
Boyce.
          p.   cm.
Rev. ed. of : Inside AutoCAD / Daniel Raker and Harbert
Rice. 5th ed. 1989.
 Includes index.
 ISBN 1-56205-020-6 : $34.95
  1. AutoCAD (Computer program)   I. Boyce, Jim, 1958- .
 II. Raker, Daniel. Inside AutoCAD.   III. Title.
T385.G467   1990
620'.0042'02855369—dc20

Warning and Disclaimer

This book is designed to provide tutorial information about the AutoCAD and AutoShade computer programs. Every effort has been made to make this book as complete and as accurate as possible, but no warranty or fitness is implied.

The information is provided on an "as is" basis. The authors and New Riders Publishing shall have neither liability nor responsibility to any person or entity with respect to any loss or damages arising from the information contained in this book or from the use of the disks and programs that may accompany it.

Acknowledgments

The authors wish to thank Patrick Haessly for reworking much of the old exercise material and for developing new material and graphics techniques for the fifth edition of this book.

Extreme thanks are due to Christine Steel for editing, Bill Hartman for production and page layout, Ken Billing for technical editing, Kevin Coleman for producing graphics and testing exercises, and Nancy Trotic and Susan Huddleston for proofreading.

The authors offer profuse thanks to numerous friends and colleagues at Autodesk for encouragement and support over these seven years.

The authors of the special edition owe their gratitude to Harbert Rice for his input into this edition and for making it all possible. Thanks are also due to Mark Pierce for preliminary testing and illustration work.

Special thanks to KBJ Architects, Inc. and ModelMation for their AutoCAD drawings on the front cover.

Trademarks

About the Authors

Rusty Gesner

B. Rustin Gesner is publishing director and managing editor of New Riders Publishing in Gresham, Oregon. Prior to joining New Riders, Mr. Gesner was founder and president of CAD Northwest, Inc., in Portland, Oregon. CAD Northwest was an industry leading dealer and authorized training center in the early days of AutoCAD.

Mr. Gesner is a registered architect and formerly practiced the profession in Oregon and Washington after attending Antioch College and the College of Design, Art and Architecture at the University of Cincinnati. He has used AutoCAD since Version 1.1 and writes about AutoCAD from the viewpoint of a professional user and customizer of the program. Mr. Gesner is co-author of the New Riders books *CUSTOMIZING AutoCAD* and *INSIDE AutoLISP*.

Jim Boyce

Jim Boyce is a senior instructor in the Drafting and Design Technology department of Texas State Technical Institute in Harlingen, Texas. He teaches courses in using, customizing, and programming AutoCAD and mechanical engineering software. Mr. Boyce is also a freelance writer and a full Press member of the Computer Press Association. His work appears regularly in CAD and computer magazines, including *PC Magazine*, *CADalyst*, and *CADENCE*.

Prior to joining the faculty of T.S.T.I., Mr. Boyce was with Marathon LeTourneau, a world leader in the design and manufacture of offshore oil exploration platforms. His work there included production planning, steel structure design, and CAD system administration, development, programming, and operator training. Over the past ten years, Mr. Boyce has worked with a wide variety of systems, including AutoCAD, Accugraph ACD-800, Computervision, and Autotrol.

Daniel Raker

Daniel Raker is president of Design & Systems Research, Inc., a Cambridge, Massachusetts-based management consulting firm specializing in computer graphics applications and market research. He is founder of the MicroCAD Institute™, a leading training organization serving professional users of computer-aided design systems. Mr. Raker earned his Bachelor of Arts degree from Harvard College.

Harbert Rice

Originally trained as a plant biochemist, Mr. Rice earned his Ph.D. from Harvard University. While at Harvard, he became interested in using computers to model non-linear systems. Mr. Rice gained computer software experience at ERT, an engineering consulting subsidiary of COMSAT Corp., and the Raytheon Company in Burlington, Mass., where he held research and development positions. Mr. Rice was founder and president of New Riders Publishing, the first and foremost publisher of books on AutoCAD.

Table of Contents

Part One

Part Two

AutoCAD and 3D Drawing 581

14 Getting Started With 3D 585

xix

Part Three

Introduction

SOME IMPORTANT INFORMATION

AutoCAD, the most popular computer-aided drafting program in the known universe, is a complex piece of work. But don't let its size and complexity intimidate you. Whether you are a beginner looking for an introduction to AutoCAD's basic commands, an intermediate user who needs a tutorial on a specific command sequence, or an advanced user who needs a lasting reference that covers every nuance, *INSIDE AutoCAD* belongs on your bookshelf.

INSIDE AutoCAD is three things: an introduction to the world of AutoCAD-aided drafting and drawing; an easy-going tutorial that will help you unlock AutoCAD's power to do your design and drafting work quickly and easily; and a lasting reference to keep near your computer as you work. Using the general index or the listing of commands in Appendix A, you can quickly find information and examples for everything you always wanted to know about AutoCAD but didn't know who to ask. You will see how every command in AutoCAD works and how your work can benefit from AutoCAD.

How INSIDE AutoCAD Is Organized

INSIDE AutoCAD is organized for both the beginner and the experienced AutoCAD user. The book starts out easy, with the basics of 2D CAD drafting, continues through advanced techniques, and ends with customizing AutoCAD. You do not need any prior knowledge of CAD and the book does not require you to do any programming.

1

INSIDE AutoCAD is divided into three sections:

Part One shows you how to create and display two-dimensional (2D) drawings. It demonstrates how to communicate with AutoCAD through the keyboard, pointer (mouse or digitizer), and menus. Part One takes you sequentially from setting up AutoCAD through building and editing 2D drawings.

Part Two shows you how to create and edit 3D drawings, how to use 3D surface meshes and solids modeling, and how to pass an AutoCAD 3D drawing to AutoShade for rendering.

Part Three shows you how to take control of AutoCAD and make it into your *own* drawing system. Starting with creating menus and macros, it demonstrates how to customize AutoCAD for your application and how to use AutoLISP to create new commands and automate your drawings.

INSIDE AutoCAD has three helpful appendixes. Appendix A provides a complete listing, both alphabetically and by chapter, of all the AutoCAD commands covered in the book. Appendix B provides additional help setting up AutoCAD, improving performance, and dealing with problems and errors. Appendix C covers the setup and use of AutoCAD's tablet menu, and offers a quick-reference chart of AutoCAD's system variables.

How to Use the Tutorials

Chapters are divided into a series of exercises, each teaching one or more AutoCAD commands. If you just read the text and exercises and look at the illustrations, you will learn a great deal about AutoCAD. But to make your knowledge of AutoCAD concrete, you need to sit down at an AutoCAD-equipped computer and work through the exercises. Explanatory text accompanies each exercise, putting commands and techniques into context, explaining their behavior, and explaining how to use their different options.

We suggest that you work through each part of the book in sequence. Where possible, we've organized it so you can pick and choose topics to explore. The optional *INSIDE AutoCAD* Disk (IA DISK) makes it possible to jump in at several points in each chapter. If you are in a hurry to get started, the following Quick Start Guide provides suggestions for getting started with key topics and techniques. The primary chapters which cover the topics are shown in bold type.

Note: Wherever you start, you should first do the setup (and optional IA DISK installation) exercises in Chapter 1 so that your system setup will correspond with the directions in our exercises.

Table I.1
Quick Start Guide

If You Want to:	Turn to This Chapter:
Set Up to Use the Book and IA DISK	Chapter **1**
Set Up AutoCAD	Chapters **1**, 2, and Appendixes **B** and C
Set Up Drawings	Chapters **2**, 3, 4 and **10**
Use Menus and Dialogue Boxes	Chapters **1** and **2**
Use Various Forms of Input	Chapters **1**, 2, and **3**
Use the User Coordinate System (UCS) in 2D	Chapters **3**, 8, 9, and 10
Use the User Coordinate System (UCS) in 3D	Chapters **14**, 15, 16, and **18**
Use Multiple Views (Viewports) in 2D	Chapters **4** and **10**
Use Multiple Views (Viewports) in 3D	Chapters **14**, **15**, 16, and 18
Use Paper Space Viewports in 2D	Chapters **4** and **10**
Use Paper Space Viewports in 3D	Chapters **14**, 15, 16, and **18**
Learn 2D Drawing Commands	Chapters **5**, 7, 8, and 9
Use 2D Drawing Commands to Create 3D	Chapter **14**
Learn 3D Drawing Commands	Chapters **14**, **15**, and **18**
Learn 3D Solids Modeling	Chapter **18**
Edit 2D Drawings	Chapters 6, **7**, and 8
Edit 3D Drawings	Chapters **14**, **15**, and 18
Create 2D Drawings From 3D	Chapters **14**, 15, and **18**
Plot 2D and 3D Drawings	Chapters **10** and 16
Compose Paper Space Drawing Sheets to Plot	Chapter **10**
Use Blocks (Symbols and Parts) in Drawings	Chapters **9** and 13
Externally Reference One Drawing From Another	Chapter **9**
Add Attribute Information to Drawings	Chapter **13**
Dimension Drawings	Chapter **12**
Use Associative Dimensions and Dimstyles	Chapter **12**
Control 3D Views and Perspectives	Chapter **16**
Render 3D Drawings With AutoShade	Chapter **17**
Customize AutoCAD Menus and Macros	Chapter **19**
Use AutoLISP to Automate Drawing	Chapter **20**
Look Up AutoCAD Commands	Appendix **A**
Look Up System Variables	Appendix **B**

The Optional IA DISK

To help you save time and effort, and allow you to pick and choose topics, *INSIDE AutoCAD* has an optional diskette, the IA DISK. The IA DISK will save you from doing repetitive drawing setup sequences. It contains starting and intermediate drawing files for most of the chapter exercises, as well as menu macros and AutoLISP routines used in the customization chapters in Part Three.

You don't need the disk to work through the book. We've designed all the example exercises so that you can do them from scratch, but the disk makes it easier to get to the heart of the topic at hand. Using drawings from the IA DISK insures accuracy and lets you concentrate on learning what you need to know about AutoCAD when you want to know it.

You'll find an order form for the *INSIDE AutoCAD* drawing disk (IA DISK) inside the back of the book. See the instructions in Chapter 1 for backing up and installing the disk.

Note to Instructors

If you are using *INSIDE AutoCAD* for classroom instruction, you will want to know what AutoCAD commands and techniques each chapter covers. Early in each chapter, we specify what tools, techniques, and groups of commands will be covered.

Read This — It's Important

AutoCAD has grown to become a complex program, but we've made *INSIDE AutoCAD* as easy to use and follow as possible. To avoid errors and misunderstandings, please read the following sections before jumping into the book. And be sure to do the setup exercises in Chapter 1 before doing the other exercises.

Chapter 1 explains how to set up your hard disk directories for use with *INSIDE AutoCAD*. We've designed the book's setup and exercises so that they won't interfere with any AutoCAD settings or other work that you may already be doing with AutoCAD. Chapter 1 also shows you how to install the drawing and support files on the IA DISK, if you have it.

How the Exercises Look and Work

The following is a typical exercise. Don't try to work through this exercise; it's only a sample to show you what to expect. Each exercise is illustrated to show you what you should see on your screen when you do the exercise. In our exercise format, AutoCAD's screen display text and your input are in computer-style type on the left of the exercise. Comments and instructions are given on the right.

Example Exercise Format

Command: <Snap on>	Toggle snap on with the <F9> key.
Pull down **[Draw]** *Select* **[Circle >]**	Select CIRCLE command.
CIRCLE 3P/2P/TTR/<Center point>:	Pick point ① in the upper right of screen (see fig. I.1).
Diameter/<Radius>:	Drag a radius of 1 inch and pick a point.

Set the PLAN layer current and set color to red.

Command: **LINE**	Draw a line.
From point: **@0,-1**	Enter point one unit below last point.
To point: **2,3**	Enter point at specified coordinates.
To point: **<RETURN>**	Exit LINE command.

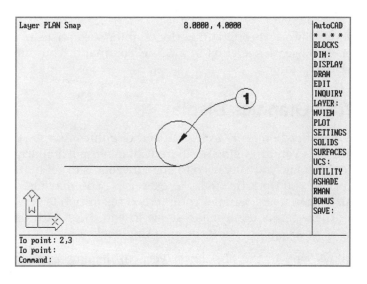

Figure I.1:
A sample exercise
illustration.

When you see *Pull down*, you select the indicated pull-down menu. *Select* means to pick the menu item shown. The bracketed items are menu items, labels, or boxes. In the example above, you select [Draw] from the pull-down menu bar at the top of the screen and then select [CIRCLE >] to use the CIRCLE command. To select an item, you highlight its label and press your mouse or digitizer pointer pick button. You can also execute commands by typing them at the keyboard and pressing <RETURN> (also known as the <ENTER> key). LINE (in the example above) is a typed command.

Each exercise shows all necessary commands, prompts, and input at the left-hand side of the page. (In later exercises, we abbreviate or drop repetitive prompts.) The input you need to enter as you work through the exercises is shown in boldface type. The <RETURN> is shown only when it is the sole input on the line; otherwise you should automatically press <RETURN> following any boldface input shown.

Type input exactly as shown (followed by <RETURN>), watching carefully for the difference between the number 0 and the letter o. The @ is the @ character, above the 2 on your keyboard. Keyboard keys are shown in angle brackets, like <RETURN>. <F9> is a function key and <^C> stands for the Control-C key combination.

The right-hand section provides our *in-line* comments in the book's normal text font. These comments will give you instructions and extra pieces of information to guide you. We sometimes use this font at the left to give abbreviated instructions for familiar commands.

Except for exercises in early chapters which specifically show the use of the menus, we just show commands as you would type them. However, you may use any form of selection you like, as long as you end up with the right command! (Caution: some pull-down menu commands are modified and act differently from typed commands.)

We don't expect that you will work through an entire chapter's exercises in a single sitting. Wherever an exercise sequence ends in a SAVE command, you may safely end the drawing and reload it later.

Exercises and Your Graphics Display

Our illustrations were developed on an EGA (Enhanced Graphics Adaptor) display with 640 x 350 resolution. If you are using a different display, particularly a CGA (Color Graphics Adaptor) display, you may need to do more zooms to get better views of your screen display when you work through the exercises. You may also need to adjust your aperture size when using osnap if your screen resolution is very high or very low. If a couple of these terms don't make sense to you, bear with us. You'll understand them soon as you begin to work through this book.

Because different displays vary in the horizontal/vertical display area ratio, you may need to zoom slightly to get the views illustrated when loading drawings from the IA DISK. If your display is configured for a white background, the color that AutoCAD calls white will appear black on your screen.

Note: For clarity, we omit the AutoCAD grid from most of our illustrations, but you should keep your grid on.

Exercises and the IA DISK

In the exercises that reference the IA DISK, we've marked certain instructions with special symbols. These show you what to do if you have the disk.

Disk Symbols	
	Do this if you have the IA DISK.
	Do this if you don't have the IA DISK.

What You Need for the Book

To work with *INSIDE AutoCAD*, you need a system that can run AutoCAD Release 10, 11, or a later release. You should have about 1Mb of free disk space (2Mb if you are using the IA DISK). See Appendix B for more information on system requirements.

We assume that you:

- Can use the basic features and utility commands of your operating system.
- Have a copy of AutoCAD Release 10 or 11 installed and configured.
- That you have a graphics display and a mouse or digitizer tablet, all configured for AutoCAD.

Release 10 vs. Release 11

This special edition of *INSIDE AutoCAD* has been substantially rewritten for AutoCAD Release 11. If you are using Release 10, don't be alarmed. We give alternative instructions at all critical points. Everything possible in this edition of *INSIDE AutoCAD* is perfectly usable with Release 10 and exceptions are identified. However, some of your menus, dialogue boxes, and a few command prompts will differ slightly from those shown in the exercise sequences and illustrations.

The fifth edition of *INSIDE AutoCAD*, which specifically supports Release 10, is also available from New Riders Publishing — see the order form in the back of the book. An international version, *INSIDE AutoCAD-Metric Edition*, is also available.

We assume that you are using AutoCAD fresh out of the box, but it is a highly adaptable and malleable program. If someone has installed AutoCAD on your system and altered its command or menu structure, your prompts, screen menus, and tablet menu may be slightly different from those represented in the book. If so, get a copy of the original ACAD.MNU file from the SOURCE directory or from the original AutoCAD disks and use the MENU command to load it into the ACAD drawing we create in Chapter 1.

DOS vs. Other Operating Systems

You may see minor differences in AutoCAD's screen display, but all of AutoCAD's files (and our IA DISK files) are usable on any system that runs AutoCAD. To use the IA DISK on non-DOS systems, you may need to install the files on a DOS system and then use a network or alternative disk format to transfer them to your system. (You can use a DOS window to install the IA DISK on OS/2 systems.) If you're using Unix, use lower-case letters to enter all filenames shown in the book's exercises.

Should Problems Occur

- Try again, and go back to the previous exercises to see if you made an error that did not immediately show up.
- Check defaults such as snap, osnaps, aperture, layer, and visibility.
- See Appendix B.
- Check your AutoCAD Reference Manual.
- Call your AutoCAD dealer. If you have no current dealer, Autodesk can find you one.
- Try the ADESK forum on CompuServe, the world's largest CAD user group and most knowledgeable source of support.
- If you have the IA DISK, see the UPDATE.TXT file for any possible updated information.
- If there is a specific problem in the book, particularly with an exercise, you can call New Riders Publishing at (503) 661-5745. Have a specific *INSIDE AutoCAD* page reference ready — we cannot give general AutoCAD support.
- If you have a problem installing the IA DISK and if the instructions packaged with the disk do not help, call us.

Now, let's get started.

Part One

Working in 2D With AutoCAD

HOW TO GET ACCURATE, PROFESSIONAL DRAWINGS

Basic Drawing Tools

Two-dimensional (2D) drawings are the workhorses of drafting and design. To get good 2D drawings from AutoCAD, you need to know the basics about setting up drawings, creating and editing objects, inserting drawing symbols, dimensioning, and preparing drawings for plotting and presentation. We've designed Part One of *INSIDE AutoCAD* to teach you the basics for producing accurate, professional-looking 2D drawings. You will find all the commands, drawing and editing techniques, tips, and tricks you need for the high quality drawings you want and expect from AutoCAD.

How Part One Is Organized

Part One has thirteen chapters that will take you from starting your program, through two-dimensional drawing and editing, to dimensioning and adding attribute tags to your drawings. These chapters fall into five categories:

- Setup and display controls
- Drawing and editing
- Blocks (symbols) and reference files
- Presentation and plotting
- Dimensioning and attributes

9

Why Setup and Display Controls Are Important

Whether you work in 2D or 3D, an efficient working environment will help you learn AutoCAD and cut down on drawing time. The first four chapters take you from setting up your files through controlling your display.

Chapter 1 teaches the basics of setting up your system for the book's exercises, and creating and saving drawing files. It teaches you how to communicate with AutoCAD and use menus. By the chapter's end, you will be able to create an AutoCAD drawing file on disk, add lines and text to the drawing, correct errors, and save the drawing for future use.

Chapter 2 explains how to prepare a drawing by specifying a drawing scale and sheet size, and setting up electronic layers with colors and linetypes. You'll also learn to use dialogue boxes for input. Chapter 3 shows how to make precise drawings using AutoCAD's object snaps and other electronic aids. You'll learn to control where you are in your drawing file and how to create your own coordinate system (UCS).

Knowing how to control your display will save you countless hours and frustration when you work with more complex drawings. Chapter 4 shows you how to work with single and multiple viewport displays and to control what you display on the screen with zooms and pans. The chapter demystifies paper space — the bridge between your computer and the paper. By the chapter's end, you will be able to create lines, polylines, circles, and text, and display your work in multiple viewports. You will know how to save both your drawing views and your viewports for future use.

Drawing and Editing

In Chapters 5, 6, 7, and 8, you will learn how to create and edit two-dimensional drawings. Chapter 5 shows how to use *every* 2D drawing command. Chapters 6 and 7 teach you how to edit your drawings. Chapter 6 contains the basics for moving, copying, rotating, arraying, and mirroring entities in your drawings. Chapter 7 covers more exotic editing commands for extending, stretching, trimming, scaling, and offsetting objects. Chapter 7 also explains how to edit polylines to get continuous drawing lines. This is a prelude to 3D editing. If you want a quick look at creating a 3D drawing, take a look at Chapter 7's 2D polyline editing section.

All the drawing and editing chapters have tips and tricks. Chapter 8 is a pure techniques chapter; it shows how to combine construction lines, electronic point filters, and editing commands to quickly build accurate drawings. It also shows how to place editing marks and controls in your editing sequences so that you can try different edits without wasting time. As you apply AutoCAD's drawing and editing commands to your drawings, you will begin to recognize patterns in your own command usage. The trick to improving your productivity is to learn the drawing and editing commands that let you build fast, accurate drawings, then incorporate these editing sequences and techniques in your everyday use. If you are looking for some advanced editing techniques, you will have them by the time you work through the chapters on editing.

Using Symbols and Reference Files

AutoCAD calls symbols blocks. Learning how to use blocks in your drawings saves drawing time and file space. Chapter 9 will show you how to use blocks, and how to update your drawings quickly and easily by redefining blocks.

You will also learn how to create drawings that reference the contents of other drawing files. Reference files coordinate the cooperative editing of a master drawing by letting several people simultaneously work on parts of it. They make drawings smaller by allowing those parts to exist in their own drawing files, yet the master file is automatically updated.

Getting Presentable

Chapter 10 shows how to get plotted output just the way you want it. You will learn how and when to use paper space to compose drawings and to make multi-view plotting a cinch. You'll also discover dozens of plotting tips. Chapter 11 contains techniques for hatching, linetypes, and freehand sketching. This chapter winds up with AutoCAD's inquiry commands that tell you what, where, and when you're drawing.

Dimensioning and Attributes

In Chapters 12 and 13, you will learn how to add dimensions and other nongraphic information to your drawings. Chapter 12 will guide you through AutoCAD's dimensioning settings and commands. It covers associative dimensions and how to use dimensioning styles to control and standardize dimensioning. Chapter 13 describes how to add text data to your drawings, and how to extract this information in a report. You can use these techniques to create bills of materials, specifications, schedules, and other data lists.

Getting From 2D to 3D

We've all heard about the importance of learning the basics. Part One will give you the 2D basics that you need for 3D, which is covered in Part Two. Among other things, you need to know how to control your own coordinate system (UCS) and how to control multiple viewports (VPORTS) to work in 3D. All the basic 2D drawing and editing commands that you learn in Part One can be used in Part Two.

Instead of talking about it, let's see AutoCAD in action. Turn to Chapter 1 to get started *INSIDE AutoCAD*.

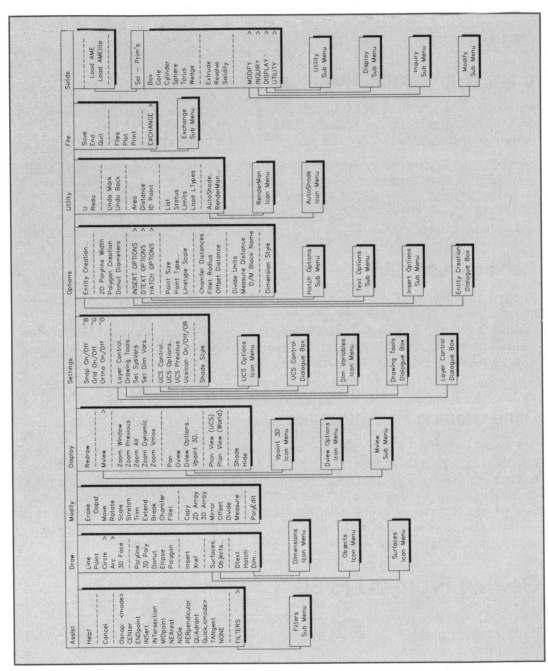

Figure:1.1:
Pull-down menu map.

Getting Started

The Lay of the Land

This book is a tutorial about AutoCAD. In this chapter we cover the basics on how to set up the program, how to turn it on, and how to draw. By the end of the chapter you will have created an electronic CAD drawing file, played around by drawing a few lines, typed some text, and saved your drawing.

The Benefits of Learning How AutoCAD Works

The benefits of learning how to set up and store an electronic drawing file are obvious. Your real drawing benefits will come from learning about AutoCAD's command structure (see fig. 1.1) and how you can interact with AutoCAD to produce the drawings you want. By learning to communicate with AutoCAD, you will unlock AutoCAD's power and versatility for your own use.

Think about learning AutoCAD in the same way that you learn to navigate your way around a big city. You know where you want to go — you just need to get a few basic routes down pat. Then you can explore the byways at your leisure. And before you start exploring AutoCAD, you need to set up a directory to do your exploring from.

13

Setting Up AutoCAD for Exercises in This Book

Let's get a few chores out of the way. *INSIDE AutoCAD* comes with an optional disk called the IA DISK. The book and disk are designed for use on your AutoCAD workstation. Setting up for *INSIDE AutoCAD* requires that you set aside space on your hard disk to create a directory called IA-ACAD. Even if you don't have the IA DISK, this setup insures that any AutoCAD settings used for the exercises in the book won't interfere with any other AutoCAD settings or projects that you or your co-workers may have under way.

Directories

We assume that you are using the DOS operating system, running AutoCAD on a hard disk called C:, and that you have a directory structure similar to the one shown in the following exercise.

> **Note:** If your drive letter or subdirectory names vary from those shown, you need to substitute your drive letter and directory names wherever you encounter the C: or the directory names in the book. If you are using an operating system other than DOS, your directory creation and setup will differ slightly from what is shown below.

Making the IA-ACAD Directory

We also assume that you will work in the IA-ACAD directory. You need to make this directory, then copy your AutoCAD configuration files to this directory. By copying the files, you set up a self-contained AutoCAD environment. You should be in the root directory of your hard disk. Make the IA-ACAD directory.

Making the IA-ACAD Directory

`C:\> MD \IA-ACAD`   Creates the directory.

Take a look at your directory names. Get into the root directory of drive C: and type:

`C:\> DIR *.`

Your computer will respond with:

```
Volume in drive C is DRIVE-C
Directory of C:\
ACAD    <DIR> 12-01-88  11:27a
DOS     <DIR> 12-01-88  11:27a
IA-ACAD <DIR> 12-01-88  11:27a
```
AutoCAD program, configuration, and standard support files.
All of the DOS files.
INSIDE AutoCAD configuration and support files.

> ### Making the IA-ACAD Directory—continued
>
> Your disk may show other directories, like:
>
> ```
> 123      <DIR> 12-01-88   11:27a          Lotus 123 directory.
> DBASE    <DIR> 12-01-88   11:27a          dBASE III files.
> 5 File(s)  8753472 bytes free             Your list will be different.
> ```

Setting Up AutoCAD Configuration Files

AutoCAD requires a configuration file (and four overlay files with 640K DOS versions). These files are created when AutoCAD is first run. We assume that AutoCAD's configuration files are in the ACAD directory. By copying these files to the IA-ACAD directory, you establish a separate AutoCAD configuration for this book. (If you are using an operating system other than DOS or are using the 386 DOS version of AutoCAD, skip the steps for copying the .OVL files in the following exercise.)

> ### Copying AutoCAD Files to the IA-ACAD Directory
>
> ```
> C:\> CD \ACAD <RETURN>                    Change to the ACAD directory.
> C:\ACAD> COPY ACADP?.OVL \IA-ACAD\*.*     Do this for 640K DOS or DOS 286
>                                           version.
> ACADPL.OVL                                Plotter overlay file.
> ACADPP.OVL                                Printer/plotter overlay file.
> 2 File(s) copied
> C:\ACAD> COPY ACADD?.OVL \IA-ACAD\*.*     Do this for 640K DOS version only.
> ACADDS.OVL                                Display (video) overlay file.
> ACADDG.OVL                                Digitizer (or mouse) overlay file.
> 2 File(s) copied
> C:\ACAD> COPY ACAD.CFG \IA-ACAD\*.*       General AutoCAD configuration file.
> 1 File(s) copied
> ```

> **Note:** If your AutoCAD directory is not named ACAD, you will have to make sure that you can find the AutoCAD support files and copy them to the IA-ACAD directory.

See Appendix B for more help on setting up AutoCAD's system environment and configuring AutoCAD.

Installing the IA DISK

Now you are ready to install the IA DISK files. If you have the optional disk, install it. If you don't have the disk yet, see the order form in the back of the book on how to get a copy. Besides saving you typing and drawing setup time, the disk provides starting drawings for many of our exercises, letting you skip material you already know. For example, if you want to learn about dimensioning, but don't want to first create a drawing to dimension, you can jump right into dimensioning a preset drawing from the disk.

Installing the IA DISK

Put the IA DISK in your disk drive A: Change directories, and type A:IA-LOAD.

```
C:\> CD \IA-ACAD
C:\IA-ACAD> A:IA-LOAD
```

For more complete instructions on installing the IA DISK, or if you have any problems, see the instruction sheet packaged with the disk.

All that's left to do is create a simple batch file that will start AutoCAD without conflicting with your current AutoCAD setup and will keep your drawing exercise files in one place. The batch file calls AutoCAD directly from your ACAD directory to avoid conflict with any possible ACAD.BAT batch file that you might have. It does this by using AutoCAD's environment variables. These are labels that you can tell DOS to equate with a directory. AutoCAD checks with DOS when it starts, to see if these variables have been set. Two of AutoCAD's environment variables are named ACAD and ACADCFG. The easiest way to set environment variables so that they are correct every time you start AutoCAD is in a batch file. Let's make a batch file named IA.BAT to use environment variables with the directory you've created for the IA DISK.

Starting AutoCAD

After you create the IA.BAT batch file, you can start AutoCAD from any directory by typing \IA. The batch file will make sure the ACAD and ACADCFG settings are cleared, automatically change to the IA-ACAD directory, start AutoCAD, and then return you to the root directory when you exit AutoCAD. The simplest form of the IA.BAT file requires only four lines:

```
SET ACADCFG=
SET ACAD=
\acad\ACAD %1 %2
CD \
```

However, if you are using any AutoCAD ADI device drivers (perhaps for your video board or digitizer), you need to add the command to execute the device driver(s) to your IA.BAT file just before the \acad\ACAD line. Similarly, if you already have AutoCAD set up with a startup batch file that makes any memory or swap disk configuration settings, you need to add them to your IA.BAT file also. But don't add any additional lines beginning with SET ACAD= or SET ACADCFG=. Examples of typical device driver and configuration lines are:

```
DS800R11 -I -X
SET DGPADI=DIGIDRV
SET ACADFREERAM=24
```

The %1 and %2 in the third line of IA.BAT are known as replaceable parameters. They are used in batch files as place holders for any optional parameters that a program might take. Since AutoCAD can take two optional parameters (which you'll learn about later), we've included two place holders. See the *AutoCAD Installation and Performance Guide* (the IPG) for more information.

Note: If your AutoCAD program files are not in a directory named acad, then substitute your directory name for acad where shown in lower-case letters in the listing above and the exercise below. If you are using an operating system other than DOS, you can create a similar shell file instead of the batch file. See the AutoCAD IPG.

The best way to create your batch file is to use a word processor or text editor in ASCII text mode; however, you can use the copy technique shown below if you need to. Add any ADI or configuration lines you need.

Creating the IA.BAT Batch File

Return to the root directory.

`C:\> COPY CON IA.BAT`	To create a file from keyboard input.
`CD \IA-ACAD`	To change directory to IA-ACAD.
`SET ACADCFG=`	
`\acad\ACAD %1 %2`	To call the AutoCAD program.
`CD \`	To return to the root directory after exiting AutoCAD.
`^Z`	Hold down the control key while you type a Z, then <RETURN> to end the IA.BAT file.
`1 File(s) copied`	The IA.BAT file is written to disk.

Now, you can start an *INSIDE AutoCAD* session from anywhere in your hard drive simply by typing \IA. For more information on settings in the startup batch file, see Appendix B.

With these file-handling chores out of the way, it is time to start up AutoCAD.

Starting AutoCAD

`C:\> \IA`

As soon as you type \IA from the operating system, the batch file takes control of your computer. It changes the directory to IA-ACAD, and the AutoCAD program displays the main menu for you (see fig 1.2). The main menu gives you the choice of creating or editing drawings, plotting drawings, installing (configuring) AutoCAD, and a whole list of special utilities.

Figure 1.2:
Main menu with op-
tion 1 selected.

```
            A U T O C A D (R)
Copyright (c) 1982-90  Autodesk, Inc.  All Rights Reserved.
Release 11 (10/18/90) 386 DOS Extender
Serial Number:  000-00000000
Licensed to:    New Riders Publishing
Obtained from:  Autodesk, Inc.

Main Menu

   0.  Exit AutoCAD
   1.  Begin a NEW drawing
   2.  Edit an EXISTING drawing
   3.  Plot a drawing
   4.  Printer Plot a drawing

   5.  Configure AutoCAD
   6.  File Utilities
   7.  Compile shape/font description file
   8.  Convert old drawing file
   9.  Recover damaged drawing

Enter selection: 1

Enter NAME of drawing: ACAD=
```

If you are like most CAD enthusiasts, you face the first screen with anticipation. The first time around, we all really want to get at drawing. There is that nagging urge to get in the drawing editor, thinking, "Can I get away with entering a few commands just to see what happens?" Before you satisfy that urge, you need to insure that your *INSIDE AutoCAD* sessions are set to the default settings.

When you begin a new drawing, AutoCAD looks for a drawing called ACAD.DWG. AutoCAD uses this drawing as a *prototype* to establish the default settings for each new drawing. For the purposes of this book, we assume your prototype drawing is the same as when you took AutoCAD out of the box. In order to make sure this is true, you need to create a new prototype drawing (ACAD.DWG) in your IA-ACAD directory. The following exercise creates the new prototype drawing. The equal sign following the drawing name tells AutoCAD to make the ACAD.DWG with its original default settings. You will learn more about the settings in the ACAD.DWG prototype in the next chapter.

Creating a Prototype Drawing

Enter selection: **1**	From main menu.
Enter NAME of drawing: **ACAD=**	

The AutoCAD drawing screen appears.

Command: **END**	Saves the drawing and exits the drawing editor.

The Drawing Editor

We can come back later and explore the main menu options; for now let's jump right back into the drawing editor. You get into the drawing editor by selecting option 1 from the main menu. Begin a new drawing file by giving it the name CHAPTER1. AutoCAD will set up a new drawing file called CHAPTER1 in the IA-ACAD directory on drive C:. Then AutoCAD puts you into the drawing editor, clears the screen of text, and sets you up for drawing.

Loading a New Drawing File

Enter selection: **1**   Begin a NEW drawing.
Enter NAME of drawing: **CHAPTER1**   The drawing screen and menu appear.

Note: For your drawing names, you can use characters, numbers, and most symbols, but no spaces. AutoCAD adds a filename extension of .DWG when it stores the drawing on disk, creating drawing names like CHAPTER1.DWG. AutoCAD takes care of the .DWG extension (.DWG) so you should not enter it.

Getting Familiar With the Screen Menus

AutoCAD's first drawing screen displays a graphics drawing area and its screen menu down the right side of the screen. The first screen menu is called the root menu. It has "AutoCAD" at the top of the menu. If you look at the bottom of the AutoCAD screen, you'll see one to three command prompt lines. This is AutoCAD's communication channel. You will learn to keep an eye on the command prompt line to see your input and to read messages from AutoCAD. If you have a dual screen system, you may have a single command line, or no command line, and you'll have to watch your text screen for your input or messages.

As you move your pointing device across the desk top, pad, or tablet, the crosshairs on the screen move too. Make your pointer move the crosshairs towards the items listed in the root menu. When the crosshairs pass into the menu area, a menu item lights up. Now move the pointer up and down to highlight different menu items (see fig. 1.3).

Using the [DRAW] and [LINE:] Menus

You can select a menu item from the screen by pressing your pointer's pick button. Select [DRAW]. As soon as you do, you get a new menu (see fig. 1.4). Now select [LINE:]. When you do this, both the screen menu and the prompt line change. Move

Figure 1.3:

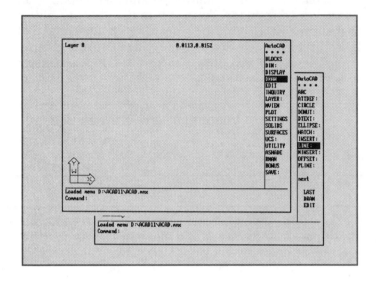

Figure: 1.4:

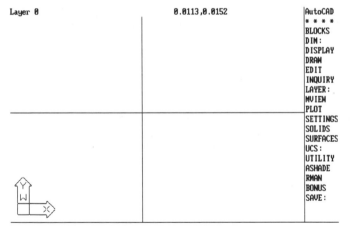

Drawing Your First Line

Select **[DRAW]**	[DRAW] screen menu appears.
Select **[LINE:]**	Select from screen menu.

The LINE command starts and prompts for the first point.

Command: LINE From point:	Pick the first point (see fig. 1.5).

Move the crosshairs and see the beginning of a line trailing behind them.

To point:	Pick a second point (see fig. 1.5).
To point: **<RETURN>**	End the LINE command.

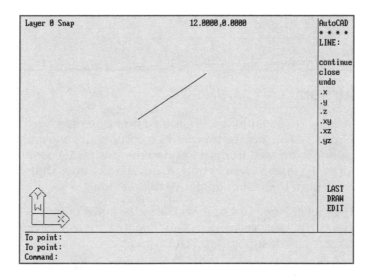

Figure 1.5:
Beginning a line.

Continue your line by repeating the LINE command with a <RETURN>.

Continuing the LINE Command

Command: **<RETURN>**	<RETURN> repeats the previous command.

Draw a second set of connecting lines.

LINE From point: **<RETURN>**	<RETURN> starts line at last point of first line.
To point:	Pick a point (see fig. 1.6).
To point:	Pick a point (see fig. 1.6).
To point: **<RETURN>**	End the LINE command.

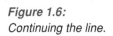

Figure 1.6:
Continuing the line.

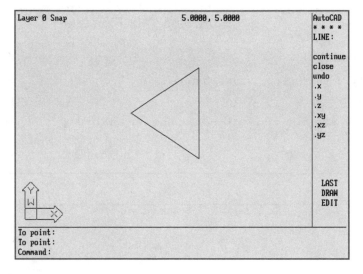

Rubber Band Cursor

You've seen that AutoCAD's LINE command is simple and straightforward. Issuing the LINE command to AutoCAD begins the process of recording the two endpoints of a line segment. Once a line is created from two endpoints, AutoCAD assumes that you want to continue drawing lines. Not only that, AutoCAD assumes that you want to continue drawing lines from the last endpoint of the previous line.

You can keep on drawing segments every time you see a To point prompt. AutoCAD helps you visualize where the next segment will be located by *rubber-banding* or trailing a segment between your last point and the cursor.

Tip: A CANCEL or <^C>, a <RETURN>, or a <SPACE> (pressing the space bar) ends the LINE command and returns the command prompt.

AutoCAD's Pull-Down Menus

At the top of the screen, AutoCAD has a set of pull-down menus in addition to the screen menus found on the right side of the screen. These pull-down menus are quite similar to the screen menus. If your video hardware supports pull-down menus, you will see a menu bar when you move your pointing device to the top of the graphics screen. The menu bar presents a list of titles indicating the selections available in each pull-down menu (see fig. 1.7).

Pull-down menus require a video board which supports the AUI (Advanced User Interface). If you are uncertain about whether your workstation supports pull-down menus, try the following test by typing the word shown in bold.

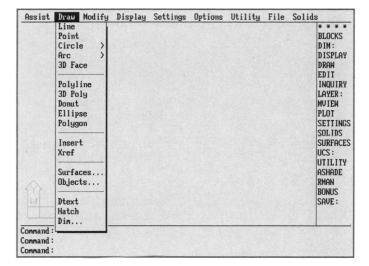

Figure 1.7:
The [Draw] pull-down menu.

Testing for Support of Pull-Down Menus

Command: **SETVAR**   Access the system variables.
Variable name or ?: **POPUPS**
POPUPS = 1 (read only)

If you got a 1, you can use AutoCAD's pull-down and icon menus. If you got a 0, you need a new video driver from your board manufacturer, or you need a new video board and driver that support the pull-down menus. If you got *Unknown variable name,* you have an earlier version of AutoCAD that doesn't support pull-down menus. If you can't use pull-down menus, you can follow the exercises by using similarly named screen menus, or by typing the commands.

Using Pull-Down Menus

To open a pull-down menu, you *highlight* the menu bar title and press the pick button on your pointing device. Then you are presented with a list of items that you highlight and pick to select. When you make a selection, the pull-down menu closes and the selection executes exactly like the screen menu items.

In the following exercise, try selecting from the pull-down menus as we type in some text and zoom in closer to see it. Enter the text and coordinate values shown in bold and complete the entry with <RETURN>s. If your workstation does not support pull-down menus, you can select the same menu items from the screen menu.

Using the [Draw] Pull-Down Menu

Pull down **[Draw]** *Select* **[Dtext]**	Select from pull-down menu.
Align/Fit/Center/Middle/Right/TL/TC/TR/ML/ MC/MR/BL/BC/BR: **C**	Center text.
DTEXT Justify/Style/<Start Point>: C	
Center Point: **7.25,4.5**	Enter coordinates.
Height <0.2000>: **.05**	Set the text height.
Rotation angle <0>: **<RETURN>**	
Text: **Welcome To INSIDE AutoCAD**	<RETURN> twice to finish the DTEXT command.

So where is the welcome? Let's zoom in to see it.

Pull down **[Display]** *Select* **[Zoom Window]**	Select from pull-down menu.
Command: 'zoom	Magnify an area to read text.
All/Center/Dynamic/Extents/Left/Previous/ Vmax/Window/<Scale(X/XP)>: **w**	
First corner:	Pick a point at ① (see fig. 1.8).
Other corner:	Pick a point at ② and you see it (see figs. 1.8 and 1.9).
Command: **<RETURN>**	Repeat the ZOOM command.
ZOOM	
All/Center/Dynamic/Extents/Left/Previous/ Vmax/Window/<Scale(X/XP)>: **ALL**	
Regenerating drawing.	Returns to the full magnification.

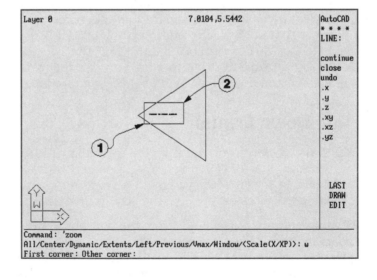

Figure 1.8:

Small text prior to [Zoom Window].

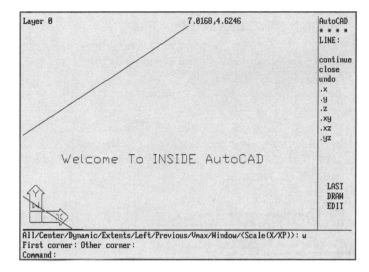

Figure 1.9:
Magnified text after
[Zoom Window].

Tip: When you select menu items from the screen, it is a good idea to glance at the command prompt line at the bottom of your screen to make sure that you and AutoCAD are communicating. Then watch the center of the graphics screen for the action.

You have loaded a new drawing file and created some lines and text using AutoCAD's screen menus. Why not complete your first pass through the drawing editor by saving your first effort?

Saving a File

AutoCAD provides two saving commands. Both save your work to a .DWG file and secure it by renaming your previous drawing file on disk with a .BAK extension.

- The SAVE command makes a .DWG file and returns you to the drawing editor to work on your current file. Saving gives you the option of saving your current drawing editor session under the current name or under a filename of your choice.

- The END command makes a backup file from your previous (last) file, stores the up-to-date copy of your file, and exits the drawing editor. The END command assumes the current drawing filename.

When you use any command that prompts for a filename, such as the SAVE command, AutoCAD presents you with a filename dialogue box (unless you have Release 10). Dialogue boxes are discussed later in this chapter — for now just press <RE-TURN> to save the drawing with its original name.

Using SAVE to Save Your File

Command: **SAVE**   Type or select from screen menu. The dialogue box
                               appears (or the Release 10 prompt File name
                               <CHAPTER1>:).

Press <RETURN> to save the drawing with its original name.

As we promised, you have just navigated the most basic route with AutoCAD. You
have started a new drawing file, done some drawing, and saved it. Now let's take a
more leisurely look at AutoCAD's drawing screen.

How AutoCAD Communicates
With You (and Vice Versa)

Why is it so easy to draw in AutoCAD? You boot the program, get into the drawing
editor, and start entering points. It doesn't matter whether you enter points by
picking them with your pointer or by entering them at the keyboard (as you did to
center your "Welcome" text). The reason, of course, is that AutoCAD knows its
geometry and has a default Cartesian coordinate system set up and ready for your
use.

World Coordinate System

When you enter the drawing editor, you enter a coordinate system called the world
coordinate system. When AutoCAD asks you to enter a point, you either locate the
point with your pointing device or enter the point's coordinates from the keyboard.
The system's coordinates consist of a horizontal X displacement and a vertical Y
displacement (and a positive Z displacement for 3D). These are called absolute
coordinates. Although it is conventional to specify absolute coordinate points with
parentheses (3,4), when you type coordinates for AutoCAD at the keyboard you
separate the X and Y values with a comma and omit the parentheses: 3,4. Both the
X and Y are measured from a zero base point that is initially set at the lower left
corner of your screen. This base point's coordinates are 0,0.

The UCS — User Coordinate System

If you look at the lower left corner of your screen, you will see that there is an icon
at point 0,0. This is the UCS (User Coordinate System) icon (see fig. 1.10). UCS
means that you can establish your own coordinate system and shift your base point
in your drawing by changing the position of the coordinate system. You will make
extensive use of the UCS when you work in 3D, but for now we will leave it at the
default position.

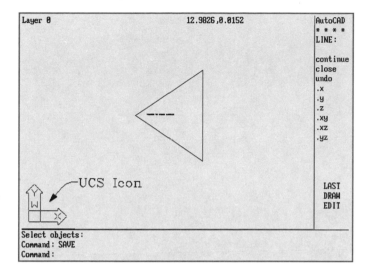

Figure 1.10:
Screen with UCS icon.

The default X axis is horizontal, left to right, and the Y axis is vertical, down to up. If you look closely at the UCS icon, you will see that the X arrow points to the right on the X axis, and the Y arrow points up the Y axis. The "W" on the Y arrow means that you are currently in the default world coordinate system. The UCS icon displays other information about where you are in 3D. For example, the UCS icon displays a "+" when it is shown at the UCS origin (0,0). And the box in the corner indicates the Z axis direction, which we will cover in the 3D section. If you find the UCS distracting when you are working in 2D, you can always turn it off. Here is how you turn it off and on.

Turning the UCS Icon Off and On

Command: **UCSICON**	Turn icon off.
ON/OFF/All/Noorigin/ORigin <ON>: **OFF**	
Command: **UCSICON**	Turn it on again.
ON/OFF/All/Noorigin/ORigin <OFF>: **ON**	

The Status Line

If you look at the top of your graphics screen, you will see a line of text. This line is called the status line. Here you'll find information about how AutoCAD is set up, and how it will react when you issue certain commands. Think of the status line as a medical monitor that gives you AutoCAD's vital signs. Figure 1.11 shows the layer name and other types of settings that you see on the status line. We won't go into detail now for all the signs, but we will have you check a few to see how they work.

Figure 1.11:
Status line.

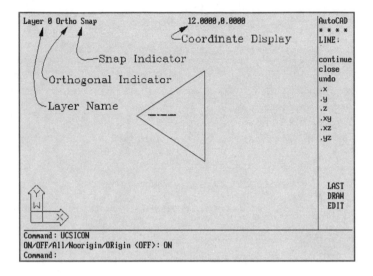

If you look at the status line area, you will see several numbers to the right. These numbers represent the latest crosshairs coordinate position. When you move the pointer around, these numbers don't change. They're stuck at the last point you officially entered as part of a command.

Using the Coords Toggle for Cursor Digital Readout

To make the status line coordinates readout follow your cursor's position, press <^D> (pronounced Control-D — the control key and D pressed at the same time). The <F6> function key does the same thing on most systems. This turns on the continuous update and display of the cursor's position on the coordinates readout. We refer to it as the coords toggle.

Now move your cursor around the screen. The coordinates readout will keep up with you and always let you know where you are. Move the cursor's position to the lower left corner and you will see the coordinates approach 0,0. You can disable the continuous coordinates display by pressing <^D> (or <F6>) again.

The Command Line — Keeping Track of AutoCAD

As you work with the AutoCAD program, you'll come to know what it expects from you and how it reacts when you do something. Many AutoCAD commands set up new drawing environments to receive additional commands. As we said a little earlier, AutoCAD uses the bottom part of the screen to tell you what it's doing. This communication channel is called the *command line*. The command line is usually three lines, depending on your video hardware, and shows you AutoCAD's prompts and your responses or input. It keeps track of your latest communication with AutoCAD.

AutoCAD has a flexible command and menu structure. You can issue an AutoCAD command by typing the command name at the keyboard in response to the command prompt. You have already executed several system commands at the keyboard in this fashion, turning the UCS icon off and on, and testing whether your system supports pull-down menus.

As you type, the letters appear following the command prompt. In order to execute any typed command, you must press the <RETURN> key on your keyboard to let AutoCAD know that you're finished typing. On some systems this is the <ENTER> key, on others it is a broken arrow ↵. If AutoCAD doesn't understand what you've typed, it will let you know after you press <RETURN>.

Command Line Exercise

```
Command: LI
Unknown command.  Type ? for list of commands.

Command: LINE                                 Execute the LINE command.
From point:                                   Pick any point.
To point:                                     Pick any point.
To point: <RETURN>                            End LINE command.
```

Note: In the exercise above and throughout the rest of the book, we show the <RETURN> only when it is the only input on a line. However, you must press <RETURN> or <ENTER> to enter your input, such as the LINE command, above. Unless AutoCAD is expecting a text string, such as for the TEXT command, you can use the <SPACE> or <TAB> keys in place of <RETURN>.

The Flip Screen

In addition to the command line, AutoCAD can display a full screen of text to show you more information. On a single-screen system, use the Flip Screen function to display the text screen instead of the graphics screen. It is usually the <F1> key, or occasionally the <HOME> key. Press the key and the graphics drawing area goes away (along with the screen menu) and a text page appears (see fig. 1.12). On a two-screen system, this text is shown on your second monitor, so using the <F1> key is unnecessary. However, if you accidentally press the <F1> key on a two-screen system, you may need to press it again to return command line response to the graphics screen.

Figure 1.12:
Flipped text screen.

```
All/Center/Dynamic/Extents/Left/Previous/Vmax/Window/<Scale(X/XP)>: W

First corner: Other corner:
Command:
ZOOM
All/Center/Dynamic/Extents/Left/Previous/Vmax/Window/<Scale(X/XP)>: ALL
Regenerating drawing.

Command: UCSICON

ON/OFF/All/Noorigin/ORigin <ON>: OFF

Command: UCSICON

ON/OFF/All/Noorigin/ORigin <OFF>: ON

Command: LI
Unknown command.  Type ? for list of commands.

Command: LINE
From point:
To point:
To point:

Command:
```

Flip Screen Exercise

Command: **<F1>**	Use your Flip Screen key.
	The graphics screen goes away and a page of text appears.
Command: **<F1>**	Flip back to graphics.

If you look closely at the text, you will see the last sequence of commands you typed (or picked from the screen menu). Using this text screen, you can look back through a set of command lines to see where you've been. If you get interrupted with a phone conversation, using the Flip Screen is an easy way to pick up your place. Some commands (like HELP) automatically flip you to the text screen.

What to Do About Errors and How to Get HELP!

AutoCAD is very forgiving. The worst thing that can happen when you mis-type a command name is that AutoCAD warns you that it does not understand what you want to do. It gives you another chance or prompts you to get help.

What if you catch a typing error before you hit <RETURN>? Using the <BS> (backspace) key on the keyboard erases the characters. Pressing <^X> displays *Delete*, ignores all previous characters on the line, and gives you a blank new line to enter what you intended. What if you start the wrong command and it is already showing on the command line? Press <^C> one or more times to cancel any command and return you to the command prompt.

Using the ERASE Command

What do you do if you draw something that you don't want, or put an object in the wrong place?

You can remove it using the ERASE command, and try again. When you use ERASE, the crosshairs change to a *pick box*. You move the pick box until it touches the entity that you want to remove. Select the entity by clicking on it with your pointing device's pick button. There are other ways to select entities and other ways to salvage errors without erasing. We will explore them in later chapters. For now, ERASE is enough to get you out of a jam if you get stuck with a screen full of lines that you don't want. Try erasing the "Welcome..." text on your screen, or draw something new to erase. You will find ERASE on the [EDIT] screen menu and on the [Modify] pull-down menu.

Using ERASE to Erase an Entity

```
Command: ZOOM                                   Use a window to zoom in on the text.
All/Center/Dynamic/Extents/Left/Previous/Vmax/Window/<Scale(X/XP)>: W
First corner:                                   Pick first corner point.
Other corner:                                   Pick second corner point.
Select [AutoCAD]                                Return to the root menu.
Select [EDIT]                                   Displays [EDIT] menu.
Select [ERASE:]                                 Starts the ERASE command.
Command: ERASE                                  Move cursor into drawing area. The
                                                crosshairs turn into a pick box (see
                                                fig. 1.13).
Select objects:                                 Click to pick the text.
1 selected, 1 found.
Select objects: <RETURN>                        The text is gone (see fig. 1.14).
```

Using the U Command to Undo

Sometimes, you will discover you have executed a lot of commands and that your drawing isn't turning out quite right. It's like the proverbial fork in the road. If you had turned left back at some command instead of right, things would have turned out okay. Well, you can use AutoCAD's U (undo) command to step back one command at a time. Using undo can be more helpful than just erasing, because the command undoes not only entities, but zooms and screen settings that you may have changed along the way.

Figure 1.13:
Text with pick box.

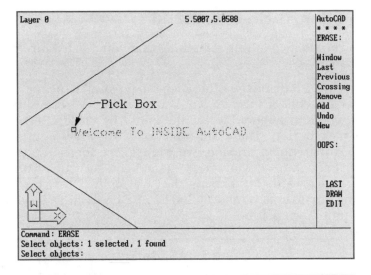

Figure 1.14:
Text is gone.

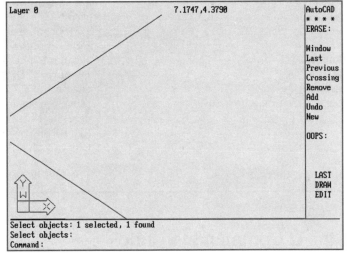

Error Handling With Undo

Command: **U**	Undoes the erased text from previous exercise. Undo shows what command was undone.
GROUP	Menu items are *grouped*.
Command: **U**	You can keep undoing steps.
ZOOM	Undoes the Zoom.
Command: **REDO**	Undoes the undo. The zoom is restored.

Error Handling With Undo—continued

```
Command: REDO
```
Previous command did not undo things   But you only can redo one step.
```
Command: LINE
```
Try canceling a command.
```
From point:
```
Pick any point.
```
To point: *Cancel*
```
Press <^C> to cancel line and return to
the command prompt.
```
Command:
```

If you get lost, what do you do?

Type ? or HELP. AutoCAD always gives you more information.

Help!

Help is almost always available in AutoCAD. You can get a complete listing of available commands or more information about a specific command.

If you are at the command prompt, you can either type HELP or ? to invoke AutoCAD's friendly help. AutoCAD will prompt you for what you want help with. Enter a <RETURN> for a list of all the available commands as well as point input information. Or you can enter a command name to get detailed information about a specific command. When HELP has shown you all it knows, it returns you to the command prompt.

You can usually type '? or 'HELP while you are in the middle of another command to receive help about the command. This type of help is called *transparent* help. With Release 11, transparent help usually gives help for the specific prompt of the current command — this is called *context-sensitive* help. With Release 10, transparent help gives the same information as regular help.

Try getting some help by looking at the COPY command.

Using HELP to Get Help

```
Command: HELP
```
Or enter a ?
```
Command name (RETURN for list):
```
You can enter a command name for help on a specific command, or...
```
Command name (RETURN for list): <RETURN>
```
<RETURN> for general help.

A help text screen appears with an alphabetical listing of commands (see fig. 1.15).
```
Press RETURN for further help. <RETURN>
```

Using HELP to Get Help—continued

Another screen of help appears...and more <RETURN>s display several more screens.

`Command: COPY`	Start the COPY command.
`Select objects: '?`	Enter apostrophe and ? for transparent help (See fig. 1.16).

A help screen for object selection is displayed. (Or general COPY help in Release 10.)

`>Do you want more help for the COPY command? <N> Y`	Ask for more help.

More help on COPY appears.

`Press RETURN to resume COPY command. <RETURN>`

`Resuming COPY command.`

`Select objects: *Cancel*`	Cancel the COPY command.
`Command:`	Press the Flip Screen key to get back to the graphics screen.

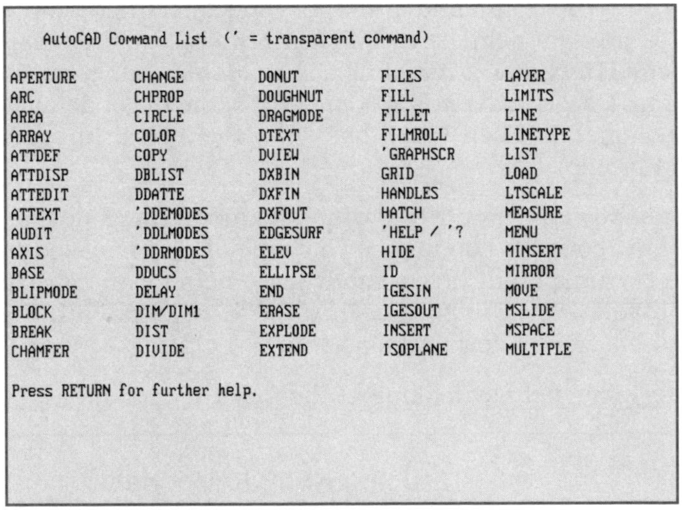

Figure 1.15:
Help screen.

```
AutoCAD Command List  (' = transparent command)

APERTURE    CHANGE      DONUT       FILES       LAYER
ARC         CHPROP      DOUGHNUT    FILL        LIMITS
AREA        CIRCLE      DRAGMODE    FILLET      LINE
ARRAY       COLOR       DTEXT       FILMROLL    LINETYPE
ATTDEF      COPY        DVIEW       'GRAPHSCR   LIST
ATTDISP     DBLIST      DXBIN       GRID        LOAD
ATTEDIT     DDATTE      DXFIN       HANDLES     LTSCALE
ATTEXT      'DDEMODES   DXFOUT      HATCH       MEASURE
AUDIT       'DDLMODES   EDGESURF    'HELP / '?  MENU
AXIS        'DDRMODES   ELEV        HIDE        MINSERT
BASE        DDUCS       ELLIPSE     ID          MIRROR
BLIPMODE    DELAY       END         IGESIN      MOVE
BLOCK       DIM/DIM1    ERASE       IGESOUT     MSLIDE
BREAK       DIST        EXPLODE     INSERT      MSPACE
CHAMFER     DIVIDE      EXTEND      ISOPLANE    MULTIPLE

Press RETURN for further help.
```

Quitting the Drawing Editor

Of course there are those occasions when you may get hopelessly muddled up in a drawing. In that case, you can make a dignified retreat by quitting your drawing. Unlike the SAVE command, if you quit your drawing using the QUIT command, AutoCAD does not update your drawing (.DWG) file. After you confirm that you really want to quit, AutoCAD discards your drawing and returns you to the main menu.

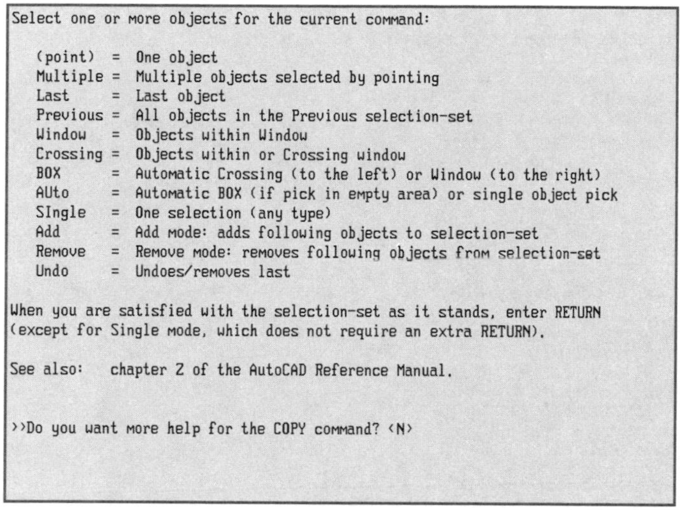

```
Select one or more objects for the current command:

  (point)  =  One object
  Multiple =  Multiple objects selected by pointing
  Last     =  Last object
  Previous =  All objects in the Previous selection-set
  Window   =  Objects within Window
  Crossing =  Objects within or Crossing window
  BOX      =  Automatic Crossing (to the left) or Window (to the right)
  AUto     =  Automatic BOX (if pick in empty area) or single object pick
  SIngle   =  One selection (any type)
  Add      =  Add mode: adds following objects to selection-set
  Remove   =  Remove mode: removes following objects from selection-set
  Undo     =  Undoes/removes last

When you are satisfied with the selection-set as it stands, enter RETURN
(except for Single mode, which does not require an extra RETURN).

See also:   chapter 2 of the AutoCAD Reference Manual.


>>Do you want more help for the COPY command? <N>
```

Figure 1.16:
COPY help screen.

Follow the prompts below to clear the screen and leave the drawing editor. AutoCAD will diplomatically ask if you want to discard all your changes to your drawing.

Using QUIT to Quit a Drawing

Command: **QUIT**
Really want to discard all changes to drawing? **Y**   Returns to the main menu.

If you have saved your drawing before quitting, the saved copy remains on disk even after you quit.

Comparing AutoCAD's Menus

Where are we? Where are we going? Let's take that second look at AutoCAD's main menu, then get an overview of how AutoCAD's menu systems work.

The Main Menu

The main menu header gives information ranging from your AutoCAD version and serial number to your current default drawing name. It also tells who owns your program's license and what dealer it was obtained from — this is the dealer who is required to provide you with support (see fig. 1.17).

Here's a listing of what each main menu selection does.

Figure 1.17:
AutoCAD's main
menu.

```
          A U T O C A D (R)
Copyright (c) 1982-90  Autodesk, Inc.  All Rights Reserved.
Release 11  (10/18/90) 386 DOS Extender
Serial Number:  000-00000000
Licensed to:   New Riders Publishing
Obtained from:  Autodesk, Inc.
Current drawing:  CHAPTER1

Main Menu

   0.  Exit AutoCAD
   1.  Begin a NEW drawing
   2.  Edit an EXISTING drawing
   3.  Plot a drawing
   4.  Printer Plot a drawing

   5.  Configure AutoCAD
   6.  File Utilities
   7.  Compile shape/font description file
   8.  Convert old drawing file
   9.  Recover damaged drawing

Enter selection:
```

Main Menu Options

Option 0 (Exit AutoCAD) gets you back to the operating system. You will use this option every time you finish an AutoCAD session. Typing \IA <RETURN> at the DOS prompt starts the batch file that gets you in; option 0 gets you out.

Options 1 (Begin a NEW drawing) and 2 (Edit an EXISTING drawing) are where you create, edit, and store your drawings in AutoCAD. You will spend the majority of your AutoCAD hours inside the drawing editor. The drawing editor is the AutoCAD equivalent of your drafting board — the interactive part of the program that lets you create and modify drawings.

There are two ways to get into the drawing editor. If you are starting a new drawing file, type 1 <RETURN> in response to the main menu selection prompt. AutoCAD will prompt you for the name of a NEW drawing file. If you want to edit a drawing that already exists, type 2 <RETURN>, and AutoCAD will prompt you for the name of the existing disk file you want to work with.

Options 3 (Plot a drawing) and 4 (Printer Plot a drawing) are where you can print and plot your drawings.

Option 5 (Configure AutoCAD) steps you through AutoCAD's interactive utility to let the ACAD program know what hardware you are using. You can find more details about this option in Appendix B.

Option 6 (File Utilities) lets you perform disk file maintenance operations just as if you were using the operating system. You can use the AutoCAD file utility to per-form housekeeping chores on your files. If you feel more comfortable using the commands directly from the operating system prompt, there is no harm in doing so — they perform the same tasks:

```
AutoCAD File Utility Options       DOS Equivalent
0. Exit file utility menu
1. List drawing files             DIR *.DWG
2. List user specified files      DIR
3. Delete files                   DEL
4. Rename files                   REN
5. Copy file                      COPY
6. Unlock file                    none
```

Note: If you get a Waiting for file: ... Locked by ... Press Ctrl-C to cancel. message, check to be sure no one else is using the file. If you are sure no one else is using it, it may have been left locked accidentally. If so, you can use item six to unlock it. File locking enhances security on networks and is not included in Release 10.

You also can access the AutoCAD file utility from within the drawing editor by typing FILES at the command prompt.

Options 7 (Compile shape/font description file) and 8 (Convert old drawing file) are special situations and will not be covered in this book. See *CUSTOMIZING AutoCAD* (New Riders Publishing) or the *AutoCAD Reference Manual* for details.

Option 9 (Recover damaged drawing) is for salvaging a drawing file in which AutoCAD detects an error and will not load (not included in Release 10.)

Let's get back into the drawing editor for an overview of AutoCAD's commands and menus. You can reload your previous drawing file from the main menu. (If you exited to the operating system, start up AutoCAD again by typing \IA.)

Loading an Existing Drawing

```
Enter selection: 2
Enter NAME of drawing (default CHAPTER1): <RETURN>
```

AutoCAD's Six Standard Menu Types

AutoCAD has more than 150 commands and numerous subcommands. Most of these commands relate to specific functions such as drawing, editing, or dimensioning. Because many of us are somewhat handicapped when it comes to typing,

AutoCAD provides an ACAD.MNU file which contains six alternate ways to enter commands with menus:

- Screen Menu
- Pull-Down Menu
- Dialogue Box
- Icon Menu
- Tablet Menu
- Button Menu

You have already used the screen menu and a pull-down menu. Menus provide a convenient way to organize and group commands into screen *pages* so they can easily be selected and executed. A screen, icon, or pull-down *menu page* is a listing of commands, options, and branches. A *branch* is our name for an item which activates another AutoCAD submenu. The groupings of menu pages are for convenience only and have no effect on AutoCAD's command structure. AutoCAD doesn't care how you tell it what to do.

When you select a menu item, it changes menu pages or sends a command, option, or a series of commands to AutoCAD for execution. This command execution is the same as if you had typed the input.

Note: Most menu items begin with several <^C>s to cancel any previous commands.

AutoCAD's standard menus give you many different ways to execute some of the same commands. Figure 1.18 shows all the different ways that you can execute the END command to end a drawing.

You should try all the types of menus available to you to see which menu method you prefer. Feel free to experiment with the menus as you read on. If you get lost, just select [AutoCAD] at the top of any screen menu. This returns you to the initial screen menu, called the *root menu,* and restores the initial pull-down menu bar. We'll explain menus more fully and give you practice using the various menus in the next chapter. Later in the book, you will learn how to change these standard menus and create your own custom menu selections.

The Screen Menu

The most commonly used menu is the screen menu. You saw the screen menu on the right side of the display screen when you first entered the drawing editor. Recall that you make your screen menu selections by highlighting the item with your pointing device and pressing the pick button.

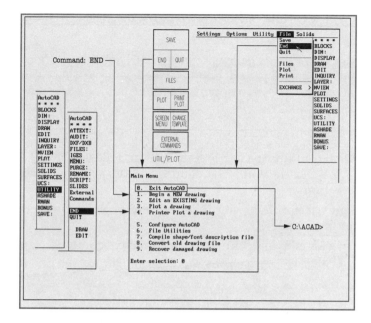

Figure 1.18:
Summary of the
menu options to end
a drawing.

Keyboard Access to the Screen Menu

You can also access the screen menu from the keyboard. The keyboard offers two methods of screen menu selection. The first method is to press the menu cursor key (usually <INS>) to highlight a menu selection. Use the up and down arrows to move the highlighted bar to the menu item you want and press <INS> again (or <RETURN>) to execute the selection.

The second method is to start typing characters of the menu selection at the command prompt. As you type, the menu label beginning with the characters you type becomes highlighted. Most selections can be highlighted by typing one or two characters, then you press <RETURN> or the <INS> key to execute the selection.

Screen Menu Conventions

As you move through the screen menus, you will notice some selections are followed by colons, [DIM:], [LAYER:], [UCS:] and [SAVE:]. These selections not only branch to a new menu page, but also start the command. Any selection which automatically starts a command has a colon after the menu label. Many commands require subcommands in order to complete their chores. These subcommands are usually listed in lower-case letters. As you flip through menu pages, remember you can always return to the root menu by selecting [AutoCAD] at the top of the menu page.

At the bottom of most menu pages are shortcut branches that let you return to your [_LAST_] menu page or to the [DRAW] and [EDIT] menu pages. Some menu pages offer more selections than can fit on one page. In such cases, the [next] and [previous] selections flip forward and back through pages to access all the selections available.

Finally, every menu page has [* * * *] below the [AutoCAD] selection. Choosing this selection presents you with a menu page of options called osnaps. These are aids for drawing objects. We will cover the osnap options later in Chapter 3 when we look at drawing basics.

To summarize the screen menu conventions:

- Commands are listed in upper-case letters and are followed by a colon. They usually both begin the AutoCAD command and present a page of subcommand selections.
- Selections without a colon following them are either subcommands or branches to other menu pages.
- Subcommands are usually listed in mixed or lower-case letters.
- Selecting [AutoCAD] at the top of the menu page will always return you to the root menu.
- Selecting [* * * *] will present a selection of osnap options.
- The bottoms of most menu pages have a selection of shortcut branches: [__LAST__], [DRAW], and [EDIT].
- Some menu pages present you with [next] and [previous] selections in order to display all the menu item selections available.

Pull-Down Menus

AutoCAD's pull-down menus are similar to screen menus. You have already tested your video hardware for pull-down support. If you have pull-down menus, you will see a menu bar when you move your pointing device to the top of the graphics screen. (If you do not have a pointing device, you cannot access the pull-down menus.) The menu bar presents a list of titles indicating the selections available in each pull-down menu. You can have up to ten pull-down menus available, but the standard AutoCAD menu bar uses only nine. (Release 10 uses eight.) All nine choices are shown in figure 1.19 below.

Many pull-down menu selections open a screen menu page to help with subcommand selection (see fig. 1.20). Some AutoCAD pull-down menus present dialogue boxes for commands with multiple settings, and groups of related commands. Many people find pull-down menus easier to use than screen menus because each submenu occupies a different spot on the screen. Pull-down menus are also a little quicker than screen menus since you don't have to return to the root menu as often. The complete set of pull-down menus is shown in the facing page illustration at the beginning of the chapter (see fig. 1.1).

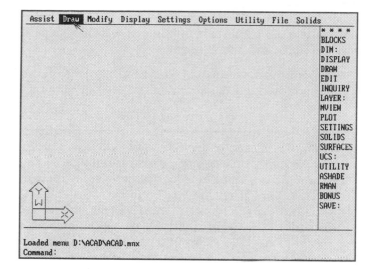

Figure 1.19:
The menu bar.

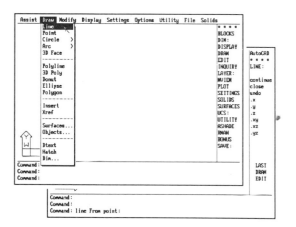

Figure 1.20:
Pull-down menu
calling a screen
menu.

Pull-down menus have their own conventions — they don't follow the upper-case, lower-case, and colon convention of screen menus. Most pull-down menu items are capitalized.

▪ Pull-down selections followed by three dots, such as [Vpoint 3D...], call a dialogue box, icon menu, or AutoLISP program.

▪ Upper-case selections followed by an angle bracket, such as [HATCH OPTIONS >], do not execute commands, but call submenus which replace their menu's position in the pull-down menu bar.

■ Lower-case selections followed by an angle bracket, such as [Circle >], both execute commands and call options submenus which replace their menu's position in the pull-down menu bar.

Many pull-down menu selections, such as the [Line] or [Ellipse] items on the [Draw] menu, both execute a command and call a screen menu page of options for that command.

Note: Some commands act a little differently depending on whether you type them from the command line, use screen menus, or use pull-down menus. For example, the pull-down menu [Point] and [Erase] items automatically repeat until canceled. If you type them from the command line, they only execute once. Several selections, such as [Insert] and [Dtext] on the [Draw] menu, are AutoLISP-modified commands. These items require you to set defaults on the [Settings] or [Options] menus before using them. Then, these menu items will execute their commands with those defaults and not prompt you for the options you preset.

Dialogue Boxes

AutoCAD's dialogue boxes offer a unique and convenient way to view and adjust certain AutoCAD settings, to enter and edit text strings, and to enter filenames. Like pull-down menus, dialogue boxes require AUI video support. Although dialogue boxes are actually brought up by commands beginning with DD, such as DDEMODES, you can also access them through menu selections which contain their commands. Table 1.1 lists the commands that use dialogue boxes.

When a dialogue box pops up on the screen, it shows a list of settings and their current values. Some settings are on/off toggles with a check mark in a box to indicate when they're on. You click on the box with the pick button on your pointer to turn it on or off. Other settings display values such as names, colors, or distances. You change these settings by highlighting and editing them or entering a new value. Some values, such as file or layer names, are presented in lists which may be too long to fit on screen at one time. These have scroll bars at the right side to scroll up and down the lists (see fig. 1.21).

Although dialogue boxes duplicate the functions of other commands, they provide clearer and more convenient control over complex commands or groups of commands. We'll more fully explain and practice using dialogue boxes in the next chapter.

The Icon Menu

If your hardware supports pull-down menus, it also supports a third type of screen menu called an icon menu. An icon menu displays menu selections as graphic images. AutoCAD uses slide files to construct these icon menus, displaying four, nine, or sixteen images at one time. After displaying an icon menu, you select a menu item by highlighting the small square to the left of the image and pressing the pick button on your pointing device. AutoCAD executes the corresponding selection like any other menu selection. Icon menus can page through other icon menus the same way screen menus page through other menu pages. AutoCAD has a number of preset icon menus such as for hatch patterns and text styles (see fig. 1.22).

Table 1.1
Dialogue Box Commands

Command	Pull-down	Purpose
DDEMODES	[Entity Creation...] (DDEntityMODES)	Set layer, color, linetype, and other default properties for new entities.
DDLMODES	[Layer Control...] (DDLayerMODES)	Create layers, set their default properties, and control visibility.
DDRMODES	[Drawing Tools...] (DDdRawingMODES)	Control snap grid axis and isometric settings.
DDATTE	none (DDAttributeEditing)	Easily edit attributes in blocks.
DDUCS	[UCS Control...]	Control User Coordinate Systems.
DDEDIT	none	Easily edit text entities or attribute definitions.
all file commands	various	Display and scroll through lists of filenames.

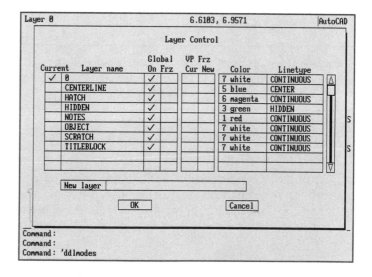

Figure 1.21:
The layer control
dialogue box.

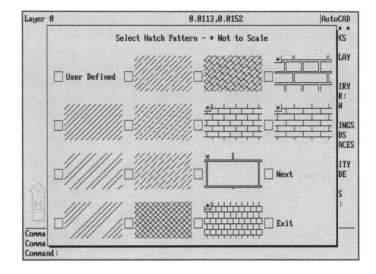

Figure 1.22:
The hatch pattern icon menu.

Menus are a powerful tool within AutoCAD, giving you flexibility in command entry. With a little practice, you will soon find your preferences. Many users prefer to use a tablet menu.

The Tablet Menu

AutoCAD comes with a standard tablet menu that performs many of the same functions as the screen and pull-down menus. Figure 1.23 shows the complete tablet menu. The tablet menu offers a few advantages over the other menu options. It's easy to remember where to find tablet menu selections and they're always available without flipping through menu pages. The tablet menu also includes graphic images to help you identify the selection. Many selections from the tablet menu call the appropriate screen menu pages to help you in your subcommand option selections.

> **Note:** Bringing up AutoCAD's standard tablet menu requires running through a small set of configuration steps. See Appendix C to help you configure the AutoCAD standard tablet menu.

The Buttons Menu

We all use some type of pointing device with AutoCAD, usually a tablet puck or a mouse (see fig. 1.24). AutoCAD reserves one button on the puck or mouse for picking points and selecting screen and tablet menu items. This is the button that tells AutoCAD to pick a point or select an object where the cursor or crosshairs are positioned on the screen. A mouse usually has two or three buttons, and a puck can have up to sixteen buttons. The position of the pick button varies with the device. The second button acts like a <RETURN> key. Most of the other buttons are assigned to the same toggles as the function keys and control settings we'll explore in the next chapter.

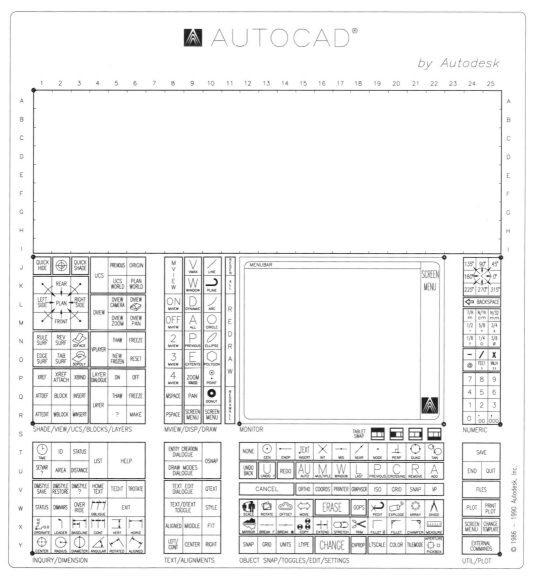

Figure 1.23:
AutoCAD tablet menu.

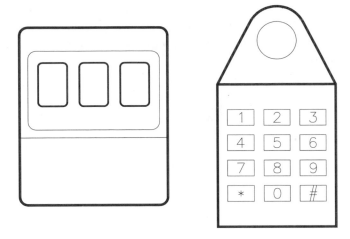

Figure 1.24:
Mouse and tablet pointing devices.

You can assign the buttons to execute other menu selections by creating a custom button menu. For details on creating button menus, see *MAXIMIZING AutoCAD, Volume I* (New Riders Publishing).

Keyboard Commands vs. Menus

Many users think that keyboard command entry can be just as fast if not faster than using menus. This is particularly true with AutoCAD's *command alias* feature (not available prior to Release 11). A command alias is an abbreviation that you can use instead of typing the entire command name. When you use an alias, AutoCAD replaces it with the full command name and executes the command normally. For example, to execute the CIRCLE command with a menu, you pull down the [Draw] menu or select the [DRAW] screen menu, then select the [Circle] or [CIRCLE] items. Or, you can merely type a C, press <RETURN> and be done with it. AutoCAD's standard abbreviations are:

Abbrev.	Command	Abbrev.	Command
A	Arc	LA	LAyer
C	Circle	M	Move
CP	CoPy	P	Pan
DV	DView	PL	PolyLine
E	Erase	R	Redraw
L	Line	Z	Zoom

While these abbreviations cover only a few of AutoCAD's many commands, it is quite easy to create your own abbreviations by modifying the ACAD.PGP file. This is explained in Appendix B, and a more comprehensive IA-ACAD.PGP file is included on the optional IA DISK. We recommend you use it, or create your own custom ACAD.PGP file for your most frequently used commands.

AutoCAD offers a similar keyboard shortcut for command options. Instead of flipping through menus for command options, virtually any command option can be abbreviated to the one or two letters that are unique for that option at the current command prompt. For example, recall the ZOOM command prompt:

```
All/Center/Dynamic/Extents/Left/Previous/Vmax/Window/<Scale(X/XP)>:
```

Earlier, the [Zoom Window] menu item you used responded to this prompt with merely a W, not with the entire word WINDOW. You need only type the characters that are shown as upper-case in AutoCAD prompts to execute an option.

When to Use the Keyboard or Menus

In the next chapter, you'll use a lot of menus, but in most of the book we'll just show commands as entered from the keyboard. The purpose of the book is to thoroughly teach you AutoCAD, so we want you to become intimately familiar with its commands. After you learn the commands, you can decide if keyboard entry or menus are better for you.

AutoCAD's standard menus are general purpose, but you may do specific types of drawings for which custom menus would be much more efficient. You can purchase custom menus for many different applications. See the *AutoCAD Sourcebook*, published by Que Corporation, for a listing. Or you can create your own custom menus, as explained later in this book and comprehensively covered in *CUSTOMIZING AutoCAD* from New Riders Publishing.

We recommend using command abbreviations and options from the keyboard for ordinary, commonly used commands, and creating or purchasing a custom menu for using AutoCAD more efficiently with your particular application.

One More Utility — Ending Your Work

You have already seen that AutoCAD provides a quick way out of the drawing editor through QUIT. Quitting is fast, but does not save anything. Save your work now using the END command. Remember, ending makes a backup file from your previously saved file, stores the up-to-date copy, and exits the drawing editor. The END command saves the drawing to the current drawing filename.

Using END to Save a Drawing

Command: **END**   You've completed your first
                                                        AutoCAD session.

Exit AutoCAD with a 0 from the main menu.

Tip: At times, you may need your drawing files to be as small as possible for archiving or exchanging with others. You can sometimes reduce the size of an AutoCAD drawing file by ending twice. That is, end your drawing once, reload it, and end it a second time. When you erase objects in a drawing, they aren't actually removed from the drawing database until the drawing is loaded the next time. Double-ending a drawing will completely purge it of deleted entities. This can save disk space, especially after an extensive editing session.

Summing Up

You've had a chance to set up AutoCAD and play around with the drawing editor by entering a few commands. Surprise! It does not bite, and it does not laugh when you make mistakes. AutoCAD is cooperative. It only takes action when you tell it to do something. AutoCAD lets you know that it's waiting for your input with the command prompt or other prompts on the prompt line. Help is always available to you if you type HELP or ? at the command prompt, or if you type 'HELP or '? when you are in commands. If you get stuck drawing, you can always undo a command, erase your drawing, or quit the drawing and start over.

Now that you know your way in and out of AutoCAD, you can move on to organizing AutoCAD's drawing environment and experimenting with using menus.

2

Setting Up an Electronic Drawing

PREPARING TO DRAW

Preparing to draw in AutoCAD is much like preparing to draw on a drafting board. In manual drafting, you select your drawing tools to fit your particular drawing — you might select a 1/16" scale for instance. In AutoCAD, you set up parameters to fit your particular drawing — creating, in effect, custom tools. You set up the right units, scale, linetype, sheet size, and text. Then you are ready to begin drawing.

A little advance preparation before you start each drawing makes AutoCAD easier and faster to use in the long run. While it takes a little more time to set up, you can save your settings and use them in your next drawing. Setting up is like the old adage: "Once right is better than twice wrong." You will save time and grief later on.

This chapter will show you how to get set up for drawing, and how to save those settings in a prototype drawing. As we promised in the last chapter, we'll also explore and further explain the use of AutoCAD's various menus.

Organizing Your Drawing Setups

While organizing an electronic drawing is similar to organizing a manual drawing, there are differences. You have to adjust your way of thinking about scale, layers, and drawing entities. Before you prepare an electronic drawing sheet, take a moment to become familiar with the concepts behind scale, layers, and entities.

49

How Full Scale Electronic Drawings Work

Inside AutoCAD, drawing elements are stored in real-world units. AutoCAD can track your drawing data in meters, millimeters, feet, inches, fractions, decimals, or just about any unit system that you want to use.

When drawing on a drafting board, you usually create the drawing to fit a specific sheet size or scale. The text, symbols, and line widths are generally about the same size from one drawing to another.

In AutoCAD this process is reversed. You always draw the image at actual size (full scale) in real-world units. The only time you need to worry about scale is for plotting. You scale your full-size electronic drawing up or down to fit the plot sheet. You have to plan ahead for this and make settings that adjust the scale of the text, symbols, and line widths so that they plot at an appropriate size.

A bolt which is two inches long may look one foot when it's blown up on the screen, but AutoCAD thinks of it as two inches no matter how you show it or plot it. To help you get comfortable with electronic scale, we will take you through some setups with different units and sheet sizes in a few pages.

How Electronic Layers Work

Even in manual drafting, almost everything you design and draw can be thought of as separated into layers. Printed circuit boards have layers. Buildings are layered by floors. Even schematic diagrams have information layers for annotations. In AutoCAD, unlimited electronic layers give you more flexibility and control in organizing your drawing.

Perhaps you have used overlay drafting to actually separate your drawings into layers. Think of AutoCAD's electronic layers in 2D as sheets of clear acetate laid one over the other. When you are working in 2D, you are looking down through a stack of sheets (see fig. 2.1). You can see your whole drawing built from the superimposed sheets. You can pull a single sheet out to examine or work on, or you can work with all the layers at once.

In 3D, layers become more of an organizational concept and have less physical resemblance to overlays. Any layer may contain any group of objects, which may be superimposed in space to coexist with other objects on other layers see (fig. 2.2). Think of 3D layers as containing classes of objects. You can look at all layer groups together, or you can look at any combination, by specifying the layers you want to see.

Each layer can have any color and linetype associated with it. When you set up your AutoCAD layers, you need to determine what parts of your drawing you are going to place on each layer, and what color and linetype you are going to use on each layer. You can make as many, or as few, layers as you need.

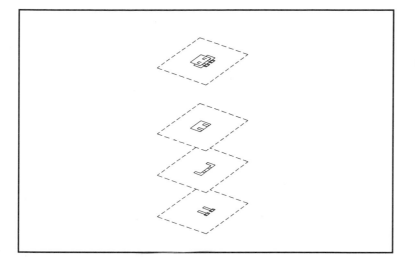

Figure 2.1:
2D layer .

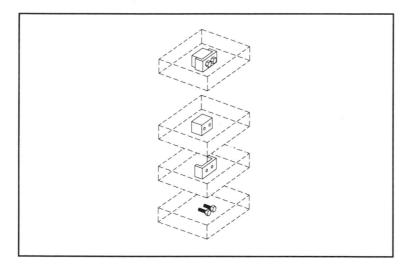

Figure 2.2:
3D layer .

Electronic Entities and Properties

When you use AutoCAD's drawing tools to draw on one of these electronic layers, you create a *drawing entity*. A line segment is an entity, circles and text are entities. Besides its geometric location, each entity has an associated color, layer, linetype, and thickness (for 3D). AutoCAD calls these associations *properties*. Color is commonly used in AutoCAD to control the line weight of entities when they are plotted. You can preset the color and linetype for each layer.

Part of the organization process is to determine how you're going to group entities on layers and what colors and linctypes you are going to use when you construct your drawing entities. The simplest (and in many cases the best) organization is to use your layers to control the properties of your entities. If you are going to draw a red gizmo with dashed lines, then you draw it on the red dashed-line layer. Many of these decisions are determined by drawing standards that you may have already established. If you need to make exceptions, AutoCAD lets you change the properties of any entity, regardless of its layer. (If you are not using color in your plotted and printed output, you may want to consider using it to control line weight in your plots.)

The Drawing Setup Tools

You will find most of the setup tools you need on the two pages of the [SETTINGS] screen menu, or the [Settings] and [Options] pull-down menus (see fig. 2.3).

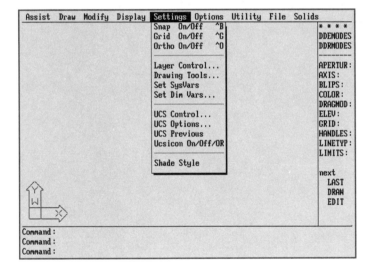

Figure 2.3:
Settings screen and
pull-down menus.

Setting Up a Drawing

When you begin a new drawing, AutoCAD makes several assumptions about drawing setup, including display and input units, scale, and linetype. These pre-established settings are called *defaults*.

ACAD.DWG — AutoCAD's Prototype Drawing

AutoCAD sets up many default settings by reading a prototype drawing stored on your hard disk. AutoCAD's standard prototype drawing, which comes with your

AutoCAD software, is called ACAD.DWG. You created a fresh copy of it in your IA-ACAD directory in Chapter 1 (if you didn't, you should before proceeding).

The standard ACAD.DWG assumes you want to draw entities on layer 0. By default, layer 0 has white, continuous lines. (These may *appear* inverted as black lines on a white background on some systems, but AutoCAD still thinks of them as white lines.) ACAD.DWG also assumes a default system of measurement display (called units) that uses decimal units and initial drawing *limits* of 12 units in the X direction and 9 units in the Y direction. The drawing limits define your intended drawing area.

When you set up your drawing, you are actually modifying settings that were passed by AutoCAD from the prototype drawing into your new drawing. As you work through your drawing setups, AutoCAD lets you know what defaults are set by showing you default values in brackets in the command prompt. You can accept the default value that AutoCAD offers by just pressing <RETURN>. You can also tell AutoCAD what prototype drawing to use. You will see how to change a prototype drawing and tailor it for your own use in the book's last part (Part Three) on making AutoCAD more productive.

Determining a Scale Factor and Drawing Limits

How do you work out your scale? First, you establish your system of units. Then, you determine a *scale factor* so you can calculate the AutoCAD settings which will allow you to draw at actual size (full scale) and produce a plot at the size you want. You set your electronic sheet so that you can draw at full scale.

We'll start tailoring AutoCAD settings by taking a case study approach to scale. First, we will take you through setting up an architectural drawing. Second, we will work through an engineering drawing. Then, we will show you how to set up layers using a simple one-to-one scale drawing.

Scale Factor Settings

When you determine a drawing scale factor, it affects several AutoCAD settings. These include:

- Sheet size (limits)
- Line width
- Text height
- Symbol size
- Linetype scale

Sheet size is the most important. AutoCAD's electronic equivalent of sheet size is limits. You set your limits during your initial drawing setup. You set the other drawing effects later.

Determining Scale Factor and Sheet Size

Sheet size is calculated in much the same way as in manual drafting, except you use the resulting scale ratio to scale your sheet size up to fit around the full scale size of what you are drawing instead of scaling the drawing down to fit within the sheet. Then you scale everything back down by the same factor when you plot it.

Take an architectural calculation as your first case. You have a floor plan that is 75 feet x 40 feet, and you want a drawing scale at 1/4 inch = one foot (12 inches). What is your scale factor, and what size electronic sheet are you going to use? The size of your electronic sheet is set by the limits that you choose. These are the X,Y values of the lower left and upper right corners of your electronic sheet.

If you convert your drawing scale to a ratio of 1:*n*, then *n* is your scale factor. If you already have selected a drawing scale, it is easy to determine the scale factor. For example, if you had selected a drawing scale of 3/8" = 1'-0", your drawing scale factor would be 32.

```
3/8:12/1 converts to 1:96/3 or 1:32 for a scale factor of 32.
```

You currently are working at 1/4" = 1'-0", so your scale factor is 48.

```
1/4:12/1 converts to 1:48/1 or 1:48 for a scale factor of 48.
```

Calculating a Sheet Size for a Known Scale and Object Size

From your scale factor, you determine your electronic drawing limits by running some test calculations on possible plotting sheet sizes. You set your limits by multiplying the sheet size that you select by your scale factor. Here is a sample set of calculations.

```
Size of floor plan          75' x 40'
Scale                       1/4" = 12"
Determine scale factor      48
```

Test a 17" x 11" sheet:

```
17" x 48 = 816" or 68'
11" x 48 = 528" or 44'
A 17" x 11" sheet equals 68' x 44' at 1/4" to 12" scale.
```

This sheet size is too small. Test a 36" x 24" sheet:

```
36" x 48 = 1728" or 144'
24" x 48 = 1152" or 96'
A 36" x 24" sheet equals 144' x 96' at 1/4" to 12" scale.
```

This should work with plenty of room for dimensions, notes, and a border.

In this example, you determined your limits by the number of units that fit across a standard sheet (D size, 36" x 24", for 144' across 36" at 1/4" = 12"). If you have to fit the drawing to a predetermined sheet size, you start with that size and the size of what you are drawing, and then calculate the scale factor from them.

Setting your limits doesn't actually limit how big your drawing can be. Think of AutoCAD's limits as an *electronic fence* which AutoCAD can use to warn you if you draw outside your boundary. This boundary is an ideal way to represent a sheet size. It gives you a frame of reference for zooming or plotting. If you draw outside your electronic sheet, you can expand the sheet by resetting the limits.

How do you get these settings into AutoCAD? You can set limits explicitly, or you can use an AutoCAD setup routine that will automatically set limits by stepping you through the calculations for your sheet size and scale, based upon your chosen limits. First, we'll use the automatic limits set up on an architectural sheet, then we'll use the UNITS and LIMITS commands to set up an engineering drawing.

Setting Limits Automatically

The [MVSETUP] item on the [BONUS] screen menu (or [Setup] on the Release 10 root screen menu) loads and executes an AutoLISP program that sets up your limits. It also draws a border around the drawing, or inserts a complex title block (title block not available in Release 10). The border is drawn as a reference line that matches your limits, around the perimeter of the sheet. This border is not intended to be plotted, but shows you your sheet edges. [MVSETUP] also includes another option that sets up the drawing in paper space with optional viewports (both topics of Chapter 4), and inserts a complex title block. Figure 2.4 shows the menu selection sequence for [MVSETUP].

To get started, you need to start AutoCAD and create a new drawing with the main menu. Try stepping through the setup sequences in the following exercise.

Using [MVSETUP] to Prepare an Architectural 1/4" Scale Drawing

Load AutoCAD with your IA.BAT batch file to get the main menu.

```
Enter selection: 1
Enter NAME of drawing: ARCH
```

Select **[BONUS]**   Displays the [BONUS] menu.
Select **[next]**
Select **[MVSETUP]**   Displays the following prompt.

```
Paperspace/Modelspace is disabled. The old setup will be
invoked unless it is enabled. Enable Paper/Modelspace? <Y>: N
```

With Release 10, you skip all of the above and simply select [Setup] from the root menu.

```
Select the Units from the screen menu: 4          Select [archtect].
Select the Scale from the screen menu: 48.0       Select [1/4"=1'].
Select the Paper size from the screen menu: 36.0 24.0   Select [24X36], completing
                                                         the setup.
```

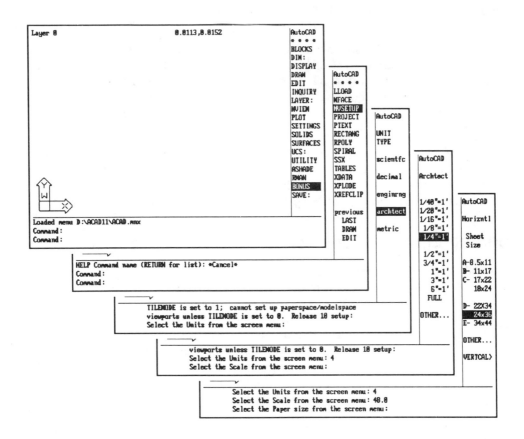

Figure 2.4:
Architectural setup menu sequence.

A border is drawn around the screen and the coordinates at the top of the screen are 1728.0000,1152.0000, which, in inches, is 144' x 96' at 1/4"=1' scale. But the automatic setup didn't set the units to feet and inches.

Setting Units

AutoCAD offers units suitable for nearly any normal drawing practice. If you normally use architectural units, then use AutoCAD's architectural units. Select your system of units with the UNITS command. Setting units does two things for your drawing. First, it sets up the input format for entering distances and angles from the keyboard. Second, it sets up the output format AutoCAD will use when displaying and dimensioning distances and angles.

When you use the UNITS command, your screen flips to text mode and AutoCAD prompts you for units information. For this example, you'll select architectural units: feet and inches with 1/64" as the smallest fraction displayed.

> **Tip:** Even though you may not need finer fractions than 1/2" at this scale, setting it to 1/64" will ensure precision. If you set it to 1/2", everything drawn will be rounded to 1/2" when displayed, even if not accurate. Individual errors in drawing will be less likely to show up, but may cause cumulative errors. Setting it to 1/64" will make drawing errors more likely to show up — if a coordinate displays as 49/64" when you know it should be 1", you know it is not drawn correctly.

AutoCAD prompts you through setting angle measurements and angle display, giving examples for each system setting. The default screen setting for zero angle is usually to the right or *east*. The default setting for angle measurement is *counter-clockwise*. Use these default settings in your setup. You can type the UNITS command or use the menu selection sequence shown (see fig. 2.5).

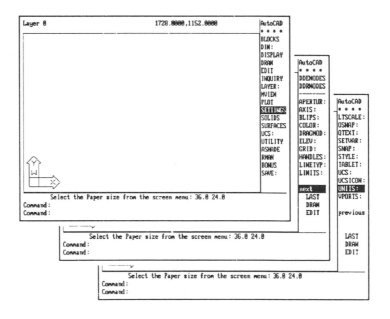

Figure 2.5:
Menu selection sequence for units.

Using UNITS to Set Architectural Units for a Drawing

```
Select [SETTINGS] [next] [UNITS:]                    AutoCAD flips to text screen.
System of units:                (Examples)
1. Scientific                   1.55E+01
2. Decimal                      15.50
3. Engineering                  1'-3.50"
4. Architectural                1'-3 1/2"
5. Fractional                   15 1/2
```

```
With the exception of Engineering and Architectural formats,
these formats can be used with any basic unit of measurement.
For example, Decimal mode is perfect for metric units as well
as decimal English units.
```

```
Enter choice, 1 to 5 <2>: 4                          Architectural.
Denominator of smallest fraction to display
(1, 2, 4, 8, 16, 32, or 64) <16>: 64                 1/64".
```

```
System of angle measure:        (Examples)

1. Decimal degrees              45.0000
2. Degrees/minutes/seconds      45d0'0"
3. Grads                        50.0000g
4. Radians                      0.7854r
5. Surveyor's units             N 45d0'0" E
```

```
Enter choice, 1 to 5 <1>: <RETURN>
Number of fractional places for display of
  angles (0 to 8) <0>: 2
Direction for angle 0.00:
East    3 o'clock = 0.00
North  12 o'clock = 90.00
West    9 o'clock = 180.00
South   6 o'clock = 270.00
Enter direction for angle 0.00 <0.00>: <RETURN>
```

```
Do you want angles measured clockwise?
  <N>: <RETURN>
```

```
Command: <F1>                    Flip screen to get back to the
                                 graphics screen.
Command:                         Pick a point near the top right
                                 corner of the border.
Command: END                     Saves the drawing and exits.
```

After you set the units, the coordinates display shows feet, inches, and fractions. If the format of the current coordinate is too long to fit in the coordinates display area, it displays in scientific units, like 1.704450E+03,95'-9 51/64". When you pick a point, the coordinates change to a point near but not exactly at 144'-0",96'-0", verifying that the limits were set correctly.

We'll see how to precisely control pick points in the next chapter.

Usually, you set units only once for a drawing, but you can change units in mid-stream should the need arise.

Fractional units represent inches by default, but the inch marks (") are not shown. You can use fractional units for units other than inches by adjusting dimensioning and plot setups.

Entering and Displaying Values in Various Units

No matter what your units are set to, you can enter values in integer, decimal, scientific, or fractional formats (only decimal or scientific in Release 10). When you are using architectural or engineering units, you can input values as feet, inches, or both. AutoCAD assumes the value is in inches unless you use a foot mark (') to indicate feet, so you can omit the inches mark ("). In fact, you do not need to type the inches value at all if it is zero. 2'0" or 2'0 or 2' or 24" are all equivalent in engineering units. No space is allowed between the foot and inch value, just the foot mark, like 1'3". The inch mark (") is optional; you can enter 1'3" or 1'3.

A dash is used to separate fractions, as in 1'3-1/2. Fractions must be entered without spaces, like 1-3/4 instead of 1 3/4, because AutoCAD reads a space as a <RETURN>. The input format and display format differ. You input 1'3-1/2" but it displays as 1'-3 1/2". However, in Release 11, you can force feet and inches, angles, and fractions to display in the same form as entered by setting the UNITMODE system variable to 1. To do so, just type UNITMODE at the command prompt.

Now, let's look at setting limits manually .

Using the LIMITS Command

You have used AutoCAD's automatic limits setup. Try stepping through a setup sequence for the engineering sheet using AutoCAD's individual settings commands for units and limits.

Determining a Scale for a Known Object and Sheet Size

Take an engineering example as a second case for setting limits. Say you want to draw a 24-inch manhole cover on an 8 1/2" x 11" plotting sheet. Okay, this isn't quite a full engineering case, but you get the idea. How do you compute your scale factor and determine your electronic limits? You need to do a little trial and error:

```
Size of manhole cover      24" diameter
Sheet size                 11" x 8 1/2"
```

Test 1/2" = 1" scale (1 unit = 2 units) scale factor of 2:

```
11"    x 2 = 22"
8 1/2" x 2 = 17"
```

This scale factor gives 22" x 17" limits — too small.

Test 1/4" = 1" scale (1 unit = 4 units) scale factor of 4:

```
11"    x 4 = 44"
8 1/2" x 4 = 34"
```

These 44" x 34" limits should work.

For this example, you'll select engineering units: feet and inches with the inch as the smallest whole unit. Engineering fractions are decimals of an inch. We'll abbreviate the prompts since you've already seen them.

Using UNITS to Set Engineering Units for a Drawing

`Enter selection: 1`	Begin a NEW drawing.
`Enter NAME of drawing: ENGR`	
`Command: UNITS`	Or select from the [SETTINGS] screen menu.
`System of units:          (Examples)`	
`3. Engineering           1'-3.50"`	
`Enter choice, 1 to 5 <2>: 3`	Engineering.
`Number of digits to right of decimal point`	
`   (0 to 8) <4>: 2`	
`System of angle measure:     (Examples)`	
`1. Decimal degrees        45.0000`	
`Enter choice, 1 to 5 <1>: <RETURN>`	
`Number of fractional places for display of`	
`   angles (0 to 8) <0>: 2`	
`Enter direction for angle 0.00 <0.00>: <RETURN>`	
`Do you want angles measured clockwise?`	
`  <N>: <RETURN>`	
`Command: <F1>`	Flip screen to get back to the graphics screen.

Setting Limits

Next, you'll set your drawing file sheet boundaries with the LIMITS command. You can type the command or select it from the [SETTINGS] screen menu. AutoCAD shows you <0'-0.00",0'-0.00"> as a default prompt for the lower left-most corner —

home base. It is telling you that the lower left-most boundary of your intended drawing area is X = 0,Y = 0. You can enter a new lower left corner by typing new X,Y coordinates or by accepting the default with a <RETURN>. You'll enter your estimated limits of 44",34" for the upper right corner.

▶ Setting Limits for an Engineering Drawing Sheet

```
Select [SETTINGS] [LIMITS:]
Command: LIMITS
Reset Model space limits:
ON/OFF/<Lower left corner ><0'-0.00",0'-0.00">: <RETURN>
Upper right corner <1'-0.00",0'-9.00">: 44",34"
```

Manually setting limits doesn't insert a border, so how can you see where your limits are? One easy way to see your drawing limits is to set a drawing grid, then extend your screen image using the ZOOM command. A grid is also useful for eyeballing coordinate values and distances. You can type GRID or select [GRID:] from the [SETTINGS] menu, and type ZOOM or select [ZOOM:] from the [DISPLAY] menu in the exercise sequence that follows.

▶ Seeing Your Limits With a Grid

```
Select [SETTINGS] [GRID:]                         Set grid to 1".
Command: GRID
Grid spacing(X) or ON/OFF/Snap/Aspect <0'-0.00">: 1

Select [DISPLAY] [ZOOM:]                          Zoom so the limits and
                                                  grid cover the screen.
Command: 'ZOOM
All/Center/Dynamic/Extents/Left/Previous/Vmax/
   Window/<Scale(X/VP)>: A
Regenerating drawing.
Select [DISPLAY] [ZOOM:]                           Zoom so limits and grid
                                                   cover 75 percent of
                                                   screen.
Command: 'ZOOM
All/Center/Dynamic/Extents/Left/Previous/Vmax/
   Window/<Scale(X/VP)>: .75
Regenerating drawing.
```

Your screen should look like the screen in figure 2.6. The area covered by the grid is your defined limits, representing an 11" x 8 1/2" plotting sheet. If you drew outside the grid, you would actually be drawing outside the area that represents your intended plot area.

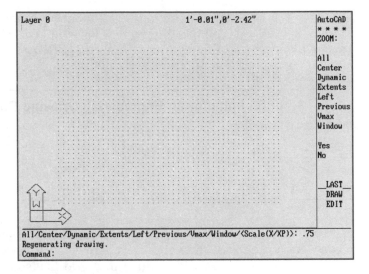

Figure 2.6:
Limits shown by grid.

Tip: When you set drawing limits to match your plotting sheet size, remember that plotters grip a portion of the sheet's edge during plotting. Make sure your drawing allows enough room at the borders for your plotter. A safe margin varies from 1/4" to 1 1/4", depending on the plotter brand and on which edge it grips.

Turning the Limits Warning On

You may have noticed the ON/OFF prompt or [ON] and [OFF] menu selections for the limits. When you turn limits checking on, AutoCAD will not allow you to draw outside the limits. Let's try it in the next exercise.

Drawing Full Scale on a Small Sheet

Although your limits represent a plot area of 11" x 8.5", they cover 44" x 34" in real-world units. Try drawing a 24-inch diameter circle to represent the manhole cover and see that it fits within your limits. Type CIRCLE or select it from the [DRAW] screen menu or [Draw] pull-down menu. If you use the pull-down, you can ignore the [CIRCLE] submenu that appears; it will disappear when you enter a point. If you use the screen menu, you need to select the [CEN,RAD:] option from the [CIRCLE] submenu to actually execute the CIRCLE command in its default center point and radius mode.

Testing Your Drawing Scale Factor and Limits

Command: **LIMITS**
Reset Model space limits:
ON/OFF/<Lower left corner> <0'-0.00",0'-0.00">: **ON**

Select **[DRAW] [CIRCLE] [CEN,RAD:]**   Draw a circle at 22,17 with
                                                          a 12" radius.

CIRCLE 3P/2P/TTR/<Center point>:   Try to pick a point outside
                                                          the grid.

**Outside limits

3P/2P/TTR/<Center point>: **22,17**   Type it.
Diameter/<Radius>: DRAG **12**

Your manhole should fit neatly on your drawing, as shown in figure 2.7.

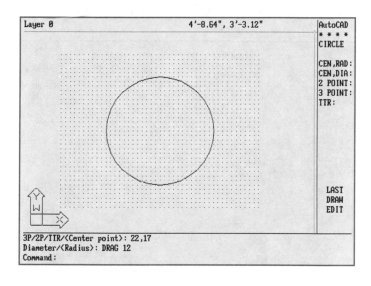

Figure 2.7:
Manhole drawn with a
circle.

Setting Other Drawing Effects

Settings such as text height and symbol scale are a matter of drawing standards. If you have an established standard, you should adjust AutoCAD's settings to your normal standard. Just as you set your electronic sheet size to accommodate the manhole cover, you adjust your text, symbols, and line width in proportion to your sheet size. Once you have a drawing scale factor, this is a simple procedure. You determine the size you want your text, symbols, and other elements to be when the drawing is plotted, then multiply that size by the scale factor.

Here are some examples for the manhole cover.

Plotted Size	x	Scale Factor	=	Electronic Size
0.2" Text height	x	4	=	0.8"
1/2" Bubble	x	4	=	2" diameter
1/16" Line width	x	4	=	1/4"

AutoCAD also provides a variety of linetypes, such as hidden and dashed linetypes. You adjust linetypes by the scale factor, with the LTSCALE command. Like text and symbols, LTSCALE should be set for the plotted appearance, not how it looks on the screen. Linetype scale is largely a matter of personal preference, but setting it to your scale factor is a good starting point. Linetype selection is discussed later in this chapter.

Try applying some of the examples to the manhole drawing, creating the bubble with a circle and the number 1. You will find [LINETYPE] and [LTSCALE] on the [SETTINGS] menu. Use the following illustration (see fig 2.8) as a guide for the exercise.

Figure 2.8:
Manhole with text,
symbol, and a
linetype.

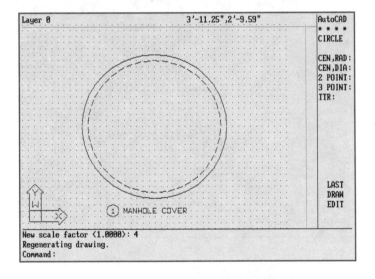

► Setting Text Height, Symbol Size, and Linetype Scale

```
Command: ZOOM
All/Center/Dynamic/Extents/Left/Previous/
  Vmax/Window/<Scale(X/VP)>: A
Regenerating drawing.
Command: <F6>                          Or <^D> to toggle continuous coordi-
                                       nate display on.

Command: DTEXT
```

Setting Text Height, Symbol Size, and Linetype Scale—continued

```
Justify/Style/<Start point>: M          M is for middle justification. (The
                                         Release 10 prompt is a little dif-
                                         ferent, but you still enter M.)

Middle point: 22,3
Height <0'-0.20">: .8
Rotation angle <0.00>: <RETURN>
Text: MANHOLE COVER
```

Move text cursor by using coordinate display to pick approximate point 1'-3.00", 0'3.00" with your pointer.

```
Text: 1
Text: <RETURN>                           Ends the command.
Command: CIRCLE                          Draw a circle at 15,3 with a 1"
                                         radius.
3P/2P/TTR/<Center point>: 15,3
Diameter/<Radius>: 1

Command: LINETYPE                        Set current linetype to hidden.
?/Create/Load/Set: S                     Set.
New entity linetype (or ?) <BYLAYER>: HIDDEN
?/Create/Load/Set: <RETURN>

Command: CIRCLE                          Draw a circle at 22,17 with an 11"
                                         radius.
```

The circle has a hidden linetype, but you need to adjust the linetype scale to see it.

```
Command: LTSCALE
New scale factor <1.0000>: 4             Set linetype scale to scale factor.
```

As you can see from the exercise, it is relatively simple to adjust text height and linetype scale by using a drawing scale factor. The important thing to remember is that this drawing scale factor is *external* to AutoCAD. It is not an internal AutoCAD setting. You apply a scale factor to get your initial drawing limits, then you apply it to individual commands, like DTEXT, to adjust your text proportionately by setting your text height.

Tip: A linetype scale range of 0.3 to 0.5 times your drawing scale factor yields the best plotted output, but may not be visually distinguishable on screen. You may need to set one linetype scale when drawing and reset it for plotting.

We'll save this drawing before moving on. When we save, we'll take a closer look at using dialogue boxes, particularly the file selection dialogue box.

Using Dialogue Boxes

The efficiency of dialogue boxes can't be beat for settings where you need to view or change several items at a time, or for filenames where you need to see a list of files (not available in Release 10). We'll examine the file dialogue box — it contains all dialogue features except on/off toggles. On/off toggles are check boxes that appear next to key words of items that can only be on or off. If a check mark appears in the box, it is on; if the box is blank, it is off. You click on the box with your pointer to turn it on or off (see fig. 2.9).

Figure 2.9:
Layer 0 on, layer floorplan off.

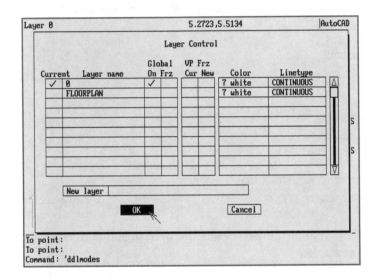

You use *input buttons* in dialogue boxes to enter text and values such as file, color, or layer names, or distances or scale factors. In the file dialogue box, the long, rectangular boxes immediately to the right of the [Directory], [Pattern], and [File] labels are input buttons. You can highlight an input button by moving your cursor over it. Then, if you start typing, what you type replaces the current value and the input button expands. An input button expands with a [Cancel] button and an [OK] button, which you use to close and cancel or accept the new value. If you want to edit the current value instead of replacing it, you can click on the input button before you start typing. However you enter the value, you can use the left and right arrow cursor keys, backspace, and delete, as well as typing new characters. The <RETURN> key and <^C> are alternatives to the [OK] and [Cancel] buttons (except in Release 10). If AutoCAD won't accept your new value, it is invalid and you'll have to edit it or cancel. If the value is too long to fit into the button, it will scroll to the left or right, using an angle bracket to indicate that it overflows (not available in Release 10). Some input buttons, such as the color buttons in the layer control dialogue box, open into other dialogue boxes, which you use to enter a new value from a list.

Note: If you accidentally press an arrow key when not in edit mode, your cursor may appear to lock up. Press the <END]> key to free it.

Some lists are too long to see in their entirety. These lists have *scroll bars* at the right for moving up and down through the list (Release 10 has up, down, page up and page down buttons instead). The file list in the file dialogue box is a typical example of a list with a scroll bar. Imagine that your file dialogue list has 50 filenames. The list displays one page full of names at a time. The elevator box, initially near the top of the scroll bar, shows you where in the list the currently displayed page is. You can move up or down a page at a time by clicking on the bar above or below the box. You can move up or down a line at a time by clicking on the boxed arrows at the top and bottom of the scroll bar. Some input buttons, such as the [File] button on the file dialogue box, are associated with scroll bar lists. You select a name from the list by clicking on it. When you do so, the associated input button's value changes.

Dialogue boxes also include *action buttons*, which execute the action indicated by their labels when you click on them. The [OK], [Cancel], [Type it] and [Default] buttons at the right of the file dialogue box are typical action buttons. Figure 2.10 shows the different types of buttons and a scroll bar.

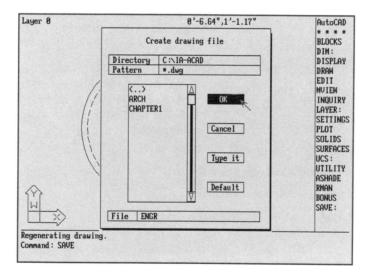

Figure 2.10:
The file dialogue box for save.

Using the File Dialogue Box

The input buttons of the file dialogue box show the current defaults for the directory, wildcard filename filter pattern and filename. These defaults reset themselves each time you enter the file dialogue box; any changes you make are not saved as defaults. When you change the directory or pattern, the file list is redisplayed. The pattern uses a wildcard convention similar to common Unix systems and offers more wildcard characters than the DOS command line does. See Chapter 13 for a complete list.

When you know exactly what filename you want, it may be quicker to type than to find and select it from a long list of names. You could click on [Type it], or you could turn the automatic file dialogue feature off. To turn it off, you set FILEDIA to 0. With the file dialogue box turned off, file commands prompt for the filename on the command line, but you can easily pop up the file dialogue box when you want to use it. To pop it up, you just enter a tilde (~) when prompted for a filename. After we save our drawing, let's turn FILEDIA off, and leave it off for the rest of the book.

Let's save the drawing and try out the file dialogue box at the same time.

Saving an Architectural Sheet With the File Dialogue Box

Command: **SAVE**   The file dialogue box appears.

(In Release 10 you just get the File name <ENGR>: prompt. Enter ENGR<RETURN> and skip to the QUIT at the end of this exercise.)

Open **[Pattern]**   Open it by clicking on the [*.dwg] box to the right.

Enter ***.***   Change the pattern filter to *.* and click on [OK]. The file list now shows your entire IA-ACAD directory.

Open **[Directory]**   Open it by clicking on the directory box to the right. Change it to your AutoCAD directory (probably \ACAD) and <RETURN> for OK. The file list now shows your entire ACAD directory.

Click on the scroll bar, under the box, to page down the list.

Click on the scroll bar, above the box, to page up the list.

Click on the down arrow box to scroll down one line.

Click on any filename. It appears in the [File] input button.

Select **[Default]**   Restores the ENGR default.
Select **[Type it]**   The dialogue box disappears and you get a filename prompt.

File name <ENGR>: **ENGR**   Type ENGR and then enter it with <RE-TURN>.

Command: **FILEDIA**
New value for FILEDIA <1>: **0**   Turns automatic file dialogue boxes off.
Command: **SAVE**   See, no file dialogue box appears.

Saving an Architectural Sheet With the File Dialogue Box—continued

File name <ENGR>: ~	Enter a tilde, and then the dialogue box appears.
Select **[Cancel]**	Cancels it.
Command: **QUIT**	Quit the drawing to start over fresh.

Now, and for the rest of the book, the file dialogue box will only appear when we call it up with a tilde.

As a quick aside related to the file dialogue box, let's look at file-naming conventions before we jump back into scaling, units, and limits.

File-Naming Conventions

As you work in AutoCAD, it helps to think ahead about how you are going to name and organize your drawing files. If you already have a naming convention, try adapting it to AutoCAD. While you can have up to 254 characters in your drawing names with some operating systems, MS-DOS is still limited to eight characters. Try to anticipate how you are going to sort your files in MS-DOS. PROJ01 and PROJ02 sort in order with PROJ??, but PROJ1 sorts after PROJ02.

As you invest time in your drawings, they become more valuable and you need to save them frequently. Use SAVE to record your work-in-progress. Adopt a temporary naming convention that lets you save as you go, PTEMP01, PTEMP02, etc. Your work isn't secure until it is saved to file on your hard disk (and copied to a backup disk or tape).

Now that we've saved the drawing, let's plot it.

Getting a Quick Printer Plot

If you have a printer configured for plotting in AutoCAD, you can do the following exercise to get a hard copy of the manhole drawing. Don't be too concerned about the sequence of the exercise. We will explain plotting in detail in the plotting chapter. The plotted drawing will show how all the calculations that you made provide a plotted drawing at 1/4-inch scale. If you don't have a printer that can do an AutoCAD printer plot but do have a plotter, you can use it instead. All of the prompts will be quite similar.

```
                    Making a Quick Printer Plot
Command: PRPLOT
What to plot — Display, Extents, Limits, View, or Window <>: L
Plot will NOT be written to a selected file
Sizes are in Inches
Plot origin is at (0.00,0.00)
Plotting area is 7.99 wide by 11.00 high (MAX size)
Plot is NOT rotated
Hidden lines will NOT be removed
Scale is 1=1.00

Do you want to change anything? <N> Y
Write the plot to a file? <N> <RETURN>
Size units (Inches or Millimeters) <I>: <RETURN>
Plot origin in Inches <0.00,0.00>: <RETURN>

Standard values for plotting size
Size    Width   Height
MAX     7.99    11.00

Enter the Size or Width,Height (in Inches)
   <MAX>: <RETURN>
Rotate plot 0/90/180/270 <0>: 90              (Respond Y to the similar
                                               Release 10 prompt.)

Remove hidden lines? <N> <RETURN>

Specify scale by entering:
Plotted Inches=Drawing Units or Fit or ? <1=1.00>: 1=4
Effective plotting area:  7.99 wide by 11.00 high
Position paper in printer.
Press RETURN to continue: <RETURN>

Processing vector: nnn                         AutoCAD cycles through
                                               whole drawing.

                                               Plotting takes place.

Printer plot complete.
Press RETURN to continue: <RETURN>

Command: QUIT                                  To start a fresh drawing.
```

You should be able to take a drafting scale to your printout and measure a 24-inch circle at 1/4 scale and 0.2-inch-high text with a 0.25 bubble. Figure 2.11 shows how your plot should look.

Setting Up Layers, Colors, and Linetypes

Next, we'll set up a new drawing using engineering units and limits for an 8 1/2" x 11" sheet with a drawing scale factor of one (full scale). We will use this setup to create a set of layers and to set colors and linetypes.

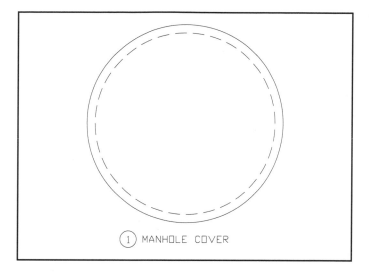

Figure 2.11:
Plotted manhole
drawing.

(1) MANHOLE COVER

Setup Drawing for Layers

Enter selection: **1**	Begin a new drawing.
Enter NAME of drawing: **CHAPTER2**	
Command: **UNITS**	Set units to engineering with 2 decimal places of accuracy and 2 fractional places for angles. Default all other settings.
Command: **LIMITS**	Set your limits for 8.5" x 11".
ON/OFF/<Lower left corner ><0'-0.00",0'-0.00">:**<RETURN>**	
Upper right corner <1'-0.00",0'-9.00">: **11,8.5**	
Command: **ZOOM**	
All/Center/Dynamic/Extents/Left/Previous/Vmax/	
Window/<Scale(X/VP)>: **A**	Zoom all.

Layers

Layers help you control your drawing and keep it organized. If your drawing becomes too dense or complicated, you can turn selected layers off. If you neglect to anticipate drawing certain parts, you can create new layers for those parts.

We have compared layers to acetate sheets. In effect, you create your drawing by building it on a family of sheets. Each sheet has a name, a default color, and a linetype. You can work on any layer. Editing commands, such as ERASE, work on any number of layers at once. But you can only *draw* on one layer at a time.

The active layer is called the *current* layer. When you draw an entity, it is attached to the current layer. Your current layer name is displayed on the status line (see fig. 2.12). In the new drawing you just started, your current layer is the default layer 0 from the prototype drawing.

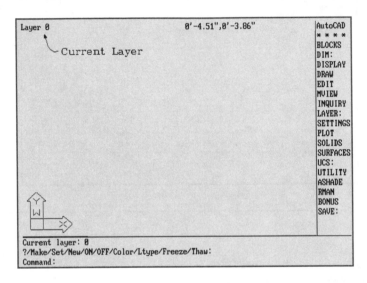

Figure 2.12:
The status line shows the current layer.

You set up and control your layers using the LAYER command or the layer control dialogue box. You use LAYER to switch from layer to layer, and to turn layer visibility on and off. You can type the LAYER command or select [LAYER:] from the root screen menu.

You can see the properties associated with your layers by having AutoCAD display the layer status with the LAYER command or with the dialogue box. Using the LAYER command, you respond to the first prompt by typing a question mark. The <*> in the default layer name prompt is a *wildcard*, meaning "Tell me about every layer." You can also use question marks or any of the other wildcard pattern matches that AutoCAD supports to select groups of layers. Let's try it.

Displaying Layer Information

Command: **LAYER**   Type or pick from screen menu.
?/Make/Set/New/ON/OFF/Color/Ltype/Freeze/Thaw: **?**
Layer name(s) for listing <*>: **<RETURN>**

AutoCAD responds by flipping to the text screen and displays:

Layer name	State	Color	Linetype
0	On	7 (white)	CONTINUOUS

Current layer: 0
?/Make/Set/New/ON/OFF/Color/Ltype/Freeze/Thaw:

As you might have anticipated, you have AutoCAD's default drawing properties: layer 0 with white, continuous lines. Layer 0 is fine for playing around and has some special properties that you will see later, but for most drawing work, you will want to set up your own layers.

Layering Conventions

Well, how do you go about setting up layers? Like setting other drawing effects, setting up layers is a matter of standard practice and style. The most common-sense approach to layers is to use them to separate different types of objects in your drawing. For example, put drawing components on one layer and their dimensions on another. Try to anticipate the number of types that you want to separate. Here is an example set:

Objects on Layer	Layer Names
Components	OBJ01
Dimensions	DIM01
Symbols & Annotations	ANN01
Text	TXT01
Title Sheets	REF01

You can create an unlimited number of layers, but for most applications, 10 to 20 layers is more than enough. When you name your layers, it helps to apply DOS-type naming conventions and use *wildcards* to organize them. Layer names can be up to 31 characters long. However, the status line will only show the first eight characters of the layer name. You can use letters, digits, dollar signs ($), hyphens (-), and underscore (_) characters. AutoCAD converts all layer names to upper case.

There are many different layer-naming schemes in use. Some code the color, linetype, and line weight. Others specify the trade and work location, like ARCH-FLR01 or ELEC-CLG03. One popular convention codes layers with the CSI material code. Whatever scheme you use, there are three important considerations. First, coordinate with those with whom you may be trading drawings, such as consultants and subcontractors. Second, whatever types of information you code in your names, always put the same type of information in the same column (character position) so you can select groups of layers by wildcard. For example, ARCH-FLR01 and ARCH-FLR03 allows you to select all floor plan layers with ????-FLR?? or all architectural layers with ARCH*. But if you name the second floor A-2NDFLR, you can't select it with the same wildcards. Third, make the scheme extensible — capable of growth. Even if you're drawing a three-story building, use two characters for floor numbers so the naming scheme will be compatible with the 33-story building you do next year.

Using the LAYER Command

Think about what having separate layers means operationally. You need a way to let AutoCAD know which layer you want to draw on. The LAYER command lets you tell AutoCAD which layers you want to set current and which layers you want to turn on. Then AutoCAD prompts you for the name(s) of the layers you want this property applied to. You can only operate on one property at a time, but you can apply one property to several layers in one pass with wildcards, or by naming several layers on one line.

The LAYER command sets the following properties:

LAYER Properties

ON   Makes the layer visible.

OFF   Makes the layer invisible.

Color   Defines a single default color so that anything drawn directly on that layer will take on the color unless specifically overridden with an entity color.

Ltype   Defines a single default linetype. Lines (and other drawing elements) drawn on a layer will take on the linetype unless you specifically override it.

Freeze Makes the layer invisible and all entities are ignored during a regeneration, increasing the performance of AutoCAD searches and screen displays.

Thaw   Unfreezes layers.

The LAYER command also offers these options:

LAYER Options

?   Lists all the layers in your current drawing including their status and default properties.

Make   Creates a new layer and sets it current.

Set   Makes the layer current or active for drawing.

New   Creates a new layer, but doesn't make it current.

Creating New Layers

AutoCAD provides two options for creating layers. The Make option creates one layer and automatically sets it as the current layer. If you want to make more than one layer, use the New option, and then use Set to specify the current layer.

Right now, there is only one layer in the drawing file. We'll put in several more, set them up, and then save them for future use. The target layers are shown in the following table.

Table 2.1
Layer Configuration Table

Layer Name	State	Color	Linetype
0	On	7 (white)	CONTINUOUS
CIRCLE	On	3 (green)	CONTINUOUS
PARAGRAM	On	5 (blue)	CONTINUOUS
SQUARE	On	2 (yellow)	CONTINUOUS
TEXT	On	4 (cyan)	CONTINUOUS
TRIANGLE	On	1 (red)	CONTINUOUS
Current layer: 0			

The following exercise shows how to create the new layers with the LAYER command.

Creating New Layers

Continue with the LAYER command.

?/Make/Set/New/ON/OFF/Color/Ltype/Freeze/Thaw: **N**   Type NEW or
                                                                        just N.

New layer name(s): **TRIANGLE, SQUARE, CIRCLE, TEXT, PARAGRAM**

?/Make/Set/New/ON/OFF/Color/Ltype/Freeze/Thaw: **?**   Displays layer
                                                                        information.
Layer name(s) for listing <*>: **<RETURN>**   See the list.

Your text screen should look like figure 2.13. Notice that AutoCAD presents the layers in alphabetic order (except in Release 10).

You can enter as many names as you want on the New layer name(s): line. Separate layer names with commas because a space or <RETURN> ends your input. If you input a space, AutoCAD thinks you are trying to end the input line just like a <RETURN>.

Take a look at the layers information. Since you didn't set any properties for the new layers, AutoCAD automatically set them with the same defaults as layer 0. Each layer is color 7 (white) with a continuous linetype. Next we'll change the layers to the desired properties, starting with color.

```
----------------- --------- ------------- ------------
0                       On          7 (white)    CONTINUOUS

Current layer: 0

?/Make/Set/New/ON/OFF/Color/Ltype/Freeze/Thaw: N

New layer name(s): TRIANGLE,SQUARE,CIRCLE,TEXT,PARAGRAM
?/Make/Set/New/ON/OFF/Color/Ltype/Freeze/Thaw: ?

Layer name(s) to list <*>:

     Layer name        State       Color        Linetype
----------------- --------- ------------- ------------
0                       On          7 (white)    CONTINUOUS
CIRCLE                  On          7 (white)    CONTINUOUS
PARAGRAM                On          7 (white)    CONTINUOUS
SQUARE                  On          7 (white)    CONTINUOUS
TEXT                    On          7 (white)    CONTINUOUS

TRIANGLE                On          7 (white)    CONTINUOUS

Current layer: 0

?/Make/Set/New/ON/OFF/Color/Ltype/Freeze/Thaw:
```

Setting Layer Color

A layer has only one color, but several layers can have the same color. Color is assigned to layers by names or numbers (up to 255 different colors — limited by your hardware, not AutoCAD). Colors are commonly used to assign plotting line weights to objects in the drawing. AutoCAD uses the following naming and numbering conventions for seven standard colors:

AutoCAD's Seven Standard Colors

1 - Red	5 - Blue
2 - Yellow	6 - Magenta
3 - Green	7 - White
4 - Cyan	

Note: Colors above number seven do not have names and their availability varies depending on your video card and display. You can see them by loading the CHROMA or COLORWH drawings, on the AutoCAD SAMPLE disk and probably in your SAMPLE subdirectory. CHROMA can also be seen by viewing the slide named ACAD(CHROMA) and COLORWH can be seen by viewing the slide named COLORWH. The VSLIDE command is explained later in the book. Be cautious in your use of colors above number 15 because they all plot the same as color 15. These colors are primarily intended for 3D work.

When you assign a color to a layer, you can use a color number or a color name for the standard seven colors. Actually, you need only the first character of the name, like R for Red. Each color requires a separate execution of the color subcommand, but you can make several layers the same color by entering more than one layer name on the prompt line. AutoCAD prompts you with the current layer name as a default. Assigning a color automatically turns the specified layers on, but assigning a negative color, like -7, turns them off.

Setting Layer Color

```
Continue with the LAYER command.
?/Make/Set/New/ON/OFF/Color/Ltype/Freeze/Thaw: C
Color: 1
Layer name(s) for color 1 (red) <0>: TRIANGLE
?/Make/Set/New/ON/OFF/Color/Ltype/Freeze/Thaw: C
Color: YELLOW                                            Or just type Y.
Layer name(s) for color 2 (yellow) <0>: SQUARE
?/Make/Set/New/ON/OFF/Color/Ltype/Freeze/Thaw: C
Color: 3
Layer name(s) for color 3 (green) <0>: CIRCLE
?/Make/Set/New/ON/OFF/Color/Ltype/Freeze/Thaw: C
Color: C                                                Or type CYAN.
Layer name(s) for color 4 (cyan) <0>: TEXT
?/Make/Set/New/ON/OFF/Color/Ltype/Freeze/Thaw: C
Color: 5
Layer name(s) for color 5 (blue) <0>: P*                Abbreviate. It's the only
                                                        name starting with P.
?/Make/Set/New/ON/OFF/Color/Ltype/Freeze/Thaw: ?       Check the colors.
Layer name(s) for listing <*>: <RETURN>                 See previous Layer Con-
                                                        figuration Table.
```

Setting Layer Linetype

The LTYPE subcommand sets your layer linetype. CONTINUOUS is always offered as a default. When you specify a non-continuous linetype, AutoCAD first looks in its linetype library (the ACAD.LIN file) to see if it has a linetype definition that matches your request (see fig. 2.14). If it finds your linetype, everything is okay. If not, you have to select another.

In addition, each of the linetypes shown above has corresponding double scale and half scale linetypes, such as DASHED2 for a half scale dashed line and DASHEDX2 for a double scale dashed line. The half scale linetypes all end in 2 and the double scale ones end in X2.

Set the layer linetypes shown in the previous Layer Configuration Table.

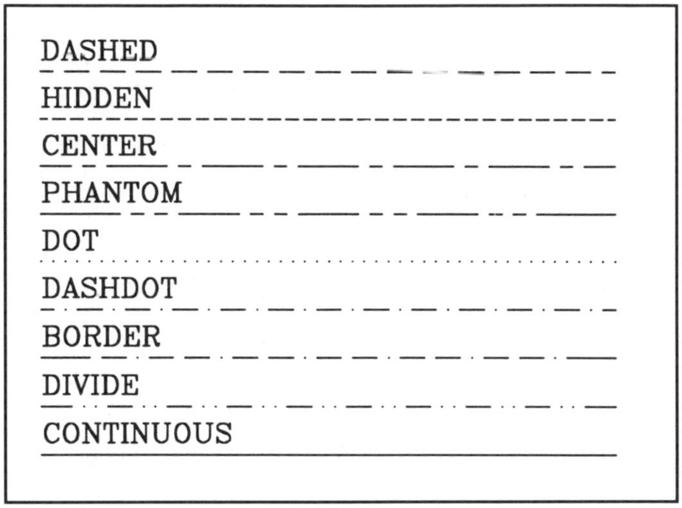

Figure 2.14:
Standard AutoCAD
linetypes.

DASHED

HIDDEN

CENTER

PHANTOM

DOT

DASHDOT

BORDER

DIVIDE

CONTINUOUS

Setting Layer Linetype

```
Continue with the LAYER command.
?/Make/Set/New/ON/OFF/Color/Ltype/Freeze/Thaw: L
Linetype (or ?) <CONTINUOUS>: DASHED
Layer name(s) for linetype DASHED <0>: CIRCLE
?/Make/Set/New/ON/OFF/Color/Ltype/Freeze/Thaw: L
Linetype (or ?) <CONTINUOUS>: HIDDEN
Layer name(s) for linetype DASHED <0>: PARAGRAM
?/Make/Set/New/ON/OFF/Color/Ltype/Freeze/Thaw:
```

Tip: You can create your own custom linetypes with the LINETYPE command — see Chapter 11 for details.

You now have a complete set of layers. You can modify their other properties by indicating the layers that you want to modify.

Next we'll look at setting the current layer and modifying layer visibility.

Setting the Current Layer

You can only draw on the current layer. Use the Set option to tell AutoCAD which layer you want as the current layer. The Set subcommand will show the current layer name as the default in the prompt. If you want to leave the current layer alone, just press <RETURN>. Setting a new current layer automatically makes the *old* current layer inactive.

Make the SQUARE layer the current layer.

Setting the Current Layer

Continue with the LAYER command.
```
?/Make/Set/New/ON/OFF/Color/Ltype/Freeze/Thaw: S
New current layer: SQUARE
?/Make/Set/New/ON/OFF/Color/Ltype/Freeze/Thaw: <RETURN>
Regenerating drawing.
```
The changes take effect.

Look at the layer name on the screen status line (see fig. 2.15) to see that SQUARE is the current layer.

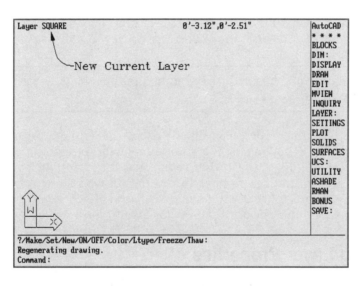

Figure 2.15:
The status line shows the new current layer.

You can change layer settings at any time while you are in the drawing. If you alter the properties of layers on the screen (like linetype or color), AutoCAD regenerates the screen image to reflect these changes when you exit the LAYER command.

Making Layers Invisible

Try turning a layer on and off. Both work the same way. If you turn the current layer off, AutoCAD will ask if you are sure you want to. Remember you have to see what you are drawing!

Draw a square with lines, then turn the SQUARE layer off, then on again.

Setting Layer Visibility

Command: **LINE**   Draw a square
                                                                                  with lines.

Command: **LAYER**
?/Make/Set/New/ON/OFF/Color/Ltype/Freeze/Thaw: **OFF**
Layer name(s) to turn Off: **SQUARE**
Really want layer SQUARE (the CURRENT layer) off? <N> **Y**
?/Make/Set/New/ON/OFF/Color/Ltype/Freeze/Thaw: **<RETURN>**   It disappears.
Command: **<RETURN>**   Repeats the
                                                                        command.
LAYER ?/Make/Set/New/ON/OFF/Color/Ltype/Freeze/Thaw: **ON**
Layer name(s) to turn On: **SQUARE**
?/Make/Set/New/ON/OFF/Color/Ltype/Freeze/Thaw: **<RETURN>**

Remember you can use a wildcard (* or ?) to turn collections of layer names on or off. However, you can't use wildcards with the Make, Set, or New options.

> *Tip:* If you are drawing but you can't see anything happening, check to see if you've turned the current layer off.

Freezing also turns a layer off. When a layer is frozen, the entities on it do not display, regenerate, or print. This means that your screen will refresh more quickly after you invoke a command (like ZOOM) that requires a regeneration. The disadvantage to freezing layers is that layers have to regenerate when you thaw them. Thawing takes a little longer to do, so use it instead of off and on when you know you won't need to display, regenerate, or print a layer (or layers) for a while.

Testing Drawing Layer Properties

During the last few minutes, you have created a working drawing file with real units, limits, and a foundation of layers. It would be nice to know that all these layers really work. You just saw the yellow square on layer SQUARE. Set your CIRCLE layer current, and draw a circle to see how entities adopt other layer settings. After you have drawn the circle, your screen should look like figure 2.16.

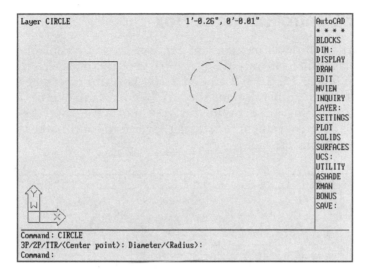

Figure 2.16:
Square on SQUARE
and circle on CIRCLE
layer.

Testing Your Drawing Layers

```
Command: LAYER                                              Set layer CIRCLE current.
?/Make/Set/New/ON/OFF/Color/Ltype/Freeze/Thaw: S
New current layer <SQUARE>: CIRCLE
?/Make/Set/New/ON/OFF/Color/Ltype/Freeze/Thaw: <RETURN>

Command: CIRCLE
3P/2P/TTR/<Center point>:                                  Pick a point centered in
                                                           the upper right quarter of
                                                           the screen.
Diameter/<Radius>:                                         Drag a radius of about 1
                                                           inch and pick a point.
```

You should have a yellow square and green dashed circle. Save your drawing by naming it to a new file called WORK. You will use this drawing as the prototype drawing in the next chapter on drawing accuracy.

Saving the WORK Drawing

```
Command: SAVE
File name <CHAPTER2>: WORK                                  Save with new name, WORK,
                                                           for use in Chapter 3.
```

Now that you have put WORK safely to rest, you can experiment a little further with creating and modifying layers with a dialogue box.

Using the Layer Control Dialogue Box

If your display supports pull-down menus, you can use the layer control dialogue box (called the modify layer dialogue box in Release 10) to do all the layer setups that we have just done (see figs. 2.17, 2.18, 2.19 and 2.20). You can create new layers, rename layers, and use all the other options the LAYER command offers. Using the dialogue box offers the advantage of seeing all the layer information and the settings as they are made. This is a convenient way to set layer data and makes it much easier to keep track of your layers.

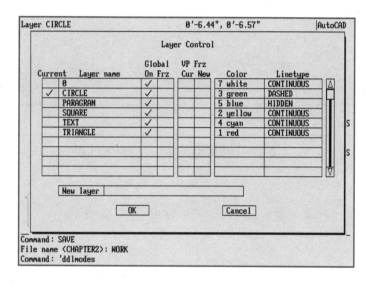

Figure 2.17:
Dialogue box showing current settings.

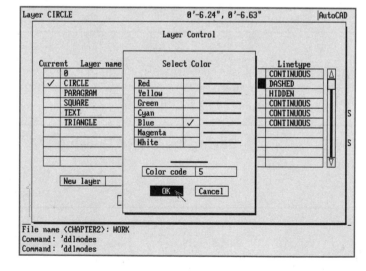

Figure 2.18:
Color dialogue box showing current settings.

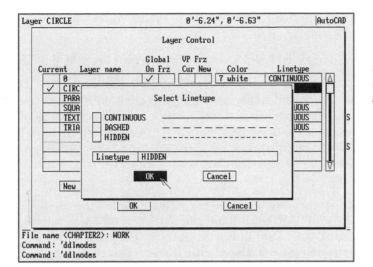

Figure 2.19:
Linetype dialogue box.

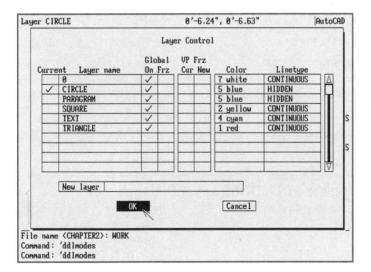

Figure 2.20:
Dialogue box showing new settings.

The layer control dialogue box is found with the [Layer Control...] item on the [Settings] pull-down menu or by typing the DDLMODES command at the command line. DDLMODES is a *transparent* command, meaning you can use it when you are in the middle of most other commands by prefacing it with a single quote: 'DDLMODES.

Each row in the layer control dialogue box controls the settings for one layer. There are three groups of settings. In the first group (the block at the left), you control the current layer, on/off visibility, and freeze/thaw regeneration. To set a new current layer, just click next to its name in the Current column. Only one layer can be current, indicated by the check mark. Click in the On or Frz columns to toggle a layer between on/off or freeze/thaw. Any number of layers can be on or frozen at one time, with a check mark indicating on or frozen.

In Release 11, the second (middle) block controls the current layer and default layer creation in individual viewports. Viewports are a topic of Chapter 4.

The third block controls color and linetype. When you click on a layer's row in the Color or Linetype column, it brings up a select color or select linetype dialogue box, illustrated above. To set colors or linetypes, you click in the column next to the color or linetype name, or you can open the color code or linetype input button. You must use the input button for colors above number seven. Input buttons were described earlier in this chapter.

Only currently loaded linetypes are displayed. You have to use the LINETYPE command or LAYER command to load additional linetypes. If there are more linetypes than can be displayed at once, a scroll bar appears at the right side of the select linetype dialogue box. (In Release 10, use the up/down buttons.)

There is also a permanent scroll bar at the right side of the layer control dialogue box, because most real drawings will have more layers than can be displayed at one time.

Each of the layer names is an input button, which you can use to change its layer name. But, don't try to create a new layer with a blank input button — it may seem to work, but it won't. You have to use the new layer input button to create new layers.

Use the following exercise to practice changing color and linetype for the TRIANGLE layer.

Using the DDLMODES Layer Dialogue Box

Pull down [Settings] Select [Layer Control...]	The dialogue box is displayed.
Select [3 green]	The color dialogue box opens.
Select [Blue]	Change color to blue.
Select [OK]	Or <RETURN> to close the color dialogue box.
Select [DASHED]	The linetype dialogue box opens.
Select [HIDDEN]	Change linetype to hidden.
Select [OK]	Close the linetype dialogue box.

The dialogue box shows the changes to the CIRCLE layer.

Select [OK]	Or <RETURN> to regenerate with the changes.

The circle is now blue and hidden (smaller dashes).

Command: U	Undoes the changes.

If you can modify a layer so easily, it will come as no surprise that you can individually modify the color and linetype properties associated with any drawing entity.

Setting Color and Linetype by Entity

You've seen how to control an entity's color or linetype by drawing it on an appropriate layer. You also can set color and linetype explicitly by *overriding* the layer's defaults and setting an entity's color and linetype with separate commands.

How an Entity Gets its Color

The COLOR command is in charge of making sure an entity gets the color you want. Entities set to specific colors (instead of BYLAYER), by the COLOR command, are referred to as having *explicit* colors. Explicit colors are not affected by the layer the entity is on or by changes to the layer. When a new entity is created, AutoCAD checks the current setting of COLOR, and assigns that color to the new entity. Existing entities are not affected by the COLOR command, only entities created after the color is set.

You can set color to any valid color name or number. (Remember you can have 1 to 255 colors, but only the first seven have names.) Setting color by layer is AutoCAD's default condition. When color is set to BYLAYER, AutoCAD doesn't store new entities with a specific color. Instead, it gives new entities the color property by layer, which causes entities to adopt the color of whatever layer the entity is on.

> *Tip:* There is also a BYBLOCK color. We will cover BYBLOCK assignments when we get to the blocks chapter.

Take a look at the color setting right now. Change the color to red using the COLOR command. You will see that the default color is set to BYLAYER. After you change the color, draw another circle to see how the explicit color settings override the layer setting.

Using the COLOR Command

Select **[SETTINGS] [COLOR:]**	Or just type COLOR.
Command: COLOR	
New entity color <BYLAYER>: **RED**	New entities will be red.
Command: **CIRCLE**	Draw a circle below the first circle.

Your drawing should show a red dashed circle in addition to your green dashed circle and yellow square (see fig 2.21).

Figure 2.21:
Second circle is color red.

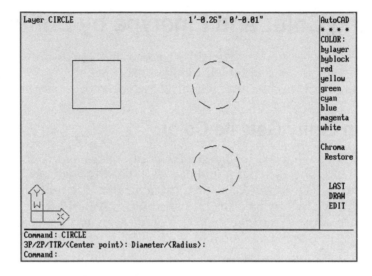

```
Layer CIRCLE                    1'-0.26", 0'-0.01"         AutoCAD
                                                          * * * *
                                                          COLOR:
                                                          bylayer
                                                          byblock
                                                          red
                                                          yellow
                                                          green
                                                          cyan
                                                          blue
                                                          magenta
                                                          white

                                                          Chroma
                                                          Restore


                                                          LAST
                                                          DRAW
                                                          EDIT

Command: CIRCLE
3P/2P/TTR/<Center point>: Diameter/<Radius>:
Command:
```

How an Entity Gets its Linetype

After this colorful discussion, you might have guessed that linetype settings have a similar control. Take a look at the LINETYPE command. The Set option lets you set an explicit linetype that overrides the layer's default for all entities that you create after you change the setting. Linetype can also be set to BYLAYER to use the layer's default.

LINETYPE Options

?   Displays a listing of all the linetypes currently defined in the drawing.

Create Allows user to create a linetype.

Load   Loads linetype from a user-specified file. The default ACAD.LIN file has 27 linetype definitions.

Set   Sets the linetype to be used for all new entities until reset.

Using the LINETYPE Command

```
Command: LINETYPE
?/Create/Load/Set: S
New entity linetype (or ?) <BYLAYER>: CONTINUOUS
?/Create/Load/Set: <RETURN>
Command: CIRCLE                                    Draw another circle.
```

You should have three circles. The last one is drawn with a red continuous line, even though it is on the CIRCLE layer which is set to green and dashed (see fig. 2.22).

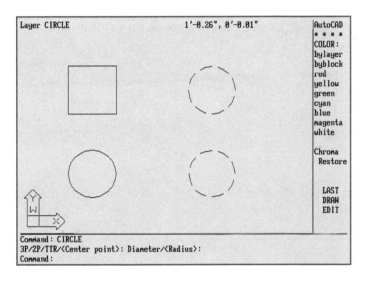

Figure 2.22:
Third circle is red and continuous.

Tip: Explicit color and linetype settings stay in effect even when you change current layers. We do not generally recommend mixing explicit color and linetype settings with layer settings — it can get too confusing. Try to stick with one system of control or the other, with few exceptions.

Changing Entity Properties

The COLOR and LINETYPE commands only change the properties for new entities drawn *after* you change the color and linetype settings. However, you can change the properties of existing entities by using the CHPROP (CHange PROPerties) command. After you select the objects to change, AutoCAD prompts you for the properties to modify. You can change the following properties with CHPROP:

- Color
- Layer
- Linetype
- Thickness

Thickness is a property associated with 3D — more about that in a later chapter.

Try changing a circle using CHPROP.

Using CHPROP to Change Layers and Color

```
Command: CHPROP                               Select or type.
Select objects:                               Select the green (first) circle.
1 selected, 1 found.
Select objects: <RETURN>
Change what property (Color/LAyer/LType/
   Thickness) ? LA
New layer <CIRCLE>: SQUARE                    Circle has layer SQUARE prop-
                                              erties.

Change what property (Color/LAyer/LType/
   Thickness) ? C
New color <BYLAYER>: 1                         1 is the color number for red.
Change what property (Color/LAyer/LType/
   Thickness) ? <RETURN>                      Circle turns red.
```

Obviously, you can't always determine how an entity will be created by looking at the layer name on the status line. You need a way to check the current settings. You have two ways: the entity creation modes dialogue box and the STATUS command.

Controlling Properties With the DDEMODES Dialogue Box

The entity creation modes dialogue box, accessed by [Entity Creation...] on the [Options] pull-down menu or the DDEMODES command, can be used to view or change the current color, layer name, linetype, text style, elevation, or thickness (see fig. 2.23). (In Release 10, it's [Entity Creation...] from the [Settings] pull-down menu.) It can be used transparently during most commands, like 'DDEMODES. Each of the modes has its own input button.

We will use this dialogue box later in the book when we begin working with blocks and drawing symbols.

For a more complete listing of everything you wanted to know about your drawing but were afraid to ask, try the STATUS command.

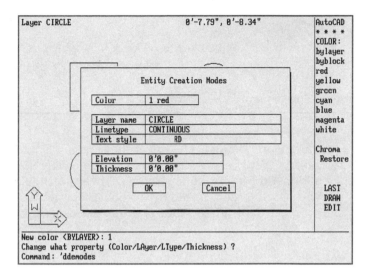

Figure 2.23:
Entity creation modes dialogue box.

Using the STATUS Command

You can check your current entity properties defaults with the STATUS command, but it can't change them. The STATUS command flips to the text screen. Try it now; type STATUS in response to the command prompt. Your screen should look like figure 2.24.

```
11 entities in CHAPTER2
Model space limits are X:  0'-0.00"   Y:  0'-0.00"  (Off)
                        X:  0'-11.00"  Y:  0'-8.50"
Model space uses        X:  0'-2.00"   Y:  0'-1.52"
                        X:  0'-8.98"   Y:  0'-7.00"
Display shows           X:  0'-0.00"   Y:  0'-0.00"
                        X:  1'-0.27"   Y:  0'-8.50"
Insertion base is       X:  0'-0.00"   Y:  0'-0.00"   Z:  0'-0.00"
Snap resolution is      X:  0'-1.00"   Y:  0'-1.00"
Grid spacing is         X:  0'-0.00"   Y:  0'-0.00"

Current space:      Model space
Current layer:      CIRCLE
Current color:      1 (red)
Current linetype:   CONTINUOUS
Current elevation:  0'-0.00"  thickness:  0'-0.00"
Axis off  Fill on  Grid off  Ortho off  Qtext off  Snap off  Tablet off
Object snap modes:  None

Free disk: 14403584 bytes
-- Press RETURN for more --
```

Figure 2.24:
Status screen display.

Using STATUS to Get a Drawing Status Report

Command: **STATUS**   Flips to text mode and shows a
                                                 screen full of information.

− Press RETURN for more −

Press the <RETURN> key, then hit the Flip Screen key to get back to graphics.

Command: **QUIT**   After examining the screen,
                                                 quit.

Exit AutoCAD with a 0 from the main menu.

The status report shows your drawing limits at the top of the screen. About halfway down, it lists the current layer, current color, and current linetype. The status text screen carries additional information about your settings. These settings will become more important to you as you read through the book. For now, just feel comfortable knowing that you can look at the information and that AutoCAD is keeping track of all that stuff for you.

If entity properties seem a bit confusing, don't worry — just start with simple controls. Use layers with the default BYLAYER setting to control your drawing color and linetype. Wait until you start editing complex drawings, then use COLOR, LINETYPE, and CHPROP sparingly for exceptions where you need more flexibility.

Summing Up

What you've seen so far is typical of AutoCAD setup commands. AutoCAD begins new drawings by reading many default settings from a prototype drawing named ACAD.DWG. Setting up a drawing file requires setting up units, limits, and a working set of layers as a good foundation for future drawing. AutoCAD tries to save you time by offering defaults and wildcard options in place of elaborate keyboard entry during your setup.

There are several keys to establishing a good drawing setup. Use drawing scale factor to set your drawing limits for your electronic sheet size. You also can use AutoCAD's automatic setup routines to select your final sheet size and to set your limits. You can scale text, linetype, and symbols using your drawing scale factor.

Organize your layers for different object types. Adopt a layer-naming convention that lets you organize your names with wildcards. The current layer is the active drawing layer. The status line always shows the current layer. Default drawing properties for color and linetype are set BYLAYER. You can explicitly override BYLAYER color and linetype with the COLOR and LINETYPE commands. You can also change properties associated with existing entities by using the CHPROP command. If you are uncertain about what properties are current in your drawing, use the entity creation modes dialogue box or STATUS command to help you keep track.

Setting up is well and good, but we're getting anxious to try out some drawing basics.

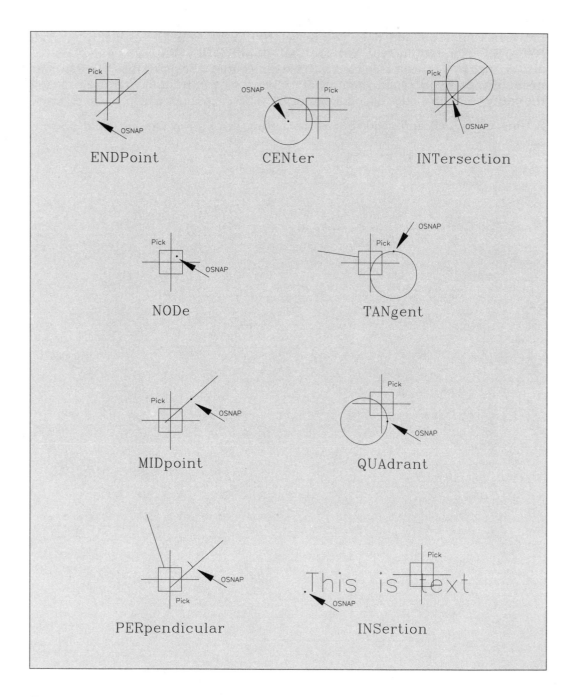

Figure 3.1:
OSNAP targets and the points they pick.

3

Drawing Accurately

COORDINATE ENTRY AND CONTROL

Given a straight edge and a rule, a draftsperson can locate a point on a drawing sheet with some degree of accuracy and use that point as a location for drawing more objects. In this chapter, you will learn how AutoCAD's electronic tools replace the draftsperson's manual tools for locating points and maintaining drawing accuracy.

Some benefits from using AutoCAD's tools stand out immediately: no eraser shavings, always having the right scale ruler, never having to borrow your 30-60 triangle back from your neighbor. Other benefits, however, are not as apparent: 100 percent accurate straight edges and triangles, precise mathematically defined curves, and electronically flexible graph paper to trace over as a guide.

Electronic Drawing Aids

The first step in getting accurate drawings is to locate your drawing points. How do you locate your drawing points accurately? One way is to type your coordinates in. You might know some of the coordinate values to start a drawing. However, you rarely have such complete information that you can type in all your drawing points. Besides, this would be grueling, tedious work and prone to typing errors.

Most of the time you *pick* your drawing points. As you saw in the last chapter, it's hard to pick accurately without some kind of help. AutoCAD gives you two ways to control the movement of your pointer so you can select accurate pick points. The first method is to use the *grid* and *snap* functions, and the second is to use the *object snap* functions, commonly called osnap (see fig. 3.1).

How Grid and Snap Work

If you pick your drawing points without some form of control, AutoCAD must approximate the coordinates of your pointer location. These are generally numbers like 2.3754,4.6835. Even if you visually align the crosshairs with the grid or other objects, you can seldom accurately locate the point that you want. Grid acts as a visible template on your screen showing you where a set of points are located, but it does not round the input points to accurate locations. Snap acts as an invisible grid template that controls the points that you can select with your pointer. If you set snap to 0.5, then you can only select points that fall on 0.5 increments.

You control your pick points by coordinating your grid and snap. If you set them equally, then you can only select grid points. If you set your snap increments to half your grid increments, then you can only select grid points or points halfway between grid points. You control the accuracy of your point selection with snap and visually keep track of where you are snapping with your grid.

Object Snap Points

As your drawing becomes more complex, not all drawing points are going to fall on grid and snap points. Points on arcs, circles and intersections of angled lines are obvious examples. AutoCAD offers osnap (Object SNAP) as a means to control pick points on objects. Osnap is sometimes called geometric snap. It helps to think of drawing objects as having *attachment* points. Lines have mid and endpoints; circles have center, quadrant, and tangent points. When you draw, you often *attach* lines to these points.

AutoCAD's osnaps are geometric filters that let you select your drawing attachment points. For example, if you want to draw to an intersection of two lines, you set the osnap to filter for intersections, and pick a point close to the intersection. The point will snap to the intersection of the lines, not something close to the intersection, but *the* intersection! While it takes a little time to get used to setting osnaps, they are the best way to maintain geometrically accurate drawings.

Tools for Making Accurate Drawings

You will find the GRID, AXIS, SNAP, and OSNAP commands on the [SETTINGS] screen menu. The current settings of these commands can be toggled on and off with function and control keys. The [Settings] pull-down menu also contains toggles for snap and grid, and the [Assist] pull-down menu includes the OSNAP command and all of its options (see fig. 3.2). Snap, grid, and axis can also be controlled with the DDRMODES (DRawMODES) command and its drawing tools dialogue box on the [Settings] pull-down menu (see fig. 3.3). DDRMODES is a transparent command, so you can make these settings in the middle of other commands.

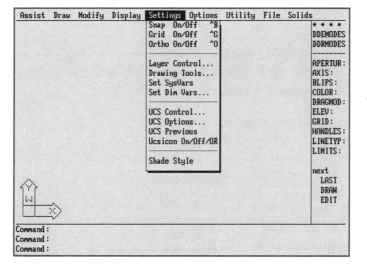

Figure 3.2:
Settings screen and
pull-down menus.

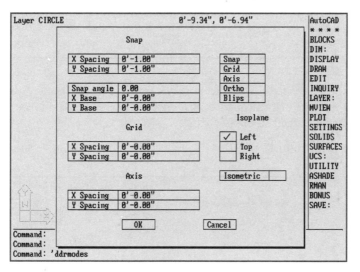

Figure 3.3:
DDRMODES drawing
tools dialogue box.

Using Drawing Aids

We are going to use the WORK drawing we saved in Chapter 2 to help us learn how to use AutoCAD's drawing aids. Use your IA.BAT file to get back into the AutoCAD drawing editor. If you are using the IA DISK, you'll use a technique of starting a new drawing equal to one of the drawings from the disk. This is similar to the equal sign you used to create a new prototype drawing in Chapter 1 with AutoCAD's original defaults, except this time your new drawing will use the defaults from another drawing. AutoCAD will essentially begin with a copy of the other drawing and give it the new name you specify. As you make your way through the drawing exercises, you can select from the screen or pull-down menu items, or type the commands as you need them.

Reloading the WORK Drawing File

 Begin a NEW drawing named WORK=IA6WORK.

 Use the WORK drawing from Chapter 2.

Load AutoCAD with your IA.BAT batch file to get the main menu.

Enter selection: **2**	Edit an EXISTING drawing.
Enter name of drawing: **WORK**	
Command: **ERASE**	Clean up any stray entities, like the four lines of the square.
Select objects:	Click on each entity to select, leaving only the green circle at upper right.
Select objects: **<RETURN>**	
Command: **LAYER**	Use the ? option to verify that your drawing settings are the same as those shown in the table below.

Your screen should look like figure 3.4, showing a single circle in the upper right of your graphics drawing area. Verify that your drawing settings are the same as those shown in table 3.1. Your current layer is CIRCLE.

Let's start by drawing a few points on the CIRCLE layer.

Figure 3.4:
WORK drawing.

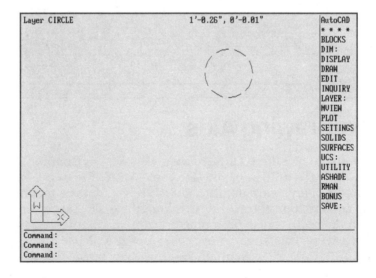

Table 3.1
WORK Drawing Settings

UNITS Engineering, 2 decimal places, 2 fractional places for angles, defaults all other settings.

LIMITS 0,0 to 11,8.5

Layer Name	State	Color	Linetype
0	On	7 (white)	CONTINUOUS
CIRCLE	On/Current	3 (green)	DASHED
PARAGRAM	On	5 (blue)	HIDDEN
SQUARE	On	2 (yellow)	CONTINUOUS
TEXT	On	4 (cyan)	CONTINUOUS
TRIANGLE	On	1 (red)	CONTINUOUS

Controlling Drawing Points

The POINT command is the simplest drawing command that inputs a drawing point. Try it with the coordinate values shown below. To see the actual point entity, you need to redraw your screen after you enter the point.

Using the POINT Command

Select: [DRAW] [next] [POINT:]   Or type POINT to make the point.
Command: POINT Point: **3,6.25**   In the upper left quarter of your screen.
                                     A small blip appears at that point.
Command: **REDRAW**   Leaves only a dot.

First, a mark appeared on your screen at the coordinate values you input. This mark was actually larger than the point that you placed. It was the construction marker (blip) for the point. Your redraw cleared the construction marker and left a small green dot on the screen. (It may be hard to see if your screen has a white background.) This is a true drawing point you can osnap to. You can be certain of its location because you input the *absolute* coordinate values. Absolute coordinates are explicitly entered coordinates.

How Accurate Are Pick Points?

When you pick a point on the screen with your pointer, it is much more difficult to get accurate points. To help track your pointer, turn on your coords by pressing the <F6> key or <^D>. Take a look at the status line and see what the digital readout of your coordinates says. Move your pointer around; the status line should display the current X,Y location of your crosshairs. Figure 3.5 shows where the coordinate readout is displayed.

Figure 3.5:
Coordinate readout.

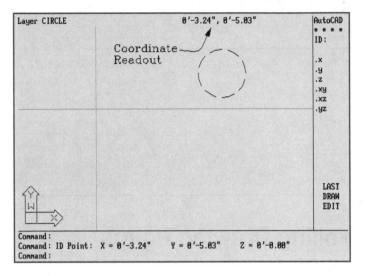

Now, try the following exercise to see how accurately you can pick your drawing points. To test your pick point, use an inquiry display command called ID. Select [ID:] from the [INQUIRY] screen menu or type it in. Then *try* to pick the point given in the exercise.

Using ID to Test Pick Points

Make sure your coords are toggled on with <^D> or <F6>.

Select: **[INQUIRY] [ID:]**	Use coordinate readout to position your crosshairs.
ID Point:	Try picking a point at exactly 0'-3.25",0'-5.00".
X = 0'-3.24" Y = 0'-5.03" Z = 0'-0.00"	Your pick points may be different.

The ID command shows the X, Y, and Z position of your pick point. Try a few more points. You will quickly find it's nearly impossible to pick the point you want accurately. Without some form of controlling your picks, a drawing can quickly turn into a sea of inaccurate points.

Note: Even if ID and the coordinates display claimed the point was exactly at 3.25,5.00, if you changed your units to six or eight decimal places, you would find that it was really rounding off an inaccurate point.

Grid and Axis Displays

The first step to getting accurate points is to set up templates that help you see points on the screen. AutoCAD has two such templates: the grid and the axis display. Both grid and axis can be set and toggled on/off with the DDRMODES drawing tools dialogue box. The most useful of these two tools is the grid.

Setting Up a Grid

A grid is a frame of reference, a series of construction points that appear on the screen but are not part of the drawing file itself. You set up a grid with the GRID command. Set up a one-inch grid, then prove to yourself that grid points do not actually control input points by moving your crosshairs around and trying to pick one with ID.

Using GRID to Set Up a Grid

Select: **[SETTINGS] [GRID:]**	Or type GRID.
GRID Grid spacing(X) or ON/OFF/Snap/Aspect <0'-0.00">: **1**	(see fig. 3.6).
Command: **ID**	
Point:	Try to pick 7.00,6.00.
X = 0'-6.99" Y = 0'-5.99" Z = 0'-0.00"	Still not precise.

Grid is just a visual aid. It doesn't affect point entry or the movement of the pointer. When you set your grid spacing, avoid setting dense grids. A too-dense grid gets in the way and redraws slowly.

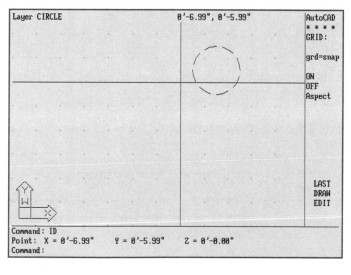

Figure 3.6:
My first grid.

> **Tip:** Turning a grid on not only helps you visualize distances on the screen, it also shows your drawing limits.

You are not limited to creating rectangular grids. You have several options in setting up your grid. You can, for example, change your grid spacing to give different X,Y aspect ratios. Figure 3.7 shows a grid with a 2X:1Y aspect ratio.

Figure 3.7:
Grid with 2X:1Y
aspect ratio.

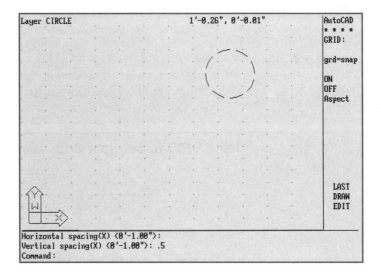

Here are your options for setting the GRID command.

GRID Options

ON   Turns grid on.

OFF   Turns grid off.

Snap   Changes the grid spacing to match the current snap setting.

Aspect   Allows different spacing for vertical and horizontal.

spacing (X) A value followed by an X creates a grid that is a multiple of the current snap setting.

> **Note:** A <^G> or <F7> acts as an on and off toggle for the grid.

> **Tip:** If your grid takes too long to redraw, it's too dense. Try a coarsely spaced grid coordinated with a finely spaced axis.

AutoCAD's Axis Ruler

Another way to help you eyeball accurate screen locations is to use an axis ruler. An axis acts like a manual drafting machine, giving you tick marks across the bottom and right side of your screen.

You can select [AXIS:] from the [SETTINGS] menu, use the AXIS command, or use the drawing tools dialogue box. The axis prompt, shown in figure 3.8, is virtually identical to grid, and the command behaves the same way.

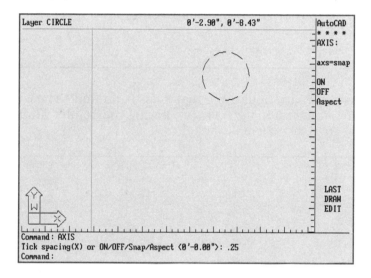

Figure 3.8:
AutoCAD's axis.

Notice that the lower and right boundaries of the screen have a built-in ruler with tick marks at .25-inch spacing and a longer tick at every inch. Use these ruling lines to help you locate your crosshairs movement. It's best to coordinate your grid and axis spacing. For example, set grid to one and axis to .125 to help you eyeball 1/8-inch increments between grid points. Although axis helps keep track of where you are, it does not affect point entry itself. An axis provides reference marks only at the screen edges and won't work in viewports. Using a grid is the easiest and most popular way to locate drawing points.

A grid provides a good set of reference points, but you still can't *pick* the point you want accurately. This is about to change. This may be the last time you'll see freely moving crosshairs. To whip the pointer into shape, you need *snap*.

Setting Snap Points

Snap sets up the smallest increment AutoCAD will recognize when you move the pointer around. When you set snap on and set a spacing value, notice that your screen cursor has a jerky motion. It jumps from snap point to snap point instead of tracking smoothly. Think of setting snap as setting your smallest drawing increment. When you set your snap spacing values, all drawing pick points are forced to multiples of your snap values.

It's good practice to set your snap to some fraction of your grid spacing. AutoCAD normally aligns your snap points with the grid. It's easy to eyeball the 1/4 or 1/5 points between grid points as you draw. Try setting your snap to 0.25 inch, or 1/4 your grid spacing.

Using SNAP to Set Snap Points

Select: [SETTINGS] [next] [SNAP:]
Snap spacing or ON/OFF/Aspect/Rotate/Style <0'-1.00">: **.25**

Now, the status line says "Snap," indicating that snap is on and the coordinates readout is rounded to 1/4 inch (see fig. 3.9). Try moving the pointer around. The crosshairs jump to the snap increments.

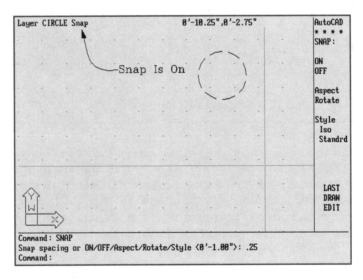

Figure 3.9:
The status line shows snap on.

Note: Snap has a toggle: <^B> or <F9>. You'll find this toggle helpful when you are trying to get to a point that is not snappable. Use <^B> in the middle of other commands when you want to turn snap off (or on).

Using Snap Points to Draw Objects

Once you set your snap, you can draw accurately as long as what you want to draw is on a snap point. The status line will show the correct crosshairs position as it rounds the X,Y values to 0.25 inches.

Let's draw a 2" x 2" square with the lower left corner at 0'-7.50",0'-1.00". Use the coords readout to help you pick the points given in the exercise below.

Using Snap to Draw a Square

Command: **LAYER**	Set layer SQUARE current.
Command: **LINE**	Watch the coords display.
From point:	Pick absolute point 7.50,1.00.

The coords display now shows a distance and angle, which we'll play with soon. But for now, toggle coords with <F6> or <^D> to show crosshairs position as X,Y.

To point:	Pick absolute point 9.50,1.00.
To point:	Pick absolute point 9.50,3.00.
To point:	Pick absolute point 7.50,3.00.
To point:	Pick absolute point 7.50,1.00.
To point: **<RETURN>**	End LINE command.

When you are done, your screen should look like figure 3.10.

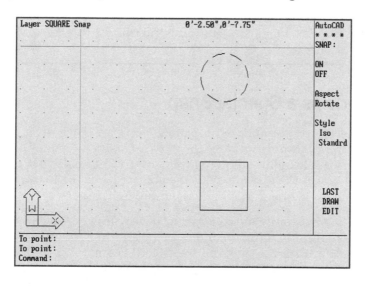

Figure 3.10:
A square drawn with snap.

As you work with grid and snap, you will find that you need to adjust your grid and snap settings as you zoom to work in greater detail. If you start with a snap at 1 unit and a grid at 5 units on a whole drawing, you may need to reset your snap to 0.25

units and your grid to 1 unit when you zoom to work on a portion of the drawing. You can coordinate your snap and grid spacing to suit your needs. Make it a practice to set your grid and snap and leave them on most of the time. If you don't pick your drawing points with snap (or osnap) on, you won't get accurate drawings.

You have several options in setting your snap spacing. Here is the list:

SNAP Options

Snap spacing	A value indicating the snap setting.
ON	Turns snap on.
OFF	Turns snap off.
Aspect	Allows a different increment spacing for the vertical and horizontal snap.
Rotate	Changes the angle and base point (origin) of the snap. Also changes the grid and axis to match.
Style	Provides a standard or isometric snap.

Note that Style provides a standard snap and an isometric snap. You can use isometric snaps to control isometric drawing planes. We will show you how isometric snaps work later in this chapter.

> **Note:** We won't show the grid in most of the illustrations in this book, but you should generally keep it on.

Using Ortho Mode as a Special Snap

When you are drawing horizontal and vertical lines, you can place an additional constraint on your pointer movements by setting a special *ortho* mode on. Ortho stands for *orthogonal*, and limits your pointer movement to right angles from the last point. This means that any lines you enter with the pointer when ortho is on will be aligned with the snap axes. In effect, you can only draw right angles.

Ortho is easy to use and handy any time you are faced with drawing sets of horizontal and vertical lines. Try turning ortho on and drawing another square around the square you just drew. To turn ortho on, type the ORTHO command, or use either <^O> or <F8> as toggles. You can also use the drawing tools dialogue box. After you draw the square, undo it and toggle ortho off; you will use this drawing later on to try out osnaps.

Using Ortho to Draw a Square

Toggle ortho on with <^O> or <F8> and snap off with <F9>.

Command: **LINE**

From point: Pick ① near 7.00,0.50. (see fig. 3.11)

To point: Pick ② near 10.00,0.50.

To point: Pick ③ near 10.00,3.50.

To point: Pick ④ near 7.00,3.50.

To point: **C**   C closes series of lines and ends command.

Command: **U**   Undo removes the four lines you just drew.

Toggle ortho off with <^O> or <F8>.

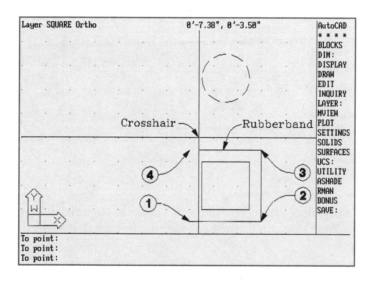

Figure 3.11:
Drawing a square
with Ortho.

When you turn ortho on, Ortho appears on the status line and <Ortho on> shows on the prompt line. As you draw the square, you find that your cursor is limited to vertical and horizontal movement, making it easy to get true 90-degree corners. The rubber band cursor that normally trails from the last point to the intersection of the crosshairs instead goes from the last point to the nearest perpendicular point on the X or Y crosshairs.

Note: If you toggle a mode like ortho, snap, or grid in the middle of a command, and later undo the command, the toggled setting is also undone.

Checking Your Drawing Aids Settings

While you have used individual axis, grid, and snap commands to help you construct these shapes, you can also set these drawing aids using the DDRMODES command. Check your settings by comparing them to figure 3.12.

Figure 3.12:
The drawing tools
dialogue box.

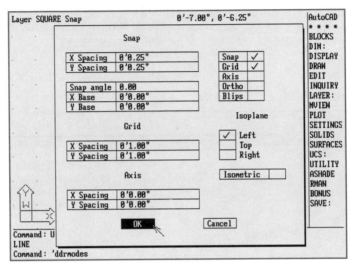

Coordinate Entry

When you enter coordinates from the keyboard, they override the snap and ortho drawing controls, but not object snap. You often use coordinate entry when you are setting up drawings or when you are drawing at specific points or known distances relative to known points.

Note: The Z distance or Z angle is always assumed to be zero unless it is specified with another value.

Absolute Coordinates

When you know the exact coordinates of your point or its distance and angle from the 0,0 drawing origin, you can simply type in the coordinates in one of several formats. These are all known as absolute or explicit coordinates.

Absolute Cartesian coordinates treat coordinate entry as X and Y displacements from 0,0 (or X,Y,Z from 0,0,0 in 3D). For example, 6,5,4 places a point 6 units along the positive X axis, 5 units along the positive Y axis, and 4 units along the positive Z axis from the 0,0,0 base point. The default position for 0,0 is at the lower left of your limits and drawing screen, but you can set it anywhere you like with the UCS command. If your displacement is positive, you don't need to use a + sign. Negative displacement is left and down on the screen. You must use a - sign for negative displacements. In figure 3.13, Cartesian points are located using the distances X, Y, and Z.

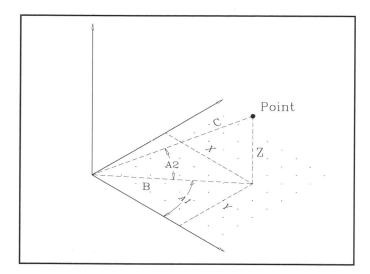

Figure 3.13:
Various forms of absolute coordinate entry.

Absolute Polar coordinates also treat coordinate entry as a displacement from 0,0 but you specify the displacement as a distance and angle. For example, 2<60 is 2 units from 0,0 along a line at 60 degrees from the X axis in the X,Y plane. The distance and angle values are separated by a left angle bracket (<). Positive angles are counterclockwise relative to 0 degrees as a horizontal extending to the right of 0,0. Ninety degrees is vertically above, 180 degrees is horizontally left (see fig. 3.14).

Absolute Spherical coordinates are 3D polar coordinates, specified as a distance and two angles. The first angle is from 0,0 in the X,Y plane and the second angle is the angle towards the Z axis up or down from the X,Y plane. In figure 3.13, a point is located using spherical coordinates by distance C and angles A1 and A2. For example, 2<60<45 specifies a point 2 units from the 0,0,0 origin along a line at 60 degrees from the X axis in the X,Y plane and at 45 degrees up towards the Z axis from the X,Y plane.

Absolute Cylindrical coordinates are also for 3D use. They're like polar coordinates plus a height in the Z axis above or below the X,Y plane. As indicated in figure 3.13, a point is located using cylindrical coordinates by distance B, angle A2, and distance Z. For example, 2<60,3 specifies a point 2 units from the 0,0,0 origin along a line at 60 degrees from the X axis in the X,Y plane that angles up to a point 3 units vertically above the X,Y plane.

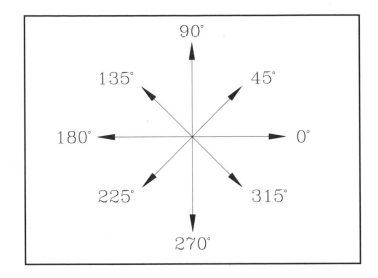

Relative Coordinates

Very often, the point you want to enter has a known X,Y or X,Y,Z distance or known distance and angle from a previous point, but its relative displacement from 0,0 is unknown. Any of the above methods of entering coordinates can also be used *relative* to the last previous point entered in your drawing instead of relative to 0,0. To enter a relative point, you simply enter an @ symbol before the first number.

Relative Cartesian coordinates treat the last point of coordinate entry as a temporary 0,0. If you want to add a horizontal line segment that is two units in the X direction and one in the Y from the previous point, you type @2,0. Relative polar coordinates also treat the last point as 0,0, but you specify your point displacement with a distance and angle. For example, @2<60 is 2 units at 60 degrees.

If you want to enter a new point at the last point, you could use a zero distance, like @0,0 or @0<*nn* (where *nn* could be any angle). This is the same as the last point. But there is a simpler way. You can just enter the @ sign without any number or angle and AutoCAD interprets it as specifying the last point.

Tip: You often want to draw relative to a point that is not the last point used in the drawing. Just use the ID command to pick the point you want to work relative to and it will become the new last point. You can also check and change the last point with the LASTPOINT system variable.

Using Absolute Coordinates

Let's review absolute Cartesian coordinates, which you've already used several times, and try absolute polar coordinates as we draw a triangle at the upper left of the screen (see fig. 3.15).

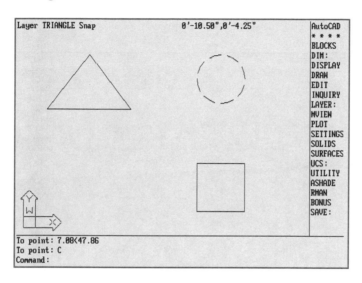

Figure 3.15:
Triangle drawn with
absolute coordinates.

Specifying Absolute Points

Continue working in the WORK drawing.

Command: **LAYER**	Set layer TRIANGLE current.
Command: **LINE**	
From point: **1.25,5.25**	Absolute Cartesian.
To point: **3,7.5**	Absolute Cartesian.
To point: **7.08<47.86**	Absolute polar. (Release 10 users enter 4.75, 5.25).
To point: **C**	Closes it.
	Toggle snap on with <F9>.

These were simple points. In a real drawing, they'd be harder to calculate and we wouldn't be there to give them to you. And if you examined the drawing database closely, you'd find that the third point (five times the square root of 2 at 45 degrees) doesn't exactly align with the first. Absolute coordinates are great for locating the first point of an object in the drawing, but relative coordinates usually serve you better for subsequent points. And, often, relative polar coordinates can be easily picked with the cursor.

Tracking and Picking Polar Coordinates

Often, the precision of the snap, grid, and ortho tools is sufficient for accuracy, but it would be easier to draw if you knew how far the cursor is from the last point. You can use the pointer to pick polar coordinates. You track your pointer movements for polar input by toggling coords into polar readout mode with <F6> or <^D>. Figure 3.16 shows where the polar coordinates are displayed.

Figure 3.16:
Displaying polar
coordinates.

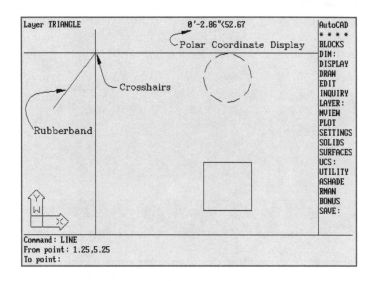

Coords has three modes. The default mode is static coordinates, or off. Static coordinates display an X,Y point, which is updated only when a new point is picked.

When you toggle <F6> once, you get the second mode where the X,Y display is constantly updated as you move the cursor. This second, constantly updated mode has a split personality in most commands. When the crosshairs pull a rubber band line around, such as in a LINE command, the second mode automatically switches into a polar *dist<angle* readout relative to the last point. This is the most frequently used mode because it lets you pick the initial point for a command with absolute X,Y coords and pick subsequent points with relative polar points.

The third mode locks the coords into X,Y display. This works only within a command that shows a polar readout. Then, pressing <F6> once more locks it into X,Y mode. If this sounds confusing, it is! Do what we do, which is toggle once or twice until we get the coords display we want.

Drawing With Relative Coordinates

Let's try relative, Cartesian, and polar coordinate entry by drawing a parallelogram. We'll use both keyboard and cursor to specify relative polar coordinates. Use the following exercise sequence for your input values. When you are done, your screen should look like figure 3.17.

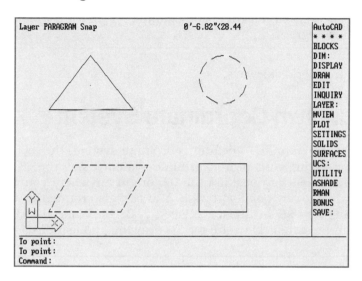

Figure 3.17:
Parallelogram using
relative coordinates.

Using Relative Coordinates to Draw

Continue from the previous triangle exercise. You'll work relative to its last point.

Command: **LAYER**   Set layer PARAGRAM current.
Command: **LINE**

Toggle coords once if needed with <F6> or <^D> so they update the X,Y display as you move.

From point: Use the coords to pick absolute Cartesian
                                             coordinates 0'-4.25",0',1.00".

The coords change to polar display. Toggle once more so they lock into X,Y mode.

To point: **@2.25<60**   Relative polar coordinates.
To point: **@-3,0**   Relative Cartesian coordinates.

Toggle coords twice more so they track in polar mode.

To point: Using the coords, pick relative polar coordi-
                                             nates @ 0'-2.25"<240.00.
To point: Using the coords, pick relative polar coordi-
                                             nates @ 0'-3.00"<0.00.

To point: **<RETURN>**

> *Note:* Don't let the coords readout fool you. It displays with as much or as little precision as you set in the UNITS command. A polar readout is rarely precise at angles other than 90-degree increments. For example, 2.10<60 is more likely 2.0976325 at 60.351724 degrees.

Let's turn and look at the world sideways.

Creating Your Own Coordinate System

So far you have been using AutoCAD's default coordinate system, the *world* coordinate system. You can create your own coordinate system using the UCS command. The UCS command lets you position the 0,0 origin anywhere you wish, so that you can work relative to any point you wish. You can also rotate the X,Y (and even Z) axes to any angle in 2D or 3D space (see fig. 3.18). While the UCS was developed for 3D, it can be extremely useful for 2D drawing applications.

Figure 3.18:
User coordinate system and world coordinate system.

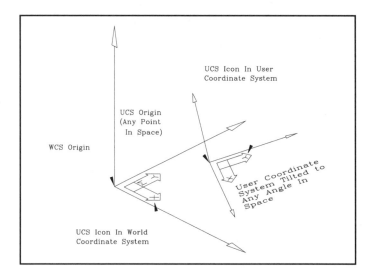

We will show you two examples. The first uses UCS to change the location of the 0,0 origin point and the direction of the X and Y axes in your drawing. The second changes the location of 0,0, keeping the X and Y directions the same as the default directions. Drafting in 2D, you frequently encounter cases where you have drawing data relative to 0,0 positions. Large sets of offset data or datum-dimensioned work are common examples. To handle this type of drawing, you can set your UCS, input the drawing data, then return your UCS to its original (default) world setting.

You can modify or change the current UCS with either the UCS command or the UCS control dialogue box, the DDUCS command (see fig. 3.19). The [UCS:] item on the root screen menu brings up a menu of UCS options, which includes [DDUCS:].

The [UCS Control...] item on the [Settings] pull-down menu also brings up the dialogue box. The [Define new current UCS] button on the UCS control dialogue box brings up the sub-dialogue box (see fig. 3.20). The [Settings] pull-down menu includes several other UCS-related items. [UCS Options...] is an icon menu of preset 3D UCS orientations. [UCS Previous] restores the most recent previous UCS. And [Ucsicon On/Off/OR] toggles the UCS icon through its settings.

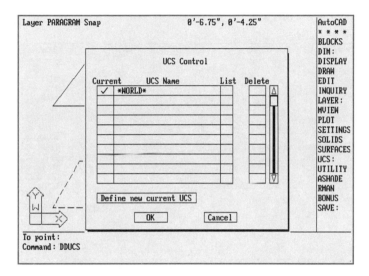

Figure 3.19:
UCS control
dialogue box.

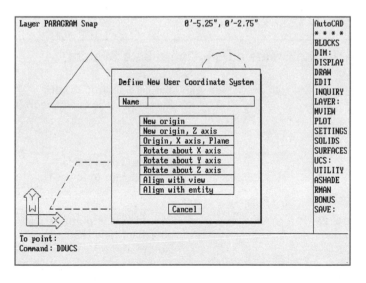

Figure 3.20:
Define a new current
UCS dialogue box.

The UCSICON (the X,Y arrow at the lower left) helps you keep track of the UCS. It shows the orientation of the X,Y axes. It can be set to appear aligned on the 0,0,0 origin of the UCS, if there is room on screen. A plus mark appears in the UCS icon at the origin, when the icon is set to the origin and it can fit there. If it can't fit on screen at the origin, it will appear at the lower left, without a plus mark. The UCS icon's appearance is controlled by the UCSICON command.

Make sure your UCSICON (the X,Y arrow at the lower left) is on, then use the UCS command to rotate your drawing's coordinate system 90 degrees and set the 0,0 origin near the lower right corner (see fig. 3.21). When you specify the coordinates of a new UCS, you specify them in terms of the current coordinate system. Use the coords display to pick the new origin.

Figure 3.21:
The new user coordi-
nate system.

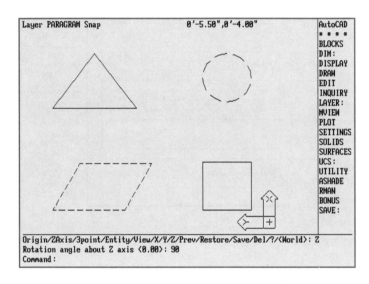

Using UCS to Create a User Coordinate System

```
Command: UCSICON
ON/OFF/All/Noorigin/ORigin <ON>:OR            Set UCS icon to origin.
Command: ZOOM                                 Zoom out to see UCS icon jump to
                                              origin.

All/Center/Dynamic/Extents/Left/Previous/
  Vmax/Window/<Scale(X/XP)>: .9
Command: U                                    Undo to zoom back.
Command: UCS                                  Move Origin to lower right corner.
Origin/ZAxis/3point/Entity/View/X/Y/Z/Prev/
  Restore/Save/Del/?/<World>: O
Origin point <0,0,0>: 10.25,.5               Pick absolute point 10.25,.5 as
                                              coords of new UCS.
Command: UCS                                  Rotate about the Z axis 90 degrees.
Origin/ZAxis/3point/Entity/View/X/Y/Z/Prev/
  Restore/Save/Del/?/<World>: Z
Rotation angle about Z axis <0.00>: 90
```

To see the effect of the changed origin, move your crosshairs around and watch your coords display. They should show 0,0 at the lower right corner, a *vertical* X direction and a *horizontal* Y direction.

While offsetting the origin is straightforward, you might ask what rotating the UCS around the Z axis has to do with your 2D drawing. Imagine that you're standing on the X axis, looking down at your drawing, with your left arm extended to the left to grip a pole rising up from 0,0. Walk forward through 90 degrees, kicking the X axis along with you. You just rotated about the Z axis 90 degrees.

Try out the new UCS by making a border around your drawing. Use the following sequence as a guide.

Drawing a Border in a UCS

```
Command: LAYER                                   Set layer TEXT current.
Command: LINE
From point: 0,0                                  Lower right corner of border.
To point:                                        Pick relative polar coords @
                                                 7.50<0.00.
To point:                                        Pick relative polar coords @
                                                 9.75<90.00. Notice "up" is left
                                                 now! (see fig. 3.22)
To point:                                        Pick relative polar coords @
                                                 7.50<180.00.
To point:                                        Pick relative polar coords @
                                                 9.75<270.00.
To point: <RETURN>                               End the line.
Command: UCS                                      Set UCS back to World, the de-
                                                 fault.

Origin/ZAxis/3point/Entity/View/X/Y/Z/Prev/
   Restore/Save/Del/?/<World>: <RETURN>
```

Try changing the location of your UCS origin to about midway up your drawing, then input some text.

Using UCS to Demonstrate Changed Origin Point

```
Command: UCS                                      Set UCS to center of drawing.
Origin/ZAxis/3point/Entity/View/X/Y/Z/Prev/
   Restore/Save/Del/?/<World>: O
Origin point <0,0,0>: 5.5,4.25                   The current coordinates of the
                                                 new UCS.

Command: DTEXT
Justify/Style/<Start point>: C
Center point: 0,0
```

Using UCS to Demonstrate Changed Origin Point—continued

```
Height <0'-0.20">: .25
Rotation angle <0.00>: <RETURN>
Text: Welcome To INSIDE AutoCAD                Our favorite text.
Text: <RETURN>
Command: REDRAW                                Clean up the display.
Command: UCS                                   Set UCS back to the world
                                               coordinate system.

Origin/ZAxis/3point/Entity/View/X/Y/Z/Prev/
   Restore/Save/Del/?/<World>: <RETURN>
Command: LAYER                                 Set layer 0 current.
Command: SAVE                                  Save with the name BASIC, for
                                               later use, then quit.
```

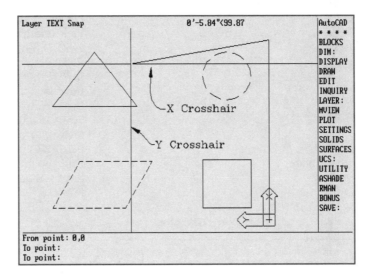

Figure 3.22:
Border in progress.

Check your drawing. Your screen should look like figure 3.23. Each shape should be on its appropriately named layer, with the color and linetype of the layer. Your grid should be one unit and snap .25 units. If needed, make corrections and save it again as BASIC. We'll use this drawing again in the following exercises and in the next chapter on display controls.

As you can tell by looking at the command prompt line, the UCS command is one of the more complex commands and has several options. We will show you how to use all of these options when we discuss 3D in Part Two. Meanwhile, here is a subset of the options that will get you through most two-dimensional applications.

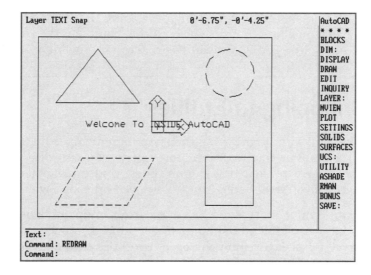

Figure 3.23:
Text centered at
current UCS origin.

Subset of UCS Options (for 2D Applications)

Origin   Lets you specify a new X,Y,Z origin point relative to the current origin.

Z   Lets you rotate the X,Y axes about the Z axis.

Prev   Lets you step back to the previous UCS, up to ten previously used UCSs.

Restore   Sets the UCS to a previously saved UCS.

Save   Stores the current UCS under a name that you specify.

Del   Removes a saved UCS.

?   Displays a list of saved UCSs by name, point of origin, and orientation.

<World>   The default, sets the UCS to the world coordinate system.

Here are the UCSICON command options to control the display of the UCS icon.

UCSICON Options

ON   Makes the UCS icon visible.

OFF   Removes the UCS icon.

All   Displays the UCS icon in all viewports see the next chapter.

Noorigin   Displays the UCS icon in the lower left corner of viewport instead of at the origin.

ORigin   Displays the UCS icon at the point of origin (0,0,0).

If you want to take a coffee break, this is a good stopping point. In fact, whenever we save or quit a drawing, you can figure that's a safe breaking point. For the rest of the chapter, we are going to use the BASIC drawing as a scratch drawing to see how osnaps work.

Osnaps — Snapping to Entities

Snap is great when what you want to draw fits the snap increments. And, between the various ways for absolute or relative coordinate entry, you can draw almost anything. But when you need to align new points, lines, and other objects with geometric points on entities you've already drawn, you need an easier way.

For example, let's say you want to start a new line at the exact endpoint of one of the lines on the screen and it doesn't fall at a snap point. Or what if you want to pick a tangent point to a curve? Or pick the intersection of two lines that don't fall on a snap point? You need osnap! The OSNAP command lets you precisely edit existing entities or precisely add new entities to existing entities by providing a choice of geometric points that you can *osnap* to.

Using OSNAP to Pinpoint a Crosshairs Location

AutoCAD's OSNAP command and filter modes calculate the *attachment* points you need to make accurate drawings. You tell AutoCAD which osnap attachment mode(s) to use, such as INT for INTersection. Then, when you pick a point or enter coordinates near the geometric point you want, AutoCAD osnaps to the precise attachment point.

In a dense drawing, there might be several suitable attachment points close to your pick point. When osnapping to an INTersection, AutoCAD may indeed find an intersection, but not necessarily the intersection you want. Osnap uses a tolerance or *target* box for identifying the points it considers (see fig. 3.24). This tolerance is controlled by an *aperture* box, an electronic bull's-eye that homes in on osnap points. AutoCAD only considers the osnap for objects that fall within the aperture. Just how large you should set the aperture depends on what you are selecting, how you are zoomed, your display resolution, and your drawing density.

Note: Some display adapters, those that use display list (virtual screen technology) to provide instantaneous pans and zooms, take over control of the aperture setting. See your display adapter manual for information if this is the case.

Figure 3.1 shows you all the filter modes for picking different attachment points on objects. The basic geometric shapes in your BASIC drawing will let you exercise all these osnap options.

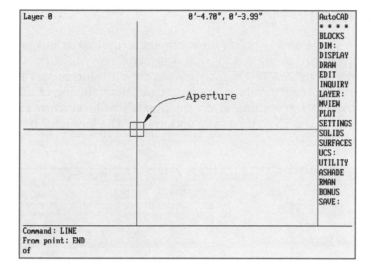

Figure 3.24:
OSNAP turns the crosshairs into a target.

Setting the Aperture and Picking a Point

Let's get started by setting the aperture to control the size of the crosshairs bull's-eye that osnap uses to zero in on target objects. You can type the APERTURE command or use the [APERTUR:] selection from the [SETTINGS] screen menu. While you are at it, change your current layer to layer 0, using it as a scratch layer.

Using APERTURE to Set the Osnap Target

Edit an EXISTING drawing named BASIC=IA6BASIC.

Edit an EXISTING drawing named BASIC.

Command: **APERTURE**
Object snap target height (1-50 pixels) <10>: **5**

A pixel is the smallest *dot* that can be displayed on your screen. Four or six pixels (the default value is ten) give a good target size. The size is measured from the center, so five pixels make a ten-pixel high aperture box. Try a few different values to see how comfortable you feel with larger and smaller apertures.

> **Note:** A small aperture size finds points faster and more accurately in crowded drawings, but the crosshairs are harder to line up. A large aperture is easy to line up, but is slower and less accurate in a crowded drawing. If you have 1024 x 768 or greater screen resolution, you may want to set the aperture size to eight or ten instead of the five specified in the exercise above.

Overrides vs. Running Mode

You can use osnaps as single pick *override* filters, or set a *running* osnap mode that remains in effect until you are prompted for object selection or you turn it off. You select osnaps as *overrides* (which interrupt the current running mode) from the [Assist] pull-down menu, or the [* * * *] item that appears near the top of the screen menu. You can find the OSNAP command on the [Assist] pull-down or the [SETTINGS] screen menu (see fig. 3.25). The osnap options are the same for both interrupts and running modes.

Figure 3.25:
[Assist] and [* * *]*
Osnap menus.

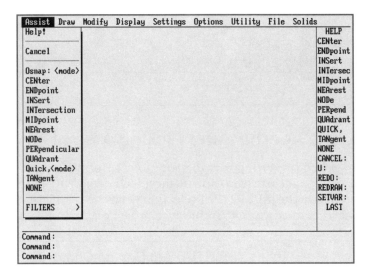

Tip: If you type the osnap modifiers, you just type the first word or first three or four characters like ENDPoint or PERpendicular. When using ENDPoint, get in the habit of typing ENDP, not END, to avoid accidentally ENDing your drawing.

Using OSNAP as a Single Pick Filter

To learn how overrides work, use NODe and ENDPoint to draw a line from the point entity (your first point) in the triangle to the corner of the triangle. NODe osnaps to a point entity, not the triangle's geometric node. The resulting drawing will look like the OSNAP NODe and ENDPoint illustrations. Pick the osnap options from the [Assist] pull-down menu, tablet menu, [* * * *] screen menu, or type them at the keyboard.

Using OSNAP NODe and ENDPoint

Command: **SNAP**	Turn snap off.
Command: **LINE**	
From point: **NOD**	Type NOD for node.
of	Pick point ① near point entity in triangle. (see fig. 3.26).
To point: **ENDP**	Type ENDP for endpoint.
of	Pick point ② near corner of triangle (see fig. 3.26).
To point: **<RETURN>**	

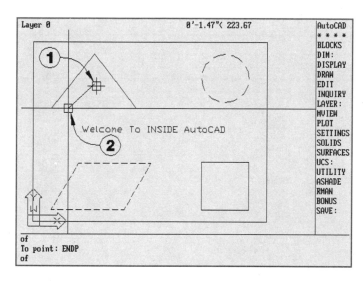

Figure 3.26:
OSNAP NODe and
ENDPoint.

Congratulations! You've successfully osnapped (see fig. 3.27).

Continue the exercise to see how the remaining osnaps work. Use figure 3.28 for this portion of the exercise.

Completing the OSNAP Options

Command: **LINE**	
From point: **@**	Starts line from last point.
To point: **INT**	Type INT for intersection.
of	Now pick ① near intersection of parallelogram.
To point: **MID**	Type MID for midpoint.
of	Pick ② or anywhere on base line of triangle.
To point: **PER**	Type PER for perpendicular.
of	Pick ③ or anywhere on right side of triangle.
Select: **[****] [INSert]**	Try the screen menu of OSNAPs.
To point: INSERT of	Sets mode and the menu changes back.
	Pick ④ or anywhere on the text.

Completing the OSNAP Options—continued

See figure 3.29 for the following points.

```
To point: TAN                 Type TAN for tangent.
of                            Pick ⑤ on upper left side of circle.
To point: CEN                 Type CEN for center.
of                            Pick ⑥ or anywhere on circle.
To point: QUA                 Type QUA for quadrant.
of                            Pick ⑦ near bottom of circle.
To point: NEA                 Type NEA for near.
of                            Pick ⑧ or anywhere on line from text to circle.
To point: <RETURN>
```

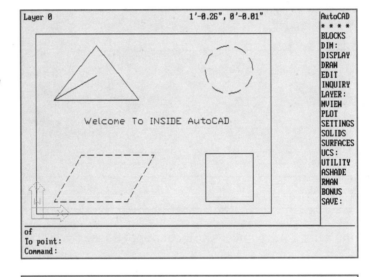

Figure 3.27:
Completed osnapped
line.

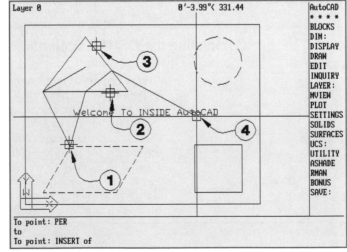

Figure 3.28:
OSNAP INTersection,
MIDpoint,
PERpendicular,
and INSert.

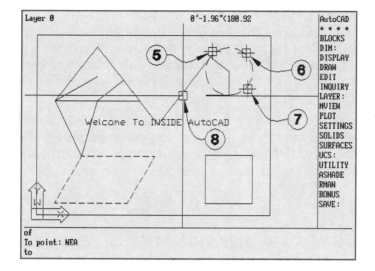

Figure 3.29:
OSNAP TANgent,
CENter, QUAdrant,
and NEAr.

Your drawing should look like figure 3.30.

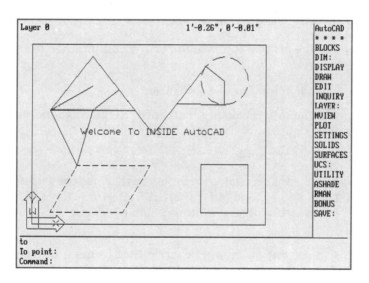

Figure 3.30:
Completed osnaps.

Using QUIck to Optimize OSNAP

AutoCAD goes through a lot of work trying to find the correct object to osnap to when you are using an OSNAP command. In fact, AutoCAD searches every object on the screen to find all objects crossing the aperture box. Then it calculates potential points for all of these objects to find the *best* (closest) fit for your osnap request. This can take a bit of time when you have a lot of objects.

You can optimize or shorten the osnap search process by keeping the aperture reasonably small to keep extraneous objects out of the target. Or you can use the QUIck osnap option. QUIck lets AutoCAD take the most recently created object that meets your osnap criteria instead of doing an exhaustive search and comparison to find the closest. You invoke QUIck by using it as a prefix for other osnap option(s), like QUI,INT for a quick intersection.

QUIck may sometimes let you down if the first fit that AutoCAD finds is not the one you want. In that case, simply cancel what you are doing and start the osnap process again without the quick modifier. Here is the complete osnap options list, including the QUIck modifier.

OSNAP Options

CENter	Snaps to the center of an arc or circle.
ENDPoint	Snaps to the nearest endpoint of a line or arc.
INSert	Snaps to the origin of text, attributes and symbols (block or shape) that have been inserted into the drawing file. More about blocks, shapes, and attributes later.
INTersection	Snaps to the nearest intersection of any combination of two lines, arcs or circles.
MIDpoint	Snaps to the midpoint of a line or arc.
NEArest	Snaps to the nearest point on an entity. This will generally be an endpoint, tangent, or a perpendicular point.
NODe	Snaps to a point entity.
PERpendicular	Snaps to a point on a line, arc, or circle that, for the picked entity, would form a perpendicular (normal) line from the last point to the picked entity. The resulting point need not even be on the entity.
TANgent	Snaps to a point on an arc or circle that forms a tangent to the picked arc or circle from the last point.
QUAdrant	Snaps to the closest 0-, 90-, 180-, or 270-degree point on an arc or circle.
QUIck	Forces all other osnap options to quickly find the first potential target, not necessarily the closest. QUIck finds the potential point that is on the most *recent* qualified object in the target box.
NONe	Removes or overrides any running osnap.

> *Note:* In the above list, *line* and *arc* don't refer to only line and arc entities, but include each edge or segment of solid, trace, 3Dface, viewport, polygon mesh, or polyline entities. Polylines are treated as if they have zero width. Some of these entities may not be familiar to you, but we'll cover them in later chapters.

In the exercises, you used OSNAP as an override in the middle of the line command to fine tune your line endpoints. This override mode temporarily sets up an osnap aperture condition to complete a task at hand. Often, you'll repeatedly use the same mode or combination of modes so AutoCAD lets you set running modes.

Using a Running Mode Osnap

Setting up osnap conditions to be in effect until you change them is called a *running mode.* You set a running mode with the OSNAP command. Running mode osnaps remain in effect until you replace them with another running mode setting or temporarily override them. Unlike SNAP, GRID, and ORTHO, the OSNAP command is not transparent, but, fortunately, overrides are. Use the NONe override to temporarily suppress a running mode.

> *Note:* If a running osnap is on, the crosshairs will have a bull's-eye aperture during your point entry and object selection.

Try putting a diamond in the square using a running osnap mode. Use figure 3.31 as a guide for the following exercise.

Using a Running Osnap to Put a Diamond in a Square

```
Command: OSNAP
Object snap modes: MID          Type MID for midpoint.

Command: LINE
From point:                     Pick point ① on the top line.
To point:                       Pick point ② on the right line.
To point:                       Pick point ③ on the bottom line.
To point:                       Pick point ④ on the left line.
To point:                       Pick point ⑤ on the top line.
To point: <RETURN>
```

You can specify two or more modes at once and AutoCAD will find the calculated point of whichever is the closest to the crosshairs. Specify multiple modes by separating them with commas, like END,MID,CEN.

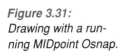

Figure 3.31:
Drawing with a run-
ning MIDpoint Osnap.

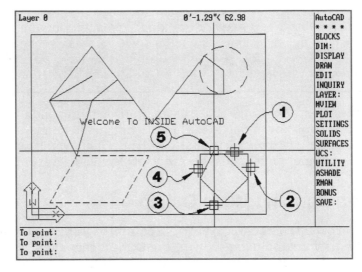

Tip: INT,END,MID will cover most cases.

Use the override mode whenever the need arises. Set up a running osnap when you know that you will be repeatedly using the same osnap mode(s).

REDRAW and BLIPMODE for a Clean Screen

As you worked through the osnap exercises, you probably noticed that when you enter a point on the screen (either with a pointer or keyboard entry), AutoCAD places a small cross (blip) on the screen. As you draw, filling up the screen area with real drawing entities (like lines and circles), you also get a screenful of clutter from construction markers. A few blips are great for keeping an eye on where you've been (or might want to go again), but they are a distraction when they accumulate. You will also find as you draw, erase, and move entities, that pieces of lines and entities seem to disappear. Usually, they're still there, but when you erase or move an entity that overlaps another, it leaves a gap in the underlying entity's screen representation.

Use the REDRAW command to clean up the screen, redraw underlying entities and get rid of blips. Let's try it.

Using REDRAW to Clear Up the Screen

Command: **ERASE**
Select objects: Pick point on line from triangle to the center of text.

Select objects: **<RETURN>**   It's gone. So is part of the triangle — or is it (see fig. 3.32)?

Command: **REDRAW**   The screen redraws, the blips are gone and the triangle's okay (see fig. 3.33).

Command: **QUIT**   You don't need to save this drawing.

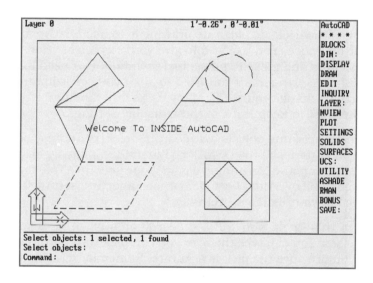

Figure 3.32:
Display screen after ERASE, before REDRAW.

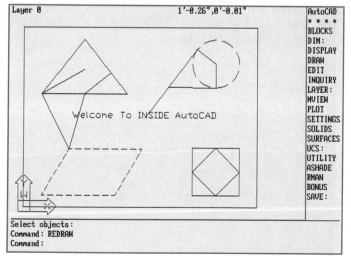

Figure 3.33:
Display screen after REDRAW.

> **Tip:** If the grid is visible, you can do a redraw without typing or picking the command. Toggling grid twice with <^G> or <F7> causes a redraw. You also can issue a transparent redraw with 'REDRAW.

If you find you just don't need blips, you can use the BLIPMODE command to suppress construction markers. You can keep AutoCAD from drawing these temporary markers by typing BLIPMODE OFF or selecting [BLIPS:] from the [SETTINGS] screen menu.

Summing Up

You have seen that one of the tricks to accurate drawing is to use relative and polar points, with coords for reference. You use grid to give you a frame of reference and snap to limit your crosshairs and picks to preset increments. If you need to draw at 90-degree increments, toggle ortho on. If you need to align your coordinate system with your drawing, you can change your UCS. Many users find it helpful to jot down notes or make up a checklist to keep track of these display settings.

To construct geometrically accurate objects, use coordinate entry and use osnap for snapping to objects. You can invoke the OSNAP command temporarily as an override to any point-picking command. A running osnap mode sets up a full-time mode and aperture that you can still override. Try to find a good aperture setting to control the reliability and speed of your osnap searches.

Throughout the rest of this book, you will see coordinates given in response to prompts with the exercises. You can type them, or you can pick the coordinates with the pointing device if you are sure the pick is accurate. Remember crosshairs position is only accurate with snap on, or with osnap. Use osnap at every opportunity you can. Your drawing productivity will improve and you can be confident that your work is accurate. Now that you've had a chance to play around with osnaps, you can move on to learning how to get around in AutoCAD.

4

Getting Around

MAKING A SMALL DISPLAY SCREEN DO THE WORK OF A BIG PIECE OF PAPER

Whether you've set your drawing limits to represent 2 by 3 feet or 2000 by 3000 feet, your display screen is not large enough to give you a one-to-one view of your drawing file. In this chapter, you will learn to use AutoCAD's set of electronic tools to control where you are in your display, where you are going, and how you will get there. Your display becomes a *viewport* into your drawing, zooming in, out, and around. You will learn to use *multiple viewports* (see fig. 4.1) to see several parts of your drawing simultaneously, and to scale the viewports to different sizes for eventual plotting.

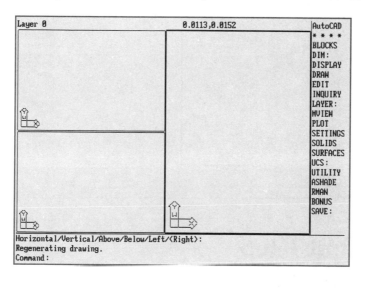

Figure 4.1:
Screen divided into
three viewports.

The Benefits of Getting Around

AutoCAD's display controls make your drawing life easier. AutoCAD's basic display controls, like *zoom* and *pan*, function just as they do in photography. The ZOOM command lets you magnify your drawing to do detailed work. PAN lets you slide your drawing from side to side so that you can work on large objects without having to return to a full screen view to find where you are. Simple controls, like *redraw* and *regen*, let you clean up your screen or display the most current view of your drawing.

To make working on your drawings easier, you can open multiple viewports on the screen to display your model at different scales and from different viewpoints. You can also use these viewports to display areas of your model that would normally not be visible on the screen together, such as both ends of a long part. For example, you can see your entire object in a single window while you zoom in to work on a drawing detail in a second window. Or you can keep a parts schedule in one window while you check your drawing annotations in another. You can even set many of AutoCAD's settings, such as snap, grid, and ucsicon (and even layers in Release 11) differently in each viewport. When you save your drawing, your viewport setup is saved with it so you don't have to create the viewports each time.

You will find the view control tools on the [DISPLAY] screen menu and the [Display] pull-down menu (see fig. 4.2).

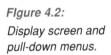

Figure 4.2:
Display screen and pull-down menus.

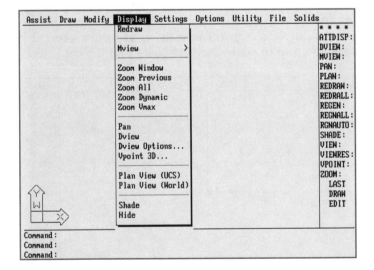

Display Control Setup

You don't need an elaborate drawing to get a feel for display controls; the simple geometric shapes in the BASIC drawing you saved in Chapter 3 will work well enough to get you around the display screen. If you are using the IA DISK, you have the BASIC drawing as IA6BASIC.DWG.

Table 4.1
BASIC Drawing Settings

AXIS	GRID	SNAP	ORTHO	UCS	UCSICON
Off	On	On	Off	World	On

UNITS Engineering, 2 decimal places, 2 fractional places for angles, defaults all other settings.

LIMITS 0,0 to 11,8.5

Layer Name	State	Color	Linetype
0	On/Current	7 (white)	CONTINUOUS
CIRCLE	On	3 (green)	DASHED
PARAGRAM	On	5 (blue)	HIDDEN
SQUARE	On	2 (yellow)	CONTINUOUS
TEXT	On	4 (cyan)	CONTINUOUS
TRIANGLE	On	1 (red)	CONTINUOUS

Display Control Setup

 Begin a NEW drawing named BASIC=IA6BASIC.

 Edit an EXISTING drawing named BASIC from Chapter 3, and make sure the drawing has the settings shown in the BASIC Drawing Settings table.

Your screen should look like figure 4.3.

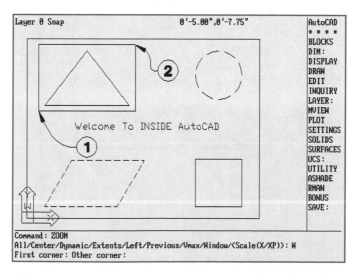

Figure 4.3: BASIC drawing.

Controlling Screen Display With ZOOM

Suppose you want to look more closely at the triangle on the screen. To do this, you need to *zoom* in on the drawing. The most common way to tell AutoCAD what part of the current screen you want to enlarge is to show a box or *window* around the area of interest. ZOOM Window zooms in on your drawing.

Using ZOOM Window to Look More Closely

Step through a zoom window example. Use the illustration as a guide to picking your window corners. You don't need to pick exact coordinates; just show a rough area you want to see in more detail.

Using ZOOM Window

```
Command: ZOOM
All/Center/Dynamic/Extents/Left/Previous/Vmax/
  Window/<Scale(X/XP)>: W
First corner:                          Pick point ①. (see fig. 4.4)
Other corner:                          Pick point ②. (see fig. 4.4)
```

Figure 4.4:
ZOOM window box.

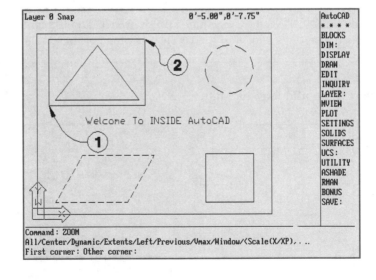

Notice that after you pick the first corner, instead of the normal crosshairs, your cursor changes to a *rubber band* box. As soon as you pick the other corner, AutoCAD repaints the screen with the area you enclosed in the window (see fig. 4.5). The corners that you picked guide AutoCAD in setting up the zoomed-in display. This display will usually not be exactly the same shape as your original window because AutoCAD maintains its X and Y screen ratio regardless of your corner locations.

Try zooming closer to the upper point of the triangle, picking two more window corners, and letting AutoCAD redraw the screen. Use figures 4.6 and 4.7 as your guide.

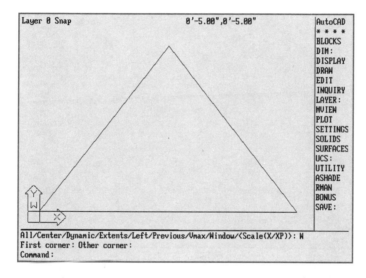

Figure 4.5:
Magnified screen.

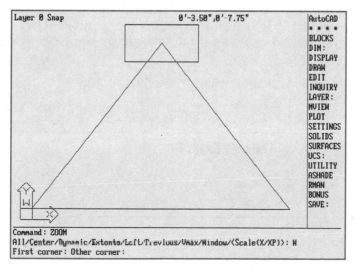

Figure 4.6:
Second ZOOM window.

Picking a ZOOM Window

```
Command: ZOOM                                          Zoom to upper point of tri-
                                                       angle.

All/Center/Dynamic/Extents/Left/Previous/
  Vmax/Window/<Scale(X/XP)>: W
First corner:                                          Pick the lower left corner.
Other corner:                                          Pick the upper right corner.
```

Figure 4.7:
Magnified top of
triangle after zoom.

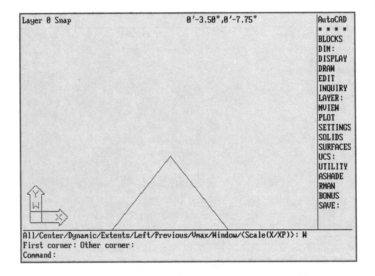

How far can you zoom in? Let's say you drew the entire solar system at full scale — it's about seven billion miles across. If you drew it with enough detail, you could zoom in far enough to read this book on your desk, thanks to AutoCAD's 14 significant digits of precision. Try zooming in on your drawing if you want, before we zoom back out.

Okay, you can get in. How do you get back out? Use ZOOM All.

ZOOM All is the easiest way to get back to the full display of your drawing file.

Using ZOOM All

```
Command: ZOOM
All/Center/Dynamic/Extents/Left/Previous/Vmax/Window/<Scale(X/XP)>: A
Regenerating drawing.
```

Your screen should be back to where you started. When AutoCAD does a ZOOM All, it regenerates and repaints the screen with everything in the drawing file. If you have drawn within your drawing limits, ZOOM All takes you to your limits. If you have exceeded your limits, ZOOM All zooms beyond the limits to display everything in your drawing file.

Other ZOOM Options

ZOOM Window and ZOOM All will get you in and out, but you have several other zoom options at your fingertips. Here's the complete list.

ZOOM Options

All
Zooms out to limits, or everything in the drawing file, whichever is greater. ZOOM All always regenerates the drawing, sometimes twice.

Center
Magnifies the screen around a center point with a given height or magnification factor.

Dynamic
Temporarily displays the whole drawing (or as much as it can without a regen), letting you graphically select any portion of the drawing as your next screen view.

Extents
Gives the tightest possible view of everything in the drawing file.

Left
Scts a new lower left corner and zooms to a height or by magnification factor.

Previous
Restores the last zoom setting. Remembers up to ten previous magnifications.

Vmax
Zooms out as far as possible without causing a regen. (Not in Release 10.)

Window
Uses a rectangular window to select a drawing area to display on the screen.

<Scale(X/XP)>
Uses a numeric zoom factor to determine magnification. A magnification factor of 1 displays a view of the drawing limits. A value less than 1 zooms out from the limits, and greater than 1 zooms in. The magnification X modifier gives zooms relative to your current view. For example, 2X gives a display twice as large as the last display. The XP modifier (not in Release 10) scales the view relative to paper space. Paper space is covered in detail later in this chapter.

Note: Zooms will occasionally require a drawing regeneration. ZOOM All and Extents always cause a drawing regeneration. If you can use a ZOOM Previous or ZOOM Vmax, you will avoid the regeneration.

Keeping Track of Zoom Displays

Every time you zoom in or out, AutoCAD keeps track of the previous display. In fact, AutoCAD remembers up to ten zooms. Try the Left and Center options, then use Previous to step back out.

Using ZOOM Left, Center, and Previous

```
Command: ZOOM

All/Center/Dynamic/Extents/Left/Previous/
   Vmax/Window/<Scale(X/XP)>: L
Lower left corner point:
```
Use the Left option to zoom an area surrounding the text.

Pick absolute point 2.50,2.00 (see fig. 4.8).

```
Magnification or Height <0'-8.50">: 4.5
Command: ZOOM
All/Center/Dynamic/Extents/Left/Previous/
   Vmax/Window/<Scale(X/XP)>: C
Center point:
Magnification or Height <0'-4.50">: .5
Command: ZOOM
```
Zoom Center on the W in Welcome.

Pick a point on the W (see fig. 4.9).

Zoom Previous to return to the complete text.

```
All/Center/Dynamic/Extents/Left/Previous/
   Vmax/Window/<Scale(X/XP)>: P
Command: ZOOM
```
Use Previous again to return to the start.

```
All/Center/Dynamic/Extents/Left/Previous/
   Vmax/Window/<Scale(X/XP)>: P
```

If all went well, you should end up where you started. Your screen should show a zoomed-out view of your drawing.

Note: Previous does not necessarily zoom out. It zooms to the previous zoom view setting.

You may have noticed a speed difference in zooms that regenerate the screen and those that do not. In a complex drawing, this can be a considerable time difference. To control when it occurs, you need to understand how zoom works.

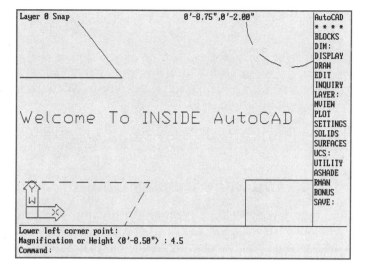

Figure 4.8:
ZOOM left.

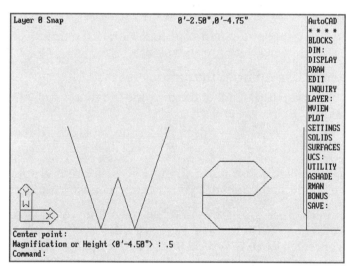

Figure 4.9:
ZOOM center.

Zoom, Regen, Redraw and the Virtual Screen

To understand the ZOOM command, you need to understand the relationship of redraw, regen, and the virtual screen. When you load a new drawing or use the REGEN command, AutoCAD recalculates the current view to its full 14 places of precision. It calculates this as if it were a 32,000 x 32,000 pixel display screen, the *virtual screen*. This is a *regen*. Then it translates this calculated image to your actual display screen and *redraws* the screen. AutoCAD can do a redraw very quickly, several times as quickly as a regen. This translation is all that occurs when you use the REDRAW command, toggle the grid, turn on layers, or change other settings that cause a redraw.

Many zooms require only a redraw, not a regen. As long as you do not zoom outside of the current virtual screen, or zoom so far into tiny detail that AutoCAD can't accurately translate from the virtual screen, it won't regenerate. When a zoom occurs without a regen, it occurs at redraw speed.

The key to fast zooming is to avoid regens. Zooming in is usually no problem, but the easiest way to control this when zooming out is to use ZOOM Dynamic.

ZOOM Dynamic Gives You More Display Control

You have used the basic two-step process of zooming in on your drawing with a window and zooming back out with a ZOOM All. But what if you want to magnify a small portion of your drawing while you are already zoomed in to a different section? There is another option called ZOOM Dynamic that lets you control and display your zoom window in a single step without having to do a ZOOM All.

There are really three display subsets. When you work with a dynamic zoom, these subsets are shown on your screen. Here are the display sets:

- The drawing extents. Everything in the drawing file.
- Generated area. A portion (up to all) of the drawing file that AutoCAD has regenerated. This is the virtual screen.
- The current screen view. A portion (up to all) of the generated data that currently appears on the screen.

When you select a dynamic zoom, you can see all three of these areas graphically on the screen before making a decision on what your next screen view will be.

Take a look at the sample screen in figure 4.10. You see four rectangular areas outlined on the diagram. The first three show the entire drawing extents (white or black), the currently generated virtual screen (four red corners), and the current view screen (green or magenta). (The extents will be the limits unless you have drawn beyond the limits.)

The fourth rectangular area is a dynamic window (white or black) that moves with your pointer. Use this dynamic window to select the next screen view you want to see.

If you select your next screen view from within the area bounded by the *generated* data, the next screen view will appear on the screen in redraw speed. If you select your next screen view to include data from outside the currently generated data, your zoom will require a regeneration of the entire drawing file as AutoCAD calculates the part of the drawing file you want to see in your next view. When you move the pointer outside the generated drawing file area, a little hourglass appears on the

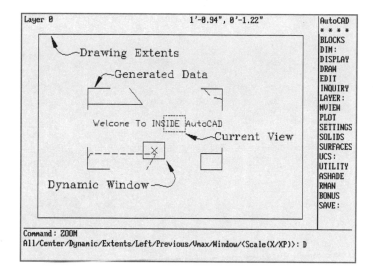

lower left part of the screen indicating that regeneration will occur. If you zoom in beyond about 50X, AutoCAD must regenerate the drawing.

Try a ZOOM Dynamic. First zoom All and then zoom in to magnify your drawing three times. This ensures we all start out the same. Then call up the ZOOM Dynamic display.

Using ZOOM Dynamic

```
Command: ZOOM                                    Zoom All.
Command: ZOOM                                    Use a scale factor of 3 to
                                                 magnify display.

All/Center/Dynamic/Extents/Left/Previous/
   Vmax/Window/<Scale(X/XP)>: 3                  (see fig. 4.11).

Command: ZOOM                                    Now get the dynamic zoom
                                                 display on the screen.

All/Center/Dynamic/Extents/Left/Previous/
   Vmax/Window/<Scale(X/XP)>: D
```

Your screen should look like figure 4.12. When you move your pointer around, it *drags* the dynamic viewing window around the screen as if it were held by the X handle in the middle of the window. Your pointer also controls the size of the window. When you press your pointer button, you get an arrow that controls the size of your window. Then, when you move the arrow to the right, you make the window larger. Left makes it smaller.

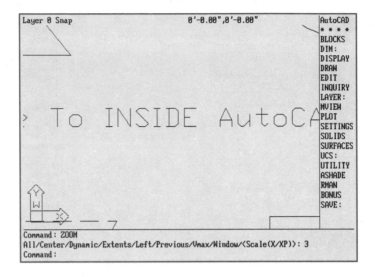

Figure 4.11:
Screen magnified three times.

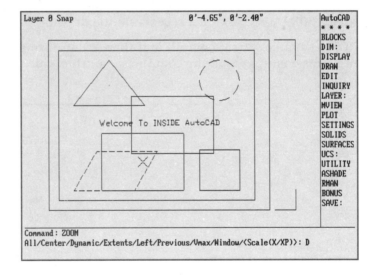

Figure 4.12:
Beginning of ZOOM Dynamic.

When the dynamic window is the size you want, press the pointer button again to lock in the size. You can toggle between controlling the dynamic window size and its location with the pointer button.

Once you have windowed the next viewing screen that you want, press the <RETURN> key while holding the dynamic viewing window in place to select it. AutoCAD will zoom. Use the illustrations as a guide in the exercise sequence.

Controlling a ZOOM Dynamic

`All/Center/Dynamic/Extents/Left/Previous/Vmax/Window/<Scale(X/XP)>: D`

Move the dynamic window around with the X handle ① (see fig. 4.13).
Press the pointer button to switch to dynamic window size.

Stretch or shrink the dynamic window by moving horizontally ② (see fig. 4.14).
Press the pointer button to switch to dynamic window location control.

Line up the dynamic viewing window to enclose the circle ③ (see fig. 4.15).
Hold the pointer in place and press the <RETURN> key. AutoCAD zooms (see fig. 4.16).

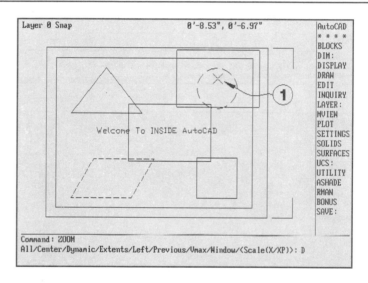

Figure 4.13:
Moving current view screen.

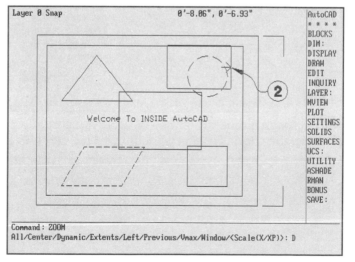

Figure 4.14:
Resizing current view screen.

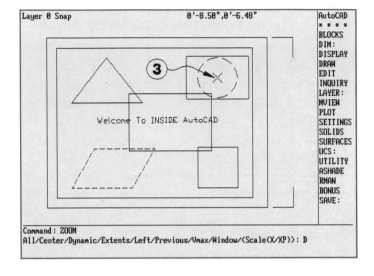

Figure 4.15:
Viewing window
enclosing the circle.

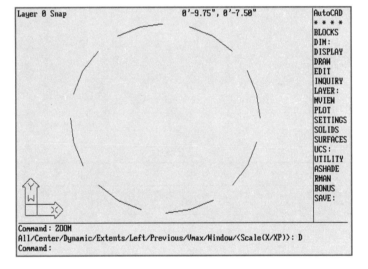

Figure 4.16:
Display after dynamic
zoom.

Note: It is possible to shrink the dynamic window so far that you see only the arrow or X. You will have to enlarge the window with the pointer to regain control.

> **Tip:** You can do your own style of dynamic zoom by simply using the normal zoom options and cutting them short. For example, you can start a ZOOM Previous and cut it short with a <^C> as soon as you see enough to decide where to go next. Then follow it with your intended zoom.

When you are done, try zooming back out with a ZOOM Extents. ZOOM Extents and All both zoom out as far as needed, even beyond the limits, to display everything in the drawing file. Unlike All, which never zooms to a smaller area than the limits, ZOOM Extents zooms to the smallest area possible that will display all entities in the drawing.

Using ZOOM Extents

```
Command: ZOOM
```
ZOOM Extents magnifies screen to edge of border.
```
All/Center/Dynamic/Extents/Left/Previous/
  Vmax/Window/<Scale(X/XP)>: E
```

Your screen should look like figure 4.17.

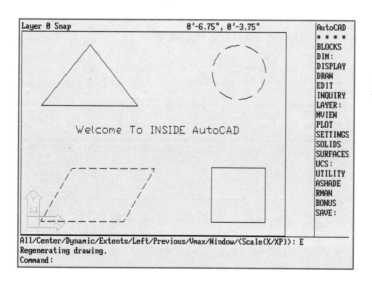

Figure 4.17:
ZOOM Extents.

> **Tip:** Always use a ZOOM Extents just before you end your drawing session. It will act as a check to let you know if you have drawn anything outside your limits. You can cut it short with a <^C>.

As you may have noticed, you can use ZOOM Dynamic to move your current view from side to side without changing the magnification. This is called *panning*. There is also a PAN command just for panning.

Using PAN to Slide a View

Frequently, you will need to move your drawing sideways (or up, or down). Say you are working on a zoomed-in area and want to see the part of the drawing file that is just a little to the left. What view control do you use? Use PAN. PAN acts just like a camera pan. It lets you move around the drawing file at your current magnification.

To make PAN work, you need to supply AutoCAD with a *displacement*. You define a displacement by specifying two points. These two points determine a vector giving the distance and direction of your pan. When you give two points to identify a displacement, you specify a point where AutoCAD will pick up the drawing (first displacement point) and then specify another point where the drawing will be placed (second displacement point). Your display crosshairs trail a line from the first to the second displacement point, showing you the pan path (see fig. 4.18).

Use PAN to isolate the square in the upper left corner of your screen. When you are done, your screen should look like the View After Pan illustration (see fig. 4.19).

Using PAN for Display

```
Command: PAN
Displacement:                          Pick first point in square.
Second point:                          Pick second point in triangle.
```

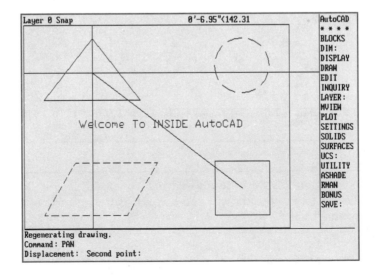

Figure 4.18:
Pan showing displacement.

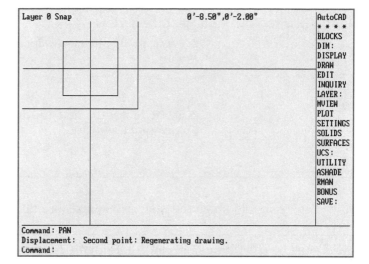

Figure 4.19:
View after pan.

> **Note:** Using ZOOM Dynamic with a constant window size functions like the PAN command. You can also do limited panning with the Center and Left zoom options by defaulting the height.

Using VIEW to Name and Save Working Displays

As you work on a drawing, you will find that your zooms and pans frequently return to the same few drawing views. It would certainly save time if you could save and recall your zooms and pans.

Suppose that you are going to concentrate your work on the square for the next few hours. Periodically, you will want to zoom out to work in other areas, but most of the time you will be zoomed in to the square. Rather than having to show a window around the square every time you want to zoom to this area, you can store this window, give it a name, and call it up whenever you need it.

A stored window is called a *named view.* To store a window, use the VIEW command to name and store it. You can select [VIEW:] from the [DISPLAY] screen menu, or you can type it at the keyboard. Here's an exercise to test AutoCAD's VIEW command and to save SQUARE as a named view.

Using VIEW to Save and Restore a View

```
Command: ZOOM                              Zoom to an area just surrounding the
                                           square.
Command: VIEW
?/Delete/Restore/Save/Window: S
View name to save: SQUARE
Command: ZOOM                              Zoom All to test the view (see fig. 4.20).
Command: VIEW                              Now restore it.
?/Delete/Restore/Save/Window: R
View name to restore: SQUARE
```

When you are done, your display should show the restored square (see fig. 4.21).

Tip: Useful named views would be L for Limits or A for All. Both are quick and easy to type and can be used instead of ZOOM All to avoid regens. Use a view called PLOT for consistency in plotting.

Figure 4.20:
After ZOOM all.

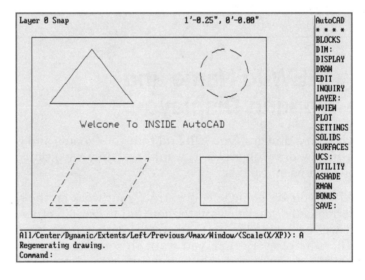

The VIEW command has five options.

VIEW Options

?
Displays a list of all named views, and whether they exist in paper space (P) or model space (M). Paper space and model space are covered later in this chapter.

Save   Lets you name the current view and stores its size and center point.

Restore   Redisplays the named view that you specify.

Delete   Prompts you for the name of a view to delete from the library of named views.

Window   Lets you name and save a view that you specify with a window (not necessarily the current display).

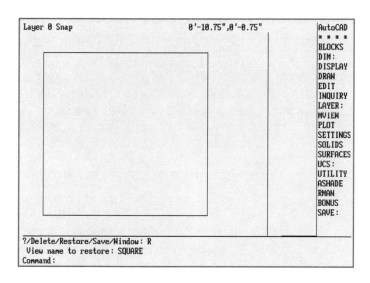

Figure 4.21:
Saved and restored
view named
SQUARE.

Note: You can rename an existing view with the RENAME command.

Tip: If you zoom Center .8X, then save the view as A or ALL, you will give yourself a margin of safety in avoiding zoom and pan regenerations. Then use VIEW Restore All instead of ZOOM All.

Keeping the Right Image Generated

As your drawing files become larger, you will need to control the screen size and resolution of your drawing. This means that you have to be conscious of just how much of your drawing you want AutoCAD to keep active at any one time. In using dynamic zooms, you have seen that AutoCAD keeps three different sets of drawing data active: the drawing extents, generated data, and the screen view.

When your drawing file is small and uncomplicated, all these subsets are usually one and the same. But as your drawing file gets larger, only portions of the file are generated, and it is more efficient to show only portions of your drawing on the screen. Going from one screen view to another within the generated portion of the drawing file with a PAN or ZOOM is usually done with redraw (fast) speed. However, calling up a screen view that contains non-generated data requires a regen of a different set of data and takes more time.

VIEWRES Controls Smooth Curves and Regeneration

The AutoCAD VIEWRES (VIEW RESolution) command controls the speed of your zooms and regenerations in two ways. First, it turns *fast zoom* on and off. Fast zoom means that AutoCAD maintains a large virtual screen so it can do most pans and zooms at redraw speed. If fast zoom is off, all pans and zooms cause a regen. Second, it determines how fine to generate curves. When circles or arcs are tiny, AutoCAD needs only a few straight lines on the screen to fool your eye into seeing smooth curves. When arcs are larger, AutoCAD needs more segments (or vectors) to make a smooth arc. The VIEWRES circle zoom percent tells AutoCAD how smooth you want your curves, and AutoCAD determines how many segments are needed to draw what is to be shown on the screen.

Try altering the smoothness of the circle on the screen by generating fewer segments. To see the effect, you need to change the circle's layer to a continuous linetype. Figures 4.22 and 4.23 demonstrate the effect of VIEWRES on circles.

Figure 4.22:
Before first VIEWRES.

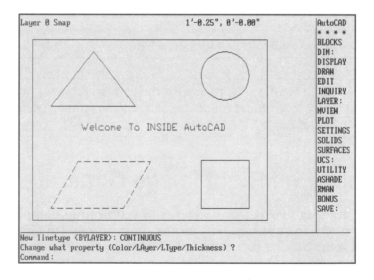

```
Layer 0 Snap                    1'-0.25", 0'-0.00"        AutoCAD
                                                          * * * *
                                                          BLOCKS
                                                          DIM:
                                                          DISPLAY
                                                          DRAW
                                                          EDIT
                                                          INQUIRY
                                                          LAYER:
                                                          MVIEW
                                                          PLOT
           Welcome To INSIDE AutoCAD                      SETTINGS
                                                          SOLIDS
                                                          SURFACES
                                                          UCS:
                                                          UTILITY
                                                          ASHADE
                                                          RMAN
                                                          BONUS
                                                          SAVE:
New linetype <BYLAYER>: CONTINUOUS
Change what property (Color/LAyer/LType/Thickness) ?
Command:
```

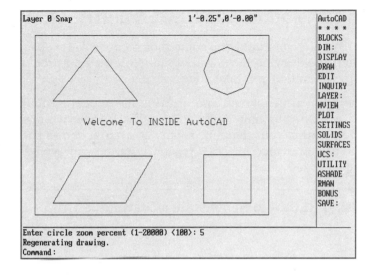

Figure 4.23:
After first
VIEWRES.

Using VIEWRES to Control Resolutions

Command: **ZOOM**	Zoom All.
Command: **CHPROP**	Change the circle's linetype to continuous.
Command: **VIEWRES**	
Do you want fast zooms? <Y>: **<RETURN>**	
Enter circle zoom percent (1-20000) <100>: **5**	
Regenerating drawing.	
Command: **VIEWRES**	Set zoom percent back to 100.

The trade-off for fast zoom is that when a regen is required, it will take longer than if fast zoom is off, because it regenerates a larger area.

Note: If you turn fast zoom off, ZOOM Dynamic and all other pans and zooms will always cause a drawing regeneration. Although turning fast zoom off is rarely advisable, it may be more efficient when zooming large text-filled drawings or doing work that often causes regens even if fast zoom is on. Also, if set to a high number, VIEWRES may cause slow regenerations.

Controlling Data Generation With REGEN and REGENAUTO

You've seen that the VIEWRES command and some zooms cause AutoCAD to regenerate the drawing. When the drawing file is full of many entities, particularly text, arcs, and circles, this regeneration will take a long time.

You can force a regeneration of the screen and drawing file with the REGEN command. You might choose to do so to make AutoCAD recalculate the virtual screen at a particular current view so that your dynamic zoom screen just shows the portion of the drawing that you are interested in. Try a regeneration now by typing REGEN or selecting it from the [DISPLAY] menu.

Using REGEN to Regenerate a Drawing

```
Command: REGEN
Regenerating drawing.
```

Tip: Freezing layers keeps extraneous data from being regenerated. Thaw the layers when you need them.

Using REGENAUTO to Control AutoCAD's Regeneration

When you zoom, pan, or view, you usually want AutoCAD to make sure that everything in the drawing file is represented accurately on the screen. However, since regeneration in large drawings may take a long time, you may not want AutoCAD to regenerate when you are busy drawing or editing.

You can control when AutoCAD regenerates the drawing with the REGENAUTO command. When REGENAUTO is off, AutoCAD avoids regeneration unless absolutely necessary. When necessary, AutoCAD will first stop and ask if you want to regenerate. However, the REGEN command always overrides REGENAUTO and forces a regeneration.

The disadvantage to turning REGENAUTO off is that reset linetype scales, redefined symbols, and changed text styles won't automatically display with their new settings until you regenerate. Once you are comfortable with these items in AutoCAD, this is a small penalty to pay for the time savings of keeping REGENAUTO turned off in complex drawings.

Note: QTEXT is a command that displays text on the screen as only a box outline so that the screen will regenerate quickly. We will show you how QTEXT works in the chapter on text entities.

Transparent PAN, ZOOM, and VIEW

You can use the PAN, ZOOM, and VIEW commands, as well as REDRAW, while you are in the middle of most other AutoCAD commands. These *transparent* commands are triggered by a leading apostrophe ('). Recall that you can get transparent 'HELP the same way.

Draw a line and try a transparent 'VIEW and 'ZOOM. Look for the double angle bracket at the command prompt line. The double bracket shows that the current command is suspended (see fig. 4.24).

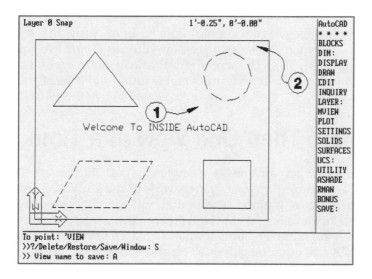

Figure 4.24:
Line suspended by
transparent view.

Using Transparent VIEW and ZOOM

Command: **ZOOM**	Zoom All.
Command: **LINE**	Pick any point in the triangle.
To point: **'VIEW**	Type a leading apostrophe for transparency.
	Note the > prompt indicating that another command is suspended.
>?/Delete/Restore/Save/Window: **S**	
>View name to save: **A**	Saves the current view as A for All.
Resuming LINE command.	
To point: **'ZOOM**	Transparently window the circle.
>Center/Dynamic/Left/Previous/Vmax/ Window/<Scale(X/XP)>: **W**	
>First corner:	Pick first corner point ① (see fig. 4.24).
>Other corner:	Pick second corner point ② (see fig. 4.24).

Using Transparent VIEW and ZOOM—continued

```
Resuming LINE command.
To point:                              Pick any point within the circle.
To point: 'VIEW                        Restore the view A for All.
>?/Delete/Restore/Save/Window: R
>View name to restore: A               Back to the whole view, without a regen.
Resuming LINE command.
To point: <RETURN>

Command: QUIT                          Leave the drawing unchanged.
```

So far, all the display controls you've used have looked in on your drawing with a single viewing screen or viewport. Next, we'll see how you can create multiple views of your drawing and display them on the screen simultaneously. In effect, you divide your screen into windows called *viewports* and display different views of your drawing in each of them.

Displaying More Than One View at a Time

You've been working in a viewport all along — a single viewport that covers the entire drawing area of your screen. Multiple viewports work just as if you divided your drawing screen into rectangles, making several different drawing areas instead of one. You can have up to 16 viewports visible (and create as many as you want) at one time. (In Release 10, you are limited to four viewports created and displayed on DOS machines, or 16 on UNIX and other machines.) You still retain your screen and pull-down menus and command prompts area.

You can work in *only* one viewport at a time. This is called the *current* viewport. You set the current viewport by clicking on it with your pointer. When a viewport is current, its border will be thicker than the others. When you work within a viewport, use your normal display controls just as if you were working with a single screen. You can zoom and pan, set a grid and snap, and those settings are retained for that viewport. The key point, however, is that the images shown in multiple viewports are multiple images of the same data. You're not duplicating your drawing — just putting its image in different viewports.

Because the viewports look onto the same *model* or drawing, you *can* draw from viewport to viewport. You can start a line in one viewport, click to set another viewport current, and then complete the line. AutoCAD will rubber-band your line segment across the viewports.

Multiple viewports are essential in 3D modeling to give you concurrent views of your model from different viewpoints. For example, you can display plan, elevation, and isometric views of your model on the same screen. Viewports also offer advantages over a single view display in some common 2D drafting situations. When you are faced with the problem of detailing different areas of a large drawing or you need to keep one area of your drawing (like a title block or bill of materials) in constant view, use viewports to divide your screen.

There are two types of viewports available in AutoCAD — *tiled* viewports (see fig. 4.25) and untiled (*paper space*) viewports (which are actually entities). (Release 10 is limited to tiled viewports.) Since untiled viewports (see fig. 4.26) offer several advantages over tiled viewports, let's first take a look at the environment in which untiled viewports work. It's called paper space.

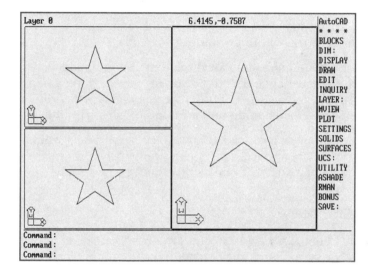

Figure 4.25:
Tiled viewports.

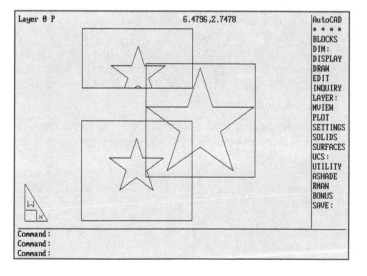

Figure 4.26:
Untiled paper space viewports.

Understanding and Using Paper Space and Model Space

Model space is the drawing environment that exists *in* any viewport, whether it is a single full-screen viewport, one of several tiled viewports, or a viewport entity in paper space. Model space was the only drawing environment that was available for drawing in AutoCAD Release 10. Release 11 adds a new environment called *paper space*. Think of paper space as an infinitely large sheet of paper upon which you can arrange viewports that look onto your model. While model space is a three-dimensional environment, paper space is a two-dimensional environment for arranging views of your model for drawing within or plotting.

Whether you are creating two-dimensional or three-dimensional models, you will do most of your drawing in model space. You'll draw in paper space when you add standard items like title blocks and sheet borders and some types of dimensioning or annotation. Paper space dimensioning and annotation is essential in 3D work.

There is no way to view paper space other than in plan view, which reinforces the two-dimensional nature of paper space. You can actually draw 3D objects in paper space, but with no way to view them, it makes little sense to do so.

Working in Paper Space

Along with paper space comes a new type of viewport — paper space viewports. Paper space viewports can be any size; they do not have to touch (be tiled), and they can even overlap one another. Think of viewports as glass windows into your drawing that can either be opened or closed. If you are in paper space, the window is closed and you can't reach through it to make changes to the entities behind it. But you can move and edit the window frame itself. When you are in model space, the current viewport window is open and you can get at the entities shown inside to edit them or draw more. But you can no longer make changes to the window frame — just to the entities inside. And, you can't have more than one of those windows open (current) at a time.

You can draw anything in paper space that you can draw in model space, except that 3D objects will look flat. Paper space is like another semi-independent drawing that overlays your entire group of viewports. What you draw in paperspace appears *over*, but not *in*, your viewports. You can osnap from paper space to the model-space contents of the underlying viewports, but you cannot osnap from model space to paper space.

When you are working in paper space, viewports are like any other entity. For example, you can edit the boundary of the viewport itself. Indirectly, that can affect the view of the model shown in the viewport. If you make the paper space viewport larger by stretching it, you might see more of the model. If you make the paper space viewport smaller, some of the model might disappear behind the boundary of the viewport. You can use the MOVE command to grab a viewport and move it around on the screen without affecting other viewports. You can change the color of a viewport's boundary box using CHPROP, and you can erase a viewport just like any other AutoCAD entity. But all this happens in paper space.

When you drop back into model space, you can select individual viewports and edit individual entities that show up in those viewports. But, you can't edit the viewport frame's size, color, or other attributes.

Paper Space Viewports vs. Tiled Viewports

So what's so special about paper space viewports? You can work on simultaneous multiple views of your drawing in tiled viewports. But there are restrictions on how you can size tiled viewports, while you can resize and place paper space viewports however you like. Paper space viewports also allow you to selectively control layers by viewport, rather than globally in all tiled viewports. This lets you freeze a layer in one viewport while leaving it thawed in another.

Because paper space viewports let you do everything that tiled viewports do, and then some, we recommend going directly to paper space.

The Command Set for Paper Space Viewports

We'll use three primary commands and one system variable to enter and use viewports in paper space. The TILEMODE system variable must be set to 0 (off) to take you into paper space. Then use the MSPACE command to create viewports. To enter model space so you can work within these viewports, use the MVIEW command. And, to return to paper space to edit viewports, add title blocks or annotation, or set up for plotting, use the PSPACE command.

Entering Paper Space and Creating Viewports

When you begin a drawing in AutoCAD, the display shows a single viewport by default, unless you are using a prototype drawing that has been set up for multiple viewports. The system variable TILEMODE is set to 1 (on) by default, which gives you only tiled viewports. To enter paper space, TILEMODE must be set to 0. If you are in paper space, setting TILEMODE back to 1 will place you back in model space with one or more tiled viewports.

To switch to paper space, select the [Mview] option from the [Display] pull-down menu. Selecting [Mview] changes from the [Display] pull-down menu to the [Mview] pull-down menu. It also sets TILEMODE to 0 (meaning paper space viewports), and executes the MVIEW command. You can also access the MVIEW command from the [DISPLAY] screen menu or type it from the command line.

Let's take a look at an example using the BASIC drawing from Chapter 3 or IA6BASIC.DWG from the IA DISK. We'll enter paper space, create a few paper space viewports, then draw some lines and experiment with object selection in paper space.

Creating Viewports in Paper Space

 Begin a NEW drawing again named BASIC=IA6BASIC.

 Edit an EXISTING drawing named BASIC, and make sure the drawing has the settings shown in the BASIC table near the start of this chapter.

Command: **TILEMODE**   (TILEMODE is set automatically
                                                        when you select [Mview]).

New value for TILEMODE <1>: **0**
Entering Paper space. Use MVIEW to insert
  Model space viewports.
Regenerating drawing.

The drawing has disappeared because there are no paper space viewports to display it in yet.

Command: **MVIEW**   Fit a single viewport to the full
                                                        screen.

ON/OFF/Hideplot/Fit/2/3/4/Restore/<First
  Point>: **F**   The screen looks like before
                                                        you started, except for a trian-
                                                        gular *paper space icon*, a P on
                                                        the status line, and a border
                                                        around the single viewport.

Command: **ZOOM**   Zoom Center with center point
                                                        12,0 and height 19.
                                                        You see the viewport like a
                                                        window surrounded by paper
                                                        space, as illustrated in figure
                                                        4.27.

Command: **MVIEW**   Let's make some more view-
                                                        ports, as shown in figure 4.28.

ON/OFF/Hideplot/Fit/2/3/4/Restore/<First
  Point>: **2**

Creating Viewports in Paper Space—continued

```
Horizontal/<Vertical>: H
Fit/<First Point>: INT
of                                          Pick upper right corner of
                                            viewport.

Second point: 24,-9
Regenerating drawing.
Command: SAVE                               Save the drawing.
Command: LINE                               Draw a few lines across the
                                            screen. They cut right across
                                            viewports.
Command: ERASE
Select objects:                             Select the lines.
Select objects:                             Try to select the circle or text.
                                            You can't.
Select objects: <RETURN>
```

Note: You don't have to be in paper space to use MVIEW. If you are in model space, AutoCAD temporarily switches to paper space to create the viewports.

The MVIEW command gives you other options for creating and controlling viewports in paper space. Here is a listing of them.

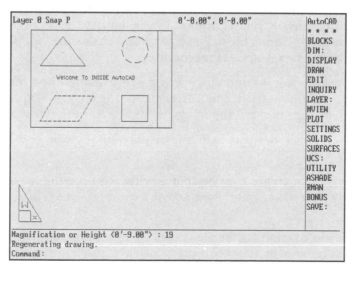

Figure 4.27:
First paper space
viewport.

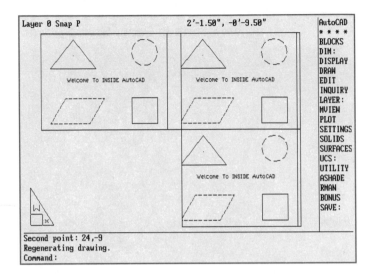

Figure 4.28:
Three paper space
viewports.

MVIEW Options

<First Point> The default option lets you create a viewport using two points. You pick two points to define a rectangular boundary, and the viewport is created to fill that area.

ON Turns on the model view inside the viewport. When on, the default, AutoCAD displays the model and includes the viewport when it regenerates.

OFF Turns off the model view inside the viewport. When the viewport is off, you can move, resize, and otherwise edit the viewport in paper space without having the model view visible inside the viewport. This saves time when AutoCAD regenerates.

Hideplot Turning Hideplot on in a viewport causes a hidden-line removal to occur on that viewport when it is plotted from paper space. This doesn't change the way the model is displayed in the viewport.

Fit Creates a single viewport to fill the display, however large it happens to be.

2 Allows you to create two viewports within a rectangular area you specify, either horizontal (one above the other), or vertical (side by side).

3 Allows you to create three viewports in a rectangular area, making them side by side, stacked on top of each other, or with a larger viewport above, below, to the left, or to the right of two smaller ones.

4   Creates four viewports in a rectangular area, either by specifying the area, or fitting the four viewports to the display.

Restore   Translates a tiled viewport configuration created with the VPORTS command into individual paper space viewports.

Note: The viewports created with the Fit option will appear tiled, but you can move them apart and resize them using commands such as STRETCH and MOVE.

Note: The MVSETUP bonus program included with AutoCAD can set up multiple viewports, adjust limits, and insert a title block. It can be accessed from the [BONUS] screen menu if you select [BONUS] [next] and [MVSETUP].

Well, now you have multiple viewports. What do you do with them?

Drawing in Multiple Viewports

We'll try a simple exercise, entering model space and setting the upper left viewport current. Then we'll zoom to get a better view of the triangle and draw a line from the center of the triangle to the circle on the right. We'll traverse the rest of the drawing, drawing to the approximate center points of the square and parallelogram, and close the line up to the triangle.

If you have Release 10, you can still do this exercise. Just do the exercises in the Using Tiled Viewports section at the end of this chapter, then come back and try this. Your screen won't quite match the illustrations, but will be similar.

Drawing With Multiple Viewports

Continue in the BASIC drawing.

Command: **MSPACE**   You enter model space. (Skip this command in Release 10.)
The paper space icon disappears and each viewport gets a UCS icon.
The upper right was created last, so it is current and has a fat border.

Move the cursor. Notice it's a crosshair when over the current viewport, but an arrow elsewhere.

Pick a point in the upper left viewport, making it current.

Command: **ZOOM**   Use a window to magnify triangle and a bit of the text (see fig. 4.29).

Command: **GRID**   Set grid to .25.

Drawing With Multiple Viewports—continued

```
Command: LINE
From point:                          Start line from approximate center of
                                     triangle.
```

Pick a point in the upper right viewport, making it current.

```
To point: 'ZOOM                      Do a transparent zoom window around
                                     circle.
Resuming LINE command.
To point:                            Continue line to approximate center of
                                     circle (see fig. 4.30).
```

Make bottom right viewport current.

```
To point:                            Continue line to approximate center of the
                                     square (see fig. 4.31).
To point:                            Continue line to approximate center of the
                                     parallelogram (see fig. 4.32).
To point: C                          Line closes in the triangle.
```

When you are done, the upper viewports should show portions of the completed lines and the bottom viewport should show it all.

We just kind of slapped those viewports up on screen. They're fine for drawing, but we could edit them to make better use of our screen's space.

Figure 4.29:
Left viewport zoomed,
with small grid.

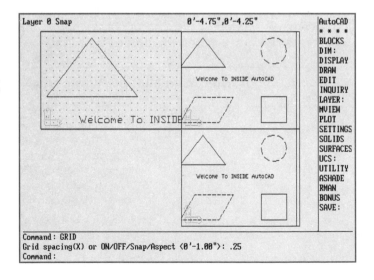

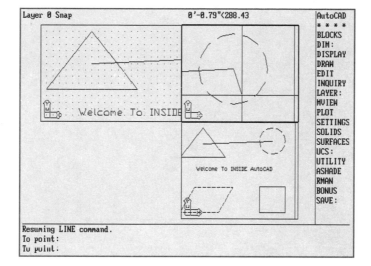

Figure 4.30:
Upper right viewport with first line.

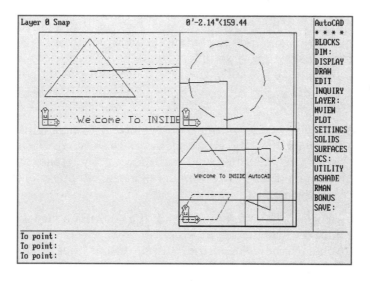

Figure 4.31:
Bottom right viewport with continuing line.

Editing Paper Space Viewports

In model space, any actions you take such as erasing, copying, and so on, affect the model in the current viewport, not the viewport itself. When you are working in paper space, the only entities you can access are the boundary boxes around each viewport, and any entities you may have created or inserted in paper space itself. That's the key to understanding viewports in paper space: when you are working in

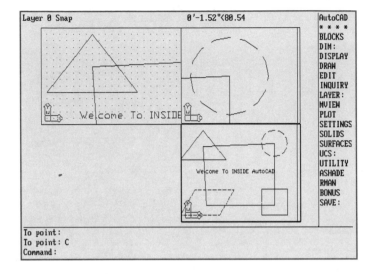

Figure 4.32:
Complete line in
viewports.

paper space you can't make any changes to the model — just to the viewport. To make changes to the model, you have to re-enter model space. But there are times when you will want your edit commands to change the viewport itself, rather than the model that is displayed inside it. For example, you might have created a viewport that isn't quite large enough to display all of the view that is supposed to appear in it to a certain scale. So, you would use AutoCAD's STRETCH command to resize the viewport while in paper space.

AutoCAD recognizes the boundary box around the viewport as a single entity. If you select one line of the boundary box, the entire viewport is selected. Because the viewports are recognized as single entities, you can move, copy, erase, and scale them. (These editing commands will be covered in detail in the chapter on editing — for now just follow the exercise steps.)

You can also place the viewports on different layers. If the color for a viewport is set to BYLAYER, the boundary box will display at whatever color has been assigned to the layer. Or, you can change the color of the boundary box lines by using the CHPROP command and providing an explicit color for the viewport. Changing the layer or color of the boundary does not affect the image inside the viewport, just the boundary box. If you want to plot a drawing without plotting the viewport boundary boxes, place the boundaries on a layer that can be turned off for plotting.

Let's go back to the BASIC drawing that was modified in the last exercise, and use AutoCAD's editing commands to change the viewports. If you have already quit the drawing, load it in again using option 2 from the main menu. Use figure 4.33 for your pick points, when the exercise is completed, your screen should resemble figure 4.34.

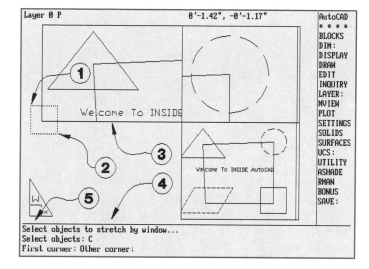

Figure 4.33:
Paper space
viewports unedited.

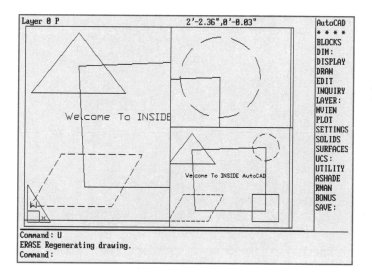

Figure 4.34:
Edited paper space
viewports.

Editing Paper Space Viewports

Continue in the BASIC drawing.

Command: **PSPACE**   Make sure you are in paper space.

Command: **STRETCH**
Select objects to stretch by window...
Select objects: **C**
First point: Pick point ① near left viewport.

Editing Paper Space Viewports—continued

Second point:	Pick point ②, enclosing bottom left corner of viewport.
Select objects: **<RETURN>**	
Base point:	Pick point ③ on bottom edge, by which to stretch viewport boundary.
New point:'	Stretch the viewport down to make it twice its original size and click on ④ aligned with ttom of bottom right viewport.
Command: **MOVE**	Move all the wports into positive X,Y coordinate space.
Select objects:	Select all three viewports by picking each on one boundary box line.
Select objects: **<RETURN>**	
Base point or displacement:	Pick point ⑤ outside bottom left of left viewport.
Second point of displacement: **0,0**	
Command: **ZOOM**	All.
Command: **CHPROP**	Change color of upper right viewport's boundary box.
Select objects:	Pick the boundary box for the viewport.
Select objects: **<RETURN>**	
Change what property (Color/LAyer/ LType/Thickness) ? **C**	
New color <BYLAYER>: **RED**	
Change what property (Color/LAyer/ LType/Thickness) ? **<RETURN>**	
Command: **ERASE**	Erase the bottom right viewport.
Select objects:	Pick viewport No. 3.
Select objects: **<RETURN>**	
Command: **U**	Undo the erasure.
Command: **SAVE**	Save the drawing.

You can see how easy it is to change paper space viewports. Just remember that if you want to change the viewport, you have to be in paper space. If you want to change the model, you have to be in model space.

Controlling Layer Visibility With VPLAYER

Normally, freezing a layer makes that layer disappear from every viewport on the screen. That's because the LAYER command affects layers globally. With paper space viewports (not tiled viewports), you can control the layer visibility in individual viewports, using the VPLAYER (ViewPortLAYER) command.

Unlike freezing layers with the LAYER command, VPLAYER only affects how layers appear in a single viewport. This allows you to select a viewport and freeze a layer in it, while still allowing the contents of that layer to appear in another viewport. VPLAYER settings only affect the visibility of layers in viewports when TILEMODE is set to 0 (paper space viewports). If you switch back to a single or tiled model view by setting TILEMODE to 1 (model space), the global layer settings take precedence over any VPLAYER settings.

The VPLAYER command can be executed from either paper space or model space. If you are in model space and use the select option, it temporarily switches to paper space so you can select a viewport. We'll try it from model space to demonstrate.

Let's use the BASIC drawing again to experiment a little with the VPLAYER command. If you have already quit the drawing, reload it. At the end, we'll set TILEMODE back to 1 (on) and see the screen change back to a single tiled viewport, as it was before we started on our paper space journey.

Controlling Layer Visibility with VPLAYER

Continue in the BASIC drawing, or reload it. Make sure you're in model space.

```
Command: VPLAYER
?/Freeze/Thaw/Reset/Newfrz/Vpvisdflt: F          Freeze.
Layer(s) to Freeze: CIRCLE
All/Select/<Current>: S                          Select.
Switching to Paper space.
Select objects: 1 selected, 1 found             Select upper right viewport.
Select objects: <RETURN>
Switching to Model space.
?/Freeze/Thaw/Reset/Newfrz/Vpvisdflt: F
Layer(s) to Freeze: PARAGRAM
All/Select/<Current>: S
Switching to Paper space.
Select objects: 1 selected, 1 found             Select lower right viewport.
Select objects: <RETURN>
Switching to Model space.
?/Freeze/Thaw/Reset/Newfrz/Vpvisdflt: F
Layer(s) to Freeze: TEXT
All/Select/<Current>: S
Switching to Paper space.
Select objects: 1 selected, 1 found             Select left viewport.
Select objects: <RETURN>
Switching to Model space.
?/Freeze/Thaw/Reset/Newfrz/Vpvisdflt: <RETURN>
Regenerating drawing.
Command: TILEMODE                                Set to 1 and you'll revert to a
                                                 single tiled viewport.
Command: SAVE
```

Compare your display with the illustration. Notice that even though a layer is frozen in each of the viewports, the data on it still appears in the other viewports.

The VPLAYER command gives you a number of options for selectively controlling layer visibility, as well as creating new layers. The following is a list of options available in VPLAYER.

VPLAYER Options

?   If you enter a question mark, AutoCAD prompts you to select a viewport, then displays the names of layers in that viewport that are frozen. If you happen to be in model space, AutoCAD will switch temporarily to paper space to let you select a viewport.

Freeze   Allows you to specify one or more layers to freeze in the selected viewport. You can answer the prompt with a single layer name, a list of layer names, or a wildcard specification to affect a number of similarly named layers.

Thaw   Allows you to thaw a layer, turning its display back on again. As with Freeze, Thaw lets you respond with single or multiple layer names, as well as wildcard specifications.

Reset   Restores the default visibility setting for one or more layers in the selected viewport. See the following explanation of Vpvisdflt for more information on default visibility settings.

Newfrz   Gives you a quick way to create layers without exiting the VPLAYER command. By default, layers you create this way are frozen and you must thaw them with the Thaw option before they will be visible.

Vpvisdflt   Lets you set the default visibility of one or more layers. Say you freeze a layer in several viewports and thaw the same layer in others. The Vpvisdflt setting for that layer determines the initial display mode (frozen/thawed) of that layer in any new viewports you create from that point on.

Dialogue Box Viewport Layer Control

You can also use the layer control dialogue box, the DDLMODES command, to control layers in paper space viewports (see fig. 4.35).

The VP Frz Cur (ViewPort FReeZe CURrent) column controls the freeze/thaw status of layers in the current viewport. If you are in paper space, the change applies to the paper space view itself, not to any of the viewports within. A check mark means the layer is frozen. Click to change it.

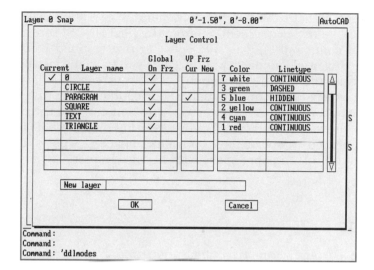

Figure 4.35:
Layer control dialogue box.

The VP Frz New column controls how layers will be in newly created viewports. If checked, the layer(s) will automatically be frozen in subsequently created viewports. You might choose to do this when setting up several new viewports in a complex drawing.

Next, let's take a look at tiled viewports and converting them to paper space viewports.

Using Tiled Viewports

Most, if not all, of your modeling and drawing can be done using paper space viewports. However, there may be times when you want to use AutoCAD's tiled viewports for model space work. And, if you are using Release 10, tiled viewports are all you have! Bear in mind when you go through the following exercises that all of the drawing features found in tiled viewports, like the ability to draw from one viewport to another, are also inherent in paper space viewports.

The VPORTS command controls tiled viewports. It divides the AutoCAD graphics screen into windows. Like paper space viewports, each tiled viewport contains a unique view of the drawing. Unlike paper space viewports, however, tiled viewports must touch at the edges, and they can't overlap one another. You can't edit, rearrange, or turn individual tiled viewports on or off. The other limitation of tiled viewports is in layer visibility — VPLAYER and the VP Frz columns of the layer control dialogue box don't work in tiled viewports. You have to use the LAYER command or Global column of the layer control dialogue box to freeze layers in tiled viewports, and the corresponding layers in all viewports will be affected.

Tiled viewports are created with the VPORTS command. The TILEMODE system variable must be set to 1 (on). Select [VPORTS:] from the [SETTINGS] screen menu. VPORTS offers several command options that you can use to build your screen display by adding, deleting, and joining viewports. Once you have the viewports you want, you can save and name the group. A group of viewports is called a *configuration*. Use the same naming conventions to name your configuration that you use for layer names. You can have up to 31 characters, and you can use three special characters ($, -, and _) in your names. Saving and restoring named tiled viewports are the only advantages tiled viewports have over paper space viewports, but we'll tell you how to get around this in paper space later in this chapter.

Here are the command options.

VPORTS Options

Save   Stores the current viewport configuration under the name that you specify.

Restore   Redisplays a saved viewport configuration.

Delete   Removes a named viewport configuration.

Join   Combines two adjoining viewports into a single viewport.

SIngle   Makes the current viewport into a single screen.

?   Displays a detailed description of the current viewport in the drawing.

2   Divides the current viewport in half vertically or horizontally.

3   Divides the current viewport into three viewports. You can choose from several configuration options.

4   Divides the current viewport into quarters.

Creative use of the 2, 3, 4, and Join options is often needed to get the arrangement you want. Try using VPORTS to divide your screen into three viewports using the BASIC drawing from Chapter 3 or IA6BASIC.DWG from the IA DISK. First, start a new drawing, or set TILEMODE to 1 in your current drawing. Then divide your screen in half. Next, divide the top half into three viewports. Finally, join the top three viewports into two viewports so that you end up with a configuration of two up and one below. Use figures 4.36 through 4.39 and the exercise sequence below as guides.

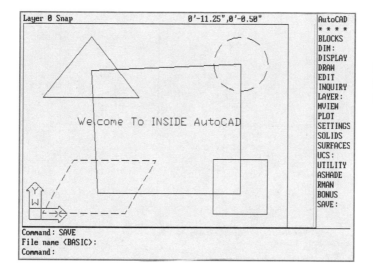

Figure 4.36:
Screen before
viewports.

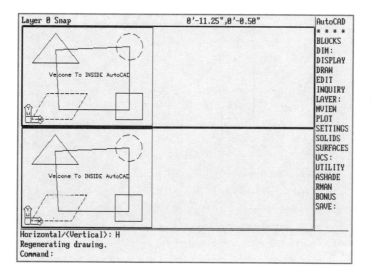

Figure 4.37:
Screen with two
viewports.

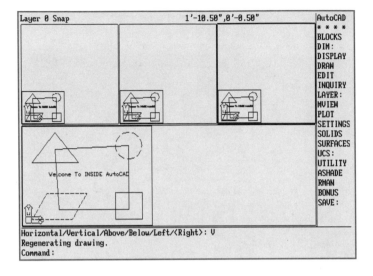

Figure 4.38:
Top viewport divided
three times.

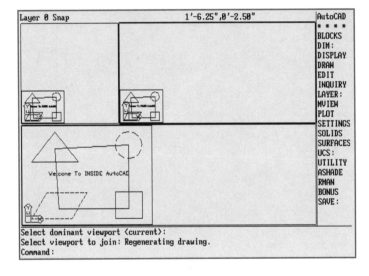

Figure 4.39:
Screen with two
viewports joined.

Using VPORTS to Get Multiple Views

 Begin a NEW drawing named TILEVP=IA6BASIC.

 Edit an EXISTING drawing named BASIC (see fig. 4.36), or continue from the previous exercise.

Command: **TILEMODE**

If continuing with Release 11, make sure it's set to 1 (on). Divide screen in half horizontally (see fig. 4.37).

Command: **VPORTS**

Save/Restore/Delete/Join/SIngle/?/2/<3>/4: **2**
Horizontal/<Vertical>: **H**
Regenerating drawing.
Command: **VPORTS**

Divide top half into three viewports (see fig. 4.38).

Save/Restore/Delete/Join/SIngle/?/2/<3>/4: **3**
Horizontal/Vertical/Above/Below/Left/<Right>: **V**
Command: **VPORTS**

Join the top left and center viewports (see fig. 4.39).

Save/Restore/Delete/Join/SIngle/?/2/<3>/4: **J**
Select dominant viewport <current>: **<RETURN>**
Select viewport to join:

Pick top center viewport.

Now, save your viewport configuration, return your display to a standard single-screen display, and restore the named viewport configuration.

Saving a VPORT Configuration

Command: **VPORTS**

Save the viewport configuration.

Save/Restore/Delete/Join/SIngle/?/2/<3>/4: **S**
?/Name for new viewport configuration: **BASIC**
Command: **VPORTS**
Save/Restore/Delete/Join/SIngle/?/2/<3>/4: **SI**

Set viewport to single screen.

Command: **VPORTS**

Restore the viewport configuration.

Save/Restore/Delete/Join/SIngle/?/2/<3>/4: **R**
?/Name of viewport configuration to restore: **BASIC**
Regenerating drawing.
Command: **SAVE**

If you're using Release 10, you can use this configuration and drawing to do the earlier *Drawing With Multiple Viewports* exercise.

Note: You can translate previously saved tiled viewports into paper space viewports. This is primarily for Release 10 users who are switching to Release 11. To do so, use the Restore option of the MVIEW command while in paper space.

The time it takes to name and save standard working views and viewport configurations is worthwhile if you are using multiple views. As your drawings become more complex, named views will save you time in editing and plotting.

Saving and Restoring Paper Space Viewports

Neither the VPORTS command nor the VIEW command can save and restore paper space viewports. When you save and restore named views in paper space, any viewports currently in the views will be visible, just like any other entity. But if the arrangement of viewports has changed since the view was saved, the former arrangement is not restored. However, you can save and restore paper space viewports by using the BLOCK, INSERT, and MVIEW commands. The BLOCK and INSERT commands are covered in detail in Chapter 9, but here are the steps. We'll try saving and restoring viewports in Chapter 5.

To save an arrangement of viewports: while in paper space, you make a block of the viewport entities you want to save, using an insert base point of 0,0 and any name you like.

To restore a previously saved (blocked) arrangement of viewports: while in paper space, you insert the saved block of the viewport entities using an insert point of 0,0 and prefacing the name with an asterisk. Then you use the MVIEW command to turn them on (they insert turned off), selecting all of the viewports. Of course, before inserting the saved viewports, you would probably want to erase any current viewports.

To save an arrangement of viewports for use in other drawings, you use the WBLOCK command instead of the BLOCK command. To import them into other drawings, use the INSERT and MVIEW commands as previously described. You can also create several groups of viewports in paper space, and pan around to the set you want to work in.

Note: Some early copies of Release 11 may create an extraneous viewport when you reinsert wblocked viewports. If you see an extra image, zoom out, and erase the extra viewport frame, then zoom Previous.

Using REDRAWALL and REGENALL

When you are using multiple viewports and you want to redraw or regenerate all the ports, use the REDRAWALL or REGENALL commands. The standard REDRAW and REGEN commands only affect the current viewport. REDRAWALL can also be performed transparently.

> **Note:** You can delete the BASIC and TILEVP drawings; we won't be using them again.

Summing Up

There are many ways to get around an AutoCAD display screen. Display commands frame different aspects of your drawing, while viewports give you multiple views. Here are a few summary tips from experienced users.

Zoom gives you more (or less!) detail. The most common zoom-in method is Window. It is the most intuitive and convenient way to specify what the next screen view will contain. The most common zoom-out methods are All and Previous, or named views. When zooming out, use ZOOM Dynamic or a view named ALL to get you there in a single step. ZOOM Dynamic lets you choose your next zoom display screen. ZOOM Extents gives you the biggest view possible of your drawing file. Use ZOOM Extents at the end of a drawing session to make sure that you haven't drawn outside your limits.

A PAN displacement gives a nearby view while you are still at the same magnification. When getting from one side of the drawing file to another, use ZOOM Dynamic to get the *whole* view and help you locate your next screen view. ZOOM Dynamic is more intuitive than PAN and gives you feedback on how long it will take to generate your requested image. The VIEW command saves and restores zoomed-in windows. Take the time to use names and store views for drawing efficiency.

Watch how and how often you regenerate your drawing file. Doing a REDRAW cleans construction marks off the screen and *refreshes* the image without regenerating the drawing. Remember VIEWRES optimizes display generation by trading looks for speed. The REGEN command gets you the latest look at what's in the drawing file. Automatic drawing regeneration is controlled with REGENAUTO.

Use paper space viewports to get multiple views of your drawing. Use multiple viewports when you need to do detailed (zoomed-in) work while still looking at your whole drawing, or to see a schedule or reference part of your drawing.

Let's get out of our viewing chairs and climb inside AutoCAD. In the next chapter, we'll find out how AutoCAD's drafting tools work, and how they speed up drawing creation.

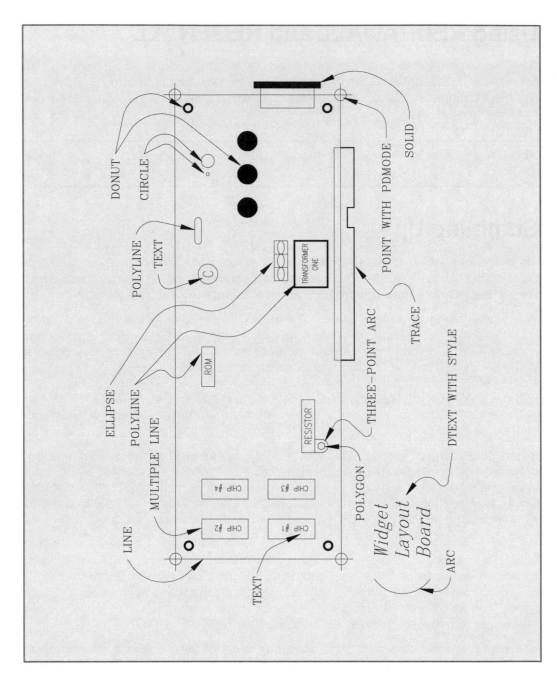

Figure 5.1:
Entities used in WIDGET drawing.

5

Graphic Entities

Setup and display controls are really just tools for creating an environment in which to draw. Just as you'll find collections of tools around a manual drafting board for making lines, text, and curves, you will find AutoCAD gives you a collection of electronic tools to perform similar functions. In this chapter, you will learn about the drawing commands — the drawing tools. You will use these tools to build the drawing shown in figure 5.1. Each command creates an entity, the most fundamental piece of a drawing. The LINE command creates a line entity; the ARC command creates an arc entity. These drawing entities are sometimes called *graphic primitives* (see fig. 5.2). Primitives are the primary entities from which more complex components, symbols, and whole drawings are built. For example, you might make an annotation bubble symbol from primitive line, circle, and text entities.

On paper, your drawing is static. In AutoCAD, graphic entities are *dynamic*. An AutoCAD arc has handles for hauling it around. Text has changeable height, width, and slant. Lines have two endpoints, but when two lines cross, AutoCAD can find the exact intersection.

Note: In addition to the entities illustrated in figure 5.2, AutoCAD has several 3D primitives which are covered in the 3D chapters of the book. Other entities are blocks, attributes, and shapes (covered in Chapter 9) and dimensions (in Chapter 12). You've already learned about viewport entities in Chapter 4.

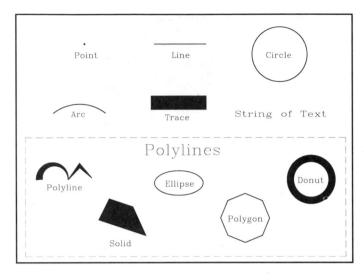

Drawing Tools

In the course of setting up your drawing environment, you have already used a core set of drawing commands, the POINT, LINE, CIRCLE, and DTEXT commands. We will formally re-introduce them and their associates, the ARC, PLINE, DONUT, POLYGON, ELLIPSE, TRACE, TEXT, and SOLID commands.

You will find all the drawing commands by selecting [DRAW] on the root screen menu. The [DRAW] screen menu has two pages of commands. Use [next] to get to the second page. [DRAW] appears near the bottom of most screen menus as a convenience to get to the [DRAW] menu. You also can select drawing commands from the [Draw] pull-down menu (see fig. 5.3), or from your tablet menu. In this chapter, we will show the commands to use. Type them or select them by whatever means you prefer.

Note: Several of the command items on the [Draw] pull-down menu are modified commands for which you can preset parameters with the [Settings] or [Options] pull-down menus.

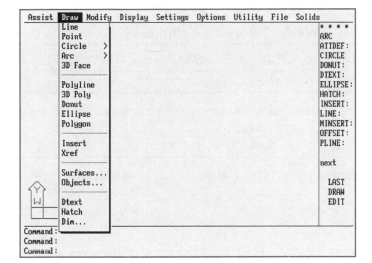

Figure 5.3:
The Draw screen and pull-down menus.

Drawing Goals

The goals for this chapter are two-fold. The first is to learn about the different graphic entities and how they're used. The second is to begin work on a real drawing. You will use graphic entities to build a design, which we call a widget. Then, in the next chapter, you'll use AutoCAD's powerful editing commands to manipulate your drawing by moving, copying, and changing entities quickly and easily.

By the end of the next chapter, you should have a complete widget layout on your screen and a complete understanding of AutoCAD's drawing and editing commands. The widget may show only faint resemblance to a real board layout, but it does contain *all* of AutoCAD's 2D entities. Again, figure 5.1 shows the entities that you will use to create the widget drawing.

Setup for Drawing Entities

To get started, you need to create a new drawing. If you are using the IA DISK, use the IA6WIDGE drawing and name it WIDGET. If you are not using the disk, create the WIDGET drawing with the settings shown in table 5.1. After you finish your setup, create three viewports, and save your viewport configuration as 3VIEW.

Table 5.1
WIDGET Drawing Settings

AXIS	COORDS	GRID	SNAP	UCSICON
Off	On	.5	.1	ORigin

UNITS	Engineering, 2 decimal places, 2 fractional places for angles, default all other settings.
LIMITS	0,0 to 11,8.5

Layer Name	State	Color	Linetype
0	On/Current	7 (white)	CONTINUOUS
BOARD	On	2 (yellow)	CONTINUOUS
HIDDEN	On	1 (red)	HIDDEN
PARTS	On	4 (cyan)	CONTINUOUS
TEXT	On	3 (green)	CONTINUOUS

Setup for WIDGET Drawing

 Begin a NEW drawing named WIDGET=IA6WIDGE.

 Begin a NEW drawing named WIDGET and set it up with the settings shown in table 5.1.

Command: **ZOOM**   Zoom All.

If using Release 11, skip the following VPORTS commands. Pick up the exercise again with the TILEMODE command.

Command: **VPORTS**   (If using Release 10, set up three viewports.)

Save/Restore/Delete/Join/SIngle/?/2/<3>/4:
  <RETURN>
Horizontal/Vertical/Above/Below/Left/<Right>: **A**
Regenerating drawing.

Command: **VPORTS**   (If using Release 10, save viewport configuration and skip rest of this exercise.)

Save/Restore/Delete/Join/SIngle/?/2/<3>/4: **S**
?/Name for new viewport configuration: **3VIEW**

If using Release 11, set up the viewports in paper space as shown below.

Command: **TILEMODE**   Set to 0 (off).

Setup for WIDGET Drawing—continued

```
Command: MVIEW
ON/OFF/Hideplot/Fit/2/3/4/Restore/<First Point>: 3
Horizontal/Vertical/Above/Below/Left/<Right>: A
Fit/<First Point>: F
Regenerating drawing.
Command: BLOCK                              Save the viewport setup.
Block name (or ?): 3VIEW
Insertion base point: 0,0
Select objects: C                           A crossing window (explained
                                            in Chapter 6).
First corner:                               Pick a point in lower left
                                            viewport.
Other corner:                               Pick a point in right half of
                                            upper viewport.

3 found
Select objects: <RETURN>

Command: INSERT                             Restore the viewports.
Block name (or ?): *3VIEW
 Insertion point: 0,0
 Scale factor <1>: <RETURN>
 Rotation angle <0.00>: <RETURN>

Command: MVIEW                             Turn the viewports back on.
ON/OFF/Hideplot/Fit/2/3/4/Restore/<First
   Point>: ON
Select objects: C                          A crossing window.
First corner: Other corner:                Pick the same corner points as
                                           above.

3 found
Select objects: <RETURN>
Regenerating drawing.
Command: MSPACE                            UCS icons appear in each
                                           viewport. You're in model
                                           space.

Command: SAVE                              Save the drawing.
```

When you are done, your screen should look like figure 5.4. Your current layer should be layer 0. The crosshairs cursor should be active in the upper viewport because it is current.

From this point on in this chapter, it makes no real difference in the viewports whether you're using Release 10 or Release 11.

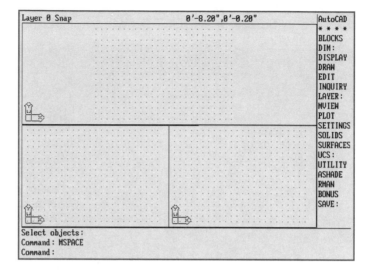

Figure 5.4:
Drawing with
viewports 3VIEW.

Using a Scratch Layer to Experiment

Each exercise in the chapter shows you how to use one or more drawing command options for each graphic entity. As you work through this chapter's exercises, you will use each drawing command. Some commands like ARC, PLINE, and DTEXT have several options that you may want to explore on your own. If you wish, you can make a layer named SCRATCH to experiment on; it will not be used in the basic widget drawing. If your practice entities get in the way, turn layer SCRATCH off.

Using Snaps and Osnaps

The drawing entity exercises show absolute or relative coordinate values for drawing or picking points. These are all snappable (or osnappable) points. You can pick the points on the screen by using your snap and grid, and by following your coords readout. If you are unsure about a coordinate value, you can always pick or type in the value shown in the exercise. If you type the values, omit any trailing zeros or inch marks we show.

The Point's Point

Start with the point. The lowly point is the *most* fundamental drawing entity. Points play a helpful role in building a drawing file. You can use points as drawing reference points. The point itself is sometimes hard to see, but you can control the point display to make points more visible. Lay out the four reference points for the widget board using POINT, and then we'll show you how to use the PDMODE system variable to set a point *type* that is easier to see.

A Word About System Variables

AutoCAD stores a long list of system variables with each drawing. System variables give you the opportunity to set defaults for many commands, which AutoCAD stores in the system variable list. You can use the SETVAR command to update the system variable list. This can take less time than changing the default through the command. And some settings can only be changed directly by the system variables. In Release 11, you can either enter the SETVAR command at the command prompt or just enter the variable name as if it were a command. AutoCAD will recognize the system variable by its name and show the current default. Use the SETVAR command to see a list of all the system variables and their current settings by responding with a question mark (?) at the variable name prompt and an asterisk (*) at the variables to list prompt. Release 10 owners cannot enter system variable names directly at the command prompt and must use the SETVAR command.

Now let's make the point.

Using PDMODE to Set a Point Type

Command: **POINT**	Starts the POINT command.
Point: **2.50",3.30"**	Puts a small blip at the point.
Command: **REDRAW**	Leaves only a hard-to-see dot.
Command: **PDMODE**	(Release 10 users should use the SETVAR command to set PDMODE.)
New value for PDMODE <0>: **34**	Displays points as a circle with a cross in them.
Command: **POINT**	Put points at 2.50,5.80 — 9.50,5.80 — 9.50,3.30.
Command: **REGENALL**	Force a regen to see the first point.
Regenerating drawing.	
Command: **ZOOM**	Use Window to fill top viewport with the points.

Your screen display should look like figure 5.5. When you drew the first point, a mark appeared on the screen. This mark was actually larger than the point that you placed — it was simply the construction marker (blip) for the point. The REDRAW cleared the construction marker and left a small, white dot on the screen. That's the default point type.

Resetting your point display mode gave you the circle-with-cross points. You can set about 20 combinations of point types with PDMODE, as figure 5.6 shows. This illustration is an AutoCAD slide which can be displayed with the [Point Type...] selection on the [Options] pull-down menu or the [Complex Points example:] item on the [POINTS] screen menu (select [POINTS:] from the [DRAW] screen menu to get to the [POINTS] menu page). You can also display it with the VSLIDE command; the slide name is ACAD(POINTS). After displaying it with the screen menu or command, use the REDRAW command to restore your screen.

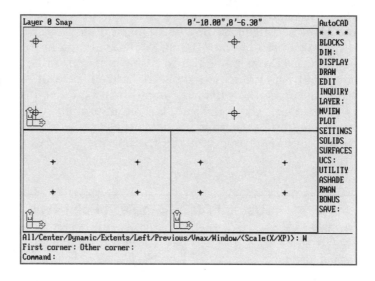

Figure 5.5:
Changing point styles with PDMODE.

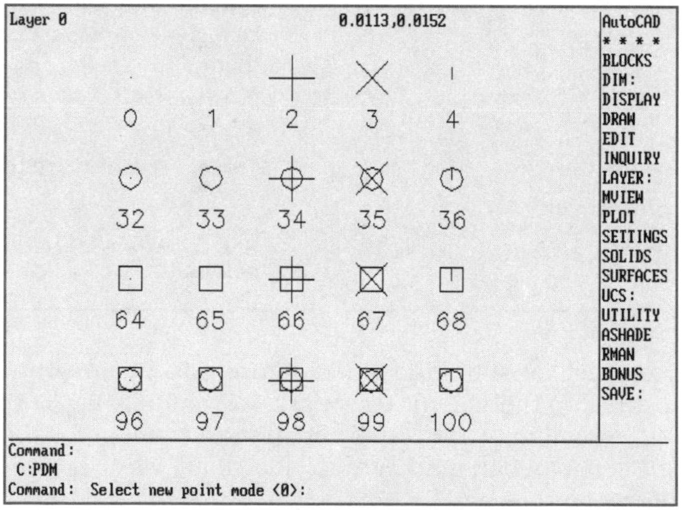

Figure 5.6:
Some of the point styles available in AutoCAD.

The [Point Type...] selection also prompts for the new PDMODE, or you can type PDMODE or select it from the [POINTS] screen menu.

You control the size of the points with the PDSIZE system variable. Setting PDSIZE to a positive number sets its height in current drawing units. Setting it to a negative number makes its point size a consistent percentage of screen or current viewport height, regardless of zoom. For example, 8 will make points eight units high while -8 will make points 8 percent of the screen or current viewport height. You can use the [Point Size] selection from the pull-down menu, [PDSIZE:] from the screen menu, or just type PDSIZE to change it. (Type SETVAR PDSIZE in Release 10.)

Setting up a reference layer with points or a few lines can help you organize your drawing file for placing other elements. When you are all through with your placements, turn the reference layer off. You can also osnap to a point, which makes them useful to include as osnap nodes in blocks. Blocks are covered in Chapter 9.

The LINE Command — How Two Points Make a Line

You've already used the LINE command several times. Issuing the LINE command to AutoCAD begins a process of recording the two endpoints of a line segment. The two points you identify define a line segment. Remember, there are several ways to enter points.

- Use the pointer and crosshairs to pick points.
- Use SNAP, ORTHO, and OSNAP commands to control your point picking.
- Type coordinates at the keyboard: absolute or relative, Cartesian, polar, spherical, or cylindrical.

In the following exercises, we'll practice using osnaps and the various forms of typed and picked coordinate entry from Chapter 2.

Once a line is created from two endpoints (however they are entered), AutoCAD assumes that you want to continue drawing lines until you end the LINE command and return to the command prompt.

The LINE Command's Options

The LINE command has three useful options: continue, Undo, and Close. The continue option lets you pick up the last point of the most recent line to start a new line segment. A <RETURN> entered in response to the From point prompt lets you continue. Undo eliminates the last line segment of the current command and backs up one point to let you try the line segment again. Close makes a polygon by taking your last endpoint and *closing* it to your first point. Undo and Close are achieved by typing a U or a C at the To point prompt.

Here's a little line exercise. Select [LINE] from the [DRAW] screen menu and draw the perimeter of the widget board using osnaps and the Close option. When you are done, your screen should resemble figure 5.7.

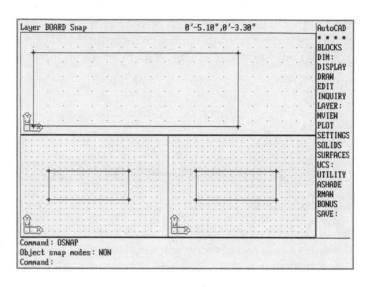

Figure 5.7:
The completed widget board layout.

Using LINE With Osnap NODe and the Close Option

Command: **LAYER**	Set layer BOARD current.
Command: **OSNAP**	
Object snap modes: **NOD**	Sets a running osnap for the points.
Command: **LINE**	
From point:	Pick each of the point entities, in order.
To point: **C**	Close to complete rectangle.
Command: **OSNAP**	
Object snap modes: **NON**	Sets running osnap back to none.

Any time you have drawn a few line segments and want to make them into a polygon, use Close. A C<RETURN> is all you need from the keyboard in response to the To point prompt.

Next, let's use the LINE command's Continue and Undo options. We'll add a port to the widget's right side to see the effects of the Close option.

Using LINE's Undo and Continue Options

Command: **LINE**	
From point:	Pick absolute point 9.30,3.70.
To point: **<Coords>**	Toggle coords to X,Y mode and pick absolute point 9.30,4.50.
To point:	Pick any random point.
To point: **U**	Oops, wrong point. A U undoes it.
To point: **<RETURN>**	Ends command.
Command: **<RETURN>**	A <RETURN> repeats the command.
LINE From point: **<RETURN>**	Another continues from last point of last line drawn.
To point:	Pick absolute point 9.60,4.50.
To point:	Pick absolute point 9.60,3.70.
To point:	Pick absolute point 9.30,3.70.
To point: **<RETURN>**	Ends command.

Your screen now should look like figure 5.8.

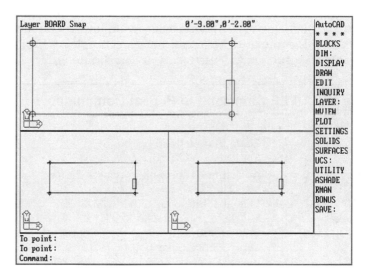

Figure 5.8:
The widget board with the port added.

Here is a summary of the LINE options.

LINE Options

<RETURN>   Pressing <RETURN> at the From point prompt starts a new line from the endpoint of the last line or arc drawn.

Close   Uses the From point of the first line segment in the current LINE command as the next To point, making a closed polygon out of the connected segments and ending the command.

Undo   Lets you wipe out mistakes without leaving the LINE command. If you make a mistake, you can undo the last point by picking the screen menu undo selection, or by typing U at the keyboard, then reissuing your next point.

> *Note:* You can keep undoing as long as you are in the LINE command and have not exited the command with a <RETURN>, <SPACE>, or <^C>.

You've seen how a <RETURN> repeats the previous command. You can also have AutoCAD automatically repeat commands.

The MULTIPLE Command

You can automatically repeat commands by preceding them with the MULTIPLE command. Try filling up the left side of the board by drawing four rectangles, using MULTIPLE to repeat the LINE command. We'll call these rectangles RAM chips. As we draw the RAM chips, we'll practice various forms of coordinate entry.

Using the MULTIPLE Command to Repeat Commands

Click in the bottom left viewport to make it current.

Command: **ZOOM**	Zoom in on left side of board.
Command: **LAYER**	Set layer PARTS current.
Command: **MULTIPLE LINE**	No command prompt is reissued after MULTIPLE.
From point:	Pick absolute point 2.80,3.70.
To point: **<Coords><Coords>**	Toggle to polar display. Pick relative polar point @ 0.70<90.00.
To point: **@.3<0**	Type relative polar point.
To point:	Pick relative polar point @ 0.70<270.00.
To point: **C**	Closes line and MULTIPLE automatically starts a new line.
LINE From point:	Pick absolute point 2.80,4.70.
To point: **@0,.7**	Type relative Cartesian point.
To point:	Pick relative polar point @ 0.30<0.00.
To point: **@.7<-90**	Type relative polar point (-90=270).
To point: **C**	
LINE From point: **3.4,4.7**	Type absolute point.

Using the MULTIPLE Command to Repeat Commands—continued

To point:	Pick or type relative polar points @.7<90 to @.3<0 to @.7<270 and type C to close it.
LINE From point:	From absolute point 3.4,3.7 to @.7<90 to @.3<0 to @.7<-90 and C to close.
LINE From point: *Cancel*	Press <^C> to cancel MULTIPLE LINE.
Command: **SAVE**	

Your screen should look like figure 5.9.

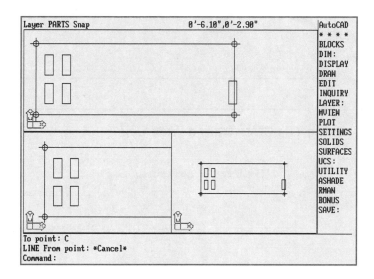

Figure 5.9:
The widget board with RAM chips added.

TRACE Is a Fat Line

TRACE is a distant cousin of LINE. You draw traces just like you draw lines, with a From point and a To point. But AutoCAD first asks you how wide you want the trace. You can create traces as wide as you want (see fig. 5.10). When drawing traces, AutoCAD lags one segment behind in displaying the trace, calculating the miter angle between the previous trace segment and the next.

Try using TRACE to draw a connector on the lower right side of the widget, typing or picking the points.

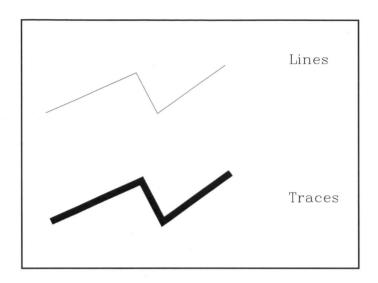

Figure 5.10:
A line and a trace.

Lines

Traces

Using TRACE to Draw a Wide Line

Make the top viewport current.

Command: **LAYER**	Set layer BOARD current.
Command: **TRACE**	
Trace width <0'-0.05">: **.01**	
From point: **5.5,3.3**	
To point: **@.2<270**	
To point: **@2<0**	
To point: **@.1<90**	
To point:	Continue with @.3<0 to @.1<270 to @.9<0 to @.2<90.
To point: **<RETURN>**	
Command: **LINE**	Add interior line from 5.50,3.30 to @.1<90 to @3.2<0 to @.1<-90.
Command: **ZOOM**	Zoom in close to see difference between line and trace.
Command: **U**	Undo the zoom.

You should see a noticeable thickness to the trace (see fig. 5.11). If your drawing has numerous wide traces, it will slow down regens, redraws, and plots. Read about the FILL command, later in this chapter, to see how to temporarily turn off the interior filling of traces and speed things up.

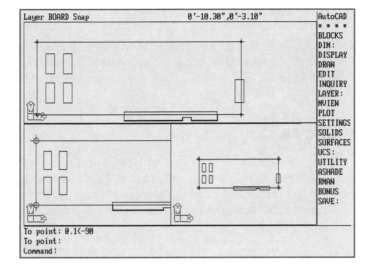

Figure 5.11:
The connector, drawn with TRACE.

Traces do have some limitations:

- You can't curve a trace.
- You can't close a trace.
- You can't continue a trace.
- You can't undo a trace segment.

Okay, so TRACE isn't much like LINE, but you get the idea. To create thick lines, we recommend that you use either color assignment to thick plotter pens or the PLINE command (covered later in this chapter), except when you *need* mitered ends.

Tip: To get a finished end with a miter, draw an extra segment and erase it. The remaining segment will have a mitered end, depending on the direction of the trace that followed.

Note: Traces are stored like four-sided solids, so osnapping to them is limited. Osnap INT and ENDP both find the corners. Osnap MID finds the middle of any side; you can use it (not ENDP) on the end of a trace to find the original From and To points.

Arcs and Circles

Unlike lines, arc and circle entities require more than two simple endpoints. You can create arcs and circles in at least a dozen different ways. Regardless of the parameters (like endpoints, angles, directions, or chords) that you enter to create the entity, arcs and circles are stored as the simplest possible geometry. A circle is stored as a center point and a radius. An arc is a center point, a radius, a start angle, and an end angle. Using this geometric information, AutoCAD can regenerate curves at the best possible resolution and smoothness that your system can display or plot.

Getting to Know Circles

If you select [CIRCLE] from the screen menu, you will get another screen menu listing five circle creation methods. Why so many? Different drafting tasks provide different information about where circles should go. Most often you know the center point and the radius or diameter. In these cases, you use this information to create the circle. Here are the circle options.

CIRCLE Options

2P   Lets you pick the two points of the circle's diameter.

3P   Lets you pick any three points on the circumference of a circle.

TTR   Lets you pick two tangent points and a radius. If a circle can exist through these two points, AutoCAD will generate it for you.

<Center point> Lets you pick the center of the circle and then either use the radius default or diameter option to complete it.

You can create a circle in at least five ways (see fig. 5.12). Which one do you choose? If you know ahead of time whether you have a radius, diameter, or points, you can pick the correct option from the screen menu. If you haven't thought that far ahead, AutoCAD lets you pick your options in midstream, using keyboard entry.

Note: Notice the difference between Center point/Diameter and 2P. Both let you specify a diameter, but if you pick the second point with Center point/Diameter, it merely shows the diameter's distance and the circle does not draw through the point. When you pick two points with 2P, you see a circle appear between those two points with the distance as the diameter. 2P lets you draw a diameter circle the way most people intuitively think about diameter.

We'll draw three circles, using MULTIPLE to repeat the command. Try using the default center point/radius, 2P, and center point/diameter options to draw a capacitor near the center of the board and a knob and a small contact (more contacts to follow, next chapter) for a switch on the right side of the board.

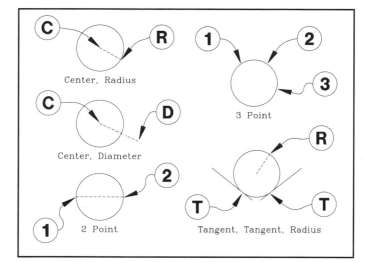

Figure 5.12:
AutoCAD enables you
to draw circles in five
different ways.

Using CIRCLE to Draw Capacitors

Command: **LAYER**	Set layer PARTS current.
Command: **MULTIPLE CIRCLE**	Use Center point/radius for capacitor.
3P/2P/TTR/<Center point>: **6.80,5.30**	Center point.
Diameter/<Radius>: **0.15**	The radius.
CIRCLE 3P/2P/TTR/<Center point>: **2P**	Use 2P for center of switch.
First point on diameter: **8.40,5.30**	
Second point on diameter: **8.60,5.30**	
CIRCLE 3P/2P/TTR/<Center point>: **8.30,5.30**	Use Center point/diameter for contact of switch.
Diameter/<Radius>: **D**	
Diameter: **.05**	
CIRCLE 3P/2P/TTR/<Center point>: **<^C>**	Cancel the command.

Your screen should resemble figure 5.13.

When you pick a center point, AutoCAD gives you the option of selecting a radius or diameter. If you pick a coordinate as the radius, as you did in the example, you will get a circle through the radius point. A D<RETURN> response instead will show the diameter prompt. Then a pick coordinate will give you a circle by the Center point/ diameter method.

Typing 2P, 3P, or TTR <RETURN> will get you one of those options, and AutoCAD will prompt you for the necessary points to complete the circle.

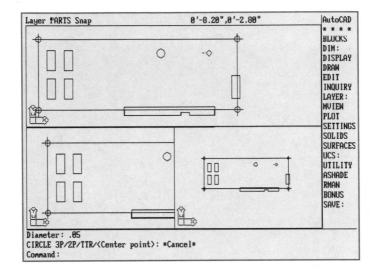

Figure 5.13:
Some capacitors
drawn with circles.

Using Three-Point Arcs

If you thought there were a lot of ways to create circles, there are even more ways to create arcs. AutoCAD offers nearly every possible geometric method to create arcs.

The most straightforward way to enter arcs is with the three-point default of the ARC command. It works about the same way as a three-point circle. The first point is the arc's beginning; the second and third points define the arc's curve. The last point and first point define the chord of the arc. AutoCAD automatically drags the arc, unless you have turned drag off (with DRAGMODE).

Try a three-point arc, to be part of a future logo (see fig. 5.14). Locate the arc just to the lower left of the board, zoomed into your right viewport.

Using ARC With Start Point, End, and Direction

Make bottom right viewport current.

Command: **LAYER**	Set layer TEXT current.
Command: **ZOOM**	Zoom to the lower left quarter of viewport.
Command: **SNAP**	Set to 0.05 units.
Command: **ARC**	Three-point.
Center/<Start point>:	Pick absolute point 2.2,2.8. at ①.
Center/End/<Second point>:	Pick second point 2.0,2.35 at ②. Drag automatically comes on.
End point:	Pick 2.2,1.9 at ③.

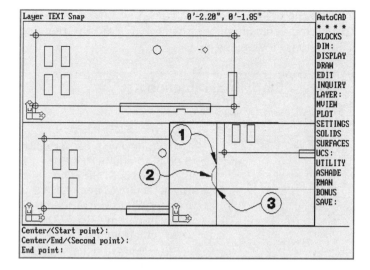

Figure 5.14:
A three-point arc for a future logo.

Figure 5.15 shows a zoomed view of the new arc.

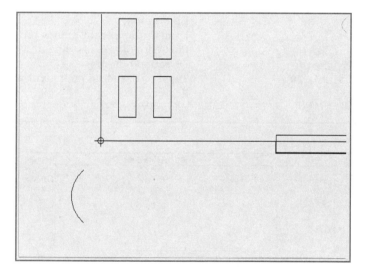

Figure 5.15:
Detail of a lower right viewport.

Make sure you feel comfortable with the way AutoCAD uses drag to help you decide where the three-point arc is going to fall. After the first two points are entered, drag is automatically turned on. Do you understand why the arc can flip around depending on the third point's placement? Push the pointer around until you do.

Drawing an arc with a start point, an endpoint, and a starting direction (tangentially from the start point) is useful for connecting two parallel lines with an arc. Draw a resistor on the widget using the LINE command. Then use LINE and ARC to draw the mounting tab on the bottom left side of the resistor. Locate the resistor next to the RAM chips in your lower left viewport.

Using a Start, End, Direction Arc

Make bottom left viewport current.

Command: **LAYER**	Set layer PARTS current.
Command: **ZOOM**	Use Window with corner points at 3.90,3.40 and 5.10,4.20.
Command: **VIEW**	Save view as RESISTOR.
Command: **LINE**	Draw rectangle from 4.1,3.9 to @.8<0 to @.2<270 to @.8<180 and close it.
Command: **LINE**	Draw line from 4.10,3.60 to @.1<90.
Command: **LINE**	Draw line from 4.30,3.60 to @.1<90.
Command: **ARC**	A Start,End,Direction arc, using osnaps.
Center/<Start point>: **ENDP**	Use endpoint osnap.
of	Pick endpoint of first line at ① (see fig. 5.16).
Center/End/<Second point>: **E**	End option.
End point: **ENDP**	Drag automatically comes on.
of	Pick endpoint of last line at ②.
Angle/Direction/Radius/<Center point>: **D**	Direction option.
Direction from start point: **270**	Type, or drag and pick point at 270 degrees.
Command: **ZOOM**	Zoom Previous.

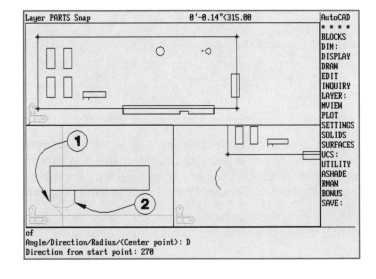

Figure 5.16:
A resistor with a
Start,End,Direction
arc.

There are ten options for the ARC command, which we've grouped by common functions (see fig. 5.17).

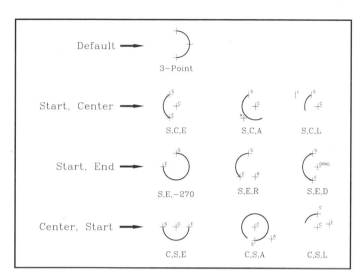

Figure 5.17:
AutoCAD lets you draw arcs in ten different ways.

ARC Options

Default   Creates an arc that passes through three selected points. A further default, invoked by a <RETURN> at the first arc prompt, starts a new three-point arc tangent to the last endpoint of the last line or arc drawn. Similarly, a <RETURN> at the first prompt of the LINE command will start a new line at the end of the last arc. Try some of these arc options on your SCRATCH layer.

Start,Center   Requires an arc starting point and the center point of the radius of the arc. This option group has a third parameter which determines the arc by specifying an endpoint, an angle, or a length of chord.

Start,End   Lets you define the starting and ending points of the arc first, then define how the arc will be drawn. You define the arc with an angle, radius, direction, or center point.

Center,Start   Allows you to first pin down the center of the arc, then the start point. The arc is completed by supplying an angle, length of chord, or endpoint.

You can select any of the ten arc options from the arc, screen, or tablet menus. The options are abbreviated by mnemonic letters. If you're keying arc commands from the keyboard, you'll find the commands have common beginnings according to their class (Start,Center: Start,End, etc.).

You can choose your options midstream and select one arc creation method over another by entering ARC and the options from the keyboard. Beginning an arc with a picked point will narrow your construction methods to those that begin with Start; beginning with C will restrict you to options that accept the center point first, and so on.

Polylines Are Sophisticated Lines

You have explored the most common entities—the line, arc, and circle. Given what you already know about entities, how would you create thic ; lines or thick, tapered lines other than by using the trace command? How would you draw a continuous series of lines and arcs? Can you make a closed polygon with three straight sides (lines) and one curved side?

Before you spend too much time making basic graphic entities work too hard, consider the polyline, or *pline* for short. Instead of creating multiple lines to get a thick one, or creating independent arcs and then connecting them to lines, you can create a polyline.

Polylines vs. Lines

Polylines are different from independent line entities that visually appear to be joined by continuing the LINE command. AutoCAD treats a multi-segment polyline as a single drawing entity. Polylines can include both line and curve segments connected at vertices (endpoints). Information such as tangent direction and line width is stored at each vertex.

Polylines offer two advantages over lines. First, as figure 5.18 demonstrates, polylines are versatile. They can be straight or curved, thin or wide, one width or tapered. For example, you could draw a curved leader with an arrowhead as a single polyline.

Second, the fact that a polyline is a single entity makes editing operations easier and reduces errors when doing crosshatching and 3D work. You can edit a polyline by selecting any segment, since selecting any segment selects all segments. By contrast, if you wanted to copy one of the RAM chip rectangles made up of four individual line entities in the widget drawing, you would have to select each individual line segment. When you crosshatch or create 3D objects from 2D lines, you must have edges that truly connect. (Objects drawn with lines and arcs may appear connected but still have tiny gaps which will cause hatch or 3D errors.) Use polylines to draw any closed or connected object or polygon, particularly if you anticipate hatching it or working with your drawing in 3D.

Using PLINE, try to create another widget rectangle, the ROM chip, in the center of the board.

Figure 5.18:
You can create many
kinds of polylines.

Using PLINE to Draw a ROM Chip

Make bottom right viewport current.

Command: **PAN**   Pan or zoom to fill viewport
                                              with center of the board.
Command: **PLINE**   Create a ROM chip.
From point: **5.10,5.20**
Current line-width is 0'-0.00"
Arc/Close/Halfwidth/Length/Undo/Width/
  <Endpoint of line>: **@0,0.2**
Arc/Close/Halfwidth/Length/Undo/Width/
  <Endpoint of line>: **@.6<0**
Arc/Close/Halfwidth/Length/Undo/Width/
  <Endpoint of line>:   Pick point @.2<270.
Arc/Close/Halfwidth/Length/Undo/Width/
  <Endpoint of line>: **C**

Your screen now should look like figure 5.19. This new rectangle looks similar to the RAM chips on the left. In the next chapter, you will see that this single ROM chip entity includes all four segments, while the other rectangles are each actually four separate entities.

Since PLINE can draw two basic kinds of segments, straight and curved, you will find that some prompts are similar to the line and arc prompts. When you draw straight polyline segments, you get prompts like Endpoint, Close, and Undo. Check out the possibilities on the PLINE prompt line.

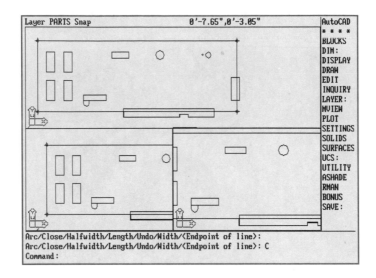

Figure 5.19:
A ROM chip drawn
with PLINE.

PLINE Options

Arc	Changes prompt to display arc options.
Close	Draws a straight line segment back to the first point of the polyline.
Halfwidth	Accepts values for half the polyline width for the start and endpoints of the following segment.
Length	Specifies a length of line to be drawn at the same angle as the previous segment. Used immediately after an arc segment, it will produce a tangent line.
Undo	Removes the last segment added to the polyline.
Width	Prompts for the starting and ending width of the following polyline segment. The ending width becomes the default width for all subsequent segments until changed with the Width/Halfwidth option.
<Endpoint of line>	Accepts the next point as the endpoint of the current polyline segment.

Selecting the Arc option presents another set of options, including some familiar arc prompts like Angle/CEnter/Radius, as well as Second pt and Endpoint of arc.

PLINE Arc Options

Angle	Prompts for the included angle of the current arc segment.
CEnter	Prompts for the center point of the current arc segment.
CLose	Draws an arc segment back to the first point of the polyline.
Direction	Allows you to override the default tangent direction.
Halfwidth	Accepts values for half the polyline width for the start and endpoints of the following segment.
Line	Changes prompt to display line options.
Radius	Accepts a radius value for the following arc segment.
Second pt	Accepts the second point of the arc.
Undo	Removes the last segment added to the polyline.
Width	Prompts for the starting and ending width of the following polyline segment. The ending width becomes the default width for all subsequent segments until changed with the Width/ Halfwidth option.
<Endpoint of arc>	Accepts the next point as the endpoint of the current polyline segment.

Drawing lines and arcs with PLINE is similar to drawing the equivalent elements with the basic LINE and ARC commands. But there are several important differences. First, you get all the prompts every time you enter a new polyline vertex. Second, there are additional prompts that control the width of the segment, like Halfwidth and Width. When a polyline has width, you can control the line fill by turning FILL on or off. (We will show you how fill works a little later in this section.) Third, you can switch back and forth from straight segments to curved segments, adding additional segments to your growing polyline.

Using PLINE to Draw Arcs and Wide Lines

Try using these extra polyline features by putting two more objects on your widget. Create a diode (a little narrow object with arcs on both ends) by combining line and arc segments. Then, draw a rectangular transformer using a wide polyline. Locate the diode between the circles at the top and the transformer near the bottom center of the board. Continue working in your right viewport. When you start PLINE, the first prompt is for drawing straight segments.

Using PLINE to Draw a Diode and Transformer

```
Command: PAN                              Pan or zoom if needed.
Command: PLINE                            Draw the diode.
From point:                               Pick absolute point 7.30,5.40.
Current line-width is 0'-0.00"
Arc/Close/Halfwidth/Length/Undo/Width/
  <Endpoint of line>: @0.30,0
Arc/Close/Halfwidth/Length/Undo/Width/
  <Endpoint of line>: A                   Arc.
Angle/CEnter/CLose/Direction/Halfwidth/Line/
  Radius/Second pt/Undo/Width/<Endpoint
  of arc>: A                              Angle.
Included angle: 180
Center/Radius/<Endpoint>: @0.10<90
Angle/CEnter/CLose/Direction/Halfwidth/Line/
  Radius/Second pt/Undo/Width/<Endpoint
  of arc>: L                              Line.
Arc/Close/Halfwidth/Length/Undo/Width/
  <Endpoint of line>: @0.30<180
Arc/Close/Halfwidth/Length/Undo/Width/
  <Endpoint of line>: A                   Arc. .
Angle/CEnter/CLose/Direction/Halfwidth/Line/
  Radius/Second pt/Undo/Width/<Endpoint
  of arc>: CL                             Close.
```

You can zoom in for a better look, if you wish. Then undo or zoom Previous.

```
Command: <RETURN>                         Repeat command. Draw the
                                          transformer with wide polyline.
PLINE From point:                         Pick absolute point 6.60,3.50.
Current line-width is 0'-0.00"
Arc/Close/Halfwidth/Length/Undo/Width/
  <Endpoint of line>: W                   Width.
Starting width <0'-0.00">: .02
Ending width <0'-0.02">: <RETURN>         Defaults to starting width.
Arc/Close/Halfwidth/Length/Undo/Width/
  <Endpoint of line>: @0.50<90.00
Arc/Close/Halfwidth/Length/Undo/Width/
  <Endpoint of line>: @0.70<0.00
Arc/Close/Halfwidth/Length/Undo/Width/
  <Endpoint of line>: @0.50<270.00
Arc/Close/Halfwidth/Length/Undo/Width/
  <Endpoint of line>: C
Command: SAVE
```

Figure 5.20 shows the board with the newly created diode and transformer in place.

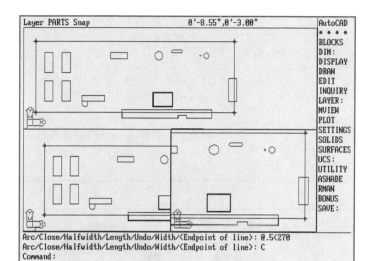

Figure 5.20:
*A diode and a trans-
former drawn with
PLINE.*

Note: Because you can create complex objects with polylines, there is a companion command, PEDIT, that lets you modify a polyline without redrawing it from scratch. We will cover PEDIT in the next chapter.

Polylines in Disguise — Donuts, Polygons, and Ellipses

As you might imagine, the DONUT command creates a donut-looking entity. Donuts can have any inside and outside diameter you like. In fact, a donut with a 0 inside diameter is a filled-in circle and makes a good dot (see fig. 5.21).

Get a cup of coffee and try the donuts! Try putting three filled dots on the right of the board. Then, put regular donuts at each corner of the widget as ground holes.

Using DONUT to Create Donuts

```
Command: DONUT
Inside diameter <0'-0.50">: 0
Outside diameter <0'-1.00">: .3
Center of doughnut:                    Pick absolute point 8.80,4.70.
Center of doughnut:                    Pick absolute point 8.30,4.70.
Center of doughnut:                    Pick absolute point 7.80,4.70.
```

Using DONUT to Create Donuts—continued

```
Center of doughnut: <RETURN>

Command: <RETURN>                          Repeat the command.
DONUT Inside diameter <0'-0.00">: 0.1
Outside diameter <0'-0.30">: 0.15
Center of doughnut:                        Pick absolute point 9.30,5.60.
Center of doughnut:                        Pick absolute point 9.30,3.50.
```

Make the top viewport current.

```
Center of doughnut:                        Pick absolute point 2.70,3.50.
Center of doughnut:                        Pick absolute point 2.70,5.60.
Center of doughnut: <RETURN>
```

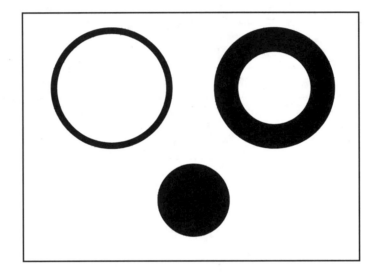

Figure 5.21:
Some DONUT
examples.

Figure 5.22 shows the results of this command sequence.

As you can see, DONUT keeps on prompting for the center of the donut until you press <RETURN> to exit the command. DONUT or DOUGHNUT, AutoCAD doesn't care which way you spell it.

The donut that AutoCAD constructs is not a new primitive. It is actually a polyline that has the following three polyline properties: it is made of arc segments, it has width (you set the widths by entering the inside and outside diameter), and it is closed.

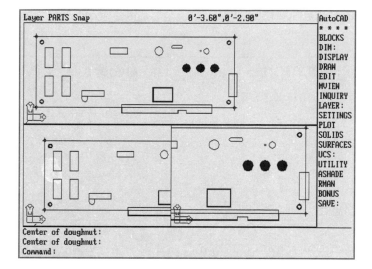

Figure 5.22:
Adding parts with
DONUT.

Drawing Regular Polygons With POLYGON

If you want multi-segmented polygons with irregular segment lengths, use polylines or closed lines. But if you want nice, regular polygons, take a look at the POLYGON command. A polygon is actually another polyline in disguise. POLYGON gives you two ways to define the size of your figure (see fig. 5.23). You can show the length of one of the edges or define it relative to a circle. The polygon can then be inscribed in or circumscribed around the circle.

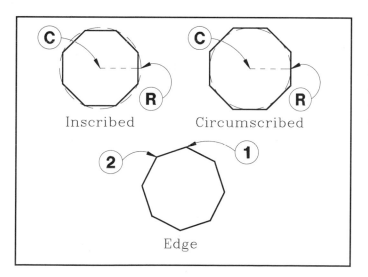

Figure 5.23:
AutoCAD lets you
draw polygons in two
basic ways.

Six-sided polygons make good hex nuts. Let's put a six-sided polygon in the mounting tab on the bottom of the resistor.

Using POLYGON to Draw Regular Polygons

Make the bottom left viewport current.

Command: **VIEW**	Restore view RESISTOR.
Command: **POLYGON**	
Number of sides: **6**	
Edge/<Center of polygon>: **CEN**	Osnap to the center.
of	Pick anywhere on the arc.
Inscribed in circle/Circumscribed about circle (I/C): **C**	
Radius of circle: **.05**	

Figure 5.24 shows the result of this command sequence.

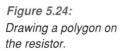

Figure 5.24:
Drawing a polygon on
the resistor.

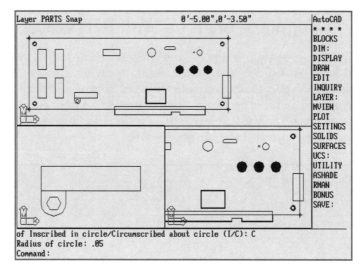

When you know the center point, the inscribed or circumscribed method is probably what you need. You'll find the edge method handy for aligning an edge of the polygon with existing objects. The edge method generates a polygon continuing counterclockwise from the two edge endpoints you select.

If you want to see a *slow circle*, do a polygon with 1000 edges.

Last — But Not Least — The Ellipse

The ELLIPSE command creates a polyline in disguise. AutoCAD first prompts you for the major axis, defined by two endpoints or the center and one endpoint. Then you can define the minor axis by distance or rotation, dragging the ellipse if you pick the point or angle. Use figure 5.25 as a guide to help you make your ellipses.

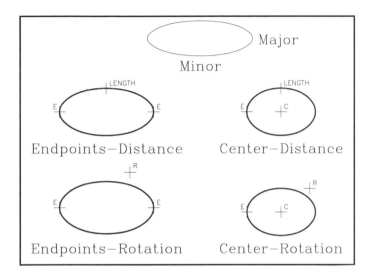

Figure 5.25:
Some ellipse
examples.

Create a rectangle just above the transformer and put three ellipses in it. We'll call the part a jumper.

Using ELLIPSE to Draw a Jumper	
Make the bottom right viewport current.	
Command: **ZOOM**	Zoom in close, just above the transformer.
Command: **PLINE** From point: **6.70,4.10** Current line-width is 0'-0.02" Arc/Close/Halfwidth/Length/Undo/Width/ <Endpoint of line>: **W**	Set width to zero. Draw to @0.2<90 to @0.6<0 to @0.2<270 and close.
Command: **LINE**	Snap in two lines, dividing the rectangle in thirds.
Command: **ELLIPSE**	Draw center,distance ellipse in left box.
<Axis endpoint 1>/Center: **C**	Center option.
Center of ellipse:	Pick absolute point 6.80,4.20.
Axis endpoint:	Pick polar point @0.10<0.00.
<Other axis distance>/Rotation:	Pick polar point @0.05<270.00.

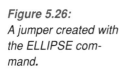

Using ELLIPSE to Draw a Jumper—continued

```
Command: ELLIPSE                        Draw ends,distance ellipse in
                                        center box.
<Axis endpoint 1>/Center:               Pick absolute point 6.90,4.20.
Axis endpoint 2:                        Pick polar point @0.20<0.00.
<Other axis distance>/Rotation:         Pick polar point @0.05<270.00.
Command: ELLIPSE                        Draw ends,rotation ellipse in
                                        right box.
<Axis endpoint 1>/Center:               Pick absolute point 7.10,4.20.
Axis endpoint 2:                        Pick polar point @0.20<0.00.
<Other axis distance>/Rotation: R
Rotation around major axis: 60
Command: SAVE
```

Figure 5.26 shows the results of this command sequence.

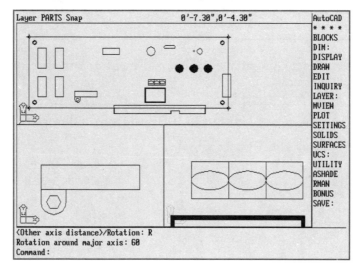

Figure 5.26:
A jumper created with
the ELLIPSE com-
mand.

Ellipse is the last of the polyline family. If you want to try more polylines, use your SCRATCH layer as an exploratorium.

SOLID Is a Polygon Filled With Ink

The SOLID command creates a polygon filled with ink or pixels. It's that simple. A solid is a two-dimensional boundary filled with color.

Creating Solids

The SOLID command lets you create a solid filled area. This area is defined by three or four points forming either a triangular or quadrilateral shape. You can construct more complex shapes by continuing to add vertices. The order in which you enter vertices, and the spatial relationship between these points, determines what the solid will look like (see fig. 5.27). You have to be careful not to get a bow tie shape from four points when you really want a quadrilateral. Nine times out of ten, users first create bow ties and butterflies instead of quadrilaterals.

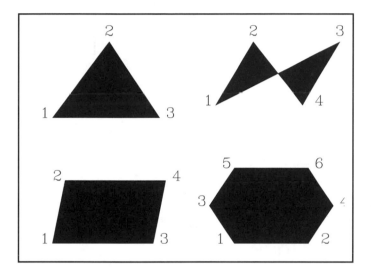

Figure 5.27:
Examples of solids.

Use SOLID to create a vertical solid at the outer edge of the port on the right side of the widget. Here's the prompt sequence.

Using SOLID to Make a Solid Shape	
Command: **ZOOM**	Use Dynamic to magnify an area around the port.
Command: **SNAP**	Set snap to 0.1.
Command: **SOLID**	
First point:	Pick absolute point 9.60,4.60.
Second point:	Pick absolute point 9.70,4.60.
Third point:	Pick absolute point 9.60,3.60.
Fourth point:	Pick absolute point 9.70,3.60.
Third point: **<RETURN>**	

Figure 5.28 shows the results of this command sequence.

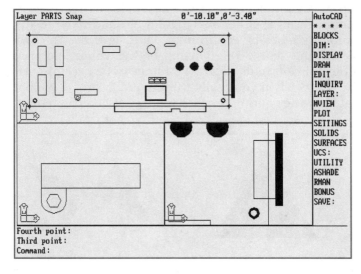

Figure 5.28:
*Enhancing the port
with SOLID.*

Once they are created, solids and traces are identical except in name. They osnap
and fill the same way.

Using FILL Control With Solids,
Traces, and Polylines

When turned off, the FILL command temporarily reduces solids, polylines, and
traces to single-line outlines of their boundaries. When fill is on, solids, polylines,
and traces are filled-in or shaded on the screen and at plotting time. Having fill off
decreases redraw, regeneration, and plotting time (you can use off for check plots).

Fill is a *toggle*. It is either on or off. Turn the widget's filled entities on and off.

Using the FILL Command

```
Command: FILL
ON/OFF <ON>: OFF
```
It doesn't affect existing entities until you regenerate.

```
Command: REGENALL
```

```
Command: FILL
```
Turn FILL back on.

```
Command: END
```
End drawing and take a break, or save, regenerate,
and continue.

Notice the pie-shaped sections in the donuts (see fig. 5.29). When fill is off, each polyline segment shows as an outline.

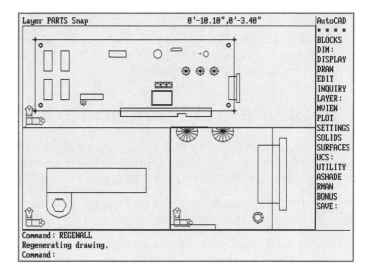

```
Layer PARTS Snap          0'-10.10",0'-3.40"   AutoCAD
                                               * * * *
                                               BLOCKS
                                               DIM:
                                               DISPLAY
                                               DRAW
                                               EDIT
                                               INQUIRY
                                               LAYER:
                                               MVIEW
                                               PLOT
                                               SETTINGS
                                               SOLIDS
                                               SURFACES
                                               UCS:
                                               UTILITY
                                               ASHADE
                                               RMAN
                                               BONUS
                                               SAVE:

Command: REGENALL
Regenerating drawing.
Command:
```

Figure 5.29:
Fill off.

This is a good resting point. There is one more entity to cover — text. If you have the time, move on. If you are pressed for time, take a break.

A Word About Text and Style

AutoCAD's text has a set of default parameters that define how text is placed and stored. You have to select a beginning point for your text, a height for the characters, and how the text is to be placed and formatted. Then, you key in the characters. You've already used AutoCAD's text in its default form. Before you proceed further with text, you should consider style.

Style Settings

S is for Style, and AutoCAD has it. Think about this: if you had to draw the letter A, you would need 7, 19, or more line strokes, depending on the font. Rather than storing each stroke of each character in each string of text, AutoCAD stores characters as references to their definitions in special files called shape files. Shape files very efficiently store each character definition as a series of *vectors* (line offsets). These shape files are compiled into even more efficient binary SHX files, from which AutoCAD can rapidly extract character information for display. In translating text from the compiled shape files to your screen or plotter, AutoCAD passes the text through several filters to get it to come out the way you want. Text *style* is a set of parameters AutoCAD uses in translating text from a shape into strokes on the plotter or characters on the screen. A text style is a particular named collection of instructions in the current drawing and does not change the original shape file font definition.

As you have seen, AutoCAD supplies you with several default settings. The default style is called STANDARD. This style is defined with the simple TXT font and with default width, rotation angle, and justification (alignment).

Using STYLE to Create and Maintain Text Styles

Use the STYLE command to create new styles or change the parameters for existing styles. Setting your style is really part of the setting up process. We recommend that you set your styles early in the drawing before you get into any intensive text input.

The default TXT font used in the STANDARD style is a bit clunky. Use the following exercise to respecify the font used with your STANDARD style.

Using STYLE to Modify a Text Style

 Begin a NEW drawing named WIDGET=IA6WIDG2.

 Edit an EXISTING drawing named WIDGET or continue from the previous exercise.

```
Command: STYLE
Text Style name (or ?) <STANDARD>: <RETURN>        Change the default style.
Existing style.
Font file <txt>: ROMANS
Height <0'-0.00">: <RETURN>
Width factor <1.00>: .8                            Make it a little skinny.
Obliquing angle <0.00>: <RETURN>
Backwards? <N>: <RETURN>
Upside-down? <N>: <RETURN>
Vertical ? <N>: <RETURN>
STANDARD is now the current text style.
```

Now your STANDARD style will use the ROMANS font and be slightly narrower than normal.

To help you graphically select fonts, AutoCAD has three pages of icon menus to select your text styles from. The first two pages are shown in figures 5.30 and 5.31. The third is a set of symbols, and also includes the STANDARD style, as the TXT font item. All of AutoCAD's standard fonts are included in the [Text Font...] icon menus. Selecting a font from the icon menus creates a new style, with the same style name as the font.

To get to these icon menus, select [Dtext Options >] from the [Options] pull-down menu, and then select [Text Font...].

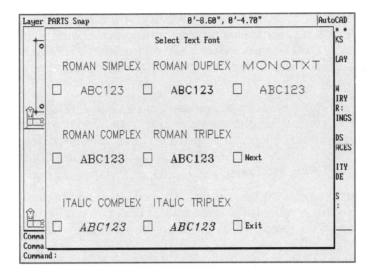

Figure 5.30:
The first icon menu
for creating text
styles.

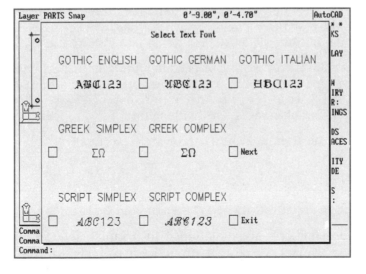

Figure 5.31:
The next icon menu
for creating text
styles.

Here are the text style options.

STYLE Options

Name   Just a name to help you remember how text drawn in this collection of style parameters will look.

Font   A file of vectors that define letters and symbols with a certain style. When you respecify an existing style with a new font, AutoCAD will regenerate your screen (unless REGENAUTO is off) and replace all the occurrences of that style with the new style. This only affects the font used, not any other options in the style.

Height   The default is zero, which means the TEXT or DTEXT commands will control text height. However, if you set style height to greater than zero, text placed using this style will always default to the height you give here. You will not get a height prompt in the TEXT and DTEXT commands.

Width   A multiplier, normally set to 1, that adjusts the width of characters. With a style width greater than one, you will have fat characters. With a style width less than one, the type will look narrow (see fig. 5.32).

Obliquing Angle   Normally, characters are upright, with obliquing angle = 0. But you can oblique your characters, making them lean forward with a positive slant or backward with a negative one. Be careful: a small angle like 15 or 20 degrees causes a dramatic slant.

Upside-down and **backwards** settings   If you like mirror writing or need to annotate the bottom of something, you can set up a style with upside-down or backwards writing. This also is useful for transparencies or the backs of printed circuit boards. Or just for fun!

Vertical   Any of the standard fonts can be styled vertically.

Notes on STYLE

Here are some notes on using AutoCAD's STYLE command.

- AutoCAD's style definitions are maintained in a tables section of the drawing database file. You can store many styles in a single drawing file. They affect only the current drawing.

- When using the STYLE command, a ?<RETURN> in response to the text style name prompt will give you a list of the styles currently defined and stored in the drawing file.

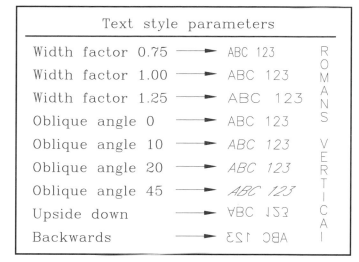

Figure 5.32:
Examples of text
styles.

- When you give a new name in response to the text style name prompt, AutoCAD creates a new style in the style library.

- When you give an existing style name in response to the text style name prompt, AutoCAD assumes you want to change or edit the existing style. It prompts you for all the style parameters using the old settings as default prompts.

- When you change the Font or Vertical option of a style that is currently defined in the drawing file, AutoCAD regenerates the screen. Any existing text of that style is updated with the new style definition. Changes to all other options are ignored for existing text.

Tip: You needn't bother to define a standard set of styles each time you start a new drawing. You can add your standard styles to your standard prototype drawing (see Chapter 19). Or, you can save them as part of another drawing file and insert them as a block (this won't override any existing definitions in an existing drawing). See Chapter 9.

Once you have created the styles you want for your drawing, AutoCAD offers two ways to input the text.

Dynamic Text vs. Regular Text

AutoCAD has two text commands, DTEXT and TEXT. Either command places text. The only difference is that DTEXT (you might have guessed it) does it *dynamically*, letting you see each character in the drawing as it is typed.

If you use TEXT, AutoCAD waits for all your text characters and then places the text on the screen when you exit the TEXT command.

To get started with TEXT (and to see the new style definition), let's label the resistor in the lower left part of the widget.

Using TEXT to Add Labels

Make the bottom left viewport current.

Command: **LAYER**	Set layer TEXT current.
Command: **TEXT**	Label the resistor.
Justify/Style/<Start point>: **J**	Enter J for the full justification prompt.
Align/Fit/Center/Middle/Right/TL/TC/TR /ML/MC/MR/BL/MC/BR: **M**	Use Middle option.
Middle point:	Pick absolute point 4.50,3.80.
Height <0'-0.20">: **.1**	
Rotation angle <0.00>: **<RETURN>**	
Text: **RESISTOR**	The text doesn't appear until you press <RETURN>.
Command: **SAVE**	

Figure 5.33 shows the result of this operation.

Notice the prompt options are the same as for the DTEXT command you used earlier. Let's examine them.

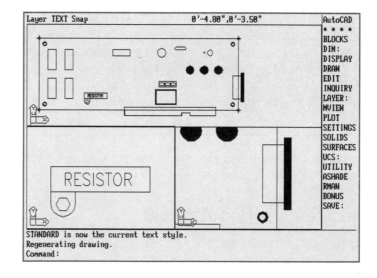

Figure 5.33:
The resistor, labeled with TEXT.

Text Formatting Options

The first thing AutoCAD wants to know about the text is how you want to format it. You have several options for formatting your text.

DTEXT/TEXT Options

Start Point   Left-justified is the default. Just respond to the prompt by picking a point for left-justified text. The point picked is the left end of the *base line* (the base of upper-case characters or characters without *descenders*) of the text string. Descenders are the lower part of characters like j or g.

Justify   Displays a menu of all of the available text justification options.

Style   Lets you select from various styles you have previously set. The default is the last STYLE used by text or set by the STYLE command.

Text Justification

Justification (or alignment) specifies how the text is aligned relative to the start and optional endpoint(s) you give it. You've used Middle, Center, and the default Left justifications. The justification prompt shows the complete list:

```
Align/Fit/Center/Middle/Right/TL/TC/TR/ML/MC/MR/BL/BC/BR:
```

Figure 5.34 presents a graphical depiction of each option. The following section examines these options.

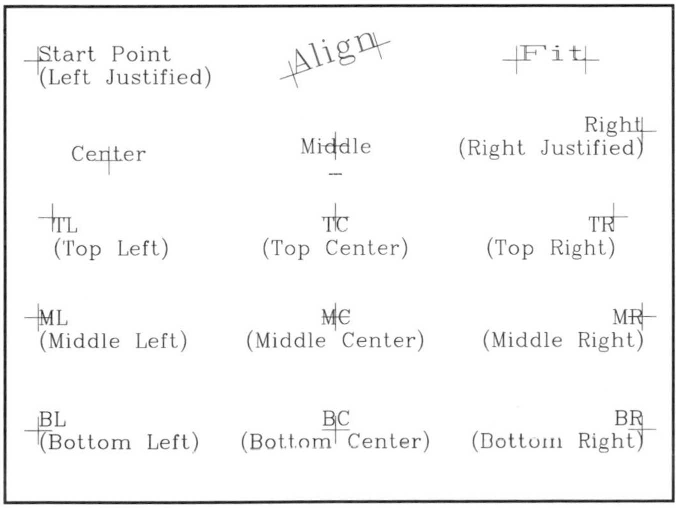

Figure 5.34:
Text justification
options.

Justification Options

Align
Give the start and endpoint of the text location. AutoCAD determines the base line angle from your points and fills the distance between the two points with the text string you enter. Align maintains the style's width proportion and adjusts the text height to fit the distance. It overrides the style's height, if set.

Fit
Like Align, you pick the starting point and endpoint of the text string. However, Fit uses the text height you specify and adjusts the text width to fit the distance between the two points. Fit overrides the style's width setting.

Center
The midpoint of the text base line is placed at the point you pick.

Middle
Places the center point of an imaginary rectangle around the text on the point you pick. The vertical position of the text base line will vary, depending on whether the specific text string includes upper-case letters or letters with ascenders (like h and f), or descenders, or both.

Right
Like the left-justified default, except it uses the right justification point you pick as the ending point, at the right end of the base line.

TL (Top/Left)
The top left corner of the first text cell is positioned at the point you pick. The *text cell* is a rectangle enclosing an imaginary character with both ascenders and descenders, or an imaginary upper-case character which also has descenders.

TC (Top/Center)
The point you pick is vertically positioned at the top of the text cells like TL, but the string is horizontally centered on the point.

TR (Top/Right)
The top right corner of the last text cell is positioned at the point you pick.

ML (Middle/Left)
The point you pick is vertically centered on the *upper-case character cell*, at the left end of the string. Regardless of the actual text string, it is calculated as if it contained only upper-case text.

MC (Middle/Center)
The point you pick is vertically centered on the upper-case character cell, at the midpoint of the string.

MR (Middle/Right)
The point you pick is vertically centered on the upper-case character cell, at the right end of the string.

BL (Bottom/Left)   The bottom left corner of the first text cell is positioned at the point you pick.

BC (Bottom/Center) The point you pick is vertically positioned at the bottom of the text cells like BL, but the string is horizontally centered on the point.

BR (Bottom/Right)   All text characters are placed entirely above and to the left of the point picked.

The TL, TC, TR, ML, MC, MR, BL, BC, and BR justifications are simply the nine possible combinations of the Top, Middle, and Bottom vertical justifications and the Left, Center, and Right horizontal justifications. The default Left and the simple Center and Right justifications are all base line justifications, which could have fit into this same matrix if B wasn't already taken by Bottom! Fit, TL, TC, TR, ML, MC, MR, BL, BC, and BR justified text cannot be used with vertical text styles; the others work vertically or horizontally.

Unlike middle-justified text, which floats vertically depending on the particular character string, TL, TC, TR, ML, MC, MR, BL, BC, and BR justified text maintain their vertical positions regardless of the string entered. Middle is designed to always be centered in both axes, for use in bubbles and similar applications. The other justifications are designed to be consistent for most other applications. (The vertical justification of TL, TC, TR, ML, MC, MR, BL, BC, and BR is not correctly described in early versions of the Release 11 *AutoCAD Reference Manual*, because they were redesigned as the initial manuals were being printed.)

Tip: If you respond to the DTEXT (or TEXT) start point prompt with a <RETURN>, the new text will start one line below the last text you entered in the drawing. The new text will assume the height, style, and justification of the previous text, even if you have used intervening AutoCAD commands.

We'll practice several of these justifications as we experiment with the DTEXT command.

Placing Text With DTEXT

DTEXT is easier to use than TEXT. Input for DTEXT is always shown left-justified on the screen regardless of the chosen format. The justification is corrected when the command is finished. You also can reposition the box cursor on the screen at any point during text entry by picking a new point with your pointing device. This lets you place text throughout your drawing with a single DTEXT command. The trade-off for this flexibility in picking new points is the disabling of menus during the DTEXT command.

What happens if you make a mistake entering text? If you are using DTEXT, you can backspace and correct your errors as you type. If you do not realize that you have a mistaken text entry until you see it on the screen, don't panic — all is repairable. We will show you how to edit text in the next chapter. For now, just undo and try again.

We'll try more text input with DTEXT by labeling other parts of the widget. Add text by entering the justifications and starting points shown, and either typing or dragging answers to the height and angle prompts. We'll start on the left, labeling the RAM chips with Middle/Left text.

Using DTEXT to Label the Widget Drawing

`Command: ZOOM`	Zoom Dynamic to enclose RAM chips.
`Command: SNAP`	Set to 0.05.
`Command: DTEXT`	
`Justify/Style/<Start point>: J`	Enter J for the full justification prompt. (Release 10 users pick 3.00, 3.80).
`Align/Fit/Center/Middle/Right/TL/TC/TR/` `   ML/MC/MR/BL/BC/BR: ML`	Middle/Left text. (Release 10 users skip this step.)
`Middle/left point:`	Pick 2.95,3.8. (Release 10 users skip this step.)
`Height <0'-0.10">: .08`	
`Rotation angle <0.00>: 90`	
`Text: CHIP #1`	And move cursor by picking point 2.95,4.8. (Release 10 users pick 3.60, 4.80).
`Text: CHIP #2`	And move cursor by picking point 3.55,3.8. (Release 10 users pick 3.60, 3.80).
`Text: CHIP #3`	And move cursor by picking point 3.55,4.8. (Release 10 users pick 3.00, 4.80).
`Text: CHIP #4`	
`Text: <RETURN>`	Ends DTEXT and redisplays justified text.

Figure 5.35 shows the newly labeled chips in detail.

Whenever you need reminding, you can enter a J at the first text prompt to see the full justification prompt. However, you don't need the full prompt to use any of its justifications. You can enter any of them at the first prompt. Next, try the Middle, Fit, Center, and Middle/Center justifications.

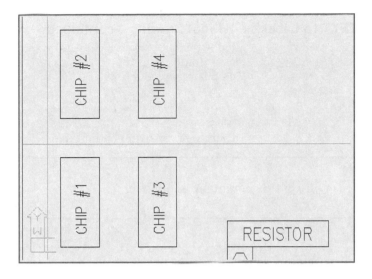

Figure 5.35:
Detail of chip labels.

Using DTEXT to Label the Widget Drawing—continued

Command: **ZOOM**	Pan or zoom Dynamic to the center of the board.
Command: **DTEXT**	Label the capacitor circle.
Justify/Style/<Start point>: **M**	Middle.
Middle point: **CEN**	Osnap to center of circle.
of	Pick any point on the circle.
Height <0'-0.08">: **.15**	
Rotation angle <90.00>: **0**	
Text: **C**	
Text: **<RETURN>**	
Command: **DTEXT**	Label the transformer.
Justify/Style/<Start point>: **F**	Fit.
First text line point:	Pick absolute point 6.65,3.80.
Second text line point:	Pick polar point @0.60<0.00.
Height <0'-0.15">: **.08**	
Text: **TRANSFORMER**	Text is redrawn, squeezed between points.
Text: **<RETURN>**	
Command: **DTEXT**	
Justify/Style/<Start point>: **C**	Center.
Center point:	Pick absolute point 6.95,3.65.
Height <0'-0.08">: **<RETURN>**	
Rotation angle <0.00>: **<RETURN>**	
Text: **ONE**	
Text: **<RETURN>**	
Command: **DTEXT**	Add label to ROM chip.

Figure 5.36 shows the results of this command sequence.

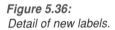

Figure 5.36:
Detail of new labels.

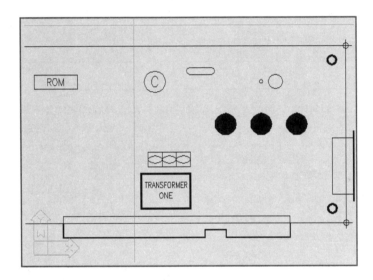

AutoCAD never forgets. Its default prompts during the text commands show your previous parameter settings. You can speed parameter entry by accepting defaults with <RETURN>s.

You also can use snaps and osnaps to help you place your text.

Placing Successive Lines of Text

DTEXT will automatically line up successive lines of text one under the other when you press <RETURN> after each line. If you press <RETURN> at the first text prompt, it will line up under the previous text entered. Let's try it, but first change your text style to one with an oblique slant, to give the widget drawing a title with a unique look.

Defining an Oblique Text Style

Make the bottom right viewport current.

```
Command: ZOOM                                    Zoom Dynamic to the logo in
                                                 the lower left corner of the
                                                 board.

Command: STYLE                                   Create a new style for the title.
Text Style name (or ?) <STANDARD>: TITLE         Name it.
Font file <ROMANS>: ROMANC
Height <0'-0.00">: .2                             Give it a fixed height.
Width factor <1.00>: .8                           Make it a little skinny.
Obliquing angle <0.00>: 15                        Slant it 15 degrees.
Backwards? <N>: <RETURN>
Upside-down? <N>: <RETURN>
Vertical ? <N>: <RETURN>
TITLE is now the current text style.
```

Now use the TITLE style and have DTEXT automatically line up the words "Widget," "Circuit," and "Board" under one another. When you are done, change your display to a single view and zoom for a good look.

Creating Successive Lines of Text

```
Command: DTEXT
Justify/Style/<Start point>:                     Pick absolute point 2.50,2.60.
Rotation angle <0.00>: <RETURN>
Text: Widget
Text: Layout
Text: Board
Text: <RETURN>
```

Make the top viewport current.

```
Command: VPORTS                                  (If using Release 10, set VPORTS to SI for a
                                                 single screen view.)

Command: TILEMODE                                (If using Release 11, set to 1 [on] for a single
                                                 screen view.)

Command: ZOOM                                    Zoom Extents to fill the screen.

Command: SAVE
```

Your final screen should look like figure 5.37.

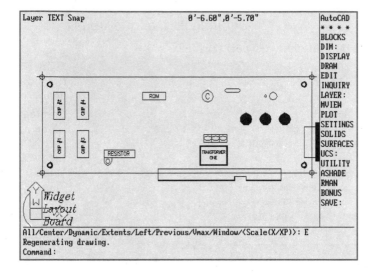

Figure 5.37:
A zoomed widget
board with text.

We have two more special, quick text topics. But first, here are some tips on text entry.

> **Tip:** Often you can set height and angle once (say when you are setting up your drawing file), and simply use these defaults for all future text use.

> **Tip:** To add a line to existing text, use DTEXT with osnap mode INSert and enter only a space on the first line. Then a <RETURN> will space you down for the next line.

> **Tip:** You can enter text upside down by using an angle definition to the left of the starting point (180 degrees).

> **Tip:** The default height shown in the TEXT command is rounded off to your units setting and may not accurately display its true value.

Using Special Text Characters

Occasionally, you may need to use special symbols, or angle text on a drawing. This section describes how to create some common special texts. If you want to try some of the special text examples, use your SCRATCH layer to practice on.

> **Note:** If your special text needs exceed those shown here, see *MAXIMIZING AutoCAD, Volume I* from New Riders Publishing for instructions on creating your own fonts and characters.

Text Underscore and Overscore

Underscores, superscripts, and special symbols are used regularly in text strings on drawings. You will not find these symbols on standard keyboards. Figure 5.38 shows some special text. The underscored and overscored text in the illustration was typed into the DTEXT command as follows:

```
Text: %%u88%%u %%o88%%o
```

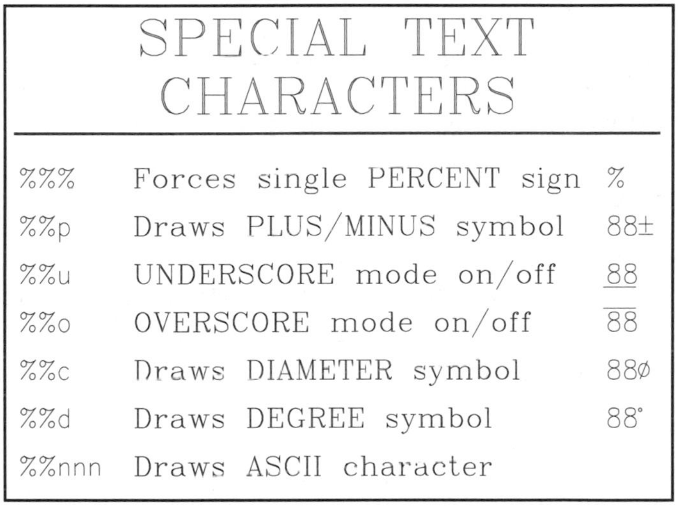

Figure 5.38:
Examples of
special text.

SPECIAL TEXT
CHARACTERS

%%%	Forces single PERCENT sign	%
%%p	Draws PLUS/MINUS symbol	88±
%%u	UNDERSCORE mode on/off	88
%%o	OVERSCORE mode on/off	88
%%c	Draws DIAMETER symbol	88⌀
%%d	Draws DEGREE symbol	88°
%%nnn	Draws ASCII character	

You can enter the special character switches, %%u (underline) and %%o (overscore), any time you are typing a text string in response to the text prompt.

Angled vs. Vertical Text

Most text reads horizontally from left to right. Sometimes, however, you may want text which is not horizontal.

Usually, you just use the normal DTEXT or TEXT parameters to rotate or align your text at any angle. But occasionally, you want your text to read vertically. You can create a style and give it a vertical orientation. A vertical orientation aligns characters one below the other. You can give all standard AutoCAD fonts a vertical orientation.

Quick vs. Fancy Text

As your drawing file fills up with drawing entities, it takes longer and longer to zoom, redraw, or regenerate the screen. Sooner or later, you'll want to cut down the regeneration time. AutoCAD offers two options for speeding up text display. First, you can do all your text work in a simple font such as TXT while you are creating the drawing and for test plots. When it comes time for final plotting, you can enhance the drawing by replacing the simple font with a more elegant one such as ROMANC. You save time during initial drawing editor work, but your drawings still come out well with the last-minute font change.

> **Note:** Font character definitions differ in width, and font respecification doesn't attempt to compensate, so you may find the new fancy text will not fit where you placed the old simple text.

A second option (and one we recommend to speed regeneration time) is to use AutoCAD's QTEXT command. QTEXT (for Quick TEXT) lets you temporarily replace the screen display of text with a rectangle outlining its position.

The QTEXT Command

QTEXT is available from the keyboard or from the [SETTINGS] screen menu. It does not replace text until the next regeneration. Try *qtexting* the widget drawing.

Looking at QTEXT

```
Command: QTEXT
ON/OFF <Off>: ON
Command: REGEN            The text is replaced with boxes (see fig. 5.39).
Regenerating drawing.
Command: QTEXT            Turn QTEXT off.
Command: END
```

The text will regenerate when you reload the drawing in the next chapter.

Notice that QTEXT did not accurately represent the justification and text line lengths. To do so, AutoCAD would have to do the full text display calculations, and that would save little time over normal text display.

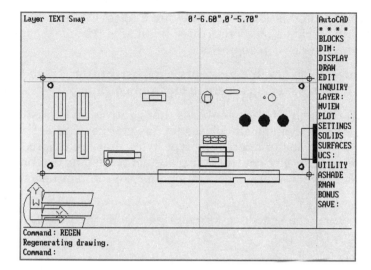

Figure 5.39:
The widget after
QTEXT is turned on.

Summing Up

In this chapter you've covered a lot of material. Congratulate yourself on a whirlwind tour of graphic entities. Screen and tablet menus are becoming friends, like road signs in a new town. While the number of side streets for different drawing commands may seem endless, you're beginning to understand how the primary drawing commands will get you almost all the way to your destination.

You may put aside learning additional commands and options until you need them or have some extra time to explore AutoCAD further. If you like Sunday drives into the country, AutoCAD lets you wander through some of the less frequently used commands without letting you go too far astray. We invite you to master the ten different ways to create an arc!

Here are some reminders about entities you have used.

Points are useful reference locaters for a later osnap. They can be displayed in various sizes and styles.

Lines are the pillars of the drawing community. Connected lines are the norm; a <RETURN> stops a connected line run. Continue starts a line at the last endpoint. Close makes a polygon by returning a connected line series to the first point. Take advantage of TRACE's mitered edge to get angled ends for fat lines. Otherwise, you will find PLINE superior to TRACE for every other purpose.

CIRCLE requires minimal information to generate full circles. Center point/radius is the most common circle creation method. A three-point arc is the most convenient to create. The start,center series is also useful.

Polylines let you create single graphic elements composed of linear and curved segments. Donuts, polygons, and ellipses are made from polylines.

Text gets to the screen through a filtering process that controls style, justification, height, and rotation. DTEXT dynamically places text as you key characters at the keyboard. Style gives you flexibility in creating typestyles that are tailored to your needs. The justification options give control over placement. Keeping text on its own layer or using QTEXT keeps redraw and regeneration times to a minimum as drawing files expand.

You can think ahead about the sequence for entering SOLID vertices. But we bet you'll get a bow tie anyway!

Onward

In this chapter you began earnest work on a real drawing. You will be relieved to know that every entity that you used here works the same in a 3D drawing, although AutoCAD has a few more graphic entities especially designed for 3D which you will see in a later chapter.

While widgets may not be your thing, you have already mastered setting layers, drawing lines and circles, and inserting text. By the end of the next chapter, this drawing will be a complete, four-layer, full-color widget layout drawing.

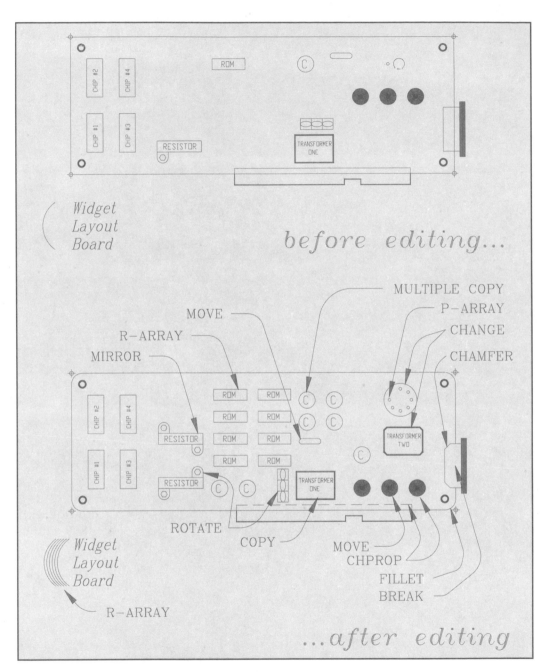

Figure 6.1:
Widget drawing before and after editing.

6

Introduction to Editing

IF AT FIRST YOU DON'T SUCCEED, TRY EDITING

You Edit More Than You Create

As you go through the book's examples, you may feel like saying, "Give me a drafting board, a straight edge, and a compass and I can beat this CAD system in a flash!"

It just isn't so. While some draftspeople may be able to create original linework faster than AutoCAD, it is safe to say that no human can revise and print new clean drawing sets faster than AutoCAD (and an organized user). The one certainty in the drawing business is *change*. Change this! Change that! Drawing revision numbers keep mounting! Becoming familiar with AutoCAD's editing functions is critical to your successful use of AutoCAD.

So far you have spent most of your tutorial time creating new drawing entities. Beginning with this chapter, you'll see how easy it is to modify your drawing with AutoCAD's editing commands. You may find yourself spending more time editing existing drawings than creating new ones.

The benefits of editing are pure and simple. Editing allows you to quickly and easily stay on top of changes, and to create multiple objects with minimal original entry. Figure 6.1, for example, shows how simple editing techniques can enhance a drawing. You will make these changes to the widget drawing in this chapter.

Editing Activities — Changing, Copying, and Erasing

What types of activities will you encounter in editing a drawing?

229

Three basic activities stand out: changing, copying, and erasing. You can change an existing entity's location, layer, and visual properties like color and linetype. You also can *break* entities, deleting portions of line and arc segments. You can copy entities, either one at a time or in a swoop (array) of creation. You can erase entities, getting rid of previous mistakes.

There are more advanced editing functions, like trimming, extending, stretching, and scaling, as well as some editing *construction* techniques. We will cover these advanced functions in the following chapters. And, we will cover 3D variations on these editing commands in the book's 3D chapters.

The Editor's Toolkit

Most of the editing commands you will use are gathered on the [EDIT] screen menus and the [Modify] pull-down menu (see fig. 6.2). There are also settings for the CHAMFER, FILLET, DIVIDE, and MEASURE commands on the [Options] pull-down menu.

Figure 6.2:
The [EDIT] screen and the [Modify] pull-down menus.

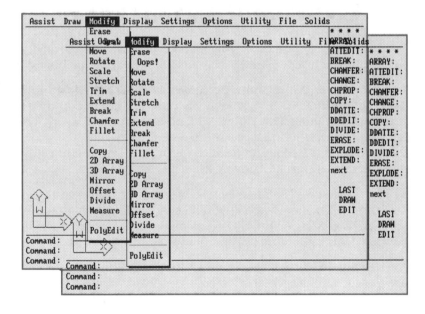

This chapter covers the basics of editing. You'll change both the spatial (location) and appearance (color and linetype) properties of existing entities. We have broken down the basic editing commands into two groups. The first group includes MOVE and ROTATE, which relocate entities; COPY and MIRROR, which duplicate entities; and ARRAY, which makes multiple copies. The second group includes the BREAK, CHAMFER, and FILLET commands. These commands delete portions of objects. In addition, we will review how to delete whole entities with ERASE.

How Editing Commands Work

Most editing commands involve a four-step process. You have to think about what kind of edit you want to do, which objects you want to edit, and how you want to edit them. The process works this way:

- Select the editing command
- Select the entities
- Enter parameters and pick points
- Watch the edit occur

Selecting an editing command puts you in an object selection mode. To get the objects you want, most commands require you to group one or more objects. This group is called the *selection set*.

The Selection Set

There are about a dozen ways to collect objects for editing, including picking individual objects and using a window. If you make an error at the select objects prompt, AutoCAD will prompt you with all the available modes. As you select objects, AutoCAD sets up a *temporary* selection set and highlights the objects on the screen by temporarily changing their color, blinking them, or giving them dotted lines. This way you can confirm what you've selected to edit. Once you have selected all desired objects, a <RETURN> continues the editing command. One of the goals for this chapter is to give you practice using a variety of the myriad options available for collecting selection sets.

Basic Selection Set Options

Object pick   The default is to select by picking individual objects. Picking finds the most recently created object that falls within or crosses the pick box. If snap and osnap are used together, AutoCAD snaps first, then osnaps from that snapped point.

Window   Pick the corners of a window to group the objects you want and it selects only those objects that are totally enclosed in the window.

Last   Adds the last object created to the selection set.

Crossing   Works like Window, except it also includes any object which is partially within (or crossing) the window. If your display hardware supports pull-down menus, Crossing will use a dashed or highlighted box.

Remove	Switches to Remove mode, so you may select objects to be removed from the selection set (not from the drawing).
Add	Switches from the Remove mode back to normal, so you may again add to the selection set.
Multiple	Lets you pick multiple objects in close proximity and speeds up selection by allowing multiple selections without highlighting or prompting. An extra <RETURN> is required to complete the multiple selection and return to normal object selection.
Previous	Selects the entire previous selection set (from a previous command) as the current selection set.
Undo	Undoes or reverses the last selection operation. Each U undoes one selection operation.

When do you use which mode? Object picking is quick and simple, even for picking three or four objects, and it requires no mode setting. Last and Undo are obvious. Previous is great for repeated operations on the same set of objects, like a copy and rotate operation.

Choose between Window and Crossing, depending on which will best extract the group you want from the crowd. Sometimes selecting more objects than you want is inevitable; that is why the Remove mode exists. And Add just gets you back to normal.

> **Note:** The Window selection process ignores the portions of objects that fall partly outside the current viewport or screen display. If all *visible* portions of an object are within the Window box, it will be selected.

AutoCAD has a preference for finding the most recently created object. Sometimes objects are so close to each other that you can't pick the one you want; AutoCAD just keeps finding the same most recently created object over and over again. In those cases, you can use Multiple to pick repeatedly and it will only find the recent object once. Then you can use Remove to remove the recent object if you don't want it.

> **Note:** There are a number of editing commands, such as FILLET (which you will see later in this chapter), and TRIM and EXTEND (next chapter), that require individual entity selection part or all of the time. In these cases, you must select your objects by picking them.

There are three other selection set options: BOX, AUto, and SIngle. These are designed primarily for use in menus and offer no real advantages over the above when specifying modes from the keyboard.

Advanced Selection Set Options

BOX   Combines Window and Crossing into a single selection. Picking the points of your box (window) from left to right is the same as a Window selection; right to left is the same as a Crossing selection.

AUto   Combines individual selection with the BOX selection. This selection acts just like BOX except if the first pick point finds an entity, that single entity is selected and the BOX mode is aborted.

SIngle   Works in conjunction with the other selection options. If you precede a selection with SIngle, object selection will automatically end after the first successful selection, without the <RETURN> normally required to exit object selection.

When specifying modes from the keyboard, you obviously know how you intend to select the object(s), so you can use Window, Crossing or just pick the object rather than use BOX or AUto. And it's easier to just hit that last <RETURN> from the keyboard than to enter SI<RETURN> in advance.

Tip: Create a button menu with AUto object selection programmed onto a button and you can do all of your object selection without using the keyboard or other menus. See Chapter 19 or, for greater detail, get *MAXIMIZING AutoCAD, Volume I* from New Riders Publishing.

Setting Up for Editing

This chapter uses the WIDGET drawing that you created in the last chapter, or IA6WIDG3.DWG from the IA DISK. You'll create a new file called WIDGEDIT in which you'll try out the editing options.

Setup for Editing the WIDGEDIT Drawing

 Begin a NEW drawing named WIDGEDIT=IA6WIDG3.

 Begin a NEW drawing named WIDGEDIT=WIDGET and confirm the settings shown in table 6.1.

Command: **ZOOM**   Zoom Center with a height of 6 for a little elbow room to work in.

Table 6.1
Setup for Editing the Widget Drawing

AXIS	COORDS	GRID	SNAP	UCSICON
Off	On	.5	.1	OR

UNITS	Engineering, 2 decimal places, 2 fractional places for angles, default all other settings.
LIMITS	0,0 to 11,8.5
ZOOM	Zoom Center, height 6"
VIEW	Saved as RESISTOR

Layer Name	State	Color	Linetype
0	On	7 (white)	CONTINUOUS
BOARD	On	2 (yellow)	CONTINUOUS
HIDDEN	On	1 (red)	HIDDEN
PARTS	On	4 (cyan)	CONTINUOUS
TEXT	On/Current	3 (green)	CONTINUOUS

You should have a full screen view of the widget. The following exercises do not make use of the viewports stored with the widget drawing, but you can use viewports in the exercises if you want to. You can restore Release 10 viewports with VPORTS or Release 11 viewports with TILEMODE=0. Your current layer is not important to the exercises. Editing commands work on any layer! If you want additional practice using individual editing commands, use a layer named SCRATCH, set it current, create some new entities to practice on, and practice the editing command. When you are done, undo, erase, or freeze the SCRATCH layer and take up again where you left off.

MOVE — Some Quick Moves With AutoCAD

Making a move is quite simple. You grab what you want, and move it where you want it. Try moving the solid donuts using a Window selection. When you are prompted for a *base point* or *displacement,* pick a base point. After you pick this point, you can *drag* the selection set with your pointer and pick a second displacement point to place the objects.

Selecting and Windowing Donuts to Move

```
Command: MOVE                              Crosshairs change to a pick box.
Select objects: ?                          Any wrong input gives you a full
                                           prompt.

*Invalid selection*
Expects a point or Window/Last/Crossing/
  BOX/Add/Remove/Multiple/
Previous/Undo/AUto/SIngle
Select objects:                            Pick the far left donut.
1 selected, 1 found.
Select objects: W                          Put window around the two right
                                           donuts.

First corner:                              Pick first corner at ① (see fig. 6.3).
Other corner:                              Pick second corner at ②.
2 found.                                   All the donuts are highlighted.
Select objects: <RETURN>                   This tells AutoCAD you are through
                                           selecting.

Base point or displacement:                Pick any point near the donuts.
Second point of displacement:              Pick polar point @1.00<270.00 and
                                           the move takes place (see fig. 6.4).
```

As you can see, moving is easy. In the default Select Objects mode, the crosshairs cursor changes to a small square pick box. A selection window is similar to a zoom window. After you collect your donuts with a window, they are highlighted. You tell AutoCAD you're through collecting by pressing <RETURN> in response to the select objects prompt. When you are through selecting, pick your displacement points and your donuts are moved.

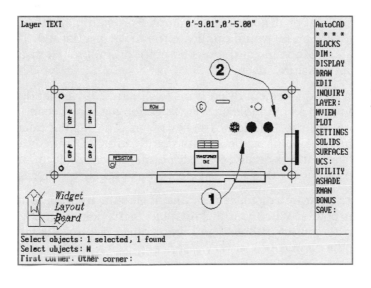

Figure 6.3:
Selecting donuts with a window for MOVE.

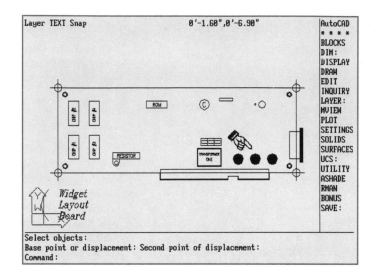

Figure 6.4:
The donuts after
being moved.

Tip: You can change the pick box size by changing the system variable PICKBOX. Just type PICKBOX (or use the SETVAR command in Release 10). You can also change it transparently in the middle of a command with 'SETVAR or 'PICKBOX, but the change won't take effect until the second following pick.

Displacement and Drag

When you change the location of objects that you have collected in a selection set, you use a displacement. If you know the absolute X,Y or polar displacement, you can enter it at the base point or displacement prompt. For example, either 0,-1, or 1<270 (don't preface it with an @) would duplicate the move we just did. Then you enter a <RETURN> instead of a value at the second point prompt to tell AutoCAD to use the first value as an absolute offset.

Often you want to show a displacement by entering two points, as we just did. Think of the first point (base point) as a *handle* on your selection set. The second point is where you are going to put the handle of the set down. The displacement is an imaginary line from the base point to the second point. AutoCAD calculates the X and Y differences between the base and second points. The new location of the object(s) is determined by adding this X,Y displacement to its current location.

AutoCAD does not actually draw a displacement line; it gets the information it needs from the displacement points. When you pick displacement points on the screen, AutoCAD shows you a temporary rubber band line trailing behind the crosshairs from the first point to the second.

As you just saw when you moved the donuts, an image of the selection set also follows the crosshairs. This is called *dragging*. It provides a visual aid to help you pick your second displacement point. Without dragging, it sometimes can be difficult to see if the selection set will fit where you want it.

When you set up a selection set handle to drag, try to pick a base point that is easy to visualize (and remember). If the base point is not in, on, or near the contents of the selection set, it will appear that you are carrying the selection set around magically without touching it. Sometimes you will osnap the points to a different but related object. Otherwise, it's a good idea to make this drag anchor (base displacement point) a reference point, like an osnap point on one of the objects.

Using DRAGMODE

When you edit very large selection sets, you may wish to control dragging. You can turn drag on or off using the DRAGMODE command. The default for DRAGMODE is Auto, which causes AutoCAD to drag everything that makes sense. If you want to be selective about what you drag, you can turn DRAGMODE on. If DRAGMODE is on and you want to drag in the middle of a command, type DRAG <RETURN> before picking the point that you wish to drag. Off turns DRAGMODE off entirely and ignores a typed DRAG <RETURN>.

Adding and Removing Modes for the Selection Set

Sometimes you put too many objects into a selection set and you need to take some out. AutoCAD has two modes for handling selection set contents: the default Add mode and a Remove mode. In Add mode, you get the default select objects prompt. Picking individual objects or using any other object selection mode, such as Window or Last, puts the objects into the selection set.

You also can type R for Remove in response to the normal Add mode prompt. You will get the remove objects prompt. Remove objects from the selection set by using any type of object selection in the Remove mode. Type A to return to Add mode.

Using a Crossing Window

There is a second type of window object selection called a *crossing window*. Crossing selects everything that either falls within your selection window or crosses the boundary of the window. You will find Crossing handy when you want to select objects in a crowded drawing. AutoCAD also knows the difference between objects within the window and objects crossing the window. Some advanced editing commands, like the STRETCH command, treat selected objects in the window differently from those crossing the window boundary.

Use the next example to combine a crossing window and the Remove mode to move the ROM chip, using a polar displacement. Select the capacitor and the ROM chip together with Crossing, then remove the capacitor from the selection set. The capacitor is the circle with a C in it.

Using Crossing, Add, and Remove Selection Set Modes

Command: **MOVE**	
Select objects: **C**	Select ROM chip and capacitor.
First corner:	Pick first corner point at ① (see fig. 6.5).
Other corner:	Pick second corner point at ②.
4 found.	Highlighting indicates they are selected.
Select objects: **R**	Remove mode.
Remove objects:	Select the circle.
1 selected, 1 found, 1 removed	The circle is removed from the selection set.
Remove objects:	Select the character C.
1 selected, 1 found, 1 removed	The C is removed from the selection set.
Remove objects: **\<RETURN\>**	
Base point or displacement: **1.1<270**	A polar displacement. (Release 10 users enter 0, -1.1).
Second point of displacement: **\<RETURN\>**	Use previous input as displacement.

As figure 6.6 shows, this operation moves the chip and leaves the capacitor in its original location.

Figure 6.5:
Using a crossing window to move objects.

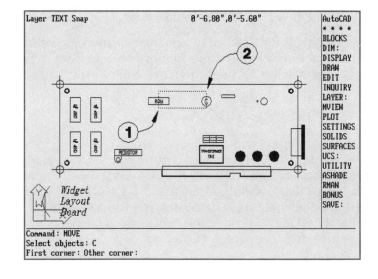

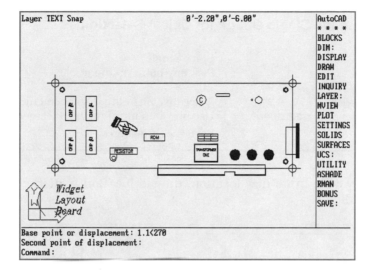

Figure 6.6:
The ROM chip in its
new location.

What's in the Selection Set?

In a complex drawing, you may notice the time it takes AutoCAD to search through the drawing file for entities that qualify for the selection set. Every time you select more objects for the selection set, AutoCAD lets you know how many you selected and how many it actually found. These numbers are not always the same for two reasons. First, you can select objects that do not qualify for editing. Second, you may have already selected that entity. In the latter case, AutoCAD lets you know it found a duplicate. In all cases (except Multiple mode selections), AutoCAD uses the highlighting feature to show you what is currently in the selection set.

> **Tip:** To speed up the selection of complex selection sets, you can turn the HIGH-LIGHT system variable off. Type HIGHLIGHT (in Release 10, use SETVAR) and set it to 0 (off).

Using the SIngle Option for Object Selection

Menu items that expect you to select exactly one object may use the SIngle mode of object selection. As soon as an object (or group of objects) is selected, object selection ends without your having to enter a <RETURN>. Try SIngle and an absolute displacement to move the diode from the top of the widget down to the left. Remember that the diode was made with a polyline, so it selects and moves as a single entity.

Using the SIngle Option for Object Selection

```
Command: MOVE
Select objects: SI                        SI for SIngle.
Select objects:                           Pick any point on diode.
1 selected, 1 found.
Base point of displacement: -.6,-.9       A negative absolute displacement.
Second point of displacement:<RETURN>     Use previous input as displacement.
Command: SAVE                             Save the drawing.
```

Figure 6.7 shows the diode in its new location; the old location is marked by the ghosted image of the diode.

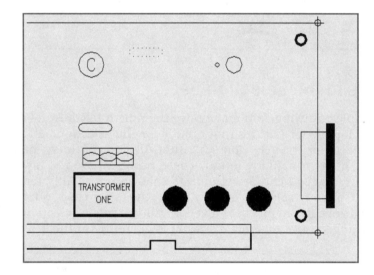

Figure 6.7:
The diode's new
location.

SIngle was designed for use in menu macros. You can precede any of the object selection modes with SI for SIngle.

Previous Selection Set Option

You will find the Previous selection option helpful when you cancel an editing command or use several commands on the same selection set. Previous object selection reselects the object(s) that you selected in your previous editing command.

Previous lets you edit the previous set without having to individually select its objects again. Previous is different from the Last option, which selects the last created object visible on the screen. Previous does not work with some editing commands (like STRETCH) where a window, crossing, or point selection is specifically required.

Tired of moving? Let's take a look at copying.

The COPY Command

The basic COPY command is similar to the MOVE command. The only difference between a copy and a move is that COPY leaves the original objects in place.

We'll copy the widget's transformer, using a BOX selection. BOX combines a window and a crossing window. If you make your box left to right, it acts like a window. Right to left acts like a crossing window. Try canceling the command and using Previous to reselect the selection set to copy.

Using the COPY Command and BOX Mode

```
Command: COPY
Select objects: BOX                          Enclose transformer and text
                                             right to left for crossing.
First corner:                                Pick first corner at ① (see fig.
                                             6.8).
Other corner:                                Pick second corner at ②.
3 found.
Select objects: <RETURN>
<Base point or displacement>/Multiple: <^C>  Cancel it.
Command: COPY
Select objects: P                            Previous.
3 found.
Select objects: <RETURN>
<Base point or displacement>/Multiple: INT   Intersection.
of                                           Pick lower left corner of trans-
                                             former.
Second point of displacement: 8.20,4.30
```

Figure 6.9 shows the board with the newly copied transformer.

Remember, you can always use osnap and snap functions as modifiers to help you get an exact displacement location, or to help select objects for the selection set.

COPY Options

The COPY command options are similar to the MOVE options. They include displacement points identification, object selection options, and a new one — Multiple (for multiple copies, not to be confused with Multiple object selection).

Figure 6.8:
Selecting the trans-
former.

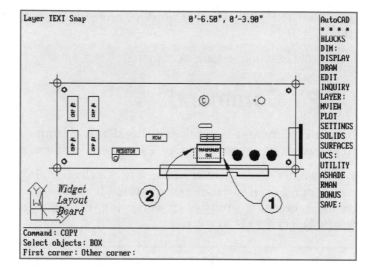

Figure 6.9:
The copied trans-
former.

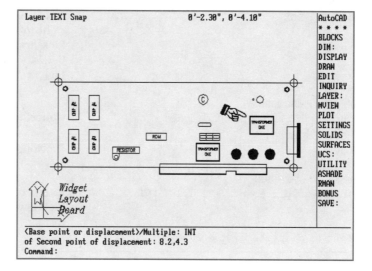

COPY Multiple Option

The Multiple option of the COPY command lets you copy the contents of your selection set several times without having to respecify the selection set and base point. If you respond with M to the base point prompt, AutoCAD will reprompt for base point, then repeatedly prompt you for multiple <Second point of displacement> points. A simple <RETURN> response gets you out of the Multiple loop.

Try making multiple copies of the capacitor. Put three copies next to the original capacitor. Put one copy between the transformers. Finally, put two more copies next to the resistor on the bottom of the board. The polar coords shown are for your reference; they are all snap points for accuracy.

Using COPY Multiple to Make Copies of the Capacitor

```
Command: COPY
Select objects: W                               Put a window around the capacitor
                                                (see fig. 6.10).
First corner:                                   Pick first corner point.
Other corner:                                   Pick second corner point.
2 found.
Select objects: <RETURN>
<Base point or displacement>/Multiple: M
Base point:                                     Pick center of capacitor.
Second point of displacement:                   Pick polar point @0.40<270.00.
Second point of displacement:                   Pick polar point @0.50<0.00.
Second point of displacement:                   Pick polar point @0.64<321.34.
Second point of displacement:                   Pick polar point @2.26<225.00.
Second point of displacement:                   Pick polar point @1.94<235.49.
Second point of displacement:                   Pick polar point @1.41<315.00.
Second point of displacement: <RETURN>
```

Figure 6.11 shows the copies.

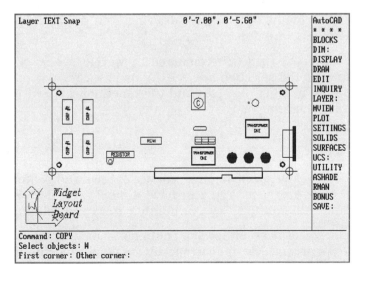

Figure 6.10:
Before the multiple copy.

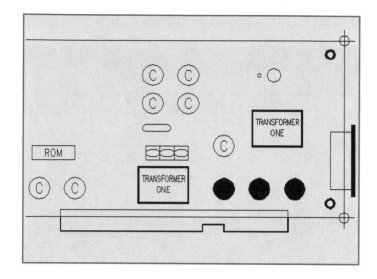

Figure 6.11:
The completed mul-
tiple copy.

Let's look at another type of multiple copying — making *arrays*.

ARRAY — Making Multiple Copies in a Pattern

Often, you want to make multiple copies of an object or group of objects in a regular pattern. For example, suppose you have a rectangle that represents a table in a cafeteria. It would be useful if AutoCAD had some way of placing that table repeatedly every nine feet in the X direction and every fourteen feet in the Y direction to make five rows and eight columns of tables. Or drawing evenly spaced bolt holes around the circumference of a tank top.

The ARRAY command works like the COPY command. However, instead of making individually placed copies of the selection set, ARRAY makes a regular pattern of entities. You determine the number of copies and the repetition pattern. The two basic patterns are rectangular and polar.

Rectangular Arrays

You make a rectangular array by specifying the number of rows and columns that you want and an X,Y offset distance. You can have a single row with multiple columns, a single column with multiple rows, or multiple rows and columns.

You can show the displacement between rows or columns by picking two points at the distance between rows prompt. Or you can specify the offsets by entering positive or negative offset values (see figs. 6.12 and 6.13). The offset distance is the X and Y direction from the original selection set. Entering negative values will produce an array in the negative X and/or Y directions. A positive X value gives columns to the right. A negative X value gives columns to the left. A positive Y gives rows up. A negative Y gives rows down.

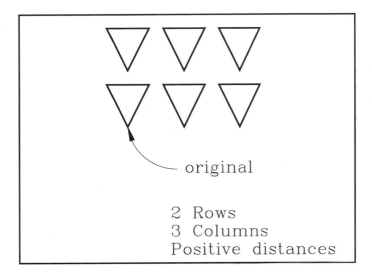

Figure 6.12:
Positive array offsets.

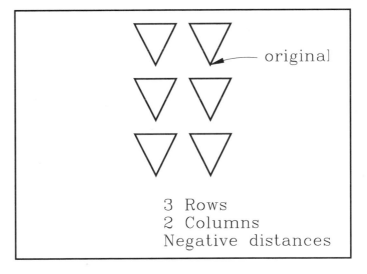

Figure 6.13:
Negative array off-
sets.

Try making a rectangular array using the ROM chip.

Using ARRAY to Make a Rectangular Array

```
Command: ARRAY
Select objects:                                Pick the ROM chip and its text.
2 selected, 2 found.
Select objects: <RETURN>
Rectangular or Polar array (R/P): R            Rectangular.
Number of rows (---) <1>: 4
Number of columns (||||) <1>: 2
Distance between rows (---): 0.40
Distance between columns (||||): 0.80          The array draws (see fig. 6.14).
```

Figure 6.14:
The completed rect-
angular array.

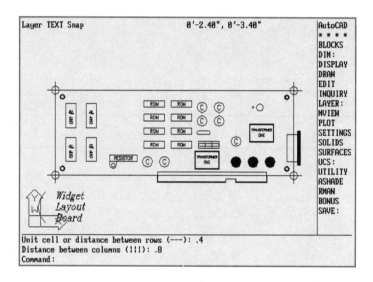

If you set up a big array (many rows and columns), AutoCAD will ask if you really want to repeat the selection set so many times. If it gets out of hand, you can stop it with a <^C> and then reverse it with a U for Undo.

Tip: ARRAY is useful even if you want to make only one row or column of entities. It is quicker than COPY Multiple.

Try making a set of logo arcs next to the widget layout text at the bottom left of your drawing. This is the single-row array of arcs shown in the next example.

> ### Making a Single-Column Array
>
> ```
> Command: ARRAY
> Select objects:                                Pick the logo arc.
> 1 selected,  1 found.
> Select objects: <RETURN>
> Rectangular or Polar array  (R/P): R
> Number of rows (---) <1>: <RETURN>            One row.
> Number of columns (||||) <1>: 6
> Distance between columns (||||): 0.05         The array draws (see fig. 6.15).
> ```

Figure 6.15:
Detail of the logo after the array.

Polar Arrays

In polar arrays, you place the entities in the selection set around the circumference of an imaginary circle or arc. Polar arrays are useful for creating mechanical parts like gear teeth, or bolt patterns. Figures 6.16 and 6.17 show examples of regular and rotated circular arrays.

When you form a polar array, you specify the number of items you want in the array, the angle you want to fill, and whether you want the items rotated. One item is one copy of the selection set to be arrayed. When you count your items, remember to include the original. You can array around a full circle or part of a circle. If you array around part of a circle, you will need one more item than the total arc angle divided by the incremental angle. For example, if you are arraying 90 degrees and you want the items at 30 degree increments, you will need 90/30 + 1 = 4 items.

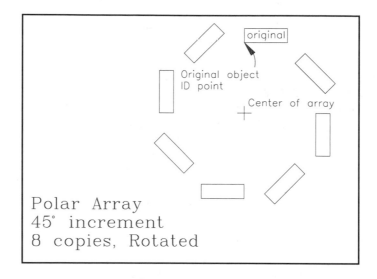

Figure 6.16:
A rotated polar array.

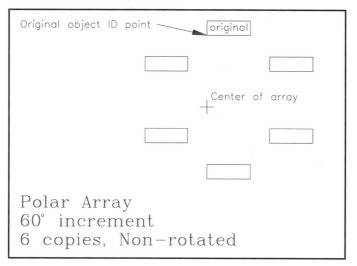

Figure 6.17:
A nonrotated polar array.

The following exercise shows how to array the contact around part of a circle. The contact is the small circle to the left of the switch (large circle) on the right side of the widget.

Using Polar Array on Switch Contacts

```
Command: ARRAY
Select objects:                              Select small circle ① to left of
                                             switch.
1 selected, 1 found.
Select objects: <RETURN>
Rectangular or Polar array (R/P): P          Polar.
Center point of array: CEN                   Osnap it.
of                                           Pick any point on large circle.
Number of items: 7                           That's 270/45 + 1.
Angle to fill (+=ccw, -=cw) <360>: 270
Rotate objects as they are copied? Y <RETURN>   It doesn't matter for circles!
```

Figure 6.18 shows a zoomed view of this array.

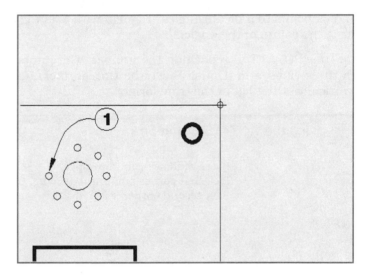

Figure 6.18:
Detail view of the
switch after the array.

Tip: Polar arraying a line twice around its midpoint or four times around its end-point will create a cross. A large number of items will create a sunburst.

If an array can rotate entities, you must be able to rotate entities individually.

The ROTATE Command

The ROTATE command lets you turn existing entities at precise angles. Like MOVE, you specify a first point as a base point. This rotation base point doesn't need to be on the object that you are rotating. You can put it anywhere and AutoCAD will turn your selected entities relative to the base point. But be careful — it's easy to become confused with rotation base points (like bad drag handles) that are not on the entities you intend to rotate. After you specify the base point, give a rotation angle. Negative angles produce clockwise rotation, positive angles produce counter-clockwise rotation (with the normal direction setting in units).

As an alternative to specifying an angle, you can use a reference angle. You can change the angle of an entity by giving AutoCAD a reference angle that should be set equal to the new angle. In effect you say, "Put a handle on 237 degrees (for example) and turn it to 165." This is often easier than calculating the difference (72 degrees clockwise) and typing that number at the prompt. You need not even know the actual angles; you can pick points to indicate angles. To align with existing objects, use osnaps when picking the points of the angle(s).

Try two rotations. First, use ROTATE to reposition the jumper. The jumper is the rectangular thing with three ellipses in it, just above the transformer. Rotate the jumper into position vertically at the left of the transformer.

Using the ROTATE Command

```
Command: ROTATE
Select objects: W                    Place window around jumper.
First corner:                        Pick first corner point at ① (see fig. 6.19).
Other corner:                        Pick second corner point at ②.
6 found.
Select objects: <RETURN>
Base point: 6.45,4.3.
<Rotation angle>/Reference: -90
```

Figure 6.20 shows the rotated jumper.

Next, combine a COPY command and a ROTATE command to place another mounting tab nut and flange on top of the resistor. This COPY/ROTATE technique is an efficient trick.

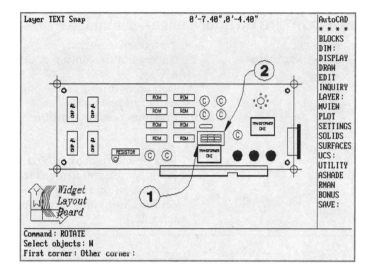

Figure 6.19:
Selecting the jumper
with a window.

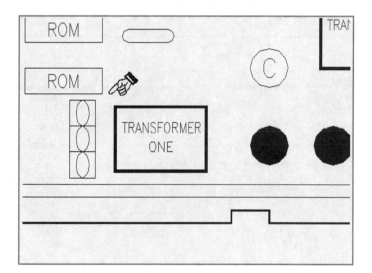

Figure 6.20:
The jumper after
being rotated.

Using the COPY/ROTATE Technique

Command: **VIEW**	Restore view RESISTOR.
Command: **COPY**	
Select object: **W**	Select the mounting tab.
First corner:	Pick first corner point at ① (see fig. 6.21).
Other corner:	Pick second corner point at ②.
4 found.	
Select objects: **<RETURN>**	

Using the COPY/ROTATE Technique—continued

`<Base point or displacement>/Multiple: `**`0,0`**	Zero displacement.
`Second point of displacement: `**`<RETURN>`**	Copies entities on top of themselves.
`Command: `**`ROTATE`**	Rotate mounting tab to opposite corner of resistor.
`Select objects: `**`P`**	Previous reselects entities.
`4 found.`	
`Select objects: `**`<RETURN>`**	
`Base point:`	Pick absolute point 4.50,3.80.
`<Rotation angle>/Reference:`	Drag cursor 180 degrees to left and pick. Rotation takes place again.
`Command: `**`REDRAW`**	Shows the complete resistor (see fig. 6.22).

Note: This exercise shows how handy COPY and ROTATE can be for avoiding redrawing entities in new positions.

Figure 6.21:
Selecting a resistor nut with window.

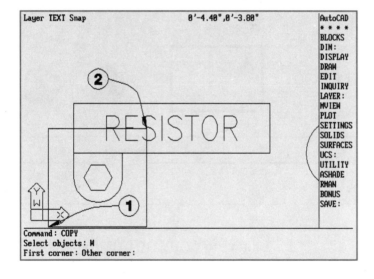

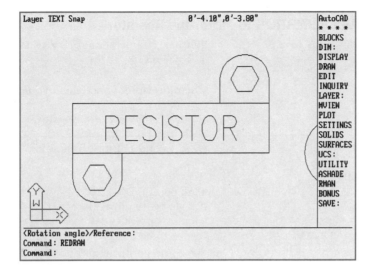

Figure 6.22:
A nut after copy and rotate.

MIRROR — Copying Through the Looking Glass

The MIRROR command creates a mirrored copy of objects. You can mirror the contents of a selection set at any angle. MIRROR prompts you to identify a selection set in the usual manner. Then comes the mirror twist. AutoCAD prompts you for the beginning and endpoint of a mirror line. The line can be any direction. If you want a straight 180-degree flip, use ortho to help you get a straight mirror line. If you want mirroring at a precise angle, use relative polar coordinates, @8<60 for example, or use a rotated snap or UCS.

Finally, AutoCAD asks if you want to keep the original entities in place or to delete them. Think of this as either copying or moving the contents of the selection set through the mirror.

If you have text in your selection sct (as our cxample does), you need to consider whether you want to pass the text through the mirror unchanged or mirrored. If you do not want text mirrored, you can set the MIRRTEXT system variable to 0, allowing mirror-inverted graphics, but letting text come out reading the way it goes in.

Mirror the resistor you have been working on. Set MIRRTEXT to 0 so text is not mirrored. Mirror the resistor by flipping it 180 degrees. Keep the original in place.

Using MIRROR to Mirror the Resistor

Command: **MIRRTEXT**	Release 10 users use SETVAR to set MIRRTEXT.
New value for MIRRTEXT <1>: **0**	
Command: **ZOOM**	Zoom Previous to see the layout board.
Command: **MIRROR**	
Select objects: **W**	Place window around resistor.
First corner:	Pick first point at 4.00,3.40.
Other corner:	Pick second point at 5.00,4.20.
13 found.	
Select objects: **<RETURN>**	
First point of mirror line:	Pick point 5.00,4.20.
Second point: <Ortho>	Toggle ortho on with <^O> or <F6> and pick any point to left.
Delete old objects? <N> **<RETURN>**	
Command: **SAVE**	Save and continue or end and take a break.

Figure 6.23 shows a zoomed view of the mirrored resistor and the location of the mirror line.

Figure 6.23:
Detail view of the resistor after being mirrored.

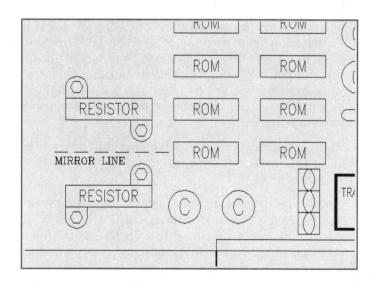

If you need to take a break, end your drawing. So far, the editing commands that you have worked with are variations on a theme — moving or copying single entities, or making multiple copies of entities. The next group of editing commands involves deleting portions of entities, or, in the case of ERASE, deleting entire entities.

ERASE and Its Sidekick, OOPS

Like a hammer, ERASE can be a constructive tool. But, like a hammer, watch out! The ERASE command has been the scourge of many a good drawing file.

The following exercise uses ERASE, but adds a good friend, the OOPS command. You will find OOPS prominently displayed on the [ERASE] screen menu and the [Modify] pull-down menu (and also available by typing it). OOPS asks no questions — it just goes about its business of restoring whatever you just obliterated with ERASE.

Let's get rid of the original resistor and the diode with an ERASE. You can reload your WIDGEDIT drawing, or continue from the previous exercise. In either case, your drawing now should resemble figure 6.24.

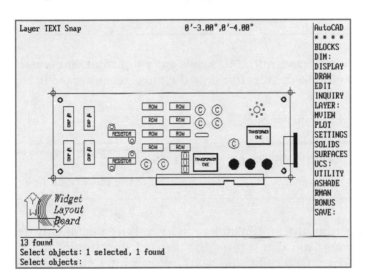

Figure 6.24:
The layout board before erasing.

Using ERASE

Edit an EXISTING drawing named WIDGEDIT, or continue from previous exercise.

```
Command: ERASE
Select objects: W                    Window the original resistor. (If continuing, you
                                     can use Previous instead.)

13 found.
Select objects:                      Pick the diode.
1 found.
Select objects: <RETURN>             The deletion takes place (see fig. 6.25).
```

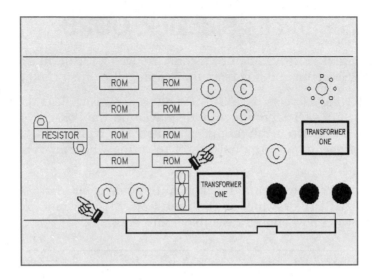

Figure 6.25:
The completed erase.

Every time you execute an erase, AutoCAD keeps a copy of what you erased in case you want to oops it back into the file. But only the most recent erase is kept oops-ready!

Try OOPS now to get your objects back.

Using OOPS on Your Last Erase

Command: **OOPS**   Here come the resistor and diode.

OOPS lets you recover from the unthinkable. After you have mistakenly deleted an entity from your drawing, you can recover the last deletion (under most circumstances) with OOPS. The OOPS command won't recover after you plot or end and then resume a drawing.

Using BREAK to Cut Objects

BREAK cuts existing objects into two or erases portions of objects. Use any of the standard selection set techniques to let AutoCAD know which entity you want to break. Picking is usually the safest way to get the object you want. AutoCAD uses the pick point as the start of the break and prompts you for the second point. Crossing, Window, or Previous will break the most recently selected entity. Unless you select by picking, you will then be prompted for the first point (the start of the break) and second point (the end of the break). If you pick the same point again,

AutoCAD cuts your object into two at the selected point, but does not delete any of it.

Picking doesn't work as well when breaking between intersections, because AutoCAD may select the wrong entity. You can use another object selection method or pick the object to be broken at another point, then respecify the first break point. To do this, enter an F at the initial second point prompt and AutoCAD will reprompt you for the first point.

Here's the prompt sequence for breaking out the line at the port on the right side of the widget.

Using BREAK to Break a Line

```
Command: BREAK
Select object:                                    Pick line of widget board at ① (see
                                                  fig. 6.26).
Enter second point (or F for first point): F      Reprompt for first point.
Enter first point:                                Use OSNAP INT to pick first point at
                                                  ②.
Enter second point:                               Use OSNAP INT to pick second point
                                                  at ③.
```

Figure 6.27 shows the result of this sequence.

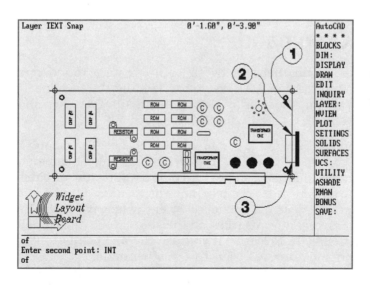

Figure 6.26:
The board before breaking.

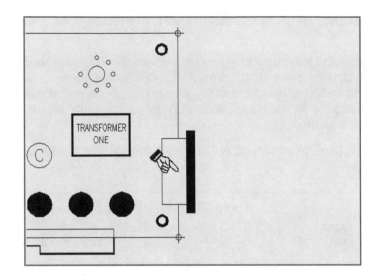

Figure 6.27:
The board after
breaking.

BREAK works on lines, arcs, circles, traces, and polylines (including polygons and donuts). Take care to select the first and second points in counterclockwise order when breaking circles. Closed polylines need a little experimentation. BREAK's effects will depend on the location of the polyline's first vertex. The break cannot extend across this vertex. If a point is off the entity, it acts as if you used osnap NEArest. If one point is off the end of an arc, line, trace, or open polyline, that end is cut off instead of breaking the entity into two.

The FILLET Command

A fillet is a tangent arc swung between two lines to create a round corner. The FILLET command is simple; AutoCAD asks you to identify the two lines that you would like joined. You identify the lines by picking them. AutoCAD then shortens or extends the lines and creates a new arc for the fillet corner.

You can specify the radius of the arc to create the fillet corner. The default radius is <0>. The fillet radius you set becomes the new default. The most common use for FILLET is to round corners, but using a fillet with a zero radius (the original default) is good for cleaning up under- or overlapping lines at corners. FILLET with a zero radius creates a corner, but does not create a new entity (see fig. 6.28). In Release 10, if the two lines intersect, AutoCAD trims off the shorter end of each line picked and retains the longer ends. In Release 11, you use the pickpoints to identify the ends you want retained and AutoCAD trims off the other ends.

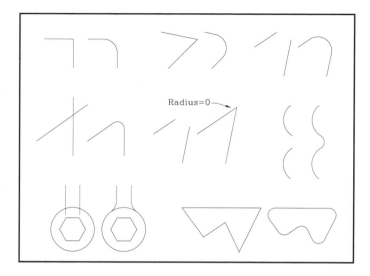

Figure 6.28:
Examples of fillets.

FILLET works on any combination of two arcs, circles and non-parallel lines, or on a single polyline. You can select lines or a polyline by Window, Last, or Crossing, but the results may be unpredictable. Selection by picking is safer, and is required for arcs or circles. Arcs and circles have more than one possible fillet, so they are filleted closest to the pick points.

Try filleting the four corners of the layout board.

Using FILLET to Round Corners

```
Command: FILLET
Polyline/Radius/<Select first object>: R
Enter fillet radius <0'-0.00">: .2
Command: FILLET                          Fillet a corner of the layout
                                         board.
Polyline/Radius/<Select first object>:   Pick the two lines that make
                                         up the corner.

Repeat the FILLET command for the remaining corners.
Command: REDRAW                          Refresh the screen.
```

Your board's corners should resemble the one shown in figure 6.29.

Tip: When you are faced with a task where the fillets have the same radius arc (like the exercise above), you can speed up the edit by using the MULTIPLE command to make multiple fillets.

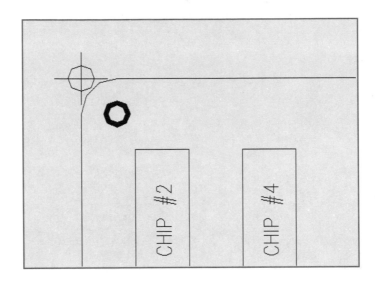

Figure 6.29:
Detail of a filleted
corner.

Filleting Polylines

There are two ways to fillet polylines: one vertex or all vertexes. If you select the polyline by Window, Crossing, or Last, the most recent vertex will be filleted. If you pick two points on adjacent segments, the vertex between those segments will be filleted. If you enter a P at the first fillet prompt, you will be prompted to select a polyline and all of its vertexes will be filleted.

The CHAMFER Command

A chamfer is a beveled edge. Adding a chamfer is easy. As you might expect, the CHAMFER command works like FILLET. CHAMFER works only on two lines or a single polyline. To get the chamfer, you supply a chamfer distance along each line that you want to join, rather than an arc radius. The distance that you supply is the cut-back distance from the intersection of the lines (see fig. 6.30).

Try two sets of chamfers. Chamfer all four corners of the second transformer polyline with 45-degree chamfers (equal distances). Then chamfer two corners on the right side port.

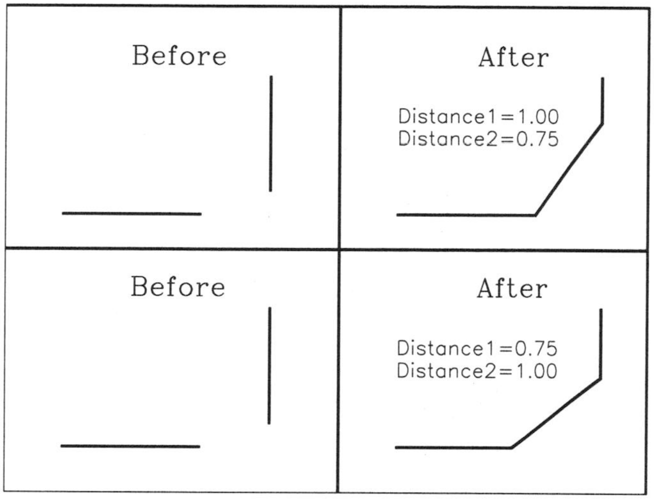

Before | After

Distance1=1.00
Distance2=0.75

Before | After

Distance1=0.75
Distance2=1.00

Figure 6.30:
Examples of
chamfered line
intersections.

Using CHAMFER on the Layout Board

```
Command: CHAMFER
Polyline/Distances/<Select first line>: D
Enter first chamfer distance <0'-0.00">: .05
Enter second chamfer distance <0'-0.05">: <RETURN>          Defaults to equal first.
Command: <RETURN>
CHAMFER Polyline/Distances/<Select first line>: P
Select 2D polyline:                                        Pick the transformer
                                                           polyline on the right.
4 lines were chamfered
Command: <RETURN>
CHAMFER Polyline/Distances/<Select first line>: D
Enter first chamfer distance <0'-0.05">: .1
Enter second chamfer distance <0'-0.10">: <RETURN>
Command: <RETURN>
CHAMFER Polyline/Distances/<Select first line>:            Pick top horizontal port
                                                           line.
Select second line:                                        Pick vertical port line.
Command: <RETURN>
CHAMFER Polyline/Distances/<Select first line>:            Pick bottom horizontal
                                                           port line.
Select second line:                                        Pick vertical port line.
```

As you can see from the exercise, it is easy to chamfer polylines. All four corners were modified at the same time (see fig. 6.31).

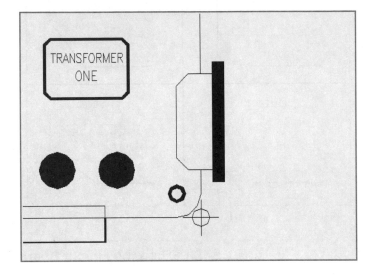

Figure 6.31:
The transformer and
port after chamfering.

Let's look at two more commands that modify existing entities.

The CHANGE Command

CHANGE can selectively edit one or more parameters that give a drawing entity its identity, location, and appearance in the drawing file. We recommend that you use CHANGE in 2D drawings to modify entity points, text, or attribute definitions (see Chapter 13) and use a second command, called CHPROP (see below), to modify appearance. CHPROP works in both 2D and 3D.

When you select objects to change, AutoCAD prompts you for the points and parameters that are changeable for the entities that you select. These vary with the type of entity.

How CHANGE Affects Different Entities

- Lines. CHANGE point changes the endpoint of a line. If several lines are selected, their nearest endpoints will converge at the change point picked. If ortho is on, they will be forced parallel instead of converging — a good trick to try.
- Circles. CHANGE point changes the circumference of an existing circle, forcing it to pass through the change point, while keeping the same center point.

■ Text (and attribute definitions). Changes location, rotation angle, height, style, and/or text string. CHANGE acts as a second chance to reset your text parameters.

■ Blocks (see Chapter 9). CHANGE lets you change the insertion point or rotation angle.

If you select several different entities, even different types, CHANGE will ignore any change point you pick and instead cycle through the entities in the order selected, prompting for the appropriate changes.

Try CHANGE to change the text of the second transformer from "ONE" to "TWO." Then, change the diameter of the switch circle on the right side of the board. Figure 6.32 shows the board before these changes are made.

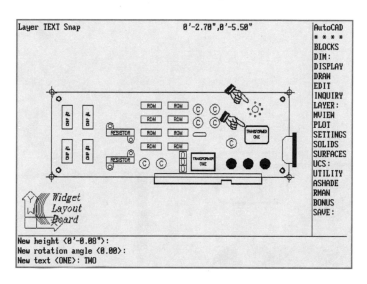

Figure 6.32:
Text and circle before changes.

Using CHANGE to Modify the Layout Board

```
Command: CHANGE                          Change text in transformer on
                                         the right.
Select objects:                          Select text string ONE.
1 selected, 1 found.
Select objects: <RETURN>
Properties/<Change point>: <RETURN>
Enter text insertion point: <RETURN>
Text style: STANDARD
New style or RETURN for no change: <RETURN>
New height <0'-0.08">: <RETURN>
New rotation angle <0.00>: <RETURN>
```

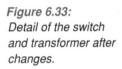

Using CHANGE to Modify the Layout Board—continued

```
New text <ONE>: TWO                    Change ONE to TWO.
Command: CHANGE                        Change diameter of switch.
Select objects:                        Pick the center switch circle.
1 selected, 1 found.
Select objects: <RETURN>
Properties/<Change point>:             Pick absolute point 8.20,5.30
                                       as the new circumference
                                       point.
```

Figure 6.33 shows a zoomed view of the changed switch and transformer.

Figure 6.33:
Detail of the switch and transformer after changes.

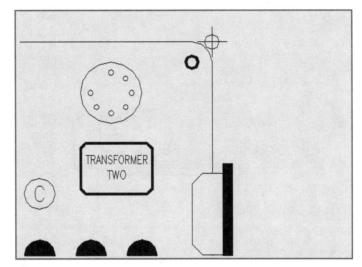

You also can use CHANGE to modify the properties of entities. Using CHANGE to modify properties in 2D drawings works fine, but it may not always work in 3D drawings. That is why AutoCAD has the CHPROP command, which always works.

Tip: When you redefine an existing text style with STYLE, only changes to the font and vertical orientation affect existing text. But you can use the CHANGE command to force existing text to reflect modifications to width, height, obliquing angle, etc. Entering a style name at the new style prompt will update all text parameters, even if the style name entered is the same as the currently defined style. Pressing <RETURN> leaves all parameters unchanged.

Using CHPROP to Change Properties

CHPROP changes properties in a 2D or 3D drawing. So far you have changed the location, size, or shape of entities already in place. Let's see how to change their properties.

Entity Properties

If you recall our earlier discussion on entities (Chapter 2), all entities have properties that you can edit. These are:

- Color
- Elevation
- Layer
- Linetype
- Thickness

When you created the lines in your widget drawing, you gave them a color and linetype. You might not have thought about it at the time. It may seem like a lot of edits ago! You created the individual widget parts on the layer PARTS with both entity color and linetype BYLAYER (PARTS has a cyan [4] default color and a continuous default linetype). When you created the parts, these entities picked up their characteristics from the layer defaults. While you were editing these lines, they retained their BYLAYER color and linetype. (At this point, the widget's entities have 0 elevation and thickness. These properties apply to 3D drawings. You will learn about them in Part Two, which covers 3D drawing and editing.)

Using CHPROP is the best way to change the properties of entities that you have already drawn. Use CHPROP to change the interior connector line's layer property to the HIDDEN layer. The object selection prompts are abbreviated in this and most of the remaining exercises, leaving you on your own for selection method. Once you select the objects, you will get a prompt for the property that you want to change.

Using CHPROP to Change Layers

```
Command: CHPROP                            Change lines to the HIDDEN
                                           layer.
Select objects:                            Select the connector lines.
Change what property (Color/LAyer/LType/
   Thickness) ? LA
New layer <BOARD>: HIDDEN
Change what property (Color/LAyer/LType/
   Thickness) ? <RETURN>
```

Your drawing should show a red hidden connector line (see fig. 6.34). The linetype and color properties are still BYLAYER.

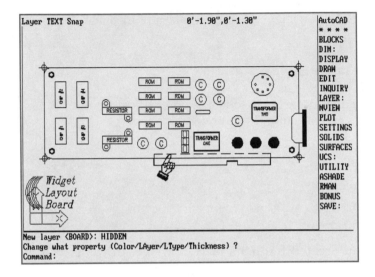

Figure 6.34:
The connector after
the layer change.

Entity color and linetype properties can be independent of layer. In fact, an entity can have any color or linetype. Try using CHPROP to change the color of the solid donuts. Then take one last look at your widget layout drawing with all its edits, and end it.

Using CHPROP to Change the Color of Donuts

```
Command: CHPROP                          Change the entity color of the
                                         solid donuts.
Select objects:                          Select the three solid donuts.
Change what property (Color/LAyer/LType/
  Thickness) ? C
New color <BYLAYER>: 6                    Change color to magenta.
Change what property (Color/LAyer/LType/
  Thickness) ? <RETURN>
Command: ZOOM                            All to get a full view.
Command: END
```

Now the donuts are magenta, overriding the cyan PARTS layer default.

CHPROP provides an easy method for changing entity properties. But for organized controlled drawings, it is usually best to deal with color and linetype by layer settings. Instead of changing color and linetype properties, try expanding and redefining the layers you set up in your drawings.

As we promised, you now have a full four-color widget layout board (see fig. 6.35). Save this drawing; you can use it later when we take up plotting in Part Two.

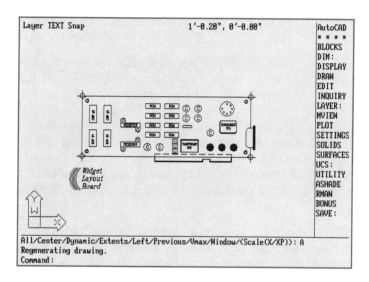

Figure 6.35:
The completed
WIDGEDIT drawing.

Note: You can now delete the WIDGET, PSPLOT, MVPLOT, and VPLAYER drawings; you no longer need them.

Summing Up

Now you can see how important editing is in constructing a drawing. In the beginning of the chapter on graphic entities, we said that drawings are dynamic. With a first course in editing under your belt, you can see just *how* dynamic a drawing can be.

Are you ready for the next engineering change order? Here's an Editor's Guide to Editing to keep you prepared.

Editor's Guide to Editing

Plan ahead for editing. When you first set up a drawing, think about how you are going to use your layers. Having everything on one layer complicates editing, so plan to use multiple layers. Think about repetitive features. Draw it once, copy it forever. Think about your building blocks. Start by defining your basic components and building your drawing up from there.

You should not have a favorite edit command. Use them all. Use snap, ortho, and osnaps to set up your MOVE and COPY displacements. MIRROR and ARRAY can help you complete a repetitive drawing in a hurry. Be careful with ERASE. To avoid disasters, there's always OOPS and Undo.

Learn to use all of the object selection options including the Remove option. All the selection set options have their roles. Last and Previous are used all the time when you realize that AutoCAD did what you said, not what you meant. The object picking method is best for detail work, especially with osnap. Window is powerful, but it doesn't do it all. Remember, what you see in the window is what goes into the selection set. You can use Crossing like a knife to slice out a selection set. BOX and SIngle are best for menu macros, as we shall see when we get to customization. AUto is a good habit. You can use it like a window, a crossing, or just to select an object. Previous saves time in repetitive editing. Don't forget, a U undoes the last object selection operation.

Think ahead about individual edits. Use display control to keep your field of view small and your concentration level high. Don't get caught setting up the base point of a displacement only to find that the second point is off the screen (if that happens, cancel, zoom, and try again). Don't underestimate the power of CHANGE. It really is an effective tool. Changing an endpoint is easier than erasing and adding a new line segment. Changing text is almost always easier than retyping text. AutoCAD prompts you for every change. CHPROP allows you to change the layer, color, and linetype properties of existing entities.

Stay informed about what AutoCAD is up to. Watch the current layer name on the status line. Create entities on the layers you want them on. Watch the prompt line for edit prompts — it is easy to start creating a selection set window while the prompt line is waiting for you to enter W to initiate the window selection. Use the Flip Screen key to see what's going on.

On to More Editing

So far, you've looked at some of AutoCAD's basic editing commands. Let's move on to more advanced editing commands and see how you can combine them with some electronic drafting techniques to get more productivity out of editing your drawings.

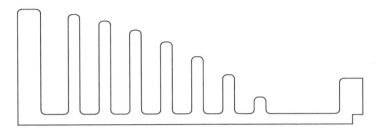

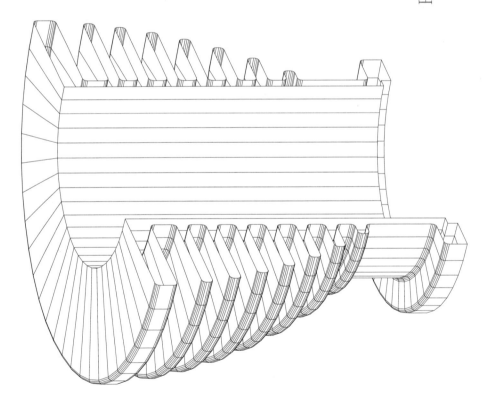

Figure 7.1:
3D piston cylinder and profile

7

Advanced Editing

PUTTING DRAWINGS TOGETHER — CAD STYLE

To take full advantage of AutoCAD's power, you need to combine AutoCAD's editing commands with CAD drafting techniques. While the editing commands you learned in the last chapter will help you speed up your drafting, the editing commands and techniques you learn in this chapter will change the way you create your drawings. These advanced editing commands, like EXTEND, STRETCH, TRIM, and OFFSET, go beyond copying and moving entities. They build on AutoCAD's geometrical knowledge of the entities in your drawing. By combining these commands with construction techniques, setting up construction lines, parallel rules, and construction layers, you can rough out a drawing quickly, then finish it perfectly.

Besides construction techniques, we want to emphasize how to get *continuity* in your two-dimensional drawings by using polylines and by editing with PEDIT. Continuous polylines are important to AutoCAD's hatch patterns and 3D. Polylines provide continuity when you form three-dimensional faces and meshes. If your two-dimensional drawing has breaks in its line profile, you will not be able to form a complete three-dimensional surface. Figure 7.1 shows the effect of taking a continuous polyline and forming a 3D mesh.

Drawing polylines and modifying them with PEDIT, or converting or joining existing entities into new polylines with PEDIT, are basic 2D skills that you want to master before working in 3D. The exercises in this chapter will show you how to use PEDIT and the other advanced editing commands to combine entity creation and CAD construction techniques into a single drawing process.

Advanced Editing Tools

The editing commands covered in this chapter's exercises are found on the [EDIT] screen menu and the [Modify] pull-down menu. These commands include EXTEND, OFFSET, SCALE, STRETCH, TRIM, and PEDIT. The PEDIT command, labeled [PolyEdit] on the pull-down menu, has an extensive set of options for global PEDITs, and options to edit individual vertexes of polylines. The trick to using these advanced editing commands is to plan ahead. The operations of commands like EXTEND, STRETCH, and TRIM can involve a number of entities. PEDIT requires continuity to join lines and arcs. These commands require more setup and more planning for how you are going to use them.

Setting Up the Cylinder Drawing

The drawing that you will create in this chapter's exercises is the piston cylinder profile (see fig. 7.2). The full cylinder is approximately 10 inches high by 14.60 inches wide.

Figure 7.2:
A cylinder profile
target drawing.

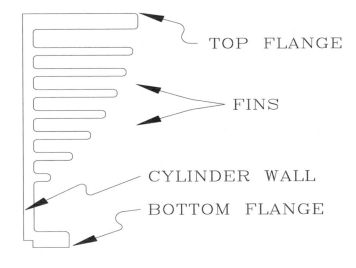

Here are our sample calculations for estimating a drawing scale factor and setting a sheet size.

```
Finned Piston Cylinder Wall                14.60" x 10.00"
Plot sheet size                            11" x 8 1/2"
Test 1/2" = 1" scale is a scale factor of 2.
    11" x 2 = 22" and 8 1/2" x 2 = 17"     22" x 17" limits
```

Create a new drawing called CYLINDER. Use the default decimal units, each unit representing one inch. If you were to dimension this drawing, you could have AutoCAD's dimensioning automatically add inch marks. Set your limits at 22 x 17. Use the settings shown in table 7.1 to help you complete your setup. If you are using the IA DISK, begin your CYLINDER drawing by setting it equal to IA6CYLIN.

Setup for CYLINDER Drawing

Begin a NEW drawing named CYLINDER=IA6CYLIN.

 Begin a NEW drawing named CYLINDER and complete the setup shown in the Cylinder Drawing Settings table. Set the 2D layer current.

Table 7.1
Cylinder Drawing Settings

AXIS	COORDS	GRID	SNAP	ORTHO
Off	On	1	0.1	ON

UNITS	Default decimal units, 2 digits to right of decimal point, default all other settings.
LIMITS	0,0 to 22,17
ZOOM	Zoom All.

Layer Name	State	Color	Linetype
0	On	7 (white)	CONTINUOUS
2D	On/Current	1 (red)	CONTINUOUS
3D	On	3 (green)	CONTINUOUS

If you want to practice individual editing commands, you can use a layer named SCRATCH. Create some entities, try out some editing variations, then freeze your SCRATCH layer and pick up again where you left off with the exercise sequences.

Using Lines and Polylines to Rough-In a Drawing

Let's start by roughing-in the section profile of the cylinder (see fig. 7.2). First, use a polyline to draw the top, side, and bottom of the cylinder. Then, draw one line and array it to form the construction lines for what will later become the cylinder fins.

Finally, draw an arc on the right side as a construction line to help form the ends of the fins. Your current layer is 2D. Your drawing should resemble the one shown in figure 7.3.

Figure 7.3:
The rough construc-
tion lines of a cylinder
wall.

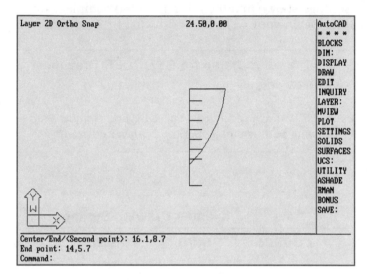

```
Layer 2D Ortho Snap                    24.50,0.00              AutoCAD
                                                               * * * *
                                                               BLOCKS
                                                               DIM:
                                                               DISPLAY
                                                               DRAW
                                                               EDIT
                                                               INQUIRY
                                                               LAYER:
                                                               MVIEW
                                                               PLOT
                                                               SETTINGS
                                                               SOLIDS
                                                               SURFACES
                                                               UCS:
                                                               UTILITY
                                                               ASHADE
                                                               RMAN
                                                               BONUS
                                                               SAVE:

Center/End/<Second point>: 16.1,8.7
End point: 14,5.7
Command:
```

Using PLINE, LINE, and ARC to Rough-In the Cylinder Wall

Command: PLINE	Draw a profile of the cylinder wall and flanges.
From point:	Pick absolute point 17,12.
Current line-width is 0.00	
Arc/Close/Halfwidth/Length/Undo/Width/ <Endpoint of line>:	Pick @3<180.
Arc/Close/Halfwidth/Length/Undo/Width/ <Endpoint of line>:	Pick @8<270.
Arc/Close/Halfwidth/Length/Undo/Width/ <Endpoint of line>:	Pick @1<0.
Arc/Close/Halfwidth/Length/Undo/Width/ <Endpoint of line>: **<RETURN>**	
Command: **LINE**	Draw a line from 14.00,11.00 to @1<0.
Command: **ARRAY**	Array the fin lines from the line.
Select objects: **L**	L selects the last entity.
1 found.	
Select objects: **<RETURN>**	
Rectangular or Polar array (R/P): **R**	

▶ **Using PLINE, LINE, and ARC to Rough-In the Cylinder Wall—continued**

```
Number of rows (– – –) <1>: 7
Number of columns (| | |) <1>: <RETURN>
Unit cell or distance between rows (– – –): -.8
Command: ARC                          Draw three-point arc from
                                      17,12 to 16.1,8.7 to 14,5.7.
```

Your arc should extend down from the polyline endpoint on the top right, intersect the first line that you drew, and intersect the polyline on the left a little more than halfway between the bottom and the intersected line. This arc will act as a construction line boundary to form the cylinder fins. The fin lines will be formed by extending them to the arc.

Extending Entities

To extend the lines to the arc, the command we turn to is EXTEND. You use EXTEND to extend lines, polylines, and arcs. The command is straightforward. The boundary edge(s) can be lines, polylines, arcs, circles, and viewport entities (when in paper space). Use normal object selection to select the boundary edge(s) that you want to extend to, then pick the objects you want to extend. The main thing to remember is that you have to individually pick each object to extend. You cannot use other modes to fill a selection set full of objects that you want extended, and then extend them all at once. Objects to extend are ignored unless EXTEND can project them to intersect a boundary object.

Use EXTEND when you are faced with the problem of not knowing (or not wanting to calculate) drawing intersection points. In these cases (and in the current exercise), it is easier to use a construction line, and extend your entities. There are a few constraints on using EXTEND: you cannot extend closed polylines and you cannot use EXTEND to shorten objects. That's a job for TRIM.

Try using EXTEND to lengthen the fin lines until they meet the construction arc (see fig. 7.4).

▶ **Using EXTEND to Extend Lines to an Arc**

```
Command: ZOOM                         Get into a closer working area.
Command: EXTEND
Select boundary edges(s)...
Select objects:                       Pick the arc.
1 selected, 1 found.
Select objects: <RETURN>
<Select object to extend>/Undo:       Pick each of the upper six arrayed lines.
```

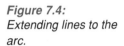

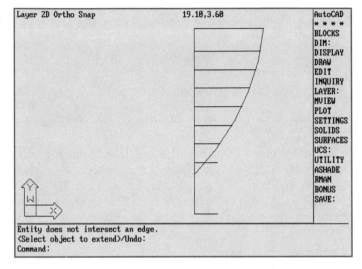

Figure 7.4:
Extending lines to the arc.

The seventh line already crosses the arc, so EXTEND can't adjust it. We could use TRIM, but we'll save it for a STRETCH exercise and use TRIM later for something more complicated. Now we need to add some thickness to the fins.

The OFFSET Command

Each of the cylinder fins as well as the cylinder wall itself is made up of parallel lines. The command you use to duplicate parallel drawing lines is OFFSET. You have to individually pick each entity that you want to offset and AutoCAD creates a parallel copy.

There are some types of entities that you cannot offset. The legal offset list is line, arc, circle, and 2D polyline. Polyline includes donuts, ellipses, and polygons. Each offset creates a new entity with the same linetype, color, and layer settings as the original entity. Polylines will also have the same width and curves.

You have two ways to offset. You can provide an offset distance and then indicate the side where you want the offset to go. You can input values or pick a point to show the offset distances, but you *must* use a pick to show the side for placement. Offset distances cannot be negative. Or, you can pick the entity you want to offset and then pick a point for it to be offset *through*. This Through option is the default. If the through point falls beyond the end of the new entity, the offset is calculated as if the new entity extended to the through point, but is drawn without that imaginary extension.

Use OFFSET with a through point to create a double cylinder wall and with a distance to double the lines that will form the fins (see fig. 7.5). Then draw lines to close the ends of the wall and fins (see fig. 7.6).

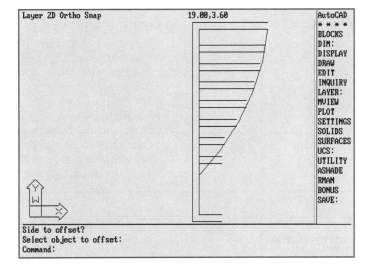

Figure 7.5:
The cylinder after offset.

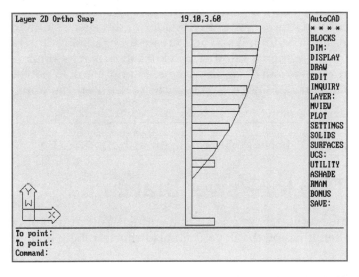

Figure 7.6:
The cylinder with connecting lines.

Using OFFSET to Create Wall and Fin Lines

Command: **OFFSET**	
Offset distance or Through <Through>: **<RETURN>**	Through.
Select object to offset:	Pick polyline on left.
Through point:	Pick any point 0.3 (3 snap units) to left of polyline.
Select object to offset: **<RETURN>**	
Command: **<RETURN>**	
OFFSET Offset distance or through <Through>: **.3**	Use a distance.
Select object to offset:	Pick one of the fin lines.

Using OFFSET to Create Wall and Fin Lines—continued

`Side to offset?`	Pick any point above the line.
`Select object to offset:`	Continue to offset the fin lines, placing each offset line above the selected line.
`Command:` **`OSNAP`**	Set running osnap to ENDPoint.
`Command:` **`LINE`**	Draw vertical lines between ends of each pair of fin lines.
`Command:` **`OSNAP`**	Set running osnap to NONe.
`Command:` **`SAVE`**	Save the drawing.

While this exercise has shown how to offset lines and polylines, you can also use OFFSET to form concentric circles.

Note: OFFSET forms a new entity by drawing the entity parallel to the original entity. OFFSET will fail to form a new entity inside an arc or circle if the offset distance exceeds the original radius. (You can't create a negative radius.) Donuts, polygons, and arc or short segments in other polylines are treated similarly. OFF-SET makes a logical attempt at small zig-zag segments and loops in polylines, but you may get confused results. Use PEDIT to clean the offset up if you don't like the results.

Let's thicken the flanges and shorten that bottom fin with STRETCH.

Using STRETCH for Power Drawing

The STRETCH command lets you move *and* stretch entities. You cannot only stretch entities in the sense of lengthening them, you can also shorten them and alter their shapes.

The key to STRETCH is to use a crossing window. After you select your objects with a crossing window (see fig. 7.7), you show AutoCAD where to stretch your objects with a displacement, a base point and a new point. Then, everything inside the crossing window you selected is moved, and entities crossing the window are stretched. Inside the window means that all of an object's endpoints or vertex points are within the window. Crossing the window means one or more points are inside and one or more points are outside the window.

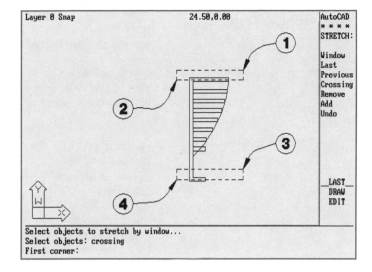

Figure 7.7:
Crossing windows to stretch flanges.

The STRETCH command is built around the crossing window selection set. (A window will only move, but not stretch, entities.) If there are objects within the crossing window that you want left untouched, you can use the Remove mode to remove them from the selection set. However, you can only add objects you want moved to the selection set with a window. But, because STRETCH only recognizes the last Crossing or Window selection used, using Crossing or Window to add or remove entities will generally not get the results you want.

STRETCH interacts differently with different entities. Try your hand at using STRETCH on lines and polylines, widening the top and bottom of the cylinder. When you are done, your drawing should resemble the one shown in figure 7.8.

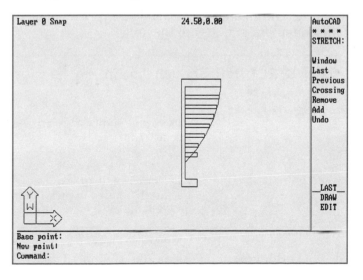

Figure 7.8:
Top and bottom flanges after stretch.

Using STRETCH to Widen the Flanges

```
Command: STRETCH                              Stretch the top flange up.
Select objects to stretch by window
Select objects: C                            Use Crossing.
First corner:                                Pick upper right corner at ①.
Other corner:                                Pick lower left corner at ②.
3 found
Select objects: <RETURN>
Base point:                                  Pick any point on the screen.
New point:                                   Pick a point @.3<90 degrees.
Command: <RETURN>                            Repeat to stretch the bottom
                                             flange up.

STRETCH Select objects to stretch by window
Select objects: C                            Use Crossing.
First corner:                                Pick upper right corner at ③.
Other corner:                                Pick lower left corner at ④.
2 found
Select objects: <RETURN>
Base point:                                  Pick any point on the screen.
New point: @.3<90
```

Note: STRETCH won't accept absolute X,Y or polar displacements, like MOVE and COPY do. Recall that an X,Y or @dist<angle value at the first prompt becomes an absolute displacement if you <RETURN> at the second point prompt in MOVE and COPY. Picking any point for the base point and then typing relative coordinates, such as @0,-7.5, is STRETCH's equivalent to an absolute displacement.

Use STRETCH again to shorten the fin lines that extend beyond the construction arc on the right, bringing the bottom fin in line with the arc.

Using STRETCH to Shorten the Fin

```
Command: STRETCH
Select objects to stretch by window...
Select objects: C                            Pick corner points between ① and ②
                                             (see fig. 7.9).
4 found.
Select objects: <RETURN>
Base point:                                  Pick corner of fin at ③.
New point:                                   Use an INT osnap to pick intersection of
                                             arc and line at ④.
```

When you are finished, the bottom fin should look like the one detailed in figure 7.10.

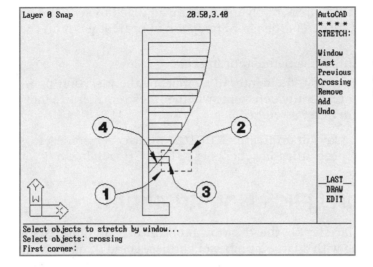

Figure 7.9:
A crossing window for stretching the fin.

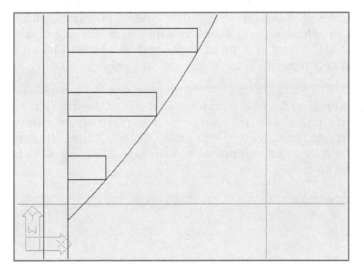

Figure 7.10:
A detail of stretched fin.

As you worked through this stretch, you may have noticed that the construction arc was highlighted by the crossing window but was not changed by the stretch. The arc was not moved or stretched because its endpoints were not enclosed in the window. STRETCH operates differently with different entities.

Some of the significant points for entities with STRETCH are:

- The endpoints or vertex points of lines, arcs, polyline segments, viewports, traces, and solids determine what is stretched or moved.

- The center points of arcs or polyline arcs are adjusted to keep the sagitta (altitude or distance from the chord midpoint to nearest point on the arc) constant.

- Viewport contents remain constant in scale.

- The location of a point, the center of a circle, or the insertion point of a block, shape, or text entity determine whether these entities are moved or not, but they are never stretched.

We encourage you to play around with STRETCH to discover some of its quirks. Once you get used to these little idiosyncrasies, STRETCH will do what you expect.

Using TRIM in Quick Construction

Frequently, you are faced with the drawing problem of trimming existing lines. When you are working with a large number of entities, going in and breaking individual entities is tiresome and cumbersome. You can get the same results faster using TRIM. Like EXTEND, TRIM makes use of boundary entities. Also like EXTEND, TRIM's boundaries may include lines, arcs, circles, polylines, and, in paper space, viewports. The entities that you select as your boundary edge become your *cutting edge*. Once you select your cutting edge, you pick the individual entities that you want to trim. You can trim lines, arcs, circles, and polylines. Other objects to trim are ignored.

Figure 7.11 demonstrates the effects of trimming; notice that the interior lines of the top three cylinder fins have been trimmed out. Compare those fins with the untrimmed ones. Then use TRIM to cut the interior lines of all the cylinder fins; the results are shown in figure 7.12. You'll probably have to toggle snap off to be able to pick the lines you want to trim.

Figure 7.11:
A cylinder with three fins trimmed.

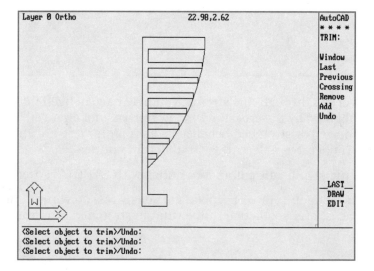

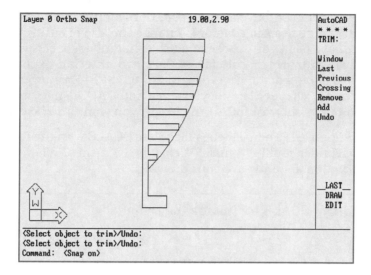

Figure 7.12:
A cylinder after trim.

Using TRIM to Cut Fin Lines

Command: **TRIM**	
Select cutting edge(s)...	
Select objects:	Use Window to select all the entities in the drawing.
26 selected, 26 found	
Select objects: **<RETURN>**	
<Select object to trim>/Undo: <Snap off>	Toggle snap off with <F9> or <^B> and pick a point on cylinder wall between fin lines.
<Select object to trim>/Undo:	Continue picking until all cylinder wall fin lines are trimmed.
<Select object to trim>/Undo: <Snap on> **<RETURN>**	Toggle snap on and end command.

Note: The same entity can be in the cutting edge boundary and be cut as an object to trim.

The SCALE Command

While we don't like to admit it, occasionally we get our drawing symbol and text scale wrong, or we have to change an object's size in mid-drawing. SCALE lets you shrink or enlarge objects that you have already placed in your drawing. When you rescale drawing objects, you use a scale factor to change the size of entities around a given base point. The base point you choose remains constant in space; everything around it grows or shrinks by your scale factor. You can enter an explicit scale factor, pick two points to show a distance as a factor, or tell SCALE you want to use a reference length. To use a reference length, you show AutoCAD a length (generally on an entity) and then tell or show AutoCAD the length you want it to become.

The piston cylinder is supposed to be 10 inches high. Use SCALE with the Reference option to change the cylinder profile to make it exactly 10 inches. When you are done, erase the construction arc and save your drawing.

Using SCALE to Enlarge the Cylinder

Command: **ZOOM**	Zoom All.
Command: **SCALE**	
Select objects:	Select every entity.
Base point:	Pick corner of wall at ① (see fig. 7.13).
\<Scale factor>/Reference: **R**	The Reference option.
Reference length \<1>:	Pick corner of wall at ①.
Second point:	Pick corner of wall at ③.
New length: **10**	Type or drag and pick a new 10-inch length.
Command: **ERASE**	Erase the construction arc.
Command: **SAVE**	Save the drawing.

At this point, your drawing should look like figure 7.14. The cylinder should be exactly ten inches high.

Figure 7.13:
A cylinder profile
before scale.

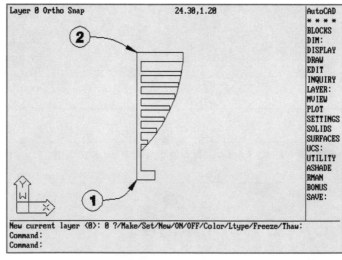

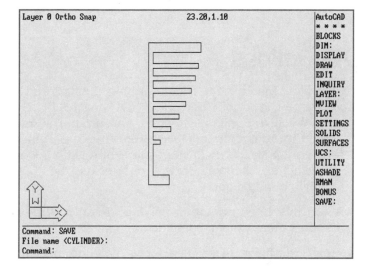

Figure 7.14:
A cylinder profile after
scale.

> **Tip:** The scale base point is also the base point of the new length in the Reference option. If you want to show the length on another object by picking, place your base point there, scale the selection, then adjust its location with MOVE Previous.

This drawing is a mixture of polylines and lines. Let's turn our attention to polyline editing. In the next section, you will do some simple polyline edits like changing polyline width, and you will form a new polyline by joining the individual entities which make up the cylinder profile.

PEDIT Gives Ultimate Control Over Polylines

Since polylines can be a complex, continuous series of line and arc segments, AutoCAD provides a command called PEDIT just for editing polylines. As you think about polyline properties, you are probably already imagining the list of PEDIT subcommands. To manage the list, AutoCAD divides PEDIT into two groups of editing functions. The primary group of functions works on the whole polyline you are editing. The second group works on vertexes connecting segments within the polyline.

There are more restrictions on using the PEDIT command when you edit three-dimensional polylines, as you will see in Part Two on 3D. For now, we will concentrate on editing two-dimensional polylines. However, we will show you how to revolve the final cylinder drawing at the end of this chapter to demonstrate how a three-dimensional polyline mesh is formed from two-dimensional polylines.

Here are the PEDIT options.

Primary PEDIT Options

Close/Open   Close will add a segment (if needed) and join the first and last vertexes to create a continuous polyline. PEDIT toggles between open and closed. When the polyline is open, the prompt shows Close; when closed, the prompt shows Open. A polyline can be open even if the first and last points coincide and it appears closed. Unless you use the Close option when you draw it, or later use the PEDIT Close option, a polyline will be open,

Join   Lets you add arcs, lines, and other polylines to an existing polyline. Their endpoints must exactly coincide to be joined.

Width   Sets a single width for all segments of a polyline, overriding any individual widths already stored.

Edit vertex   Presents a set of options for editing vertexes and their adjoining segments.

Fit curve   Creates a smooth curve through the polyline vertexes.

Spline curve   Creates a curve controlled by, but not usually passing through, a framework of polyline vertexes. The type of spline and its resolution are controlled by system variables.

Decurve   Undoes a Fit or Spline curve back to its original definition.

Undo   Undoes the most recent editing function.

eXit   As you might imagine, the default <X> gets you out of PEDIT and returns you to the command prompt.

Using PEDIT Join to Create a Polyline

Use PEDIT to join the cylinder lines into a single closed polyline. Use a window to select all the entities that you want to join. After you have created the polyline, increase its width to .02 inch (see figs. 7.15 and 7.16). Then, exit the PEDIT command and use FILLET to fillet all the corners in the polyline profile.

Using PEDIT to Join and Change a Polyline

```
Command: ZOOM                                    Zoom in closer.
Command: PEDIT
Select polyline:                                 Select the bottom line of one of
                                                 the middle fins.
```

Using PEDIT to Join and Change a Polyline—con tinued

```
Entity selected is not a polyline                    If it isn't a polyline, you can
                                                     make it into one.

Do you want to turn it into one? <Y> <RETURN>
Close/Join/Width/Edit vertex/Fit curve/Spline
   curve/Decurve/Undo/eXit <X>: J
Select objects:                                      Select all of the entities with a
                                                     window.
Select objects: <RETURN>                             End selection and the polyline is
                                                     created and closed.

35 segments added to polyline
Open/Join/Width/Edit vertex/Fit curve/Spline
   curve/Decurve/Undo/eXit <X>: W
Enter new width for all segments: .02
Open/Join/Width/Edit vertex/Fit curve/Spline
   curve/Decurve/Undo/eXit <X>: <RETURN>

Command: FILLET                                      Set a radius of 0.125.
Command: <RETURN>
FILLET Polyline/Radius/<Select first object>: P
Select 2D polyline:                                  Pick polyline.
36 lines were filleted
```

Figures 7.17 and 7.18 show the results of the FILLET routine.

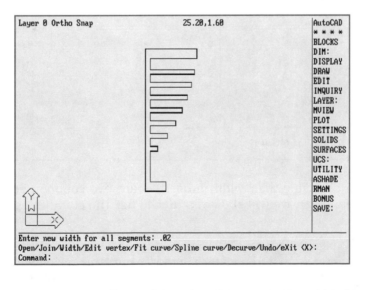

Figure 7.15:
A joined polyline with changed width.

Note: Like linetype scale, polyline width is set for a good plot appearance. It may look irregular on screen, or not show its width at some zoom levels or display resolutions.

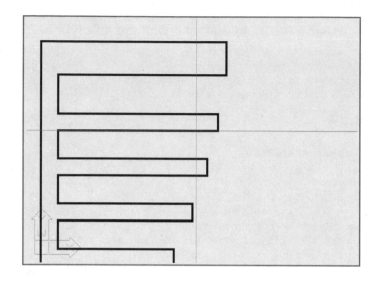

Figure 7.16:
Detail of a widened
polyline.

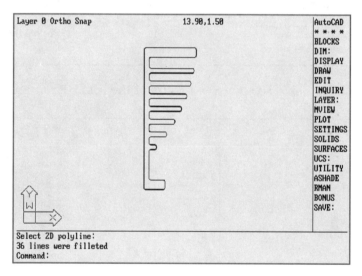

Figure 7.17:
A polyline after being
filleted.

Joining polylines and changing their width properties are two common edits that you will use frequently. Later, we will show you how to use the curve fit options.

Tip: Joining becomes tricky and may fail if the endpoints of the entities do not coincide exactly. Not using snap and osnaps when drawing, and occasional round-off discrepancies can all cause problems. Edit or replace stubborn entities, osnapping to the adjacent endpoints, and pedit again. Using FILLET with a zero radius is a good way to make endpoints coincide.

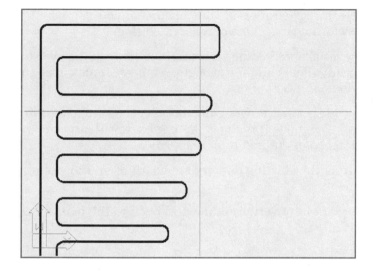

Figure 7.18:
Detail of a filleted
polyline.

Right now, let's look at how you edit individual segments or vertexes within a polyline. Knowing that each polyline segment belongs to and is controlled by the preceding vertex helps you understand how PEDIT works. The Edit vertex option gets you into a separate set of Edit vertex subcommands where the first vertex of the polyline is marked with an X. This X shows you what vertex you are editing. Move the X until you get the vertex you want to edit.

Here are the options.

PEDIT Edit Vertex Options

Next/Previous   Next/Previous gets you from one vertex to another by moving the X marker to a new current vertex. Next is the initial default.

Break   Splits the polyline into two or removes segments of a polyline at existing vertexes. The first break point is the vertex where you invoke the Break option. Use Next/Previous to get to another vertex for the second break point. Go performs the break. (Using the BREAK command is usually more efficient than using a PEDIT Break unless curve or spline fitting is involved.)

Insert   Adds a vertex at a point you specify following the vertex currently marked with an X. This can be combined with Break to break between existing vertexes.

Move   Changes the location of the current (X-marked) vertex to a point you specify.

Regen   Forces a regeneration of the polyline so you can see the effects (like width changes) of your vertex editing.

Straighten   Removes all intervening vertexes from between the two you select, replacing them with one straight segment. It also uses the Next/ Previous and Go options.

Tangent   Lets you specify a tangent direction at each vertex to control curve fitting. The tangent is shown at the vertex with an arrow, and can be dragged or entered from the keyboard.

Width   Controls the starting and ending width of an individual polyline segment.

eXit   Gets you out of vertex editing and back to the main PEDIT command.

Using PEDIT Edit Vertex Options

Once you have formed a polyline, you often need to move a vertex or straighten a line segment. Try exercising these two editing functions by removing two of the fillets. Remove one at the top left of the cylinder profile and another on the bottom flange. After you get into the PEDIT Edit Vertex option, you need to move the X to get the right segment (see figs. 7.19 and 7.20). Then, use the Move option to move the top left vertex to the corner. This will create a bump at the corner from the existing fillet arc segment (see fig. 7.21). You can use a transparent 'ZOOM if you want to see the bump. Use the Straighten option to make a 90-degree corner and eliminate the bump.

Figure 7.19:
Location of the edit X
before the move.

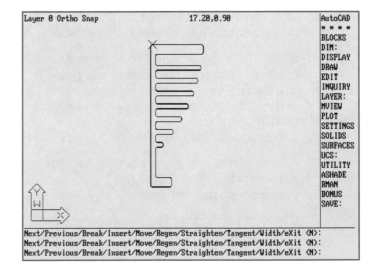

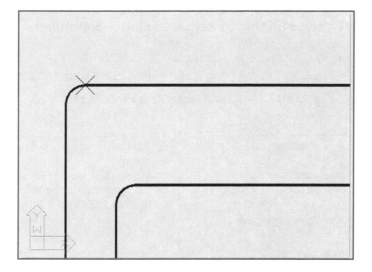

Figure 7.20:
Before the move.

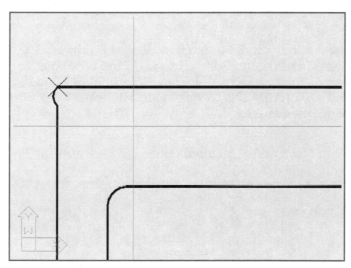

Figure 7.21:
After the move.

Using PEDIT Vertex Editing to Remove Fillets

```
Command: PEDIT
Select polyline:                                        Select the polyline.
Open/Join/Width/Edit vertex/Fit curve/Spline
  curve/Decurve/Undo/eXit <X>: E
Next/Previous/Break/Insert/Move/Regen/
  Straighten/Tangent/Width/eXit <N>: <RETURN>
```

An X appears on the polyline. Repeat <RETURN> until Next moves the
X to match figure 7.19.

Using PEDIT Vertex Editing to Remove Fillets—continued

```
Next/Previous/Break/Insert/Move/Regen/
    Straighten/Tangent/Width/eXit <N>: M
Enter new location:
```
Pick polar point @0.125<180.

Now straighten the bump. Use 'ZOOM if you want to see it, then zoom back out.

```
Next/Previous/Break/Insert/Move/Regen/
    Straighten/Tangent/Width/eXit <N>: S
Next/Previous/Go/eXit <N>: <RETURN>
```
Next moves the X below the bump.

```
Next/Previous/Go/eXit <N>: <RETURN>
Next/Previous/Go/eXit <P>: G
```
Moves X to match figure 7.22.
Go straightens the line (see figures 7.23 and 7.24).

```
Next/Previous/Break/Insert/Move/Regen/
    Straighten/Tangent/Width/eXit <N>:
```

Stay in the command for the next exercise.

Tip: If you make a mistake, exit the Edit vertex mode to the primary PEDIT mode and use the Undo option. Then re-enter Edit vertex mode and redo your work. Undo will undo all operations of the Edit vertex session. When doing a long sequence, occasionally exiting and re-entering Edit Vertex mode will protect the work you've done so far from subsequent mistakes.

You can repeat the above Move and Straighten options to clean up the lower right corner.

Figure 7.22:
The location of X
before straightening.

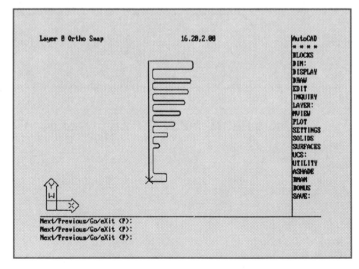

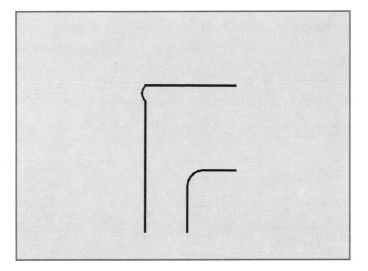

Figure 7.23:
Before straightening.

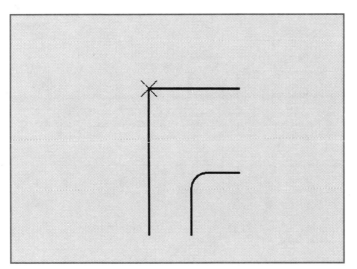

Figure 7.24:
After straightening.

Straightening the Lower Right Corner

Press <RETURN> three times and Next moves the X to match figure 7.25.

```
Next/Previous/Break/Insert/Move/Regen/
    Straighten/Tangent/Width/eXit <N>: M
Enter new location: @0.125<0                    Type in polar coordinate.
Next/Previous/Break/Insert/Move/Regen/
    Straighten/Tangent/Width/eXit <N>: S
Next/Previous/Go/eXit <N>.                      <RETURN> twice to move X to
                                                match figure 7.28.
```

Straightening the Lower Right Corner—continued

```
Next/Previous/Go/eXit <N>: G                          Go straightens the line.
Next/Previous/Break/Insert/Move/Regen/
   Straighten/Tangent/Width/eXit <N>:
```

Figures 7.25 through 7.30 show the progress of this operation. Stay in the command for the next exercise.

Figure 7.25:
The location of edit X before the second move.

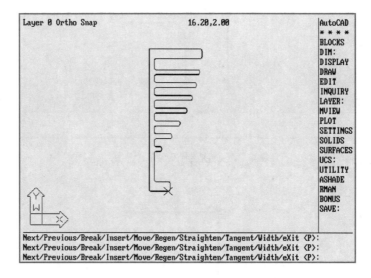

Figure 7.26:
Before the move.

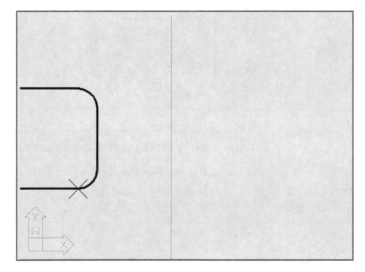

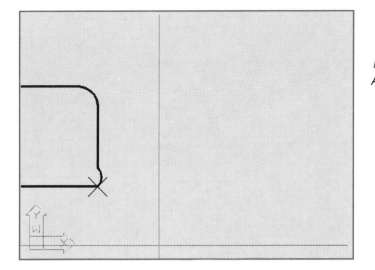

Figure 7.27:
After the move.

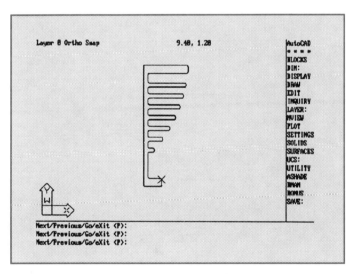

Figure 7.28:
The location of X
before the second
straightening.

You can add a vertex to an existing polyline. Try adding a notch to the lower left corner of the cylinder profile. The following editing sequence uses the Insert and Move vertex options.

Figure 7.29:
Before straightening.

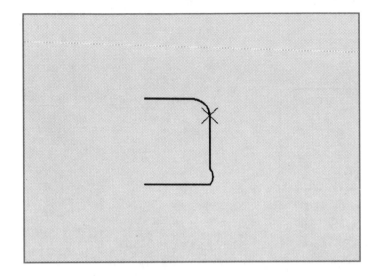

Figure 7.30:
After straightening.

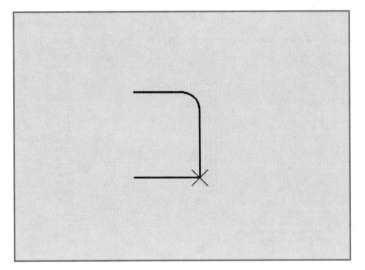

Using PEDIT to Add a Notch

```
Next/Previous/Break/Insert/Move/Regen/
   Straighten/Tangent/Width/eXit <N>: P
```

Press <RETURN> again to move the X to match figure 7.31.

```
Next/Previous/Break/Insert/Move/Regen/
   Straighten/Tangent/Width/eXit <P>: M
Enter new location: @0.175<90                    Move up to make .3" notch.
```

Using PEDIT to Add a Notch—continued

```
Next/Previous/Break/Insert/Move/Regen/
   Straighten/Tangent/Width/eXit <P>: I
Enter location of new vertex:                    Pick polar point @0.30<0
Next/Previous/Break/Insert/Move/Regen/
   Straighten/Tangent/Width/eXit <P>: N
Next/Previous/Break/Insert/Move/Regen/
   Straighten/Tangent/Width/eXit <N>: <RETURN>
Next/Previous/Break/Insert/Move/Regen/
   Straighten/Tangent/Width/eXit <N>: M
Enter new location: @0.175<0
Next/Previous/Break/Insert/Move/Regen/
   Straighten/Tangent/Width/eXit <N>: X
Open/Join/Width/Edit vertex/Fit curve/Spline
   curve/Decurve/Undo/eXit <X>: <RETURN>
Command: SAVE
```

Figures 7.31 through 7.39 show the progress of this command sequence.

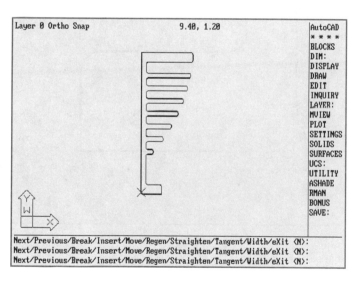

Figure 7.31:
The location of X
before the move.

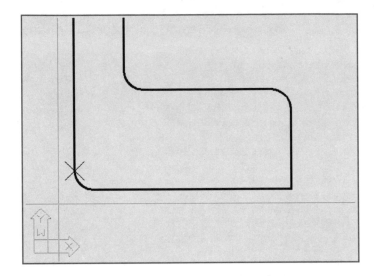

Figure 7.32:
Before the move.

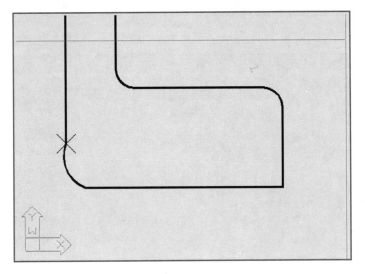

Figure 7.33:
After the move.

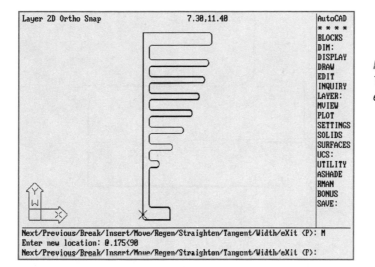

Figure 7.34:
The location of the
edit X before insert.

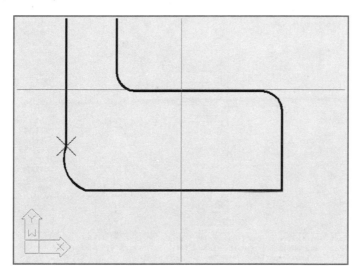

Figure 7.35:
Before the insert.

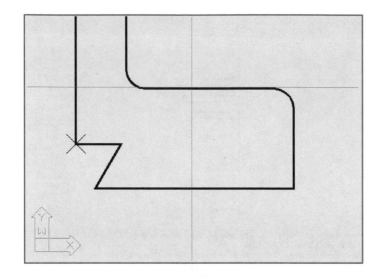

Figure 7.36:
After the insert.

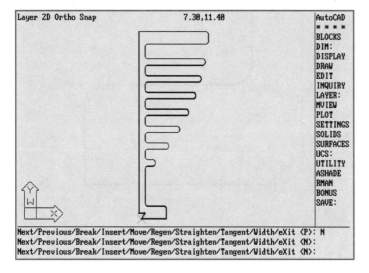

Figure 7.37:
The location of the edit X before the second move.

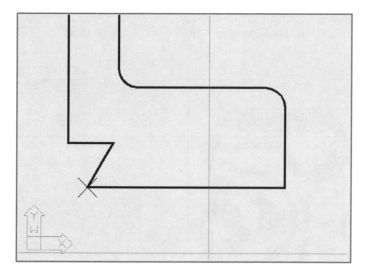

Figure 7.38:
Before the move.

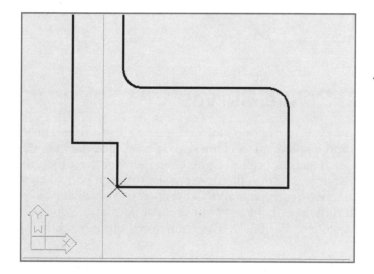

Figure 7.39:
After the move.

Using EXPLODE on Polylines

If you are faced with extensive edits on polylines, it's hard to know whether it's easier to edit the vertexes or to explode the polyline into individual segments, do your edits, then re-join the segments. EXPLODE is the command you use to break a polyline into its individual segments. There are drawbacks to exploding polylines. They lose their width and tangent information. EXPLODE locks in curves and splines by converting the polyline to many arcs or small straight lines. Wide polylines come out of an explosion looking like shaved poodles, with only their center lines showing (see fig. 7.40). If you were to explode the cylinder's polyline, you would get 72 entities.

Polyline before...   ...and after EXPLODE

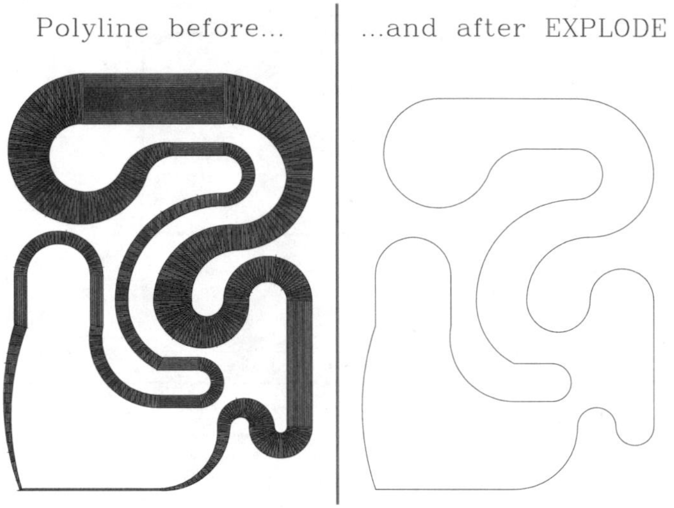

Figure 7.40:
A polyline before and
after explosion.

PEDIT Fit and Spline Curves

The PEDIT command provides two options for making polyline curves through control points: a fit curve and a spline curve. One reason we chose the cylinder profile to demonstrate pedits is that this profile dramatically shows the different results between fit curves and spline curves. A fit curve passes through your vertex control points. Fit curves consist of two arc segments between each pair of vertexes (see fig. 7.40). A spline curve interpolates between your control points but doesn't usually pass through the vertexes (see fig. 7.41). The framework of vertexes is called the *spline frame*.

PEDIT spline curves create either arcs or short line segments approximating the curve of the arc. To help you visualize your spline curve, AutoCAD provides a system variable called SPLFRAME. You can set SPLFRAME on 1 to show you the reference frame and vertex points for a spline curve. The fineness of the approximation and type of segment is controlled by the SPLINESEGS system variable. The numeric value controls the number of segments. A positive value generates line segments while a negative value creates arc segments. Arcs are more precise, but slower. The default is 8.

You can generate two kinds of spline curves, controlled by the SPLINETYPE system variable. The types are a quadratic b-spline (type 5) or a cubic b-spline (the default, type 6).

Try both fit and spline curves using the cylinder fins as your control points. After you have generated the spline curve, turn SPLFRAME on to see the reference frame for the curve. The exercise sequence will show you how to regenerate the drawing within the PEDIT command to make the frame visible (see fig. 7.42). When you are done, use the Undo option to restore the original cylinder profile (see fig. 7.43). Be careful with the Decurve option; it will remove the fillets in the drawing. If you try it, undo to recover.

Using PEDIT to Make a Fit and a Spline Curve

```
Command: PEDIT                              Try a fit curve, then a spline
                                            curve.
Select polyline: L                          Last.
Open/Join/Width/Edit vertex/Fit curve/Spline
   curve/Decurve/Undo/eXit <X>: F           Creates a fit curve, as shown in
                                            figure 7.41.

Open/Join/Width/Edit vertex/Fit curve/Spline
   curve/Decurve/Undo/eXit <X>: S           Creates a spline curve, as shown
                                            in figure 7.42.

Open/Join/Width/Edit vertex/Fit curve/Spline
   curve/Decurve/Undo/eXit <X>: 'SPLFRAME   (Release 10, use 'SETVAR to set
                                            SPLFRAME.)
>New value for SPLFRAME <0>: 1              Turns on frame.
Resuming PEDIT command.                      The frame won't show until you
                                            use Edit vertex to regenerate.

Open/Join/Width/Edit vertex/Fit curve/Spline
   curve/Decurve/Undo/eXit <X>: E
Next/Previous/Break/Insert/Move/Regen/
   Straighten/Tangent/Width/eXit <N>: R     Regenerates image to display the
                                            frame (see fig. 7.43).

Next/Previous/Break/Insert/Move/Regen/
   Straighten/Tangent/Width/eXit <N>: X
Open/Join/Width/Edit vertex/Fit curve/Spline
   curve/Decurve/Undo/eXit <X>: U
Open/Join/Width/Edit vertex/Fit curve/Spline
   curve/Decurve/Undo/eXit <X>: X
Command: U                                  Undo the PEDIT, restoring the
                                            cylinder profile.
```

Figure 7.41:
A piston cylinder after
fit curve.

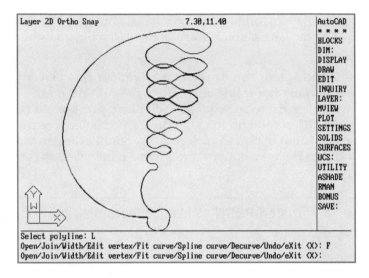

Figure 7.42:
A piston cylinder after
spline curve.

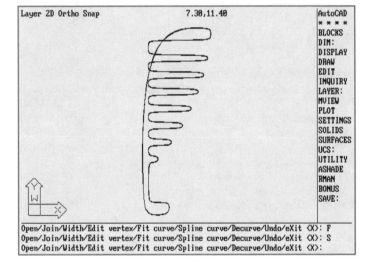

When you displayed the reference frame for spline curves, it showed the original cylinder profile and points. If you are editing a spline curve and you need to know where your control points are located, use the SPLFRAME system variable to get your frame of reference back.

After undoing your curve fitting, your screen should look like the Original Cylinder After Undo illustration (see fig. 7.44). Although you have moved, stretched, curved, and pummeled the poor polyline, it is still a *continuous* polyline.

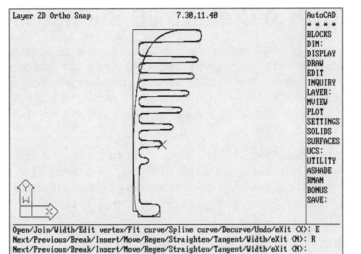

Figure 7.43:
A spline curve with
frame.

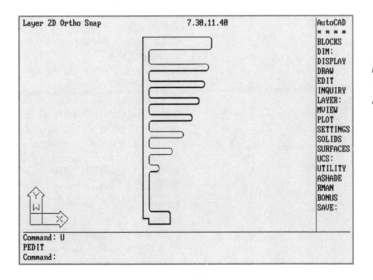

Figure 7.44:
The original cylinder
after the undo.

> **Note:** The BREAK and TRIM commands make curve- and spline-fitting permanent. The PEDIT Break option and EXTEND command allow subsequent PEDITs to decurve and refit curves or splines. Curve- and spline-fit polylines get complex. See the *AutoCAD Reference Manual* for quirks and interactions with other editing commands.

Using REVSURF to Create a 3D Surface Mesh

Use your cylinder profile to get a 3D surface mesh. The following exercise sequence will guide you through a quick 3D setup, giving you a 3D viewpoint that looks down at the cylinder so that you can see the surface mesh as it is formed. You will use a 3D entity command called REVSURF to form the surface mesh. REVSURF forms a polyline surface mesh from the two-dimensional polyline making up the cylinder profile.

Don't worry about the commands or the sequence used to create the 3D cylinder. Just try the exercise to see how easily a complex 3D part is created. If the results whet your appetite, you will be pleased to know that there is much more to come in Part Two on 3D. When you are done, save your drawing as 3DCYLIND.

Using REVSURF to Make a Quick 3D Mesh

Continue from the previous exercise.

Command: **\<Grid off>**	Turn grid off with \<F7> or \<^G>.
Command: **ZOOM**	Zoom All.
Command: **LINE**	Draw from absolute point 10,15 to polar point @13<270. This is a rotation line.
Command: **LAYER**	Set layer 3D current.
Command: **SURFTAB1**	Set vertical mesh value to 24 (Release 10, use SETVAR SURFTAB1).
Command: **SURFTAB2**	Set horizontal mesh value to 4 (Release 10, use SETVAR SURFTAB2).
Command: **WORLDVIEW**	Set to 0 for viewpoint change (Release 10, use SETVAR WORLDVIEW).
Command: **REVSURF**	Create 3D half section of piston cylinder.
Select path curve:	Pick the polyline.
Select axis of revolution:	Pick the rotation line near the bottom.
Start angle <0>: **\<RETURN>**	
Included angle (+=ccw, -=cw) \<Full circle>: **180**	
Command: **LAYER**	Freeze layer 2D.
Command: **UCS**	Rotate the X axis -90 degrees.
Origin/ZAxis/3point/Entity/View/X/Y/Z/Prev/ Restore/Save/Del/?/\<World>: **X**	
Rotation angle about X axis <0>: **-90**	
Command: **VPOINT**	Move to a better viewpoint.

> **Using REVSURF to Make a Quick 3D Mesh—continued**
>
> Rotate/<View point> <0.00,1.00,0.00>: **R**
> Enter angle in X-Y plane from X axis <270>: **215**
> Enter angle from X-Y plane <0>: **17**   Your view should look like the
>   one shown in figure 7.45.
>
> Command: **SAVE**   Save as 3DCYLIND.

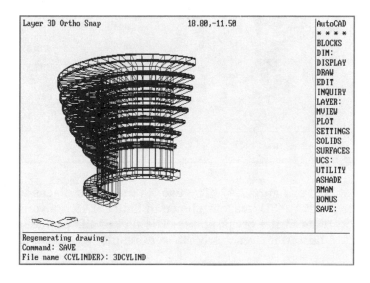

Figure 7.45:
A 3D half section of a cylinder.

To cut down on computing time, the exercise only created a half section of the cylinder. You could revolve the polyline 360 degrees to get the full cylinder. If you have six minutes to an hour to kill (depending on your machine's speed), you can do a HIDE to let AutoCAD sort through all those lines and generate a more realistic image by getting rid of the hidden lines.

> **Using HIDE to View Cylinder**
>
> Command: **HIDE**   Start your timer! Figure 7.46 shows the results of the
>   HIDE command.
> Command: **QUIT**   When you're done, quit. You already saved the
>   drawing in 2D and 3D.

You can get some sense of how powerful 3D editing commands are by how easy it is to create the complex cylinder surface mesh from the two-dimensional polyline of your cylinder profile. We mentioned how important continuity becomes in 3D. To show the effect of discontinuity, we have gone back and *nicked* the cylinder polyline in two places. Then, we revolved the cylinder again with REVSURF to get a 3D surface mesh.

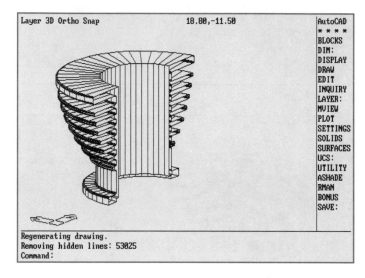

Figure 7.46:
A piston cylinder after HIDE.

The nicked profile is shown in figure 7.47. The two Xs mark the places where we broke the polyline. The resulting 3D image is shown in figure 7.48. As you can see, the 3D mesh formation halts at the break points. The nicked 2D profile looks the same as your original profile, but it gives vastly different results when you form a 3D surface image.

Note: You can erase the CYLINDER drawing; you won't need it again.

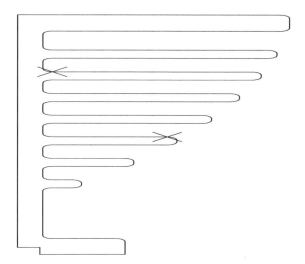

Figure 7.47:
A broken 2D polyline.

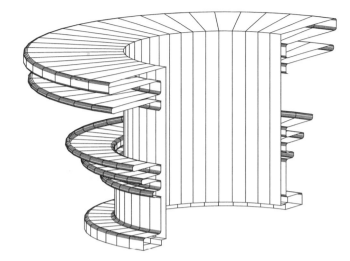

Figure 7.48:
A 3D half cylinder
with a nicked polyline.

Summing Up

We said that when you start editing, your drawings become dynamic. Now, with an advanced editing course under your belt, you may sense that the drawing process itself can give you added power and control. The editing commands, EXTEND, OFFSET, STRETCH, TRIM, SCALE, and PEDIT, are *new* tools. They don't have exact counterparts in the manual world. All of these editing commands operate on multiple entities. When you combine these advanced editing tools with the electronic equivalent of construction lines, you can create fast, accurate drawings.

The trick to using these commands is to plan ahead. Don't get trapped into traditional thinking. It would have been a laborious process to draw the cylinder profile line by line and point by point. Plan on using EXTEND, OFFSET, STRETCH, and TRIM to rough-in your drawing. Then, get the details that you want using PEDIT.

A second trick to using these new editing commands is to think about *how* the drawing is constructed. As you work with the more complex commands, the behind-the-scenes construction is almost as important as the appearance of the final drawing. You saw how two little nicks in a 2D polyline can have a drastic effect on a 3D object.

There are two more editing techniques that we want to show you in the next chapter. These are using XYZ point filters as super fast invisible construction lines, and undo marks, a way to mark your drawing file so that you can backtrack and try different editing paths as you draw.

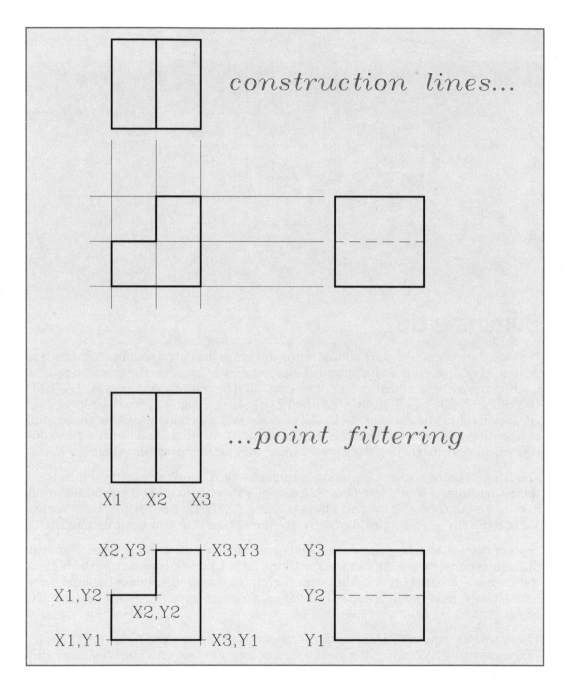

Figure 8.1:
Construction lines and point filter techniques.

Drawing Construction Techniques

QUICK WAYS TO BUILD WHOLE DRAWINGS

Advanced Construction Methods

This is a methodology chapter. It will show you how to combine the drawing and editing commands that you learned in the previous chapters with construction lines, point filters, and undo marks. You will learn how to use these powerful tools to rapidly construct drawings.

Point Filters and Construction Lines

Point filters are construction tools. The best way to visualize point filters is to think of them as invisible construction lines. Figure 8.1 compares construction lines and point filters. Construction lines are as important in CAD as they are in manual drafting. When you use a construction line to help draw an entity, you are really looking for the coordinate values of an intersection point, say an X value and a Y value. Point filters give you the advantages of construction lines without any extra work ahead of time. When you use point filters, you indicate the coordinate values that will give you the intersection point, eliminating the need to actually draw a construction line. Once you get the hang of using point filters, they will increase your drawing productivity. They are a fast on-the-fly tool.

311

To get a handle on drawing construction techniques, we will build a new drawing called MOCKUP. If you are using the IA DISK, you have the MOCKUP drawing setup stored as the IA6MOCK drawing. A second drawing on the disk, IA6MOCK2, has the completed left view of the flange. Point filters are used to help construct the section view on the right. If you want to jump directly to the section on point filters, turn to *Using XYZ Point Filters for Section Construction* in the last third of the chapter and use the IA6MOCK2 drawing as your starting drawing.

Undo Marks

You have seen the simple use of U or UNDO to reverse the effects of a command that botches up your drawing file. As you design and draft, you often try alternatives that may or may not work out. These often involve a long series of commands. You can always undo repeatedly to back up and try again. But it would be easier if you could place a *mark* in your drawing session at the beginning of the alternative branch, so that you could backtrack to that editing point in a single step. Well, you can. Undo marks are like editing checkpoints in your drawing. After placing a mark, you can try an editing sequence, then go back to your mark if it doesn't work and try an alternate sequence.

You place a mark with the UNDO command. Each time you start an editing session, AutoCAD keeps track of every command you execute by writing it to a temporary file on disk. This temporary file records all your moves whenever you are in the drawing editor. You won't find this file on disk when you're done with an editing session because it is a hidden file. At the end of a session, AutoCAD wipes it out and cleans up the disk. However, while you are in an editing session, you can play this sequence in reverse, undoing each command, or if you undo too much, you can redo parts of your past command sequence.

Tip: If you have a printer hooked up to your system, you can get a hard copy of all your command prompt lines by pressing <^Q> to start your printer printing, or select the PRINTER TOGL on the tablet menu. It will print everything that scrolls by on the text screen. Another <^Q> turns off printing.

After you master this chapter, don't expect AutoCAD to do all your work for you. However, you can look forward to a better division of drafting labor — you can do the thinking and setting up, and AutoCAD can do the bulk of the carrying out.

Advanced Editing Tools

The editing commands that you will use are on the [EDIT] screen menus and the [Modify] pull-down menu. Selecting [FILTERS >] from the [Assist] pull-down menu replaces the [Assist] pull-down menu with a [Filters] pull-down. You can also find the filters on the [POINTS] screen menu, via the [DRAW] menu, but you can probably type them faster. [UNDO:], on the second [EDIT] screen menu page, leads to an [UNDO] menu. Several undo items are also on the [Utility] pull-down menu.

This chapter's exercises also use the OFFSET, ARRAY, TRIM, FILLET, CHAMFER, CHANGE, CHPROP, and PEDIT editing commands. If you need to review these commands, refer to the two previous editing chapters.

Setup for the Mockup Drawing

The mockup is actually a plan and section drawing of a flange. Like the now-familiar widget drawing, you don't have to know or care about flanges to learn the basic concepts of undo marks, construction lines, and point filters. The dimensions needed to create the drawing are shown in figure 8.2.

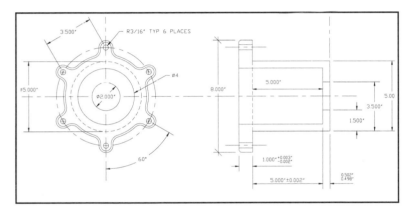

Figure 8.2:
A dimensioned mockup target drawing.

Although in reality this would probably be drawn in decimal units, we'll set up the MOCKUP drawing with fractional units for variety (see table 8.1). Set your drawing limits to 34 inches by 22 inches. The scale factor is 1:2 for a 17" x 11" final drawing.

Setting Up the Mockup Drawing

 Begin a NEW drawing named MOCKUP=IA6MOCK.

 Begin a NEW drawing named MOCKUP and set up your drawing to match table 8.1.

Table 8.1
Mockup Drawing Settings

COORDS	GRID	LTSCALE	ORTHO	SNAP
On	1	1	ON	.5

UNITS	Set UNITS to 5. Fractional, 64ths denominator. Default the other Units settings.
LIMITS	Set LIMITS from 0,0 to 34,22.
ZOOM	Zoom All.
VIEW	Save view as A.

Layer Name	State	Color	Linetype
0	On	7 (white)	CONTINUOUS
CENTER	On/Current	1 (red)	CENTER
DIMS	On	2 (yellow)	CONTINUOUS
HIDDEN	On	4 (cyan)	HIDDEN
PARTS	On	3 (green)	CONTINUOUS

Using Construction Lines

The first step in making the mockup is to rough-in some construction lines (see figs. 8.3 and 8.4). Notice that there are two center lines and a circle center line in the illustration. Create these lines, using your CENTER layer as a background layer to help you lay in the two major sections of the drawing. Then, you can use the PARTS layer to draw the flange and its section view.

Figure 8.3:
Offset on a line.

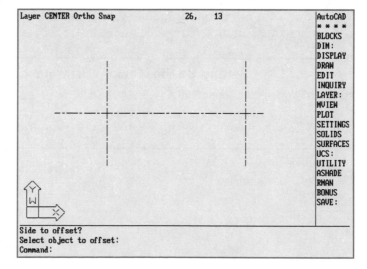

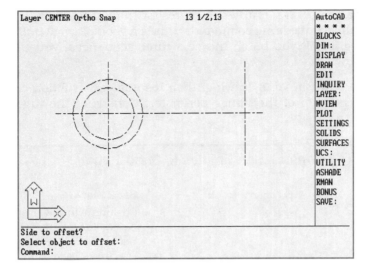

Figure 8.4:
Offset on a circle.

Using OFFSET to Create Construction Lines

Command: **LINE**	From absolute point 4,13 to polar point @24<0.
Command: **LINE**	From absolute point 10,7 to polar point @12<90.
Command: **CIRCLE**	Draw a 3" radius circle at absolute point 10,13.
Command: **OFFSET** Offset distance or Through <Through>: **16** Select object to offset: Side to offset? Select object to offset: **<RETURN>**	Pick vertical line. Pick any point to the right of line.
Command: **<RETURN>** OFFSET Offset distance or Through <16>:	Offset circle to outside with distance 1 to create a 4" radius circle.

The two circles on your screen are temporary construction lines to help you form the complex entity that makes up the perimeter of the flange.

Placing an Undo Mark

Look at figure 8.2 again. The perimeter of the top flange is a polyline with six lugs sticking out. It would be difficult to draw this entire perimeter as a single polyline. The next three exercises will show you how to create one-sixth of the perimeter, array this sixth to get the basic perimeter, then form a polyline by joining the arrayed entities.

Since you will be creating several entities to represent the top flange and you will also be using several different editing commands, this is a good place to put an undo mark in your drawing file. If you botch the next three sequences, you can easily come back to this point.

Use UNDO to place a mark in your drawing, then resume construction of the lug that sticks out from the top of the flange perimeter. Construct the lug on your PARTS layer.

Using Construction Entities to Draw a Lug

```
Command: UNDO
Auto/Back/Control/End/Group/Mark/<number>: M          Set a mark.
Command: ZOOM                                         Position window around
                                                      circles for a better view.
Command: LAYER                                        Set layer PARTS current.
Command: CIRCLE                                       Use 2P to draw a 1" diameter
                                                      circle.
3P/2P/TTR/<Center point>: 2P
First point on diameter:                              Pick first point at ① (see fig.
                                                      8.5).
Second point on diameter:                             Pick second point at ②.
Command: <RETURN>
CIRCLE 3P/2P/TTR/<Center point>:                      Pick center of last circle.
Diameter/<Radius>: D                                  Draw a 3/8" diameter circle.
Diameter: 3/8
Command: LINE                                         Use osnap QUAdrant to add
                                                      the lines of the flange cut.
From point: QUA
of                                                    Pick a point on the circle at
                                                      ③ (see fig. 8.6).
To point:                                             Pick any point below the
                                                      circle at 270 degrees.
To point: <RETURN>
Command: <RETURN>
LINE From point:                                      Repeat for line at ④.
Command: SAVE                                         Save the drawing.
```

Let's pause for a moment and look at undoing and redoing command sequences.

Controlling AutoCAD's UNDO

There are three basic commands that control undos in your draw and edit sequences. These are U, UNDO, and REDO.

You may be thinking, "I already know how to use the ERASE Last command to delete the last entity that I drew. If I make an erase mistake, I can even use OOPS to restore the last item erased. And I already know how to use U."

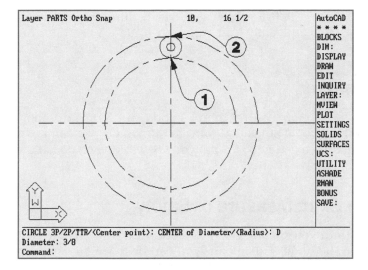

Figure 8.5:
Lug construction after circles.

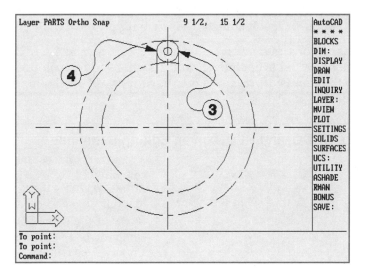

Figure 8.6:
Lug construction after lines.

However, erasing the last item you drew is only part of going back through your drawing file. When you decide to go back, it is often to undo a whole sequence of draw and edit commands. Here is where the Undo set of commands comes in handy.

The U Command

The U command is a mini-undo which backs up by one step or command. Whatever you did immediately before issuing the U command will be undone when you type U. But, unlike the OOPS command, U works any number of times, stepping back through each previous *last* command, one by one. In this sense, U is similar to the

Undo option within LINE or PLINE which gets rid of line or polyline segments by going back one segment at a time. You can even undo an OOPS or an ERASE with a U.

The UNDO Command

The UNDO command offers more control than U. You can UNDO <number>, where <number> equals the number of steps you want to return. Or you can set marks or group a series of commands together so if what you are working on doesn't work out, you can undo the whole series at once.

REDO Gives an Extra Measure of Safety

Say you undid more than you planned. If you issue REDO immediately after any undo, REDO will undo the undo. This means you can be daring if you are not sure how far back you want to go. You can do something drastic like UNDO 20, then recover with a REDO. You can even *play back* your drawing sequences with UNDO, and then use REDO to show or teach someone else what you have done.

Use the following illustrations and exercise sequence to test the U, UNDO, and REDO commands. When the test is complete, your drawing should look the same as it does now. Type the commands; if you use a menu, your results will differ because UNDO groups menu items.

Using U, UNDO, and REDO on an Editing Sequence

Command: **U**	A simple U undoes the last command.
SAVE	AutoCAD shows the last command it undid.
Command: **REDO**	Reverses the U command.
Command: **UNDO**	Undo the last four commands.
Auto/Back/Control/End/Group/Mark/<number>: **4**	Undoes the last four commands (see fig. 8.7).
SAVE LINE LINE CIRCLE	
Command: **REDO**	Reverse the UNDO command.
Command: **UNDO**	Undo back to the mark set at the beginning of the exercise.
Auto/Back/Control/End/Group/Mark/<number>: **B**	Undoes back to the previously set mark (see fig. 8.8).
SAVE LINE LINE CIRCLE CIRCLE LAYER ZOOM Mark encountered	
Command: **REDO**	Reverse the UNDO command.

If you accidentally undo too much and can't recover, just reload your saved drawing. Although UNDO showed SAVE as an undone command, commands that write to the disk are never actually undone. The UNDO Back that you used is only one of six options that control UNDO. Here is the complete list.

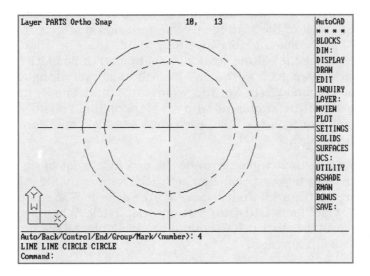

Figure 8.7:
Mockup after an
UNDO 4.

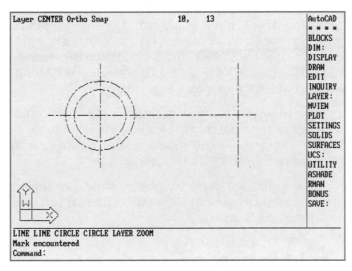

Figure 8.8:
Mockup after an
UNDO back.

UNDO Options

<number>   If you enter a number, AutoCAD steps back by that many steps.

Auto   is an on/off setting. Auto affects menu items only. Sometimes a single menu item creates or edits many entities. Normally, everything done by one command is one step back in UNDO.

Setting Auto ON (the default) causes an entire menu item to be treated as a single step by making it an undo *group*.

Back and **Mark**   An UNDO Back will undo all the way back until it comes to the beginning of the editing session, an undo mark, or a PLOT or PRPLOT command (because they re-initialize the undo file as if beginning the editing session at that point). If no mark has been placed, you get a warning, "This will undo everything. OK <Y>." You respond Yes or No. You set an undo mark simply by executing the UNDO command with the Mark option. You may mark as many times as you like, each time setting a stop for the next UNDO Back.

Control   Creating the temporary undo file can take a lot of disk space. Control lets you specify how active the temporary file will be with three options All/None/One. All is the default. None turns UNDO off. One limits UNDO to just one step back. When set to One, none of the other UNDO options are available. All restores UNDO to its full function.

Group and **End**   Like Back and Mark, Group and End put boundaries on series of commands in the temporary file so that you can undo the series in one step. You begin a group with the Group option, end the group with the End option, and continue doing work. Later you step back with U or UNDO <number>. When the backstep gets to an End, the next UNDO step will wipe out everything between the End and Group markers as a single step.

Watch out for undoing more than you want. Any settings during a command, including toggles (such as snap) or transparent commands, will be undone along with the main command. UNDO has the power to wipe out your entire drawing in one step, but if you catch it *immediately* with REDO, you can save it.

In the rest of the book, and in your own work, try placing your own undo marks to give yourself additional checkpoints in the editing session. Then, if you need to retry a sequence, you can easily step back and do it.

Using Array Techniques to Construct the Flange Perimeter

Let's resume drawing the flange. First, finish the lug using the TRIM command. This is easier than trying to calculate the exact arc and line lengths that make up the lug. It also insures that all the endpoints match.

Using TRIM to Draw First Lug of Flange

```
Command: <Snap off>                 Toggle snap off with <^B> or <F9>.
Command: TRIM
Select cutting edge(s)...
Select objects:                     Pick the 3" diameter circle on the CENTER layer.
1 selected, 1 found.
Select objects:                     Pick the first lug line.
1 selected, 1 found.
Select objects:                     Pick the second lug line.
1 selected, 1 found.
Select objects: <RETURN>
<Select object to trim>/Undo:       Pick the bottom right half of 1" diameter circle.
<Select object to trim>/Undo:       Pick bottom end of right lug line (see fig. 8.9).
<Select object to trim>/Undo:       Pick the bottom half of 1" diameter circle again.
<Select object to trim>/Undo:       Pick bottom end of left lug line.
<Select object to trim>/Undo:
  <Snap on><RETURN>                 Toggle snap back on, exit TRIM.
```

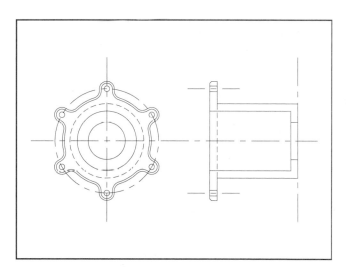

Figure 8.9
A lug after first circle and line trim.

The first lug is complete (see fig. 8.10). The perimeter in the target drawing showed the lug in six places. You could array the lug now and draw the remaining entities between the arrayed lugs, but it is more efficient to create one-sixth of the perimeter and then do the array.

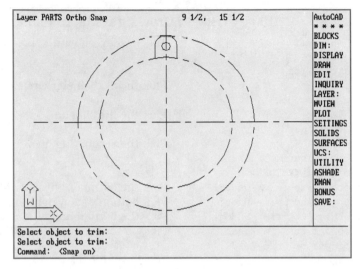

Figure 8.10:
A completed lug after
trim.

Completing a One-Sixth Portion to Array

Here we will rely on AutoCAD's editing commands to do the calculation and construction. Use the ROTATE command to set up a one-sixth segment of the circle. Then use the ARC and FILLET commands to complete the segment.

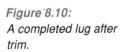

Using ROTATE and ARC to Construct a Perimeter Segment	
Command: **ROTATE**	
Select objects:	Select short lug line on the right.
1 selected, 1 found.	
Select objects: **<RETURN>**	
Base point:	Pick center of circles at absolute point 10,13.
<Rotation angle>/Reference: **60**	Lug line is rotated (see fig. 8.11).
Command: **ARC**	
Center/<Start point>: **ENDP**	
of	Pick endpoint of left lug line ① (see fig. 8.12).
Center/End/<Second point>: **C**	
Center: **INT**	
of	Pick intersection of center lines ②.
Angle/Length of chord/<End point>: **ENDP**	
of	Pick endpoint of rotated lug line ③.

Now, fillet the perimeter segment.

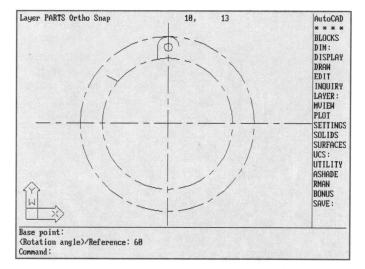

Figure 8.11:
The rotated lug line.

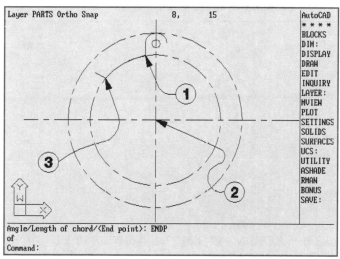

Figure 8.12:
The arc completes a one-sixth segment.

Using FILLET to Complete the Perimeter Segment

Command: `<Snap off>`	Toggle snap off with `<^B>` or `<F9>`.	
Command: **FILLET**	Set fillet radius to 1/2 inch.	
Command: **FILLET**	Pick arc at ① and line at ② (see figs. 8.13 and 8.14).	
Command: **FILLET**	Pick line at ③ and arc at ④.	
Command: `<Snap on>`	Toggle snap back on.	

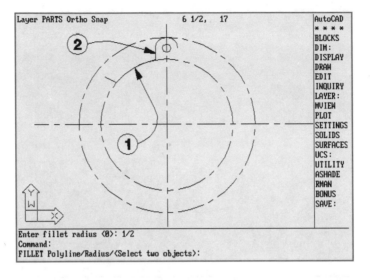

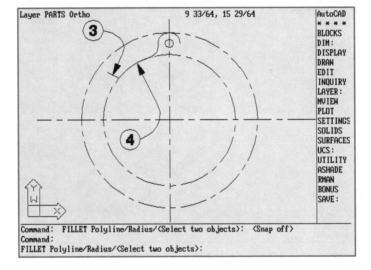

Figure 8.14:
Picks for the second
fillet.

Now you are ready to create the perimeter by arraying the one-sixth segment. If you followed the construction sequence, all the entity points will line up. Notice that you have made only one trivial calculation: dividing the circle into sixths (60 degrees). By using osnaps and editing commands, you have let AutoCAD do all the hard calculations and locations.

Using ARRAY and PEDIT to Create the Perimeter

Use a polar array to replicate the one-sixth segment to complete the perimeter of the flange. Then, use PEDIT Join to group the entity segments into a single polyline. After you have joined the segments, create two circles in the interior of the flange.

Using ARRAY and PEDIT to Complete the Flange

```
Command: ARRAY
Select objects: W
First corner:
Other corner:                              Put window around all flange
                                           entities on the PARTS layer.

7 found.
Select objects: <RETURN>
Rectangular or Polar array (R/P): P
Center point of array: INT
of                                         Pick intersection of center lines
                                           at absolute point 10,13.

Number of items: 6
Angle to fill (+=ccw, -=cw) <360>: <RETURN>
Rotate objects as they are copied? <Y> <RETURN>    The array is created (see fig.
                                                   8.15).

Command: PEDIT
Select polyline:                           Pick first arc created on top
                                           flange.

Entity selected is not a polyline
Do you want to turn it into one? <Y> <RETURN>
Close/Join/Width/Edit vertex/Fit curve/Spline
  curve/Decurve/Undo/eXit <X>: J
Select objects: W
First corner:                              Make the window as large as
                                           you like.
Other corner:                              As long as it includes all the
                                           top flange entities,
44 found.                                  Join will ignore extra entities.
Select objects: <RETURN>
35 segments added to polyline
Open/Join/Width/Edit vertex/Fit curve/Spline
  curve/Decurve/Undo/eXit <X>: <RETURN>
Command: CIRCLE                            Draw 4" diameter circle for
                                           inside wall of flange.

Command: CIRCLE                            Draw 2-1/2" diameter circle for
                                           center hole in bottom of part.
                                           Your drawing should now
                                           resemble figure 8.16.
```

The PEDIT Join requires that each entity endpoint matches the adjacent endpoint exactly. If you did not get a join, undo, and try again.

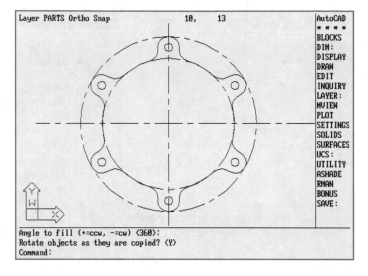

Figure 8.15:
Top flange after array.

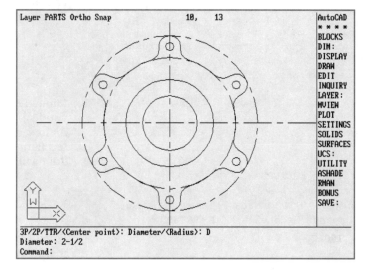

Figure 8.16:
Circles complete the
top flange.

> *Tip:* You can use a far-off drawing corner or a scratch UCS for background construction, putting together pieces of a drawing that you can later move, copy, or array into place.

Editing by Recycling Entities

Frequently, you can save a little drawing time by recycling the now-surplus construction circles rather than creating new ones. Change the inner construction circle's layer (linetype) and radius to make a hidden line for the outer wall, and change the outer circle's radius to make a bolt ring center line.

Using CHPROP and CHANGE to Complete Top View

```
Command: CHPROP
Select objects:                          Select inner center line construction circle.
Change what property (Color/LAyer/
  LType/Thickness) ? LA
New layer <CENTER>: HIDDEN
Change what property (Color/LAyer/
  LType/Thickness) ? <RETURN>
Command: CHANGE
Select objects: P                        Previous reselects the circle.
Properties/<Change point>: <RETURN>
Enter circle radius: 2.5                 Remember you can type decimal entry
                                         even in fractional units (see fig. 8.17).

Command: CHANGE                          Change the radius of the outside circle to
                                         3-1/2" (see fig. 8.18).
Command: REGEN                           Regenerate drawing to verify changes.
Command: END                             Save as default drawing.
```

The plan view of the flange is finished. This is a good point to take a break. The next section uses XYZ point filters to construct the section view of the flange.

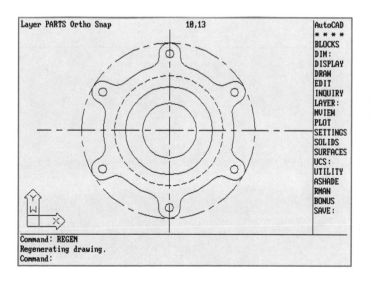

Figure 8.17:
Changing the construction circle layer and radius.

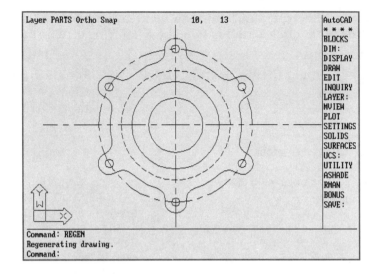

Figure 8.18:
The changed
construction circle
radius.

Using XYZ Point Filters for Section Construction

If you look at figure 8.19, you will see that most of the geometry you need to draw the section view on the right already exists in the plan view. You can draw an accurate section quickly by aligning the new section lines with intersections of the lines and entities making up the plan view. However, you cannot draw the lines by simply aligning your cursor crosshairs because some of the intersection points are not on snap increments (for practice, we'll pretend none of the points are snappable).

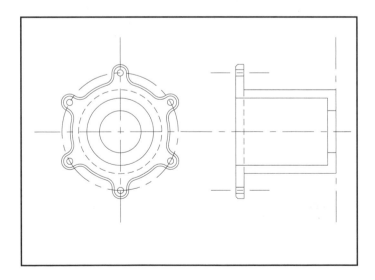

Figure 8.19:
A mockup target
drawing.

Using XYZ point filters makes this alignment easy. Point filters let you pick X, Y, and Z coordinates independently. Because we are drawing in two dimensions, we are only concerned with X and Y coordinates. Don't worry about Z filtering for now.

If you are resuming your MOCKUP drawing, re-check your setup with the table at the front of the chapter. If you are using the IA DISK and jumping in at this point, use the IA6MOCK2 drawing. This drawing contains the completed plan view of the flange. Your current layer should be PARTS. Restore View A to start the drawing.

Setting Up for XYZ Point Filters

 Begin a NEW drawing named MOCKSECT=IA6MOCK2.

 Begin a NEW drawing named MOCKSECT=MOCKUP and use VIEW to restore view A.

To use point filters, precede a point that you pick (or type) with a .X or .Y (pronounced dot-X or dot-Y). The dot (period) distinguishes the point filter from some command options that begin with an X or Y. AutoCAD will then take only the specified coordinate from the following point, and reprompt you for the other coordinate values. For example, when you specify a .X value, you pick a point or osnap to an entity that has the X value that you want, then AutoCAD will tell you that you need a Y value. You can pick, type or use an osnap to get your Y value, giving you the X,Y intersection point.

Since the flange is symmetrical, you only need to draw half of the section view, then mirror the other half. Use the next exercise sequence with X and Y filters to create the lower half of the section.

Using XYZ Point Filters to Draw a Section View

Command: **ZOOM**	Zoom into area shown.
Command: **OSNAP**	Set a running osnap to INT,END.
Command: \<Snap off\>	Toggle snap off.
Command: **APERTURE**	Set to 6.
Command: **LINE**	
From point: **.X**	Build the first line.
of	Pick anywhere on vertical base line at ① (see fig. 8.20).
(need YZ):	Pick intersection of hole and vertical center line at ②.
To point: @-.5,0	
To point: **.X**	Build the second line.
of	Pick left side of last line drawn at ③.
(need YZ):	Pick inside of flange circle and vertical center line at ④.
To point: @-5.5,0	Draw the third line (see fig. 8.21).
To point: **.X**	Build the fourth line (see fig. 8.22).

Using XYZ Point Filters to Draw a Section View—continued

of	Pick left side of last line drawn at ⑤.
(need YZ):	Pick intersection of arc and vertical center line at ⑥.
To point: @1/2,0	Draw the fifth line.
To point: .X	Build the sixth line.
of	Pick right side of last line drawn at ⑦ (see fig. 8.23).
(need YZ):	Pick intersection of hidden circle and vertical line at ⑧.
To point: PERP	Use PERP to override running osnap.
to	Pick anywhere on vertical base line at ⑨.
To point: C	Close to beginning point.

Figure 8.20:
The first and second lines of the section.

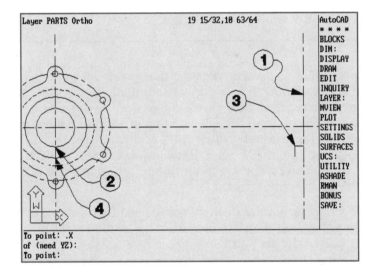

Figure 8.21:
The third line of the section.

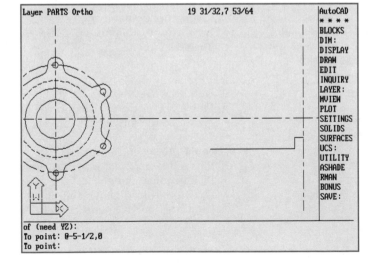

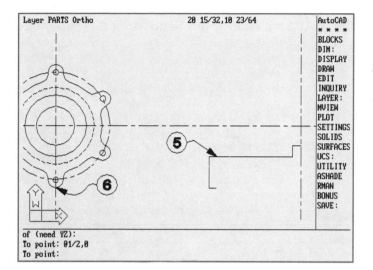

Figure 8.22:
The fourth and fifth lines of the section.

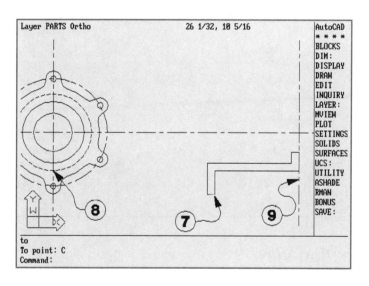

Figure 8.23:
A completed section.

Your screen should now show half a section view of the mockup part. Complete the section half by using XYZ filters to add the lines for the hole in the top flange.

Using XYZ Filter to Draw a Hole in the Section View

```
Command: LINE
From point: .X        Build first line of hole.
of                    Pick line of top flange in the section view at ① (see fig.
                      8.24).
(need YZ):             Pick where the drilled hole and center line intersect at
                      ②.
```

Using XYZ Filter to Draw a Hole in the Section View—continued

```
To point: PERP
to                              Pick line in the section view at ③.
To point: <RETURN>
Command: LINE                   Repeat the process for second hole bottom line.
Command: LINE
To point: .X                    Build center line for hole.
of                              Pick a point 1" to the right of the bottom flange at ④
                                (see fig. 8.25).
(need YZ):                      Pick center of lug hole at ⑤.
To point:                       Pick a point 1" to the left of the top flange at ⑥.
To point: <RETURN>
Command: CHPROP                 Change last line to the CENTER layer.
```

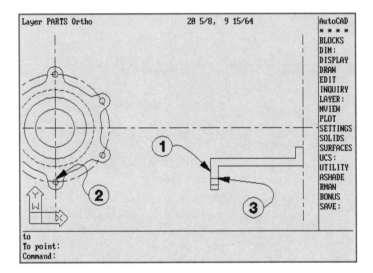

Figure 8.24:
A section view with
hole lines.

Mirroring the Section View

All you need to do to get the rest of the section view is to mirror the lower half, and add four more lines. Here is the exercise sequence.

Using MIRROR to Complete the Section View

```
Command: MIRROR
Select objects: W               Enclose the entire section image.
First corner:                   Pick first corner point.
Other corner:                   Pick second corner point.
11 found.
Select objects: <RETURN>
```

Using MIRROR to Complete the Section View—continued

First point of mirror line: Pick intersection of center lines at ① (see fig. 8.26).
Second point: Select any point 180 degrees to the left.
Delete old objects? <N> **<RETURN>**

Command: **LAYER**   Set HIDDEN layer current.
Command: **LINE**   Draw hidden line from ② to ③ (see fig. 8.27).
Command: **LAYER**   Set PARTS layer current.
Command: **LINE**   Draw the three lines at ④ to complete the section.
Command: **OSNAP**   Set to NONe.
Command: **SAVE**   Save to the default drawing.

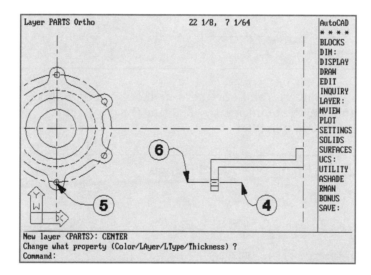

Figure 8.25:
A center line through hole.

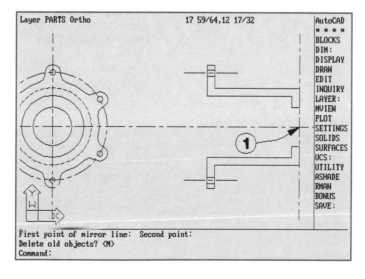

Figure 8.26:
The section after mirroring.

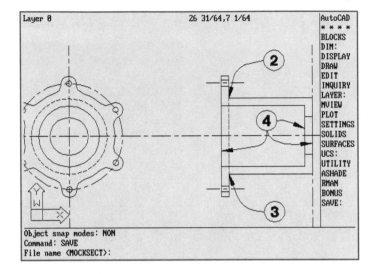

Layer 0   26 31/64,7 1/64   AutoCAD

Figure 8.27:
The completed sec-
tion.

The target flange has a chamfer. Take one more moment to chamfer the section view, then add the chamfer to the plan view by offsetting the perimeter. Here are two illustrations and a sequence to help you.

Chamfer Edge of Flange

Zoom to view shown.

```
Command: CHAMFER
Polyline/Distances/<Select first line>: D
Enter first chamfer distance <0>: 1/8
Enter second chamfer distance <1/8>: <RETURN>

Command: <RETURN>
CHAMFER Polyline/Distances/<Select first line>:     Pick top flange line at ① (see
                                                    figs. 8.28 and 8.29).
Select second line:                                 Pick end flange line at ②

Command: <RETURN>
CHAMFER Polyline/Distances/<Select first line>:     Pick top flange line at ③.
Select second line:                                 Pick end flange line at ④.

Command: OFFSET
Offset distance or Through <Through>: 1/8
Select object to offset:                            Pick any perimeter point on the
                                                    top flange in the plan view.
Side to offset?                                     Pick a point inside the
                                                    perimeter.

Select object to offset: <RETURN>

Command: END                                        Save your work and exit.
```

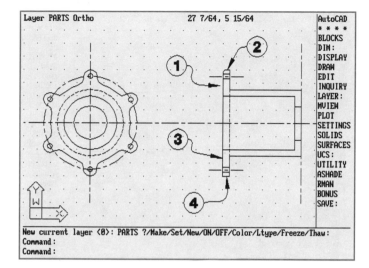

Figure 8.28:
The section after
chamfering.

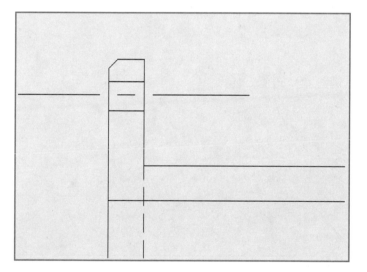

Figure 8.29:
Detail of the chamfer.

Figures 8.30 and 8.31 show the plan view of the flange with the new offset.

You will use this MOCKSECT drawing later when we practice dimensioning

Note: You can delete the MOCKUP drawing, which is no longer needed.

Figure 8.30:
Top view after offset-ting.

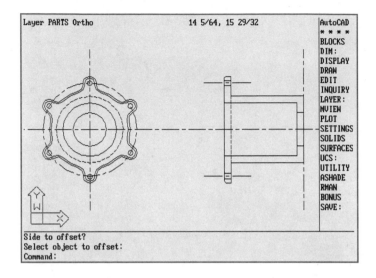

Figure 8.31:
Detail of the offset.

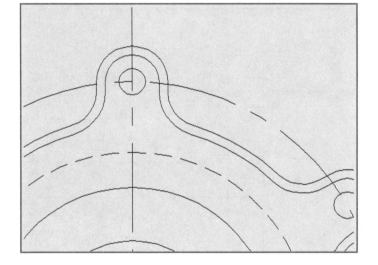

Summing Up

AutoCAD's drawing construction tools are as much a frame of mind as a framework of commands and options. In the course of constructing the mockup, you have learned how to drop construction lines, use a construction underlayer, and trace over construction lines. You also have learned how to use point filters, combining them with osnaps to create a section view.

There is never just one way to build an AutoCAD drawing. In fact the opposite is true — there are always many ways to build the same drawing. The trick is to find the methods that work most intuitively and efficiently for you. Planning ahead can save you many unnecessary steps. Recycling entities can save erasing and drawing anew. Try to envision the commands you will use well in advance. If you can visualize the construction technique ahead of time, your drawing productivity will increase dramatically.

Use point filters and construction lines to line up entities. Use construction lines for center lines, base lines and lines to align large numbers of points. Use point filters for everyday on-the-fly alignments. Use osnaps to help you pick filtered points. Set up one or more layers for your construction lines. Construction lines don't need to be linear — use arcs and circles for angular or curved tracing. A few extra construction lines never hurt and can make your drawing life easier.

Use UNDO to protect your work sequences. Use REDO for a rescue — but only immediately after an undo. Marks and Groups help control undos and make going back easier. Watch out for PLOT and PRPLOT when you plan to undo! Going back to a mark is no substitute for saving regularly. Saving is still the best way to protect your drawing file.

On to Blocks

Talk about saving — wouldn't it be useful if you could save the contents of the selection set and use it as a rubber stamp whenever you need it? You can — with blocks. We'll show you how in the next chapter.

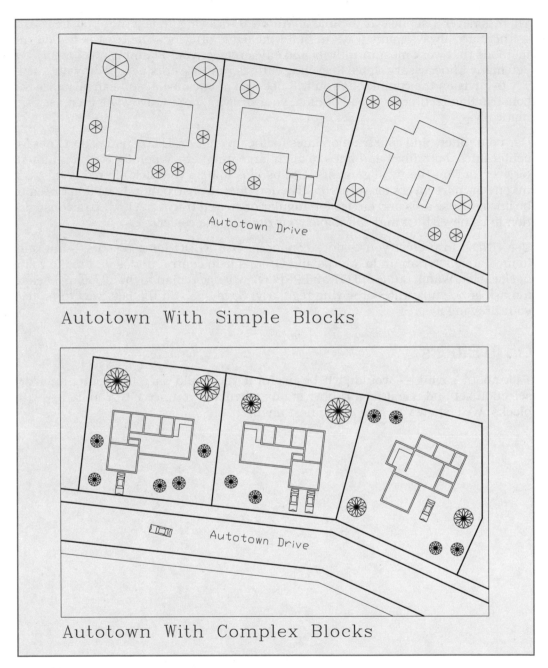

Autotown With Simple Blocks

Autotown With Complex Blocks

Figure 9.1:
The Autotown drawing with simple and complex blocks.

Grouping Entities Into Blocks

DRAWING WITH PARTS AND SYMBOLS

The Benefits of Using Blocks and Xrefs

In this chapter, you will learn how to create, store, and use blocks. Blocking entities into groups allows them to be repeated easily and efficiently within one or more drawing files, or made into permanent symbols in a symbol library.

You will also learn how to work with xrefs (not available in Release 10), which are similar to blocks. Xrefs make workgroup drafting (in which several people work on different parts of the same drawing) simple and error-free. They are the key to effective distributed design. Xrefs are more efficient than blocks, and automatically update drawings when changes are made. We'll cover xrefs as a separate topic after we explore blocks.

Blocks: Parts and Symbols

Figure 9.1 illustrates how an entire town can be created from different types of drawing *blocks*. Blocks group individual entities together and treat them as one object. Symbols and drawing parts are typical candidates for such groupings (see fig. 9.2). We consider *parts*, such as a car or a desk, to represent real objects, drawn full size or at one-unit scale. *Symbols*, such as section bubbles, electrical receptacles and weld symbols, are symbolic objects, scaled appropriately for plot size.

To move or copy symbol objects as individual drawing entities, you collect the individual entities into a selection set. However, as drawings become crowded, it becomes

339

more difficult to select the entities that you want. It is much easier if the entities are grouped together as a block. A block is saved with a name and can be later reused in the same drawing or in other drawings.

AutoCAD blocks let you operate on the group as a whole. Entities in blocks stick together; move one part of the block and the whole block moves. You can, of course, break up a block by *exploding* it if you need to edit it.

Figure 9.2:
Some common symbols and parts.

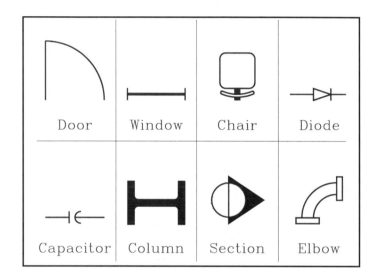

Block Speed and Versatility

Building up libraries of frequently used blocks will speed up drawing creation. A library can consist of: many individual drawing files, each used as a single block; a few files, each containing many blocks; or a combination of both. Building such a library takes time, but it dramatically reduces your design time later on.

Besides their convenience, blocks provide additional drawing and editing benefits. It's a lot faster to insert a block than to redraw the same objects 20 times in 20 different drawings, or copy them 20 times in the same drawing. When you insert blocks into your drawing file, you can change their scale and rotation. Instead of using multiple instances of the block, you can use one block, such as a window or bolt head, to represent many different sizes of the same object. This allows you to build your drawing quickly and easily by modifying simple blocks. You can also globally replace one block with another, revising an entire drawing with a single command.

Block Efficiency and Storage

One of the biggest advantages to using blocks is that they help keep your drawing file sizes to a minimum. A smaller file takes up less disk space and uses less memory when it loads. For example, when you draw 100 lines, you add 100 entities to your drawing. When you make a block containing 100 lines, AutoCAD creates a block definition containing 100 entities. Block definitions are stored in the drawing file. When you insert a block in your drawing, you only add one new entity — a reference to the block definition. So if you insert a block containing 100 lines into your drawing in 12 places, you only have 112 entities for AutoCAD to store: 100 lines in the block definition and 12 block references for the visible inserts. Without blocks, if you draw and copy 12 groups of 100 lines, you add 1200 entities to your drawing file. It's easy to see that blocks can save huge amounts of disk space.

How the Block Exercises Are Organized

You can use this chapter's exercises in several ways. First, the exercises in the early part of the chapter guide you through the basic block commands, including writing blocks to disk files and redefining blocks in a drawing. If you don't have the IA DISK, you'll need these blocks for the final Autotown exercise.

Second, the section on xrefs guides you through creating, attaching, detaching, controlling, and converting xrefs. This section can be done independently from the rest of the chapter, if you like.

This chapter's last section, the final Autotown block exercises, creates the AUTOTOWN drawing. This section uses blocks created in the first section. This will give you more extensive practice working with blocks and xrefs in a simple but realistic drawing. It also shows other drawing techniques, such as using a UCS to locate drawing objects within each building lot and inputting distance<angle measurements in surveyor's units for the site plan.

Block Editing Tools

Grouping entities into blocks is really very simple. You use BLOCK to create a block definition, INSERT to place a block reference in a drawing, and WBLOCK to store a block's entities permanently as a separate drawing file on disk. These commands are on the [BLOCKS] screen menu, along with two other block commands, BASE and MINSERT. You will also find an [Insert] menu item on the [Draw] pull-down menu (see fig. 9.3).

Besides these block commands, we will introduce three additional commands that you use with blocks. These are the EXPLODE, DIVIDE, and MEASURE commands. You will find these commands on the [EDIT] screen menus. The [Modify] pull-down

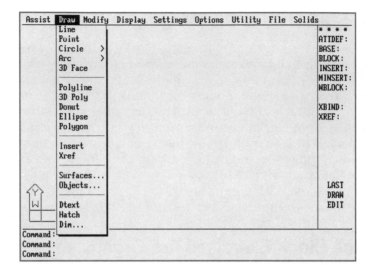

Figure 9.3:
The blocks screen
menu and the draw
pull-down menu.

menu also includes [Divide] and [Measure] items, for which you can preset options with the [Options] pull-down menu.

Note: AutoCAD has another type of symbol entity called a SHAPE. Text is a special form of the shape feature. To learn more about shapes, see *MAXIMIZING AutoCAD, Volume I* from New Riders Publishing.

Setup for Blocks

Let's set up a drawing to create some blocks that you'll use later in Autotown. Autotown is our version of a site plan. It encompasses three building lots along an elegant street, "Autotown Drive." The drawing uses feet and decimal inches. Set your drawing limits at 360 feet by 240 feet — a 36" x 24" D-size sheet plotted at 1" = 10'.

Setting Up Blocks Exercises

Begin a NEW drawing named IABLOCKS and set up the layers and settings shown in table 9.1.

Your current layer should be layer 0. Before you can do anything, you need to draw some objects on layer 0 to make into blocks.

Table 9.1
Blocks Drawing Settings

AXIS	COORDS	GRID	SNAP	UCSICON
Off	ON	10'	6"	OR

UNITS	Engineering, 2 decimal places, decimal degrees, default all other settings.
LIMITS	0,0 to 360',240'

Making Some Objects

Trees and cars can be found in most subdivisions. Draw a car and a tree using the dimensions shown in figures 9.4 and 9.5. (Don't worry if the tree looks a little sparse. We'll spruce it up later.)

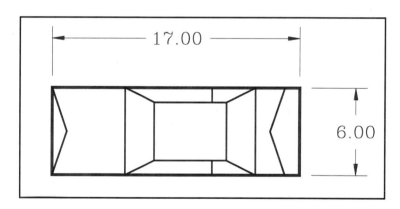

Figure 9.4:
A car for the block exercise.

Making a Car and Tree Symbol

Command: **ZOOM**   Zoom in to center of screen with height 15'.

Draw the car using the dimensions shown in figure 9.4.

Command: **ZOOM**   Zoom in below the car with a height of 8".

Set snap to .25 and draw a 1" (yes, one inch) diameter tree.

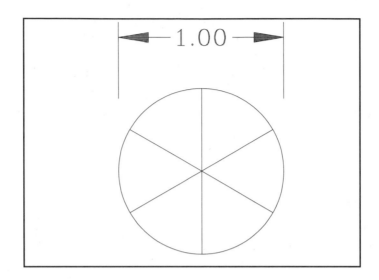

Figure 9.5:
A tree for the block
exercise.

The car is drawn and inserted full size, but the tree is drawn tiny (one unit in diameter) so it can be easily scaled to make different sized trees when inserted.

The BLOCK Command

Now, turn the car and tree into blocks. When you execute the BLOCK command, AutoCAD will first ask you for the block name that you want to use. Name the blocks TREE1 and CAR2. Then, AutoCAD will ask you for an insertion base point. This is the reference point that you will later use to put the block in a new location. After you identify a base point, select the entities that will form the blocks.

Using BLOCK to Create Your First Blocks

```
Command: BLOCK
Block name (or ?): TREE1
Insertion base point:               Pick the center of tree.
Select objects:                     Select all entities of the tree (see fig. 9.6).
Select objects: <RETURN>            And they're placed in memory as a block.

Command: ZOOM                       Previous.
Command: SNAP                       Set back to 6".

Command: BLOCK
Block name (or ?): CAR2
Insertion base point: MID           Use MIDpoint osnap.
of                                  Pick the front of the car at ① (see fig. 9.7) with
                                    crossing window.
Select objects:                     Select all entities of the car.
Select objects: <RETURN>
```

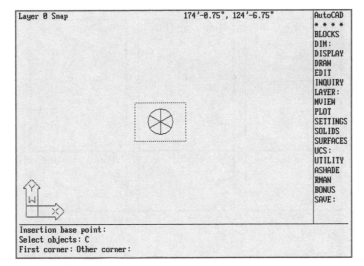

Figure 9.6:
The tree block.

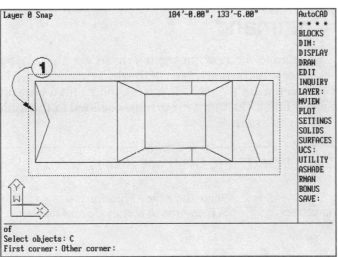

Figure 9.7:
The car block.

You should now have a blank screen. After being selected, your entities disappeared. They are not lost. The entities are safely stored away in memory as two blocks named CAR2 and TREE1.

Where are they? AutoCAD keeps track of all blocks in an invisible part of the drawing file called the block table. When you used the BLOCK command, it created a definition of the car and the tree and stored the definitions in the block table (see fig. 9.8). Each block definition defines the entities associated with the block name. When you save the drawing, they will be stored as part of the drawing file.

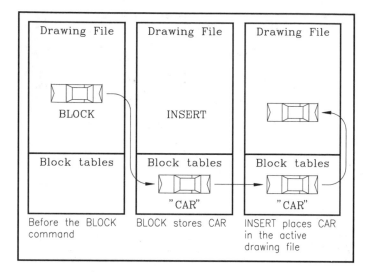

Figure 9.8:
BLOCK and INSERT
with a block table
area.

The INSERT Command

We will leave the tree in storage for now (in memory). To get the car back, you INSERT it from the block table into the active part of the drawing file. First, AutoCAD wants to know which block you want to insert. If you respond with a question mark, AutoCAD lists the names for all blocks that are currently defined in the table area of your drawing. Take a look at the names.

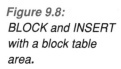

Using INSERT ? to Get Block Names

```
Command: INSERT
Block name (or ?): ?                      Show the defined blocks.
Block(s) to list <*>: <RETURN>            Screen flips to text mode and displays:
Defined blocks.
  CAR2
  TREE1
User     Unnamed
Blocks   Blocks
   2        0                             When you've seen the list, press <F1> to do a
                                          flip screen.
```

Now, insert your car. After you supply the block name, CAR2, you can drag the block to insert it, or you can give coordinates for the insertion point. AutoCAD will also ask for scale and rotation factors. Default these factors. After you insert the car, copy it.

Using INSERT to Insert the Car Block

Command: **ZOOM**	Zoom left corner 168',110' with height 40'.
Command: **INSERT**	
Block name (or ?): **CAR2**	
Insertion point:	Drag car and pick point 174',118'.
X scale factor <1>/Corner/XYZ: **<RETURN>**	Defaults to 1:1.
Y scale factor <default=X>: **<RETURN>**	Defaults to 1:1.
Rotation angle <0.00>: **<RETURN>**	Car is inserted with 0 rotation.
Command: **COPY**	Select by picking car and copy with polar displacement @30'<0.

The results of these two operations are shown in figures 9.9 and 9.10.

Your car came back on the screen with the insertion. But this car is not the same individual entities as your original car. When you copied the car, you selected it with a single object pick. Once you have inserted a block in your drawing, you can move and copy it as a single entity.

What took place behind the drawing insertion? INSERT did three things: it created a block reference to the block definition; it left the original block definition in the block table area; it drew an image representing the entities which make up the block definition.

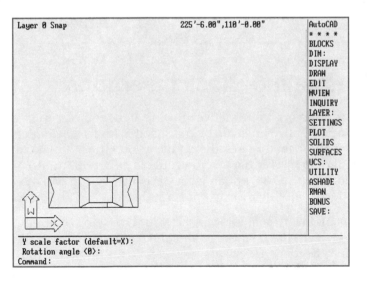

Figure 9.9:
The inserted car.

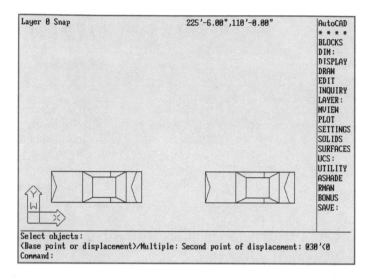

Figure 9.10:
A copied car.

Note: Not only can you insert blocks that you have created in the current drawing, but you can also insert any drawing file that you have saved on disk. A previously saved drawing inserts as a block in the current drawing. The saved drawing's origin becomes the insertion base point unless you have set another base point with the BASE command (discussed later in this chapter). Inserting a drawing creates a new block definition containing all of that drawing's entities. If AutoCAD cannot find a block that you know you have on disk, check its location against the list of directories AutoCAD searches in Appendix B.

Scaling and Rotating Block Insertions

When you insert a block reference in the active drawing area, you can enter different values for its scale and rotation. You scale by inputting X and Y scale factors. The default scale prompt for the Y factor uses the X factor you enter to make it easy to scale your drawing symbol to a 1:1 ratio. Or, you can use different X and Y scales by entering different responses (the XYZ option is for 3D control). You can also give an angle of rotation by entering an angle or by dragging the rotation and picking.

Try two modified car block insertions. First, insert your car using different X and Y scales. Use the values given in the following command sequence to elongate the car like a stretch limousine. Second, insert another car at an angle. If you make a mistake, use UNDO or ERASE Last to remove the block insertion.

Using INSERT With Scale and Rotation Changes

```
Command: INSERT
Block name (or ?) <CAR2>: <RETURN>
Insertion point:                                         Pick point 174',128'.
X scale factor <1>/Corner/XYZ: 1.5
Y scale factor <default=X>: 1
Rotation angle <0.00>: <RETURN>
Command: INSERT
Block name (or ?) <CAR2>: <RETURN>
Insertion point:                                         Pick point 205',128'.
X scale factor <1>/Corner/XYZ: <RETURN>
Y scale factor <default=X>: <RETURN>
Rotation angle <0.00>: 45
```

The results of these two sequences appear in figures 9.11 and 9.12.

What happened behind the insertion scenes this time? Again, INSERT made references to the block table, this time modified by the scale and rotation values, that it applied to the image of the car in the active drawing (see fig. 9.13).

Tip: A handy trick for inserting objects that are normally horizontal or vertical is to use your pointer to pick a rotation angle with ortho <^O> turned on. This limits the rotation angle to 0, 90, 180, or 270 degrees.

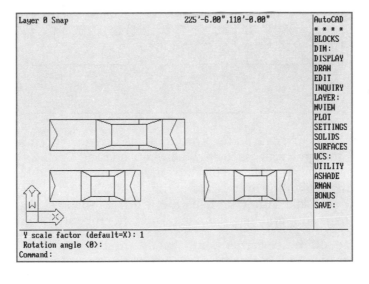

Figure 9.11:
A stretched limousine.

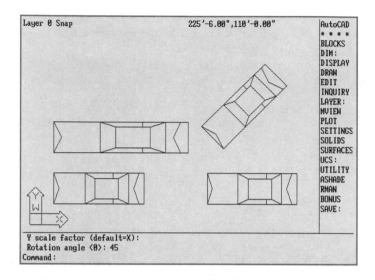

Figure 9.12:
An angled car.

Layer 0 Snap   225'-6.00",110'-0.00"   AutoCAD
                                                                   * * * *
                                                                   BLOCKS
                                                                   DIM:
                                                                   DISPLAY
                                                                   DRAW
                                                                   EDIT
                                                                   INQUIRY
                                                                   LAYER:
                                                                   MVIEW
                                                                   PLOT
                                                                   SETTINGS
                                                                   SOLIDS
                                                                   SURFACES
                                                                   UCS:
                                                                   UTILITY
                                                                   ASHADE
                                                                   RMAN
                                                                   BONUS
                                                                   SAVE:
Y scale factor (default=X):
Rotation angle <0>: 45
Command:

Figure 9.13:
A car drawing in-
serted with changes.

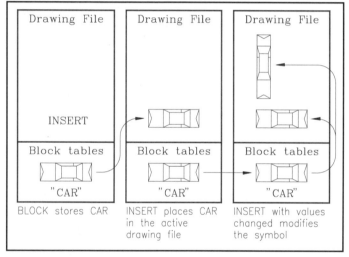

While you were inputting your scale values, you may also have noticed a second option, called Corner, to input scale factors. When you use the Corner option to input your scale values, you can scale the block by indicating the X and Y size of a rectangle. The insertion point is the first corner of the rectangle. Drag and pick the other corner to determine scale. AutoCAD uses the width as the X scale and the height as the Y scale. The width and height are measured in current drawing units.

You do not need to type a C to use corner point scaling. Just pick a point at the X scale prompt and then pick another point. The Corner option is used in menus because it limits scale input to corner point picking and issues an Other corner: prompt.

Note: Whether you use keyboard scale entry or the Corner option, you can specify negative scale factors to mirror the block's insertion, turn it upside-down, or both.

Be careful with corner point scaling! The dragged scale is relative to *one unit* (1") square. It works great if your block definition is about one unit in size. But if your block definition is many drawing units in size, like CAR2, even a small rectangle will give a large scale factor.

When using corner scale input, use snap or osnap to control accuracy. It is most useful when inserting unit scale blocks such as parts (see figs. 9.14 and 9.15).

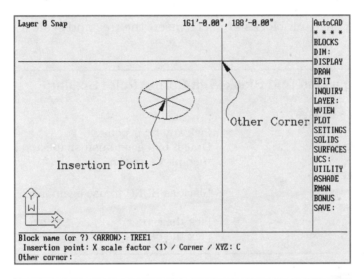

Figure 9.14:
A one-unit tree block inserted with corner scaling.

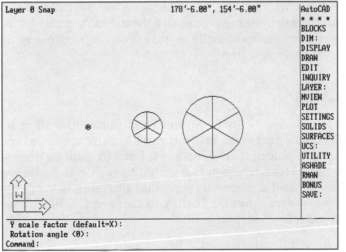

Figure 9.15:
A one-unit tree inserted at 12", 6' and 12'.

Using Unit Scale to Make Flexible Blocks

At first you may think that you will use insertion scale and rotation only occasionally. Nothing could be further from the truth! Being able to scale and rotate blocks during insertion is a valuable feature.

The trick is to create your parts in a *1 x 1 unit cell*. Then, when you insert a block, you can stretch or shrink it to fit. The block is good at any scale with any insertion scale factor. For example, you can store a door or window part so that the endpoints are on the left and right edges of the unit cell. Then insert the symbol with appropriate scale factors to fill the area you need. Remember, you draw a unit block at 1 inch, so to insert it scaled to 3 feet, you use a scale factor of 36, not 3.

To show how versatile one-unit blocks are, let's insert the tree and scale it down to a bush.

Inserting a One-Unit Block With Corner Point Scaling

```
Command: INSERT
Block name (or ?) <CAR2>: TREE1
Insertion point:                   Pick any clear point.
X scale factor <1> / Corner / XYZ: Drag it to a good bush shape and size,
                                   then pick a corner.
Rotation angle <0>: <RETURN>
Command: BLOCK                     Block as BUSH to use again later.
Block name (or ?): BUSH
Insertion base point:              Pick the center.
Select objects:                    Pick the bush.
```

One-unit blocks are very useful. You can create libraries full of one-unit parts, then insert them at different sizes depending on the situation. Don't create whole libraries full of different sizes of windows or bolts — just create a single one-unit part, then insert it to whatever scale you need.

Using Preset Scales

So far, you have inserted blocks by giving an insertion point first, then specifying scale and angle. This is quick and easy, but you can't see the angle or how big the block is until after you have placed it. This makes it hard to visually drag scaled or rotated blocks into place. Fortunately, you can preset the scale and rotation. When you preset the block's scale and angle, insertion point dragging is suspended until you have completed your preset options. Then, you can see the block's scale and angle as you drag it to pick the insertion point.

Try making one more stretch limousine using preset values.

Using INSERT With Preset Scales

```
Command: INSERT                         Insert a stretched car rotated 180 degrees.
Block name (or ?) <TREE1>: CAR2
Insertion point: X                      Preset the X scale.
X scale factor: 1.3
Insertion point: Y                      Preset the Y scale.
Y scale factor: 1
Insertion point: R                      Preset the rotation angle.
Rotation angle: 180
Insertion point:                        Drag it around, then pick point 196',138.'
```

The newly inserted car appears in figure 9.16.

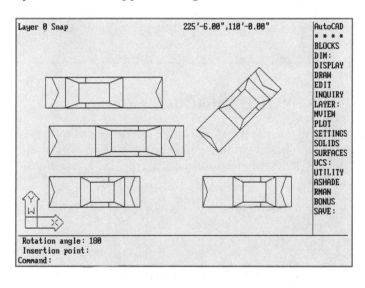

Figure 9.16:
A stretch limousine inserted with preset scale.

Presets offer several options, but they are not shown in the insert prompt. Here is a complete list.

Preset Scale and Rotation Options

Scale and **PScale** will prompt for scale factor which will be preset to X, Y, and Z axes.

Xscale and **PXscale** only preset an X scale factor.

Yscale and **PYscale** only preset a Y scale factor.

Zscale and **PZscale** only preset a Z scale factor.

Rotate and **PRotate** preset rotation angle. Enter from the keyboard or by picking two points.

Just type the first one or two characters of the preset option to tell AutoCAD what you want to preset.

P stands for preliminary, not preset. Options prefixed with a P establish a preliminary scale and rotation value to aid in insertion. After the insertion point is selected, the normal prompts are displayed to let you change the preset values.

Preset scale factors have limitations. You cannot mix fixed presets, like Xscale, with preliminary presets, like PYscale. If you try to mix them, the preliminary presets become fixed, and you will not be reprompted for their values.

> *Note:* Preset options work best when you use them in menu macros. These macros can transparently apply preset options, making dragging while in the INSERT command natural and easy to do.

When Is a Block Not a Block?

You use the BLOCK command to collect entities into a single group. When you insert the block in a drawing file, the insertion is a single entity. When you erase a block, the whole block (but not its stored definition) is erased. The same holds true for moving and copying blocks.

When is a block not a block? A block is not a block when it is *inserted or exploded.

Using *INSERT

Sometimes you want to be able to individually edit the different entities that make up a block after you insert them. But, individual entities lose their identities when they are stored as a block.

What if you want to edit a block after you insert it? To edit individual pieces of a block after insertion, AutoCAD provides an option for the INSERT command. Placing an asterisk (*) in front of a block name at insertion time tells AutoCAD to break the block back into its individual entities. This is commonly called an *insert-star* or *star-insertion*. A *insertion does not insert a block reference; it duplicates the original entities of the block definition. However, unlike duplicating entities with COPY, a *insertion allows you to modify the scale and rotation of the copy.

Inserting a separate drawing file into the current drawing creates a block in the current drawing unless you *insert it. *Insertion inserts only individual entities, without creating a block.

Let's zoom in and insert the car in the clear area of the screen. Then to prove the new car is really a collection of separate entities, we'll change it into a sports car. Use some editing commands on the *inserted car and create a car as complex as you like, making sure it looks different from the original. It will be used in a later exercise.

Using *INSERT to Break Blocks Into Components

Command: **ZOOM**	Zoom in to a height of 15' in a clear area.
Command: **INSERT**	
Block name (or ?) <CAR2>: ***CAR2**	
Insertion point:	Pick a point, and default scale and rotation.
Command: **ERASE**	Erase the windshield line and two lines on the trunk and hood.
Command: **STRETCH**	Stretch the rear glass towards the back.
Command: **STRETCH**	Make the roof smaller.
Command: **ARC**	Draw a new windshield.
Command: **FILLET**	Round the corners of the car.
Command: **ZOOM**	Previous.
Command: **SAVE**	

The *inserted car block is shown in figure 9.17. The newly created sports car appears in figure 9.18.

When you use the star option to insert a block, AutoCAD restricts your flexibility in rescaling the objects as they are placed. You can only specify a single, positive scale factor in the * mode. Negative and unequal X and Y scales are not allowed. But you can rescale your *inserted blocks with STRETCH, SCALE, EXTEND, and other editing commands after insertion.

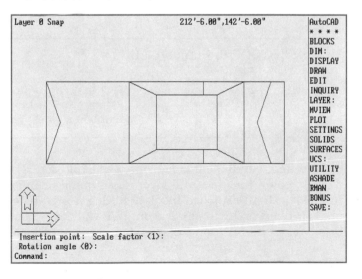

Figure 9.17:
An *inserted car.

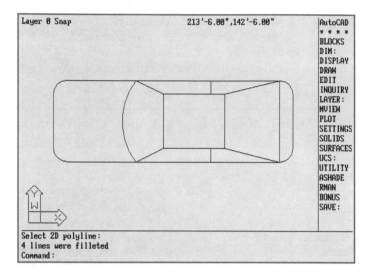

The figure shows an AutoCAD screen with:

```
Layer 0 Snap                    213'-6.00",142'-6.00"        AutoCAD
                                                             * * * *
                                                             BLOCKS
                                                             DIM:
                                                             DISPLAY
                                                             DRAW
                                                             EDIT
                                                             INQUIRY
                                                             LAYER:
                                                             MVIEW
                                                             PLOT
                                                             SETTINGS
                                                             SOLIDS
                                                             SURFACES
                                                             UCS:
                                                             UTILITY
                                                             ASHADE
                                                             RMAN
                                                             BONUS
                                                             SAVE:

Select 2D polyline:
4 lines were filleted
Command:
```

> **Tip:** If you place a complex *inserted block in the wrong place, use Undo to get rid of all the pieces.

What if you want to modify a block after it has already been inserted? Explode it.

The EXPLODE Command

You can achieve the same effect on an existing block that you get with a *insertion. AutoCAD gives you the EXPLODE command to separate a block back into its original entities. Try exploding the first car you inserted on the far bottom left of your drawing.

Using EXPLODE to Explode a Block

Command: **EXPLODE**
Select block reference, polyline, dimension, or mesh: Pick first car in the lower left corner. The block is redrawn as it explodes.

The exploded car pieces look identical to the image before the explosion. There may be exceptions where byblock, color, linetype, and layer assignments can come undone when you explode a block. If an exploded block includes nested blocks, only the outer level of nesting is broken up by the explosion. (We will cover nesting and byblock properties a little later in this section's discussion of block properties.)

There are some things that you cannot explode. You can't explode an *inserted block because it already is exploded. You can't explode a *minserted* block. And, you can't explode mirrored blocks or a block with differing X and Y (and Z) scale factors.

The MINSERT Command

A block is more than a block when it is minserted. Suppose you wanted to put a whole bunch of cars (or desks, or printed circuit board drill locations, or any other symbol you might have blocked away) in your drawing. You could insert one copy of the block and then use ARRAY to make several columns and rows.

MINSERT provides another option. Think of MINSERT (Multiple INSERTion) as a single command that combines insertion and rectangular arrays (no polar arrays with MINSERT). However, there is a difference. Each entity that the ARRAY command generates is an individual entity in the drawing file — it can be edited, deleted, copied, or even arrayed individually. Each component of the block that MINSERT generates is part of a single minserted block. You cannot edit the individual component blocks. (You also cannot *minsert blocks.)

Use MINSERT to fill your screen with cars. Pan to the right side of your drawing to get a clear space. After you have minserted the cars, use an ERASE Last to get rid of them.

Using MINSERT to Insert a Block

Command: **PAN**	Pick a point and pan by a displacement of @60'<180.
Command: **MINSERT**	
Block name (or ?) <*CAR2>: **CAR2**	
Insertion point:	Pick a point in the lower left.
X Scale factor <1>/Corner/XYZ: **\<RETURN>**	
Y Scale factor <default=X>: **\<RETURN>**	
Rotation angle <0.00>: **\<RETURN>**	
Number of rows (− − −) <1>: **4**	
Number of columns (| | |) <1>: **2**	
Unit cell or distance between rows (− − −): **8'**	
Distance between columns (| | |): **19'**	Eight cars appear, arranged in two columns (see fig. 9.19).
Command: **ERASE**	Use Last to prove that all are tied to one another.

Note: When you specify a rotation in MINSERT, the array is rotated, along with the individual blocks within it.

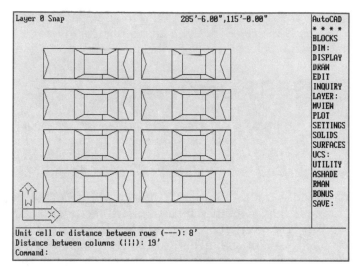

Figure 9.19:
Some minserted cars.

MINSERT is an efficient way to place multiple copies of a block in a drawing file. In an array, every entity occurrence takes up disk space. In a minsert, the block reference occurs only once and includes information about the number of rows, columns, and spacing of elements.

There are two additional commands that you can use to insert multiple copies of a block. These are the DIVIDE and MEASURE commands.

The DIVIDE Command

Frequently, you are faced with the problem of placing blocks in a drawing at a set interval. You can use the DIVIDE command to divide an entity, say a polyline, into equal length parts, and insert a block at the division points. DIVIDE does not actually break the polyline (or other entity), it only marks the divisions. You can divide lines, arcs, circles, and polylines.

Create a new car block from CAR2 in the space where you erased your minserted cars. Call this new car block CAR3 and change its insertion point so that the cars will set back from the polyline when they are inserted. Next, create a polyline. The direction in which you drew the polyline determines which side the cars insert on. Then use DIVIDE to divide the polyline into five segments and insert the new car blocks.

Using DIVIDE to Insert a Car Block

```
Command: INSERT
Block name (or ?) <CAR2>: <RETURN>
Insertion point:                        Pick a point in the center and default the
                                        scale.
Rotation angle <0.00>: -90              We want it at right angles to the polyline.
Command: BLOCK
Block name (or ?): CAR3
Insertion base point: @0,3'             Makes insert point 3' in front of car.
Select objects: L
1 found.
Select objects: <RETURN>                CAR3 is now a nested block containing
                                        CAR2.
Command: PLINE                          Draw a polyline from 275',133' to @22'<180
                                        to @ 17'<-90.
Command: FILLET                         Fillet corner with a 12' radius. The result-
                                        ing polyline appears in figure 9.20.
Command: DIVIDE
Select object to divide:                Pick the polyline.
<Number of segments>/Block: B
Block name to insert: CAR3
Align block with object? <Y> <RETURN>
Number of segments: 5
```

After you are done, your screen should have four cars, one between each of the five segments (see fig. 9.21). Each inserted block is a separate entity.

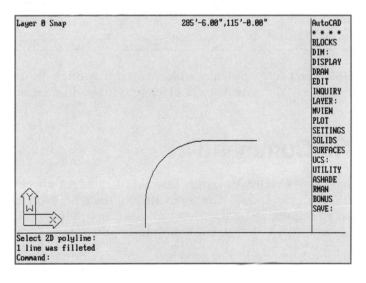

Figure 9.20:
A polyline for DIVIDE.

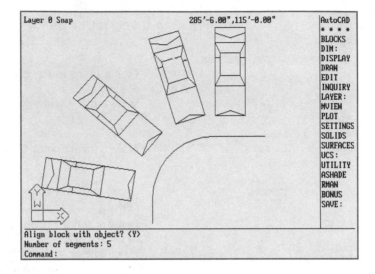

Figure 9.21:
Some cars inserted
with DIVIDE.

You can divide a line or polyline even if you do not use blocks. DIVIDE will insert point entities to which you can osnap with NODe. You can make them display more visibly with PDMODE and PDSIZE.

When you use DIVIDE to insert blocks (or points), AutoCAD saves the inserted entities as a Previous selection set. You can get the group again for editing by using the Previous selection set option. For example, if you want to change the layer of the cars, you can select them all simply by using the Previous option when prompted to select objects in CHPROP.

> *Tip:* You can use a construction entity for your block insertions, then erase it after you do your DIVIDE (or MEASURE) insert.

DIVIDE (and MEASURE) don't let you scale a block. If you wanted to insert the original one-unit size trees, you'd create a larger block and insert it, or rescale each block after insertion.

The MEASURE Command

MEASURE works much like DIVIDE. However, instead of dividing an entity into equal parts, MEASURE lets you specify the segment length. Once you specify a block name to insert and a segment length, either by inputting a value or by picking two points, AutoCAD inserts them at segment length intervals.

Are you getting tired of seeing just cars? For good measure, try adding some bushes to the parking area, using the BUSH block that you made in the one-unit block exercise.

Using MEASURE to Insert Bush Blocks

```
Command: MEASURE
Select object to measure:                    Pick the polyline.
<Segment length>/Block: B
Block name to insert: BUSH
Align block with object? <Y> <RETURN>
Segment length: 5'                           Place a bush every five feet.
```

As figure 9.22 shows, your parking area is beginning to look more realistic.

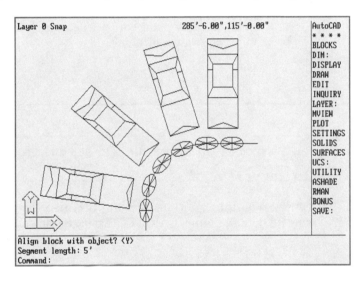

Figure 9.22: Some bushes inserted with MEASURE.

Like DIVIDE, MEASURE works with blocks or points, and forms a Previous selection set that you can use for subsequent editing.

WBLOCK — The Write BLOCK Command

So far, the blocks you have created and stored in the block table have been self-contained in the current drawing file. They will be stored in this drawing when you save or end it. Whenever you work in this drawing file, these block definitions will be there. However, sooner or later you will want to use them in another drawing.

Sending Blocks to Disk as Drawing Files

WBLOCK lets you save any block in your current drawing as a separate drawing file on disk. Or you can select a set of entities and write them to a separate drawing file without making them into a block in the current drawing. Any block or selection set can be stored as a separate drawing file, and any drawing file can be inserted as a block.

The drawing file created by WBLOCK is a normal drawing containing the current drawing settings and the entities that make up the block definition. The entities are normal drawing entities and are not defined as a block in the new file.

Try storing CAR2 as a separate file called CAR2.DWG, and TREE1 as TREE1.DWG.

Using WBLOCK to Write a Block to Disk

```
Command: WBLOCK
File name: CAR2                  AutoCAD automatically adds the .DWG.
Block name: =                    Responding to Block name with = tells AutoCAD the
                                 block name equals the filename.

Command: WBLOCK
File name: TREE1
Block name: =
```

Tip: If a block is really useful, wblock it to a disk file. Periodically group your wblocked symbols into library files.

To later insert (or *insert) CAR2.DWG into another drawing file, use the INSERT command and call the file using its disk filename, CAR2. Figure 9.23 shows how this process works.

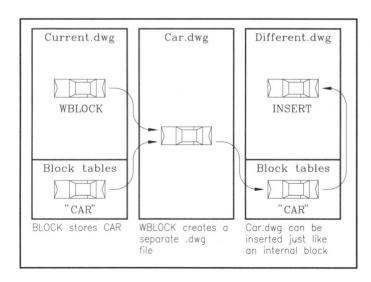

Figure 9.23:
WBLOCK and IN-
SERT.

Using Entity Selection to Wblock a File

You can wblock a file without creating a block first. If you enter a <RETURN> instead of giving an existing block name in response to a block name prompt, you will be prompted for an insertion base point and object selection. You can use any of the standard object selection techniques to select items for wblocking. When you finish selecting with a final <RETURN>, the entities are copied to the disk file you specified.

The entities are not defined as a block in the current drawing unless you also insert them. The drawing file created by WBLOCK is a normal drawing containing the selected entities and current drawing settings. The entities are not defined as a block in the new file.

Wblock the sports car to the filename MY-CAR. When you use BLOCK or WBLOCK, the selected entities are erased. OOPS will restore them, just like it restores entities deleted by the ERASE command. After you create the drawing file, undo or oops the entities back.

Creating a Block Drawing File With Entity Selection

```
Command: ZOOM                    Zoom Previous, Dynamic, or pan to the sports car.
Command: WBLOCK
File name: MY-CAR
Blockname: <RETURN>
Insertion base point:            Pick front midpoint of car.
Select objects:                  Select all entities of sports car.
Select objects: <RETURN>
Command: OOPS                     Return the car to the drawing.
```

Just as you can insert an entire drawing file as a block, you can wblock an entire current drawing to disk as a new file.

Remember, the drawing file created by WBLOCK is just like any other drawing file. WBLOCK doesn't create *any* blocks. It creates a drawing file that contains the entities that you select or that make up an existing block.

WBLOCK * Writes the Entire Drawing — Almost

If you respond to the WBLOCK block name prompt with an asterisk, then it writes almost the entire current drawing to a disk file. We say almost because it does not write any *unused* named things that are referenced by entities, such as blocks, text styles, layers, or linetypes. Drawing environment settings for UCSs, views, and viewport configurations are written, however.

Using WBLOCK* to Write it All

Command: **WBLOCK**   Wblock your entire drawing.
File name: **AUTOCITY**
Block name: *****   It writes the drawing to a new file on disk.

Tip: WBLOCK * is often used as an alternative method to purge unused blocks. (You can also purge them with the PURGE command.) If you wblock * to the same filename as the current drawing, it will ask if you want to replace it. If you answer yes, then quit the current drawing, you will have saved the current drawing, but without any unused blocks. This trick is commonly called a wblock star. But use it with caution because it will also delete unused layers, linetypes, and text styles.

The PURGE Command

As you work with blocks, you can build up extraneous blocks in the block table by inserting them, then later deleting them. Use the PURGE command to remove unused block definitions from the block table of the current drawing file.

PURGE only works in an editing session *before* you modify your drawing database either by creating a new entity or by editing an existing entity. PURGE is selective and prompts you extensively, giving you information about what blocks are stored in the block table area and asking you explicitly if you want to clean them out. You can also use PURGE to clean out unused layers, views, or styles — anything that you named during a drawing editor session. Using PURGE is a good habit before backing up a drawing on diskettes. To use PURGE, load your drawing and issue PURGE as the first command.

When you create other drawing files that you may later use as blocks, you need an easy way to control their insertion base points.

The BASE Command

The BASE command creates an insertion base point in a drawing file so you can control where it inserts into another file. The base point is an insertion handle just like the insertion base point on a regular block. (The base point is not an entity or visible point.) If you make a drawing, store it on disk, and later insert it in another drawing, it defaults to 0,0 as the insertion base point unless you specify the base point. Figure 9.24 shows how the BASE command works.

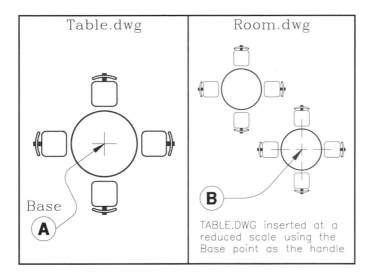

Figure 9.24:
Inserting a drawing
into another drawing.

Naming Conventions for Blocks

As your list of blocks and wblocked drawing files grows, you will find that you need some organization and structure in naming your blocks. We recommend that you give your blocks useful names. CAR1 and CAR2 are better than C1 and C, but not as descriptive as VWBUG and PORSCHE.

Try to make your block names the same number of characters or fewer than your operating system allows for filenames. You may want to wblock them later, and having a block name that is an allowable filename lets you specify = for the filename instead of typing it. You may also want to use common prefixes for similar classes of blocks (and drawings) to make it easy to use wildcards. Keep an alphabetical log of block names in a disk text file and print it out as it changes. This way you won't accidentally call the wrong block or duplicate block names.

Block Structure

Blocks are powerful tools. Their use can make your drawing life easier. There are two additional block properties that you should be aware of when you use blocks: blocks can include other blocks, and blocks can include entities on different layers.

Nesting Blocks

A block can be made up of other blocks. This is called nesting. You can place a block inside a block inside a block. AutoCAD does not place a limit on the number of block nesting levels, although editing nested blocks can get confusing if you go more than a few levels deep. When you created the BUSH block, it contained the TREE1 block as a nested block.

To include a block in another block, you simply select the first block when you block the second. You can use standard editing commands, like ARRAY, COPY, and MOVE, on nested blocks just as on normal blocks.

Nested blocks further increase the efficiency and control of blocks. The BUSH block contains only one entity (the TREE1 block) instead of one circle and three lines. In figure 9.25, we've made the chair a nested block so that the outer TABLE block need only contain four block references instead of all of the entities that make up each chair. It also allows the CHAIR block to be redefined (changed) easily and independently of the TABLE block definition.

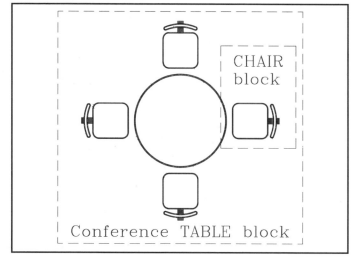

Figure 9.25:
An example of a nested block.

Blocks and Layers

When dealing with blocks and layers, we are primarily concerned with what layers the entities in the block definition are on. So far, entities of all the blocks you have used have been entities drawn on layer 0. You can, however, create a block with entities on different drawing layers (see fig. 9.26). For example, you can create a block with graphic entities on layer ABC, and text on layer XYZ. When you create the block, AutoCAD will store the entities inside the block on their appropriate layers.

When you insert multiple-layer blocks, each entity in the block will display according to its rules of color and linetype as they were at the time of the entity's creation. Entities included in the block at the time of block creation can have color or linetype specification set BYLAYER (the default), BYBLOCK, or by explicit color or linetype settings. If the current drawing file does not contain all of the needed block's layers, insertion will create the layers in the current drawing. Figure 9.27 shows a normal block insertion where the entity retains its original explicit color when inserted on a different active layer.

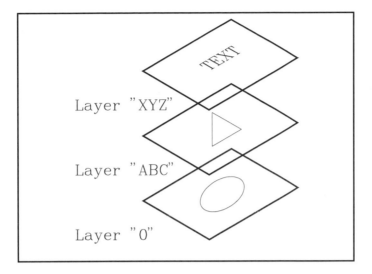

Figure 9.26:

A block can have entities on many layers.

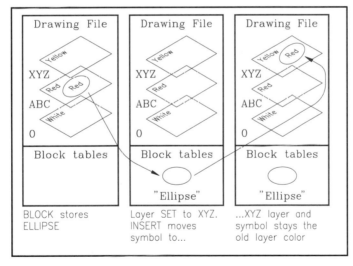

Figure 9.27:

An example of a color layer insertion.

Layer 0's Special Block Insertion Properties

If you create entities on layer 0, store them in a block, and then insert the block on a different active layer, the entities will move to the layer of insertion. If they had explicit color or linetype, they will retain them. However, if they had color and/or linetype set BYLAYER, they will adopt the default layer settings of their layer of insertion (see fig. 9.28). Blocks made from layer 0 BYLAYER entities act like chameleons.

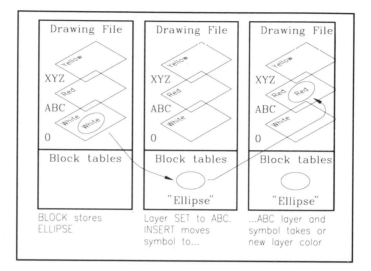

Figure 9.28:
An example of a layer insertion.

Note: Any entities that were on layer 0 at the time of block creation will go back to layer 0 and return to their original color and linetype when you use a *insertion or explode them.

Using BYBLOCK Colors and Linetypes

You can get a similar effect to layer 0 entities by creating them with the BYBLOCK property (or by changing existing entities to BYBLOCK with CHPROP). These BYBLOCK entities will take on the current color and linetype settings of the layer upon which the block is inserted. Unlike blocked layer 0 BYLAYER entities, which are predestined to assume the default layer color and/or linetypes of the layer upon which the entities were drawn, BYBLOCK entities in blocks are completely flexible. They assume the settings of the insertion layer at the time of insertion, whether explicit (like red), BYLAYER, or even BYBLOCK (for nesting).

Blocks and Frozen Layers

Sooner or later, we all have the experience of inserting a block with multiple-layer entities on a layer, freezing the layer, and suddenly having the block disappear from view. How does this happen?

When you give AutoCAD an insertion base point, that invisible reference point is defined in the block at the time of creation. The reference point anchors the block into the drawing file by its insertion point coordinates. When you insert a block, AutoCAD does not actually insert all the information that makes up the block, but only a block reference back to the invisibly stored block definitions. This means that whatever layer you use to insert the block will contain the block reference at the insertion point. When you freeze the layer, you suppress the block reference, even though the block has entities on other layers that you haven't frozen.

Block Substitution and Redefinition

All of these properties sound good in theory, but what about some practical techniques? We would like to wrap up this first section on blocks by showing you two useful block techniques: using substitute blocks, and redefining blocks. The Autotown block exercises will show you how to substitute working blocks and do block redefinitions.

Substituting Working Blocks

As you insert a block, you can assign a different block name by using an equal sign. You use an assignment such as IA-TREE=TREE1 to tell AutoCAD to use the graphic information stored in the TREE1.DWG file on disk. The TREE1 symbol will then be inserted in your drawing as the working block IA-TREE. Substituting the IA-TREE name within your current drawing provides you with a safety step that makes it difficult to overwrite blocks in your drawing.

Redefining Blocks

If the block name already exists in your drawing, then reinserting it with an equal sign will redefine all existing insertions of the block.

To see how block redefinition works, try replacing all your CAR2 blocks with MY-CAR blocks (the sports car you saved to disk). You can use the INSERT command to replace blocks as well as to insert them. You do not have to actually complete the INSERT command to redefine existing blocks. Just cut it short with a <^C>, and the redefinition will occur.

Using INSERT to Redefine Blocks

Zoom or pan as needed to view all cars.

```
Command: INSERT
Block name (or ?) <CAR2>: CAR2=MY-CAR
Block CAR2 redefined
Regenerating drawing.
Insertion point: *Cancel*                    Type <^C> to cancel command.
Command: END
```

Figure 9.29 shows the redefined blocks.

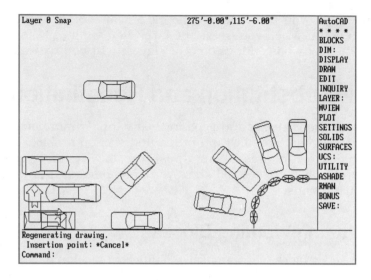

Figure 9.29:
CAR2 blocks
redefined as
MY-CAR blocks.

You should have sports cars all over the place. Replacing a few cars with a few different cars may seem like a trivial exercise. But, if you have a minor revision to make on a block that occurs several hundred times in a drawing, it is no trivial matter! You can globally replace all your blocks with a revised block in a single insertion redefinition.

Tip: If you are satisfied with a part of a drawing (or a part on a layer) and you won't be working on that part for a while, block it and replace it with a simple block to improve redraw speed and reduce screen clutter. When you are ready, put the drawing back together again by inserting the block with an equal sign.

External References (Xrefs) Give You Distributed Design

Let's say your building design team consists of four people — one is working on the building's structure and floor plan, one on the electrical system, one on the plumbing and other facilities, and the last is working on the interior design.

Everyone needs to know what the basic outline of the building is and where walls, doors, windows, and other features are. They can't wait for the floor plan to be finalized and completely drawn — they have to get to work right away to stay on top of the project. If a change is made to the floor plan, the rest of the team needs to know it right away.

The perfect solution is for each person on the team to insert the floor plan into his drawings as an xref. Every time he loads his drawing to work on it, the very latest revision of the floor plan will automatically be incorporated. If a wall has moved, he will know it right away and can respond to the change.

Even if you don't design buildings, this should give you an idea for incorporating xrefs into your own application.

Xrefs (external references) are collective entities similar to blocks. They can contain multiple entities (lines, arcs, and so on); you can insert them in your drawing like blocks; and you can select them as a single entity whether they contain one entity or a hundred.

The big difference between a block and an xref is that while blocks reduce multiple drawing entities in your drawing file down to a single case, xrefs remove those entities from the drawing file altogether.

When you create a block that contains 100 lines, your drawing database contains an entry for each of those lines, including each line's layer setting, color setting, linetype, and so on. You can't see a listing of that data, even if you list the drawing database's contents. The data is buried in the block definition table, but it's still there — for all 100 lines. When you insert more copies of your block onto your drawing, you duplicate only the block reference, not the original data. But the original lines always have to be in the block definition table for the block to exist.

Xrefs for Efficiency

Xrefs remove the need to store block data in the drawing at all. Xrefs do exactly what their name implies — they reference external drawings. When you insert an xref, you are inserting only its name and a few other bits of information that AutoCAD needs to be able to display the image of the xref on the screen. The entities that make up the image are still located on disk in the drawing file referenced by the xref. The drawing file saves only a reference to the external reference file.

Xrefs are like ghost images of other files. You can use them to insert images of parts and symbols into your drawing without actually inserting the data that makes up the part or symbol. And, like blocks, you can osnap to objects within the xref. If your blocks are complex, containing hundreds of drawing entities, using an xref instead of a block could remove those hundreds of entities from each drawing file that uses them, making file sizes much smaller.

Xrefs for Control

Another, and perhaps even more significant, reason to use xrefs is the control they offer. When several people work on parts of the same drawing, assembling them into one master drawing as xrefs insures that every time that master drawing is loaded or plotted, the latest revisions to the referenced drawings automatically get used. The TABLET.DWG and its three referenced drawings (TABLET-A B and S) on the Release 11 sample disk are an example of this.

Using xrefs assures that parts get automatically updated throughout an entire library of drawings. If you have parts that change from time to time, and they need to be updated to the latest revision in a number of existing drawings, you could use block redefinition, one block and one drawing at a time. But if you instead inserted them as xrefs, they would automatically update whenever a drawing was loaded or plotted.

Using Xrefs

Xrefs best lend themselves to cases where you are inserting common parts that could still be revised during your project. Because they always reflect the most current revision of the data they reference, xrefs can significantly reduce the errors normally associated with copying data from one drawing to another. If you make a change to the xref's source file, that xref will be updated in every drawing in which it is referenced.

Let's briefly examine the command options available with XREF, then run through several exercises using these options. Here is a list of the options:

XREF Options

?
Allows you to list the names of xrefs that have already been attached to your drawing. AutoCAD will prompt you for a name to list, and you can specify an individual name, enter multiple names separated by commas, or use wildcard characters to list multiple names. If you press <RETURN> in response to the prompt, AutoCAD will list all of the xrefs currently attached to the drawing.

Bind
Converts the xrefs you specify by name into standard blocks, binding them to the drawing as permanent entities.

Detach
Removes an xref from your drawing. If the xref is currently being displayed as part of the drawing, it will disappear when you detach it.

Path
Allows you to change the path to the xref's source file. Because an xref references an external file, AutoCAD needs to keep track of what disk and directory the xref's source file is on. Using the Path option, you can change the directory path associated with the xref.

Reload
Causes AutoCAD to reload the xref from disk. If a change has been made to the xref's source file, the change will become apparent after a reload. You can specify a single xref or multiple xrefs to reload.

Attach
This option attaches a new xref to your drawing. If the xref has already been attached, AutoCAD will inform you and remind you that you can reload it to update its definition.

The commands for using xrefs are found as [XREF:] and [XBIND:] on the [BLOCKS] screen menu, and [Xref] on the [Draw] pull-down menu.

Let's attach an xref to a drawing. We'll begin a new drawing named XSYMBOL. Then we'll draw a new symbol on a layer called SYMLAYER (see fig. 9.30). After we save the drawing and return to the main menu, we'll attach it as an xref in a new drawing.

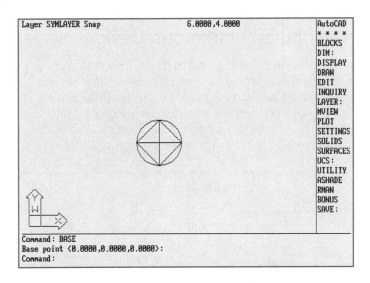

Figure 9.30:
A symbol on layer
SYMLAYER in
XSYMBOL drawing.

Attaching an Xref to Your Drawing

Begin a NEW drawing named XSYMBOL.

Command: **LAYER**   Make a red layer named SYMLAYER and set it current.

Turn snap on and draw the symbol shown with 1" radius.

Command: **BASE**   Set insertion base point at center.
Command: **END**

Begin a NEW drawing named XTEST and turn snap and coords on.

Command: **XREF**   Attach the XSYMBOL drawing as an xref.

?/Bind/Detach/Path/Reload/<Attach>: **<RETURN>**
Xref to Attach: **XSYMBOL**
Attach Xref XSYMBOL: XSYMBOL
XSYMBOL loaded.   The rest of the prompts are identical to INSERT.

Insertion point: **5,5**
  X scale factor <1> / Corner / XYZ: **<RETURN>**
  Y scale factor (default=X): **<RETURN>**
  Rotation angle <0>: **<RETURN>**
Command: **END**   End the drawing to save it.

You can see that attaching an xref is a lot like inserting a block. Xrefs act a lot like blocks. If you select any part of the xref with the ERASE command, the entire xref is deleted, just as if it were a block. You can't explode an xref to edit its entities, but you can edit the external source file. This is one way in which xrefs are very different from blocks. When you update an xref's source drawing file, you will affect every drawing in which that file is referenced. Usually, that's a good thing.

Using Xrefs for Distributed Workgroup Design

One of the main reasons xrefs were designed was to facilitate workgroup design. You can allocate different parts of a large project to members of your design team and have all the pieces come together at the end to make up the final project. Let's use the XSYMBOL drawing you just created as an example of xref's ability to provide automatic updates. Load it, then add two more circles to it and save the drawing. Then, load XTEST again to see XSYMBOL automatically update.

Updating an Xref

Edit an EXISTING drawing named XSYMBOL.

`Command:` **CIRCLE**	Add two concentric circles around the symbol.
`Command:` **END**	End the drawing to save it.

Edit an EXISTING drawing named XTEST.

`Resolve Xref XSYMBOL: XSYMBOL`	The current revision is loaded when you load the drawing.
`XSYMBOL loaded.`	

When you load a drawing that contains xrefs, AutoCAD automatically reloads any external references. You loaded XSYMBOL, changed it, then ended it. When you loaded the drawing that contained XSYMBOL as an xref, the updated version of XSYMBOL appeared in the file automatically.

But if you are part of a design team, you are probably on a network with the rest of the designers. What happens to your xrefs if someone edits the source file you have referenced in your drawing while you are still working on the drawing? Nothing happens, unless you reload the xref.

Reloading Xrefs

There are two ways to reload xrefs. The first way, which you just used, is to load the drawing again. The other way is to use the XREF Reload option. When AutoCAD asks you which xrefs you want to reload, you can specify one or more xrefs by name, or simply type * to reload them all.

We'll change the original XSYMBOL external file by drawing and wblocking a new square symbol to its filename. Then reload XSYMBOL in your XTEST drawing to update it. XTEST should still be loaded.

Reloading an Xref After its Source File Has Changed

```
Command: LAYER
```
Make layer named SYMLAYER, color yellow and linetype dashed. Set it current.

Draw a 2" square symbol with an X through it, as illustrated in figure 9.31.

```
Command: WBLOCK
```
Wblock square symbol to filename XSYMBOL, overwriting existing file. Use the center of the square as the insertion point.

```
Command: XREF
?/Bind/Detach/Path/Reload/<Attach>: R
Xref(s) to reload: *
   Scanning...
Reload Xref XSYMBOL: XSYMBOL
XSYMBOL loaded.   Regenerating drawing.
```
Asterisk updates all xrefs (see fig. 9.32).

When you reload xrefs, AutoCAD scans your drawing for xrefs and rereads the XSYMBOL drawing file from disk. Then it updates the symbol in the current drawing.

We created a new SYMLAYER layer before wblocking the symbol to make its layer name match the original xrefs. Let's examine how xrefs handle layers.

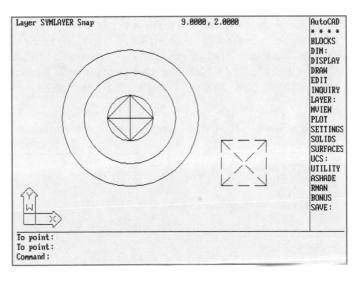

Figure 9.31:
The new square symbol before wblocking.

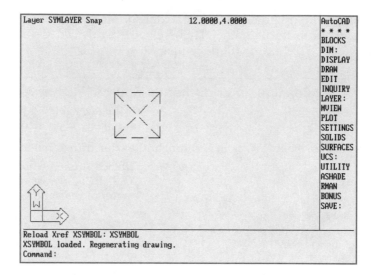

Figure 9.32:
The xref symbol after
updating.

Xrefs and Their Layers

When you insert a block into a drawing, any layers in the block's definition are added to the drawing. (If a layer in a block already exists in the drawing, and the entities are set BYLAYER, the block's entities take on the characteristics of the existing drawing layer.)

Xrefs work a little differently. When you attach an xref that contains layers other than layer 0, AutoCAD modifies the xref layer names to avoid duplication. It prefixes the layer names with the name of the xref using a *pipe*, a vertical bar (I), to separate the prefix from the layer name. You created the XSYMBOL data on layer SYMLAYER. When you attach XSYMBOL as an xref, AutoCAD renames SYMLAYER to XSYMBOL|SYMLAYER in the drawing in which the xref is attached. Renaming the layers prevents the xref's entities from taking on the characteristics of existing layers in the drawing.

Let's check the layers in XTEST to see that the layer has been renamed.

Listing Xref Layers

```
Command: LAYER
?/Make/Set/New/ON/OFF/Color/Ltype/Freeze/Thaw: ?
Layer name(s) to list <*>: <RETURN>
    Layer name        State        Color         Linetype
  ----------------  --------   -------------   --------------
0                     On       7 (white)        CONTINUOUS
SYMLAYER              On        2 (yellow)       CONTINUOUS
XSYMBOL|SYMLAYER      On        2 (yellow)       XSYMBOL|DASHED   Xdep: XSYMBOL
```

> **Listing Xref Layers—continued**
>
> ```
> Current layer: SYMLAYER
> ?/Make/Set/New/ON/OFF/Color/Ltype/Freeze/Thaw:          Set layer 0 current.
> Command: SAVE
> ```

Layer 0 is the exception to layer renaming by xrefs. As with block insertions, any data in the xrefs source file that resides on layer 0 comes in on layer 0 in the current drawing, and assumes any layer settings you have assigned to layer 0.

Now you know how to attach an xref to your drawing, and you also know what happens to the xref's layers when it is attached. But what if you no longer need the xref and want to remove it completely?

Removing Xrefs From Your Drawing

If you erase an xref, the reference to the external file is still in your drawing, just as a block's definition remains in memory even after all visible insertions are erased. When the drawing is reloaded, AutoCAD will still look for the external file, even though it won't visibly appear.

Use XREF's Detach option to get the xref out of your drawing. To see how that works, use Detach to remove XSYMBOL from your XTEST drawing.

> **Detaching an Xref from a Drawing**
>
> ```
> Command: XREF
> ?/Bind/Detach/Path/Reload/<Attach>: D
> Xref(s) to Detach: XSYMBOL
>     Scanning...                          The xref disappears; it's no
>                                          longer part of your drawing.
> ```

Bind Makes Xrefs Into Permanent Blocks

There may be times when you want to make your xref data a permanent part of your drawing instead of a reference to another external file. Otherwise, when you finish a project and want to archive it, you have to archive all of the xref source drawings along with the main drawings. If the xref source drawings are not available when you try to load your drawing, AutoCAD will give you an error message saying it can't find the xrefs. If it can't find them, it can't load and display them as part of the drawing. Binding the xrefs converts the xrefs into permanent blocks in the drawing file.

Any time you are removing a drawing from its original environment (including copying it onto diskette for distribution to a client or contractor), you must either bind the xrefs, or include the xref source drawings. Binding the xrefs is usually the safest method. However, if you are sending drawings to a consultant as work in progress, you may need to leave them as xrefs until the project is complete.

Let's go back into the XTEST drawing and use the Bind option to make the xref XSYMBOL a permanent part of the drawing.

Using Bind to Make an Xref Permanent

```
Command: XREF
?/Bind/Detach/Path/Reload/<Attach>: <RETURN>
Xref to Attach: XSYMBOL
Attach Xref XSYMBOL: XSYMBOL
XSYMBOL loaded.
Insertion point: 5,5
 X scale factor <1> / Corner / XYZ: <RETURN>
 Y scale factor (default=X): <RETURN>
 Rotation angle <0>: <RETURN>
Command: XREF
?/Bind/Detach/Path/Reload/<Attach>: B
Xref(s) to bind: XSYMBOL
    Scanning...
```

The Bind option attaches the xrefs to the drawing file in which they are contained. The xref becomes a standard block within the drawing. After it's attached, you can explode it and manipulate it just as you can any other block created or inserted directly in the drawing. To prove the XSYMBOL is now an ordinary block, you can explode and edit it, or list it with the BLOCK or INSERT command ? option.

Bind also makes a change to the layers that belong to xrefs. It replaces the vertical bar (|) in the layer name with n, where n is a number. If you list your layers again, you'll see that the layer XSYMBOL|SYMLAYER has been renamed to XSYMBOL0SYMLAYER. When AutoCAD renames the layers in this way, it tries to use 0 for the number. If a layer name by that name already exists, it tries a 1. It continues trying higher numbers until it comes up with a unique layer name. You can use the RENAME command to change these strange layer names to whatever you like.

Tip: If you want to insert a drawing as a block into your current drawing but you know they have conflicting layer names, attach it as an xref first, then bind it as a block. This will preserve the incoming block's unique layers.

In addition to insuring unique layer names, AutoCAD prevents xrefs and blocks from having the same names.

Controlling Xref Names and Block Conflicts

If you try to attach XSYMBOL again, you will get an error message:

```
** Error: XSYMBOL is already a standard block in the current drawing. *Invalid*
```

If you need to attach the xref again, you can substitute a working name in the current drawing like you do for blocks. (Or you can use RENAME to rename the XSYMBOL block to remove the conflict.) To see what filename is referenced by an xref already loaded under a substitute name, use the ? option of XREF. You can also use the ? option of the BLOCK command to get information on blocks and xrefs.

Let's re-attach XSYMBOL using the name XSYM2=XSYMBOL. Then, list it with the ? option of XREF, with the ? option of BLOCK, and with the ? option of LAYER.

Attaching an Xref With a Substitute Name

```
Command: XREF
?/Bind/Detach/Path/Reload/<Attach>: A
Xref to Attach <XSYMBOL>: XSYM2=XSYMBOL
Attach Xref XSYM2: XSYMBOL                    XSYM2 is the xref name and
                                             XSYMBOL is the external filename.

XSYM2 loaded.
Insertion point:                             Pick 9,5 and default the scale and
                                             rotation.
Command: XREF                                List all xrefs with ? and *.
     Xref Name               Path
----------------------    -------------
   XSYM2                    XSYMBOL
Total Xref(s): 1
Command: BLOCK                               List all blocks and xrefs with ? and *.
Defined blocks.
   XSYM2                    Xref: resolved
   XSYMBOL
User    External   Dependent   Unnamed
Blocks  References Blocks      Blocks
   1        1          0           0
Command: LAYER                               List all layers with ? and *.
   Layer name      State    Color      Linetype
----------------  --------  ---------  ------------
0                  On       7 (white)   CONTINUOUS
SYMLAYER           On       2 (yellow)  DASHED
XSYM2|SYMLAYER     On       2 (yellow)  XSYM2|DASHED  Xdep: XSYM2
XSYMBOL$0$SYMLAYER On       2 (yellow)  XSYMBOL$0$DASHED
```

When you listed the xrefs with XREF and BLOCK, they showed XSYM2 as the xref name in the current drawing and XSYMBOL2 as its path, the externally referenced filename.

Although you can attach an xref with an equal sign, you can't redefine an existing xref as you can for blocks. You *can* rename an xref using the Block option of the RENAME command. If you do so, RENAME will warn you:

```
Caution! XSYM2 is an externally referenced block.
Renaming it will also rename its dependent symbols.
```

What are dependent symbols anyway? And what do XSYM2 | DASHED linetype and Xdep: XSYM2 mean in the layer listing above?

Xref's Dependent Symbols

Layers, linetypes, text styles, blocks, and dimstyles are symbols in the sense that they have arbitrary names representing things like layers or styles (not to be confused with graphic symbols like your TREE1). The symbols which are carried into a drawing by an xref are called dependent symbols because they depend on the external file, not the current drawing, for their characteristics. Dependent symbols are prefixed in the same manner as XSYM2 | SYMLAYER and XSYM2 | DASHED to avoid conflicts. The only exceptions are unambiguous defaults like layer 0, and linetype CONTINUOUS. But, text style STANDARD can be varied, so it gets prefixed.

This prefixing is carried to nested xrefs; if the external file XSYMBOL included an xref named TITLEBLK, it would get the symbol name XSYMBOL | TITLEBLK if XSYMBOL was attached to another drawing. If TITLEBLK included the layer LEGEND, it would get the symbol XSYMBOL | TITLEBLK | LEGEND.

Note: If xrefs are nested deeply (one xref contains another, which contains another, and so on) or a drawing contains a lot of xrefs, things can get complex. So AutoCAD maintains a log file in ASCII text format that you can refer to. It's stored in the same directory as your drawing and its name matches your drawing name, with an .XLG filename extension. It continues to grow as the drawing is edited over many sessions, so you may want to delete all or part of it to save disk space.

What you can do to these dependent symbols in your current drawing is limited to protect the integrity of the xref. For example, you cannot make one of an xref's layers current and draw on it like you can with a standard drawing layer. However, you can modify an xref's appearance by changing the color, linetype, and visibility of an xref's layer. Any changes you make are only temporary; they will revert to their original states when the xref is reloaded. That's true even if you save the drawing after making changes to an xref's layer settings.

However, you can selectively import these dependent symbols into your current drawing.

XBIND — Binding Dependent Symbols of an Xref

When you used the Bind option of XREF to convert XSYMBOL from an xref to a block, AutoCAD converted the entire xref. All layers and data in the xref's source file became part of the new block.

You can also use the XBIND command to bind only portions of the xref to the drawing. If you only want to bring in text style, a block, or a layer defined in the xref without binding the entire xref, you can do so.

To see how XBIND works, bind only the SYMLAYER layer in XSYMBOL, not the entire xref. The data drawn on that layer will not be bound, only the layer itself.

Binding Only Parts of an Xref With XBIND

```
Command: XBIND
Block/Dimstyle/LAyer/LType/Style: LA
Dependent Layer name(s): XSYM2|SYMLAYER
    Scanning...
Also bound linetype XSYM2$0$DASHED:
it is referenced by layer XSYM2$0$SYMLAYER.
1 Layer(s) bound.
```

Use DDLMODES or LAYER to check to see that the layer and linetype have been bound and renamed with (0) instead of (|).

```
Command: END
```

Linetypes and other symbols that are dependent upon being bound, such as blocks or layers, are automatically bound. The entities (lines, etc.) contained in the xref are not bound to the drawing. But, if you bind a block, you can then use INSERT to insert it in the current drawing.

Tip: You can extract blocks and other symbols from one drawing and use them in your current drawing. Just attach the drawing on disk as an xref, bind what you need, and detach the xref.

Use BIND if you want to bind the entire xref, making it a block. Use XBIND if you only want to bind layer, linetype, dimension styles, nested blocks, or text styles without binding any actual entities in the xref.

The following Autotown exercise makes use of the BLOCK, INSERT, WBLOCK, and XREF commands that you learned in this chapter's first two sections. The exercise uses a set of simple blocks to place houses and trees on three lots in the Autotown site plan, then replaces them with more complex symbols to create the final drawing (see figs. 9.33 and 9.34).

Figure 9.33:
Autotown with simple symbols.

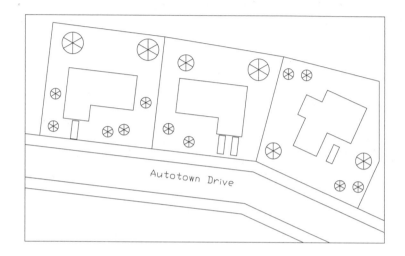

Figure 9.34:
Autotown with com-plex symbols.

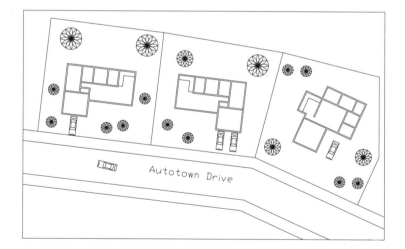

Autotown Block Exercises

Because the Autotown exercises involve several other techniques in addition to further exploration of blocks and xrefs, we give you several options with the IA DISK. If you don't have the disk, you'll need to do the whole sequence in order.

First, whether you have the disk or not, you need to set up and save the AUTOTOWN drawing file as instructed in the next exercise.

The exercise sequence beginning with *Laying Out Autotown Drive and Lots* lays out the site plan and offers drawing input techniques in surveyor's units. If you have the IA DISK, you have this site plan layout already. If you don't want to try surveyor's units, you can skip it.

Do the sequence, *Attaching the Site Layout as an Xref,* whether you have the IA DISK or not. In it, you'll edit the AUTOTOWN drawing you saved and attach the site plan layout drawing file as an xref (or as a block, if you're using Release 10).

The *Creating Blocks for Autotown* sequence creates a set of simple and complex blocks for subsequent exercises. You'll need the CAR2 and TREE1 blocks from the beginning of this chapter. If you have the IA DISK, you can create the additional blocks or use blocks from the disk.

Finally, beginning with *Aligning Working Blocks With a UCS,* you'll get more block insertion practice, from substituting working block names and setting temporary UCSs to align their insertion, to redefining blocks.

Setting Up Autotown

You are going to start a site plan layout drawing named ATLAYOUT. The drawing uses feet and decimal inches and surveyor's angles. Set your drawing limits at 360 feet by 240 feet. The drawing is sized to fit a 36" x 24" D-size sheet plotted at 1" = 10'.

Set up the AUTOTOWN drawing according to the settings in table 9.2.

Table 9.2
ATLAYOUT Drawing Settings

AXIS	COORDS	GRID	SNAP	UCSICON
Off	ON	10'	6"	OR

UNITS	Engineering, 2 decimal places, angles in surveyor's units, default all other settings.
LIMITS	0,0 to 360',240'
ZOOM	Zoom ALL
VIEW	Save view as All

Layer Name	State	Color	Linetype
0	On	7 (white)	CONTINUOUS
SITE	On/Current	3 (green)	CONTINUOUS
PLAN	On	5 (blue)	CONTINUOUS

Next add a border and the street using polylines, OFFSET, and TRIM. Your drawing
should resemble the one shown in figure 9.35.

Figure 9.35:
The Autotown border
and drive.

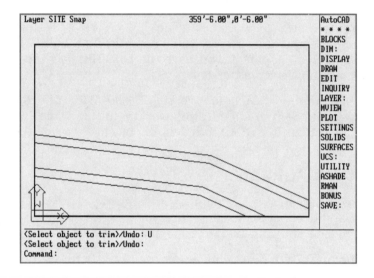

In manual drafting, converting and using surveyor's units is always a nuisance. Let AutoCAD do it for you.

Using Surveyor's Angles

Autotown's setup contains surveyor's angles. AutoCAD will still accept normal decimal angle input for surveyor's angles, and let you enter a simple N, S, E, or W for 90-, 270-, 0-, and 180-degree angles. You can specify angles in survey nomenclature, like N14d52'00"E for North 14 degrees, 52 minutes and 00 seconds East. Use surveyor's angles to draw the lot lines for the three lots. Use the osnap modes shown below when you pick your drawing points.

Using Surveyor's Angles to Draw Autotown's Lot Lines

```
Command: LINE
From point: INT                       Use intersection osnap.
of                                    Pick bend in the road at ① (see fig. 9.36).
To point: @100'2.5<N14d52'E
To point: @112'5.5<N80d47'W
To point: PER                         Use perpendicular osnap.
to                                    Pick north side of road at ②.
To point: <RETURN>

Command: LINE
From point: INT                       Use intersection osnap.
of                                    Pick northwest corner of center lot at ③.
To point: @105'<N82d57'W
To point: PER                         Use perpendicular osnap.
to                                    Pick north side of road at ②.
To point: <RETURN>

Command: LINE
From point: INT                       Use intersection osnap.
of                                    Pick northeast corner of center lot at ④.
To point: @91'8<S76d7'E
To point: @74'<S
To point: PER                         Use perpendicular osnap.
to                                    Pick north side of road at ⑤.
To point: <RETURN>
```

Next, label the road with DTEXT as shown above, using this tip:

Tip: To align text with an existing object, use an osnap to set the text angle, then pick the real location to put the text.

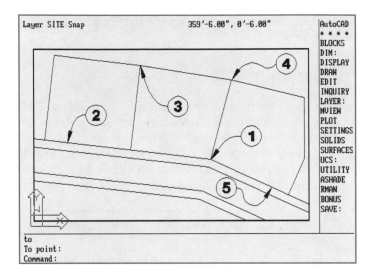

Figure 9.36:
Autotown with sur-
veyed lot lines.

Using DTEXT to Label the Road

```
Command: SNAP               Set snap to 1'.
Command: DTEXT              Use INT to pick the southwest corner of the center lot.
Height <0.2000>: 6'
Rotation angle <E>: INT
of                         Pick southeast corner of center lot.
Text:                      Pick absolute point 133',75' for the real location.
Text: Autotown Drive
Text: <RETURN>
Command: SNAP              Set snap back to 6".
Command: END              End the drawing.
```

Figure 9.37 shows the site. That finishes the site layout — unless the planning commission turns down your zoning appeal.

Using the Site Layout as an Xref

You'll use the AUTOTOWN setup drawing you saved in the first Autotown exercise and attach the site layout drawing to it as an Xref. If the planning commission denies your appeal and you have to modify the site layout, the changes will automatically be reflected in the finished Autotown drawing. If you have the IA DISK, you can use its site drawing instead of the ATLAYOUT we did earlier. (If you are using Release 10, insert the layout as a block instead of an xref.)

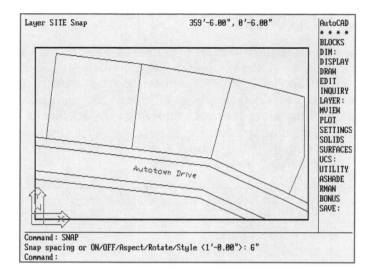

Figure 9.37:
A completed
Autotown Drive with
text.

Attaching the Site Layout as an Xref

Edit an EXISTING drawing named AUTOTOWN.

Command: **UNITS**   Set angles back to decimal
                                                            degrees.

Command: **LAYER**   Set layer 0 current.

Command: **XREF**
?/Bind/Detach/Path/Reload/<Attach>: **<RETURN>**
Xref to Attach: **~**   Use the tilde to bring up the
                                                            file dialogue box.

 Select IA6ATLAY.

 Select ATLAYOUT.

Attach Xref ATLAYOUT: ATLAYOUT
ATLAYOUT loaded.
Insertion point: **0,0**
  X scale factor <1> / Corner / XYZ: Default scale and rotation
                                                            angle.

Command: **SAVE**

Now it's time to do some house siting studies. First you need to set up eight blocks.

Preparing Autotown's Blocks

To study siting options, you might insert and arrange houses and site improvements as blocks. Throw in a car or two to dress up your presentations. It doesn't make much difference with only three lots, but if Autotown had three dozen lots, the complexity of the blocks used would make a big difference in regen and redraw speeds. The solution is to use matching pairs of simple and complex blocks and use redefinition to swap them. Use the simple blocks during site design, then substitute the complex ones for presentation plots. Figure 9.38 illustrates the simple and complex blocks you will use in the following exercises.

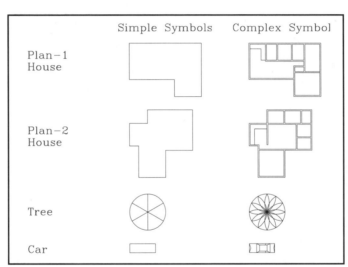

Figure 9.38:
Simple and complex blocks.

You already have two blocks, CAR2 and TREE1. Unless you have the IA DISK, you need to create the other six blocks now. If you have the disk and still want to do the block creation exercises, you'll overwrite the disk blocks when you wblock your creations. Start with a floor plan.

Creating Blocks for Autotown

Command: **ZOOM**   Zoom in on one of the lots as a construction area.

Draw the SIMPLE1 floor plan with the dimensions shown in figure 9.39.

Command: **WBLOCK**   Wblock the floor plan as SIMPLE1.

Command: **OOPS**   Oops the floor plan back.

Edit the SIMPLE1 floor plan to draw the COMPLEX1 floor plan. Make it as complex as you like, or use figure 9.40 as a guide. Hint: OFFSET comes in handy here.

Command: **WBLOCK**   Wblock the floor plan as COMPLEX1.

Draw, wblock, and oops the SIMPLE2 floor plan with the dimensions shown.

Draw and wblock the COMPLEX2 floor plan by modifying the SIMPLE2 floor plan (see figs. 9.41 and 9.42). Make it as complex as you like.

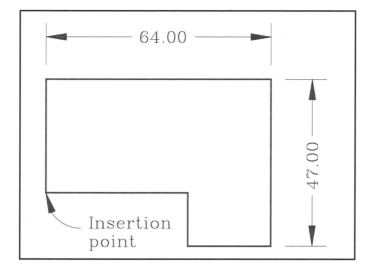

Figure 9.39:
Floor plan SIMPLE1.

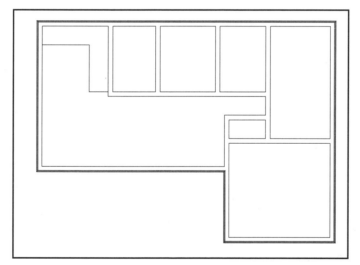

Figure 9.40:
Floor plan
COMPLEX1.

Creating Blocks for Autotown—continued

Continue by making a simple car and complex tree. You already have CAR2 and TREE1 from an earlier exercise.

Draw the CAR1 symbol with the dimensions shown in figure 9.43.

Command: **WBLOCK**   Wblock the car symbol as CAR1.

Zoom in and set snap to .125 to draw the TREE2 tree symbol one unit (1") in diameter (see fig. 9.44).

Command: **WBLOCK**   Wblock the tree symbol as TREE2.
Command: **VIEW**   Restore view All.

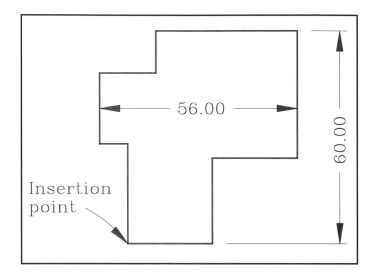

Figure 9.41:
Floor plan SIMPLE2.

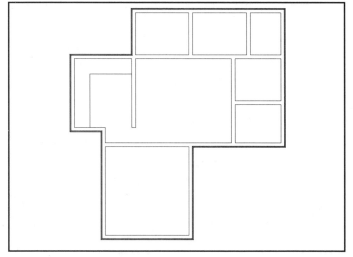

Figure 9.42:
Floor plan COM-
PLEX2.

Now that the blocks are done, the screen should be clear. It's time to build the subdivision. We'll use a temporary UCS to help position the houses in the subdivision.

Using a UCS to Insert Blocks

To insert the houses, set a UCS at the corner of each lot. This helps align the house plan in relationship to the lot. As you insert each block, substitute a working name (such as PLAN-1=SIMPLE1). That will tell AutoCAD to use the SIMPLE1.DWG drawing file on disk, but it will name the block PLAN-1 within the drawing.

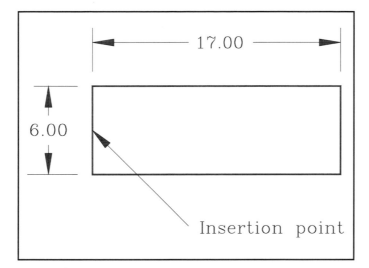

Figure 9.43:
The CAR1 simple car symbol.

17.00

6.00

Insertion point

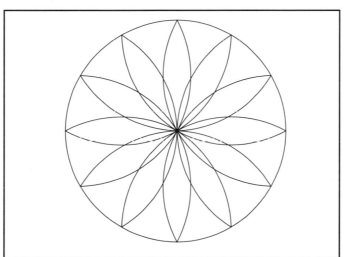

Figure 9.44:
The TREE2 complex tree symbol.

Aligning Working Blocks With a UCS

Command: **LAYER**	Set layer PLAN current.
Command: **UCS**	Set a three-point UCS on the center lot.
Origin/ZAxis/3point/Entity/View/X/Y/Z/Prev/ Restore/Save/Del/?/<World>: **3**	
Origin point <0,0,0>:	Pick lower left corner of lot at ① (see fig. 9.45).
Point on positive portion of the X-axis <130'- 7.69", 101'-4.86", 0'-0.00">:	Pick lower right corner of lot at ②.

Aligning Working Blocks With a UCS—continued

Point on positive-Y portion of the UCS X-Y plane <130'-6.78", 101'-5.86", 0'-0.00">:	Pick upper left corner of lot at ③.
Command: **INSERT**	Insert SIMPLE1 plan on center lot.
Block name (or ?): **PLAN-1=SIMPLE1**	Make the block name PLAN-1.
Insertion point: **17',36'**	And default scale and rotation.
Command: **UCS**	Use Origin option to set UCS on left lot at lower left corner ④.
Command: **INSERT**	Use a -1 X scale to insert a flipped PLAN-1 on west lot. You don't need an = sign because the previous insertion defined PLAN-1 in your drawing's block table.
Insertion point: **88',36'**	
X scale factor <1> / Corner / XYZ: **-1**	The -1 flips it.
Y scale factor (default=X): **1**	
Rotation angle <E>: **<RETURN>**	
Command: **UCS**	Set origin for east lot at lower left corner ⑤ (see fig. 9.46).
Command: **UCS**	Use Z option to rotate about Z axis, making X axis parallel to front lot line.
Origin/ZAxis/3point/Entity/View/X/Y/Z/Prev/ Restore/Save/Del/?/<World>: **Z.**	
Rotation angle about Z axis <0.0>:	Pick lower left corner of lot at ⑤
Second point:	Pick lower right corner of lot at ⑥.
Command: **INSERT**	Insert PLAN-2=SIMPLE2 on east lot at 25'6,28' with rotation E.

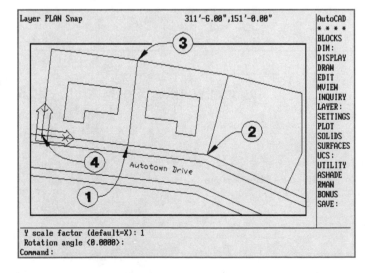

Figure 9.45:
Autotown with the first two floor plans.

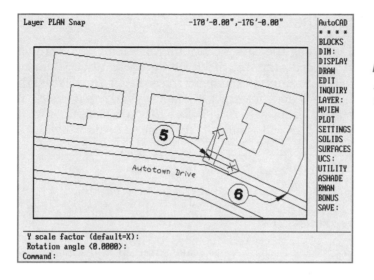

Figure 9.46:
Autotown with the last floor plan.

No subdivision is complete without a few cars scattered around. Insert some simple cars with CAR=CAR1. Pick your own insertion points, default or stretch the scales, and drag the angles.

Using INSERT to Insert Car Blocks

Command: **UCS**	Set UCS to World.
Command: **INSERT**	Insert CAR=CAR1 for the first car.
Command: **INSERT**	Insert CAR for the remaining cars.

Figure 9.47 shows how you might arrange the cars.

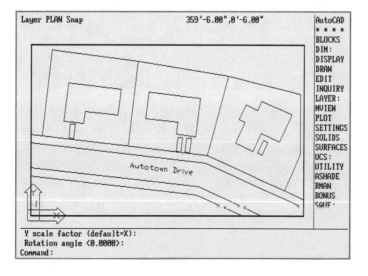

Figure 9.47:
Autotown with some inserted cars.

Using Preset Scale Insertions

After you have finished inserting the cars, spruce up the subdivision with variously sized trees. Remember, you drew the tree block with a one-unit (1") diameter. Use different scale values to create different diameter trees. Enter the desired diameter in inches because scale doesn't accept feet, only a factor by which it scales. It would be hard to accurately place 1" trees with drag before they are scaled, so we'll preset the scale factors. That way, they will display at the desired scale while dragging.

Using Preset Scale to Insert Trees

Command: **LAYER**	Set layer SITE current.
Command: **INSERT**	
Block name (or ?) <CAR>: **TREE=TREE1**	
Insertion point: **SCALE**	Apply a scale factor before insertion.
Scale factor: **240**	Make a tree 20' in diameter.
Insertion point:	Pick a point.
Rotation angle <0.00>: **<RETURN>**	

Continue the sequence above to insert more trees with different diameters. Figure 9.48 shows how you might arrange the trees.

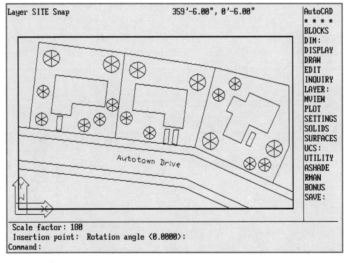

Figure 9.48:
Autotown with some trees.

Autotown with simple symbols is complete. If you were to try different arrangements, your regens would be quick because the blocks are simple. Before we redefine them with the complex blocks for presentation, let's review the blocks in your drawing and on your hard drive.

Displaying Blocks and Drawing Files

Use BLOCK and a ? (INSERT and a ? will also work) and DIR to look at your drawing directory files. (The DIR command is defined in AutoCAD's support disk file called ACAD.PGP. ACAD.PGP must be in your AutoCAD directory, or where AutoCAD can find it.) If DIR doesn't work, you can use the FILES command, located on the [UTILITY] screen menu.

Displaying Blocks and Drawing Files

```
Command: DIR                                          Display flips to text screen.
File specification: *.DWG
Volume in drive C is YOURDISK
Directory of  C:\IA-ACAD
SIMPLE1  DWG   1998 12-02-90    3:31p
SIMPLE2  DWG   3537 12-02-90    4:14p
AUTOCITY DWG   8085 12-02-90    9:06a
ATLAYOUT DWG   7549 12-02-90    9:34a
XSYMBOL  DWG   3848 12-02-90    8:45a
XTEST    DWG   6576 12-02-90    8:50a
AUTOTOWN DWG   3530 12-02-90   12:24p
COMPLEX1 DWG   2077 12-02-90    3:33p
COMPLEX2 DWG   3952 12-02-90    5:34p
CAR1     DWG   1863 12-02-90    3:29p
CAR2     DWG   2917 12-02-90    5:29p
MY-CAR   DWG   3313 12-02-90   11:52p
TREE1    DWG   1971 12-02-90    3:34p
TREE2    DWG   3003 12-02-90    5:24p
    ## File(s)   7501824 bytes free
```

Your DIR list will include other files. Your order, volume, directory names, numbers, and dates will differ from our list.

```
Command: BLOCK
Block name (or ?): ?
Block(s) to list <*>: <RETURN>
Defined blocks.
  ATLAYOUT                    Xref: resolved
  CAR
  PLAN-1
  PLAN-2
  TREE
  User     External    Dependent    Unnamed
  Blocks   References   Blocks       Blocks
    4          1           0            0
```

As you can see, each working block has two corresponding wblocked drawing files. The working blocks in the current drawing have simple PLAN-1, PLAN-2, TREE and CAR names because you used an equal sign when inserting them (as in PLAN-1=SIMPLE1). Maintaining the wblocked files separately makes it easy to keep track of both the simple and complex symbols. The BLOCK command also lists the xref site layout.

Now you can replace the simple blocks with the complex ones.

Block Redefinition

To redefine the blocks, we'll again use the equal sign option of the INSERT command. You do not have to actually complete the INSERT command. Just cut it short with a <^C> and the redefinition will occur.

Using INSERT = to Redefine Blocks

```
Command: INSERT
Block name (or ?) <TREE>: PLAN-1=COMPLEX1
Block PLAN-1 redefined
Regenerating drawing.
Insertion point: *Cancel*                       Press <^C>.
```

The existing block PLAN-1 was updated. Your drawing should look like figure 9.49.

Figure 9.49:
Updating PLAN-1 in
Autotown.

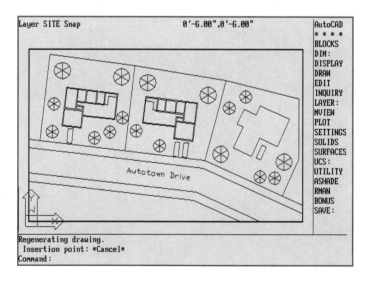

> **Tip:** If you have a lot of redefinitions to do, waiting for the regeneration each time is a nuisance. Turn REGENAUTO off and use a single regeneration when you finish.

Redefine the rest of the working blocks to match figure 9.50.

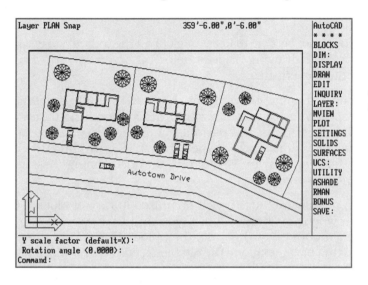

Figure 9.50:
A finished Autotown
with complex blocks.

Completing the Block Redefinitions With REGENAUTO Off

Command: **REGENAUTO**	
ON/OFF <On>: **OFF**	
Command: **INSERT**	Insert PLAN-2=COMPLEX2 and cancel insert.
Command: **INSERT**	Insert TREE=TREE2 and cancel insert.
Command: **INSERT**	Insert CAR=CAR2 and cancel insert.
Command: **REGENAUTO**	Turn it back on.
Regenerating drawing.	It automatically regenerates.
Command: **LAYER**	Set layer PLAN current.
Command: **INSERT**	Insert a CAR and place it on the road.
Command: **END**	

All the blocks are now redefined in the drawing, so the last insertion used the new CAR=CAR2 block definition.

Take one last look at Autotown. Your finished Autotown drawing has about 200 entities. If you had created the drawing without blocks and xrefs, it would have about 1000 entities. This gives you some idea of how efficient blocks and xrefs can be.

> **Note:** You can now delete all of the files created in this chapter except AUTOTOWN and ATLAYOUT.

Summing Up

Without blocks, you would not be able to keep track of all the individual components that make up even a simple drawing. Blocks help you organize your drawing by grouping useful collections of entities.

Xrefs help you carry that grouping convenience over into multiple drawings. Xrefs are most useful for keeping file size to a minimum, and for ensuring that a drawing has the most up-to-date revision of the parts it contains. Xrefs behave a lot like blocks, so you can consider them a special type of block. If controlling the proliferation of common data, keeping drawing size down, and decreasing disk usage are critical problems, then xrefs are for you.

A well-planned system usually includes a well-organized library of blocks. Don't be afraid to create blocks when you need them. If you find that you are copying the same group of unblocked objects all the time, then block them. If you need a new block similar to an existing block, explode the old block, edit it, and block it to a new name.

Use drag to see how a block is going to fit as you insert it. Use preset scale and rotation to see the block accurately as you drag it. Try to plan ahead to make groups of insertions so you can use AutoCAD's insertion default prompts instead of typing block names and options over and over.

Use MINSERT, MEASURE, and DIVIDE to place many blocks with one command. Use a *INSERT or EXPLODE to convert your blocks back into their individual entities.

Block redefinitions can be a big time saver. If you are doing a project which requires that a schematic or simple layout precede a more accurate and detailed drawing, a global replacement can automate an entire drawing revision cycle. You can also update a drawing by redefining obsolete blocks, or using xrefs instead of blocks.

Be careful when you insert from a disk file. Existing named symbols and objects and their parameters take precedence over incoming ones. When you do an insertion from a disk file, all named objects and symbols in the outside file get copied into the receiving file. If a layer (or style) already exists in the receiving drawing, it takes precedence. This may change text styles in the newly inserted parts or add to the current drawing file. To avoid that possibility, insert your parts as xrefs. Any duplicate layer names or other dependent symbols in the incoming drawing will be renamed, avoiding duplication. Then, if you need the data to become a permanent part of your drawing, use XREF Bind or XBIND to make it permanent.

Use PURGE or a WBLOCK *, QUIT sequence to keep your drawing file clean. PURGE is selective but WBLOCK *, QUIT will wipe out all unused blocks. To remove unused xref definitions, use XREF Detach.

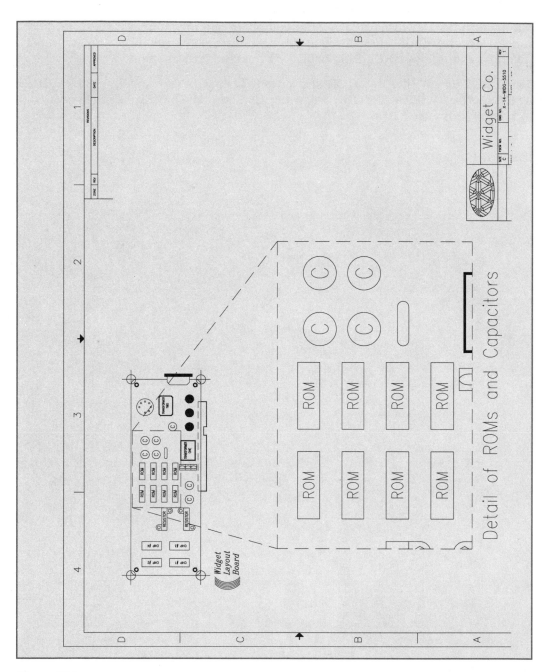

Figure 10.1:

A detail viewport and layout plotted from paper space sheet.

Sheet Composition, Scaling, and Plotting

COMPOSING AND PLOTTING A FINISHED DRAWING

How Plotting and Printing Work

You don't create a drawing in AutoCAD in the same way you draw with paper and pencil. Instead, you use AutoCAD's graphics editor to build a collection of data in memory. When you save your drawing, that data — lists and tables full of coordinates, numbers, and other cryptic information — is stored in a file on disk. Visually, the data has no resemblance at all to a drawing. When you edit the drawing, AutoCAD converts this data into a screen image by reading the database and issuing instructions that convert it into the image you see.

Generating a plot is similar to representing a drawing on the screen. But, instead of converting the data into pixels on your monitor, AutoCAD translates it into commands a plotter can understand. After initially setting up the plotter, these commands usually amount to little more than moving a pen up and down, and from one coordinate to another on the paper. If the pen is down when the move command is issued, a line is drawn. Lots of little line segments combine to plot arcs and text.

Luckily, AutoCAD takes care of translating the data in your file into plotter commands. All you have to do is set up the plotter, select the drawing, tell AutoCAD what to plot, and watch it plot. There are so many plotters available that it would be impossible to cover the configuration and setup of each one, especially since most plotters control many of the plotting parameters and functions from the plotter, rather than through AutoCAD. This chapter focuses on composing your drawing for plotting and actually creating plots.

There is no significant difference in the Release 10 and Release 11 plot process, except the plot rotation prompt is slightly different. However, Release 10 lacks the significant plot composition and scaling advantages of Release 11's paper space (see fig. 10.1).

Getting Ready to Plot

There is more to plotting than just issuing the PLOT command. When you install AutoCAD, you have to tell it what type of plotter you have, how it is connected, and what default settings to use. When you draw, you have to compose your finished drawing for plotting. When you plot, you have to load paper into the plotter, put in the right type of pens for the plotting media you are using, and make sure the plotter is ready to start receiving information. When you finally issue the PLOT command, you have to check each of its parameters to make sure they are correct for that particular plot. With the drawing file ready to plot, you access the PLOT or PRPLOT command, which passes the data through a sort of filter that controls the size and appearance of the finished plot, converts the data into plotter commands, and sends them to the plotter.

Configuring AutoCAD for Your Plotter

If you have not configured AutoCAD for your plotter, you should do so now. Consult your plotter manufacturer's instructions and your AutoCAD *Installation and Performance Guide*. To configure AutoCAD, select option 5 from AutoCAD's main menu. Then, select option 5, for plotter, from the configuration menu. Select the type of plotter you have from AutoCAD's list of plotters, using all of the default settings for now. If you do not have a plotter, but will be using a printer instead, or if you have both, follow the same procedure for configuring a printer, using option 6 in the configuration menu.

If you have already used your plotter or printer, chances are good that your settings no longer match the defaults. In the following exercises, we assume you are starting with the default settings, so go through the configuration routine described above. When asked whether you want to select a different plotter, answer yes, then re-select the same plotter as before. Then set all the plot parameters to their default values. The plotting examples in this chapter are based on a generic D-size (34 x 22) plotter and a generic printer. Your default pen speed, sheet size, and linetypes may vary from the examples in the book, but these settings will not affect the exercises.

The following checklist outlines items you should check when you initially configure your plotter:

First-Time Checklist

- Is the plotter plugged in?
- Is the plotter connected to the correct port on the computer?
- Does the interface cable between the plotter and computer match the connections shown in the AutoCAD installation manual?
- Has the plotter been configured in AutoCAD?
- Are the software configuration settings correct?
- Does the plotter self-test run properly, and does the drawing output look okay?
- Is the paper alignment correct, and do the pens operate properly?

If you are using a printer instead of a plotter, or a smaller plotter, most of the discussion in this chapter will still apply. For printers, substitute the PRPLOT command sequences for the PLOT command in the exercises and examples. In either case, adjust your paper size and scale accordingly. Some printers (such as PostScript printers) are configured as plotters. If you don't have a printer or plotter, but can carry a diskette to a system with one, you can plot to a disk file and then copy it to the plotter. This process is covered later in this chapter.

If your plotter or printer requires an ADI driver for AutoCAD, see the manufacturer's instructions and be sure to add any required commands to your IA.BAT or AUTOEXEC.BAT files.

There are two phases to plotting: setting up the plotter to run, and readying your drawing file with the proper scale and other plotter assignments in AutoCAD. Once you have configured the plotter in AutoCAD, you will only need to check and adjust parameters such as paper size and pen selection when you plot. Here's a checklist:

Every-Time Checklist

- Is the paper or other media loaded and properly aligned in the plotter? Does it move freely without striking the wall, cables, or other obstructions?
- Is the plotter adjusted for that size of paper?
- Are the pens in the holder? Are they primed and flowing freely? If the plotter uses removable carousels, is the correct carousel in the plotter? Does the carousel type match the pen type? Are the correct pens for the media being used, and is the speed set so they work without skipping?
- If the plotter shares a single COM port with another device such as a digitizer, has the selection switch been switched to the plotter, or has the cable been connected to the plotter?

■ Does the plotter need to be in Remote mode to sense incoming commands?

Now that you are ready, let's see how a plot works.

Accessing the PLOT Commands

There are a number of ways to access the PLOT and PRPLOT commands in AutoCAD. You can plot or print from the main menu by selecting option 3 or 4, from the [PLOT] menu item in the screen menu, from the [File] pull-down menu (see fig. 10.2), or by typing the command at the command prompt.

Figure 10.2:
The Plot pull-down and screen menus.

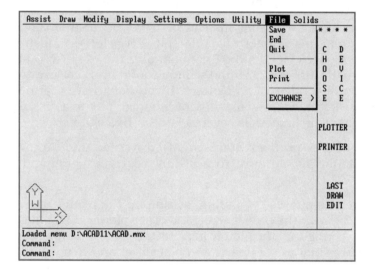

You can also use scripts to run plots automatically. The SCRIPT command is located in the [UTILITY] screen menu. Plotting from a script file is covered later in this chapter.

A Checkplot to Fit the Paper

When you plot a drawing to fit, AutoCAD calculates a ratio between the width of the drawing area you specify and the width of the plotting area. It performs the same calculation for the height of the drawing area and the height of the plotting area. The larger of the two will determine the actual size of the plot. Because the drawing will be plotted in proportion to its true size, some blank space may be left on the plot either for the width or height, depending on which proportion was smaller.

We'll first plot the drawing limits, fitting them to the sheet, rather than scaling the drawing to a specific size. Plotting using the Limits and Fit options will cause the area bounded by your drawing limits to be plotted as large as possible on the paper. We'll use the WIDGEDIT drawing from Chapter 6. If you didn't create that file, you can use any drawing since it will be plotted to fit the paper.

Then, select option 3 from the AutoCAD main menu, and follow the command sequence in the following exercise.

Plotting Limits to Fit the Paper

Select option 3, Plot a drawing, from the main menu and enter WIDGEDIT for name of drawing.

```
Specify the part of the drawing to be plotted by
    entering:
Display, Extents, Limits, View, or Window <>: L        Limits.
Plot will NOT be written to a selected file
Sizes are in Inches
Plot origin is at (0.00,0.00)
Plotting area is 33.00 wide by 21.00 (MAX size)       May be different on your
                                                      plotter.

Plot is NOT rotated
Pen width is 0.010
Area fill will NOT be adjusted for pen width
Hidden lines will NOT be removed
Plot will be scaled to fit available area
Do you want to change anything? <N> <RETURN>          Accept defaults, if they match
                                                      ours. Or answer Y and set
                                                      them to match.

Effective plotting area: 31.50 wide by 21.00 high
Press RETURN to continue or S to Stop for
    hardware setup <RETURN>
```

Make sure your plotter and paper are ready, then press <RETURN>.

```
Processing vector: nn                                 Processes each drawing vector
                                                      as plotting takes place.

Plot complete.
Press RETURN to continue: <RETURN>                    Main menu reappears.
```

If you used the WIDGEDIT drawing, your plot should resemble the one shown in figure 10.3. If the drawing didn't plot completely, check the limits in the drawing to ensure that they enclose the entire drawing. If it plotted sideways, you'll see later how to rotate it to fit the sheet.

If you have a printer, let's try it next.

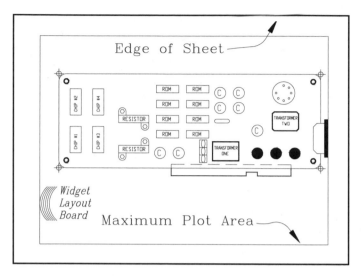

Figure 10.3:
The WIDGEDIT draw-ing, plotted with limits to fit.

Using Printer Plots

You can plot with a printer by using the PRPLOT command from within the drawing editor, or by using option 4 on the main menu. Since the printer is a simpler device, you have fewer prompts to step through. Printer plot the limits of the WIDGEDIT drawing.

Printer plot the WIDGEDIT drawing from the main menu, printing it to fit on your printer. In our example, we assume you are using a wide-carriage printer. If you have a narrow-carriage printer, the drawing will naturally print smaller.

Printer Plotting WIDGEDIT to Fit

Select option 4, Printer plot a drawing, from the main menu, and enter WIDGEDIT for name of drawing.

```
Specify the part of the drawing to be plotted by entering:
Display, Extents, Limits, View, or Window <>: L
Plot will NOT be written to a selected file
Sizes are in Inches
Plot origin is at (0.00,0.00)
Plotting area is 13.59 wide by 11.00 high (MAX size)
Plot is NOT rotated
Hidden lines will NOT be removed
Plot will be scaled to fit available area
Do you want to change anything? <N> <RETURN>
```
Accept the defaults, if they match ours. Or answer Y and set them to match.

Printer Plotting WIDGEDIT to Fit—continued

```
Effective plotting area:  13.59 wide by 8.69 high
Position paper in printer.
Press RETURN to continue:
Processing vector: nn                        AutoCAD cycles through the
                                             drawing.

Printer Plot Complete.
Press RETURN to continue <RETURN>
```

Tip: Take advantage of your printer plotter by using it to make easy and inexpensive checkplots. If it has high enough resolution, it is also useful for 11" x 8 1/2" detail prints.

That's basically what it takes to get a plot or printer plot. But you should compose your plot before you even turn on the plotter.

Composing and Finishing a Drawing for Plotting

The WIDGEDIT drawing makes a nice plot, but it isn't a finished drawing. A finished drawing is composed with a title block and usually includes more than one view of the object it represents. Often detailed views are included — views that may be at different scales than the original drawing. A finished drawing often includes annotations and dimensions. Some layers, like construction layers for example, may be turned off. Finished drawings usually include more than one line weight — usually controlled by plotting with different pens.

In the plot and printer plot we just did, we used AutoCAD's defaults for all of the plotting control parameters. Most finished drawings require changing one or more of those parameters for each plot. These include:

- Select the Part of the Drawing to Plot. Select how much of the drawing to plot by specifying Display, Extents, Limits, View, or Window.
- Select the Plotting Area. Specify a sheet size, such as C, D, and so on, for plotting area. Or specify a custom plot size by plot length and width if you are using an odd-sized sheet or need the plot to be a certain finished size.
- Select the Plot Scale. Choosing Fit will scale the drawing to fill the plotting area, proportional to the model, but not to any certain scale. To plot to a specific scale, enter a value in the form *Plotted Inches=Drawing Units*.

In Release 11, paper space makcs it easy to finish and compose a drawing for plotting. You simply treat paper space as an electronic sheet of paper sized to match your plotter media and compose your drawing in it. When you plot it, what you see on screen is what you get in the plot — at the precision and resolution of your plotter.

Finishing and composing a drawing without paper space is more complicated. Model space is the only drawing mode found in AutoCAD prior to Release 11. It is the environment in which you model your design, whether 2D or 3D. In model space, you can only plot the current viewport. In Release 11, this would be like plotting in tilemode viewports or in model space. Even if you have Release 11, try it. It's useful for quick checkplots, and will make your finished plots in Release 11 seem like a breeze by comparison.

> ***Tip:*** Think ahead about leaving room for a border and a title block. Make your limits your paper size, sizing and positioning your title block and border margins to compensate for the area the plotter needs to grasp the paper.

The first consideration to finishing and composing a drawing is deciding what to plot.

Controlling What to Plot

Many times, whether from model space or paper space, you will want to plot only a portion of your drawing. For example, you may need a checkplot of only one viewport, or of part of a viewport. If you use layers and colors to segregate your data, you might wish to plot only certain layers or colors. Both the PLOT and PRPLOT commands allow you to specify how much of the drawing to include in the plot, and to control how layers and colors plot. Combining this with the ability to move the location of the plot on the paper, scale the plot, and fit it to the paper gives you very fine control over the finished plot, even without paper space.

Plotting Different Areas of the Drawing

There are five options that control how much of the drawing will plot. When you first enter either the PLOT or PRPLOT commands, you are prompted to enter a selection for Display, Extents, Limits, View, or Window. Anything that falls outside the selected area is clipped and not plotted. Here is what each choice does:

PLOT and PRPLOT Options

Display   Selecting Display tells AutoCAD to use the image currently displayed on your screen to determine what to plot. Everything inside the area of the current viewport is plotted. (Remember, paper space itself or a single full-screen view in tilemode are considered viewports.) If you use PLOT or PRPLOT from the main menu, AutoCAD plots the display that was active in the current viewport when the drawing file was last saved.

Extents   Selecting Extents will cause AutoCAD to plot the extents of your drawing. Used in coordination with Fit, this will plot everything in the file to fit the paper.

Limits   Specifying Limits causes AutoCAD to plot everything within the drawing limits.

View   Selecting View plots a named view that you have previously saved. You can save a number of different views with different names, then use VIEW to plot each one by name. Saving an appropriate view named PLOT in every drawing makes plotting easy to standardize.

Window   Selecting Window allows you to define a rectangular window around the area of the drawing you wish to plot. Normally, you would use the Window option only when you are plotting or printing from within the drawing editor. However, if you select Window when plotting or printing from the main menu, AutoCAD will prompt you for the coordinates of the opposing corners of the window to determine what to plot.

Setting the Plotting Scale

In the first exercise, you plotted the WIDGEDIT drawing to fit the paper in the plotter. While this gave you a plotted image proportional to the original model, it wasn't set to any specific scale. Most of the time your drawings do need to be plotted to scale.

In paper space, you compose your drawing in paper space limits that equal your sheet size and plot it at full scale.

In model space or with Release 10, sizing your plot to a particular scale is more involved but fairly straightforward. It involves finding a ratio between the actual size of the model and the scale at which you want it to plot. For example, let's say you have a house plan drawn actual size, and want to plot it at a scale of 1/4" = 1'-0". When you specify a plot scale in the PLOT command, you simply type the corresponding scale in units that AutoCAD can interpret, instead of typing Fit. In this case you could type either 1/4"=1'0 or 1=48, and the drawing would plot to that scale. Optionally, you could enter the same value in decimal form, such as .25=12, or .020833=1. This scales the model correctly, but what about scaling the annotations?

Scaling Annotations, Symbols, and Dimensions

How can you determine what size your text, bubbles, and dimensions will plot? The key is to understand that everything in your model is related to model space, or real-world dimensions. You nearly always draw objects actual size, and scale them when it is time to plot. In the previous example, the house plan would have been drawn actual size. Let's say you wanted your text to plot 1/8" high. If you were to create your text and other annotations at 1/8", the dimensions and notes would be so small relative to the house plan itself that you couldn't read them. It would be like standing 200 feet above the house while trying to read a newspaper resting on the ground.

When you create your dimensions and text, you need to know at what size you will eventually plot the drawing. In this case (1/4" = 1'-0"), you need to find a relationship between 1/8" on the paper and the size of the text in the model. If 1/4" on paper equals 12" in the model, then 1/8" equals 6", so text and dimensions should be drawn 6" high in the drawing to plot 1/8" on paper at this scale. Dimension text and symbols are scaled similarly.

Let's take one more example. Say you find that your house plan is too big to fit on the paper at 1/4" = 1'-0", so you decide to scale it to 3/16" = 1'-0" instead. But, you still want all of the text to plot 1/8" high. 1/8" is two-thirds of 3/16" (2/16 compared to 3/16) and 8" is two-thirds of 12", so you need 8" text to get 1/8" high characters on paper.

These same scales apply to text and annotations that you put on your model in model space viewports even if you compose the final drawing in paper space. Later, we'll explore some paper space alternatives.

Table 10.1 shows the model text size needed to achieve a specific plotted text size at some common scales.

Composing a Title Block in Model Space

Drawing in full scale brings up the problem of how to place a D-size sheet border and title block around a model that may be a hundred feet wide. The answer is simple: You create the title block full size (34 x 22 or 36 x 24 for a D-size sheet). Then you insert it as a block in your drawing, using the inverse of the scale that you would use to plot the drawing. Let's look at an example and see why.

Table 10.1
Common Text Sizes at Various Scales

Scale	Plotted Text Size	Text Size (Model)
1/8"=1'-0"	1/8"	12"
	3/16"	18"
	1/4"	24"
3/16"=1'-0"	1/8"	8"
	3/16"	12"
	1/4"	16"
1/4"=1'-0"	1/8"	6"
	3/16"	8"
	1/4"	12"
1/2"=1'-0"	1/8"	3"
	3/16"	4.5"
	1/4"	6"
1"=1'-0"	1/8"	1.5"
	3/16"	2.25"
	1/4"	3"
1 1/2"=1'-0"	1/8"	1"
	3/16"	1.5"
	1/4"	2"
1:2	.125"	.25"
	.1875"	.3875"
	.25"	.5"
1:10	.125"	12.5"
	.1875"	18.75"
	.25"	25"
2:1	.125"	.0625"
	.1875"	.09375"
	.25"	.125"

We'll take the same example we used before — a house plan drawn actual size that needs to go on a D-size sheet at a scale of 1/4" = 1'-0". You'd draw the house plan and enter a scale of 1/4"=1'0 (equal to 1:48) when prompted for a scale in PLOT. Your title block is drawn actual size also, only 34" or 36" wide. When you insert the title block using the BLOCK command, you'd have to scale it up proportionally to the model. So if you insert the title block drawing into the model, and scale it 48 times larger to fit around the plan of the house, it will scale back to its original size when the drawing is plotted.

A Model Space Alternative: Faking Paper Space

Another approach would be to scale the model drawing down and insert it into the title block *before* you plot. This has the advantage of always plotting at a standard 1=1 scale, and it lets you preview the *what you see is what you'll plot* image on screen. It also makes it much easier to combine multiple scales of details in a single drawing. There are two ways to do this.

You can do it in a single drawing file. First, create a block of your entire drawing and don't OOPS it back. Next, insert your title block at 1=1 scale on its own layer and zoom to the title block. Then, insert your entire drawing into the title block on the title block layer at the scale that you would have used to plot it in the previously discussed method. In this example, you'd simply insert it at 1/48. If you later need to make changes to the drawing model, freeze the title block layer, *INSERT the drawing block at 1=1 scale, zoom out and make changes, and reblock it to the same name. When you thaw and zoom back to the title block layer, you'll find the changes due to the block redefinition.

Or, you can create a separate 1=1 scale title block drawing and insert the model drawing file into it at the appropriate scale. If you make changes to the model drawing file, reinsert it with an equal sign to redefine it in the title block.

In either case, you plot the results at full scale. If you need to add annotations or title text, you do it at the real-world scale you want it to be in the plot. This method makes multiple model views or detail with varying scales in one drawing easier, but it is not as easy as using paper space.

Plotting Multiple Model Views or Details

Composing multiple model views or details with varying scales in one drawing is easy in paper space. Basically, you just set up each desired view or detail in its own viewport, scale it, and plot everything at once from paper space. We'll cover the full process later in this chapter.

You can fake the paper space technique by inserting a block for each desired view or detail into your 1=1 title block. Scale each insertion as if you were plotting it to scale by itself. As you will see in the 3D chapters, you can use UCSs when you wblock your blocks to disk to create varying viewpoints of the same model. Then you can insert these into a single title block.

A third alternative is to scale and plot each view or detail separately, but all on the same sheet of paper. This requires the ability to position each plot where you want it on the plotter sheet.

Positioning the Plot on the Paper

However you compose and scale your plot, whether you plan to plot it all at once or plot separate views or details on the same sheet of paper, your next decision is how to place the plot on the paper.

All plotters have a limit to how wide a drawing they can plot, and cut sheet plotters are also limited in how long a plot they can produce. Roll plotters (plotters that use a roll of plotting media instead of cut sheets) are limited as to width, but can often plot a drawing as long as the length of the media on the roll. Since cut sheet plotters are much more common than roll plotters, we'll concentrate on cut sheet plotters.

Plot Origin vs. Area-to-Plot Origin

A plotter's starting pen position is the plotter origin. The plot places the lower left corner of the area to plot (display, extents, limits, view, or window) at the plotter origin. On a pen plotter, the plotter origin is usually at or near the lower left corner of the paper. For a printer plotter, it is the upper left corner. If you tell AutoCAD to rotate the plot, the origin changes. The rectangular boundary that defines the maximum plotting area for a plotter is called its hard clip limits. If you place a point in each of the opposite corners of the hard clip limits, one of the points will be the plotter origin.

You can determine your plotter's origin and hard clip limits by separately plotting a vertical line and a horizontal line (length is unimportant). Plot them on the same sheet, using Extents and Fit. They will both start at the plotter origin and extend to the X or Y limits.

Normally, AutoCAD places the lower left corner of the part of the drawing you specify to plot at the plotter origin. To plot the drawing at a particular point on the sheet, as you would to separately plot multiple views, you can tell AutoCAD to move the plotter origin. Do this by specifying an X,Y displacement in plotter units at the plot origin prompt. By specifying a different displacement for each view or detail, you can plot multiple images on a sheet, one at a time.

Plot Standardization

Even normal plots (one per sheet) are easier if you standardize the relationship of the plotter origin to the lower left corner of the area you specify to plot. We standardized the book's drawings by setting limits to the sheet size (in drawing units). If your plotter can plot the full sheet from edge to edge, you can plot limits at the default plot origin (home position at the lower left corner of the sheet). But most plotters grip a portion of the paper during the plot. This means the lower left corner of the paper is not at the plotter origin, so you can't plot limits to scale. You can still get an accurately scaled plot by doing a window plot or plotting a named view. Set the lower left corner of the window or view in the drawing at an offset from the lower left corner of the limits. This offset should be equal to the distance from the lower left corner of the sheet to the plotter origin for your plotter. Unless you are plotting at full scale, you need to convert this offset to drawing units (offset times scale factor). Set the upper right corner to encompass the area you want to plot; anything outside the window or view (or outside your plotter's hard clip limits) will be clipped. Make sure any title block you use fits in the window or view and is within your plotter's hard clip limits.

Using a view named PLOT, you can standardize plotting at the appropriate scale at the default plotter origin. You can further standardize your plotting by combining this technique with using paper space or the fake paper space method. That way, you would always plot a view named PLOT at full scale at the default plotter origin.

Plotting a Standard View Named PLOT to Scale

To see how this works, and to practice plotting a drawing to scale, let's plot the WIDGEDIT drawing from Chapter 6 again. WIDGEDIT was created with 11" x 8.5" limits, matching an A-size sheet at 1=1 scale or a C-size (22 x 17) sheet at 2=1 scale (twice real size). We'll plot it at 2=1 scale. If you didn't create the drawing, substitute the WIDGET drawing from Chapter 5, the IA6WIDG3 drawing from the IA DISK, or any other drawing with 11" x 8.5" limits.

We'll assume that our generic plotter's origin is offset 1/2" in the X axis and 3/4" in the Y axis from the lower left corner of the sheet. This makes your offset .25,.375 (.5,.75 divided by a 2:1 plot-to-drawing scale). Placing the lower left corner of your PLOT view at .25,.375 will place the 0,0 point of your limits precisely at the corner of the plot sheet. If your plotter origin offset is different, substitute your X,Y offset divided by 2. If you're using a printer plotter or if your maximum sheet size is smaller than C-size, plot to a smaller scale and adjust your offset to match.

Plotting WIDGEDIT to Scale, and Moving the Origin

Edit an EXISTING drawing named WIDGEDIT.

Command: **Zoom**	Zoom All.
Command: **VIEW**	
?/Delete/Restore/Save/Window: **W**	
View name to save: **PLOT**	
First corner: **.25,.375**	Or substitute your calculated offset.
Other corner: **11,8.5**	
Command: **PLINE**	Draw border, no larger than half your hard clip limits.

Plotting WIDGEDIT to Scale, and Moving the Origin—continued

Command: **POINT**   Place a point at your calculated
                                                            offset point.

Command: **PLOT**
Specify the part of the drawing to be plotted
    by entering:
Display, Extents, Limits, View, or Window <L>: **V**
View name: **PLOT**
Plot will NOT be written to a selected file
Sizes are in Inches
Plot origin is at (0.00,0.00)
Plotting area is 44.72 wide by 23.30 high
    (MAX size)   Yours may be different.
Plot is NOT rotated
Pen width is 0.010
Area fill will NOT be adjusted for pen width
Hidden lines will NOT be removed
Plot will be scaled to fit available area
Do you want to change anything? <N> **Y**

For now, ignore the color, linetype, and pen parameters that display.

Do you want to change any of the above
    parameters? <N> **<RETURN>**
Write the plot to a file? <N> **<RETURN>**
Size units (Inches or Millimeters) <I>: **<RETURN>**
Plot origin in Inches <0.00,0.00>: **<RETURN>**
Standard values for plotting size
Size   Width   Height
A   10.50   8.00
B   16.00   10.00
C   21.00   16.00
D   33.00   21.00
MAX   44.72   22.30
Enter the Size or Width,Height (in Inches)
    <MAX>: **C**   Or your maximum, if less than C.
Rotate plot 0/90/180/270 : **<RETURN>**   Answer 90 for a printer plotter.
Pen width <0.010>: **<RETURN>**
Adjust area fill boundaries for pen width?
    <N> **<RETURN>**
Remove hidden lines? <N> **<RETURN>**
Specify scale by entering:
Plotted Inches=Drawing Units or Fit or ?
    <0.25=12>: **2=1**   Or your scale, if smaller.
Effective plotting area: 21.00 wide by 16.00 high
Position paper in plotter.   Make sure your plotter and paper
                                                            are ready.

▶ **Plotting WIDGEDIT to Scale, and Moving the Origin—continued**

```
Press RETURN to continue or S to Stop for
   hardware setup  <RETURN>
Processing vector: nn                            Processes each drawing vector.
```

Plotting takes place.

```
Plot complete.
Press RETURN to continue: <RETURN>              Drawing reappears.
```

The widget should have plotted at twice its real-world size, with the lower left corner of the border exactly at your plotter origin and the lower left limits at the sheet corner (see fig. 10.4).

Figure 10.4:
Plot offset for
WIDGEDIT at 2=1
scale.

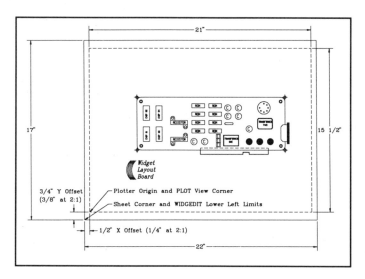

If your plotter offset is too large and your hard clip limits are too small to accommodate your standard title sheet, perhaps you can expand them.

Expanding the Plotting Area

There are times when your drawing doesn't fit within the hard clip limits, perhaps by a fraction of an inch. With many plotters, the hard clip limits can be expanded. In some cases, this can increase the plot area half an inch or more. Check your plotter documentation to see if yours offers an expanded mode. Usually, expanded mode is controlled by a small switch on the plotter. Expanded mode moves the location of the 0,0 plotter origin to the corner of the expanded area.

Sometimes, the expanded plotter origin comes too close to the pinch wheels that hold the paper against the plotter drum, sometimes even moving past the wheels. If this happens with an ink plot, the wheels will smear anything drawn inside their area. To eliminate this problem, you can adjust the plotter origin away from the pinch wheel. To do so, enter a small offset at the Plot origin in Inches <0.00,0.00>: prompt.

If you have AutoCAD Release 11, you'll find that composing a plot in paper space is even easier than using our fake paper space technique.

Composing a Plot in Paper Space

One of paper space's primary functions is to make plotting easier, particularly in 3D work. The process you go through each time you take your drawing from the design stage to a finished plot is pretty much the same. Here's a checklist that will give you an idea of what steps to take after your design is drawn:

- Enter PSPACE and use MVIEW to create as many viewports as you need for the various views and details you want to plot. If your viewports exceed 15, turn them on 15 at a time and plot twice on a single sheet, or put details in separate drawing files and insert them or attach them as xrefs in paper space before plotting. You can also create and draw in viewports that you don't intend to plot, to work on the main or master model from which the other views are derived. You can do the bulk of your design work now or after planning the arrangement of views in the title sheet.

- Insert your title sheet into paper space at full scale, or attach it as an xref. Put it on its own layer so you can freeze it as you work on your drawing. Plan how the viewports to be plotted are to be arranged and scaled in the title sheet. You can draw construction lines on a layer that won't be plotted to keep track of your arrangement. Freeze the title sheet layer.

- Enter model space and create or finish drawing your views and details. Compose each view that will be plotted as if it were a separate drawing in its own viewport. You don't need to have the viewports in their final arrangement as you work — arrange and size them for drawing convenience. But keep the planned scale and size of each in mind, particularly as you add annotations. You can control layers independently in each viewport so annotations for one won't show up in others. Finish the model, complete with most dimensions, notes, and other details.

- Enter paper space and thaw your blank title sheet. Erase or freeze the layers of viewports that won't be plotted.

- Resize, stretch, and move the viewports to be plotted to match your planned arrangement in the sheet.

■ Enter model space and use the ZOOM command's *n*XP option (where *n* is your scale value) to scale each view or detail to the correct plotted scale. This is covered in the next section.

■ Re-enter paper space. Add any annotations or dimensions that you wish to do in paper space (dimensions can be automatically scaled to the viewport's contents). Insert any details or attach any xrefs that are stored as separate drawing files. (These could be ordinary blocks or blocked viewports. If viewports, you'll have to turn them on.) Fill in your title block information.

■ Create a view named PLOT with its lower left corner offset to match your plotter's offset. Restore the view. What you see is what you'll get. Make any final layer on/off or freeze/thaw adjustments.

■ Use the PLOT (or PRPLOT) command to plot the PLOT view at full scale.

> **Note:** If you plot using the Display option and have multiple viewports set, you get a plot of whatever is displayed in the current viewport.

The procedure outlined above introduced something new: zooming relative to paper scale.

Scaling Viewports Relative to Paper Scale

In the ZOOM command, entering a scale factor followed by XP will cause the image to display relative to your paper scale. (The XP stands for "times paper scale.") If you enter a factor of 1XP, the viewport will display the image at full scale (1=1) relative to your paper. When you plot the drawing at full scale from paper space, the viewport will plot at the scale factor specified by ZOOM XP. Entering a zoom factor of .5XP would cause the image in the viewport to display at half size.

You determine the ZOOM XP scale as a decimal scale factor in the same manner you would figure scale if you were plotting that viewport by itself. For example, if you want a view of your model at 1/4" = 1'-0", which is 1:48, divide 1 by 48 to get 0.020833 and type 0.020833XP in the ZOOM command as your scale factor.

After you use ZOOM XP, be careful not to do other zooms in or out in model space. Pan is safe and good for fine-tuning the view. If you use ZOOM Dynamic for panning, be sure that you don't change the size of the zoom box.

> **Note:** Scaling a viewport like this only makes sense if you are working in model space (MSPACE). ZOOM XP still works in paper space or tilemode viewports, but its effect is identical to ZOOM X in those cases.

Setting Up Paper Space Views for Plotting

Whether you used tiled or untiled viewports, you will model your design in one or more model space viewports, then compose your title block sheet in paper space for plotting as outlined above.

If you need more than one title sheet to contain all of your views and details, you can insert more than one copy of your title block, then open viewports accordingly on each sheet. You can define plot views with names like PLOT1, PLOT2, and so on. If you have more than 15 total viewports, you will have to use MVIEW to turn them on and off as you plot the different plot views. This keeps you from having to duplicate the model in separate files for each sheet.

There is more to composing a sheet than haphazardly opening viewports on the page and scaling the views inside them. You can overlap viewports if you wish. You can turn viewport frames off by layer control if you don't want them to plot. Their contents will still plot unless their appropriate layers are frozen.

Let's compose a new plot and arrange the viewports. We'll use the WIDGEDIT drawing from Chapter 6 again, or you can substitute the WIDGET drawing from Chapter 5, the IA6WIDG3 drawing from the IA DISK, or any other drawing with 11" x 8.5" limits. We'll compose two viewports on a 22" x 17" sheet and plot it at full scale. If you don't have a C-size plotter, compose it on an 11" x 8.5" sheet and reduce all the scale factors by half. We'll just draw a simple polyline border to represent the title block sheet that we'd normally insert or attach. When you start out, your drawing should look like the one shown in figure 10.5.

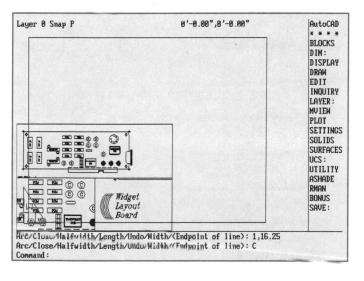

Figure 10.5:
Widget in paper space before rearranging the viewports.

Composing a Plot in Paper Space Viewports

 Begin a NEW drawing named PSPLOT=IA6WIDG4.

Begin a NEW drawing named PSPLOT=WIDGEDIT.

Begin a NEW drawing named PSPLOT=WIDGEDIT.

Command: **TILEMODE**	
New value for TILEMODE <1>:	Set to 0.
Entering Paper space. Use MVIEW to insert Model space viewports.	

The three viewports from Chapter 5 reappear. Ignore them for now.

Command: **LIMITS**	Set from 0,0 to 22,17 for a 1=1 scale C-size plot. Notice that paper space limits are independent from model space.
Command: **GRID**	Set to 1.
Command: **ZOOM**	Zoom All.
Command: **PLINE**	Draw a border from 1,.75 to 21,.75 to 21,16.25 to 1,16.25 and close it.

Now we need to arrange the viewports in the border. First, the top viewport:

Command: **MOVE**	Use osnap INT to move upper left corner of top viewport to upper left corner of border.
Command: **STRETCH**	Use a crossing window and osnap INT to stretch lower right corner of top viewport to point 18,9.

Maybe it would be easier to erase the viewports and insert the last one with MVIEW.

Command: **ERASE**	Erase lower left and lower right viewports.
Command: **MVIEW** ON/OFF/Hideplot/Fit/2/3/4/Restore/<First Point>: **7,2**	
Other corner:	Use osnap INT to pick lower right corner of upper viewport.
Command: **MSPACE**	Now we'll pan and scale the viewport contents.

Select upper viewport and toggle its grid off.

Command: **ZOOM** All/Center/Dynamic/Extents/Left/Previous/ Vmax/Window/<Scale(X/XP)>: **1XP**	Scale the image to 1=1.

Composing a Plot in Paper Space Viewports—continued

Command: **PAN**   Center the image.

Select lower right viewport and toggle its grid off.

Command: **ZOOM**   Zoom it 4XP to scale its image
                                                           to 4=1.

Command: **ZOOM**   Use Dynamic to pan to eight
                                                           ROMs and four capacitors
                                                           without changing size of zoom
                                                           box.

Command: **PAN**   Fine-tune to center them in the
                                                           view.

The results of this command sequence are shown in figure 10.6.

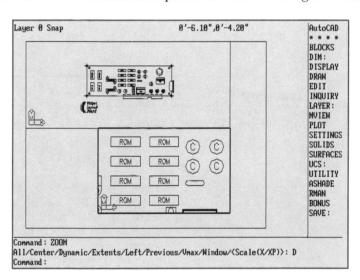

Figure 10.6:
Widget viewports
arranged and scaled.

Normally, you would add annotations and other finishing touches to each viewport, using unique layers to prevent visibility in other viewports. Let's assume you've done that. You may also want to add annotations in paper space. You can use osnaps when in paper space to snap to objects within viewports. This helps align and position your paper space objects and annotations.

Tip: Use the MVIEW Hideplot option in 3D work to specify which viewport(s) should have hidden lines removed when plotted.

Let's turn the viewport frames off and tie the 4X scale viewport to the full image with two dashed rectangles and dashed zoom lines (see fig. 10.7). This will show the reader of the plot where the 4X image comes from.

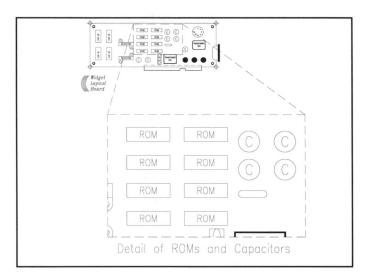

Figure 10.7:
The plotted widget with two viewports.

Annotating in Paper Space

Command: **PSPACE**

Command: **LAYER** Create layer DONTPLOT and turn it off.
Create layer DASHED and make it linetype DASHED. Set it current.

Command: **PLINE** Use osnap INT to trace dashed rectangle over frame of bottom viewport.

Command: **CHPROP** Select both viewports and change to layer DONTPLOT.
You'll have to select the dashed polyline also, then remove it from selection set with Remove mode.

Command: **REDRAW**

Command: **COPY** Copy Last (the polyline) with a 0,0 displacement.

Command: **SCALE** Scale Last, pick any base point, and enter .25 as scale factor.

Command: **MOVE** Move Last to the area of the board that matches the 4X view.

Command: **REDRAW**

Annotating in Paper Space—continued

Command: **LINE**   Use osnap INT,QUI to connect
                                           two rectangles with diagonals.

Command: **DTEXT**   At this point you might also add
                                           annotations and title text.
                                           Just set your text height to what
                                           you want in the plot.

Command: **VIEW**   Window a view and name it
                                           PLOT. Set lower left corner to
                                           match your plotter offset.

Command: **PLOT**   Plot a view named PLOT at 1=1
                                           scale on a C-size sheet.

```
Specify the part of the drawing to be plotted
   by entering:
Display, Extents, Limits, View, or Window <L>: V
View name: PLOT
Plot will NOT be written to a selected file
Sizes are in Inches
Plot origin is at (0.00,0.00)
Plotting area is 21.00 wide by 16.00 high (C size)
Plot is NOT rotated
Pen width is 0.010
Area fill will NOT be adjusted for pen width
Hidden lines will NOT be removed
Scale is 1=1.00"
Do you want to change anything? <N>
```
Check your scale.
Answer yes if you need to
change anything
to match the settings shown
here. Plot the drawing.

Command: **QUIT**

The advantage of annotating in paper space is that you don't have to scale it. You work at real size and plot it at 1=1. The disadvantage is that the annotation is not tied to the viewport contents.

Now that you know how to set up your title block and viewports manually, you'll appreciate the fact that AutoCAD can automate the creation and insertion of title blocks and viewport configurations.

Automating Your Plot Setup With MVSETUP.LSP

The MVSETUP.LSP routine is an AutoLISP program located on the [BONUS] screen menu. If you chose not to install all files when you installed AutoCAD, you may not have MVSETUP.LSP on your system. If not, copy the file MVSETUP.LSP from your original AutoCAD BONUS disk into your AutoCAD directory, your IA-ACAD directory, or the directory where you keep your AutoLISP files.

To use MVSETUP.LSP, select [BONUS] from the main screen menu, then select [MVSETUP]. The first time you use MVSETUP will take longer than subsequent uses, because MVSETUP sets itself up on your system. The first time each title block size is used also takes longer because it builds the title block from scratch. The routine offers you the option of wblocking the title blocks to disk, so it can fly through your sheet layout in subsequent uses. After you initially load MVSETUP, you can execute it as a command with the name MVS.

MVSETUP has options for aligning, creating, and scaling viewports, and inserting a title block. Not all of these apply to your initial setup, so you will probably use MVSETUP more than once on each drawing. We'll start by loading the WIDGEDIT drawing, then use MVSETUP to insert a title block and viewports. We'll save the ANSI-C title block it creates for use later in the book.

Setting Up a Widget Plot With MVSETUP

Begin a NEW drawing named MVPLOT=WIDGEDIT.

Select **[BONUS] [next] [MVSETUP]**	From the screen menu.
MVSetup loaded. Type MVS to set up your drawing. Command:	MVS is executed automatically.

Paperspace/Modelspace is disabled. The old setup
   will be invoked unless it is enabled. Enable
   Paper/Modelspace? <Y>: **<RETURN>**	

Entering Paper space. Use MVIEW to insert Model space viewports.	
Regenerating drawing.	The three existing viewports appear.
Align viewports/Create viewports/Scale viewports/Title block/Undo: **C**	Create.
Delete objects/Undo/<Create viewports>:**D**	Delete.
Select the objects to delete:	Select all existing viewports.
Delete objects/Undo/<Create viewports>: **<RETURN>**	
Add/Delete/Redisplay/<Number of entry to load>: **<RETURN>**	
Align viewports/Create viewports/Scale viewports /Title block/Undo: **T**	Title block.
Delete objects/Origin/Undo/<Insert title block>: **<RETURN>**	Insert title.
Available title block options:	
0: None 1: ANSI-V Size	

Setting Up a Widget Plot With MVSETUP—continued

```
2:      ANSI-A Size
3:      ANSI-B Size
4:      ANSI-C Size
5:      ANSI-D Size
6:      ANSI-E Size
7:      Arch/Engineering (24 x 36)
Add/Delete/Redisplay/<Number of entry to
   load>: 4
```
Enter 4 to insert a C-size title block (see fig. 10.8).

```
Create a drawing named ansi-c.dwg?
  <Y>: <RETURN>
```
Saves it for later.
```
Align viewports/Create viewports/Scale
  viewports/Title block/Undo: C
Delete objects/Undo/<Create viewports>: <RETURN>

Available Mview viewport layout options:

0:      None
1:      Single
2:      Std. Engineering
```
Sets up top, front, right, and 3D isometric viewports.
```

3:      Array of Viewports
Add/Delete/Redisplay/<Number of entry to
   load>: 3
```
Array.
```
Bounding area for viewports.  First point: 1,16
Other point: 16,2.5
Number of viewports in X. <1>: 2
Number of viewports in Y. <1>: 2
Distance between viewports in X. <0.0>: .5
Distance between viewports in Y. <0.5>: <RETURN>

Align viewports/Create viewports/Scale
  viewports/Title block/Undo: S
```
Scale.
Select the upper right viewport.
```
Select the viewports to scale:
Select objects: 1 selected, 1 found

Select objects: <RETURN>

Enter the ratio of paper space units to model
  space units...
Number of paper space units. <1.0>: 2
```
Scale the view to 2:1.
```
Number of model space units. <1.0>: <RETURN>

Align viewports/Create viewports/Scale viewports/
  Title block/Undo: <RETURN>
```

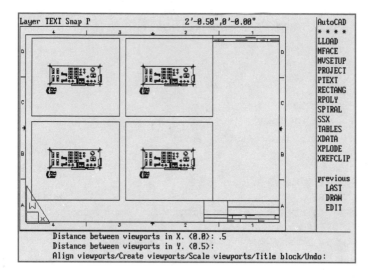

Figure 10.8:
A title block inserted
by MVSETUP.

You now have a title block that shows four viewports of WIDGEDIT, with the upper right viewport at a plot scale of 2:1 (see fig. 10.9). But that's not all MVSETUP can do. You can use MVSETUP to automatically align images in two different viewports.

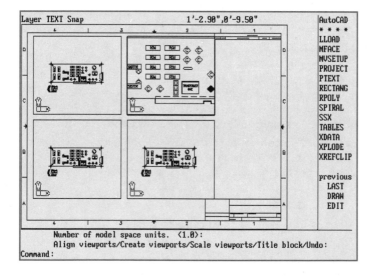

Figure 10.9:
Viewports created
and scaled by
MVSETUP.

Aligning Viewport Images

Often, you want common elements in adjacent views of your drawing to line up with each other. This is particularly important in multiview 3D plots. While you can do this manually, MVSETUP makes it much easier. To use MVSETUP to align your images, start in paper space and zoom in on the two bottom viewports. Enter model space and misalign the bottom left viewport with PAN (see fig. 10.10). Then use MVSETUP to realign the image between the two viewports. When you finish the following command sequence, your screen should look like the one shown in figure 10.11.

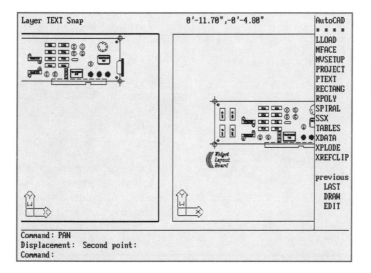

Figure 10.10:
Misaligned images.

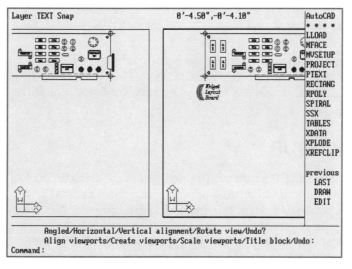

Figure 10.11:
Images realigned by
MVSETUP.

Realigning Views With MVSETUP

```
Command: PSPACE
Command: ZOOM                                    Zoom in on adjacent halves of
                                                 the two bottom viewports.

Command: MSPACE

Select the bottom left viewport.

Command: PAN                                      Pan the image in the bottom
                                                  left viewport up a little.

Now, use MVSETUP to realign the two views.

Command: MVS                                      Type it or select [MVSETUP]
                                                  from the [BONUS] menu.

Align viewports/Create viewports/Scale viewports/
   Title block/Undo: A                            Align.
Angled/Horizontal/Vertical alignment/Rotate
   view/Undo? H
Basepoint: ENDP of                                Pick endpoint of a line in the
                                                  left viewport.
Other point: ENDP of                              Pick endpoint of a correspond-
                                                  ing line in the right viewport.
Angled/Horizontal/Vertical alignment/Rotate
   view/Undo? <RETURN>
Align viewports/Create viewports/Scale viewports/
   Title block/Undo: <RETURN>
Command: QUIT
```

Now, your viewport images should be lined up again. When pan, zoom, and other functions misalign views and change the scale of a drawing you have already composed for plotting, realign and rescale all of your views as the last thing you do before plotting.

Customizing MVSETUP

You can customize the MVSETUP setup routine to use your own title blocks, custom viewport layouts, and more. Its defaults are contained in an ASCII file named MVSETUP.DFV, which contains instruction on how to customize it. The easiest form of customization is to simply edit the standard title block drawings it creates, making them conform to your standards and adding your standard title text.

We've made several references to controlling layer visibility when plotting. Let's look into it.

Controlling Layer Visibility in Plots

You've seen how you can place paper space viewports on layers which you turn off to prevent their plotting. And we've discussed how AutoCAD works like overlay drafting, turning on and off combinations of layers to view the drawing data you need to see. This layer control gives you great flexibility in getting a number of finished plots out of a single drawing file. Whatever layers are on and thawed get plotted, and those that are off or frozen don't get plotted. Layer control is more sophisticated in paper space viewports than in tilemode or model space, so we'll examine paper space first.

Layer Control in Paper Space

The ability to control your plot by layer is one of the most important aspects of plotting. Used properly, this technique can save you from duplicating work and filling up your disk with duplicate drawings. To see why, we'll use a facilities plan as an example, but the same concept applies to nearly any type of drawing you create in AutoCAD.

We'll assume we have a site plan and a floor plan, as well as electrical, piping, and equipment layouts. This master facilities plan will be used to create five separate plots — one for each of the areas listed. We could make five copies of the drawing, erasing everything except what is needed in each, but that presents some major problems. If a change is made to the facility, all five drawings will have to be revised. Plus, if you make a change to one of the drawings, it will be difficult to see how it affects the other areas if they are detailed on separate drawings. But that doesn't have to be a problem, if we plan ahead.

The five different systems on the master drawing are all separated onto different layers. When you work on the drawing, you can leave all of the layers turned on so all of the pertinent information gets displayed on the screen. Any change to the electrical system, for example, shows conflicts with the other systems.

To plot the finished drawings, you can create five different title sheets in paper space and named plot views, one for each finished plot. Then, opening model space viewports on each sheet, you would position and scale the model images for each, adding any additional notation or details needed. Use the LAYER command to freeze the unnecessary layers for each sheet when you plot it. Freezing a layer in one viewport freezes it in all. Of course, all that freezing and thawing as you go from view to view to work or plot becomes a nuisance. To get around that problem, you can use the VPLAYER (View Port LAYER) command to selectively freeze layers in one viewport without affecting other viewports.

The same principles apply to any multiview drawing, where you have annotations and dimensions that are specific to the views in each viewport. You simply use VPLAYER to freeze those annotation layers in all other viewports.

Let's use our trusty WIDGEDIT drawing in the next exercise to see how the VPLAYER command works (see fig. 10.12). While we're there, we'll also create a new layer on which to place the viewport boundary boxes, and turn off the boxes by freezing the layer. When you finish the following command sequence, your screen should resemble the one shown in figure 10.13.

Figure 10.12: WIDGEDIT before freezing layers.

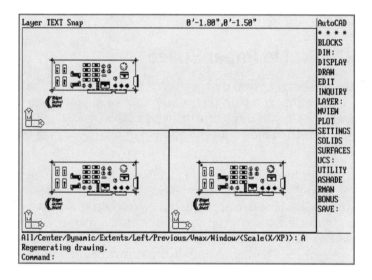

Figure 10.13: WIDGEDIT after freezing layers.

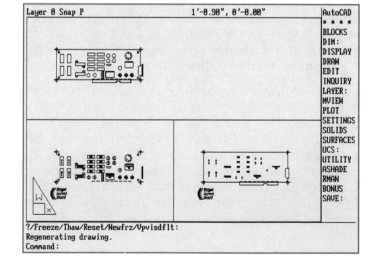

> ### Freezing Layers Selectively With VPLAYER
>
> Begin a NEW drawing named VPLAYER=WIDGEDIT.
>
> Command: **TILEMODE**   Set to 0 to enter paper space.
>   The drawing regenerates with
>   the three existing viewports.
>
> Enter model space and zoom All in each of the lower viewports.
>
> Command: **DDLMODES**   Review the layer names and
>   set layer 0 current.
>
> Select the lower right viewport.
>
> Command: **VPLAYER**
> ?/Freeze/Thaw/Reset/Newfrz/Vpvisdflt: **F**   Freeze.
> Layers(s) to Freeze: **PARTS**
> All/Select/<Current>: **<RETURN>**
> ?/Freeze/Thaw/Reset/Newfrz/Vpvisdflt: **<RETURN>**   The parts disappear.
> Command: **PSPACE**   VPLAYER works equally well
>   in paper space.
>
> Command: **VPLAYER**
> ?/Freeze/Thaw/Reset/Newfrz/Vpvisdflt: **F**
> Layers(s) to Freeze: **BOARD**
> All/Select/<Current>: **S**
> Select objects: Select the lower left viewport.
> Select objects: **<RETURN>**
> ?/Freeze/Thaw/Reset/Newfrz/Vpvisdflt: **F**
> Layers(s) to Freeze: **TEXT**
> All/Select/<Current>: **S**
> Select objects: Select the upper viewport.
> Select objects: **<RETURN>**
> ?/Freeze/Thaw/Reset/Newfrz/Vpvisdflt: **<RETURN>**

Although you have frozen each of the main layers in one of the viewports, those layers are still visible in the other two viewports. The boxes around the viewports disappear when you change them on the VPBOXES layer, which is frozen. Here is a recap of VPLAYER options.

VPLAYER Options

?   Displays the layer names that are frozen in a viewport that you select.

Freeze   Freezes layers in a viewport that you select.

Thaws   Thaws layers in a viewport that you select.

Reset   Restores the default settings for the specified layers in selected viewports.

Newfrz   Creates a new layer which is frozen in all viewports.

Vpvisdflt   (ViewPort VISibility DeFauLTs) Controls whether specified layers are frozen or thawed in newly created viewports.

You can also use the DDLMODES Layer Control dialogue box to control layers in viewports. The VP FRZ Cur column controls the freeze/thaw status of layers in the current viewport, and the VP FRZ New column controls whether layers will be frozen or thawed in the newly created viewports.

Even without paper space viewports, you can achieve control over layers nearly as well, albeit with more effort.

Controlling Layers in Model Space or Tilemode Viewports

In model space, you can only control your layers globally — a change to a layer's visibility affects all views. To compose your drawing for plotting, make sure the data you want to plot is on a different layer from the data that you don't want. Using the facilities plan example, you would start with the same model (each of the different systems for the facility would be on separate layers). You can use the LAYER command to turn on/off or freeze and thaw the correct layers for each desired combination of layers when you plot it. The key to doing this successfully is in knowing what to separate from what. It's usually better to err on the side of having too many layers rather than too few. Let's take a closer look.

To create a title block for each sheet, put the blank title block and common text on a layer by itself. Create unique layers for title block text that differs from sheet to sheet. Place common data such as the building outline on a layer by itself, and turn it on for all plots. Make sure that any data that is unique to a certain sheet is either on the layer for its system, or on a layer by itself. That allows you to turn it on or off when you need it to plot. You can ease that nuisance of turning layers on or off, freezing and thawing, by naming layers to allow you to substitute wildcard characters.

The last form of plot control is using colors to control pens, line weights, and linetypes.

Controlling Pens, Line Weights, and Linetypes

Until now, we've ignored any color settings you may have had in the original drawing and plotted everything with a single pen, line weight, and plotter linetype. But, many drawings require different line weights or colors to communicate the content of the drawing. Many new CAD users settle for a single line weight, not realizing they can use different pens on one plot even with a single-pen plotter. If you use a single-pen plotter, AutoCAD will prompt you to change pens.

You can control three factors with drawing colors. You can plot with different pens (for different colors or sizes of pens), with different plotter linetypes, and with different pen speeds. (A *plotter linetype* is defined internally in the plotter, independently of AutoCAD's *software linetypes*.) Controlling any of these three factors is simple, because AutoCAD separates the plot data by color. Everything that is the same color on your drawing will plot using the same pen number, plotter linetype, and pen speed. If you have not organized specific parts of the drawing by entity or layer color, use the CHPROP command to regroup them.

Pen Color

If you use the PLOT command to assign pen No. 1 to the drawing color red, everything that is red in your drawing will plot with pen No. 1. Then you place a red pen in pen slot No. 1 (or place a red pen in the pen holder when prompted to do so for single-pen plotters). If you want pen No. 1 to plot with thick black lines, put a thick black pen in slot No. 1. Drawing colors don't necessarily have to match plot colors. Plotting with different sizes of pens is exactly the same as plotting with different colors of pens. Just use drawing color as a logical alias for line weight, and assign the same pen number to each color that needs to be plotted at the same line weight. You can assign more than one drawing color to a particular pen number. For example, you could assign blue as well as red to pen No. 1. Then, anything in the drawing that is either blue or red would plot with pen No. 1. To avoid frequent swapping of pens, AutoCAD's plot optimization sorts by pen number as it generates the plot data.

Plotter Linetype

The second plot factor you can control with drawing color is plotter linetype. Many plotters can generate internal plotter linetypes. They don't have anything in common with AutoCAD's linetypes, so don't confuse the two. You can assign a linetype for each drawing color in the PLOT command. The linetype is specified by a number. Plotter linetype 0 is continuous, the default. Entering a linetype number for a certain drawing color will plot all entities with that drawing color using that plotter linetype. Be careful to avoid plotting entities that have a software linetype other than continuous with a plotter linetype other than continuous; the result will be an inconsistent combination of the two. We'll compare the pros and cons of software vs. plotter linetypes after the exercise. Plotter linetypes are assigned to drawing color independently of pen numbers, so more than one pen can use the same linetype, and one pen can use more than one plotter linetype. Some plotters have internally programmable linetypes/pen assignments that override AutoCAD's plot settings.

Pen Speed

The final plot factor you can control with drawing color is pen speed. The best speed
varies with the pen type, size, type of ink, and plotting media. Use trial and error to
set the fastest speeds that plot consistently. Pen speed is assigned to drawing color
independently of pen numbers and plotter linetypes. The pen speed numbers are in
cm/second. Some plotters have internally programmable speed/pen assignments
that override AutoCAD's settings.

Plotting With Different Colors, Line Weights, and Linetypes

For a multi-pen plotter, place different colored pens or different size pens in slots 1, 2, and
3. For a single-pen plotter, place a pen in the plotter and you will be prompted to change
pens at the appropriate time. Prepare the plotter for plotting. We'll just plot Limits to Fit,
and not worry about the size of your plotter or printer.

Select option 3, Plot a drawing, from the main menu and enter WIDGEDIT for name of
drawing.

```
Specify the part of the drawing to be plotted by entering:
Display, Extents, Limits, View, or Window <V>: L
Plot will NOT be written to a selected file
Sizes are in Inches
Plot origin is at (0.00,0.00)
Plotting area is 21.00 wide by 16.00 (C size)
Plot is NOT rotated
Pen width is 0.010
Area fill will NOT be adjusted for pen width
Hidden lines will NOT be removed
Scale is 1=1.00"
Do you want to change anything? <Y> <RETURN>
```

You must respond
yes to get to pen and
linetype selections.
Also check and reset
any parameters that
don't match the
above listing.

Entity Color	Pen No.	Line Type	Pen Speed	Entity Color	Pen No.	Line Type	Pen Speed
1 (red)	1	0	36	9	2	0	36
2 (yellow)	1	0	36	10	2	0	36
3 (green)	1	0	36	11	2	0	36
4 (cyan)	1	0	36	12	2	0	36
5 (blue)	1	0	36	13	2	0	36
6 (magenta)	1	0	36	14	2	0	36
7 (white)	1	0	36	15	2	0	36
8	1	0	36				

▶ Plotting With Different Colors, Line Weights, and Linetypes—continued

```
Line types   0 = continuous line
```
It shows a crude representation of the plotter's linetypes.

```
                  1 = .......................
                  2 = ----    ----    ----    ----
                  3 = -----   -----   -----   -----
                  4 = ------. ------. ------. ------.
                  5 = ---- -  ---- -  ---- -  ---- -
                  6 = --- - - --- - - --- - - --- - -
Do you want to change any of the above parameters? <N> Y
Enter values, blank=Next value, Cn=Color n, S=Show
   current values, X=Exit
Entity      Pen Line  Pen
Color       No. Type  Speed
1 (red)     1   0     36    Pen Number <1>: <RETURN>     Defaults.
1 (red)     1   0     36    Line Type <0>: <RETURN>
1 (red)     1   0     36    Pen Speed <36>: <RETURN>
2 (yellow)  1   0     36     Pen Number <1>: 2           Assigns pen No. 2.
2 (yellow)  2   0     36     Line Type <0>: 2            Assigns linetype 2,
                                                         dashed.
2 (yellow)  2   2     36    Pen Speed <36>: <RETURN>
3 (green)   1   0     36     Pen Number <1>: 3           Pen No. 3.
3 (green)   3   0     36     Line Type <0>: 4            Dash-dot.
3 (green)   3   4     36    Pen Speed <36>: <RETURN>
4 (cyan)    1   0     36     Pen Speed <36>: X           Exits.
Write the plot to a file? <N> <RETURN>
Size units (Inches or Millimeters) <I>: <RETURN>
Plot origin in Inches <0.00, 0.50>: 0,0
Standard values for plotting size
Size   Width     Height
A      10.50      8.00
B      16.00     10.00
C      21.00     16.00
D      33.00     21.00
MAX    44.72     22.93
Enter the Size or Width, Height (in Inches) <C>: <RETURN>   Or your MAX size, if
                                                            smaller.
Rotate plot 0/90/180/270 : <RETURN>                         Answer 90 for a
                                                            printer plotter.
Pen width <0.010>: <RETURN>                                 See the discussion
                                                            following exercise.

Adjust area fill boundaries for pen width? <N> <RETURN>
Remove hidden lines? <N> <RETURN>
Specify scale by entering:
Plotted Inches = Drawing Units or Fit or ? <F>: F
```

Plotting With Different Colors, Line Weights, and Linetypes—continued

```
Effective plotting area: 21.00 wide by 16.00 high
Position paper in plotter.
Press RETURN to continue or S to Stop for hardware
   setup <RETURN>
Processing vector: nn
```

With a multi-pen plotter, AutoCAD plots the pens you preloaded.

With a single-pen plotter, replace the pen each time AutoCAD prompts you like this:

```
Install pen number 2, color 2 (yellow)
Press RETURN to continue: <RETURN>
Processing vector: nn
Install pen number 3, color 3 <green>
Press RETURN to continue: <RETURN>
Processing vector: nn

Plot complete.
Press RETURN to continue: <RETURN>
```

Your plotted drawing should look like the one shown in figure 10.14.

Figure 10.14:
The widget plotted
with plotter linetypes
and line weights.

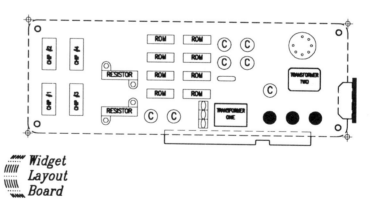

The color, pen, linetype, and speed dialogue has three options we didn't use. If you enter an S, it redisplays the settings made up to that point. If you enter C*n* where *n* is a color number, the dialogue jumps to that color number. Entering C with no number jumps to the next color. If you enter an asterisk in front of a pen number, linetype number, or pen speed, like *3 for pen 3, it assigns that setting to the current color and all higher numbered colors.

Plotter Linetypes vs. Software Linetypes

Plotter linetypes have advantages and disadvantages over software linetypes. Plotter linetypes are independent of scale, while you have to calculate and set an appropriate linetype scale for software linetypes. We generally recommend AutoCAD's software linetypes, but only lines, circles, arcs, and two-dimensional polylines accept software linetypes. Short polyline segments or spline and curve fit polylines generally plot continuous, because the distance between vertex endpoints is usually too short to break the line. AutoCAD linetypes intelligently adjust to balance between endpoints, so corners are always closed. Plotter linetypes often fail to close at corners, but do work well for polylines with short segments or curves. Consider using plotter linetypes when you need curved polyline linetypes, or a special effect like applying a linetype to 3D meshes or even text. If you use a plotter linetype, make sure your entities are drawn in a unique color for that linetype only.

> **Note:** Plotter settings allow only 15 colors; if your drawing has more than 15 colors, any color number over 15 will default to the same as color 15.

The pen width setting (default 0.010) in the plot dialogue does not directly affect the pen selections. This setting controls the spacing of the closely spaced lines that AutoCAD plots to fill wide polylines, solid entities, and traces. Set it to match the smallest pen that will be used to plot these entities to avoid gaps. It also affects text. If plotted text shows partial skips in characters, or if characters run together, check your pen width plot setting. Too large a value causes these symptoms.

> **Tip:** The *line weight* of PostScript printers (which are configured as plotters) is controlled by the pen width setting; 0.005 works well for 300 dpi printers.

Pen Motion Optimization

To minimize pen changes and time spent in pen-up moves (between the end of one line and the start of the next), AutoCAD includes configurable plot optimization. The settings are:

0. No optimization.
1. Adds endpoint swap.
2. Adds pen sorting.
3. Adds limited motion optimization.
4. Adds full motion optimization.
5. Adds elimination of overlapping horizontal or vertical vectors.
6. Adds elimination of overlapping diagonal vectors.

The default is 4: endpoint swap, pen sorting, and full motion optimization. Some plotters do their own internal optimization, which may be more efficient. Items 5 and 6 (Release 11 only) are primarily for 3D, where you may have many overlapping lines in a plot. You can adjust the level of optimization by reconfiguring your plotter, after first selecting item 2. Allow detailed configuration from the configuration menu. See your AutoCAD *Installation and Performance Guide* for details.

We've covered a lot of plot settings. Changing them each time you plot can be time-consuming — it would be nice if you could save settings and reuse them.

Saving Default Plot Settings

AutoCAD maintains your most recent PLOT (and PRPLOT) parameters from plot to plot and from one AutoCAD session to the next in its ACAD.CFG file. This is convenient; you don't have to reset all of the settings if it takes several attempts to get a plot correct, or if you use the same settings day in and day out. We've given you some suggestions for standardizing your plotting as much as possible. But you may need several different sets of standard settings, or you may need to use more than one type of plotter. AutoCAD provides two ways to save and restore settings and plotter configurations.

You can use configuration subdirectories to save and use several sets of defaults. At the beginning of the book, we created such a directory — named IA-ACAD. You can create as many configuration directories as you like, in exactly the same manner as you created IA-ACAD. Create a startup batch file similar to the IA.BAT file for each configuration. Then you can use one configuration for each plotter or set of standards, and AutoCAD will remember the settings from plot to plot.

You can also use *scripts* to store and execute standard plot setups. Scripts give you a way to make AutoCAD push its own buttons. Scripts are like the macros you find in many other programs — they're really nothing more than automated input that simulates strings of keystrokes. Scripts are covered more fully in Part Two, where they are used for presenting a series of slides. AutoCAD users often overlook the fact that scripts can start and run plots. Scripts have the unique property of being able to run outside the drawing editor. You can use a script, for example, to load a drawing, create some entities, then end the drawing. You can use any input for scripts that you can use in your drawings or in AutoCAD's main and configuration menus. You can reconfigure plotters with scripts. You can end one drawing and start another, edit it, plot it, end it and so on. If you have a specific set of operations to run on a group of drawings, you can use a script file to batch process the drawings.

How to Use Scripts to Run Plots

You can also run a script from inside a drawing file. Say that you have four standard plotting sequences, each requiring resetting parameters in the plot dialogue. You can simply create four standard scripts, one for each setup. If you set up a standard view to plot named PLOT, your script might look like the following example. This script is provided on the IA DISK as DPLOT.SCR. It plots to a D-size sheet at a 1=1 scale. (The right-hand comments are not part of the script file.)

Table 10.3
A Standard PLOT Script

PLOT	The PLOT command.
V	View.
PLOT	Plot name.
Y	Yes, change some parameters.
N	No, don't change pen/color/linetypes.
N	No, don't plot to file.
I	Inches.
0,0	Origin.
D	Size.
N	No, don't rotate.
0.01	Pen width.
N	No, don't adjust for pen width.
N	No, don't hide.
1=1	Scale.
And a blank line to start the plotter.	
And a blank line to return to the drawing.	

If you named the above script DPLOT.SCR, running it from the command prompt would look like:

```
Command: SCRIPT
Script file <SCRTEST>: DPLOT
```

AutoCAD would run through the plot dialogue, plot the drawing, and return to the drawing editor after the plot is complete. If you have the IA DISK, examine (and modify) the script to adapt it to your own use. If you don't have the disk, you can create the script with your text editor. If you do, don't input our comments on the right in the above example.

What if you don't have a plotter? Or you are at home and the plotter is at work? Or you need to create a plot file to import into a desktop publishing program?

Plotting to a File and Spooling

There are times when you may want to plot your drawing to a file, rather than to a plotter or printer. When you plot to a file, AutoCAD issues the same plot commands that it would if you were plotting to a plotter. The only difference is that AutoCAD redirects those commands to a file on disk, instead of to the plotter.

For example, you may have a plot spooling program (more on that in a minute) that allows you to plot multiple drawings one after the other without user intervention. In that case, you would plot your drawing to a file, instead of sending it to the plotter. Then, the plot spooler could pick up the file and send it to the plotter.

Another occasion when you may want to plot to a file is when you are transferring your drawings to other programs, like desktop publishing programs or presentation graphics programs. Many programs import HP-GL or PostScript plot files. HP-GL files contain plot commands for Hewlett-Packard plotters. Even if your plotter is not a Hewlett-Packard plotter, you can configure AutoCAD for an HP plotter and plot an HP-GL file to disk. Then, you can import your plots into PageMaker, Ventura Publisher, and other graphics programs.

Plotting to a file is simple. When you issue the PLOT or PRPLOT command, one of the questions AutoCAD asks you is whether you want to plot to a file or not. If you answer yes, AutoCAD will redirect the plot commands to the filename you specify. If you need a special type of file, such as an HP-GL file, remember to first select the correct plotter using the Configure option from the main menu.

Using a Plot Spooler

A plot spooler is a program that can control access to a plotter by one or more workstations, and queue multiple plot requests through a single plotter. Because there are as many different possibilities for spooling as there are spoolers, we can't go into much depth about the subject. However, we can give you a brief idea of what a spooler can do for you.

SPOOL is an acronym for Simultaneous Peripheral Output On-Line (at least it spells something!). On a single-user system, the spooler receives your plot as fast as AutoCAD can send it and trickles it out to the plotter, so you can go on working instead of waiting for the plotter to finish. Plot and print spoolers also let several people access a single device. The spooler logs their requests and schedules their plot or print into a queue to be printed when the device is available. Spooling is an integral part of UNIX, as well as most other multi-user/multi-processing operating systems and networks. There are also third-party programs available for DOS systems that can handle spooling. Depending on the spooler you are using, you may need to plot your drawing to a file first, then direct the file to the spooler as a job request. See the documentation that comes with your spooler for specifics on installing and using it.

General Plotting Tips

Plotting Media

The type of media you use depends on the plotter, the project, and whether you need a checkplot or finished drawing. For checkplots, you can usually use the least expensive type of paper you can put through the plotter. Large cut sheets are relatively inexpensive if you purchase them in 1000 sheet quantities. But to really save money, buy a roll of butcher paper from your local paper supplier. Roller-ball pens or fiber-tip pens are usually best for checkplots. Butcher paper is not very smooth, so roller-ball pens work better than fiber-tips, which tend to bleed.

The types of vellum and mylar depend mainly on personal preference and the type of projects. Some types of vellum and mylar do not work well with the inks used in plotter pens. Major drawing media suppliers have special vellum and mylar for use in plotters.

Pen Type, Speed, and Force

There are three common types of pens for plotting: roller-ball, fiber-tip, and ink pens. Roller-ball and fiber-tip pens are disposable, and ink pens are available in both disposable and refillable types. There are four factors that affect the efficiency of your pens — speed, acceleration, force, and point quality. With most plotters you can change the speed, as well as the force that's applied to the pen against the media. Many plotters default speed and force settings for the type of pen it thinks is installed. But you can override those settings to fine-tune your plot.

Pen speed is typically expressed in inches per second (ips) or centimeters per second (cps or cm/sec). Acceleration is stated in G-force. Acceleration is important because with short segments, text, and curves, the pen has little room to get up to full speed. Roller-ball pens offer the fastest acceleration, which is why they are ideal for checkplots. Roller-ball pens can go as high as 60 cps with good results. Fiber-tip pens often work best around 40 to 50 cps, and slowing their speed doesn't affect the quality much, either. With ink pens though, fine-tuning the speed and acceleration often makes a difference. Normally, ink pens will plot well anywhere from 10 cps to 30 cps. Jewel tips outwear tungsten or ceramic, which outwear stainless, but all will wear out eventually. Mylar wears tips much faster than vellum. Cross-grooved tips (not single grooved) can plot at higher speeds than plain tips.

Keeping Your Plotter and Pens Working

Most plotters are fairly maintenance-free (see your manufacturer's instructions for specifics). However, here are a couple of things to do every month or so for preventive maintenance. The first is to keep the roller and pinch wheels clean. The pinch wheels press the paper against the roller, and the roller moves the paper in and out of the plotter. Keep them clean of paper particles with a stiff toothbrush. The other item to check is the paper sensors, if your plotter uses photo-diodes to measure the ends of the paper when you load it. If so, there will be two holes in the plate over which the paper moves, one in back and one in front. These will have glass covers to keep dust and paper fibers out. When the covers get dirty, you will have problems loading the paper. Use a cotton-tipped swab with a little alcohol on it to clean these.

The secret to pen maintenance is to keep them capped, even if your pens normally sit in a pen carousel. Ink pens sometimes need a little extra care. The disposable pens usually come with caps that have a small rubber cushion inside, which keeps it from drying out and clogging. Even so, you may want to place capped pens in a carousel or sealed container with a damp sponge. Then a quick tap of the top end of the pen (not the tip!) should get it running again. Finally, don't try to refill disposable pens; the nibs wear out too soon to make reusing them worthwhile.

Solving Plotter Problems

The following are a few common plotter problems and possible solutions.

Computer and Plotter Not Communicating

If you issue the PLOT command and AutoCAD gives you an error message saying the plotter is not responding, it usually means the computer can't make contact with the plotter. If this happens, check for the obvious first and use the checklist from the beginning of this chapter. If it still fails to plot, you may have a bad cable. Although it doesn't happen very often, cables do sometimes just go bad. Or someone might have accidentally pulled the cable and disconnected one of the contacts in the connector at one end of the cable. Having a spare pretested cable around lets you confirm or rule out cabling problems with a simple swap.

Paper Jams

Paper jams are usually caused by misalignment of the paper or by having one of the pinch wheels half-on, half-off the sheet. If one pinch wheel is completely off the paper, it will jam for sure. Make sure the edges of the sheet are square with each other or the plotter won't be able to measure it properly and may try to run it out past the pinch wheels, causing a jam. Check and adjust or replace worn rollers.

Replotting When You Run Out of Ink or a Pen Skips

Okay, this is the *most* irritating thing that can happen when you plot. If it happens, don't remove the sheet from the plotter. You can replot over the original. The obvious next step is to get the pens working again. You might as well check them all while you are at it. If the plot is a relatively short one, just issue the PLOT command again and let AutoCAD plot over the entities. If you are plotting a drawing that takes a long time to plot, resave the drawing, then erase the entities that plotted the first time. Then, reissue the PLOT command to finish the plot.

Linetypes Aren't Right

If lines plot with a completely different linetype than you expected or if the scale of dashed linetypes seems wrong, check to see if plotter linetypes are specified in the plotter dialogue. If the linetype for a color is anything other than 0, those entities will plot using the plotter's internal linetypes instead of AutoCAD's linetypes. If the scale of your lines is off, check the drawing's LTSCALE setting and adjust it for correct plotting.

Summing Up

Think ahead about plotting. Plan your scale, pen types, and colors. When you set up your drawing file, you should have an idea about how it eventually will be plotted out. We don't recommend plotting scale to fit for final drawings. Set a standard plot = drawing scale.

If you are running Release 11, use paper space as much as possible for composing your plots. Also, use xrefs or blocks for common details, sections, and title blocks. Composing your plot in paper space (or faking paper space in Release 10) lets you plot what you see and avoid time-consuming replots.

Take advantage of the MVSETUP.LSP routine provided by AutoCAD. It can automate and customize your viewport layouts, title blocks, and generally make your plots easier to standardize.

Use the VPLAYER command to selectively freeze layers in one viewport without affecting the others. Controlling your plotting by layers is a powerful technique that can save you from duplicating work and wasting disk space.

For high speed plotting, try cross-grooved tungsten or jeweled pen points. For good no-fuss plots, use disposable liquid ink pens. For everyday checkplots, use disposable fiber-tip or roller-ball pens. Cap pens when not in use; they dry out quickly. Worse, they can get partially clogged and skip in the last minute of a one-hour plot.

Plotter maintenance is essential. Pen plotters are mechanical beasts. Keep your paper and pen supplies stored in the right humidity. A dust-free environment helps keep pens from clogging. Keep the paper path clean. Brush the paper or mylar before plotting. Finger prints can cause skips. Rubbing alcohol removes finger prints. For final copies, it may pay to slow the plotter down to improve line definition. Once slow is better than twice fast.

Above all, plotting is an art. Experiment and learn what works best for you.

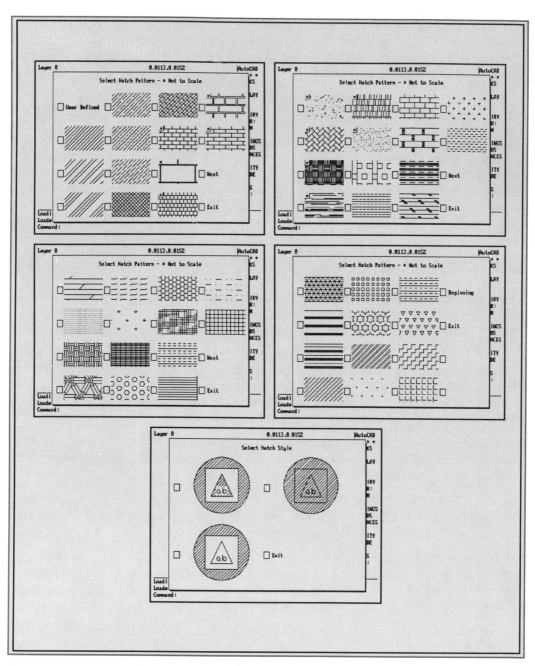

Figure 11.1:
AutoCAD's hatch patterns and styles.

Drawing Enhancements

MAKING DRAWINGS MORE PRESENTABLE

Creating Professional Drawings

Up to this point, our drawings have been simple. If you would like to make your drawings look more presentable and professional, you can enhance them with patterns, shading, annotation, dimensioning, and linetypes. You might also need to sketch in freehand or traced lines, such as contours in the Autotown site plan. You've already learned text annotation, and dimensioning is the topic of the next chapter. The rest you'll learn in this chapter.

We will also show you how to use AutoCAD's inquiry commands to get information about your drawings and their entities. You've already used the ID, HELP, and STATUS commands. We'll cover the ID, AREA, DBLIST, DIST, LIST, and TIME commands in this chapter.

Drawing Inquiry and Enhancement Tools

You will find AutoCAD's inquiry commands on their own [INQUIRY] screen menu. Both [SKETCH:] and [HATCH:] are on the [DRAW] screen menu. The SKETCH command lets you make freehand line entry. HATCH draws pattern fills. [Hatch] is also on the [Draw] pull-down menu. The [HATCH OPTIONS >] item on the [Options] pull-down menu leads to the [HATCH] options pull-down menu. You use this menu to preset the options before using the [Hatch] item on the [Draw] pull-down menu, which uses the preset options instead of prompting you. The [Hatch Pattern...] and [Hatch Style...] items on the [HATCH OPTIONS >] pull-down menu lead to the five

445

pages of icon menus shown in figure 11.1. [LINETYPE:] and [LTSCALE:] are on the [SETTINGS] screen menu, and [Linetype Scale] is on the [Options] pull-down menu. Figure 11.2 shows the [HATCH OPTIONS >] pull-down menu and the [INQUIRY] screen menu.

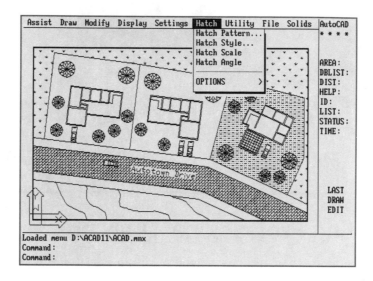

Figure 11.2:
Hatch options pull-
down and inquiry
screen menus.

Hatches Are Blocks

We deferred talking about hatching drawings until after the blocks chapter because AutoCAD's hatch patterns are really blocks. When you use the HATCH command to place a pattern, say a brick pattern in a walkway area, you are really inserting a block with the brick pattern.

Hatches are specialized blocks. They do not share the efficiency or easy insertion point control of normal AutoCAD blocks, and they require some care in setting up boundaries. Getting good results may take a little practice.

Otherwise, the basic scaling and rotating techniques that you have learned in inserting blocks also apply to placing hatch patterns. AutoCAD's standard hatch patterns are sized as unit blocks. When you insert these patterns in your drawing, you scale and rotate the pattern. If you are composing your drawing in paper space, you can have AutoCAD automate hatch scaling.

Because you generally will want to fit these patterns within predefined areas in your drawing, the focus of the chapter is to give you a set of techniques that will help you define the polygon boundaries that control the insertion of the hatch block.

Setting Up for Drawing Enhancements

The hatching and sketching exercises are a suburban renewal project for Autotown. You're going to pave the road and plant some yards with hatching, and improve the drainage by sketching some contour lines.

You can use the IA6HATCH drawing from the IA DISK, or recycle the AUTOTOWN drawing that you saved at the end of Chapter 9. Add two more layers called SCRATCH and HATCH and check the other settings in table 11.1. You'll also need the xrefed ATLAYOUT (or IA6ATLAY from the IA DISK) drawing, unless you're using Release 10. You'll bind it to the current drawing and explode it so you can select its component entities when you hatch.

Setting Up for Enhancing Autotown

 Begin a NEW drawing named AUTOTOWN=IA6HATCH, replacing your previous AUTOTOWN drawing.

 Edit an EXISTING drawing named AUTOTOWN. Create the HATCH and SCRATCH layers and check the other settings shown in table 11.1. (If you're using Release 10, you won't have the ATLAYOUT0 layers.) Set layer SCRATCH current.

```
Command: XREF              Use Bind option to turn ATLAYOUT into block.
Command: EXPLODE           Explode layout into individual entities.
```

Your starting drawing should look similar to figure 11.3.

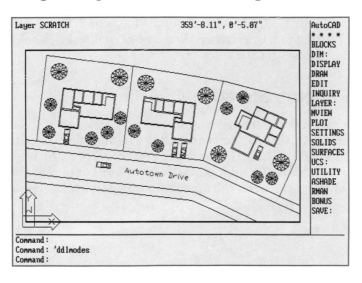

Figure 11.3: The Autotown drawing.

Table 11.1:
Autotown Drawing Settings

APERTURE	COORDS	GRID	SNAP	ORTHO	UCSICON
5	On	10	1	OFF	OR

UNITS	Engineering units, 2 decimal places, decimal degrees, 4 places, default angle 0.
LIMITS	0,0 to 360',240'
ZOOM	Zoom All.
VIEW	View saved as ALL.

Layer Name	State	Color	Linetype
0	On	7 (white)	CONTINUOUS
ATLAYOUT0PLAN	On	5 (blue)	CONTINUOUS
ATLAYOUT0SITE	On	3 (green)	CONTINUOUS
HATCH	On	6 (magenta)	CONTINUOUS
PLAN	On	5 (blue)	CONTINUOUS
SCRATCH	On/Current	7 (white)	CONTINUOUS
SITE	On	3 (green)	CONTINUOUS

Hatching often requires building boundaries to control your hatch inserts. We're starting with the SCRATCH layer current, and we'll build our hatch boundaries there. You can also use it as a pure scratch layer to play with any of the predefined hatch patterns that may catch your fancy.

Wouldn't Autotown look better if the road had some character? The good citizens have been thinking of putting in a brick road. Maybe not a yellow brick road, but at least a brick road. Where do we get the bricks?

Examining the Patterns Stored in ACAD.PAT

AutoCAD comes with over 50 predefined patterns (40 in Release 10). These are stored in a disk file named ACAD.PAT. You can find the names of these patterns by using the ? inquiry option of the HATCH command. You then enter the name of the pattern to list or use wildcards to list multiple patterns. (The ? option alone lists all patterns in Release 10.) The text screen will appear, listing pattern names with brief descriptions.

Let's look through the listing.

HATCH Icon Menus

Instead of reading text descriptions of the hatch patterns, you can use the [Hatch Pattern...] item on the [HATCH] options pull-down menu to graphically display the hatch patterns. You can use the icon menu in the middle of the HATCH command if you type the command or select it from the screen menu, but the [Hatch] item on the [Draw] pull-down menu requires presetting the pattern and other options. When you select from the icon menu to preset options or just use it at the command prompt, it will display the pattern name on the command line. We'll use the icon menu in the next exercise.

The HATCH Command

Well, you've got the bricks. How do you hatch Autotown Drive? The trick to hatching is to define the boundary for the hatch. The HATCH command wants to see the world as a series of closed polygons. To use the HATCH command to fill an area, you must completely define a closed boundary. Watch out for overlaps and gaps at corners and for open-ended polygons or your pattern will spill out of them.

Using a polyline to trace over the perimeter of the area you want to hatch is the simplest method. This gets around the uncertainty of whether your drawing has any questionable endpoints (like the endpoints where Autotown drive meets the border line), or whether your fill area is open or closed. Create such boundaries on a scratch layer so they won't affect the rest of the drawing.

Let's create a boundary for Autotown Drive by tracing over the road perimeter with a polyline. Use osnaps to help pick the endpoints. You can select the brick pattern from the icon menu, or type your input.

Using HATCH to Insert a Brick Pattern

```
Command: PLINE          Trace the perimeter of the area of the road.
                        Use osnaps and Close to create an accurate
                        closed boundary.

Command: LAYER          Set HATCH current.
Command: HATCH
```

Using HATCH to Insert a Brick Pattern—continued

```
Pattern (? or name/U, style):          Pulldown [Options], select [Hatch Options >], then
                                       [Hatch Pattern] to bring up the icon menu. Select
                                       [Next] and third icon in top row, or just type BRICK.
Scale for pattern <1.0000>: 120        Our drawing scale factor.
Angle for pattern <0.0000>: 45
Select objects:                        Select polyline boundary, text, and car in road.
Select objects: <RETURN>               The hatch is drawn (see fig. 11.4).
Command: <Grid off> ZOOM               Toggle the grid off to better see the hatch, and
                                       zoom in on the car (see fig. 11.5).
```

Look closely at your bricked drive. What's wrong with the car?

The Hatch Donut and Hole Problem

The brick hatch pattern drew directly over the car in the road. Putting bricks on cars will never do, but it is a classic hatching problem. We call this the donut and hole problem. If you select something as simple as a circle or rectangle, hatch will fill it in, stopping the pattern at the edges. If you want to fill in a more complex boundary that contains other objects, you need to tell HATCH not to flow the hatch pattern across them.

HATCH tries to decide what is the donut and what is the hole when it is figuring out where to hatch. In the Autotown Drive case, the text is a hole, but the car is a number of holes. (Text is treated as if surrounded by an invisible boundary.) AutoCAD normally hatches by starting the pattern at the perimeter boundary and

Figure 11.4:
Autotown with a
bricked drive.

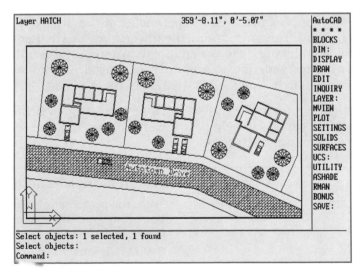

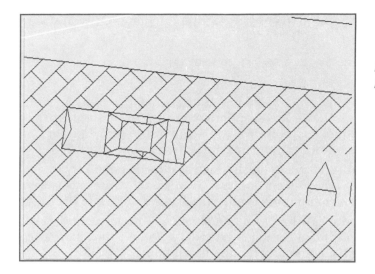

Figure 11.5:
Detail of the car.

stopping at the next boundary, and then starting again at the next boundary. The car is made up of many lines, creating many interior boundaries, so the pattern filled over parts of the car. HATCH offers three hatch style options to help with this problem.

As you work with hatches, you will also need to set the scale and angle to get the effects that you want. Here is a list of the HATCH command prompts and options that you have to work with.

HATCH Prompts and Options

Pattern   Determines the type of hatch pattern to use. Responding with a name from ACAD.PAT calls up that pattern and gets it ready for use. A U lets you define your own simple user-defined pattern with lines. A ? lists the available pattern names stored in ACAD.PAT.

Scale   Sets the size of the pattern elements. Pattern insertion is just like block insertion. You can scale the pattern as you insert it. Most of the standard patterns are scaled to look good when plotted at full scale. (Patterns identified with asterisks in the icon menus are not scaled consistently with the other standard patterns.) Typically, you'll use your drawing scale factor as the hatch scale. In Autotown, 1"=10' equals 1=120, so we used 120. If you have composed your drawing for plotting, in paper space viewports, you can enter a scale with an XP. For example, if your viewport is sized to 1"=10' relative to paper space, entering a scale of 1XP will scale the hatch to 120. The spacing between lines of a user-defined pattern scales in the same manner.

Angle The standard patterns have a horizontal orientation. If you want to slant your patterns, adjust the angle.

Style There are three styles used to control how hatch patterns see and use boundaries.

- ■ **Normal** is the default. Normal means that the pattern is drawn alternately from the outside boundary inward. It stops at the first interior boundary, then turns on again at the next interior boundary. It goes off-on until it runs out of nested boundaries.

- ■ **Outermost** produces a hatch from the outside boundary to the first interior boundary it encounters. You get the Outermost effect by appending a comma and O after the hatch name, like BRICK,O.

- ■ **Ignore** produces a hatch that ignores any interior boundaries, creating a totally filled perimeter boundary. You get the Ignore effect by appending a comma and I to the hatch name, like BRICK,I.

Using HATCH Outermost

Try the Outermost option to repave the road. HATCH only considers the entities you select when it calculates the interior boundaries, so be sure to select all interior objects you don't want hatched.

Using HATCH Outermost to Hatch Around Objects

Command: **ZOOM**	Previous.
Command: **ERASE**	Erase Last to get rid of the previous hatching.
Command: **HATCH**	
Pattern (? or name/U, style) <brick>: **BRICK,O**	
Scale for pattern <120.0000>: **<RETURN>**	
Angle for pattern <45.0000>: **<RETURN>**	
Select objects:	Reselect the polyline, car, and text.
Select objects: **<RETURN>**	

Figures 11.6 and 11.7 show the results of this command sequence.

Breaking Existing Entities for a Hatch Boundary

Creating a separate layer for hatching and tracing your boundaries is a good method, although this may be more work than is really necessary. You may encounter cases where it is easier to edit your drawing, breaking (or trimming) existing lines to get the boundaries that you need.

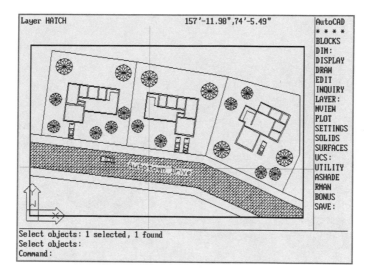

Figure 11.6:
Autotown Drives,
properly bricked.

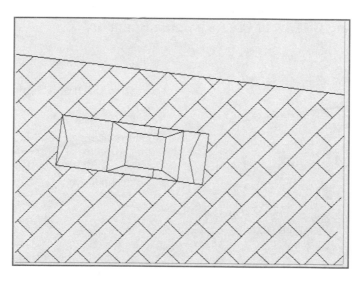

Figure 11.7:
Detail of the car.

In the Autotown drawing, we want to place a grass pattern between the three lot lines and the drawing border. In this case, it is easier to break the four intersections where the border and the outer lot lines meet Autotown Drive than to trace the entire lot and border perimeters.

Try using BREAK to pick the segments as the hatch boundary and fill the area with a grass pattern. Figure 11.8 and the following command sequence show the break points on Autotown Drive's polyline.

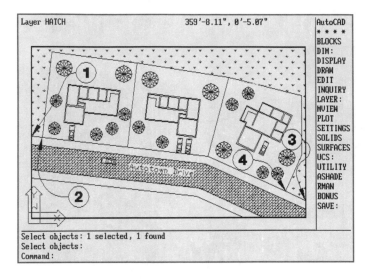

Figure 11.8:
Inserted grass pattern
in Autotown.

Using BREAK to Create a Hatch Boundary

```
Command: BREAK
Select object:                                    Pick the border near point ①.
Enter second point (or F for first point): F
Enter first point:                                Use osnap ENDPoint to pick point
                                                  ①.
Enter second point: @                             Repicks the first point.
Command: BREAK                                     Repeat BREAK for road at point ②,
                                                  border at point ③, and road at
                                                  point ④, using F for first point and
                                                  ENDPoint osnaps.


Command: HATCH
Pattern (? or name/U,style) <BRICK,O>: GRASS
Scale for pattern <120.0000>: <RETURN>
Angle for pattern <45.0000>: 0
Select objects:                                   Border polyline, two broken ends
                                                  of road, and all six lot lines.
Select objects: <RETURN>                          Hatch occurs.
```

You may notice that the grass slightly overlaps the wide border polyline. HATCH hatches to the center line of wide polylines.

If you place a pattern with the wrong scale or angle, you can always Erase Last or U to get rid of it and try again. A <^C> will stop a pattern fill in progress. But any editing of hatches gets more complicated.

Editing Hatch Patterns

You probably noticed that the single ERASE Last wiped out the first hatch pattern. Hatch patterns are *unnamed blocks*, with insertion points at 0,0. Normal editing commands like MOVE, COPY, and ARRAY operate on the entire pattern just like on a block. If you hatch multiple areas in a single HATCH command, and then try to move them individually, the hatches will move as a group.

If you want to edit individual lines within a pattern, explode it or use the asterisk option before the pattern name when you hatch it. *BRICK, for example, works just like the *insertion. A *hatch creates lots of little lines, so an Undo is the best way to get rid of an erroneous hatch.

> **Note:** The 0,0 insertion point causes a problem with STRETCH. STRETCH ignores hatch patterns, blocks, and text unless the insertion point is included in the selection window. For hatches, this means that you must include 0,0 in your window to get STRETCH to move it.

There are several items worth noting when deciding whether to explode hatches or insert them with an asterisk (*HATCH). Exploding hatches sends the bits and pieces flying to layer 0, making it easy to select and modify the entities if you keep layer 0 clean. A *HATCH goes on the current layer. A normal hatch creates an unnamed block definition containing all the hatch's lines and a block reference. When you explode it, the drawing will temporarily contain twice as much data. You get a new set of individual lines, but the block definition remains until the drawing is ended and reloaded. A *HATCH creates a set of individual lines, but no block definition, so it uses less data.

Because HATCH uses blocks simply to group the lines as one entity, every use of the HATCH command creates a unique block definition. Normally, blocks save data storage space through multiple insertions of the same object. But simultaneously hatching identical multiple areas with the same pattern does not save data space. However, if you copy a hatch, the copy will use the same block definition and save space.

> **Tip:** When hatching several identical areas, hatch one and copy it several times to save data storage space.

Hatching Complex Areas

Next, we want to show some mud on the east lot. (It was built too close to the swamp, a common problem in Autotown.) This is a more difficult hatch problem since we want to fill around the house, tree, and car blocks. This lot can only be hatched by tracing boundaries around the objects in the lot. But you're welcome to try Outermost instead; we thought it would work too.

Hatching Complex Boundaries

Command: **LAYER**	Set SCRATCH current.
Command: **ZOOM**	Zoom in on east (right) lot.
Command: **BREAK**	Break road at corner ① using F for first point and osnap ENDPoint (see fig. 11.9).
Command: **PLINE**	Trace perimeters of house and car using osnap INT.
Command: **CIRCLE**	Draw circles around each tree using osnaps INS and QUA.
Command: **LAYER**	Set HATCH current.
Command: **COLOR**	Set color to YELLOW.
Command: **HATCH**	
Pattern (? or name/U, style): <GRASS>: **MUDST**	
Scale for pattern <120.0000>: **<RETURN>**	
Angle for pattern <0.0000>: **<RETURN>**	
Select objects:	Select lot lines and interior boundary lines only.
Select objects: **<RETURN>**	
Command: **COLOR**	Set color back to BYLAYER.
Command: **SAVE**	

The result appears in figure 11.10.

You can see that hatching complex areas can be a lot of work.

Tip: When creating blocks you are likely to hatch around, draw a boundary on a scratch layer before you make them into blocks. When you insert the blocks, they will already have boundaries included with them. Turn layers on and off as needed to get just the boundary visible, and then hatch.

Tip: When creating simple and complex block pairs for redefinition, make sure you have good clean hatch boundaries in the simple blocks. Then you can hatch before you redefine simple blocks with complex blocks.

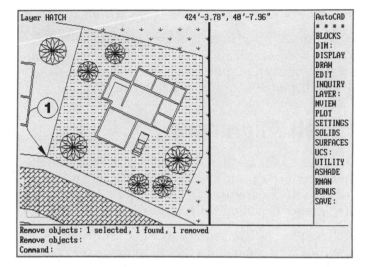

Figure 11.9:
Imperfect HATCH
outermost.

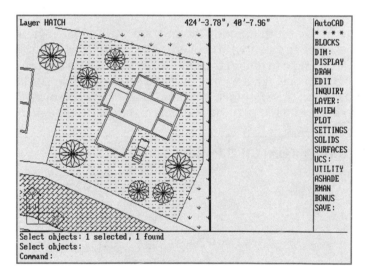

Figure 11.10:
Perfect HATCH with
traced boundaries.

So far, you have used both the Normal and Outermost hatch styles. The third style option ignores any interior boundary. If you want to test Ignore, change to your SCRATCH layer and try it.

User-Defined Hatches

Hatch has one more style trick up its sleeve. Say that you want to use some simple parallel lines as a shading pattern to fill a boundary. Immediately after you invoke the HATCH command, you can screen pick, tablet pick, or type U. U stands for *U design it.* This hatch option lets you create parallel or perpendicular crossed line patterns.

The U option with zero or 90-degree rotation is good for ruling or gridding areas such as pavement, ceiling plans, or section cuts. We'll use the U option in the next exercise, in which we'll also explore controlling hatch alignment.

Controlling Hatch Alignment

So far we have used hatches to fill an area and indicate a type of material. The precise alignment of the pattern relative to objects in the drawing isn't important in these uses. However, when hatches are used to lay out patterns such as for pavement, floor tile, or ceiling grids, the alignment is critical.

The base point of a hatch pattern's alignment is at 0,0 of the current UCS. You can relocate your UCS or use the SNAP command's Rotate option to relocate your hatch insertion point, rather than letting it default to 0,0. We recommend relocating the UCS.

Let's say you live in the house on the muddy lot and you want to turn your garage into a family room. You want to tile it with a user-defined hatch of 36 x 36 carpet tiles. If you just set a hatch angle to match the family room angle, its alignment with the walls will be purely by chance. A better method is to set the UCS to the lower left corner of the family room, and then hatch it. You'll probably have to adjust the UCS and redo the hatch to center the tile pattern and balance the cut-edge pieces.

Aligning a HATCH U Pattern With a UCS

Command: **ZOOM**	Zoom in to the garage/family room.
Command: **LAYER**	Set SCRATCH current.
Command: **PLINE**	Use osnap INT to trace closed boundary inside room (the house is a block).
Command: **LAYER**	Set HATCH current.
Command: **UCS**	Use three-point option with osnap INT to set UCS in corner of room, picking ①, ②, and ③ (see fig. 11.11).

Command: **HATCH**
Pattern (? or name/U,style) <MUDST>: **U**
Angle for crosshatch lines
   <0.0000>: **<RETURN>**   UCS is aligned with walls.
Spacing between lines <1.0000>: **36**   36 x 36 carpet tiles.
Double hatch area? <N> **Y**
Select objects: Select the polyline boundary.
Select objects: **<RETURN>**

With snap on, move crosshairs and check coords display of points ④ and ⑤. They are 21',21' and 22',23'.

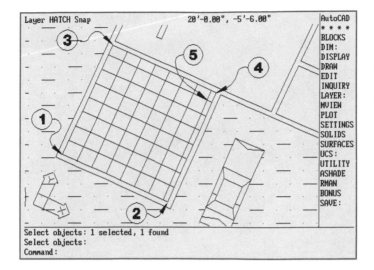

Figure 11.11:
First try hatching tiles
in the family room.

The hatch is aligned but not centered. The X,Y offset of the two points you checked is 1',2'. To center the pattern, you could adjust your UCS by either half of that offset (6",12") or by half plus 18" in the X axis (24",12"). Six-inch tile edge pieces should be avoided, so we'll offset the UCS by 24",12" and redo the hatch.

Realigning a HATCH With an Adjusted UCS

Command: **ERASE**	Erase Last.
Command: **UCS**	Use Origin option and enter 24,12 as new origin.
Command: **HATCH**	Default settings to values in previous exercise and reselect polyline to rehatch it.
Command: **SAVE**	Save and continue or end and take a break.

The newly balanced tiles appear in figure 11.12.

Tip: User-defined hatches are not restricted to simple patterns. Try hatching in different linetypes and at different linetype scales to generate some interesting patterns.

Creating Custom Hatch Patterns

You can create your own hatch patterns in a fashion similar to the linetype we're about to create. Creating hatch patterns is much more complex than creating linetypes — you can learn how to create hatch patterns in *MAXIMIZING AutoCAD, Volume I* (New Riders Publishing).

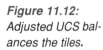
Figure 11.12:
Adjusted UCS bal-
ances the tiles.

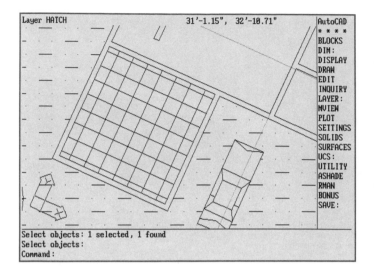

Using Linetypes and Linetype Scales

We often overlook the opportunity to enhance drawings by using AutoCAD's standard linetypes, or by creating and using our own custom linetype patterns. Every linetype is a pattern of spaces, short line segments, and/or dots. You create your own patterns using the LINETYPE command. Linetype affects only lines, arcs, circles, and polylines, and those entities within blocks.

Recall that you can use the LINETYPE or LAYER commands to set different linetypes. You can control the overall scale of these patterns with LTSCALE. The easiest way to select linetypes is with the DDLMODES layer control dialogue box and the DDEMODES entity creation modes dialogue box, on the [Settings] and [Options] pull-down menus. Both dialogue boxes bring up a select linetype dialogue box (see fig. 11.13), which graphically displays all currently loaded linetypes. However, you have to use the LINETYPE command or the Ltype option of the LAYER command to load linetypes before they show up in the dialogue box. The LINETYPE command has a ? option to let you list any or all linetypes in any linetype file.

LTSCALE Controls Line Pattern Spacing

You've used the LTSCALE command to adjust linetype scales. If you can't remember how LTSCALE works, review the examples below.

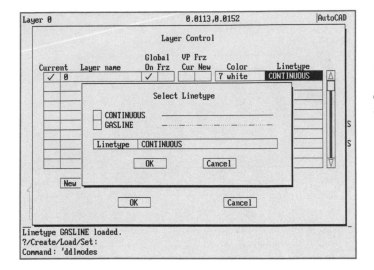

Figure 11.13:
The select linetype
dialogue box with
GASLINE linetype.

Each standard line pattern is defined to look good when plotted at full scale when LTSCALE is set to 1, the default. By setting LTSCALE to the desired scale factor, you can condense or stretch the pattern. Use your drawing scale factor as a starting scale, although you may need to adjust it slightly to personal preference or standards. You set LTSCALE for the plot appearance, not the screen appearance. Whatever setting meets your standards, remember to adjust it for your drawing scale for other than 1=1 plots. For example, a 1/4" = 1'-0" plot with a 0.375 standard linetype scale yields 48 x .375 = 18 as the actual setting.

You can only have one linetype scale, which is applied to all linetypes. However, each of the standard linetypes comes in three variants (not in Release 10), a standard scale pattern with a name such as PHANTOM, a half-scale pattern with a name such as PHANTOM2, and a twice-scale pattern with a name such as PHANTOMX2. Many users find the half-scale variants best for most purposes. Figure 11.14 shows how several of the standard, half-scale, and twice-scale linetypes look at different linetype scales.

Note: If your lines generate slowly or appear continuous instead of broken, try resetting LTSCALE higher.

Tip: In complex drawings with a lot of patterned linetypes, your regenerations may get rather slow. To speed things up, you can temporarily use continuous linetypes while drawing, and then change them to the correct linetypes before plotting.

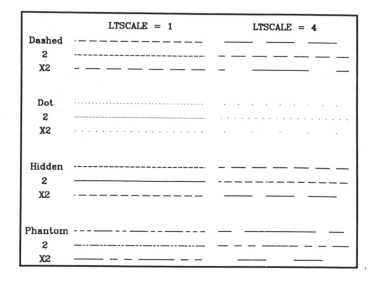

Creating Your Own Linetypes

Autotown is getting a new gas line. Rather than use a standard linetype to draw it, the next set of exercises will show you how to make your own linetype (named GASLINE), scale it, and then use it to draw the gas line.

The LINETYPE command lets you define your own dot and dash pattern, and store that pattern in a linetype file. AutoCAD's standard linetypes are stored in a disk file named ACAD.LIN. You can add linetypes to ACAD.LIN or create your own file, like the MYLINES.LIN file in this exercise.

Let's create a new linetype, GASLINE, and store it.

Using LINETYPE to Create a Linetype

```
Command: LINETYPE
?/Create/Load/Set: C
Name of linetype to create: GASLINE
File for storage of linetype <acad>: MYLINES
Creating new file
Descriptive text: GASLINE _____ ..... _____ .....    Use underscores and periods.
Enter pattern (on next line):
A,.4,-.1,0,-.1,0,-.1,0,-.1,0,-.1,0,-.1                Use five zeroes for five dots.
New definition written to file.
?/Create/Load/Set: <RETURN>
```

The linetype has been created and stored, but is not yet loaded.

What went on in the linetype definition sequence? Here is an explanation of the prompts and responses.

Linetype Creation Options

Name of linetype to create This is the name of the linetype you want to create. Use a good descriptive name to label your linetype so that later you can figure out what it is.

File for storage of linetype This is the name of the disk file where the linetype definition will be stored. It's safer to store linetype definitions in your own file rather than to use the ACAD.LIN file where AutoCAD stores the standard linetypes. If you want them all in one file, copy the ACAD.LIN file to your name, and then add your linetypes to it.

Descriptive text This is what you will see when you issue a ? query to list the named linetypes. It is a dot and dash representation of the linetype that shows on a text screen. Just type underscores (__) and periods (. . .) as descriptive text.

Enter pattern (on next line) Here AutoCAD is asking for the actual definition of the linetype pattern to repeat when it draws the line. You separate values with commas. The pattern codes include:

- The A — is entered for you. A is the alignment code to balance the pattern between endpoints. There are no other alignments currently supported.
- A positive number — like .4. The positive number gives the unit length of a pen down stroke. The first stroke must be pen down; it is the maximum line length that will appear as the first segment.
- A negative number — like -.1. The negative number gives the unit length of a pen up stroke. In other words, it is the length of the blank space.
- A zero — represents a dot.

Once you have stored one or more linetypes in a linetype file, you can load the linetypes for use. You call these linetypes up for active duty with the Load option of the LINETYPE command. You can list several names with commas between names. Use wildcards, such as * and ?, to load several or all linetypes at once. Loading a linetype doesn't set it current. You use the LAYER command to set it for layers or the LINETYPE Set option to set it as an explicit entity linetype.

Let's try loading and setting GASLINE.

Using LINETYPE to Load a Linetype

```
Command: LINETYPE
?/Create/Load/Set: L
Linetype(s) to load: *                          A * is quicker than typing
                                                 GASLINE.
File to search <MYLINES>: <RETURN>
Linetype GASLINE loaded.
?/Create/Load/Set: S
New entity linetype (or ?) <BYLAYER>: GASLINE
?/Create/Load/Set: <RETURN>
```

Once loaded, a linetype is stored in the drawing, and, unlike text font and xref files, the drawing file does not need to reference the linetype file in order to use it.

Any entities that you create now will show the new GASLINE linetype. Try drawing the gas line between the curb and setback property line on the south side of Autotown Drive.

Testing and Scaling a Linetype

Command: **UCS**	Set to World.
Command: **VIEW**	Restore ALL.
Command: **LAYER**	Set SCRATCH current and freeze HATCH.
Command: **PLINE**	Draw line between curb and property lines, border to border. The line looks as if it is continuous.
Command: **LTSCALE** New scale factor <1.0000>: **120** Regenerating drawing.	Try adjusting it to the drawing scale factor. The linetype is still too small to be sure it's right (see fig. 11.15).
Command: **ZOOM**	Use Center, pick a point on line and enter 30' for height. Now it looks okay (see fig. 11.16). It should plot fine at 1"=10'.
Command: **ZOOM**	Previous.
Command: **ERASE**	Last.
Command: **SAVE**	

Just like text, properly scaled linetypes are not always legible when you are working on your drawing. When you are zoomed way out or in, they may appear continuous or invisible.

Tip: If you can't discern linetypes on screen in large-scale drawings, you may want to set a temporary linetype scale for screen appearance. Just remember to set it back to the correct scale before plotting.

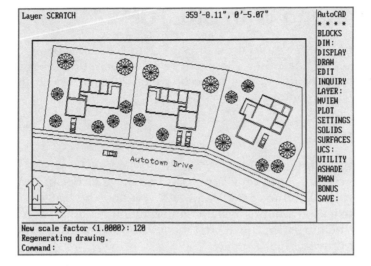

Figure 11.15:
GASLINE at
LTSCALE 120.

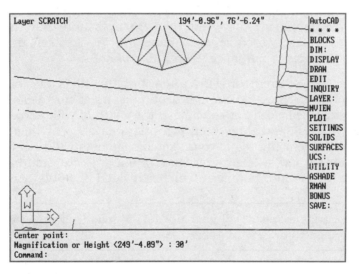

Figure 11.16:
GASLINE zoomed.

Tip: Like replacing blocks and styles, loading a new definition of a linetype will cause a regeneration and replace old linetypes with new unless you suppress regeneration with REGENAUTO. Adjustments to LTSCALE do not affect existing entities until after a regeneration.

We want to wrap up the Autotown drawing by sketching some contour lines between the road and the lower border, to redirect the drainage away from the east lot and its new family room.

Freehand Drawing With SKETCH

The SKETCH command allows you to draw lines freehand, without being bothered by From points, To points, and other alignment or input parameters. You sketch just as you would doodle or draw on a piece of paper. Sketch is also useful for tracing free curves such as contour lines.

How Sketch Works

AutoCAD stores sketch entities in the drawing file as successive short line segments. It draws wherever you move your cursor, as you move it. Because AutoCAD doesn't know where your sketching may lead, both you and the program have to take precautions not to let the amount of sketch information get out of hand. Just a few quick motions of the cursor in the sketch mode can create a huge number of short segments in the drawing file.

To help AutoCAD keep sketch information under control, you tell it how short a line segment to use for storing your sketch data. This is known as the *record increment*. AutoCAD stores a new segment every time your pointer moves more than the record increment away from the last stored segment endpoint. Try to keep the record increment as large as possible to minimize the number of lines.

The record increment is in current drawing units, but the effect on your input coordination also depends on the area your mouse or tablet puck has to move within and on your currently zoomed view. For example, if the width of your screen represents 300 feet (3600 inches), and the screen pointing area on your digitizer is 6 inches wide, a 60-inch increment means your sketch segments will be 5 feet, and that AutoCAD will record a new segment every time you move your pointing device about one-tenth of an inch (6 inches times 60 inches divided by 3600 inches).

Note: Mice that have variable speed will vary in their mouse-to-screen scaling — move them at a steady speed for best results.

You also have to let AutoCAD know when to consider the sketching pointer up (off the paper) or down (sketching). AutoCAD keeps all sketch input in a temporary buffer until you enter an R to record it into the drawing file database. You can enter an E to erase sketched lines before you record them. Recording sketched lines turns them into regular line (or polyline) entities.

Using SKETCH to Make Contour Polylines

Try making some contour lines with the SKETCH command. We chose this example because it is a common and extremely useful application of SKETCH. To get good smooth contour curves, you need to sketch with polylines rather than with lines (the default). Use the SKPOLY system variable to switch SKETCH from lines to polylines. If SKPOLY is 0, SKETCH will draw lines. If it is 1, it draws polylines.

> **Note:** Polylines can be easily stretched and edited, but their biggest advantage is that you can curve fit polylines and get a smooth curve. When you set SKPOLY to sketch polylines, set your record increment larger than you would when you sketch with lines. Use an increment one-half the smallest radius or turn that you will sketch. This may seem too large until you curve fit it.

Try sketching the contour lines. It takes a little time to get the hang of sketching, so don't be shy about undoing or erasing and trying again. Don't worry if your sketch ends slop over the drive and border lines. You can trim the loose ends later. We'll set the linetype back to continuous, because broken linetypes don't work well for short line segments such as SKETCH creates. Set up SKETCH in the following exercise sequence, and then sketch and edit the contour polylines.

Using SKETCH and SKPOLY to Draw Contour Lines

Command: **ZOOM**   Zoom to area shown in figure 11.17.
Command: **LINETYPE**   Set to CONTINUOUS.
Command: **SKPOLY**   Set to 1 to draw polylines. (Release 10, use SETVAR SKPOLY.)

Command: **SKETCH**   Draw one of the contour lines illustrated.

Record increment <0'-0.10">: **60**
Sketch. Pen eXit Quit Record Erase Connect.
<pen down>   Click to put pen down and move cursor to sketch.

<pen up>   Click to pick pen up.
R   Press an R to record the lines.
1 polyline with 14 edges recorded. You are still in sketch mode.

Repeat the pen down, pen up, record process to sketch the next contour.

X   Press X to exit.
Command: **PEDIT**   Smooth the sketch polyline.
Select polyline: **L**
Close/Join/Width/Edit vertex/Fit curve/Spline
  curve/Decurve/Undo/eXit <X>: **F**
Close/Join/Width/Edit vertex/Fit curve/Spline
  curve/Decurve/Undo/eXit <X>: **<RETURN>**

Draw the remaining contours shown and curve fit them.

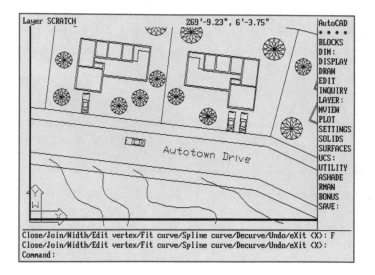

Figure 11.17:
Autotown with
sketched contours.

When you are in the SKETCH command, all other input is ignored except for the sketch mode controls (and toggles like ortho <F8> and snap <F9>). The following options, entered without a <RETURN>, control SKETCH.

SKETCH Options

Pen   Is a toggle that tells AutoCAD the pointer is up or down. Just type P, without a <RETURN>, to change the toggle. Clicking also toggles the pen up/down.

eXit   Records the sketch segments you have been creating in the drawing file and gets you back to the command prompt. A <SPACE> or <RETURN> will do the same thing.

Quit   Leaves SKETCH without storing the segments you have been creating. A <^C> will do the same thing.

Record   Keeps you in SKETCH, but stores the segments you have been creating so far in the drawing file. It is just like a save, but once you record, segments that get stored are not available for Erase from within SKETCH.

Erase   Is somewhat like an undo but erases any unrecorded segment from a point you pick to the last segment drawn.

Connect   Connects the pen to the end of the last endpoint of an active sketch chain. You can also use normal AutoCAD editing techniques to connect finished sketch lines to other elements after you finish the sketch.

Now, trim any loose sketch ends that you have. The finished lines should resemble those shown in figure 11.18.

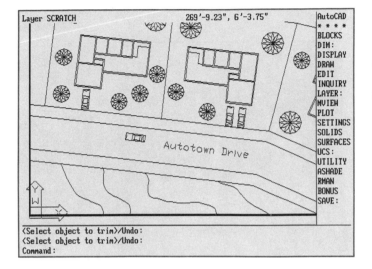

Figure 11.18:
The sketched lines
after trimming.

Using TRIM to Trim Sketch Polylines

```
Command: TRIM
Select cutting edge(s)...
Select objects:                          Select the road and border lines.
Select objects: <RETURN>
<Select object to trim>/Undo:            Select the overlapping ends of the sketch lines.
Command: VIEW                            Restore ALL.
Command: LAYER                           Thaw HATCH if you want to view the complete
                                         drawing.
Command: END                             Return to the main menu.
```

The added contour lines were the last step in Autotown's suburban renewal. Your drawing should now resemble figure 11.19.

Not everyone feels confident about freehand drawing skills. If you'd rather trace, AutoCAD provides a way to trace contours (or any kind of data) from an existing paper drawing.

Tablet Tracing and Sketching

If you have a digitizer tablet, you can use it to trace and digitize drawings into AutoCAD. The tablet has two modes: the screen pointing mode you usually use, and a calibrated digitizing tablet mode. You use the calibrated tablet mode to establish a relationship between points on a drawing taped to the tablet and points in your

Figure 11.19:
Enhanced Autotown.

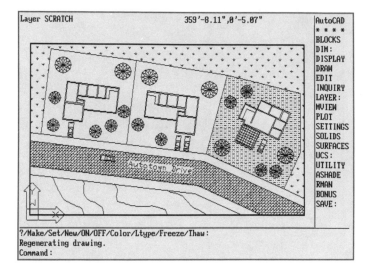

AutoCAD drawing. Once that relationship has been calibrated, you can fairly accurately pick points in the AutoCAD drawing by digitizing the corresponding points on the paper drawing. While this is not as accurate as creating a new drawing entirely from accurate coordinate and measurement data, it is often the only efficient way to import existing drawing data.

Tablet tracing is well-suited to tracing contours, which don't demand absolute precision, with sketched lines. But, tablet tracing isn't limited to sketching. You can use the full range of drawing commands and controls, even inserting blocks at datum points picked on the tablet.

To trace, you first use the Calibrate option of the TABLET command. It prompts you for two known points on the paper drawing and for the drawing coordinates to assign to them. It is best to use points that are horizontally or vertically aligned, to control skew. Once calibrated, the relationship between the drawing and tablet is maintained even if you pan and zoom. The X and Y axes are calibrated with equal scales. If the tablet drawing is distorted (as many paper drawings are), you can compensate after tracing by blocking the results and inserting them with differing X and Y scales. If your paper drawing won't fit within the tablet menu's screen pointing area, you can reconfigure the tablet to use its full area for tracing. To exit the calibrated tablet mode, use the TABLET command's OFF option; to re-enter tablet mode, use ON. You can also toggle between tablet mode and screen pointing mode with the <F10> key or <^T>.

We are not going to change the Autotown drawing any more, but we will use AutoCAD's inquiry commands to take another look at it. Autotown has defined distances and areas that make it a good practice drawing for retrieving information.

Using Inquiry Commands

AutoCAD's inquiry commands are useful for providing information about drawings. When lines are placed into a drawing file, they often represent distances and locations with real world relationships. Helping the drawing reader understand these spatial implications is part of creating a good drawing.

You've used the ID, HELP, and STATUS commands in earlier chapters. With these and other inquiry commands, you can measure, identify, and generally find out what's in a drawing file. AutoCAD already has much of the spatial information that you may need built into the drawing file. The distance and area commands, for example, return line distances and polygon area values from the entities that you have already placed in the drawing.

Just for fun, we'll start our inquiry session with a look at AutoCAD's timing features, and set the clock to see how long this last section of the chapter takes to examine.

Using TIME to Track Your Drawing Time

Unlike the other inquiry commands, TIME is really a management tool. TIME gives you a listing of times and dates about your drawing and editing sessions. These include: the current system time; the date and time a drawing was created; the date and time of the last update; time in the editor; and elapsed time.

Select the TIME command, and set time ON. This will act as an elapsed timer that you can check at the end of these inquiry exercises to measure your time spent in the drawing editor.

These inquiry exercises can use any version of the Autotown drawing, as long as it has the lot lines in it. If you are starting after a break, reload your AUTOTOWN drawing. If you are jumping into the chapter at this point, do the quick *Setting Up for Enhancing Autotown* exercise at the beginning of the chapter, and then the following exercise. We'll start by turning on an elapsed timer built into the TIME command.

Using TIME to Track Your Drawing Time

Edit an EXISTING drawing named AUTOTOWN.

```
Command: TIME
Current time:             06 Nov 1990 at 19:57:00.570
Drawing created:          05 Nov 1990 at 17:25:29.630
Drawing last updated:     06 Nov 1990 at 18:17:00.670
Time in drawing editor:   0 days 14:42:39.980
Elapsed timer:            0 days 14:42:39.980
Timer on.
```

Using TIME to Track Your Drawing Time—continued

```
Display/ON/OFF/Reset: R                          Reset the elapsed timer.
Timer reset.
Display/ON/OFF/Reset: <RETURN>
```

You can also access the time data with AutoLISP, allowing you to create drawing time management and billing programs

We'll check the elapsed time after we look at the other inquiry commands. The simplest inquiry, ID, deserves a second look.

The ID Command

You have used ID before to locate points. Recall that ID returns the X,Y,Z location of a point.

> *Tip:* The ID command is useful for resetting the last point without drawing anything, so you can use relative coordinates from the reset point. The last point is stored as the system variable, LASTPOINT.

Let's use ID to reset the last point.

Using ID to Reset LASTPOINT

```
Command: LAYER                              Set layer 0 current and freeze
                                            SCRATCH and HATCH layers.
Command: LASTPOINT                          (Release 10, use SETVAR
                                            LASTPOINT.)
New value for LASTPOINT <168'-6.00",
  46'-6.00",0'-0.00">: <RETURN>             Yours may vary.
Command: ID
Point: ENDP                                 Use osnap ENDPoint to pick point at
                                            ① (see fig. 11.20).
of  X = 142'-5.95"    Y = 205'-0.89"
                 Z = 0'-0.00"               Returns exact location.
Command: LASTPOINT
New value for LASTPOINT <142'-5.95",
  205'-0.89",0'-0.00">: <RETURN>            Reset by ID.
```

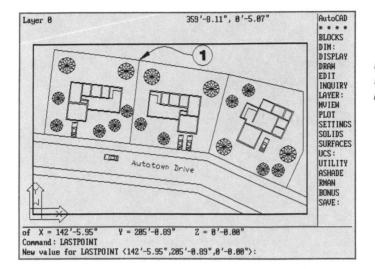

Figure 11.20:
ID corner point
between lots.

Using DIST to Get Line Lengths — and More

DIST gives the 3D distance between two points, its angles in and from the X,Y plane, and the X, Y, and Z offset distances. The measured distance is stored as the system variable, DISTANCE.

Say you need to check the length of the lot line between the east lot and the middle lot. Use the osnaps for accuracy and DIST will get you this information.

Using DIST to Get a Lot Line Length and Angle

Command: **DIST**
First point: Use ENDPoint to pick corner of
                                                lot at ① (see fig. 11.21).
Second point: Use ENDPoint to pick corner of
                                                lot at ②.

Distance = 100'-2.50", Angle in X-Y Plane =
   255.1333, Angle from X-Y Plane = 0.0000
Delta X = -25'-8.53", Delta Y = -96'-10.25",
   Delta Z = 0'-0.00"

If units were set to surveyor's angles, DIST would return the angle as S 14d52'0" W.

Let's survey the perimeter and areas.

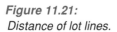

Figure 11.21:
Distance of lot lines.

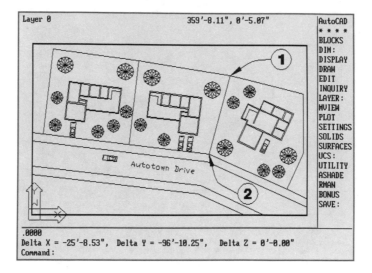

Using AREA to Get Area and Perimeter Values

AREA will give you the area surrounded by a straight-sided polygon defined by temporary points that you pick. Or, you can select an entity such as a polyline or circle, and AREA will automatically calculate its area, including curves. AREA keeps a running total that you can add to or subtract from to calculate complex areas or groups of areas. In the Add or Subtract mode, the AREA command stays active until you exit it with a <RETURN>. Add and Subtract only accumulate in the current command; each use of the AREA command restarts from 0. The area is stored as the system variable, AREA, and the calculated perimeter is stored as the system variable, PERIMETER.

Try surveying the area and perimeter of the east lot, using osnaps for your pick points.

Using AREA to Calculate a Lot and Perimeter Area

```
Command: OSNAP                          Set running osnap to INT,END.
Command: AREA
<First point>/Entity/Add/Subtract:      Pick corner of the lot at ① (see fig.
                                        11.22).
Next point:                             Pick corner of the lot at ②.
Next point:                             Pick corner of the lot at ③.
Next point:                             Pick corner of the lot at ④.
Next point:                             Pick corner of the lot at ⑤.
Next point: <RETURN>                    <RETURN> closes the boundary.
Area = 1634309.43 square in. (11349.3710
   square ft.), Perimeter = 418'-2.67"
```

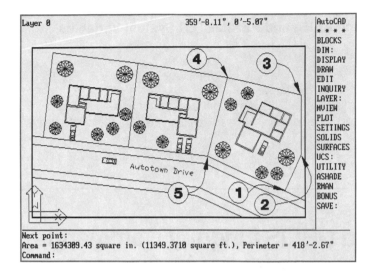

Figure 11.22:
Getting the area of
the east lot.

You can also get an area just by picking an entity. AREA recognizes polylines and circles. Use the Entity option when you need the area of an existing or curved boundary. Trace a temporary polyline over your drawing if you need to define the boundary.

If you hatched the muddy east lot, try getting the area of the east house by picking the hatch boundary you drew around it earlier.

Using AREA to Find Area of the East House

| Command: **OSNAP** | Set osnap to NONe. |
| Command: **LAYER** | Thaw layer SCRATCH. |

Command: **AREA**
<First point>/Entity/Add/Subtract: **E**
Select circle or polyline: Select polyline boundary
                                                         around house.

Area = 340992.00 square in. (2368.0000
   square ft.), Perimeter = 232'-0.00"

Note: An area is always a closed calculation. AutoCAD assumes a closure line between the first and last pick points of your area boundaries. Likewise, when you select an open polyline, AREA treats it as if it were closed.

You can access the last-calculated area, distance, and perimeter values using the SETVAR command.

Using the AREA and PERIMETER System Variables

```
Command: SETVAR                        AREA is both a command and system
                                       variable name, so you have to use
                                       SETVAR to check it.

Variable name or ? <LASTPOINT>: AREA
AREA = 340992.00 (read only)           In square inches.

Command: DISTANCE                      (Release 10, use SETVAR DISTANCE.)
DISTANCE = 100'-2.50" (read only)

Command: PERIMETER                     (Release 10, use SETVAR PERIMETER.)
PERIMETER = 232'-0.00" (read only)
```

The LIST and DBLIST Inquiry Commands

There are two other inquiry commands that we should mention: LIST and DBLIST. LIST gives a complete listing of entities that you select, including where the entities are located. Listing a closed polyline will give its area, including curves.

LIST is often used to check the block name, dimension style, color, layer, or pertinent coordinate points of existing entities so you can use this information for drawing new entities. Let's list a block and a polyline.

Listing Entity Data

```
Command: LIST
Select objects:                        Select car and polyline border
                                       around it in east lot.
        POLYLINE   Layer: SCRATCH      The polyline begins.
                   Space: Model space
        Closed
  starting width 0'-0.00"
    ending width 0'-0.00"

        VERTEX     Layer: SCRATCH      Polyline continues with four
                                       vertexes.
                   Space: Model space
     at point, X=297'-3.17" Y=108'-8.77"  Z= 0'-0.00"
  starting width 0'-0.00"
    ending width 0'-0.00"
```

Three more vertexes are listed, then:+

```
                   END SEQUENCE  Layer: SCRATCH   The polyline ends.
                        Space: Model space
      area  15120.00 sq in (105.0000 sq ft)      Saved in AREA system vari-
                                                 able.
```

> ### Listing Entity Data—continued
>
> ```
> perimeter 47'-0.00"                              Saved in PERIMETER system
>                                                  variable.
>             BLOCK REFERENCE Layer: PLAN          The block data.
>                 Space: Model space
>         CAR                                      The block name.
>     at point, X=300'-0.00"  Y=107'-6.00"  Z= 0'-0.00"
>         X scale factor    1.0000
>         Y scale factor    1.0000
>     rotation angle 245.7723
>         Z scale factor    1.0000
> ```

The color and linetypes are also listed when they are anything other than the default BYLAYER.

DBLIST gives a complete data listing on every entity in the drawing file. Once you do a DBLIST, you will never do it again. It scrolls through the entire database. Cancel with <^C> to get out if you get stuck in it.

Using TIME to Get Elapsed Editing Time

Time is coming to an end for this inquiry session. Finish up by looking at TIME again to see how long you spent in this editor session.

> ### Using TIME to Get Elapsed Drawing Time
>
> ```
> Command: TIME
> Current time:             06 Nov 1990 at 20:09:56.420
> Drawing created:          05 Nov 1990 at 17:25:29.630
> Drawing last updated:     06 Nov 1990 at 18:17:00.670
> Time in drawing editor:   0 days 14:46:35.830
> Elapsed timer:            0 days 00:12:52.060          About 13 minutes.
> Timer on.
> Display/ON/OFF/Reset: <RETURN>
> Command: END
> ```

When we tested these inquiry features, we spent about 13 minutes in the drawing editor.

Summing Up

AutoCAD provides nearly limitless possibilities for enhancing drawings. In this chapter, we've covered the essentials to get you started. Here are some other reminders on hatching and sketching.

AutoCAD needs fully closed boundaries for hatching; use polylines to create closed continuous boundaries. Standard AutoCAD patterns are designed to be scaled by your drawing scale factor. Use HATCH U when you just want a quick hatch. A <^C> will terminate hatching in progress. An ERASE Last will get rid of hatch patterns as a block. When hatching, take time to find the patterns that work best for your drawings. Don't overlook the ability to create your own hatch patterns and linetypes to give your drawings a unique look.

Be careful with SKETCH. It's fun to play around with, but before you turn the pointer over to your kids, make sure you have plenty of free disk space. Use it with a relatively large increment, set SKPOLY to 1, and curve fit with PEDIT for smooth efficient curves. Use the calibrated tablet mode when you need to sketch or trace data from existing paper drawings.

Use AutoCAD's inquiry commands to measure, identify, and generally find out the status of entities and what's in a drawing file. Consider using the TIME command as a management tool. Use ID to identify coordinates and reset the last point. Use DIST for distances and angles. Use AREA for areas and perimeters. Use LIST to check coordinates and properties of existing entities. Don't forget the system variables that store these data.

12

Dimensioning

ADDING "SMARTS" TO YOUR DRAWING

The Importance of Dimensions

To communicate designs, drawings need to convey more information than just graphic entities and annotations. Many drawings require dimensions, tolerances, and other key information to define the design completely enough for manufacturing or building. This information is often as important or even more important than the graphics. If something is drawn a little out of scale, it might not affect the project as long as the dimensions are correct. But put down a wrong dimension, and your chances of an error in production go way up.

This chapter will show you how to dimension your drawings in AutoCAD, defining spatial relationships between objects. You'll learn how to control the style and placement of dimensions, and to create dimension styles to speed up dimensioning. You will also learn how to use different types of dimension text, and how to make dimensions update automatically when you change the geometry of your design.

How Dimensioning Works

AutoCAD takes as much work out of dimensioning as possible: distances are calculated for you automatically; dimension arrows are consistently sized; standards for such things as extension line offsets are maintained and applied to your drawing; and the entities that make up a dimension are created automatically.

479

But the key to accuracy in dimensioning relies more on how you draw than how you dimension. Because AutoCAD calculates dimensions based on the points you specify, the accuracy of your drawing controls the accuracy of your dimensions. If you draw something out of scale or to an incorrect size, your dimensions will reflect that error unless you override them. Having to override your dimensions eliminates much of the advantage of letting AutoCAD calculate dimensions for you. So, drawing accurately makes dimensioning much easier.

AutoCAD can create dimensions in many different styles and to nearly any standard. The default style of dimensioning will work, but won't likely suit your standards. To dimension in AutoCAD, you usually create a group of standard settings that control the appearance and placement of your dimensions. Then, you select the type of dimension and the points or entities to dimension, and AutoCAD does the rest. System variables called *dimension variables* (sometimes called dimvars) give almost complete control over size, placement, and appearance of dimensions. You set dimension variables with SETVAR or by entering their variable names in dimensioning mode. (Table 12.1 lists AutoCAD's dimension variables. Those shown in bold type are not available in Release 10.)

You usually have several standard sets of dimension variables that you use. You can save these as *dimension styles* (dimstyles). Dimstyles are groups of settings that you can save and recall by name, to easily set up different styles for different applications. Dimension styles are not available in Release 10. Here are a few of the characteristics you can control with dimension variables (and dimension styles):

- The appearance and size of your dimension arrows (or what you use instead of arrows).
- The size and style of the dimension text.
- What, if any, tolerance ranges will be included with the text.
- Where the dimension text will go relative to the dimension line.
- The layer on which arrows, text, and extension lines are placed (to control plotted line weight by color — not available in Release 10).

After you tell AutoCAD how to draw dimensions, you identify what to measure. You usually pick endpoints, arcs, or other points of existing entities, often using osnaps for accuracy. Then, you pick a location for the dimension line and text. Finally, you either accept AutoCAD's measurements as dimension text, or type in your own text.

How the Dimensioning Exercises Are Organized

The exercises in this chapter are organized into three major groups.

The first group shows how to use the dimensioning commands by placing center, radius, diameter, angular, and linear dimensions. You will also learn how to set a

Table 12.1
AutoCAD Dimension Variables

VARIABLE NAME	DEFAULT SETTING	DEFAULT MEANING	DESCRIPTION
DIMALT	0	OFF	Use alternate units ON=1 OFF=0
DIMALTD	2	0.00	Decimal precision of alternate units
DIMALTF	25.4000		Scale factor for alternate units
DIMAPOST	""	NONE	Suffix for alternate dimensions **<RO>**
DIMASO	1	ON	Associative=1 Line,Arrow,Text=0
DIMASZ	0.1800		Arrow size=Value (also controls text fit)
DIMBLK	`\"\"`	NONE	Block name to draw instead of arrow or tick **<RO>**
DIMBLK1	`\"\"`	NONE	Block name for 1st end, see DIMSAH **<RO>**
DIMBLK2	`\"\"`	NONE	Block name for 2nd end, see DIMSAH **<RO>**
DIMCEN	0.0900	MARK	Center mark size=Value Add center lines=Negative
DIMCLRD	0	COLOR	Dimension line, arrowhead, and dim line leader color
DIMCLRE	0	COLOR	Dimension extension line color
DIMCLRT	0	COLOR	Dimension text color
DIMDLE	0.0000	NONE	Dimension line extension=Value
DIMDLI	0.3800		Increment between continuing dimension lines
DIMEXE	0.1800		Extension distance for extension lines=Value
DIMEXO	0.0625		Offset distance for extension lines=Value
DIMGAP	0.0900		Gap between text and dimension line
DIMLFAC	1.0000	NORMAL	Overall linear distance factor=Value
DIMLIM	0	OFF	Add tolerance limits ON=1 OFF=0
DIMPOST	`\"\"`	NONE	User-defined dimension suffix (eg: "mm") **<RO>**
DIMRND	0.0000	EXACT	Rounding value for linear dimensions
DIMSAH	0	OFF	Allow separate DIMBLKS ON=1 OFF=0
DIMSCALE	1.0000		Overall dimensioning scale factor=Value
DIMSE1	0	OFF	Suppress extension line 1 Omit=1 Draw=0
DIMSE2	0	OFF	Suppress extension line 2 Omit=1 Draw=0
DIMSHO	0	OFF	Show associative dimension while dragging
DIMSOXD	0	OFF	Suppress dimension lines outside extension lines Omit=1 Draw=0
DIMSTYLE	*UNNAMED		Current dimension style **<RO>**
DIMTAD	0	OFF	Text above dimension line ON=1 OFF(in line)=0
DIMTIH	1	ON	Text inside horizontal ON=1 OFF(aligned)=0
DIMTIX	0	OFF	Force text inside extension lines ON=1 OFF=0
DIMTM	0.0000	NONE	Minus tolerance=Value
DIMTOFL	0	OFF	Draw dim. line even if text outside ext. lines
DIMTOH	1	ON	Text outside horizontal ON=1 OFF(aligned)=0
DIMTOL	0	OFF	Append tolerance ON=1 OFF=2
DIMTP	0.0000	NONE	Plus tolerance=Value
DIMTSZ	0.0000	ARROWS	Tick size=Value Draw arrows=0
DIMTVP	0.0000		Text vertical position
DIMTXT	0.1800		Text size=Value
DIMZIN	0		Controls leading zero (see AutoCAD manual)

<RO> indicates read only. Bold variable names are not in Release 10.

few of the dimensioning variables. If you are just starting with dimensions, you should work through these exercises.

The second group of exercises, beginning with the section *Dimension Variables Explained*, goes deeper into dimension variables and shows how to create and save sets of dimension variables as dimension styles. Using dimension styles, you can quickly set up dimensioning environments for different applications. You will also learn how to create chained (continued), baseline, and ordinate dimensions, and how to dimension in paper space. If you are already familiar with AutoCAD's basic dimensioning features, you might start with this section. But first do the *Setting Up for Dimensioning* and *Setting DIMTXT, DIMASZ, and DIMSCALE* exercises in the first section.

The third section shows you how to use associative dimensions, which allow you to update dimensions simply by changing the geometry they are associated with. Along the way, you will learn to use more dimensioning variables to create complex dimensions such as tolerances and to customize various aspects of dimensioning. You'll also learn to use AutoCAD's dimension utility commands to change existing dimensions and dimension text.

Dimensioning Tools

Take a look at AutoCAD's dimensioning tools. You will find the complete set of dimensioning commands, options, and variables available from the [DIM:] selection on the root screen menu. In all, AutoCAD has nine screen menu pages for dimensioning. The pull-down menu is also extensive and easy to use — the [Dim...] item on the [Draw] pull-down menu leads to four icon menus and there are twelve more icon menu pages for setting dimension variables (see fig. 12.1). You also will find dimensioning commands located at the lower left of your tablet menu.

Because dimensioning has so many options, it has its own command mode and prompt, accessed through the DIM: and DIM1: commands.

Dim Mode, the Dim Prompt, and Dim Commands

When you enter the dimensioning mode (dim mode), you see a new prompt, Dim:, instead of the usual AutoCAD command prompt. The DIM command puts you in dim mode and leaves you there. The DIM1 command automatically exits dim mode after one dimensioning command. All dimensioning is done in dim mode. When you are in dim mode, you can't execute the regular AutoCAD commands, but toggle keys, osnap overrides, and most transparent commands and dialogue boxes work okay. When you are finished dimensioning, you exit the dimensioning mode and return to the regular command prompt. You can abbreviate any dimensioning command to the fewest characters that are unique to that command, like HOR for

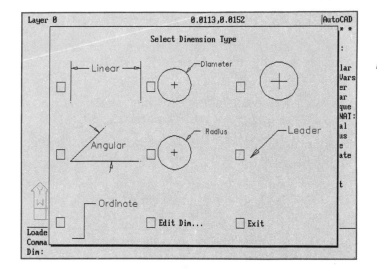

Figure 12.1:
The first page of
[Dim...] icon menus.

Horizontal. Six commands require three characters: HORizontal, HOMetext, REStore, REDraw, STAtus, and STYle. Six others can be abbreviated to one character: Baseline, Diameter, Newtext, Exit, Leader, and Undo. All others can be abbreviated to their first two characters. We'll just standardize the exercises to show the first three characters.

Dimensioning has a vocabulary all its own and AutoCAD has its own dialect. Figure 12.2 and the following list offer a quick primer in AutoCAD dimensioning vocabulary.

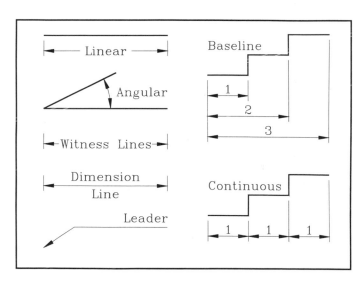

Figure 12.2:
Dimensioning
vocabulary examples.

Dimension Vocabulary Primer

Linear
A set of dimension lines, extension lines, arrows, and text that shows the distance between two (or more) points in a straight line.

Angular
A set of dimension lines, extension lines, arrows, and text that shows the measurement of an angle.

Extension Line
A short line segment that shows the drawing reader what is being dimensioned (also called witness line).

Leader
A special single dimension line that joins dimension text with the element being dimensioned or annotated.

Dimension Line
A line that shows what distance or angle is being dimensioned. It usually has an arrow at one end.

Baseline Dimensions
A series of successive linear dimensions starting at the same extension line.

Continuing Dimensions
A series of successive linear dimensions that follow one another. They are also referred to as chained dimensions.

Associative Dimension
A dimension created as a single entity instead of individual lines, arrows (solids), arcs, and text. Associative dimensions can be moved, scaled, and stretched along with the entities being dimensioned, and the dimension text will adjust automatically. This is the default dimensioning mode.

Arrow
Also called terminator. This is the block attached to the end of a dimension line. Other entities such as ticks, dots, and user-defined blocks may also be used for terminators.

Dimension Text
The text string that displays the dimension value. You can use AutoCAD's default value or enter your own value to override the default.

Tolerances
Plus and minus amounts that can be attached to your dimension text. To use tolerance dimensions, you must first set their values with dimension variables.

Limits
Another form of tolerance dimensioning, limit dimensions show a high and low dimension range limit for a dimension, rather than a single value.

Alternate Units
Dimensions in which two measurement systems are used, such as inches and metric units.

Center Mark / Center Line	Lines that identify the center point of a circle. AutoCAD's dimensioning commands draw these automatically.
Dimension Variables	A set of user-definable variables, sometimes called dimvars, that control size, style, location, and appearance of dimensions.
Dimension Styles	A named group of dimension variable settings that can be stored to disk. Once you fine tune your dimension variable settings, you can save that setup by name for future use.

Dimensioning Setup

In this chapter we are going to reuse the MOCKSECT drawing that you created in Chapter 8. We'll be using this drawing to explore a wide variety of dimensioning features, so we'll take some liberties from what is considered usual dimensioning for this type of drawing. When you are done, your completed drawing should resemble figure 12.3. If you are using the IA DISK, you can use the IA6MOCKD.DWG file.

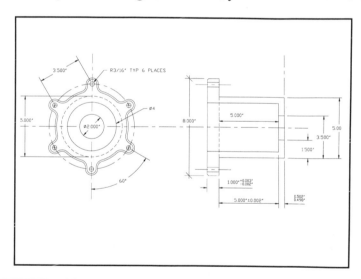

Figure 12.3:
The MOCKSECT drawing with a potpourri of dimensions.

Setting Up for Dimensioning

 Begin a NEW drawing named MOCKDIM=IA6MOCKD.

Begin a NEW drawing named MOCKDIM=MOCKSECT and check the settings shown in table 12.2. Make sure the current layer is DIMS and restore view A.

Table 12.2
MOCKDIM Drawing Settings

COORDS	GRID	LTSCALE	ORTHO	SNAP	OSNAP
On	1	1	On	.25	NONe

Layer Name	State	Color	Linetype
0	On	7 (white)	CONTINUOUS
DIMS	On/Current	2 (yellow)	CONTINUOUS

Your MOCKDIM drawing should look like figure 12.4.

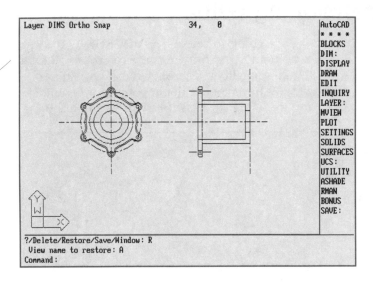

Figure 12.4:
The starting
MOCKDIM drawing.

We'll assume that MOCKDIM will be scaled 1 = 2 (a half scale factor) when plotted or composed in a paper space sheet. Let's look at scaling dimensions.

How to Set Up and Scale Dimensions

AutoCAD makes assumptions about dimension setup parameters, including the scale of your dimension text and arrows. The defaults may be okay for a drawing that will be plotted at full scale, but if your drawing will be scaled, the default settings may make your dimensions huge or nearly invisible. In a 60-foot by 100-foot facilities planning drawing, for example, the default arrow of 0.18 inches is invisible at almost any drawing scale and sheet size. Setting a scale factor for sizing dimensions is similar to setting a scale for annotating your basic drawing.

You could reset all your dimension variables to get the right size. But, AutoCAD has a better answer, and it's called DIMSCALE. Every scalar dimension variable is multiplied by DIMSCALE before it is applied to the drawing. DIMSCALE does not affect the measured value of the dimension, just its physical size relative to your drawing. You can use DIMSCALE to change all your dimensioning variables with a single scale factor. The default for DIMSCALE is 1.0000. You set it to the drawing scale factor (drawing units divided by plot or paper space sheet units). If you scale your drawing down, you need to scale the dimensions back up to their intended size. If you scale a drawing up when you plot, you need to scale the dimensions down. MOCKDIM will be plotted at half scale (1 plotted inch = 2 drawing units), so the drawing scale is 2.

You set the scalar dimension variables, such as dimension text and arrow size, to the actual sizes you want in your plotted output. DIMTXT is for text and DIMASZ is for arrows. Their settings get multiplied by DIMSCALE, so a .125 DIMTXT setting will be .25" in the drawing (.125 x 2), but will plot half that size (.125).

Let's set these values. Set DIMTXT for your text, set DIMASZ for your arrows, and then set DIMSCALE to 2, making your dimension scale offset your drawing scale.

Setting DIMTXT, DIMASZ, and DIMSCALE to Scale Dimensions

```
Command: DIM                                    Puts you in dim mode.

Dim: DIMTXT
Current value <3/16> New value: .125            Makes text 1/8" high.

Dim: DIMASZ
Current value <3/16> New value: 0.14            Sets the arrowhead size.

Dim: DIMSCALE
Current value <1> New value: 2                  Sets DIMSCALE to 2.

Dim: EXIT                                        Exit to command prompt with EXIT or
                                                <^C>.

Command: SAVE
```

Tip: Be careful when you undo after you exit the dimensioning mode if you have set variables. A command prompt level Undo or U will undo everything in the preceding dim mode session as a single Undo step. This makes it easy to accidentally undo dimension variable settings. Make a practice of exiting dim mode immediately after you set dimension variables, then re-enter dim mode. This will protect them from an accidental undo.

You can exit dim mode with the EXIT command, abbreviate it with just an E (in Release 10, use EXIT where we show only an E), or use a <^C>.

Using Undo in the DIM Command

Using DIM's Undo is similar to using an undo in the line command. DIM's Undo removes *all* entities (extension lines, arrows, text, etc.) from the last dimension try. You type U to undo at the Dim: prompt. You can also undo dimensions with the normal Undo command from the Command prompt, but one Undo will then wipe out an entire dimensioning session.

Dimensioning the MOCKDIM Plan View

To start dimensioning, we'll use the plan view (the left side) of the MOCKDIM drawing to test most of the basic dimensioning commands. Figure 12.5 shows the dimensions covered in this first section. We will work through the different dimension types one at a time so that you can see how they're done.

Figure 12.5: Some dimension examples.

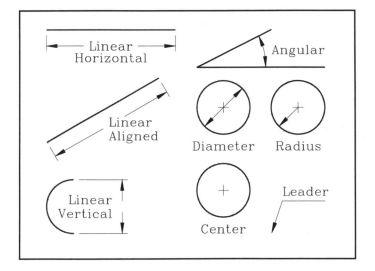

Dimensioning With Center Marks

The plan view has a series of small circles in the lugs on the flange's edge. Start your dimensioning sequence by placing center marks in these circles with the CENTER command. CENTER puts a cross at the center of an arc or circle.

Make sure you are at the dim prompt, and then type CENTER, or select it from the screen, icon, or tablet menus. Put the first mark in the circle at the top, and then work your way around the flange.

Using DIM CENTER to Place a Center Mark

Command: <Snap off>	Toggle snap off with <F9> or <^B>.
Command: **ZOOM**	Zoom in on top view.
Command: **DIM**	Type, or select [DIM:] from the root screen menu. Notice the dim prompt.
Dim: **CEN**	Type, or select [radial], then select [center].
Select arc or circle:	Pick a point on the hole's circumference at ① (see fig. 12.6). A center mark appears.
Dim: **<RETURN>**	
CEN Select arc or circle:	Add center marks to the five remaining holes.

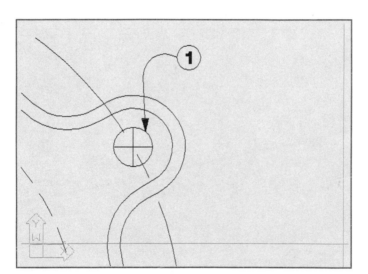

Figure 12.6:
Detail of a center mark.

Note: The DIMCEN dimension variable sets the size of the center marker. If you give it a negative value, center lines extending beyond the circumference are added to the center mark. In either case, the value of DIMCEN is half the width of the cross it creates.

Dimensioning a Radius

Next, try placing a radius dimension in the inner flange circle. The RADIUS command measures from an arc or circle center point to a circumference point. In the following example, the dimension text will not fit inside the circle. Drag the dimension outside the circle and place it by picking a point. The point determines the leader length, not its endpoint.

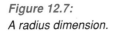

Using DIM RADIUS to Place a Radius Dimension

Dim: **RAD**	Type, or select [radial], then select [radius].
Select arc or circle:	Select the inner circle at point ① on the circumference (see fig. 12.7).
Dimension text <1 1/4>: **<RETURN>**	
Enter leader length for text:	Pick point outside circle to set leader length.

Figure 12.7:
A radius dimension.

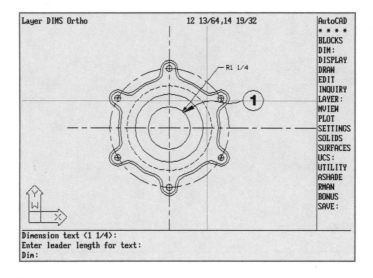

AutoCAD measured the radius for you, and drew the correct dimension with default text. You can always input your own text instead of using the default dimension text. The dimension lines, arrow, and text wouldn't fit inside the circle, so AutoCAD asked you for a leader length. You are not limited to picking a point; you can also type a value for the length. But the leader angle is always determined by the center of the circle and the point picked to select the circle.

Forcing the Text Inside the Circle or Arc

Text size and your pick point determine whether the dimension will fit in the circle. What do you do if you want the radius dimension inside the circle, no matter what? AutoCAD gives you a variable to control that. With radial dimensions, the variable DIMTIX ON forces the value inside the circle or arc, even if AutoCAD would normally prompt you to place it outside. DIMTIX OFF forces it outside. (DIMTIX does not affect radial dimensions with Release 10. AutoCAD decides where to put it based on its size.)

To see how this works, undo this first radius, and put in another radius dimension. Then, set DIMTIX on and execute the radius command again. This time, select the circle by picking at about the 85-degree point on the circumference.

Using DIM RADIUS to Force a Radius Dimension Inside a Circle

Dim: **U**	Undo the first radius dimension.
Dim: **DIMTIX**	Type, or select [Dim Vars], then [dimtix] from third menu page.
Current value <Off> New value: **ON**	
Dim: **EXIT**	To protect from undo.
Command: **DIM**	
Dim: **RAD**	
Select arc or circle:	Pick circle at point ① (see fig. 12.8).
Dimension text <1 1/4>: **<RETURN>**	
Dim: **EXIT**	
Command: **SAVE**	

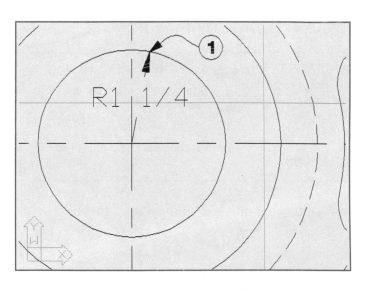

Figure 12.8:
Detail of a radius dimension.

The dimension text was placed in the circle, and you weren't prompted for leader length.

> **Tip:** You can use a text style with a width factor of 0.75 if you need to condense your dimension text into less space.

AutoCAD always writes dimension text horizontally, even for angular dimensions, unless you change it with dimension variables.

> **Note:** You will run into problems if your current text style is vertical when you enter dimensioning mode. Reset your text to a horizontal style before executing the dim commands.

Dimensioning a Diameter

Now that we know that the text fits in the circle, let's replace the radius with a diameter dimension. Diameter measures between two diametrically opposed points on the circumference of a circle or arc. Placing a diameter is similar to placing a radius. When you select the circle that you want to dimension, DIAMETER uses the point you pick as a diameter endpoint. AutoCAD automatically figures out where the second endpoint goes. (If the text does not fit, a leader will also stem from this first picked point.) Diameter dimension text placement is controlled by DIMTIX, just like radius dimensions.

Undo the radius and put in a diameter dimension. Because DIMTIX is still on, the dimension will automatically be placed inside the circle.

Using DIM DIAMETER to Place a Diameter Dimension

```
Command: U                                  Undo twice to undo the previous dimension
                                            command.
Command: DIM
Dim: DIA
Select arc or circle:                       Pick the circle at point ① (see fig. 12.9).
Dimension text <2 1/2>: <RETURN>
```

AutoCAD determines everything and draws the dimension.

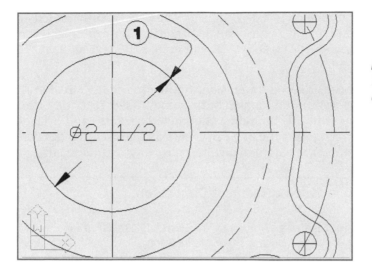

How to Force an Inside Dimension Leader

You've noticed that DIMTIX ON forces the text and leader inside the arc or circle and OFF forces them outside. When the leader and text are outside, no leader or arrows are drawn inside. Your dimensioning standards may require a radius or diameter leader drawn from or through the center to the pick point, even if the text is outside. The DIMTOFL dimension variable controls the inside leader (not in Release 10). To force AutoCAD to draw outside text with both an outside and inside leader, set DIMTOFL ON and DIMTIX OFF. DIMTOFL OFF (the default) suppresses the inside leader. If the inside leader is drawn, the arrows are drawn inside. (In Release 10, you can force text outside by adding a series of blank spaces before or after your dimension text. They won't show up, but will trick AutoCAD into thinking the text won't fit inside.)

Adding Text to a Default Dimension

You may have noticed that AutoCAD precedes the radius and diameter text with an R or a diameter symbol, but it doesn't put a space between the symbol and the measured text. How can you force a space between them? How can you add other text to a dimension? Or override the measured dimension if you have not drawn to scale?

When you create a dimension, AutoCAD measures the value and displays it for you as a default. Pressing <RETURN> at the default will cause AutoCAD to use that value. But there are times when you want to add text to the dimension, or change it altogether. To do so, type the desired text at the default dimension text prompt. If you want the default dimension text to appear along with your added text, you represent it in what you type by a pair of angle brackets. For example, if the default is <2 1/2">, then typing <> NOT TO SCALE will create the text as 2 1/2" NOT TO SCALE.

Let's try adding text to a measured dimension. Return to the lug circle at the top of the flange and place a radius dimension with some added text. Use the prompt sequence to get your text input, including the angle brackets, and a leader offset value. Since AutoCAD recognizes the angle brackets as representing the default text value, the text will include the calculated value, plus any text added after the <>.

Adding Text to a Dimension

```
Dim: DIMTIX
Current value <ON> New value: OFF          Turn DIMTIX off to force pick for text
                                           location.
Dim: RAD                                   Use RADIUS to dimension the outer
                                           flange holes.
Select arc or circle:                      Pick the top small hole at point ① (see
                                           fig. 12.10).
Dimension text <3/16>: <> TYP 6 PLACES     Type the input.
Enter leader length for text:              Pick a point outside the arc.
Dim: *Cancel*                              Exit dim mode with a <^C>.
Command:
```

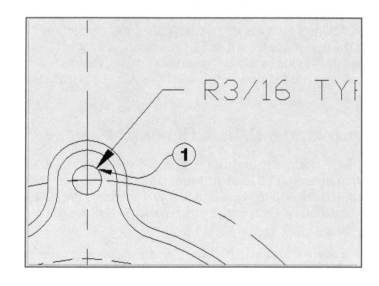

Figure 12.10:
Detail of a radius
dimension.

Your drawing should look like figure 12.11.

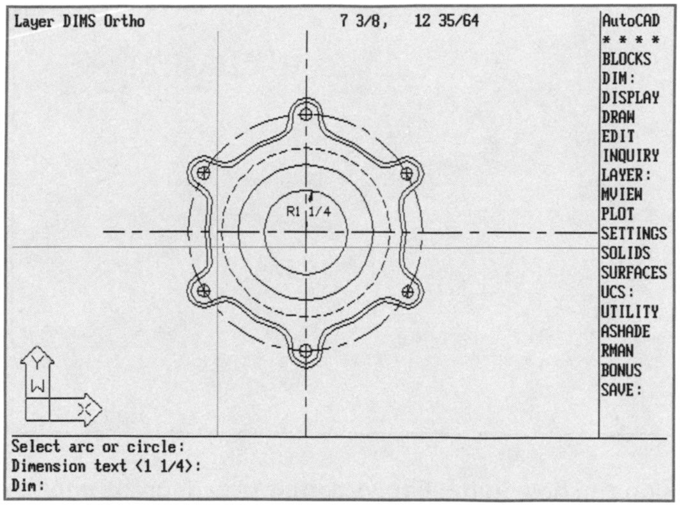

Figure 12.11:
A radius dimension
with added text.

Table 12.3 shows some other text examples.

Table 12.3
Alternative Text Examples

When AutoCAD offers:	Type this	To get this
Dimension text <2.5000>:	<SPACE>	
Dimension text <2.5000>:	Not important	Not important
Dimension text <2.5000>:	about <>	about 2.5000
Dimension text <2.5000>:	roughly <>"	roughly 2.5000"

Dimensioning With Leader Dimensions

In both the radius and diameter dimensions, you saw a leader used to place text outside the circle (or arc). LEADER is like a combination of an arrow block insert, the line command, and the text command. It lets you create a *call out* to point text to a specific location. You use LEADER to create an arrow with one or more continuous line segments to place text away from the entities you are dimensioning (see fig. 12.12).

Figure 12.12:
Some leader
examples.

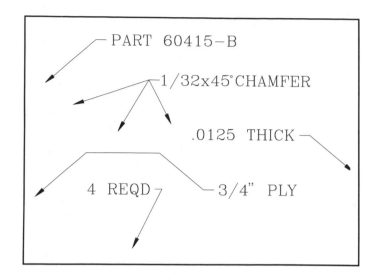

PART 60415-B

1/32x45°CHAMFER

.0125 THICK

4 REQD   3/4" PLY

Use a leader to dimension the hole in the flange. AutoCAD will prompt for a starting point for the leader line. You don't need to pick a point for the leader's short horizontal extension line — AutoCAD will automatically place a horizontal extension onto the end of the leader for your text.

Using DIM LEADER to Place a Leader Dimension

Command: **DIM**	
Dim: <Ortho off> <Snap on>	Toggle ortho off with <F8> and snap on with <F9>.
Dim: **LEA**	Type, or select [leader] from the screen menu.
Leader start: **NEA**	Osnap it.
to	Pick right side of the large circle at point ① (see fig. 12.13).
To point:	Pick point ②.
To point: **<RETURN>**	
Dimension text <3/16>: **%%C4**	Input text with %%C for the diameter character.
Dim: **EXIT**	Or just type E to exit dim mode.

This gives you the same effect as if you had dimensioned the hole with the DIAMETER dimensioning command. But, you can use leaders to annotate any feature with a note — not just circles and arcs — and you can use them to snake multi-segmented leaders through dense drawings.

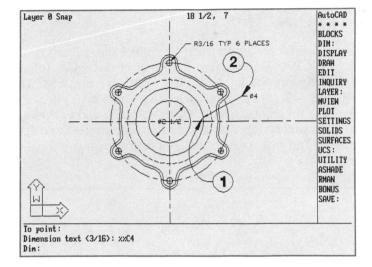

Figure 12.13:
Creating a leader
dimension.

Usually, you type new text each time you create a leader. After you locate the points for the leader and press <RETURN>, you are prompted for the text. After you type in the text and press <RETURN>, the LEADER command places the text at the end of the leader (near the last point indicated). If the last segment of the leader line is pointed toward the right, the text will be left justified. If the last leader segment points left, the text will be right justified. This prevents the text from overwriting the leader itself.

If you're using Release 11, you've probably noticed that the leader dimension is a different color—white. It was created with color BYBLOCK. We'll explore the reasons for this when we get into dimension styles and associative dimensions. You may have also noticed that AutoCAD offers the default text value of the previous radius dimension as the default leader text. It is possible to use a previous dimension value as all or part of the leader text.

Tip: Use CHPROP to change the color of leaders and center marks from BYBLOCK to BYLAYER.

How to Put Measured Dimension Values on a Leader

To use a previous dimension value, execute any dimension, say a DIAMETER dimension, and cancel it at the text prompt. Then execute the LEADER dimension, and accept the default dimension or use angle brackets with added text.

Dimensioning an Angle

Say that you want to measure the angle between two of the outer flange holes. This is an angular dimension. ANGULAR measures the inner or outer (acute or obtuse) angle between two specified nonparallel lines, the angle of an arc, or the angle between three points (see fig. 12.14). You can select an arc, circle, line, or polyline entity to dimension, or pick three points for the vertex, start, and endpoints of the angle, giving you enough flexibility for virtually any situation. (Release 10 doesn't allow picking three points, but you can draw temporary construction lines and dimension them instead.)

Figure 12.14:
Angular dimension
examples.

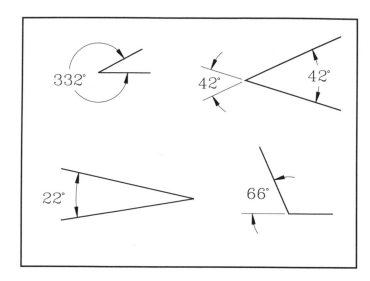

Dimension the angle between the two outer holes at the lower right of the flange. Use DIM1, which lets you do a single command and then exits dim mode. Use osnaps to pick the points, zooming in if needed.

Release 10 users will have to draw a line from the center of the hole at point <161> before dimensioning the angle. Erase the line after the dimension is in place.

Using DIM ANGULAR to Place an Angular Dimension

```
Command: DIM1
Dim: ANG
Select arc, circle, line, or RETURN: <RETURN>
Angle vertex: INT
of                                          Pick center of part at ① (see fig. 12.15).
First angle endpoint: CEN
of                                          Pick hole in tab at ②.
```

Using DIM ANGULAR to Place an Angular Dimension—continued

```
Second angle endpoint: END
of                                        Pick bottom end of vertical center line
                                          at ③.

Enter dimension line arc location:        Pick ④.
Dimension text <60>: <RETURN>
Enter text location: <RETURN>             Defaults to same as arc location.
Command:                                  DIM1 automatically exited.
```

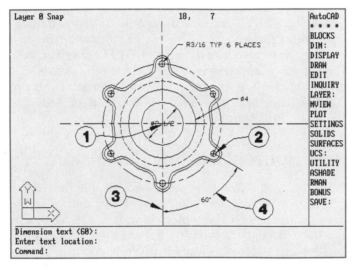

Figure 12.15:
Creating an angular
dimension.

The Many Ways to Draw Angular Dimensions

The ANGULAR command gives you a number of options. If you select an arc, it dimensions the arc from endpoint to endpoint, prompting you to place the dimension text. It calculates the included angle of the arc automatically, using the arc's center and its two endpoints. If you select a circle, AutoCAD assumes you want to measure from the pick point to the next point you pick on the circle. The angle is then measured from the center of the circle. If you select a line, AutoCAD assumes you want to dimension the angle between two lines and prompts for a second line. Or you can press <RETURN> instead of selecting an entity, as we did above. This way, you can use three points to measure and dimension any angle. Usually, you osnap the points to existing entities.

However you choose to do it, the result is an arc angle between two points about a center point. For every such set of points, there are two angles: one obtuse angle and one acute angle. Which angle gets dimensioned depends on where you pick your dimension line arc location. If you pick it between the two points, you get an acute angle with a small dimension arc, as we did above. If you pick it outside the two points, you get an obtuse angle with a large dimension arc.

Dimensioning With Linear Dimensions

Linear is a group of dimensioning commands (HORIZONTAL, VERTICAL, ALIGNED, ROTATED, BASELINE, and CONTINUE) that measure between two points. The points can be endpoints, intersections, arc chord endpoints, or any two points you can identify, usually by selecting an entity or osnapping.

Most of these are obvious: HORIZONTAL creates horizontal dimension lines; VERTICAL creates vertical dimension lines; ALIGNED creates dimension lines that are aligned (parallel) to an object or two specified points. ROTATED creates dimension lines rotated to a specified angle, not necessarily aligned with the points. BASELINE creates a series, with each dimension using the previous dimension's second extension line as the new dimension's first extension. CONTINUE creates a series of dimensions, all from the same first extension line.

Making Vertical and Horizontal Linear Dimensions

VERTICAL and HORIZONTAL work exactly the same, except one dimensions vertically and the other horizontally. With either, you can pick two points as the origins of two extension lines, or you can select an object (like a line, arc, or circle) and automatically dimension the full length or breadth of that object. The dimension line and text are drawn between the extension lines if there is room or if you set the dimension variables to force it.

Try dimensioning the dashed (hidden line) circle. Use the second option of VERTICAL and select the circle, which will select the circle's top and bottom quadrant points as starting points for your extension lines. Once you've selected the circle, AutoCAD will prompt you for the location of the dimension line. Place the dimension line about one unit to the left of the circle. When you are done, your results should look like figure 12.16.

Using Linear VERTICAL to Place a Vertical Dimension

Command: **DIM**	Get back in dim mode.
Dim: **VER**	Type, or select from [linear] screen menu.
First extension line origin or RETURN to select: **<RETURN>**	
Select line, arc, or circle:	Pick any point on the hidden circle.
Dimension line location:	Pick absolute point at about 4-1/2,15.
Dimension text <5>: **%%C<>**	Add the diameter symbol to the text.

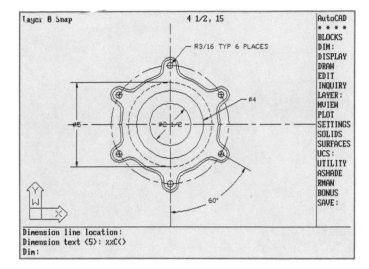

Figure 12.16:
*A linear vertical di-
mension on a circle.*

The text conflicts with the center line. The dimension text location is automatically set, but you can control it with dimension variables or change it after placement, as you will see in the associative dimensioning section of this chapter.

Aligned Dimensions

Now try dimensioning a distance that is neither horizontal nor vertical, such as the distance from the center of one of the outer flange holes to the center of another outer flange hole. A vertical dimension would measure only the Y axis distance from the first hole to the second hole. What you want is the actual distance between the two holes. This is what you get from ALIGNED. ALIGNED works like any linear dimension; you have the option of picking points to locate your dimension lines or of selecting an object. The dimension is drawn parallel to the two points or object. Try it on the two holes at the upper left of the flange.

Using Linear ALIGNED to Place an Aligned Dimension

Dim: **ALI**   Type, or select from the [linear] screen
                                                                    menu.

First extension line origin or RETURN to
   select: **CEN**   Osnap.
of   Pick the center of hole at ① (see fig.
                                                                    12.17).

Second extension line origin: **CEN**
of   Pick the center of hole at ②.
Dimension line location: Pick absolute point 8,18.
Dimension text <3 1/2>: **<RETURN>**   Accept AutoCAD's default text.

Figure 12.17:
An aligned
dimension.

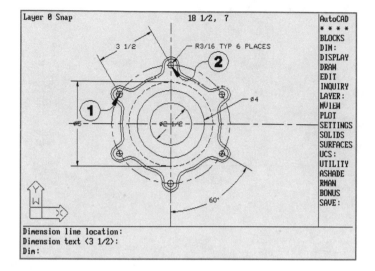

Voilà! You've got an aligned dimension. Of course, if your origin points align vertically or horizontally, an aligned dimension produces identical results to vertical or horizontal.

Creating Rotated Dimensions

There are times when you don't want the dimension line to align with the two points you are dimensioning. AutoCAD provides a type of linear dimension called rotated dimensions for just such occasions.

The rotated linear dimension is similar to the other linear dimensions except you must first specify the angle of the dimension line. In fact, you can use ROTATED for vertical and horizontal dimensioning by specifying an angle of 90 or 0 degrees.

Let's try a rotated dimension. Let's say you want to dimension the distance between the lower right flange hole perpendicular to a line from the center of the 2 1/2" circle through the upper right flange hole. The dimension line should be at 120 degrees.

Using Linear ROTATED to Place a Rotated Dimension

`Dim:` **ROT**	Type, or select from the [linear] screen menu.
`Dimension line angle <0>:` **120**	
`First extension line origin or RETURN to`	
`  select:` **CEN**	
`of`	Pick center of 2 1/2" circle.
`Second extension line origin:` **CEN**	

Using Linear ROTATED to Place a Rotated Dimension—continued

of	Pick center of lower right flange hole.
Dimension line location: **16.5,15.5**	
Dimension text <3 1/32>: **<RETURN>**	
Dim: **E**	Exits dim mode (Release 10, use EXIT or <^C>).
Command: **END**	

Your drawing now should resemble figure 12.18.

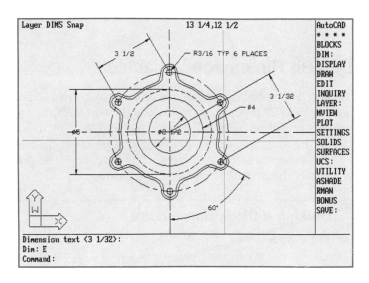

Figure 12.18:
A rotated dimension.

This completes a quick tour through the basics of dimensioning. While the dimensioning commands may seem complex, the basics are quite simple. First, you tell AutoCAD what it is you want to dimension, then you tell it where to place the dimension entities. Getting the effects you want may take some practice. If you'd like, use the MOCKDIM drawing to try some variations before you proceed to the next section.

In the next section, we'll explore controlling dimension appearance with more dimension variables, and work with sets of dimension variable settings using dimension styles. As we go, we'll dimension the section view using more horizontal and vertical dimensions, and three kinds of dimensioning commands that string a number of dimensions in a series: ORDINATE, CONTINUE, and BASELINE. We'll use ordinate dimensioning to explore dimensioning in paper space.

Dimension Variables Explained

From the few dimension variables you've already changed, you can see the effect on the appearance of certain dimensions. There are over 40 dimension variables, which you can set in different combinations to create dimensions that match nearly any standard. You will likely use several different combinations in your own work; you can save and restore these sets as named dimstyles.

The dimension variable names are rather cryptic acronyms for what they do. You should be able to decode them from the listing shown on the facing page of this chapter or the listing that the STATUS dim command gives you. You'll find it easier to remember the acronyms if you think of them in terms of their functions. Let's look at a few of the default dimension variables.

Looking at the Default Dimension Variables

We'll look at the dimension variables using two different commands and in two different units. We'll use the SETVAR command with the default decimal units and the STATUS dimensioning command with fractional units, like the units in the MOCKDIM drawing. If you have a printer, you can print out these lists for easy comparison. We won't show the complete lists below, only several of the dimension variables that we have already discussed or will discuss below.

Looking at Dimension Variables

Begin a NEW drawing named DIMVARS.

```
Command: <Printer echo on>                          Toggle printer on with <^Q>, if
                                                    you have one.

Command: SETVAR
Variable name or ?: ?
Variable(s) to list <*>: DIM*                       All dimension variables begin
                                                    with DIM, so use wildcard *.

DIMASZ      0.1800
DIMCEN      0.0900
DIMDLI      0.3800
DIMEXE      0.1800
DIMEXO      0.0625
DIMGAP      0.0900
DIMSCALE    1.0000
DIMSTYLE    "*UNNAMED"      (read only)
DIMTIX      0
DIMTOFL     0
DIMTXT      0.1800
```

Looking at Dimension Variables—continued

```
Command: UNITS                                     Set to Fractional, denominator
                                                   64, default the rest.

Command: DIM1
Dim: STATUS                                         Lists the current settings.

DIMASZ       3/16              Arrow size
DIMCEN       3/32              Center mark size
DIMDLI       3/8               Dimension line increment for continuation
DIMEXE       3/16              Extension above dimension line
DIMEXO       1/16              Extension line origin offset
DIMGAP       3/32              Gap from dimension line to text
DIMSCALE     1.000000          Overall scale factor
DIMSTYLE     *UNNAMED          Current dimension style (read-only)
DIMTIX       Off               Place text inside extensions
DIMTOFL      Off               Force line inside extension lines
DIMTXT       3/16              Text height
Command: <Printer echo off>                         Toggle printer off with <^Q>, if
                                                    you have one.

Command: QUIT
```

As you can see, the dim STATUS listing is more informative. Both methods display in current units; we changed units to make the following point.

Caution: The current units mislead you when the listing rounds off the default settings. Take DIMTXT, for example: STATUS with fractional units *shows* it as 3/16 but .1800 is still its actual value. The values displayed as defaults are rounded to the drawing units settings. This difference becomes important when you mix annotations generated by the dimension commands with ones created with TEXT, DTEXT, and other drawing commands. Your text heights won't match and you'll have trouble lining things up. So, we recommend changing all scalar dimension variables to exact fractional values when using any system of units that doesn't display true values. If you enter 3/16 as a new value for DIMTXT, it will become .1875; however, if you press <RETURN> at the default <3/16> prompt, it will be unchanged and remain .1800.

We'll reset all scalar dimension variables to precise decimal equivalents of these fractions as we look at several ways to set dimension variables.

Using the Dimensioning Icon Menus

You can set dimension variables with the SETVAR command, or by typing the name of the dimension variable at either the command prompt or the dim prompt. You can also set the dimension variables by selecting [Dim Vars] from the dimensioning screen menu. You'll get a list of dimension variables menu items covering three full screen menu pages.

Because the dimension variable names are cryptic and sometimes hard to remember, AutoCAD has devoted twelve icon menus to setting dimension variables and creating dimension styles. Each icon menu shows a graphic representation of what it affects. The [Set Dim Vars...] item on the [Settings] pull-down menu brings up the main [Select to Set Dimension Variables] icon menu (see fig. 12.19) from which you can access most of the other menus. You can jump back and forth between the different menus, setting the dimension variables to your needs.

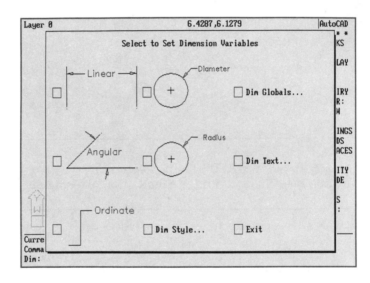

Figure 12.19:
[Select to Set Dimension Variables] icon menu.

The dimensioning icon menus make it easier to set the effects you want. But using the dimension variables directly is probably faster if you know what to set. We'll show both the dimension variable names and values as well as the icon menu instructions for setting them in the following exercise. As you make icon menu selections, try to watch the command line to see what dimension variables are affected. You can exit and flip to the text screen or turn printer echo on with <^Q> to see them more easily. In this way, you'll gradually learn the dimension variables so you can set them manually if you wish to. The quick way to exit a dimension variable icon menu is to use <^C> or <ESC>; the settings made up to that point will remain set.

Let's continue in the MOCKDIM drawing and reset the scalar dimension variables to precise fractions. We'll also show the icons for the DIMTIX and DIMTOFL settings we made earlier. If you are using Release 10 or your system can't use icons and pull-downs, enter the dimension variable names and values at the dim mode prompt instead. Some dimension variables, such as DIMTXT, have no icons; just type them or use the screen [Dim Vars] menu.

Note: The format for the following exercise is a little different from the format you've seen so far. We've omitted the prompts and set the dimension variable names and values in bold on the left and put the icon menu instructions on the right. For example:

> Dim: **DIMTIX**
>
> Current value <On> New value: **ON**

will be abbreviated as:

> **DIMTIX** <On>: **ON**

The icons are numbered for this exercise, starting with #1 in the upper left corner, working left to right, top to bottom.

Continue in the MOCKDIM drawing and reset the scalar dimension variables to precise fractions. If you use Release 10 or can't use icons enter the values at the prompt instead. Some dimension variables have no icons; just type them or use the screen menu. When you enter numerical values, type them — if you just press <RETURN>, the rounded off defaults won't be changed.

Setting Dimension Variables With Icon Menus

 Begin a NEW drawing named MOCKDIM=IA6MOKD2

 Edit an EXISTING drawing named MOCKDIM.

Select **[Settings] [Set Dim Vars...]** From the pull-down menu.

Select diameter, icon #2 from [Select to Set Dimension Variables] icon menu.

First, just to see what icon sets diameter and radius the way we first used them:

DIMTOFL <On>: **ON**	Select icon #3 to force an inside dimension line with outside leader and text.
DIMTIX <Off>: **OFF**	Set by above.
DIMCEN <3/32>: **3/32**	Select icon #5 to set the center mark size.

Now, the icon that sets diameter and radius the way we most recently used them:

DIMTIX <Off>: **ON**	Select icon #1 to force inside text (which overrides DIMTOFL).

Select [Previous...], then select icon #1, linear, from [Select to Set Dimension Variables] icon menu.

◄ | **Setting Dimension Variables With Icon Menus—continued**

`DIMEXO <1/16>:` **1/16**   Select icon #10. Sets offset of extension lines from their origin points.

`DIMEXE <3/16>:` **3/16**   Select icon #9. Sets extension of extension lines above dimension line.

`DIMDLI <3/8>:` **5/8**   Select icon #12 to set the spacing between each continued and baseline dimension line. Set it to a larger value, 5/8.

Select the [Dim Globals...] icon to change to the [Set Global Dimension Variables] icon menu.

`DIMSCALE <2>:` **2**   Select icon #10 for DIMSCALE, set earlier in the chapter.

Select [Dim Text...] then [Next...] to change to [Set Dimension Text Variables -2-] icon menu.

`DIMGAP <3/32>:` **3/32**   Select icon #9 to set text gap in dimension line.

`Dim:` **<ESC>**   Use your escape key to make a quick exit: the settings remain.

`Dim:` **DIMTXT**   Set to 1/8. There is no icon to set text size.

`Dim:` **E**   Exit dim mode.
`Command:` **SAVE**

You could have used the [Exit] icon and selected the [Do Not Save Dimension Style] icon to exit, but <ESC> is quicker if you aren't saving the settings as a dimension style.

Saving Sets of Dimension Variables as Dimstyles

Even with the icon menus to help, setting dimension variables can be a nuisance. Many effects you want to achieve don't depend on a single setting, but rather on many dimension variable settings working together. To remember all of the combinations necessary for the variety of dimensioning in the typical drawing is difficult. Yet the dimensioning in a typical drawing can usually be grouped into a few types. So Release 11 includes the dimstyle feature to let you save sets of dimension variable settings. (All settings except DIMASO and DIMSHO get saved.) With dimension styles, you can easily save as many different groups of settings for as many types of dimensioning as you need, and restore any style at will.

If you use associative dimensioning, dimstyles are saved with the dimension entities. This protects the style of the associative dimension from accidental changes while you edit the drawing. It also allows you to set a style current just by selecting a dimension entity that uses it. Associative dimensions are described in detail later in the chapter.

The next dimension exercise requires changing a few dimension variables, so let's first save the current settings as a style.

> **Note:** If you are using Release 10, skip to the section on Dimensioning With Continued Dimensions. The intervening sections cover dimstyles, ordinate dimensions, and dimensioning in paper space and model space, which are not available in Release 10.

Saving a Dimstyle

Saving the current dimension variable settings as a dimstyle is very simple. You can use the SAVE dimensioning command or use the icon menus. Both the [Save as NEW Dimension Style] icon on the [Dimension Style Options] icon menu and the [Save NEW Dimension Style] icon on the [Save Dimvar Changes Before Exit?] icon menu will save the current settings as a style. The latter menu comes up when you use an [Exit] icon to exit the dimension variable icon menus, if you've made any changes in the icon session.

When you save a style, you need to give it a name. The default style name is *UN-NAMED, which is not saved in associative dimension entities. Any time you change a dimension variable, it creates a new *UNNAMED style. If you want to be sure that your dimensions are protected from change, you should make sure you always have a named style current when you create new dimensions.

Let's save the current settings as a style named MOCK2I (named for half scale, Inside text because DIMSCALE and DIMTIX were the only significant deviations from the defaults).

Saving the Current Dimension Variables as Dimstyle MOCK2I

```
Command: DIM
Dim: SAVE
?/Name for new dimension style: MOCK2I
Dim: SAVE                                    You can also check to see what
                                             dimstyles have been saved.
?/Name for new dimension style: ?
Dimension style(s) to list <*>: <RETURN>
```

Saving the Current Dimension Variables as Dimstyle MOCK2I—continued

```
Named dimension styles:
  MOCK2I
?/Name for new dimension style: <RETURN>
Dim: E
Command: SAVE
```

Saving dimstyles is that simple. Dimension styles are restored by the RESTORE dimensioning command. They are defined and saved in the drawing, not as separate files on disk like text fonts or linetypes are. However, later in the chapter we'll show you ways to save text fonts and linetypes in drawing files that you can treat as if they were dimstyle files.

Creating a Dimstyle for Paper Space Dimensioning

Sometimes you may want to dimension objects in a model space viewport while you are finishing up and getting ready to plot in paper space. Most of the preparation is the same as in the plotting chapter, where we composed a paper space plot sheet. We told you then to set up your viewport(s) and scale their contents relative to the paper space sheet with ZOOM XP.

Two things make dimensioning model space objects from paper space possible. First, you can osnap to model space from paper space. Second, a special feature of the DIMLFAC dimension variable adjusts the dimensions measured in model space to the scale factor of the viewport. DIMLFAC is a factor by which all measurements are multiplied before dimension text is generated. This global scale factor allows dimensioning at scales other than the current units. It is normally set to 1. When set to a negative value, it multiplies all paper space dimensions by the absolute value of that value. (Model space dimensioning ignores a negative setting and uses 1, so you don't have to create a separate dimstyle for this purpose.) To make it easy to set for paper space, the DIMLFAC dimension variable allows you to select a viewport and calculates the value for you.

Let's set up to dimension the section from paper space.

Setting Up for Paper Space Dimensioning

```
Command: TILEMODE          Set to 0 to enter paper space.
Command: MVIEW             Pick 3,2 and 10,8 to define a viewport.
Command: MSPACE
```

Setting Up for Paper Space Dimensioning—continued

Command: **ERASE**	Erase the 3 1/32 rotated dimension to make room.
Command: **ZOOM**	Zoom .5XP for a half scale image.
Command: **PAN**	Pan to match figure 12.20.
Command: **DDLMODES**	Create magenta layer PSDIMS and set it current.
	Freeze layer DIMS in Current VP Frz column.
Command: **PSPACE**	
Command: **DIM**	
Dim: **DIMLFAC**	Set to scale relative to viewport scale factor.
Current value <1.000000> New value (Viewport): **V**	Viewport.
Select viewport to set scale:	Pick viewport.
DIMLFAC set to -2.000000	The inverse of the ZOOM XP factor.
Dim: **SAVE**	Save as dimstyle MOCK2I again.
Dim: **E**	
Command: **SAVE**	Save the drawing.

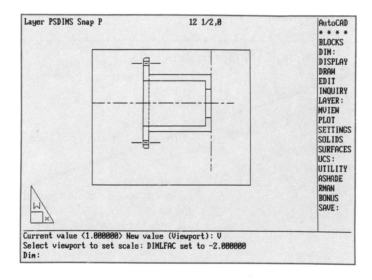

*Figure 12.20:
A paper space
viewport set up for
dimensioning.*

Note: One disadvantage of dimensioning in paper space is that associative dimensions are not tied to the model space objects and will not automatically update when the drawing is edited.

Now we're ready to do ordinate dimensioning of the section.

Placing Ordinate Dimensions

Ordinate dimensions (sometimes called *datum dimensions*) are series of offset dimensions from a common base point, without dimension lines. They have only one extension line, a leader where the dimension text is placed. The dimension text is always aligned with the leader, regardless of the values of the dimension variables DIMTIH and DIMTOH. (The ORDINATE dimension command is not in Release 10.) Ordinate dimensions measure the X datum or Y datum of the point you specify from the current 0,0 origin. You use UCS to place the current origin at your desired base point and osnap to ensure accurate datum points. Usually, you make sure ortho is on to ensure straight leader lines. Otherwise, if you pick a point for the end of your leader that isn't in line with the dimension point, AutoCAD draws a dogleg in the leader. Doglegs can be useful for avoiding overlapping dimension text in closely spaced dimensions.

Let's add a few ordinate dimensions to the section view. First set your UCS, using XYZ point filters to get the bottom left corner at the chamfer. Pick all the dimension leader endpoints so they'll line up nicely. We'll toggle ortho off for the last dimension, to keep it clear of the top one.

Placing Ordinate Dimensions

Command: **ZOOM**	Zoom to fill screen with viewport.
Command: **SNAP**	Set to 1/8.
Command: <Ortho on>	Make sure ortho is on.
Command: **UCSICON**	Set to ORigin.
Command: **UCS**	Set to lower left corner of section.
Origin/ZAxis/3point/Entity/View/X/Y/Z/ Prev/Restore/Save/Del/?/<World>: **O**	
Origin point <0,0,0>: **.X**	.X point filter.
of	Pick point on face of flange with osnap NEA or INT.
(need YZ):	Pick point at bottom of section with osnap NEA or INT.
Command: **DIM**	
Dim: **ORD**	Dimension the base point.
Select Feature: **0,0**	The UCS base point.
Leader endpoint (Xdatum/Ydatum):	Pick @1<180 for end of dimension leader.
Dimension text <0>: **<RETURN>**	
Dim: **ORD**	Use osnap INT to dimension point ① (see fig. 12.21).

Placing Ordinate Dimensions—continued

Dim: **ORD**	Use .X and .Y point filters and osnaps to dimension top left corner of section.
Dim: **ORD**	Dimension the hole at top.
Select Feature: **END**	
of	Pick point ② at end of center line.
Leader endpoint (Xdatum/Ydatum):	
\<Ortho off\>	Toggle ortho off and pick point ③.
Dimension text \<7 1/2\>: **\<RETURN\>**	
Dim: **E**	Exit the DIM command.

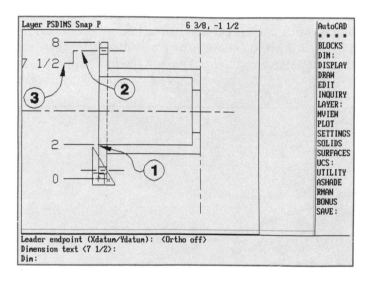

Figure 12.21:
Ordinate dimensions
in paper space.

AutoCAD rounds off the angle between your first and second points to 90-degree increments to determine whether to calculate the X datum or Y datum. The Xdatum and Ydatum options of ORDINATE let you override AutoCAD and specify whether you want an X coordinate or Y coordinate.

More often than paper space, you will dimension in model space.

Dimensioning the Section View in Model Space

When you dimension in model space, you need to make sure DIMSCALE is appropriately set for your final plotting scale. The whole point of composing a drawing in a paper space sheet is so that the sheet then gets plotted at full scale. If you compose your sheet before you dimension, you can set DIMSCALE relative to paper space scale. DIMSCALE has a special feature to do this for you. If you set DIMSCALE to 0, then it calculates an appropriate scale value relative to the scale of the current viewport in paper space. This is the inverse of the ZOOM XP scale value used for that viewport. When you are in paper space, or using tilemode viewports, the 0 setting is ignored and treated as if set to 1.

We'll set up a viewport and use DIMSCALE in the following exercise.

Setting Up for Dimensioning the Section View

We'll create and zoom the viewport for half scale. We also need to set two other dimension variables to get the dimension appearance we want. If you look at figure 12.22, you'll see that the 1" and 1/2" dimensions at the bottom of the view have no text or dimension lines between the extension lines. You need to turn DIMTIX and DIMTOFL off to allow the text outside and suppress the inside dimension line when the text is placed outside. We'll save the changes as a new dimstyle. You can use the icon menus or enter the dimension variables at the dim mode prompt. We'll use the same modified prompt format as in the earlier dimension variable icon exercise.

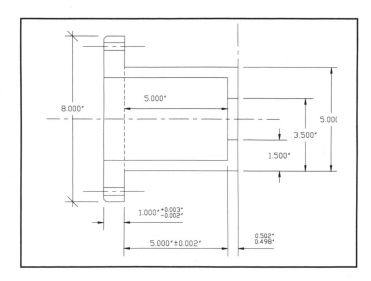

Figure 12.22:
The MOCKDIM
section view target
drawing.

Setting Up for Dimensioning the Section View in Model Space

Command: **PSPACE**
Command: **UCS**   Set to World.
Command: **ERASE**   Erase the ordinate dimensioning and viewport.
Command: **LAYER**   Set DIMS current.
Command: **MVIEW**   Enter points .5,.5 and 12,8 to create a new
                                         viewport.

Setting Up for Dimensioning the Section View in Model Space—continued

Command: **ZOOM**	Zoom to fill screen with viewport.
Command: **MSPACE**	
Command: **ZOOM**	Zoom .5XP for half scale.
Command: **DIMSCALE**	Set to 0.
Command: **PAN**	Pan the image as illustrated.
Command: **PSPACE**	
Select [**Settings**] [**Set Dim Vars...**]	From pull-down menu to display [Select to Set Dimension Variables] icon menu.
Dim:	Select [Dim Text...] icon to change to [Set Dimension Text Variables -1-] icon menu.
DIMTOFL <On>: **OFF**	Select icon #8, which suppresses line between extension lines when text is outside.
Dim:	Select [Next...] icon to change to [Set Dimension Text Variables -2-] icon menu.
DIMTIX <On>: **OFF**	Select icon #3, which allows text outside extension line.
Dim:	Select the [Exit] icon to change to the [Save Dimvar Changes Before Exit?] icon menu.
Dim:	Select icon #1 and save new dimension style as MOCK2O (the letter o, not zero, named for 1/2 scale with Outside text and dimension lines).
Dim: **E**	Exit the DIM command.
Command: **MSPACE**	Ready to dimension (see fig. 12.23).
Command: **SAVE**	

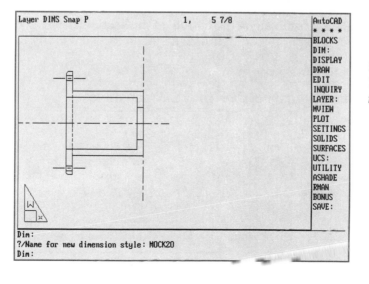

Figure 12.23:
The viewport, ready to dimension.

Even though you only changed three dimension variables, including DIMSCALE, the last exercise shows how easy it is to modify a dimension style and create a new one. The DIMSCALE 0 setting for model space dimensioning and the earlier DIMLFAC -2 setting for paper space dimensioning are compatible — this style can now be used for either.

> **Caution:** If you need to zoom an image, don't zoom in model space. It will throw off the DIMSCALE sizing of the dimension relative to paper space. Instead, enter paper space and zoom, and then re-enter model space.

Let's take another look at figure 12.22. The linear dimensions along the bottom form a set of continuing dimensions; the dimensions on the right are baseline dimensions.

Dimensioning With Continued Dimensions

You start with a normal linear dimension. Then CONTINUE strings subsequent dimensions together in a series, starting a new dimension line where the last dimension line left off. If it needs to clear the previous text, it offsets the new dimension line by the DIMDLI value. We set it to 5/8 earlier. CONTINUE uses the previous extension line as the first extension line for the new dimension.

> **Note:** If you're using Release 10 and picking up again at this point, set DIMTIX and DIMTOFL off, erase the 3-1/32 dimension, and pan to the view in the following illustration before doing the exercise.

Let's draw a horizontal dimension along the bottom of the section view and continue by adding new extension lines (to the right). Remember to use osnaps to ensure accuracy.

Using Horizontal CONTINUE Dimensions

```
Command: DIM
Dim: HOR
First extension line origin or RETURN to select:    Pick point ① (see fig. 12.24).
Second extension line origin:                       Pick point ②.
Dimension line location:                            Pick absolute point 21,8.
Dimension text <1/2>: <RETURN>                      Accept AutoCAD's text
                                                    default.

Dim: CON                                            Type, or select [continue] from
                                                    the screen menu.
```

> ### Using Horizontal CONTINUE Dimensions—continued
>
> | | |
> |---|---|
> | `Second extension line origin or RETURN to select:` | Pick the next point at ③ (see fig. 12.25). |
> | `Dimension text <5>:` **`<RETURN>`** | Accept AutoCAD's text. |
> | `Dim:` **`CON`** | Pick next point at ④ and accept default text. |

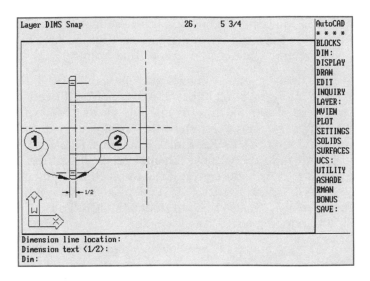

Figure 12.24:
First horizontal dimension.

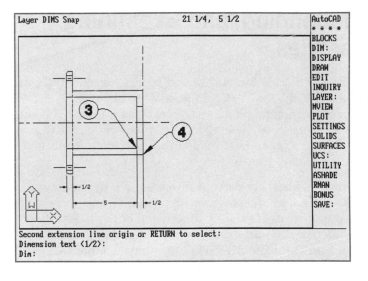

Figure 12.25:
Continued horizontal dimensions.

Notice that the new dimensions are scaled the same as the earlier dimensions done with DIMSCALE 2. AutoCAD put the 1/2 of the first dimension outside the extension line because it could not fit into the dimensioned space. To put the text on the left side, just reverse the pick order of the two points.

AutoCAD automatically put the continued dimension line below the first one. The distance between the two dimension lines is controlled by DIMDLI. If the first horizontal dimension, 1/2, had been drawn right to left, its text would have been on the left and all three dimension lines would have been drawn in-line.

The default for CONTINUE is to string dimensions from the last linear dimension drawn in the current drawing session. The Return to select option (not in Release 10) lets you select an existing linear dimension to continue from.

Next, we'll do a series of vertical baseline dimensions. Like continue dimensions, baseline dimensions start from an existing linear dimension. You'll need a normal vertical dimension to start with. If you use the current dimstyle as it is, it will put the text outside the extension lines, but you won't know this until you try it. So we'll try a vertical dimension, undo, reload the MOCK2I dimstyle, change DIMSCALE to 0 for model space and save it, and redo the vertical dimension. We'll use the MOCK2I dimstyle because it sets DIMTIX on, to force AutoCAD to place the dimension text within the dimension lines. We'll need to turn DIMTOFL off to prevent it drawing a dimension line through the text. We'll also need to update MOCK2I's DIMSCALE to 0 for model space scaling to paper space.

(If you are using Release 10, skip ahead to the *Dimensioning With Baseline Dimensions* section.)

Restoring, Redefining, and Examining Existing Dimstyles

The primary dimension commands for working with existing dimstyles are SAVE, RESTORE, and VARIABLES. (We will also look at the UPDATE and OVERRIDE commands in the associative dimensioning section of this chapter.) You can use the SAVE command to save changes you make to a style, which redefines that style. Use caution in redefining existing dimstyles, because that will change all the drawing's existing dimension entities using that style.

The RESTORE command changes the current dimstyle to a previously saved style. You enter a dimension style name to restore, or press <RETURN> to view dimension options and adopt the dimstyle of an existing dimension entity. Restoring dimstyles by selecting existing dimensions is an excellent way to prevent errors — what you see is what you get. You can enter the DIMSTYLE system variable as a command to see what the current style name is, but you can't change it that way. You can, however, rename an existing dimstyle with the RENAME command (it's not a dim mode command).

The VARIABLES command lists the dimension variable settings of any saved dimstyle. It lists them in the same format as the STATUS dimensioning command lists the settings of the current dimstyle.

The SAVE, RESTORE, and VARIABLES commands each have an inquiry option. If you enter a question mark, they will list existing style names. You can use wildcards, such as an asterisk, for a listing of all styles.

Let's try that vertical dimension we need. Then undo it and use RESTORE to reload the MOCK2I dimstyle and adjust its DIMSCALE and DIMTIX settings. We'll redo the dimension in a subsequent exercise. Remember, changing any dimension variable changes the current dimstyle to *UNNAMED, so use SAVE to redefine the style and set it current before using it.

Restoring and Redefining a Dimstyle

```
Dim: VER
First extension line origin or RETURN to select:      Pick corner at ① with osnap INT
                                                      (see fig. 12.26).
Second extension line origin:                         Pick corner at ② with osnap INT.
Dimension line location:                              Pick absolute point 28,11.
Dimension text <1-1/4>: <RETURN>                      Places the text outside, with a
                                                      leader.
Command: U

Dim: RES                                              Restore.
Current dimension style: MOCK2O
?/Enter dimension style name or RETURN to
  select dimension: MOCK2I
Dim: DIMSCALE                                         Reset from 2 to 0 to automatically
                                                      scale to paper space.
Dim: DIMTOFL                                          Set to OFF to suppress dimension
                                                      line inside extension lines.
Dim: SAVE
?/Name for new dimension style: MOCK2I
That name is already in use, redefine it? <N>: Y
```

Now the vertical dimension will fit within the extension lines when you redo it in the next exercise.

You can also use the [Dimension Style Options] icon menu to select, save, restore, list, and redefine dimstyles. To get to it, select [Set Dim Vars...] from the [Settings] pull-down menu, and then select the [Dim Style...] icon. The menu's icons make their functions pretty clear. When you try them out, some of them seem to leave you at the dim mode prompt; press <RETURN> to get back to the icon menu. (We'll look at the [Dimension Style Override] later in the chapter.)

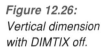

Figure 12.26:
Vertical dimension
with DIMTIX off.

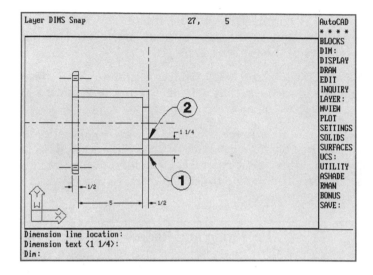

There are two ways you can save dimstyles and reload them from separate disk files.

Saving and Reloading Dimstyles From Disk Files

Just as you create a library of blocks, you can create a library of dimstyles. One way is to define all of the dimstyles you need in a prototype drawing. Then, if you start new drawings equal to the prototype (*newname=prototypename*) or set it as your default prototype with the AutoCAD configuration menu, new drawings will already contain those dimstyles.

The other method is to create a drawing file containing one or more dimension styles and insert it as a block into any drawing where you need to use those styles. There are several ways to do this. You can wblock the dimension entities which use those styles to a new file. Then, when you insert it as a block, cancel the insertion before the entities themselves become part of your drawing. Or, you can define the styles in an empty drawing and insert it without needing to cancel it. You can also create a style-laden empty drawing by erasing dimension entities from a wblocked drawing. In any case, the insertion will make any dimstyles in the inserted file a part of your current drawing.

Dimensioning With Baseline Dimensions

Now that the first vertical dimension line is in place, use the BASELINE command to continue it. BASELINE is like a cross between continue and ordinate dimensioning.

It works like CONTINUE, except it uses the first extension line (base extension line) as the origin for all successive dimension calculations and line placements. This means that each successive dimension line is offset by the DIMDLI setting.

Using BASELINE for a Series of Vertical Dimensions

If using Release 10, set DIMTIX on and DIMTOFL off.

Dim: **VER**	Repeat previous dimension, picking points ① and ② with osnap INT and dimension line at 28,11 (see fig. 12.27).
Dim: **BAS**	Type, or select [baseline] from the screen menu.
Second extension line origin or RETURN to select:	Pick corner point at ③ (see fig. 12.28).
Dimension text <3 3/4>: **<RETURN>**	Accept the default text.
Dim: **BAS**	Pick second extension line origin at ④ and <RETURN> for default text.
Dim: **E**	Return to command prompt.
Command: **SAVE**	Save and continue or end and take a break.

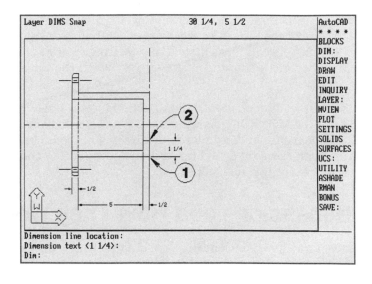

Figure 12.27:
The first vertical dimension for BASELINE.

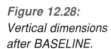

Figure 12.28:
Vertical dimensions
after BASELINE.

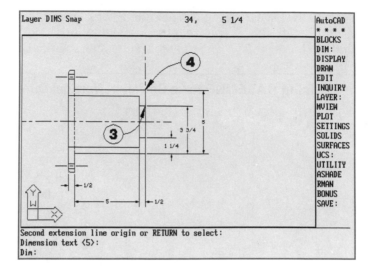

Save your drawing, because the next set of exercises will stretch, scale, and update it.

The Efficiency of Dimstyles

It may seem as if dimstyles add more work to dimensioning. Why not just set the dimension variables and be done with it? That might be easier for a few dimensions. But when you do several types of dimensions over and over, you will be constantly resetting dimension variables as you switch between types. With dimstyles, you can just restore the style to switch between types instead of resetting several dimension variables. In the long run, they are faster and easier — well worth the time it takes to set them up.

You've been creating associative dimensions all along, whether you knew it or not. In the next section we'll use the MOCKDIM drawing to take a closer look at associative dimensions. You'll also learn to further tailor your dimensions to include tolerances, change the terminator (arrow) type, and use dimensioning utility commands to edit the characteristics of existing dimensions.

Associative Dimensions and How They Work

An associative dimension is a dimension entity — a single entity. We call them *asodims*. You can move, scale, and stretch them along with the entities being dimensioned, and the dimension text will adjust automatically. Associative dimensioning is the default dimensioning mode. If the DIMASO dimension variable is on,

AutoCAD creates asodims (except for leader dimensions, which are always individual entities). If DIMASO is off, AutoCAD draws dimensions with individual lines, arrows (solids), arcs, and text entities. If you have not changed the default from <ON>, you have been creating associative dimensions all along!

An asodim is a special kind of unnamed block. Exploding an asodim creates individual lines, arrows (solids), arcs, and text entities which *look* the same as the original dimension entity. The individual components of asodims can only be edited by special associative dimensioning commands or by STRETCH. Exploded asodims or dimensions created with DIMASO OFF can be edited as ordinary entities.

The dimstyle name current at the time of creation is stored with an associative dimension entity. If it is a named dimstyle, this protects the asodim from being affected by any subsequent changes to dimension variables (unless the dimstyle is redefined). If the current dimstyle is *UNNAMED when you create a dimension, then the asodim will change to reflect whatever dimension variables are current if it is edited or updated. This has the usually undesirable effect of changing its appearance. Accidentally updating asodims is easily done with the STRETCH or SCALE commands as well as several dimensioning commands. To protect the integrity of your dimensions, you should be careful to make sure a named dimstyle is current whenever you create a dimension. (Release 10 asodims always behave as if they had *UNNAMED dimstyles, because Release 10 has no dimstyle feature.) Whenever asodims are updated, they assume the current dimstyle (or all dimension variables in Release 10), text style, and units settings.

Asodims are drawn with the current text style and units. There are no dimension variables to control these. You can use the normal AutoCAD UNITS command to set units and the dim mode STYLE command or the normal AutoCAD STYLE command to set text style. The dim mode STYLE command is limited to setting styles; it can't define a style. Using a named dimstyle does not protect the text style or units from accidental updating. The safest thing is to limit your dimensions to a single text style. If you need more than one type of units, keep one type set with the UNITS command and create the other(s) with the dimension variables DIMALT, DIMALTD, DIMALTF, DIMPOST, and DIMLFAC.

When you use associative dimensioning, you are creating *definition points* (defpoints). Asodims use defpoints to control their rescaling and updating. Defpoints are kept on a special layer called DEFPOINTS. They won't plot but are always visible if their dimension is visible. Exploding an asodim converts defpoints to point entities on layer DEFPOINTS. The defpoint locations vary with the type of dimension; for linear dimensions, there is one at each extension line origin and one at the dimension line intersection with the second extension line. You can osnap to defpoints with osnap NODe, even though frozen. You can also osnap NODe to the midpoint of the asodim text, although it is not a true defpoint.

Subentities of asodims respond to the osnap modes just like subentities of ordinary blocks. For example, you can snap to the end of a dimension arrow using osnap ENDPoint.

How to Use Associative Dimensions

Associative dimensions make it easy to update and rescale a fully dimensioned drawing. In the following exercises, we will show you three ways to use asodims: to update dimension variables, including redefining and reassigning dimstyles; to stretch dimensions to relocate dimension text; and to stretch and rescale drawing entities and their associated dimensions to automatically update measurements.

There are seven dimensioning commands for editing existing associative dimensions. (Only HOMETEXT, NEWTEXT, and UPDATE are in Release 10.) Here is a complete listing.

Associative Dimensioning Commands

HOMETEXT   Restores asodim text to its default (home) position.

UPDATE   Reformats asodims to the current dimstyle.

NEWTEXT   Allows editing of asodim text, or restores the default measurement as text.

OBLIQUE   Changes extension lines to an oblique angle.

OVERRIDE   Allows overriding (changing) one or more dimension variable settings of the current dimstyle and applying them to one or more selected asodims, as dimstyle *UNNAMED.

TEDIT   Changes the position of dimension text.

TROTATE   Allows you to change the rotation of dimension text.

Appending a Units Suffix to Dimension Text

If you look closely at your current drawing, you will see that your dimension text does not show any units. We are using the multipurpose fractional style of units. You can set an automatic dimension suffix with DIMPOST to append any text character or string to dimensions. You set it to a period to clear the suffix. Commonly used suffixes or prefixes include ', ", cm, fathoms, R (radius), or the diameter symbol %%C. We'll use " to add inch marks to the dimensions. Occasionally, you may want to add a suffix, prefix, or both by typing your custom characters before or after < > at the dimension text prompt, and AutoCAD will insert your characters and replace < > with its calculated text.

Controlling Extension Line Offset From Objects

While you are setting dimension variables, reset DIMEXO to increase the offset for extension lines. The default 1/16 is too small to clearly separate extension lines from objects. After setting the dimension variables, we'll use UPDATE to apply the changes to the existing dimensions.

Updating Associative Dimensions

UPDATE updates selected asodims by applying the current dimstyle (or all dimension variables in Release 10), text style, and units settings to them. You should make sure a current named dimstyle exists before using it, or the asodim will adopt an *UNNAMED dimstyle. All non-asodim entities are ignored even if they are part of the selection set, so window and crossing selections are easy and convenient.

We'll update all the asodims with DIMPOST and DIMEXO. First, for simplicity, return to a single TILEMODE viewport and reset DIMSCALE to 2. Update the current MOCK2I dimstyle first, and then repeat the process for MOCK2O. (If you're using Release 10, skip the TILEMODE setting and the SAVE and RESTORE dimensioning commands.)

Updating Dimensions With Suffix Text and
Increased Extension Line Origin Offsets

 Begin a NEW drawing named MOCKDIM=IA6MOKD3 to replace the old MOCKDIM.

 Edit an EXISTING drawing named MOCKDIM.

Command: **TILEMODE**	Set to 1. (Release 10, just zoom instead.)
Command: **ZOOM**	Zoom to the view shown.
Command: **DIM**	
Dim: **DIMEXO**	Set extension line offset to 1/8".
Dim: **DIMPOST**	
Current value <> New value: `"`	Set suffix to ".
Dim: **DIMSCALE**	Set to 2.
Dim: **SAVE**	Save as MOCK2I again. It immediately redefines vertical baseline asodims with added " and larger extension origin offsets.
Dim: **UPD**	Update the rest of the inside dimensions in top view.
Select objects:	Select all the dimensions of the top view with a window. (Release 10, select the vertical baseline asodims also.)

**Updating Dimensions With Suffix Text and
Increased Extension Line Origin Offsets—continued**

`34 found.`	All objects except asodims will be ignored.
`Select objects: `**`<RETURN>`**	An " gets added and the extension origin offset increases.
`Dim: `**`RES`**	Restore and repeat process for MOCK2O dimstyle.
`Current dimension style: MOCK2I`	
`?/Enter dimension style name or RETURN to`	
`  select dimension: `**`<RETURN>`**	
`Select dimension:`	Pick one of the horizontal continue asodims.
`Current dimension style: MOCK2O`	

Set DIMEXO 1/8", DIMPOST suffix type to ", DIMSCALE to 2, and SAVE as MOCK2O dimstyle again to redefine horizontal continue asodims. (If using Release 10, also set DIMTIX off.)

`Dim: `**`UPD`**	Select the R3/16" TYP 6 PLACES dimension to update. (Release 10, select the horizontal continue asodims also.)
`Dim: `**`E`**	

Now all the dimension text except the 60-degree radius dimension have inch marks (see fig. 12.29). Angular dimensions ignore DIMPOST. With DIMEXO at 1/8, the dimensions are separated more clearly from the objects they dimension. But, the extension lines on the 5" diameter vertical dimension at the left still look too close because of the large radius of the circle. We'll fix that in a minute, but first take a quick look at other controls for dimension line and extension line appearance.

Controlling Dimension and Extension Lines

Don't confuse DIMEXO with the similar sounding DIMEXE, which controls how far extension lines extend beyond the dimension line. Other useful dimension variables for controlling dimension and extension line appearance are DIMDLE, DIMGAP, DIMTAD, DIMSE1, and DIMSE2. Here's what they do:

DIMDLE Extends the dimension line through tick marks by its value when DIMTSZ is on (non-zero).

DIMGAP Controls the gap between text and the break in the dimension line. (It's not in Release 10.)

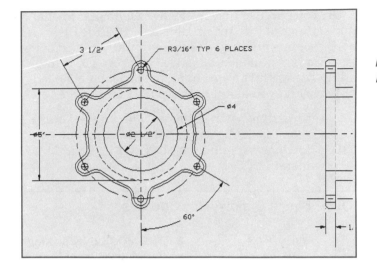

Figure 12.29:
Detail of a top view.

DIMTAD Puts text above the dimension line, with no break, when on. How far above is controlled by DIMTVP.

DIMSE1 Suppresses drawing of the first extension line. An on/off toggle switch. Suppression off means draw the line; suppression on means omit the line.

DIMSE2 Suppresses drawing of the second extension line.

DIMSE1 and DIMSE2 are commonly used as exceptions to various dimstyles. Often you need to draw a dimension where the extension line would overlap the object itself or another existing extension line. With nonassociative dimensions, this creates extra entities and extra data in the drawing file. This doesn't hurt anything except it will slow down regenerations and may not plot neatly. The overlapping lines will each plot, which may show differently from other plotted lines. You can suppress this with plot optimization (not in Release 10). If the extraneous extension line overlaps a dashed or hidden line, you will definitely need to suppress DIMSE1 or DIMSE2.

Sometimes, in odd cases like suppressing DIMSE1 or DIMSE2 or putting an extra large DIMEXO on a curve, it is more expedient to override one or two dimension variables for a single dimension rather than create another special dimstyle. (In Release 10, you just use UPDATE for everything.) We'll try a DIMSE1 and DIMEXO override in the next exercise.

Overriding Dimension Styles

There are two ways to override a dimstyle. You can simply change one or more dimension variables before drawing the odd dimension, and then restore the style and continue working. Or, you can use the OVERRIDE command to change one or more dimension variable settings of the current dimstyle. OVERRIDE then prompts you to select one or more asodims and updates them to the modified set of dimension variables. If the asodim has a named dimstyle, you can ask it to be updated (redefining it for all entities using it). The current dimstyle is not changed, unless it is also the asodim's dimstyle and you ask it to be updated.

Let's alter the 5" diameter vertical dimension at the left with an even larger DIMEXO and draw a horizontal dimension inside the flange hole on the section with DIMSE1 on. (Because Release 10 lacks dimstyles, just use UPDATE instead of OVERRIDE and skip the RESTORE command.)

Overriding a Dimstyle for Odd Cases

Command: **DIM**	
Dim: **RES**	Restore MOCK2I by picking the vertical dimension of the circle.
Dim: **OVE**	Override. (Release 10, set DIMEXO to 1/2 and use UPDATE.)
Dimension variable to override: **DIMEXO**	
Current value <1/8> New value: **1/2**	
Dimension variable to override: **<RETURN>**	
Select objects:	Select the vertical dimension of the circle.
Modify dimension style "MOCK2I"? <N>	
<RETURN>	Leave it unchanged.
Dim: **DIMSE1**	Set to ON to suppress first extension line.
Dim: **HOR**	Pick extension line origins at ① on hidden line, ② inside hole, and dimension line at ② (see fig. 12.30).
Dim: **RES**	Restore MOCK2I.
Dim: **E**	
Command: **SAVE**	

Now the offset should be quite distinct. You can see no first extension line from the new horizontal dimension over the hidden line. You should be able to see the second extension line in yellow, overlapping the green bottom line of the hole.

Override with caution. Whether you use OVERRIDE or you change dimension variables, draw a dimension, and then restore the style, you'll get the same results. The difference between OVERRIDE and UPDATE is that OVERRIDE assigns dimstyle *UNNAMED to the asodim(s) (unless you ask it to update the dimstyle), so they are not protected from accidental updating. UPDATE assigns the current dimstyle, named or unnamed.

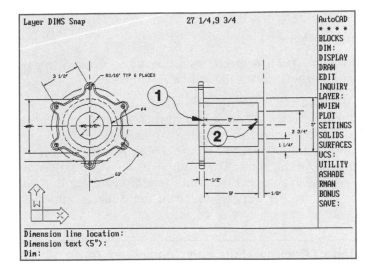

Figure 12.30:
Dimension on a circle
before override.

Tip: If the asodims have the current dimstyle, answering yes to update the dimstyle with OVERRIDE is equivalent to first changing dimension variables and then redefining the current dimstyle with SAVE.

Until now, we have been using fractional units. Dimensioning will use whatever units are current. Drawings like this are usually done in decimal units, so let's try updating to them.

Controlling Units

Controlling units is simple and automatic — the current drawing units are used in the dimensioning text. Almost as simple is applying a round-off factor with the DIMRND dimension variable. If DIMRND is non-zero, all measurements (except angular dimensions) are rounded to the nearest increment of its value. For example, if set to .5, the dimension text would be rounded to the nearest half unit. DIMRND does not truncate trailing zeros; the number of decimal places and display of zeros are controlled by the UNITS command and the DIMZIN dimension variable.

With DIMZIN, controlling units begins to get tricky. There are several possible ways to format many measurements. For example, in feet and inches, 1/4", 8" and 3' might also be formatted 0'0 1/4", 0'8", and 3'0". This is controlled by setting DIMZIN to 1, 2, 3, or 4.

- A setting of 0 suppresses both zero feet and zero inches (the default).
- A setting of 1 includes both zero feet and zero inches.

- A setting of 2 includes zero feet but suppresses zero inches.
- A setting of 3 suppresses zero feet but includes zero inches.

If there are fractional inches, then zero inches are not suppressed, regardless of setting. This avoids hard-to-read values like 6'1/2".

DIMZIN also controls decimal zeros, using settings of 4 and 8. These are additive settings; you can use them both for a sum of 12 and you can add them to the 0,1, 2, or 3 settings for feet and inches control. A value of 4 (or 5, 6, or 7) suppresses all leading zeros. For example, 0.7500 would become .7500. A value of 8 (or 9, 10, or 11) suppresses (truncates) trailing zeros. For example, 0.7500 would become 0.75. A value of 12 (or 13, 14, or 15) suppresses both leading and trailing zeros. For example, 0.7500 would become .75. Let's try updating our dimensions with decimal units and suppressing some zeros.

Updating to Decimal Units and Controlling Zeros

Command: **ZOOM**	Window 16,6 to 34,18.
Command: **UNITS**	Set to 2, decimal units, 3 decimal places, and default the rest.
Command: **DIM**	

If using Release 10, set DIMTIX on and DIMEXO to 1/8.

Dim: **UPD**	Select all vertical asodims and they become decimal. The DIMPOST " suffix remains.
Command: **RES**	Restore dimstyle MOCK2O. (Release 10, set DIMTIX off instead.)
Dim: **UPD**	Select all horizontal asodims and they become decimal.
Dim: **OVE**	Override. (Release 10, set DIMZIN to 12 and use UPDATE.)
Dimension variable to override: **DIMZIN**	Set to 12.
Dimension variable to override: **<RETURN>**	
Select objects:	Select the horizontal dimensions.
Modify dimension style "MOCK2O"? <N>	Answer no for each selected dimension.

Examine the dimensions, then undo the DIMZIN override:

Dim: **U**	(Release 10, undo twice, for DIMZIN and UPDATE.)
Dim: **OVE**	Override the 5" horizontal dimension inside the hole with DIMSE1 ON. (Release 10, set DIMSE1 on and use UPDATE.)
Dim: **E**	
Command: **SAVE**	Save the drawing.

Figure 12.31 shows the section before DIMZIN; figure 12.32 shows the dimensions after DIMZIN.

Experiment with different units and DIMZIN settings for other combinations you may need in your work.

You can also alter the linear scale of units and combine two alternate forms of units in one dimension.

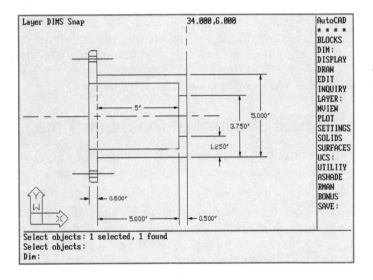

Figure 12.31:
Decimal dimensions
before DIMZIN.

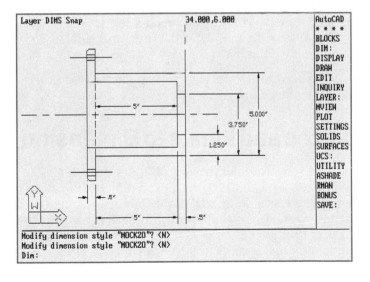

Figure 12.32:
Decimal dimensions
after DIMZIN.

Dimensioning With Alternate Units

Normally, AutoCAD uses the units settings and actual distances you set up when you draw entities to calculate dimensions. If these units are not the lengths you want shown in dimensioning, you can apply a standard multiplier to alter the default AutoCAD calculations. You might use this to dimension an inserted scaled-down or metric detail.

To get AutoCAD to multiply all linear default dimensioning measurements by a standard factor, you set the DIMLFAC dimension variable. When DIMLFAC is non-zero, AutoCAD uses the factor as a multiplier when calculating the dimension text. DIMLFAC has no effect on angular dimensioning. For example, if the measured dimension is 7.05" you could set DIMLFAC to 2.54 to generate the metric equivalent (17.907). Then to make it read as 17.907cm, set DIMPOST to cm.

Using Two Measurement Systems at the Same Time

To get AutoCAD to display alternative dimension text strings on a dimension line, set DIMALT on. When you do, AutoCAD formats the dimension like *number* [*alternate number*] on the dimension line.

The first number is the standard dimension measurement (multiplied by DIMLFAC if it is non-zero). The alternate number, shown in brackets, is the first number multiplied by DIMALTF (dim alternative factor). The alternate number of decimal places is set by DIMALTD (dim alternative decimals). The default for DIMALTF is 25.4, the number of millimeters in an inch. The default for DIMALTD is two decimal places. The optional alternative suffix is set by DIMAPOST. For example, if the measured dimension is 7.05, to have the text line read 7.05" [17.907cm], set these dimension variables: DIMAPOST to cm: DIMALT on; and DIMALTF to 2.54. (DIMALTD is already 2 places by default.)

A common reason for using alternative units is so you can include tolerances in your dimensions. AutoCAD makes it easy.

Adding Tolerances and Limits to Dimension Text

The dimension variables that control tolerances and limits are DIMTOL, DIMLIM, DIMTM, DIMTP, and DIMTFAC. The DIMRND round-off dimension variable is also useful. DIMTOL ON turns tolerances on and DIMLIM ON turns limits on. They are mutually exclusive; turning one on turns the other off. DIMTP is the plus tolerance/limit value and DIMTM is the minus value. DIMTFAC controls the size of the plus and minus tolerance and limits text strings (relative to DIMTXT size).

If you have only a couple of tolerance or limits dimensions in a drawing, you may want to use OVERRIDE. If you use frequent tolerances and limits, you'll want to create dimstyles for them. A convenient compromise is to have tolerance and limits dimstyles that you can override for specific DIMTP and DIMTM values, but that will sacrifice the dimstyle protection against accidental changes.

Tolerances and limits work the same whether you update existing dimensions or create new ones with their settings. We'll update the existing horizontal asodims below the section. We'll set DIMTOL on, DIMTP to .003, DIMTM to .002, and DIMTFAC to .8 (.8 x .125 DIMTXT = .1 text), and save a new dimstyle. We'll also set DIMTAD on to place dimension text above unbroken dimension lines. Then we'll override those settings to update one asodim with equal DIMTP and DIMTM values and update another with DIMLIM on. You can use the dimension variables directly or the dimvar icon menus. The [Dim Text] icon on several of the dimvar icon menus brings up the [Set Dimension Text Variables -1-] icon menu, which contains four easy-to-use icons. They lead to equally easy-to-use icon menus for setting tolerance and limits values.

Creating and Using Tolerance and Limits Dimensions

```
Command: DIM
Dim: DIMSTYLE                                MOCK2O should be current. (Release 10,
                                             DIMTIX should be off.)

Dim: DIMTAD                                  Set on for text above the dimension line.
Dim: DIMTOL                                  Set tolerances on.
Dim: DIMTP                                   Set .003 for plus tolerance.
Current value <0.000> New Value: .003
Dim: DIMTM                                    Set .002 for minus tolerance.
Dim: DIMTFAC                                  Set to .8 for .125 x .8 = .1" text.

Dim: SAVE                                     Save as dimstyle MOCK2OTP3M2
                                             (DIMSCALE 2 Outside Tolerance Plus
                                             .003 Minus .002).

Dim: UPD                                      Select bottom three horizontal dimensions
                                             to update them, as shown in figure 12.33.

Dim: DIMTP                                    Set to .002, same as DIMTM.
Dim: UPD                                      Update 5.000" horizontal toleranced
                                             dimension to override its style.

Dim: DIMLIM                                   Set to on, which turns DIMTOL off.
Dim: UPD                                      Update 0.500" horizontal toleranced
                                             dimension to override its style, as shown
                                             in figure 12.34.

Dim: E
Command: SAVE
```

Figure 12.33:
Horizontal dimensions above a line with tolerances.

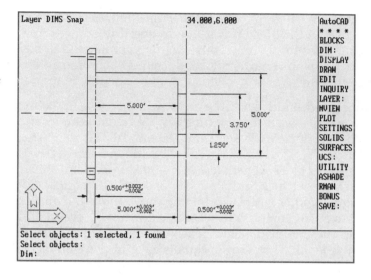

Figure 12.34:
Horizontal dimensions with tolerances and limits.

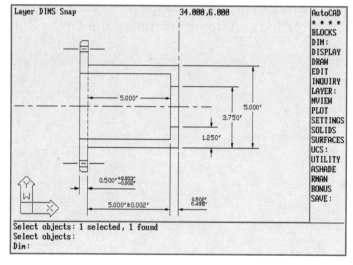

The left-most horizontal dimension should read 0.500" +0.003"/-0.002", the middle one 5.000" ±0.002", and the right-most one 0.502"/0.498".

> ***Note:*** For more complete coverage of geometric dimensioning and tolerancing to ANSI Y14.5M standards, see *STEPPING INTO AutoCAD*, also from New Riders Publishing.

Besides the settings we've used, like units, tolerances, limits, and size, there are several other ways to control dimension text.

Controlling Dimension Text

In addition to those we've already covered, there are several other important commands and dimension variables that affect dimension text:

HOMETEXT   Restores asodim text to its default (home) position.

NEWTEXT   Allows editing the contents of asodim text, or restores the default measurement as text if you enter <>. Embedded <> measurements and text are legal.

TEDIT   Changes location of dim text without affecting its contents. You can justify it left or right, pick a new location, restore it to its home position, or change its angle. Or you can use the STRETCH command instead. TEDIT includes the features of HOMETEXT, NEWTEXT, TROTATE, and STRETCH, but can only edit one asodim at a time.

TROTATE   Allows you to change the rotation angle of dimension text.

DIMTIH   Keeps text that is inside extension lines horizontal when on (the default). When off, the angle of the text takes on the angle of the dimension line.

DIMTOH   Same as DIMTIH, but places text outside the extension lines.

DIMCLRT   Assigns a color to asodim text, for plotting pen line weight control.

STRETCH   The regular command, not a dimension command, is useful for relocating dim text to locations not allowed by the TEDIT command.

Let's use STRETCH to relocate the 0.500" +0.003"/-0.002" horizontal section view dimension. When selecting dim text with STRETCH, the crossing window only needs to catch the node point in the center of the dim text. Then use TEDIT to relocate the 5.000" horizontal dimension in the hole of the section view and the 5" vertical dimension text on the far left of the flange top view. The 5" vertical dimension text is located on top of the flange center line, so we'll move it up a little. While we're editing the dimensions, break the center lines going through the inner circle's 2 1/2" diameter dimension. We'll also set DIMCLRT to red, both to try it out and to use it as a visible flag to see which dimension text values are changed by the TEDIT and STRETCH commands.

Relocating Text and Controlling Color
With TEDIT, STRETCH, and DIMCLRT

Command: **PAN**	Or zoom D, to view illustrated in figure 12.35.
Command: **DIM**	
Dim: **RES**	Restore dimstyle MOCK2I. (Release 10, set DIMTOL and DIMTAD off and DIMTIX on.)
Dim: **UPD**	Select all asodims in top view (except R3/16) to update to decimal.
Dim: **DIMCLRT**	Set to red. (Not in Release 10.) Now dimstyle is *UNNAMED.
Dim: **E**	
Command: **STRETCH**	Select 0.500" +0.003"/-0.002" horizontal dimension ① with Crossing (see fig. 12.35).
Base point:	Pick the midpoint of the text with osnap NODe.
New point: <Ortho on>	Drag to left of extension lines and pick point to place it with ortho on.
Command: **STRETCH**	Stretch the 5.000" horizontal dimension ② slightly to the left and clear above the dimension line with ortho off (see fig. 12.35).
Command: **DIM**	
Dim: **DIMSHO**	Set to off to suppress updating dimensions while dragging.
Dim: **TEDIT**	(Release 10, use STRETCH instead.)
Select dimension:	Pick the 5" diameter dimension at the far left.
Enter text location (Left/Right/Home/Angle):	Pick new location above center line.
Dim: **E**	
Command: **BREAK**	Break the center lines to clear the 2.500" diameter dimension.
Command: **SAVE**	

Figure 12.36 shows the results of this command sequence.

Setting DIMCLRT made the current dimstyle *UNNAMED. However, the first STRETCH and the TEDIT didn't change their dimension's text values because they had named dimstyles stored with them. The second STRETCH, of the 5" horizontal dimension, updated it to the current dimension variable settings and changed its color because it was an *UNNAMED asodim to begin with. (If using Release 10,

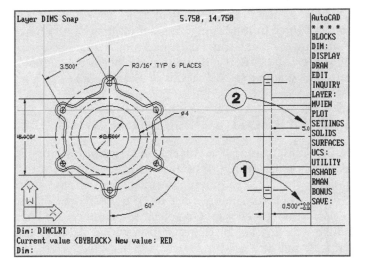

*Figure 12.35:
MOCKDIM before
STRETCH and
TEDIT.*

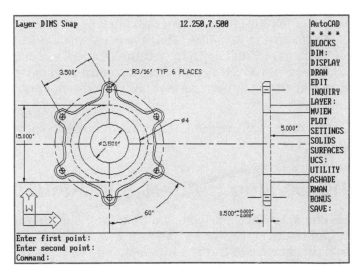

*Figure 12.36:
MOCKDIM after
STRETCH and
TEDIT.*

without dimstyles, they all changed to current settings.) As you saw, when you stretch an asodim's text out of the dimension line, the line heals itself. The HOMETEXT command makes the asodim text snap back to its default home.

Did you notice a difference in dragging with DIMSHO off? If DIMSHO is on, AutoCAD recalculates the dimension value and updates the dimension while dragging; if off, it doesn't. DIMSHO ON may be jerky and slow on slower computers; if so, turn it off. DIMSHO is not stored in the dimstyle, so changing it doesn't change the current dimstyle to *UNNAMED.

Editing other objects, such as center lines, may be the easiest way to clear up conflicts. When you have a choice in modifying an asodim, it's usually better to use dimensioning utility commands rather than normal AutoCAD commands. Instead of using STRETCH to move text, use TEDIT. Instead of exploding a dimension so you can edit its text or change its color, use NEWTEXT or DIMCLRT.

Controlling Dimension Color (and Line Weight)

In addition to using the DIMCLRT dimension variable to set color for dimension text, you can use DIMCLRD to set color for dimension lines, arrows, and leaders. DIMCLRE similarly controls the color of extension lines. You can set them to any color, or to BYLAYER or BYBLOCK. They are set to BYBLOCK by default, so the entities within the dimension take on current color settings when created or changed with CHPROP. This is also why the leader dimension is white. Leaders and center marks are not asodims; they act like asodims that have been exploded.

Try using EXPLODE on an asodim. Undo is the only way to restore associativity. EXPLODE changes an asodim to individual entities with linetype BYLAYER and the color set by the DIMCLRx dimension variables. That's because asodims are really special forms of blocks. So, with default DIMCLRx settings, leaders are drawn with color BYBLOCK, which appears white. Change them by setting colors or using CHPROP. (Release 10 sends all the dimension parts to layer 0 with color and linetype set BYBLOCK.)

The STRETCH and SCALE commands are the links to maintaining associativity of dimensions as you edit drawing objects.

Stretching and Scaling Entities and Asodims

Remember that asodims contain invisible defpoints at their extension line origins. If you select a dimension when using SCALE or catch a defpoint in the crossing window when stretching, the dimension text will automatically be recalculated.

To see how this works, use STRETCH to double the flange thickness from .5" to 1" on the left side of the section view. Then use SCALE and STRETCH to resize the inner circle's hole diameter from 2.5" to 2" in both the plan view and the section view. (Release 10 text won't show tolerances anymore.)

All of the associated dimensions should have been selected and updated to match the stretched and scaled entities — the drawing is still accurate after editing (see fig. 12.38).

Using STRETCH and SCALE to Edit Objects and Their Asodims

```
Command: ZOOM                          Zoom to view illustrated.
Command: DIM
Dim: RES                               Pick asodim at flange bottom in section to
                                       restore MOCK2OTP3M2. (Except Release 10.)
Dim: HOMETEXT                          Send dimension at bottom of flange back to
                                       home position.
Dim: E
Command: STRETCH
Select objects to stretch by window...
Select objects: C                      Select crossing window points at ① and ② (see
                                       fig. 12.37).
Base point:                            Pick any point on flange face.
New point: @-.5,0                      Increase thickness by .5".
Command: SCALE
Select objects:                        Pick the 2 1/2" dimension and circle.
Select objects: <RETURN>
Base point:                            Pick the exact center of the circle.
<Scale factor>/Reference: R
Reference length <1>: 2.5
New length: 2
Command: STRETCH                       Crossing ③ and ④ to stretch edge of hole and
                                       vertical 3.750" dimension to 3.500".
Command: STRETCH                       Crossing ⑤ and ⑥ to stretch other edge of hole
                                       and vertical 1.250" dimension to 1.500".
Command: SAVE
```

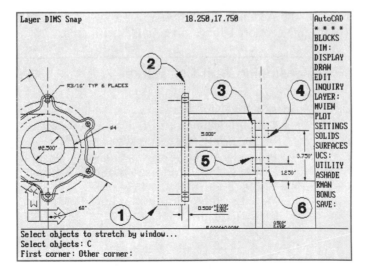

Figure 12.37:
Crossing windows for
changing the flange.

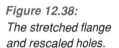

Figure 12.38:
The stretched flange
and rescaled holes.

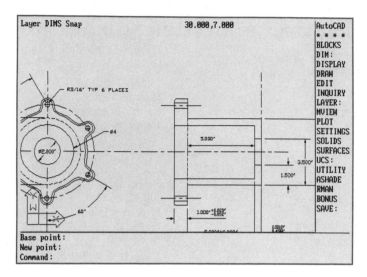

Changing the Dimension Terminator (Arrow)

A terminator is the symbol placed at the intersections of the dimension line with the extension lines. The default terminator is an arrow, but AutoCAD lets you substitute ticks or dots simply by setting dimension variables. Whenever DIMTSZ (dimension tick size) has a value greater than 0 (the default), ticks of that size are drawn instead of arrows.

Let's set DIMTSZ to a value of .125 for the tick size. Also set DIMDLE to .125 to extend the dimension line through tick marks. Then place a vertical dimension using tick marks instead of the normal dimension line arrows. Draw the overall vertical dimension of the flange section 1 inch to the left of the face.

Dimensioning With Tick Marks

Command: **DIM**	
Dim: **RES**	Restore MOCK2I.
Dim: **DIMTSZ**	Turn on tick marks with a value of 0.125".
Dim: **DIMDLE**	Set to .125 to extend the dimension line.
Dim: **VER**	Pick extension line origins ① and ②, dimension line location at 18,12 and accept the default text (see fig. 12.39).
Dim: **TEDIT**	Move text up to clear center line. (Release 10, use STRETCH.)
Dim: **E**	
Command: **SAVE**	

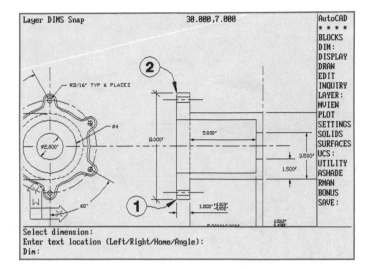

Figure 12.39:
A vertical dimension
with tick marks.

Instead of changing your arrow terminators to ticks, you can use dots or any drawing or block as a customized dimension terminator (okay, within reason).

Customizing Dimension Arrows and Terminator Symbols

You can easily set the size of your dimension arrows with the DIMASZ dimension variable. In addition to controlling the size of AutoCAD's default arrowhead or using ticks, you can substitute dots, your own style arrow, or any symbol you wish. If the DIMBLK (dimension block) dimension variable contains the name DOT, AutoCAD will create a block named DOT and use it as a terminator. If DIMBLK contains the name of any other block, AutoCAD will use that block in place of the default arrow (unless overridden by a non-zero DIMTSZ).

Once you create a custom symbol oriented for the right end of the dimension line, AutoCAD can flip it 180 degrees for the left side and rotate it for angular dimensions. Dimension blocks can be any shape you want. A few examples are shown in figure 12.40.

Tip: Make your symbol one drawing unit wide. AutoCAD will draw the dimension line or leader up to one unit away from the extension line. If your symbol is not one unit wide, there will be a gap between the symbol and the dimension line. Point the symbol or arrow to the right and make the symbol or arrow's tip the block insertion base point. If you do not plan to use a filled symbol, include a one-unit line from the insertion point to where the symbol will join the dimension line.

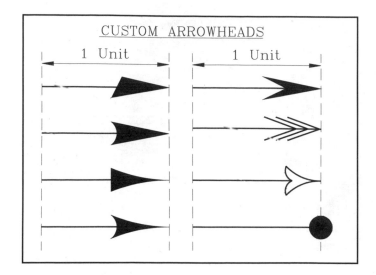

Figure 12.40:
Some DIMBLKS
examples.

You can create different dimblocks for the right and left sides. To use them, set the DIMBLK1 dimension variable to the name of the left side dimension block and DIMBLK2 to the name of the right side dimension block. Then, turn the DIMSAH dimension variable on to tell AutoCAD to use the separate blocks. (In Release 10, these affect only linear dimensions.)

Note: You can erase the MOCKSECT and DIMVARS drawing. You won't need them again.

Summing Up

Asodims are one of the most useful features of any CAD system, if you use them properly. Asodims ensure that your dimension values always reflect the current size of the objects in your drawing. If you change the objects, you don't need to change the dimensions — they will update automatically. Associative dimensions also make it easier to make global changes to your dimensions. The following are some of the keys to using associative dimensioning effectively:

Keep your drawing accurate, so your dimensions will be accurate. Don't draw out of scale unless you absolutely have to.

When you modify your drawing by stretching or scaling, make sure you include the dimensions in the selection set so they will update.

Let AutoCAD do the work of making changes by using the asodim utility commands such as NEWTEXT, TEDIT, and TROTATE.

Use named dimstyles to protect asodims from accidental updating. Standardize your dimensioning into as few dimstyles as possible. Save those dimstyles in a prototype drawing or in a drawing you can insert like a block. Use the selection option of RESTORE to set the current dimstyle by selecting existing dimensions. Seeing what you are setting the dimstyle to reduces the chance of error.

Use overrides to named dimstyles sparingly and check instances of their use before plotting to be sure they haven't accidentally changed.

Put your dimensions on a separate layer with a different color from the main body of your drawing. Use the DIMCLRx set of dimension variables to assign colors to parts of dimensions so you can plot different line weights. This way, extension lines and dimensions stand out and are not mistaken for actual drawing elements.

Adjust dimension text to the same height as your annotation text for consistency and to make text changes and additions easier.

Attributes Are Next

We've explored adding graphic intelligence to drawings with dimensioning. Next, we'll add nongraphic intelligence, or as AutoCAD calls them, attributes.

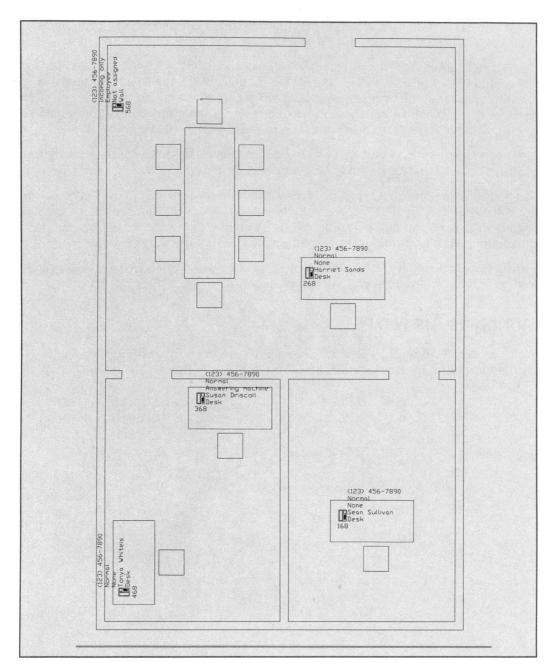

Figure 13.1:
A facility drawing with phone attributes.

13

Attributes and Data Extraction

ADDING INFORMATION TO BLOCKS
AND GETTING IT OUT AGAIN

Nongraphic Intelligence

Every drawing so far has been based on graphic entities or on spatial relationships between graphic entities. However, AutoCAD is capable of producing fully intelligent drawings. For example, in the Autotown subdivision you created, you could have added "House Model Name," "House Size (Sq. Ft.)" and "House Exterior Finish" data to each house block to give the drawing reader even more information about the real-world objects represented by the graphic blocks.

Attributes are like the paper tags attached to merchandise with a string. They can contain all kinds of information about the item they are tied to: manufacturer, model number, materials, price, stock number, etc. The information stored is the attribute's value.

In this chapter, you will learn how to add text *attributes* to blocks to give drawings a richer vocabulary for communicating information, and you will learn how to extract this data in report form. Just think of the convenience of tagging entities with attributes. You can extract automatic bills of materials, schedules, and other tabular lists of data, or you can view the information in graphic form. You don't need to clutter your drawing with attribute data you don't want to display. You can store it invisibly in the drawing file until you're ready to turn it into a report.

How Attributes Work

You store an attribute, such as a name, in a block much the same way you store graphic entities in a block. Just as you create and carefully lay out graphic entities before inclusion in a block, you define attributes prior to creating an attribute-laden block.

Tagging Blocks With Attributes

AutoCAD provides an attribute definition command called ATTDEF. You use ATTDEF to create attribute definitions (*attdef* entities) which define how and what kind of attribute values will be stored. Then, you use the regular BLOCK command to group graphic entities *and* attdefs to form a block. In effect, you sweep the attdefs into the same block definition as the graphic entities.

Frequently, you will want to tag a group of graphic entities that are already in a block. For example, if you design printed circuit boards, you may want to assign text to an integrated circuit (IC) chip by labeling manufacturer and pin assignments. If you're a facilities manager, you may want to tag each desk with an employee's name, title, department, phone number, and workstation description, as shown in figure 13.1. Chances are the desk (or IC chip for the PC board) is already stored as a block. In such cases, you can explode and reblock or form a new (nested) block by including the attdef tags and the original block in the new block definition.

After you form an attribute-laden block, you insert it into your drawing using the standard INSERT command. You control attribute display and attribute editing with three commands and two dialogue boxes:

ATTDISP Controls visibility of attributes in the drawing.

ATTEDIT Lets you change attribute values once they have been inserted in your drawing.

ATTEXT Extracts attribute values and block information that can be formed into a report.

DDEDIT Brings up the Attribute Definition Editing dialogue box (see fig. 13.2) when you select an attdef that has not been blocked. (The same command brings up the text editing dialogue box when you select a text entity.)

DDATTE Brings up the Edit Attributes dialogue box (see fig. 13.3) that you can use to edit attribute values in blocks after insertion. This same dialogue box comes up during block insertion, for initial attribute data entry, if the ATTDIA system variable is set to 1 (default is 0).

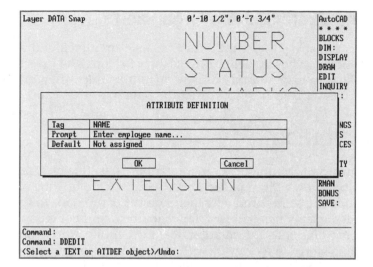

Figure 13.2:
The DDEDIT attribute definition editing dialogue box.

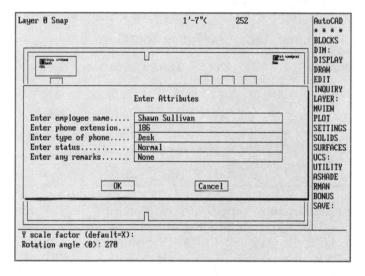

Figure 13.3:
The DDATTE edit attributes dialogue box.

An *attdef* is the attribute definition entity before it is blocked; an *attribute* entity exists only as a subentity within a block insert.

The attribute commands are scattered throughout different screen menus (none are on pull-downs). [ATTDEF:] is on the [BLOCKS] screen menu: [ATTDISP:] is on the [DISPLAY] menu; [ATTEDIT:], [DDEDIT:], and [DDATTE:] are on the [EDIT] menu; and [ATTEXT:] is on the [UTILITY] menu.

How the Attribute Exercises Are Organized

The attribute exercises are straightforward. First, we'll set up a facility drawing to work in. Then we will show you how to define attdefs, how to block and insert a block with attributes, and how to display and edit the attributes once they are in the drawing. Finally, we will show you how to extract the data in a text report.

Setup for Attributes

Facility management drawings commonly employ attributes. In this chapter, imagine that you are working in the offices of the Acme Tool Co. One of your responsibilities is to maintain drawings and produce reports on the equipment in the office. This equipment includes telephones, copiers, fax machines, and computers. Each piece of equipment in the office has information, like an identification number and name assignment, that is stored in a drawing with attributes. Your drawing-for-the-day is to show the telephone equipment for a small section of the office complex, and to extract a telephone report. Here is the information that you will store and extract.

Telephone Report for Acme Tool Co.

Name	Number	Ext	Type	Status	Remarks
Not Assigned	(123) 456-7890	586	Wall	In only	Employee
Tonya Whiteis	(123) 456-7890	486	Desk	Normal	None
Susan Driscoll	(123) 456-7890	386	Desk	Normal	Ans.Mach.
Harriet Sands	(123) 456-7890	286	Desk	Normal	None
Shawn Sullivan	(123) 456-7890	186	Desk	Normal	None

In this chapter, you will be more concerned with manipulating the attributes associated with the graphics than with manipulating the graphic entities. But you still need a drawing. Create a new drawing called OFFICE, using architectural units. The drawing scale factor is 24 for a scale of 1/2" = 1'-0", sized to plot on a 36" x 24" sheet.

If you are using the IA DISK, the IA6OFFIC.DWG file contains the basic office layout drawing. You will also find a graphic block drawing called PHN-BLK.DWG and a text file called PHONE.TXT that you will use in the data report. If you are not using the disk, you need to create the office drawing, which includes a simple floor plan. You also need to create the phone symbol before you begin your attribute definitions.

Setting Up the Office Drawing

Begin a NEW drawing named OFFICE=IA6OFFIC.

Begin a NEW drawing named OFFICE and make the settings shown in table 13.1. Make sure layer PLAN is current.

Table 13.1
Office Drawing Settings

COORDS	GRID	ORTHO	SNAP	FILL	UCSICON
ON	24	ON	3	OFF	OR

UNITS	Set UNITS to 4 Architectural, default the rest.
LIMITS	Set LIMITS from 0,0 to 72',48'
ZOOM	Zoom All.
VIEW	Save view as A.

Layer Name	State	Color	Linetype
0	On	7 (white)	CONTINUOUS
PLAN	On/Current	3 (green)	CONTINUOUS
DATA	On	7 (white)	CONTINUOUS

Your current layer is layer PLAN. If you have the IA DISK drawing, your screen will show the drawing in figure 13.4.

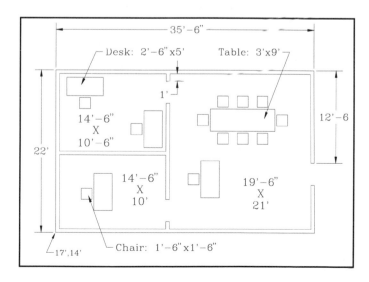

Figure 13.4:
The floor plan for office attributes.

If you need to create the drawing, change your layer to PLAN, and use the dimensions given in the illustration to draw the plan. When using SOLID, remember to pick the points in an X pattern to avoid drawing bow tie shapes.

Creating the Office Floor Plan and Furniture Symbols

You already have the floor plan. Just read this exercise.

Complete the floor plan in this exercise.

Command: **PLINE**	Draw walls — try using a single closed polyline.
Command: **SOLID**	Draw a table, chair, and desk.
Command: **COPY**	Copy chairs and desks.
Command: **ROTATE**	Rotate copied desks.

If you don't have the phone symbol, you need to create it (a simplified version is fine). If you are using the disk, insert *PHN-BLK. After you draw or insert the telephone symbol, set your UCS at its lower left corner. This will be your insertion base point.

Creating the Telephone Symbol

Command: **LAYER**	Set layer 0 current, turn layer PLAN off.
Command: **ZOOM**	Zoom Center with a height of 36".

Set snap to .25 and grid to 2".

Insert *PHN-BLK.

Draw telephone as shown in figure 13.5.

Command: **UCS**	Use Origin to put at lower left corner of telephone symbol.
Command: **SAVE**	

You are now ready to add attdefs.

Using the ATTDEF Command to Define Attributes

To create an attribute, you first use the ATTDEF command. We'll start by defining the EXTENSION attribute for the phone. Attributes have several definition modes. We have made the EXTENSION attribute a variable attribute. This is the normal (default) mode.

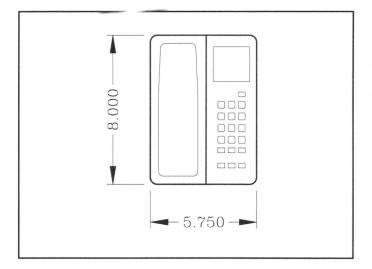

Figure 13.5:
The telephone
symbol.

Variable Attributes

Variable simply means that the attribute value can vary. A variable attribute is an attribute that is *not* constant. A variable attribute's value is usually entered when its attribute block is inserted, but it can be changed later. You can define a value to be offered as a default when you insert the block into the drawing. In addition, you set attribute definition modes and set text parameters to show how the attribute will appear on the screen (and in the drawing).

All of this sounds more complicated than it really is. Let's just try it so you can see the ATTDEF command in action, then we'll explain it all before defining the other attdefs.

Using ATTDEF to Define a Variable Attdef

```
Command: ATTDEF                                    The EXTENSION attribute is to
                                                   be verified.
Attribute modes — Invisible:N  Constant:N
  Verify:N  Preset:N
Enter (ICVP) to change, RETURN when done: V        Turn Verify on.
Attribute modes — Invisible:N  Constant:N
  Verify:Y  Preset:N
Enter (ICVP) to change, RETURN when done:
  <RETURN>
Attribute tag: EXTENSION
Attribute prompt: Enter phone extension
Default attribute value: <RETURN>
```

> **Using ATTDEF to Define a Variable Attdef—continued**
>
> ```
> Justify/Style/<Start point>: C
> Center point: 2.875,-5                    Centered under the telephone.
> Height <0'-0 3/16">: 3                    This will create 1/8" high text
>                                           at 1/2"=1'-0".
> Rotation angle <0>: <RETURN>
> ```

Your screen should show the extension attribute tag centered under the telephone (see fig. 13.6).

Figure 13.6:
The telephone with
EXTENSION Attdef.

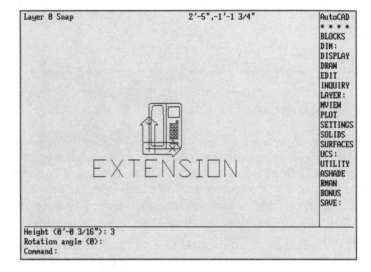

Before AutoCAD asks how you want to control the appearance of the attribute text, it prompts you for several attribute modes. These modes control attribute visibility and treatment of block insertion.

Attribute Modes

Invisible   Turns attribute visibility off. Invisible mode is useful when you want to store a lot of data in the drawing, but you don't want to display or plot all the data, or wait for it to regenerate.

Constant   Creates attributes with a fixed text value. Constant mode is helpful when you want to write boilerplate notes with attribute text. You can't edit a constant attribute once it is inserted as a block without redefining the block. The default is Constant:N, which means the attribute will be variable. **Variable** attributes can be edited after insertion with the ATTEDIT command or the DDATTE dialogue box

Verify Lets you check variable attribute values before inserting them into the drawing file. If an attribute has the Verify mode, AutoCAD will display the attribute value on the prompt line after you type it. AutoCAD will wait for a <RETURN> before inserting the text. You can see what you've typed, check for errors, and correct them before the attribute is inserted.

Preset Lets you create attributes that automatically accept their default value. When the block is inserted, attribute values are not requested. Preset is the most flexible mode. Preset attributes act like Constant attributes, except you can edit them after insertion with the ATTEDIT command or the DDATTE dialogue box.

Attributes can be Constant, Invisible, Preset, and Verified at the same time, or in any combination. The initial defaults are N (no) for all modes. To toggle one of the ATTDEF modes, you simply type I, C, V, or P followed by a <RETURN>. AutoCAD will redisplay the mode's prompt with a Y (yes) or N next to the item. The last settings will be saved as new default modes for the next use of ATTDEF.

How to Define Attributes

You define your attribute by giving it a tag name, an optional prompt, and an optional default or constant text value. The default value is what goes in the drawing, unless you enter a new value when you insert the attribute block. After you define the default value, you set its location, style, alignment, height, and angle, exactly as you do for the TEXT and DTEXT commands.

Attribute Tag — No Blanks Allowed

Each attribute has a tag. "Name," "Employee-No.," "Extension," and "Part-Numbers" are all valid tags. Think of the tag as the name of the attribute value that you will insert (like block names). The only restriction on tag names is that they cannot include blanks. Use a hyphen in place of a blank (like Employee-No.) to separate the tag name elements. AutoCAD translates all tags into upper-case letters whether you type in capitals or not.

Attribute Prompt

In addition to naming the attribute, you can assign an instructional prompt to use at insertion time. For example, you might assign the prompt, "Enter the Part Number of this widget here", to the tag name, "Part-Numbers."

You can use anything you want for prompts. "Gimme the number now, Dummy" is as valid as "Would you please enter the number here...." If you feel that the attribute tag name says it all, you don't need to add a prompt. The attribute tag name is the default prompt if you do not enter a prompt. Press <RETURN> to default the attribute prompt to the tag name.

Default Attribute Value

When you define the attribute, AutoCAD asks you for the default value. Useful defaults for variable attributes are "Not Yet Entered" or "XXX.NN". Remember, these will show up in the drawing if you accept the default with a <RETURN> instead of entering an attribute value at the time of insertion. Constant and Preset attributes insert automatically, without showing you their default values.

Attributes Display Just Like Text

After assigning the attribute value, AutoCAD prompts you for information about how to display attribute value text and store it in the drawing file. This series of AutoCAD prompts is identical to the standard text prompts. Once you've set all the text parameters, AutoCAD will draw the attribute on the screen just as it draws text. You can edit attdefs before they are blocked with the CHANGE command or DDEDIT dialogue box.

Creating a Block With Many Attributes

You have defined the extension attribute as a variable attribute. Before you build the complete phone block, you need to analyze the other attribute data types that you will include in your phone report. Here's another look at our Telephone Report as a guide to the attribute definitions that follow.

Telephone Report

Name	Number	Ext	Type	Status	Remarks
Not Assigned	(123) 456-7890	586	Wall	In only	Employee
Tonya Whiteis	(123) 456-7890	486	Desk	Normal	None
Susan Driscoll	(123) 456-7890	386	Desk	Normal	Ans.Mach.
Harriet Sands	(123) 456-7890	286	Desk	Normal	None
Shawn Sullivan	(123) 456-7890	186	Desk	Normal	None

Since all of the telephones have the same number, the telephone number is an obvious candidate for a Constant attribute with the value "(123) 456-7890." The rest of the attribute tags have different values, so make them Variable or Preset. The status and remarks attributes are likely to change infrequently, so define them as Preset to accept their defaults and avoid the prompt on insertion.

The extension, telephone type, and the name of the employee are important to today's project, so keep them visible. But the telephone number, status, and remarks are not pertinent to our report. We'll define them as Invisible so the data will be available for other reports.

Creating the Rest of the Attdefs

We'll create the rest of the attdefs in the following exercise. Change your layer to DATA. This will give you the option of displaying or plotting the drawings with only the extension visible (on the layer of insertion), or of including the type and name on layer DATA.

Look for the different attribute modes, tags, and defaults in the exercise sequence. Notice that you can repeat the ATTDEF command to get the next line of text just below the first, just like for the TEXT command. Answer all the attribute-specific prompts first. Then, when the start point prompt appears, AutoCAD will highlight the last attribute-defined line on the screen. If you simply press <RETURN>, the current attdef will go immediately below the old one.

Using ATTDEF to Define Attributes

```
Command: LAYER                                Set layer DATA current.
Command: ATTDEF                               Make the NUMBER attribute
                                              Constant and Invisible.

Attribute modes — Invisible:N  Constant:N
  Verify:Y Preset:N
Enter (ICVP) to change, RETURN when done: V   Turn Verify off.
Attribute modes — Invisible:N  Constant:N
  Verify:N Preset:N
Enter (ICVP) to change, RETURN when done: I   Turn Invisible on.
Attribute modes — Invisible:Y  Constant:N
  Verify:N Preset:N
Enter (ICVP) to change, RETURN when done: C   Turn Constant on.
Attribute modes — Invisible:Y  Constant:Y
  Verify:N Preset:N
Enter (ICVP) to change, RETURN when done:
  <RETURN>
Attribute tag: NUMBER
Attribute value: (123) 456-7890
Justify/Style/<Start point>: 6.75,20
```

Using ATTDEF to Define Attributes—continued

```
Height <0'-3">: <RETURN>
Rotation angle <0>: <RETURN>
Command: <RETURN>
ATTDEF                                              Make the STATUS attribute
                                                   Invisible and Preset.

Attribute modes - Invisible:Y Constant:Y
  Verify:N Preset:N
Enter (ICVP) to change, RETURN when done: C        Turn Constant off.
Attribute modes - Invisible:Y Constant:N
  Verify:N Preset:N
Enter (ICVP) to change, RETURN when done: P        Turn Preset on.
Attribute modes - Invisible:Y Constant:N
  Verify:N Preset:Y
Enter (ICVP) to change, RETURN when done:
  <RETURN>
Attribute tag: STATUS
Attribute prompt: Enter status
Default attribute value: Normal
Justify/Style/<Start point>: <RETURN>
Command: <RETURN>
ATTDEF                                              Make the REMARKS attribute
                                                   Invisible and Preset.

Attribute modes - Invisible:Y Constant:N
  Verify:N Preset:Y
Enter (ICVP) to change, RETURN when done:
  <RETURN>
Attribute tag: REMARKS
Attribute prompt: Enter any remarks
Default attribute value: None
Justify/Style/<Start point>: <RETURN>
Command: <RETURN>
ATTDEF                                              Make the NAME attribute
                                                   normal.

Attribute modes - Invisible:Y Constant:N
  Verify:N Preset:Y
Enter (ICVP) to change, RETURN when done: I        Turn Invisible off.
Attribute modes - Invisible:N Constant:N
  Verify:N Preset:Y
Enter (ICVP) to change, RETURN when done: P        Turn Preset off.
Attribute modes - Invisible:N Constant:N
  Verify:N Preset:N
Enter (ICVP) to change, RETURN when done:
  <RETURN>
Attribute tag: NAME
Attribute prompt: Enter employee name
```

Using ATTDEF to Define Attributes—continued

```
Default attribute value: Not assigned
Justify/Style/<Start point>: <RETURN>
Command: <RETURN>
ATTDEF

Attribute modes — Invisible:N  Constant:N
  Verify:N  Preset:N
Enter (ICVP) to change, RETURN when done:
  <RETURN>
Attribute tag: TYPE
Attribute prompt: Enter type of phone
Default attribute value: Desk
Justify/Style/<Start point>: <RETURN>
Command: PAN


Command: SAVE
```

Also make the TYPE attribute normal.

Pan, if needed to see every-thing.

An attdef displays the attribute tag; when blocked and inserted, the attribute value will display instead. Your screen should now show all six attribute definitions even though some attributes will become invisible when you block the phone (see fig. 13.7).

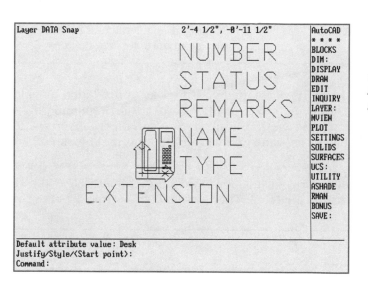

Figure 13.7:
A telephone with all attribute definitions.

Using BLOCK to Group Graphics and Attdefs

The next step is to group all the graphic entities (lines, polylines, etc.) and nongraphic entities (attdefs) together using the BLOCK command. Once the attdefs are blocked, you cannot edit the definitions without a block redefinition. Right now, you can edit the attdefs with the CHANGE command or DDEDIT dialogue box, just as you would edit strings of text. You can also erase the attdefs and replace them with ATTDEF if you need to make major changes.

Block your telephone symbol, using the lower left corner as an insertion base point. The order in which you select attdefs is *important* because the selection order controls the prompting order when you insert the block. Name the block PHONE.

Using BLOCK to Group Graphics and Attdefs Into a Block

```
Command: BLOCK
Block name (or ?): PHONE
Insertion base point: 0,0        Pick the UCS point of origin .
Select objects:                  Pick the NAME attdef first.
Select objects:                  Pick the EXTENSION attdef.
Select objects:                  Pick the TYPE attdef.
Select objects:                  Pick the NUMBER attdef.
Select objects:                  Pick the STATUS attdef.
Select objects:                  Pick the REMARKS attdef.
Select objects:                  Pick entities for the PHONE block.
Select objects: <RETURN>         All graphic elements and attdefs disappear,
                                 just as in normal block creation.
```

Congratulations! You have just formatted your first attribute-laden block! There is nothing special about attribute block creation, other than remembering to order your attdef pick sequence the way you want it. You can block, insert, wblock, and redefine an attribute block the same way you would a normal block.

Note: If you use a Window or Crossing object selection, the attdefs will be found in the order of most recently created first. This is probably the opposite of the order you want.

Using INSERT to Insert Attribute Blocks

Locate the telephones in the offices by inserting them at the appropriate places in the floor plan. Start by inserting the employee telephone on the wall in the conference room on the right.

Using INSERT to Insert Attribute Blocks

Command: **LAYER**

Set layer 0 current, turn layer PLAN on.

Command: **ZOOM**

Zoom to view shown.

Command: **UCS**

Set UCS to World.

Set snap to 6", grid to 2', and turn UCSICON off.

Command: **INSERT**

Start by inserting the employee telephone.

Block name (or ?): **PHONE**

Insertion point:

Pick in upper right corner of conference room (see fig. 13.8).

X scale factor <1> / Corner / XYZ: **<RETURN>**
Y scale factor <default=X>: **<RETURN>**
Rotation angle <0>: **<RETURN>**
Enter attribute values
Enter employee name <Not assigned>: **<RETURN>**
Enter phone extension: **586**
Enter type of phone <Desk>: **Wall**
Verify attribute values
Enter phone extension <586>: **<RETURN>**

Command: **ZOOM**

Zoom in for a look (see fig. 13.9), then zoom P.

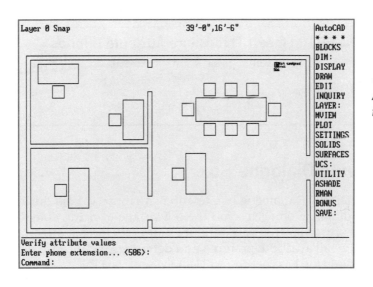

Figure 13.8:
An inserted employee telephone.

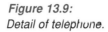

Figure 13.9:
Detail of telephone.

The PHONE block should appear on the screen with all the attributes in their correct positions. The NUMBER, STATUS, and REMARKS attributes are invisible. They are stored in the correct position, but not displayed. If you turn layer DATA off, only the phone symbol and extension attribute, which were created on layer 0, will be visible.

Repeat the insertion process for the next three telephones using the following data and figure 13.10 for telephone location and rotation.

Using INSERT to Insert Three More Attribute Phones

	Rotation	Name	Ext	Type
Command: **INSERT** at ①	0	Tonya Whiteis	486	Desk
Command: **INSERT** at ②	270	Susan Driscoll	386	Desk
Command: **INSERT** at ③	270	Harriet Sands	286	Desk

Using the Attribute Dialogue Box

You can also use the DDATTE dialogue box to enter attribute values during block insertions. Using the dialogue box gives you the advantage of being able to edit or change the defaults in any order that you want, including the preset attributes. The dialogue box will display all attribute prompts and defaults except those defined as Constant. To use the dialogue box, set the ATTDIA system variable to 1. Then when you insert blocks with attributes, the dialogue box will appear.

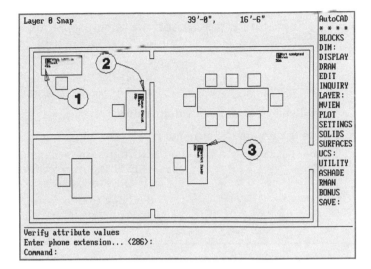

Figure 13.10:
Three more
telephones inserted in
the office.

Try inserting the last telephone (Shawn Sullivan) using the attribute dialogue box, as shown in figure 13.11. His telephone goes on the desk in the lower left office. After you insert the block, toggle the dialogue box back off. If your display does not support dialogue boxes, insert the last telephone the same way you did in the previous exercise.

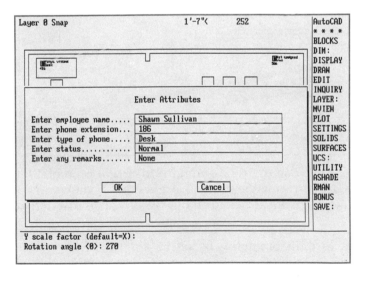

Figure 13.11:
A DDATTE dialogue
box.

Using the Attribute Dialogue Box to Insert an Attribute Block

Command: **ATTDIA**   Set to 1. (Release 10, use
                                       SETVAR ATTDIA.)

Command. **INSERT**   Insert the PHONE block at ①
                                       at 270 (see fig. 13.12).

The dialogue box automatically displays to accept attribute values.

Highlight the input fields next to the prompts shown and type in the following data:

Enter employee name..... **Shawn Sullivan**   <RETURN> or select: [OK].
Enter phone extension... **186**   <RETURN> or select: [OK].
Select: **[OK]**   Or <RETURN>.

Command: **ATTDIA**   Set back to 0 to turn DDATTE
                                       dialogue box off.

Command: **SAVE**

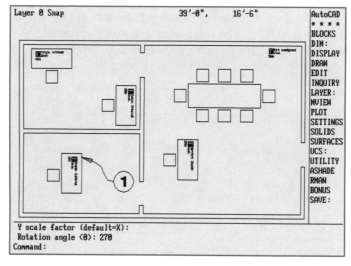

Figure 13.12:
A telephone inserted
with a dialogue box.

The dialogue box is easier to use than the standard insertion prompts. It lets you accept defaults and verify entries without any overt action on your part. Later, we will show you how to use the dialogue box to change values of an inserted attribute.

Tip: You can suppress attribute prompting by setting the ATTREQ system variable to 0. This will force block insertion to accept all the attribute defaults, but will allow normal attribute editing at a later time. This makes variable attribute block insertions act as if preset.

> **Tip:** If you use the DDATTE dialogue box, keep your attribute prompts to less than 24 characters or they will be truncated.

Your screen should now show the floor plan with all five PHONE blocks (see fig. 13.13).

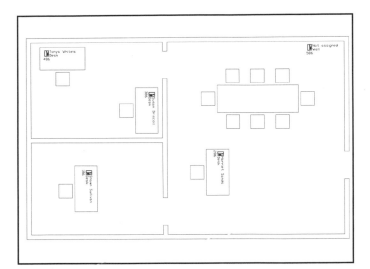

Figure 13.13: The floor plan showing five PHONE blocks.

> **Tip:** It is possible to form an attribute block that has no graphic entities in it. Simply create a block with nothing but attributes and insert it in the drawing. You can use these nongraphic blocks to automate drawing text entry, and to associate invisible or nongraphic information in a drawing. Be sure at least one attribute has a visible value when inserted, or you can get an invisible block of attributes.

Using ATTDISP to Control Attribute Display Visibility

You can control an attribute's visibility by using the ATTDISP (ATTribute DISPlay) command. ATTDISP temporarily reverses visibility, turning invisible attributes on, or visible attributes off. To return to the default condition that was set by the ATTDEF command, set ATTDISP to N for normal.

Use ATTDISP to turn all the attributes off, back to normal, then on. ON will force all the attributes to display. When the screen is regenerated, you'll see how you have stored the STATUS, REMARKS, and DATA attributes.

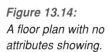

Using ATTDISP to Control Attribute Visibility

Command: **ZOOM**   Zoom in on upper left office.

Command: **ATTDISP**
Normal/ON/OFF <Normal>: **OFF**
Regenerating drawing.   Screen regenerates, turning off all
                                                     attributes (see fig. 13.14).
                                                     Now set it back to Normal.

Command: **<RETURN>**
ATTDISP Normal/ON/OFF <Off>: **N**
Regenerating drawing.   Back to normal display.

Command: **<RETURN>**   Now set it to ON.
ATTDISP Normal/ON/OFF <Normal>: **ON**
Regenerating drawing.   Screen regenerates, showing all invis-
                                                     ible attributes (see fig. 13.15).

Figure 13.14:
A floor plan with no
attributes showing.

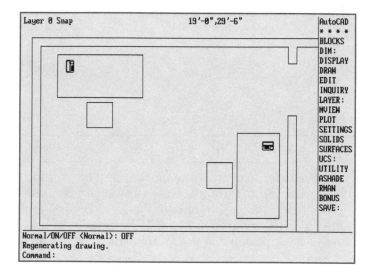

Using Layers to Control Attribute Display

You can extend your control of attribute visibility by putting your attribute data on
different layers. Insert or define the attribute on the layer that you would normally
keep it on, then use normal layer visibility controls to turn data on and off. Don't
forget that in paper space, viewports can have independent layer visibility settings.

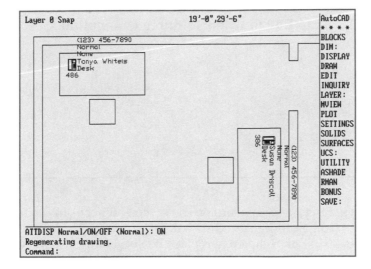

Figure 13.15:
A floor plan with all
attributes showing.

Attribute Editing With ATTEDIT

Well, as sure as the sun rises, you can bet there will be changes in the old telephone layout. No sooner is the layout complete, than you find out that Shawn really spells his name Sean. What do you do? Edit the attribute, of course!

The ATTEDIT (ATTribute EDIT) command is the change command for attributes. Using ATTEDIT, you first form a selection set for editing the attributes. ATTEDIT provides additional filters to help you select attributes. (We will explore these in more detail later.) For now, try a simple pick selection to take care of Sean.

An attribute must be displayed in order to be edited. It can be set back to normal as soon as all the editing has been completed.

Using ATTEDIT to Edit Individual Attributes

```
Command: PAN                                        Pan down to Shawn's office.
Command: ATTEDIT
Edit attributes one at a time? <Y>: <RETURN>
Block name specification <*>: <RETURN>
Attribute tag specification <*>: <RETURN>
Attribute value specification <*>: <RETURN>
Select Attributes:                                  Pick the text string Shawn
                                                    Sullivan. It doesn't highlight
                                                    until you press <RETURN>.

1 attribute selected.
```

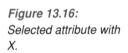

Using ATTEDIT to Edit Individual Attributes—continued

```
Value/Position/Height/Angle/Style/Layer/Color/
   Next <N>: V
Change or Replace? <R>: C
String to change: Shawn

New string: Sean
Value/Position/Height/Angle/Style/Layer/Color/
   Next <N>: <RETURN>

Command: SAVE
```

Note: you can't use wildcards here.

Notice two nice features. First, an X appears on the screen adjacent to the attribute to be edited (see fig. 13.16). Second, AutoCAD asks if you want to change part of the attribute value text string or completely replace it. You changed part of it (see fig. 13.17).

Figure 13.16:
Selected attribute with X.

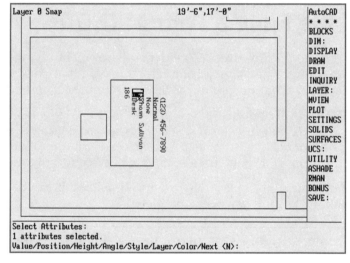

You can change much more than the text value when you edit attributes individually. Frequently, you will find that you have attributes overlapping graphic objects. For the invisible attributes, this may not be a concern. But the appearance of visible attributes will be important in your final drawing. You can use ATTEDIT to fine tune your attributes' appearance. You can change the text position and angle, or for that matter, text style, height, layer, and color.

Taking care of Sean was a simple change. But what about global changes like changing the 86 in all the extensions to 68? Or, selectively changing 86 to 68 only on employee phones throughout the building?

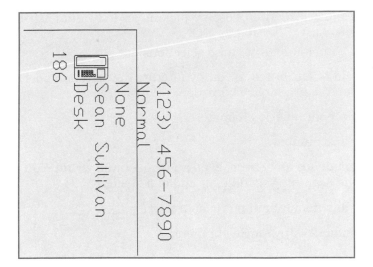

Figure 13.17:
Detail of a corrected
attribute.

Making Global Attribute Edits With ATTEDIT

Your facility drawing only has five telephones; individually picking each attribute for editing would not be a problem. But a whole office complex could have five hundred telephones. Think about editing five hundred attributes! You could gather all the tags named EXTENSION and do the replacement in one window. Or could you? You could if you were able to tell AutoCAD exactly which characters in the EXTENSION attribute you wanted to edit. In other words, you need to set up a selection set filled with just the precise group. Regular selection set techniques are not intelligent enough for this type of task.

Using Wildcards to Selectively Edit Attributes

Rather than individually picking attributes from the screen, you can use a combination of wildcard filters and standard selection set options to select your attributes. Here are some common scenarios.

- Select all attributes within blocks with a name you specify, using wildcards if you like. Use * to select all blocks.

- Select all attributes matching a tag name you specify, using wildcards if you like. Use * to select all tag names.

- Select all attributes matching a specified value, using wildcards if you like. A * selects all values.

- Further narrow the selection process by picking an individual attribute object, or Window, Last, Crossing, or BOX.
- Use any and all combinations of these selections.

You can narrow the field of attributes to edit by filtering the selection specification with wildcards. Here are the available wildcards:

@   *At* matches any alphanumeric character.

Pound matches any number.

*   *Star* or *asterisk* matches any string, even an empty (null) string. You can use an asterisk at the beginning, middle, or end of a string.

.   *Period* matches any nonalphanumeric character.

?   *Question mark* matches any single character.

~   *Tilde* matches any character but the one that follows the tilde, like ~?86 to match any telephone extension except those ending in 86.

[ ]   *Brackets* matches any single instance of any of the characters you enclose between the brackets, like [xyz] to match either an x, y, or z.

[~]   *Brackets tilde* matches anything but any one of the characters enclosed.

-   *Hyphen* matches a range of characters when used in brackets, like [1-5] to match 1,2,3,4, or 5.

`   *Reverse* or *back quote* matches the special character that follows, like `? matches a ? instead of using the ? as a wildcard.

You can use individual wildcards or combine them. Don't let the possibilities overwhelm you; you'll usually just use the question mark and asterisk (that's all Release 10 has). But the others are there if you need them.

Using Tag Selection to Edit Attributes

Once you have selected and filtered your attributes, AutoCAD prompts you to edit them. If you ask for individual editing (the default), AutoCAD prompts for your changes one at a time. As you have seen, you can tell which attribute you are editing by looking for the highlighting or X on the screen.

Try to tap some of AutoCAD's attribute-editing power by changing the wall phone status from "Normal" to "Incoming only." Narrow your selection by specifying the STATUS attribute to edit, then select all five workstations with a window. Watch the screen to know which attribute AutoCAD wants you to edit. Use the <N>, (Next default), to skip to the wall phone status. Change the text value of the wall phone status. Then, use the <N> to skip past the rest, or terminate ATTEDIT with a <^C>.

Using an Attribute Tag to Specify an Attribute Edit

Command: **ZOOM**	Zoom to view whole office plan.
Command: **ATTEDIT** Edit attributes one at a time? <Y>: **<RETURN>**	
Block name specification <*>: **<RETURN>**	Use asterisk for all.
Attribute tag specification <*>: **STATUS** Attribute value specification <*>: **<RETURN>**	
Select Attributes:	Select with window around all phones.
5 attributes selected. Value/Position/Height/Angle/Style/Layer/ Color/Next <N>: **<RETURN>**	Use N four times to get X mark to wall phone (see fig. 13.18).
Value/Position/Height/Angle/Style/Layer/ Color/Next <N>: **V**	Value.
Change or Replace? <R> **<RETURN>**	Replace.
New attribute value: **Incoming only**	
Value/Position/Height/Angle/Style/Layer/ Color/Next <N>: *cancel*	Exit with <^C> or <RETURN>.

Zoom in to examine (see fig. 13.19), then zoom P.

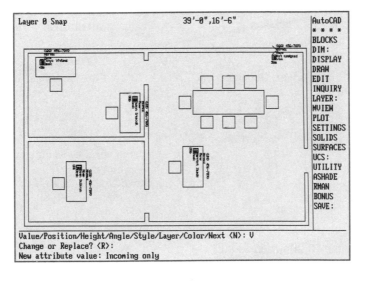

Figure 13.18:
Editing the wall phone by its tag.

Figure 13.19:
Detail of the wall
phone.

The preceding editing sequence is convenient if you are making selective changes to many attributes. But if you have a change that applies to all or a filterable subset of a large group of attributes, you can use a global selection.

Try a division-wide reorganization changing the last two digits in all the telephone extensions from "86" to "68." Use the default <*> wildcard and a window to get all your telephone extensions. Here's the prompt sequence.

Using ATTEDIT for a Global Edit

```
Command: ATTEDIT
Edit attributes one at a time? <Y>: N                     Edit all attributes — globally.
Global edit of Attribute values.
Edit only Attributes visible on screen? <Y>: <RETURN>
```

Even though all the attributes are on the screen, it's nice to know that you have the option to include those offscreen!

```
Block name specification <*>: <RETURN>
Attribute tag specification <*>: EXTENSION
Attribute value specification <*>: <RETURN>
Select Attribute: W                                       Use a window to collect all the
                                                          telephones.
5 attribute selected.                                     AutoCAD highlights the at-
                                                          tributes.
String to change: 86
New string: 68
```

Zoom in to examine (see fig. 13.20), then zoom P.

All your extensions should now end in 68. If you had wanted to change all but the wall phone, extension 586, you could have entered ~586 at the attribute value specification prompt.

Using the Attribute Dialogue Box to Edit Attributes

You can use the DDATTE dialogue box to edit attributes. It presents the same dialogue box that you used when you inserted the last PHONE block. You can edit several attributes at once, but you can only use the dialogue box to edit their text string values, one block at a time. If you use a window selection, it will only edit the most recent, the first found.

Try using the dialogue box to edit two preset REMARKS attributes.

Using the DDATTE Dialogue Box to Edit Attributes

Command: **DDATTE**
Select the wall phone
Highlight input field next to Enter any remarks.... and type in **Employee**, then <RETURN>
or select [OK] to accept (see fig. 13.21).

Select: **[OK]**
Or <RETURN> to exit dialogue box.

Command: **<RETURN>**

DDATTE
Select Susan's phone.
Highlight input field next to Enter any remarks....
and type in **Answering machine**, then <RETURN> or
select [OK] to accept.

> **Using the DDATTE Dialogue Box to Edit Attributes—continued**
>
> | | |
> |---|---|
> | *Select:* **[OK]** | Or <RETURN> to exit dialogue box. |
> | Command: **ATTDISP** | Set back to Normal. |
> | Command: **END** | Or save and try a plot before ending and exiting AutoCAD. |

Figure 13.21:
Editing attributes with the dialogue box.

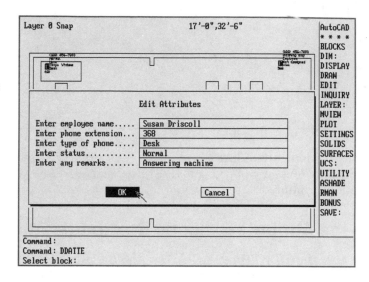

If you want to see how attributes plot, try making a quick plot of your office plan.

Plotting the Office Drawing

There are four ways to plot the drawing data:

- Turn all the attributes off.
- Plot the extension number, employee name and phone type (Normal).
- Plot the extension number only (layer 0).
- Turn all the attributes on.

We've completed the last attribute editing exercise, so end your drawing to save it. You will need it again to practice extracting the attribute data. We will also use this office drawing in Part Two of the book when we extrude it into a 3D drawing.

The next step is to extract the data to format a telephone report, something like a simple telephone directory or part of an equipment report.

Using the ATTEXT Command to Extract Attributes

The ATTEXT command sounds like some kind of text operation, but it stands for ATTribute EXTraction. ATTEXT provides a way to extract attribute information from the drawing file and print that information in a text report.

Setting Up an Attribute Report

In setting up the facility drawing, we listed the data for the employee names, status, remarks, type, and extension for each of the five telephones in a simple tabular form. While our example shows a telephone report, similar kinds of tables form the basis for bills of materials (BOM), listings, schedules, and specifications that regularly accompany professional drawings. These tables organize the data scattered around drawing files.

AutoCAD provides three ways to extract attribute values from a drawing file and format them in a disk file. You can print these lists or operate on the data in other programs, like dBASE III or IV, Lotus 1-2-3, or your favorite word processor. You can also put the list into a table and bring it back into your drawing. The ATTEXT formats are templates that define how the data will be formatted in the extracted text file.

ATTEXT Formats

CDF (Comma Delimited Format) CDF is easy to use with BASIC programs or with dBASE's "APPEND FROM . . . DELIMITED" operation. (See the example below.)

SDF (Standard Data Format) for FORTRAN and other programs that read a dBASE "COPY . . . SDF" file, or a dBASE "APPEND FROM . . . SDF" operation. (See the example below.)

DXF (Drawing Interchange Format) a subset of AutoCAD's full DXF file format that is used by many third-party programs.

You can extract data in whatever format is suitable for your application. Many users (and vendors of third-party software) now have applications built around AutoCAD using one or more of these data extraction interfaces.

Extracting Attribute Data with CDF or SDF

CDF creates a file that has commas separating the data fields in the attribute extraction. A simple example is:

CDF Format

```
'Name1','Type1','Extension1'
'Name2','Type2','Extension2'
  . . .
  . . .
  . . .
'Name9','Type9','Extension9'
'Name10','Type10','Extension10'
```

Formatting extract files gets down to the nitty-gritty placement of alphanumeric characters, commas, and spaces. In the CDF format, each data field is separated by a comma, and the spacing of the data field is dependent on the data width within the field. Name10 in the example above will take up more room than Name9.

The SDF format creates a file similar to CDF, but without commas and with a standard field length and spacing.

SDF Format

```
Name1           Type1           Extension1
Name2           Type2           Extension2
  . . .           . . .           . . .
  . . .           . . .           . . .
Name9           Type9           Extension9
Name10          Type10          Extension10
```

Here, the data field length is standardized. It is preformatted to a standard value, regardless of the data value length. If the data exceeds the length, the data is truncated.

How to Create an Attribute Report Template File

Before you can extract attributes, AutoCAD needs a template file in order to create the SDF or CDF file. The template file is a format instruction list telling AutoCAD what to put where in the extract data file. The IA DISK contains a template file called PHONE.TXT. This file provides an SDF template for the telephone data. If you are using the disk, you can use this file to create the report.

If you are not using the disk, create the file as an ASCII text file using a line editor or word processor. See Appendix B if you need help selecting a suitable text editor. ATTEXT is touchy. Use spaces, not tabs. Make sure you end the last line of your file with a <RETURN>. Also, make sure you do not have any extra spaces at the end of lines, or extra <RETURN>s after the last line of text.

If you don't feel like making the file, just read through the next two exercises and you will get the sense of how a report is generated.

Here is the PHONE.TXT file format for your example telephone data. The template assumes that NAME comes first, TYPE second, and EXTENSION third. The NUMBER, STATUS, and REMARKS will not be included in the report.

Creating an SDF Template File

 Examine the PHONE.TXT file from the disk.

 Use a text editor or word processor to create a plain ASCII file named PHONE.TXT with the following lines. Make sure you end the last line with a <RETURN>.

```
BL:NAME        C011000        Type BL:NAME, not the actual block name.
BL:X           N006002
DUMMY1         C002000
BL:Y           N006002
DUMMY2         C002000
NAME           C015000
TYPE           C008000
EXTENSION      N005000
```

If you look at the right column, you can easily decipher the formatting information. The first C or N says this is a character or a number. The next three digits (011 in the BL:NAME line) tell how many spaces to leave for the data. The final three digits specify the number of decimal places for floating point (decimal) numeric data. Integer data have 000 in the last three columns.

The BL:X and BL:Y are not blocks or attributes. They extract the X,Y coordinate values for the block.

DUMMY1 and DUMMY2 only appear in the template file. They are not blocks or attributes; they are used to provide space in the report. These dummy lines force a two-space blank between the X,Y coordinates (BL:X,BL:Y) and a two-space blank between the Y coordinate and the NAME, making the output easier to read.

The complete list of kinds of data that ATTEXT can extract is shown in the following table.

Table 13.2
ATTEXT Template Fields

FIELD	DATA TYPE	DESCRIPTION	FIELD	DATA TYPE
BL:LEVEL	integer	Block nesting level	BL:XSCALE	decimal
BL:NAME	character	Block name	BL:YSCALE	decimal
BL:X	decimal	X insert coord	BL:ZSCALE	decimal
BL:Y	decimal	Y insert coord	BL:XEXTRUDE	decimal
BL:Z	decimal	Z insert coord	BL:YEXTRUDE	decimal
BL:NUMBER	integer	Block counter	BL:ZEXTRUDE	decimal
BL:HANDLE	character	Entity handle	*attribute*	integer
BL:LAYER	character	Insertion layer	*attribute*	character
BL:ORIENT	decimal	Rotation angle		

Integer fields are formatted Nwww000, floating point (decimal) fields are Nwwwddd, and character fields are Cwww000 where www is overall width such as 012 for 12 characters wide, 000 is 000, and ddd is width to the right of the decimal point.

Extracting the Data File

Once you have the template file, you can extract data for all or some of the attributes. If you have the PHONE.TXT file, get back into AutoCAD. Load your office drawing, and extract the attribute data into a file called PHN-DATA.

Using ATTEXT to Create an SDF Data File

Edit an EXISTING drawing named OFFICE.

```
Command: ATTEXT
CDF, SDF, or DXF Attribute extract (or Entities) <C>: S
Template file: PHONE
Extract filename <OFFICE>: PHN-DATA              AutoCAD writes
                                                 PHN-DATA.TXT to disk.

5 records in extract file.
Command: QUIT
```

If you had entered an E for entities, AutoCAD would have prompted for object selection to extract data from specific blocks, and then reprompted for CDF, SDF, or DXF.

> **Note:** Don't use the same name for your template file as for your extract file, or the extract file will overwrite the template.

The extracted SDF report file is shown in the section below. You can examine the file with your text editor or word processor after exiting AutoCAD. Take a look at your data text file.

SDF Report Example

PHONE	408.33	435.79	Not assigned	Wall	568
PHONE	60.00	441.00	Tonya Whiteis	Desk	468
PHONE	198.00	396.00	Harriet Sands	Desk	268
PHONE	303.00	318.00	Susan Driscoll	Desk	368
PHONE	123.00	294.00	Sean Sullivan	Desk	168

Notice that the extracted data gives useful spatial information about this drawing as well as the attribute data. The X and Y data fields give the X and Y insertion points of each PHONE block. Your X,Y fields will vary from ours, depending on where you inserted the blocks. The PHONE column is set up to print the name of the block acting as the attribute data source. The PHONE column has character data (see the C in the template), and an 11-character print width.

The next two columns give the X and Y locations of the block insertion point in numeric form (see N in the template). (Your data will vary from the example.) The X and Y data have two decimal places and the decimal point in a six-character print width. The X and Y fields and the employee name would all run together if not for the two-character dummy fields. The other extracted attribute fields are in the last two columns, a character field and a numeric field. If an employee had an unusually long name, you can see that it would be truncated by the print width.

DXF, DXB, and IGES Drawing Data

AutoCAD provides additional methods for extracting spatial and graphic data from the drawing file. Block layers and block levels (levels of nesting for nested blocks, block rotation, and scale) are extractable. These spatial attributes are useful for handing data off to engineering programs where the block orientation or relationship among drawing entities is as critical as the text or numeric data associated with the block.

DXF, AutoCAD's Drawing Interchange Format, is used in many third-party enhancements and for drawing file exchange. You use the DXFOUT command to extract the DXF file from a drawing. An ATTEXT DXF includes block reference and attribute information only, but the DXFOUT command exports either the full drawing file or selected entities. A full DXFOUT creates a complete ASCII text description of the drawing. It also has a binary option to create a more compact binary file for faster processing by sophisticated third-party programs.

Another command, DXFIN, imports a DXF file. A full DXFIN requires a totally new drawing file, created by starting a new drawing equal to nothing, like *NAME* = <RETURN>. You can use DXFIN to import into an existing drawing, but you will get the message "Not a new drawing — only ENTITIES section will be input." In such a partial DXFIN, data such as block definitions and layer information won't be imported. A partial DXFIN behaves like an insert, where the current drawing definitions override the imported definitions.

The IGES format is another drawing exchange format. You get data in and out by using the IGESIN and IGESOUT commands. IGES is not perfect, and editing of the resulting drawing is typically required. IGESOUT loses attdefs and solid fills, and 3D data may be represented differently. When you register your AutoCAD program, you will receive a detailed IGES Interface Specifications document.

DXB is another file format used by AutoCAD. This is a binary drawing file format. DXBIN imports binary drawing files. You can output a limited (everything converted to straight line segments) DXB format file by configuring your plotter as an ADI plotter and selecting AutoCAD DXB file as the output format.

To learn more about attributes, DXF, and other types of file processing with AutoCAD, see *Maximizing AutoCAD, Volume II* from New Riders Publishing.

This is the last on the subject of attributes. It is time to move on to the world of 3D. If you want a quick peek at your office in 3D, take a look at figure 13.22, which shows the facility drawing extruded into 3D.

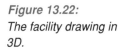
Figure 13.22:
The facility drawing in 3D.

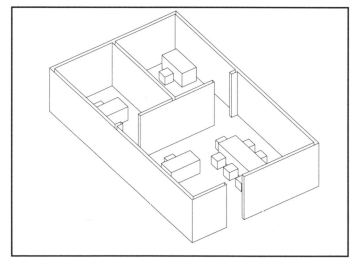

Summing Up

Attributes provide power and flexibility for annotating your drawings and producing reports. When you use attributes, you make AutoCAD manage both graphic and nongraphic information. Here are some tips for using and organizing attributes.

Design your report formats before you define attributes. Scratch out a rough table to plan ahead for field name, size, and prompting. Good layout and design of attribute fields is critical to creating a useful attribute file. Test your extraction before you fill up your drawing with information in a format you can't use.

Place your attdefs on different layers or create them with different colors to distinguish them from regular text. The names you use for tags are important, so keep them brief but explanatory. The tag name is the default prompt when no other prompt is given, and it is used in attribute edits and extracts. Break your attribute data into useful fields. Use enough fields to capture all the variable information you need. Avoid fields that are filled with extra long strings of output.

ATTEDIT is an extremely flexible and powerful command. But check your results before you go past the point of being able to undo if you create global havoc in an ATTEDIT error. You can have AutoCAD prompt you for all the changes if you take advantage of grouping attributes by layer, tag name, value, and so on.

Use attributes in place of normal text for standardized boilerplate entries and title blocks. Attributes offer more input control, automation, and sophisticated editing than regular text.

This Is the End of Part One

Are you ready to create your own drawing files, attributes, and reports? You now have the tools, you just need some practice. In Part One, you have gone from drawing setup to assigning attributes and extracting data in 2D. If you took the time, you may have turned the polyline cylinder profile into a 3D half-section by revolving the cylinder with a 3D mesh command.

Now it is officially time for 3D. Turn to Part Two to learn about full 3D, including how to draw and edit in 3D, how to do dynamic views, how to create solid models and extract 2D sections and profiles, and how to shade your images with AutoShade.

Figure PT2.1:
Table and Chair in a Two-Dimensional Office

Part Two

AutoCAD and 3D Drawing

Making the Transition From 2D to 3D

Commands like ARRAY, OFFSET, TRIM, EXTEND, and STRETCH significantly increase your AutoCAD productivity over what you can do manually with triangles and a pencil.

AutoCAD's 3D modeling features can increase your productivity even more. In many applications, 3D modeling is essential. But 3D modeling is not the answer for everything. If you are drawing flat patterns or facilities plans, the added complexity of 3D will slow you down without adding any benefit. If you are drawing mechanical parts, however, 3D may be the best way for you to easily and accurately make the leap from idea to finished drawing.

3D Modeling Benefits

Up to now, you have worked with two-dimensional images on your screen, much like you would on paper. But drawing on paper is hopelessly inadequate when it comes to 3D object manipulation. In AutoCAD, you can draw, edit, rotate, scale, and stretch 3D objects much as you work with 2D objects (see fig. PT2.1). You can move your viewpoint around the 3D model, using different views of it to help visualize, create, and present the design. If you need a side view, you just move your viewpoint around to that side. If you need to see the underside of the model, you simply move your viewpoint again. This visualization can solve many difficult design problems.

581

You can use 3D models to create complex shapes or find intersections and other design relationships that would be difficult or impossible to draw manually. And with AutoCAD's solid modeling extension (AME), creating a 3D model is a lot like manufacturing the actual product — you just use AutoCAD commands to build the model in the computer instead of using machine tools.

The Building Blocks of 3D

Building a 3D model isn't difficult if you take it one step at a time. You use simple shapes like cubes, spheres, surfaces, and cones to build more complex shapes. You might use 2D entities like lines, polylines, and circles to build part of your model, then switch to 3D entities and objects like faces, surfaces, spheres, cubes, and cylinders. Solid modeling jumps up another level to give mass to those same 3D objects. But no matter how you put your model together, you simply make small parts and assemble them to form larger, more complex parts.

How Part Two Is Organized

Part Two leads you step by step through the entire process of building 3D models. The explanations and exercises in Part Two will take you from building simple 3D shapes with 2D entities, to full 3D surface modeling, to solid modeling, to creating presentations and AutoShade renderings.

Chapter 14 will teach you to manipulate the user coordinate system (UCS) to position construction planes anywhere in 3D space. You'll draw on these construction planes using standard 2D AutoCAD drawing commands. You'll see how to use UCSs to move, rotate, and tilt your X,Y,Z axes to create a 3D model from extruded 2D entities. You'll use your viewports in new ways to visualize your model in 3D. We'll also show you how to see a more realistic view of your model with hidden lines removed.

Chapter 15 will introduce you to new entities like 3D polylines, 3D faces, and 3D surface meshes. We'll model an office chair by creating 3D parts and inserting them as blocks to assemble the chair. In addition to the basic surface commands, you'll use AutoLISP-defined commands that create 3D objects such as boxes, wedges, cones, and spheres. We'll also compare surface shading (with AutoCAD's SHADE command) to hidden line removal for viewing your model quickly and clearly.

Chapter 16 will show you how to dynamically adjust your 3D viewpoint and create perspective views, using the DVIEW command as a single 3D substitute for the VPOINT and ZOOM commands. We'll present advanced 3D viewing techniques to make 3D drawing easier and help you plan and preview 3D presentations. You'll learn how to put dynamic views, slides, and scripts together to create a *walk-through* of successive views in a simple 3D office model.

Chapter 17 will explain how to use AutoShade to create surface-shaded images. We will show you how to pass AutoCAD images into AutoShade, then set camera, target, and lights to produce realistic shaded images. With AutoShade and Autodesk RenderMan, you can even add textures for photorealism.

Chapter 18 will teach you to use AutoCAD's optional AME solid modeling program. If you haven't purchased AME, you can use AMElite to do many of the exercises in this chapter. AMElite is included with AutoCAD. You'll use simple 3D solid shapes to build complex models by adding them together, subtracting one from another, and finding the intersections of solids. We'll show you how to add substance to your 3D model. You can give it mass, specify material type, and set other volumetric properties. Once you've defined solids, you can extract information such as surface area, moment of inertia, and weight from them. You'll also learn to use solid models to create 2D drawings by automatically generating 2D sections and profiles of a 3D model.

When to Use 3D

One of our goals in this 3D section is to help you assess when 3D modeling will be useful to you, and when it will not be. Many projects don't require 3D modeling — simple plans, diagrams, and flow charts are good examples.

On the other hand, much of what you design and build is three-dimensional, and 3D modeling can be the most natural way to create and document your design. But 3D modeling sometimes adds time and complexity to the design process. The next five chapters will help you understand the advantages of 3D modeling and decide when it is worth the added time and effort.

As you look through the chapters and think about your own applications, don't take our examples too literally. The extruded entities in Chapter 14's table and the surfaces in Chapter 15's chair could also be applied to architectural models, piping and machinery design, topographic models, and package design, to name but a few. The dynamic viewing, rendering, and presentation techniques in Chapters 16 and 17 apply equally well to nearly any application. For precision in mechanical parts design, you *need* solid modeling. Surfaces are only approximations but solids are mathematically precise enough to far exceed the abilities of NC machines. And solids aren't only for machine parts design. They are useful for architectural mass models, for designing details and extracting sections, and for graphically calculating complex intersections that you need to represent in 2D drawings.

In any case, once you've seen how easy 3D can be, you will probably find *some* indispensable use for it in your everyday work.

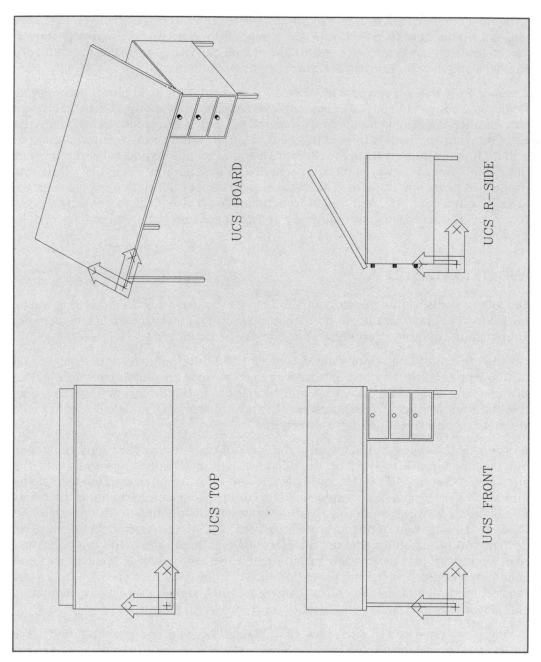

UCS BOARD

UCS R–SIDE

UCS TOP

UCS FRONT

Figure 14.1:
The table drawing with UCS icons.

14

Getting Started With 3D

WORKING IN A 3D WORLD

In 3D, what you see on your screen is just one of many possible views of the 3D model you create and store in AutoCAD. The distinction between the model and a view of the model is important. AutoCAD has certain tools for building 3D models and other tools for viewing them. Before we turn to look at the tools, let's look at the key concept behind 3D in AutoCAD, the *UCS* (User Coordinate System).

The UCS Concept — User Coordinate System

You've been working in 2D UCSs. The base coordinate system is the *WCS* (World Coordinate System), but you can create as many UCSs as you want. UCSs can be at any angle and location in 3D space. The X,Y plane of a UCS is its default *construction plane*. A construction plane is like a transparent sheet of plastic upon which you can draw with standard 2D or 3D AutoCAD commands. You can rotate and align that transparent sheet to any orientation in 3D space using the UCS command. The Z elevation of points defaults to the construction plane, unless explicitly specified. (The Z elevation of the construction plane can be set with a non-zero elevation, but we do not recommend that approach. Instead, relocate the UCS.)

Look at the table drawings in figure 14.1. The four views are of a single table drawn in 3D. Each view has an associated UCS that lets you work on a different plane as if it were a 2D X,Y plane. In the course of this chapter, you will create and edit this table using 2D drawing entities and editing commands! Learning how to locate your UCS in your drawing is the key to using 3D.

585

You can draw 2D entities in any UCS construction plane, and extrude them in their Z axis. The drawing board, for example, is drawn at a 30-degree angle to the table top. It was drawn by first placing the UCS on the table top, then rotating the UCS X axis angle 30 degrees to the top of the table. The board was given a thickness by extruding it in the Z plane. All 2D drawing and editing commands work for drawing and editing in any construction plane, set by the UCS anywhere in 3D space. Learning how to locate and use your UCS gives you an immediate leg up on 3D because it lets you use everything you already know about 2D drawing and editing to create work in 3D.

What This Chapter Covers

This chapter will give you the basics for working in 3D. The type of drawing that you will create is called a wireframe drawing. Sequentially, the chapter will take you through:

- Using VPOINT to control the angle from which you view your 3D model
- Using viewports for 3D
- Moving and rotating your UCS
- Drawing and editing in 3D with extruded 2D entities
- Using HIDE to remove hidden lines for a more realistic 3D image
- Blocking and inserting 3D blocks into your drawing
- Composing multiple 3D views in your drawing

The chapter focuses on using the UCS and 2D entities to create 3D geometry. There are two ways 2D entities can represent 3D objects: by their position in space, and by extruding them in the Z axis.

Finding Your 3D Tools

Working in a 3D world is a mix of drawing and editing, and of setting up views and viewports to display what you are doing and what you have done. You can find the tools for these activities in the screen menu, the pull-down menus, or the tablet menu. Here is a quick list of where to find your main display and UCS controls on the screen and pull-down menus.

Viewpoint and Viewport Controls

The commands for working with 3D displays are on the [Display] pull-down menu and on the [DISPLAY] and [SETTINGS] screen menus. On the [DISPLAY] screen menu, you will find [VPOINT:] and [MVIEW:]. An extra [MVIEW:] selection appears on the root screen menu. [VPOINT:] sets your viewing position in 3D space, and [MVIEW:] controls the configuration of your screen display viewports in paper space. (In Release 10, you will use the VIEWPORTS command to set up viewports. You can type the command as VPORTS or VIEWPORTS.)

You can access customized versions of these commands with [Vpoint 3D...] and [MVIEW >] on the [Display] pull-down menu. [Vpoint 3D...] brings up an icon menu of preset viewpoints. [MVIEW >] replaces the [Display] pull-down with an [Mview] menu. You can also use the [MVSETUP] item on the [BONUS] screen menu to automate viewport setup and control, as discussed in Chapter 10. In addition, you will find the PLAN command on both the pull-down [Display] and the screen [DIS-PLAY] menus. PLAN will return you to a top-down view (from a point on the Z axis looking down at the X,Y plane) in whatever coordinate system you specify.

Finding the UCS Commands

The [SETTINGS] screen menu includes all of the UCS and UCSICON command options and access to the VPORTS command, if you prefer to use tiled viewports instead of paper space. The [Settings] pull-down menu gives you four options for controlling the UCS and the UCSICON through dialogue boxes and toggle commands.

Drawing and Editing Commands

Most of the 3D drawing and editing commands are the familiar tools you've been using throughout this book. You will use some commands, like CHPROP and PEDIT, more frequently, to change an entity's Z thickness value. You'll also use the THICK-NESS system variable (not command) to preset the Z extrusion thickness of new entities.

Setting Up for a 3D Drawing

In this chapter, you will draw a drafting table in 3D. At first you will draw a few simple 3D entities and move around them to get familiar with viewpoints in 3D space. Begin by setting up a new drawing called TABLE using settings from table 14.1. The table is drawn 42 inches high, 62 inches long, and 31.5 inches deep.

Setting Up the 3D Table Drawing

Begin a NEW drawing named TABLE and make the settings shown in table 14.1. Set the SCRATCH layer current.

Table 14.1
Table Drawing Settings

COORDS	FILL	GRID	ORTHO	SNAP	UCSICON
ON	OFF	2	ON	.25	OR

UNITS	Use defaults for all UNITS settings.
LIMITS	Set LIMITS from 0,0 to 68,44.
ZOOM	Zoom All.

Layer Name	State	Color	Linetype
0	On	7 (white)	CONTINUOUS
SCRATCH	On/Current	7 (white)	CONTINUOUS
TABLE	On	7 (white)	CONTINUOUS

If you are using Release 10, make sure the FLATLAND system variable is 0, off.

> *Tip:* If you encounter problems in any exercise, check your current UCS, thickness, and osnap settings.

Getting Around in Simple 3D Drawings

Every entity we have drawn so far has been in the same plane as the WCS construction plane. The X and Y values of the entities have been in a flat plane and the Z value for all of these entities has been 0. But just as you have control over X and Y locations for entities, AutoCAD gives you Z axis control for creating 3D objects.

You can draw some entities directly in 3D. There is no reason a point or line has to lie flat on the X,Y construction plane. Adding a Z coordinate when you pick point coordinates is the simplest way to give 3D life to your drawing. The ubiquitous LINE command and the full 3D entity commands, 3DPOLY, 3DFACE, and 3DMESH, as well as several surfacing commands, accept Z input for any point. Other 2D entity commands accept a Z coordinate for their first point only, which is applied to the rest of their points to create them parallel to the current construction plane.

While many 3D objects look complex, they are easy to draw. Try a simple exercise using all three coordinates to create lines in 3D space.

Using LINE to Make 3D Lines

Command: **ZOOM**	Zoom Center, 0,0 for center point and 3 for height.
Command: **COLOR**	Set color to red.
Command: **LINE**	Draw line along Y axis from 0,0,0 to 0,1,0.
Command: **COLOR**	Set color to yellow.
Command: **LINE**	Draw line along X axis from 0,0,0 to 1,0,0.
Command: **COLOR**	Set color to green.
Command: **LINE**	Draw line along Z axis from 0,0,0 to 0,0,1.

Notice that you used three values for coordinate entry. The third value is for the Z axis. While the first two lines did not actually require a Z value, we added the Z coordinates to clarify the exercise.

Take a look at your screen. You will see two lines and the UCS icon. Although you drew three lines, only the two lines in the X,Y plane are clearly visible (see fig. 14.2). From your current viewing direction, you cannot see the third line because you are looking directly down at its endpoint. It is as if the line is coming directly out of the screen at you, so you see it as a single point. What you need is a way to view the drawing from a better angle. Fortunately, AutoCAD gives you the VPOINT command.

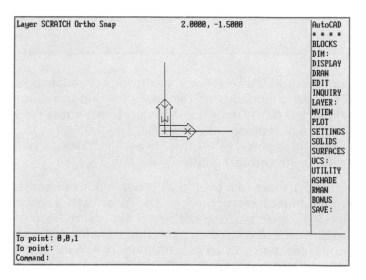

Figure 14.2:
Three lines in 3D
space.

Using VPOINT to Get Around

Until now, your screen has represented the X,Y plane only. Your vantage point in front of the screen is actually some distance above the X,Y plane, looking down along the Z axis. If the plane of the screen represents flat ground, you are looking at that flat ground from a perch atop a flagpole. Figure 14.3 shows you how the real-world X, Y, and Z are oriented on your screen in a normal plan view.

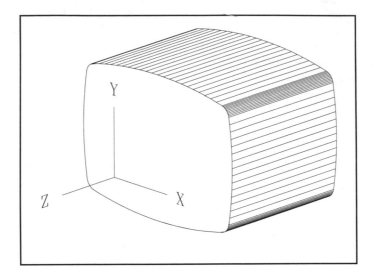

Figure 14.3:
Orientation of X, Y, and Z axes relative to screen.

In AutoCAD, the direction from which you view your drawing or model is called the viewpoint. AutoCAD's VPOINT command controls this direction in relation to the drawing. The default VPOINT is 0,0,1, implying that your viewpoint is directly over the X,Y origin. Your line of sight is along a line from 0,0,1 to 0,0,0 (the origin). This is called the *plan view*. So long as you are directly above your drawing looking down the Z axis, everything you create with 2D entities looks flat.

In order to see 3D, you have to move to a point that is not looking straight down at your model. Your viewpoint must have a non-zero X or Y, or both. For example, a 1,1,1 setting gives you a 45-degree angle in the X,Y plane and a 45-degree angle above the X,Y plane, looking back at 0,0,0 where your lines are located. You can set VPOINT to any X, Y, and Z location you please. Although you can type values to locate your viewpoint, the easiest way to use VPOINT is through its predefined icon selections, or by using the viewpoint globe icon.

Using the VPOINT Globe Icon

The viewpoint globe icon looks like crosshairs in a bull's-eye. You can get the viewpoint globe icon on your screen in four ways: by selecting [Vpoint 3D...] from the [Display] pull-down menu, then selecting the globe from the icon menu; by using the axes option in the [VPOINT:] screen menu; by picking the globe icon from your tablet; or by pressing <RETURN> in response to the VPOINT command's first prompt.

To understand VPOINT, consider your drawing to be located at the center of a transparent globe. The default viewpoint is sitting at the north pole, looking down to the center at your drawing. The concentric circles on the screen represent the globe, with the center point being the north pole, the inner circle representing the equator, and the outer circle representing the south pole. When you move the cursor around the globe icon, you move around the outside of the globe's sphere. If the cursor is in the inner circle, as shown in figure 14.4, you are above the equator, looking down on your model (in the northern hemisphere). If the cursor is in the outer circle, you are looking from *under* your drawing, or from the southern hemisphere. The horizontal and vertical lines represent the X and Y axes, dividing the globe into four quadrants, just as the screen X and Y axes divide your drawing world.

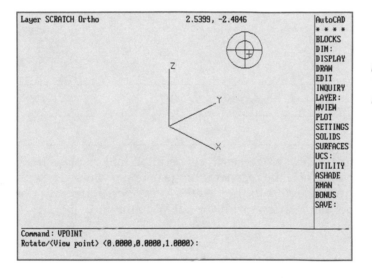

Figure 14.4:
The VPOINT screen icon.

The dynamically moving XYZ axes icon shown on your screen reflects the position of your viewpoint as you move the cursor. For some people, this is an intuitive way to select a viewpoint. Get the VPOINT globe on screen, use the following illustrations and exercise to position your cursor in the concentric circles, then pick your viewpoint. Your drawing will regenerate to reflect your VPOINT position.

Using the VPOINT Screen Icon

Command: **VPOINT**

Rotate/<View point> <0.0000,0.0000,1.0000>: **<RETURN>**

Move your pointing device until it matches figure 14.4; press the pick button.

Command: **PAN**   Pan to a clear view of axis lines.

Your drawing should match the axes of the X, Y, Z axes icon as shown in figure 14.5.

Figure 14.5:
Lines after VPOINT
and PAN.

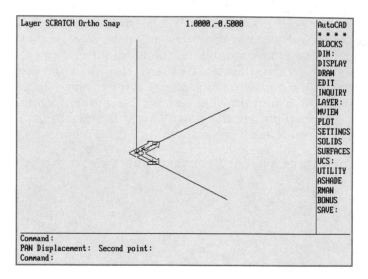

```
Layer SCRATCH Ortho Snap            1.0000,-0.5000        AutoCAD
                                                          * * * *
                                                          BLOCKS
                                                          DIM:
                                                          DISPLAY
                                                          DRAW
                                                          EDIT
                                                          INQUIRY
                                                          LAYER:
                                                          MVIEW
                                                          PLOT
                                                          SETTINGS
                                                          SOLIDS
                                                          SURFACES
                                                          UCS:
                                                          UTILITY
                                                          ASHADE
                                                          RMAN
                                                          BONUS
                                                          SAVE:

Command:
PAN Displacement:  Second point:
Command:
```

Tip: The VPOINT command always causes a regeneration and displays the image as a zoom Extents. You can cancel the regeneration as soon as you see how the drawing will be displayed and zoom in to the desired view. For frequently used viewpoints, save and restore named views with the VIEW command.

Using Menus to Select a Viewpoint

AutoCAD provides a series of menu boxes with predefined viewpoint directions for selecting viewpoints (see fig. 14.6). To use them, select [Display] and [Vpoint 3D...] from the pull-down menu, or use the 3D section on your tablet menu.

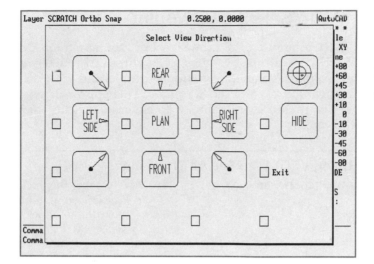

Figure 14.6:
The VPOINT icon
menu.

Look at the eight boxes surrounding [PLAN]. The [PLAN] box sets VPOINT to 0,0,1, the plan view. The other eight boxes position you away from your drawing at the sides indicated. As soon as you pick a line-of-sight direction, you get a screen menu that asks you to select an angle from which to view your drawing (see fig. 14.7). After you select a direction and an angle, AutoCAD calculates the viewpoint from your selections and regenerates the drawing.

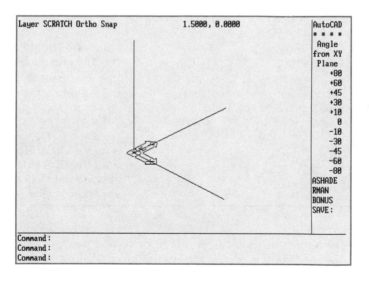

Figure 14.7:
The VPOINT screen
menu.

Using Polar Angles to Select a Viewpoint

If you looked at the VPOINT prompt on the command line, you saw a Rotate option. You can also set VPOINT by inputting two angles. The first angle determines the rotation in the X,Y plane from the X axis (X axis equals 0 angle) and the second angle determines the Z angle (inclination) from the X,Y plane. This approach seems more natural to many users. Use the following exercise to experiment with the VPOINT options to see which you like.

Using VPOINT to See All Three Lines

Pull down **[Display]** *Select* **[Vpoint 3D...]**	Try using the icon menu.
Select	Select icon with arrow pointing to upper right.
Select **[+30]**	Select 30 degrees from the screen menu (see fig. 14.8).
Regenerating drawing.	
Command: **VPOINT**	Try using coordinate values.
Rotate/<View point> <-2.5110,-2.5110,2.0503>: **1,1,.5**	
Regenerating drawing.	Your view should resemble figure 14.9.
Command: **VPOINT**	Try the Rotate option.
Rotate/<View point> <1.0000,1.0000,0.5000>: **R**	
Enter angle in X,Y plane from X axis <45>: **200**	
Enter angle from X,Y plane <19>: **50**	
Regenerating drawing.	Your view should now resemble figure 14.10.
Command: **VPOINT**	Use Rotate to view from the bottom.
Rotate/<View point> <-0.9060,-0.3298,1.1491>: **R**	
Enter angle in X,Y plane from X axis <200>: **<RETURN>**	
Enter angle from X,Y plane <50>: **-50**	
Regenerating drawing.	Notice the box is gone from the UCS icon. It appears only when you are above it (see 14.11).

Practice with VPOINT for a few minutes to get a feel for how it works. VPOINT will make sense if you remember that you are always looking through the specified viewpoint towards 0,0,0 (and beyond). You move around the drawing, not the other way around.

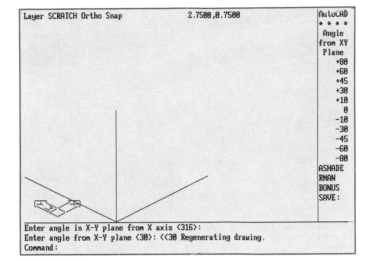

Figure 14.8:
A viewpoint
established with
icon menu.

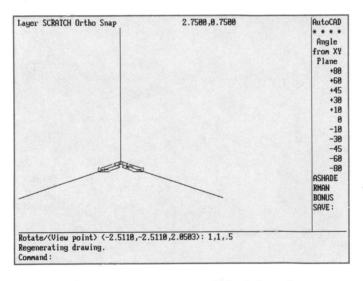

Figure 14.9:
A viewpoint
established with
coordinate values.

As you try the different options, you will find that the XYZ axes icon matches your three lines. The lines' three colors and their intersection at 0,0,0 should help you identify your vantage point. If you happen to select a viewpoint parallel to the current X,Y construction plane, you will see the UCS icon turn into a *broken pencil* icon. This means point selection on the screen may be meaningless (more about UCS icons soon).

Figure 14.10:
A viewpoint
established with
rotate values.

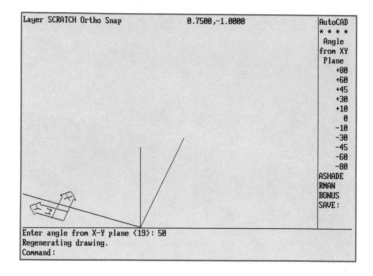

Figure 14.11:
A bottom view using
rotate option.

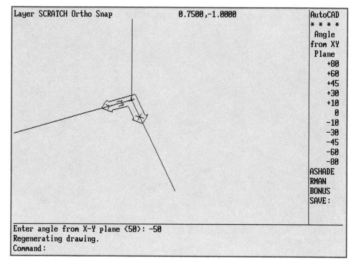

Tip: If you are having trouble picking a viewpoint, try to pinpoint the angle in the X,Y plane first and then adjust the inclination.

WORLDVIEW System Variable

By default, VPOINT always bases your views on the world coordinate system, not the current UCS. The WORLDVIEW system variable controls whether VPOINT bases the view on the WCS or UCS. The default WORLDVIEW of 1 bases your view on the WCS. If you set WORLDVIEW to 0, your coordinates and viewpoint rotation angles are interpreted by VPOINT in the current UCS instead of the WCS. If you need to enter coordinates relative to the WCS while a UCS is current, prefix the coordinate with an asterisk, and the UCS will be ignored.

We recommend working with WORLDVIEW set to 1 (the default). It provides a constant viewpoint reference to the world coordinate system, and makes it easier not to get lost in space. Regardless of WORLDVIEW setting or current UCS, you are always looking through your viewpoint and drawing at the WCS origin.

Using the PLAN Command

What do you do if you get lost in space? The PLAN command will take you home at warp speed. PLAN is a fail-safe option for reorienting lost viewers. It automatically resets the viewpoint to 0,0,1 in the current UCS (default), the WCS, or a named UCS you have saved.

Try using a quick PLAN command.

Using PLAN to Return to a Plan View	
Command: **PLAN**	Select or type.
<Current UCS>/Ucs/World: **<RETURN>**	The current UCS is also the WCS.
Regenerating drawing.	
Command: **ZOOM**	Zoom Center at 0,0,0 with a height of 2.
Command: **SAVE**	Save and continue or end and take a break.

The simple drawing exercise you did a few moments ago showed that you can use AutoCAD's basic LINE command in 3D space. In the next section, we'll use some other 2D commands in the 3D drawing world.

Drawing 2D Entities in 3D Space

You can draw most of AutoCAD's basic 2D entities with a Z coordinate value. But 2D entities such as polylines, circles, arcs, and solids are constrained to the X,Y plane of the UCS. For these entities, the Z value is accepted only for the first coordinate to set the elevation of the 2D entity above or below the current plane.

When picking entity coordinates on the screen, AutoCAD assumes a Z value of 0 (unless you osnap). This is equivalent to drawing all entities in the X,Y plane — as you have been until you began this 3D section of the book. However, picking coordinates above or below the X,Y plane (when a Z value is allowed) is as easy as adding a Z value when AutoCAD asks for a point. When you pick a point using an OSNAP mode, it assumes the Z value of the point to which you osnapped.

Here are a few tips for making 3D objects from familiar 2D entities.

- Circles are best for making closed cylinders. Donuts make good open-ended cylinders with thick walls.

- Solids are good and quick for rectilinear closed objects. Keep FILL turned off to speed up regenerations.

- Lines and polylines make good open rectilinear objects. Polylines show their width.

- Lines can approximate any object in wireframe, but can't hide anything unless extruded.

- Solids, wide polylines, and traces fill only in plan view, and do not plot filled in other views.

Three-Dimensional Thickness

You can do a lot by positioning *flat* 2D entities at various angles in 3D space. But to quickly create more realistic 3D models, you can *extrude* entities such as lines, polylines, arcs, circles, and solids by giving them a thickness in their Z direction. Think of thickness as a wall rising from an entity in its Z direction. For example, if you draw a line on the X,Y plane, its thickness will appear as a wall stretching from the line itself to the height of the thickness given it. Figure 14.12 shows how a 3D object "grows" from flat 2D entities.

Figure 14.12: Growing a 3D drawing from 2D entities.

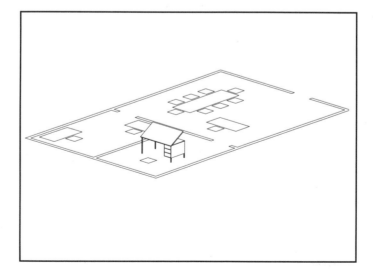

You can create new entities with thickness by first setting a value for the THICK-NESS system variable. All entities created when THICKNESS is non-zero get that thickness. You can also edit the thickness of an existing entity with the CHPROP command.

> **Note:** Thickness can be positive (up in the Z direction) or negative (down in the Z direction). Thickness is relative to the Z axis of 2D entities, even if applied by CHPROP with the current UCS in a different orientation. For 3D entities that can accept thickness, such as points and lines, thickness is always relative to the current UCS. They will appear oblique if they do not lie in or parallel to the current UCS. If thickness is added to a line drawn directly in the Z direction, it will appear that the line extends beyond its endpoint in the positive or negative thickness direction.

Using THICKNESS to Draw Table Legs

Let's draw the table. Begin by setting the layer TABLE current and by setting a thickness for the extruded height of the legs. Draw one table leg with lines and a second with a polygon, then copy both to create the table's other two legs.

Using the THICKNESS Variable to Extrude a 2D Entity

Edit the existing drawing named TABLE, or begin a NEW drawing named TABLE and make the settings shown back in table 14.1.

Command: **LAYER**	Set layer TABLE current and layer SCRATCH off.
Command: **ZOOM**	Zoom All.
Command: **THICKNESS** New value for THICKNESS <0.0000>: **25**	(Release 10, use SETVAR THICKNESS.) This will be the length of the legs.
Command: **COLOR**	Set color to yellow.
Command: **LINE**	Draw a 1" square with the lower left corner at 4,7.5.
Command: **POLYGON**	Draw a four-sided polygon at 51.5,8 circumscribed about a .5 radius circle.
Command: **COPY**	Copy the two legs up 29" along the Y axis.

You have what appears to be four squares for table legs (see fig. 14.13). You need to view the legs from a different viewpoint to see the thickness. The recurring problem of drawing in 3D is that you can't see what you've done without changing your viewpoint. You need multiple views of your drawing in order to work effectively in 3D.

Figure 14.13:
Table legs drawn with
THICKNESS.

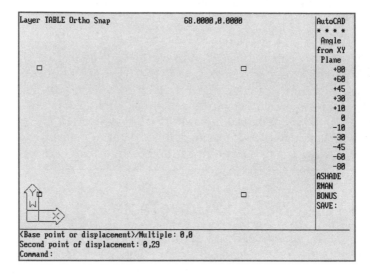

Using Multiple Viewports to Control Screen Display and 3D Viewing

With several viewports, each can have different snap, grid, zoom, and viewpoint settings. MVIEW and VPORTS are the commands that create multiple viewports.

Using Multiple Viewports in 3D

You have already used MVIEW and VPORTS to set up and control 2D drawing viewports in Chapters 4 and 10. Recall that VPORTS divides the AutoCAD graphics screen into as many as 16 tiled viewports, and MVIEW creates up to 15 paper space viewports. (One viewport number is reserved by the system for the main model space viewport in paper space.)

Remember that you can work in only one viewport at a time, the current viewport. You make the viewport current by clicking on it with your pointer. When you work within a viewport, you can use all your normal zoom display controls just as if you were working with a single screen. As you draw or edit in one viewport, your drawing is updated in all viewports.

When you work in 3D, we recommend setting up three viewports as a starting configuration. Set up one viewport for your UCS plan view. Use a second as a 3D viewport for visualizing and building your 3D model. Use the third viewport to hold a WCS view or a second 3D view of your drawing.

Using Viewports to View 3D Table Construction

In the next exercise, we're going to set up three viewports so you can see the 3D table construction as you draw it. Split the screen into a large top view for construction and two smaller views below. The lower left viewport gives you a left-front 3D view of the table from above. The lower right viewport gives you a right-front 3D view of the table from below. The top view is your plan view. The table you are building will appear in each viewport. When your views are set up, save the viewport configuration as TABLE.

Using MVIEW to Set Three Viewports

Command: **VPORTS**	(Release 10 only.)
Save/Restore/Delete/Join/SIngle/?/2/<3>/4: **3**	
Horizontal/Vertical/Above/Below/Left/<Right>: **A**	
Regenerating drawing.	
Command: **TILEMODE**	Release 11 only: set to 0 to enter paper space.
Command: **MVIEW**	Release 11 only.
ON/OFF/Hideplot/Fit/2/3/4/Restore/<First Point>: **3**	
Horizontal/Vertical/Above/Below/Left/<Right>: **A**	
Fit/<First Point>: **F**	Fit three viewports to the screen.
Command: **MSPACE**	Release 11 only.
Click in the bottom left viewport to make it active.	
Command: **VPOINT**	Set VPOINT to -.6,-1,.8.
Select the lower right viewport.	
Command: **VPOINT**	Set VPOINT to -1,-1,-.4.
Command: **PAN**	(Release 10, select top viewport and center table.)
Command: **VPORTS**	(Release 10, save as TABLE.)
Select bottom left viewport.	
Command: **VPORTS**	(Release 10, set to SIngle, save as 3D VPORTS.)
Command: **VIEW**	Save 3D view as TABLE.
Command: **VPORTS**	(Release 10, restore TABLE.)
Command: **PSPACE**	Release 11 only.
Command: **VIEW**	Release 11 only: save three-viewport view as TABLE.

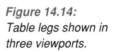

Using MVIEW to Set Three Viewports—continued

Command: **ZOOM**	Release 11 only: fill screen with 3D image in lower left viewport.
Command: **VIEW**	Release 11 only: save this paper space view as 3D-P.
Command: **ZOOM**	Release 11 only: zoom Previous.
Command: **MSPACE**	Release 11 only: back to model space.
Command: **SAVE**	Save the drawing.

The table legs should be visible in all three viewports (see fig. 14.14). Their thickness makes them 25 inches high.

Figure 14.14:
Table legs shown in
three viewports.

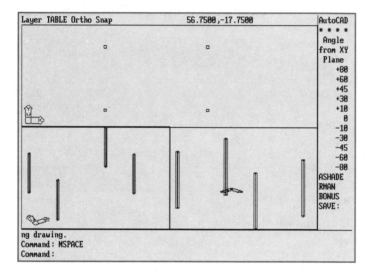

Note: When you are using multiple viewports and you want to redraw or regenerate *all* viewports, use the REDRAWALL or REGENALL commands.

Using SOLID to Make a 3D Object

Now we are ready to put a top on the table. We want the table top to show as a solid surface, so we will make it a SOLID entity. The top is 0.5 inches thick; we can extrude the top by assigning a thickness to it. The only constraint on using SOLID in 3D is that all the extruded Z points must lie in a plane parallel to the X,Y plane.

Using XYZ Filters in 3D

How do you get the table top up on top of the legs? You have two choices. You can assign a thickness of 0.5 inches for your table top, then begin your solid at the Z height of 25 inches above the current UCS construction plane, or you can set a new UCS 25 inches above the current one so that Z=0 is the top of the legs, beginning your solid from there.

We'll use the first method in the following exercise, which shows you how to start the solid at the right Z height using XYZ filters. First set THICKNESS to 0.5 inches. Then, use SOLID to create the table top, typing the Z value.

Using SOLID and XYZ Filters to Make 3D Table Top

Click in the top viewport to make it active.

Command: **THICKNESS**	Set THICKNESS to .5 (Release 10, use SETVAR THICKNESS).
Command: **OSNAP**	Set to ENDPoint.
Command: **SOLID**	
First point: **.XY**	Use XYZ filters for first point.
of	Pick corner of leg at ① (see fig. 14.15).
(need Z): **25**	Type in Z value.
Second point:	Pick corner of leg at ②.
Third point:	Pick corner of leg at ③.
Fourth point:	Pick corner of leg at ④.
Third point: **<RETURN>**	
Command: **OSNAP**	Set to NONe.
Command: **SAVE**	Save the drawing.

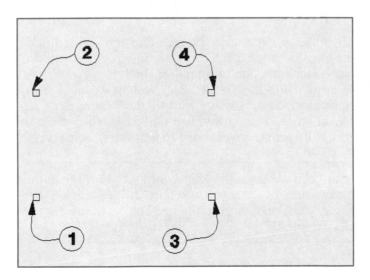

Figure 14.15:
Detail of pick points.

Figure 14.16 shows the table top added to the legs.

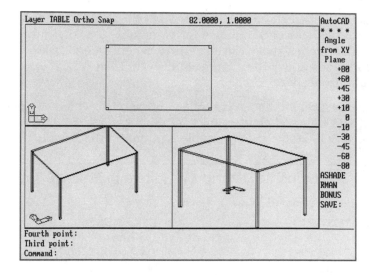

Figure 14.16:
The table top, added with SOLID.

Note that after you entered the Z value for the first coordinate point, AutoCAD assumed the same Z value for the three remaining points.

> **Tip:** XYZ point filters are efficient for creating entities at various Z elevations without changing your UCS. You can osnap the XY point to an existing object and type in a Z value, or osnap Z in a different viewport.

How to Keep an Eye on Z Values and Thickness

You made a simple 3D table by extruding the legs and top, assigning thickness values, and drawing the entities at the Z height you wanted. When you draw in 3D, remember that the draw commands don't prompt for thickness. You can check the current thickness setting by using the THICKNESS system variable. You can find the Z value and thickness of an existing entity with the LIST command. If you want to change the thickness of an existing entity, use CHPROP. You select the entity, respond with thickness as the property you want to edit, then input a new value.

> **Note:** The ELEV command can assign a thickness value, but we recommend using the THICKNESS system variable. ELEV can also set an ELEVATION variable, but we do not recommend its use. ELEV may eventually be eliminated, and it can be confusing to use along with varying UCSs.

> *Tip:* Text ignores the thickness setting when created. If you want text with a 3D thickness, use the CHPROP command to set a thickness after creating the text.

You now have a good-looking 3D drawing of a simple table! Before we move on to more 3D drawing and editing, take a minute to check your table drawing with hidden lines removed.

Using HIDE for Hidden Line Removal

The different views of the table in the bottom viewports are *wireframe* representations. All of those wire edges help you visualize just how the table appears in 3D space. When AutoCAD generates a wireframe image, it does not stop to think whether a line would be visible from your viewpoint if the objects on the screen were solid. Instead, AutoCAD shows it as if it were transparent or constructed of wires. This is the quickest way the program can get the view on the screen.

Once you get a view that you like, you can make it look more realistic by using the HIDE command to remove lines that should be hidden. While the HIDE command is simple to use (all you do is type HIDE), calculating a hidden line removal in a complex drawing can take a very long time. AutoCAD tells you that it is processing hidden lines with a number count. Don't despair; eventually you will get your hidden line view.

Try hiding the table — it's simple, so it will be quick.

Using HIDE to Remove Hidden Lines in the Table

Click in the bottom left viewport to make it active.

```
Command: HIDE
Regenerating drawing.
Removing hidden lines: 50                 It displays a count as it works.
```

Now the table top obscures the back leg (see fig. 14.17).

What Gets Hidden With HIDE?

Here's a way to think about hidden lines. If you were to cover your 3D wireframe model with a tight-fitting piece of cloth, you would only see the sides of the cloth facing you, and nothing behind the cloth. In effect, AutoCAD attempts to hide all wireframe edges from view that would be on the back side of the cloth.

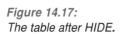

Figure 14.17:
The table after HIDE.

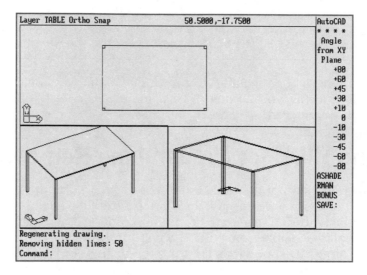

It helps to know how AutoCAD treats various entity surfaces when it calculates hidden line removal. AutoCAD puts an opaque cap on the bottom and top of most graphic entities that surround an area. For example, circles and solids have top and bottom surfaces that hide lines enclosed within or behind them. (You saw the effect of the solid table top in your table view.) A polyline (or trace) only hides what is behind its thickness extrusion or concealed by its width. Areas *enclosed* by closed polylines are not hidden because they have no top or bottom. Remember, polygons, ellipses, and donuts are really polylines. Other 2D extruded entities hide only what is behind their extrusions.

> **Note:** The HIDE command includes entities on layers that are turned off when it calculates what to display. This can result in invisible objects hiding visible ones. Use frozen layers instead to suppress unwanted objects when hiding.

Using Hidden Layers to See Hidden Lines

What happens to all those hidden lines? AutoCAD throws them away until the next regeneration. If you want, you can save them on a separate layer. Let's say you build your plan view 3D model entities on a layer named STUFF. If you also create a layer named HIDDENSTUFF, all hidden line vectors will get put on the HIDDENSTUFF layer when you use HIDE. Any layer in your drawing file can have a hidden line counterpart, even layer 0 (HIDDEN0). To create a hidden layer, just use the same name as your drawing layer, with a HIDDEN prefix.

You can control hidden layers, turning them on (the default) and off, and giving them colors. However, hidden layers ignore layer linetype settings — lines placed there retain their original linetypes. However, these hidden vectors are not real entities and you cannot edit them. The vectors regenerate with each HIDE.

Try creating a hidden layer for the table. Make it any color you like. Then try another HIDE.

Using HIDE With a Hidden Layer

Make the bottom left viewport active.

Command: **DDLMODES**	Or use LAYER to create a new layer named HIDDENTABLE with color of your choice, but don't set it current.
Command: **HIDE**	Hidden lines are still visible, on HIDDENTABLE layer.

A popular use for hidden layers is to set their colors to alternate plotter pens so that when you hide a plot of a 3D view, the hidden lines plot in a different color, line weight, or plotter linetype. Another use is to show hidden lines on screen in a different color.

Tip: All normal editing commands work on 3D-generated displays, but a regeneration or any zoom will unhide the drawing. When you edit a hidden line display, turn REGENAUTO off to avoid accidentally regenerating the drawing.

Tip: Freeze layers that contain extraneous information before doing a HIDE. Don't have AutoCAD spend time removing hidden lines unnecessarily.

Tip: If you have created top and bottom objects from entities that do not hide lines behind them, try solidifying the surface boundaries with circles, solids, or wide polylines.

Don't let familiarity breed contempt; all the editing tools you have learned so far can also be applied to 3D.

Note: HIDE hides one entity when it is behind another. If two entities intersect or coincide in the same plane, small roundoff errors make it impossible to predict which will hide the other. When two entities intersect, cut a tiny slide out of one at the intersection. If they coincide, move one a tiny distance in front of the other.

The Familiar Editing Commands Are 3D Tools Too

The editing commands that reposition entities are valuable in 3D drawing. Often, it is easier to draw an entity in the current UCS and then move, copy, or rotate it than to use more advanced 3D techniques. The COPY and MOVE commands accept 3D points or displacements. COPY Multiple is useful for positioning several identical entities at different points in 3D space. The ROTATE command will only rotate objects parallel to the current UCS, but by setting different UCSs you can rotate objects to any orientation in space.

Using MOVE as a 3D Construction Tool

We need to construct a cabinet on the table's right side. It will overlap the legs. Later, we'll shorten the legs and add drawers. We'll draw the cabinet at the UCS origin and then move it into place rather than pick the corner points in space. Set a new color to distinguish the cabinet from the table. (We used cyan.) Use SOLID to draw the cabinet and extrude it in the Z direction with an 18.5-inch thickness.

Drawing and Moving the Cabinet in 3D

Command: `<Ortho off>`	Turn ortho off.
Command: **COLOR**	Set color to cyan.
Command: **THICKNESS**	Set to 18.5 (Release 10, use SETVAR THICKNESS).
Command: **SOLID**	Draw cabinet at UCS origin.
First point: **0,0**	
Second point:	Pick or type 14,0.
Third point:	Pick or type 0,30.
Fourth point:	Pick or type 14,30.
Third point: **\<RETURN\>**	
Command: **ZOOM**	Zoom in close on upper right corner of table top.
Command: **MOVE**	Move cabinet to below top at right front corner.
Select objects:	Select the cabinet in lower right viewport.

Drawing and Moving the Cabinet in 3D—continued

`Base point or displacement: ` **`ENDP`**	Use osnap ENDP to pick point ① (see fig. 14.18).
`Second point of displacement:`	Use osnap ENDP to pick point ② (see fig. 14.19).
`Command: ` **`ZOOM`**	Zoom Previous.
`Command: ` **`SAVE`**	Save and continue, or end and take a break.

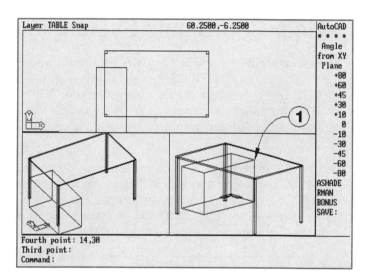

Figure 14.18:
The table with the cabinet at UCS origin.

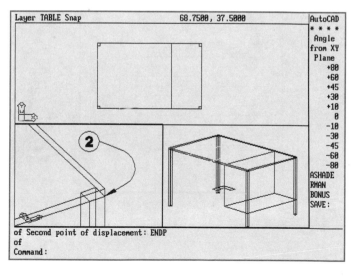

Figure 14.19:
The table with the cabinet moved below top.

If all went well, you should have a good solid cabinet mounted under the right side of the table, as shown in figure 14.19.

While using THICKNESS settings, Z coordinate values, osnap, and the editing commands are useful for constructing 3D drawings, they cannot handle all the 3D construction tasks that you will encounter. In the next set of exercises, you will add drawers and a drawing board at a 30-degree slant on top of the table. Think about how you would draw these with what you have used so far. The drawers are pretty simple, but the slanted drawing board will be easier to do with a reoriented UCS.

Establishing a User Coordinate System in 3D

Let's start this section by taking a closer look at the UCS command and the UCS icon. So far, you have been using AutoCAD's WCS, the default coordinate system, and UCSs that share its X,Y plane. You can create your own coordinate system using the UCS and UCSICON commands. These commands were developed for 3D to let you work with 2D entities and editing commands by locating your coordinate system anywhere in 3D space.

You can establish or modify a UCS with the UCS command, the [UCS:] screen menu, the [UCS:] item on the [SETTINGS] screen menu, or with several items in the [Settings] pull-down menu. The [UCS Control...] pull-down item brings up the DDUCS UCS Control dialogue box (see fig. 14.20), and the [UCS Options...] selection brings up an icon menu with a group of predefined UCSs (see fig. 14.21).

Figure 14.20:
The UCS control
dialogue box.

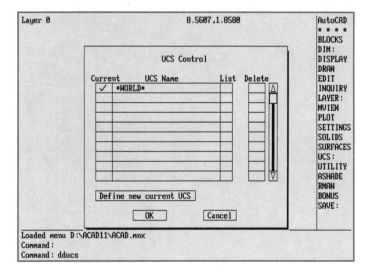

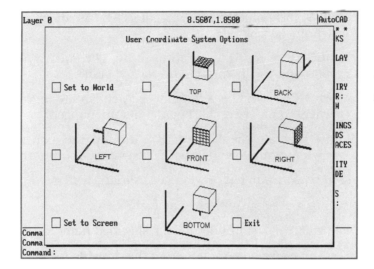

There are just four basic ways to establish a new UCS in 3D.

- Specify a new origin, a new X,Y plane, or a new Z axis.
- Copy the orientation of an existing entity.
- Align the new UCS to your current view.
- Rotate the current UCS around any one, or all X, Y, or Z axes.

You can set a UCS by any one of these methods, or you can combine them by executing the UCS command several times in succession. It's easier to visualize a complex UCS move in several steps. You can define any number of UCSs by naming and saving them. However, only one UCS can be current at any one time. The current UCS defines all coordinate input. If you are using multiple viewports, they all share the current UCS.

As we construct the rest of the table, we will show you how to use most of the command options to define, name, and save UCSs. Here is a complete list of the options. We will give you more details when we work with them.

UCS Command Options

Origin   Establishes the X and Y axes at a new point of origin.

ZAxis   Sets a new point of origin and Z axis direction.

3point   Specifies a new origin and a new X,Y plane orientation. You input or pick three points: the origin, a point on the positive X axis, and a point on the positive Y portion of the new X,Y plane. This is the most flexible method for defining a new UCS.

Entity	Sets a new UCS by selecting an existing entity. The entity type determines the origin and the orientation of the X,Y plane.
View	Defines a new UCS with the X,Y plane perpendicular to your view direction (parallel to the screen). The origin is unchanged.
X/Y/Z	Three options to rotate the current UCS around the axis that you specify. You pick the rotation angle with two points, or input the value.
Prev	Lets you step back, up to ten previous coordinate systems.
Restore	Sets the UCS to a previously saved named UCS.
Save	Stores a coordinate system under a user-specified name.
Del	Removes a saved coordinate system from the drawing.
?	Displays saved coordinate systems by name, origin, and orientation.
<World>	Sets the UCS to the WCS (world coordinate system).

> **Note:** The X,Y plane of the current UCS is also the current construction plane unless the ELEV command has set a non-zero elevation. A non-zero elevation creates a current construction plane above or below the UCS X,Y plane and can make drawing in 3D confusing. That is why we do not recommend setting elevations with ELEV. For brevity and simplicity, we often use the term UCS in lieu of construction plane.

Let's get back to the table. We'll define and save two UCSs to work from.

Defining a 3Point UCS and Saving It

Let's establish two more UCSs, first at the front of the table, then on the right side. We'll use the 3point option for the front UCS. You can use 3point to establish *any* possible UCS. If you don't pick up all the options immediately, this is the option we recommend learning first. You define the UCS by entering three coordinate points. The first point defines the origin, the second point defines the positive X axis from the new origin point, and the third point defines the X,Y plane. The third point need not be on the Y axis, but it defines the direction of the positive Y axis. The only constraint for 3point is that all three points cannot lie in a straight line. The prompts for each of the points present defaults that would leave that point or axis the same as in the current UCS.

Use the following exercise to define the UCS at the base of the table's left front leg. Pick the first origin point on the front lower left corner of the leg, the second on the right leg and the third on the front edge of the top. After you pick the points, save the UCS as FRONT. We'll also return to a single viewport and set a larger grid, so you can more easily see the osnap points and UCS icon as you work.

Using 3point to Create a UCS

Edit an EXISTING drawing named TABLE, and select bottom left viewport.

Command: **PSPACE**	Release 11 only.
Command: **VIEW**	Release 11 only: restore view 3D-P.
Command: **MSPACE**	Release 11 only.
Command: **VPORTS**	(Release 10, set to SIngle.)
Command: **UCSICON**	Make sure UCSICON is set to OR (origin).
Command: **GRID**	Set to 6.
Command: **ZOOM**	To the view shown.
Command: **UCS**	Create the front UCS with 3point.

```
Origin/ZAxis/3point/Entity/View/X/Y/Z/Prev/
   Restore/Save/Del/?/<World>: 3
Origin point <0,0,0>:
```
Use osnap INT to pick point ① at front left leg (see fig. 14.22).

```
Point on positive portion of the X-axis <5.0000,
   7.5000,0.0000>:
```
Use osnap INT to pick point ② on front right leg.

```
Point on positive-Y portion of the UCS X,Y plane
   <4.0000,8.5000,0.0000>:
```
Use osnap MID to pick point ③ on front edge of top.

```
Command: UCS
```
Save UCS as FRONT.
```
Origin/ZAxis/3point/Entity/View/X/Y/Z/Prev/
   Restore/Save/Del/?/<World>: S
?/Desired UCS name: FRONT
```

Now, your UCS icon origin should be on the base of the front left leg with the X axis pointing towards the right leg and the Y axis pointing vertically up the left leg towards the top. Notice that setting the UCS did not change your view of the drawing.

While we are at it, let's define the second UCS on the right side.

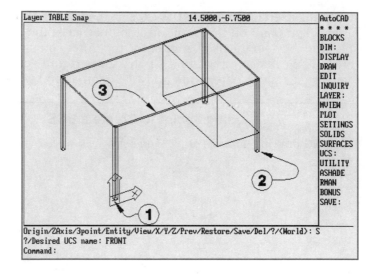

Figure 14.22:
The table with a
3point UCS at the
front.

Using the ZAxis Option to Define a UCS

We'll use the ZAxis option to move our UCS to the right leg, with the X,Y plane on the table's right side. The ZAxis option lets you specify a new positive Z axis by picking an origin and a point on the Z axis. This rotates the X,Y plane based on your new Z axis. Again, this is a quick and easy option to use.

We want the new Z direction to face outward from the right side of the table. After you pick your origin point, pick the second point with relative polar coordinates at 0 degrees. Save the new UCS as R-SIDE.

Using ZAxis to Create Right Side UCS	
`Command:` **UCS**	Create the right side UCS with ZAxis.
`Origin/ZAxis/3point/Entity/View/X/Y/Z/Prev/` `  Restore/Save/Del/?/<World>:` **ZA**	
`Origin point <0,0,0>:`	Use INTersection to pick ① right front leg.
`Point on positive portion of Z-axis <48.0000,` `  0.0000,1.0000>:` **@1<0**	
`Command:` **UCS**	Save the UCS as R-SIDE.
`Command:` **SAVE**	Save the drawing.

Your new UCS icon origin should be at the base of the right front leg with the Z axis pointing toward the right rear leg (see fig. 14.23).

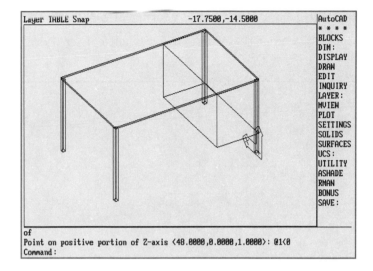

Figure 14.23:
The table with UCS at
the right side.

Keeping Track of UCS Orientation With the UCSICON

You will come to rely heavily on the UCS icon as a reminder of your construction plane orientation, and to confirm that you have defined your UCS the way you want it.

Looking closely at your screen, you will see that the icon's X and Y axes point along the axes of the table. The + on the icon means that it is located at the origin of the current UCS. The W on the Y axis is missing, indicating that your current coordinate system is not the WCS. The box at the icon's base means you are viewing the UCS from above (a positive Z direction). No box means that you are looking at the icon from below (a negative Z direction). Figure 14.24 shows a collection of icon views that you will encounter. When you see a *broken pencil* icon, your view is within one degree of parallel (edge on) to the current UCS and point picking is unreliable. When you see the paper space icon, you will know to switch to model space to draw.

The following list reviews the UCSICON options for controlling its display.

UCSICON Options

ON   Makes the UCS icon visible.

OFF   Removes the UCS icon.

All   Displays the UCS icon in all viewports.

Noorigin   Displays the UCS icon in the lower left corner of viewport.

ORigin   Displays the UCS icon at the origin (or lower left corner if origin is not visible or is too close to edge).

Figure 14.24:
Some different UCS
icon views.

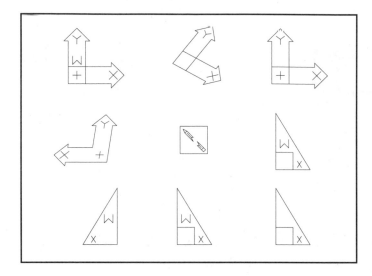

When you are working with three viewports, AutoCAD displays the UCS icon in each. You can set different display settings for the icon in each viewport.

Setting UCS Origin and a Plan View

Depending on what you are doing, a 3D viewpoint or a plan view of the current UCS may be clearer to draw in. Use PLAN to set a plan view if it's easier to find your pick points that way.

We'll restore the FRONT UCS, then use the UCS Origin option to set the UCS at the lower left corner of the cabinet. Then use PLAN to set a plan view for constructing the drawers. Draw the first (lower) drawer on the cabinet face with a 2D polyline, then use COPY Multiple to add the next two drawers. When done, restore your 3D view named TABLE.

Using UCS in Plan View to Add Drawers to the Table	
Command: **COLOR**	Set color to red.
Command: **THICKNESS**	Set THICKNESS to .01 (Release 10, use SETVAR THICKNESS).
Command: **UCS**	Restore the FRONT UCS (see fig. 14.25).

Using UCS in Plan View to Add Drawers to the Table—continued

Command: **UCS**	Move UCS to lower left corner of cabinet with Origin.
Origin/ZAxis/3point/Entity/View/X/Y/Z/ Prev/Restore/Save/Del/?/<World>: **O**	
Origin point <0,0,0>:	Use osnap ENDP to pick lower left corner of cabinet.
Command: **UCS**	Save the UCS as CABINET.
Command: **PLAN**	View the front of the desk in plan to the cabinet UCS.
Command: **ZOOM**	Zoom in on the cabinet.
Command: **PLINE**	Draw from .5,.5 to @13<0 to @5.5<90 to @13<180, then close.
Command: **COPY**	Copy Multiple to place two drawers above the original.
Select objects:	Select the drawer polyline.
<Base point or displacement>/Multiple: **M**	Multiple copies.
Base point:	Pick absolute point 0,0.
Second point of displacement:	Pick polar point @6<90.
Second point of displacement:	Pick polar point @12<90.
Second point of displacement: **<RETURN>**	This ends the COPY command. Your cabinet should have three drawers, as shown in figure 14.26.
Command: **VIEW**	Restore view TABLE (see fig. 14.27).
Command: **SAVE**	

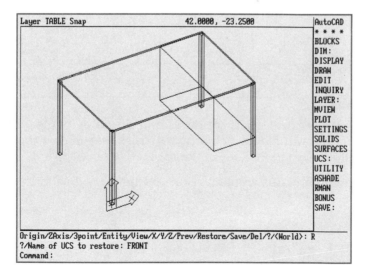

Figure 14.25:
The table with UCS
FRONT.

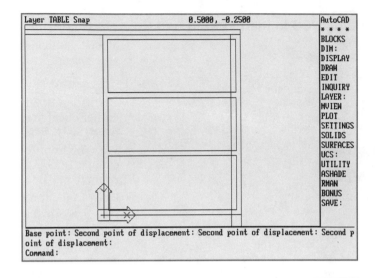

Figure 14.26:
The cabinet in a plan
with drawers and
UCS.

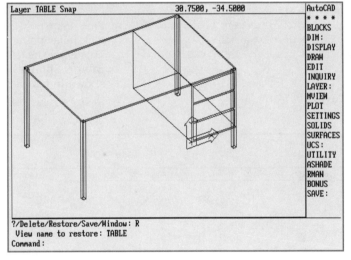

We set a thickness of .01 because when entities are in the same plane, you can't always predict which entity will hide which. The .01 thickness makes the drawer polylines protrude slightly beyond the face of the cabinet.

Besides the Origin, 3point, and ZAxis options that you have used so far, there are several other ways to set a UCS.

Setting a UCS With the X/Y/Z, View, and Entity Options

The X/Y/Z options let you rotate the current UCS around either the X, Y, or Z axis. The angle of rotation is relative to the specified axis of the current UCS through the right-hand rule of rotation. The right-hand rule of rotation is that if you close your right fist and extend your thumb to point in the positive direction of the specified axis, your curled fingers point in the direction of positive rotation. Figure 14.28 shows the direction of rotation angles. If you want to rotate more than one axis, simply re-execute the UCS command to rotate the second (or third) axis. (We will use the X/Y/Z options in some of the remaining exercises.)

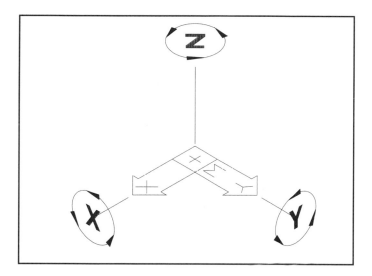

Figure 14.28:
Rotation angles from
viewpoint 1,1,1.

The View option is simple. It sets the X,Y plane of the UCS parallel to the orientation of the screen. The origin is not changed. The Entity option is a bit more complex.

Using Entity Selection to Establish a UCS

You can define a new UCS by selecting an existing entity. Doing so aligns the UCS with the entity. We'll use entity selection in the next set of exercises when we create and insert a block to form the drawing board. If you select an entity, the entity type and your pick point determine the new UCS. There are two entity types you can't use: 3D polylines and 3D meshes. (You will see these two entities in the next chapter.) Here is the official list of how the entities specify a new UCS.

ARC
The arc's center is the new origin point, and the X axis goes through the endpoint nearest your pick point.

CIRCLE
The center is the new origin point, and the X axis passes through your pick point.

LINE
The endpoint nearest your pick point is the new origin, and the second endpoint is on the positive X axis. (The second point's Y coordinate is 0.)

POINT
The point is the new origin point.

2D POLYLINE
The polyline's start point is the new origin point, the X axis lies along the line to the first vertex point. (The first vertex Y coordinate is 0.)

SOLID
The first point is the new origin point, and the X axis lies along the line between the first two points.

TRACE
The first point of the trace is the new origin point, and the X axis lies along the trace's center line.

3DFACE
The first point determines the new origin point, the X axis lies along the first and second points, and the positive Y axis is determined by the first and fourth points.

DIMENSION
The new origin is the middle of the dimension text, and the X axis is parallel to the X axis in effect when the dimension text was drawn.

TEXT, ATTRIBUTE, ATTDEF, SHAPE, INSERT
The new origin is the entity's insertion point. The X axis is defined by the entity's rotation about the extrusion direction (Z axis). In effect, the entity that you select will have a zero rotation angle in the new UCS.

For all of these entities, the positive Z axis of the resulting UCS is parallel to the Z extrusion direction of the selected entity. Since each entity type behaves differently, you should play with each to see how it behaves when you establish a new UCS. Set an undo mark and use your SCRATCH layer to draw and test any entity type that catches your fancy, then use it to define a new UCS. When you are done, undo back and resume with the next exercise on blocks.

Well, you have a table with a decent set of drawers. The last item to add to the drafting table is the drawing board.

Using BLOCK and INSERT to Insert Blocks in 3D

The drawing board is 1.25 inches thick and overlaps the table top on all sides by 1 inch. The next two exercises will show you how to make the drawing board and insert it as a block, slanted at a 30-degree angle.

You can insert 3D blocks into a drawing the same way you insert 2D blocks. The standard INSERT command accepts a 3D insertion point and gives you the option of X-scaling, Y-scaling, *and* Z-scaling the block's entities. The current UCS defines the X,Y plane for the block when it is created.

Using BLOCK to Create a Unit 3D Block

As in 2D, unit-scaled blocks are versatile in 3D. As the first step in making the drawing board, use SOLID to build a 1x1x1 block and name it CUBE. We'll extrude the solid in the Z direction by setting thickness to 1. The resulting block can be inserted with various scales to represent any rectilinear 3D box.

Use the UCS Entity and Z options to set the construction plane on the table top to build the block. Save the UCS as TOP, then make the block.

Making a Solid Building Block

Command: **UCS**	Use Entity selection to see how it works.
Origin/ZAxis/3point/Entity/View/X/Y/Z/Prev/ Restore/Save/Del/?/<World>: **E**	
Select object to align UCS:	Select the table top solid anywhere.
Command: **UCS**	Try the Z option to rotate the X and Y axes.
Origin/ZAxis/3point/Entity/View/X/Y/Z/Prev/ Restore/Save/Del/?/<World>: **Z**	
Rotation angle about Z axis <0>: **-90**	
Command: **UCS**	Save as TOP.
Command: **COLOR**	Set color to BYLAYER.
Command: **ZOOM**	Zoom Center to height 3 in a clear area in the drawing.
Command: **GRID**	Set to 1.
Command: **LAYER**	Set to 0 so CUBE will assume properties of layer inserted on.
Command: **THICKNESS**	Set THICKNESS to 1 (Release 10, use SETVAR THICKNESS).
Command: **SOLID**	Draw a 1" square.
Command: **BLOCK**	Block solid as CUBE.

Making a Solid Building Block—continued

Block name (or ?): **CUBE**	
Insertion base point:	Pick point ① at lower front left corner (see fig. 14.29).
Select objects:	Select the solid, then press <RETURN>.
Command: **THICKNESS**	Set thickness to 0.
Command: **ZOOM**	Zoom Previous.
Command: **GRID**	Set back to 6.

Figure 14.29:
A 1x1x1 building
block with insert point.

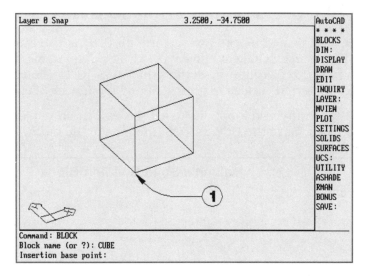

The cube is now safely defined and tucked away in your drawing.

Using INSERT to Insert a 3D Block

Use the INSERT command to insert the cube into the drawing, stretching its scale into a drawing board. When you insert a 3D block, the block's X,Y plane is aligned *parallel* to the current UCS.

The TOP UCS is the current UCS. To slant the drafting board 30 degrees, use the UCS X option and rotate the UCS 30 degrees about the X axis. Offset the insertion by one inch to provide the overlap at the front of the table. The INSERT XYZ scale option tells INSERT to prompt for all three scale factors. If you do not provide a Z scale value, INSERT will default the Z scale to the X scale. We have purposely used an X scale value that will extend the board 12 inches beyond the right side of the table. (We will come back to the table later and edit it to make it fit.)

Using INSERT to Insert a 3D Block for a Drawing Board

```
Command: LAYER                              Set layer TABLE current.
Command: UCS                                Use X option to rotate 30
                                            degrees about X axis, and save
                                            UCS as BOARD.

Command: INSERT
Block name (or ?): CUBE
Insertion point: -1,-1                      Start point is 1" from 0,0 to get
                                            1" overlap.
```

Drag it around with your cursor to get a feel for it.

```
X scale factor <1> / Corner / XYZ: XYZ      Prompt for all three scales.
X scale factor <1> / Corner: 62             Drawing board length.
Y scale factor (default=X): 31              Drawing board width.
Z scale factor (default=X): 1.25            Drawing board thickness.
Rotation angle <0>: <RETURN>
Command: ZOOM                               Zoom Extents.
Command: SAVE                               Save the drawing.
```

When you finish, the drawing board will lie in the same X,Y plane as your X-rotated UCS. The UCS icon should appear to lie just under the drawing board at the lower left corner of the table (see fig. 14.30). The Z scale value of 1.25 scaled the board's thickness in the positive Z direction from the rotated UCS icon. We could also have rotated the block. When you provide a rotation angle, it rotates the block in the current X,Y plane around the insertion point.

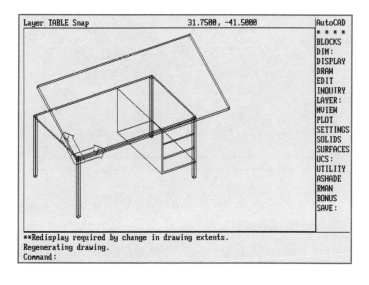

Figure 14.30:
The table with drawing board.

Building a Library of 3D Blocks

As you work in 3D, you can build a library of blocks like the CUBE — a wedge, a pyramid, a cone, various roof shapes, and a pipe elbow are examples of useful shapes that you can easily insert and scale in different drawings. Using the same blocks over and over helps you create drawings quickly and reduces the size of drawing files.

AutoCAD also provides a set of AutoLISP routines that create primitive shapes made up of 3D meshes. These are on icon menus accessed from the [Objects...] and [Surfaces...] selections on the [Draw] pull-down menu (see figs. 14.31 and 14.32). They are documented in the *AutoLISP Programmer's Reference*, but you don't need to be a programmer to use them. The routines form custom shapes from 3D meshes. Although they are not blocks, they behave somewhat like blocks. You can select an entire primitive with a single pick, just like a block. And, you can explode them into individual 3DFace entities. Unlike multiple occurrences of scaled blocks which all reference the same block definition, each occurrence of these mesh objects is composed of separate data. If you use the same primitives frequently, you can block and insert them for greater efficiency. We will make and use 3D meshes in the next chapter.

Figure 14.31:
The 3D mesh objects icon menu.

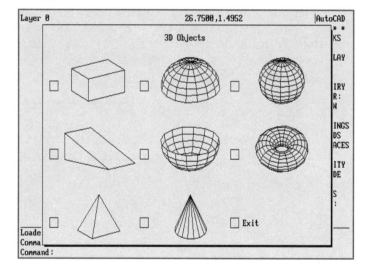

Editing in 3D

Meanwhile, back at the table, the drawing looks a bit funny. The board overhangs on the right, and the two right legs extend up through the cabinet. You guessed it — it must be time for 3D editing.

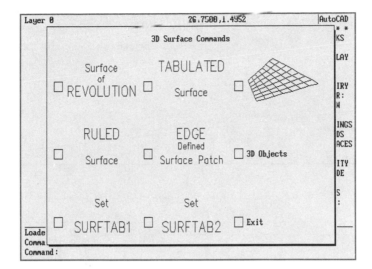

Figure 14.32:
The 3D mesh sur-
faces icon menu.

Wireframes can quickly become confusing. As you edit, there are several things that you can do to avoid mis-picking entities or getting lost in 3D space. First, use color extensively to help identify entities. Second, keep track of the UCS that you used when you created an entity. Many of the problems that you encounter result from picking objects that are at an oblique angle to the UCS. Several 2D editing commands only work for entities parallel to the current construction plane. In these cases, you need to adjust your UCS to match the entity's UCS. The easiest way to do this is to use the UCS Entity option. If you have any doubts about the outcome of your edits, work in multiple viewports.

You've already used MOVE and COPY in 3D. In the following section, we'll examine CHPROP, STRETCH, TRIM, EXTEND, BREAK, FILLET, CHAMFER, and OFFSET. We'll also try HATCH, another drawing command. First, CHPROP.

Using CHPROP to Edit an Entity's Thickness

The CHPROP command works on any entity with any current UCS setting. It's often easier to create or copy entities with the current settings and then use CHPROP to alter them, than to change settings, create an entity, and change the settings back. CHPROP is the only way to give a thickness to text, shape and attdef entities.

Try fixing the right two legs of the table by changing their thickness with CHPROP.

Using CHPROP to Edit Entity Thickness

```
Command: CHPROP                              Select the two right legs at the
                                             cabinet.
Change what property (Color/LAyer/LType/
    Thickness) ? T                           Thickness.
New thickness <25.0000>: 6.5                 New value.
Change what property (Color/LAyer/LType/
    Thickness) ? <RETURN>
Command: REDRAW
```

Figures 14.33 and 14.34 show the table before and after the change to the right legs.

Figure 14.33:
The original table legs.

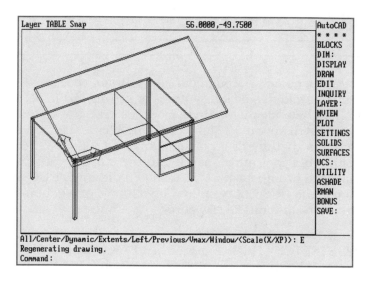

> *Note:* The CHANGE command is pickier than CHPROP. Several of its options require that selected entities be parallel to the current UCS, so it won't select nonparallel entities. Use CHPROP instead whenever possible.

Using STRETCH to Edit in 3D

The results of STRETCH depend on the entity and current UCS. Fully 3D entities such as lines (and 3D meshes) can be stretched from and to any point in 3D space regardless of current UCS. For 2D and extruded 2D entities, it's safest when all of the entities being stretched are aligned with the STRETCH displacement. Otherwise, entities' construction planes may be changed by STRETCH and the results may be hard to predict.

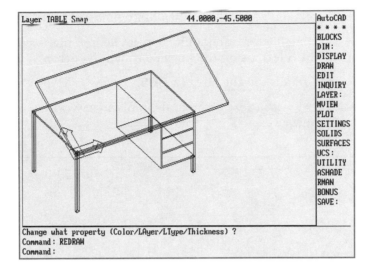

Figure 14.34:
The table legs after being edited.

Let's stretch the table to fit the length of the drawing board. All of the entities align with the X axis of the current BOARD UCS. Stretch the cabinet, drawers, top and right legs 12 inches along this X axis.

Making the Table Longer With STRETCH

Command: **STRETCH**
Select objects: **<RETURN>**   Use crossing window with first corner at ① and
                                                 second corner at ② (see fig. 14.35).
Base point: **@**   Selects last point (any point would do).
New point: **@12<0**   Twelve inches along X axis from last point.
Command: **REDRAW**   Clean up the display. Your table should now look
                                                 like the one in figure 14.36.
Command: **SAVE**

Like CHANGE and STRETCH, several other editing commands require more care and attention in 3D.

2D Editing Commands Requiring Special Attention

The following editing commands work correctly only for entities where the current UCS is in or parallel to the construction plane of their entity coordinate system(s). The easiest way to use them is to use the UCS Entity option to set your UCS parallel to the entities you want to edit.

BREAK   Projects the entity and break points to the current UCS.

TRIM   Projects the trim edge and entities to the current UCS.

EXTEND   Projects the extend edge and entities to the current UCS.

FILLET and   All objects being filleted or chamfered must lie in a plane parallel to
CHAMFER   the current UCS (extrusion thickness parallel to current Z axis).

OFFSET   is performed relative to the current UCS.

You may find it easiest to work with these commands in plan view, while observing the results in multiple 3D viewports.

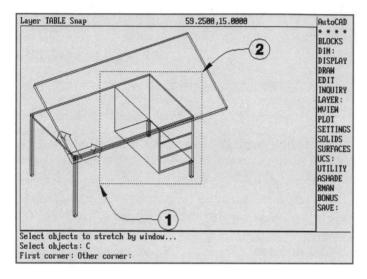

Figure 14.35:
A crossing window for
STRETCH.

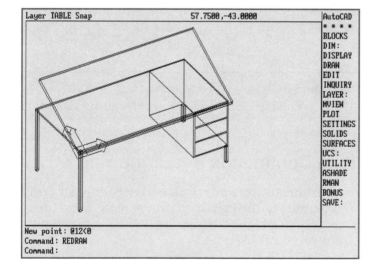

Figure 14.36:
The table after
STRETCH.

Using FILLET to Edit in 3D

To see how FILLET behaves in 3D, try filleting the polylines of the cabinet drawers using a 0.5 radius. First, try it in the current UCS to see the type of error messages that you will encounter.

Using FILLET to Fillet Drawers in 3D

```
Command: FILLET                              Set radius to .5".
View is not plan to UCS. Command results
   may not be obvious.
Polyline/Radius/<Select first object>: R
Enter fillet radius <0.0000>: .5

Command: FILLET
View is not plan to UCS. Command results
   may not be obvious.
Polyline/Radius/<Select first object>: P    Drawers are polylines.
Select 2D polyline:                          Pick a drawer.
   Entity not parallel with UCS.
Select 2D polyline: *cancel*                 Use <^C> to cancel fillet.

Command: UCS                                 Restore the CABINET UCS that you
                                             used to create drawers.
Command: FILLET                              Try it again. Use Polyline option and
                                             select the first drawer.
Command: FILLET                              Fillet the second drawer.
Command: FILLET                              Fillet the last drawer.

Command: ZOOM                                Zoom in for a look (see fig. 14.37),
                                             then zoom Previous.
```

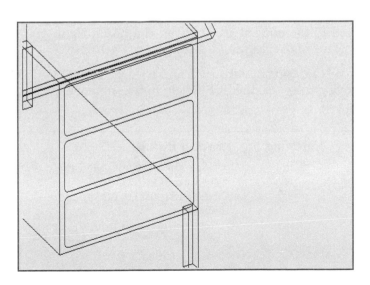

Figure 14.37:
The filleted drawers.

If you are wondering why your CABINET UCS icon seems to be floating in space, remember that you stretched the table 12 inches to the right, away from the UCS origin. The FRONT UCS would also have worked for these fillets.

Hatching in 3D

You can spruce up your 3D images by filling their surfaces with hatch patterns. You will generally have to set the UCS on the surface to be hatched and draw new boundary edges to hatch in. HATCH projects the hatch boundaries onto the X,Y plane of the current UCS where the hatch itself is drawn.

Let's try it both ways. Create a boundary with lines on layer 0 and try to hatch the board.

Trying to Hatch the Drawing Board

Command: **LAYER**	Set layer 0 current.
Command: **COLOR**	Set color to BYLAYER.
Command: **LINE**	Use osnap INT to draw four lines bounding top of drawing board. You'll probably have to transparently zoom in on front left corner to pick it.
Command: **HATCH**	
Pattern (? or name/U,style): **LINE**	
Scale for pattern <1.0000>: **6**	
Angle for pattern <0>: **<RETURN>**	
Select objects:	Select the four boundary lines.
Select objects: **<RETURN>**	The hatch is drawn (see fig. 14.38).

The hatch was projected to the current UCS. To get the hatch right, you need to locate the UCS on the plane of the drawing board surface.

Erase your first hatch, restore your BOARD UCS and try again. The BOARD UCS is on the underside of the board, so use the UCS Origin option to move the origin 1.25 inches up to the board top.

Hatching the Drawing Board

Command: **ERASE**	Erase the previous hatching.
Command: **UCS**	Restore BOARD UCS.
Command: **UCS**	Set Origin to 0,0,1.25 to move UCS to top of board.
Command: **HATCH**	Repeat the hatch from the previous exercise.
Command: **SAVE**	

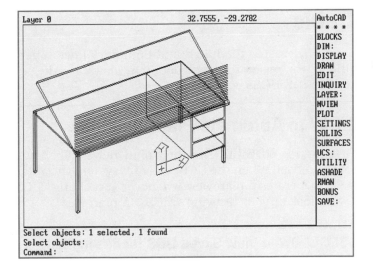

Figure 14.38:
The table with an
incorrect hatch

Your table should have a hatch on the plane of the drawing board (see fig. 14.39).

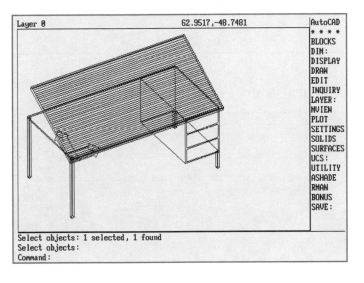

Figure 14.39:
The table with a
correct hatch.

Both the TRIM and EXTEND commands behave similarly to HATCH, projecting their boundary edges and entities onto the construction plane of the current UCS to calculate the trim or extension. However, the trimmed or extended entities remain in their own planes after modification.

> ***Note:*** As you edit in 3D, you will find that it usually pays to name and save your UCSs. If you forget what you have, you can always get a listing with the first UCS command or DDUCS dialogue box.

Viewing the Table

We'll clean up the drawing by erasing the hatch and boundary lines. Then, before putting the table drawing to rest, review its construction by looking at the plan views of the TOP, FRONT, and R-SIDE UCSs you saved.

Using UCSFOLLOW to Automate Plan Views

Viewing the TOP, FRONT, and R-SIDE UCSs in their plan views will show the top, front, and right sides of the model. When the UCSFOLLOW system variable is set to 1, AutoCAD automatically generates a plan view whenever you change UCSs. Let's set UCSFOLLOW to 1, and look at your drawing's UCSs in plan view.

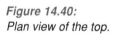

Using UCSFOLLOW to View Saved UCS Planes in Plan	
Command: **ERASE**	Erase the hatch and boundary lines on layer 0.
Command: **UCSFOLLOW**	Set to 1. (Release 10, use SETVAR UCSFOLLOW.)
Command: **UCS**	Restore TOP UCS.
Command: **UCS**	Restore FRONT UCS.
Command: **UCS**	Restore R-SIDE UCS.
Command: **UCSFOLLOW**	Set to 0 (off).

The various views are shown in figures 14.40 through 14.42.

Figure 14.40:
Plan view of the top.

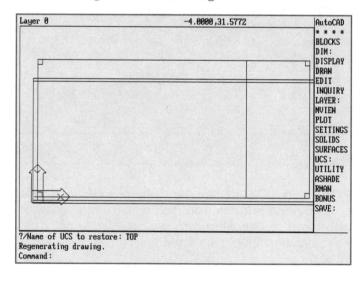

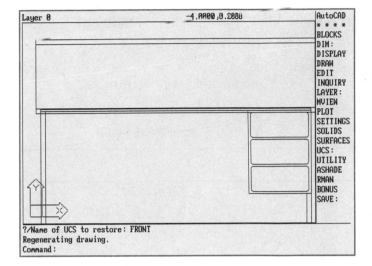

Figure 14.41:
Plan view of the front.

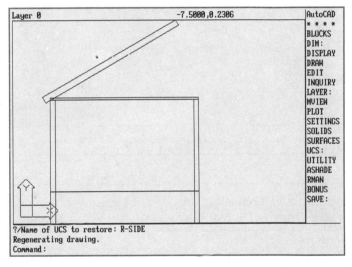

Figure 14.42:
Plan view of the right side.

After you've reviewed your drawing, restore your 3D view and hide the table. We'll also set up some settings for later. Then, end the drawing.

Using HIDE to View Hidden Table

Command: **PSPACE**	Release 11 only.
Command: **ZOOM**	Release 11 only: zoom All.
Command: **ERASE**	Release 11 only: erase all three viewports.
Command: **TILEMODE**	Release 11 only: set to 1 to return to single tilemode viewport.

> ### Using HIDE to View Hidden Table—continued
>
> | Command | Description |
> |---|---|
> | Command: **VIEW** | Restore 3D view. |
> | Command: **ZOOM** | Zoom Extents. |
> | Command: **GRID** | Set to 4. |
> | Command: **LAYER** | Turn off layer HIDDENTABLE. |
> | Command: **HIDE** | Take a look at a hidden view (see fig. 14.43). |
> | Command: **UCS** | Set UCS to World. |
> | Command: **END** | That's it for creating the table. |

Figure 14.43:
The hidden table.

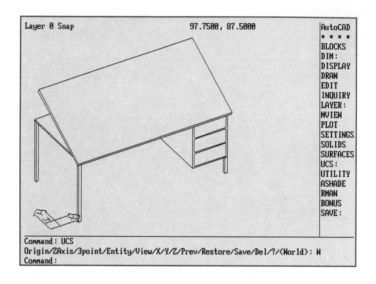

```
Layer 0 Snap                    97.7500, 87.5000        AutoCAD
                                                        * * * *
                                                        BLOCKS
                                                        DIM:
                                                        DISPLAY
                                                        DRAW
                                                        EDIT
                                                        INQUIRY
                                                        LAYER:
                                                        MVIEW
                                                        PLOT
                                                        SETTINGS
                                                        SOLIDS
                                                        SURFACES
                                                        UCS:
                                                        UTILITY
                                                        ASHADE
                                                        RMAN
                                                        BONUS
                                                        SAVE:

Command: UCS
Origin/ZAxis/3point/Entity/View/X/Y/Z/Prev/Restore/Save/Del/?/<World>: W
Command:
```

> **Tip:** When you edit 3D views which have had hidden lines removed, the hidden lines may reappear. If so, just execute HIDE again when you are through editing.

Congratulations! You've created (and edited) a 3D table from start to finish. We hope you have gained a feel for the power and ease built into 3D drafting. Once you get the hang of it, using a UCS is still just like 2D drafting. The only difference is that, like a fly, you can climb all over your drawing.

To document the results of your 3D designs, you will want to create assembly drawings. The next section shows how to assemble a multiview drawing.

Creating 3D Multiview Drawings

Once you have a basic 3D drawing, it is easy to create a multiview drawing. The next two exercises will show you two ways to get a plan, top, right side, and 3D view in the same drawing. The first method is for users with Release 10, or for Release 11 users working in the default drawing environment: a single tilemode viewport. The second method of composing each view in a separate paper space viewport can only be done with Release 11.

Creating 3D Multiview Drawings in Tilemode or Release 10

If you are working with Release 10, model space is the only environment you have. The trick to displaying multiple views is to make a block of the model and use the UCSs you made to orient one copy for each desired view. Blocks get defined relative to the UCS that was current when blocked, and they get inserted relative to the UCS that was current when inserted. It's simplest to block most objects in the WCS. There are two approaches to getting them inserted and oriented. You can insert them in the WCS and rotate them into place by changing the UCS. Or you can set up the UCS first and then insert the block. The first approach is easiest for positioning blocks in the drawing. Let's try it.

Assembling a 3D Multiview Drawing in Model Space

 Begin a NEW drawing named MV-TABLE=IA6MVTBL.

 Begin a NEW drawing named MV-TABLE=TABLE.

Command: **BLOCK**	Block everything to name TABLE1, picking base point at bottom front left corner of front left leg with osnap INT.
Command: **LIMITS**	Reset to 176,136 (22 x 17 at 1=8 scale).
Command: **PLAN**	Set to current UCS or WCS — they're the same.
Command: **ZOOM**	Zoom All.
Command: **INSERT**	Insert TABLE1 four times, at 16,16 for front view, 16,92 for top view, 108,16 for right view and 92,88 for isometric view. Default scale and rotation.

First, re-orient the front view.

Command: **UCS**	Restore UCS R-SIDE.
Command: **ROTATE**	Select the lower left block.
Base point:	Use osnap INS to pick insertion point of block.
<Rotation angle>/Reference: **-90**	

Assembling a 3D Multiview Drawing in Model Space—continued

Next, the right side view.

Command: **UCS**	Restore FRONT.
Command: **ROTATE**	Select the lower right block.
Base point:	Use osnap INS to pick insertion point of block.
<Rotation angle>/Reference: **90**	
Command: **UCS**	Restore the WCS.
Command: **ROTATE**	Rotate again, -90 degrees, osnap INS base point.

Last, the 3D isometric view.

Command: **ROTATE**	Rotate upper right block -45 degrees about insertion point.
Command: **UCS**	Restore UCS R-SIDE.
Command: **ROTATE**	Rotate upper right block -55 degrees about insertion point.
Command: **UCS**	Restore the WCS.
Command: **END**	

All you have done is inserted the same block for each view, then rotated the block to view it from a particular direction. The TOP view was already inserted in plan view, so you didn't adjust it. The ROTATE command only rotates in the X,Y plane about the Z axis, so you set a UCS perpendicular to the orientation you are trying to achieve. To visualize this, take a small cardboard box and mark the UCSs on it. Then take a smaller box, book, or block of wood and mark the views. Then try rotating the view block in the UCS box.

Release 11 offers the paper space alternative.

Assembling a 3D Multiview Drawing in Paper Space

By far the best way to compose a multiview drawing from a 3D model is to use paper space. Not only does paper space give you a means of quickly and easily generating and plotting different views of your model, but it does it without duplicating data. All views are views of the same entities. This is an advantage in editing, whereas the previous method requires *inserting, editing, and redefining blocks.

Setting up a multiview drawing is easy. All you have to do is enter paper space, insert your title block (if you have one), and open up as many viewports as you need to contain the different views of your model. Then you orient the views by simply setting the desired UCS in each and using PLAN. Let's do it.

Assembling a Multiview Drawing in Paper Space

 Begin a NEW drawing named PV-TABLE=IA6MVTBL.

 Begin a NEW drawing named PV-TABLE=TABLE.

Command: **TILEMODE**   Set TILEMODE to 0 to enter
                                         paper space.

Command: **LIMITS**   Reset paper space limits 0,0 to
                                         22,17.

Zoom All and set grid to 2.

Command: **MVIEW**   Open four viewports.
ON/OFF/Hideplot/Fit/2/3/4/Restore/<First Point>: **4**
Fit/<First Point>: **1,2**
Second point: **20,15**
Command: **ZOOM**   Zoom to fill screen with
                                         viewports (see fig. 14.44).

Command: **MSPACE**

Select the upper left viewport.

Command: **PLAN**   Set the view plan to the WCS.
Command: **ZOOM**   Zoom .125XP (1=8 scale).

Select the lower left viewport.

Command: **UCS**   Restore UCS FRONT.
Command: **PLAN**   Set the view plan to the current
                                         UCS.
Command: **ZOOM**   Zoom .125XP (1=8 scale).

Select the lower right viewport. Restore UCS R-SIDE and use PLAN to set the view to the
current UCS. Zoom .125XP (1=8 scale).

Select the upper right viewport. It already has the 3D view.

Command: **ZOOM**   Zoom .6 (not .6XP).

Command: **PSPACE**
Command: **LAYER**   Or use DDLMODES to set layer
                                         TABLE current and freeze layer
                                         0. The viewport borders
                                         disappear (see fig. 14.45).

Command: **END**

That's all there is to it! You now have four different views of your table, and you
didn't have to copy or insert anything to do it. To get it ready for plotting, see
Chapter 10.

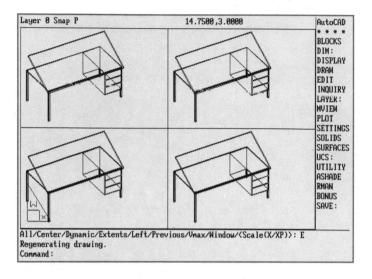

Figure 14.44:
Paper space
viewports before
reorienting views.

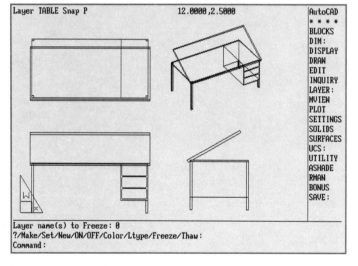

Figure 14.45:
The completed
multiview table in
paper space.

Summing Up

Good layer and color management can greatly ease and speed 3D work. Colors help clarify a mass of overlaid wireframe images. Layers allow you to turn objects off to help with picking points in heavy traffic, and to freeze unneeded layers to speed up regenerations and hidden line removal. Paper space gives you individual layer visibility control in each viewport.

Use multiple viewports when drawing in 3D. It is sometimes hard to select objects and pick points in a single viewport, particularly when osnapping to an existing object. Remember that you can use XYZ point filters, and even switch viewports midstream. For example, you can select your objects in one or more viewports, pick your XY point in another viewport, and then switch to a third viewport to osnap the Z value.

A standard set of named UCSs, views (viewpoints), and viewports makes jumping around in 3D a breeze. Don't forget, each viewport can have its own set of snap and grid settings. Save your settings in a 3D prototype drawing. Use the UCS Entity option for quick edits to existing entities, or to add new entities parallel to existing ones. The X,Y orientation may look unusual, but it seldom matters.

For 2D entities that are constrained to be parallel to the current UCS, you need not change the UCS just to place them above or below the current UCS. A Z value entered for their first coordinate point will establish their position in 3D space. Don't confuse things by setting elevation or using the ELEV command.

Remember that you can use editing commands in 3D. For example, COPY and MOVE can place any entity up and down in the current Z axis.

3D Entities

There is more 3D to come. The next chapter shows you how to work with 3D entities. Now that you have a drafting table, you need a chair — a 3D chair.

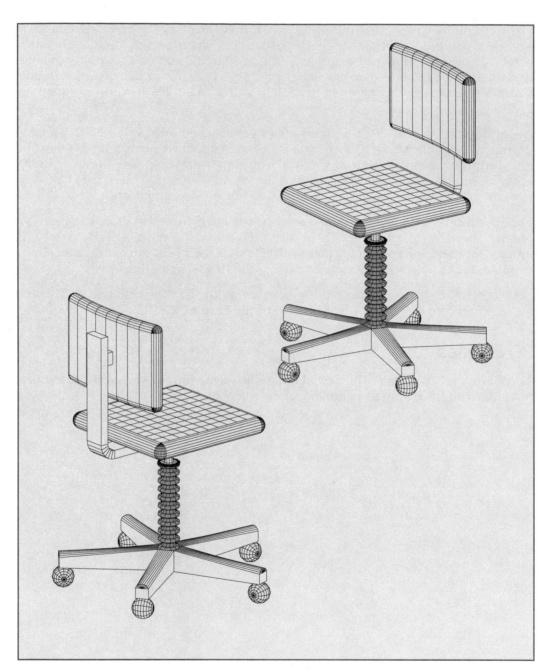

Figure 15.1:
The 3D chair.

15

Using 3D Entities

3D Graphic Entities

In the last chapter, you used 2D entities and extrusions to build a table in 3D space. In this chapter, you will learn how to draw and edit objects using true 3D entities and surface meshes. You can use these 3D entities to construct complex shapes by creating meshes on flat and curved surfaces. You can combine these into complex assemblies by making and inserting blocks of 3D entities to build a drawing.

Since you have a table, you need a comfortable chair to sit in while you watch AutoCAD do all this 3D work. (Okay, maybe it's not that comfortable, but we don't want to make it too complicated.) The chair, shown in figure 15.1, uses all of AutoCAD's 3D entities.

3D Entities and Meshes

There are only four true 3D entities in AutoCAD: points, lines, 3Dfaces, and a family of special polylines. The simplest of the polylines is the 3D polyline: a polyline without width or curvature whose vertexes can be at any X, Y, or Z coordinate in space. The 3Dface entity is much like a 2D solid entity except that each of its three or four corners can be at any X, Y, and Z coordinate in space, while a solid is planar. The sides of the chair's legs are constructed of 3Dfaces. Although you can create multiple 3Dfaces in a single 3DFACE command, they exist as individual entities. More efficient and versatile are the polyline mesh entities.

Most of the 3D commands you will work with in this chapter construct faceted surface meshes. The chair's seat, back, and pedestal have multiple faces. While you could build these surfaces using individual 3Dfaces, AutoCAD's 3D mesh commands automatically generate surface meshes that can approximate any possible surface in 3D space. They can be either planar, like the square center of the seat, or curved like the pedestal, back, edges, corners, and casters.

There are two types of polyline meshes: polygon meshes and polyface meshes. Polyface meshes are extremely versatile, and can be arbitrarily irregular. They are created by the PFACE command, and can have any number of edges and vertexes and any number of visible or invisible interior divisions. Polygon meshes are created by several commands. They can be warped and distorted, but they must have four *sides* (any line or curve). Opposite sides must have the same number of subdivisions, although a *side* can converge to a single point.

3D Drawing Tools

AutoCAD provides a number of commands and AutoLISP routines for constructing polyline meshes. You'll find the 3D drawing commands, 3DFACE, 3DPOLY, PFACE, 3DMESH, EDGESURF, REVSURF, RULESURF, and TABSURF, on the [SURFACES] screen menu or with [3D Surfs] on the [DRAW] menu. The [3d] and [objects] selections call a menu of AutoLISP routines that automatically create geometric objects like spheres, cones, and tori from the surface meshes. These are also found on the [3D Objects] icon menu with the [Objects...] selection on the [Draw] pull-down menu. The [Draw] pull-down menu also includes [3D Poly] and [Surfaces...] choices, which bring up an icon menu of surfacing commands (see figs. 15.2 and 15.3).

Figure 15.2:
The [3D objects] icon menu.

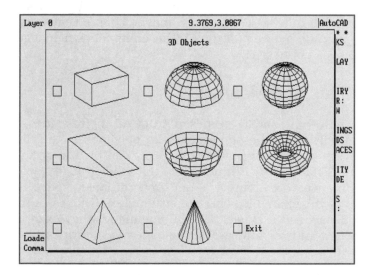

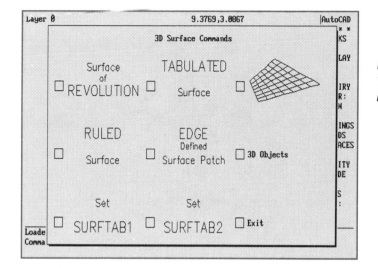

Mesh Generation Concepts

Think of a mesh as a skin that you can wrap around a surface. The PFACE and 3DMESH commands can create irregularly shaped surfaces, but most surfaces have some form of symmetry or regularity about or within which a mesh can be generated. The RULESURF command generates a surface defined by ruling lines between two edges, which are defined by lines or curves. The EDGESURF command generates a mesh that fills the area bounded by four lines or curves.

Generating a mesh often involves specifying the profile of the mesh and line it is to be rotated about or translated (moved) along. The REVSURF command makes a circular mesh when you specify a *path profile* and an axis of rotation. The path profile is a cross section of the surface that you want. If you rotate the profile 360 degrees, you get a cylindrical or globular surface, like the chair's pedestal or casters.

You can also generate a mesh with TABSURF, translating a *direction vector* along a path profile. The results of TABSURF look like the results of extruding a 2D entity into 3D, except that TABSURF can create oblique or skewed surfaces. Figure 15.4 shows how these 3DMESH commands are used to create our chair.

You can control the fineness of meshes with system variable settings. That's all there is to meshes: defining edges, path profiles, direction vectors or rotation axes, and a few system variable settings.

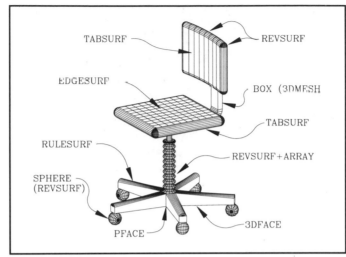

How to Use the Chair Exercises

We'll take you through each 3D drawing command as we build the parts of the chair. Along the way, you'll get some practice and tips on using UCSs to draw and edit entities in 3D space. We'll also show you how to edit some of the chair's meshes with PEDIT. As you create the parts, you'll make them into 3D blocks. Then you'll assemble the chair by inserting the casters on the legs, the legs on the pedestal, the pedestal on the seat, and so on. Using 3D blocks is simply applying the standard BLOCK and INSERT commands.

Since the chair is built in parts, you can do it all, or pick and choose the commands that you want to learn by working on particular components. If you are using the IA DISK, you have the component blocks. You can still assemble the chair even if you choose not to draw all the parts. We'll set up the drawing to use the upper right viewport as a scratch viewport and a SCRATCH layer where you can practice any of the 3D commands. When done, restore the previously current layer and freeze SCRATCH.

Setup for Using 3D Entities

The CHAIR drawing uses two layers, CHAIR and BUILD, with default drawing units and limits large enough to contain the chair at full scale. The chair is 35 inches high and about 25 inches wide at the base, with varied entity colors to help your viewing in 3D.

If you are using the IA DISK, you have the drawing setup in the IA6CHAIR.DWG file. Load it and skip the rest of the setup below. Otherwise, create a new CHAIR drawing, make the settings as shown in table 15.1 and set up your viewports. The initial setup uses three viewports: a full-height viewport on the left where you will spend most of your time building the chair; a lower right viewport with a plan view of the chair; and an upper right viewport to use as a scratch viewport.

Table 15.1
3D Chair Drawing Settings

COORDS	FILL	GRID	SNAP	UCSICON
ON	OFF	Off	.25	OR

UNITS	Use defaults for all settings.
LIMITS	0,0 to 68,44

Layer Name	State	Color	Linetype
0	On	7 (white)	CONTINUOUS
BUILD	On	1 (red)	CONTINUOUS
CHAIR	On/Current	7 (white)	CONTINUOUS
SCRATCH	On	4 (cyan)	CONTINUOUS

Setting Up for 3D Entities

Begin a NEW drawing named CHAIR=IA6CHAIR.

 Begin a NEW drawing named CHAIR and make the settings shown in table 15.1.

```
Command: VPOINT                              Set to -1,-1,0.5.
Command: VPORTS                              (Release 10 only, create three
                                             viewports.)

Save/Restore/Delete/Join/SIngle/?/2/<3>/4: 3
Horizontal/Vertical/Above/Below/Left/<Right>: L
Command: VPORTS                              (Release 10 only, save viewport
                                             configuration as BUILD.)

Command: TILEMODE                            Release 11 only: set TILEMODE
                                             to 0 to enter paper space.
Command: MVIEW                               Release 11 only: create three
                                             viewports.

ON/OFF/Hideplot/Fit/2/3/4/Restore/<First Point>: 3
Horizontal/Vertical/Above/Below/Left/<Right>: L
```

Setting Up for 3D Entities—continued

`Fit/<First Point>:` **F**	Fit three viewports to the screen.
`Command:` **MSPACE**	Release 11 only.
Select upper viewport to make it active.	
`Command:` **ZOOM**	Zoom Center at 0,0 and a height of 10.
`Command:` **UCSICON**	Turn icon off.
`Command:` **VIEW**	Save view as CHAIR.
Make left viewport current.	
`Command:` **UCS**	Set origin to 0,88,0 and save as HUB.
`Command:` **ZOOM**	Zoom Center at 0,0 and a height of 20.
`Command:` **VIEW**	Save view as BUILD.
Make lower right viewport current.	
`Command:` **PLAN**	Go to plan view of current UCS.
`Command:` **ZOOM**	Zoom Center at 0,0 and a height of 5.
`Command:` **SAVE**	

Your screen should look like figure 15.5, with layer CHAIR current and the UCS icon in the center of the left and lower right viewports. The lower right viewport should be current.

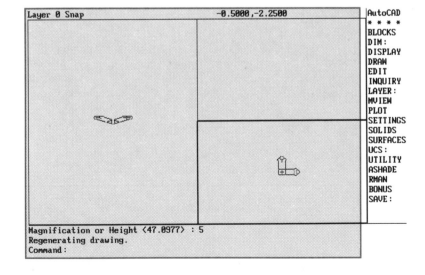

Figure 15.5:
Viewports for the
chair.

Creating 3D entities requires preparation. Drawings can become complex and difficult to visualize. Your ability to visualize and select entities easily will depend on your display resolution. These exercises will specify the required zoom, snap, ortho, and osnap settings, but you should also use these freely as needed in the exercises. Use the illustrations as guides to the use of zoom.

Using the [3D Objects] Icon Menu

We could extrude a 2D polyline to create the chair's hub, but we'd rather find a way to create it as a true 3D surface. The hub is a pentagon. Let's see if we can use one of the AutoLISP 3D mesh drawing commands from the [3D Objects] icon menu to draw it. If your display doesn't have icon menu capability, you can load the following AutoLISP commands by entering (load "3D") at the command prompt. Then you can use them like normal AutoCAD commands. They are: CONE, WEDGE, TORUS, SPHERE, PYRAMID, MESH, DOME, DISH, and BOX. This 3D AutoLISP file also defines a command named 3D that you can use to access any of these commands. It issues the prompt:

```
Box/Cone/DIsh/DOme/Mesh/Pyramid/Sphere/Torus/Wedge:
```

so you can select the surface shape you want. These are documented in your *AutoLISP Programmer's Reference*, but they're so easy to use you shouldn't need to look them up.

There isn't a pentagon among these commands, but that won't deter us. With a little creativity, we can make CONE work for us.

Using a Cone to Construct the Chair's Hub

The AutoLISP CONE command is versatile. It lets you specify a top as well as bottom diameter if you want to truncate your cone. If the diameters are equal, you get a cylinder. You can also specify the resolution (number of segments) that it uses to represent the cone or cylinder. Five segments will generate a pentagon.

Let's use CONE to create the hub of the chair.

Drawing a Five-Sided "Cone"	
Command: **COLOR**	Set color to yellow.
Command: **(load "3D")**	Type, or select [3D Objects...] from the [Draw] pull-down menu.
Command: **CONE**	Type it if you loaded 3D manually, otherwise select the cone icon to load the 3D commands and execute CONE.

> **Drawing a Five-Sided "Cone"—continued**
>
> Base center point: **0,0,-2.5**   We want it below the UCS.
> Diameter/<radius> of base: **1.55**
> Diameter/<radius> of top <0>: **1.55**
> Height: **2.5**
> Number of segments <16>: **5**

You should have a plan view of the hub polygon in your right viewport, and a 3D view of it in your left viewport (see fig. 15.6).

Figure 15.6:
The hub of the chair.

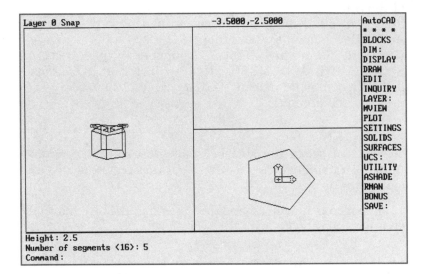

Next, we are going to create the chair's leg with 3DFACE entities.

Using the 3DFACE Command

3Dfaces are defined by three or four edges (they always have four corner points, but the third and fourth may coincide). A solid is confined to a single plane (in any UCS), but the edges and points of a 3Dface can be anywhere in space. The 3DFACE command prompts are similar to those for a 2D solid, but the pick point order is more natural. You can pick clockwise or counterclockwise instead of in a criss-cross bow tie. An unextruded 2D solid and a 3Dface may look the same if they both lie in the same plane, but they will have different edge and transparency properties. If all points and edges of a 3Dface lie in a single plane, HIDE treats it as opaque. But, if it is not planar, it is transparent and won't hide. Unlike a solid, you can't extrude a 3Dface, and it always has zero thickness.

Use 3Dfaces when you want to draw simple three- or four-point planar faces. For the chair leg, we want an end cap, an underside, and two simple planar sides.

Using 3Dfaces to Create Chair Leg

Create a four-sided 3Dface as the leg's end cap, working in the left viewport. It's easiest to create it at the origin, then move it where you want it. After you create and move the end cap, use 3DFACE again to create the bottom and the two sides, osnapping to endpoints on the cap and hub. We'll leave the top open for now.

Using 3DFACE to Make First Leg	
Make left viewport current.	
Command: **3DFACE**	Create end cap of leg at the UCS origin (see fig. 15.7).
First point: **0,0**	
Second point: **0,0,1.25**	
Third point: **0,1.5,1.25**	
Fourth point: **0,1.5,0**	
Third point: **\<RETURN\>**	
Command: **MOVE**	Move the 3Dface with a displacement of -12.5, -.75,-2.
Command: **PAN**	Pan to view shown to see end cap (see fig. 15.8).
Command: **OSNAP**	Set running osnap mode ENDP to draw the leg faces.
Command: **3DFACE**	Draw leg's left face first, then remaining faces in clockwise order. Select points ① through ⑧ in sequence, then \<RETURN\> to exit (see fig. 15.9).
Command: **OSNAP**	Set osnap back to NONe.
Command: **HIDE**	Try a quick HIDE to confirm what you've drawn (see fig. 15.10).
Command: **SAVE**	Save the drawing.

3Dfaces With Invisible Edges

By using multiple adjoining 3Dfaces with invisible edges, you can create what appears to be a single surface. The SPLFRAME system variable controls whether the invisible edges display or not. (This is the same variable that you use to control the frame points for a curve fit polyline in 2D.) When SPLFRAME is 0, invisible edges are invisible; when SPLFRAME is 1, all edges are visible. To draw 3Dfaces with invisible edges, you precede the first pick of each edge you want invisible with an I and a \<RETURN\>.

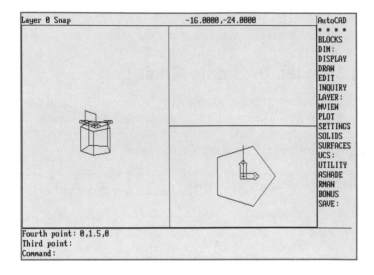

Figure 15.7:
The end cap of the
leg at UCS origin.

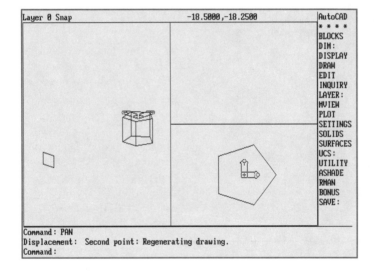

Figure 15.8:
The end cap of the
leg moved into place.

We can use invisible edges to make the top of the chair hub look like one piece. Use 3DFACE to create a triangular surface that we can later array with the leg to complete the chair base. Use SPLFRAME to make invisible edges visible to confirm the results.

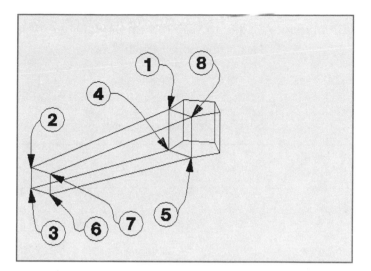

Figure 15.9:
Detail of pick points.

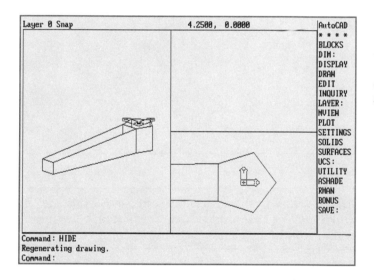

Figure 15.10:
The chair leg constructed with 3Dfaces.

Using 3DFACE With Invisible Edges to Cap the Chair Hub

Make lower right viewport current.

Command: **3DFACE**	Remember to precede all picks with I<RETURN>.
First point: **I**	Pick first corner of polygon at ① with osnap ENDP (see fig. 15.11).
Second point: **I**	Pick second corner of polygon at ② with osnap ENDP.

Using 3DFACE With Invisible Edges to Cap the Chair Hub—continued

Third point: **I**	Pick center of polygon at ③ or type 0,0.
Fourth point: **<RETURN>**	Make it three-sided.
Third point: **<RETURN>**	It's there, but invisible!
Command: **SPLFRAME**	Set to 1, on. (Release 10, use SETVAR SPLFRAME.)
Command: **REGEN**	Now you see it.
Command: **SAVE**	Save the drawing.

Figure 15.11:
Detail of edges and pick points.

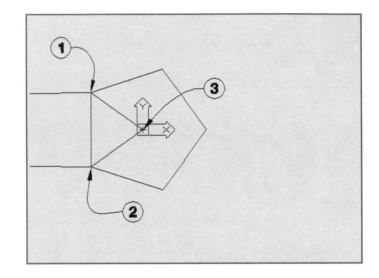

Tip: If you create a 3Dface with all edges invisible and SPLFRAME off, AutoCAD won't select it, even with Window or Last, and you may even forget it's there. It's best to leave SPLFRAME on until you hide or end.

Tip: The AutoCAD Sample disk includes the EDGE.LSP AutoLISP program, which is probably installed in your ACAD\SAMPLE directory. It edits the visibility of existing 3Dface edges. Enter (load "\\ACAD\\SAMPLE\\EDGE") to load it and EDGE to use it as a command.

So far, you have used simple, flat 3D entities. The rest of the chair construction involves curves and contours. Let's look at the mesh tools for such 3D surface constructions. Then, we'll come back to the chair leg and put a *ruled* surface on top of it.

3D Polyline Meshes

There are only two 3D mesh entities, both polyline variants: polyface meshes, created by the PFACE command, and polygon meshes, for which there are five drawing commands. All of the mesh commands except PFACE create meshes of *n* rows by *m* columns. The basic polygon mesh command is 3DMESH. While 3DMESH generates a mesh directly, point by point, the other four commands rely on existing entities to establish the edges, directions, paths, and profiles of the resulting surface. Here is a listing of the commands.

3DMESH   Is a wireframe rectilinear *blanket* composed of *m* column lines by *n* row lines passing through a matrix of *m* x *n* 3D points in space. You have complete control over *m*, *n*, and the coordinate location of each of the 3D points.

RULESURF   Creates a ruled surface. It's like stretching and bending a ladder in 3D space. You select any two lines, polylines, or curves that make up the rails, and AutoCAD fills in the ladder with straight rungs. If you select a point, the rungs will converge to that point.

TABSURF   Is short for tabulated surface. AutoCAD sweeps or translates a line you select (called a direction vector or generatrix) along any curve you select (called the directrix) to define the surface. For example, if you translate a straight line along a circle, you create a cylinder.

REVSURF   Creates a surface of revolution. AutoCAD sweeps any curve you select about an axis of revolution. For example, if you sweep a 90-degree arc about a line through one of its endpoints, you create a bowl shape.

EDGESURF   Is the *flying carpet* of 3D entities. You select four boundary lines or curves, and AutoCAD fills in *m* x *n* column and row lines to define the surface.

PFACE   Constructs a mesh of any topology you desire. You specify arbitrary locations of vertexes and then specify which vertexes are part of which face. You can have any number of edges, and any number of faces, each with any number of sides or vertexes. Any side can be any color, on any layer, or be invisible.

Figure 15.12 shows examples of these entities.

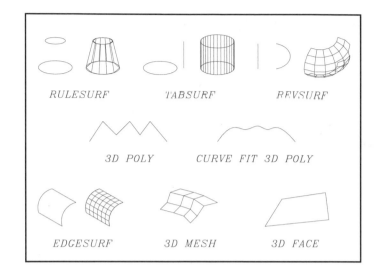

Figure 15.12:
Mesh entity
primitives.

The 3DMESH Command

You will rarely use the 3DMESH command unless you are using AutoLISP to automatically generate mesh points. 3DMESH is made up of rows and columns, where m and n are indices specifying the number of rows and columns that make up the mesh, up to 256 x 256. These indices determine the number of vertexes required in the mesh. Once you set m and n, you input each vertex as X,Y,Z coordinates. Meshes can be open or closed depending on whether the mesh joins in either the m or n direction, or both.

Figure 15.13 shows an example of a 3D mesh, showing the m and n directions. This is an open mesh. A donut mesh would be an example of a mesh closed in both directions. An example of a mesh closed in m and open in n would be a tube, while an auto tire (without a rim) is open in m and closed in n. Later, when we edit a mesh, we'll identify the vertexes to see how the mesh vertex information is displayed.

3DMESH is difficult to use because the points must be entered in rigid row-by-row, column-by-column order. PFACE is more flexible.

The PFACE Command

Like the 3DFACE command, PFACE can create surfaces with invisible interior divisions. Unlike the other meshes, you can specify any number of vertexes, and create any number of faces using PFACE. First, you pick all of your vertex points, remembering the numbers of their order, then you create your faces by entering the vertex numbers that define their edges. To make an edge invisible, you respond to the first

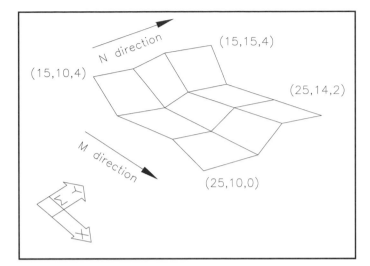

Figure 15.13:
A 3D mesh example.

vertex prompt of that edge with a negative instead of a positive vertex number. Like 3Dfaces, invisible polyfaces are visible when SPLFRAME is set to 1 and invisible when it is 0. You can also assign a color or layer by responding to any `Face n, vertex n:` prompt with C for color or L for layer. Then it will reprompt for the vertex number. If you do so, the current face and all subsequent faces will get that color or layer until you specify otherwise.

Although PFACE is capable of making more complex surfaces, we could have used it in place of 3DFACE to cap the hub. Let's use it to put a bottom on the hub, for comparison. Use osnap ENDP to pick all but the center vertex point. SPLFRAME is set to 1 so all edges will be visible until we set it to 0 and regenerate. (Release 10 doesn't include PFACE, so skip this exercise.)

Putting a Bottom Surface on the Hub With PFACE

Make left viewport current, zoom in on the hub, and set running osnap to ENDP.

```
Command: PFACE
Vertex 1: 0,0,-2.5             The center vertex (see fig. 15.14).
Vertex 2:                      Pick ②.
Vertex 3:                      Pick ③.
Vertex 4:                      Pick ④.
Vertex 5:                      Pick ⑤.
Vertex 6:                      Pick ⑥.
Vertex 7: <RETURN>
Face 1, vertex 1: -1           Negative makes following edge invisible.
Face 1, vertex 2: 2            Positive makes outside edge visible.
Face 1, vertex 3: -3           Negative makes following edge invisible.
```

Putting a Bottom Surface on the Hub With PFACE—continued

Face 1, vertex 4: **<RETURN>**	No more edges for face 1.
Face 2, vertex 1: **-1**	
Face ?, vertex 2: **3**	
Face 2, vertex 3: **-4**	
Face 2, vertex 4: **<RETURN>**	
Face 3, vertex 1: **-1**	Specify -1, 4, and -5 for vertexes 1, 2, and 3, then <RETURN>.
Face 4, vertex 1: **-1**	Specify -1, 5, and -6 for vertexes 1, 2, and 3, then <RETURN>.
Face 5, vertex 1: **-1**	Specify -1, 6, and -2 for vertexes 1, 2, and 3.
Face 5, vertex 4: **<RETURN>**	No more edges for face 5.
Face 6, vertex 1: **<RETURN>**	No more faces (see fig. 15.15).

Set SPLFRAME to 0, and regenerate to see the edges become invisible.

Set osnap back to NONe, set SPLFRAME back to 1, and zoom Previous.

Command: **SAVE**

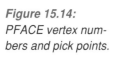

Figure 15.14:
PFACE vertex num-
bers and pick points.

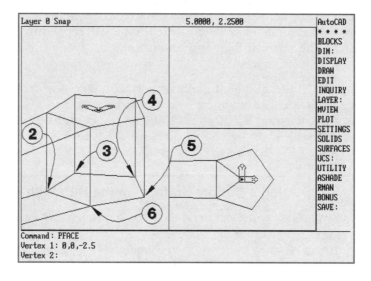

In most of your constructions, you generally will not know all of the surface points. Instead, you will find yourself using the four SURF commands to generate your 3D surfaces based on boundaries, curves, and direction vectors.

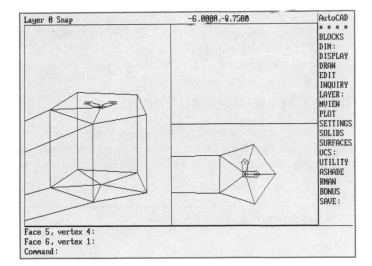

Figure 15.15:
A completed PFACE
bottom of a hub.

Tip: The IA DISK includes an AutoLISP command named PFACE2. You load it with (load "pface2") and use it in place of the PFACE command. It displays numbered markers at the vertexes during the command to make it easier to keep track of them. The AutoCAD Sample disk includes the MFACE.LSP AutoLISP program, which is probably installed in your ACAD\SAMPLE directory. It lets you enter only the perimeter vertexes and generates a polyface with invisible interior edges. Enter (load "\\ACAD\\SAMPLE\\MFACE") to load it and MFACE to use it as a command.

System Variables Used in Mesh Construction

Although you probably will not often use the 3DMESH command, you still need to set the system variables that control the m and n indices to control mesh density in the other commands. The SURFTAB1 system variable sets the m index, and SURFTAB2 sets the n index. While you can use values up to 256 for either, we recommend using the lowest values that generate acceptably smooth surfaces. Values of 8 to 16 are suitable for most purposes. Dense meshes will significantly increase your drawing processing time. If you don't like the mesh you get, you can't respecify these variables for an *existing* mesh. You have to erase the mesh, reset your SURFTAB values, and create a *new* mesh.

The RULESURF Command

RULESURF creates a ruled surface between two boundaries of nearly any type. RULESURF creates a 2 x m polygon mesh between the two boundaries; that is, it defines a one-way mesh of straight ruled lines between them. The entities that define the boundaries can be points, lines, arcs, circles, 2D polylines, or 3D polylines. (If you use a point, only one edge can be a point.) You only need to set the SURFTAB1 system variable, which controls the spacing of the rules.

Using RULESURF to Create the Leg Top

We'll use RULESURF to finish the leg's top surface and add a little arched cap to the end. The top surface will run as a ruled surface from an arc drawn above the end cap to the top edge of the hub top. To create the arc, use the UCS Entity option to set the UCS in the plane of the end cap.

Preparing for RULESURFs

Make the left viewport current.

Command: **LAYER**	Set layer to BUILD.
Command: **COLOR**	Set color to BYLAYER.
Command: **UCS**	Use Entity option and pick end cap at ① to avoid selecting the 3Dface sides (see fig. 15.16).
Command: **PDMODE**	Set to 66 to make points visible. (Release 10, use SETVAR PDMODE.)
Command: **POINT**	Use osnap MID to draw a point at ①.
Command: **LINE**	Use osnap ENDP to draw line from ② to ③.
Command: **ARC**	Use osnap ENDP to draw start, end, angle (135 degrees) arc from ④ to ⑤.
Command: **UCS**	Restore UCS to HUB.

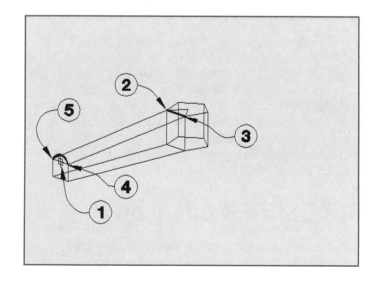

Figure 15.16:
Detail of curves.

Once you've defined the curves for RULESURF, you can begin the surfacing. The arc defines a curve for the top of the leg *and* the space at the end cap. Once you draw the top mesh surface, it will be impossible to pick the arc for the arched end cap surface, because the top surface will get in the way. To use the arc for both surfaces, we'll temporarily erase the top mesh. After making the arched mesh, we'll use OOPS to bring the top mesh back.

Using RULESURF to Complete the Leg

Command: **LAYER**	Set layer CHAIR current.
Command: **COLOR**	Set color to yellow.
Command: **SURFTAB1**	Set to 8. (Release 10, use SETVAR SURFTAB1.)
Command: **RULESURF**	
Select first defining curve:	Select line at ① (see fig. 15.17).
Select second defining curve:	Select arc at ② and the surface is drawn.
Command: **ERASE**	Temporarily erase the top surface.
Command: **RULESURF**	
Select first defining curve:	Select the point at ③ with osnap NODe.
Select second defining curve:	Select arc at ②.
Command: **OOPS**	Restores the erased top surface.
Command: **SAVE**	Save the drawing.

Figure 15.18 shows the completed leg surfaces.

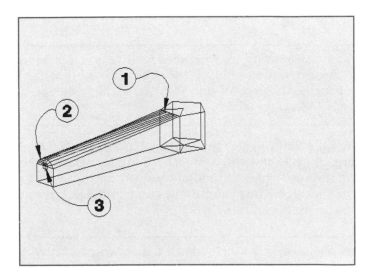

Figure 15.17:
Detail of RULESURF.

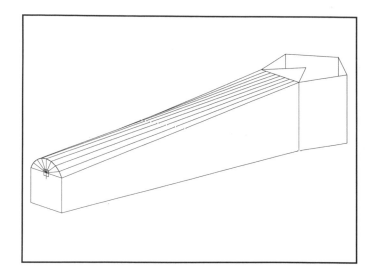

Figure 15.18:
*The completed leg
surfaces.*

When you work with RULESURF, your pick points can be important. If your edge curves are open, the rule is built from the endpoint nearest your pick point on each entity. The ruled surface can twist if you don't pick the nearest endpoints on the edge entities. You can also get a twist with closed entities. The generated mesh starts from the 0-degree point of circles and from the starting vector of closed polylines. If you are generating a mesh between two circles or a circle and closed polyline, make sure that your zero points and first points are aligned to avoid a twist in the mesh.

Tip: You may often want to use RULESURF between a circle and a polyline ellipse. It is almost impossible to align the zero point on the circle with the starting vector of the ellipse. The easiest method for controlling RULESURF alignment is to create both entities with the ELLIPSE command.

The mesh commands require that you pick the entities that will be used to create the ruled surface. When creating meshes with a common boundary entity, you need to get the first mesh out of the way to pick the boundary entity for the second mesh, or it's almost impossible to pick it. Putting your profiles on a different layer also helps you control the selection of profile entities.

Tip: Besides temporary erasures, other methods for temporarily removing an entity are blocking it to a temporary name and doing an *insert later, or moving it to another location and back again later.

Completing and Blocking the Base Assembly

To complete the base, we need a caster, then we'll duplicate the leg and caster to make the other four legs. The caster is a case where you can take advantage of one of the AutoLISP 3D mesh drawing commands from the [3D Objects] icon menu. The sphere that we will use to make the caster for the chair is generated by an AutoLISP routine that uses the REVSURF command to revolve an arc about an axis line.

Using a 3D Sphere to Construct the Chair's Casters

You can select either [3d] or [objects] from the [SURFACES] screen menu, then select [Sphere]; or select [Objects...] from the [Draw] pull-down menu and select the sphere icon; or enter (load "3D") and then SPHERE as a command. You will be prompted for the sphere's center point and radius. The routine will automatically clean up after it is done, erasing the arc and axis line.

Using the AutoLISP SPHERE Command to Make a Caster

Command: **UCS**	Rotate the X axis 90 degrees.
Command: **COLOR**	Set color to red.
Select **[Sphere]**	Select from screen or icon menu, or enter (load "3D") and SPHERE.
Please wait... Loading 3D Objects. nil	
Command: Sphere	The SPHERE command is started.
Center of sphere: **0,0**	
Diameter/<radius>: **1.25**	
Number of longitudinal segments <16>: **12**	
Number of latitudinal segments <16>: **12**	The sphere draws (see fig. 5.19). Zoom in for a closer look, if you like.
Command: **UCS**	Set to previous UCS.
Command: **MOVE**	Move the caster with displacement -12,0,-3.25 (see fig. 15.20).
Command: **REDRAWALL**	

Now, one leg is complete.

Arraying the Legs for the Chair Base

We can array this leg and caster to complete the chair's base, then block the base as a finished component. Use the standard ARRAY command to array the leg and BLOCK to create the BASE block.

Figure 15.19:
The chair caster
before move and
UCS previous.

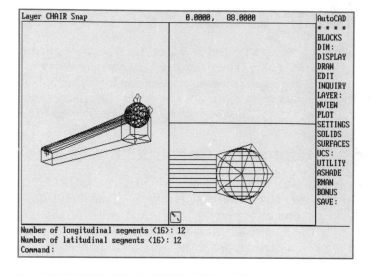

Figure 15.20:
The chair caster after
move.

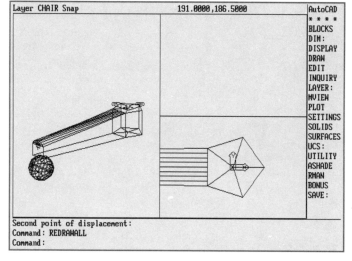

Arraying the Legs to Complete the Base

Make the lower right viewport current.

Command: **ZOOM**	Zoom Center at 0,0, with a height of 28.
Command: **LAYER**	Turn layer BUILD off.
Command: **ARRAY**	Polar array all but hub and bottom cap, about center point 0,0 — 5 items to fill 360 degrees and rotate as copied (see fig. 15.21).

Arraying the Legs to Complete the Base—continued

Try a HIDE, if you have a few minutes.

Command: **BLOCK**   Block everything to name BASE with insert base point 0,0.

Command: **SAVE**   Save and continue, or end and take a break.

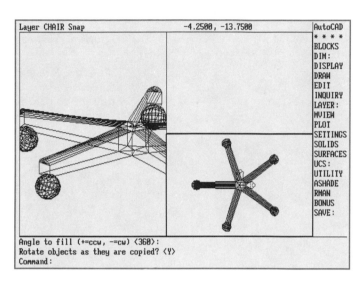

Figure 15.21:
The completed base
after array.

The BASE block is stored in your current CHAIR drawing. If you are using the IA DISK, you will also have the base stored on disk as BASE.DWG. Next, we'll build the pedestal with REVSURF.

The REVSURF Command

You saw REVSURF in action, generating the sphere. REVSURF creates a surface by revolving a path curve around an axis of revolution. You can select a line, arc, circle, or 2D or 3D polyline as the path curve. You can select a line or open polyline to specify the axis of rotation. Then, you enter the angle that you want the surface rotated, 360 degrees for a full cylinder or sphere. You can offset the start angle if you don't want to start from a 0-degree angle.

Using REVSURF to Construct the Pedestal

We'll use REVSURF to create a more complex surface — the chair's pedestal cover, which is accordion-shaped to cover the shaft as it goes up and down. The pedestal mesh is made up of two different revolved shapes. Create a single pleat at the bottom and the top closure as two polyline profiles, then revolve them into 3D surfaces with REVSURF. You'll array the bottom piece vertically to complete the pedestal.

In this exercise, we'll set up a UCS and create a vertical axis line of revolution and a polyline path profile for the bottom pleat. We'll use PEDIT to add tangent and curve fitting to the bottom profile so it will smoothly meet adjoining sections.

Preparing Axis and Bottom Path Curve for REVSURF

Make left viewport current, set color to BYLAYER, set layer BUILD current, and erase the leftover arc, line, and point.

Command: **UCS**	Rotate the X axis 90 degrees.
Command: **LINE**	From 0,0 to 0,13 for axis of revolution.
Command: **PLAN**	Set the plan view to current UCS.
Command: **ZOOM**	Zoom in on bottom half of the line.
Command: **PLINE**	Draw from 1.25,0 to .75,.5 to 1.25,1.

```
Command: PEDIT
Select polyline: L
Close/Join/Width/Edit vertex/Fit curve/ Spline curve/
   Decurve/Undo/eXit <X>: E
Next/Previous/Break/Insert/Move/Regen/Straighten/
   Tangent/Width/eXit <N>: T
Direction of tangent: 90
Next/Previous/Break/Insert/Move/Regen/Straighten/
   Tangent/Width/eXit <N>: <RETURN>
Next/Previous/Break/Insert/Move/Regen/Straighten/
   Tangent/Width/eXit <N>: <RETURN>
Next/Previous/Break/Insert/Move/Regen/Straighten/
   Tangent/Width/eXit <N>: T
Direction of tangent: 90
Next/Previous/Break/Insert/Move/Regen/Straighten/
   Tangent/Width/eXit <N>: X
Close/Join/Width/Edit vertex/Fit curve/Spline curve/
   Decurve/Undo/eXit <X>: F
Close/Join/Width/Edit vertex/Fit curve/Spline curve/
   Decurve/Undo/eXit <X>: <RETURN>
```

The results appear in figure 15.22.

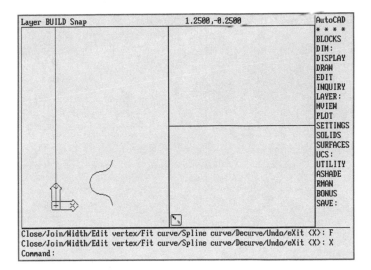

Figure 15.22:
The bottom path
curve and axis for
REVSURF.

The top of the pedestal will terminate with a shaft. Draw the second path curve to establish the top shaft profile and a closure where it meets the arrayed bottom piece. This shaft profile combines polyline arc and line segments.

Creating Top Path Curve for the Shaft Top

```
Command: ZOOM                                    Zoom Dynamic to top half of line.
Command: PLINE
From point: .5,13
Current line-width is 0.0000
Arc/Close/Halfwidth/Length/Undo/Width/<Endpoint of line>: @0,-2.75
Arc/Close/Halfwidth/Length/Undo/Width/<Endpoint of line>: @.5,0
Arc/Close/Halfwidth/Length/Undo/Width/<Endpoint of line>: A          Arc.
Angle/CEnter/CLose/Direction/Halfwidth/Line/Radius/Second pt/
   Undo/Width/
<Endpoint of arc>: @.25,-.25
Angle/CEnter/CLose/Direction/Halfwidth/Line/Radius/Second pt/
   Undo/Width/
<Endpoint of arc>: <RETURN>
```

The results appear in figure 15.23.

Now, complete the shaft with REVSURF. Set your SURFTAB1 and SURFTAB2 settings. When you execute REVSURF, pick your profile entity first, then the axis line. Default the start angle and the included angle for a full circle. After you have revolved the bottom, repeat REVSURF for the top. Finish the pedestal by using a rectangular array to create nine copies (ten rows, one column) of the bottom piece. When done, reset your UCS and block it as PEDESTAL.

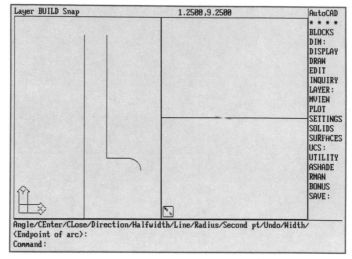

Figure 15.23:
The top path curve for the pedestal shaft top.

Using REVSURF to Make the Pedestal Surface

Command: **VIEW**	Restore BUILD view.
Command: **ZOOM**	Zoom Dynamic to see both path pro-files.
Command: **LAYER**	Set layer CHAIR current.
Command: **COLOR**	Set color to cyan.
Command: **SURFTAB1**	Set to 12. (Release 10, use SETVAR SURFTAB1.)
Command: **SURFTAB2**	Set to 4. (Release 10, use SETVAR SURFTAB2.)
Command: **REVSURF**	Revolve top pedestal shaft.
Select path curve:	Select top profile ① (see fig. 15.24).
Select axis of revolution:	Select axis ②.
Start angle <0>: **<RETURN>**	
Included angle (+=ccw, -=cw) <Full circle>: **<RETURN>**	
Command: **SURFTAB2**	Set to 6. (Release 10, use SETVAR SURFTAB2.)
Command: **REVSURF**	Select bottom profile at ③ as path curve and line at ② as axis of revolution, and revolve bottom pedestal full circle (see fig. 15.25).
Command: **ARRAY**	Array the bottom piece with 10 rows at 1 unit, and 1 column.
Command: **UCS**	Restore UCS HUB to set up for blocking.
Command: **LAYER**	Turn layer BUILD off.

Using REVSURF to Make the Pedestal Surface—continued

Command: **ZOOM**

Zoom in on lower right viewport for a better look.

Command: **BLOCK**

Block to PEDESTAL with insert point at 0,0.

Command: **SAVE**

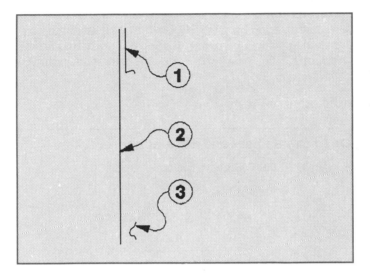

Figure 15.24:
Detail of REVSURF pick points.

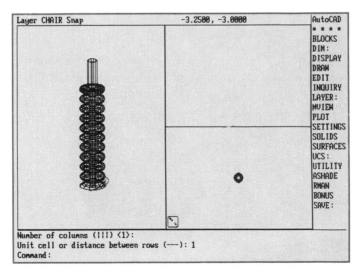

Figure 15.25:
The completed pedestal.

The pedestal used the default (full circle) rotation. The next exercise uses a partial, 90-degree REVSURF, connecting rectangular frames made with BOX, one of the AutoLISP 3D mesh drawing commands. We'll make the frames first, then connect them with a partial REVSURF.

Using the BOX AutoLISP Command

BOX is one of the AutoLISP 3D mesh drawing commands on the [3D Objects] icon menu. You can select [objects] from the [SURFACES] screen menu or [Objects...] from the [Draw] pull-down menu to get to the BOX command, or enter (load "3D") and then BOX as a command. You will be prompted for the starting corner, length, width, height, and rotation angle. You can enter the values or pick points. There is also a cube option.

Let's use BOX to draw the three frame pieces.

Using BOX to Create Seat and Back Support Frames

The left viewport and layer CHAIR should still be current.

Command: **COLOR**	Set color to green.
Select **[Box]**	Select from screen or icon menu, or enter (load "3D") and BOX.
Please wait... Loading 3D Objects. nil	
Command: Box	Create seat support base (see fig. 15.26).
Corner of box: **-1.5,-1.25**	
Length: **10.5**	
Cube/<Width>: **2.5**	
Height: **1**	
Rotation angle about Z axis: **0**	
Command: **ZOOM**	Zoom viewports to views shown.
Command: **BOX**	Create back support upright (see fig. 15.27).
Corner of box: **10,-1.25,2**	
Length: **1**	
Cube/<Width>: **2.5**	
Height: **13**	
Rotation angle about Z axis: **0**	
Command: **BOX**	Create back support spacer with corner 9.25,-1.25,11.5, length .75, width 2.5, height 1.5 and 0 rotation.

Next, we'll connect the frames by revolving a 3D polyline with REVSURF.

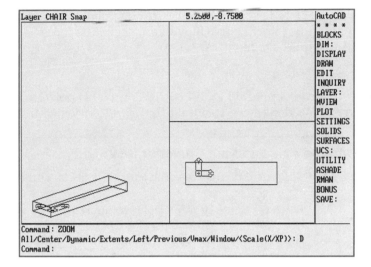

Figure 15.26:
The seat support,
made with BOX.

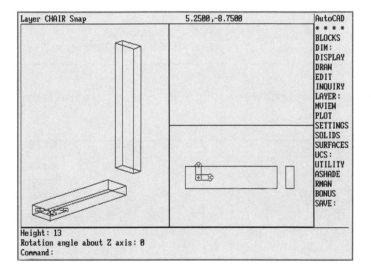

Figure 15.27:
The back support,
made with BOX.

Using 3D Polylines

Use 3D polylines when you need to traverse a 3D space in multiple planes. 3DPOLY draws polylines with independent X,Y, and Z axis coordinates. 2D polylines can exist in any 3D construction plane, but the vertexes of 3D polylines are not bound to a single plane. Unlike 2D polylines, 3D polylines have only straight line segments with no thickness. You can spline fit 3D polylines with PEDIT, but the curve will be made of short, straight segments.

Editing a 3D polyline with PEDIT is similar to editing a 2D polyline, but with fewer options. 3D polylines cannot be joined, curve fit with arc segments, or given a width or tangent. The PEDIT prompt looks like this:

```
Close/Edit vertex/Spline curve/Decurve/Undo/eXit <X>
```

We'll use LINE to draw the axis of rotation for REVSURF, and a 3D polyline to create a rectangular path curve. You don't need to adjust the UCS to draw with 3DPOLY.

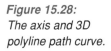

Creating the Axis and Path Curve for REVSURF

Set color BYLAYER, set layer BUILD current, and erase the leftover pedestal entities on the BUILD layer.

Command: **LINE**	Draw axis of revolution from 9,1.25,2 to @0,-2.5 (see fig. 15.28).
Command: **3DPOLY**	Osnap a rectangle around end of seat support.
From point:	Pick endpoint at ① (see fig. 15.29).
Close/Undo/<Endpoint of line>:	Pick endpoint at ②.
Close/Undo/<Endpoint of line>:	Pick endpoint at ③.
Close/Undo/<Endpoint of line>:	Pick endpoint at ④.
Close/Undo/<Endpoint of line>: **C**	CLOSE completes the rectangle.

Now that you have the axis and polyline path profile, connect the two frames with a partial REVSURF.

Figure 15.28:
The axis and 3D polyline path curve.

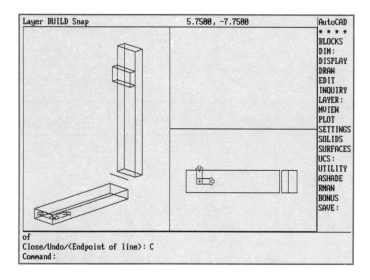

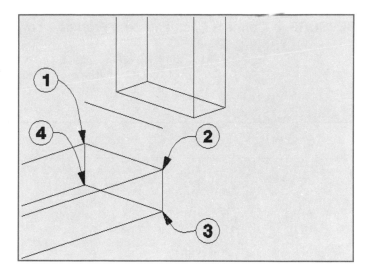

Figure 15.29:
Detail of 3DPOLY
pick points.

Partial REVSURFs and the Direction of Rotation

The direction of surface rotation for REVSURF is determined by your pick point on the axis of rotation and the *right-hand rule*. When you pick an axis of rotation, the end nearest your pick point is considered the origin of that axis. Recalling the right-hand rule of rotation from Chapter 14, if you curl your fingers around that axis and point with a straight thumb away from the origin, the fingers point in the direction of positive rotation. Assigning a non-zero start angle will offset the mesh in this direction, and a partial rotation will sweep in this direction from the starting angle.

Revolve the 3DPOLY profile through a 90-degree arc to create a mesh section that connects the two frames. When you get the supports connected, block the frames and the mesh as a block named SUPPORT. As you do the REVSURF, visualize the right-hand rule.

Using a 90-Degree REVSURF to Connect Back and Seat Frames

Set color to green, and set layer CHAIR current.

Command: **SURFTAB1**	Set to 6. (Release 10, use SETVAR SURFTAB1.)
Command: **REVSURF**	
Select path curve:	Select rectangle on near side edge at ① (see fig. 15.30).
Select axis of revolution:	Select axis line at ②.
Start angle <0>: **<RETURN>**	

Using a 90-Degree REVSURF to Connect Back and Seat Frames—continued

```
Included angle (+=ccw, -=cw) <Full circle>: -90
Command: LAYER                              Turn off layer BUILD.
Command: BLOCK                              Block everything as SUPPORT
                                            with base point at 0,0.

Command: SAVE
```

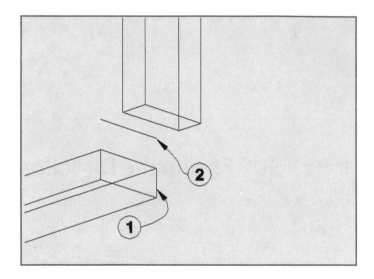

Figure 15.30:
Detail of REVSURF
pick points.

Figure 15.31 shows the connected supports.

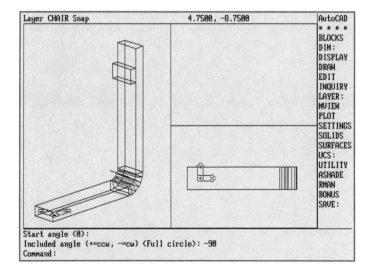

Figure 15.31:
The supports after
REVSURF.

The seat and back support construction involved simple surfaces. In the next section, we will encounter curved surfaces and corners that require more complex meshes.

Combining 3D Surfaces for Complex Mesh Construction

Many 3D objects are made by combining different 3D meshes. We need to make a curved back cushion with curved corners and edges. We're going to create the backrest with seven mesh entities. When you deal with multiple mesh entities, you will frequently encounter cases where the edges coincide. Recall when you added the arched ruled surface mesh to the end cap of the chair leg. You temporarily erased the previous mesh from the top of the leg to get it out of the way. In dealing with several meshes at once in the following exercises, we'll use the alternate technique we mentioned earlier of temporarily moving meshes out of our way.

In plan view, the main body of the chair back is slightly curved and 1.5 inches thick with semicircular ends. We'll create its profile as a polyline by drawing a large arc, offsetting it 1.5 inches and closing the ends with two small arcs. We'll create a major axis line at the center of the large arc for later surfacing commands to use. The top, bottom, and corners of the back are also curved, so we'll create another small arc and minor axis at one corner for the surfacing commands for use in defining them. We'll build these profiles and axes in plan view in the lower right viewport.

Creating a Polyline Path Curve of Back Cushion

Make the lower right viewport current, and zoom Center at 0,0 with height 20.

Set color to BYLAYER, set layer BUILD current, and erase leftover entities from BUILD layer.

```
Command: ARC                                    Draw arc for inside profile of back.
Center/<Start point>: 0,-7
Center/End/<Second point>: E
End point: 0,7
Angle/Direction/Radius/<Center point>: A
Included angle: 20

Command: LINE                                   Draw direction vector and rotation
                                                axis line from osnapped center of arc
                                                to @0,0,-9 in the Z direction.
```

Make left viewport current and zoom Extents to see line, then make lower right viewport current again.

```
Command: OFFSET                                 Offset arc 1.5 to the right to create
                                                outside profile of back.
```

Creating a Polyline Path Curve of Back Cushion—continued

Command: **ARC**   Connect end of large arcs with a start, end, angle arc, using osnapped start point ②, osnapped endpoint ①, and 180-degree included angle (see fig. 15.32).

Command: **PEDIT**   Join all three arcs into single polyline and close to create fourth arc segment at other end of large arcs (see fig. 15.33).

Make left viewport current to draw small arc and axis shown below, for path curve of both rounded corner and top surfaces.

Command: **ZOOM**   Zoom to left end of polyline.

Command: **LINE**   Osnap ENDP to connect small arc segment ends at ① and ② (see fig. 15.34).

Command: **UCS**   Use Entity option and select line just drawn.

Command: **UCS**   Rotate 90 degrees about X axis.

Command: **ARC**   Draw start, end, angle arc, using osnapped start point ②, osnapped endpoint ①, and 180-degree included angle.

Command: **ZOOM**   Zoom out with Extents or Dynamic to see major axis line and profile paths (see fig. 15.35).

Command: **SAVE**   Save the drawing.

Figure 15.32:
Detail of arc pick points.

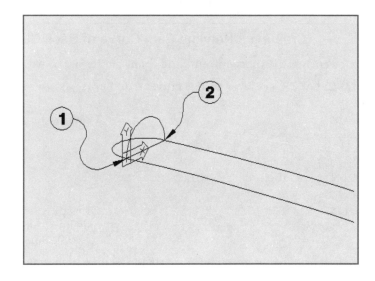

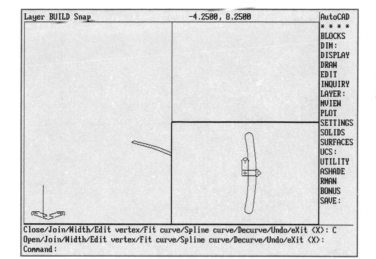

Figure 15.33:
The backrest profile
and axis line.

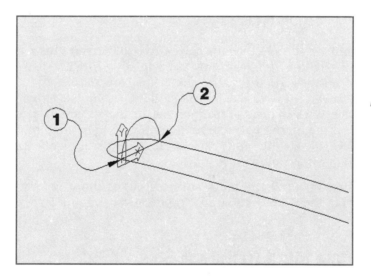

Now we're ready to create the mesh entities, starting with TABSURF for the main body of the backrest.

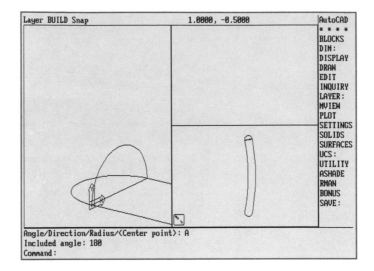

Figure 15.35:
An axis and path
curve for rounded
edges and corners.

```
Layer BUILD Snap          1.0000, -0.5000        AutoCAD
                                                 * * * *
                                                 BLOCKS
                                                 DIM:
                                                 DISPLAY
                                                 DRAW
                                                 EDIT
                                                 INQUIRY
                                                 LAYER:
                                                 MVIEW
                                                 PLOT
                                                 SETTINGS
                                                 SOLIDS
                                                 SURFACES
                                                 UCS:
                                                 UTILITY
                                                 ASHADE
                                                 RMAN
                                                 BONUS
                                                 SAVE:

Angle/Direction/Radius/<Center point>: A
Included angle: 180
Command:
```

The TABSURF Command

TABSURF creates a *tabular* surface using a path curve (directrix) and a direction vector (generatrix). Like RULESURF, you only need to set SURFTAB1. TABSURF uses the usual set of entities for the path curve: line, arc, circle, or 2D or 3D polyline. After you select the entity to use for the path curve, you select your direction vector. The surface lines it creates are parallel to the direction vector. The direction vector need not be on the path curve; it simply defines the direction and distance in which TABSURF extrudes your path profile. The direction of extrusion is away from the direction vector pick point.

As we mentioned earlier, we'll need to move surfaces out of the way as we create them. We'll move them to the WCS in the upper right viewport using a special form of coordinate input.

Forcing Coordinate Input to the WCS

Prefixing any coordinate value with an asterisk makes AutoCAD interpret the coordinate value in the WCS. Using MOVE with a first point of 0,0 (in the current UCS) and a second point of *0,0 will move the mesh surfaces to the WCS coordinate point that corresponds to their current UCS locations.

Let's use TABSURF to create the main part of the chair's back and *0,0 to move it out of the way so that you can create the top and corner meshes.

Using TABSURF and *0,0 to Create and Move the Back

Command: **LAYER**	Set layer CHAIR current.
Command: **COLOR**	Set color magenta.
Command: **SURFTAB1**	Set to 8. (Release 10, use SETVAR SURFTAB1.)
Command: **TABSURF**	Draw the main body of the back.
Select path curve:	Pick the joined polyline profile.
Select direction vector:	Pick top of major axis line at ① (see fig. 15.36).
Command: **MOVE**	Move the mesh from 0,0 to *0,0 (see fig. 15.37).
Command: **REDRAWALL**	

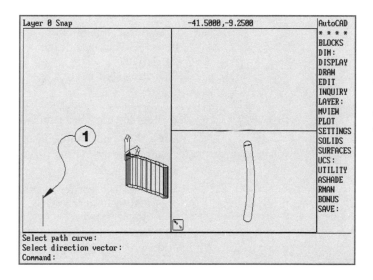

Figure 15.36:
The TABSURFed body of the back before move.

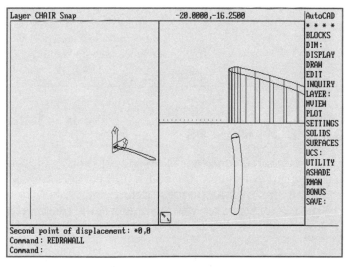

Figure 5.37:
Body of the back moved to WCS.

REVSURF Revisited

We'll use our old friend, REVSURF, to surface the top edge and a corner of the backrest. First, do a 20-degree partial REVSURF, revolving the small arc at the corner about the major axis to create the top edge of the back. Then move it to the WCS. Finally, use a 90-degree REVSURF to create the first rounded corner with the same arc, but revolve it about the short axis between its endpoints.

Using REVSURF to Surface Top Edge and Corner of Backrest

Command: **SURFTAB2**	Set to 8. (Release 10, use SETVAR SURFTAB2.)
Command: **REVSURF**	Create top edge of chair back.
Select path curve:	Select the last arc drawn at ① (see fig. 15.38).
Select axis of revolution:	Pick the axis line at ③ (see fig. 15.39).
Start angle <0>: **<RETURN>**	
Included angle (+=ccw, -=cw) <Full circle>: **20**	20 degrees matches profile angle.
Command: **MOVE**	Move the mesh from 0,0 to *0,0.
Command: **ZOOM**	Zoom in on left end of polyline as shown below.
Command: **REVSURF**	Make the first corner of the backrest (see fig. 15.40).
Select path curve:	Pick the arc at ①.
Select axis of revolution:	Pick the short line connecting arc ends at ②.
Start angle <0>: **<RETURN>**	
Included angle (+=ccw, -=cw) <Full circle>: **90**	
Command: **MOVE**	Move two meshes in upper right viewport from *0,0 back to 0,0.
Command: **ZOOM**	Zoom to fill left viewport with back surfaces (see fig. 15.41).
Command: **SAVE**	

Mirroring to Duplicate 3D Meshes

You've got all the entities you need to complete the backrest. You could work your way around the backrest creating the remaining edges and corners the same way, but it is much easier to mirror the existing entities. Before you mirror the entities, change the UCS to make the mirroring easy. After completing the backrest with two MIRRORs, block everything to the name BACK.

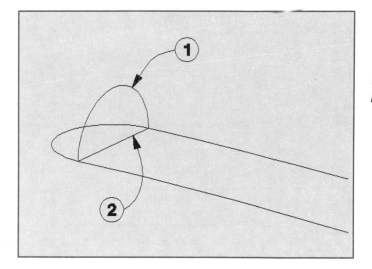

Figure 15.38:
Detail of path curve
pick point.

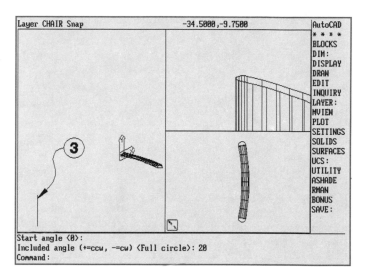

Figure 15.39:
Surface on the top
edge of the backrest.

Using MIRROR to Complete the Backrest

Make the lower right viewport current.

Command: **UCS**	Restore UCS HUB to return UCS to top front center of backrest.
Command: **MOVE**	Move the center midpoint of main back to UCS origin.
Select objects:	Select everything.

Figure 15.40:
Surface the corners.

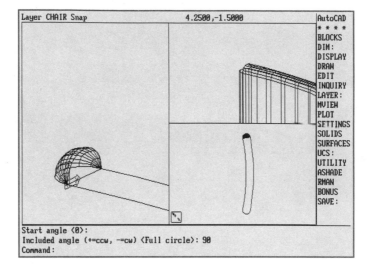

Figure 15.41:
A backrest with three
mesh entities.

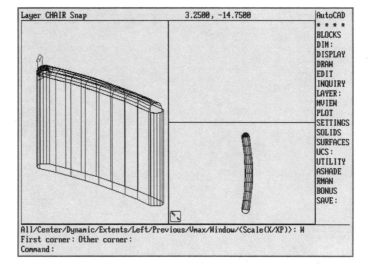

Using MIRROR to Complete the Backrest—continued

Base point or displacement: Use osnap ENDP to pick middle of back side at
    ① in lower right viewport (see fig. 15.42).

Second point of displacement: `0,0,4.5`   Moves the back up 4.5".

Command: **UCS**   Rotate -90 degrees around Y axis (see fig. 15.43).

Command: **MIRROR**   Mirror corner mesh to other side.

Select objects: Select corner mesh.

First point of mirror line: **0,0**

Second point: **1,0**

Using MIRROR to Complete the Backrest—continued

Delete old objects? <N> **<RETURN>**	Draws corner on opposite side of top (see fig. 15.44).
Command: **MIRROR**	Mirror top edge and both corners down across mirror line from 0,0 to 0,1 and don't delete old objects (see fig. 15.45).
Command: **UCS**	Restore HUB.
Command: **LAYER**	Turn layer BUILD off.
Command: **BLOCK**	Block everything to name BACK with base point 0,0.
Command: **SAVE**	Save and continue, or end and take a break.

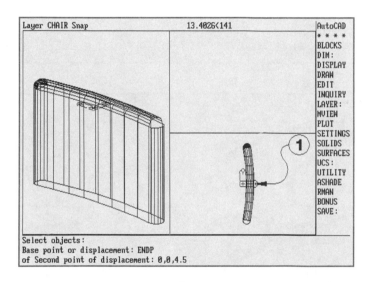

Figure 15.42:
The back midpoint moved 4.5" above HUB UCS origin.

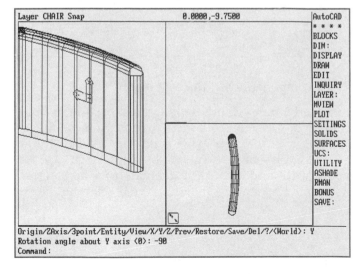

Figure 15.43:
UCS oriented for mirroring.

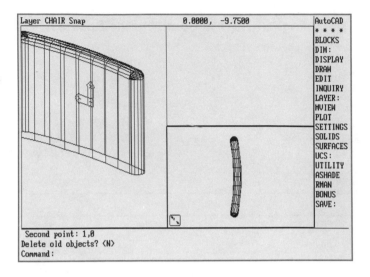

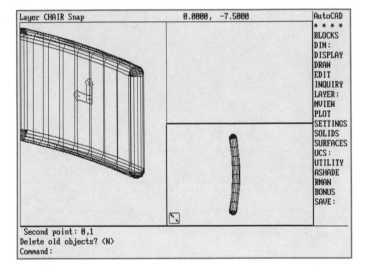

You now have all the chair components but the seat itself.

In the next section, we will create the chair's seat and explore the use of PEDIT to change the surface contours of the seat. With PEDIT, you can move mesh vertexes and smooth meshes by spline fitting. First, we'll do the body of the seat with EDGESURF. Later, we'll finish the seat construction by using a 3DFACE for the seat bottom, and by using REVSURF and TABSURF to create rounded edges and corners. Finally, we will assemble the chair by inserting the blocks that store its component parts.

The EDGESURF Command

EDGESURF creates a polygon mesh from four adjoining edges. The edges can be lines, arcs, or open 2D or 3D polylines, but the four edges must touch at their endpoints. A polyline is a single edge no matter how many vertexes it has. You need to set SURFTAB1 and SURFTAB2 to specify your *m* and *n* mesh density. Executing EDGESURF is quite simple; you just select the four edge entities. The first pick sets the SURFTAB1 *m* mesh direction along the edge picked.

Using EDGESURF to Create Seat Surface

We'll create four lines to define the planar edges of the top surface of the seat cushion, then use EDGESURF to fill it in with a 10 x 10 mesh. Pick the edges where shown so your *m* and *n* directions will match ours. We'll temporarily go back to a single viewport so you can better see the results when we experiment with PEDIT mesh smoothing. The cushion is 2 inches thick, so begin by drawing the line edges with a Z value of 2.

Using EDGESURF to Create the Top Surface of the Seat Cushion

Make sure left viewport is current.

Command: **TILEMODE**	Release 11 only: set to 1 to return to single viewport.
Command: **VPORTS**	(Release 10 only, set to SIngle.)
Command: **ZOOM**	Zoom Center at 0,0,3 with height 15.

Set color to BYLAYER, set layer BUILD current, and erase leftover entities.

Command: **SURFTAB1**	Set to 10. (Release 10, use SETVAR SURFTAB1.)
Command: **SURFTAB2**	Set to 10. (Release 10, use SETVAR SURFTAB2.)
Command: **LINE**	Draw from 7,7,2 to 7,-7,2 to -7,-7,2 to -7,7,2, and close.

Set color to magenta, and set layer CHAIR current.

Command: **EDGESURF**	Create a 10 x 10 mesh 2" above seat bottom.
Select edge 1:	Pick line at ① (see fig. 15.46).
Select edge 2:	Pick line at ②.
Select edge 3:	Pick line at ③.
Select edge 4:	Pick line at ④.
Command: **SAVE**	

Figure 15.47 shows the mesh.

You can change the surface contours of a 3D polyline polygon mesh by editing the 3D vertex points with PEDIT.

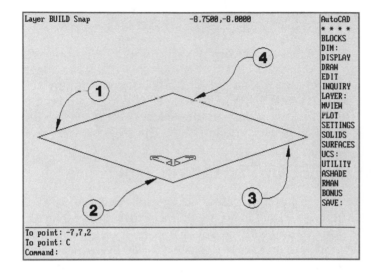

Figure 15.46:
Creating the seat
edges.

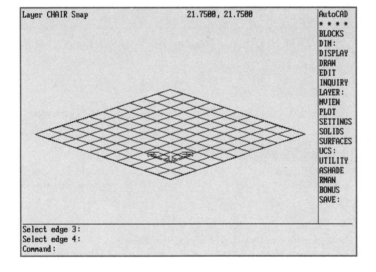

Figure 15.47:
The EDGESURF
mesh.

Using PEDIT to Edit 3D Meshes

PEDIT is an intelligent command. When you select a mesh, PEDIT will only prompt with the options available for editing meshes. (The options also change with 2D or 3D polylines, but polyface meshes can't be edited.) You can use PEDIT to move a mesh vertex point by identifying the vertex point and entering a new 3D coordinate. You can also *smooth* and *desmooth* the mesh by spline fitting the vertex mesh points.

When editing meshes, PEDIT has several options for moving the vertex editing X marker from vertex to vertex in addition to the familiar Next and Previous options. Look at the prompt line in the following exercise. The X starts at the corner nearest the first pick point used in EDGESURF. The Vertex (*m,n*) prompt indicates your current vertex, where the X is. You move the X up (away from the starting corner) and down the *m* direction or right (away from the starting corner) and left in the *n* direction. Next initially moves in the right direction.

To get a feel for editing vertexes and spline fitting meshes, try the following exercise. It exaggerates the movement of the vertex points so that you can see the effects of different curve fits. Watch the (*m,n*) prompt and X mark as you work. We'll also set an undo mark so we can easily undo our experiments.

Using PEDIT to Edit Mesh Vertex Points

```
Command: UNDO                                      Set an undo mark.
Command: PEDIT
Select polyline:                                   Pick mesh.
Edit vertex/Smooth surface/Desmooth/Mclose/Nclose/Undo/eXit <X>: E
Vertex (0,0). Next/Previous/Left/Right/Up/Down/Move/REgen/
   eXit <N>: <RETURN>
Vertex (0,1). Next/Previous/Left/Right/Up/Down/Move/REgen/eXit <N>: R
Vertex (0,2). Next/Previous/Left/Right/Up/Down/Move/REgen/eXit <R>: U
Vertex (1,2). Next/Previous/Left/Right/Up/Down/Move/REgen/
   eXit <U>: <RETURN>
Vertex (2,2). Next/Previous/Left/Right/Up/Down/Move/REgen/
   eXit <U>: <RETURN>
Vertex (3,2). Next/Previous/Left/Right/Up/Down/Move/REgen/eXit <U>: R
Vertex (3,3). Next/Previous/Left/Right/Up/Down/Move/REgen/eXit <R>: M
Enter new location: @0,0,3                         Moves vertex 3" in the Z direc-
                                                   tion.
Vertex (3,3). Next/Previous/Left/Right/Up/Down/Move/REgen/
   eXit <R>: <RETURN>
Vertex (3,4). Next/Previous/Left/Right/Up/Down/Move/REgen/eXit <R>: M
Enter new location: @0,0,2                         Moves vertex 2" in Z.
```

Go to vertex (4,4) with Up option and move it 2" in Z with @0,0,2.

Go to vertex (4,3) with Left option and move it 2" in Z with @0,0,2.

Go to vertex (7,4) with Up Up Up Right and move it 1" in Y and 9" in Z with @0,1,9.

Go to vertex (8,5) with Up Right and move it -5" in Z with @0,0,-5 (see fig. 15.48).

```
Vertex (8,5). Next/Previous/Left/Right/Up/Down/Move/REgen/eXit <R>: X
Edit vertex/Smooth surface/Desmooth/Mclose/Nclose/Undo/
   eXit <X>: <RETURN>
```

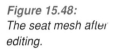

Figure 15.48:
The seat mesh after editing.

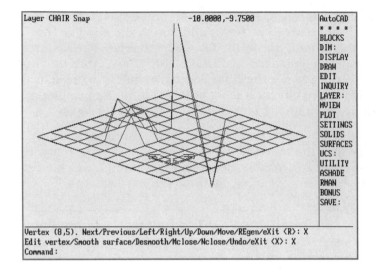

```
Layer CHAIR Snap                        -10.0000,-9.7500        AutoCAD
                                                                * * * *
                                                                BLOCKS
                                                                DIM:
                                                                DISPLAY
                                                                DRAW
                                                                EDIT
                                                                INQUIRY
                                                                LAYER:
                                                                MVIEW
                                                                PLOT
                                                                SETTINGS
                                                                SOLIDS
                                                                SURFACES
                                                                UCS:
                                                                UTILITY
                                                                ASHADE
                                                                RMAN
                                                                BONUS
                                                                SAVE:

Vertex (8,5). Next/Previous/Left/Right/Up/Down/Move/REgen/eXit <R>: X
Edit vertex/Smooth surface/Desmooth/Mclose/Nclose/Undo/eXit <X>: X
Command:
```

The smooth surface option allows three types of spline fitting. Each type produces a different blended smooth surface based on formulas that produce a surface passing near the vertex points. You control the type of spline fit by setting the SURFTYPE system variable. Two other system variables, SURFU and SURFV, control the fineness of the fit in the *m* and *n* mesh directions. You use the SPLFRAME system variable to control whether the spline fit or original mesh will display. A 0 (off, the default) displays the spline fitting, if any, and 1 (on) displays the original mesh and vertexes regardless of spline fitting.

Smooth Surface Options

The three smooth surface options and the variables to set them are:

- Cubic B-spline curve — SURFTYPE 6 (AutoCAD's default).
- Quadratic B-spline curve — SURFTYPE 5.
- Bézier curve — SURFTYPE 8.

Try all the smoothing options on the mesh to see the effect each has. Use the exercise that follows to get your SURFU, SURFV, and SURFTYPE settings.

Using PEDIT to Smooth Mesh Surface Fitting

Command: **SURFU**	Set to 24. (Release 10, use SETVAR SURFU.)
Command: **SURFV**	Set to 24. (Release 10, use SETVAR SURFV.)
Command: **PEDIT**	Try cubic B-spline surface, with default SURFTYPE 6.

Using PEDIT to Smooth Mesh Surface Fitting

```
Select polyline:                                  Select mesh.
Edit vertex/Smooth surface/Desmooth/
  Mclose/Nclose/Undo/eXit <X>: S
Edit vertex/Smooth surface/Desmooth/
  Mclose/Nclose/Undo/eXit <X>: <RETURN>
```

Oops, nothing happened — remember, we had SPLFRAME set to 1 for polyface and 3Dmesh visibility.

Command: **SPLFRAME**	Set to 0 to show spline fitting. (Release 10, use SETVAR SPLFRAME.)
Command: **REGEN**	Regenerate drawing to see spline fit mesh (see fig. 15.49).
Command: **SURFTYPE**	Set to 5. (Release 10, use SETVAR SURFTYPE.)
Command: **PEDIT**	Select mesh and use smooth again for quadratic B-spline surface (see fig. 15.50).
Command: **SURFTYPE**	Set SURFTYPE to 8.
Command: **PEDIT**	Select mesh and use SMOOTH again for Bézier surface (see fig. 15.51).
Command: **UNDO**	Use UNDO Back to restore flat mesh seat surface.

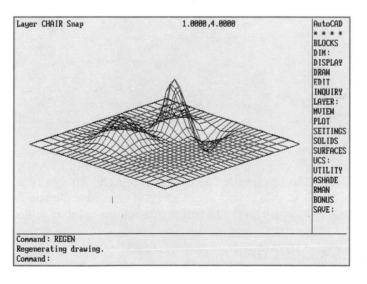

Figure 15.49: SURFTYPE 6 smoothing.

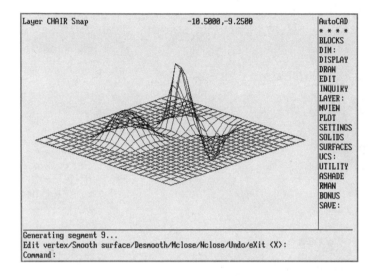

Figure 15.50:
SURFTYPE 5
smoothing.

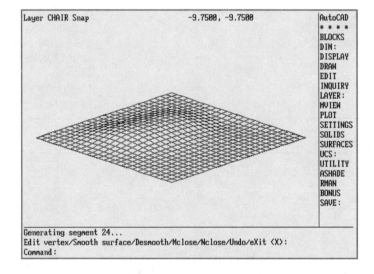

Figure 15.51:
SURFTYPE 8
smoothing.

You have to look closely to see the difference between SURFTYPEs 5 and 6, but 8 is dramatically smoother. You can regenerate to see the effects of a SPLFRAME change, but you have to use PEDIT to resmooth the mesh to see the effects of changing SURFTYPE, SURFU, or SURFV. When you are done, you should have the flat starting mesh restored. If you like, you can try to edit it into a comfortable seat contour.

Other PEDIT Mesh Options

The Mclose and Nclose options control whether a mesh connects the first vertex to the last vertex of the mesh. A mesh in the shape of a dish (half a sphere) is closed in the M direction and open in the N direction. If you were to open the dish in the M direction by selecting Mclose, the dish would be redrawn with a wedge segment missing. Likewise, if you closed the dish in the N direction, the dish would be redrawn with a mesh going from the edge to the center of the dish, creating a cone inside the dish. The M and N options display either close or open prompts depending on the current status of the mesh being edited.

Let's finish the seat.

3DFACE, TABSURF, and REVSURF Revisited

We'll make a simple seat bottom with 3DFACE, then use REVSURF to make curved corners and TABSURF to close the curved edges.

After drawing the seat bottom with 3DFACE, we'll create the arc and axis for REVSURF. We'll also move the existing mesh out of the way so we can select one of its edge lines when we TABSURF the arc. These are the same techniques that you used to build the backrest.

▶ Using 3DFACE and Creating Arc Path and Axis for REVSURF and TABSURF

Command: **TILEMODE**	Release 11 only: set to 0 to return to three paper space viewports.
Command: **VPORTS**	(Release 10 only, restore BUILD viewport configuration.)

Make left viewport current, and zoom Center 0,0 to height 36.

Command: **3DFACE**	Draw seat bottom from 7,7 to 7,-7 to -7,-7 to -7,7, then <RETURN> to exit.

Set color to BYLAYER, and set layer BUILD current.

Command: **LINE**	Draw from -7,7 to @0,0,2 as axis for REVSURF.
Command: **MOVE**	Move seat top mesh from 0,0 to *0,0 (to WCS in upper right viewport).
Command: **ZOOM**	Zoom top right viewport with center point *0,0 with height 16.
Command: **UCS**	Use Entity option and pick line in left viewport to put UCS at bottom of line.
Command: **UCS**	Rotate -90 degrees about Y axis.
Command: **ARC**	Draw start, end, angle arc, from start point 2,0 to endpoint 0,0 with included angle 180 degrees, for seat corner REVSURF and edge TABSURF.

The progress of this command sequence is shown in figures 15.52 and 15.53.

Figure 15.52:
The seat with a 3Dface bottom.

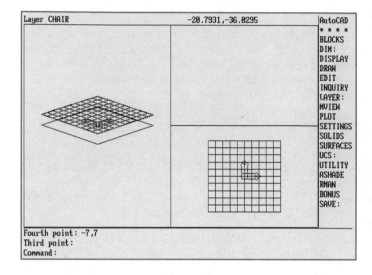

Figure 15.53:
Arc and construction lines ready for surfacing.

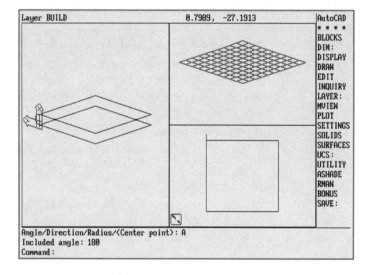

Now we can use REVSURF and TABSURF to create the first corner and edge. Then, a polar array will complete the seat cushion. Using ARRAY takes advantage of the fact that the seat is symmetrical and saves mirroring or individually creating the edges and corners.

Using REVSURF, TABSURF, and ARRAY to Complete the Seat

Command: **LAYER**	Set layer CHAIR current.
Command: **COLOR**	Set color magenta.
Command: **REVSURF**	Revolve arc to surface corner.
Select path curve:	Pick arc at ① (see fig. 15.54).
Select axis of revolution:	Pick line at ②.
Start angle <0>: **<RETURN>**	
Included angle (+=ccw, -=cw) <Full circle>: **90**	
Command: **UCS**	Restore UCS HUB.
Command: **MOVE**	Move corner from 0,0 to *0,0.
Command: **REDRAW**	
Command: **TABSURF**	Create edge of seat cushion.
Select path curve:	Pick arc at ①.
Select direction vector:	Pick line at ③.
Command: **MOVE**	Move meshes back from upper right viewport, from *0,0 to 0,0.
Command: **LAYER**	Turn layer BUILD off.
Command: **ARRAY**	Polar array edge and corner mesh to create 3 remaining sides.
Select objects:	Select TABSURF edge mesh and REVSURF corner mesh (see fig. 15.55).
Rectangular or Polar array (R/P): **P**	
Center point of array: **0,0**	
Number of items: **4**	
Angle to fill (+=ccw, -=cw) <360>: **<RETURN>**	
Rotate objects as they are copied? <Y> **<RETURN>**	
Command: **BLOCK**	Block everything to name SEAT with base point 0,0.
Command: **SAVE**	Save and continue, or end and take a break.

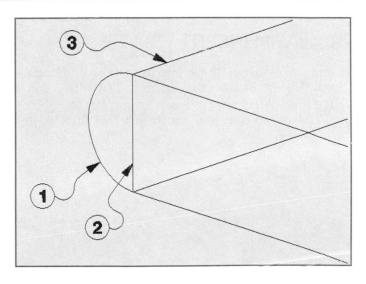

Figure 15.54:
Detail of pick points.

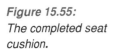

Figure 15.55:
The completed seat
cushion.

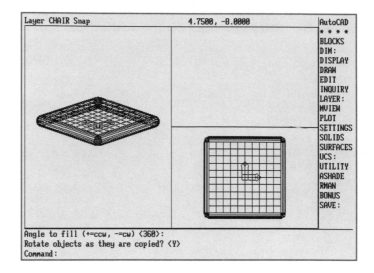

Congratulations! You now have all your chair components tucked away in your drawing as blocks.

Inserting 3D Blocks

In 3D, building complex parts as a series of smaller blocked parts offers several productivity benefits. First, you only have to deal with a limited number of entities on the screen for a particular part. This makes construction and editing less confusing because other parts will not get in your way. This also makes redraws, regenerations, and interim hidden line removals faster. Another benefit is that you can change the components quite easily. For example, with a variety of seat, back, pedestal, and base blocks, you could use block redefinition to quickly build a different chair from other parts.

Assembling the Chair With INSERT

Use the INSERT command to construct the chair from the components you've blocked. If you didn't create all the blocks, they're on the IA DISK. You can still insert them if you have the disk. When all parts are inserted, use BASE to set an insertion base point at floor level so that you can insert this drawing into other drawings.

Using INSERT to Assemble the 3D Chair

 Continue in the CHAIR drawing, or begin a NEW drawing named CHAIR=IA6CHAIR, replacing your previous CHAIR drawing.

 Continue in the CHAIR drawing.

Command: **TILEMODE**	Release 11 only: set TILEMODE to 1 to return to single viewport.
Command: **VPORTS**	(Release 10 only, select left viewport and set to SIngle.)
Command: **UCS**	Set Origin to 30,22,0.

Turn on all layers, do a zoom Extents, and erase any leftover entities.

Command: **ZOOM**	Zoom Center at 0,0,18 with a height of 42.
Command: **INSERT**	Insert BASE at 0,0,4.5 with default scale and rotation.
Command: **INSERT**	Insert PEDESTAL at 0,0,4.5 with default scale and rotation.
Command: **INSERT**	Insert SUPPORT at 0,0,17.5 with default scale and rotation.
Command: **INSERT**	Insert SEAT at 0,0,18.5 with default scale and rotation.
Command: **INSERT**	Insert BACK at 9.25,0,30 with default scale and rotation.
Command: **BASE**	Set base point 0,0,0 for future insertions.
Command: **SAVE**	

Now the chair is complete (see fig. 15.56). Take a good look at it with the HIDE and SHADE commands.

HIDE vs. SHADE for Viewing Images

You've already used the HIDE command to remove hidden lines from wireframe images. You can do a HIDE of the chair, but it will take anywhere from six minutes to an hour, depending on the speed of your system. Release 11 offers a much quicker viewing alternative: the SHADE command. SHADE produces four types of surface renderings, and only takes about as long as it would take to do two regenerations. On the chair, this is less than a minute on most systems. SHADE is faster because it is a screen display-based process, while HIDE considers every vector in the drawing datbase. The type of rendering created by SHADE is controlled by the SHADEDGE system variable.

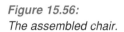

Figure 15.56:
The assembled chair.

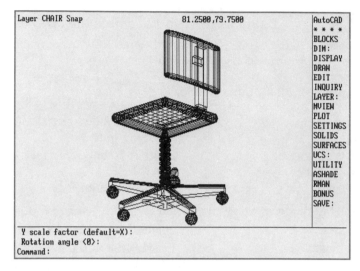

> **Note:** The relative speed of SHADE versus HIDE depends on the complexity of the drawing. HIDE may be faster for simple drawings, but SHADE is faster for complex surfaces like the chair.

If you have a 256-color display that uses AutoCAD's standard color scheme, you can create two types of *shaded* images. Shading means it renders the surfaces as if a single light source behind your eyes is illuminating the model, assuming you are looking at it from directly in front of the screen. The default lighting assumes 70 percent direct light reflecting from this source and 30 percent ambient background light. These percentages are controlled by the SHADEDIF system variable. Its settings can range from 0 to 100, with a default of 70. Higher values increase reflectivity and contrast. The intensity of the shading on a particular face is greatest if it's perpendicular to the light source and decreases as the angle of the face increases. This shading can be done with edges highlighted in the background screen color (SHADEDGE 1), or without highlighted edges (SHADEDGE 0), which usually looks best. The results of shading without highlighted edges look like the image on the facing page of Chapter 18, although that is actually an AutoShade image.

With any display, two types of unshaded surface renderings can be produced. The default (SHADEDGE 3) draws faces filled with their original colors and highlights edges in the background screen color. This looks best on simple images. On images with a lot of small faces, like the chair, the edges break up the image too much. The last type of rendering is a simulated hidden line removal (SHADEDGE 2). It displays faces in the background screen color and draws edges in the original colors of their faces. This looks as good as a slow HIDE. However, HIDE still has two advantages over SHADE. You can select entities after a HIDE, but you must regenerate after a SHADE before you can select entities. HIDE can also put the hidden lines on a special layer for viewing or plotting.

Let's sit back and use VPOINT to look at the chair from all sides. Our favorite view is shown below. When you get a view you like, try the SHADE or the HIDE command to view it. Finally, end your drawing.

Shading or Hiding the Chair

Command: `<Grid off>`	Toggle your grid off for a clear image.
Command: **SPLFRAME**	Set to 0 to hide invisible edges. (Release 10, use SETVAR SPLFRAME.)
Command: **VPOINT**	Rotate to 240 degrees in X,Y plane and 19 degrees from X,Y plane.
Command: **ZOOM**	Zoom Center at 0,0,18 with a height of 42.
Command: **HIDE**	Try it while you take a break (or use SHADE with Release 11).
Command: **SHADE**	Release 11 only: try the default, with SHADEDGE 3 (see fig. 15.57).
Command: **SHADEDGE**	Set to 2 for simulated hidden line removal (see fig. 15.58).
Command: **SHADE**	Release 11 only.
Command: **MSLIDE**	Make a slide, if you want to view it again later.
Command: **END**	Put your chair away.

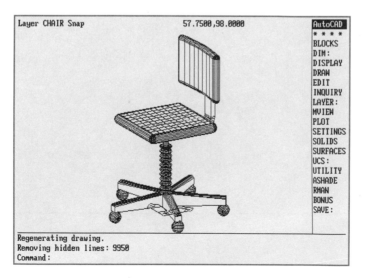

Figure 15.57:
The chair with HIDE, or shaded with SHADEDGE 3.

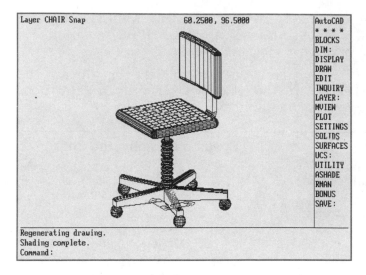

Figure 15.58:
The chair shaded with
SHADEDGE 2.

You have to regenerate a SHADE before you can pick entities. Both shaded and hidden images disappear with a regeneration, but making slides is a good way to save them for later viewing. You can't plot a shaded image, so AutoCAD still has to use the hidden line removal process for plotting.

Figure 15.59 shows the finished chair, along with the table you drew in chapter 14.

Figure 15.59:
The table and chair.

Summing Up

When you construct a 3D drawing, use the entities and commands that fit your purpose. Meshes may not always be the most efficient way to go. Extruded 2D entities take less space in memory and on disk — use them if they adequately represent what you need to show.

You should generally use a mix of 2D extruded entities and 3D mesh entities. If you are building a complex drawing, we recommend using the approach taken in this chapter: build your drawing in components and assemble it using the BLOCK and INSERT commands.

When you do use meshes, set reasonable surface mesh density with SURFTAB1 and SURFTAB2. Keep track of these settings — if you forget to set the values you want, you have to erase your mesh and create a new one. Keep your mesh profile entities on a separate layer so they don't conflict with your 3D model entities. If you have meshes with common edges, use temporary blocks, moves, or erasures to get one mesh out of the way to pick the edge entity for the second mesh. If you really want to control your meshes, create some AutoLISP routines. In the next chapter, we'll take a walk through a 3D office. You'll generate perspectives and partial hides, and dynamically view an office drawing.

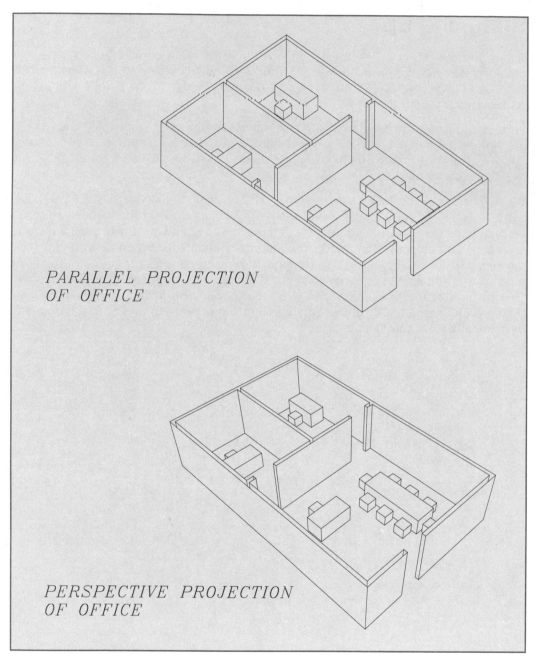

PARALLEL PROJECTION
OF OFFICE

PERSPECTIVE PROJECTION
OF OFFICE

Figure 16.1:
Parallel and perspective projections of an office.

16

Dynamic 3D Displays

CONTROLLING YOUR 3D IMAGES

Dynamic Viewing for Drawing, Presentation, and Perspectives

In the past two chapters, you've learned to draw 3D models. In the next chapter, you'll learn to create rendered 3D presentations with AutoShade. When you create a presentation, you use a variety of views in 3D space. Even our simple chair looks impressive revolved in space. This chapter is a bridge, a presentation of advanced 3D viewing techniques that will make drawing in 3D easier, as well as help you plan and preview your 3D presentations. The key to this is the DVIEW command. DVIEW dynamically displays your model as you adjust your viewpoint, much like ZOOM Dynamic does for zooms.

This chapter will show you how to use DVIEW as an interactive 3D substitute for the VPOINT and ZOOM commands — plus display perspectives in AutoCAD! We'll also show you how to create slides of these views and how to present a slide show using a script file.

By combining DVIEW with paper space viewports, you can draw and annotate a single drawing with any combination of views you like, including perspectives. By combining DVIEW, the SHADE command, slides, and scripts, you can quickly and easily create preliminary or simple presentations. Then, you can go on to create impressive full motion video presentations with AutoShade, Autodesk RenderMan, 3D Studio, AutoFlix and/or Autodesk Animator (all Autodesk products).

699

DVIEW vs. VPOINT and ZOOM Commands

DVIEW is like an enhanced VPOINT *and* ZOOM command. The DVIEW dynamic display of your drawing as you adjust your viewpoint is a dramatic improvement over VPOINT, and you can zoom and adjust your viewpoint in a single command. Unlike VPOINT, DVIEW provides either parallel (orthographic) or perspective views. Figure 16.1 shows both parallel and perspective views of an office. In the perspective view, lines recede from your view to a vanishing point. In the parallel view, lines always remain parallel. VPOINT is limited to parallel views, which may seem un-natural to your eyes because you are accustomed to lines converging to a vanishing point.

VPOINT always zooms to the drawing extents, but DVIEW gives you full control over the zoomed display of your view. With VPOINT, you always look *through* the entire drawing towards 0,0,0. DVIEW lets you look from any point to any point and you can clip the foreground or background to avoid seeing objects that would obscure what you want to see.

DVIEW utilizes an intuitive camera and target metaphor to control your drawing view. To select a view, you *point* the camera at a target in your drawing. Think of the line from the camera to the target as a line of sight. You can move the camera and target to get different views. The camera metaphor is carried further in perspective views, to let you change your field of view by changing the *lens* length. You can also get cut-away sections of your drawing by *clipping* the front or back plane of your view. This is helpful when you want to look at an office interior in a building plan, or create a section view of a part.

All this gives you more control over your drawing views, but the most important point is that DVIEW is interactive, unlike the trial-and-error method that VPOINT often requires. DVIEW works with a selection set to improve speed in complex drawings. You can rapidly adjust your viewpoint using only selected entities, then regenerate the view with everything. You can select and *drag* the entities that will make up your view, adjust your camera and target settings, and see a screen pre-view.

The Chapter's Goals in Perspective

This chapter takes you from working in 3D views to preparing 3D presentations. Most of the chapter is devoted to the DVIEW command. We'll use a simple office plan, but the DVIEW controls apply equally to any 3D application. This chapter will take you through:

- Setting up dynamic views.
- Locating camera and target points.
- Panning a camera.

- Getting perspective and hidden views, including clipped views.
- Creating and scripting a slide show.
- Editing a perspective view using viewports.
- Preparing a 3D view for rendering.

Often, the right 3D view can save you time and money. Systematically revolving a drawing in 3D space may reveal an unanticipated design condition, such as interference between machinery and a wall. Learning to use tools like DVIEW and AutoShade can help you win projects with better presentations.

The IA DISK drawing for this chapter includes saved views that correspond to this chapter's three series of exercises. The first series starts at the beginning of the chapter. The series continues at the *Rotating the View With the Target Option*, and at the *Making a 3D Slide Presentation* sections. You can use the disk to start in any of these sections.

Dynamic Display, Slide, and Script Tools

You'll find [DVIEW] on the [DISPLAY] screen menu and [Dview] on the [Display] pull-down menu. You can also use the [DVIEW Options] icon menu (see fig. 16.2) by selecting [Dview Options...] on the [Display] pull-down menu.

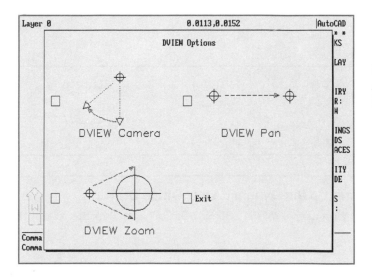

Figure 16.2:
A [DVIEW options]
icon menu.

In addition to DVIEW, we'll use the SCRIPT, MSLIDE, and VSLIDE commands. MSLIDE and VSLIDE are commands for making and viewing slides. These are on the [UTILITY] screen menu.

Setting Up for DVIEW

This chapter uses the office plan from Chapter 13 that you saved as OFFICE.DWG. We chose this drawing because you can get a variety of perspective views from the different rooms and because it will regenerate quickly in the exercises. This is an admittedly simple drawing, but it illustrates a time-saving technique. You can work with simple shapes like those in this drawing, then replace them with complex blocks before plotting or presenting your work.

If you are using the IA DISK, you have IA6OFF3D.DWG already extruded and ready for the first DVIEW exercise. If you do not have a copy of the OFFICE drawing, you can quickly create it by doing the first two exercises from Chapter 13.

After loading the drawing, we'll freeze the attributes layer since we only need the floor plan for this chapter's exercises. Then, we'll extrude the plan into a 3D drawing by giving height to the walls, tables, and chairs.

Table 16.1:
Dynamic View Office Drawing Settings

COORDS	GRID	ORTHO	FILL	SNAP	UCSICON
ON	2'	OFF	OFF	3"	ON and OR

UNITS	Set to 4 Architectural, default the rest.
LIMITS	Set LIMITS from 0,0 to 72',48'.
VIEW	Restore saved view named A.

Layer Name	State	Color	Linetype
0	Frozen	7 (white)	CONTINUOUS
PLAN	On/Current	3 (green)	CONTINUOUS
DATA	Frozen	7 (white)	CONTINUOUS

Setting Up the Dynamic View Office Drawing

Begin a NEW drawing named OFFICE3D=IA6OFF3D and skip the rest of this exercise.

 Begin a NEW drawing named OFFICE3D=OFFICE and make sure the current settings match table 16.1.

Command: **LAYER**   Set layer PLAN current and freeze layers 0 and DATA (see fig. 16.3).

Setting Up the Dynamic View Office Drawing—continued

Command: **EXPLODE**	Explode polylines used to draw walls, if you used polylines.
Command: **CHPROP**	Change thickness of all walls to 8'.
Command: **CHPROP**	Change thickness of desks and tables to 30".
Command: **CHPROP**	Change thickness of all chairs to 18".
Command: **ZOOM**	Zoom Window 16',13' to 34',26' (see fig. 16.4).

After you zoom, you should see the lower left room of the floor plan, with a primitive chair and table in the center of the room. You should be in the WCS with the UCS icon showing in the lower left corner of your screen. You won't see the thickness of the extrusions until you do your first dynamic view.

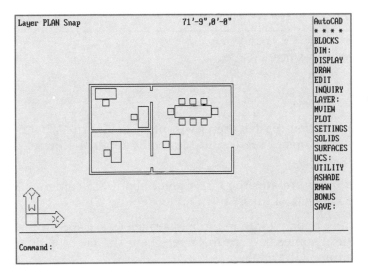

Figure 16.3:
The office with primitive tables and chairs.

The DVIEW Command

DVIEW is a complex command with twelve options, but it is easy to use once you learn them. DVIEW asks for a selection set, then you set your point of view (camera) and the focus (target) point of view by picking or setting points. You can refine the view by zooming, panning, clipping, or hiding. When you have the view you want, you exit DVIEW and it regenerates the drawing from that viewpoint. DVIEW's default view is parallel projection; perspective is set with the Distance option.

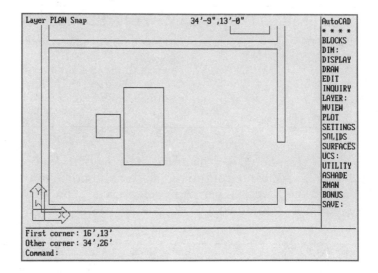

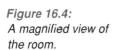

Figure 16.4:
A magnified view of
the room.

The options for controlling DVIEW are:

DVIEW Options

CAmera   The CAmera option rotates the viewpoint. It is like the VPOINT Rotate option, except CAmera rotates the viewpoint about the target point instead of about 0,0.

TArget   The TArget option rotates the target point about the camera viewpoint. This is the opposite of the CAmera option.

Distance   The Distance option switches from parallel to perspective view and changes the distance camera to target along the current line of sight without changing the angle.

POints   The POints option sets the camera position (viewpoint) and target point. These are the points you are looking from and to.

PAn   The PAn option moves both the camera and target points, parallel to the current view plane. Both points change but their angles and distance don't.

Zoom   The Zoom option zooms in and out on the image without changing perspective.

TWist   The TWist option rotates the image about the line of sight. You can even turn it upside down.

CLip   The CLip option removes foreground or background objects from the image, as if sliced off by a giant knife.

Hide   The Hide option performs a temporary hidden line removal in the DVIEW command. The image is regenerated when you exit DVIEW.

Off   The Off option turns off perspective mode and returns to parallel projection.

Undo   The Undo option undoes the other options.

eXit   The eXit option exits back to the AutoCAD command prompt and regenerates all drawing entities except portions that are clipped or outside of the current DVIEW view. If in perspective mode, it regenerates in perspective.

Note: You can't use transparent commands or flip screen when you are in DVIEW; however, you can use toggles such as snap, ortho, and coords. You can't use ZOOM, PAN, SKETCH, or pick points from a perspective generated by DVIEW.

Setting a Line-of-Sight View With Points

Try setting your first DVIEW with the POints option. Select the entire room to view. Then set the camera position in the upper left corner of the room at approximately eye level, looking at a target point on the center of the table top. Locate the target point first, then the camera point with XYZ point filters. After you pick the target point, you'll see a rubber-band line from the target point to the camera point to help you visualize the line of sight. Figure 16.5 shows your screen after you input the points. Figure 16.6 shows what you'll see when you exit DVIEW.

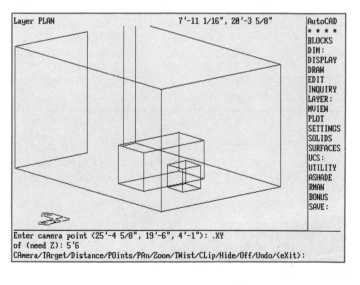

Figure 16.5:
The DVIEW screen after point selection.

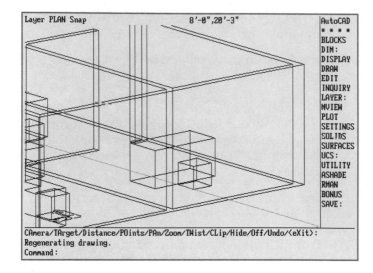

Figure 16.6:
Offices viewed from
the corner of the
room.

Using Points to Set the DVIEW Camera Line of Sight

```
Command: DVIEW
Select objects:                               Use Window to select room
                                              and contents.

CAmera/TArget/Distance/POints/PAn/Zoom/
   TWist/CLip/Hide/Off/Undo/<eXit>: PO
Enter target point <26'-5 1/8", 19'-6", 4'-0">: .XY
of                                            Pick point in middle of table
                                              top with XY point filter.
(need Z): 3'6
Enter camera point <26'-5 1/8", 19'-6", 4'-1">: .XY
of                                            Pick upper left corner of
                                              room with XY point filter.
(need Z): 5'6                                 About eye level.
CAmera/TArget/Distance/POints/PAn/Zoom/
   TWist/CLip/Hide/Off/Undo/<eXit>: <RETURN>
```

Your screen regenerates when you exit DVIEW. It should show a view of the table, with the office doorway in the left background. The table and chairs are primitive, but you get the idea. (Some of our local office wags refer to this drawing as Fred Flintstone's office.)

> ***Tip:*** DVIEW automatically turns snap off, but you can toggle it back on for snapping to points with <F9> or <^B>. You can also use osnap overrides to pick points.

> **Note:** Your default target and camera points that DVIEW prompts with, as well as other default values and your pick points, will vary from ours. The exact defaults and points depend on your display and on the locations of your tables and chairs.

DVIEW's Undo Option

Like other complex commands, DVIEW has an Undo option to step back through the settings, angles, and point changes made during the current DVIEW command. If you have exited DVIEW, you can use the UNDO command to undo an entire DVIEW operation.

The DVIEW House Icon

If you press <RETURN> in response to the DVIEW object selection prompt instead of selecting objects, you will see a 3D *house* icon to orient you in space during DVIEW. As you adjust your DVIEW settings, the house icon dynamically moves. When you exit DVIEW, your drawing regenerates with the icon's latest viewpoint. You can customize the icon by defining a block named DVIEWBLOCK. DVIEW scales the icon to fit your drawing and aligns it to the axes of your current UCS, so create your block as a 1 x 1 x 1 unit block aligned with the X,Y,Z axes, with an origin point at the front lower left corner. Using an icon block instead of selecting complex objects makes DVIEW quick and efficient.

> **Tip:** Create an easily recognizable DVIEW block with a unique top, bottom, left, right, front, and back side to help your visual orientation. Keep the block simple so it will drag efficiently in DVIEW.

Changing the Camera Location

The CAmera option rotates your point of view about the target point. The CAmera option is like the VPOINT Rotate option, except the order of the angle prompts is reversed. The first CAmera prompt asks for the angle from the X,Y plane. This angle rotates the camera up and down. The second prompt asks for the angle from the X axis (in the X,Y plane). This angle moves the camera from side to side. You can input the angles from the keyboard or drag and pick them with *slider bars*. The slider bar for the angle from the X,Y plane appears at the right of your screen, the slider for the angle in the X,Y plane appears at the top.

> **Note:** The angles in DVIEW are always in the WCS unless you set the WORLDVIEW system variable to 0. If you have a UCS current and WORLDVIEW is 1 (the default), AutoCAD switches to the WCS during DVIEW, then switches back to the UCS. A camera angle of 0 from the X,Y plane looks edge-on to the UCS or WCS construction plane.

Try the CAmera option, changing the angle in the X,Y plane to a view from the lower left corner of the room looking back at the table. The office doorway will appear on the right. Leave the angle above the X,Y plane unchanged.

Using CAmera Option to Locate DVIEW Camera

```
Command: DVIEW
Select objects:                            Use Previous to select walls of
                                           room, table, and chair.

CAmera/TArget/Distance/POints/PAn/Zoom/
   TWist/CLip/Hide/Off/Undo/<eXit>: CA
Enter angle from X-Y plane <14.36>: <RETURN>    Keep the current angle.
Enter angle in X-Y plane from X axis
   <141.95>: -135                          Type, or drag and pick approx.
                                           angle with slider bar (see fig.
                                           16.7).

CAmera/TArget/Distance/POints/PAn/Zoom/
   TWist/CLip/Hide/Off/Undo/<eXit>: X
```

As you move the slider bar, AutoCAD updates an angle display on the status line in place of the coordinates display. The resulting view appears in figure 16.8.

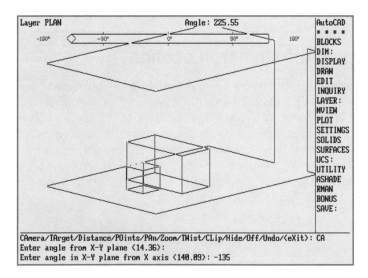

Figure 16.7:
The DVIEW screen during camera selection.

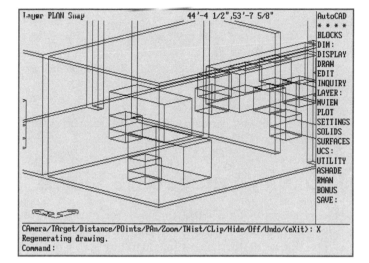

Figure 16.8:
The camera moved to
the lower left corner.

Note: When you select an option that uses slider bars, the initial image depends on your current cursor location. Our illustrations show the cursor and slider at their current default positions.

How to Use Slider Bars

Typed input is good for accuracy, but slider bars are better for getting the right image without trial and error. The right side slider bar goes from 90 degrees (plan view) to -90 degrees (upside-down plan). The top slider bar goes from -180 degrees (on the left) to 180 degrees. At 0 degrees, you are looking along the X axis. To pick from the bar, move your cursor along it until you get the angle (and view) that you want, then pick. As you move your cursor, you'll see rubber-band lines tracking from the current setting to a moving diamond at your pending setting. AutoCAD updates the angle display and the image as you move your cursor. Similar slider bars are provided for other settings, such as distances. The disadvantage to slider bars is that precise values are hard to pick.

Tip: For precise angles, use snap, or use the sliders to approximate the angle, then type in an exact value.

> *Tip:* DVIEW turns snap off. If you toggle it back on, the angle slider bar moves in a snap increment, but it varies with the axis and with your display. For EGA and VGA displays, a snap setting of .005556 moves the right slider in one-degree increments and for EGA, a snap setting of .0044562 moves the top slider in one-degree increments. You can find the settings for your display by trial and error.

If you want to play with the slider bar, try moving the camera around. When you are done, undo to return the camera to -135 degrees.

Setting a Distance for Perspective Views

You switch from parallel to perspective view with the Distance option. AutoCAD will prompt you for a new distance from the camera to the target, with your current distance as the default. The line of sight will remain unchanged. You can enter a distance or use the top slider bar. The slider values range from 0X (on the left) to 16X (on the right). 1X is your current distance factor. Moving to the right is farther away from the target; 2X is twice the distance. You will see a continuous update of your distance on the status line. Remember, the default prompt and status lines show the distance, but the slider is a multiplication factor, not a distance.

When you select the Distance option, you will also see your UCS icon replaced with a perspective icon (a small cube) in the lower left corner of your screen. This is a reminder that you are in perspective mode. To turn perspective off, use the DVIEW Off option.

Try setting a new camera/target distance to get a perspective view. The current distance is about seven or eight feet. First, press <RETURN> to default the distance so you can see the table in perspective at the current distance. Then, increase the distance to about 19 feet (about 2.7X). When done, use VIEW to save it as a named view so that you can return to it later.

Using Distance Option to Create a Perspective View

```
Command: DVIEW
Select objects:                          Use Previous to select walls of
                                         room, table, and chair.

CAmera/TArget/Distance/POints/PAn/Zoom/
  TWist/CLip/Hide/Off/Undo/<eXit>: D
New camera/target distance <8<|>'-0 13/16">:
    <RETURN>                             Your screen should resemble
                                         figure 16.9.

CAmera/TArget/Distance/POints/PAn/Zoom/
  TWist/CLip/Hide/Off/Undo/<eXit>: D
```

> ### Using Distance Option to Create a Perspective View—continued
>
> ```
> New camera/target distance <8<|>'-0 13/16">: 19'
> ```
> Type or select approximate distance. Your screen should resemble figure 16.10.
>
> ```
> CAmera/TArget/Distance/POints/PAn/Zoom/
>   TWist/CLip/Hide/Off/Undo/<eXit>: X
> Command: VIEW
> ```
> Save the view with name OFFICE1.
>
> ```
> Command: SAVE
> ```
> Save and continue, or end and take a break.

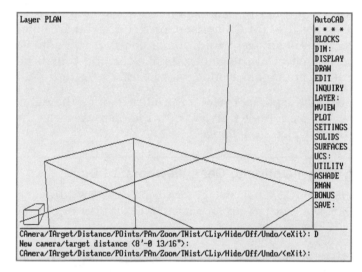

Figure 16.9:
The table at a distance of 8<|>'-0 13/16".

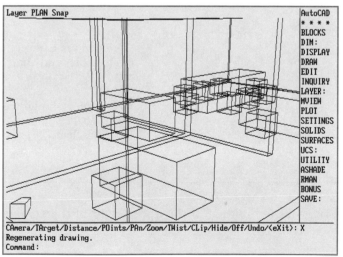

Figure 16.10:
The table at a distance of 19<|>'-0".

Changing the distance changes the perspective. You can magnify an image with the Zoom option without changing distance. Zoom acts like switching or zooming a camera lens. Once you are in perspective, the POints, CAmera, and Target options can also be used to change the perspective by changing points.

In the next section, leave perspective on and change the target point.

Rotating the View With the TArget Option

One frustration of the VPOINT command is that it always looks at the WCS origin point. But, DVIEW's POints and TArget options allow you to move the target point. The TArget option prompts are similar to the CAmera prompts. The first prompt is for a new angle from the X,Y plane, the second for a new angle in the X,Y plane from the X axis. The effect is opposite of the CAmera option's effect; you are changing the target's angles relative to your vantage point (camera point). If you adjust only the angle in the X,Y plane, the effect at the camera is like turning your head to look around the room (or rotating the room around your head).

Use the TArget option to aim the point of view at the office door on the right. Change the target angle in the X,Y plane to get a view with the doorway near the center. Leave the angle from the X,Y plane unchanged.

Using TArget Option to Get a Viewpoint of Door

 Continue in the OFFICE3D drawing, or begin a NEW drawing named OFFICE3D=IA6OFF3D, replacing your previous OFFICE3D drawing. Then use VIEW to restore the OFFICE1 view.

 Continue in the OFFICE3D drawing, or reload it and use VIEW to restore the OFFICE1 view.

```
Command: DVIEW
Select objects:                              Use Previous to select walls of
                                             room, table, and chair.

CAmera/TArget/Distance/POints/PAn/Zoom/
  TWist/CLip/Hide/Off/Undo/<eXit>: TA
Enter angle from X-Y plane <-14.36>: <RETURN>   Your screen should resemble
                                                figure 16.11.
Enter angle in X-Y plane from X axis <45.00>: 22   Type or select.
CAmera/TArget/Distance/POints/PAn/Zoom/
  TWist/CLip/Hide/Off/Undo/<eXit>: X
```

You should see the corner of the building in the upper right of the screen (see fig. 16.12).

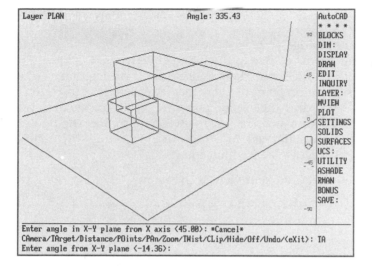

Figure 16.11:
The DVIEW target option with slider.

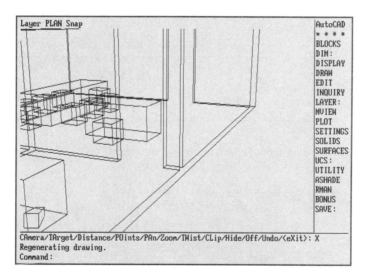

Figure 16.12:
The room with a new target.

Selection Sets and Dragging in DVIEW

As you adjust these perspective images, you'll get a feel for your system's performance in updating DVIEW's preview image. Complex images slow the responsiveness. If your entities are extremely complex (with 3Dmeshes), you may not get a fully formed preview. The solution is to select only enough entities to orient you in the drawing while you are in DVIEW. Remember, the whole drawing will be regenerated with the view when you exit DVIEW.

Using the PAn Option to Center the Room View

The PAn option lets you change your view by moving the camera and target point side to side and up and down relative to the plane of your current view. The target and camera points both change, but their angles and distance don't. You pan by picking a base point and second point to show the displacement. AutoCAD dynamically drags the image as you drag the second point. In parallel projection, this is just like the effect of the PAN command. The entire image shifts, but the relative visual positions of objects remain unchanged. In perspective projection, the relative visual positions shift in the perspective as the image pans.

Try centering the table in your current view of the room.

Centering the Room With PAn

```
Command: DVIEW
Select objects:                              Use Previous to select walls of
                                             room, table, and chair.

CAmera/TArget/Distance/POints/PAn/Zoom/
   TWist/CLip/Hide/Off/Undo/<eXit>: PA
Displacement base point:                     Pick any point near the table.
Second point:                                Drag table to center of screen
                                             and pick.

CAmera/TArget/Distance/POints/PAn/Zoom/
   TWist/CLip/Hide/Off/Undo/<eXit>: <RETURN>
```

You should have a perspective view with the table centered in the room (see fig. 16.13).

Figure 16.13:
Panned to the center
of the room.

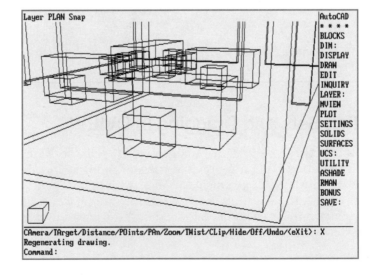

> **Tip:** Sometimes it is difficult to have the perspective view pan to fill the screen. But you should be able to achieve the effect you want by using a combination of PAn and Distance. For example, first use PAn to center your view on the screen, then use the Distance slider bar or try entering different distances to get the view you want.

Organizing Your Views

After all the trouble of setting up perfect perspectives, it would be nice if you could save and later restore them. You can, with the VIEW command. In the Distance option exercise, we saved the original perspective view as a view named OFFICE1. We'll use VIEW to restore it in the next exercise. VIEW can name and save perspective views just like normal views. VIEW Save stores all of the current DVIEW settings so you can go about your work and later use VIEW Restore to return your perspective to the current viewport.

You can also save a collection of views including perspectives in multiple viewports. You use the VPORTS Save option in Release 10 or model space, or the block technique to save paper space viewports. See Chapter 4 for details.

Previewing Hidden Line Removal With the Hide Option

DVIEW's Hide option has two purposes. The first is to check your clipping settings while you are in DVIEW. (We'll do clipping in the next section.) The second is to preview a selection of objects and get the view you want before doing a time-consuming complete hidden line removal. DVIEW Hide works like the HIDE command, except you see the hide in perspective. However, DVIEW Hide is temporary and affects only the entities selected. Exiting DVIEW regenerates the drawing without the hide. To hide the full drawing, use the HIDE command.

We want to work with the original perspective view that you saved as the OFFICE1 view, so use VIEW to restore it. Then, try the Hide option.

Using DVIEW's Hide

```
Command: VIEW                              Restore view OFFICE1 (see fig.
                                           16.14).

Command: DVIEW
Select objects:                            Use Previous to select walls of
                                           room, table, and chair.

CAmera/TArget/Distance/POints/PAn/Zoom/
  TWist/CLip/Hide/Off/Undo/<eXit>: H
CAmera/TArget/Distance/POints/PAn/Zoom/
  TWist/CLip/Hide/Off/Undo/<eXit>: <RETURN>
```

Now, that gives new meaning to hide: as figure 16.15 shows, you can't see anything but the nearest corner of the wall! Let's clip it away to see what's inside.

Figure 16.14:
The original
perspective restored.

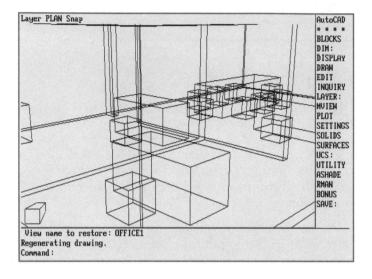

Figure 16.15:
The completely
hidden DVIEW
perspective.

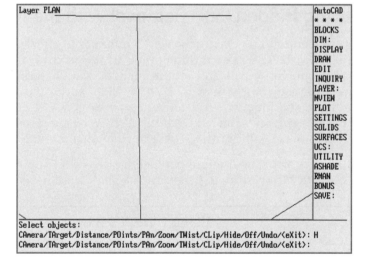

Using DVIEW to Clip Away Obstructions

When you hid the office, the two walls forming the nearest corner obstructed your view. To present your drawing, you often need to show what is behind the foreground objects. As you work in complex 3D wireframes, you also need a way to get foreground or background objects that clutter the image out of your way. The DVIEW CLip option lets you place a front and a back clipping plane (or both) to get these effects. A back clipping plane obscures everything behind it; a front plane removes everything in front of it from your view. Clipping works in both parallel and perspective projection.

Clipping planes are perpendicular to the line of sight between the camera and the target. You place clipping planes by specifying their distances from the target. A positive distance puts the plane between the target and the camera (or behind the camera), while a negative distance puts it beyond the target. You can also set the front clipping plane to be at the camera with the CLip Front Eye option sequence. The CLip option gives you a Back/Front/<Off> prompt, which you use to set the back or front clipping distances, or turn clipping off. Off turns both planes off, but the Back option also has an independent on/off option to control it.

If you paid close attention to the first perspective before you set the camera-to-target distance to 19 feet, you may have noticed the front plane clipping effect. When you switch perspective mode on, it turns the front clip on and defaults its location to the current camera position (like the Eye option).

Try clipping the nearest corner and background. Put your front clipping plane at about two and a half feet from the target. Then, try Hide again for an unobstructed view of Flintstone's table and chair. Before exiting DVIEW to see the full drawing, set the back clipping plane at about minus 10 feet (just beyond the room) to clip out the background clutter. Then you can try a SHADE or HIDE command.

Using CLip to See Into the Room and Remove Background Clutter

Command: **DVIEW**	
Select objects:	Use Previous to select walls of room, table, and chair.
CAmera/TArget/Distance/POints/PAn/Zoom/ TWist/CLip/Hide/Off/Undo/<eXit>: **CL**	
Back/Front/<Off>: **F**	
Eye/<Distance from target> <19'-0">: **2'8**	See figure 16.16.

Now try the Hide option again. You'll see into the room this time.

CAmera/TArget/Distance/POints/PAn/Zoom/ TWist/CLip/Hide/Off/Undo/<eXit>: **H**	See figure 16.17.
CAmera/TArget/Distance/POints/PAn/Zoom/ TWist/CLip/Hide/Off/Undo/<eXit>: **CL**	
Back/Front/<Off>: **B**	Now try a Back clip. B turns the back plane on.
ON/OFF/<Distance from target> <4'-0">:	Move slider bar to see the clipping move forward and back. Position it just beyond the back corner at about -10' and pick. See figure 16.18.
CAmera/TArget/Distance/POints/PAn/Zoom/ TWist/CLip/Hide/Off/Undo/<eXit>: **X**	
Command: **SHADE**	See figure 16.19.

Figure 16.16:
During DVIEW with front clipping to see into a room.

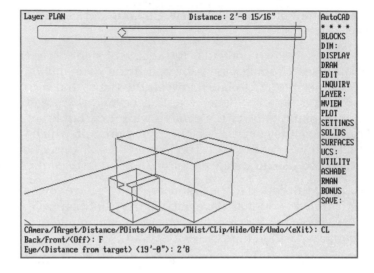

Figure 16.17:
Hide with the nearest corner clipped.

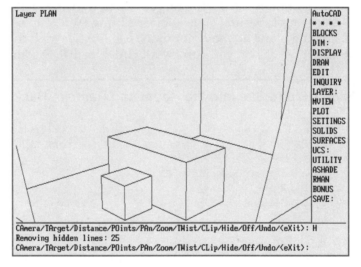

Now you can see what you want to present, and working in the drawing is easier because most of the extraneous background clutter is gone. A little clutter remains in front of the back clipping plane.

> **Note:** In simple drawings like this, HIDE is faster than SHADE, but in complex drawings, SHADE is much quicker.

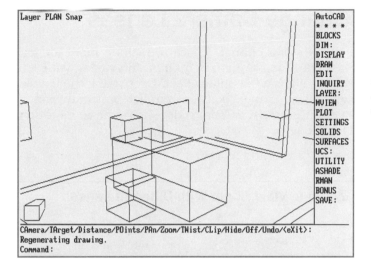

Figure 16.18:
Regenerated with the front and background clipped.

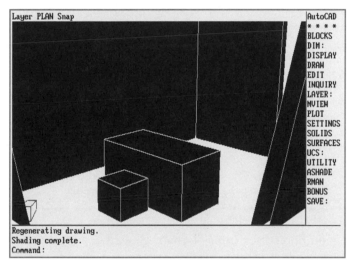

Figure 16.19:
The clipped room with SHADE.

Note: Watch your clipping values! They remain in effect when you exit DVIEW. If you think you've suddenly lost portions of your drawing, you probably left clipping on. If so, turn DVIEW CLip off.

You can't use the ZOOM command in a perspective view, but as we mentioned earlier, you can use DVIEW to change your field of view.

Zooming to Change Camera Lenses

The DVIEW Zoom option lets you change lenses to include more (or less) of the image in your view. The default lens length is 50 mm. Increasing your lens length (105 mm in the next exercise) has a telephoto effect. Decreasing the lens length (35 mm) gives a wide angle effect. Using Zoom on parallel projection acts just like AutoCAD's standard ZOOM Center. The Zoom slider shows the zoom ratio while the status line shows the lens length.

Use your current view to try switching lenses.

Using Zoom to View Room With Different Lenses

```
Command: DVIEW
Select objects:                              Use Previous to select walls,
                                             table, and chair.

CAmera/TArget/Distance/POints/PAn/Zoom/
   TWist/CLip/Hide/Off/Undo/<eXit>: Z
```

Try dragging the slider to see that the perspective doesn't change, only the image scale.

```
Adjust lens length <50.000mm>: 105           Try a telephoto lens (see fig.
                                             16.20).

CAmera/TArget/Distance/POints/PAn/Zoom/
   TWist/CLip/Hide/Off/Undo/<eXit>: Z
Adjust lens length <105.000mm>: 35           Try a wide angle lens (see fig.
                                             16.21).

CAmera/TArget/Distance/POints/PAn/Zoom/
   TWist/CLip/Hide/Off/Undo/<eXit>: X
Command: VIEW                                Save as OFFICE2.
Command: SAVE                                Save and continue, or end and
                                             take a break.
```

The 35mm lens is a good choice for interior room views because its wider angle encompasses more of the room.

Contrary to popular belief, the lens length does not affect perspective. Only the distance and angle from camera to target determine perspective. The lens length only determines the width of the view. Many people think lens length affects perspective because wide angle (short) lenses coincidentally tend to be used for close distances and telephoto (long) lenses are used for distant subjects. Unlike real lenses (especially very short fish-eyes), AutoCAD's lenses are perfect with no distortion. They always yield a geometrically true perspective.

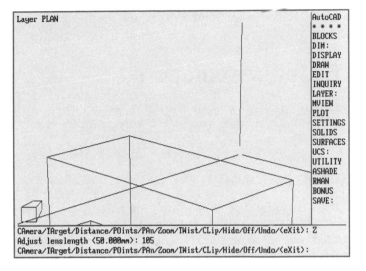

Figure 16.20:
View with a 105 mm lens.

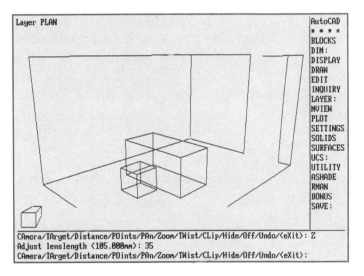

Figure 16.21:
View with a 35 mm lens.

TWist, the Other Option

DVIEW has one more option, called TWist. As its name implies, TWist lets you rotate your view *around* your line of sight by specifying an angle. TWist uses the right-hand rule of rotation, so a positive angle is counterclockwise. If you try a twist, you can see how easy it is to turn the room upside down. If you try it, undo to restore the current view.

As you develop a set of views, you may want to capture them as slides for later reference or presentation.

Making a 3D Slide Presentation

Slides have been the mainstay for AutoCAD presentations since their early use in computer shows. When you make a slide, you save a screen image that AutoCAD can quickly recreate on the screen.

Using MSLIDE to Make a Slide

The MSLIDE (Make SLIDE) command creates a disk file with the extension .SLD. AutoCAD does not store all the drawing file information in the .SLD file. It only stores the display vector list and colors needed to paint the screen quickly. AutoCAD cannot edit slides. If you want to change a slide, you must first edit the drawing file that was used to create the slide, then create a new one.

Try making a slide of your current office view. You must be exited from DVIEW and use HIDE or SHADE to get a hidden or shaded view. Then use MSLIDE to make a slide named VIEW-1.

Using MSLIDE to Create a Slide of the Office

 Continue in the OFFICE3D drawing, or begin a NEW drawing named OFFICE3D=IA6OFF3D, replacing your previous OFFICE3D drawing. Then use VIEW to restore the OFFICE2 view.

Continue in the OFFICE3D drawing, or reload it and use VIEW to restore the OFFICE2 view.

Command: **HIDE**	(Release 10 only, use HIDE before creating the slide.)
Command: **SHADEDGE**	Release 11 only: set to 2 to simulate HIDE.
Command: **SHADE**	Release 11 only: use SHADE before creating the slide (see fig. 16.22).

```
Command: MSLIDE
Slide file <OFFICE3D>: VIEW-1
```

Your image is now stored on disk as VIEW-1.SLD.

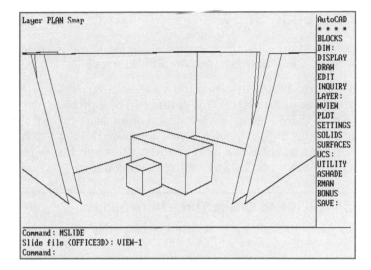

Figure 16.22:
View of the office for slide.

Using VSLIDE to Display a Slide

The VSLIDE (View SLIDE) command recalls the .SLD file from the disk and displays the slide image. When you display a slide, it temporarily takes over the screen. It leaves whatever you were working on intact and active, but invisible.

To see how this works, put a plan view (WCS) of the office back on your screen, then display the VIEW-1 slide.

Using VSLIDE to View the Slide	
Command: **PLAN**	Go to the WCS plan view.
Command: **VSLIDE**	Display the slide, the same image as shown in figure 16.22.
Slide file <OFFICE3D>: **VIEW-1**	
Command: **REDRAW**	Redraw removes the slide.

After you redraw the screen, you should be back in plan view.

Note: Slides appear over your actual drawing. Any attempt at drawing or editing the slide will actually wind up on the drawing which is obscured by the slide.

Tip: Use a viewport to display a slide for reference while you work in another viewport.

Making Slides for a Slide Show

Next, we want to produce a slide show, but we need at least three more slides. (A slide show with one slide isn't enough, even for the Flintstones!)

Create three more perspective views, and make a slide of each. These next three views will take you around the office plan. VIEW-2 and VIEW-3 provide two views of the large room on the right. VIEW-4 gives a view of the office with two tables in the upper left. Use the exact values shown because we'll compare these DVIEW images to corresponding AutoShade images in the next chapter. After you have created the slides, end the drawing and exit AutoCAD to create a script file.

Using MSLIDE to Create Three More Slides

Command: **DVIEW**   Select representative sampling of walls, tables, and chairs.
Use CLip off to turn clipping off.
Use POints to set target to 33',33',2' and camera to 51'6,21'6,5'6 for VIEW-2 slide.
Use Distance and accept default to turn on perspective.
Use Zoom to set lens to 35mm, then exit.

Command: **HIDE**   Or use SHADE before creating the slide.

Command: **MSLIDE**   Make slide with name VIEW-2 (see fig. 16.23).

Command: **DVIEW**   Select Previous objects and use POints to set VIEW-3 target to 52',35'6,0' and camera to 33',14'6,6', then exit. Perspective and lens remain set.

Do SHADE or HIDE and make slide with name VIEW-3 (see fig. 16.24).

Command: **DVIEW**   Select Previous objects and use POints to set VIEW-4 target to 38',33'6,0' and camera to 17'6,25',6', then exit.

Do SHADE or HIDE and make slide with name VIEW-4 (see fig. 16.25).

Command: **PLAN**   Return to WCS plan view of office.

Command: **ZOOM**   Zoom All.

Command: **END**   End drawing and exit AutoCAD to create script.

You have the slides. Now, how do you make a script?

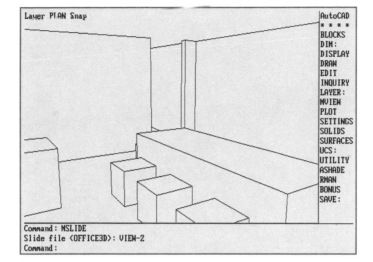

Figure 16.23:
Slide VIEW-2.

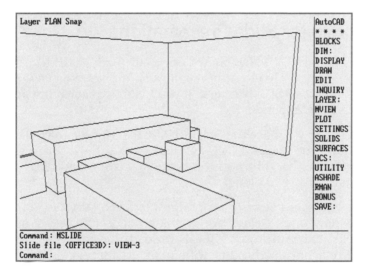

Figure 16.24:
Slide VIEW-3.

Automating Slide Shows With Script Files

SCRIPT is a utility command for hands-free operation. A script file is a listing of commands, input, and responses that is stored in a text file and *played* character for character exactly as if it were typed directly at the keyboard. Like slides, scripts were designed for self-running demonstrations of AutoCAD at presentations and shows.

Figure 16.25:
Slide VIEW-4.

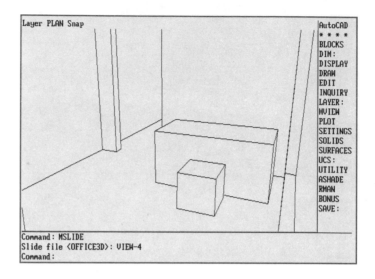

Making a Script File for Slide Presentations

Scripts were designed to control VSLIDE shows. Script files are ASCII text files and have an .SCR extension. In order to create or modify a script, you need a text editor or word processor that creates ASCII text files. If you need help selecting or setting up a suitable text editor, see Appendix B.

If you are using the IA DISK, you have the SLIDSHO.SCR script file to run the four-slide show. If you do not have the IA DISK, you can create the script with a text editor. Type it in exactly as it is shown in the next exercise. If you don't want to create the script, you can just read along.

The SCRIPT command loads and starts a script. Scripts use a DELAY command to control each slide's display time. Delays are in milliseconds (2000 is 2 seconds). Scripts can use a preloading feature of VSLIDE to load the next slide while the current one displays. Prefacing a slide name with an asterisk preloads it to shorten any time gap between slides. There is also an RSCRIPT command which repeats a script.

The SLIDSHO.SCR script (below) controls the display of the slides, VIEW-1 through VIEW-4, by stringing together a series of VSLIDE and DELAY commands. The final RSCRIPT command loops the script to start over. After you create the file, move on to the next exercise to run it.

Creating a Script for a Slide Show

 You have SLIDSHO.SCR. Look at it if you like, then test it in the next exercise.

Create the SLIDSHO.SCR text file, then test it in the next exercise.

`C:\IA-ACAD>NE SLIDSHO.SCR`   NE starts our editor, Norton's Editor. Use *your* editor to create or look at SLIDSHO.SCR. Don't use tabs or any trailing spaces. Use a <RETURN> to end the last line.

Enter the following:
```
vslide view-1
vslide *view-2
delay 2000
vslide
vslide *view-3
delay 2000
vslide
vslide *view-4
delay 2000
vslide
delay 2000
rscript
```
Save SLIDSHO.SCR and exit your editor.

Other Uses for Scripts

Scripts can do other things besides run slide shows. Scripts offer three unique advantages. First, you can run them outside the drawing editor from the operating system prompt. Second, they can end a drawing, run through the main menu, the configuration menu, the plot or printer plot dialogues, and go back into a drawing. The third advantage is that scripts can loop indefinitely. Scripts are sometimes used to modify or plot a batch of drawing files. See Chapter 10 on plotting for details.

Using SCRIPT to Run a Slide Show

You now have a script for AutoCAD's SCRIPT command to run. Get back into AutoCAD and load your OFFICE3D drawing (or any drawing). Run the script, sit back, and enjoy the slide show. The slides will show on the screen, cycling through in sequence and repeating until you cancel the script with a backspace or <^C>.

Using SCRIPT to Run the Slide Show

Edit an EXISTING drawing named OFFICE3D (any drawing would do).

```
Command: SCRIPT
Script file <OFFICE3D>: SLIDSHO
```

`Command: vslide`	The script commands scroll by on the command line.
`Slide file <OFFICE3D>: view-1`	And the slides display.
`Command: delay Delay time in milliseconds: 2000`	Other script commands and slides appear on the screen.
`Command: rscript`	RSCRIPT repeats the script sequence.
`Command: vslide`	
`Slide file <OFFICE3D>: view-1`	
`Command: vslide`	
`Slide file <OFFICE3D>: *view-2`	
`Command: delay Delay time in milliseconds: 2000`	
`Command: vslide`	
`Command:`	Type <^C> to exit script.
`Command: QUIT`	Quit to discard any changes you may have made.

If a script has an error, it will stop and return to the command prompt. You can correct it with your text editor. Look for the error following the last command that executed correctly.

After you run the slide show, you can adjust the delay or slide name sequence to alter the show. If you want to show slides of your own, substitute your own names and extend the script by repeating the vslide *name*, delay, vslide pattern.

Stopping and Resuming Scripts

You can stop a script with <BACKSPACE> or <^C>. It will finish its current command and return to the command prompt. You can do some work and then pick up where you stopped the script by using the RESUME command.

Slide Library Files

Although slides were invented for presentations, they now have an important use as images for icon menus. To avoid cluttering your disk with dozens of slide files, you can group and store slides in slide library (.SLB) files.

To display a slide from a library, use the format *libraryname(slidename)* as the slide name in your script or with VSLIDE at the command prompt. When you display an icon menu, you are displaying slides from the standard ACAD.SLB slide library file.

Making a Slide Library File

You can create your own slide library files using AutoCAD's SLIDELIB.EXE program. Creating a slide library is a three-step process.

- Make all the needed slides.
- Create an ASCII text file (as an example call it SLDLIST.TXT), listing each slide name (without the .SLD extension) on a separate line. Do not include any extra <RETURN>s or <SPACE>s. Make sure that you <RETURN> after the last name.
- Run the SLIDELIB.EXE program to create a .SLB library file from your *slidelist*.TXT file and the listed slide files.

  Assuming that the slides and a slide list file named SLDLIST.TXT are in your current IA-ACAD directory, and that the SLIDELIB.EXE program is in the ACAD directory, the command line format to create a slide library named IA-LIB.SLB is:

  ```
  C:\IA-ACAD>\ACAD\SLIDELIB IA-LIB <SLDLIST.TXT
  ```

AutoFlix, the Low-Cost Animator

If you like slide shows, you should look into AutoFlix, another Autodesk program. AutoFlix can combine AutoCAD and AutoShade slides with text files and even simple musical notes to create a *movie*. AutoFlix includes AutoLISP programs to automate the production of slides and shaded images. It can even follow animation sequences. You can make the movies self-running or interactive. Interactive movies prompt the user for a choice and then branch to various movie subsections or even run external programs. AutoFlix requires an EGA (or VGA) standard video card. The AutoFlix program is *shareware*, meaning that you can copy and distribute it freely. But if you find AutoFlix useful, you are required to pay $35 to Autodesk for it.

If you are a member of CompuServe, you can download AutoFlix from the Autodesk Forum. It's available in a file called AFLIX.ARC in the Animation/Graphics section of the files library. AutoFlix is also included with the AutoShade program.

Using Autodesk Animator for Creating Presentations

Sometimes, putting together a group of slide files using AutoFlix or a script file isn't an impressive enough presentation. Maybe you need to add a splash of color, add text and titling, use special effects such as dissolves and wipes, or even add real character animation. For those times, Autodesk has another answer — Autodesk Animator.

Animator gives you all the features we just mentioned, and more. Animator can add color, special effects, and titles to your animation to achieve professional quality animated sequences.

In addition to AutoCAD slides and AutoShade rendering files, Animator can import GIF images. GIF is the popular graphic format standardized by CompuServe. With additional hardware, you can even incorporate videotaped sequences and photographs in your presentation and export presentations to videotape. For an in-depth look at Animator, see *INSIDE Autodesk Animator* from New Riders Publishing.

Drawing and editing commands work normally in parallel projection views created by VPOINT or DVIEW, with or without clipping. But drawing and editing are restricted in perspectives.

How to Edit, Annotate, and Plot Perspectives

How do you edit perspective drawings? The big limitation in perspective is not being able to pick points. Several commands do not allow entity selection in perspective because they *require* picking by point. These include BREAK, FILLET, CHAMFER, TRIM, EXTEND, the UCS Entity option, and DIM by entity picking, but you can still use these commands by typing coordinates or picking in other viewports. Normal object selection, including entity picking, still works with some exceptions.

The PAN, ZOOM, and SKETCH commands are not allowed in perspective. These commands will cancel themselves and AutoCAD will prompt, "This command may not be invoked in a perspective view." Instead of PAN and ZOOM, use DVIEW's PAn and Zoom options. These limitations are not severe, largely because you can easily use DVIEW in multiple viewports.

Using Viewports to Work With Perspective Views

Rather than trying to work directly in a perspective view, we recommend using multiple viewports. Enter points in one while you observe your perspective in another. Any command that you execute in a normal viewport is reflected in the perspective viewport. As you modify your drawing, the perspective view updates to match the changes.

Let's set up three viewports and use one for a DVIEW perspective, another for editing in parallel projection, and a third for plan view editing. We'll do a HIDE in the perspective viewport because you can't select objects after the SHADE command.

Editing a Perspective in Viewports

 Continue in the OFFICE3D drawing, or begin a NEW drawing named OFFICE3D=IA6OFF3D, replacing your previous OFFICE3D drawing.

 Continue in the OFFICE3D drawing.

Command: **VIEW**	Restore the OFFICE2 view.
Command: **TILEMODE**	Release 11 only: set to 0 to enter paper space.

Editing a Perspective in Viewports—continued

Command: **MVIEW**	Set three viewports with Right default and Fit. (Release 10, use VPORTS.)
Command: **MSPACE**	Release 11 only.
Command: **HIDE**	Hide right viewport.
Command: **DVIEW**	Use Off option to return top left viewport to parallel view.
Command: **PLAN**	Set bottom left viewport plan to WCS.
Command: **ZOOM**	Zoom Center 25',20' with height 12' in bottom left viewport. Your screen should resemble figure 16.26.

Make right viewport current.

Command: **MOVE**

Select objects:	Select table and chair. Object selection works fine.
Base point or displacement:	Try to pick a point in perspective.
Pointing in perspective view not allowed here.	

Make upper left viewport current.

Base point or displacement:	Use osnap INT in top left viewport to pick right-most bottom corner of table.

Make lower left viewport current.

Second point of displacement:	Drag and pick in lower left viewport to place table in upper right corner.

As you dragged the table and chair in the lower left viewport, the images dragged with you in all viewports (see fig. 16.27). A REDRAW will clean up the upper left viewport, but the right viewport requires re-hiding. If the right viewport wasn't hidden to start with, a REDRAW would also clean it up.

Sooner or later, you will want to enhance or annotate a 3D perspective image.

Annotating and Plotting Perspective Drawings

You can plot a single perspective image by plotting the current viewport. What you see is what you get, except for any hides or shades. You can use the PLOT command's hidden line removal option if you like.

But you may want to plot the perspective on a sheet with a title or other images, or with annotations, or do a bit of rendering to it before plotting. Adding title text, annotations, or drawing a border around a perspective view is practically impossible in 3D. Placing 3D trees and shrubs around a building perspective is impractical and makes the drawing slow to regenerate. You need to turn the perspective view into a 2D representation that you can annotate and add rendering details to. Then you can use all of AutoCAD's commands to enhance the drawing. There are two practical ways to do this.

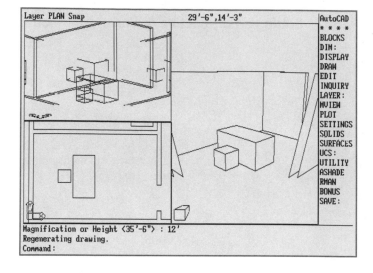

Figure 16.26:
The three viewports
before editing.

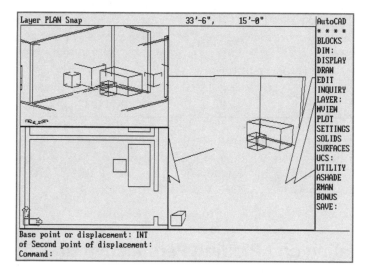

Figure 16.27:
The three viewports
after editing.

The best way to compose and annotate a perspective is to use paper space in Release
11. Treat a perspective view in a paper space viewport just like any other viewport.
You can add 2D annotation and other details to the view in paper space, and plot the
results. When you plot in paper space, the view(s) that are current at plot time,
parallel or perspective, clipped or not, are what get plotted. To have the plot remove
hidden lines in a particular viewport, select it with the MVIEW Hideplot option. See
Chapter 10 for details on composing and plotting in paper space.

With Release 10, you will have to plot your perspective to a DXB file. You can make
a 3D image into a 2D image by plotting to a DXB file and importing it into a 2D
drawing for annotation and subsequent plotting to a real plotter. Use the configura-

tion menu (main menu item 5) to reconfigure your plot device as an ADI plotter, and select AutoCAD DXB file as the output format. The rest of the plot parameters, plot scaling, and settings are the same as for a real plotter. Scale the plot to the size that you want in the final drawing. The drawing will be plotted to a file with the extension .DXB. The DXB file can then be imported into a new 2D drawing where you can add titles, annotation, and any kind of details you like. You use the DXBIN command to import it. When imported, it becomes a 2D image of the perspective made up of lots of little lines. Use any of AutoCAD's normal commands to edit it. When finished, plot the resulting drawing to a real plotter.

> **Note:** You can delete OFFICE.DWG, which you no longer need, but keep OFFICE3D.DWG for the next chapter.

Summing Up

Don't get carried away with 3D and perspectives. Use them for what you need, but 2D is simpler and quicker if 3D is not really required.

Here are some techniques for speed and efficiency when you use DVIEW:

- Use the DVIEW house icon (or your own custom icon) instead of selecting complex entities.
- Select a representative subset of entities to use in DVIEW.
- Use block redefinition, substituting simple blocks for complex ones until you get it right, then swapping them back for the final presentation images.
- Use osnaps and point filters to set points in DVIEW instead of using trial and error (unless in perspective). If you know where you want to look from (camera point) and what you want to look at (target point), then you can use osnaps and XYZ point filters to align them with known geometry. If setting perspectives, get the points ahead of time with the ID command.
- Use sliders for dynamic image adjustment, then type in exact values if you need precision in your views.
- Use named views to save and restore your perspectives and other DVIEW settings after you get them right.

AutoShade Is Next

You have created a series of 3D perspective views, but they don't represent the most realistic images that you can present of your drawings. Take one step further and create images with surface shading and lighting effects. The next chapter, on AutoShade, will show you how to create more realistic shaded images by rendering the same simple (and now familiar) office that you used in this chapter.

Figure 17.1:
The 3D shaded chair.

17

Inside AutoShade

ENHANCING 3D WITH SHADED RENDERINGS

The AutoShade program renders 3D AutoCAD drawings, letting you light and shade your images to achieve more realistic 3D effects. Renderings on a 256-color display are absolutely impressive. Using AutoShade's tools, you can adjust camera angles and set multiple light sources to bring your drawings to life. For example, just look at the shaded version of the chair you created in Chapter 15 (see fig. 17.1). Think of AutoShade as a photo studio for your AutoCAD drawings. Whether you just use AutoShade, or you also use RenderMan to add photorealistic textures and reflections, you'll impress your clients with improved presentations.

Scenes and Filmroll File

AutoShade runs as a program separate from AutoCAD. After you create your 3D drawings in AutoCAD, you pass the drawings to AutoShade via a filmroll file. AutoCAD creates the filmroll file, and AutoShade processes, displays, and prints the film.

The *scene* is the key element in the filmroll file. When you make a filmroll file, you *shoot* scenes in AutoCAD. A scene is made up of a 3D drawing, a camera, and one or more light sources. Making a scene is like setting up a real-world scene for a still or motion picture. In fact, the scene icon is a miniature clapper board just like you find on the movie set. When you create your scene in AutoCAD, you set your camera position, distance, angle, and lighting, then you execute the SCENE command. Think of a scene as an individual frame of film. You can create as many scenes as you like before developing your filmroll.

735

Assumptions About AutoShade

This chapter is designed to show you the interface between AutoShade and AutoCAD and to give you a feel for AutoShade's capabilities. The exercises are written as if you had AutoShade. However, if you don't have AutoShade yet, the exercises provide enough information so that you can follow along easily. The rendered illustrations speak for themselves!

Our emphasis is on the AutoCAD side of the AutoCAD-to-AutoShade interface. Since you don't create your 3D drawings in AutoShade, how you prepare your drawings in AutoCAD has a big impact on the appearance and efficiency of your AutoShade renderings. Seemingly slight differences between 2D or 3D commands, extruded 2D entities or 3D surfaces, and the order of entity creation in AutoCAD can make a big difference in the results you get in AutoShade. You set your cameras and lighting *within* AutoCAD before you pass the drawings to AutoShade. Using the 3D tools provided within AutoCAD and working out good lighting schemes are keys to creating efficient AutoShade-bound 3D drawings in AutoCAD.

> *Note:* The realism of your shaded images depends on the number of colors that AutoShade can use. Your display card may require an ADI driver for AutoShade to get 256 colors. See the manufacturer's instructions for details.

AutoShade Tools in AutoCAD

You will find the AutoShade tools that you need through the [ASHADE] menu item (see fig. 17.2) on the root screen menu. [ASHADE] loads a set of AutoLISP functions and calls a page of AutoShade menu items. They are [LIGHTS:], [CAMERA:], [AC-TION], and [CAMVIEW:]. The [ACTION] menu item calls a menu with the [SCENE:] and [FLMROLL:] menu items. You can also use an AutoShade icon menu accessed by the [AutoShade...] item on the [Utility] pull-down menu. Out of all these tools, only FILMROLL is an AutoCAD command. The rest (SCENE, LIGHT, CAMVIEW, and CAMERA) are defined in AutoLISP and can't be typed as commands until loaded. They are loaded by the [AutoShade...] pull-down and [ASHADE] screen menu selections, or you can enter (load "ASHADE") at the command prompt.

Setting Up for AutoShade

If you have AutoShade, we assume that AutoShade and its supporting files are installed in your AutoCAD directory. These supporting files include ASHADE.LSP,

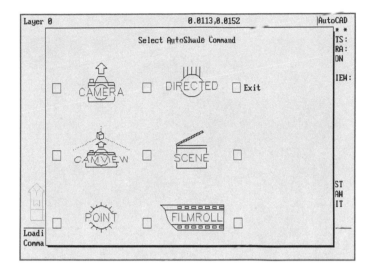

Layer 0   0.0113,0.0152 |AutoCAD
                          Select AutoShade Command   * *
                                                                        TS:
                                                                        RA:
                                                                        DN

              CAMERA   □ DIRECTED □ Exit   IEW:

              CAMVIEW   □ SCENE   □

                                                                        ST
                                                                        AW
                                                                        IT
              POINT   □ FILMROLL □
Loadi
Comma

Figure 17.2:
The AutoShade icon
menu.

the CAMERA.DWG camera block, the OVERHEAD.DWG and DIRECT.DWG light block drawings, and the CLAPPER.DWG and SHOT.DWG scene block drawings. We also assume you have gone through the *AutoShade User Guide* tutorial and can find your way around the AutoShade commands and menus. The exercises will not show every little step in AutoShade, but they do emphasize the major points. Key sequences are captured and shown in the illustrations.

Creating a Filmroll File

Before you can use AutoShade, you must have a drawing from which to create the filmroll file. The exercises in this chapter use the handy chair that you created in Chapter 15, and the handy (but humble) office that you worked with to get some dynamic views in Chapter 16.

Let's start with the chair and do a fast shade. To see your chair in AutoShade, you need to get into AutoCAD and create a filmroll file to pass into AutoShade. Load your CHAIR drawing from Chapter 15 (see fig. 17.3). If you do not have the CHAIR drawing but do have the IA DISK, you can quickly assemble the chair by doing the *Using Insert to Assemble the 3D Chair* exercise near the end of Chapter 15. Or, you can just read along and start with the office drawing in the *Preparing 3D Drawings for AutoShade* section. After you load your chair drawing, set VPOINT and use FILMROLL to create the chair filmroll file.

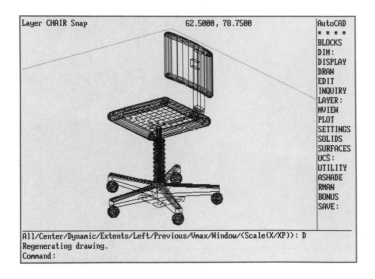

Figure 17.3:
The view of the chair
for AutoShade.

Creating a File With FILMROLL

Edit an EXISTING drawing named CHAIR from Chapter 15.

```
Command: VPOINT                              Set VPOINT to -.75,-1,.5.
Command: ZOOM                                Zoom Dynamic to fill screen.

Command: FILMROLL                            Make CHAIR.FLM.
Enter filmroll file name <CHAIR>: <RETURN>
Creating the filmroll file
Processing face: 257                         AutoCAD processes the filmroll.
                                             See note below.

Filmroll file created
Command: END                                 End drawing and exit AutoCAD.
```

Note: Early versions of Release 11 have a bug with polyfaces. The filmroll processing may pause for 2 to 20 minutes and create an unusable file that will crash AutoShade. If this happens, *insert the BASE block in a clear area, turn SPLFRAME on (1), regenerate, erase the polyface from the bottom of the hub, turn SPLFRAME off, and block the remaining entities to redefine the BASE block.

AutoCAD creates a filmroll file of all the objects in the drawing. AutoShade processes this file into rendered images. A filmroll can contain many different viewpoints, called scenes. Each scene gets rendered individually. This first chair exercise does not have any defined scenes, so your current AutoCAD viewpoint for the 3D drawing becomes the default viewpoint for the scene. You can use this approach to get a quick rendering of a 3D drawing to see how it will look before you commit to a full-blown filmroll with different camera positions and multiple light settings in several scenes.

Now let's go into AutoShade and use the Fast Shade option. We assume AutoShade is in the ACAD directory. Even a fast shade is a lengthy process. After you select the Fast Shade option, it can take from 15 seconds to 10 minutes for AutoShade to process the chair drawing, but read on with us while it processes.

Using Fast Shade

C:\IA-ACAD>**CD \ACAD**	Change to the ACAD directory.
C:\ACAD>**SHADE**	Get into AutoShade by typing SHADE.
Pull down **[File]**	
Select **[Open]**	AutoShade opens a Filmroll dialogue box displaying the current directory and filmroll files (see fig. 17.4).

Highlight box next to Directory and change to IA-ACAD directory, or click in the boxes to get to IA-ACAD in the directory list.

Select **[CHAIR]**	Click box next to CHAIR and CHAIR is displayed in the [File] box.
Select **[OK]**	Click the [OK] box or simply press <RETURN>.
Pull down **[Display]**	See figure 17.5.
Select **[Fast Shade]**	AutoShade processes the rendering.

Before the image is displayed, AutoShade displays the percentage of completion for each task it performs as it processes the rendering.

Pull down **[File]**
Select **[QUIT]**

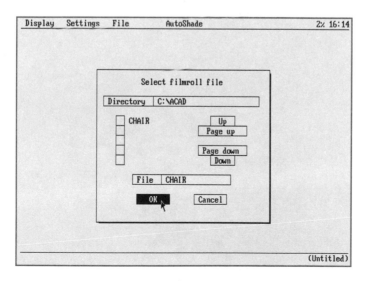

Figure 17.4:
The filmroll file dialogue box.

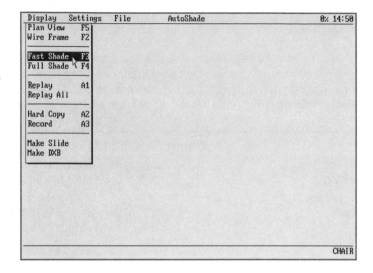

Figure 17.5:
The fast shade option on the [Display] pull-down menu.

Fast Shade gives a quick preview of the chair, showing the effects of the default (ambient) light and shading (see fig. 17.6). Fast Shade performs a rendering, but it does not check for overlapping faces. If you look closely at the screen image, you will see overlapping faces that give unusual shaded patches to the chair. The casters are showing through some of the legs and the back support appears to come out of the seat. The chair may also appear quite dark. This darkness is due to default lighting conditions assumed by AutoShade and the colors the chair was drawn in. Despite these limitations, Fast Shade gives you a quick check method for previewing a rendering. A Fast Shade is much quicker than a Full Shade (which we will explore a little later). A Full Shade checks for overlapping faces and will give a correct rendering, but it takes much longer to process.

Figure 17.6:
The first chair rendering.

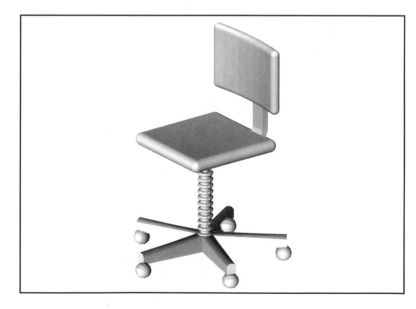

Note: Exit AutoShade in an emergency or apparent lockup by holding down the <ALT> key and typing CRASH. But don't assume it's locked up just because a complex drawing takes many hours to process.

Tip: When it becomes necessary to overlap or nest entities, small changes in Z values or thickness can control the final order and appearance of your image.

Preparing 3D Drawings for AutoShade

Any of AutoCAD's entities can be used in a 3D wireframe image drawing. However, AutoShade ignores all entities without surfaces or thickness. It only recognizes the following entities:

- Circles, solids, traces, donuts, and wide polylines
- 3Dfaces and 3D polyline meshes
- Extruded entities
- AME solids (which must be surfaced by SOLMESH)

Tip: Be careful when you construct 3Dfaces. In AutoShade, *front* faces obscure *back* faces. Faces whose vertexes are in a clockwise order from the current viewpoint are considered front faces, while counterclockwise faces are considered back faces. You can set UCS to Entity to check an existing face. If the Z axis points toward the camera, it's a front face. The MIRROR command will flip a face. The wrong order can create a rendering where the back faces obscure the front faces. The [Back norm is neg] check box on the Expert Specifications dialogue box of the [Settings] pull-down menu will reverse the order of the rendering if you get the wrong order.

If your shaded images have missing areas, they may have been created as wireframe lines, which AutoShade does not recognize. You need to go back and reconstruct your 3D drawing with extrusions or surfaces.

Sprucing Up the Drawn Image

AutoShade renders each face with a single shade of color, which may cause a large surface to look wrong when it is rendered. For example, a long wall receding away from your point of view should normally become darker as it recedes. However, since AutoShade applies a single shade of color, you can only get this shading effect by making the wall's surface out of many smaller faces. Try to anticipate the need for mesh surfaces where you want complex or graduated surface effects. You can control the number of faces on curved surfaces by adjusting VIEWRES and the surface system variables SURFTAB1, SURFTAB2, SURFU, and SURFV.

> **Tip:** Hatches can add texture to 3D drawings. The hatch must be exploded and given a small thickness. You can apply a small thickness to other entities like lines and points so they will be recognized by AutoShade.

Creating AutoShade-bound drawings will usually require more work and more entities to define objects with surfaces. The more faces you use in constructing your drawing, the better your AutoShade rendering will look. However, there is a trade-off. The more faces you have, the larger the drawing file will be, and both AutoCAD's and AutoShade's processing time will increase. For example, a Full Shade rendering of the chair drawing takes anywhere from one minute to three hours, depending on your hardware and version of AutoShade.

Using Perspective in AutoShade

AutoShade renders in perspective by default. Smaller objects may not display the perspective well. You can enhance perspective views and show relative scale by adding foreground and background objects in AutoCAD. In architectural scenes, these objects could be walls, trees, and vehicles. You can enhance mechanical drawings by adding contrasting surfaces in the background of the view. You will find that AutoShade's perspective works the same way as DVIEW within AutoCAD. In fact, the perspective tools for setting a target distance, camera, camera angle, and clipping were in AutoShade before they were added to AutoCAD. AutoShade has a few more capabilities than AutoCAD, such as side, top, and bottom clipping.

The rendered chair looks good, although it is floating in space. Let's move on to work with the office drawing. The remainder of the exercises will use the office drawing to show you how to control cameras and lighting in making shaded scenes. We will also show you how to prepare a presentation by running a series of AutoShade renderings with a script file. These perspective renderings will match the perspective view slides that you created with DVIEW.

Lights, Camera, and Action

Before you can get anything onto a roll of film, you need a camera and lights. You shoot a scene in AutoShade as you would with a camera. AutoShade provides a camera block, two types of light blocks, and AutoLISP-defined commands (in the ASHADE.LSP file) to establish scenes in your drawing. You place the camera and light blocks and name them with unique (attribute) names in your drawing. Once you have placed the camera and lights, you can create one or more scenes by inserting scene blocks. When you make your filmroll, all these scenes will be recorded for rendering in AutoShade. All the AutoShade blocks are automatically placed on a layer named ASHADE to help with your drawing organization.

Options for Making Scenes of the Office Drawing

You have two options for working with the office drawing. You can either work with the simple, rather primitive, office drawing from Chapter 16, or create a more realistic office by inserting the CHAIR drawing from Chapter 15 and the TABLE drawing from Chapter 14 into the corner office of the office drawing. The table and the chair contain a lot of faces and will require substantial processing time in AutoShade. If you don't want to tie up your workstation processing complex AutoShade images, we recommend that you use the simple office drawing to do the following exercises. Then, to create the more complex and realistically shaded images, you can come back later, substitute the complex table and chair, and redo the filmroll and rendering.

This is a good technique to remember: use a simple drawing to get your cameras, lights, and perspectives right, then substitute complex 3D objects for the final filmroll and renderings. Our exercise illustrations will show both the simple and complex drawings.

Using CAMERA to Place Cameras

We will create two scenes of the floor plan by placing two cameras in the drawing. To use a camera, you need to select a target point, locate the camera, and give the camera a name. You need to name the camera because you can have more than one camera in the drawing.

We'll point the first camera at the office chair and set it at about eye level. Point the second camera at the right corner of the room, also at eye level. The coordinates are given in the exercise sequence. Make sure that AutoCAD can find ASHADE.LSP and that the AutoShade blocks are in your ACAD directory.

You'll need the OFFICE3D drawing from Chapter 16. If you don't have the OFFICE3D drawing, you can quickly create it from the Chapter 13 OFFICE drawing by doing the *Setting Up the Dynamic View Office Drawing* exercise near the beginning of Chapter 16. If you have the IA DISK, you can use the IA6OFF3D drawing instead.

Using CAMERA to Locate a Camera for AutoShade

Get into AutoCAD.

     Begin a NEW drawing named OFIC-SHD=IA6OFF3D.

     Begin a NEW drawing named OFIC-SHD=OFFICE3D, using OFFICE3D from Chapter 16.

Using CAMERA to Locate a Camera for AutoShade—continued	
Command: **ZOOM**	Zoom lower left office with chair and table to fill screen (see fig. 17.7).
Select **[ASHADE]**	Select from screen menu, or [AutoShade...] from [Utility] pull-down menu.
Command: Loading ashade.lsp (v1.1)...loaded.	It's loading.
Command: **CAMERA**	Select or type CAMERA.
Enter camera name: **CAMERA1**	Your first camera.
Enter target point: **21'6,19'6,1'6**	Center of the chair seat.
Enter camera location: **17'6,14'6,5'6**	Lower left corner of the room.
Accept the defaults for the remaining prompts.	
Command: **CAMERA**	
Enter camera name: **CAMERA2**	Your second camera.
Enter target point: **32'6,14'6,0**	Lower right corner of the room.
Enter camera location: **17'6,24'6,5'6**	Upper left corner of the room.
Accept the defaults for the remaining prompts.	

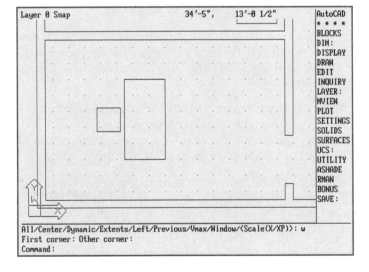

Figure 17.7:
The office room for shading.

When you finish selecting your locations and other parameters, a camera icon with the camera name appears at each location, directed toward the target point. The 5'-6" height in the Z axis places the camera at approximately eye level.

Using CAMVIEW to Check a Camera View

The icons are shown in plan view, so you can't really tell what you will see through the lens. The ASHADE.LSP file has another command called CAMVIEW. CAMVIEW is an AutoLISP-defined command that uses DVIEW to show you a wireframe view of what the camera will see in AutoShade. While you are still in AutoCAD, try the CAMVIEW command on CAMERA1.

Using CAMVIEW to Check a Camera View

Command: **CAMVIEW**	Select or just type.
Select the camera:	Pick camera one.
Command: **U**	Undo back to the plan view.
GROUP Regenerating drawing.	

Figure 17.8 shows the camera's view of the simple Flintstone chair and table. Figure 17.9 shows the 3D chair and drawing table.

Using CAMVIEW is like looking through a camera's viewfinder at your drawing. If you don't like the view, you can erase the camera and put in a new one. Alternatively, you can wait and position it in AutoShade, but we recommend using CAMVIEW to get a good starting view. Camera settings in AutoCAD are saved in the drawing and rendering files, but camera changes in AutoShade version 1.1 are temporary and not saved. AutoShade version 2.0, however, can write out your camera changes to a script file along with other changes that you will be making a little later. We'll discuss script files near the end of this chapter.

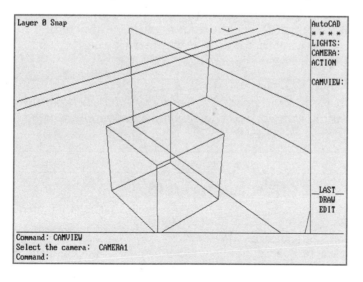

Figure 17.8:
The simple view through the lens of CAMERA1.

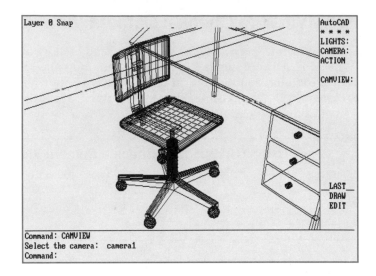

Figure 17.9:
The complex view
through the lens of
CAMERA1.

Using LIGHT to Set Lights

To design your lighting, AutoShade provides two types of light sources: point sources and directed lights. A point source is a light that radiates in all directions. A bare light bulb or an overhead light is a good example of a point source. A directed light provides parallel rays in a given direction. Think of directed light as light from a spotlight, a flashlight, or direct sunlight through a window. The sun is a point source in the scale of the solar system, but to objects on earth, it is directed.

You place lights the same way you place cameras. A light requires a location and a name. A direct source also needs an aim point. Place four lights in the drawing to represent an overhead light (point); a light from a window (directed); and a flash (directed) aimed from each camera towards the camera's target. Again, use the location values given in the exercise sequence.

Note: If you receive additional prompts from the LIGHT command, your ASHADE.LSP is compatible with AutoShade version 2.0. Simply accept the additional defaults offered.

Using LIGHT to Locate Lighting Types

Command: **LIGHT**	Type or select LIGHT from menu.
Enter light name: **POINT**	
Point source or Directed <P>: **<RETURN>**	
Enter light location: **26'0,19'6,10'0**	A ceiling light in the middle of the room.

Using LIGHT to Locate Lighting Types—continued

Accept the defaults for the remaining prompts.

```
Command: LIGHT
Enter light name: WINDOW
Point source or Directed <P>: D
Enter light aim point: 21'6,19'6,1'6        Middle of the chair seat.
Enter light location: 26'0,14'6,6'0         A window in the wall.
```

Accept the defaults for the remaining prompts.

```
Command: LIGHT
Enter light name: DIRECT1                    One flash.
Point source or Directed <P>: D
Enter light aim point: 21'6,19'6,1'6        Middle of the chair seat.
Enter light location: 17'6,16'6,6'0         Near CAMERA1.
```

Accept the defaults for the remaining prompts.

```
Command: LIGHT
Enter light name: DIRECT2                    The other flash.
Point source or Directed <P>: D
Enter light aim point: 32'6,14'6,6'0        Lower right corner of the room.
Enter light location: 17'6,23'0,6'0         Near CAMERA2.
```

Accept the defaults for the remaining prompts.

After you place the lights, the light icons appear with their names (see fig. 17.10). Each direct light source is pointing at its aim point.

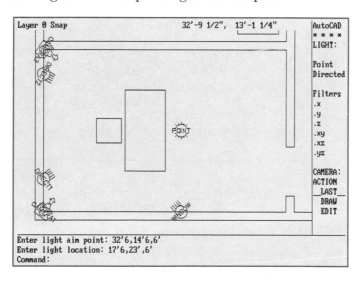

Figure 17.10:
An office with lights.

> **Tip:** Use XYZ point filters for camera and light placement.

> **Tip:** You can construct complex lights, like linear and fluorescent lights, by using many small lights. In AutoShade, you can adjust the intensity of each light, its color, and other parameters.

Action!

All that remains to do in AutoCAD is to group your cameras and lights into a scene. A scene consists of one camera and as many lights as you want. Try creating two scenes using the window and ceiling lights in both, and each camera's flash in its scene. When you place the scene's clapper icon block, pick a convenient point in your drawing. The location of the scene block is not critical.

Using SCENE to Set a Scene

```
Command: SCENE
Enter scene name: SCENE1
Select the camera:                 Pick the CAMERA1 icon.
Select a light:                    Pick the POINT light source.
Select a light:                    Pick the WINDOW light source.
Select a light:                    Pick the DIRECT1 light source.
Select a light: <RETURN>
Enter scene location:              Pick a point in an open area.
Scene SCENE1 included
Command: SCENE
Enter scene name: SCENE2
Select the camera:                 Pick the CAMERA2 icon.
Select a light:                    Pick the POINT light source.
Select a light:                    Pick the WINDOW light source.
Select a light:                    Pick the DIRECT2 light source.
Select a light: <RETURN>
Enter scene location:              Pick a point below SCENE1.
Scene SCENE2 included
```

The scene blocks are shown to indicate how many scenes the drawing contains and what cameras and lights go with each scene (see fig. 17.11). Once you have established all the scenes, you make the filmroll.

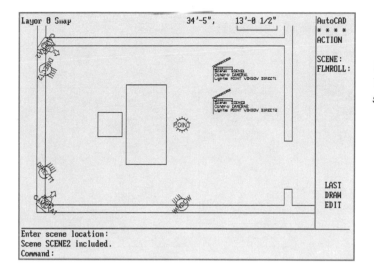

Figure 17.11:
The office with
scenes created.

Roll 'Em

```
Command: FILMROLL                                    Make OFFICE.FLM.
Enter filmroll file name <OFIC-SHD>: OFFICE
Creating the filmroll file
Processing face: 257                                 AutoCAD processes filmroll.
Filmroll file created

Command: END                                         End drawing and exit
                                                     AutoCAD.
```

Your filmroll now contains SCENE1 and SCENE2. Get ready to render these scenes in AutoShade.

AutoShade's Display and Pull-Down Menus

You have already made one quick pass through AutoShade to get a Fast Shade of the chair. Let's take a second look at the AutoShade screen display and menu system (see fig. 17.12). The first display you see is an interactive screen which can display wireframe images. The top line contains the menu bar with three pull-down menu headers, an area to display the amount of memory that has been used, and a digital clock.

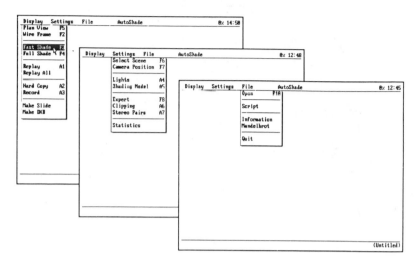

Figure 17.12:
AutoShade pull-down
menus.

The bottom line displays messages indicating the current activity and the name of the current filmroll file. The center of the screen is where the pull-down menus and dialogue boxes are displayed along with wireframe images. You use your pointing device to control the arrow pointer, to highlight selections, and to make menu choices. Most of the selections you make from the menus will present you with a dialogue box. Dialogue boxes are your primary means of control in AutoShade.

Using Full Shade to Render the Office Scenes

Return to AutoShade to examine your scenes of the office. Load your office filmroll, then select the [Full Shade] option to render the two scenes.

Using Full Shade to Render a Scene

Change to the ACAD directory and get into AutoShade.

Pull down **[File]**

AutoShade opens a Filmroll dialogue box displaying current directory and filmroll files. Make sure directory is set to \IA-ACAD.

Select **[OFFICE] [OK]**	Click the box next to OFFICE and load filmroll. A Select Scene dialogue box is presented showing SCENE1 and SCENE2 for selection.
Select **[SCENE1] [OK]**	Select [SCENE1] and [OK] (see fig. 17.13).
Pull down **[Display]**	
Select **[Full Shade]**	AutoShade processes the rendering.

> ### Using Full Shade to Render a Scene—continued
>
> AutoShade displays the percentage of completion for each task it performs as it processes the rendering.
>
> Examine the rendering and process SCENE2.
>
> *Pull down* **[Settings]**
> *Select* **[Select Scene]**   Select SCENE2.
> *Pull down* **[Display]**
> *Select* **[Full Shade]**

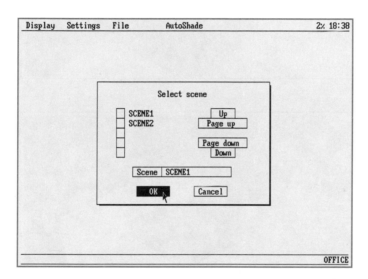

Figure 17.13:
The select scene dialogue box.

Your scenes should look like figures 17.14 through 17.17. Each scene is displayed with the lighting and camera angles you set up in AutoCAD.

The rendering in SCENE1 is fine, although the camera has cut off the top of the table. Let's see if we can improve on SCENE2, where there is relatively little contrast between the table top and the walls behind it. Also, it may be possible to get a better camera angle. AutoShade gives you a set of tools to adjust your lighting and camera settings.

Using Lighting and Shading to Enhance Images

You can adjust your lighting in AutoShade. The [Settings] pull-down menu provides two dialogue boxes for adjusting the lighting appearance.

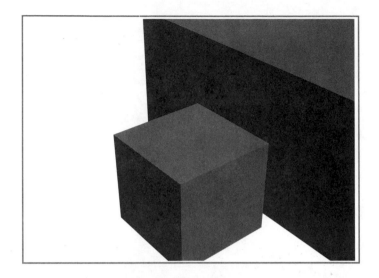

Figure 17.14:
A simple rendering
of SCENE1.

Figure 17.15:
A complex rendering
of SCENE1.

The Set Light Intensities dialogue box, accessed by the [Lights] selection, shows all the lights available for the current scene. The box shows the light's name, type, and intensity. You can make a scene's lights brighter or dimmer by increasing or decreasing the intensity value. A zero value is the same as turning the light off. In fact, a negative value can actually subtract light (like a black hole).

AutoShade does not let you add lights or adjust the type and location of existing lights. If you need to change or add lighting, you must return to your drawing in AutoCAD, make the lighting adjustments, and create a new filmroll. We recommend providing more lights than you think you will need when you create your scenes in

Figure 17.16:
A simple rendering
of SCENE2.

Figure 17.17:
A complex rendering
of SCENE2.

AutoCAD. Then, you can turn off the lights you don't need. This approach is similar to lighting a stage where you try to anticipate a variety of light schemes. This lets you try different lighting effects in AutoShade without having to return to AutoCAD.

In real life, objects appear to get darker as their distance from you increases. AutoShade does not depict shading differences relative to distance from a light source unless it has been told to do so. The Shading Model dialogue box offers a number of ways to adjust your lighting. These settings adjust how the light will reflect from the objects in your drawing. The settings affect the look and texture of the rendering. Changing the settings can give surfaces a shiny or a matte-like finish.

You can also control visual depth by having AutoShade make objects with the same color brighter in the foreground than in the background. You can choose other options to set a background color, preview black and white output according to NTSC standards, and create black and white or color separations.

> **Tip:** You can give faces the effect of different colors on each side of the face by duplicating the entity with an extremely small distance separating the face and the duplicated face, and then changing the color of the duplicated face. Use COPY, SCALE, or MOVE, and then the LAYER or COLOR command.

The factors we will adjust in the next exercise include the ambient factor (controlling overall light level), and the diffuse and specular factors (controlling reflectivity). The [Ambient factor] setting uniformly controls the brightness of stray light (such as is bounced off walls, ceilings, and all objects in the real world) as opposed to light from specific sources. An ambient setting of 0 contributes no stray light (unrealistic) and a maximum setting of 1.0 floods all surfaces equally, so light sources have no effect. While the ambient factor controls *how much* light hits the surfaces, other factors control how it is reflected.

The [Diffuse factor] setting controls (from 0 to 1.0) the diffuse reflection of all surfaces. Diffuse reflection is light reflected equally in all directions, relative to the *amount* of light striking the surface, regardless of the direction of the source. The specular settings control directional reflections.

The [Specular factor] setting controls (from 0 to 1.0) the amount of shiny surface reflection versus diffuse reflection. The sum of the ambient, diffuse, and specular factors should equal 1.0. The [Specular exponent] setting controls how perfect the shine is. A perfect mirror receiving a perfect parallel beam would reflect a perfect parallel beam. In reality, shiny surfaces reflect an imperfect cone of light. A low specular exponent, such as 3, reflects a wide cone. A high value, such as 20, reflects a narrow beam. If the cone is too narrow, none of the specular light from angled surfaces will reach the camera, and the surfaces will appear dark.

Try enhancing the room in SCENE2 with some lighting and shading model adjustments. You will also turn stretch contrast off in the shading model. If stretch contrast is on, AutoShade renders the image as if it were a picture taken with automatic exposure, and adjusts lighting based only on the ambient factor, ignoring all light intensity settings.

Using Lights and Shading Settings to Enhance Contrast

Pull down **[Settings]**	
Select **[Lights]**	Open Set Light Intensities dialogue box.
Select **Point [Intensity]**	Set value to 3 to increase intensity.
Select **Window [Intensity]**	Leave value at 1.

> ### Using Lights and Shading Settings to Enhance Contrast—continued
>
> | | |
> |---|---|
> | *Select* **Direct? [Intensity]** | Set value to 3 to increase intensity. |
> | *Select* **[OK]** | Close dialogue box. |
> | *Pull down* **[Settings]** | |
> | *Select* **[Shading Model]** | Open Shading Model dialogue box. |
> | *Select* **[Ambient factor]** | Set value to 0.2 to decrease background light. |
> | *Select* **[Diffuse factor]** | Set value to 0.8 to increase the reflectivity of drawing. |
> | *Select* **[Specular exponent]** | Set to 12 to adjust reflection from shiny surfaces. |
> | *Select* **[Stretch contrast]** | Turn off so shades are computed at absolute intensities. |
> | *Select* **[OK]** | Close dialogue box. |
> | *Pull down* **[Display]** | |
> | *Select* **[Full Shade]** | AutoShade processes the rendering. |

When you are done, your screen should show an image with differing contrasts (see figs. 17.18 and 17.19).

Figure 17.18:
A simple SCENE2
rendered with new
settings.

The new light and shading model settings show AutoShade's flexibility. With practice, you can make settings to simulate actual lighting situations. Take a look at SCENE1 to see the effect of the light changes. Experiment with different settings. Try your own hand at using a wide variety of values to see new effects. The best way to understand lighting is to experiment.

Figure 17.19:
A complex SCENE?
rendered with new
settings.

Shading Model Distance Factors

Several factors adjust the shading of surfaces relative to their distance from light sources or from the camera. *Inverse square* causes light intensity to decrease as the square of the distance from the light source to the object face. *Linear lighting* causes light intensity to decrease linearly from the light source to the object face. Linear lighting does not produce distance shades of color as dark as inverse square. *Inverse contrast* is used in conjunction with linear lighting to produce an effect similar to fluorescent lighting. *Z shading* produces a rendering with the foreground brighter than the background. Light placements, intensities, and shading factors (except stretch contrast) are ignored. This is adequate for most quick studies, and easier than setting linear and inverse factors.

Compare figures 17.20 and 17.21 to see the effect of inverse square.

Using Camera Position Settings to Improve an Image

You have seen how lighting affects the appearance of a rendering; now try other camera positions to get a new perspective. AutoShade gives you a lot of flexibility for setting a camera's position and target point. However, any changes you make to the camera are only set for AutoShade. If you want to permanently set a new camera setting, you need to change those values in your AutoCAD drawing.

Figure 17.20:
Shading with inverse
square.

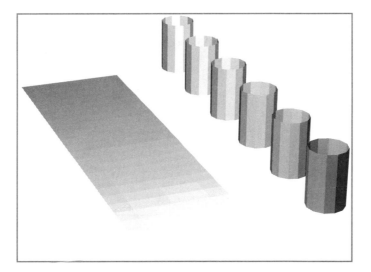

Figure 17.21:
Shading without
inverse square.

Setting New Camera Positions

The Camera Specifications dialogue box displayed by the [Camera Position] menu item provides three types of settings: you can adjust the camera angle from the X axis in the X,Y plane, and up from the X,Y plane; you can change the camera distance from the target; and you can change the camera's lens length. AutoShade treats the camera as if it were a normal 35mm camera with a 50mm lens (standard on most cameras). You can change the lens in the same manner as a regular camera, with the same results. Changing to a 35mm lens will give you a wide angle view, whereas changing to a 135mm lens will act like a telephoto lens producing a zoomed-in view of the target.

Let's return to SCENE2, keeping the lighting changes you made in the previous exercise, and change the camera settings to get a bird's-eye view of the office.

Using Camera Position to Set a New Camera View

Pull down **[Settings]**

Select **[Camera Position]**   Opens Camera Specifications dialogue box.

Select **[Distance]**   Set value to 480, moving camera 40 feet away from target.

Select **[Lens in mm]**   Change to a 35mm lens for a wide angle view.

Select **[Degrees up]**   Set degrees to 45 to get a view looking down on the office.

Select **[OK]**   Close dialogue box.

Pull down **[Display]**

Select **[Full Shade]**   AutoShade processes the rendering.

Your new view of SCENE2 should look much different from the original scene. You are looking down on the office (see figs. 17.22 and 17.23). The perspective should be more evident. See Chapter 16 on AutoCAD's DVIEW command for a more complete discussion of perspective.

Using Expert and Clipping Controls

Your drawings may require more than camera and lighting adjustments to get a good rendering. AutoShade's Expert and Clipping Specifications dialogue boxes offer you more sophisticated controls over your renderings.

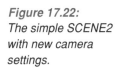

Figure 17.22:
The simple SCENE2 with new camera settings.

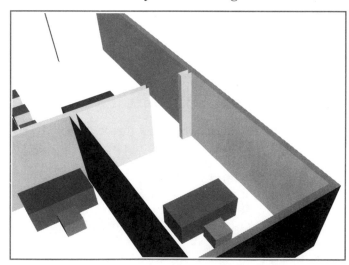

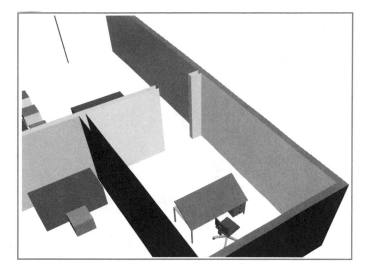

Figure 17.23:
The complex
SCENE2 with new
camera settings.

The Expert Specifications dialogue box gives you additional control over camera placements. You can adjust the camera's target position as well as the camera's position. These positions are shown as X,Y,Z values. You should record these values so you can match the changes you made in AutoShade when you go back to your drawing in AutoCAD. If your drawing contains faces that intersect, you will have to turn [Intersections] on to get a correct rendering. [Intersections] is off by default because intersection checking takes a lot of time. A number of other settings are available for more advanced control of depth, intersections, and rendering order.

The [Perspective] setting lets you override perspective rendering. With perspective off, AutoShade will use a parallel projection to create an orthographic wireframe and rendering, like the views you get with AutoCAD's VPOINT command.

The current view of SCENE2 focuses on one office. We'll use the Expert Specifications dialogue box to move the camera's target for a better view of all three offices (see figs. 17.24 and 17.25). Change the Target Y value to move the camera's aim point from the lower right corner of the current office to the lower right corner of the other small office. The values in the dialogue box are shown in inches, so we will enter a value of 300 to move the camera's target 25 feet in the Y direction.

Using the Expert Box to Change Camera Positions

Pull down **[Settings]**	
Select **[Expert]**	Open Expert Specifications dialogue box.
Select **[Target Y]**	Set value to 300 to move target to lower right corner of upper office.
Select **[OK]**	Close dialogue box.
Pull down **[Display]**	
Select **[Full Shade]**	AutoShade processes the rendering.

Figure 17.24:
The simple offlce viewed with a new target.

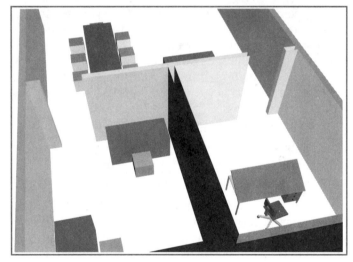

Figure 17.25:
The complex office viewed with a new target.

You are through with SCENE2.

Let's return to SCENE1 and set up for clipping. We'll recreate the office clipping view that you created using DVIEW in Chapter 16. Start by moving the camera 19 feet (228 inches) from the center of the chair. Use a 35mm lens. When you get into SCENE1, all of the settings will remain from SCENE2, except those involving camera position and light intensities.

Positioning the Camera for Clipping

Pull down [Settings]	
Select [Select Scene]	Select SCENE1.
Select [OK]	Close dialogue box.
Pull down [Settings]	
Select [Lights]	Open Set Light Intensities dialogue box.
Select Point [Intensity]	Set value to 3 to increase intensity.
Select Window [Intensity]	Leave value at 1.
Select Direct1 [Intensity]	Set value to 3 to increase intensity.
Select [OK]	Close dialogue box.
Pull down [Settings]	
Select [Camera Position]	Open Camera Specifications dialogue box.
Select [Distance]	Set value to 228, moving camera 19 feet away from target.
Select [Lens in mm]	Make sure lens is set to 35mm.
Select [OK]	Close dialogue box.
Pull down [Display]	
Select [Full Shade]	AutoShade processes the rendering.

Your rendering should show only the outside corner of the office drawing. Like DVIEW, AutoShade defaults to clipping at the camera, which you moved outside the office (see fig. 17.26). You need to adjust clipping so that the corner of the room is clipped, allowing a view into the office.

Figure 17.26:
Shade of the office
from a new camera
position.

Clipping the View

The camera sees everything in your drawing, but you may not want to render everything. You can determine how much of the drawing you want rendered by adjusting values in the Clipping Specifications dialogue box to clip foreground and background images perpendicular to your line of sight. You can also set the size and shape of your viewing frame by adjusting the top, bottom, left, and right clipping values.

Let's set clipping values to open up the office.

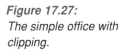

Using Clipping to Enhance the Office Image	
Pull down **[Settings]**	
Select **[Clipping]**	Open Clipping Specifications dialogue box.
Select **[Clip at camera]**	Turn clip at camera off.
Select **[Front clip Z]**	Set front clip to 30".
Select **[OK]**	Close dialogue box.
Pull down **[Display]**	
Select **[Full Shade]**	AutoShade processes the rendering.

Your screen should show the corner of the wall clipped perpendicular to your view, revealing the office with table and chair (see figs. 17.27 and 17.28). This view is the shaded equivalent of the clipped office view that you made in Chapter 16 with DVIEW. AutoShade's clipping tools work the same as those in DVIEW except AutoShade has more clipping options. The left, right, top, and bottom clips can be thought of as cropping values.

Figure 17.27:
The simple office with
clipping.

Figure 17.28:
The complex office
with clipping.

Unlike DVIEW, where your desired perspective may force the image to be small and off-center, you can crop your AutoShade display. AutoShade always adjusts its display to fill the screen with the current image. But remember, like front and back clipping, the cropping is perpendicular to your line of sight. If you want to experiment, try some more clipping values.

If you were to quit AutoShade now, all the changes you made to SCENE1 would be lost. Before we leave AutoShade, let's look at what AutoShade offers for saving your finished scenes.

Saving and Printing AutoShade Renderings

If you have a PostScript printer or AutoShade ADI hard copy device installed and configured, you can make a printed copy by opening the [Display] pull-down menu and selecting [Hard Copy]. Then, do a Full Shade. Rather than producing a rendering on the screen, AutoShade will prompt you for a PostScript print filename. After the file is created (with the file extension .EPS or .PS), you can send it to your printer with the DOS print command. If you were wondering how we produced the shaded images in this chapter, they were output as PostScript files and printed on a standard 300 dpi PostScript printer.

Note: AutoShade version 1.1 directly creates .EPS (Encapsulated PostScript) formatted files. Earlier versions require slight modification to the print file by an ASCII text editor if you need an .EPS file. You must change the first line to read `%!PS-Adobe-2.0 EPSF-1.2` to change the version. You must move the `%%BoundingBox` line from the end of the file and insert it as the second line. Then insert a new line that reads

---

> `%%EndComments` directly after the last comments line (usually the `%%Pages` line). All comments begin with %%.

The most common method for saving scenes is to select [Record] from the [Display] pull-down menu. AutoShade will then prompt for a rendering filename each time a shade rendering is made. The rendering is written to a file as well as displayed on the screen. Rendering files have an .RND extension. You can view them in AutoShade at any time by selecting [Replay All] or [Replay] and entering a filename. These renderings are displayed much faster than the original shade because they do not require reprocessing. In this chapter's last set of exercises, we will show you how to create rendering files and run them with a script.

> **Note:** Rendering files are display device-specific. Files created with one type of video configuration cannot be displayed on any other type of video.

AutoShade Scripts

You can also display renderings using the [Script] selection from the [File] pull-down menu. You create scripts with an ASCII text editor, the same way you create them for AutoCAD. You can use scripts to view renderings and to run demonstrations. You can also use scripts to automate AutoShade processing. As you may have noticed, rendering a drawing can take a long time. If you have many scenes to process, you can create a script to do the tedious processing: stepping through each scene, adjusting camera settings, and recording or printing the rendering. Run the script at night, and your renderings will be ready for viewing in the morning!

Making and Saving Wireframe Images

The last two methods for saving scenes are the [Make Slide] and [Make DXB] selections on the [Display] pull-down menu. If you make a slide, you can view it in AutoCAD. You can also import a .DXB file into AutoCAD with DXBIN. Both the slide and .DXB files are created as wireframe images of the current view. These images will look like the perspective wireframe images that you obtain with DVIEW in AutoCAD; however, you have the advantage of AutoShade's cropping ability.

Let's try making a quick wireframe image of the current view and look at a plan view to verify camera and light placement.

Getting a Wireframe Image in AutoShade

Pull down **[Display]**
Select **[Wire Frame]** Produces a wireframe image of the current scene (see fig. 17.29).

This is a good way to preview the shaded image.

Select **[Plan View]** Produces a wireframe plan view of the current scene (see fig. 17.30).

Pull down **[File]**
Select **[Quit]** Exit AutoShade.

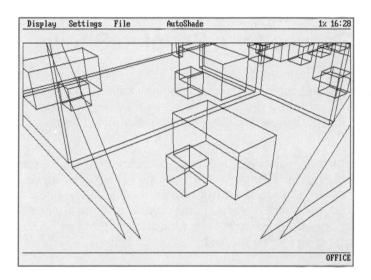

Figure 17.29:
A wireframe view of the office.

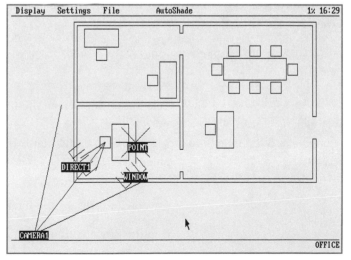

Figure 17.30:
A plan view of the office.

Selecting [Wire Frame] is the quickest way to verify a new camera location before doing a shade. The [Plan View] selection also provides a quick wireframe view of the current scene. In addition to the drawing, the current scene locations of camera and lights are shown.

Tip: Use [Plan View] to refresh your memory if you have done many camera and target moves.

In the next section, we'll go back to AutoCAD and set up four final scenes to create renderings of the office plan. These renderings will correspond to the perspective views that you developed with DVIEW.

Developing Scenes for a Scripted Show

So far, you have explored AutoShade's camera and lighting settings to get a desired rendering. The office with the chair and table are small objects and you can control their renderings easily. Larger and more complex drawings require more control in AutoShade, and more forethought when you create your camera, lights, and scenes in AutoCAD.

Let's return to the simple office drawing in AutoCAD and recreate the camera positions from the DVIEW exercise in Chapter 16. We'll create a set of renderings which will be replayed similarly to the slide show in Chapter 16. The difference this time is that each image will be fully shaded. First, make a new drawing named RENDER from the simple office plan and prepare it for a filmroll. Use figure 17.31 and table 17.1 to create the four scenes for the filmroll.

Creating Four Scenes and a Filmroll for a Rendering Show

 Begin a NEW drawing named RENDER=IA6OFF3D.

 Begin a NEW drawing named RENDER=OFFICE3D.

Command: **ZOOM**	Zoom All.
Select **[ASHADE]**	Select from the screen menu.
Command: Loading ashade.lsp (v1.1)...loaded	It's loading.

Use table 17.1 to place cameras and lights, and to create scenes to match figure 17.32.

Command: **FILMROLL**	Make RENDER.FLM.
Enter filmroll file name <RENDER>: **<RETURN>**	
Creating the filmroll file	
Processing face: 257	AutoCAD processes the filmroll.
Filmroll file created	
Command: **END**	End the drawing and exit AutoCAD.

Table 17.1
Settings for Office Scenes

SCENE1	Target Location	Icon Location
CAMERA1	23'9,19'6,3'6	10'9,6'6,8'6
POINT1 (point)		25'6,19'6,10'0
DIRECT1 (direct)	23'9,19'6,3'6	14'6,5'6,8'6

SCENE2	Target Location	Icon Location
CAMERA2	33'0,33'0,2'0	51'6,21'6,5'6
POINT2 (point)		43'0,25'0,10'0
DIRECT2 (direct)	33'0,33'0,2'0	49'0,18'0,5'6

SCENE3	Target Location	Icon Location
CAMERA3	52'0,35'6,0'0	33'0,14'6,6'0
POINT2 (same as above)		43'0,25'0,10'0
DIRECT3 (direct)	52'0,35'6,0'0	37'6,15'6,6'0

SCENE4	Target Location	Icon Location
CAMERA4	38'0,33'6,0'0	17'6,25'0,6'0
POINT3	(point)	25'6,30'0,10'0
DIRECT4 (direct)	38'0,33'6,0'0	19'6,27'6,6'0

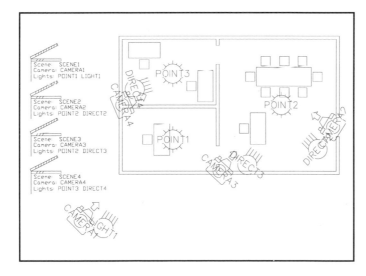

Figure 17.31:
The RENDER
drawing ready for
FILMROLL.

Now that you have the four scenes safely stored in the filmroll file, return to AutoShade and create a render file for each scene.

Rendering the Four Scenes

Change to the ACAD directory and get into AutoShade.

Pull down **[File]**
Select **[Open]**   AutoShade opens a Filmroll dialogue box display-
                                                 ing current directory and filmroll files. Make sure
                                                 directory is \IA-ACAD.
Select **[RENDER] [OK]**   Click box next to RENDER and select [OK].
Select **[SCENE1]**   Start with scene one.

Clip at camera off, set lens to 35mm, and Front clip Z to 30.

Select **[Display]**
Select **[Record]**   Select record.
Select **[Full Shade]**   Open dialogue for filename.
Select **[File name]**   Create a file named \IA-ACAD\RENDER-1.

Repeat the record sequence above for the remaining three scenes. Leave clipping set at
camera and set the lens to 35mm for each scene.

Name each rendering \IA-ACAD\RENDER-2 through RENDER-4.

Once you have all the rendering files created, you can replay them individually or by
directory. [Replay All] displays all .RND files found in the currently selected directory. Let's use the replay function to see all of the renderings.

Replaying the Rendering Files

Select **[Display]**
Select **[Replay All]**
Select **[OK]**   Make sure the directory is \IA-ACAD and select
                                                 [OK]. Renderings are displayed on the screen.
<^C>   Stops the replay.
Pull down **[File]**
Select **[QUIT]**

The renderings are displayed in sequence, with a one-second delay between each
(see figs. 17.32 through 17.35).

The following script file would produce the same display as [Replay All] did, except
the delay would be 15 seconds.

```
replay render-1
delay 15
replay render-2
delay 15
replay render-3
delay 15
replay render-4
delay 15
rewind
```

Figure 17.32:
Rendering of
SCENE1.

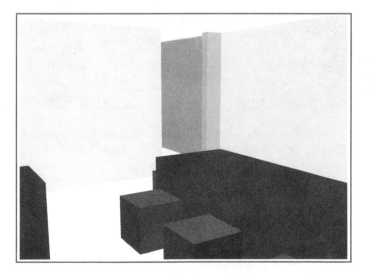

Figure 17.33:
Rendering of
SCENE2.

Figure 17.34:
Rendering of
SCENE3.

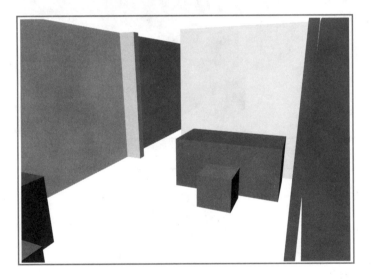

Figure 17.35:
Rendering of
SCENE4.

The advantage of a script is that it can control which renderings to display, the order of display, and give different delays as needed. A script can also be started at the DOS prompt. Use these command line options at the operating system prompt to bypass the AutoShade screen and menus for single shot preset renderings, or to start scripts:

SHADE -S<*filename*>	Runs a script file after loading AutoShade.
SHADE -B -S<*filename*>	Runs a script file without loading AutoShade screen and menus.

| SHADE -R | Reconfigures AutoShade. |
| SHADE -? | Displays the command line options. |

Additional AutoShade Features

Fractals! Yes, AutoShade has fractals and a few more interesting and entertaining features. You will find fractals (and an information box) on the [File] pull-down menu.

[Mandelbrot] Displays a dialogue box of settings to create displays of the Mandelbrot set (fractals).

[Information] Displays a box with the AutoShade version number.

You will also find a facility for creating stereo pairs, and a scene statistics selection on the [Settings] pull-down menu.

[Stereo Pairs] Presents a dialogue box to generate two separate images side by side for stereoscopic viewing.

[Statistics] Displays a box of information to inform you about the size of the rendering in faces and triangles, and the extents of the rendering. This information can be used to estimate the amount of memory required for a rendering.

Photorealism With AutoShade 2.0 and RenderMan

A recently updated version of AutoShade, version 2.0, offers many new enhancements that make rendering easier, faster, and better looking. Although we've kept our AutoShade exercises simple enough to be used with the earlier versions, AutoShade 2.0 users will want to take advantage of the program's:

- DOS extender technology for faster performance on 386 or 486 computers.
- New AutoLISP commands for inserting cameras and lights that automatically assume the 3D location and direction of the current view.
- An improved user interface with scroll bars like AutoCAD Release 11.
- A new Quick Shade option that gives you most of the quality of Full Shade rendering in less time.
- Smooth shading (Gouraud) that eliminates the faceted look of curved surfaces in 3D models.

- Scripts that can automatically store all your AutoShade settings for easy restoration. The script language has been greatly expanded.
- Seamless integration with Autodesk RenderMan.

When AutoCAD drawings are used with Autodesk RenderMan, AutoShade can produce lifelike rendered images that rival photographs. Autodesk RenderMan produces high-resolution, anti-aliased (no jaggies) images of models. You have full control over shading and shadow casting, and you can assign textures, materials and surface properties in AutoCAD.

AutoShade can produce quality shaded images but requires some patience and a good understanding of how lighting, reflection, and shading is calculated. Trial and error will focus you on the settings you will use most of the time, but experimenting with the more obscure settings and studying the *AutoShade User Guide* will help you get an even better understanding and produce better renderings.

> **Note:** You can delete OFFICE.DWG, RENDER.DWG, *.FLM and *.RND from your IA-ACAD directory.

Summing Up

From planning and creating your 3D model in AutoCAD, to using the ASHADE.LSP commands to prepare lights, cameras, and scenes for the filmroll, to taking the filmroll from AutoCAD to AutoShade, to finetuning the image in AutoShade, to rendering it on the screen or printer — remembering a few tips will make the process quicker and the results better.

Use simple entities to get your scenes right and test the shading, then substitute complex meshed objects for final renderings.

Plan and create your 3D model with extrusions, surfaces, and surfaced solids, or objects won't show up in AutoShade. Create 3Dfaces in a counterclockwise order (the AutoLISP 3D objects commands ensure the right order).

When setting colors in AutoCAD, consider how they will appear after shading darkens and lightens them.

Use osnaps, XYZ point filters, and DVIEW to plan your scenes before putting in lights and cameras.

Balance the efficiency of entities in AutoCAD versus smoothness of shading in AutoShade. Simple extrusions and low mesh densities regenerate and process faster, but fine surface meshes create smoother shading.

Use AutoCAD and AutoShade scripts to automate filmroll and rendering production. AutoFlix and the Autodesk Animation Tool Kit (ATK) include AutoLISP routines that can automate creating a series of scenes for your filmroll. *INSIDE Autodesk Animator*, from New Riders Publishing, includes a chapter on using the ATK to create an animated movie of AutoShade renderings. The ATK is available from your AutoCAD or Animator dealer, in AutoShade 2.0, or from the Autodesk forum on CompuServe. See the end of Chapter 16 for information on Animator, AutoFlix, and CompuServe.

If you're using the standard 640K DOS or DOS 286 version of AutoShade, creating a RAM disk and setting environment variables to use can improve rendering speed. See the *AutoShade Installation and Performance Guide* for details.

What you see on screen isn't necessarily what you get in hard copy, particularly with black and white printers. It may be necessary to adjust your colors in AutoCAD to get the effects you want. We had to set all colors to white to get our Fast Shade-rendered chair illustration to look right in print.

On to Real 3D

Wireframes, surface meshes, and shaded surfaces — all are useful approximations of 3D objects. But sometimes you need more precision and mass in your 3D objects. Let's move on to AutoCAD's AME and create a *solid* model with real-world properties like density, yield strength, linear expansion coefficient, centroid, and moment of inertia.

18

Inside Solid Modeling

ADDING SUBSTANCE TO YOUR 3D MODELS

Understanding Solid Modeling

In the 3D work you did in previous chapters, you used two 3D modeling techniques — wireframe and surface modeling. AutoCAD Release 11 also includes the third type — solid modeling. To understand exactly what solid modeling is and how to use it, let's take a quick look at how it differs from wireframe and surface modeling.

The Three Types of 3D Modeling

Not only are wireframe models often the hardest to create, they convey the least amount of information. All a wireframe can describe is that two 3D coordinates are connected by a line or other 2D entity. With enough coordinates and lines, you can create a respectable *looking* 3D image. However, the wireframe is ambiguous in representing where surfaces exist between lines and intersections. You can make some visual assumptions, but the model lacks associative information that is useful in design. And, without surface data, wireframes can't be shaded and used for visualization.

Surface models add another layer of complexity to the model by associating entities with surfaces, and maintaining relationships between surfaces (like edge-to-edge intersection). This lets you model much more complex designs and shade them. But even with that added associativity, surface models do not convey substance — the presence of mass (solids), or the absence of mass (voids).

Solid modeling adds those properties to the model. Using a solid model, you can calculate such mass properties as weight, center of gravity, moments of inertia, and so on. One of the best aspects of solid modeling is the fact that it is usually easier to accomplish than the other two types of 3D modeling. That is because you build a solid model in much the same way you would actually manufacture the item being modeled. For example, you can start with a block, punch holes in it (subtract a cylinder), and perform other modeling operations that mimic the actual manufacturing operation.

Who Needs Solid Modeling?

Although solid modeling has generally been the province of mechanical designers, AutoCAD's solid modeling features are also useful to spatially oriented designers such as architects and to drafters of many disciplines. With solids, you can resolve complex intersections and penetrations that might take arduous calculations in 2D drafting. Solids can quickly demonstrate conflicts and interferences between components. Architects can use solids to mock up mass studies of models, then transfer the results to 3D surfaces for presentation drawings or to 2D for drawing development. Just pretend that the mechanical parts in this chapter's exercises are mass models for a strange-looking building!

Getting Started in Solid Modeling

Everything you have learned about 3D modeling in previous chapters applies to solid modeling. You use the same types of coordinate systems (UCSs) and many of the same basic techniques. AutoCAD helps by providing special functions to create solid primitives (simple geometric solids), as well as functions to add solids together, subtract them from each other, and analyze mass properties.

If you have not purchased the Advanced Modeling Extension (full AME) option, you won't have access to many of the utility commands that let you modify and combine solid primitives. But even with the basic software (called AMElite), you can create solid primitives and perform many of the utility commands. The differences between AME and AMElite are identified throughout this chapter. Some versions of AutoCAD Release 11 may run on systems that are not capable of running AME or AMElite. If you are using a version of AutoCAD prior to Release 11, you won't have any of the solid modeling functions. You might find this chapter interesting reading anyway.

The exercises in this chapter are grouped into three sections. In the first, we show you how to create simple primitives and combine them to form more complex models. We also show you how to create revolved and extruded solids, and how to use many of the solid editing functions. In the second section, we show you how to list, manipulate, and change many of the properties of your completed model. In the final section, we show you how to take a solid model and translate its information into a 2D drawing.

Setting Up a 3D Solid Modeling Environment

Since the best way to learn is by doing, let's use AutoCAD's AME functions to create a simple mechanical part in a new drawing called 3D. The first thing you will do is create the viewports and User Coordinate Systems you'll need for working in 3D (see fig. 18.1). Then, save the drawing as a prototype to use in the rest of the exercises. This prototype is called IA6-3D on the IA DISK.

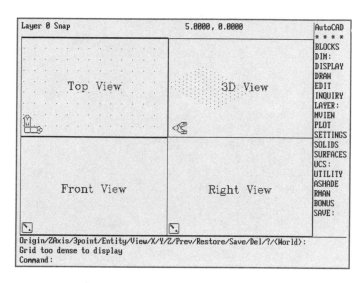

Figure 18.1:
The 3D prototype drawing setup.

Setting Up the Modeling Environment

 Copy IA6-3D.DWG to 3D.DWG and skip this setup.

 Begin a NEW drawing named 3D and continue.

Set snap to 0.25, grid to 1, and turn coords on.

Command: **LINETYPE**   Load the HIDDEN
                                                          linetype.

Command: **TILEMODE**
New value for TILEMODE <1>: **0**
Entering Paper space. Use MVIEW to insert Model space viewports.
Regenerating drawing.

Command: **MVIEW**
ON/OFF/Hideplot/Fit/2/3/4/Restore/<First Point>: **4**
Fit/<first point>: **0,0**
Second point: **36,24**
Regenerating drawing.

Command: **ZOOM**   All.

▶ **Setting Up the Modeling Environment—continued**

Command: **MSPACE**   Enter model space.

Use the VPOINT command to set up each of the four views.

Select lower left viewport to set up front view.

Command: **VPOINT**
Rotate/<View point> <0.0000,0.0000,1.0000>: **R**
Enter angle in X-Y plane from X axis <270>: **270**
Enter angle from X-Y plane <90>: **0**

Select the lower right viewport to set up the right side view.

Command: **VPOINT**
Rotate/<View point> <0.0000,0.0000,1.0000>: **R**
Enter angle in X-Y plane from X axis <270>: **0**
Enter angle from X-Y plane <90>: **0**

Select the upper right viewport to set up a 3D isometric view.

Command: **VPOINT**
Rotate/<View point> <0.0000,0.0000,1.0000>: **R**
Enter angle in X-Y plane from X axis <270>: **315**
Enter angle from X-Y plane <90>: **30**

Select the right side view.

Command: **UCS**   Set to current view.
Origin/ZAxis/3point/Entity/View/X/Y/Z/Prev/Restore/
  Save/Del/?/<World>: **V**
Command: **UCS**   Save it.
Origin/ZAxis/3point/Entity/View/X/Y/Z/Prev/Restore/
  Save/Del/?/<World>: **S**
?/Desired UCS name: **RIGHT**

Select the front view.

Command: **UCS**   Set to current view and
                                                       save it as FRONT.

Select the top view.

Command: **UCS**   Set to World.

Command: **END**   End the drawing to save
                                                       it as a prototype.

Making Something From Nothing — Almost

Like any complex operation, solid modeling is made up of many smaller, simpler operations. When you bring all of those simple operations together, you have a complex model. AutoCAD's solid modeling commands give you tools to create simple solids (primitives) and merge them together to quickly create complex models. These functions are similar to the AutoCAD functions for creating surface primitives that were covered in previous chapters.

For example, there are commands to create solid boxes, cylinders, cones, spheres, toruses, and wedges. You can use these primitives to construct complex designs from simple geometric shapes. You might start with a box or extrusion, and add other primitives to it. Or you might start with a complex extrusion and use utility commands to remove material from it.

Let's take a look at AutoCAD's solid modeling commands, and use them to create a few simple primitives. Then, we'll merge those primitives into a more complex part.

AutoCAD's Solid Modeling Tools

AutoCAD groups all of the solid modeling functions into a module called the Advanced Modeling Extension. Although the AME commands act like an integral part of AutoCAD, they are actually a separate program which is loaded into AutoCAD and run through the ADS and AutoLISP. The AME functions are located in the [Solids] pull-down menu and in the [SOLIDS] screen menu. If you haven't loaded the functions into memory yet, you will see two options — Load AME, and Load AMElite — when you select the [Solids] pull-down menu. The full AME requires that you purchase the AME option. When you purchase the AME option, all you get is an authorization code; the program is on your original AutoCAD disks but won't run without the code. AMElite is a subset of AME that is included with the AutoCAD program and needs no authorization code.

You can load either AME or AMElite after you start a new drawing by selecting [Load AME] or [Load AMElite] from the pull-down or screen menu. AutoCAD will load the solid modeling functions and initialize the 3D environment for modeling. You only have to load it once in each AutoCAD session, no matter how many drawings you create or edit. The very first time you load the full AME, you have to enter your authorization code. If you want to load AME or AMElite without using a menu, you can enter `(xload "AME")` or `(xload "AMELITE")` at the command line.

Creating a Simple Model Using Primitives

Many solid models can be created from little more than boxes, cylinders, and other simple shapes. AutoCAD provides six commands for creating 3D solid primitives. Here is a list:

SOLBOX   Lets you create a box shape by picking diagonally opposite corners and supplying a height. You can also specify a box by length, width, and height, or use the Cube option to create a cube of a specified size.

SOLCONE   Creates a circular or elliptical conic solid. If circular, you provide a center point, radius or diameter, and height. For elliptical cones, you specify two axes, as you do for the ELLIPSE command, along with the height.

SOLCYL Creates a solid cylinder given a center point, radius or diameter, and a height. It may be elliptical; the prompts are identical to SOLCONE.

SOLSPHERE Creates a solid sphere, given a center point and radius or diameter.

SOLTORUS This command works exactly like its surface counterpart in AutoCAD's 3D menu. You specify the center point, radius or diameter of the torus, and radius or diameter of the tube.

SOLWEDGE Lets you create a wedge by specifying opposite corners and the height of the wedge, or by specifying the width, length, and height. The first point picked identifies the thick end of the wedge.

You can use all of the above commands with either AME or AMElite, but you must have AME to do elliptical cones or cylinders. The height of these solids is parallel to the Z axis. The bases of wedges and boxes are always parallel to the X and Y axes of the current UCS, so to create rotated wedges or boxes, you must first adjust your UCS.

You can control the Z elevation of these primitives by presetting an elevation with the ELEV command or ELEVATION system variable; however, setting ELEVATION and adjusting UCSs can lead to confusing combinations. We recommend controlling elevation with UCSs or by specifying a Z value as part of the first coordinate. Specifying a Z value (relative to the current UCS) as part of the first coordinate is the easiest method; the solid will be created relative to that point.

Let's use figure 18.2 along with the SOLBOX and SOLCYL commands to rough out your first solid model.

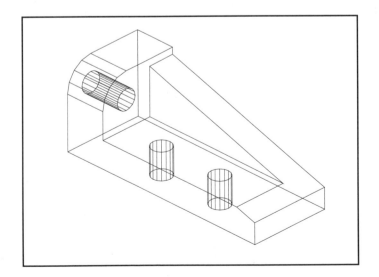

Figure 18.2:
The finished guide
block 3D model.

Creating Your First Solid Model

Begin a NEW drawing named GUIDBLOK=3D.

Select the 3D isometric (upper right) viewport.

```
Command: ZOOM
```
Zoom Center, point 3,3 and height 8.

```
Command: UCS
```
Restore UCS RIGHT.

Select [Load AME] (or [Load AMElite]) from the screen or pull-down menu. Wait while it loads.

```
Command: SOLBOX
Initializing Advanced Modeling Extension.
Corner of box: 0,0
Cube/Length/<Other corner>: 3,3
Height: 1.5
Phase I - Boundary evaluation begins.
Phase II - Tessellation computation begins.
Updating the Advanced Modeling Extension database.
```

```
Command: UCS
```
Restore UCS FRONT.

```
Command: SOLBOX
Corner of box: 1.5,0,-3
Cube/Length/<Other corner>: L
Length: 6.5
Width: 2.75
Height: 1
```
Try length, width, and height.

Boundary evaluation and tessellation occur.

```
Command: UCS
```
Set to World.

```
Command: SOLBOX
Corner of box: ENDP of
Cube/Length/<Other corner>: ENDP of

Height: 1
```
Pick points ① and ② to locate opposite corners of horizontal plate (see fig. 18.3).

Boundary evaluation and tessellation occur.

```
Command: UCS
```
Restore UCS RIGHT.

```
Command: SOLCYL
Elliptical/<Center point>: 1,2,-1
Diameter/<Radius>: .375
Height of cylinder: 3
```

Boundary evaluation and tessellation occur.

```
Command: UCS
```
Set to World.

```
Command: SOLCYL
Elliptical/<Center point>: 3,1,-1
Diameter/<Radius>: .375
Height of cylinder: 3
```

Creating Your First Solid Model—continued

Boundary evaluation and tessellation occur.

```
Command: SOLCYL
Elliptical/<Center point>: 4.5,1,-1
Diameter/<Radius>: .375
Height of cylinder: 3
```

Boundary evaluation and tessellation occur.

```
Command: ZOOM
```
Zoom each of the other views as illustrated in figure 18.3.

Figure 18.3:
The roughed-out
guide block model.

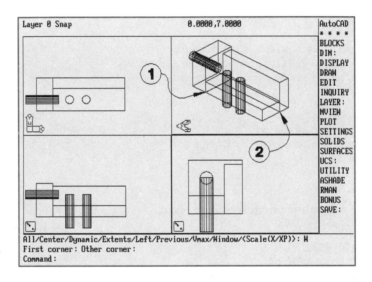

Your model should look like figure 18.3. But, there is one mistake in the model. The last cylinder you created was located at the wrong coordinate. It should be 1 inch farther away from cylinder number 2. To show that solids can be edited like any other type of entity, use the standard AutoCAD MOVE command to move it over 1 inch along the X axis.

Moving Solids With the MOVE Command

Select the 3D isometric viewport.

```
Command: MOVE
Select objects:                          Select the right-most cylinder.
Base point or displacement: 1,0          Enter a displacement.
Second point of displacement: <RETURN>   Use first point as displacement.

Command: REDRAWALL
Command: SAVE                            Save the drawing.
```

You can also use other editing commands to change solids. For example, you can use ROTATE to rotate them in 3D space. Or, you could have simply copied the second cylinder to create the third.

Boolean Operations — AutoCAD's Solids Modifiers

Operations that combine solids, subtract one solid from another, and find the intersection of solids are called *Boolean operations*. AutoCAD includes three Boolean functions for performing those three tasks: SOLUNION, SOLSUB (SOLid SUBtraction) and SOLINT (SOLid INTersection). You must have the full AME to use these commands. If you don't, skip the next exercise and rejoin us when we create and rotate a wedge.

Adding two solids together to form a single homogeneous solid is called a union. AutoCAD provides the SOLUNION command to do just that. The SOLSUB command is used to subtract one solid from another, such as subtracting a cylinder from a box to form a hole. Finally, the SOLINT command allows you to find the intersection of two solids (the common space shared by the two solids).

When you use the SOLUNION command, you build a selection set of solids. Then you press <RETURN> to finish the set, and AutoCAD combines all of the individual solids in the set to form a composite solid.

The SOLSUB command acts a little differently. SOLSUB prompts you to select entities in two sets. The first set of entities comprises the main group of solids. The second set of entities are the entities to be subtracted from the main group. So, if you want to subtract a cylinder from a box to form a hole, select the box first (as the main group), then select the cylinder as the second set.

SOLINT finds the intersection between two solids. We'll use it a little later in the chapter. For now, let's use the SOLUNION and SOLSUB commands on the guide block to join the boxes and create the holes. These solid utility commands are located in the [Solids] pull-down menu under [MODIFY >]. Or, you can find them in the [SOLIDS] screen menu.

Using SOLUNION and SOLSUB to Modify Solids

```
Command: SOLSUB
Source objects...
Select objects:                              Select the bottom horizontal box ① (see
                                             fig. 18.4).

1 selected, 1 found
Select objects: <RETURN>
1 solid selected.
Objects to subtract from them...
```

Using SOLUNION and SOLSUB to Modify Solids—continued

```
Select objects:
Select objects: <RETURN>
2 solids selected.
```
Select the two vertical cylinders.

Boundary evaluation and tessellation occur.

```
Command: SOLSUB
Source objects...
Select objects: <RETURN>
1 solid selected.
Objects to subtract from them...
Select objects:
Select objects: <RETURN>
1 solid selected.
```
Select the left vertical box ②.

Select the horizontal cylinder.

Boundary evaluation and tessellation occur.

```
Command: SOLUNION
Select objects:
Select objects: <RETURN>
3 solids selected.
```
Select the three box shapes.

Boundary evaluation and tessellation occur.

```
Command: SAVE
```

As figure 18.5 shows, there are no longer lines on the right side and front dividing the horizontal box from the vertical box. It is all one solid entity now.

Figure 18.4:
The guide block
before subtraction
and union.

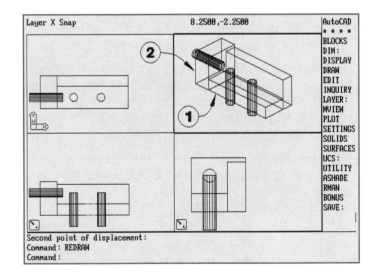

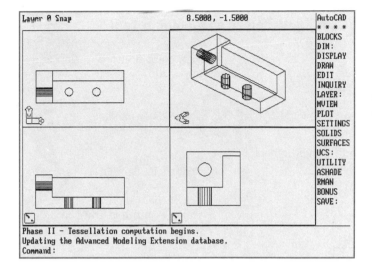

Creating Solid Tools for Removing Material

In manufacturing, you use different tools to remove material from stock to create a finished part. Drill bits (cylinders) are used to form holes, milling cutters can be used to cut rectangular shapes from stock, and broaches (extruded shapes) can be used to form keyways, keyseats, and other broached shapes.

The same concept applies in solid modeling, and that's why using a solid modeler is one of the easiest ways to model in 3D. Many of the operations you perform to create your design are just like the operations you would perform in the shop to manufacture the part. You don't have to learn a new way of doing things.

If you need to punch a slot in your model, you can create the outline of the slot, extrude it to a solid, then subtract it from the main body, forming a void. If you need to mill a circular pocket out of your model, draw the profile of the pocket and rotate it to form a solid, then subtract it from the main body. In both cases, you are making tools out of 2D geometry that can be used to modify your model.

In the real world, two bodies can't coexist in the same space at the same time. Inside the computer, it's different. You can create two solids and put one inside the other. The main, or outside, solid is still completely solid — at least as far as the computer is concerned. But when you subtract the inside solid from the main body, you form a void where the interior solid used to be.

Let's use that technique on the guide block. Create a wedge using the SOLWEDGE command. Then, position the wedge in the same space as the guide block, using it as a subtraction tool to form a sloped surface. If you only have AMElite, you can create, move, and rotate the wedge, but you won't be able to subtract it.

Using a Wedge as a Machining Tool

```
Command: SOLWEDGE
corner of wedge:                          Pick point 0,-1.5 (location is not actually
                                          important).

Length/<Other corner>: L
Length: 9
Width: 3
Height: 2.75
```

Boundary evaluation and tessellation occur.

```
Command: UCS                              Restore UCS FRONT.
Command: ROTATE
Select objects:                          Select the wedge.
Base point:                              Pick a point near front middle of base of
                                         wedge.

<Rotation angle>/Reference: 180

Command: ZOOM                            Zoom Extents if you need to see better.

Command: MOVE
Select objects:                          Select the wedge.
1 selected, 1 found
Select objects: <RETURN>
Base point or displacement: ENDP         Pick left rear endpoint of wedge at ①
                                         (see fig. 18.6).
Second point of displacement: ENDP       Pick rear vertical box at ②.
Command: SOLSUB                          Select rear vertical box and subtract
                                         wedge.

Command: ZOOM                            Previous, if you zoomed Extents above.
Command: SAVE                            Figure 18.7 shows the results.
```

Figure 18.6:
The wedge, ready to move and subtract.

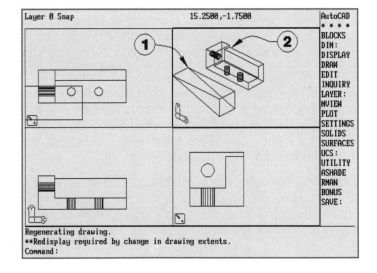

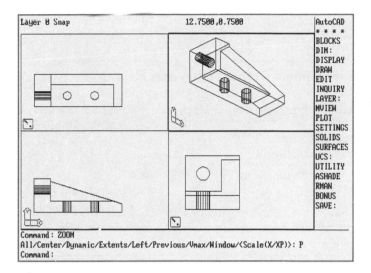

Figure 18.7:
The wedge removed
from guide block.

If your finished profile required a more complex shape, you could draw the shape in 2D, extrude it to form a solid, then subtract it from the main body. Extrusions are covered a little later in the chapter.

Creating Fillets and Chamfers on Existing Solids

When you draw fillets and chamfers in 2D, it is often easier to draw rectangular shapes, then fillet the corners afterwards. You can also do the same thing with 3D solids using the SOLFILL and SOLCHAM utility commands. They are both located in the solids [MODIFY >] menu. Both of these commands require the full AME.

SOLCHAM can add to the solid to chamfer an inside edge or subtract from it to bevel an outside edge. SOLFILL can also fill an inside edge or round off an outside edge. Both SOLFILL and SOLCHAM will work on straight, convex, or concave edges of a solid. Where two or more edges come together at a corner, SOLFILL and SOLCHAM will correctly resolve the corner.

When you use SOLCHAM, AutoCAD first prompts for a *base surface*, then for the edge(s) to chamfer. Then, you specify the distance to chamfer back along the base surface (that's why you specify a base surface). Finally, you specify the distance to chamfer along the second surface. If you pick an edge that is not adjacent to the base surface, it won't be chamfered. When you press <RETURN>, AutoCAD creates a primitive called a chamfer and automatically subtracts or unions (adds) it to the solid.

Because a fillet is symmetrical along an edge, SOLFILL prompts only for the edge(s) you want to fillet. You can select one or more edges. Then, you specify the radius of the fillet. AutoCAD calculates the resulting fillet primitive, then subtracts or unions it to the solid.

Use SOLFILL to finish up the guide block model by filleting the corner of the left vertical box.

Filleting a Corner Using SOLFILL

Command: **SOLFILL**
Select edges to be filleted (Press ENTER when done):   Pick left vertical plate at ①
                                                            (see fig. 18.8).

1 edges selected. **<RETURN>**
Diameter/<Radius> of fillet< 0.00>: **1**

Boundary evaluation and tessellation occur.

Command: **SAVE**   Figure 18.9 shows the
                                                            finished guide block.

Figure 18.8:
The guide block be-
fore the fillet.

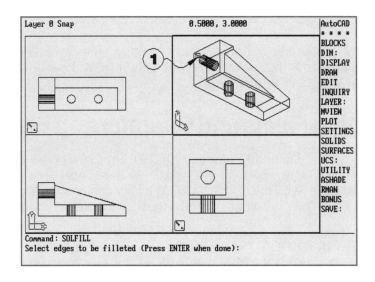

There is one thing to keep in mind when you are creating multiple fillets on a model. If you select a single edge to fillet, then come back and fillet an edge that intersects the fillet, you will get the effect shown in figure 18.10. If you want the two edges to fillet together smoothly, as shown in figure 18.11, pick both edges within the same SOLFILL command. For example, if you wanted to fillet all twelve edges of a cube to model a die (as in pair of dice), you would have to select all twelve edges in the same operation.

By now, you may wish you could remove hidden lines and view your solid clearly. You can, but you need to prepare your model before you can use the HIDE command on it.

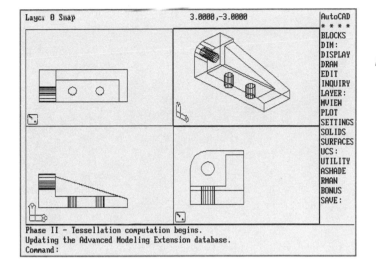

Figure 18.9:
The guide block after
the fillet.

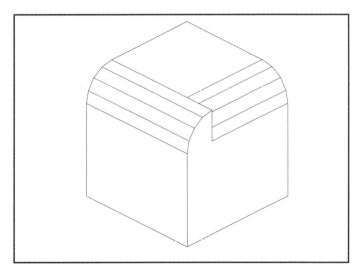

Figure 18.10:
Non-simultaneous
fillets.

Controlling How Solid Models Display

You can choose to display your solids in wireframe (the default), or with surface meshes. The two methods don't produce much difference in how the model looks. But when you perform a hidden line removal with the HIDE command or shade your model with SHADE, it won't display properly unless you first put a surface mesh on it.

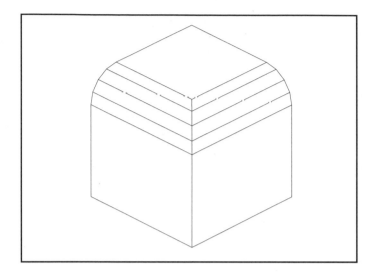

Figure 18.11:
Simultaneous fillets.

AutoCAD provides commands to convert solids between wireframe and mesh representations, and to control the resolution of your wireframe or surface mesh. The resolution can be set by command, or by setting a variable. Here's a listing of some of the commands that control solid model display:

SOLWIRE   Allows you to select and display a solid as a wireframe.

SOLMESH   Allows you to select and display solids using a surface mesh. Solids must have a surface mesh for the HIDE and SHADE commands to work properly.

SOLWDENS   (SOLid Wire DENSity) This command sets the wire density (number of tessellation lines) for curved surfaces of wireframes, and the mesh density of meshes. It can be a number from 1 to 8. Higher numbers give higher resolutions, and take longer to calculate images.

SOLVAR   Like the SETVAR command, SOLVAR lets you assign values to variables. SOLVAR controls only variables that relate to solid modeling. You can set wire density with either the SOLWDENS command, or by using SOLVAR to set the variable SOLWDENS.

You can use any of these commands with either the full AME or AMElite. They are located in the [Solids] pull-down menu under [Display], or you can access them from the [Display] option in the [SOLIDS] screen menu.

These settings affect only how solids display — internally, they are still calculated as solids with complete precision, unlike AutoCAD 3D surface entities, which are only approximations.

The choice of wireframe or mesh has other effects beyond how it displays. Meshes and wireframes are both specially controlled blocks, and only one can display at a time. A mesh explodes into pface entities while a wireframe explodes into lines and polylines. You can use osnaps such as TAN, CEN, and QUA on arcs and circles in a wireframe, but you will be restricted to osnaps such as ENDP, INT, and MID in mesh representations.

Let's use the solid display functions to place a mesh on the guide block model, then use HIDE to perform a hidden line removal on the isometric view.

Checking the Model With HIDE

```
Command: SOLMESH
Select solids to be meshed ...
Select objects:                              Select the solid.
1 solid selected.
```

Boundary evaluation, tessellation, and meshing occur.

```
Creating block for mesh representation...
Done.
Command: HIDE
Regenerating drawing.
Removing hidden lines: nn                    Your drawing should resemble
                                             figure 18.12.

Command: END                                 Save drawing for later in this
                                             chapter, and exit.
```

To round out our tour of solid primitives, let's look at spheres and toruses.

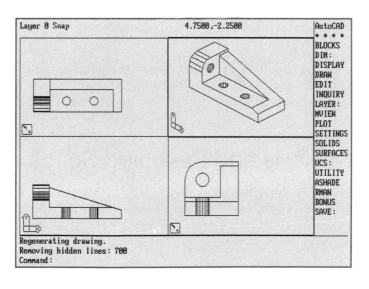

Figure 18.12:
The finished guide block, with HIDE.

Creating Toroidal and Spherical Primitives

AutoCAD's AME and AMElite modules include functions to create toruses and spheres. Both functions work much like the functions for creating toroidal and spherical surfaces that you can access from the [3D] menu, but they create solid primitives rather than a surface mesh.

The SOLSPHERE command prompts you for a center point, which can be picked or typed in (see fig. 18.13). Then, you supply either a radius value or diameter value.

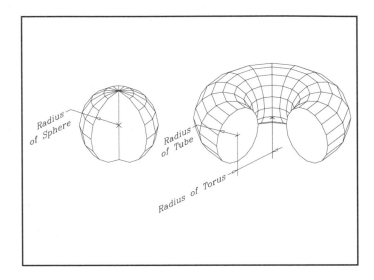

Figure 18.13:
OLSPHERE and
SOLTORUS
examples.

The SOLTORUS command prompts you to specify the center of the torus, the radius or diameter of the torus, and the radius or diameter of the tube (see fig. 18.13). As with the TORUS surface mesh command, you can pick points for the distance values, or type them in.

If you specify a radius for the tube that is greater than the radius of the torus, you create a self-intersecting torus. A self-intersecting torus has no center hole and looks like an apple. If you specify a negative torus radius, the resulting solid will have a football shape.

Creating Extrusions and Revolved Solids

Often, you model three-dimensional solids using a two-dimensional pattern as a basis. This might be the 2D profile of a part that you extrude, or a cross section that you revolve to form a solid. AutoCAD AME and AMElite provide SOLEXT for extrusions and SOLREV for revolved solids. Both use 2D geometry as a basis for the solids.

The SOLEXT command will extrude polylines, polygons, circles, ellipses, and 3D polylines. If the polyline you select has a width associated with it, SOLEXT ignores the width and extrudes the shape from the center line of the polyline. There are other limits to what SOLEXT can do. The geometry must consist of at least two line segments. If the polyline isn't closed, SOLEXT assumes it to be closed by a line from the first segment to the last. If the polyline has segments that intersect (whether real or assumed by SOLEXT), SOLEXT will not extrude the shape.

Extrusions can be straight or tapered, but tapered extrusions require the full AME. The extrusion taper angle must be zero or greater, and must be less than 90 degrees, so the 2D base will always be larger than the tapered end of the extrusion. In other words, you can't taper out from the base — only in.

Let's use the SOLEXT command to create the basic solid that will be used to model the hinge block shown in figure 18.14. Begin a new drawing, setting it equal to your 3D prototype drawing, draw the polyline profile, and extrude it.

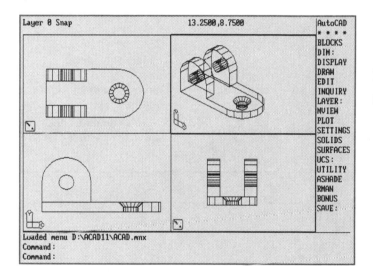

Figure 18.14:
The finished hinge block 3D model.

Using an Extruded Solid to Create HINGBLOK

Begin a NEW drawing named HINGBLOK=3D.

Select the front (lower left) view.

Command: **UCS**	Restore UCS FRONT.
Command: **ZOOM**	Zoom Left corner -1,-1 with height 5.
Command: **PLINE**	Draw front profile with lower left corner at 0,0 as shown in figure 18.15. Use line and arc options, and close it.

Using an Extruded Solid to Create HINGBLOK—continued

```
Command: SOLEXT                              Extrude polyline to 3" thick.
Select polylines and circles for extrusion...
Select objects:                              Select the polyline.
1 selected, 1 found
Select objects: <RETURN>
Height of extrusion: 3
Extrusion taper angle from Z <0>: <RETURN>

Command: UCS                                 Set to World.
Command: MOVE                                The hinge block extruded into
                                             negative coordinates. Move it
                                             with a displacement of 0,3.
```

Zoom each of the viewports to match figure 18.14.

Select the top view.

```
Command: CIRCLE                              Draw .375 radius hole in hori-
                                             zontal plate at 4.5,1.5,-1.

Command: SOLEXT
Select polylines and circles for extrusion...
Select objects:                              Select the circle.
Height of extrusion: 2
Extrusion taper angle from Z <0>: <RETURN>   Your drawing should resemble
                                             figure 18.16.

Command: SOLSUB                              Select the main body and sub-
                                             tract the cylinder (see fig. 18.17).

Command: SAVE
```

Figure: 18.15.
The front profile of a hinge block.

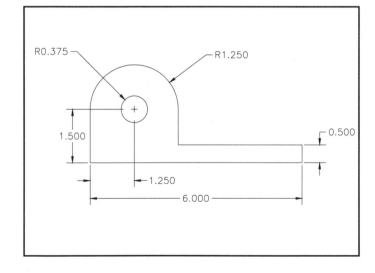

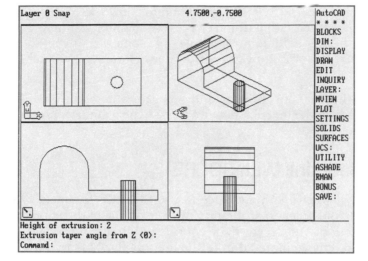

Figure 18.16:
The hinge block before SOLSUB.

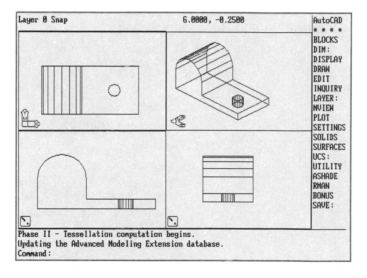

Figure 18.17:
The hinge block after SOLSUB.

Before you finish modeling the hinge block, let's take a side trip to one of the utility commands called SOLSEP.

Separating Joined Solids With SOLSEP

When you take two solids and perform a union on them you are joining them together. When you subtract one solid from another, you are still joining them together in the sense that both original primitives still exist, although one exists as a void.

AutoCAD's full AME provides the SOLSEP command to allow you to separate solids that have been joined together with a union or subtraction. For example, if you had subtracted a cylinder from a solid to form a hole only to find that the hole should have been countersunk, you would need to separate the original cylinder from the rest of the model.

Let's go back into the hinge block drawing and separate the hole in the horizontal plate from the main body of the model. Then, we'll erase the cylindrical solid and put in the countersunk hole.

Creating a Countersink With SOLREV

The next exercise will also give you a chance to use SOLREV to create a revolved solid. Separate the original hole, erase it, and draw the profile of the countersink as you would see it in section. Then revolve the countersink to create a solid counter-sink tool to be used to remove material from the main body. This requires the full AME module.

Separating and Revolving Solids

`Command: SOLSEP`	
`Select objects:`	Select the solid.
`1 selected, 1 found`	
`Select objects: <RETURN>`	
`1 solid selected.`	
`Command: ERASE`	Select the cylinder.
Select the front view.	
`Command: UCS`	Restore UCS FRONT.
`Command: PLINE`	Draw profile of countersink from 4.5,0,-1.5 to @.375,0 to @0,.25 to @.25,.25 to @-.625,0 and close (see fig. 18.18).
`Command: UCS`	Set to World.
`Command: SOLREV`	
`Select polyline or circle for revolution...`	Select polyline profile of counter-sink.
`Axis of revolution - Entity/X/Y/<Start point of axis>: ENDP`	Select the bottom point of counter-sink at center line.
`End point of axis: ENDP`	Pick the top center point.
`Included angle <full circle>: <RETURN>`	

Separating and Revolving Solids—continued

Select the isometric view.

Command: **SOLSUB**

Select the main body and subtract the countersink. Your drawing should now resemble figure 18.19.

Command: **SAVE**

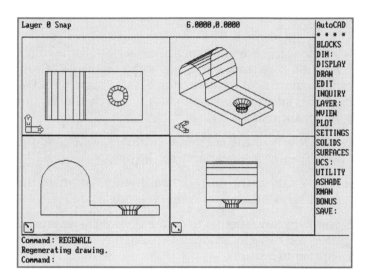

Figure 18.18:
The hinge block after revolving the counter-sink.

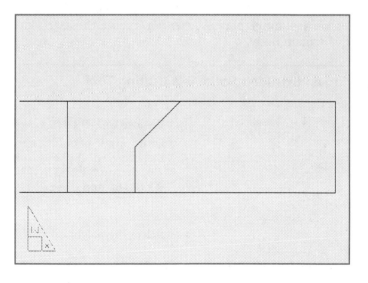

Figure 18.19:
Detail of the counter-sink profile.

Okay, if you caught us, we'll admit that you could have just used a SOLCHAM on the original cylinder. But, then, you wouldn't have an excuse to use SOLSEP and SOLREV.

More on Revolved Solids

The last exercise showed you how to create a revolved solid from 2D geometry. SOLREV provides four options for defining the axis of revolution.

SOLREV Options

Entity   Allows you to select a line or single-segment polyline to use as the axis of rotation. You cannot use one of the segments of your profile geometry as the axis of rotation. If necessary, osnap a 2D line over the segment you want as the axis, then pick the 2D line when prompted for the axis entity.

X   Defines the X axis of the current coordinate system as the axis of revolution. The axis passes through the origin.

Y   Defines the Y axis of the current coordinate system as the axis of revolution. The axis passes through the origin.

<Start Point>   Allows you to pick two points to define the axis of revolution. Using this option, you can pick endpoints of segments in your profile, or pick any other two points.

You have the basic blank stock for the hinge block, along with the countersunk hole. Next, switch to the right side view and create a rectangular tool to cut the material out between each of the vertical hinge plates. After you create the extruded cutting block, subtract it from the main body.

Using an Extruded Solid as a Cutting Tool

Select the right side view.

```
Command: UCS                                    Restore UCS RIGHT.

Command: PLINE                                  Draw profile of cutout between
                                                the two vertical plates from point
                                                .75,.5,-2 to @1.5<0 to @3<90 to
                                                @1.5<180 and close.

Command: SOLEXT
Select polylines and circles for extrusion...
Select objects:                                 Select the polyline.
Height of extrusion: 6
```

> ### Using an Extruded Solid as a Cutting Tool—continued
>
> `Extrusion taper angle from Z <0>:` **`<RETURN>`**
>
> `Command:` **`SOLSUB`**
>
> The cutting tool should appear as shown in figure 18.20.
>
> Select the main body of the model and subtract the block (see fig. 18.21).

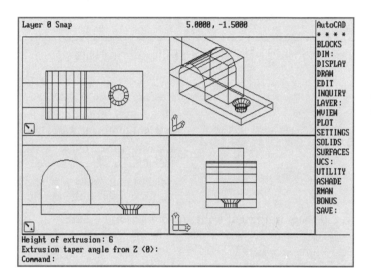

Figure 18.20:
An extruded block as a cutting tool.

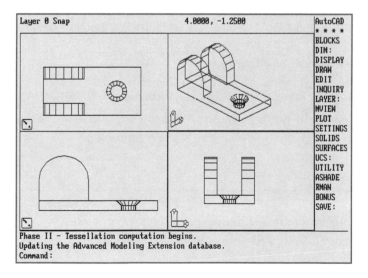

Figure 18.21:
The hinge block after the block is removed.

Finishing the Hinge Block With Fillets and Holes

To finish the hinge block, we'll add holes and round off the end of the horizontal plate with two fillets. Instead of creating a cylinder and subtracting it from the main body to get the holes, draw circles and extrude them. Then, subtract the resulting solids.

Pick both corners of the horizontal plate and fillet them at the same time. Finally, place a mesh on the finished model and perform a hidden line removal on the isometric view to check it.

Finishing the Hinge Block With Fillets and Holes

Select the front view.

Command: **UCS**	Restore UCS FRONT.
Command: **CIRCLE**	Draw .375 radius circle for hole in vertical plates at 1.25,1.5,-4.
Command: **SOLEXT**	Extrude the circle to a height of 6" (see fig. 18.22).
Command: **SOLSUB**	Select main body of model and subtract resulting cylinder.

Select the isometric view and zoom in to right front end of horizontal plate.

Command: **SOLFILL**
Select edges to be filleted (Press ENTER
    when done):   Select vertical edges of plate at ①
                                                    and ② and <RETURN>.

2 edges selected.
Diameter/<Radius> of fillet< 0.00>: **1.5**   Figure 18.23 shows the filleted
                                                    plate.

Boundary evaluation and tessellation occur.

Command: **UCS**	Set to World.
Command: **ZOOM**	Previous.

Finally, you'll check the model by putting a mesh on it and doing a hide.

Command: **SOLMESH**	Select the solid.
Command: **HIDE**	
Command: **END**	

That takes you through all of the modeling primitives except cones. Let's take a quick look at the SOLCONE command, and use it and SOLINT to find the intersection of two solids.

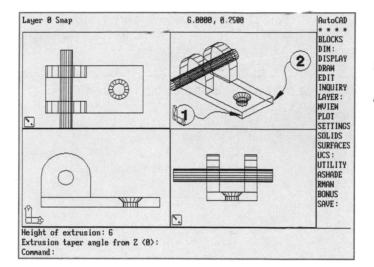

Figure 18.22:
The extruded cylinder
and fillet pick points.

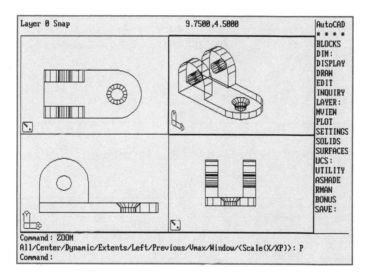

Figure 18.23:
Subtracted holes and
the filleted plate.

Intersections, Interferences, and SOLINT

AutoCAD's full AME module includes a Boolean function called SOLINT that allows you to model the intersection of two or more solids. The intersection is the common mass shared by the solids you select. You can use SOLINT to check for conflicts and interferences between two parts. Or use it to do such things as take a slice out of a cone. In fact, that's just what you're about to do!

Start a new drawing and set it equal to 3D. Create a cone with a diameter of 4" and a height of 6". Then, create a box 6" high to use as a tool to cut the slice out of the cone.

Finding the Intersection of a Cone and Box

Begin a NEW drawing named CONE=3D.

Select the top (upper left) viewport and set the UCS to World.

```
Command: SOLCONE
Elliptical/<Center point>:                    Pick a point in the middle for center of cone.
Diameter/<Radius>: 2
Height of cone: 6
Command: SOLBOX
Corner of box:                                Draw the box to intersect the cone as shown
                                              in figure 18.24.
Cube/Length/<Other corner>:
Height: 6
Command: SOLINT
Select objects: 1 selected, 1 found           Pick the cone.
Select objects: 1 selected, 1 found           Pick the box.
Select objects: <RETURN>
2 solids selected.
Command: REDRAW
Command: QUIT
```

As figure 18.25 shows, SOLINT finds the material that is common to both solids and subtracts the rest.

Figure 18.24:
The cone and box
before intersection.

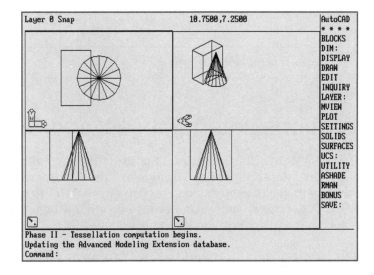

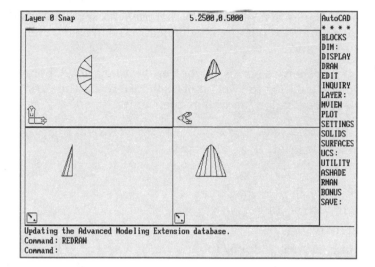

Figure 18.25:
Common material
shared by the cone
and box.

This is a good place for a break. You've covered all of the solid primitives and most of the utility commands. Most of what you have covered so far is not very different from basic 3D surface modeling.

In the next section, you will learn how to specify material types for your model, how to change the material specification, and how to determine some of the mass properties of your model. You will also learn to use a few more of the solids utility commands.

Adding Properties to Your Solid Model

Although creating a 2D drawing from a 3D solid model is one of the easiest ways to draw a complex part, the emphasis in solid modeling has traditionally been on designing rather than drafting. A large part of design involves not only defining the geometry of a part, but also defining and determining other characteristics such as weight, center of gravity, surface area, and moments of inertia.

AutoCAD's AME and AMElite allow you to determine those properties and others by first specifying certain parameters, like the type of material from which the solid would be made. Then, after setting a few variables to control the accuracy of your calculations, you can evaluate the design with a single command.

Adding a Material Specification With SOLMAT

Both AME and AMElite include the SOLMAT command as the [Material] selection on the solids [UTILITY >] pull-down menu, for controlling a solid's material properties.

SOLMAT lets you choose from a list of common materials to set a solid's default material. If the material you need is not already defined, you can easily create, save, and load your own material specifications.

All of the defined material properties are used when evaluating a solid. For example, the density is used when calculating the weight of a solid. Here are the variables you can assign in a material specification, as well as their units:

- Density, kg/cu_m
- Young's Modulus, GN/sq_m
- Poisson's ratio
- Yield strength, MN/sq_m not,
- Ultimate strength, MN/sq_m
- Thermal Conductivity
- Linear expansion coefficient, alpha/1e6
- Specific heat, kJ/(kg deg_C)
- Convection Coefficient

SOLMAT Options

The SOLMAT command lets you manipulate most properties of a solid's material definition. Here are the options available with SOLMAT.

Change   Allows you to change the material assigned to a solid.

Edit   Lets you edit specific properties of a material.

eXit   Exits the SOLMAT command.

LIst   Displays the current property settings of a material.

LOad   Allows you to load a material definition from an external ASCII file.

New   Creates a new material definition.

Remove   Removes a material definition from the current model.

Save   Saves a material definition in an external file.

Set   Sets the default material definition of newly created solids.

?   Displays a listing of all materials currently defined in your model.

Before you calculate the properties of a solid, remember to first assign the correct material to the solid. The default material is MILD_STEEL.

Calculating the Properties of a Solid

SOLMASSP is a full AME command for calculating the mass properties of solids in your models. After you have assigned a material definition to the solid, you use SOLMASSP to calculate and display all of the available properties. SOLMASSP calculates mass, volume, bounding box (3D extents), centroid, moments of inertia, products of inertia, radii of gyration, and principal moments of a solid. When AME is finished calculating those values, you have the option of writing them to a file. You can select SOLMASSP as [Mass Property] from the solids [INQUIRY >] pull-down menu.

Changing the Characteristics of a Solid

Standard AutoCAD editing commands, such as STRETCH, do not work on solids, and cannot change the size and shape of individual features in a solid. A composite solid is much like a block — you cannot get at the individual entities that make it up, which prevents you from accessing the individual primitive features. You need a way to change solids and their features. One of the most important utility commands for editing solids is the SOLCHP command, which requires the full AME. SOLCHP lets you change many characteristics of solid primitives. What makes it so important is the fact that you can use the command to change primitives that are part of a larger, composite solid. Here's why.

When you perform a union on two solids, AutoCAD calculates the resulting union and displays the result. But, the original primitives that were unioned still exist in memory, and AutoCAD maintains these along with the composite solid. You can't see the original primitives, but they are still there and can be accessed by the SOLCHP command.

This lets you perform such edits as changing the color of a hole, moving a hole in a solid (by relocating the cylinder that created it), deleting a hole, or changing its size. You can even use SOLCHP to change the overall size of the main body. Before using the SOLCHP command, take a look at its options for editing your solids.

SOLCHP Options

Color   Changes the color assigned to a primitive.

Delete   Deletes a primitive from the model. If it is a stand-alone primitive (not part of a composite solid), the primitive is deleted altogether. If it is part of a composite, it is deleted from the CSG tree, but you have the option of retaining it as a stand-alone primitive. (The CSG tree is defined following this list.)

Evaluate   Causes a re-evaluation of the CSG tree, updating the solid. This is similar in concept to a drawing regeneration.

Instance   Creates a copy of the primitive you select, in the same location as the original. This is most useful when you want to copy or replace a feature.

Move   Lets you move a primitive around in the solid. For example, you can relocate a hole (subtracted cylinder) using the Move option.

Next   Cycles through the solid to the next primitive in the composite solid.

Pick   Similar to Next, but this option lets you pick the primitive to be edited.

Replace   Replaces the selected primitive with another solid. For example, you can create a rectangular solid and replace a hole in a solid with a square cutout simply by replacing the hole's defining cylinder with the new rectangular primitive.

Size   Gives you control over the size of a selected primitive. You can resize individual components of a composite solid, such as changing the diameter of an existing hole. Size can change the size of a box; the x radius, y radius, and height of a cone; the radius of a sphere; the major and minor radii of a torus; the shape, height, and taper of an extrusion; and the included angle of a revolved solid.

eXit   Exits the SOLCHP command and returns you to the command prompt.

CSG stands for *Constructive Solid Geometry*. The CSG tree is a hierarchical structure of the Boolean operations, like union and subtraction, that were used to create a composite solid. At the top of the tree structure is the composite solid. In descending levels under that are the Boolean operations that make up the composite, and the primitives that help define the composite. You can think of the CSG tree as the parts list and instructions for building a composite solid.

Let's use the SOLCHP command to make a few changes to the guide block model you created earlier in the chapter. If you have the IA DISK, you have the GUIDBLOK drawing as IA6GUID.DWG. Load the drawing, change the size of the outermost hole in the horizontal plate, and move the hole half an inch toward the matching hole. This requires the full AME.

Changing the Size and Shape of a Composite Solid Model

Begin a NEW drawing named GUIDBLK=IA6GUIDB.

Begin a NEW drawing named GUIDBLK=GUIDBLOK.

Command: **UCS**   Set to World.

> ### Changing the Size and Shape of a Composite Solid Model—continued
>
> Select upper right viewport.
>
> Load AME.
>
> Command: **SOLCHP**   An XYZ icon appears.
> Select Solid: Select the solid.
>
> Each primitive flashes as it updates.
>
> Boundary evaluation, tessellation, and meshing occur.
>
> Select Primitive: Select any of the primitive fea-
>   tures.
>
> Color/Delete/Evaluate/Instance/Move/Next/
>   Pick/Replace/Size/eXit <N>: **<RETURN>**
>
> Use <RETURN>s to cycle through primitives until right-most vertical cylinder is high-
> lighted.
>
> Color/Delete/Evaluate/Instance/Move/Next/
>   Pick/Replace/Size/eXit <N>: **S**
>
> Specify x radius <0.375>: **.25**
> Specify y radius <0.25>: **<RETURN>**
> Specify height <3>: **<RETURN>**
>
> Boundary evaluation and tessellation occur.
>
> Color/Delete/Evaluate/Instance/Move/Next/
>   Pick/Replace/Size/eXit <N>: **M**   Move the cylinder .5" toward
>   the other hole.
> Base point of displacement: **-.5,0**   Enter displacement, like for
>   MOVE command.
> Second point of displacement: **<RETURN>**   See figure 18.26.
> Color/Delete/Evaluate/Instance/Move/Next/
>   Pick/Replace/Size/eXit <N>: **X**
>
> Boundary evaluation, tessellation, and meshing occur.

If we had wanted to change both of the holes in the horizontal plate, we could have changed both within the same SOLCHP command.

Let's take a look at another change. Say you have a hole that you want to highlight, to identify a special tolerance consideration. One way to do that would be to change the color of the hole to make it plot differently from the rest of the composite. Because the hole is really a primitive that is buried inside a composite solid, you cannot use the standard AutoCAD CHANGE and CHPROP commands. Instead, use the Color option of SOLCHP.

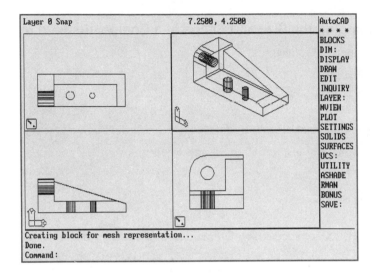

Figure 18.26:
The guide block after
resizing and moving
the hole.

Changing the Color of Primitives in a Composite Solid

Change the color of the last hole to red.

```
Command: SOLCHP
Select Solid:                              Select the composite solid.
Select Primitive:                          Select the smaller vertical cyl-
                                           inder.

Color/Delete/Evaluate/Instance/Move/Next/Pick/
  Replace/Size/eXit <N>: C
New color <7 (white)>: RED
Color/Delete/Evaluate/Instance/Move/Next/Pick/
  Replace/Size/eXit <N>: X
```

Boundary evaluation and tessellation occur.

```
Creating block for mesh representation...
Done.
```

Not only does the primitive change color, but so does the inside face of the hole. If you perform a HIDE on the view, the hole will still retain its new color.

Deleting Features From a Composite Solid

As with other changes to a composite solid, erasing a feature cannot be accomplished with the standard AutoCAD ERASE command. But, SOLCHP lets you delete primitives from the composite. Let's use it to delete the last hole from the model.

> ### Deleting Primitives From a Composite Solid
>
> Delete the last hole (the red one).
>
> ```
> Command: SOLCHP
> Select Solid:                                     Select the composite.
> Select Primitive:                                 Select the red cylinder.
> Color/Delete/Evaluate/Instance/Move/Next/Pick/
>   Replace/Size/eXit <N>: D
> Retain detached primitive? <N>: <RETURN>
> Color/Delete/Evaluate/Instance/Move/Next/Pick/
>   Replace/Size/eXit <N>: X
> ```
>
> Boundary evaluation, tessellation, and meshing occur.
>
> ```
> Creating block for mesh representation...
> Done.
> Command: REDRAW
> ```

The primitive is removed and the change is reflected when the model is updated. If you had answered yes to the question about retaining the detached primitive, AME would have separated the cylinder from the composite, but would not have deleted it from the drawing.

Replacing Features in a Composite Solid

Another operation you often need to perform on a solid involves updating the geometry of some of the features. You may need to change a slope, change the shape of a cutout, or change a hole to a square slot. The SOLCHP Replace option lets you do that. To see how it works, replace the remaining hole in the horizontal plate with a square slot.

> ### Replacing Primitives in a Composite Solid
>
> ```
> Command: PLINE                Draw a 1 x 1 square and close
>                               it.
> Command: SOLEXT               Extrude the square to a height
>                               of 4" with no taper.
> Command: SOLCHP
> Select Solid:                 Select the composite.
> Select Primitive:             Select the remaining vertical
>                               cylinder (see fig. 18.27).
> Color/Delete/Evaluate/Instance/Move/Next/
>   Pick/Replace/Size/eXit <N>: R
> Select solid to replace primitive:   Select the extruded square.
> Retain detached primitive? <N>: <RETURN>
> ```

▶ **Replacing Primitives in a Composite Solid —continued**

```
Color/Delete/Evaluate/Instance/Move/Next/
   Pick/Replace/Size/eXit <N>: X
```

Boundary evaluation, tessellation, and meshing occur.

```
Creating block for mesh representation...
Done.
```

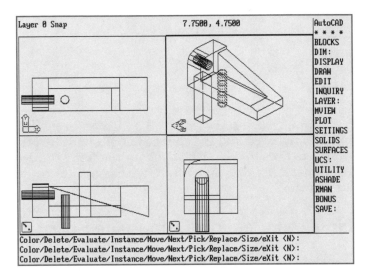

Figure 18.27:
Selecting a cylinder to
replace with a square.

What happened to the square? It disappeared. It became a part of the composite solid, but because it doesn't touch the rest of the solid, you can't tell that it has been subtracted.

The Replace option does not automatically place the new primitive in the same location as the original. If you don't position the new primitive before you execute the Replace, you can use the Move option to move the new primitive into position. Let's try that with the square.

▶ **Moving a Primitive Into Position**

```
Command: SOLCHP                              Select the composite.
Select Solid:                                Select any primitive.
Select Primitive:
Color/Delete/Evaluate/Instance/Move/Next/
   Pick/Replace/Size/eXit <N>: <RETURN>      Use <RETURN>s to cycle
                                             through primitives until the
                                             extruded square is selected.
```

Moving a Primitive Into Position—continued

```
Color/Delete/Evaluate/Instance/Move/Next/
    Pick/Replace/Size/eXit <N>: M
Base point of displacement:                    Pick a corner point on square.
Second point of displacement:                  Pick a point inside base of
                                               composite to place it.

Color/Delete/Evaluate/Instance/Move/Next/
    Pick/Replace/Size/eXit <N>: X
```

Boundary evaluation, tessellation, and meshing occur.

```
Creating block for mesh representation...
Done.                                          See figure 18.28.
Command: END                                   Save the model and exit.
```

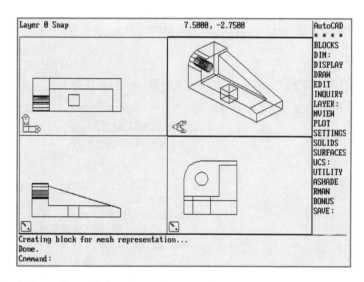

Figure 18.28:
The square moved into position.

That's it! Now the solid is complete, and you had an opportunity to use most of the options for SOLCHP. SOLCHP gives you a way to modify existing 3D solids. But what about modifying other types of 3D data, like polylines that have a thickness assigned to them? Let's take a look.

Turning Non-Solid 3D Geometry Into Solids

Sometimes it's easier to create models by adding thickness to 2D entities such as polylines. Or, you may need to take existing 3D models you have created with previous versions of AutoCAD and turn them into solid models.

AutoCAD's AME and AMElite include the SOLIDIFY command, which converts several types of AutoCAD objects into solids. The entities can be polylines, polygons, circles, ellipses, traces, donuts, or solids (standard AutoCAD *solid* entities, not AME solid models). Any polyline width is ignored. The object must have a non-zero thickness, because its thickness becomes the extruded height of the resulting solid object. A positive thickness extrudes up; negative extrudes down.

The results of SOLIDIFY are almost exactly like those of SOLEXT. But SOLIDIFY requires a predefined thickness while SOLEXT prompts for thickness, ignoring any preset thickness. SOLEXT also allows taper, while SOLIDIFY does not. Like the SOLEXT command, if the object is not closed, SOLIDIFY assumes a closing line from the end of the last segment to the beginning of the first segment. And, the object cannot have intersecting segments, whether real or assumed.

Try out the SOLIDIFY command in a new drawing. To test SOLIDIFY, set thickness to 4. Then, draw a closed polyline of any shape. Draw another polyline inside the first. Solidify both polylines, then subtract the second from the first one to prove that they are now solids.

Turning 3D Wireframes Into Solids With SOLIDIFY

Begin a NEW drawing named SOLIDIFY.

`Command:` **VPOINT**   Rotate angle in X,Y plane to 315, angle
                                             from X,Y plane to 30.

Toggle grid on.

`Command:` **THICKNESS**
`New value for THICKNESS <0.0000>:` **4**

`Command:` **PLINE**   Draw first polyline and close it.
`Command:` **PLINE**   Draw second closed polyline inside the
                                             first. Figure 18.29 shows what your
                                             polylines might look like.

Load AME, if not already loaded.

`Command:` **SOLIDIFY**
`Select objects:`   Select the first and second polylines.
`Command:` **SOLSUB**   Select the outside solid and subtract
                                             the inside solid.

Check the results by meshing the model with SOLMESH and doing a HIDE (see fig. 18.30).

`Command:` **QUIT**

Use SOLIDIFY when you need to update 3D models that were created before Release 11, or that were created without the benefit of the AME module. This allows designing on multiple stations that don't have access to AME, then bringing all of the models onto one station that does have AME to convert 3D shapes to solids.

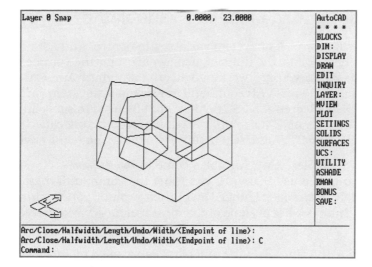

Figure 18.29:
Sample polylines
before solidifying.

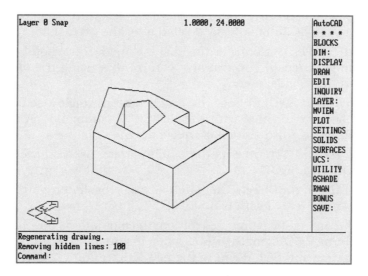

Figure 18.30:
Meshed solid with
Hide.

Listing Solids Information and Controlling Variables

Let's finish up this section of the chapter by covering the variables that the solid modeling module adds to AutoCAD. Also, we'll cover a command that allows you to list information about a solid, and one that lets you find the surface area of a solid.

Setting and Listing Solid Modeling Variables

The AME module uses its own set of system variables to control and list parameters such as the wire density of solids, the units of measurement for the volume of a solid, and the display mode. When you are working with the standard AutoCAD drawing environment, you can use the SETVAR command to list and set system variables like PDMODE and TILEMODE. Regrettably, SETVAR cannot be used to set solid modeling system variables. AME and AMElite include a similar command called SOLVAR, which works very much like SETVAR. Use it to tailor your solid modeling environment.

Like standard system variables, AME variables come in two types — read only, and ones that you can change. To use SOLVAR, you issue the command, then the name of the variable you wish to change. AutoCAD will then prompt you to supply a new value for the variable. Here is a list of some of the most common variables you will set with SOLVAR:

SOLAReau   (SOLid AREA Unit) Sets the unit of measure used in area calculations. AutoCAD maintains a list of valid unit types in the file ACAD.UNT.

SOLDELent   (SOLid DELete ENTity) Controls whether a 2D entity used as the basis for extrusion is automatically deleted after the extrusion takes place.

SOLDIsplay   (SOLid DISPLAY) Controls the display mode of a solid, whether wireframe or mesh. You can also control this using the display options in the [Solids] menu.

SOLHAngle   (SOLid Hatch ANGLE) Sets the hatch pattern angle used to crosshatch sections created with the SOLSECT command. SOLSECT is covered in the third section of this chapter.

SOLHPAT   (SOLid Hatch PATtern) Sets the hatch pattern used on sections created with SOLSECT.

SOLHSize   (SOLid Hatch SIZE) Sets the hatch size of crosshatch patterns used on sections created with SOLSECT.

SOLLength   Sets the unit of measure used for length calculations of solids. When you change SOLLength, AME asks if you also want to update SOLVolume and SOLAReau to the new length unit.

SOLMASs   Sets the unit of measure for the mass of the solid.

SOLVolume   Sets the unit of measure for volume calculations of solids.

?   Like a help request in other AutoCAD commands, this lists the SOLVARs along with their current settings.

The SOLAREA command uses the SOLLength variable to calculate surface area, then converts the results into SOLAReau units.

Listing Information Attached to a Solid

Like other entities in AutoCAD, solids have data attached to them that you don't normally see. The SOLLIST command allows you to extract and display that information. If you have the full AME, you can list information associated with an edge or face of a solid; with either AME or AMElite, you can list the CSG tree for a solid.

You can use the Edge option of SOLLIST to display such information as the type of edge (line, circular, and so on), its endpoints, center point, and radius. The Face option lists the type of surface, such as planar, cylindrical, conical, spherical, or toroidal. Depending on the type of surface, you will get other information such as radius, direction of the outward normal vector (direction away from the solid), and center point if it is a spherical or toroidal surface.

Finding the Surface Area of a Solid

Whether you are calculating the amount of surface finish required for a part or some other surface-related value, you will sometimes need to find the surface area of a solid you have created. AME and AMElite include a command called SOLAREA to do that. One caution: the area is computed as the sum of the areas of the mesh faces used to represent the solid. It is an approximation, so a higher SOLWDENS setting will increase accuracy.

Let's run through a quick exercise and calculate the surface area of the guide block. Calculate the surface area in square centimeters first (the default), then recalculate in square inches.

Calculating the Surface Area of a Solid

 Begin a NEW drawing named GUIDBLOK=IA6GUIDB, replacing your old GUIDBLOK drawing.

 Edit an EXISTING drawing named GUIDBLOK.

```
Command: UCS                                              Set to World.
```
Select upper right viewport.

Load AME.
```
Command: SOLLENGTH
Lenght units <cm> IN
Change area and volume units also <N>? Y
Command: SOLAREA
Select solids for surface area computation ...
Select objects:                                          Select the solid.
Updating solid.
Surface area of solids is 100.2 sq in
Command: SOLVAR
Variable name or ?: SOLAREA
Area units <sq cm>: SQ IN
Command: SOLAREA
Select solids for surface area computation ...
```

Calculating the Surface Area of a Solid—continued

```
Select objects:                                    Select the solid again.
Surface area of solids is 646.7 SQ cm
Command: QUIT
```

That wraps up the utility and inquiry commands. In the last section of the chapter, we'll show you how to turn a 3D solid model into a 2D drawing using a few more of the AME commands. You'll cut a section through a solid, transfer the profile of a solid to a 2D representation, and transfer a face or edge of a solid into 2D.

Turning Your Solid Model Into a Finished Drawing

There are really two sides to solid modeling — the design side and the documentation side. Some users need solid modeling to facilitate design, while others use it to help generate 2D drawings of complex 3D parts. Whichever your case, you will probably want to turn your solid model into a finished 2D drawing, complete with notes, dimensions, and other annotation. AutoCAD's full AME and paper space make this easy.

Starting Your 2D Drawing With Profile Views

When you begin laying out a 2D drawing, you normally start by drawing the outline of your design in three orthographic views. AutoCAD's full AME provides SOLPROF to automatically extract the profile of a solid.

SOLPROF is most useful in conjunction with paper space; in fact, it won't work in tiled viewports. You model your design in model space, use SOLPROF to create a profile for each view, then create a named block out of each profile. Enter paper space, insert your title block, insert each view in its correct orientation, and add annotations and dimensions.

SOLPROF does a hide on the current viewport and creates new 2D entities on new layers to represent the hidden view. You can then erase entities that you don't need in the final view. SOLPROF has an option to automatically place hidden lines on a layer separate from visible lines. If the HIDDEN linetype is loaded, it will automatically be set for the layer containing the hidden lines so hidden lines will display properly on your finished drawing.

There are two important points to remember when creating profiles. First, the profile is created relative to your current viewport. SOLPROF takes the viewpoint of that viewport into account when it determines which lines should be visible and which lines should be hidden. The number of that viewport determines how it names the layers it creates. These new layers will not show up in other viewports unless you thaw them there.

The other point is that the profile is created relative to the current UCS. You should set the UCS normal to the view before you create the profile. This makes it easy to insert the views into your final drawing in their correct orientations.

Use the hinge block model to create profiles of each of the top, front, and right side views of HINGBLOK. The next three exercises will take you through creation of each of these profiles and have you write them to disk so you can insert them into your final drawing.

Creating a Front Profile of Hinge Block

 Begin a NEW drawing named HINGBLOK=IA6HINGB, replacing your old HINGBLOK drawing.

 Edit an EXISTING drawing named HINGBLOK.

Select the front view.

Command: **UCS**	Restore UCS FRONT.
Command: **SOLPROF**	
Select objects:	Select the solid.
1 selected, 1 found	
Select objects: **\<RETURN>**	
Display hidden profile lines on separate layer ? \<N> **Y**	
Updating, evaluation, and hidden line removal occur.	
Command: **DDLMODES**	Turn off layers 0 and 0-PH-4, which contain your solid and hidden lines. Change layer 0-PV-4 to yellow, 0-PH-4 to blue and AME_FRZ to cyan (see fig. 18.31).
Command: **ZOOM**	Zoom in and examine the profile (see fig. 18.32).
Command: **DDLMODES**	Turn off 0-PV-4, and turn on 0-PH-4, to see hidden lines.

Notice that AME and SOLPROF have created several new layers. AME_FRZ is the layer AME uses to store the primitives that make up the solid. You will normally keep it off and should never need to use it directly. The SOLPROF command creates two layers, one for hidden lines (in this case, 0-PH-4) and one for visible lines (0-PV-4). It names the layers by combining the original layer name (0), a hyphen, PV (for ProfileVisible) or PH (ProfileHidden), another hyphen, and the viewport number (in this case, 4). If the HIDDEN linetype is loaded in the drawing, it automatically sets it for the PH layer. The check marks in the VP Frz New column of the layer control dialogue box show that these new layers are automatically frozen in new viewports so the profiles won't interfere with other entities.

Figure 18.31:
DDLMODES shows
new layers.

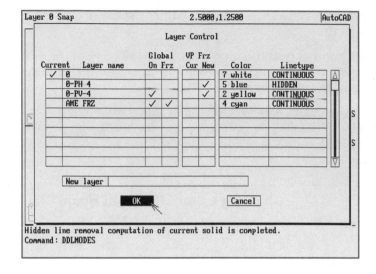

Figure 18.32:
The hinge block pro-
file.

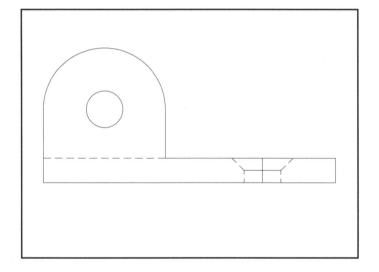

The visible and hidden profiles are created as blocks on their respective layers. You probably noticed that the hidden profile contained lines that you would not normally draw as hidden because they would be behind the visible profile lines. In your normal work, you may want to explode its block and erase the extra lines. When you explode it, the lines will take on color BYBLOCK, so you will want to reblock the remaining lines or use CHPROP to change them to BYLAYER.

Now let's write the profile to disk as the drawing file HING-F for later insertion into our final drawing.

Saving the Profile as a Drawing File

Command: **DDLMODES**	Turn on layer 0-PV-4.
Command: **WBLOCK**	Select both hidden and visible profiles and write to file HING-F with insertion base point at lower left corner of profile.
Command: **DDLMODES**	Turn on layer 0.

WBLOCK saved the front profile in its own file. Next, create the profile of the right side view (see fig. 18.33), the top view (see fig. 18.34), and the 3D view.

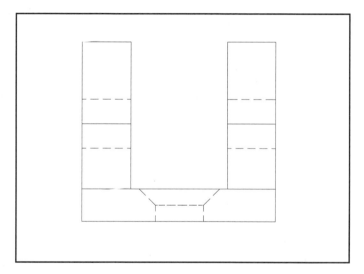

Figure 18.33:
The hinge block's right profile.

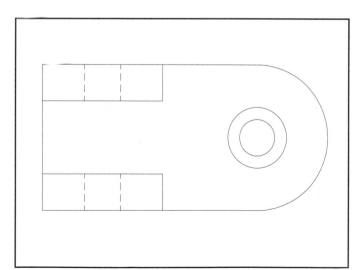

Figure 18.34:
The hinge block's top profile.

Creating the Right Side and Top Profiles of Hinge Block

Select the right side viewport.

Command: **UCS**	Restore UCS RIGHT.
Command: **SOLPROF**	Select solid and create profile with separate hidden layer.
Command: **DDLMODES**	Turn off layer 0. Set new PV layer to yellow, PH layer to blue.
Command: **WBLOCK**	Select both hidden and visible profiles and write to file HING-R with insertion base point at lower left corner of profile.
Command: **DDLMODES**	Turn on layer 0.

Select the top (plan) viewport.

Command: **UCS**	Set to World.
Command: **SOLPROF**	Select solid and create profile with separate hidden layer.
Command: **DDLMODES**	Turn off layer 0. Set new PV layer to yellow, PH layer to blue.
Command: **WBLOCK**	Select both hidden and visible profiles and write to file HING-T with insertion base point at lower left corner of profile.
Command: **DDLMODES**	Turn on layer 0.
Command: **SAVE**	

At this point, you could load each of the drawings you just created and clean them up before inserting them into your final drawing. But, we'll leave the task of composing the final drawing for a little later. For now, let's use the two other commands that AME provides for converting your solid model into a drawing. We'll start by cutting a section.

Cutting a Section Through a Solid

Documenting a design requires more than just drawing and dimensioning three views. Many times, you need section views of your design. With a 2D drawing, or with a 3D wireframe, you would have to draw the section from scratch, laying it out like any other part of your drawing. But one of the main benefits of creating your design using solid modeling is the fact that once the geometry is created, you can cut sections through it and automatically convert that data to a 2D representation.

The full AME command SOLSECT lets you cut a section through a solid, transferring it to 2D. It doesn't create the section on a special layer, but it will automatically crosshatch the section if you set a pattern. SOLSECT uses the X-Y plane of the current UCS as the cutting plane. So, the secret to using SOLSECT is to set up the UCS so it passes through the solid where you want the section taken.

To see how the SOLSECT command works, take a vertical section through the centers of the two vertical hinge plates.

Cutting a Section Through a Solid With SOLSECT

Select the front view.

```
Command: UCS                                    Restore UCS FRONT.
Command: PLAN                                   Change view to current UCS.
Command: UCS
Origin/ZAxis/3point/Entity/View/X/Y/Z/Prev/
  Restore/Save/Del/?/<World>: 3
Origin point <0,0,0>:                           Pick the center of the hole.
Point on positive portion of the X-axis <2.2500,
  1.5000,0.0000>: @0,0,-1
Point on positive-Y portion of the UCS X-Y plane
  <1.2500,2.5000,0.0000>: @0,1,0

Command: SOLVAR
Variable name or ?: SOLHPAT                      Set your hatch pattern to STEEL.
Hatch pattern <NONE>: STEEL

Command: SOLSECT
Select objects:                                 Select the solid.
1 selected, 1 found
Select objects: <RETURN>
```

Evaluation takes place.

Select the right view.

```
Command: UCS                                    Restore UCS RIGHT.
Command: PLAN                                   Change view to current UCS.
Command: ZOOM                                   Zoom 2.

Command: WBLOCK                                 Write the hatch outline and pat-
                                                tern to disk.

File name: HING-S
Block name: <RETURN>
Insertion base point:                           Pick lower left corner.
Select objects: C                               Use Crossing to select everything.
2 found
Select objects: R                               Remove mode.
Remove objects:                                 Remove the solid model, by select-
                                                ing at ① (see fig. 18.35).

1 selected, 1 found, 1 removed
Remove objects: <RETURN>                        Writes the file.

Command: REDRAWALL
Command: SAVE
```

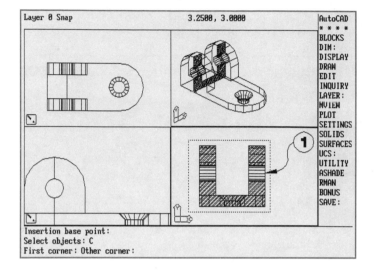

Figure 18.35:
A hatched section
through the solid.

The section is made up of two blocks: the section outline and the hatch. The two are not tied together in any way. You can change them to different layers if you want to alter their colors for plotting. You can specify the scale of the hatch pattern with the SOLHSIZE variable and the angle with the SOLHANGLE variable, using the SOLVAR command.

Copying an Edge or Face of a Solid to 2D

The last full AME command for translating your 3D solid into a 2D drawing is called SOLFEAT (SOLid FEATure). SOLFEAT is similar to the SOLPROF command, except that instead of generating an entire profile, it creates a 2D representation of a single edge or face. As with the other translation tools, SOLFEAT creates an unnamed block containing the resulting geometry and places it at the same location as the original edge or face.

When you are using the Edge option, SOLFEAT allows you to select only one edge at a time, so you can't use a window selection set. The same holds true with the Face option. You can only convert one face at a time. To select a face, you must pick one of its edges. However, every edge is an edge between two faces; AME can't tell which one you want. So the Face option lets you either accept the face that it initially highlights, or use its Next option to cycle to the adjacent face.

In either case, the 2D entity that is created by SOLFEAT becomes the last entity created, and can be accessed by the Last selection option. This makes it easy to select the 2D geometry to move it away from the solid, or to put it in a block.

Let's use the SOLFEAT command to pull a single edge, then a single face off the hinge block model.

> ### Copying Edges and Faces from a 3D Solid to a 2D Drawing
>
> Select the isometric view.
>
> | | |
> |---|---|
> | Command: **UCS** | Set to World. |
> | Command: **SOLFEAT** | |
> | Edge/<Face> : **E** | |
> | Select an edge... | Select any edge. |
> | PMESH solid. Change it to WIREFRAME for feature selection? N/<Y>: **<RETURN>** | |
> | Repeat selection: | Pick the same edge again. |
> | Command: **MOVE** | Use Last to select new 2D entity and move it off the solid. |
> | Command: **REDRAW** | |
> | Command: **SOLFEAT** | |
> | Edge/<Face> : **FACE** | |
> | Select a face... | Select arc between front vertical face and curved top of nearest hinge plate. |
> | <OK>/Next: **N** | Next highlights the P-shaped front face. |
> | <OK>/Next: **<RETURN>** | Accept the face. |
> | Command: **MOVE** | Use Last to move the face away from the solid. |
> | Command: **REDRAWALL** | |
> | Command: **ERASE** | Erase the P-shaped 2D face and 2D edge line. |
> | Command: **END** | |

When you selected the circular edge of the front face, AutoCAD selected the tops of the two vertical hinge plates, which it considers as a single face. Selecting the Next option cycled through to the next adjacent face, which was the front face.

That wraps up the translation utilities for converting 3D solids to 2D geometry. Now, let's go through one final exercise that brings those views together in paper space to make a final drawing.

Composing a Drawing from Profiles, Sections, and a 3D View

In the final 3D exercise, we'll clean up the HINGBLOK drawing, saving only its 3D viewport. Then we'll insert the ANSI-C title block created in Chapter 10 using MVSETUP, change to paper space and compose the finished drawing within it. We'll use MVIEW to tell the 3D viewport to do a hide when plotted, and change its border to a new layer which is turned off to make it invisible. Then inserting the other views and any optional annotations that you feel inspired to do will complete the project.

Composing Your Drawing From Viewports, Profiles, and Sections

 Begin a NEW drawing named HINGE=IA6HINGB.

 Begin a NEW drawing named HINGE=HINGBLOK.

Select the 3D viewport.

Turn grid off.

Command: **ZOOM**	Zoom 1XP, that's at 1:1 scale to paper space.
Command: **PSPACE**	Return to paper space.
Command: **ERASE**	Select viewport frames of top, front, and right views to erase them.
Command: **LIMITS**	Reset, 0,0 to 22,17.
Command: **GRID**	Set to 1 in paper space.
Command: **INSERT**	Insert ANSI-C at 0,0 with default scale and rotation.
Command: **MVIEW** ON/OFF/Hideplot/Fit/2/3/4/ Restore/<First Point>: **H**	Set the 3D viewport to hide when plotted.
ON/OFF: **ON**	Hideplot on.
Select objects:	Pick the top edge of the 3D viewport border.
1 selected, 1 found	
Select objects: **<RETURN>**	
Command: **MOVE**	Move 3D viewport to position 3D image to upper right of title block.
Command: **LAYER**	Make a new 3D-VP layer, turn it off, and thaw layers 0-PH-? and 0-PV-?
Command: **CHPROP**	Change frame of 3D viewport to 3D-VP layer. It disappears, but 3D image remains.
Command: **ZOOM**	Zoom All.
Command: **INSERT**	Insert HING-T (top view) at 3,11 with default scale and rotation.
Command: **INSERT**	Insert HING-F (front) at 3,4 with default scale and rotation.
Command: **INSERT**	Insert HING-R (right) at 12,4 with default scale and rotation.
Command: **INSERT**	Insert HING-S (section) at 17,4 with default scale and rotation Your drawing should resemble figure 18.36.
Command: **SAVE**	

You can dimension and annotate the drawing, or plot it as-is. Then, end it.

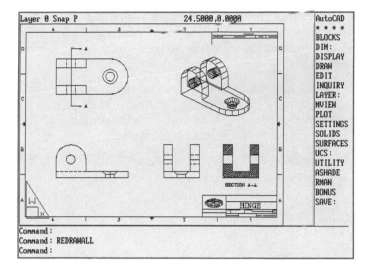

Now you can dimension your views and place notes and other annotations on the drawing to finish it. For a cleaner plot, you would want to explode the top, front, and right images and erase the extraneous hidden lines that are overlapped by visible lines. The 3D image will plot with hidden lines removed.

Note: You can safely erase the drawings 3D, GUIDBLOCK, HINGBLOCK, CONE, GUIDBLK, and HINGE if you want to. You won't need them any longer.

Summing Up

Solid modeling will probably be most useful to you if you are doing mechanical design, or a type of design related to mechanical engineering. In any case, solid modeling gives you two major benefits. The first benefit is that it makes it much easier to create a design and check it against other parts for fit and function. For example, you can model two parts, place them in their proper 3D orientation to each other, then perform a Boolean intersection on them to see if there is any interference between the two. If you end up with solids left over, you have interference between the solids.

The other benefit to solid modeling is that it makes creating a drawing for a complex part much simpler. Instead of laying out 2D geometry to make up your drawing, you can model the part as a solid, then let AutoCAD pull off profiles and sections for your drawing.

Most of the functions for creating solid primitives work virtually the same as their surface modeling counterparts do. And, working with coordinate systems and axes is no different whether you are creating wireframes, surface models, or solid models. Only your model is different.

One of the keys to using solid modeling effectively is to model your design in much the same way you would actually manufacture the part. Start with a solid that represents your blank stock, then create tools and perform union and subtraction operations to "machine" your design from that blank stock.

When you are comfortable with solid modeling, you may find it is really so much easier to create your 2D drawings from it that you may do all of your design work in 3D!

Part Three

Customizing AutoCAD

INCREASING YOUR PRODUCTIVITY

Creating a Custom Environment

For most of the book, you have been on a guided tour through AutoCAD land. By now you have covered a lot of territory, learned many commands, and explored many screen menus. The standard tour is over. The next two chapters will help you customize AutoCAD to make it your own.

Why Customize AutoCAD?

Most CAD drawings are repetitive. There are many kinds of repetition, ranging from using the same symbols and parts over and over to creating drawings with countless variations on a basic design. CAD thrives on repetition; if you just run AutoCAD by typing and picking from the standard AutoCAD menu, you're not making the most of the program's abilities.

AutoCAD's standard menu is a good starting tool, but it becomes cumbersome as you gain experience. You probably use 20 percent of the commands 80 percent of the time. The trick to improving your productivity is to capture the repetition in your drawing, to recognize patterns in what you do, then customize AutoCAD to automate the repetition. If you can see a method in what you do, you can customize AutoCAD by creating your own drawing environment, menus, and even AutoLISP programs. Your ultimate benefits are finding ways to type and pick less, and accomplish more.

827

How Part Three Is Organized

Part Three contains two chapters on customizing AutoCAD.

Chapter 19 will help you explore customization. Here, you can go beyond the standard AutoCAD working environment. Because drafting and design frequently lack universal standards, you often need to adapt AutoCAD to fit your own particular standards. Customizing at this level involves:

- Capturing complex sequences and turning them into simple macros on a menu.
- Grouping pages of macros to fit the flow of your work.
- Creating screen and tablet menu macros that ask for information and then execute commands based on the input.
- Understanding how screen, tablet, pull-down and buttons (pointing device) menus work, and tailoring them to your liking.
- Setting the system variables that work behind the scenes in the AutoCAD program.

Chapter 20 will introduce you to AutoLISP, AutoCAD's programming language. You can use AutoLISP to create new commands. AutoLISP can do calculations and run programs to execute commands, draw pictures, and create reports and databases. This last chapter will give you a hands-on look at working with menu macros and AutoLISP.

Learn by Doing

Customization is easy when you get into it. Like magic, it just seems intimidating until you see what's actually happening behind the scenes. The funny part about customizing AutoCAD is that you already know how to do a lot of it. The most important tools you will use in customization are the commands and sequences you have already used, and what you know about your unique application. When you write macros and set up custom menus, you just type commands and options that you have been using all along, adding a few special characters. When you create symbol libraries, you call on old friends like WBLOCK and INSERT. AutoLISP . . . well, that's not until the last chapter anyway — wait and see!

If you're not sure that customization can make your AutoCAD life better, these two chapters will give you a convincing overview. If you are already convinced, you may want to just skim these chapters and go into more detail with *MAXIMIZING AutoCAD, Volumes I and II* from New Riders Publishing. These books give you a thorough step-by-step approach to customization with comprehensive explanations.

19

Customizing Macros and Menus

AutoCAD YOUR WAY

Tailoring AutoCAD to Your Needs

This chapter will show you how to begin tailoring AutoCAD to meet your special needs by creating menu macros. Customizing AutoCAD does not require any elaborate effort or programming experience. The chapter's focus is to show you the *types* of things that you can do to automate your drawing procedures. Simple things, such as making a macro to automatically scale a block that you use frequently, often pay the largest dividends in time saved.

Macros and Menus Explained

Macro is shorthand for macro-command, meaning a large or long command. We use macro to mean a series of one or more AutoCAD commands and parameters strung together to perform a drafting or design task. You can make macros that pause for user input and execute any of AutoCAD's commands, or even automatically repeat commands. Here is a simple macro that executes three <^C>s:

```
[^C]^C^C^C
```

If you placed this macro in a screen menu and selected the [^C] item, it would execute three <^C>s just as if you had typed them from the keyboard. You build macros by writing keyboard command sequences in a text file. You group macros into menu files.

A menu is a text file listing each menu item or macro for every box on the screen, tablet, button, pop-up, and icon menus. AutoCAD's standard menu text file is ACAD.MNU. (The compiled menu file is ACAD.MNX.) You can make items in a menu very short, even a single character, or very complex, involving many commands. You can also use AutoLISP in menu items. We will refer to any menu item as a macro. When you create your own commands using menu macros, you automate your drawing command sequences.

Common Menu Macro Tasks

There is a common set of tasks that any custom menu performs. As you think about what procedures you can automate, use the following list as a take-off point. A custom menu system can help you:

- Standardize your drawings.
- Set up, format, and fill in data for title sheets.
- Place text on the drawing.
- Locate, draw, and insert components, assemblies, and materials.
- Dimension and annotate components.

Any or all of these tasks are candidates for creating custom menu macros.

How to Use Menu Macro Examples

We will start by showing you how to build a simple screen menu with ten macros. (If you have the IA DISK, you already have the menu.) These macros provide *examples* of the control that you can exercise over AutoCAD commands. You can do anything in a macro that you can do with AutoCAD commands. As you work with these examples, look for the *types* of macros that will help you in your own applications.

Menu and Macro Tools

You will use two commands, SHELL and MENU, that are on the [UTILITY] screen menu. MENU, as its name implies, lets you load a menu file from within the drawing editor. SHELL is one of the [External Commands] on the [UTILITY] screen menu. It lets you exit AutoCAD from within the drawing editor, execute another program or DOS level command, then resume your drawing in the drawing editor.

Creating Menu Macros

To develop a good menu, you need working macros and working symbols. Of course, good working macros (and symbols) don't appear under a pillow overnight. You get them by reading and using examples, like those you will find in this chapter, and by writing down the commands, options, and input parameters that you use when you are drawing. Your own repetitive drawing sequences are the raw material for macros. If you think you have a candidate sequence, write it down. You can then make a test macro to see if it will help you.

Getting Started With Your Editor

To write a menu macro, you must have a text editor or word processor that is able to create standard ASCII text files. We recommend installing a copy of your text editor in the IA-ACAD directory, where you are creating the drawings for this book. Or, configure your editor and system so that you can start your editor from the current directory and create files in the current directory. Either way allows you to use it interactively via the SHELL command. You can even automate editing and reloading menu files with a menu macro.

If you do not want to set up your text editor to work interactively, simply end AutoCAD when you edit the menu files. You'll have to end AutoCAD and load your text editor to read and modify the menu text files, then exit your editor and reload AutoCAD to use the modified files.

If you are not sure of your editor or need information on choosing, testing, and setting up a text editor, see Appendix B. You need a suitable editor to work with the menu files. If you do not have an editor, you can still read the exercise sequences to learn how macros work. All the macros are annotated.

We assume that you are in the directory called IA-ACAD, and your text editor is installed in the same directory.

The following exercise provides you with a test to see whether you can use the SHELL command to enter your text editor from within AutoCAD.

Using SHELL From Inside AutoCAD

 Edit an EXISTING drawing named MENUTEST=IA6MENU from the IA DISK.

 Begin a NEW drawing named MENUTEST.

```
Command: SHELL                      Executes the ACAD.PGP SHELL command.
OS Command:                         Here you can enter any valid operating system
                                    command or program.
```

If you got the OS command prompt, proceed with the next exercise to edit the IA6MENU.MNU file.

If you didn't get the OS command prompt, your ACAD.PGP file isn't where AutoCAD can find it, or your system is set up incompatibly. Find the ACAD.PGP file on your original or master backup AutoCAD diskettes and copy it to your AutoCAD program directory, or get help from your support source. (Appendix B has more information on setting up your system environment, including AutoCAD's PGP file.)

If this or the next exercise step won't work for you, end AutoCAD when you need to edit the menu file. If you end AutoCAD and start your editor in your normal manner, be sure that the menu file gets created in or copied to the IA-ACAD directory.

Use the next exercise step to edit or examine the IA6MENU.MNU file. If you are using the IA DISK, load the IA6MENU.MNU file into your text editor. If you are not using the disk, start up your editor and create IA6MENU.MNU. Either way, start your editor exactly as you would if you were creating a plain ASCII text file from the DOS (or other operating system) prompt. In the following exercises, we use NE (Norton's Editor) for our editor. Use the name that you normally use to start *your* editor.

Starting a Text Editor in SHELL

 Just examine the finished IA6MENU.MNU menu from the IA DISK.

 Create the IA6MENU.MNU file with your editor.

OS Command: **NE IA6MENU.MNU**   NE is our editor's name. You use yours.

If everything is set up right, you're now in your text editor.

Using the IA DISK IA6MENU.MNU File

If you are using the IA DISK, your text editor should automatically load the IA6MENU.MNU file. Use the next exercise as a guide to read the file with your editor. You don't have to type in any input. You'll see the complete menu file, which includes more lines than the next exercise sequence shows. When you exit your editor to return to AutoCAD, quit instead of saving so you don't change the file. Even if you have the disk, going through the editor exercises will teach you the process for creating and modifying your own menus.

Creating the IA6MENU.MNU File

If you are not using the IA DISK file, use your text editor to start a new IA6MENU.MNU file in the IA-ACAD directory. Some editors can't automatically load files. If your editor does not automatically load files, you will need to load them manually in your editor. We will assume that your editor loads the file automatically.

Create the following menu macros. Type the characters that you input exactly as the book shows them. Don't use tabs or trailing spaces. Don't put in any blank lines. End each line with a <RETURN>, including the last line.

Here is the menu sequence for IA6MENU.MNU.

Creating or Examining IA6MENU.MNU

 Examine these menu items in the file, then quit your editor.

 Type these 20 lines into the IA6MENU.MNU file.

```
[^C]^C^C^C
[]
[CIRCLE:]*^C^C^CCIRCLE
[ARC:]^C^C^CMULTIPLE ARC
[ZOOM:P]'ZOOM P
[]
[EDIT-MNU]^C^C^CSHELL \MENU ;
[]
[INSERT:S]*^C^C^CINSERT \SCALE
[PLINE:]*^C^C^CPLINE \W 0 ;
[CH:LAYER]^C^C^CSELECT AU \CHPROP P ;LAYER (getvar "CLAYER") LAYER \;
[SECT-MK: ]^C^C^CINSERT SECT-MK S (getvar "DIMSCALE") \\\ ATTEDIT ;;;;L A 0 ;
[]
[BOLT:    Pick 2 endpoints and enter scale to create a bolt.]^C^C^C^P+
LINE;\\;INSERT SCALE S \@ 0 SETVAR MENUECHO 3;+
INSERT NUT S @ CEN,QUI @ @ MID,QUI @;+
ERASE L ;MOVE L ;@ MID,QUI @ OOPS;+
ERASE QUA,QUI @ ;PEDIT MID,QUI @ Y E I ;^C+
OOPS PEDIT END,QUI @ W MID,QUI @ CEN,QUI @;;+
INSERT HEAD S MID,QUI @ CEN,QUI @ @ MID,QUI @ ERASE P ;REDRAW; SETVAR MENUECHO 0
```

Save the file in ASCII mode and exit your editor.

Note: You'll want to put a bookmark in this page and refer back as you read the following explanations of these macros.

You should be back in AutoCAD and have an IA6MENU.MNU file in the current directory. If you ended AutoCAD to run your text editor, reload AutoCAD.

To use your new menu, you must load it into AutoCAD.

How to Load Menus

AutoCAD provides two methods for loading your .MNU files and making them active within the AutoCAD drawing editor. You can use the MENU command, or select [MENU:] from the [UTILITY] screen menu. This command simply asks you for the name of the .MNU file and loads it. Or you can load any menu file in your prototype drawing instead of the default ACAD.MNU, and it will automatically load in new drawings.

You can also integrate your menu macros into another menu, even into the standard ACAD.MNU. We will show you how to load your menu with the MENU command. It will replace the standard AutoCAD menu, so you will have to do without tablet and pull-down menus for a while. Later, we will show you how to integrate macros into the standard ACAD.MNU menu.

Generally, you want to load and test your menu before you do any menu integration. Try loading your new menu with the MENU command. Use the following exercise sequence as a guide to help you test the menu. Use the comments to help you test each menu item.

Using MENU to Load the IA6MENU.MNU for Testing

```
Command: MENU
Menu file name or . for none <acad>: IA6MENU
Compiling menu IA6MENU.MNU...
```
[^C] appears at top of screen menu area, [BOLT:] at bottom (see fig. 19.1). Now, test the menu.

```
Command: ZOOM
```
Make a 6" high working area with ZOOM Center.

```
Select [CIRCLE: ]
Command: CIRCLE 3P/2P/TTR/<Center point>:
Diameter/<Radius>:
Command: CIRCLE 3P/2P/TTR/<Center point>:
Diameter/<Radius>:
Command: CIRCLE 3P/2P/TTR/<Center point>: <^C>
```
Acts like an ordinary CIRCLE.
Pick a point.
Enter a radius.
Except it repeats.

Until you <^C> to cancel it.

```
Select [ARC: ]
Command: MULTIPLE ARC Center/<Start point>:
Center/End/<Second point>:
End point:
ARC Center/<Start point>:
```
A MULTIPLE ARC command.
Pick point.
Pick point.
Pick point.
It also repeats. Start another arc.

```
Select [ZOOM:P]
```
It transparently zooms Previous.

```
To point:
```
Pick point.

> **Using MENU to Load the IA6MENU.MNU for Testing—continued**
>
> To point: **<^C>**   Until canceled.
>
> *Select* **[EDIT-MNU]**   Access your text editor.
> Command: SHELL   It issues the SHELL command.
> OS Command: **NE IA6MENU.MNU**   Type the command that starts
>   *your* text editor.
>
> Make any necessary corrections, save and end the editor, then SHELL returns you to
> AutoCAD.
>
> Where the [EDIT-MNU] continues with the menu command:
>
> Command: MENU Menu file name or . for
>   none <IA6MENU>:
> Compiling menu C:\IA-ACAD\IA6MENU.MNU...   Which reloads the modified
>   menu.
>
> Command: **SAVE**

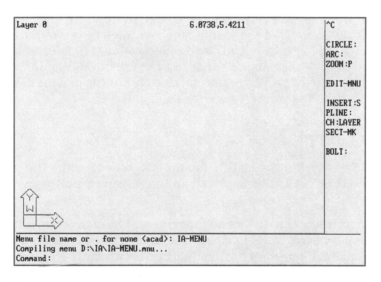

Figure 19.1:
The first screen
menu.

> **Note:** If you end AutoCAD to edit your menu, just use the MENU command to
> manually reload the menu each time you change it.

If all went well, your screen showed the IA6MENU menu screen as shown in figure
19.1, and you were able to execute the menu macros. Spend some time trying the
macros. Use Undo if you crash. Any error in a menu item crashes the rest of the
item, but Undo cleans it up. If your drawing accumulates clutter, just erase what
you don't need.

Automating Menu Editing

If you want to further automate menu editing, you can add to the [EDIT-MNU] macro. Simply insert the exact character sequence you typed to load your editor at the OS command prompt (above). For example, our line for Norton's Editor becomes:

```
[EDIT-MNU ]^C^C^CSHELL NE IA6MENU.MNU;MENU ;
```

Or, if your editor is EDLIN, the last line would be:

```
[EDIT-MNU ]^C^C^CSHELL EDLIN IA6MENU.MNU;MENU ;
```

Go ahead and change [EDIT-MNU] now if you want to automate it. But the exercises assume you'll just continue entering your editor and filename whenever you need to edit the menu.

How to Construct Menu Macros

Let's take the macros apart to show how they're made. There are really just two basic types of ingredients: AutoCAD commands and parameters, and a group of special character codes used by the AutoCAD menu (and command) interpreter. As you read through the following sections, refer back to the 20 lines of the IA6MENU you created earlier to help you follow along. You can also try out the macros again by picking the menu items from the screen to see the code in action.

Labeling Macro Commands

As you look at menu items, the first special character that you encounter is a pair of square brackets [ ]. You control what is displayed on the screen by putting a macro label in square brackets.

The square brackets signify labels to the menu interpreter. The characters after the right-hand bracket are the macro. Only eight characters display on the screen menu label, but you can make labels longer for documentation. Labels can include letters, numbers, and any displayable character. Control and extended ASCII characters are simply ignored. You can use an empty pair of brackets to make a blank menu item.

Using <^C> to Cancel

All our macros start with two or three <^C>s. Control-C is a special code in a menu that cancels a command just like canceling from the keyboard.

Since you want most macros to execute from AutoCAD's command prompt, starting a macro with three <^C>s insures that any pending commands are canceled. Why three? There are some dim recesses in AutoCAD that require three <^C>s to get you back to the command prompt. If you look at how the macros are constructed, you will see that the AutoCAD command in the macro comes after the <^C>s. In effect, you cancel everything, then start your macro.

To put a <^C> in a macro, type a caret (^) (the shifted character above the 6 on your keyboard) followed by a C. This caret character allows menus to include codes for any control character without interfering with the meaning that a real control character might have to your text editor.

Command Options and Parameters

To put options or parameters within a macro, use the same characters that you would normally type at the keyboard. For example, we use P for the Previous option in the ZOOM command in the [ZOOM:P] macro.

Using Semicolons vs. Spaces in Macros

If we look again at the macros, you will see that they have some spaces and semicolons in them.

The semicolon is the special character for a <RETURN>. In macros, spaces are like pressing the space bar and semicolons are like pressing the <RETURN> key from the keyboard. You usually can use semicolons and spaces interchangeably in macros. However, if you need a <RETURN> at the end of a macro, use a semicolon. Don't use a trailing space.

Repeating Commands and Macros

Placing an asterisk as the first character of the macro repeats the macro indefinitely. Put the asterisk immediately after the closing right bracket.

The asterisk triggers the menu interpreter to repeat the macro in its entirety. The * must be followed by at least one <^C> (or <^X>). Otherwise, it is interpreted as part of the following command or input. For example, AutoCAD would see *MOVE, not recognize it, and an error would result.

You can repeat single commands without an asterisk by using the MULTIPLE command. In the [ARC:] macro, the MULTIPLE command modifier causes AutoCAD to repeat the command until you hit a <^C> to cancel it. MULTIPLE only repeats the command, ignoring any options or parameters used in the first execution.

MULTIPLE works for simple menu items, or you can use it to repeat the last command in a macro. However, if you try to make TEXT automatically repeat a mode, like M for Middle, it will use the mode the first time, then ignore the mode thereafter. MULTIPLE is intended primarily for on-the-fly keyboard use or for single commands. We find the asterisk method works better for most macros.

Pausing for Input

Several of the macros pause for input from the user. The backslash (\) is the special character that makes a macro pause for input, then resume execution with more commands or options. The pause lets you string together multiple commands and input.

A single backslash tells AutoCAD to wait for a single piece of input. In the [INSERT:S] macro example, the macro pauses for the insert point. Without a backslash, AutoCAD would continue taking its input from the macro and would pass the next item along to the command processor. It would read the SCALE entry and cause an error. You must supply one backslash for each point that you want for input. We'll try the [INSERT:S] macro later.

> **Note:** If you use directory path names in your macros, use forward slashes (/), not the backslashes (\) that you are used to using in the DOS operating system. AutoCAD recognizes either kind of slash, but backslashes make menus pause! Some operating systems, such as UNIX, require forward slashes for paths, so using them will automatically make your macros compatible.

Transparent Commands

Transparent operations such as 'ZOOM P do not *use up* backslashes present in the macro. When you have a macro pausing for point input with a backslash, like the [INSERT:S] macro, you can use a transparent command and the macro will continue to pause while the transparent command takes place. You can either type the transparent command, or use a transparent macro like [ZOOM:P].

Osnaps and XYZ point filters are also transparent. Other common transparent commands are: 'GRAPHSCR, 'HELP, 'RESUME, 'SETVAR, 'TEXTSCR, 'PAN, and the 'DDxxxx dialogue commands.

Special Characters in Menus

You will use about a dozen special characters in macros. You have already seen the backslash for pause, semicolon for <RETURN>, square brackets for labels, asterisk to repeat, and <^C> to clear previous commands. AutoCAD automatically reads the end of a menu line as if it ended in a space, unless the line ends with a special character. But if AutoCAD encounters a special character at the end of a menu line, it *does not* read the imaginary space at the end of the line.

Table 19.1 provides a complete list of the special characters used by AutoCAD's menu interpreter. The @ (lastpoint) that we used in IA6MENU.MNU is not a special character because it does not share in the special treatment by the AutoCAD menu interpreter.

Table 19.1:
SPECIAL MENU CHARACTERS

\	Pauses for input	;	Issues RETURN
+	Continues macro to next line	[]	Encloses Label
*	Autorepeats, or marks page	^B	Toggles SNAP
	The <SPACE> character	^M	Issues RETURN
^D	Toggles COORDS	^E	Toggles ISOPLANE
^G	Toggles GRID	^H	Issues BACKSPACE
^C	*Cancel*	^O	Toggles ORTHO
^Q	Toggles Echo to Printer	^P	Toggles MENUECHO
^X	*Delete* input buffer	^T	Toggles Tablet
^Z	Does "nothing." Put at end of line to suppress automatic space.		

When you use control characters in your macros, type them into the menu file as two characters. Use a caret followed by the upper-case letter, like ^B.

How to Control Command Parameter Macros

You can do anything in a macro that you can do in an AutoCAD command. You can preset command parameters by placing values at the right point within the macro, or you can pause for input by using backslashes. Take a look at the [PLINE:] macro: it uses both methods.

Now, try the macro using the following exercise sequence as a guide.

Using Command Parameters in Macros

Select **[PLINE:]**	
Command: PLINE	It issues the command.
From point:	Pauses for input (the backslash). Pick a point.
Current line-width is 0'-0.0000"	
Arc/Close/Halfwidth/Length/Undo/Width/	
<Endpoint of line>: W	
Starting width <0'-0.0000">: 0	Forces the width to 0.
Ending width <0'-0.0000">:	Semicolon <RETURN> defaults it.
Arc/Close/Halfwidth/Length/Undo/Width/	
<Endpoint of line>:	Stays in PLINE command, ready for more points.
Command: PLINE	And it repeats.

How to Control Object Selection in Macros

You can control object selection in a macro by limiting the type of selection input, or you can open your macro to accept different types of input. The next exercise shows you how you can control object selection in macros. Look at the [CH:LAYER] macro.

[CH:LAYER] puts you in the SELECT command in AUto mode, issues the CHPROP command with a Previous selection set, then sets the objects that you selected to the current layer. The (getvar "CLAYER") is a bit of AutoLISP. You can ignore it for now. We will explain how AutoLISP works in the last chapter. Test the [CH:LAYER] macro to see how it works. First, create a layer to test it with.

Using Object Selection in Macros

Command: **LAYER**	Create layer TEST with color red and set it current.
Select **[CH:LAYER]**	
Command: SELECT	It issues the SELECT command.
Select objects: AU	With selection mode AUto.
Select objects: 1 selected, 1 found.	Select several objects.
Select objects: 1 selected, Other corner: 2 found.	
Select objects: 1 selected, Other corner: 1 found.	
Select objects: **<RETURN>**	SELECT loops at the backslash until you <RETURN>.
Command: CHPROP	Then issues the CHPROP command.
Select objects: P 3 found.	Using the Previous selection set.
Select objects:	The semicolon <RETURN> ends selection.
Change what property (Color/LAyer/LType/ Thickness) ? LAYER	
New layer <0>: (getvar "CLAYER")	It sets them to the current layer.
Change what property (Color/LAyer/LType/ Thickness) ? LAYER	
New layer <TEST>:	Making it the default. You can <RETURN>, or input another layer (the last backslash).
Change what property (Color/LAyer/LType/ Thickness) ?	The semicolon <RETURN> exits.
Command:	

Using Selection Sets With Macros

A selection set lets you control how your macro selects objects. AutoCAD editing commands always ask for a set of entities before any edit tasks begin. This limits your macro writing by allowing only a fixed number of picks. Whether you use

Window, Last, or another selection mode, you still need to predefine one backslash per pick. AutoCAD's SELECT command is indispensable in macros because it has the unique feature of pausing the macro indefinitely until the entire selection process is complete. It pauses even when other commands follow.

As you saw in the [CH:LAYER] macro, SELECT doesn't do anything except create a selection set of entities, allowing an indefinite number of picks. This is invaluable because you can use a subsequent command, like MOVE, to select that selection set with the P (Previous) selection option.

AutoCAD has three selection modes that you will find especially useful in macros. These are:

SIngle Stays in selection mode until one object or one set is successfully picked.

BOX Acts like either crossing or window, depending on the order of the two points picked.

AUto If the first point finds an object, AUto picks it. Otherwise AUto acts like BOX.

You can combine SIngle with other modes, like BOX, Crossing, or AUto. You also can use it with SELECT if you want to force the creation of a previous set with only a single selection. Although SIngle ends object selection when an object or set is picked, it doesn't suspend the rest of a macro.

We recommend using SELECT and BOX or AUto for most macros. BOX is clean and simple. Pick left to right for a window and right to left for a crossing. AUto gives the most flexibility, combining picking by point with the BOX mode. If your first point misses, you go into BOX mode, otherwise AUto selects the entity at the first pick point.

Setting Defaults in Macros

The [PLINE:] and [CH:LAYER] macros show two methods for setting defaults in macros.

[PLINE:] sets the polyline width for the macro. Since you can't predict the current default width, make your polyline macros set the width explicitly, as in W 0 ;.

The [CH:LAYER] macro forces a change based on object properties (layer). Both methods offer ways to enforce drawing standards in your macros.

Text Input in Macros

When you enter text in a macro command, all special characters except spaces act exactly the same whether they are in the middle of a text string or not. Since you must be able to type space characters between words in text strings, AutoCAD's menu interpreter treats them as true spaces in your text, not as <RETURN>s as in the AutoCAD program itself. If you want a macro to continue after text input, you need some way to tell AutoCAD that the string of text is complete. You can't use the automatic space at the end of the menu line for text, so use a semicolon.

Creating Intelligent Macros

So far, we have worked with simple macros. In the next section, we want to show you some of the power inherent in making custom macros. As you work with the next macros, think of them as models for the types of automation that you can incorporate into AutoCAD.

The [INSERT:S] macro is a simple example of controlling a block insertion with preset scale.

The [SECT-MK:] macro is a section block macro that inserts a block into a drawing, presetting scale and automatically sizing the block for insertion. This same macro also controls attribute rotation.

The last macro, [BOLT:], shows how to get and retain coordinate points. It is an example of an intelligent macro. The [BOLT:] macro is a parametric command. It draws a bolt, requiring only two input points and a scale factor.

Using Macros to Control Block Insertions

To make [INSERT:S] work, you need a block to test. If you are using the IA DISK, you already have a block named SCALE in your drawing. Any block would work with [INSERT:S], but you'll also need this block for a later exercise, so make the block now.

Making a Scale Block

 Skip this — you have the block.

Command: **LAYER**	Set layer 0 current.
Command: **CIRCLE**	Draw a one-unit radius circle.
Command: **WBLOCK**	Wblock it to name SCALE.
Insertion base point: **QUA,QUI**	Pick point at top of circle.

Now, try the macro.

Controlling Block Insertion Scale With a Macro

```
Select [INSERT:S ]
Command: INSERT Block name (or ?): SCALE          Enter the block name.
Insertion point: SCALE  Scale factor: 2           It prompts for scale.
Insertion point:                                  Pick point.
Rotation angle <0>: <RETURN>
Command: INSERT Block name (or ?) <SCALE>:        And it repeats.
```

[INSERT:S] is an improvement over the stock INSERT command for most insertions. Presetting scale lets you see your scale when dragging and picking an insertion point. You have only one scale prompt to respond to, instead of X and Y.

The next macro, [SECT-MK:], shows how preset scale can be automatically sized to the drawing, and how attribute rotation can be controlled in a macro. First, you need to make the block as shown in figure 19.2. If you are using the IA DISK, you already have the block in your drawing.

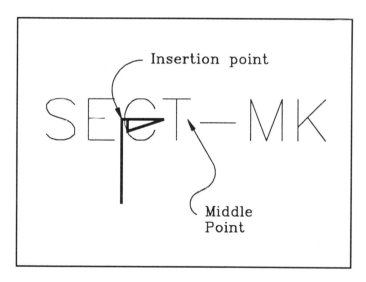

Figure 19.2:
The section mark
block.

Making a Section Mark

 Skip this — you have the block.

```
Command: PLINE
From point:                                       Pick a point in a clear area.
Current line-width is 0.0000                      Set width to .0125 units.
Arc/Close/Halfwidth/Length/Undo/Width/
   <Endpoint of line>: @0,0.375
```

> ### Making a Section Mark—continued
>
> Enter points at @0.25,0 and @-.1875,-.0625 and osnap PERP to the horizontal line.
>
> ```
> Arc/Close/Halfwidth/Length/Undo/Width/
>    <Endpoint of line>: <RETURN>
> Command: ATTDEF
> Attribute modes — Invisible:N Constant:N
>    Verify:N Preset:N
> Enter (ICVP) to change, RETURN when done:
>    <RETURN>
> Attribute tag: SECT-MK
> Attribute prompt: Enter letter
> Default attribute value: ?
> Start point or Align/Center/Fit/Middle/Right/
>    Style: M
> ```
>
> Middle point: Pick a point .16 units to the right of
>   the section marker point.
>
> ```
> Height <0'-0.125">: .25
> Rotation angle <0>: <RETURN>
> Command: WBLOCK
> ```
>   Wblock both to filename SECT-MK
>   with insertion base point at upper left
>   corner of the section marker.

Now, test the block by inserting it.

> ### Inserting the Section Mark Block
>
> ```
> Command: INSERT
> Enter attribute values
> Enter letter <?>: A
> ```
> Insert SECT-MK in a clear area.
> It prompts for the mark letter.
> Enter a character (see fig. 19.3).

The [SECT-MK:] macro is designed to insert this block at the current dimension scale, at any rotation. However, you don't want the attribute text to be rotated. The macro uses the ATTEDIT command to change the rotation of attribute text after insertion without affecting the block. Try the macro using the following exercise as a guide.

> ### Using a Macro to Control Block Scale and Rotation
>
> ```
> Command: PAN
> Command: ZOOM
> ```
> Move to clear area of the screen.
> Zoom Center, to height 3".
>
> ```
> Select [SECT-MK: ]
> Command: INSERT Block name (or ?)
>    <SCALE>: SECT-MK
> ```

Using a Macro to Control Block Scale and Rotation—continued

```
Insertion point: S                          It presets scale with the DIMSCALE
                                            system variable.

Scale factor: (getvar "DIMSCALE")
   Insertion point:                         Pick a point (the first backslash).
Rotation angle <0>:                         Pick a point below the first (the sec-
                                            ond backslash).

Enter attribute values
Enter letter <?>: B                         Enter character (third backslash).
Command: ATTEDIT                            Then it rotates the text to 0 degrees.
Edit attributes one at a time? <Y>
Block name specification <*>:
Attribute tag specification <*>:
Attribute value specification <*>:
Select Attributes: L                        The block was Last.
1 attributes selected.
Value/Position/Height/Angle/Style/Layer/
   Color/Next <N>: A                        Angle.
New rotation angle <270>: 0                 0 degrees (see fig. 19.4).
Value/Position/Height/Angle/Style/Layer/
   Color/Next <N>:
```

You have created a semi-intelligent macro. The next step in automation is control-ling points.

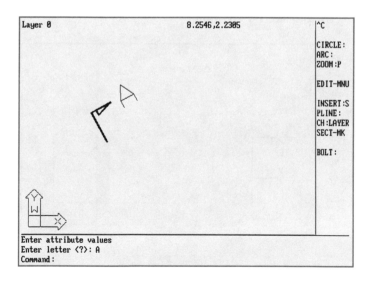

Figure: 19.3
The rotated
SECT-MK text.

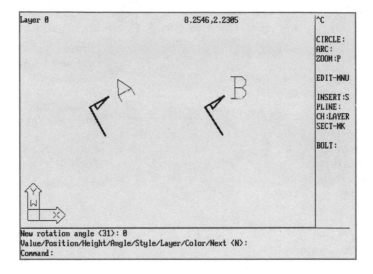

Figure 19.4:
*The non-rotated
SECT-MK text.*

How to Create a Parametric Macro

A parametric macro is a macro that is driven by input values. The [BOLT:] macro is a parametric command. It draws a bolt, requiring only two input points and a scale factor. It requires the NUT and HEAD blocks to work, and it uses the SCALE block that you created earlier. First create the NUT and HEAD blocks as shown in figure 19.5, then try it. If you are using the IA DISK, you already have the blocks in your drawing. After you have the blocks, try the macro.

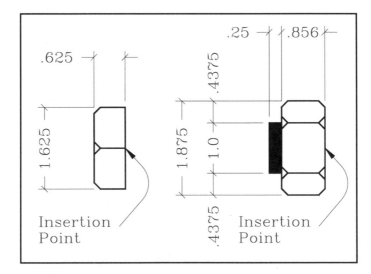

Figure 19.5:
*The HEAD and NUT
blocks.*

Using the [BOLT:] Parametric Macro

 You have the blocks.

 Create the blocks illustrated in figure 19.5.

Command: **ZOOM**   Zoom Center, to height 5".
Select **[BOLT:]**   <^P> and MENUECHO suppress
                                                           commands, input, and prompts.
Command:
From point: Pick one endpoint.
To point: Pick other endpoint.
To point:
Command: Block name (or ?) <default>:   Insertion point:
Scale factor: .5   Enter a scale.

The following scrolls by.

Insertion point: Rotation angle <0>:
Command: Variable name or ? <MENUECHO>:
New value for MENUECHO <0>:
Entity selected is not a polyline
Cancel   It cancels PEDIT and draws the bolt
                                                           (see fig. 19.6).
Command:

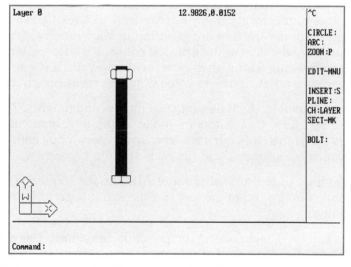

Figure 19.6:
The parametric bolt.

[BOLT:] depends on the fact that PEDIT object selection does not alter the contents of the Previous selection set. [BOLT:] uses the SCALE block as a way to store a scale value and retrieve it. It moves the block to a location where it can osnap to it, and retrieves the value by osnapping to its center point. [BOLT:] uses ERASE and OOPS to temporarily get objects out of the way so it won't find the wrong objects.

Long Macros

Menu items can get very long, especially macros that set many parameters or set up layers. You can continue a macro for many lines by ending each line with a plus sign (+).

Look at the plus signs ending the [BOLT:] macro lines. When AutoCAD sees a plus sign at the end of a line, it treats the next line as part of the same item.

You can add blank lines to a menu, each containing only a solitary plus sign. This makes menu files easier to read by providing a visual break. AutoCAD ignores the solitary plus sign, and it has no effect on the menus.

Table 19.2 shows how the [BOLT:] macro works. We've broken up the lines to explain the code, but in the menu, the lines only break at the plus signs.

Menu Macro Tips

The [BOLT:] macro is a working example of how much power you can put into a macro. To develop good macros, you need to carefully work out the drawing sequences that you want to automate. When you write menu macros, your command syntax must be exact. Use your drawing editor interactively as a testbed so that you know what options and input parameters are expected in your macros. Write your sequences down. Make your mistakes in the drawing editor. It's a lot easier to work out the sequences in the drawing editor, *then* type them into your text editor when you think you have them down pat. Here are some notes on menu macros.

Make sure you are creating simple ASCII files for your menus and macros. These are sometimes called DOS text files, programmer's mode, or nondocument files. Use existing menu items as templates. It is often easier to overtype or copy complex text containing commas, control characters, and brackets than to type anew.

Look for tricks that you have picked up using AutoCAD, like the sequence LINE:^C that resets the last point @ to the end of the last line drawn. It is great for inserting blocks at the end of a line.

Start new macros with three <^C>s to cancel the previous command. Use an asterisk (*^C^C^C) at the beginning of macros for automatic repeating. (You also can use *^X.) Use the MULTIPLE command modifier for simple single or last command repetition. Give all your menu items [LABELS], including blank labels for blank lines [ ].

Table 19.2:
The Annotated [BOLT:] Macro

`[BOLT: Pick 2 endpoints and` `    enter scale to create a bolt.]`	A long label containing comments.
`^C^C^C^P+`	<^P> suppresses commands.
`LINE;\\;`	Prompts for the two endpoints.
`INSERT SCALE S;\@ 0`	Prompts for scale and inserts the SCALE block.
`SETVAR MENUECHO 3;+`	Suppresses everything possible.
`INSERT NUT S @ CEN,QUI @`	Presets the NUT scale by osnapping to the SCALE block.
`@ MID,QUI @;+`	Insert point for NUT. Rotates it to the line's midpoint.
`ERASE L ;`	Gets the NUT out of the way.
`MOVE L ;@ MID,QUI @`	Moves SCALE to the line's midpoint.
`OOPS;+`	Restores the NUT.
`ERASE QUA,QUI @ ;`	Gets the SCALE out of the way.
`PEDIT MID,QUI @ Y E I ;^C+`	Turns line into a polyline. Resets last point to its start point.
`OOPS`	Restores SCALE.
`PEDIT END,QUI @ W MID,QUI @` `    CEN,QUI @;;+`	Changes polyline's width, osnaps to SCALE.
`INSERT HEAD S MID,QUI @ CEN,` `    QUI @ @ MID,QUI @`	Inserts HEAD like NUT.
`ERASE P ;`	Erases SCALE.
`SETVAR MENUECHO 0`	

Be careful not to leave any extra spaces at the end of lines; AutoCAD reads spaces as <RETURN>s. Watch out for extra blank lines. Never use two spaces in a row; they are too hard to count. Use one space and then semicolons for subsequent returns.

Make your macro set your defaults. You never know what was used last before your macro. It is good practice to explicitly set defaults, modes, and settings, like text styles, if they are important for your macro to function.

Use the SELECT command to automatically pause for a selection set. Use SELECT to make the set and then pass the set to other editing commands via the Previous option. Look for ways to use osnaps as tools in macros, like using rotated block insertions to get correct angles. When you use *intelligent* blocks in macros, give your blocks and macros unique yet explanatory names. DESK1 and [DESK2] don't say much. DeskEXEC and [DeskREG] are more descriptive.

How a Menu Is Put Together

So far, you have been using a simple single page screen menu for your menu macros. As you add more commands to your menu, you need a way to organize your menu system. Let's take a behind-the-scenes tour of AutoCAD's ACAD.MNU system.

Tailoring Your Menu System

You gain several productivity benefits from modifying AutoCAD's menu system or from tailoring your own menu system. You can save time and effort by simply assigning frequently used macros, like toggling an intersection osnap, to one or two buttons on your pointing device. Or you can use pages of symbols to make inserting symbols into the drawing faster and more accessible. You can improve your productivity by assigning these symbol macros to your tablet (as well as to your screen) menu. By designing your menu pages and assigning them to the appropriate device, you can group your own drawing applications by task instead of by AutoCAD functions, making your drawing more straightforward and efficient. If this convincing argument has you excited enough, you may want to jump directly to the book *MAXIMIZING AutoCAD Volume 1* (New Riders Publishing) for the complete story. Or read on for an introduction to menu structure.

Setup for Looking at Menu Systems

For much of the remainder of this chapter, we will be working with IA6ACAD.MNU, a copy of ACAD.MNU. In order to protect your standard ACAD.MNU file, make a copy of ACAD.MNU in the IA-ACAD directory with the name IA6ACAD.MNU. Find your original ACAD.MNU file so you can copy it. Look for it in your ACAD or ACAD\SOURCE directory. If it's not there, ACAD.MNU is supplied in a SOURCE subdirectory on one of your original AutoCAD support disks. By copying it to IA6ACAD.MNU, you won't modify your original menu file when you modify IA6ACAD.MNU. If you are using the IA DISK, several of the menu macro modifications are already provided as text files. Rather than create the menu macros, you only need to merge them into the IA6ACAD.MNU file, using the exercises as a guide.

Before you start AutoCAD, make a copy of ACAD.MNU and look at it.

Copying and Looking at ACAD.MNU

Quit AutoCAD and return to the operating system.

```
C:> CD \IA-ACAD
C:\IA-ACAD> COPY \ACAD\SOURCE\
  ACAD.MNU IA6ACAD.MNU          Find and copy your ACAD.MNU.
```

Copying and Looking at ACAD.MNU—continued

C:\IA-ACAD> **NE IA6ACAD.MNU**   Starts our editor, NE. Use *your* editor to
                                                  look at IA6ACAD.MNU.

Use your editor's page-up, page-down, and search commands to move around in the menu.
Be careful NOT to alter it yet.

Previously, you looked at a single page menu. Single page menus serve simple applications. Most applications need a more extensive, structured menu. While it is general purpose, not application-specific, the ACAD.MNU provides a good example of menu structure. Learn from it, and then go on to develop your own more efficient application-specific menus.

How ACAD.MNU Is Organized

ACAD.MNU is organized by devices and menu pages. Three asterisks precede device names; ***SCREEN indicates the screen as a device. Two asterisks precede a page name; **LAYER precedes the layer menu page. As you move through the following exercise examples, use your editor to search for the device and page names.

The standard AutoCAD menu begins with the ***BUTTONS (and identical ***AUX) section, followed by ***POP1 and the other pop-ups (pull-downs). Then come the ***ICON and ***SCREEN sections, followed by ***TABLET1 through ***TABLET4. AutoCAD supports 18 devices in Release 9, Release 10, and later versions. The tablet is considered as four devices, and pop-ups are up to ten devices. Take a look through the menu and see if you can find the different device sections. (It's a long file, so don't get discouraged!) The following is a list of AutoCAD's devices.

***BUTTONS	***POP5	***ICON
***AUX1	***POP6	***SCREEN
***POP1	***POP7	***TABLET1
***POP2	***POP8	***TABLET2
***POP3	***POP9	***TABLET3
***POP4	***POP10	***TABLET4

Menu Devices

The menu devices available to you in AutoCAD are the screen, tablet, buttons, pull-down (or pop-up), icon, and auxiliary devices. If you do not assign a device name in a menu file, AutoCAD assigns the macros to all devices. The buttons menu assigns macros to mouse or digitizer puck buttons. The tablet menus assign commands to your digitizer tablet. An auxiliary device is another electronic box that plugs into your computer. We are not aware of any currently being marketed. Pull-down and icon menus are treated as separate devices from the standard screen menu (device). Dialogue boxes are not part of the menu system.

The Default Device(s)

We have been treating the screen as if it were the default menu device. The truth is that the screen, tablet, and buttons are all active as defaults. Any of these devices can access as many menu items as it has lines, boxes, or buttons.

How Menu Pages Work

A menu structure is created by dividing the menu up into pages. The single page structure that you saw previously is the default. Most video displays support 20 to 30 items per screen page, but a few video displays support as many as 80 items per screen. Unless your display shows the entire menu, you will see a [NEXT] at the bottom of the screen. AutoCAD automatically pages the screen menu for you, creating a [NEXT] menu item. When you select [NEXT], another page of macros appears.

Naming Menu Pages

[NEXT] is a continuous loop with any number of pages. When you reach the last page, [NEXT] brings you to the first page. But it leaves the division of items between pages up to chance and the number of items your particular video can display. However, you can control the menu page divisions. You can break menus into named pages of commands and macros by labeling each page with a unique name. You distinguish this page name or label from other lines in a menu by using two leading asterisks, like **LAYER. The format is **pagename*, where pagename is any name you like. AutoCAD uses this label to find and activate the menu items as a set. You tell AutoCAD which page to load with the special character code $. If you are working with a screen menu, you use a $S. The format is $S=*pagename*.

Assigning Menu Pages to Devices

How do you assign menu pages to different devices? First, you break up your menu into **pages, then you assign a page, or pages, to a device with $= codes. The execution of a $= code is called a *menu call*. Each device has its own code. $S= assigns a menu page to the screen. $B= assigns a menu page to your buttons (pointing device). Table 19.3 shows all the menu device assignment codes.

A name following the device code, like $B=*pagename*, will send the named page to that device.

Table 19.3:
Menu Device Assignment Codes

CODE	ACTION
$S=	Screen menu
$P1= thru $P10=	Pull-down screen menus 1 thru 10
$B=	Buttons menu
$T1= thru $T4=	Tablet areas 1 thru 4
$I=	Icon menu
$A1=	Aux Box 1

Note: Do NOT use a semicolon as a <RETURN> following a page name call. In some cases, like $S=NAME;+, AutoCAD will not recognize it as a <RETURN>. Use a <SPACE>, like $S=NAME +.

Menu Page Order

The order of menu devices and pages is not particularly important. You can place pages in any order you want, but you need to be careful not to duplicate any page or device names in a menu file. AutoCAD will only recognize the first name. Any menu item can load or restore any page to any device. The call $S=OSNAPB will load **OSNAPB to the screen as intended, but you can just as easily write $B=OSNAPB to send the **OSNAPB page to the buttons device.

Device labels are specially reserved names that AutoCAD uses to load each device with the first page following its device label. When AutoCAD loads a menu, it looks for each device label, then loads each device with those items that follow its label, up to the next ***device or **page.

The ***SCREEN Menu

Let's examine our copy of the standard AutoCAD ACAD.MNU to see the menu device and page listings and how menu pages are directed to specific devices. If you have been browsing through the menu, return to the ***BUTTONS device section at the top of the menu. Then, search down to find the ***SCREEN section.

Looking at the ***SCREEN Menu

The top of your IA6ACAD menu should show the buttons device:

```
***BUTTONS
;
$p1=*
^C^C
^B
^O
^G
^D
^E
^T
```

Search for the characters ***SCREEN to find the screen device. You will only see blank lines where noted.

`***SCREEN`	This is the device.
`**S`	This is the default screen page named S.
`[AutoCAD]^C^C^P$S=X $S=S (setq T_MENU 0) (princ) ^P$P1=POP1`	
	Restores the screen and pull-down menus.
	Blank line.

```
[* * * *]$S=OSNAPB
[BLOCKS]$S=X $S=BL
[DIM:]$S=X $S=DIM ^C^CDIM
[DISPLAY]$S=X $S=DS
[DRAW]$S=X $S=DR
[EDIT]$S=X $S=ED
[INQUIRY]$S=X $S=INQ
[LAYER:]$S=X $S=LAYER ^C^CLAYER
```

Restores the screen menu and executes the LAYER command.

```
[MVIEW]$S=X $S=MV
[PLOT]$S=X $S=PLOT
[SETTINGS]$S=X $S=SET
[SOLIDS]^C^C^P(progn(setq m:err *error*) (princ))+
(defun *error* (msg) (princ msg) (setq *error* m:err m:err nil f nil) (princ))+
(if (null c:solbox) (progn (menucmd "S=X") (menucmd "S=SOLLOAD"))+
(progn (menucmd "S=X") (menucmd "S=SOLIDS")))) (princ);^P
[SURFACES]$S=X $S=3D
[UCS:]$S=X $S=UCS1 ^C^CUCS
[UTILITY]$S=X $S=UT
[ASHADE]^C^C^P(progn(setq m:err *error*) (defun *error* (msg)+
```

Continues with AutoShade and RenderMan setup.

The default **S screen menu (sometimes called the *root* menu) consists mostly of menu page calls. The [DRAW] item is typical. It does nothing but call the **DR (draw menu) and **X pages. Items that execute a command, like [LAYER:], are indicated by a colon. This colon is simply part of the label and is Autodesk's convention for identifying command screen macros.

Note: If you are using Release 10, your menus will differ from those shown.

Adding Menu Items to the Screen Menu

The following exercise shows you how to add your [EDIT-MNU] macro to the **EXCOMDS (EXTernal COMmanDS) menu page. The EXCOMDS page is accessed by the [UTILITY] item on the root menu, then the [External] item (in Release 10, by the [External] and [Commands] items).

First quit your text editor; don't save the file. Reload your editor with the unchanged IA6ACAD.MNU copy of ACAD.MNU. This ensures that you're working with a clean copy, and that no accidental changes were made in our travels. We'll show additions to existing menu files in bold text. If you set [EDIT-MNU] up to include your editor's name and menu filename, use the filename IA6ACAD.MNU.

Modifying the **EXCOMDS Screen Menu

Edit an EXISTING drawing named MENUTEST.

Command: **SHELL**	Access your text editor.
OS Command: **NE IA6ACAD.MNU**	Starts our editor, NE. Use *your* editor to edit IA6ACAD.MNU.

Search for **EXCOMDS.

Add your [EDIT-MNU] macro to the bottom of the page just above the ***Comments section. You'll have:

```
**EXCOMDS 3
[CATALOG:]^C^CCATALOG
[DEL:]^C^CDEL
[DIR:]^C^CDIR
[EDIT:]^C^CEDIT
[SH:]^C^CSH
[SHELL:]^C^CSHELL
[TYPE:]^C^CTYPE
```

Leave three blank labels so [EDIT-MNU] will display directly underneath the label [External] on the [UTILITY] menu after you load it. Then it's a quick double-click away.

Modifying the **EXCOMDS Screen Menu—continued

```
[]
[]
[]
[EDIT-MNU ]^C^C^CSHELL \MENU :                    Add the macro.
```

Save the IA6ACAD.MNU file and exit your editor back to AutoCAD.

Tip: If you are creating an extensive set of macros, create and test them as a small separate menu, then merge them into your big menu to save compile time.

Now, load the menu and test it.

Testing the [EDIT-MNU] Screen Menu Macro

Command: **MENU**	Load your newly modified menu.
Menu file name or . for none <IA-ACAD>: **<RETURN>**	
Compiling menu C:\IA-ACAD\IA6ACAD.MNU...	The menu recompiles and loads.
Select **[UTILITY]**	Calls the **UT page.
Select **[External]**	Calls the **EXCOMDS page.
Select **[EDIT-MNU]**	Access your text editor.
Command: SHELL	It issues the SHELL command.
OS Command: **NE IA6ACAD.MNU**	Type the command that starts *your* text editor.

Make any necessary corrections, save and end the editor, then SHELL returns you to AutoCAD.

Where the macro continues with the MENU command:

Command: MENU Menu file name or . for none <IA-ACAD>:	
Compiling menu C:\IA-ACAD\IA6ACAD.MNU...	Reloads the modified menu.
Command: **SAVE**	Save to make IA-ACAD the drawing's default menu.

Your screen should look like figure 19.7. The [EDIT-MNU] item should be at the bottom of the screen. The rest of the original screen menu pages are unaffected.

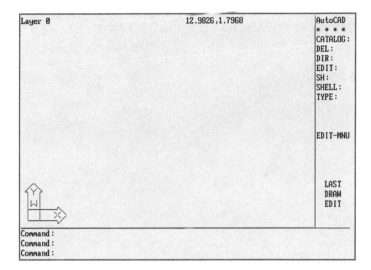

The single menu item that you added to this page could just as easily have been a call to a whole set of custom menu pages added to the screen menu. Such a menu item can call a custom page which may have items branching to other custom pages. Or, it can be a MENU command to load your own custom menu (like the IA6MENU) instead of the ACAD.MNU. Swapping items back and forth between a custom menu and the standard ACAD.MNU is a good alternative to extensive additions to the ACAD.MNU.

Note: If you end AutoCAD to edit your menu file, be sure to save or copy the menu file to the IA-ACAD directory and use the MENU command to manually reload it each time we edit it in this chapter.

The ***TABLET Menu

One of the first customization steps that many users take is to add their own customized macros to their tablet menus. In effect, you can load your symbol library onto your tablet menu. After you have done this, you can modify the standard TABLET.DWG file to create your own tablet template with your symbols to overlay your digitizing tablet.

The standard AutoCAD tablet menu sets aside one section, called ***TABLET1, for this type of customization. Let's look at ***TABLET1 and ***TABLET2 to see what the tablet menu looks like. Then we'll add a macro to ***TABLET1.

Looking at ***TABLET1 in IA6ACAD.MNU

Select **[EDIT-MNU]**   Access your text editor.
Command: SHELL
OS Command: **NE IA6ACAD.MNU**   Start *your* text editor.

Find ***TABLET1:

```
***TABLET1
[A-1]
[A-2]
[A-3]
[A-4]
[A-5]
[A-6]
[A-7]
[A-8]
```

And so on, to [A-25]. Then it starts over beginning with row B and continues through [H-25].

The standard AutoCAD tablet menu starts with 200 labeled items, inviting your customization efforts. The column numbers (1 through 25) and row letters (A through H) correspond to the markings on the standard AutoCAD tablet template.

With Release 11, you'll find many of these tablet boxes occupied. The first ten columns are used by commands for the Advanced Modeling Extension, AutoShade, and RenderMan. However, the standard AutoCAD menu has four tablet picks below the Monitor area (at [S-19] through [S-22]) which allow you to switch entire tablet areas between different menus.

When you pick the tablet area one icon, AutoCAD swaps all of the AME, AutoShade, and RenderMan menus out and replaces them with a blank ***TABLET1ALT. You can just as easily have them replaced with your own tablet menu, which could occupy the entire ***TABLET1 section. The other three tablet areas are also swapped to alternate versions that cause each menu box to act slightly differently.

The four-asterisk label [* * * *] near the top of the screen menu will display a number instead of an asterisk in the position corresponding to a tablet menu area that is currently swapped. In other words, if tablet area one is swapped, a 1 will appear where the first asterisk was. A 2 will appear instead of the second asterisk if tablet area two is swapped, a 4 if area three is swapped, and an 8 for area four. Picking a swap icon once more restores the areas to their default state, as does selecting the [AutoCAD] screen menu label. (This does not apply to Release 10.)

Find the ***TABLET2 section. See if you can identify the items where they appear on the AutoCAD template on your tablet. (If you don't have a template, see Appendix C for a tablet illustration.) They start at [J-1] with HIDE and the first row ends at [J-11] with 'REDRAW. We show the first two items.

Still in your text editor, search for ***TABLET2.

```
;                                          The last line of ***TABLET1.
***TABLET2
^C^C^P(menucmd "S=X")(menucmd "S=HIDE1")(progn (initget "Yes No")+
(setq ans (getkword "Do you want to HIDE? Y ")))(if (= ans "Yes")+
(command "HIDE")(progn (menucmd "S= ")(menucmd "S= ")))(princ);^P
$S=X $S=VPOINT VPOINT;;
```

Adding tablet macros is like putting macros in a screen menu, except you have to keep track of the tablet box numbers. Modifying them can be tricky because, unlike the ***TABLET1 section, they lack numbered labels. If you modify them and accidentally delete one or add a new line, it will throw the rest of the menu section off by one box.

Adding Macros to the Tablet Menu

Box numbers are numbered sequentially within the ***TABLET sections. They proceed row by row, starting from the top left box of each section. If you make your own fully customized menus, the number of rows and columns in each section is up to you. The standard AutoCAD menu uses arbitrary letters (A-Y) along the left side, and numbers (1-25) across the top to identify the positions on the tablet itself. Figure 19.8 shows the tablet area one of the standard tablet template drawing. It shows the [D-12] box where we are going to add a macro, safely out of the way of the AME, AutoShade, and RenderMan macros.

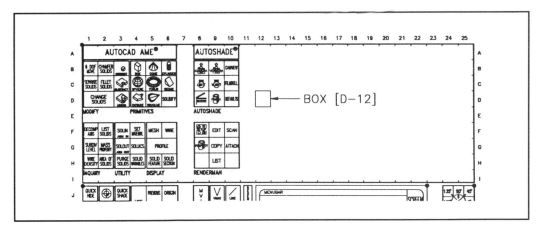

Figure 19.8:
Tablet area one template with target macro box.

The SECT-MK Block Macro

The following exercise uses the SECT-MK block from the previous chapter or from your IA DISK. Make sure that you have the SECT-MK block in your MENUTEST drawing, then add the SECT-MK macro at position [D-12]. You need to be configured for the standard AutoCAD tablet menu to *test* it. (See Appendix C to configure the standard tablet menu.)

Modifying the ***TABLET1 Menu

Still in your text editor, search for [D-12].

Edit the ***TABLET1 section as shown below.

The numbered lines not shown are left unchanged.

```
[D-11]
[D-12]^C^C^CINSERT SECT-MK S (getvar "DIMSCALE") \\\ATTEDIT ;;;;L A 0 ;
[D-13]
[D-14]
```

Save IA6ACAD.MNU and exit your editor back to AutoCAD.

```
Command: MENU Menu file name or . for
    none <IA-ACAD>:
Compiling menu C:\IA-ACAD\IA6ACAD.MNU...
```
[EDIT-MNU] continues.
And reloads the modified menu.

Testing SECT-MK on the Tablet

Select **[D-12]**   Try SECT-MK by picking the
                                                            twelfth box in the fourth row.

```
Command: INSERT Block name (or ?)
    <SCALE>: SECT-MK
```

The block insertion scrolls by. Pick insert point and angle, then:

```
Enter attribute values
Enter letter: <?>: B
```
Enter character (third backslash).

```
Command: ATTEDIT
```

ATTEDIT scrolls by and rotates the text to 0 degrees (see fig. 19.9).

When you execute the SECT-MK block macro from the tablet, it functions just like it did from the screen menu.

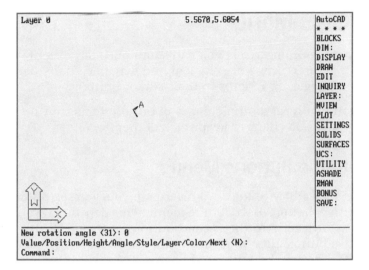

Figure 19.9:
The SECT-MK block
macro executed from
tablet.

You can easily create a mirror image section mark block and add another tablet menu item. Whether you add one symbol macro to the tablet or 200, or even design a completely new tablet, the process is the same. The design, layout, and symbols are yours. You can have multiple pages of tablet items, and change pages just as you do for screen menu items.

Adding to the Standard Tablet Template Drawing

After you have implemented your macros in the tablet menu, you can create a template or modify the standard TABLET.DWG by adding the symbol drawings that you want in the appropriate boxes. The standard menu's individual tablet boxes are 0.4" x 0.4". If you want to make your items larger, you can make each tablet menu item two boxes, or even four boxes. If you use more than one box, don't forget to add the macro to the corresponding menu item labels in the tablet menu itself. The ATTDEF, HELP, and CHANGE items on the standard menu are examples of this. If you create a custom tablet, you can make the boxes any size you want.

If you haven't looked at the tablet menu, it's TABLET.DWG on your original AutoCAD support disks. Load and modify it like any drawing.

After you have modified your tablet template, you can plot it out. If you are just modifying and using area one, plot it as a window at 1 = 1 and lay it under the clear area in the standard template. If you are modifying the entire tablet menu, plot the whole thing. Unless you change the size, location, or overall pattern of the areas, you don't need to reconfigure your tablet.

The ***BUTTONS Menu

The buttons are always at your fingertips. You can simultaneously execute a macro and pick its first point. Button menus are efficient and dynamic. Many users overlook the advantage of adding a few macros to their cursor buttons.

Like screen menus, you can have multiple pages of button items, but if you have more than a couple of pages, it's hard to keep track of them.

Adding Macros to the Buttons Menu

The following exercise shows how to add two macros to your cursor buttons. The specific digitizer (or mouse) buttons used for the menu items depend on your equipment. In the examples, we'll refer to the second button item as [B2]. Button two means the second active button after your pick button. If your normal pick button is numbered 1, then [B2] means the button numbered 3! A two-button mouse has no [B2], only a pick button and [B1]. Any items in excess of your available buttons are simply ignored.

The original ***BUTTONS section is near the top of your menu file. You saw it when you looked at the screen menu. Let's modify it by adding two new macro items to the top. The first macro picks an osnap intersection or endpoint. The second macro issues the LINE command and simultaneously picks a point.

Modifying the ***BUTTONS Menu

Select [EDIT-MNU]	Access your text editor.
Command: SHELL	
OS Command: **NE IA6ACAD.MNU**	Start *your* text editor.

Search for ***BUTTONS. Add the new lines [B1] and [B2] as shown:

```
***BUTTONS
[B1 ]INT,ENDP \                          Add first macro.
[B2 ]LINE \                              Add second macro.
;
$p1=*
^c^c
^B
^O
^G
^D
^E
^T
***AUX1
```

Save IA6ACAD.MNU and exit your editor back to AutoCAD.

> ### Modifying the ***BUTTONS Menu—continued
>
> ```
> Command: MENU Menu file name or . for
>   none <IA-ACAD>:                            [EDIT-MNU] continues.
> Compiling menu C:\IA-ACAD\IA6ACAD.MNU...     And reloads the modified
>                                              menu.
>
> Select [B2 ]                                 It issues a LINE command.
> Command: LINE From point:                    And picks the first point.
> To point:                                    Pick a few more points, and
>                                              make an intersection.
>
> To point:
> To point:
> To point: [B1] INT,ENDP of                   Pick an endpoint with [B1]. It
>                                              osnaps and picks the point.
> To point: [B1] INT,ENDP of                   Pick an INTersection with [B1].
>                                              It osnaps the point.
>
> To point: <RETURN>
> ```

Note: The INT,ENDP\ macro provides and fills its own backslash pause, so it doesn't use up any backslashes in pending menu macros. It's good for point entry in commands that are not paused, but won't work with macros expecting a specific number of points to be entered.

Pull-Down Menus — AutoCAD's Special Interface

Pull-down menus are specially implemented AutoCAD screen menus that pull down to overlay a portion of your display. They are dynamic in nature. They only appear when they are opened, and disappear as soon as another action is taken. Unlike the normal screen menu, pull-downs temporarily borrow space from the drawing.

Each of the pull-down menu positions are separate devices in the menu file. There are ten positions on the display for pull-downs, so there are ten device names: ***POP1 through ***POP10. Like other devices, the three asterisks in the labels identify the defaults. You can access any number of **pages, just like screen menus. Like the screen page code $S=, pull-downs are loaded using $P1= through $P10= page codes. The ten positions are shown in figure 19.10. (Release 10 uses eight of its ten areas.)

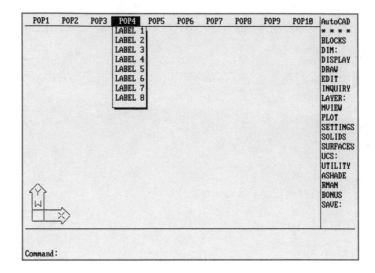

Figure 19.10:
Pull-down menu
locations.

How Pull-Downs Work

Pull-downs work differently from other devices. They need to be *opened* to be used. Using $P2=*name* loads **NAME to the P2 position, but it does not display it. You must use an asterisk in combination with a $P code to tell AutoCAD to open a pull-down. $P2=* causes AutoCAD to display whatever is currently loaded to the ***POP2 device.

Of course, you also can open a pull-down by moving the pointer up to the status area of the display and picking the pull-down currently loaded to that portion of the status line.

If your video driver supports pull-downs, you can customize them. First, find the ***POP5 device menu and take a look. It makes extensive use of transparent commands to call dialogue boxes.

Looking at Transparent Commands in the ***POP5 Menu

Select **[EDIT-MNU]**   Access your text editor.
Command: SHELL
OS Command: **NE IA6ACAD.MNU**   Start *your* text editor.

Find the ***POP5 section:

```
***POP5
[Settings]
[Snap On/Off  ^B]^B
[Grid On/Off  ^G]^G
[Ortho On/Off  ^O]^O
```

Looking at Transparent Commands in the ***POP5 Menu—continued

```
[- -]
[Layer Control... ]'ddlmodes                          Modify Layer dialogue box.
[Drawing Tools... ]'ddrmodes                          Drawing Modes dialogue box.
[Set SysVars      ]'setvar
[Set Dim Vars... ]^C^C^P(terpri)(prompt (strcat "Current dimension style: "+
(setq m:dsty (getvar "DIMSTYLE"))))(princ)^P dim $I=dimset $I=*
[- -]
[UCS Control... ]^C^Cdducs                            Modify UCS dialogue box.
[UCS Options... ]$I=ucs $I=*
[UCS Previous   ]^C^CUCS P
[Ucsicon On/Off/OR]^P(if (not m:ucsi)(defun m:ucsi (/ m:err)+
(setq m:err *error*)(defun *error* (msg)(setq *error* m:err)(princ))+
(cond ((= (getvar "UCSICON") 1)(setvar "UCSICON" 0));+
((=(getvar "UCSICON")0)(setvar "UCSICON" 3))(T (setvar "UCSICON" 1)))+
(princ)))(princ);(m:ucsi);^P
[- -]
[Shade Style    ]'shadedge \'shadedif
***POP6
```

Exit your editor back to AutoCAD.

```
Command: MENU Menu file name or . for none <IA-ACAD>: [EDIT-MNU] continues.
Loading menu C:\IA-ACAD\IA6ACAD.MNU...          And reloads the unmodified
                                                 menu.
```

Try several of the items from ***POP5 as you look at the code.

If you look at the use of transparent command macros in these menus, you will see that they do not begin with <^C>s. The <^C> cancels any pending command. If you issue a transparent command like 'DDLMODES when no other command is pending, the leading apostrophe causes no problem.

Notice that each menu page ends with a blank line. This is not required, but a blank line or even a blank [ ] *will* cause a POP menu page to end.

Adding Macros to Pull-Down Menus

Pull-downs are best for single-shot operations and settings, particularly transparent settings, because the menu disappears as soon as it is selected or as soon as any other action is taken.

Try adding a page of transparent settings to ***POP5. These macros are all variations on a transparent SETVAR; for example, setting aperture, pick box, and ortho mode. To add this menu page, you will add a menu selection to the bottom of ***POP5 that will call your new page **P5IA-ACAD. This new page will replace ***POP5 until you pick the [SETTINGS] selection to return you to the original pull-down menu. This is the same menu structure AutoCAD uses to implement multiple menu pages wherever you see selections ending with the greater than symbol (>). For example, look at the [INSERT OPTIONS >], [DTEXT OPTIONS >], [HATCH OPTIONS >], and [OPTIONS >] picks on the [Options] pull-down.

If you are using the IA DISK, you have these macros already pre-built as POP5.TXT. All you need to do is add one line to ***POP5 and merge POP5.TXT at the end of the ***POP5 menu. If you are not using the disk, you need to type in the macros. ['Setvars] is the menu bar label.

Adding Pull-Down Settings to the ***POP5 Menu

Select **[EDIT-MNU]**   Access your text editor.
Command: SHELL
OS Command: **NE IA6ACAD.MNU**   Start *your* text editor.

   Merge the POP5.TXT file into the menu as shown.

   Type in the bold text shown below.

```
[Shade Style    ]'shadedge \'shadedif          Last line of the stock menu page.
[- -]                                           Merge or enter POP5.TXT.
['SETVARS    >]$P5=P5IA-ACAD $P5=*              Loads, then displays new page
                                                Blank line.
**P5IA-ACAD
['SetVars]
['Regenauto On ]'SETVAR REGENMODE 1
['Regenauto Off]'SETVAR REGENMODE 0
['Aperture    ]'SETVAR APERTURE 6 'SETVAR ;
['Pickbox     ]'SETVAR PICKBOX 2 'SETVAR ;
[- -]
['Snap Ang/Base]'SETVAR ORTHOMODE 1 'SETVAR SNAPBASE @ 'SETVAR SNAPANG
['Snap Base   ]'SETVAR SNAPBASE @ 'SETVAR ;
['Snap Normal ]'SETVAR SNAPBASE 0,0 'SETVAR SNAPANG 0
[- -]
['OS Int,Endp ]'SETVAR OSMODE 33
['OS None     ]'SETVAR OSMODE 0
['OS Nearest  ]'SETVAR OSMODE 512
```

```
        Adding Pull-Down Settings to the ***POP5 Menu—continued
[- -]
[Highlight On  ]'SETVAR HIGHLIGHT 1
[Highlight Off ]'SETVAR HIGHLIGHT 0
[Dragmode Auto ]'SETVAR DRAGMODE 2
[Dragmode Off  ]'SETVAR DRAGMODE 0
[- -]
[SETTINGS    >]$P5=POP5 $P5=*                Restore [Settings] menu.
                                             Blank line.
***POP6                                      Beginning of ***POP6.
**p6opt
[Options]
[Entity Creation...]'ddemodes
[- -]
```

Save IA6ACAD.MNU and exit your editor back to AutoCAD.

```
Command: MENU Menu file name or . for none <IA-ACAD>:   [EDIT-MNU] continues.
Compiling menu C:\IA-ACAD\IA6ACAD.MNU...                And reloads the modified
                                                        menu.

Pull down [SETTINGS]                                    Pull down the menu by moving
                                                        the cursor up to the status
                                                        line. The pull-down line labels
                                                        should appear.

Select ['SETVARS >]                                     Your new menu page should
                                                        appear with a selection to re-
                                                        turn you to [SETTINGS] if you
                                                        desire (see fig. 19.11).
```

Try the macros.

Look at the labels. The settings with a single quotation mark in their labels are fully transparent. Notice the difference in the *greyed out* [- -] labels versus the [- -] label.

The [HIGHLIGHT] and [DRAGMODE] items use a transparent SETVAR to avoid disturbing pending commands, but they do not take effect until the next command starts. These macros are useful for dealing with large blocks and large selection sets, which drag poorly and take a long time to highlight. Use these macros to turn drag and highlight off.

The [REGENAUTO OFF] is useful if you are doing a block redefinition that otherwise forces a regeneration. The [REGENAUTO ON] macro turns regenauto back on.

Figure 19.11:
The new 'SetVars
pull-down menu page.

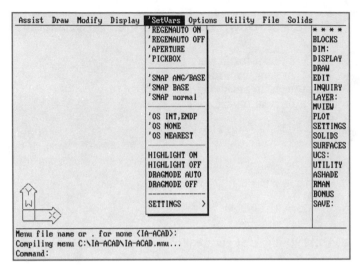

Try the ['APERTURE] and ['PICKBOX] macros during object selection. Their immediate effect is to change the pick box and aperture size in heavy traffic. The ['OS] items let you transparently reset a running osnap. Try the ['APERTURE] and ['OS NEAREST] items while you are in a drawing command to see how they suspend the command. The ['SNAP] items are macros that have the advantage of not causing a redraw as they relocate the snap base point to the last point with @, and rotate the snap angle.

Play around with the ['Setvars >] menu. If you find any macros that you like and find useful, put them in your own menu. Employ the same procedure that we used to create the **P5IA-ACAD menu to create other pull-down menu pages.

The ***ICON Menus

Let's look at icon menus. Icon menus are great for symbol libraries because they use groups of AutoCAD slides as graphic labels. (See the slides exercises in Chapter 16 if you need a refresher on slides.) Icon menus have the advantage of showing pictures to help you choose menu items. You have seen this type of menu in AutoCAD's hatch and text icon menus.

An icon menu is written just like any other pull-down menu except for its labels. You need to load the device with a $I=*pagename* and then display it with $I=*. However, icons use the label names shown in square brackets differently. Icon labels supply AutoCAD with the name of the slide to show in the box. Each label corresponds to one box on the screen. These boxes are automatically arranged in groups of 4, 9, or 16. If the label is in the form *libraryname(slidename)*, then the named slide from the named library is displayed as an icon.

If you put a space as the first character in the label, AutoCAD treats it like an ordinary label. AutoCAD displays label text in that item's screen box instead of a slide. You can use this label technique to show a More option to the user, guiding access to additional pages of icons. Examine the dim icon menu code.

Looking at the ***ICON **DRDIM Menu Code

```
Select [EDIT-MNU ]                                    Access your text editor.
Command: SHELL
OS Command: NE IA6ACAD.MNU                            Start your text editor.
```

Find ***POP2 and look at the [Dim...   ] macro.

```
[Dim...    ]^C^C$S=X $S=dim DIM $I=drdim $I=*         Loads and displays drdim icon
                                                      menu page.
```

Find ***ICON section, then skip to the **drdim page.

```
***icon
**txtalign
[Select Text Alignment]
[acad(j-tleft)]^P(setq m:ta "TLeft") ^P
[acad(j-mleft)]^P(setq m:ta "MLeft") ^P
[acad(j-start)]^P(setq m:ta "BLeft") ^P
[acad(j-bleft)]^P(setq m:ta "BLeft") ^P
```

Skip past the **txtalign and several other pages to find the **drdim page.

```
**drdim
[Select Dimension Type]
[acad1(linear)]$I=drlin $I=*
[acad1(angular)]ANG
[acad1(ordinate)]$S=X $S=DIMORD $I=drord $I=*
[acad1(diameter)]$S=X $S=DIMRADIAL DIA
[acad1(radial)]$S=X $S=DIMRADIAL RAD
[ Edit Dim...]$S=X $S=FORMAT $I=eddim $I=*
[acad1(dimcen)]CEN
[acad1(dimlea)]LEA
[ Exit]
                                                      Blank line.

**drlin
[Select Linear Dimension]
[acad1(dimhor)]$S=X $S=DIMLINEAR HOR
[acad1(dimali)]$S=X $S=DIMLINEAR ALI
```

Exit your editor back to AutoCAD.

```
Command: MENU Menu file name or . for none <IA-ACAD>:
Loading menu C:\IA-ACAD\IA-ACAD.MNX...               And reloads the unmodified
                                                      menu.
```

The macros following the icon menu labels work just as you would expect them to. The [Exit] line is an example of using a text label in an icon screen. It does nothing but clear away the icon menu and leave you at the Dim prompt.

The [Dim...] pull-down item is a menu page change. First $I=DRDIM loads the **drdim page to the icon device, then the $I=* displays it. Except for their labels, the icon macros themselves display combinations of screen and icon menus with command options and start dimensioning commands. That's all there is to it!

> *Tip:* When you make slides for icon menus, keep your images simple. Simple slides display much faster than complex ones.

Summing Up

As you consider modifying and adding to AutoCAD's standard menu, think about the types of modification that will save you time and money. Two areas that many users start with are customizing their setup procedures and adding their own standard symbols to their tablet menus. But any drawing task that will save you time is a candidate for some tailoring. You can create macros that set up, format, and fill in data for title sheets; place text in your drawing; locate, draw and insert components, assemblies and materials; automate dimension components; and annotate components. All these tasks are common to most drawing applications.

To develop a good menu, you need working macros and working symbols. Use your text editor interactively to develop and test your working macros and symbols. Your menu layout depends on what you want to achieve in your application. If you are uncertain about layout, use a simple paging structure. Use different pages for different operations. How you set up and use your pages and devices are the keys to developing a successful menu. For complete details on developing and integrating menus, see *MAXIMIZING AutoCAD, Volume I* (New Riders Publishing).

When you write complex menu items, test your command syntax extensively. Use your drawing editor as a testbed so that you know what options and input parameters are expected in your macros. Write your sequences down. Make your mistakes in the drawing editor, not in your text editor. If you think your macros are getting too complex, take a look at the next chapter on AutoLISP.

On to AutoLISP

If you followed the menu macros closely, you may have noticed that we made use of GETVAR, an AutoLISP function, in some of the menu items. The next chapter provides a closer look at AutoLISP, AutoCAD's built-in programming language. There are some commands that you can do in AutoLISP that you can't do with simple macros, and there are many macros that you can make simpler and more straightforward by using a few AutoLISP functions. It's on to AutoLISP!

20

Using AutoLISP for Drawing Automation

AutoLISP is a dialect of the LISP language (derived from XLISP) that coexists with the drawing editor within the AutoCAD program. Although the macros you created in the last chapter were powerful and complex, they were just sequences of standard AutoCAD commands. Adding AutoLISP to your macros and writing AutoLISP programs lets you create custom commands which can prompt, instruct, and provide choices and defaults just like AutoCAD's standard commands.

The Benefits of Using AutoLISP

By using AutoLISP in your menu macros, you can save data in variables, process that data, and send it back to AutoCAD. Points, distances, and other values can be stored, calculated, compared, and used to draw with. You can control your drawing environment through AutoCAD system variables by storing the system variables, prompting with drawing status, and changing and restoring the settings. You can change system settings transparently during commands for more responsiveness. You can access and extract entity data, use the data in programs, and even modify entities transparently.

You need only one tool to work with AutoLISP: your trusty text editor. Your text editor should be set up as in the previous chapter; see Chapter 19 if you need setup information. Use SHELL, as you have done previously, to take you from AutoCAD to your text editor where you can create and edit AutoLISP menu macros and AutoLISP program files.

What You Can Get From This Chapter

This chapter will give you an idea of the types of things that you can do to enhance your menu macros with AutoLISP. You can't learn AutoLISP in one chapter. In fact, there is a whole book, *Maximizing AutoCAD, Volume II* (New Riders Publishing) to teach it to you. This chapter will give you a few simple tools and techniques. But its main purpose is to give you a feel for what's involved and to encourage you to go on and learn to customize your system with AutoLISP.

There are some macros that are impossible to write without AutoLISP. As you write macros using AutoCAD's menu and command syntax, you reach a trade-off point where it is often easier to use AutoLISP to write your programs than to use the standard commands. To show you how to do this, we will use AutoLISP to rework the [BOLT:] menu macro that you used in the last chapter.

Creating an AutoLISP Command

Let's try a little AutoLISP. You are going to make a new AutoLISP command, called HOLE, by typing two lines of input at the command line. This AutoLISP command will automate the standard CIRCLE command to repeat using your specified diameters and center points.

You will see the words *Lisp returns:* in the exercise sequence. We use this line to show AutoLISP's backtalk. You won't see those same words on your screen, but you should see the line or lines that follow it on your screen.

AutoCAD recognizes AutoLISP expressions by the parentheses that surround them. Text strings are enclosed in quotation marks. Start a new drawing called LISPTEST and type the input shown in bold. Don't panic if AutoLISP returns a 1> during the input. This is just AutoLISP telling you that you need another right parenthesis. Keep typing the input as shown. After you get the response C:HOLE, try the command by typing in the command name HOLE.

Making an AutoLISP Command Called HOLE

Begin a NEW drawing named LISPTEST.

```
Command: (defun C:HOLE () (setq rad (/ (getdist "\nDiameter: ") 2))
1> (while T (command "CIRCLE" pause rad)))
Lisp returns: C:HOLE
```

Command: **HOLE**	Test the command.
Diameter: **1**	Enter a diameter.
CIRCLE 3P/2P/TTR/<Center point>:	Pick a point.
Diameter/<Radius>: 0.500000000000000	AutoLISP returns the radius.
Command: CIRCLE 3P/2P/TTR/<Center point>: **<^C>**	It repeats until canceled.

If all went well, you should have one or more holes on your screen, depending on how many points you picked (see fig. 20.1).

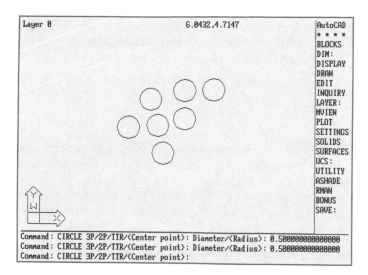

Figure 20.1:
Holes drawn with the
AutoLISP command.

In AutoLISP, opening parentheses in expressions must have matching closing parentheses. Failure to close a parenthesis will give you a prompt like 1> or 2>. The AutoLISP error prompt form is *n*> where *n* indicates how many closing parentheses are missing.

Note: If you keep getting a 1>, type a closing parenthesis and press <RETURN>, then press <^C> and try inputting the AutoLISP variables and expressions again. If you get an *n*> error prompt and adding additional parentheses doesn't help, then you left out a quotation mark. Type a single " and then type as many **))** as you need. The hardest part of AutoLISP is getting matching pairs of parentheses and quotation marks! If you have any other problems, see Appendix B.

The opening and closing parentheses allow AutoCAD to distinguish between AutoCAD commands and AutoLISP expressions. Each time AutoCAD detects an opening parenthesis, it passes the entire expression to AutoLISP. AutoLISP evaluates the expression and returns the result to AutoCAD. AutoCAD uses the result and continues.

The new HOLE command you made will remain available until you quit or end this drawing. We will explain the AutoLISP syntax used in the command and how it works. Later in the chapter, you will learn how to store an AutoLISP-made command.

AutoLISP Variables and Expressions

When AutoLISP was first introduced into the AutoCAD program, it wasn't even called AutoLISP. It was just called "Variables and Expressions" for building macros. Don't let AutoLISP intimidate you. It is often easier to think about AutoLISP as it was originally introduced, providing variables and expressions that you can use in your macros.

Variables

A *variable* is a label used to refer to a changeable value. You use variables every day. The current interest rate on your credit card is multiplied by the outstanding balance every month to see what finance charge will be added to your account. Rate and balance are variables. In AutoLISP, you can attach a value to a variable name and use it in a command or within AutoLISP expressions to perform calculations and make logical decisions.

In the HOLE example that you typed and tested, RAD (for radius) is a variable. It gets a value from the expression that divides the diameter distance in half. This value is passed to the CIRCLE command as the RAD (radius) value.

```
(defun C:HOLE () (setq rad (/ (getdist "\nDiameter: ") 2))
(while T (command "CIRCLE" pause rad)))
```

Variable Types

You can access AutoCAD's system variables and create new variables with names of your own with AutoLISP. If you look closely at the list of system variables in Appendix C, you will see three main types of variables: *string*, *integer*, and *real*. (*Points* are lists of variables.) System variables and any AutoLISP variables that you may create are one of these types.

- String variables have text values placed in quotes to identify the value as a string. For example, the system variable ACADPREFIX is currently "C:\ACAD\". The values "3.1", "FLOOR-3", "-1234", and "The quick brown fox . . ." are all strings.

- Integers are positive or negative whole numbers, without fractions, decimal places, or decimal points. AutoCAD often uses values of 0 and 1 to indicate whether a system variable toggle, like SNAPMODE or ORTHOMODE, is turned off (0) or on (1). Integers must be between -32768 and +32767. The values 1, 3234, and -12134 are valid integers.

- Reals are positive or negative numbers with decimal points. In AutoLISP, you cannot begin or end a real with a decimal point. If the value is less than 1.0, you must put a 0 before the decimal point (0.123) or you will get "error: invalid dotted pair." Examples of real system variables are

FILLETRAD, LTSCALE, and AREA. Unlike integers, you can make reals very large or very small. AutoLISP formats reals in scientific notation when the values are very large or very small. Valid reals look like 1.0, 3.75218437615, -71213.7358 and 1.234568E+17.

■ Points are really AutoLISP list variables. A list is one or more values of any variable type grouped within parentheses. The LASTPOINT system variable is a point list with a value such as: (6.500000 1.500000 0.000000).

Using system variables, you can control many AutoCAD drawing editor settings. You have changed these system settings by entering their names, or with the SETVAR command. You have used the transparent 'SETVAR command to change settings in the middle of another AutoCAD command. You can change some, but not all, of the system variable settings. Certain variables are indicated as *read only*, meaning you can only extract, not update, their values.

How to Use AutoLISP to Get and Set System Variables

You can also access AutoCAD's system variables with AutoLISP's GETVAR and SETVAR functions. GETVAR is a function, not a command. SETVAR is the name of an AutoLISP function and also the name of the AutoCAD command. In the last chapter, you used and set a system variable in the [BOLT:] macro. The flaw in that macro was the setting was left changed, with its original setting not restored when the macro was done.

With GETVAR and SETVAR, you can write macros that get, save, and restore your drawing settings.

Try some GETVAR and SETVAR functions by typing the input shown in the following exercise.

Using GETVAR and SETVAR Functions to Get and Set System Variables

Continue in your LISPTEST drawing.

Command: **LAYER**	Make a layer named OBJECTS. Leave it current.
Command: **(getvar "CLAYER")**	Get the current layer value.
Lisp returns: "OBJECTS"	The value, the layer name.
Command: **(setvar "ORTHOMODE" 1)**	Reset the ortho value.
Lisp returns: 1	
Command: **(setvar "CLAYER" "0")**	Try to reset layer.
error: AutoCAD rejected function	You can't. It's read only.
Lisp returns: (SETVAR "CLAYER" "0")	The offending AutoLISP function.

AutoCAD can cause a problem within AutoLISP when AutoCAD wants a literal text string. There are two places where AutoCAD wants a literal text string: when prompting for text, or prompting for an attribute. A system variable called TEXTEVAL controls the situation. Setting TEXTEVAL to 1 (On) forces AutoCAD to send the expression to AutoLISP for evaluation and print the results (instead of the expression itself).

Expressions

An AutoLISP expression begins with an opening parenthesis and ends with a closing parenthesis. AutoLISP expressions can contain other AutoLISP expressions, but each expression must be nested in its own pair of parentheses.

A typical AutoLISP expression has this syntax:

```
(function argument )
```

Here are the rules for the expression game:

- Every expression has opening and closing parentheses.
- Every expression begins with a function name. The name must immediately follow the opening parenthesis.
- Every expression gets evaluated (executed) and returns a result. The result may be nil, or the last evaluated value.
- Everything in AutoLISP is either True or nil. If something has no value, it's nil. If it has a value, it's True (non-nil).

Functions and Arguments

A *function* is a subroutine that tells AutoLISP what task to perform. A function may have any number of arguments or no arguments.

An *argument* provides data to the function. Arguments may be variables, constants, or other functions. Some arguments are flags that alter the action of the function. If you define a function to take an argument, you must provide the function with a value for the argument.

Using Math Functions in AutoLISP

AutoLISP has several built-in math functions. In the initial HOLE command that you typed, you used a divide function in the expression:

```
(defun C:HOLE () (setq rad (/ (getdist "\nDiameter: ") 2))
(while T (command "CIRCLE" pause rad)))
```

This expression divides the diameter distance that you gave it by two to get the radius value.

This division example has two arguments, one variable and one constant. Arguments are the data for the function. Some AutoLISP math functions, like addition, subtraction, multiplication, and division (+ - * /), can have any number of arguments. Some functions require a specific number of arguments, while others require specific arguments, but also take optional parameters. Here is a list of built-in math functions that you can use in your macros:

(/ arg1 arg2 arg3 ...)	ARG1 divided by ARG2 divided by ARG3 ...
(* arg1 arg2 arg3 ...)	ARG1 times ARG2 times ARG3 ...
(+ arg1 arg2 arg3 ...)	ARG1 plus ARG2 plus ARG3 ...
(- arg1 arg2 arg3 ...)	ARG1 minus ARG2 minus ARG3 ...
(1+ arg)	ARG plus 1
(1- arg)	ARG minus 1
(abs arg)	ABSolute value of ARG
(exp arg)	e to the ARG power
(expt base power)	BASE to the POWER
(gcd arg1 arg2)	Greatest Common Denominator of ARG1 and ARG2
(log arg)	Natural LOG of ARG
(max arg1 arg2 arg3 ...)	MAXimum of arguments
(min arg1 arg2 arg3 ...)	MINimum of arguments
(rem arg1 arg2 arg3 ...)	The REMainder only of ARG1, divided by ARG2, divided by ARG3...
(sqrt arg)	SQuare RooT of ARG

When AutoLISP evaluates a math expression, if all the arguments are integers, the results will be an integer and any fractional part will be dropped. If any argument is a real, the result will be a real.

How AutoLISP Evaluates Expressions

AutoLISP evaluates expressions at the same nesting level, left to right. When a nested expression is encountered, the entire nested expression is evaluated before the next expression on the right. One good thing about having all these parentheses is that you never write a formula that evaluates in a different order than you expect. Try some math functions and look at nesting. Type the functions in at the command line.

Using AutoLISP Math Functions

Command: **(+ 1 2.0)**   Returns a real.
Lisp returns: 3.0

Command: **(/ 3 2)**   Drops the .5 remainder.
Lisp returns: 1

Command: **(* 5 (- 7 2))**   The (- 7 2) expression is nested.
Lisp returns: 25

Command: **(setq a 1)**   Assigns the value 1 to a variable.
Lisp returns: 1

Command: **(+ (setq a (* a 3)) (+ a 2))**   Assigns variable before second expression.
Lisp returns: 8

Command: **(+ (+ a 2) (setq a (* a 3)))**   Uses variable, then reassigns it.
Lisp returns: 14

Making Your Own Variables and Expressions

You create variables by giving a value to a symbol. In the HOLE command, you gave a distance to the symbol RAD (for radius) with the expression (setq rad (getdist ...).

AutoLISP variables are completely independent of AutoCAD system variables and their names may duplicate AutoCAD system variable names. Each time you use the variable name or refer to the variable name in a macro, program, or expression, the program replaces the variable name with the most recent value assigned to that name.

Variables can be any printable combination of letters and numbers except those reserved because of their special meanings in AutoLISP. There also are some ill-advised characters that may confuse or interfere with AutoLISP when you use them in menu macros. Avoid using the following characters:

RESERVED AND ILLEGAL CHARACTERS: **. ' " ; ( )** or \<SPACE\>

AutoLISP FUNCTIONS: **~ * = > < + - /**

ILL-ADVISED CHARACTERS: **? ' ! \ ^** or any control character.

When you type your variable names, upper- or lower-case makes no difference. Try to keep your names under six characters since names over six characters require more memory. Don't begin a variable name with a number. Table 20.1 offers examples of valid and invalid variable names.

Table 20.1:
Valid and Invalid Variable Names

INVALID VARIABLE NAMES:	*VALID NAMES:*
123 (represents an integer number)	PT1
10.5 (represents a constant real value of 10.5)	txt
ANGLE (redefines the AutoLISP function ANGLE)	ANGL
A(1) (contains invalid characters)	A-1
OLD SUM (contains space)	OLD_SUM

How to Assign Values to Variables

SETQ binds a stored value to a variable name. In algebra, you write y=3, but in AutoLISP you enter (setq y 3). Both the = of the algebraic expression and the SETQ of the AutoLISP expression are functions. Each function binds (sets) the value 3 to the variable y. The opening (left) and closing (right) parentheses form the expression.

After binding a value to a variable name, you can use an exclamation point to supply that value to AutoCAD. The exclamation point identifies the word that follows as an AutoLISP symbol, usually a variable name. When AutoCAD sees the ! character, it passes the variable name to AutoLISP. AutoLISP interprets it and passes its value back to the AutoCAD command processor. You can also use the new variables in other AutoLISP expressions.

Using SETQ to Set and ! to Use AutoLISP Variables

Command: **(setq y 2)**	Set variable Y to the integer value 2.
Lisp returns: 2	
Command: **!Y**	Send Y's value to AutoCAD.
Lisp returns: 2	
Command: **(setq x 3)**	
Lisp returns: 3	
Command: **(+ x y)**	Use the values in an addition expression.
Lisp returns: 5	

Using GETxxx Functions for Macro Input

One area where AutoLISP can enhance your macros is to get (and control) the input for macro commands. Use the GETxxx family of AutoLISP functions to get drawing input. There is a GETxxx function for each major data type. All of the arguments to GETxxx functions are optional. The GETxxx functions can have a prompt argument to ask a question or to give an instruction. The prompt can be any string value. All the GETxxx functions pause for input. In a menu macro, they require backslashes.

Here is the complete list of GETxxx functions that you have to work with:

(getangle basept promptstring)	Returns angle from 2 points or typed input.
(getcorner basept promptstring)	Returns 2nd corner of a rubber-banded rectangle.
(getdist basept promptstring)	Returns distance from 2 points or typed input.
(getint promptstring)	Integer.
(getkword promptstring)	Returns one of a list of predefined key words.
(getorient basept promptstring)	Like GETANGLE but handles non-East base angle setting.
(getpoint basept promptstring)	Point.
(getreal promptstring)	Real.
(getstring flag promptstring)	String. If FLAG is True, it accepts <SPACE>s in string and requires <RETURN> to enter.

If you look at your original HOLE command yet once more, you'll see that you've used the GETDIST function.

The "\nDiameter:" is the prompt string. Try a couple of other input functions to get the hang of it. Type the input at the command line.

Using GETxxx Functions for Input to Macros

Enter selection: **1**	Begin a NEW drawing, again named LISPTEST.
Command: **(getangle "Enter angle: ")**	
Enter angle: **30**	Or pick two points to show an angle.
Lisp returns: 0.523599	AutoLISP uses and returns angles in radians, not degrees. There are 2 x PI radians in 360 degrees. One degree = 180/PI.
Command: **(* (getangle "Enter angle: ") (/ 180 pi))**	PI is predefined.
Enter angle: **30**	
Lisp returns: 30.0	
Command: **(setq pt1 (getpoint "Enter point: "))**	Save a point.
Enter point:	Pick a point.
Lisp returns: (2.0 2.0 0.0)	

Using GETxxx Functions for Input to Macros—continued

```
Command: (getangle pt1 "Enter angle: ")          Use pt1 as a basepoint for
                                                  rubber-banding.
Enter angle:                                      Pick a point.
Lisp returns: 0.96007
Command: (getangle pt1 "Enter angle: ")
Enter angle: 30                                   Or you can type it.
Lisp returns: 0.523599
Command: (getstring "Enter word: ")
Enter word: This                                  The first <SPACE> enters it.
Lisp returns: "This"
Command: (getstring T "Enter sentence: ")         T is predefined.
Enter sentence: This is a sentence.               It allows <SPACE>s.
Lisp returns: "This is a sentence."
Command: (getcorner pt1 "Enter other corner: ")   Use the base point.
Enter other corner: (5.4375 4.875 0.0)            It rubber-bands a rectangle.
```

If you followed the sequences, you noticed that the input automatically becomes the data type requested. Invalid responses that are not the requested data type are rejected.

How AutoLISP Lists Work

A list is a group of elements of any data type, treated as one expression and stored as a single variable. An AutoLISP list may contain any number of reals, integers, strings, variables, or even other lists. Anything between an opening parenthesis and closing parenthesis is a list. If this sounds hauntingly familiar, it is. An expression is a list! You use lists to organize and process groups of information. Several system variables are lists. The LIMMAX (upper right limits) system variable, for example, is a list.

Points Are AutoLISP Lists

```
Command: (getvar "LIMMAX")
Lisp returns: (12.0 9.0)                The upper right point of the limits.
```

Other examples of AutoLISP lists are ("A" "B") and ("NAME" 10.0 "DESK" "WS291A").

How to Use List Functions

AutoLISP has many list manipulation functions. LIST is simple. It just makes a list of its arguments. Since a list is a group of elements, you need a way to extract the element that you want. CAR is shorthand for the first element of a list, and CADR is the second element.

Using the QUOTE Function

The QUOTE function, which can be abbreviated as a single quotation mark, is also important. The LIST function evaluates its contents, then forms a list. The QUOTE function suppresses the evaluation of its expression(s). When it forms a list, it includes its contents literally. Let's look at LIST, CAR, CADR, the similar CDR, and at the QUOTE function. Type the input at the command line to see how these functions work.

Manipulating Lists

```
Command: (setq test (list 1 2 3.0))      Make a list.
Lisp returns: (1 2 3.0)

Command: (car test)
Lisp returns: 1                          The first element.

Command: (cdr test)
Lisp returns: (2 3.0)                    The rest of the list. All but the first element.

Command: (cadr test)                     The second element ...
Lisp returns: 2                          the CAR of the CDR.

Command: (nth 2 test)
Lisp returns: 3.0                        The third element.

Command: (setq test (list a b c))        Evaluates A, B, and C which are all unas-
                                         signed symbols (variables) with value nil.
Lisp returns: (nil nil nil)              Then it makes a list of three nils.
Command: (setq test (quote (a b c)))     Returns the unevaluated symbols.
Lisp returns: (A B C)

Command: (setq test '(a b c))            QUOTE abbreviated.
Lisp returns: (A B C)
```

AutoLISP has other functions, called CAAR, CADDR, CADAR, NTH, and more to manipulate lists. You can use the NTH function to access any element of a list, but watch the numbering. NTH counts 0, 1, 2, 3 ... (*not* 1, 2, 3 ...). This is typical computer counting. Watch your 0's and 1's carefully with AutoLISP functions. All AutoLISP functions do not count the same way.

Other List Functions

AutoLISP has several other functions that you can use to manipulate lists. These are: LAST, REVERSE, LENGTH, APPEND, and CONS. LAST will give you the last element of a list. REVERSE flips the order of the list. LENGTH returns its length. APPEND takes any number of arguments, each a list, and merges them into a single list. CONS adds a new first element to a list. See *Maximizing AutoCAD, Volume II* from New Riders Publishing to see how to use these and the other list functions.

How to Create Functions in AutoLISP

You can define your own functions in AutoLISP. You already created a new AutoLISP function called C:HOLE with DEFUN (DEFineFUNction). DEFUN defines a function by constructing a structured list of the program statements. Your AutoLISP functions create a local self-contained environment. Data passes into the function's local environment, your program statements use and manipulate the data, then pass the data back to the general AutoLISP-AutoCAD environment.

Before we define a new function, take another look at C:HOLE.

```
(defun C:HOLE ()
  (setq rad (/ (getdist "\nDiameter: ") 2))
  (while T (command "CIRCLE" pause rad))
)
```

The general form of DEFUN, using HOLE as an example, is:

```
(defun NAME (ARGs / LOCALS)
  PROGRAM STATEMENTS...
)
```

You can make the NAME of a function any name that you wish, with upper- and/or lower-case characters. Use the same rules that you use for variables.

C:HOLE has no *args* (arguments) or declared *locals*. We will look at arguments soon. Let's look at the program statements first.

Program statements like `(setq rad ... )` and `(while T ... )` are the core of your function. Program statements follow the general rules of AutoLISP evaluation, left to right and inside to out. The results of the last-evaluated statement are returned to the global AutoLISP-AutoCAD environment.

You can use your own functions the same way you use AutoLISP's built-in functions. This lets you make your programs modular, and your subroutines able to be reused. The BOLT function you are about to create is an example of a function using a subroutine, controlled by and receiving its input from another calling function.

AutoLISP's File Format

Sooner or later, you will want to store your functions for later reuse. You can store AutoLISP expressions and functions in disk files, just as you store menu files. You assign a file extension of .LSP to these files. The .LSP file may contain any number of function definitions and other expressions.

Unlike menus, you do not have to worry about devices, page sections, or <SPACE>s when you write .LSP files. Extra lines do not act like <RETURN>s and you do not need the plus sign to continue line characters. Semicolons do not cause <RETURN>s, but indicate comments you can insert for your own information.

Enhancing the [BOLT:] Macro

Create a BOLT function in a .LSP file. This BOLT function is an improvement on the [BOLT:] macro that you created in Chapter 19. The following BOLT.LSP program isn't as complicated as it looks. Half of the code (after the semicolons) is comprised of explanatory comments. We show the essential portion of the file in bold text; the semicolon comments are recommended but are not required. If you are using the IA DISK, you already have this program on disk as BOLT.LSP. You will also need the HEAD.DWG and NUT.DWG block files, either from the IA DISK, or from Chapter 19. Look at the file with your text editor, then load the file. If you are not using the disk, create the file. You can skip typing the non-boldface comments.

Making and Using an AutoLISP File

Command: **SHELL**	Start your text editor with BOLT.LSP.
OS Command: **NE BOLT.LSP**	Starts our editor, NE. Use *your* editor to create or look at BOLT.LSP.

 You have the BOLT.LSP file to examine.

 Create the BOLT.LSP file, entering the lines shown below.

```
; Draws filled bolt using HEAD and NUT blocks.
(defun BOLT (diam)
  (setq pt1 (getpoint "\nHead point: "))       ;Get Insert pt.
  (setq pt2 (getpoint pt1 "\nNut point: "))    ;Get Insert pt.
  (command "INSERT" "HEAD" "S" diam pt1 pt2    ;Insert HEAD.
        "INSERT" "NUT"  "S" diam pt2 pt1       ;Insert NUT.
        "PLINE" pt1 "W" diam "" pt2 "W" 0 "" "" ;Draw Pline shaft.
  )
);BOLT
(prompt "\nBOLT.LSP loaded.\n")
; end of BOLT.LSP
```

Save BOLT.LSP and exit to AutoCAD.

BOLT.LSP is actually quite straightforward. The diameter is fed to the function as the argument diameter. It gets the two endpoints with GETPOINT and saves them as PT1 and PT2 with SETQ. GETPOINT uses PT1 as a base point to drag a rubber-band reference line for PT2. Once it has the points and diameter, the rest of the function simply passes them to the INSERT and PLINE commands, using AutoLISP's COMMAND function.

Function Arguments

Function arguments are variable names you use to refer to the data passed into the function's environment. The number of arguments must match the number of pieces of data passed to the function. The BOLT function has only one argument, DIAM. You execute BOLT by typing `(bolt 1.25)`, or any other reasonable value, and the function sets DIAM to 1.25. Multiple arguments are assigned to input in a 1:1 order.

Local vs. Global Arguments

Arguments and other variables used within functions can be *local* or *global*. Locals are variables that you need and use only within the function. Variables must be declared (listed) in the parentheses following the function name in the DEFUN expression to be local. AutoLISP makes a small localized environment which stores values of the locally defined variables. You usually don't want your function's variables to be global. In most cases, you'll want to put all your internal variables on the local list. Arguments like DIAM are always local whether you like it or not. Local variables have no value outside their parent function, unless they were also set outside the function. If a variable with the same name as a local variable exists outside the function, its value is unaffected by the function and the function is unaffected by it. If you want an argument's value available outside the function, you have to set the argument to a different name.

Globals are variables that have a value outside of the function in which they were created, as well as within the creating function.

> *Tip:* Use a standard prefix, like #, to name global variables.

Later you'll revise BOLT to make PT1 and PT2 locals, and add a # to DIAM (making it #DIAM) as a global default value for repeated uses of the function. This will give you a working example of local and global variables.

How to Format and Document Your AutoLISP Programs

The indented format in the BOLT example is typical for typing AutoLISP programs, but AutoLISP doesn't care how you format white space. Spaces, tabs, and returns are all okay. The comments following the semicolons show how to document programs so you can still understand them next year. Programs are easier to read if all opening parentheses are either on the same line or vertically aligned with their matching closing parentheses. You can examine the sample programs included on your AutoCAD BONUS disk to see the formatting standard that Autodesk uses.

Loading an AutoLISP Function

AutoLISP's LOAD function loads the function file much like the MENU command loads menu files. While loading, AutoLISP reads the function definitions and stores them in memory. Other expressions, like the prompt (prompt "\nBOLT.LSP loaded.\n"), are executed while loading. AutoLISP's LOAD automatically assumes the file extension .LSP unless you give it another extension. (AutoLISP does not evaluate user-defined functions until you execute them.) To load the BOLT.LSP file, type (load "bolt"). Try loading and testing the BOLT function.

Using AutoLISP's Load Function	
Command: **(load "bolt")**	Load the file.
BOLT.LSP loaded.	The prompt.
Lisp returns: nil	The last-evaluated expression. PROMPT always returns nil.
Command: **(bolt 0.5)**	Execute the BOLT function, with the #DIAM argument 0.5.
Head point:	Pick point.
Nut point:	Pick point.
	The inserts and a polyline command scroll by as the HEAD and NUT are inserted and the filled shaft is drawn.
Command: **!PT1**	Look at the values of the variables.
Lisp returns: (2.37922 7.30479 0.0)	
Command: **!PT2**	
Lisp returns: (2.37922 4.43836 0.0)	
Command: **!DIAM**	
Lisp returns: nil	

If all went well, you should have a screen with an inserted head and nut (see fig. 20.2). You must type the argument as 0.5, not .5, or you will get an "error: invalid dotted pair" message.

> ***Note:*** Don't confuse AutoLISP's LOAD function with the LOAD command. AutoCAD's LOAD command loads SHAPE definitions.

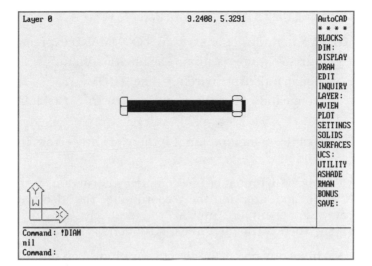

Figure 20.2:
The inserted head
and nut.

Note: AutoLISP has a feature similar to DOS's AUTOEXEC.BAT files. If AutoCAD finds an AutoLISP file named ACAD.LSP in its program directory, it automatically loads it each time you start a new or existing drawing. Any expressions in the file are executed while loading, and you can define a special S::STARTUP function to autoexecute AutoCAD commands.

AutoLISP's COMMAND Function

In the [CH:LAYER] macro, you used the AutoLISP expression (getvar "CLAYER") to return its value directly to AutoCAD. AutoLISP's COMMAND function provides a much better way of feeding AutoCAD. AutoLISP can instruct AutoCAD to draw, or to do anything else you can type. The key is the COMMAND function. It lets you run AutoCAD commands within an AutoLISP statement. COMMAND's format is:

```
(command arg1 arg2 arg3 ... )
```

AutoLISP takes each item of COMMAND's argument list and sends it to AutoCAD. If the argument is an AutoLISP variable or expression, it is first evaluated and then the results are passed to AutoCAD. Variables can be used anywhere in the statement to supply AutoCAD with data. Words within quotation marks are taken as "literal strings" by AutoCAD. Put AutoCAD commands, parameters, and text in quotes. Unquoted words are read as AutoLISP variables. You can use other built-in AutoLISP functions within the COMMAND function.

There are restrictions on using the COMMAND function:

- You cannot use GETxxx input functions within a COMMAND expression.
- You cannot precede variable names with an exclamation point.
- You cannot execute commands transparently, like 'ZOOM.
- You cannot use C: commands (see the next section) in a COMMAND expression.

Of course, AutoCAD will reject the command input if there are any errors in syntax or data type.

Each argument in the COMMAND list must be one complete instruction to AutoCAD. You cannot enter an X value, and later add the Y coordinate. You also must treat each instruction separately. For example, AutoCAD will treat (command "CIRCLE 5,5 0.25") as one erroneous instruction, not as three instructions.

You can make COMMAND functions pause for direct user input. You did this in the original HOLE command:

```
(command "CIRCLE" pause rad)
```

The function issues "CIRCLE" then pauses for the center point before issuing the value of RAD as the radius. If you use pause in a COMMAND function within a menu, you must supply the appropriate menu backslashes.

How to Add AutoLISP Commands to AutoCAD

Besides defining local and global variables, you can make your AutoLISP functions as easy to use and as clean in their screen appearance as a stock AutoCAD command. You can make AutoLISP function names into AutoCAD commands by adding the function names to AutoCAD's command list. Precede the function name with a C: to add it to the list.

Try enhancing the BOLT function. It currently requires the awkward function argument form of diameter input. The following exercise creates an enhanced BOLT command that functions like a regular AutoCAD command. It adds prompting for the diameter and saves the diameter as a +default for repeated executions. This enhanced BOLT, called EBOLT, has error handling added to its GET input functions. It is also an example of global and local variables, and a conditional if . . . then construction.

If you are using the IA DISK, this enhanced command is in the file EBOLT.LSP. If you are not using the disk, read along to see how it works. Then, come back later and type it in if you want to create and save the command. You need not type the non-boldface comments.

An Enhanced BOLT Command

Command: **SHELL**	Start your text editor with EBOLT.LSP.
OS Command: **NE EBOLT.LSP**	Starts our editor, NE.
	Use *your* editor to create or look at EBOLT.LSP.

 You have the EBOLT.LSP file to examine.

 Create the EBOLT.LSP file.

```
; Draws filled bolt using HEAD and NUT blocks.
(setq #diam 0.25)                                 ;Preset diameter to 0.25
(defun C:EBOLT (/ diam pt1 pt2 prmpt)
  (setq cmdecho (getvar "CMDECHO"))               ;saves command echo
  (setvar "CMDECHO" 0)                            ;echo off
  (if (> #diam 0)                                 ;IF #DIAM is greater than 0
    (setq diam #diam)                             ;THEN set default to it
    (setq diam 0.25)                              ;FLSE set default to .25
  )
  (setq prmpt                                     ;Set PRMPT to a string
    (strcat                                       ;combine the strings
      "Bolt diameter <"                           ;beginning of prompt string
      (rtos diam)                                 ;convert Real TO String for default
      ">: "                                       ;end of prompt string
    )
  )
  (initget 6)                                     ;initialize GET to no 0, no negative
  (if (setq #diam (getdist prmpt))                ;IF new value is entered at GETDIST
    nil                                           ;THEN do nothing - use new #DIAM
    (setq #diam diam)                             ;ELSE use old default
  )
  (setq pt1 (getpoint "\nHead point: "))          ;Get Insert pt
  (setq pt2 (getpoint pt1 "\nNut point: "))       ;Get Insert pt
  (command "INSERT" "HEAD" "S" #diam pt1 pt2      ;Insert HEAD
          "INSERT" "NUT"  "S" #diam pt2 pt1       ;Insert NUT
          "PLINE" pt1 "W" #diam "" pt2 "W" 0 "" ""  ;Draw Pline shaft
  )
  (setvar "CMDECHO" cmdecho)                      ;Restore setting
);EBOLT
(prompt "\nEBOLT.LSP loaded.\n")
; end of EBOLT.LSP
```

Save EBOLT.LSP and exit to AutoCAD.

The argument list of the DEFUN line lists the local arguments. But C: functions can't take input arguments, so #DIAM is handled by a GETDIST. This function lets #DIAM exist as a global variable so that the previous value can be used as a default in repeated uses. So before getting diameter, EBOLT checks for a default value.

```
(if (> #diam 0)             ;IF #DIAM is greater than 0
  (setq diam #diam)         ;THEN set default to it
  (setq diam 0.25)          ;ELSE set default to .25
)
```

After checking the default, EBOLT builds a prompt string that includes the default, converted to a string.

```
(setq prmpt                 ;Set PRMPT to a string
  (strcat                   ;combine the strings
    "Bolt diameter <"       ;beginning of prompt string
    (rtos diam)             ;convert Real TO String for default
    ">: "                   ;end of prompt string
  )
)
```

Then the GETDIST uses this prompt string to see if you want to specify a new diameter, using INITGET to filter the input.

```
(initget 6)                     ;initialize GETDIST to no 0, no negative
(if (setq #diam (getdist prmpt)) ;IF new value is entered at GETDIST
  nil                           ;THEN do nothing - use new #DIAM
  (setq #diam diam)             ;ELSE use old default
)
```

The rest of the function is essentially unchanged from the previous BOLT.LSP version.

You cannot use AutoLISP-defined C: commands as AutoCAD commands in a COMMAND function. You cannot enter a DEFUNed AutoLISP function when another function is active. C: functions *never* have arguments, but they can (and should) have variables declared as local variables.

Try using the enhanced BOLT command.

Using the EBOLT Command

Command: **(setq pt1 nil pt2 nil)**   Clear the old global variable values.
Lisp returns: nil

Command: **(load "ebolt")**
EBOLT.LSP loaded.
Lisp returns: nil

Command: **EBOLT**   Try it like any other command.

Bolt diameter <0.2500>: **.75**	In commands, a leading 0 like 0.75 isn't needed.
Head point:	Pick point.
Nut point:	Pick point. The PLINE draws the shaft.
Command: **EBOLT**	Try it again. See how the default diameter prompt changes.

Strings

The "Bolt diameter <0.2500>:" is the default prompt that the STRCAT function made in the example above. When you enter a value, it becomes the next default prompt. STRCAT is a function that combines (concatenates) any number of strings into a single string. All its arguments must be strings, so the function used the RTOS function to convert the real value of #DIAM to a string value. RTOS can take optional arguments to control precision and the type of units used. Otherwise, it defaults to the current units and their precision. There are several other string handling and associated functions:

ITOA	Converts Integers TO ASCII strings.
STRCASE	Converts UPPER/lower case.
SUBSTR	Extracts portions of strings.
STRLEN	Returns the length of a string.
ANGTOS	Converts ANGles TO Strings.
ATOF	Converts an ASCII string representation of a real TO Floating point (a real).
ATOI	Converts an ASCII representation of an integer TO an Integer.
ASCII	Returns the ASCII value of the first character of a string.
CHR	Converts the integer value of an ASCII character to a stringconsisting of that character.

Adding Logic to Your Macros

Every program has a flow, direction, or logic which it follows. You can use a branch in your macros to direct your AutoLISP program to execute in a predictable order. Conditional statements are the branching tools for controlling your AutoLISP programs. The following overview will give you an idea of the kinds of decisions you can have your programs make and react to.

Conditional Program Branching

AutoLISP has two branching functions, IF and COND. You used the IF in BOLT. All branching conditions need a conditional test to perform a branch. These conditional test expressions usually use *logical* and *relational* operators, like the greater than symbol in the enhanced BOLT command. A conditional test may use any AutoLISP expression, like the (setq #diam (getdist ...) in BOLT.

Using Nil and Non-Nil in Conditional Tests

Remember, everything in AutoLISP is either True or nil. If something has no value, it's nil. If it has a value, it's True (non-nil). AutoLISP's conditional functions work on a nil or a non-nil basis. Non-nil means that as long as there is some value, the condition *passes* the test. Since everything is either nil or T, any expression can act as a conditional test.

Logical Operators

A logical operator is a function that determines how two or more items are compared. Logical operators return either a T (non-nil) or a nil (false) condition. The basic functions available for logical operations are:

```
AND     OR      NOT
```

Table 20.2 gives examples for the logical operations. As you look at the table, A and B are True (non-nil) and C is nil.

Table 20.2:
Logical Operators

EXAMPLES	*RETURN*
(and a b c)	nil
(and a b)	T
(and b (getpoint "Pick: "))	Depends on input
(or c a b)	T
(or c)	nil
(not (or a b))	nil
(not c)	T

Both the AND and the OR functions can take any number of arguments. The AND function returns nil if any of its arguments are nil, otherwise, it returns T. The OR function returns True if any of its arguments are non-nil, otherwise it returns nil. Reading this carefully explains why, with no arguments, AND is T, but OR is nil!

OR stops evaluating and returns T as soon as it sees the first non-nil expression or symbol. In the same way, AND quits evaluating and returns nil as soon as it encounters a nil argument. You need to be careful when you put other functions inside AND or OR. Whether an argument is evaluated depends on the values of preceding arguments.

NOT is simple. NOT takes a single argument and returns the opposite. NOT returns T if its argument is nil, or returns nil if its argument is non-nil.

Relational Operators

A *relational* operator is a function that evaluates the relationship between two or more items. Relational operators return either a T if the expression is true (non-nil), or return nil if the expression is false. Relational operators include: less than, greater than, equal to, and not equal to.

The BOLT command used (> #diam 0) to determine whether a default value existed. The greater than and less than functions take any number of arguments. The first argument is compared to each following argument. Other relationals take only two arguments. Generally, the arguments may be any data type; the arguments are compared to see if they are numerically greater than, less than, or equal to.

In table 20.3, X is '(A B C), Y is 1.5 and Z also is '(A B C).

Table 20.3:
Relational Operators

EXAMPLE	*READ AS*	*RETURNS*
(< 2 y)	2 is less than Y — false	nil
(> 2 y 3)	2 is greater than Y or 3 — false	nil
(<= 1.5 y)	1.5 is less than or equal to Y	T
(>= 2 y)	2 is greater than or equal to Y	T
(= 1.5 y)	1.5 is equal to Y	T
(equal 1.5 y)	1.5 evaluates to same as Y	T
(eq z x)	Z is identical to X — false	nil
(equal z x)	Z evaluates to same as X	T
(/= 2 y)	2 is not equal to y	T

Except for EQ, EQUAL, =, and /=, these operations may have multiple arguments, comparing the first argument to all other arguments. Use the EQ function to test lists to see if they are bound to the same object. EQ generally is equivalent to the = and EQUAL functions for numerical and string comparisons.

How to Use the IF Structure

The simplest and most frequently used program branch is the IF structure, sometimes called *if-then-else*. In plain English, AutoLISP thinks, "*If* the condition is T, *then* execute the first expression, *else* (if it is nil) execute the second expression." Here is the BOLT example:

```
(if (setq #diam (getdist prmpt))        ;IF
    nil                                 ;THEN
    (setq #diam diam)                   ;ELSE
)
```

IF has two possible paths in the example. If you just hit a <RETURN>, GETDIST returns nil. The *If* condition test is false and the *else* is executed. The *else* execution sets #DIAM to the default DIAM. If a valid value is input, the *then* step is executed. This does nothing, leaving #DIAM set to the value input to the GETDIST.

The PROGN Structure

Limiting IF statements to only a single *then* and a single *else* statement is confining. If you want to execute several statements, AutoLISP provides PROGN. PROGN groups multiple AutoLISP expressions into one expression, notifying AutoLISP to treat the next series of statements as one statement. It always returns the value of the last expression within it. PROGN's structure is:

```
(progn arg1 arg2 arg3 ... )
```

where the arguments can be any number of valid AutoLISP expressions.

The COND Structure

COND works much like IF, except COND can evaluate any number of test conditions. Think of COND as a kind of multiple IF routine. Once COND finds the first condition that is non-nil, it processes the statements associated with that condition. COND only processes the first non-nil condition.

The general format is shown as follows.

```
(cond
  (first test-condition  first statements ... )
  (second test-condition 2nd statements ... )
  ... more tests and statements ...
  (T last-statements ... )
)
```

COND takes any number of lists as its arguments. Each argument must be a list containing a test followed by any number of expressions to be evaluated. COND interprets the first item of each list as that list's test condition. It evaluates all of the expressions within the first non-nil list.

Since COND looks for the first non-nil condition, putting your most likely non-nil conditions first increases your program's speed. The COND function is a good way to make programs branch based on a series of conditions. You can make the last test a test that is always non-nil, like the symbol T. Its expression will be evaluated if none of the others are non-nil. You can use it to issue error prompts.

Program Looping Structures

Like many other programming languages, AutoLISP has several functions for causing a series of program steps to loop, executing over and over again. You can use these looping structures to reduce the number of statements in the program, continue a routine until a user action terminates it, converge on a mathematical solution, or batch process a list of data. We will mention two of these: the REPEAT and WHILE structures.

The REPEAT Structure

AutoLISP's REPEAT is a simple looping structure. Consider using REPEAT if your macros need to repeat some task a specific number of times. All of its expressions get evaluated, once in each loop. REPEAT returns the value of the last expression on the last loop.

Here is the general format and an example.

```
(repeat number   statements to repeat ... )
```

Try a simple repeating statement at the AutoCAD command line.

Using a REPEAT Loop in AutoLISP

```
Command: (repeat 5 (prompt "\nDo some stuff"))
Do some stuff
Do some stuff
Do some stuff
Do some stuff
Do some stuffnil
Command:
```

The WHILE Program Structure

The function WHILE loops like REPEAT, except WHILE is open-ended, terminated by a conditional test. WHILE continues to loop through its series of statements until the condition is nil:

```
(while condition  statements to execute ... )
```

Unlike the IF function, WHILE does not have an alternate *else* set of statements to execute if the condition fails the test. However, like COND and REPEAT, WHILE lets you include an unlimited number of statements in the loop. WHILE allows an indefinite but controllable number of loops. Each loop of a WHILE function tests the condition and, if non-nil, evaluates each of the statements included within the closing parenthesis. WHILE returns the last evaluation of the last-completed loop. If no loops are completed, it returns nil. You used a WHILE to indefinitely repeat the HOLE command:

```
(while T (command "CIRCLE" pause rad))
```

WHILE is good for validating input, looping until the input meets the test. You also can use the function for program iteration. Iteration means that a loop is continued until the results of one or more expressions, calculated within the loop, determine whether the loop is terminated. The conditional test for an iteration usually contains some variable whose value gets changed during the course of the loop. Try a WHILE loop.

Using a WHILE Loop Function

Command: **(setq count 0)**
Lisp returns: 0

Command: **(while (< count 10) (princ count) (setq count (1+ count)))**
0123456789   And AutoLISP returns 10.

Tip: GETxxx functions are often put in a WHILE loop to test input, for example, to see if the input is a member of a list.

A Little Entity Access

Some of AutoLISP's more powerful customization features come from its access to AutoCAD's drawing database. Let's take a quick peek at AutoCAD's database, using AutoLISP's entity access.

Every AutoCAD entity, whether a line, arc, or circle, has a name that is recognized by AutoCAD. Since the names change every time a drawing is entered from the main menu of AutoCAD, you don't even want to try to remember them. Instead, use AutoLISP's entity functions to ask for the names of entities from the database. Getting entity data lets you manipulate the data directly or use the data in your macros. Type the following input at the command line.

Using ENTLAST and ENTGET Functions to Get Entity Data

Command: **LAYER**
Make layer OBJECTS and leave it current. Turn layer 0 off.

Command: **TEXT**
Enter this text at height .125 and point 8.5,2.25:

Text: **This is text.**
Command: **(setq ent (entlast))**
Get the last entity's "name" with ENTLAST.

Lisp returns: <Entity name: 60000A14>
Yours may be different.

Command: **(setq edata (entget ent))**
Look at its data with ENTGET.

Lisp returns: ((-1 . <Entity name: 60000A14>) (0 . "TEXT") (8 . "OBJECTS") (10 8.5 2.25) (40 . 0.125) (1 . "This is text.") (50 . 0.0) (41 . 1.0) (51 . 0.0) (7 . "STANDARD") (71 . 0) (72 . 0) (11 0.0 0.0 0.0) (210 0.0 0.0 1.0) (73. 0))

The entity name lets AutoLISP refer to and manipulate the entity. The ENTGET function looks up the data associated with the name you provide. You can even erase entities that you can't see by feeding AutoCAD entity names. AutoCAD's standard object selection depends on visibility, but you can bypass visibility using entity names.

Note: If you need to access entities with a handle that, unlike the entity name, is maintained from one drawing session to the next, turn HANDLES on. The AutoCAD HANDLES command can cause every entity to include a permanent identification handle in its entity data.

How Entity Data Is Stored

Entity data is returned in a list format with special groups of DXF (Drawing Interchange Format) codes that flag which type of data is contained in the sublist. Each sublist has two parts. The first part is the DXF code, and the second is the data value. The integer 0 is a code for the entity type in the example above. You can see that the type is listed as "TEXT". The 8 is a code for layer, and the layer is listed as "OBJECTS". The 10 is the code for the start (insert) point which is 8.5 2.25 and the 11 is the code for the text alignment point. For entities like lines, the 10 and 11 codes are the start and endpoints. The 40 code is the height, the 1 code is the text value, the 50 is the rotation, the 41 is the width factor, the 51 is the oblique angle, the 7 is the style, the 71 code is the mirror flag, the 72 code is horizontal justification, the 73 code is vertical justification, and the 210 is for 3D.

These codes have different meanings with different entities. Generally, any default data is not stored or listed. The leading integers in the parentheses are used to identify the type of data so that AutoLISP can process it. You can grab and manipulate any part of any drawing entity's data. The sky's the limit. That is why AutoLISP is such a powerful tool. It gives you direct access to the AutoCAD drawing database.

Extracting Entity Data

The DXF code (always an integer) allows you to access the inner parts of an entity list by association. In effect, you say, "Give me the sublist that has a 10 DXF code." AutoLISP will look at the entity list, find the sublist that has the matching 10 code, and return that sublist. AutoLISP's ASSOC function gives you the ability to associate lists. Try extracting some data:

Using the ASSOC Function to Extract Entity Data

```
Command: (assoc 1 edata)                 Get the text group.
Lisp returns: (1 . "This is text.")
Command: (cdr (assoc 1 edata))           Extract the string from the text group.
Lisp returns: "This is text."
```

Since the association list still contains the DXF code, you need to strip this code before passing the list to AutoCAD. The CDR (the list less the first item) function is perfect for this.

Getting Data From AutoCAD's Tables

AutoCAD keeps items like block, layer, style, linetype, and view names in reference tables. AutoLISP's TBLSEARCH function can look through a table and return information from it.

The TBLSEARCH function takes two pieces of information: the table to search and the name of the item to look for. Try two searches.

Using TBLSEARCH for a Quick Look at AutoLISP Table Access

Command: **(tblsearch "LAYER" "OBJECTS")**
Lisp returns: ((0 . "LAYER")(2 . "OBJECTS")(70 . 64)(62 . 3)(6 . "CONTINUOUS"))

Command: **(tblsearch "STYLE" "STANDARD")**
Lisp returns: ((0 . "STYLE") (2 . "STANDARD") (70 . 64) (40 . 0.0) (41 . 1.0) (50 . 0.0) (71 . 0) (42 . 0.125) (3 . "TXT") (4 . ""))

Command: **ERASE**   Erase the text.

Note: If you select a block insert, you get the information for the insert, not the entities within it.

The Last Exercise

Working with AutoLISP can get intense. Let's finish up with some fun. It is time to sit back, relax and look at one last AutoLISP file.

If you are using the IA DISK, get the AutoLISP file called THATSALL.LSP. It's a simple and fun example of entity modification through entity access. If you don't have the disk, you can create it or just read along.

That's All Folks

Here are the contents of the THATSALL.LSP file, if you need to create it. By now, you know how.

```
; THATSALL, an example of entity access and modification.
(defun C:THATSALL ()
  (command "TEXT" "M" (getvar "VIEWCTR")              ;Middle justified text at
                                                       screen center
    (setq ht2 0.05) (setq rot2 0) "That's All Folks!" ;Height, 0 rotation
  )
  (setq                                                ;Set variables
   edata (entget (entlast))                            ;Get entity data list
   ht (assoc 40 edata)                                 ;Get height ASSOC list
   rot (assoc 50 edata)                                ;Get rotation ASSOC list
   incang (* 0.125 pi)                                 ;1/16 of 360 degrees
  )
  (repeat 16                                           ;Increase ht and angle in 16
                                                        increments
    (setq
```

That's All Folks—continued

```
    ht2 (+ ht2 0.05)                            ;Set new height
    rot2 (+ rot2 incang)                        ;New angle
  )
  (entmod                                       ;Modify the text entity
    (subst                                      ;Substitute
      (cons 50 rot2)                            ;this new rotation ASSOC list
      rot                                       ;for this old list
      (subst                                    ;in this data list, which
        (cons 40 ht2)                           ;similarly substitutes new height
        ht                                      ;for original height list
        edata                                   ;in the original data list
    ) );close both SUBST
  );close ENTMOD
 );close REPEAT
 (repeat 17                                     ;similarly reverse height to 0
   (setq ht2 (- ht2 0.05))
   (entmod (subst (cons 40 ht2) ht edata))
 (princ)
 )
);close DEFUN
;end of THATSALL.LSP
```

To test THATSALL, just load it and run it:

Command: **(load "thatsall")**
Lisp returns: C:THATSALL
Command: **THATSALL**

And if you run it, you'll see the text spin, shrink, and grow, and you see:

```
TEXT Start point or Align/Center/Fit/Middle/Right/Style: M
Middle Point:
Height <0.0500>: 0,050000000000000
Rotation angle <0>: 0
Text: That's All Folks!
```
Lisp returns: ((-1 . <Entity name: 60000180>) (0 . "TEXT") (8 . ")") (10 6.14713 4.47 5 0.0) (40 . 1.38778e-17) (1 . "That's All Folks!") (50 . 0.0) (41 . 1.0) (51 . 0.0) (7 . "STANDARD") (71 . 0) (72 . 4) (11 6.49713 4.5 0.0) (210 0.0 0.0 1.0))
Command: **QUIT**

Your screen should resemble figure 20.3. This was the last exercise.

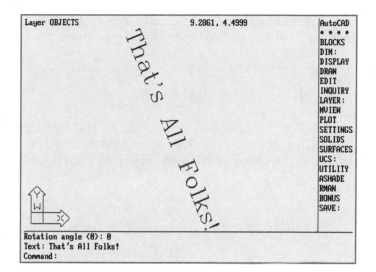

Figure 20.3:
That's all folks!

Summing Up

When you think about improving your macros with AutoLISP, feel free to convert some of our examples to your own uses. Here are a few of the ideas presented in the chapter.

You can use AutoLISP variables to eliminate menu selections that depend on drawing scale. Use AutoLISP to create intelligent macros to replace repetitive menu macros. When possible, use AutoLISP to calculate values to feed to AutoCAD commands, rather than pause the commands for input. Use AutoLISP to add prompts to menu macros to clarify the macro's use. Coordinate input with backslashes.

Use GETxxx functions to obtain user input. Use AutoLISP's COMMAND function to send instructions to AutoCAD. Remember that you can add AutoLISP C: commands to AutoCAD's command list. Use AND and OR functions for conditional prompts. Think about using WHILE to filter and validate macro input. You also can make looping programs to construct data lists using the REPEAT function.

Where to Go From Here

We've only scratched the surface of AutoLISP's capabilities, trying to give you an overview of AutoLISP's logical structure, and a quick look at using AutoLISP in menu macros and entity access. To really tap into AutoLISP's power, see *Maximizing*

AutoCAD, Volume II from New Riders. It covers the full scope of AutoLISP and will give you the tips and techniques that you need to help you customize your drawing commands.

Author's Farewell

AutoCAD is a powerful tool. But it is only that — a tool. The real inspiration and talent comes from the user. That would be you. We've explored AutoCAD's capabilities; now it's time for you to explore your own. Good luck, and good drafting!

Command Reference

APERTURE

Screen **[SETTINGS] [APERTUR:]**

The APERTURE command controls the size of the target box that appears at the intersection of the crosshairs during object snap selection. You change the aperture box's size by specifying its height in pixels (from 1 to 50). A *pixel* is the smallest visible dot that appears on screen. The default setting is <10>.

Prompt
Object snap target height (1-50 pixels) <10>:

Related System Variable
APERTURE

If you use a display list processing video driver, it may control the target box's size; the results may not be predictable if you set the pixel height in AutoCAD. Check your driver's documentation for details.

See also: OSNAP, PICKBOX

ARC

Screen **[DRAW] [ARC]**
Pull down **[Draw] [Arc >]**

The ARC command draws any segment of a circle. You can use the command in several ways. By default, the command creates an arc by three points: the starting point, a second point, and an ending point.

Prompts and Options
The ARC command offers eight options. Further, you can continue an arc tangent to the last arc, giving you a total of 11 ways to construct an arc. Prompts display the options available based on the order of the arc construction.

The eight options are Start point, Second point, End point, Center, Angle, Length of chord, Radius, and Direction.

Related System Variable
LASTANGLE

Tip
You can use X,Y,Z coordinates for the arc's first point. The Z coordinate sets the arc's elevation.

AREA

Screen **[INQUIRY] [AREA:]**
Pull down **[Utility] [Area]**

The AREA command calculates the area of an entity (such as a circle or a polyline) or a series of points that define an area. In addition to the area, the command displays the perimeter of a closed entity or the length of an open polyline. If a polyline is not actually closed, AREA calculates the value that would result if a straight line segment passed through the polyline's two endpoints. A running total may be calculated by adding and subtracting areas. The default expects you to specify three or more points to define the area that must be calculated.

Prompts
<First point>/Entity/Add/Subtract:
Next point:
Next point:

Options

First/Next point | Accepts points that define a closed area.

Entity | Determines the area of polylines and circles.

Add | Keeps a running total of the area.

Subtract | Subtracts an area from the running total.

Related System Variables
AREA, PERIMETER

Tips
You may specify 3D points when using AREA, but points and entities must lie in a plane parallel to the X,Y plane of the current UCS.

An area composed of contiguous arcs and lines may be calculated by combining the entities into a polyline (by using the PEDIT command's Join option).

See also: PEDIT (Join), LIST, DBLIST

ARRAY

Screen **[EDIT] [ARRAY:]**
Pull down **[Modify] [2D ARRAY]**

ARRAY copies entities in either a rectangular or a polar (circular) pattern.

Prompt
Rectangular or Polar array (R/P):

Options
The Rectangular option lets you designate the number of rows and columns and the distance between rows and columns for a rectangular array. You must specify at least one row or one column.

The Polar option lets you specify a center point and two of the following:

- The number of items to be arrayed
- The number of degrees to fill
- The angle between the arrayed items

In a polar array, the entities may be optionally rotated.

Tips

When setting up a rectangular array, show the row and column spacing by picking a point at the Unit cell... prompt and dragging a rectangle to indicate spacing and direction.

Create diagonal arrays by changing your UCS, the snap rotation, or the system variable SNAPANG.

See also: COPY, MINSERT

ATTDEF

Screen [BLOCKS] [ATTDEF:]
Screen [DRAW] [ATTDEF:]

Attributes enable you to store text data in a drawing—data you may use, for example, for bills of materials and schedules. ATTDEF (ATTribute DEFinition) defines the ways in which AutoCAD prompts for and stores attribute information. Attributes are saved in blocks that contain additional entities. Attribute data is specified when the block is inserted.

Prompts, Modes, and Options

Attribute modes — Invisible:N Constant:N Verify:N Preset:N

When creating attributes, you first must define them with a combination of the modes, which are set as either Yes or No. (They default to No.)

Invisible   Controls attribute visibility.

Constant   Sets a fixed, uneditable value for the attribute.

Verify   Prompts you to confirm your responses to the attribute prompt.

Preset   Establishes default values that are automatically inserted into the drawing but can still be edited.

After you set the modes, AutoCAD asks you to assign a tag, create a prompt to appear when you insert the attribute block, and assign an optional default value. (The default will appear in angle brackets at the end of the prompt.)

AutoCAD then prompts with the typical text options (text justification, insertion point, height, and rotation). Answer the text option prompts, and AutoCAD inserts the attribute tag into the drawing.

Related System Variables

AFLAGS, ATTREQ, ATTDIA

Tips

When creating a block with attributes, select each attribute individually in the order you want the prompts to appear.

If you want to edit the attribute definition, use the CHANGE, CHPROP, or DDEDIT commands before you include the attribute in a block.

Warnings

You cannot edit a constant attribute. Consider using a preset attribute instead, for greater flexibility.

When you redefine a block with attributes, constant attributes are lost in existing insertions unless the new block replaces them. The original variable attributes remain, and new variable attributes are ignored.

See also: ATTDIA (setvar), ATTDISP, ATTEDIT, ATTEXT, ATTREQ (setvar), BLOCK, DDATTE, DDEDIT

ATTDISP

Screen **[DISPLAY] [ATTDISP:]**

ATTDISP (ATTribute DISPlay) controls the display of all inserted attributes in the current drawing. ATTDISP overrides ATTDEF of invisible mode. The default is Normal (ATTDEF).

Prompt

```
Normal/ON/OFF <Normal>:
```

Options

Normal	Displays attributes the way they are defined.
ON	Makes every attribute visible.
OFF	Makes every attribute invisible.

Related System Variable

ATTMODE

Tip

You may want to create all attributes as visible and control their display by placing them on different layers. Turn the layers off or freeze them if you want the attributes to be invisible.

See also: ATTDEF, ATTEDIT, ATTEXT, ATTMODE (setvar), LAYER

ATTEDIT

Screen **[EDIT] [ATTEDIT:]**

ATTEDIT (ATTribute EDIT) lets you edit attributes individually, or globally if they have the same block names, tag names, or value. The default is to edit attributes one at a time.

Prompts

```
Edit Attributes one at a time? <Y>
Block name specification <*>:
Attribute tag specification <*>:
Attribute value specification <*>:
Select attributes:
Value/Position/Height/Angle/Style/Layer/Color/Next <N>:
```

Options

Individual

Specify the attributes to edit by their block name, attribute tag, attribute value, and selection set. If you respond with an asterisk, you can edit all attributes regardless of block name, attribute tag, and attribute value. You can edit only the attributes that currently are visible on-screen. You can edit the attribute's value, position, height, angle, style, layer, and color.

Global

Only attribute values can be edited globally. You may choose to edit only those attributes visible on-screen, or all attributes regardless of visibility. Unless REGENAUTO is off, AutoCAD regenerates the display after the command is completed. If REGENAUTO is on, you must wait until the drawing is regenerated (or use the REGEN command to force a regeneration) to see the results of your editing.

Tips

You can edit attributes more easily by using the DDATTE command's dialogue box.

You can edit a null attribute by supplying a backslash (\) as the attribute value and then editing globally.

You can use the wild-card characters **?** and * to specify the block names, tags, and values of attributes. These characters are treated literally if used within a String to change or New string prompt.

Warning

Attribute values are case-sensitive.

See also: ATTDEF, ATTDISP, ATTEXT, DDATTE

ATTEXT

Screen **[UTILITY] [ATTEXT:]**

ATTEXT (ATTribute EXTract) extracts attribute data from your drawing. This information is written to an ASCII text file in one of three possible formats—CDF, SDF, or DXF. The default format is CDF. Other programs, such as databases or spreadsheets, can read the extracted file for analysis and report generation. Either all or selected attributes can be extracted.

Prompt

CDF, SDF or DXF Attribute extract (or Entities)? <C>:

Options

The extracted data can have the following formats:

CDF	(Comma-Delimited Format). Extracts from the entire drawing.
SDF	(Standard Format). Fixed format. Extracts from the entire drawing.
DXF	(Drawing Interchange Format). Extracts from the entire drawing.
Entities	Selects specific entities to extract.

Tips

To extract a CDF or SDF file, you must create an ASCII template file. The template file specifies the type and order of data to be extracted. Each data item is listed on its own line, and specifies the field name, character width, and precision for numeric fields.

To display the data on-screen, enter **CON** when asked for an extract file name. To send the data to a printer, specify a printer port (LPT1 or PRN) when asked for an extract file name.

CDF template files can contain records to change the standard single quotation mark (') and comma (,) delimiter characters to a character of your choice.

See also: ATTDEF, ATTDISP, ATTEDIT

AUDIT

Main Menu **Option 9. Recover damaged drawing**
Screen **[UTILITY] [AUDIT:]**

The AUDIT command (Release 11 only) examines a drawing's integrity to check for errors. If you execute AUDIT from within the Drawing Editor, AutoCAD can correct errors automatically or leave them uncorrected (the default). If errors are found, AutoCAD recommends specific corrective actions.

When you execute AUDIT from the Main Menu, the program automatically corrects errors and then loads the drawing into the Drawing Editor. AutoCAD then generates an ASCII report file describing any problems found and actions taken, and places the report file in the same directory as the current drawing. The report file's name is the same as the drawing file's name, with the extension ADT.

Prompt
```
Fix any errors detected? <N>:
```

Options
When you select the No option, a report is created but errors are not fixed. AutoCAD recommends a corrective action for each error it reports.

If you select the Yes option, a report is created and errors are fixed.

Warning
This command works only with drawings that were begun with Release 11 or saved at least once within Release 11. AUDIT may not always be able to recover a corrupt drawing.

AXIS

Screen **[SETTINGS] [AXIS:]**
Pull down **[Settings] [Drawing Tools...] [Axis]**

AXIS creates ruler marks (or "ticks") on the bottom and right side of the screen. You can use these marks as visual drawing aids. The default setting is OFF with a spacing of 0.0000.

Prompt
```
Tick spacing(X) or ON/OFF/Snap/Aspect <0.0000>:
```

Options

Tick spacing	Assigns an absolute value for the ruler spacing.
0	Sets the ruler marks' spacing equal to the current snap spacing.
*n*X	Sets the ruler marks' spacing as a multiple of the current snap spacing.
ON	Displays ruler marks.
OFF	Turns off the ruler marks.
Snap	Sets ruler marks equal to the current snap spacing.
Aspect	Defines different horizontal and vertical tick spacing.

Related System Variables
AXISMODE, AXISUNIT

Tip
Use the 'DDRMODES command to activate a dialogue box, change the axis value, and toggle the AXIS command on or off.

See also: 'DDRMODES, SNAP, GRID

BASE

Screen **[BLOCKS] [BASE:]**

By default, every drawing file has a base or insertion point of 0,0,0. Any drawing can be inserted into another drawing. The BASE command sets the insertion point of the current drawing to any 2D or 3D point.

Prompt
```
Base point <0.0000,0.0000,0.0000>:
```

Related System Variable
INSBASE

See also: BLOCK, INSERT

BLIPMODE

Screen **[SETTINGS] [BLIPS:]**
Pull down **[Settings] [Drawing Tools...] [Blips]**

Blips are small crosses (+) that appear temporarily when you enter a point or select an object. BLIPMODE controls the blips' display. By default, blips are turned on.

Prompt
MODE ON/OFF <On>:

Options

ON   Generates blips.

OFF   Suppresses blips.

Related System Variable
BLIPMODE

See also: DDRMODES

BLOCK

Screen **[BLOCKS] [BLOCK:]**

The BLOCK command defines a group of entities as a single object within the current drawing. You can use the INSERT command to place copies of blocks into a drawing. You define a block by selecting one or more entities, which are deleted from the current drawing and stored as a block definition in the drawing. Each block must be assigned a name and an insertion point.

Prompts
Block name (or ?):
Insertion base point:
Select objects:

Options

Block name Up to 31 characters can be used to name a block.

?   Lists the names of blocks currently defined in the drawing in alphanumeric order. Any wild-card combinations can be used to create a more specific or partial list.

Tips
Blocks can include entities on any layers with any color or linetype. Blocks that are created from entities on layer 0 take on the color and linetype of the layer onto which they are later inserted. Blocks created with entities whose color or linetype is set to BYBLOCK take on the current explicit color or linetype setting.

Use the EXPLODE command to convert a block back into separate entities. You cannot explode blocks that have different XYZ scale values, blocks that are inserted with a negative XYZ insertion point, or blocks that are mirrored.

See also: ATTDEF, EXPLODE, INSERT, REGEN, REGENAUTO, RENAME, WBLOCK, XREF

BREAK

Screen **[EDIT] [BREAK:]**
Pull down **[Modify] [Break]**

BREAK erases portions of lines, arcs, circles, 2D polylines, and traces. When you select an object to break, AutoCAD assumes that your pick point also is your first break point.

Prompts
Select object:
Enter second point (or F for first point):

Options

Select object: AutoCAD assumes that the pick point of your object selection is the first break point, unless you enter **F** to tell AutoCAD that you want to select another first point.

First   If you enter **F**, AutoCAD prompts for first and second break points.

Tips
To break between a first point and the end of an entity, pick beyond the end of the entity rather than trying to pick the endpoint exactly.

If you enter @ (last point) for the second break point, AutoCAD uses the same coordinates as the first break point.

When you select an entity for breaking by a selection method other than picking (Window, Last, and so on.), AutoCAD automatically prompts for the first break point; otherwise, it is assumed to be the pick point. If more than one entity is included in the selection set, the last entity drawn is selected.

Warning
3D break points are projected to the X,Y plane of the current UCS. AutoCAD warns you that this may produce results you did not intend. Change the UCS to the X,Y plane of the entity before you execute the BREAK command.

See also: PEDIT, TRIM

CHAMFER

Screen [EDIT] [CHAMFER:]
Pull down **[Modify] [Chamfer]**

The CHAMFER command creates a beveled edge at the intersection of two lines or between contiguous segments of a 2D polyline. CHAMFER trims or extends two lines at a distance from their intersection point and creates a new line to connect the trimmed ends. The command requires two distance values. The first distance value is applied to the first selected line, the second to the second line. The default for distances is 0.

Prompt
Polyline/Distances/<Select first line>:

Options

Polyline   Chamfers all the intersections of a 2D polyline.

Distances   Sets chamfer distances A and B.

Related System Variables
CHAMFERA, CHAMFERB

Tips

If you want to create a 45-degree bevel, set the chamfer distances (CHAMFERA and CHAMFERB) equal to each other; to create different angles, set different chamfer distances for A and B.

The chamfered edge resides on the layer of the picked entities as long as they share the same layer; if the two entities are on different layers, the chamfered edge is placed on the current layer. The same rules apply to color and linetype.

You can establish default settings by selecting [Chamfer Distances] from the [Options] pull-down menu.

If you want the endpoints of two lines to meet, set the chamfer distance to 0 or use the FILLET command to produce the same results.

Warning

Your results will be more reliable if you use CHAMFER in plan view than if you use the command at a viewing direction that is oblique to the X,Y plane of the current UCS.

See also: EXTEND, FILLET, PLINE, TRIM

CHANGE

Screen **[EDIT] [CHANGE:]**

Use CHANGE to modify existing entities and their properties. After you issue the command, you may have to regenerate the screen to see the revisions. The CHPROP command contains the Properties option of the CHANGE command.

Prompts

```
Select objects:
Properties/<Change point>:
```

Option

Properties   Enables you to redefine any or all of the following properties: Color, LAyer, LType, and Thickness.

Change point   Redefines the location (or size) of the following entities:

- **Lines**—Relocates the endpoints of the lines closest to the new point you specify. If ORTHO is on, AutoCAD forces the lines to lie horizontal or vertical to the current UCS or snap rotation.

- **Circle**—Enables you to modify a circle's radius by picking a point to show the new circumference.

- **Block**—Enables you to relocate a block's insertion point or determine a new rotation angle.

- **Text**—Relocates text to a change point. If you press <RETURN> at the Change point: prompt, you can redefine the text style, height, rotation angle, and text string.

- **Attribute Definition**—Same as the Text option, but also enables you to change the attribute tag, prompt, and default value.

Tips

CHANGE is limited in its capability to change properties in 2D. (You should use the CHPROP command to change properties, including 3D entities. See CHPROP for a description of these properties.)

If you want to lengthen (or shorten) a group of parallel lines, make sure that ORTHO is on unless you want the lines to converge at the designated change point.

You must use CHANGE if you want to assign a thickness to text that was created with the TEXT, DTEXT, or ATTDEF commands.

It is easier and faster to use the DDEDIT command to modify attributes and text strings.

Warning

If you modify an attribute definition, existing attributes will not inherit the changes.

See also: CHPROP, COLOR, DDEDIT, DTEXT, EXPLODE, EXTEND, LAYER, LINETYPE, REGEN, REGENAUTO, STYLE, TEXT, THICKNESS, TRIM

CHPROP

Screen **[EDIT] [CHPROP:]**

Use CHPROP to redefine properties associated with existing entities. CHPROP does not include the CHANGE command's change point and text modification options. Use CHPROP instead of CHANGE to change entity properties.

Prompts

```
Select objects:
Change what property (Color/LAyer/LType/Thickness) ?
```

Options

Color	Assigns a color to an entity regardless of the entity's layer.
LType	Assigns a linetype to an entity regardless of the entity's layer.
LAyer	Moves an entity from one layer to another.
Thickness	Assigns an extrusion thickness to an entity.

Tip

If you need to enter entities on a non-current layer, you may find it quicker to stay on the current layer and use CHPROP to change the entities later. This also applies to redefining color and linetype.

See also: CHANGE

CIRCLE

Screen **[DRAW] [CIRCLE]**
Pull down **[Draw] [Circle >]**

The CIRCLE command draws circles. By default, the command lets you define a circle by specifying either its center point or its radius. If DRAGMODE is on or set to AUTO, you can pick the circle's size by dragging it on-screen.

Prompts

```
3P/2P/TTR/<Center point>:
Diameter/<Radius>:
```

Options

Center point	Specify the center point.
Diameter	Specify the diameter by inputting a value or picking two points.
Radius	Specify the radius by inputting a value or picking two points.
3P	Specify three points on the circumference.
2P	Specify two points to indicate the diameter.
TTR	Specify two points (on a line, circle, or arc) that will be tangent to the circle, then specify a radius.

Tips

To draw circles in an isometric plane, use the ELLIPSE Isocircle option.

You can use the CHANGE or SCALE commands to modify an existing circle's size.

In 3D displays, the HIDE command treats circles as a solid face.

Warning

When you use the BREAK command, the deleted portion of a circle is determined by the order of the pick points. Circles break in a counterclockwise direction.

See also: DONUT, ELLIPSE, VIEWRES

COLOR

Screen **[SETTINGS] [COLOR:]**

The COLOR command controls the color of new entities, overriding the layer's default color. To change the color of existing entities, use the CHPROP command. To control layer colors, use the LAYER command. To set a new color, respond with a color number or name. You also can set an entity's color by using the 'DDEMODES dialogue box.

Prompt

New entity color <BYLAYER>:

Options

BYLAYER   New entities inherit the color assigned to the layer on which they reside.

BYBLOCK   New entities are drawn in white until they are saved as a block. When the block is inserted, it inherits the color value set by the color command.

Color number   New entities are assigned a specific color when you specify the color's name
or name   or number. Each color has a standard number assignment, as follows:

    1 = Red   5 = Blue
    2 = Yellow 6 = Magenta
    3 = Green   7 = White
    4 = Cyan

You can use up to 255 colors, depending on your computer's graphics card.

Related System Variable

CECOLOR

Tip

You can obtain multiple line weights, linetypes, and color plots if you assign colors from your drawing to different pens on your plotter. If you use a monochrome monitor, you cannot see the colors, but the plotter acknowledges the color assignment.

Warning

Do not confuse your work by mixing colors on a single layer. Use the LAYER command to control color, and leave the COLOR command set to BYLAYER. This helps you identify an entity's layer and makes changing an entity's color a simple process of using the LAYER command to redefine the color.

See also: CHANGE, CHPROP, 'DDEMODES, LAYER, PLOT

COPY

Screen **[EDIT] [COPY:]**
Pull down **[Modify] [Copy]**

COPY creates a replica of an entity. The command lets you use standard object selection methods. The original entity or selection set remains unchanged after the copy is made.

Prompts
```
Select objects:
<Base point or displacement>/Multiple:
Second point of displacement:
```

Options

Base point	Determines a point of reference. After you locate the reference point, you can drag the selected objects to the new location at the Second point prompt.
Displacement	Type the distance for X,Y,Z and press <RETURN> at the Second point prompt.
Multiple	Enables you to copy an entity more than one time by specifying a designated reference point and responding to the Second point prompts. Press <RETURN> to end the copying process.

Tips

Use AutoCAD's object snap overrides on intersections, center points, or other logical locations to set the base point.

The base and second point do not need to be on or near the selection set.

Warning

If you accidentally press <RETURN> at the Second point prompt, your copy may end up "out in space." If this happens, it may be because you specified the X,Y,Z base point as the displacement.

See also: ARRAY, BLOCK, MINSERT, MOVE, OFFSET, SELECTION SETS

DBLIST

See LIST

DDATTE

Screen **[EDIT] [DDATTE:]**

The DDATTE (Dynamic Dialogue ATTribute Edit) command lets you edit attribute string values with the help of a dialogue box. You can edit only one block at a time.

Related System Variable

ATTDIA

Tips

Enter **MULTIPLE DDATTE** if you want to edit more than one block containing attribute information. Click on the Cancel button to end the command.

ATTDIA lets you use the dialogue box at the point of insertion if ATTDIA is set to 1.

To edit attribute values globally, use ATTEDIT to change position, height, angle, style, layer, and color.

See also: ATTEDIT, DIALOGUE BOXES, MULTIPLE

DDEDIT

Screen **[EDIT] [DDEDIT:]**

The DDEDIT (Dynamic Dialogue EDIT) command (Release 11 only) lets you edit text strings and attribute definitions. This command works only with displays that support AutoCAD's

Advanced User Interface (AUI). The command repeats until you press <^C> or the <Cancel> or <Return> key one extra time.

Prompt
```
<Select a TEXT or ATTDEF object>/Undo:
```

Options

Select a TEXT or ATTDEF object	If you select text, you can edit a text string. If you select an attribute definition, you can modify the tag, prompt, and default values.
Undo	At the Select a TEXT or ATTDEF object prompt, you can undo the last modified text string and return to the previous value. When you end the command, the Undo option undoes every modification within the command.

Tip
Use DDATTE to edit attribute values in a block.

See also: CHANGE, DIALOGUE BOXES

DDEMODES

Screen **[SETTINGS] [DDEMODES]**
Pull down **[Options] [Entity Creation...]**

The DDEMODES (Dynamic Dialogue Entity creation MODES) dialogue box shows the current settings for layer, color, linetype, text style, elevation, and thickness. You can change any of these variables. DDEMODES presents another dialogue box when you choose the layer, color, linetype, or text style options.

Options

Color	Presents a dialogue box to select a new color.
Layer	Presents a dialogue box to select a new current layer.
Linetype	Presents a dialogue box to select a new linetype. Only the linetypes currently loaded in the drawing are provided for selection.
Elevation	Assigns a new elevation value.
Text style	Presents a dialogue box to select a new current text style.
Thickness	Assigns a new thickness value.

DDEMODES uses the following default settings:

Layer	0
Color	BYLAYER
Linetype	BYLAYER
Text style	Standard
Elevation	0
Thickness	0

Related System Variables
CECOLOR, CELTYPE, CLAYER, TEXTSTYLE, ELEVATION, THICKNESS

Tips
If you need to enter entities on another layer or change the color, linetype, text style, elevation, or thickness, you may find it quicker to stay on the current layer and use CHANGE or CHPROP to edit the entities.

You can execute DDEMODES transparently by entering '**DDEMODES** within another command.

Warning

If you activate the dialogue box while in another command, the changes take place once you complete the initial command.

See also: COLOR, DIALOGUE BOXES, ELEVATION, LAYER, LINETYPE, STYLE, THICK-NESS, Transparent Commands

DDLMODES

Screen **[LAYER:]** **[DDLMODES]**

Pull down **[Settings]** **[Layer Control...]**

DDLMODES (Dynamic Dialogue Layer MODES) presents a dialogue box to control layer options. The options enable you to set the current layer, create new layers, rename layers, and modify layer properties.

Options

Current	Sets a layer as the default.
Rename	Lets you highlight a layer name and type in a new name.
GLOBAL ON	Globally controls the layer's visibility by turning it on and off.
GLOBAL Frz	Globally controls the layer's visibility by freezing and thawing.
VP Frz Cur	Freezes the selected layer in the current model space viewport.
VP Frz New	Freezes the selected layer for all new viewport entities.
Color	Assigns a color to a layer. Type in the number for any colors over number 7 in the color code box.
Linetype	Assigns a linetype. You can access only those linetypes that have previously been loaded.
New layer	Creates new layers.

DDLMODES uses the following default settings:

Layer	0
Color	White
Linetype	Continuous
On	
Thaw	

Related System Variables

CECOLOR, CELTYPE, CLAYER, TILEMODE

Tip

You can execute DDLMODES transparently by entering **'DDLMODES** within another command.

Warnings

If you activate the dialogue box while in another command, the changes will not take place until you complete the initial command.

Viewport Freeze Current and Viewport Freeze New only work if TILEMODE is off.

See also: COLOR, DIALOGUE BOXES, LAYER, LINETYPE, RENAME, Transparent Commands, VPLAYER

DDRMODES

Screen **[SETTINGS] [DDRMODES]**
Pull down **[Settings] [Drawing Tools...]**

DDRMODES (Dynamic Dialogue Drawing MODES) controls the settings of drawing aids such as Snap, Grid, Axis, and Isometric mode.

Options
DDRMODES uses the following default settings:

Snap	OFF	1.0
Snap Angle	0	
Grid	OFF	0
Axis	OFF	0
Ortho	OFF	
Blips	OFF	
Isoplane	LEFT	
Isometric	OFF	

Related System Variables
AXISMODE, AXISUNIT, BLIPMODE, COORDS, GRIDMODE, GRIDUNIT, ORTHOMODE, SNAPANG, SNAPISOPAIR, SNAPBASE, SNAPMODE, SNAPSTYL, SNAPUNIT

Tips
It is faster to use control keys and function keys to toggle settings on and off and change isoplanes.

You can execute DDRMODES transparently by entering '**DDRMODES** within another command.

Warning
If you activate the dialogue box while in another command, some changes do not take place until you complete the initial command.

See also: AXIS, BLIPMODE, DIALOGUE BOXES, GRID, ORTHO, SNAP, Transparent Commands

DDUCS

Screen **[UCS:] [DDUCS:]**
Pull down **[Settings] [UCS Control...]**

DDUCS (Dynamic Dialogue User Coordinate System) displays dialogue boxes that enable you to create, modify, and control user coordinate systems. The default UCS is the *WORLD* UCS.

Options

Current	Sets the current UCS.
UCS Name	Creates a new UCS.
Rename	Lets you rename a UCS by typing over an existing UCS name.
WORLD	Sets the current UCS to the World Coordinate System (WCS).
PREVIOUS	Returns to the previous coordinate system.
NO NAME	The current UCS is unnamed.
List	Displays the UCS' origin and the direction of its X,Y,Z axes.
Delete	Deletes the specified UCS.
Define new current UCS	Defines a new current UCS.

Related System Variables
UCSFOLLOW, UCSICON, UCSNAME, UCSORG, UCSXDIR, UCSYDIR, VIEWMODE, WORLDUCS

See also: DIALOGUE BOXES, UCS

DELAY
See SCRIPT

DIM/DIM1
Screen **[DIM:]**
Pull down **[Draw] [Dim...]**

The DIM command activates AutoCAD's dimensioning mode. When the Command: prompt changes to DIM:, only the dimensioning commands are active. The DIM1 command activates dimensioning mode for a single command and returns you to the normal Command: prompt.

By dimensioning commands, you automatically construct the appropriate dimension lines, arrow or tick marks, and extension lines, as well as dimension text to dimension drawings.

Prompts
DIM:

or

DIM1:

Dimensioning Commands
The dimensioning commands are grouped into the following four major categories: construction, edit, style (Release 11 only), and utility. These categories are supported by 42 dimension variables, the values of which you can set to control your dimensions' appearance. You can save groups of variable settings for different dimension style using unique names. You can retrieve these variable settings by using the the RESTore command.

The following is a breakdown of the four dimensioning command categories. You need to type only the capitalized letters to invoke the commands. In dimensioning mode, as in the regular command mode, you can abbreviate each command to one, two, or three characters (the fewest characters that are unique to that command).

Construction	ANgular, Leader, linear (ALigned, Baseline, COntinue, HORizontal, ROtated, VErtical), ORdinate, radial (CEnter, Diameter, RAdius)
Edit	HOMetext, Newtext, OBlique, TEdit, TRotate, UPdate
Style	OVerride, REStore, SAve, VAriables, ?
Utility	dimension variables, Exit, REDraw, STAtus, STYle, Undo

Dimensioning Command Prompts
The following prompts are commonly used in dimensioning mode. A brief description follows each prompt.

First extension line origin or RETURN to select:

You can dimension a distance either manually by picking points or automatically by selecting an object. If you pick a point, AutoCAD uses the point as the origin for the first extension line and prompts for the second extension's origin point. If you press <RETURN>, a new prompt appears.

Select line, arc, or circle:

When you select the appropriate entity, AutoCAD automatically generates extension lines.

`Dimension line location:`

At this prompt, you can specify a dimension line's location by picking a point through which the dimension line must pass.

`Dimension text <value>`

The correct measured dimension text appears as the default at the text prompt. You can press <RETURN> to accept the automatic dimension text that is in the brackets, or you can type another value. If you want to leave the dimension text blank, press <SPACE> and then <RETURN>.

If you want to enter text in addition to the default value, enter the text and include brackets at the appropriate location, such as the following:

<> YOUR TEXT or YOUR TEXT <> MORE TEXT

Tips

To dimension a polyline with a width, AutoCAD dimensions it from its centerline.

AutoCAD gives you greater dimensioning flexibility in model space than in paper space. Dimensions in paper space are not associative to entities created in model space.

Warning

You can modify the DIMTXT variable's value to set the dimension text's height. If your current text STYLE has a preset height, however, it will override the DIMTXT setting.

DIM ALigned

Screen **[DIM:] [linear] [aligned]**
Pull down **[Draw] [Dim...] [Linear] [Aligned]**

The ALigned command is an option of linear dimensioning. It draws the dimension line parallel to the extension line's origin points or to a selected entity.

Prompts

`First extension line origin or RETURN to select:`
`Select line, arc, or circle:`
`Dimension line location:`
`Dimension text:`

You can pick the first and second extension line origins, or you can press <RETURN> and pick a line, polyline, circle, or arc to dimension.

DIM ANgular

Screen **[DIM:] [angular]**
Pull down **[Draw] [Dim...] [Angular]**

The ANgular command dimensions angles. You can show angular dimensions by picking two nonparallel lines, by picking an arc or circle and another point, or by picking three points.

Prompts

`Select arc, circle, line, or RETURN:`
`Select first line:`
`Second line:`

```
Dimension text:
Enter text location:
```

Options

Arc	The center of the arc is considered the angle vertex and the endpoints become the origin points for the extension lines. You determine the location for the dimension arc and the dimension text.
Circle	The center of the circle is considered the vertex of the angle. The point used to pick the circle defines the origin of the first extension line. You are prompted for the second angle endpoint, which then becomes the origin of the second extension line.
Line	You can select nonparallel lines or polyline segments. The angle vertex is the point where the two lines intersect.
Enter (three points)	You determine the angle vertex and the angle's endpoints.

Tips

AutoCAD dimensions the complementary angle for angles over 180 degrees when two lines are picked.

If you select a circle or an arc, or pick three points to dimension an angle, the location you pick for the dimension arc determines which angle AutoCAD dimensions—the angle including the location point or its complement.

If you press <RETURN> at the text location prompt, AutoCAD automatically centers the dimension text within the dimension arc. If you pick a point and later want to place it in the center, you can use the HOMetext command.

DIM Baseline

Screen **[DIM:] [linear] [baseline]**
Pull down **[Draw] [Dim...] [Linear] [Baseline]**

Baseline dimensions multiple distances measured from a common reference point. When you create the first linear dimension, you can select the Baseline command to dimension the remainder of the distances. Each dimension will be offset from the preceding one using the same initial extension line. All you need to provide is the second extension line's origin point.

Prompts

```
Second extension line origin:
Dimension text <default>:
```

Options

The Baseline command can be used in conjunction with the ALigned, HORizontal, ROtated, and VErtical linear dimensioning commands.

Related System Variable

DIMDLI

Tip

Once you have selected the Baseline command, you can press <RETURN> to pick successive second extension line origins and to accept default dimension text values.

Warning
If you change the the value of DIMDLI, the UPdate command does not modify existing baseline dimension offsets.

See also: DIM: COntinue

DIM CEnter

Screen **[DIM:] [radial] [center]**
Pull down **[Draw] [Dim...]**
Click center mark icon

The CEnter command lets you construct a dimensioning center mark or center lines for circles and arcs.

Related System Variable
DIMCEN

Tips
When DIMCEN has a value other than 0, the Diameter and RAdius commands automatically draw center marks.

When DIMCEN is set to a positive value, AutoCAD places tick marks inside circles and arcs; when DIMCEN is set to a negative value, center lines extend outside the diameter. If DIMCEN's value is 0, the marks are omitted.

DIM COntinue

Screen **[DIM:] [linear] [continue]**
Pull down **[Draw] [Dim...] [Linear] [Continue]**

Continuous dimensioning refers to dimensions measured from the last extension line origin of the previous linear dimension. Once you have created the first linear dimension, select the COntinue option from which to dimension. Each dimension line will be drawn aligned with the last. If the dimension text does not fit, the dimension line will be placed outside the dimension. All you provide is the second extension point.

Prompts
```
Second extension line origin:
Dimension text <default>:
```

Options
You can use continuous dimensioning in conjunction with the ALigned, HORizontal, ROtated, and VErtical linear dimensioning commands:

Related System Variable
DIMDLI

Warning
When you change the value of DIMDLI, the UPdate command will not modify existing continuous dimensions.

See also: DIM Baseline

DIM Diameter

Screen **[DIM:] [radial] [diameter]**
Pull down **[Draw] [Dim...] [Diameter]**

The Diameter command enables you to dimension circles and arcs. By changing the values of the dimension variables DIMTIX, DIMTOFL, and DIMCEN, you can portray different dimensioning styles.

Prompts
```
Select arc or circle:
Dimension text:
```

Related System Variable
DIMCEN

Tip
The pick point for entity selection determines the beginning of the dimension line or leader line.

DIM Exit

Screen **[DIM:] [EXIT]**
Pull down Any **[Exit] label**

The Exit command returns you from dimensioning mode to the `Command:` prompt (or you can press <^C> to cancel).

DIM HOMetext

Screen **[DIM:] [next] [HOMETEXT]**
Pull down **[Draw] [Dim...] [Edit Dim...] [Home]**

The HOMetext command moves associative dimension text to its original location if you have used TEdit or have changed dimension variables and updated dimensions.

Prompt
```
Select objects:
```

Tip
The TEdit Home option is similar to the HOMetext option. Both options place the dimension at its original rotation angle. The HOMetext option can manipulate more than one dimension at a time, whereas the TEdit Home option modifies only one dimension at a time.

Warning
The HOmetext command works only if the dimension you are editing is associative (that is, if DIMASO is on) and is not exploded.

See also: DIM TEdit

DIM HORizontal

Screen **[DIM:] [linear] [horiz]**
Pull down **[Draw] [Dim...] [Linear] [Horizontal]**

HORizontal is a linear dimensioning option and draws the dimension line horizontally. You can pick the first and second extension line origins, or you can press <RETURN> and then pick the entity to dimension.

Prompt
```
First extension line origin or RETURN to select:
```

Tip
If you use a circle, the diameter is dimensioned. The quadrants at 0 and 180 degrees are used as the two endpoints for the extension lines. Other entities are dimensioned between their endpoints.

DIM LEAder

Screen **[DIM:] [leader]**
Pull down **[Draw] [Dim...] [Leader]**

The leader, which is made up of an arrowhead, lines, and text, is used to dimension complex areas or to add reference notes. Leaders are drawn from the point of the arrowhead to the point at which you want the dimension text or notes to be placed.

Prompts
```
Leader start:
To point:
Dimension text:
```

Tip
If you want no text to appear with the leader, press <SPACE> and <RETURN> at the prompt for dimension text.

Warnings
You can enter only one line of text for a leader. If you want to enter more than one line, use the TEXT or DTEXT command.

If the leader's length for the first segment is less than two arrow lengths long, AutoCAD does not draw the arrowhead.

Dimension editing commands do not work for any dimensions entered by the Leader command.

DIM Newtext

Screen **[DIM:] [next] [NEWTEXT]**
Pull down **[Draw] [Dim...] [Edit Dim...] [Text]**

The Newtext command lets you revise associative dimension text. Press <RETURN> to return dimension text to its default value. If you want to enter text in addition to the measured value, enter the text and include angle brackets (<>) at the appropriate location to represent the default dimension text.

Prompt
```
Enter new dimension text:
```

Warning
This feature works only if the dimension you are editing is associative (that is, if DIMASO is on) and is not exploded.

DIM OBlique

Screen **[DIM:] [oblique]**
Pull down **[Draw] [Dim...] [Edit Dim...] [OBLIQUE]**

OBlique lets you redefine the angle of existing dimension extension lines without altering the dimension value. If you press <RETURN> without specifying an angle, the extension lines return to their original angle.

Prompts
```
Select objects:
Enter obliquing angle (RETURN for none):
```

Warning
OBlique works only if the dimension you are editing is associative (that is, if DIMASO is on) and is not exploded.

DIM ORdinate

Screen **[DIM:] [ORDINAT:] [Xdatum] or [Ydatum]**
Pull down **[Draw] [Dim...] [Ordinate] [Xdatum], [YDATUM],** *or* **[Automatic]**

ORdinate dimensioning (Release 11 only) lets you dimension individual X and Y distances from a common origin 0,0. The dimension text automatically aligns with the leader line. Once you pick the feature to dimension, either point in the X or Y direction indicating the type of dimension, or select Xdatum or Ydatum.

Prompts

Select Feature:
Leader endpoint (Xdatum/Ydatum):

Options

Leader endpoint	When you are picking a point, the difference between the feature location and the leader endpoint is used to determine whether it is an X or Y dimension. If the difference in the Y axis is greater, the dimension measures the Y coordinate; if not, it measures the X.
Xdatum	Creates the X datum regardless of the length and location of the leader line.
Ydatum	Creates the Y datum regardless of the length and location of the leader line.

Tips

You should keep ORTHO on for greater control of the leader line location.

You can change the location of 0,0 by redefining the UCS.

Warning

Datum dimensions are relative to 0,0 at the time of creation. If you change the current UCS and dimension more points, the points will not be accurate relative to any dimension made while in the previous UCS.

See also: UCS

DIM OVerride

Screen **[DIM:] [next] [Override]**
Pull down **[Settings] [Set Dim Vars...] [Dim Style] [Override]**

DIM OVerride (Release 11 only) lets you override the dimension variables used to create individual dimensions without changing the variables' current values. If a selected dimension uses a named dimension style, you can update the style definition to use the new variable value. AutoCAD also updates all other dimensions that use that style.

Prompts

Dimension variable to override:
Current value <default> New value:
Dimension variable to override:
Select objects

Tip

You can pick several dimensions assigned to different DIMSTYLEs. AutoCAD asks if you want to modify the variables for each style that is represented.

Tip

You can pick several dimensions assigned to different DIMSTYLEs. AutoCAD asks if you want to modify the variables for each style that is represented.

Warning

OVerride works only if the dimension you are editing is associative (that is, if DIMASO is on) and is not exploded.

See also*:* DIM REStore, DIM SAve

DIM RAdius

Screen **[DIM:] [radial] [radius]**
Pull down **[Draw] [Dim...] [Radius]**

The RAdius command dimensions circles and arcs. By changing the values of the dimension variables DIMTIX, DIMTOFL, and DIMCEN, you can portray different dimensioning styles.

Options

The pick point for entity selection determines the location of the arrowhead and the start of the dimension line.

Prompts
Select arc or circle:
Dimension text:

Related System Variables
DIMCEN, DIMTIX, DIMTOFL

Tips

The leader line's location is determined by the pick point used during entity selection.

DIMTIX, if set OFF, forces the text outside the circle or arc at the end of an extension line.

DIMTOFL, if set ON, draws a dimension line between the extension lines.

DIM REStore

Screen **[DIM:] [next] [Restore]**
Pull down **[Settings] [Set Dim Vars...] [Dim Style...] [Restore]**

This command restores an existing dimension style as the current dimension style (Release 11 only).

Prompts
Current dimension style: default
?/Enter dimension style name or RETURN to select dimension:

Options

?	Allows you to review named dimension styles saved in the drawing. When you respond with an asterisk (*), AutoCAD displays a sorted list of all named styles. You can use any of the wild-card options to create a more specific list.
Enter dimension style name	Lets you restore an existing dimension style as the default. If you enter the name of a style that does not exist, the message Unknown dimension style appears.
Enter to select dimension	Allows you to pick a dimension that references the desired style.

Tip

If you want to compare the current style to another style, precede the style name with a tilde (~). AutoCAD lists only those variables that are different.

Warning

This command works only if the dimension you are editing is associative (that is, if DIMASO is on) and is not exploded.

See also: DIM SAve

DIM ROtated

Select **[DIM:] [linear] [rotated]**
Pull down **[Draw] [Dim...] [Linear] [Rotated]**

ROtated is an option of linear dimensioning. It draws the dimension line at any angle that you specify while keeping the extension lines perpendicular.

Prompts

Dimension line angle <0>:
First extension line origin or RETURN to select:
Select line, arc, or circle:
Dimension line location:
Dimension text:

DIM SAve

Screen **[DIM:] [next] [Save]**
Pull down **[Settings] [Set Dim Vars...] [Dim Style...] [Save NEW]**

SAve (Release 11 only) lets you save multiple dimension variable settings under one dimension style name. You can retrieve the styles by issuing the REStore command. You can modify saved styles with the OVerride command or by reissuing the SAve command after making dimension variable changes.

Prompt

?/Name for new dimension style:

Options

?   Allows you to review named dimension styles saved in the drawing. If you respond with an asterisk (*), AutoCAD displays a sorted list of all named styles. You can use any of the wild-card options to create a more specific list.

Name for new   You can enter a name for the new style. If you use the name of an existing
dimension style style, AutoCAD prompts That name is already in use, redefine it? <N>. If you answer yes, all dimensions assigned to that style will be updated.

Tip

If you want to compare the current style to another style, precede the style name with a tilde (~). AutoCAD lists only those variables that are different.

Warning

DIMASO and DIMSHO are never saved by SAve.

See also: DIM OVerride, DIM REStore, STYLE

DIM STAtus

Screen **[DIM:] [status]**
Pull down **[Settings] [Set Dim Vars...] [Dim Globals...] [Status]**

STAtus lists the current settings of all dimension variables.

Tip
To modify dimension variables, enter the name of the variable at the `Dim:` prompt or use the SETVAR command.

Warning
Make sure that you are at the `Dim:` prompt before entering the STAtus command. If you are at the `Command:` prompt, AutoCAD displays the more generalized status report of your drawing file.

DIM STYle

Screen **[DIM:] [style]**

STYle lets you select a predefined text style for your default dimensioning text.

Prompt
`New text style <default>:`

The default setting is the current text style.

Warnings
You can select only existing styles. If you need to create styles, use the STYLE command.

If you choose a style with a height set to 0, the dimension text height is determined by the DIMTXT and DIMSCALE settings. If the current text height is defined by a style with a preset height, AutoCAD ignores the DIMTXT and DIMSCALE settings.

DIM TEdit

Screen **[DIM:] [TEdit]**
Pull down **[Draw] [Dim:] [Edit Dim...] [Move]**

TEdit (Release 11 only) lets you change the location of dimension text. The default lets you dynamically drag the dimension text with your pointing device.

Prompts
`Select dimension:`
`Enter text location (Left/Right/Home/Angle):`

Options

Left   You can place the dimension text as far to the left of the dimension line as possible and still maintain a two-arrowhead-length dimension line on the left side.

Right   You can place the dimension text as far to the right of the dimension line as possible and still maintain a two-arrowhead-length dimension line on the right side.

Home   You can place the dimension text back to its original location.

Angle   This gives you a new rotation angle for dimension text.

Related System Variables
DIMSHO, DIMTAD, DIMTVP

Tips
TEdit works only if the dimension you are editing is associative (that is, if DIMASO is on) and is not exploded.

The Left and Right options work only with linear, radius, and diameter dimensions.

The position of the dimension text depends on the settings of DIMTAD and DIMTVP variables.

The TEdit Home option is similar to the HOMetext option. Both of these options place the dimension at its original location and rotation angle. The HOMetext option can manipulate more than one dimension at a time, whereas the TEdit Home option modifies only one dimension at a time.

The TEdit Angle option is similar to the TRotate option. The TRotate option can manipulate more than one dimension at a time, whereas the TEdit Angle option modifies only one dimension at a time.

Warning
Even though you can use any of the selection set options, you can edit only one dimension at a time.

See also: DIM HOMetext, DIM TRotate

DIM TRotate

Screen **[DIM:] [trotate]**
Pull down **[Draw] [Dim...] [Edit Dim...] [Rotate]**

TRotate lets you rotate existing dimension text (Release 11 only).

Prompts
```
Enter new text angle:
Select objects:
```

Tip
TRotate works only if the dimension you are editing is associative (that is, if DIMASO is on) and is not exploded.

TRotate is similar to the TEdit angle option. TRotate can manipulate more than one dimension at a time, whereas the TEdit Angle modifies only one dimension at a time.

See also: DIM TEdit

DIM Undo

Screen **[DIM:] [undo]**

When you are in dimensioning mode, you can use Undo to void the latest dimensioning operation. You can undo one step at a time until you reach the beginning of the current dimensioning session.

Warning
If you issue an UNDO at the `Command:` prompt, everything you did during the last dimensioning session will be undone. You can restore the changes by issuing the REDO command.

See also: UNDO

DIM UPdate

Screen **[DIM:] [next] [UPDATE]**
Pull down **[Draw] [Dim:] [Edit Dim...] [UPDATE]**

UPdate modifies associative dimension entities. The dimension entities are regenerated to match the current UNITS, text STYLE, dimension variables, and DIMSTYLE.

Related System Variable
DIMASO

Warnings

UPdate works only if the dimension you are editing is associative (that is, if DIMASO is on) and is not exploded.

By changing the dimension variable DIMDLI (Dimension Line Increment for continuous or baseline dimensions), you do not affect any existing dimensions created with the Baseline or COntinue dimension options.

See also: DIM VAriables

DIM VAriables

Screen **[DIM:] [Dim Vars]**
Pull down **[Settings] [Set Dim Vars...] [Dim Globals...]**
Screen **[DIM:] [next] [Variabls]**
Pull down **[Settings] [Set Dim Vars...] [Dim Style...] [List Variables]**

Dimension variables control the appearance of dimension features, such as arrowhead or tick mark size, text location, and size. Some variables set values, whereas others act as on and off switches.

You can change the different variable settings by using SETVAR, by entering the individual variable names at the the Dim: prompt, or by entering the individual variable names at the Command: prompt (Release 11 only). You also can use the UPdate and OVerride dimensioning commands to change variables after entities are dimensioned.

The VAriables command (Release 11 only) lets you select a dimension or enter the name of a dimension style to list all its individual dimension style variable settings. You can compare the current style settings to any named style, listing just those variables that are different.

Prompts

Current dimension style: *UNNAMED
?/Enter dimension style name or RETURN to select dimension:

Options

?	Activates the wild-card options for listing the names of the dimstyles defined in the drawing. When you respond with an asterisk (*), AutoCAD displays a sorted list of all dimension styles.
Enter dimension style name	If you enter a dimension style name, AutoCAD displays a list of the variables and their settings. Enter **~name** for a comparison.
RETURN to select dimension	By pressing <RETURN>, you can pick a dimension in your drawing. AutoCAD determines the assigned dimstyle and lists the variable settings.
DIMASO	DIMASO is the variable that controls associative dimensioning. DIMASO controls whether dimension entities (lines, arcs, arrows, and text) are grouped together to act as one entity or are independent of each other. DIMASO affects linear, angular, diameter, ordinate, and radius dimensioning. In addition, the dimension becomes associated with the dimensioned entity and automatically will reflect size changes if the entity is edited. If DIMASO is on when an entity is dimensioned, you can use the dimension edit commands. The default setting is ON.
ON	Dimension entities act as one (associative).
OFF	Dimension entities act individually as parts and are not directly associated to the entities that are dimensioned.

Tips

You can compare the settings of the different dimstyles by entering **~name** as the dimstyle to list at the Enter dimension style name prompt, in which *name* is the dimstyle to compare to the current one. You get a listing of only those settings that are different from the current one.

By placing your first associative dimension, you can create a layer named DEFPOINTS. DEFPOINTS (definition points) are points that link the dimension to the entity being dimensioned. Entities residing on the DEFPOINTS layer are never plotted. If you want to plot entities on this layer, you must first rename the layer. You can osnap to defpoints with the NODe option.

Warning

If you explode an associative dimension, you no longer can use the dimension editing commands on it.

See also: DIM OVerride, DIM REStore, DIM VAriables

DIM VErtical

Screen **[DIM:] [linear] [vertical]**
Pull down **[Draw] [Dim...] [Linear] [Vertical]**

VErtical is an option of linear dimensioning. It draws the dimension line vertically. You either can pick the first and second extension line origins, or you can press <RETURN> and then pick the entity to dimension.

Prompt

First extension line origin or RETURN to select:

Tip

If you select a circle, the diameter is dimensioned. The quadrants at 90 and 270 degrees are considered the two endpoints.

DIST

Screen **[INQUIRY] [DIST:]**
Pull down **[Utility] [Distance]**

DIST (DISTance) is an inquiry command that determines the direct distance between two points, the angle they form in the X,Y plane, the angle from the X,Y plane, and the distance between them along the X, Y, and Z axes.

Prompts

First point:
Second point:

Related System Variable

DISTANCE

Tip

To determine the distance between the endpoints of a line, use the LIST command.

See also: LIST

DIVIDE

Screen **[EDIT] [DIVIDE:]**
Pull down **[Modify] [Divide]**

DIVIDE places marks on an entity, "dividing" it into segments of equal length according to a quantity you specify. The divided entity is not physically separated; rather, AutoCAD places points or blocks as markers at each division point. You can divide lines, circles, arcs, and polylines.

Prompts
```
Select object to divide:
<Number of segments>/Block:
```

Options

Number of segments   Enter the number of segments for division.

Block   Divides an entity with a block currently defined in the drawing. After you provide the block name, AutoCAD prompts for the number of segments.

Tips

If you cannot see the points dividing an entity, try adjusting the PDMODE and PDSIZE system variables, then issue the REGEN command.

The Block option lets you align the block with the divided entity. An aligned block is rotated around its insertion point and drawn parallel to the divided entity. An unaligned block is drawn with a 0 rotation angle to the entity.

You can use the NODe object snap override to snap to the points created by DIVIDE.

To manipulate DIVIDE's markers as a group, use the Previous selection set option.

Warning

DIVIDE's markers are placed in the UCS of the entity being divided. They always reside on the entity, regardless of the current elevation setting.

See also: MEASURE, NODE, POINT

DONUT/DOUGHNUT

Screen **[DRAW] [DONUT:]**
Pull down **[Draw] [Donut]**

The DONUT command draws solid-filled rings and circles. DONUT entities are constructed from closed wide polyarc segments. You provide an inside diameter value (or two points) and an outside diameter (or two points). The default settings create an inside diameter of <0.5000> and an outside diameter of <1.0000>.

Prompts
```
Inside diameter <0.5000>:
Outside diameter <1.0000>:
Center of doughnut:
```

Tips

You can extrude a donut into a cylinder by assigning thickness.

You can construct a solid-filled circle by setting the donut's inside diameter to 0.

See also: FILL, PLINE, PEDIT

DRAG/DRAGMODE

Screen **[SETTINGS] [DRAGMOD:]**

DRAGMODE enables you to draw and edit entities—such as circles, arcs, polylines, and blocks—by dynamically dragging the image into position in the drawing. The default setting is <Auto>, which enables dragging for any command that supports dragging.

Prompt

```
ON/OFF/Auto <Auto>:
```

Options

ON   Allows AutoCAD to enable dragging at your request. Type **DRAG** at the `Command:` prompt when you want to drag an object.

OFF   Tells AutoCAD to ignore all requests to drag.

Auto   Automatically enables dragging for those commands that can use it.

Related System Variables

DRAGMODE, DRAGP1, DRAGP2

Tip

When you are using multiple viewports, you can watch entities being dragged only in the current viewport. If you pick entities in other viewports, you can watch them drag in the viewport from which they were chosen.

DTEXT

Screen **[DRAW] [DTEXT:]**
Pull down **[Draw] [Dtext]**

The DTEXT (Dynamic TEXT) command lets you enter text in your drawing, but gives you more control than does the TEXT command. Although the end results of DTEXT and TEXT are similar, the commands differ in several ways:

- When you use DTEXT, AutoCAD echoes the text on-screen as you type it.

- DTEXT lets you move the cursor to different parts of the drawing and enter more text without exiting from the command.

- When you use DTEXT, press <RETURN> only once to enter a second line of text; TEXT forces you to press <RETURN> twice.

Prompts

```
Justify/Style/<Start point>:
Height <default>:
Rotation angle <default>:
Text:
```

Options

Start point   Text justification is at the bottom left of the first character for each line of text.

Justify   Specify the text justification. When you select the Justify option, AutoCAD prompts you to select the type of justification you want to use for the text string. DTEXT gives you the following options:

         Align—Specify the beginning and ending point of a line of text. AutoCAD adjusts the text height to fit between these points.

         Fit—Specify the beginning and ending point of a line of text. You determine the height. AutoCAD adjusts the text width to fit between the two end-points.

         Center—Specify the center of the text horizontally and the base of the text vertically.

         Middle—Specify the middle of the text horizontally and vertically.

         Right—Text justification is at the bottom right of the last character for each line of text.

TL—Text justification is at the top left of the tallest character (Release 11 only).

TC—Text justification is at the top center of the tallest character (Release 11 only).

TR—Text justification is at the top right of the tallest character (Release 11 only).

ML—Text justification is at the middle left, between the top of the tallest character and the bottom of the lowest descender (Release 11 only).

MC—Text justification is at the middle center, between the top of the tallest character and the bottom of the lowest descender (Release 11 only).

MR—Text justification is at the middle right, between the top of the tallest character and the bottom of the lowest descender (Release 11 only).

BL—Text justification is at the bottom left of the lowest descender (Release 11 only).

BC—Text justification is at the bottom center of the lowest descender (Release 11 only).

BR—Text justification is at the bottom right of the lowest descender (Release 11 only).

Style   Change the current style default. The style must have been created with the STYLE command.

<RETURN>   If you press <RETURN>, AutoCAD highlights the last text entered, and prompts for a new text string. AutoCAD places the new text directly below the highlighted text, and applies the same style, height, and rotation as the highlighted text.

Height   Assign a text height. You are not prompted for this when using Align or a text style with a predefined height.

Rotation angle   Specify the text angle.

Text   Supply the text string.

DTEXT's Justify option uses the following default settings:

Start point	Left justified
Height	0.2000
Rotation angle	0

Special Character Codes

You can add codes to a text string to obtain the following special characters:

%%o	Toggle overscore mode on/off
%%u	Toggle underscore mode on/off
%%d	Draw degrees symbol
%%p	Draw plus/minus tolerance symbol
%%c	Draw diameter symbol
%%%	Draw a single percent symbol

When you enter text, the control characters appear in the drawing. When you end the DTEXT command, the appropriate characters replace the control codes.

Related System Variables
TEXTSIZE, TEXTSTYLE

Tips

You can preset the font, alignment, height, and rotation of text by selecting [Dtext Options >] from the [Options] pull-down menu. AutoCAD automatically activates these preset variables when you pick [Dtext] from the [Draw] pull-down menu. When you use the screen menus, the text variables are based on the last text inserted during the drawing session.

You can edit text strings by using the DDEDIT (Release 11 only) or CHANGE commands.

Warning

Base your text height on the scale at which you plan to plot the drawing. The text height you specify should be the height of plotted text multiplied by the plot scale factor.

See also: CHANGE, DDEDIT, QTEXT, STYLE, TEXT

DVIEW

Screen **[DISPLAY] [DVIEW:]**
Pull down **[Display] [Dview Options...]**

DVIEW (Dynamic VIEW) is a tool for viewing 3D models. DVIEW is similar to the VPOINT command, but DVIEW lets you dynamically drag and rotate all or part of a 3D model with the aid of slider bars. You can display a perspective view of the model and toggle between parallel and perspective views. DVIEW enables you to view a model in much the same way a camera enables you to view a target. You can set a camera point, target point, lens length, and position front and back clipping planes. DVIEW's default setting creates a parallel (not perspective) projection.

Prompts

```
Select objects:
CAmera/TArget/Distance/POints/PAn/Zoom/TWist/CLip/Hide/Off/Undo/<eXit>:
```

Options

CAmera	Pick a camera angle relative to the target. This is similar to the VPOINT rotate option. You can move your camera point up and down and around the target point.
TArget	Rotate the target point around the camera.
Distance	Determine the distance from the camera to the target. This option turns on perspective viewing
POints	Prompts you to specify a camera and target point.
PAn	Pan around the view.
Zoom	When perspective viewing is off, you can zoom in and out of the view based on the Zoom Center option. If perspective viewing is on, you can change the lens length of the camera. The default is a camera with a 50mm lens. Increasing the lens length is similar to using a telephoto lens; decreasing the lens length is similar to using a wide angle lens.
TWist	Determine the view twist angle. Rotate the camera around the line of sight to the target point.
CLip	Specify the front and back clipping planes. A clipping plane is perpendicular to the line of sight between the camera and target.
Hide	Performs a hidden line removal on the current DVIEW selection set.
Off	Turns perspective viewing off.
Undo	Reverses the last DVIEW option.
eXit	Exits the command and regenerates the drawing to reflect any changes.

Related System Variables
BACKZ, FRONTZ, LENSLENGTH, TARGET, VIEWCTR, VIEWDIR, VIEWMODE, VIEWSIZE, VIEWTWIST, WORLDVIEW

Tips
During object selection, pick only key entities to display and drag on-screen. Once you establish a viewpoint in DVIEW, exit and the rest of the drawing entities are displayed from that viewpoint.

At the Select objects: prompt, you can press <RETURN> without picking entities. A block, called Dviewblock, appears and you can pick viewpoints by watching this block rotate. When you choose a viewpoint, exit DVIEW and AutoCAD displays your drawing with the new settings.

You can customize the Dviewblock by creating your own 3D drawing with this name. Keep the geometry simple, but make sure that the different sides are unique to observe the dynamic movement of the symbol.

Use the VIEW and VPORTS SAVE options to restore perspective views. Viewports retain all the DVIEW display parameters.

Warning
You cannot issue transparent commands or editing commands when DVIEW is active.

See also: VIEW, VPOINT, VPORTS

DXBIN

Screen **[UTILITY] [DXF/DXB] [DXBIN:]**
Pull down **[File] [EXCHANGE >] [DXB In]**

DXB (Drawing Interchange Binary) is a binary drawing exchange file format. You can use the DXBIN command to import DXB files into AutoCAD. (AutoCAD cannot, however, write a DXB file on its own.) Configure AutoCAD for an ADI plotter, select the DXB file output option, and plot to a file. DXB files have the file extension DXB.

Prompt
DXB file:

Tip
If you use the DXBIN command to create a DXB plot file from a 3D drawing, AutoCAD converts the drawing to 2D. Use either VPOINT or DVIEW to set the viewpoint before plotting the drawing to a file. Once the plot is complete, you can import the file with the DXBIN command. The drawing will consist entirely of line segments, including arcs, circles, curves, and text. This process is useful for producing 2D perspective drawings.

DXFIN/DXFOUT

Screen **[UTILITY] [DXF/DXB] [DXFIN:]** *or* **[DXFOUT:]**
Pull down **[File] [EXCHANGE >] [DXF In]** *or* **[DXF Out]**

DXF (Drawing Interchange File) format is a standard ASCII text file for exchanging AutoCAD drawings with other CAD packages or specialized analysis programs. Use the DXFIN command to load drawing interchange files; use DXFOUT to write a drawing interchange file. All drawing interchange files have the file extension DXF.

Prompts
File name <*default*>:
Enter decimal places of accuracy (0 to 16)/Entities/
Binary <6>:

Options

Decimal places of accuracy	Determines the accuracy of floating-point numbers. The default value is 6.
Entities	Outputs selected entities to the DXF file.
Binary	Writes a binary drawing interchange file.

Tips

A complete DXF file loads only into a new drawing file. When entering a new drawing name at the Main Menu, enter an equal sign (=) after the name to use AutoCAD's original defaults.

You can load the DXF entities section into an existing drawing. Information such as block definitions and layering information is not included.

Use the AUDIT command to check for corrupt data after using the DXFIN command to import a DXF file. You can activate the AUDIT command from the Main Menu or at the `Command:` prompt.

See also: AMELITE

EDGESURF

Screen **[DRAW] [next] [3D Surfs] [EDGSURF:]**
Screen **[SURFACES] [EDGSURF:]**
Pull down **[Draw] [Surfaces...] [EDGE]**

EDGESURF generates a 3D polygon mesh by approximating a Coons surface patch from four adjoining edges. The edges can be made up of lines, arcs, or open polylines anywhere in 3D space. The endpoints of each entity must intersect to form a closed path. You can pick the edges in any order. The first edge or entity selected defines the M direction of the mesh. The two edges that intersect the M edge determine the N direction for the mesh. (See 3DMESH for M and N directions.)

Prompts

```
Select edge 1:
Select edge 2:
Select edge 3:
Select edge 4:
```

Related System Variables

SURFTAB1, SURFTAB2

Tips

You can use the PEDIT command to edit an entity created by EDGESURF.

When you explode an EDGESURF mesh, AutoCAD separates the mesh into individual 3D faces.

See also: 3DMESH, 3DFACE

ELEV

Screen **[SETTINGS] [ELEV:]**

The ELEV (ELEVation) command sets the elevation and extrusion thickness of entities you draw. The elevation is the entity's location along the Z axis. The extrusion thickness (negative or positive) is its height above (or below) the Z elevation. The elevation setting affects only those entities whose Z value is not otherwise specified. You also can set elevation and thickness by using the DDEMODES dialogue box.

Prompts
```
New current elevation <0.0000>:
New current thickness <0.0000>:
```
Related System Variables
ELEVATION, THICKNESS

Tip
The current UCS determines an entity's Z location or elevation. Any elevation other than 0 is applied during entity construction.

Warning
The ELEV command may be dropped in a future release of AutoCAD. Use the UCS, DDUCS, or DDEMODES command as an alternative elevation-control command. The combination of UCS and ELEV may be confusing—you may have less trouble if you use UCS only, and do not change the current elevation. Use the THICKNESS system variable to change extrusion thickness.

See also: CHANGE, 'DDEMODES

ELLIPSE

Screen **[DRAW] [ELLIPSE:]**
Pull down **[Draw] [Ellipse]**

The ELLIPSE command enables you to construct ellipses in several ways. The default method uses major and minor axes, which you specify by selecting endpoints.

Prompts
```
<Axis endpoint 1>/Center:
Axis endpoint 2:
<Other axis distance>/Rotation:
```
Options

Center   Specify a center point and one endpoint of each axis.

Rotation   Specify the rotation around the major axis. The rotation angle is between 0 and 89.4 degrees.

Isocircle   If you enable Isometric mode, the ELLIPSE prompt will include an Isocircle option. Isometric circles will be drawn in the current isoplane. You provide the center point and radius or diameter.

Tips
Ellipses are closed polylines that are made up of short arc segments. You can use all the polyline-editing commands to modify ellipses.

To construct an elliptical arc, draw an ellipse and use the BREAK or TRIM command to remove a portion of the ellipse.

You can create your own ellipse by saving a circle as a block and inserting it with different X and Y values.

See also: EXPLODE, ISOPLANE, PLINE, PEDIT

END

Screen **[UTILITY] [END:]**
Pull down **[File] [End]**

The END command saves the drawing file and exits to AutoCAD's Main Menu. The old drawing file becomes the new BAK file.

See also: QUIT, SAVE

ERASE

Screen **[EDIT] [ERASE:]**
Pull down **[Modify] [Erase]**

ERASE deletes entities from the drawing.

Prompt
Select objects:

Tip
Use the U, UNDO, or OOPS command to restore the last group of erased entities. If you executed commands after erasing entities, use the OOPS command.

See also: OOPS, UNDO

EXPLODE

Screen **[EDIT] [EXPLODE:]**

EXPLODE separates blocks, polylines, dimensions, hatches, and meshes back into their original component entities.

Prompt
Select block reference, polyline, dimension, or mesh:

Tips
Some entities may change their color and linetype after being exploded, as they return to their original layer, color, and linetype.

Exploded polylines become lines and arcs, and 3D meshes become 3D faces.

Pre-explode blocks, hatch patterns, and drawing files by inserting them with an asterisk (*) preceding their insertion name. Pre-explode dimensions by turning DIMASO off.

Warnings
An exploded polyline loses its tangent and width characteristics.

If you explode a block that contains attributes, AutoCAD replaces the attribute value with the attribute definition tag name.

You cannot explode a block with unequal X, Y, and Z scale factors, a mirrored block, a block that has been inserted with the MINSERT command, or external references and their dependent blocks.

If you explode hatches or dimensions, AutoCAD places all their entities on layer 0.

See also: DIMENSION, BLOCK, HATCH, PLINE, 3D MESH

EXTEND

Screen **[EDIT] [EXTEND:]**
Pull down **[Modify] [Extend]**

EXTEND lengthens a line, open polyline, or arc to a boundary edge. Boundary edges include lines, circles, arcs, polylines, and viewport borders (in paper space). You can have more than one boundary edge, and an entity can be both a boundary edge and an entity to extend.

Prompts
```
Select boundary edge(s) ...
Select objects:
<Select object to extend>/Undo:
```

Option

Undo   Undoes the last EXTEND operation, without exiting from the command.

Tips

The extrusion direction must be parallel to the Z axis of the current UCS.

Extending entities from another viewpoint (other than the plan viewpoint) to entities in the current viewport can produce unwanted results because boundary edges are projected to the current viewpoint. For best results, view the extending entities from their plan view.

You can select more than one boundary edge. The entities you are extending end at the first boundary. Pick the entity again, and it will extend to the next boundary edge.

Warnings

Blocks, text, and traces cannot be boundary edges or objects to extend.

Entities extend to the center of wide polylines.

See also: CHANGE, STRETCH, TRIM

FILES

Main Menu **Option 6. File Utilities**
Screen **[UTILITY] [FILES:]**

The FILES command displays the File Utility menu, which is an alternative to DOS (or your operating system) for managing your files. You also can access these file utilities from AutoCAD's Main Menu.

Options

0. Exit File Utility Menu	Return to the Main Menu or to your drawing.
1. List Drawing files	Lists AutoCAD drawing files. This is equivalent to the DOS command DIR *.DWG /W /P.
2. List user specified files	Lists files based on your specifications. You can use the wild-card options * and ? for DOS systems and *, ?, [ ] and - on UNIX systems.
3. Delete files	Specify each file to delete individually or use the wild-card options * and ?. AutoCAD prompts for comfirmation before actually deleting a file.
4. Rename files	Rename a file and place the file in a different directory at the same time.
5. Copy file	Copy a file from a drive and directory (source) into another drive and directory (destination). In addition, you can specify a different name for the copied file.
6. Unlock file	Unlock one or more files (Release 11 only). You can use the wild-card options.

Tips

When you refer to a file name, remember to include the extension (DWG for drawing files). AutoCAD will not acknowledge a drawing file unless it has the DWG extension. If you copy a file and forget to include the extension, you must use the RENAME command to supply the extension.

The Rename option copies a file from one directory to another (you can keep the same file name) and deletes the original file.

The Copy option copies a file from one drive and directory to another and renames the file at the same time. This does not delete the original file.

Warning

If you enter the File Utility menu from within a drawing file, do not delete the active drawing file, temporary files, or lock files. Temporary files have the extensions AC, AC, or $A; lock files have the extension ??K.

FILL

Screen **[DRAW] [PLINE:]** *or* **[SOLID:]** *or* **[TRACE:]**
then **[FILL ON]** *or* **[FILL OFF]**

FILL is a toggle command that determines whether polylines, solids, and traces are displayed and plotted as filled, or just the outline is displayed and plotted. FILL is on by default.

Prompt

ON/OFF <On>:

Options

ON   Polylines, solids, and traces are displayed and plotted as filled.

OFF   Only the outlines of polylines, solids, and traces are displayed and plotted.

Related System Variable

FILLMODE

Tips

You can save REGEN and REDRAW time if you keep FILL off.

You may find it faster to plot broad lines with a wider plotter pen tip rather than have the plotter try to fill in drawing entities.

Warning

When you change the FILL setting, you do not see the change until the drawing is regenerated.

See also: PLINE, REGEN, SOLID, TRACE

FILLET

Screen **[EDIT] [next] [FILLET:]**
Pull down **[Modify] [Fillet]**

FILLET lets you create an arc with a predefined radius between any two lines, polylines, circles, and arcs. If your selected entities do not meet, or if they extend past an intersecting point, FILLET extends or trims the entities until they intersect. The fillet arc is inserted according to the fillet's radius. The default fillet radius is 0.

Prompts

Polyline/Radius/<Select two objects>:
Enter fillet radius <0.00>:

Options

Polyline   Fillets all the intersections of a 2D polyline. The intersections must be contiguous segments.

Radius   Sets the fillet radius. After you set a radius, press <RETURN> or reselect the FILLET command.

Related System Variable
FILLETRAD

Tip
The fillet arc resides on the layer of the picked entities as long as they share the same layer; if the two entities are on different layers, the fillet is placed on the current layer. The same rules apply to color and linetype.

See also: CHAMFER, EXTEND, PLINE, TRIM

FILMROLL

Screen **[ASHADE] [ACTION] [FLMROLL:]**
Pull down **[Utility] [AutoShade...] [FILMROLL]**

FILMROLL produces a file containing a description of entities that can be processed into a fully shaded AutoShade rendering. The filmroll file also contains camera, lighting, and scene descriptions that are created in the drawing from tools provided in the AutoShade program.

Prompt
Enter the filmroll file name <*dwg-name*>:

GRAPHSCR/TEXTSCR

Type: **GRAPHSCR** *or* **TEXTSCR**

These two commands flip the screen between graphics mode and text mode. GRAPHSCR flips the screen to the graphics screen; TEXTSCR flips the screen to the text screen. On a DOS-based system, the <F1> key toggles between these two screens. You can issue either command transparently.

Tip
These commands are used primarily in scripts and menus to toggle the screen.

GRID

Screen **[SETTINGS] [GRID:]**
Pull down **[Settings] [Grid On/Off ^G]**

GRID displays reference dots at any user-defined increment to help you get a perspective on the drawing space and the size of your drawing entities. GRID is dynamic. You can modify the increment value and turn the setting on or off. Press <^G> (or the <F7> function key on DOS-based systems) to turn the grid on and off. The defaults are <0.0000> spacing and OFF. You also can use the DDRMODES command to set the grid spacing.

Prompt
Grid spacing(X) or ON/OFF/Snap/Aspect <0.0000>:

Options

Grid spacing(X)	Set the X and Y grid increments. If you place an X after the number, it makes the grid a multiple of the current snap value.
ON	Grid is visible.
OFF	Grid is invisible.
Snap	Grid increment equals the current snap increment. This works the same as if you set the grid equal to 0.
Aspect	Set individual horizontal and vertical grid increments.

Related System Variables
GRIDMODE, GRIDUNIT

Tips
Each viewport retains its own grid setting.

If you are working in the WCS or a UCS that is the same as the WCS, the grid is displayed to the drawing limits. If you are working in a UCS different from the WCS, the grid extends to the edges of your viewport.

If the grid is set to an increment that is too small to be shown on the screen, the message `Grid too dense to display` appears at the `Command:` prompt. If you zoom into a portion of the drawing, you can see the grid. If the grid is too dense, you can press <^C> to cancel the grid regeneration.

See also: 'DDRMODES, SNAP

HANDLES

Screen **[SETTINGS] [HANDLES:]**

The HANDLES command assigns a unique label to every drawing entity. This label is in hexadecimal format and is stored permanently in the drawing (unless you destroy it) and is used to access entities. AutoLISP programs can use handles, or you can use handles to link entities to external programs, such as databases. The default setting is OFF.

Prompts
```
Handles are disabled.
ON/DESTROY:
```

Options

ON   Assign a handle to every entity.

DESTROY   Delete all handles within a drawing. To prevent the inadvertent destruction of handle assignments, you must type in one of six random text strings that are given following the DESTROY prompt.

Related System Variable
HANDLES

Warnings
Entities within a block definition do not have handles.

If you use the WBLOCK command on a drawing file with the asterisk (*) option, AutoCAD deletes all handle assignments.

Handles are turned on automatically as long as AMElite is loaded, unless you turn them off for the current drawing.

See also: WBLOCK, AMELITE

HATCH

Screen **[DRAW] [HATCH:]**
Pull down **[Draw] [Hatch]**

The HATCH command cross-hatches or pattern-fills an area that is enclosed by existing entities. The command creates an unnamed block with the specified pattern. Hatch patterns are stored in a file named ACAD.PAT.

Prompt
```
Pattern (? or name/U,style):
```

Options

Pattern   Enter a hatch pattern name. When you specify a pattern, you must enter a scale and angle for it. When typing the hatch pattern's name, include an asterisk (*) before the name if you want the hatch block to be pre-exploded.

? or name   Lists one or all of the hatch pattern names, along with a short description. You can use wild-card characters to produce a specific list.

U   User-defined: that is you provide the pattern. AutoCAD prompts for the spacing and angle for straight lines. You also can "double-hatch" an area or create a perpendicular cross-hatch.

Style   You can specify the hatch style by appending a style code to the hatch pattern name. Separate the name and code with a comma. You have the following three choices:

- **N (Normal)**—Hatch every other boundary.

- **O (Outermost)**—Hatch only the outermost boundary.

- **I (Ignore)**—Hatch everything inside the outermost boundary.

Related System Variables
SNAPBASE, SNAPANG

Tips
Hatch lines are projected to the current construction plane defined by the USC.

If the area you want to hatch is complex, you may find it easier to draw a polyline around the perimeter and hatch the polyline. You also may want to save the polyline on a frozen layer for future reference.

If you need precise hatch pattern placement, set the system variable SNAPBASE to a point where you want the hatch pattern to originate. Be sure to reset it after hatching, because SNAP and GRID also use it.

If you explode a hatch pattern, you may consider regrouping those entities into a block. The block takes less drawing space and is easier to manipulate.

You can establish hatch defaults for the current editing session by selecting [HATCH OPTIONS >] from the [Options] pull-down menu. The settings are activated only when you select [Hatch] from the [Draw] pull-down menu.

If you hatch an area that contains text, attributes, traces, solids, or shapes, you can draw the hatch around the entity as long as you include the entity during your object selection.

To speed up your drawing regeneration and redraw time, keep hatching on its own layer, and freeze the layer until you are ready to plot.

In paper space, you can use viewport edges as hatch boundaries.

See also: BLOCK, EXPLODE, SNAP

HELP/?

Screen [Inquiry [HELP:]]
Screen [* * * *] [HELP]
Pull down [Assist] [Help!]

HELP provides information on commands and their function, and provides cross references to the AutoCAD *Reference Manual.* If you use 'HELP or '? while in another command, AutoCAD displays information on the currently active command. Otherwise, HELP lists every AutoCAD command and gives offers general help. If you want help with an individual command, type in the command name after issuing the HELP command.

Prompt
Command name (RETURN for list):

See also: Transparent Commands

HIDE

Screen **[DISPLAY] [HIDE:]**
Pull down **[Display] [Hide]**
Pull down **[Display] [Vpoint 3D...] [HIDE]**

Normally, AutoCAD displays the edges of all entities. The HIDE command calculates solid areas defined by those edges. When you issue HIDE, AutoCAD determines what should be hidden from your viewpoint and temporarily removes those edges and entities from sight. HIDE only evaluates circles, polylines (assigned a width), solids, traces, 3D faces, meshes, and extruded edges of entities assigned a thickness as opaque surfaces. Further, extruded circles, polylines (assigned a width), solids, and traces are considered solid entities and have top and bottom faces.

Tips

A regeneration causes entities to be displayed normally. Turn off REGENAUTO to suppress regenerations after using the HIDE command.

After you suppress the drawing's hidden lines, you may want to create a slide file for future reference.

You can make hidden lines visible on-screen but displayed as different colors, by creating additional layer names that are identical to the existing names, but containing the prefix HIDDEN (Release 11 only). Every time you issue the HIDE command, the hidden lines are visible and become the color of the hidden layer name. The linetype defaults to the linetype definition of the entity.

Warnings

HIDE evaluates entities residing on a layer that is turned off during the hide process. If the layer is frozen, however, HIDE does not evaluate the entities on that layer.

You may get unexpected results if you hide objects that intersect.

See also: DVIEW, SLIDE, VIEW, VPOINT

ID

Screen **[INQUIRY] [ID:]**
Pull down **[Utility] [ID Point]**

ID identifies the absolute X,Y,Z coordinates of any selected point. AutoCAD identifies the point with a blip mark if BLIPMODE is on.

Prompt
Point:

Related System Variable
LASTPOINT

Tip

ID point coordinates are stored in the LASTPOINT system variable, until you use another command that updates LASTPOINT's value.

IGESIN/IGESOUT

Screen **[UTILITY] [IGES] [IGESIN:]** *or* **[IGESOUT:]**
Pull down **[File] [EXCHANGE >] [IGES In]** *or* **[IGES Out]**

IGES (Initial Graphics Exchange Standard) is a drawing exchange file format that is supported by many CAD programs. IGESIN lets you import an IGES file into a new AutoCAD drawing. IGESOUT lets you generate an IGES file from your current AutoCAD drawing. The file extension is IGS.

Prompt
```
File name:
```

Related System Variable
FILEDIA

Warnings
Use IGESIN only in a new drawing file, before you draw any entities.

Some entities and data may not translate properly because different types of IGES translation programs are available. Be sure to compare the translated drawing with the original.

INSERT

Screen **[BLOCKS] [INSERT:]**
Screen **[DRAW] [INSERT:]**
Pull down **[Draw] [Insert]**

INSERT merges a block or drawing file into the current drawing. After you pick an insertion point, you can specify X,Y,Z scale values and a rotation angle for the inserted block. The insertion point in the drawing corresponds to the block insertion base point or a drawing's base point. By default, INSERT uses an X scale factor of 1, a Y scale factor that equals X, and a rotation angle of 0.

Prompts
```
Block name (or ?) <default>:
Insertion point:
X scale factor <1> / Corner / XYZ:
Y scale factor (default = X):
Rotation angle <0>:
```

Options

Block name	Specify the block or drawing name. An asterisk (*) before the name inserts a block or drawing as individual entities. If you insert a block with an asterisk, you can give only one scale factor for X, Y, and Z, and it cannot be negative.
?	Activate wild-card options for reviewing the names of blocks defined in the current drawing. The default, an asterisk, displays a sorted listing of all named blocks. You can use any of the wild-card options to create a more specific list.
~	Display the File dialogue box for easy selection.
X scale factor	Enter the X scale.
Corner	The Corner option can be selected at the X scale factor prompt. You specify a scale via two points that form a rubber-band box. The first point is the insertion point and the second point becomes the other corner. The X and Y dimensions of the box become the X and Y scale factors for the block.
XYZ	Initiates prompting for XYZ scale factors.
Preset Features	Preset options provide a way to establish scale and rotation prior to picking the insert point. These options are used primarily in menu macros to enable

dragging of blocks at a preset scale during insertion. The five options can be used in two ways: the first is to preset the values by entering one of the options preceded by a P at the insertion point prompt. If you prefix the option with a P, however, the values are temporary and you are again prompted for the values after the insertion point has been established. To have preset options applied after the insertion point is picked, enter the preset options without the P prefix.

Scale	Preset an XYZ scale factor.
Xscale	Preset an X scale factor.
Yscale	Preset a Y scale factor.
Zscale	Preset a Z scale factor.
Rotate	Preset a rotation angle.

Related System Variables
ATTDIA, ATTDISP, ATTREQ, EXPERT

Tips
If you respond with negative values at the scale factor prompts, AutoCAD inserts a mirrored image of the block.

Inserting a block by preceding its name with the asterisk is almost the same as exploding a block once it has been inserted. The only difference is that the BLOCK ? or INSERT ? options do not list the block name.

You can update a drawing file with a revised block definition by inserting a new block definition. Type the block name and include an = sign immediately after the last character. This tells AutoCAD to ignore the existing block definition and to use the new definition. All existing blocks will be redefined to the new block.

You can insert a block or drawing file and assign it a different name in your current drawing. At the Block name prompt, type in the block name, include an =, and enter the new block name.

Inserted blocks reside on the layer that was current when they were inserted. Entities brought in with an asterisk reside on the layers from which they were created. Exploding blocks return entities to their original layer.

Entering a P before Scale (PS), Xscale (PX), Yscale (PY), Zscale (PZ) or Rotate (PR) at the Insertion point prompt lets you temporarily preview how the block will look while it is dragged in the drawing. You cannot preview or preset values if you are inserting with the asterisk option.

You can establish default settings for the current drawing session by selecting [Options] - [INSERT OPTIONS >] from the pull-down menu. The default settings are activated only when you select [Draw] - [INSERT] from the pull-down menu.

The system variable ATTREQ, if set to 0, lets you insert attributes without prompting and applies the attribute's default values. For normal prompting, the variable is set to 1.

The system variable ATTDIA, if set to 1, will cause a dialog box (DDATTE) to appear when you insert blocks with attributes. The box displays the prompt and default value, which you can edit freely. A value of 0 causes normal attribute prompting.

Warnings
If you redefine a block, you must regenerate the drawing to see the changes.

If you modify a block containing attribute definitions and insert the modified block into a drawing containing old attributes, any constant attributes are replaced by new constant attributes. If an attribute definition is removed, attributes will be removed from existing blocks. Variable attributes remain unchanged even if their definition is omitted in the new block. New variable attributes will be included in all new insertions, but will not appear in previous block insertions.

See also: ATTDEF, ATTDIA, ATTDISP, ATTEDIT, ATTREQ, BASE, BLOCK, DDATTE, DRAGMODE, MINSERT, RENAME, WBLOCK

ISOPLANE

Screen **[SETTINGS] [next] [SNAP] [Style] [Iso]**
Pull down **[Settings] [Drawing Tools...] [Isometric]**

The ISOPLANE command lets you draw in isometric mode with the grid and crosshairs displayed isometrically. Pressing <^E> toggles to the next isoplane. The default is the left plane. You also can use the DDRMODES dialogue box to set the isoplane.

Prompt
Left/Top/Right/<Toggle>:

Options

Left   Left isoplane is active in the 90-degree and 150-degree axis pair.

Top   Top isoplane is active in the 30-degree and 150-degree axis pair.

Right   Right isoplane is active in the 90-degree and 30-degree axis pair.

Related System Variable
SNAPISOPAIR

Tips
Keep ORTHO on to help you draw in the correct plane.

You can draw isometric circles with the ELLIPSE command's Isocircle option on the ellipse submenu.

Warning
3D commands such as hidden line removal and perspective views will not work.

See also: 'DDRMODES, ELLIPSE, SNAP

LAYER

Screen **[LAYER:]**
Pull down **[Settings] [Layer Control...]**

AutoCAD layers act as transparent drawing overlays. The LAYER command is used to control layer visibility, status, color, and linetype. You draw on the current layer. When you name a layer, the name can be up to 31 characters. The LAYER command uses the following default settings:

Layer   = 0
Color   = White
Linetype   = Continuous
On
Thawed

You also can use the DDLMODES dialogue box to control layers.

Prompt
?/Make/Set/New/ON/OFF/Color/Ltype/Freeze/Thaw:

Options

? Enables you to review the names of layers defined in the drawing. The default, an asterisk (*), displays a sorted listing of the named layers. You can use any of the wild-card options to create a more specific list.

Make   Create a new layer and make it current.

Set   Make the layer current.

New   Create new layer(s).

ON   Turn layer(s) on.

OFF   Turn layer(s) off.

Color   Assign a color to layer(s).

Ltype   Assign a linetype to layer(s).

Freeze Make the layer invisible and prevents the layer from regenerating.

Thaw   Unfreeze a layer.

Related System Variables
CLAYER, TILEMODE

Tips
You cannot delete, purge, or rename layer 0. You can change its color and linetype assignment, however, including its On/Off Freeze/Thaw state.

When you create new layers, you can type more than one layer name at a time as long as they are separated by commas. The same applies to setting color and linetype.

If you set color and linetype by layer, any entities you draw default to the color and linetype of the current layer.

Blocks containing entities drawn on layer 0 adopt the current layer's properties upon insertion.

You control viewport layer visibility with the VPLAYER command (Release 11 only).

Warnings
Associative dimensioning creates a layer called DEFPOINTS (definition points). The dots are visible even though the layer is turned off. The dots do not plot unless you rename the layer.

Activating AMElite creates a layer named AME_FRZ. Do not edit entities on this layer if you plan to create, edit, or analyze AME solids.

See also: CHANGE, CHPROP, COLOR, BLOCK, 'DDEMODES, 'DDLMODES, LINETYPE, LTSCALE, PURGE, RENAME, VPLAYER

LIMITS

Screen **[SETTINGS] [LIMITS:]**
Pull down **[Utility] [Limits]**

LIMITS defines your active drawing area. This area is defined by the absolute coordinates of the lower left and upper right corners. The LIMITS command lets you modify these points and turn limits checking on and off.

Prompts
```
Reset Model space limits:
ON/OFF/<Lower left corner> <0.0000,0.0000>:
Upper right corner <12.0000,9.0000>:
```

Options

ON — Turns limits checking on; you cannot pick a point outside the limits.

OFF — Turns limits checking off (the default); you can pick a point outside the limits.

Lower left corner — Changes the lower left corner's coordinates.

Upper right corner — Changes the upper right corner's coordinates.

Related System Variables

LIMCHECK, LIMMIN, LIMMAX, TILEMODE

Tips

Set your limits to represent the drawing's full size, or even a little larger.

There are no limits in the Z direction.

If the drawing grid is on and you are in the WCS, grid dots are displayed to the drawing limits.

Model space and paper space each have their own limits.

Warning

If limits checking is enabled and you pick a point outside the limits, you receive the message `**Outside limits`, and your command may not complete.

See also: PLOT, STATUS, ZOOM

LINE

Screen **[DRAW] [LINE:]**

Pull down **[Draw] [Line]**

LINE lets you draw straight line segments. You can enter 2D or 3D points at the prompts.

Prompts

```
From point:
To point:
To point:
To point:
```

Options

Continue — At the From point: prompt, you can begin a line at the endpoint of the most recently drawn line or arc by selecting Continue or pressing <RETURN>.

Close — Enter **C** (Close) at the To point: prompt to close the line segments created during the command, connecting the last endpoint to the original start point.

Undo — Enter **U** (Undo) at the To point: prompt to undo the last line and return to the previous point.

Tips

You can save time and draw lines more accurately by using snap and object snap overrides.

If you want to draw lines with different line weights, you can use polylines or traces, or you can assign colors to the lines and plot with them pens of different weights.

Warning

Using the Undo option while in the LINE command is different from issuing an UNDO at the `Command:` prompt. When issued during the LINE command, Undo releases you to the previous point and lets you continue drawing lines. If you use the UNDO command at the `Command:` prompt, AutoCAD backsteps to the previous command.

See also: PLINE, TRACE

LINETYPE

Screen **[SETTINGS] [LINETYP:]**
Pull down **[Utility] [Load LTypes]**
Pull down **[Options] [Entity Creation...]**
Pull down **[Settings] [Layer Control...]**

LINETYPE assigns a linetype for new entities, loads linetype definitions stored in library files, and creates new linetype definitions. Linetypes are made up of dashes, dots, and spaces.

Standard linetypes include continuous, border, center, dash-dot, dashed, divide, dot, hidden, and phantom. Each linetype also has two predefined variations with twice and half the scale of the standard linetypes.

You can control the linetype of new entities individually or by their layer assignment. The default is BYLAYER. You also can set linetypes with DDEMODES and DDLMODES.

Prompt
?/Create/Load/Set:

Options

?   Display a sorted listing of the named linetype libraries. You can use any of the wild-card options to create a more specific list. If FILEDIA is set to 1, the ? displays the File dialogue box. The linetype library file extension is LIN.

Create   Create new linetypes.

Load   Load linetypes defined in existing library files. You can use any of the wild-card options to load linetypes.

Set   Set a linetype for new entities.

In addition to standard linetype names, such as HIDDEN and DASHED, you can specify BYBLOCK and BYLAYER.

BYLAYER   New entities receive the linetype of the layers on which they reside.

BYBLOCK   New entities are drawn with the continuous linetype until they are saved as a block. When the block is inserted, it inherits the linetype set by the LINETYPE command.

Related System Variables
CELTYPE, BYLAYER, FILEDIA

Tips
Only lines, circles, arcs, and 2D polylines can display broken linetypes.

You can control the scale of linetypes with the LTSCALE command or by creating new linetypes.

Some plotters can produce their own linetypes. To take advantage of these hardware linetypes and maximize display speed, use only the continuous linetype and key linetypes to different entity colors.

Warnings
You may become confused if you try to mix linetypes on a single layer. If you use the LAYER command to control linetypes, and if you leave LINETYPE set to BYLAYER, you can more easily identify the layer containing the desired entity. This also makes changing linetypes a simple process of respecifying the linetype with the LAYER command.

Some plotters do not support hardware linetypes based on an entity's color assignment. To use AutoCAD's linetypes, set your plotter to plot continuous lines at all times.

Linetypes must be loaded before they can be assigned or set.

If you change an entity's linetype, you must regenerate the screen to see the revisions.

See also: CHANGE, CHPROP, 'DDEMODES, 'DDLMODES, LAYER, LTSCALE, PLOT, RE-NAME

LIST/DBLIST

Screen **[INQUIRY] [LIST:]** *or* **[DBLIST:]**
Pull down **[Utility] [List]**

The LIST command provides detailed information on selected entities within a drawing. The DBLIST command provides information on all entities within a drawing. These commands provide different types of information, depending on the entity. If the list is long and begins to scroll off the screen, you can press <^S> or PAUSE to halt the scroll; press any key to continue the list. Press <^C> to cancel the list. If you have a printer, you can toggle on <^Q> before issuing the command and send the data directly to the printer.

Prompt
Select objects:

See also: AREA, DIST

LTSCALE

Screen **[SETTINGS] [next] [LTSCALE:]**
Pull down **[Options] [Linetype Scale]**

LTSCALE (LineType SCALE) assigns a global scale multiplier for all linetypes. The default is <1.0000>.

Prompt
New scale factor <1.0000>:

Related System Variable
LTSCALE

Tip
Use the following rule of thumb for determining a drawing's proper linetype scale: Multiply the drawing's scale factor by .375. After you plot the drawing, you can fine tune the linetype scale value.

Warning
If you change your drawing's linetype scale, you will not see a change until the drawing regenerates.

See also: LINETYPE, REGEN

MEASURE

Screen **[EDIT] [next] [MEASURE:]**
Pull down **[Modify] [Measure]**

The MEASURE command marks an entity at equal segment lengths that you specify. The entity is not physically separated, rather points or blocks are placed as markers at each segment end point. You can measure lines, circles, arcs, and polylines.

Prompts
Select object to measure:
<Segment length>/Block:
Segment length:

```
Block name to insert:
Align block with object? <Y>
```

Options

Segment length   Lets you enter the desired segment length. Segments are measured starting with the endpoint of the entity closest to the pick point you use to select an object.

Block   Allows you to measure the entity with a block currently defined in the drawing. After providing the block name, you then are prompted for the segment length.

Tips

If you cannot see points measuring an entity, try adjusting the PDMODE and PDSIZE system variables and issuing a REGEN.

You can manipulate the markers as a group by using the Previous selection set option.

Warning

Markers are placed in the UCS of the entity being measured. They always are placed on the entity regardless of the current elevation setting.

See also: DIVIDE, NODE, POINT

MENU

Screen **[UTILITY]** **[MENU:]**

The MENU option loads and displays a menu file for the current drawing. This file defines the screen, pull-down, and tablet menus, including the pick buttons if you are using a pointing device with buttons. The uncompiled source file is an ASCII text file with the extension MNU. AutoCAD compiles the menu and forms a file with the extension MNX, which it loads. The default menu is ACAD.

Prompt

```
Menu file name or . for none <acad>:
```

Options

Menu file name   Lets you enter the name of a menu file, excluding the extension MNU or MNX.

. (period)   Disables all menus. You can access the commands by typing them at the command prompt.

Related System Variables

MENUNAME, MENUECHO

Tip

All menu files have an extension of MNU. These files are compiled for speed, and a new menu file is created with the extension MNX. If an MNU file is updated, AutoCAD recognizes the file date and time and automatically recompiles and loads the new MNX file when you first start it.

Warning

The name of the last menu file used is stored in the drawing file. If you enter an existing drawing and receive the message, Enter another menu file name (or RETURN for none):, the last menu file used for that drawing cannot be located. You can type ACAD and use the menu that comes with AutoCAD. This assumes that ACAD.MNU or ACAD.MNX is located in a directory recognized by AutoCAD.

See also: TABLET

MINSERT

Screen **[BLOCKS] [MINSERT:]**
Screen **[DRAW] [MINSERT:]**

The MINSERT (Multiple INSERT) command is a combination of the INSERT and ARRAY (rectangular) commands. MINSERT lets you insert multiple copies of a block in a rectangular pattern. It has the same prompts as the INSERT command for insertion point, X,Y scaling, and rotation angle.

Prompt

Block name (or ?):

Option

?   Allows you to review the names of blocks defined in the current drawing. The default, an asterisk (*), displays a sorted listing of all named blocks. You can use any of the wild-card options to create a more specific list.

After you enter a block name, you will see the standard INSERT prompts for insertion point and scaling. MINSERT then prompts for the following rectangular array:

Number of rows (—):
Number of columns (||||):
Unit cell or distance between rows (—):
Distance between columns (||||):
You provide the number of rows and columns, and the distance between rows and columns.

Tips

When you respond with a tilde (~) when prompted for a block name, you activate the File dialogue box.

MINSERT uses less memory than inserting and arraying a block.

Warning

All the blocks making up a MINSERT array must remain intact. You cannot explode the array, nor can you minsert the block with an asterisk preceding the block name.

See also: ARRAY, BLOCK, INSERT

MIRROR

Screen **[EDIT] [next] [MIRROR:]**
Pull down **[Modify] [Mirror]**

The MIRROR command creates a mirrored replica of a selected group of entities. You can keep the original group of entities or have them deleted. The default is to not delete them.

Prompts

Select objects:
First point of mirror line:
Second point:
Delete old objects? <N>

Options

First point of mirror line   Designates the first point on an axis about which the entities are mirrored.

Second point   Designates the second point on an axis about which the entities are mirrored.

Delete old objects? <N>   If you answer yes, AutoCAD erases the entities to be mirrored.

Related System Variable
MIRRTEXT

Tips
If MIRRTEXT is set to 0, text and variable attributes are not mirrored. Text and constant attributes that are assigned to a block that is mirrored will be mirrored regardless of the MIRRTEXT setting.

You also can mirror a block by inserting it with negative X and Y values.

Warnings
You cannot explode a mirrored block.

Associative dimension text is not mirrored regardless of the MIRRTEXT setting.

See also: INSERT

MOVE

Screen **[EDIT] [next] [MOVE:]**
Pull down **[Modify] [Move]**

The MOVE command relocates entities anywhere in 3D space.

Prompts
Select objects:
Base point or displacement:
Second point of displacement:

Options

Base point	Enters a point of reference to apply the displacement distance (see next option), or by which to drag the selected entity.
Displacement	Enters the distance for X,Y,Z, or drags the entity to specify the displacement.

Tip
If you want to move entities to another layer, you must use the CHANGE or CHPROP commands.

Warning
If you accidentally press <RETURN> at the Second point prompt, your entities could end up out of view. This happens because MOVE uses the X,Y,Z base point coordinates as displacement distances.

See also: COPY

MSLIDE

Screen **[UTILITY] [SLIDES] [MSLIDE:]**

MSLIDE (Make SLIDE) creates a snapshot of your current screen display in a file with the extension SLD. The slide is of the current viewport and is independent of the drawing file from which it was created. The screen is redrawn as the slide is made. The default name for the slide is the current drawing file name. You should use the VSLIDE command to view slides.

Prompt
Slide file <default>:

Tip

Because slide files do not contain any entity data, viewing slides occurs at redraw speed.

Warning

If you save a slide file with the same name as an existing slide, you will not receive a warning message that you are overwriting the file.

See also: SCRIPT, VSLIDE

MSPACE

Pull down **[Display] [Mview >] [Mspace]**

MSPACE (Model SPACE) (Release 11 only) switches from paper space to model space. Paper space is used to annotate, dimension, compose, and plot 2D or 3D drawings created in model space.

The system variable, TILEMODE, also is used to switch between paper space and model space. The default is on. If you turn TILEMODE off (paper space current), you must create at least one viewport with the MVIEW command before you can work in model space.

Related System Variable

TILEMODE

Tips

Model space and paper space retain their own limits.

By plotting in model space, you plot only the current viewport.

See also: MVIEW, PSPACE, TILEMODE, VPLAYER

MULTIPLE

Type **MULTIPLE**

MULTIPLE is a command modifier that causes any command to repeat. Type the word MULTIPLE before a command. To end the command, press <^C> to cancel. No command prompt is issued if you enter MULTIPLE alone.

Tip

MULTIPLE saves time when editing many attributes (MULTIPLE DDATTE) and when inserting blocks (MULTIPLE INSERT).

Warning

MULTIPLE remembers and repeats the main command, but it does not retain command parameters or options.

MVIEW

Screen **[DRAW] [MVIEW]**
Pull down **[Display] [Mview >]**
[Mview *option*]

MVIEW (Make VIEW) (Release 11 only) creates and restores viewports, controls viewport visibility, and performs hidden line removal during paper space plots.

Prompt

ON/OFF/Hideplot/Fit/2/3/4/Restore/<First Point>:

Options

First point	You can create a viewport by picking two diagonal points. This new viewport becomes the current viewport.
ON	Makes all entities in the selected viewports visible.
OFF	Makes all entities in the selected viewports invisible.
Hideplot	Selects viewports for hidden line removal during plotting.
Fit	Creates a viewport the size of your graphics screen.
2/3/4	Creates viewport configurations of two, three, or four viewports.
Restore	Restores viewport configurations saved with the VPORTS command.

Related System Variables
MAXACTVP, TILEMODE

Warning
The number of viewports turned on cannot exceed the maximum allowable number of active viewports (MAXACTVP).

See also: MSPACE, PSPACE, TILEMODE, VPLAYER, VPORTS

OFFSET

Screen **[DRAW] [OFFSET:]**
Screen **[EDIT] [next] [OFFSET:]**
Pull down **[Modify [Offset]**

OFFSET lets you copy a line, arc, circle, or polyline parallel to itself by an offset distance or through a point. The default is <Through>. The OFFSET command repeats until you press <^C> to cancel.

Prompts
```
Offset distance or Through <Through>:
Select object to offset:
```

Options

Offset distance	You can enter the offset distance by typing a value or picking two points. You can pick the side to offset at the Side to offset prompt.
Through	You can pick a point to offset through.

Tip
You can establish a default by selecting [Options]—[Offset Distance] from the pull-down menu. This default is for only the current drawing session and is activated only when selecting [Modify]—[Offset] from the pull-down menu.

Warning
You can offset only one entity at a time.

See also: ARRAY, COPY, UCS

OOPS

Screen **[BLOCKS] [BLOCK:] [OOPS]**
Screen **[EDIT] [ERASE:] [OOPS]**
Pull down **[Modify] [Oops!]**

OOPS restores the last entity or group of entities that was deleted by the most recent ERASE command in the current drawing session.

Tip

You can issue the OOPS command after creating a BLOCK or WBLOCK to restore those entities.

Warning

OOPS will not restore entities erased before the PLOT or PRPLOT commands.

See also: BLOCK, UNDO, WBLOCK

ORTHO

Command: **ORTHO**

Pull down **[Settings] [Ortho On/Off ^O]**

ORTHO constrains lines, polylines, and traces to horizontal and vertical. ORTHO mode also controls the angle at which you pick the second point in many other drawing and editing commands. ORTHO is a toggle, and the default is <Off>. You also can set ORTHO with the DDRMODES dialogue box.

Prompt

ON/OFF <Off>:

Options

ON Enables ORTHO mode.

OFF Disables ORTHO mode.

Related System Variable

ORTHOMODE

Tips

Both your keyboard coordinate entry and OSNAP override ORTHO.

Keep ORTHO on when working in isometric mode.

Warning

ORTHO mode is inactive during perspective views.

See also: 'DDRMODES

OSNAP

Screen **[SETTINGS] [next] [OSNAP:]**

Pull down **[Assist] [OSNAP: <mode>]** *or specific mode*

OSNAP (Object SNAP) lets you apply one or more object snap modes to point selection. These object snap modes calculate the coordinates of geometric points on selected entities. Think of OSNAPs as snapping to attachment points on your drawing entities. When you enable an OSNAP, the cursor displays an aperture box, which must cross the entity to which to be snapped. 12 different OSNAP modes are available to you. The default is Off or NONe.

You can use the OSNAP command to set a "running" mode to be in effect for all subsequent point selections.

You can preset more than one OSNAP mode by entering a comma between each OSNAP mode without using any spaces. You can override a running mode by typing an OSNAP mode when a point is requested, or by using the pull-down menus or screen menu overrides. The screen menu overrides are displayed by the * * * * menu item on the root screen menu. The STATUS command displays the current OSNAP mode(s).

Prompt

Object snap modes:

Options
CENtcr, ENDpoint, INSertion, INTersection, MIDpoint, NEArest, NODe, NONe, PERpendicular, QUAdrant, QUIck, TANgent.

Related System Variable
OSMODE

Warning
The running OSNAPs are inactive during entity selection (Release 11 only). To apply an OSNAP, select the desired OSNAP override. Release 10 may produce unexpected results, such as selecting a circle while CENter osnap mode is active.

See also: APERTURE

PAN

Screen **[DISPLAY] [PAN:]**
Pull down **[Display] [Pan]**

The PAN command lets you scroll around your drawing without altering the current zoom ratio. It is analogous to repositioning your paper on a drafting board to reach another part of a drawing. PAN does not physically move entities or change your drawing limits. Rather, your display window moves across your drawing. PAN is a transparent command and the default is to provide a displacement in relative coordinates.

Prompts
Displacement:
Second point:

Option
Displacement   After you enter a relative X,Y distance, press <RETURN> at the Second point prompt. Or, you can enter a pair of coordinates for the Displacement and the Second point prompts.

Tips
The ZOOM Dynamic command produces the same results as the PAN command, but it can pan further in one command.

Pans become part of the ZOOM Previous queue.

Warning
You cannot perform a transparent pan while in the VPOINT, DVIEW, ZOOM, VIEW, or PAN commands, or while you are in paper space.

PEDIT

Screen **[EDIT] [next] [PEDIT:]**
Pull down **[Modify] [PolyEdit]**

The PEDIT command edits 2D or 3D polylines and 3D polygon meshes. The editing options are based on the type of polyline you chose to edit. Two basic sets of editing functions are available. The first set operates on the entire polyline and the second set lets you edit individual vertices. The default is eXit or <X> to exit the command. The default for the vertex editing options is <N> for Next vertex.

Prompts
Select polyline:
Close/Join/Width/Edit vertex/Fit curve/Spline curve/
Decurve/Undo/eXit <X>:

```
Next/Previous/Break/Insert/Move/Regen/Straighten/
Tangent/Width/eXit <N>:
```

Options

The following table shows the editing options for the three types of polyline entities. PEDIT automatically identifies the type of polyline that is being edited and adjusts its prompts accordingly. See the following explanations for individual options.

	2D Polylines	3D Polylines	Polygon Meshes
Close/Open	X	X	
Join	X		
Width	X		
Edit vertex	X	X	X
Next	X	X	X
Previous	X	X	X
Break	X	X	
Insert	X	X	
Move	X	X	X
Regen	X	X	X
Straighten	X	X	
Tangent	X		
Width	X		
eXit	X	X	X
Left			X
Right			X
Up			X
Down			X
Fit curve	X		
Spline Curve	X	X	
Decurve	X	X	
Undo	X	X	X
eXit	X	X	X
Smooth surface			X
Desmooth			X
Mclose/Mopen		X	
Nclose/Nopen		X	

The PEDIT command assumes that you want to use more than one editing option. The command will repeat itself until you choose eXit (the default) or press <^C> to cancel. (See descriptions of each PEDIT option.)

Tips

You can edit polyface meshes with the PFACE command.

To convert lines and arcs into polylines, use the join option.

To convert polylines into lines and arcs, use the EXPLODE command.

See also: EXPLODE, PLINE, POLYLINE, 3DMESH, 3DPOLY

PEDIT Close / Open

The method you use to construct polylines determines whether the polyline is considered open or closed.

An open polyline occurs when you enter the last point by typing in the coordinates or when you pick the last point on the drawing.

The system automatically closes the polyline from the starting to ending point when you select the Close option from the screen menu or enter C.

Close closes an open polyline by drawing a polyline segment from the first point of the first polyline segment to the endpoint of the last polyline segment.

Open removes the closing segment of a closed polyline.

PEDIT Join

The Join option takes individual 2D polylines, lines, and arcs, and combines them into one 2D polyline. Select the PEDIT command and at the Select polyline prompt, pick the entity to convert. If the entity is not a polyline, you will receive the following message:

`Entity selected is not a polyline. Do you want to turn it into one?`

Tips

To join entities, they must be contiguous; that is, their endpoints must meet at the same coordinates.

When using the Join option, you can use the Window or Crossing selection methods to pick the items to join. Your selection may include entities you do not want included in the selection set. As long as these entities are not contiguous with another entity, they will not join.

Warnings

You cannot join to a closed polyline.

If the endpoints do not match, the entities will not join.

PEDIT Width

The Width option redefines the width of an entire 2D polyline.

Tip

You cannot specify tapers with this option—you can give only one width to the entire polyline segment. If you want different widths between vertices, use the Width option of Edit vertex.

PEDIT Edit vertex

The Edit vertex option lets you individually edit the vertices that make up a polyline segment. An X appears at the first vertex for editing. If any of the segments are drawn with a specified tangent direction, an arrow is drawn in that direction.

Prompts

2D Polyline:
```
Next/Previous/Break/Insert/Move/Regen/Straighten/
Tangent/Width/eXit <N>:
```

3D Polyline:
```
Next/Previous/Break/Insert/Move/Regen/Straighten/eXit <N>:
```

Polyline Mesh:
```
Vertex (0,0). Next/Previous/Left/Right/Up/Down/Move/
REgen/eXit <N>:
```

Options

Next	Moves the X or arrow marker to the next vertex. The order is based on the initial construction of the polyline.

Previous   Moves the X or arrow marker to the previous vertex. The order is based on the initial construction of the polyline.

Break   Breaks a polyline between two vertices. Position the X on a vertex and select Break. Position the X on any other vertex and select Go. When you break a closed polyline segment, the segment becomes open and the closing segment is removed. Leaving the X on the same vertex for Break and Go is equivalent to using the @ last point with the BREAK command.

Insert   Inserts a new vertex. The vertex is added ahead of the X marker.

Move   Moves the vertex marked with an X to a new location.

Regen   Regenerates the polyline.

Straighten   Creates a single segment between two vertices. Any vertices that are between the two you pick are deleted.

Tangent   Attaches a tangent direction for curve fitting to the vertex marked with the X.

Width   Edits the width between two vertices. You can specify a starting and an ending width. The current polyline segment is considered to be between the X marker and the vertex found with the Next option. The polyline must be regenerated before you can see the results.

eXit   Exits the Edit vertex submenu and returns you to the PEDIT prompt. You also can use eXit to cancel the Break and Straighten routines.

Undo   Undoes the most recent Edit vertex commands one step at a time.

Go   Used during the Break and Straighten options to tell the system you are ready to break or straighten the segments between two vertices.

Left   For 3D mesh, moves you left to a previous vertex in the N direction.

Right   For 3D mesh, moves you right to the next vertex in the N direction.

Up   For 3D mesh, moves you up to the next vertex in the M direction.

Down   For 3D mesh, moves you down to the previous vertex in the M direction.

PEDIT Fit Curve

Fit curve regenerates the current polyline, placing arc segments between the vertices.

Warning

If you edit a Fit curve polyline with BREAK, EXPLODE, or TRIM, the Decurve option is no longer available.

See also: PEDIT Decurve, Spline

PEDIT Spline Curve

Spline curve uses the polyline vertices as control points for a B-spline curve. The spline passes through the beginning and ending points of the polyline and is pulled towards the other vertices, but does not pass through them. You can view the frame of the spline by setting the SPLFRAME system variable on.

Related System Variables

SPLINETYPE, SPLINESEGS, SPLFRAME

Tips

If you use the Edit vertex option, the X marker appears on the frame regardless of the current SPLFRAME setting.

The greater the value for SPLINESEGS, the more precise the curve will be, and the closer to the control points it will be. If you enter a negative number, you end up with a smoother curve. Setting SPLINESEGS to a negative number is not allowed for 3D polylines.

If the polyline is defined with arcs, the arcs are straightened when viewing the spline (SPLFRAME set to 1).

If a polyline is made up of multiple widths, the spline tapers from the beginning width definition to the ending width definition.

Warning

If you edit a spline-curved polyline with the BREAK, EXPLODE, or TRIM commands, the Decurve option will no longer be available and there will be no associated frame.

See also: PEDIT Decurve, Fit Curve

PEDIT Decurve

The Decurve option removes the curves from any polyline that is either Fit curved or Spline curved, and returns the polyline to its original state.

PEDIT Undo

The PEDIT Undo option takes you back one PEDIT option at a time. This is different from the UNDO command, which backsteps to the previous command. If you issued four PEDIT options, for example, all four PEDIT options would be reversed or undone by one use of the UNDO command or four uses of the PEDIT Undo option.

See also: UNDO

PEDIT eXit

Use eXit to leave the PEDIT command and return to the command prompt. The PEDIT command default is eXit. You also can press <^C> to cancel.

PEDIT Smooth surface / Desmooth

The Smooth option replaces a 3D mesh with a smooth surface. The Desmooth option returns a smooth 3D mesh to its original state.

Related System Variables
SURFTYPE, SPLFRAME

Warnings

Meshes that contain more than 11 vertices in either the M or N direction cannot be changed into a Bézier surface.

Cubic B-spline surfaces require a minimum control point mesh size of 4×4.

Quadratic B-spline surfaces require a minimum control point mesh size of 3×3.

The Mopen/Mclose option opens or closes a 3D mesh in the M direction. The Nopen/Nclose option opens or closes a 3D mesh in the N direction.

PFACE

Screen **[DRAW] [next] [3D Surfs] [PFACE:]**
Screen **[SURFACES] [PFACE:]**

The PFACE (PolyFACE) (Release 11 only) command creates arbitrary polyface meshes. The mesh is composed of vertices and faces that you specify. It is used mainly for AutoLISP and ADS applications.

Prompts
Vertex 1:
Face 1, vertex 1:

Options

VERTEX   Specifies the location for each vertex.

FACE   Specifies the vertex numbers that define each face.

Related System Variable

PFACEVMAX

Tips

You can make the edges of the polyface mesh invisible by entering a negative vertex number for the beginning vertex of the edge.

You can use the LAYER and COLOR commands when defining faces. Enter L or LAYER and C or COLOR when prompted to define a face. Changing the layer and color does not affect any new entities you create for subsequent commands.

Warning

You must keep track of each vertex and its number assignment in order to define the faces.

See also: EDGESURF, REVSURF, RULESURF, TABSURF, 3DFACE

PLAN

Screen **[DISPLAY] [PLAN:]**
Pull down **[Display] [Plan View (UCS)]** *or* **[Plan View (World)]**

The PLAN command displays the plan view of any defined UCS or the WCS. A plan view is defined as having a view point of 0,0,1. The default setting is <Current UCS>.

Prompt

<Current UCS>/UCS/World:

Options

Current UCS   Restores the plan view of the current UCS (the default).

UCS   Restores the plan view of a previously defined UCS.

World   Restores the plan view of the WCS.

Related System Variable

UCSFOLLOW

See also: UCS, VPOINT

PLINE

Screen **[DRAW] [PLINE:]**
Pull down **[Draw] [Polyline]**

A polyline is a series of line and arc segments that share the same vertices and are processed as a single entity. The PLINE command draws 2D polylines. It has a line mode and an arc mode, each with different prompts. You start both modes by specifying a From point. To edit polylines, you can use PEDIT and most of the regular edit commands.

Prompts

```
From point:
Current line-width is 0.0000
Arc/Close/Halfwidth/Length/Undo/Width/<Endpoint of line>:
Angle/CEnter/CLose/Direction/Halfwidth/Line/Radius/
Second pt/Undo/Width/<Endpoint of arc>:
```

Options

Arc	Switches from drawing polylines to polyarcs and activates a submenu for the polyarc options.
Angle	A polyarc option in which you specify the included angle. Because arcs are drawn counterclockwise, use a negative angle if you want to draw the arc clockwise.
CEnter	Specifies the center of the arc.
Close	Similar to the close option for lines and polylines; however, an arc is used to close the segments.
Direction	Specifies a starting direction.
Line	Switches you back into line mode.
Radius	Specifies the radius of the arc.
Second pt	Allows you to construct a three-point arc.
Close	Closes the polyline segments created during a PLINE command and connects the start point to the end point.
Halfwidth	Specifies the width from the center of a polyline to one of its edges. The number is doubled for the actual width.
Length	Lets you specify the length of a new polyline segment at the same angle as the last polyline segment. If you use this option after constructing a polyarc, the polyline will be tangent to the polyarc.
Undo	Undoes a line segment and returns you to the previous point.
Width	Creates polylines with width and mitered intersections. You can construct polyline segments with tapers by defining different starting and ending widths. Once you have drawn a tapered line segment, the next segment defaults to the ending width of the previous segment. The default width is zero.

Tips

DONUTS, ELLIPSES, and POLYGONS are created from 2D polylines.

If you draw polylines with an assigned width just to achieve line weights on the finished plot, you can get the same effect by assigning colors to represent different line weights and plotting with different pen point thicknesses.

See also: AREA, CHAMFER, FILL, FILLET, OFFSET, PEDIT, 3D POLYLINE

PLOT / PRPLOT

Main Menu **Option 3 (Plot a drawing)**
Main Menu **Option 4 (Printer Plot a drawing)**
Screen **[PLOT] [PLOTTER]** *or* **[PRINTER]**
Pull down **[File] [Plot]** *or* **[Print]**

PLOT and PRPLOT (PRinter PLOT) are the two methods you can use to get a hard copy of your drawing file. The PLOT command directs your drawing to a plotter or to a plot file. The PRPLOT command directs your drawing to a printer plotter (dot matrix or laser printer) or to a PRPLOT file.

You can plot from the Main Menu or within the Drawing Editor. If you plot from the Main Menu, you are asked which drawing file you want to plot. If you plot from within the Drawing Editor, AutoCAD assumes that you want to plot the current drawing. Only layers that are set to On and Thawed are plotted.

In model space, the plot depends on the current viewport and the chosen plotting options. In paper space, the plot depends on how much of the drawing (including viewports) falls within the chosen plotting options. Viewports turned off are not plotted.

The initial default settings for plotting are determined when you configure your plotter and printer. Changes to the default settings are stored between editing sessions.

Prompts

```
Specify the part of the drawing to be plotted by entering:
Display, Extents, Limits, View or Window <D>:
```

Options

Display   Plots what is visible in the current viewport in both model space and paper space. If you are issuing the command from the Main Menu, the last view or viewport visible when the drawing was last ended or saved is plotted.

Extents   The plot is based on the drawing extents. It takes into account all drawing entities regardless of the limits setting.

Limits   The plot is based on the drawing limits. If the current viewport is not a plan view (0,0,1), the plot is then based on ZOOM Extents.

View   Plots a previously saved view.

Window   Plots the area you designate as a Window by picking two diagonal coordinates. You can enter two coordinates with your pointing device or you can type in the absolute coordinates. If perspective is on, you cannot use this option.

After you have specified the part of the drawing to be plotted, AutoCAD asks if you want to change the current plotting parameters. If you answer yes, you are shown the following current pen assignments for each color:

Entity Color	Pen No.	Line Type	Pen Speed	Entity Color	Pen No.	Line Type	Pen Speed
1 (red)	1	0	38	9	1	0	38
2 (yellow)	2	0	38	10	2	0	38
3 (green)	3	0	38	11	3	0	38
4 (cyan)	4	0	38	12	4	0	38
5 (blue)	5	0	38	13	5	0	38
6 (magenta)	6	0	38	14	6	0	38
7 (white)	7	0	38	15	7	0	38
8	8	0	38				

Line types   0 = continuous line
1 = ...
2 = ...
3 = ------------
4 = - - - - - - -

```
Enter values, blank=Next value, Cn=Color n, S=Show current values, X=Exit
```

For each color (Entity Color), you can assign a different plotter pen (Pen No.), linetype, and pen speed depending on the plotter for which AutoCAD is configured.

blank=Next value   Once you have entered the appropriate number, press <RETURN> or <SPACE> to go to the next parameter. If you continue pressing <RETURN>, you will end up at the beginning and can begin the process all over again.

Cn=Color n	If you want to jump to the next entity color, type C. If you want to go directly to a specific entity color, type C and the number assigned to the color. If, for example, you want to go directly to Entity Color number 6, type C6.
S=Show current values	Shows the current values of pen number, linetype, and pen speed assignments.
X=Exit	When you have completed pen number, linetype, and pen speed assignments, enter an X to go to the next prompt.

After you have exited from assigning pens, you are prompted to establish the following plotting parameters.

`Write the plot to a file? <N>`

If you answer yes, AutoCAD creates a plot file. The file extension for a plotter is PLT and for a printer is LST.

If you answer no, AutoCAD plots directly to the plotter or printer.

`Size units (Inches or Millimeters) <I>:`

Establishes the plot size in inches or millimeters.

`Plot origin in Inches <0.00,0.00>:`

Plot origin in inches is based on the plotter or printer for which you are configured. The plot origin for plotters usually is located at the lower left-hand corner of the paper; for printers, the upper left-hand corner. To obtain multiple plots on one sheet of paper, you can change the plotting origin for each plot.

Standard values for plotting size

Size	Width	Height
A	10.50	8.00
B	16.00	10.00
C	21.00	16.00
D	33.00	21.00
E	43.00	33.00
MAX	64.50	36.00

`Enter the Size or Width,Height (in Inches) <MAX>:`

These values are general in nature and can change depending on the available paper size and hardware. You can enter your own set of values, which are stored to the name USER.

`Rotate plot 0/90/180/270 <0>:`

Rotates the drawing on the paper. You can answer no for 0 degrees rotation or yes for 270 degrees rotation. Rotations of 90 and 180 degrees are available in Release 11 only.

`Pen Width in Inches <0.010>:`

The pen tip width is requested so AutoCAD can optimize the number of pen strokes to fill in any polylines, solids, and traces.

`Adjust area fill boundaries for pen width? <N>`

This is used for plotting, not prplots. If you answer yes, AutoCAD will maintain dimensional accuracy when plotting with wide pens on all boundaries for polylines, solids, and traces.

`Remove hidden lines? <N>`

If your drawing is constructed with 3D entities in model space, you can have hidden edges removed during the plot. You must answer yes even if you executed the HIDE command before entering the plot command.

By using the MVIEW command's Hideplot option in paper space, you can instruct AutoCAD to perform hidden line removal on a viewport's contents during a paper space plot.

```
Plotted Inches=Drawing Units or Fit or ? <F>:
```

This prompt gives you three choices of scaling your drawing. You should draft at full scale and then scale the drawing to the paper at plot time or in paper space.

```
Plotted Inches=Drawing Units
```

Tells what scale to plot the drawing. You do this by specifying how many plotted inches equal how many drawing units. You can change the plotted scale and the paper size with each plot.

```
Fit
```

This option lets you have AutoCAD determine a plotting scale that is as large as possible to fit the selected plot area.

```
?
```

Displays a help screen that describes the plotting scale options.

```
Position paper in plotter.
Press to continue or S to Stop for hardware setup.
```

Some plotters allow you to change other settings, such as pen pressure and acceleration. If your plotter has these features, you may want to stop for additional hardware setup.

You can terminate the plot by pressing <^C> to cancel. Your plotter may have an internal or external buffer so the plotting may not cancel immediately if the buffer already has processed information.

Tips

If you want to assign the same plotting parameter (pen number, linetype, or pen speed) globally, you can enter an asterisk (*) before the value. This will update the current parameter and any that follow it.

You can create a DXB file by configuring AutoCAD for the ADI plotter driver and by selecting the DXB file output option.

Warning

AutoCAD does not retain plot settings for each drawing. It remembers only the last plotting parameters.

See also: LIMITS, VIEW, ZOOM

POINT

Screen **[DRAW] [next] [POINT:]**
Pull down **[Draw] [Point]**

The POINT command creates a point entity in X,Y,Z space. Points often are used as reference markers. You can use the POINT command to place points in your drawing. Place a point by absolute, relative, or polar coordinates, or pick a point in the drawing with your pointing device. You can osnap to points using the NODe option.

Prompt
```
Point:
```

Related System Variables
PDMODE, PDSIZE

Tip
Points that are placed on the DEFPOINTS layer by associative dimensioning are not affected by PDMODE or PDSIZE.

Warning
Unlike blips, points are part of the drawing and will plot. If you do not want the points to plot, you can erase them, create them on a layer and turn it off, or set PDMODE to 1.

See also: DIVIDE, MEASURE

Point Filters

Screen **[DRAW] [LINE:]** *or* **[DRAW] [next] [POINT:]**
Screen **[SURFACES] [3DFACE:]** *or* **[3DPOLY:]**
Screen **[INQUIRY] [ID:]**
Pull down **[Assist] [FILTERS >]**

Point filtering lets you use the coordinate components of existing points in your drawing to build a new point. You can use any combination of existing X, Y, and Z values and new values entered by the keyboard.

Options

X	Accepts the X value of the next point.
Y	Accepts the Y value of the next point.
Z	Accepts the Z value of the next point.
XY	Accepts the XY value of the next point.
XZ	Accepts the XZ value of the next point.
YZ	Accepts the YZ value of the next point.

Default XYZ

Tip
Use filters to specify a Z value when working in 3D.

See also: POINT, Point Entry

POLYGON

Screen **[DRAW] [next] [POLYGON:]**
Pull down **[Draw] [Polygon]**

The POLYGON command draws 2D regular polygons with the number of sides ranging between 3 and 1024. You can draw a polygon by inscribing or circumscribing a circle. Because polygons are closed polylines, they can be edited with the PEDIT command.

Prompts
Number of sides:
Edge/<Center of polygon>:

Options

Edge	Specifies the size by picking the endpoints of one edge.
Center of polygon	Specifies the center point about which the polygon will be drawn. All vertices are equidistant from the center point.

Inscribed in circle   Makes the vertices touch the circumference of an imaginary circle.

Circumscribed about circle   Makes the midpoint of each edge touch the circumference of an imaginary circle.

Tips

Polygons contain no tangent information and are drawn with 0 (zero) line width regardless of the default polyline width. You can use the PEDIT command and assign a width and tangents once you create a polygon.

You can establish a default by selecting [Options]—[Polygon Creation] from the pull-down menus. The defaults are available only in the current drawing session and are activated when you select [Polygon] from the pull-down menu.

See also: PEDIT, POLYLINE

PSPACE

Pull down **[Display] [Mview >} [Pspace]**

The PSPACE (Paper SPACE) command (Release 11 only) switches you from drawing in model space to paper space. The letter P appears on the status line and the paper space icon is displayed in the lower left corner of your drawing when you are working in paper space. UCSICON must be on in paper space to see the icon.

Related System Variable

TILEMODE

Tips

You have more flexibility when you dimension in model space, as well as having the advantage of associative dimensioning when editing your drawing.

Paper space and model space retain their own limits.

Warnings

The VPORTS command is disabled when you are working in paper space. Use the Save and Restore options of the VIEW command.

The system variable UCSFOLLOW has no effect in paper space.

See also: MSPACE, MVIEW, TILEMODE, UCSICON, VIEW, VPLAYER, VPORTS

PURGE

Screen **[UTILITY] [PURGE:]**

The PURGE command will delete or eliminate unused blocks, dimstyles, layers, linetypes, shapes, and text styles. You set up the command by indicating the symbol types that you want to purge. PURGE prompts you for a confirmation before purging each item.

Prompts

Purge unused Blocks/Dimstyles/LAyers/LTypes/SHapes/
STyles/All:

Options

Blocks	Deletes unused blocks.
Dimstyles	Deletes unused dimension styles.
LAyers	Deletes unused layers.
LTypes	Deletes unused lineypes.

SHapes   Deletes unused shapes.

STyles   Deletes unused styles.

All   Deletes all unused symbols. You are prompted individually for each item.

Tips

Purging is a good way to reduce drawing file size.

You cannot purge layer 0, the continuous linetype, or the text style STANDARD.

The following commands have their own Delete options: VIEW, UCS, and VPORT.

Warnings

You must issue the PURGE command before you alter the database during the current editing session.

Because blocks can be nested and drawn on multiple layers, you can purge only one reference level at a time. Once you have completed the PURGE command, you may want to end the drawing and reopen the file, then issue PURGE a second time. You may have to do this several times to purge all unused items.

QTEXT

Screen **[SETTINGS] [next] [QTEXT:]**

The QTEXT (Quick TEXT) command is a mode that displays boxes in place of text strings (including attributes) to save time redrawing or regenerating text. The box is the approximate height and length of the text string.

Prompt

ON/OFF <Off>:

Options

ON   Displays text strings as boxes.

OFF   Displays text strings normally.

Related System Variable

QTEXTMODE

Tips

If QTEXT is on, any new text you enter will display normally until the drawing regenerates.

If QTEXT is on and you use the CHANGE or DDEDIT command to edit the text, or you use the LIST command for database information, the actual text is edited or listed.

Warning

Qtext boxes may take up more space than the actual text string.

See also: REGEN

QUIT

Screen **[UTILITY] [QUIT]**
Pull down **[File] [Quit]**

The QUIT command exits the Drawing Editor without updating the drawing file. The drawing is unmodified from the last SAVE or END command.

Prompt

Really want to discard all changes to drawing?

Options

Yes   AutoCAD quits and does not update the drawing since the last END or SAVE was issued. This returns you to the Main Menu.

No   AutoCAD does not quit, but keeps you in the Drawing Editor.

See also: END, SAVE

REDEFINE/UNDEFINE

Type **REDEFINE** *or* **UNDEFINE**

UNDEFINE disables built-in AutoCAD commands so you can replace them with another command of the same name if you use AutoLISP or another programming method. REDEFINE restores the original AutoCAD command. To redefine or undefine a command, type the command name in response to the prompt.

Prompt

Command name:

Option

.(period)   Preceding an undefined command name with a period recalls the original AutoCAD command for that single condition. If you attempt to execute a command that has been undefined, you will get the message Unknown command.

Tip

REDEFINE and UNDEFINE are valid only for the current editing session.

REDRAW/REDRAWALL

Screen **[DISPLAY] [REDRAW:]** *or* **[REDRALL:]**
Screen **[* * * *] [REDRAW]**
Pull down **[Display] [Redraw]**

REDRAW cleans up the current viewport by redrawing the screen. REDRAWALL cleans up all viewports. Blips are removed and any entities or parts of entities that disappeared, or seemed erased due to editing, are redrawn. Grid dots are redrawn if the grid is on. These also can be executed transparently.

Tips

Entities are redrawn on layers that are turned off even though they are not seen; entities on frozen layers are not redrawn.

Grid density affects redraw speed.

See also: REGEN, REGENALL, TRANSPARENT, VIEWRES, BLIPMODE

REGEN/REGENALL

Screen **[DISPLAY] [REGEN:]** *or* **[REGNALL:]**

REGEN causes the current viewport to be regenerated. REGENALL regenerates all viewports. When a drawing is regenerated, all the data and geometry associated with an entity are recalculated. Changes made to some existing entities require a regeneration before they are made visible. You can stop a regeneration by pressing <^C> to cancel. You can control automatic regenerations with the REGENAUTO command. REGEN and REGENALL cannot be executed transparently.

Tip

Entities on layers that are turned off are regenerated even though they are not seen; entities on frozen layers are not regenerated.

See also: EDIT, REDRAW, REDRAWALL, REGENAUTO, VIEWRES

REGENAUTO

Screen **[DISPLAY] [RGNAUTO:]**

REGENAUTO lets you suppress some (not all) regenerations. By default, REGENAUTO is on.

Prompt

ON/OFF <On>:

Options

ON   Enables all regenerations. Turning it on creates a regeneration.

OFF   Suppresses regenerations.

Related System Variables

REGENMODE, EXPERT

Tip

If REGENAUTO is off and AutoCAD wants to regenerate, the program prompts About to regen, proceed? <Y>, unless the EXPERT system variable is set greater than 0.

See also: REGEN, REGENALL, VIEWRES

RENAME

Screen **[UTILITY] [RENAME:]**

RENAME lets you rename blocks, layers, linetypes, styles, UCS, views, and viewport configurations (Release 11 only). Use RENAME when you need to change naming standards, or when you encounter typing errors in existing named items.

Prompts

Block/Dimstyle/LAyer/LType/Style/Ucs/VIew/VPort:
Old (object) name:
New (object) name:

Tip

You can rename a layer with the DDLMODES command and a UCS with the DDUCS command.

Warning

You cannot rename layer 0, external reference layers, the Continuous linetype, or shapes.

See also: FILES

REVSURF

Screen **[DRAW] [next] [3D Surfs] [REVSURF:]**
Screen **[SURFACES] [REVSURF:]**
Pull down **[Draw] [Surfaces...] [REVOLUTION]**

REVSURF (SURface of REVolution) is one method of generating a 3D polygon mesh. REVSURF revolves a selected profile or "path curve" around an axis.

The profile or path curve can be made of a single line, arc, circle, 2D polyline, or 3D polyline. The path curve defines the N direction of the surface polygon mesh.

The axis can be a line or an open 2D or 3D polyline. If you use a polyline, the revolution axis is considered a line from the first vertex to the last vertex, omitting any other vertices. The axis defines the M direction of the surface mesh. After you specify the path curve and the revolution axis, you specify a starting angle and an included angle. The default settings are a starting angle of 0 and a 360-degree included angle (full circle).

Prompts
```
Select path curve:
Select axis of revolution:
Start angle <0>:
Included angle (+=ccw, -=cw) <Full circle>:
```

Options

Start angle   Determines the start of the surface of revolution. It can be offset from the path curve.

Included angle   Determines the distance of revolution around the axis.

Related System Variables
SURFTAB1, SURFTAB2

Tip
The direction of revolution is determined by the right-hand rule of rotation and the point used to pick the axis of rotation. In the right-hand rule, with only the thumb extended and pointing in the positive axis direction, the fingers curve in the direction of positive rotation.

See also: EXPLODE, PEDIT, 3DMESH

ROTATE

Screen **[EDIT] [next] [ROTATE:]**
Pull down **[Modify] [Rotate]**

ROTATE lets you rotate entities around a designated base. After you specify a base point, you specify a relative rotation angle or a reference angle. The default is <Rotation angle>.

Prompts
```
Select objects:
Base point:
<Rotation angle>/Reference:
```

Options

Rotation angle   The amount entities are rotated from their current orientation. A positive number creates a counterclockwise rotation; a negative number creates a clockwise rotation.

Reference   Prompts for the current reference angle and the new reference angle. The selected objects are rotated to the new angle.

See also: CHANGE, DIM TRotate, INSERT, SNAP, UCS

RULESURF

Screen **[DRAW] [next] [3D Surfs] [RULSURF:]**
Screen **[SURFACES] [RULSURF:]**
Pull down **[Draw] [Surfaces...] [RULED Surface]**

RULESURF (RULEd SURFace) generates a 3D polygon mesh depicting the ruled surface between two entities.

The two entities can be points, lines, arcs, circles, 2D polylines, or 3D polylines. If one boundary is a circle or closed polyline, then the other boundary must be closed. A point can be used with any open or closed boundary.

Prompts
```
Select first defining curve:
Select second defining curve:
```

Related System Variable
SURFTAB1

See also: EXPLODE, PEDIT, 3DMESH

SAVE

Screen **[SAVE:]**
Pull down **[File] [Save]**

The SAVE command lets you update your drawing file by saving it to disk without exiting from the Drawing Editor. The current drawing file is the default name. You can specify another directory and file name. Each time you save, the previous saved drawing is renamed as the backup (BAK) drawing.

Prompt
```
File name <default>:
```

Related System Variable
FILEDIA

Tip
If you enter a tilde (~) at the prompt, AutoCAD displays the File dialogue box if the system variable FILEDIA is set to 0.

Warning
Do not include the drawing extension DWG. It is assumed.

See also: Dialogue boxes, END

SCALE

Screen **[EDIT] [next] [SCALE:]**
Pull down **[Modify] [Scale]**

SCALE gives you the ability to change the size of existing entities. You determine the base point by which you want to scale the entities and provide either an overall scale factor or scale a specific dimension to a new distance.

Prompts
```
Select objects:
Base point:
<Scale factor>/Reference:
```

Options

Scale factor Provides a value to multiply the X, Y, and Z dimensions. A value greater than 1 enlarges the entities; a value between 0 and 1 reduces the size of the entities.

Reference Specifies an existing dimension and the new length you want the reference length to become.

Warning
You cannot scale X, Y, or Z values independently.

See also: CHANGE, INSERT, PLOT

SCRIPT

Screen **[UTILITY] [SCRIPT:]**

SCRIPT files automate routine tasks. A script file is an ASCII text file created with a text editor (such as EDLIN) that contains commands and responses in the exact order of execution. The file has the extension SCR. The script can be executed with the SCRIPT command to perform the series of commands.

You can execute script files from the operating system prompt by following the program name ACAD with a space and the drawing name, then a space and the script file name without the extension. To execute a script file while in the drawing, use the SCRIPT command. The default script name is the current drawing file name. DELAY, RESUME, and RSCRIPT are commands that control the running of the script.

Prompt
Script file <*default*>:

Options

DELAY   Creates a pause, in milliseconds, between commands. The maximum delay number is 32767, just under 33 seconds depending on the computer.

RESUME   If <^C> or <BS> is pressed, the script file is interrupted. To reactivate the script, enter the RESUME command. If the script stopped in the middle of a command, you may need to type the command with a leading apostrophe ('RESUME).

RSCRIPT   RSCRIPT (Repeat SCRIPT) is used mainly to repeat the script file during slide show presentations.

Related System Variable
FILEDIA

See also: Dialogue boxes, MSLIDE, VSLIDE

SELECT

Screen **[EDIT] [next] [SELECT:]**

SELECT lets you pick entities to be retained as the next selection set. If you are required to select entities at the next Command: prompt, you can use the Previous option to recall the selection set. You create the selection set with the standard object selection options.

Prompt
Select objects:

Tip
You cannot select model space entities when working in paper space and vice versa.

SETVAR

Screen **[* * * *] [SETVAR:]**
Screen **[SETTINGS] [next] [SETVAR:]**
Pull down **[Settings] [Set SysVars]**

The SETVAR command is used to modify system variables. Most system variables are modified through AutoCAD commands. A few system variables are "read-only."

AutoCAD saves system variables as integers, reals, points, or text strings. Most are saved in the drawing file, and a few in the general configuration file, but some are retained only for the current editing session. You can issue SETVAR transparently.

Prompts
```
Variable name or ?:
New value for varname <current>:
```

Options

Variable name   Enter the name of a variable to change.

?   Activates the wild-card options for reviewing variable settings. The default, an asterisk, displays a sorted list of all variables. You can use any of the wild-card options to create a more specific list.

Tip
If you use Release 11, you can modify most system variables by typing the variable name at the Command: prompt. Owners of Release 10 (or earlier releases) must use the SETVAR command. A variable with the same name as a command name must be changed with the SETVAR command.

SHADE

Screen **[DISPLAY] [SHADE:]**
Pull down **[Display] [Shade]**

The SHADE command produces a shaded rendering of the current viewport. SHADE (Release 11 only) produces the same results as the AutoSHADE 2.0 command Quick Shade. Only one light source is used. The only way you can control this command is by changing the settings of the system variables SHADEDGE and SHADEDIF.

Related System Variables
SHADEDGE, SHADEDIF

Tips
SHADEDGE determines the manner in which faces and edges are displayed. Some methods require a 256-color display.

SHADEDIF determines the manner in which the model is illuminated. SHADE DIFfuse defaults to 70. In other words, 70 percent of the light is diffuse reflection from the light source and 30 percent is ambient light. The value can be set anywhere from 1 to 100. A higher setting increases diffuse lighting and adds more reflectivity and contrast to the image.

Create slides of shaded viewports for later viewing.

Warning
Shaded images do not plot.

See also: MSLIDE, VSLIDE

SHAPE

Screen **[DRAW] [next] [SHAPE:]**

Shapes are an alternative to blocks. Shape definitions are stored in shape files. Each shape file can contain numerous symbol definitions. The shape file (extension SHP) must be compiled from AutoCAD's Main Menu option 7. The extension for a compiled shape file is SHX. Once the shape file is compiled, it must be loaded with the LOAD command before it can be used. The SHAPE command inserts a defined shape into the drawing.

Prompts
```
Shape name (or ?):
Starting point:
Height <1.0>:
Rotation angle <0>:
```

Options

?   Activates wild-card options for reviewing the names of shapes defined in the drawing. The default, an asterisk, displays a list of all loaded shapes. You can use any of the wild-card options to create a more specific list.

LOAD   Loads a shape (SHX) file.

LOAD ? List currently loaded shape files.

Related System Variable
FILEDIA

Tips

Shape files can be used to produce special text fonts and symbols.

Shapes regenerate much faster than the same symbols stored as blocks and take less space.

Warning

Even though shape definitions require less memory, they are not as desirable as block definitions. They cannot be exploded or scaled differently in X,Y directions. Shape files are external to the drawing file and always must accompany the drawing file in a drawing exchange.

See also: BLOCK, PURGE,

SHELL/SH

Screen **[UTILITY] [External Commands] [SH:]** *or* **[SHELL:]**

SHELL (or SH) functions as a gateway between AutoCAD, the operating system (such as DOS), and other external programs. If you press <RETURN> once after you type SHELL or SH, you can issue a single operating system command and immediately return to AutoCAD. If you press <RETURN> at the OS Command: prompt, you stay in the operating system until you type EXIT to return to AutoCAD. You can execute most operating system commands when you enter the operating system. It is also possible to access other software programs via SHELL, depending on their memory requirements.

Prompt
OS Command:

Option

It is easy to forget you have shelled out of AutoCAD and into the operating system or another program. If you are shelled to the operating system, you will see two greater-than symbols (>>) at the command prompt instead of the normal single greater-than symbol (>).

Tip

AutoCAD 386 Release 11 owners can use the SHROOM utility included with AutoCAD to release the maximum amount of memory for external programs.

Warnings

Make sure that you exit from the SHELL command from the same directory as the one you entered.

Do not issue a CHKDSK/F while you are shelled out of AutoCAD.

Do not delete any temporary AutoCAD files. They usually have a $ symbol in the file name or extension or lock files where the last character in the extension is a K (??K).

Do not load any RAM-resident programs while you work in the shell; they should be loaded before you enter AutoCAD.

Do not run programs (such as BASIC) that reset the I/O ports.

SKETCH

Screen **[DRAW] [next] [SKETCH:]**

The SKETCH command enables you to draw free-hand in contiguous short line segments with an imaginary pen. You first specify line segment length, then sketch temporary line segments. A Record option stores the line segments when you are finished. You have the option of setting a system variable (SKPOLY) to sketch either lines or polylines. The default setting is to sketch lines with a record increment of .1. You must have a pointing device, such as a mouse or digitizer, to use SKETCH.

Prompts

```
Record increment <0.1000>:
Sketch.  Pen eXit Quit Record Erase Connect.
```

Options

Pen   A toggle switch for the up or down pen position. Sketching begins when the pen is down and proceeds until you press **P** on the keyboard, or release the pick button on your pointing device.

eXit   Records temporary line segments and exits from the SKETCH command.

Quit   Discards temporary line segments and exits from the SKETCH command.

Record   Records temporary line segments and remains in the SKETCH command.

Erase   Erases temporary line segments in the opposite order in which they were entered as you move your pointing device back over the line segments.

Connect   By moving your pointing device close to the endpoint of the last temporary line segment, you can connect to that endpoint and continue sketching.

. (period)   Draws a single line segment from the last point to the current pointing device location.

You can press <^C> to cancel SKETCH.

The buttons on a pointing device are redefined during the sketch mode to the following:

Puck Command	Keyboard	Function
Pick	P	pen up/down
1		single line
2	R	record lines
3	X	exit
4	Q	quit (<^C>)
5	E	erase
6	C	connect

Related System Variables
SKETCHINC, SKPOLY

Tip
You can toggle Snap, Grid, and Ortho on and off while sketching. To get smoother sketch lines, keep Snap off.

Warning

If you sketch too fast, you may hear a beep indicating that AutoCAD is using all available memory. Slow down and then proceed with your work.

SNAP

Type **<^B>** *or* **<F9>**
Screen **[SETTINGS] [next] [SNAP:]**
Pull down **[Settings] [Snap On/Off ^B]**

SNAP is a drawing aid that restricts the crosshairs' movement to a specified increment. You can modify the increment value and turn SNAP on or off as needed. The default is a SNAP increment of 1.0000 and off. On DOS systems, <^B> and <F9> will toggle SNAP on or off. You also can change your snap settings with the DDRMODES dialogue box.

Prompt

Snap spacing or ON/OFF/Aspect/Rotate/Style <1.0000>:

Options

Snap spacing	Set the X,Y snap increment values. Changing snap settings turns SNAP On.
ON	Turn snap on.
OFF	Turn snap off.
Aspect	Set individual horizontal (X) and vertical (Y) snap increments. This option is not available if you are in isometric mode.
Rotate	Rotate the snap (and grid) by any specified angle about a base point.
Style	Allows selection of the standard or isometric styles.
Iso	Set isometric SNAP and GRID style.
Standard	Return from isometric mode to normal SNAP (and GRID) style.

Related System Variables

SNAPANG, SNAPBASE, SNAPISOPAIR, SNAPMODE, SNAP- STYL, SNAPUNIT

Tips

Typed coordinates, distances, and OSNAPs override SNAP.

Each viewport retains its own SNAP setting.

Screen crosshairs are oriented to the current snap rotation angle. ORTHO forces lines to be drawn orthogonally in relation to the crosshair orientation.

Warning

SNAP is inactive during perspective views.

See also: DDRMODES, GRID, ISOPLANE, OSNAP

SOLAREA

Screen **[SOLIDS] [INQUIRY] [SOLAREA:]**
Pull down **[Sol-Prim's] [INQUIRY >] [Solid Area]**

The SOLAREA (SOLid AREA) (Release 11 only) command calculates the surface area of solid entities. Picking more than one solid results in the sum of all solids picked.

Area calculations are derived from meshing the surfaces of the selected solids and then adding the area of the faces of the mesh. The areas of curved surfaces are only an approximation. Therefore, increasing the wire mesh density improves the accuracy.

Prompts
```
Select solids for surface area computation...
Select objects:
```

Related System Variables
SOLAREAU, SOLWDENS

Warning
When calculating curved surfaces, SOLAREA's results are only approximate.

See also: AMELITE

SOLBOX

Screen **[SOLIDS] [SOLBOX:]**
Pull down **[Sol-Prim's] [Box]**

The SOLBOX (SOLid BOX) command (Release 11 only) creates 3D solid boxes. The defaults expect you to define two diagonal corner points and a height.

Prompts
```
Corner of box:
Cube/Length/<Other corner>:
Height:
```

Options

Cube	All sides (length, width, depth) of the box are equal.
Length	You individually define the length (X axis), width (Y axis), and height (Z axis).
Other corner	Specify a diagonal corner point by entering a coordinate or by picking a point on the drawing. Once you have specified the corner point, you are asked to determine the height. If the second corner point coordinates contained a Z value, the prompt uses that Z value as its default.

See also: AMELITE

SOLCONE

Screen **[SOLIDS] [SOLCONE:]**
Pull down **[Sol-Prim's] [Cone]**

The SOLCONE (SOLid CONE) command (Release 11 only) creates a 3D solid cone. You define the center point, radius (default) or diameter, and height.

Prompts
```
Center point:
Diameter/<Radius>:
Height of cone:
```

Options

Diameter	Specify the diameter by entering a value or by picking two points.
Radius	Specify the radius by entering a value or by picking two points.

Warning
The elliptical selection [Elliptcl] on the screen menu is available only with full AME.

See also: AMELITE

SOLCYL

Screen **[SOLIDS] [SOLCYL:]**
Pull down **[Sol-Prim's] [Cylinder]**

The SOLCYL (SOLid CYLinder) command (Release 11 only) creates a 3D solid cylinder column. You specify the center point, radius (default) or diameter, and height.

Prompts
```
Center point:
Diameter/<Radius>:
Height of cylinder:
```

Options

Diameter   Specify the diameter by inputing a value or by picking two points.

Radius   Specify the radius by inputing a value or by picking two points.

Warning
The elliptical selection [Elliptcl] on the screen menu is available only with full AME.

See also: AMELITE

SOLEXT

Screen **[SOLIDS] [SOLEXT:]**
Pull down **[Sol-Prim's] [Extrude]**

The SOLEXT (SOLid EXTrude) command (Release 11 only) lets you create unique solid entities by extruding existing polyline, polygon, circle, ellipse, and 3Dpoly entities.

Prompts
```
Select polylines and circles for extrusion...
Height of extrusion:
Extrusion taper angle from Z <0>:
```

Related System Variable
SOLDELENT

Tip
The SOLDELENT system variable controls whether the selected entities are deleted (the default) or kept in the drawing file after being extruded.

Warnings
Polyline segments must contain at least three vertices. If the segments overlap, they cannot be extruded. Open polyline segments are closed automatically when extruded.

Wide polylines are extruded based on the center of the polyline. The width is converted to 0.

See also: AMELITE, SOLIDIFY

SOLID

Screen **[DRAW] [next] [SOLID:]**

SOLID draws solid filled areas. These areas can be triangular or quadrilateral. You enter points in a triangular order. The first two points are the endpoints of a starting edge. The next point defines the endpoint of a triangle, or you can enter two more points to define a second (quadrilateral) edge. If FILL or the system variable FILLMODE is on, the areas are filled.

Prompts
First point:
Second point:
Third point:
Fourth point:

Related System Variable
FILLMODE

See also: FILL

SOLIDIFY

Screen **[SOLIDS] [SOLIDIFY]**
Pull down **[Sol-Prim's] [Solidify]**

SOLIDIFY (Release 11 only) converts 2D entities (polyline, polygon, circle, ellipse, trace, donut, and solid) into unique solid entities by extruding them to the value of their thickness.

Related System Variables
SOLDELENT, SOLSOLIDIFY

Tips
The SOLDELENT system variable controls whether the selected entities are deleted (the default) or kept in the drawing file after being extruded.

The SOLSOLIDIFY system variable controls whether solid commands solidify 2D entities when encountered.

Warnings
Polyline segments must contain at least three vertices. If the segments overlap, they cannot be solidified. Open polyline segments automatically are closed when solidified.

Wide polylines are solidified based on the center of the polyline. The width is converted to 0.

See also: AMELITE, SOLEXT

SOLLIST

Screen **[SOLIDS] [INQUIRY] [SOLLIST:]**
Pull down **[Sol-Prim's] [INQUIRY >] [List Solid]**

The SOLLIST (SOLid LIST) command (Release 11 only) provides solid type, area, and material information about selected solids.

Prompt
Tree/<Solid>:

Options
Tree   Displays the definition of a solid model's Constructive Solid Geometry (CSG) tree.

Solid   Displays information about the top level of a solid's Constructive Solid Geometry (CSG) tree.

Related System Variable
SOLPAGELEN

SOLMAT

Screen **[SOLIDS] [UTILITY] [SOLMAT:]**
Pull down **[Sol-Prim's] [UTILITY >] [Material]**

The SOLMAT (SOLid MATerial) command (Release 11 only) maintains a list of materials and assigns their properties to solid entities. You can append new materials to the list and modify existing properties. The following properties are maintained for each material:

Density	kg/cu_m
Young's Modulus	GN/sq_m
Poisson's ratio	
Yield strength	MN/sq_m
Ultimate strength	MN/sq_m
Thermal conductivity	
Linear expansion coeff.	alpha/1e6
Specific heat	kJ/(kg deg_C)

Prompt
Change/Edit/<eXit>/LIst/LOad/New/Remove/SAve/SEt/?:

Options

Change	Changes the material assigned to existing solids.
Edit	Edits the definition of a material loaded in the current drawing.
eXit	Leaves the SOLMAT command and returns to the command: prompt. You also can press <^C> to cancel.
LIst	Displays the definition of a material. You can use wild-card options for reviewing the names of materials defined in the drawing or in files with the extension MAT.
LOad	Loads a material definition into the drawing from an external file.
New	Define a new material. If the material already exists in the current drawing, you are prompted to use the Change option on existing solids with that material.
Remove	Deletes a material definition from your drawing. You can enter the name or use a ? and receive a list of current material definitions.
SAve	Saves a material definition from your drawing into a file. You are warned if the material already exists in that file.
SEt	Specifies a default material for new solids.
?	Lists the materials currently defined in your drawing and external file.

SOLMESH

Screen **[SOLIDS] [DISPLAY] [SOLMESH:]**
Pull down **[Sol-Prim's] [DISPLAY >] [Mesh]**

The SOLMESH (SOLid MESH) command (Release 11 only) displays a solid object as a PFACE entity. The mesh approximates the surfaces of solids by creating multi-edged faces.

You can convert a mesh (SOLMESH) to a wireframe (SOLWIRE) and back. The solid can be displayed only only as a mesh or wireframe, however, not both at the same time.

The mesh model is considered a block reference.

Prompts
Select solids to be meshed...
Select objects:

Related System Variable
SOLWDENS

Warning

Curved surfaces are actually a series of straight edges representing the curve and therefore only are approximations.

See also: AMELITE, BLOCK, HIDE, SHADE, SOLWIRE

SOLPURGE

Screen **[SOLIDS] [UTILITY] [SOLPURG:]**
Pull down **[Sol-Prim's] [UTILITY >] [Purge Solids]**

The SOLPURGE (SOLid PURGE) command (Release 11 only) lets you decrease your drawing size and conserve memory by purging selected solid information.

Prompt

Memory/Bfile/Pmesh/<Erased>:

Options

Memory   Purge memory associated with AME.

Bfile   Purge Bfile entities on a selective basis and reduce the drawing size.

Pmesh   Purge Pmesh entities from the drawing on a selective basis.

Erased   Purge secondary entities associated with erased AME solids.

SOLREV

Screen **[SOLIDS] [SOLREV:]**
Pull down **[Sol-Prim's] [Revolve]**

The SOLREV (SOLid REVolve) command (Release 11 only) creates unique solids by revolving a polyline, polygon, circle, ellipse, or 3D polyline entity about an axis. You can revolve only one entity at a time. A polyline must contain at least three, but not more than 500 vertices.

Prompts

Select polyline or circle for revolution...
Select objects:
Axis of revolution - Entity/X/Y/<Start point of axis>:
Included angle <full circle>:

Options

Entity   The nearest endpoint of the entity becomes the origin of the axis that determines the positive direction of the rotation.

X   The positive X axis of the current UCS is the axis of revolution.

Y   The positive Y axis of the current UCS is the axis of revolution.

Start point of axis   The start point of the axis determines the positive direction of rotation.

Related System Variable
SOLDELENT

Tip

The SOLDELENT system variable controls whether the selected entities are deleted (the default) or kept in the drawing file after being extruded.

Warnings

Polyline segments must contain at least three vertices. If the segments overlap, they cannot be revolved. Open polyline segments are closed automatically when revolved.

Wide polylines are revolved based on the center of the polyline. The width is converted to 0.

SOLSPHERE

Screen **[SOLIDS] [SOLSPH:]**
Pull down **[Sol-Prim's] [Sphere]**

The SOLSPHERE (SOLid SPHERE) command (Release 11 only) creates 3D solid spheres, in which all the surface points are equidistant from the center.

Prompts
Center of sphere:
Diameter/<Radius> of sphere:

Options

Diameter   Create the sphere by specifying its diameter.

Radius   Create the sphere by specifying its radius.

SOLTORUS

Screen **[SOLIDS] [SOLTORS:]**
Pull down **[Sol-Prim's] [Torus]**

The SOLTORUS (SOLid TORUS) command (Release 11 only) creates solid 3D donut-shaped entities. After specifying the center of the torus, you enter two radius or two diameter values, one for the tube and the other for the torus.

Prompts
Center of torus:
Diameter/<Radius> of torus:
Diameter/<Radius> of tube:

Options

Diameter   Create the torus by specifying its diameter.

Radius   Create the torus by specifying its radius.

SOLVAR

Screen **[SOLIDS] [UTILITY] [SOLVAR:]**
Pull down **[Sol-Prim's] [UTILITY >] [Solvars]**

The SOLVAR (SOLid VARiables) command (Release 11 only) lets you set variables controlling the solid modeling environment, similar to the SETVAR command.

Prompt
Variable name or ?:

Options

Variable name   Enter a variable name.

?   List the variables.

Tip

You can enter the variable name directly at the command: prompt in Release 11.

SOLWEDGE

Screen **[SOLIDS] [SOLWEDGE:]**
Pull down **[Sol-Prim's] [Wedge]**

The SOLWEDGE (SOLid WEDGE) command (Release 11 only) creates a wedge. The default expects you to define two diagonal points and the height.

Prompts
```
Corner of wedge:
Length/<Other corner>:
Height:
```
Options

Length	You specify the length (X axis), width (Y axis), and height (Z axis) individually.
Other corner	Specify the opposite corner point by entering a coordinate or by picking a point on the drawing. Once you have defined the base of the wedge, you are prompted for the height. If the <other corner> coordinate contained a Z value, the prompt uses that Z value as its default.

SOLWIRE

Screen **[SOLIDS] [DISPLAY] [SOLWIRE:]**
Pull down **[Sol Prim's] [Sol-DISPLAY] [Wireframe]**

The SOLWIRE (SOLid WIREframe) command (Release 11 only) displays a solid object as a wireframe. The wireframe approximates solids by displaying the edges of faces and the tessellation lines of curved surfaces.

You can convert a wireframe (SOLWIRE) to a mesh (SOLMESH) and back. The solid can be displayed only as mesh or wireframe, but not both at the same time.

Prompts
```
Select solids to be wired...
Select objects:
```
Related System Variable
SOLWDENS

Warning
You must convert solids to a mesh (SOLMESH) before you can shade or remove hidden lines.

See also: SOLMESH

STATUS

Screen **[INQUIRY] [STATUS]**
Pull down **[Utility] [Status]**

STATUS displays information on the current drawing's limits, extents, display, drawing tool settings, and some system information.

See also: LAYER, SETVAR, UNITS

STRETCH

Screen **[EDIT] [next] [STRETCH:]**
Pull down **[Modify] [Stretch]**

STRETCH lets you dynamically lengthen or shorten entities. Place a crossing window around the endpoints of the entities that you want to stretch and then use the keyboard or a pointer to specify displacement.

You can stretch lines, arcs, traces, solids, polylines, and 3D faces. Entity endpoints that lie outside the crossing window remain fixed. Endpoints inside the window change. Text, blocks, and circles move if their definition points are within the crossing window. The definition point for blocks, shapes, and text is the insertion point. For circles, the definition point is the center point. Unlike using other editing commands, you must use a crossing window to select objects.

Prompts
```
Select objects to stretch by window...
Select objects:
First Corner:
Other Corner:
Select Objects:
Base point:
New point:
```

After you specify the base point, you can pick a new point to stretch or move the selected objects, or type an absolute or relative coordinate.

Tips

If dimension text was created with associative dimensioning (DIMASO) on, then STRETCH updates the dimension text. The definition point for dimension text is its middle center point. You can restore dimension text position with HOMETEXT.

Unless you leave one endpoint outside the crossing window, STRETCH acts just like the MOVE command.

Warning

If you pick more than one crossing window, STRETCH uses only the last crossing selection.

See also: CHANGE, EXTEND, TRIM

STYLE

Screen **[DRAW] [DTEXT:] [STYLE:]**
Screen **[DRAW] [TEXT:] [STYLE:]**
Screen **[SETTINGS] [next] [STYLE:]**
Pull down **[Options] [DTEXT OPTIONS >] [Option...]**

The STYLE command lets you create, modify, or list text styles. A style name can be up to 31 characters long. Each text style must reference a font file. Compiled font files have the extension SHX.

Prompts
```
Text style name (or ?) <STANDARD>:
Font file <txt>:
Height <0.0000>:
Width factor <1.00>:
Obliquing angle <0>:
Backwards? <N>
Upside-down? <N>
Vertical? <N>
```

Options

Style name	Create a new style or edit an existing style. Once you end the command, this style becomes the default style.
?	Activate the wild-card options for reviewing the names of styles defined in the current drawing. The default displays a sorted listing of all named styles. Use any wild-card option to create a more specific list.
Font	You supply a font name as the basis for the style. The default is <TXT>.
Height	Set a fixed height, or 0 for a variable height.

Width factor	Specify a width factor to expand or compress text.
Obliquing angle	Slant the text angle. A positive number slants towards the right; a negative number slants towards the left.
Backwards	Mirrors text horizontally.
Upside-down	Mirrors text vertically.
Vertical	Text is drawn vertically.

The STYLE command uses the following default settings:

STANDARD	Obliquing angle = 0
Font = TXT	Backwards = No
Height = 0	Upside-down = No
Width factor = 1	Vertical = No

Related System Variables
TEXTSTYLE, TEXTSIZE, FILEDIA

Tips
If you set the text height to 0, AutoCAD prompts for the text height of each text object during the DTEXT or TEXT commands.

Specify your text height based on your plotting scale factor.

Warning
Unlike blocks, font file definitions (SHX) are stored external to the drawing file and must accompany the drawing file in a drawing exchange.

See also: CHANGE, DIM, DTEXT, PURGE, RENAME, TEXT

TABLET

Screen **[SETTINGS] [next] [TABLET:]**

The TABLET command lets you configure and calibrate a digitizing tablet. By configuring the tablet, you define the tablet areas for tablet menus and the screen pointing area. By calibrating the tablet, you align the tablet to a paper drawing for digitizing. The tablet and screen menus are interactive; you can pick commands off the tablet that activate screen menus. The tablet menu supplied with AutoCAD works in conjunction with the menu file ACAD.MNX. When digitizing, use <^T> to toggle the tablet mode on and off. On DOS-based systems, you also can use the <F10> function key.

Prompt
Option (ON/OFF/CAL/CFG):

Options

ON	Enables tablet (digitizing) mode.
OFF	Disables tablet (digitizing) mode.
CAL	Calibrates the tablet with the coordinates of a paper drawing. Calibration is effective only in the space where the calibration took place.
CFG	Reserves portions of the tablet for menus and the screen pointing area. You can have a maximum of four tablet menu areas. The screen menu option [re-cfg] activates a macro to configure automatically the tablet menu supplied with AutoCAD.

Tips
When calibrating a tablet, the current UCS is the digitizing plane. You will need to recalibrate the tablet if you change the UCS, otherwise digitized points will be projected onto the UCS.

Before calibrating, configure for zero (0) tablet menu areas and enlarge the screen pointing area. This will give you more digitizing space for your paper drawing.

Warnings

You cannot change viewports or select commands from the screen while the tablet mode is on.

Tablet calibration is lost between editing sessions.

TABSURF

Screen **[DRAW] [next] [3D Surfs] [TABSURF:]**
Screen **[SURFACES] [TABSURF:]**
Pull down **[Draw] [Surfaces...] [TABULATED]**

TABSURF (TABulated SURFace) generates a 3D polygon mesh by extruding a path curve through space along a direction vector.

The path curve can be a line, arc, circle, or a 2D or 3D polyline. The direction vector can be a line or an open 2D or 3D polyline. The surface starts at the endpoint nearest your pick point on the path curve. If you use a polyline for the direction vector, only the first and last vertices are recognized.

Prompts
```
Select path curve:
Select direction vector:
```

Related System Variable
SURFTAB1

Tip
A TABSURF mesh can be exploded into individual 3D faces.

See also: EXPLODE, PEDIT, 3DFACE, 3DMESH

TEXT

Screen **[DRAW] [next] [TEXT]**

TEXT is AutoCAD's basic text command. It is an older command than DTEXT and does not dynamically show text characters on the screen as you enter them. It places a single text string when you end text input.

Prompts
```
Justify/Style/<Start point>:
Height <default>:
Rotation angle <default>:
Text:
```

Options

Start point   Default text justification is at the bottom left corner of the first character for each line of text.

Justify   Specifies one of the following text justifications:

    Align—Specifies the beginning and ending point of a line of text. The text height is adjusted to fit between these points.

    Fit—Specifies the beginning and ending point of a line of text. You determine the height. The width is controlled by the two endpoints.

    Center—Specifies the center of the text horizontally and the base of the text vertically.

Middle—Specifies the middle of the text line horizontally and vertically.

Right—Text justification is at the bottom right of the last character for each line of text.

TL—Text justification is at the top left of the tallest character (Release 11 only).

TC—Text justification is at the top center of the tallest character (Release 11 only).

TR—Text justification is at the top right of the tallest character (Release 11 only).

ML—Text justification is at the middle left, between the top of the tallest character and the bottom of lowest descender (Release 11 only).

MC—Text justification is at the middle center, between the top of the tallest character and the bottom of the lowest descender (Release 11 only).

MR—Text justification is at the middle right, between the top of the tallest character and the bottom of the lowest descender (Release 11 only).

BL—Text justification is at the bottom left of the lowest descender (Release 11 only).

BC—Text justification is at the bottom center of the lowest descender (Release 11 only).

BR—Text justification is at the bottom right of the lowest descender (Release 11 only).

Style	Changes the current style. The style must have been created with the STYLE command.
Enter	If you press <RETURN>, the last text entered is highlighted. You are then prompted for a new text string. The new text is placed directly below the highlighted text with the same style, height, and rotation as the highlighted text.
Height	Assigns a text height. You are not prompted for this when using Align or defaulting to a text style with a predefined height.
Rotation angle	Specifies the text angle.
Text	Supplies the text string.

The following are the default settings:

Start point	Left justified
Height	0.2000
Rotation angle	0

Special Character Codes

You can code your text string to obtain the following special characters:

%%o	Toggle overscore mode on/off.
%%cu	Toggle underscore mode on/off.
%%d	Draw degrees symbol.
%%p	Draw plus/minus tolerance symbol.
%%c	Draw diameter symbol.
%%%	Draw a single percent symbol.

When you are entering text, the control characters appear in the drawing. Once you end the command, the appropriate characters replace the control codes.

Related System Variables
TEXTSIZE, TEXTSTYLE

Tips
You can preset the font, alignment, height, and rotation of text by selecting [Options] - [Dtext Options >] from the pull-down menu. These preset variables are activated automatically when you pick [Draw] - [Dtext] from the pull-down menus. When using the screen menus, the text variables are based on the last text inserted during the drawing session.

Edit text strings with the DDEDIT or CHANGE commands.

Warning
You should base your text height on the scale you plan to plot the drawing. The text height you specify in AutoCAD should be the height of plotted text multiplied by the plot scale factor.

See also: CHANGE, DDEDIT, DTEXT, QTEXT, STYLE

TIME

Screen **[INQUIRY] [TIME:]**

The TIME command displays the following: the current date and time, the date and time the drawing was created, the date and time the drawing was last updated, and the amount of time spent in the current editing session. In addition, you can set an elapsed timer. The default turns the elapsed timer on.

Prompt
Display/ON/OFF/Reset:

Options
Display	Current status of the time command.
ON	Activates the elapsed timer.
OFF	Stops the elapsed timer.
Reset	Resets the elapsed timer to zero.

Related System Variables
CDATE, DATE, TDCREATE, TDINDWG, TDUPDATE, TDUSRTIMER

Tips
Time is displayed to the nearest millisecond using military format.

The date and time are based on the date and time maintained by your computer.

Warning
The time you work on a drawing will not be saved if you quit.

TRACE

Screen **[DRAW] [next] [TRACE:]**

The TRACE command, similar to the PLINE command, creates line segments with width. TRACE also automatically calculates the miter for adjacent segments, but only after the endpoint of the next segment is entered. If FILL is on, a trace is displayed as solid-filled. The default trace width is .05.

Prompts
```
Trace width <0.0500>
From point:
To point:
To point:
To point:
```

Related System Variable
TRACEWID

Tips

Polylines are much more flexible and versatile than traces.

Object snap modes treat traces the same as solid fills. You can osnap to the endpoints and midpoint of traces.

See also: FILL, POLYLINE

TRIM

Screen **[EDIT] [next] [TRIM:]**
Pull down **[Modify] [Trim]**

The TRIM command lets you clip the portions of entities that cross another entity selected as a cutting edge. You can have more than one cutting edge, and an entity can be both a cutting edge and an object to trim. Lines, arcs, circles, and 2D polylines can act as cutting edges and objects to trim. When you are working in paper space, viewport borders can be cutting edges.

Prompts
```
Select cutting edge(s)...
Select objects:
<Select object to trim>/Undo:
```

Options

Select object to trim	Select the part of the entity you want to delete.
Undo	Restore the last entity trimmed.

Tips

You can select more than one cutting edge per object. The entity will trim to the first edge and stop. Pick the object again and it will trim to the next cutting edge.

Ends of wide polylines always are square. If you trim a polyline at an angle, a portion of the polyline width may extend past the cutting edge.

Warning

Blocks, text, and traces cannot be cutting edges or objects to trim.

See also: CHANGE, EXTEND, STRETCH

UCS

Screen **[UCS:]**
Pull down **[Settings] [UCS Control...]** *or*
[UCS Options...] *or* **[UCS Previous]**

The UCS (User Coordinate System) lets you redefine the location of 0,0 and the direction of the X, Y, and Z axes. You also can set your UCS with the DDUCS dialogue boxes. The default UCS is the World (WCS).

Prompt
Origin/ZAxis/3point/Entity/View/X/Y/Z/Prev/Restore/
Save/Del/?/<World>:

Options

Origin	Specifies a new origin point while retaining the direction of the X, Y, and Z axes.
ZAxis	Specifies a new origin point and a positive Z axis.
3point	Specifies an origin with one point on the positive X axis and one point in the positive X,Y plane.
Entity	Defines a new UCS with the same orientation as a selected entity. The origin is determined by the entity type. It does not work for 3D polylines, polygon meshes, and viewport borders.
View	Defines a new UCS parallel to the screen. The point of origin is unchanged.
X	Rotates the current UCS around the X axis.
Y	Rotates the current UCS around the Y axis.
Z	Rotates the current X and Y axes about the Z axis.
Previous	Restores the previous UCS. You can backtrack up to ten previous coordinate systems for both paper space and model space.
Restore	Retrieves a previously saved UCS. Responding with a question mark (?) is the same as UCS ?.
Save	Stores the current UCS with a name you specify, up to 31 characters long. Responding with a question mark (?) is the same as UCS ?.
Delete	Deletes a saved UCS. Responding with a question mark (?) is the same as UCS ?.
?	Activates the wild-card options for reviewing the names of UCSs defined in the current drawing. The default, an asterisk (*), gives a sorted listing of the named UCS. You can use any of the wild-card options to create a more specific list. If the current UCS is unnamed, it is listed as *WORLD* or *NO NAME*, depending on its orientation.
World	Restores the WCS.

Related System Variables
UCSFOLLOW, UCSICON, UCSORG, UCSXDIR, UCSYDIR, VIEWMODE, WORLDUCS

Tips
Only one UCS can be current.

If you get lost when locating a UCS, return to the WCS and start over.

See also: DDUCS, DVIEW, PLAN, UCSICON, VPOINT

UCSICON

Screen **[SETTINGS] [next] [UCSICON:]**
Pull down **[Settings] [Ucsicon On/Off/OR]**

The UCSICON is a marker used to display graphically the origin and viewing plane of the current UCS. When the marker is L-shaped, you are in model space; when the marker is triangular, you are in paper space. The default for the icon is <ON>, Noorigin, and model space.

Prompt
ON/OFF/All/Noorigin/ORigin <ON>:

Options

ON   Displays the UCSICON.

OFF   Turns the UCSICON display off.

All   Display changes to the UCSICON in all viewports.

Noorigin   Displays the UCSICON at the lower left side of the viewport regardless of the current UCS definition.

ORigin   Displays the UCISICON at the origin of the current UCS (0,0,0). If the origin is off the screen viewing area, the icon is shown in the lower left corner.

The following are the different icon features:

W	The UCS is the same as the WCS.
+	The icon is located at the origin point of the UCS.
Box	You are viewing the UCS from a positive Z direction.
Box with a broken pencil	The X,Y plane of the UCS is perpendicular to your viewing plane.
The icon is drawn as a cube in perspective	Perspective viewing is on.

Related System Variable
UCSICON

Tips

When you select it from the pull-down menus, the UCSICON acts as a three-way toggle switch—ON/OFF/OR.

When the origin is near the edge or off the display screen, the icon is shown in the lower left corner.

See also: UCS

UNDEFINE

See REDEFINE

UNDO / U / REDO

Screen **[EDIT] [next] [UNDO:]**
Screen **[* * * *] [U:]**
Screen **[* * * *] [REDO:]**
Pull down **[Utility] [U]**
Pull down **[Utility] [Redo]**

The UNDO command lets you sequentially reverse previous commands individually, in groups, or back to the beginning of the current editing session. The default setting is the number of commands to undo at one time.

The U command is a subset of the UNDO command. U reverses the effects only of the last command. This is the same as using the UNDO command and entering the number 1.

REDO reverses the effects of the last UNDO command. You can redo only once and it must be the first command after UNDO.

Prompt
Auto/Back/Control/End/Group/Mark/<number>:

Options

Auto   Auto ON marks a menu macro as one command. Auto OFF treats each command in a menu macro as individual commands.

Back   Used in conjunction with the Mark option. You can undo to a marker with the Back option.

Control   Limits or disables the UNDO command.

All   Enables all the undo prompts and options.

None   Disables the UNDO and U commands.

One   Allows only the last command to be undone.

End   Terminates the UNDO group option.

Group   Treats a sequence of commands as one. Places an ending marker with the Mark option. This is similar to the way Auto behaves with menu macros.

Mark   Sets a marker before issuing a series of commands. You can have as many markers as you want. The Back option undoes commands back to the last marker. Once you reach the first marker, you will see the following message: This will undo everything. OK? <Y>.

Number   Enter the number of commands to undo.

Tip

Issuing a U at the DIM: prompt reverses the last dimensioning command. Issuing a U at the command: prompt after dimensioning undoes everything done while in dimensioning mode.

See also: OOPS

UNITS

Screen **[SETTINGS] [next] [UNITS:]**

The UNITS command controls the input and display format of coordinates, distances, and angles. You specify the system of units, the precision, the system of angle measure, the precision of angle display, and the direction of angles.

Options

Format   Specifies the units of measure, such as Scientific, Decimal (the default), Engineering, Architectural, or Fractional.

Precision   The number of digits past the decimal place or the smallest fraction of an inch to display. The default is 4.

Systems of angle measure   Specifies the format for angle measurements, such as Decimal degrees (the default), Degrees/minutes/seconds, Grads, Radians, or Surveyor's units.

Number of fractional places for display of angles   Selects the precision with which angles are displayed. The default is 0 (no fractions).

Direction for angle 0   Set angle 0 equal to East (the default), North, West, or South.

Do you want angles measured clockwise?   If you respond no, the angles are measured counterclockwise, which is the default. If you respond yes, the angles are measured clockwise.

Related System Variables

ANGBASE, ANGDIR, AUNITS, AUPREC, LUNITS, LUPREC, UNITMODE

Tips

You can globally update associative dimension text to show a change in units settings.

You can override the current angle format and enter angles in decimal degrees relative to AutoCAD's default orientation (zero degrees equals 3 o'clock) and direction (counterclockwise) by preceding the angle with two angle brackets (<<). By preceding the angle with three angle brackets (<<<), you override only the orientation and direction, which enables the angle to be specified in the current angle units format.

See also: SCALE

VIEW

Screen **[DISPLAY] [VIEW:]**

The VIEW command can save the current viewport or a user-definable window to a name for future retrieval. The view name can be up to 31 characters long. VIEW may be executed transparently by entering 'VIEW when you are within another command.

Prompt

?/Delete/Restore/Save/Window:

Options

?   Activates the wild-card options for reviewing the names of views defined in the drawing. The default, an asterisk (*), displays a sorted list of all named views. You can enter view names separated by commas or you can use any of the wild-card options to create a more specific list. An M (model space) or P (paper space) indicates in which space the view was defined.

Delete   Removes a defined view. You can enter view names separated by commas or you can use any of the wild-card options to create a more specific list.

Restore   Displays a saved view in the current viewport. If you restore a model space view while working in paper space, you are asked to select a viewport. The viewport must be on and active. You are then switched to model space.

        If you restore a paper space view while working in model space, you are switched to paper space. If TILEMODE is on, you cannot restore a paper space view.

Save   Saves the current viewport display.

Window   Specifies a window area to save as a view. When you restore the view, the view may be more than the windowed area up to the current display size. But when you plot the view, only the windowed area is plotted.

Related System Variables

VIEWCTR, VIEWDIR, VIEWMODE, VIEWSIZE, VIEWTWIST

Tip

You can specify a predefined view for display before beginning a drawing session. At the Enter name of drawing prompt, type the drawing name followed by a comma and the view name.

Warning

Most views can be restored transparently. You cannot execute a transparent view when working in paper space or during the following commands: VPOINT, DVIEW, ZOOM, VIEW, or PAN.

See also: REGENAUTO, RENAME, TILEMODE, VIEWRES, ZOOM

VIEWRES

Screen **[DISPLAY] [VIEWRES:]**

The VIEWRES command controls zoom speeds and the display resolution of arcs, circles, and linetypes. The default is for fast zooms. With this setting, most zooms, pans, and view restores are done at redraw speed, instead of at regeneration speed.

Prompts
```
Do you want fast zooms? <Y>:
Enter circle zoom percent (1-20000) <100>:
```

Option
When you enter a value greater than 100 for the circle zoom percent, you are given better circle and arc displays, yet regeneration times are increased. Lower values decrease the display resolution, as well as decreasing regeneration time.

Tip
Regardless of the VIEWRES setting, circles and arcs always are plotted at the plotter's resolution.

Warning
Broken linetypes can appear as continuous lines because of VIEWRES and the current zoom level. By forcing a regeneration or zooming in closer, you may display correctly the linetype.

See also: REGEN

VPLAYER

Screen **[MVIEW] [VPLAYER:]**
Pull down **[Display] [Mview] [Vplayer]**

The VPLAYER command (Release 11 only) controls layer freeze state per viewport. TILEMODE must be set to 0 (off) in order to activate this command.

Prompts
```
?/Freeze/Thaw/Reset/Newfrz/Vpvisdflt:
All/Select/<Current>:
```

Options

All	Selects *all* paper space viewports, including those that are not visible.
Select	Selects paper space viewports using standard object selection methods. If you are in model space, you are switched temporarily to paper space for viewport selection.
Current	Selects the current viewport.
?	Displays a listing of the frozen layers for the current viewport. If you are in model space, you are switched temporarily to paper space for viewport selection.
Freeze	Specifies layers to freeze. You can list layer names separated by commas or you can use wild-card characters. Once you name the layers, you can select the viewport(s).
Thaw	Selects layers to thaw. You can list layer names separated by commas or you can use wild-card characters. You also can use the DDLMODES command. Once you name the layers, you can select the viewport(s).
Reset	Restores the default visibility setting for layers based on the Vpvisdflt setting.
Newfrz	Creates new layers that are frozen in all viewports. You can create more than one layer at a time by separating each layer name with a comma.
Vpvisdflt	ViewPort VISibility DeFauLT determines layer visibility defaults before creating viewports. You can set more than one layer by using wild-card characters.

Related System Variable
TILEMODE

Warning

The VPLAYER command cannot override LAYER command settings. Layers must be thawed and on in order to be affected by the VPLAYER command.

See also: DDLMODES, LAYER

VPOINT

Screen **[DISPLAY] [VPOINT:]**
Pull down **[Display] [Vpoint 3D...]**

The VPOINT (ViewPOINT) command lets you specify the direction and angle for viewing a drawing by selecting a 3D viewpoint. The command regenerates the drawing in parallel projection from the 3D point that you specify. The default creates a plan view <0.0000,0.0000,1.0000> of the current UCS. You can define a viewpoint in the following three ways: enter X,Y,Z values; supply an angle in the X,Y plane and from the X,Y plane; or pick a point on the compass icon.

VPOINT can display only parallel projection. To generate perspectives, use the DVIEW command. VPOINT has been superseded by the DVIEW command, which lets you dynamically select and control a 3D viewpoint.

Prompt

Rotate/<View point> <0.0000,0.0000,1.0000>:

Options

Rotate   You can specify the viewpoint by entering the following two angles: the angle in the X,Y plane from the X axis, and the Z angle from the X,Y plane.

View point   Specify a view direction by entering X,Y,Z coordinates relative to 0,0,0.

              If you press <RETURN> at the prompt, a compass and axes tripod are displayed to assist in selecting a viewpoint.

Related System Variable
WORLDVIEW

Warnings

You cannot control the distance you are viewing an object, only the orientation. To control the distance, use the DVIEW command.

The viewpoint is viewed always through 0,0,0 of the WCS or UCS depending on the setting of the WORLDVIEW system variable. If you want to view your drawing through a different point, use the DVIEW command.

See also: DVIEW, PLAN

VPORTS / VIEWPORTS

Screen **[SETTINGS] [next] [VPORTS:]**

In model space, the VPORTS command lets you divide your screen into several viewing areas commonly referred to as tiled viewports. Depending on your hardware, you can define up to four or sixteen viewports at any one time. Each viewport can display a different view of your drawing and has independent Viewpoint, Snap, Grid, Viewres, Ucsicon, Dview, and Isometric settings. You can independently zoom, regenerate, and redraw in each viewport.

Model space viewports are interactive. You can begin most drawing and editing commands in one viewport and click into another viewport to complete the drawing or editing command. Only one viewport can be current at a time. The current viewport is surrounded by a wider border and the crosshairs are present only within that viewport. You can plot only the current viewport.

Paper space (Release 11 only) lets you create unlimited viewports. These viewports are not tiled; that is, the viewports can overlap one another and your crosshairs can span the entire display screen. You can control layer visibility per viewport and plot multiple viewports at multiple scales.

The following information is for model space. See PSPACE, MVIEW, and VPLAYER for more information about paper space viewports.

Prompt
Save/Restore/Delete/Join/SIngle/?/2/<3>/4:

Options

Save	Saves the current viewport configuration with a name. A viewport name can be 31 characters long.
Restore	Retrieves a saved viewport configuration. By responding with a ?, you activate the wild-card options for reviewing the names of viewports defined in the current drawing. The default, an asterisk, displays a listing of the saved viewport configurations. You can use any of the wild-card options to obtain a more specific list.
Delete	Deletes a saved viewport configuration.
Join	Combines two adjacent viewports into one viewport provided they form a rectangle.
SIngle	You can turn multiple viewports off and return to one viewport. The current viewport is the default.
?	Activates the wild-card options for reviewing the names of viewports defined in the current drawing. The default, an asterisk, gives a complete listing of all saved viewport configurations. You can use any of the wild-card options to create a more specific list.
2	Splits the current viewport into two horizontal or vertical viewports.
3	Splits the current viewport into any one of a variety of three-viewport configurations. This is the default.
4	Splits the current viewport into four viewports.

Related System Variables
CVPORT, MAXACTVP, TILEMODE

Tips
You can create viewports in paper space with the MVIEW command.

Viewports in model space are non-overlapping tiled divisions of your graphics screen. Viewports in paper space can overlap.

You can plot multiple viewports from paper space.

See also: MSPACE, MVIEW, PSPACE, REDRAWALL, REGENALL, TILEMODE

VSLIDE

Screen **[UTILITY] [SLIDES] [VSLIDE:]**

VSLIDE (View SLIDE) displays a slide file in the current viewport. A slide file has the extension SLD. You can create slides with the MSLIDE command. The default slide name is the current drawing file name. If a slide has been stored in a slide library, the format is the following: *library-name (slide-name).*

Use REDRAW or any command that causes a redraw to clear the slide. By placing an asterisk before the slide name, you cause the slide file to be read but not displayed until the next VSLIDE command. This is used in script files to load and display slides rapidly.

Prompt
Slide file <*dwg-name*>:

Related System Variable
FILEDIA

Tip
Slides can be used as an invisible "layer" to trace over onto the current drawing.

See also: DELAY, MSLIDE, SCRIPT

WBLOCK

Screen **[BLOCKS] [WBLOCK:]**

WBLOCK (Write BLOCK) writes a drawing, part of a drawing, or a block to a disk file as a new drawing. The WBLOCK is assigned to model space. This file can be inserted (using the INSERT command) into other drawings, or can be recalled from the main menu option number 2—Edit an existing drawing.

Prompts
File name:
Block name:
Insertion base point:

Options

File name	The name can be up to eight characters for DOS-based systems and include a drive and path specification. The file extension DWG is applied automatically.
Block name	Specifies the name of the block in the current drawing to be written to the disk file.
=	If you respond with an = to the Block name prompt, any existing block in the current drawing with the same name as the wblock file name is written to the file. You cannot use this method on DOS-based systems if the block name contains more than eight letters.
*	If you respond with an asterisk, WBLOCK writes the entire drawing to the disk. This purges any unused blocks, layers, linetypes, text styles, named views, UCS, viewport configurations, and unreferenced symbols. Model space entities are written to model space, and paper space entities are written to paper space.
Enter	If you do not give a Block name, you are prompted to enter an insertion base point and to select the entities to wblock. This is similar to creating a block, except the block definition is saved to disk instead of saved within the current drawing. Use the OOPS command to restore the deleted entities.

Related System Variable
FILEDIA

Tip
When you use WBLOCK in paper space, you write only those entities created in paper space. When you WBLOCK in model space, you write only those entities created in model space. When you use the * option, those entities created in model space are written to model space and those entities created in paper space are written to paper space.

Warning

You should make sure the desired UCS or WCS setting is current before wblocking entities.

See also: BASE, BLOCK, HANDLES

XBIND

Screen **[BLOCKS] [XBIND:]**

The XBIND command (Release 11 only) makes selected external reference (xref) file information a permanent part of the current drawing file. When specifying the referenced items, you can type in the name, list multiple names separated with commas, or use wild-card characters. A similar command, XREF Bind, adds the entire external reference file to your drawing.

Prompt

Block/Dimstyle/LAyer/LType/Style:

Options

Block	Adds selected xref blocks permanently to your drawing file.
Dimstyle	Adds selected xref dimstyles permanently to your drawing file.
LAyer	Adds selected xref layers permanently to your drawing file.
LType	Adds selected xref linetypes permanently to your drawing file.
Style	Adds selected xref styles permanently to your drawing file.

Tip

The added items are given names made up of the external reference file name followed by a dollar sign ($), a sequential number, and another dollar sign. The number is incremented if an item by the same name already exists.

Warning

If the XBIND command needs more than 31 characters for renaming an item, the command ends and undoes the effects of the entire XBIND command.

See also: XREF

XREF

Screen **[BLOCKS] [XREF:]**

The XREF (eXternal REFerence) command (Release 11 only) lets you attach external drawing files to your current drawing. These references are loaded into your drawing file each time you open the file for editing or request a plot from the main menu.

You cannot edit reference files indirectly, but you can osnap to referenced entities and control layer visibility, color, and linetype. Each time you make changes directly to the reference file, the latest version is loaded when you edit drawings referencing them.

You can locate referenced items easily in lists because their name is modified in the drawing reference to the file name followed by a vertical bar (|) symbol and the item name. This keeps any symbols, linetypes, styles, and so on that contain the same names in both files from conflicting with each other.

Prompt

?/Bind/Detach/Path/Reload/<Attach>:

Options

?	Lists the xrefs in a drawing file. You can use wild-card characters to specify a subset or press <RETURN> and receive a complete listing.

Bind   Makes the xref a permanent part of the drawing file. You can enter a single xref name, multiple names separated by commas, or wild-card characters. Nested xrefs also are included.

Detach Removes xrefs from the drawing. You can enter a single xref name, multiple names separated by commas, or wild-card characters. Nested xrefs also are detached.

Path   Modifies the path to search for reference file names. You can enter a single xref name, multiple names separated by commas, or wild-card characters.

Reload Reloads reference files without exiting the drawing editor. You can enter a single xref name, multiple names separated by commas, or wild-card characters. Nested xrefs also are reloaded.

Attach Attaches a reference drawing to your current drawing. This activates the File dialogue box if it is enabled and your system supports the dialogue box feature.

Related System Variable
FILEDIA

Tips
If you want to bind items selectively rather than the entire reference file, use the XBIND command.

By binding a reference file, you change the names of referenced items. The referenced items are the given names made up of external reference file names followed by a dollar sign ($), a sequential number, and another dollar sign. The number is incremented if an item by the same name already exists.

Reference files can be nested; that is, one reference file can reference another.

You can use most editing commands, such as copy, scale, and rotate, on xref objects.

You can assign another name to referenced drawings with the following format: *xref name=file name*. Xref name is the new name for the external reference only within the current drawing. The actual file name remains unchanged. You may want to do this when attaching references with the same name located in different directories or when an item exceeds the 31-character limit. You can request the File dialogue box by using the format: **xref name==.**

Warnings
Any changes you make to the color, linetype, or visibility of referenced items are retained only for the current session. To make permanent changes, open the referenced file directly and make the changes.

You cannot explode reference files.

A log file is maintained each time you use the Attach, Detach, and Reload options. This file contains a log of actions for those commands. The file (in ASCII format) has the same name as the current drawing, only with the file extension XLG. You may want to print or erase these files periodically .

Only model space entities can be referenced, whereas paper space entities are ignored.

If the Bind option needs more than 31 characters for renaming an item, the command ends and undoes the effects of the Bind up to that point.

See also: XBIND

ZOOM

Screen **[DISPLAY] [ZOOM:]**
Pull down **[Display] [Zoom Window]** *or* **[Zoom Previous]** *or* **[Zoom All]** *or* **[Zoom Dynamic]** *or* **[Zoom Vmax]**

The ZOOM command magnifies (zooms in) or shrinks (zooms out) the display in the current viewport. It does not physically change the size of the drawing; rather, it lets you view a small part of the drawing in detail or look at a greater part with less detail.

Prompt

`All/Center/Dynamic/Extents/Left/Previous/Vmax/Window/<Scale(X/XP)>:`

Options

All   In plan view, All displays the drawing to the limits or to the drawing extents, whichever is greater. In 3D, All displays the extents.

Center   Specifies a center point and a new display height or magnification in drawing units. If you pick a new center and press <RETURN>, the new point will become the center of the screen without changing the zoom magnification. Entering a magnification value is considered an absolute zoom. When you enter a magnification value followed by an X, you can zoom relative to the current factor. When you enter a magnification value followed by an XP, you can scale the magnification of the model space view relative to paper space.

Dynamic   Dynamic is a graphical combination of the ZOOM All, Pan, and Window prompts and options. The entire generated portion of your drawing is displayed with a box representing the last zoom magnification. This box can be moved around the screen to pan to another drawing area simultaneously. You can change the size of the box by toggling the pick button and moving the pointing device to resize the zoom box. Once the box size and location are satisfactory, press <RETURN>.

     If you have a color monitor, you will see a solid white or black box indicating the current drawing extents. A dotted green box depicts the area that was last displayed in the current viewport. Red lines outline four corners indicating the limits of the virtual screen that may be displayed without requiring regeneration. If an hourglass appears in the lower left corner of the monitor, regeneration is required. The hourglass appears when the zoom box is outside the red border markers (the virtual screen).

Extents   Displays all of the drawing entities as large as possible in the current viewport.

Left   Specifies a lower left corner and a new display height or magnification in drawing units. If you pick a new lower left corner and press <RETURN>, the new point becomes the lower left corner of the screen without changing the zoom magnification. A magnification value that is entered is considered an absolute zoom factor. When you enter a magnification value followed by an X, you can zoom relative to the current value. When you enter a magnification value followed by an XP, you can scale the magnification of the model space view relative to paper space.

Previous   Restores a previous ZOOM, PAN, VIEW, or DVIEW. The ZOOM command retains the last ten views for each viewport.

Vmax   (Release 11 only.) Zooms to the limits of the virtual screen's display space. This displays the maximum drawing area possible without causing a regeneration.

Window   Specifies a window area for the new display. Often you will see more than the window area because the display area is extended to fill the graphics screen.

Scale   This is the default option, but you can enter a magnification number. A scale factor of 1 displays the drawing limits, 2 displays the drawing twice as big, and .5 displays the drawing half its size.

ScaleX   Zooms relative to the current viewport display. You can enter the value followed by an *x* (times). The display center remains fixed.

ScaleXP   (Release 11 only.) Scales the magnification of a model space view relative to paper size. Tilemode must be set to 0 or off.

Related System Variables
TILEMODE, VIEWCTR, VIEWSIZE, VSMAX, VSMIN

See also: LIMITS, PAN, VIEW, REGENAUTO, VIEWRES

3DFACE

Screen **[DRAW] [next] [3DFACE:]**
Screen **[SURFACES] [3DFACE:]**
Pull down **[Draw] [3D Face]**

The 3DFACE command creates opaque objects defined by either three or four corner points, which are entered in circular fashion. You can specify varying Z coordinates for the corner points to create nonplanar faces. You can specify individual visible or invisible edges.

Prompts
First point:
Second point:
Third point:
Fourth point:

Option
I   You can enter an I before specifying the first point of an invisible edge. The I can be entered before any coordinate input, filters, or osnaps.

Related System Variable
SPLFRAME

Tips
3D faces are displayed as edges and are never filled.

Planar 3D faces are considered opaque by the HIDE command.

See also: EDGESURF, PEDIT, PFACE, REVSURF, RULESURF, TABSURF, 3DMESH

3DMESH

Screen **[DRAW] [next] [3D Surfs] [3DMESH:]**
Screen **[SURFACES] [3DMESH:]**
Pull down **[Draw] [Surfaces...]** *click 3DMesh icon*

The 3DMESH command creates open three-dimensional polygon meshes. You specify the mesh size and location in terms of the number of vertices in two directions, M and N. 3D meshes act like multiple 3D faces fused together and are treated as one entity. You specify the mesh size and the vertices as 2D or 3D points. You can close a 3D mesh by editing it with the PEDIT command. Because the 3DMESH command requires inputting individual vertex points, you should use the following automated mesh commands: EDGESURF, REVSURF, RULESURF, and TABSURF.

Prompts
Mesh M size:
Mesh N size:
Vertex (#, #):

Options

Mesh M size   Specifies the number of vertices on the M direction.

Mesh N size   Specifies the number of vertices on the N direction. The N direction is considered the direction in which you begin to define the mesh.

Tips

You can fit a smooth surface or other edits to a polygon mesh with the PEDIT command.

When you explode a 3D mesh, the result will be individual 3D faces.

See also: EDGESURF, EXPLODE, PEDIT, PFACE, REVSURF, RULESURF, TABSURF, 3DFACE

3DPOLY

Screen **[DRAW] [next] [3D Surfs] [3DPOLY:]**
Screen **[SURFACES] [3DPOLY:]**
Pull down **[Draw] [3D Poly]**

The 3DPOLY command creates a 3D polyline in which each vertex can be located anywhere in 3D space. 3D polylines cannot have arc segments, width, or taper. Use the PEDIT command to edit 3D polylines.

Prompts

```
From point:
Close/Undo/<Endpoint of line>:
```

Options

Close   Closes the polyline segments created during the command by connecting the start point to the endpoint.

Undo   Undoes the last polyline segment.

Endpoint of line   Specifies an endpoint. This is the default option. If you press <RETURN> at the endpoint prompt, the command is terminated.

Warning

3D polylines support only continuous linetypes.

See also: PEDIT, POLYLINE

Installation, Configuration, and Troubleshooting

What This Appendix Covers

This appendix explains the AutoCAD workstation and installation setup you need to be able to use the information and work through the exercises in this book. In addition, the appendix provides:

- Instructions on installing and configuring AutoCAD on your system.
- Recommendations for managing your hard drive.
- Instructions for automating your AutoCAD startup with prototype drawings and batch files.
- Directions for customizing the ACAD.PGP file to access operating system commands and programs from AutoCAD, and to create alias abbreviations for AutoCAD command names.
- A discussion of common errors involving AutoCAD and AutoLISP, along with ways to resolve them.

This appendix discusses many of the configuration settings and setup techniques you can use to control AutoCAD and improve its performance. There are too many versions, operating systems, and variables for us to cover all setups in detail. Our aim is to acquaint you with the possibilities available. If we tweak your interest and you want more detail, refer to your *AutoCAD Reference Manual, Installation and Performance Guide,* or *AutoLISP Programmer's Reference.* You should also try some experiments on your own — it's hard for us to predict what is optimal for *your* system and drawings.

Some Assumptions About Your Hardware and Software

Although there are many different operating environments for AutoCAD, most of the material in this book applies to all of the AutoCAD environments. To write the exercises, however, we've had to make certain assumptions about your operating system and your hardware. These include:

- You are running AutoCAD Release 10 or later. Emphasis throughout the book is on Release 11, with secondary emphasis on Release 10. New Riders Publishing also stocks the 5th edition of this book which fully supports Release 10.

- You are running AutoCAD in the MS-DOS or PC-DOS operating environment. However, all of the exercises and files are usable in any AutoCAD environment, with minor changes in system setup.

- You have a hard disk.

- You have a math coprocessor. Starting with Release 9, and including later versions, AutoCAD requires a math coprocessor. (80486 computers have built-in math coprocessors.)

- You are using a pointing device, such as a digitizing tablet with a stylus or puck, or a mouse.

- You have a color monitor with EGA or better resolution. The AutoShade exercises assume you have an AutoShade-supported video adapter and monitor.

- You are using a plotter for output. However, most of the plotting exercises can easily be adapted to a dot matrix or laser printer.

- You have a basic knowledge of DOS commands, allowing you to copy and erase files, change directories, and perform directory listings.

Recommended System Configuration for INSIDE AutoCAD

As with any program, how you use AutoCAD will determine the type of hardware best-suited to your application. If you use AutoCAD in an educational environment, your hardware requirements are naturally not as critical as those of a production environment.

In either case, we recommend an 80386-based system. Having a 386 will give you greater flexibility for software upgrades. If upgrading to AutoCAD 386 is not a consideration for you, and you are not using AutoCAD in a production environment, an 80286-based system will give you adequate performance as long as your drawings are not overly complex.

We recommend the following minimum configuration for the MS-DOS version of AutoCAD:

- An 80386-based system (or better) for production use, or an 80386SX-based system for educational use.
- 640K conventional memory plus at least 1Mb or more extended memory. AutoCAD 386 makes the best use of extended memory. For best performance, we recommend 4Mb of RAM. AutoCAD will also use expanded memory in addition to the extended memory required, but extended memory is faster.
- A hard disk with at least 20Mb of free disk space. This includes space to contain your AutoCAD files, along with drawing files.
- One or more diskette drives with 1.2Mb or 1.44Mb capacity.
- PC or MS-DOS Version 3.0 or later (3.3 is recommended), with program files loaded on a hard disk directory called C:\DOS.
- AutoCAD program files loaded on a hard disk directory called C:\ACAD.
- AutoCAD configuration files copied to a second hard disk directory called C:\IA-ACAD. These files are ACAD.CFG, ACADPP.OVL, ACADPL.OVL, ACADDG.OVL, and ACADDS.OVL.

Tip: Update your DOS operating system to at least version 3.1. It is easy to remember to keep AutoCAD software up to date, but it is easy to forget to update PC-DOS or MS-DOS. DOS versions 3.1 and later offer valuable features for a customized environment, including a better ability to deal with space limitations. We recommend updating your DOS to 3.3.

Installing AutoCAD

Installing AutoCAD differs slightly depending on the version you are installing. We'll cover both Release 10 and Release 11. AutoCAD 386 uses an installation routine very similar to Release 11's.

> **Important!:** Before beginning any software installation, always make a backup copy of your distribution diskettes. Always install the software from the backup set of disks, not the originals. You should also keep a backup copy of your DOS distribution diskettes.

Backing Up Your Original Diskettes

Before making backup copies of your distribution disks, place a write-protect tab on each original notched disk to prevent accidental erasure or damage to it. You will need the same number and type of backup disks as your distribution set.

Using DISKCOPY to Back Up Your Disks

If you have a single floppy drive, insert the first original (source) disk in drive A: and type:

```
C:> CD \DOS                         Change to the \DOS directory.
C:> DISKCOPY A: A:                  Then change disks when prompted.
```

If you have two diskette drives that are the same size and density (both 5 1/4" or both 3 1/2"), place the first distribution disk in drive A: and a backup (target) disk in drive B: and type:

```
C:> CD \DOS
C:> DISKCOPY A: B:                  This will copy everything on A: to B:.
```

The source disk is the disk you are copying (your original distribution disk), and the target disk is your duplicate (backup) disk. Your target disk does not have to be formatted. DISKCOPY will format it for you.

Preparing Your Hard Drive for AutoCAD Installation — All Versions

The speed by which files are accessed on your hard disk drive will significantly affect AutoCAD's performance. That is particularly true with the 640K DOS or DOS 286 versions of AutoCAD, since they must swap program overlays in and out to disk. Disk access time is also important when it comes to loading and storing drawing files, inserting blocks, and loading other files.

When DOS stores files on your hard disk drive, it must sometimes break the files up and scatter them around, rather than storing the file in contiguous (side-by-side) sectors. The more you use the disk, and the more files you store on it, the more likely that becomes. If your drive has been in use for a long time, you may want to pack the disk. Packing reorders the files, moving the data around so that your files are once again stored in contiguous sectors. Any small groups of unused sectors that were previously in between files are reallocated in larger groups.

Commercial disk management programs are available that allow you to not only pack the disk, but to check and adjust other operating parameters of your hard drive, such as the disk's interleave factor (the ordering of the sectors on the disk).

Optionally, you can choose to reformat the disk rather than pack it. Because the entire disk will be freed by reformatting, you will achieve the same effect as packing when you copy your files back onto the disk — they will be copied into contiguous sectors because you will have plenty of free space on the disk.

Packing can be done without losing data, but reformatting will destroy any existing data on your hard disk. Before you consider reformatting the hard disk, make sure you have a complete backup of all files on the drive, and that you know how to restore them after you reformat it.

Tip: Use a disk optimizer or defragmentation program frequently to speed up file access on your hard disk. See any software dealer for recommendations.

Tip: It helps to keep each program that you use, like AutoCAD, in its own subdirectory. File access is faster, you don't get files mixed up, and it is easier to install future program upgrades. Plus, it is much easier to back up your file system when programs are separated into individual directories.

Installing the 640K DOS Version of AutoCAD Release 10

All versions of AutoCAD 386 and all DOS versions of AutoCAD Release 11 include an interactive installation program. See the next section for details. However, the 640K DOS or DOS 286 versions of AutoCAD Release 10 do not include an installation program, so you will have to manually copy files to your hard disk. Refer to your DOS manual or a good DOS reference book if you need help creating directories, changing directories, copying files, and listing directories.

Begin the installation by checking the amount of free space on your hard disk. To install the 640K DOS or DOS 286 version of AutoCAD, Release 10 you will need at least 2.5Mb of free disk space. If you need more space, remove files and directories that you no longer need. When you have enough free space, type the following to create the directories to contain your AutoCAD files:

Creating an AutoCAD Directory

```
C:>PROMPT=$P$G                    Sets DOS prompt to display current drive and
                                  directory. (You should include this prompt in
                                  your AUTOEXEC.BAT file.)

C:\>MKDIR \ACAD                   Creates directory \ACAD in root directory of
                                  current drive.

C:\>MKDIR \ACAD\SUPPORT           Creates directory to hold your font files and
                                  other support files.

C:\>CD \ACAD                      Change to \ACAD directory. Your prompt
                                  should also change.

C:\ACAD>
```

The minimum files you need from your AutoCAD distribution diskettes are the program executable and overlay files, and support files. First, copy all of the files from Disk #1 to your ACAD directory. If you want to copy from drive B: instead of drive A:, substitute B for A in the following command lines.

Copying Program and Support Files

Insert Disk #1 (Overlays) into drive A:.

```
C:\ACAD>COPY A:*.*                Copies all files from A: to cur-
                                  rent directory.
```

Insert Disk #2 (Executables/Drivers) into drive A:.

```
C:\ACAD>COPY A:ACAD*.*            Copies the remaining AutoCAD
                                  program files.
```

Insert Disk #3 (Support) into drive A:.

```
C:\ACAD>COPY A:*.* \ACAD\SUPPORT  Copies all support files to
                                  \ACAD\SUPPORT.
```

Disk #3 includes a directory called SOURCE, which contains source shape description files for the standard AutoCAD fonts, the source menu file, and the source AutoShade LISP program. If you will be customizing your menu, creating your own font descriptions, or using AutoShade, you may want to copy these files to your ACAD directory.

► Copying Source Files

Insert Disk #3 in drive A:.

`C:\ACAD>`**`COPY A:\SOURCE\*.*`**

Disk #4 (Bonus) contains useful AutoLISP programs and sample drawing files. If you want, you can copy these to either the ACAD or ACAD\SUPPORT directories. Optionally, you can place them in their own directory.

► Copying Bonus and Sample Files

First, create a directory for the bonus and sample files.

`C:\ACAD>`**`MKDIR BONUS`**

Insert Disk #4 (Bonus/Sample) in drive A:.

`C:\ACAD>`**`COPY A:*.* BONUS`**

If you have the optional *INSIDE AutoCAD* diskette (IA DISK), you can install its files to the hard disk now. See Chapter 1 for details.

Installing Release 11 or AutoCAD 386 Release 10

All versions of AutoCAD 386 and all DOS versions of AutoCAD Release 11 include an installation program which automatically creates the necessary directories, copies files, and personalizes AutoCAD for you. It also lets you install only those groups of files that you want, which can save you some disk space if you don't want source, bonus, and sample files installed on your hard disk.

To install AutoCAD Release 11 or 386, first make backup copies of your distribution diskettes, then insert Disk #1 in drive A:.

You will need at least 3.3Mb of free space on your disk for executable and support files to install a minimum Release 11 configuration. If you install the sample drawings, you will need an additional 2Mb. A complete installation including the Advanced Modeling Extension (AME) will require a minimum of 8.7Mb. For AutoCAD Release 10, you will need at least 2.5Mb, and the sample drawings will take up another 750K. If you do not have enough space to install the files you have selected, INSTALL will alert you to that fact.

Since the installation program will create the necessary directories, you don't need to create them beforehand. The INSTALL program will prompt you to enter information about your installation, including your name, company name, dealer name, and dealer's telephone number. You must make an entry in each of these fields, or INSTALL will not install AutoCAD. These settings will be written to your diskette and will become a permanent part of your AutoCAD executable file.

INSTALL is fully menu-driven, so you should have no difficulty installing AutoCAD. During the installation process, INSTALL will ask if you want it to create a startup batch file called ACAD386.BAT. This file contains the minimum settings needed to start AutoCAD from the DOS prompt. Answer yes to create the batch file unless you are experienced enough to make the settings yourself.

Installing AutoCAD 386 or Release 11

Insert Disk #1 in drive A:.

`C:\>`**`PROMPT=$P$G`**	Set your prompt if you have not already done so.
`C:\>`**`A:`**	
`A:\>`**`INSTALL`**	Follow the instructions and prompts.

Your program files are copied. All that is left for you to do is run AutoCAD and configure your system. You don't need to copy the device driver files since AutoCAD can prompt you for the device driver disk during configuration. If any of your hardware requires an ADI driver, install it according to the manufacturer's instructions before configuring AutoCAD.

Configuring AutoCAD for Your Hardware

If you have just installed AutoCAD, or if you need to reconfigure AutoCAD for a different hardware device, the AutoCAD configuration menu will sequentially prompt you to identify selected parameters for your video display, digitizer, plotter, and printer/plotter which make up your workstation configuration.

You must run AutoCAD to configure it. If you haven't configured AutoCAD, it will skip to configuration automatically when you start the program. During a first-time configuration sequence, AutoCAD will automatically take you through the steps required to select your display, input device, plotter, and printer.

AutoCAD Configuration Menu

If AutoCAD has already been configured once, you can examine your configuration setup by selecting option 5 from the main menu. AutoCAD will display your current configuration and prompt you with the configuration menu.

Examining Your AutoCAD Configuration

Start AutoCAD. If you are using a startup batch file such as ACAD386.BAT, ACAD.BAT, or IA.BAT, enter ACAD386, ACAD, or IA and press <RETURN>. If your AutoCAD directory is part of your path, enter ACAD and press <RETURN>. Otherwise, change to your AutoCAD directory, enter ACAD and press <RETURN>.

If AutoCAD has not been configured, it will prompt you through the choices, then display the current configuration. To make any changes, exit to main menu and reconfigure.

To reconfigure AutoCAD, select option 5 at the main menu.

```
Configure AutoCAD.

Current AutoCAD configuration

  Video display:      Your current display.
  Digitizer:          Your current input device.
  Plotter:            Your current plotter.
    Port:             Your current plotter connection.
  Printer plotter:    Your current printer plotter.

Press RETURN to continue:

Configuration menu
  0.  Exit to Main Menu
  1.  Show current configuration
  2.  Allow detailed configuration
  3.  Configure video display
  4.  Configure digitizer
  5.  Configure plotter
  6.  Configure printer plotter
  7.  Configure system console
  8.  Configure operating parameters
Enter selection:
```

Note: For Release 11, you must enter the maximum number of users that your copy of AutoCAD is licensed for when prompted for server authorization, even if you are using it on fewer systems.

Reconfiguring Your System

Reconfiguring AutoCAD is simple and straightforward. AutoCAD asks you several questions about your hardware setup and you respond with answers or a number selection from a list of choices that AutoCAD provides. Configuration is dependent on your hardware.

To configure or change a device driver, simply select the item you want to change from the configuration menu. AutoCAD then prompts you for values to supply for each device. When you choose to configure a particular device in AutoCAD's configuration menu, AutoCAD looks on your hard drive for the appropriate driver files. If it doesn't find the driver files, it prompts you to enter the drive and directory where they are located. Insert your backup diskette that contains the drivers, and press <RETURN>. AutoCAD reads the contents of the disk and displays the drivers for you.

These driver files are only needed during configuration. During configuration, AutoCAD creates a configuration file called ACAD.CFG in the current directory. Release 10 640K DOS versions also create four files (.OVL) that contain data from the drivers. You no longer need the original driver files, so it is not necessary to copy driver files to your hard disk during installation. If you did copy the driver files, you can remove them by returning to the DOS prompt and entering:

```
C:\ACAD>ERASE *.DRV
```

This will erase all driver files from the ACAD directory. This also helps ensure the security of your program. It will not be possible for someone to copy your AutoCAD files and use them on a system with different hardware since they won't have the driver files.

Using ADI Drivers

ADI (Autodesk Device Interface) drivers are device driver programs for plotters, printers, digitizers, and video cards. There are two types of ADI drivers: real mode ADI drivers, and protected mode ADI drivers. Real mode ADI drivers are memory-resident (terminate and stay resident) programs that operate in conventional memory. If you are using a real mode ADI driver, you must install it prior to starting AutoCAD. Install this type of driver by entering its name at the DOS prompt, just like any other program. You can install an ADI driver in your CONFIG.SYS file, AUTOEXEC.BAT file, or your AutoCAD startup batch file. Examples of both files are shown in this appendix.

If you are using a protected mode ADI driver, AutoCAD loads the driver automatically into extended memory. You do not need to load it prior to starting AutoCAD. In the AutoCAD configuration menu, real mode ADI drivers are listed simply as ADI drivers. Protected mode drivers are listed as P386 ADI drivers.

Mastering the Prototype Drawing

Many readers overlook the fact that they can customize their drawing setup by starting a drawing session with a prototype drawing which they can then modify. This is a simple task that can save time-wasting setups.

Chapter 1 discusses establishing a default working environment for units, grid, and snap settings by loading a prototype drawing called ACAD.DWG. The ACAD.DWG file comes with the AutoCAD program. (All the ACAD.DWG variables and their default values are listed in the System Variables table in Appendix C.)

You can also create your own prototype drawing and use it to initialize your drawings. After you create this drawing with the defaults (and any standard graphics like a title block) that you want, you can save it on disk with a name that you choose. Then, you can either load the drawing as an option, or set up AutoCAD to load it automatically.

Use the following exercise as a guide to creating a prototype drawing file with your own default settings and standard graphics. Our example is called IA-PROTO.

For simplicity, IA-PROTO uses an 11" x 8 1/2" setup at full scale with engineering units. If you use a different scale factor and sheet size, adjust your text and dimension scales. Start your drawing with the standard defaults from the main menu by setting IA-PROTO=.

If you are using the IA DISK, you already have the drawing. You may want to read the exercise to see what is set in the IA-PROTO drawing.

Customizing a Prototype Drawing

 Edit an existing drawing named IA-PROTO.

 Begin a NEW drawing named IA-PROTO= and perform the exercise.

Make the layers and settings shown in table B.1.

Command: **STYLE**	Create a style STD with the ROMANS font and default all other options.
Command: **TEXTSIZE**	Set text size to .125. (Release 10, use SETVAR.)
Command: **LTSCALE**	Set the linetype scale factor to .375.
Command: **DIM**	Set the following dimension variables.
Dim: **DIMDLI**	Set to 0.375.
Dim: **DIMTXT**	Set to 0.125.
Dim: **DIMASZ**	Set to 0.1875.
Dim: **DIMEXE**	Set to 0.1875.
Dim: **DIMCEN**	Set to 0.0625.
Dim: **DIMEXO**	Set to 0.9375.
Dim: **EXIT**	
Command: **END**	End to save IA-PROTO for future use.

Table B.1
IA-PROTO Drawing Settings

APERTURE	AXIS	COORDS	GRID	LTSCALE	SNAP	ORTHO
6	.25	ON	.5	.375	.0625	ON

UNITS	Engineering units, default all other settings.
LIMITS	0,0 to 11,8.5
ZOOM	Scale of .75X
VIEW	Save view ALL.

Layer Name	State	Color	Linetype
0	On	7 (white)	CONTINUOUS
TITLE	On	2 (yellow)	CONTINUOUS
DIM	On	2 (yellow)	CONTINUOUS
TEXT	On	4 (cyan)	CONTINUOUS
HATCH	On	1 (red)	CONTINUOUS
CENTER	On	3 (green)	CENTER
HIDDEN	On	5 (blue)	HIDDEN
DASHED	On	2 (yellow)	DASHED
NO-PLOT	On	6 (magenta)	CONTINUOUS
OBJECTS	Current	3 (green)	CONTINUOUS

How to Optionally Load a Prototype Drawing

Now that you have preserved IA-PROTO, you can call IA-PROTO as an option by setting any new drawing equal to it. This is a technique that we use throughout the book. Let's use it now to check IA-PROTO.

Testing a Prototype Drawing

Enter selection: **1**   Begin a NEW drawing.
Enter NAME of drawing: **TEST=IA-PROTO**

AutoCAD puts you into the drawing editor and starts a new drawing identical to IA-PROTO.

If TEST is identical to IA-PROTO, it's okay.

Command: **QUIT**

How to Automate Loading a Prototype Drawing

You can set up AutoCAD to automatically use IA-PROTO for your new drawing in two ways. One is to copy IA-PROTO.DWG to the name ACAD.DWG, replacing the original default ACAD.DWG. (You should find ACAD.DWG in the same directory as your AutoCAD program files.) If you do this and you want to restore the standard ACAD.DWG prototype drawing, you just begin a new drawing in your AutoCAD directory named ACAD= and then end it as shown in Chapter 1.

The other way to automate IA-PROTO is to set it as the default prototype drawing in AutoCAD's configuration menu. Here are the steps to automating a prototype drawing by reconfiguring AutoCAD.

Automation Steps Using a Prototype Drawing

- From the main menu, select option 5, Configure AutoCAD.
- From the configuration menu, select option 8, Configure operating parameters.
- Select the operating parameter 2, Initial drawing setup.
- Enter name of default prototype file for new drawings, IA-PROTO.
- <RETURN> three times to save the changes and exit to the main menu.

Now all new drawings started with the current configuration will start up with IA-PROTO's defaults.

Checking Your AutoCAD and AutoLISP Environment

To follow the menu macros and AutoLISP exercises in this book, you need to check your AutoLISP and DOS systems' environments, and you need to check your text editor.

Selecting Text Editors

If you plan to modify your menu files, create AutoLISP programs, or customize your CONFIG.SYS and AUTOEXEC.BAT files, you will need a text editor capable of editing and saving ASCII files. Norton's Editor, Sidekick, PC Write (a "shareware" editor), Wordstar in non-document mode, the WordPerfect Library Program Editor, WordPerfect's DOS text file option, Microsoft Word in text-only format, and the DOS program EDLIN all produce the standard ASCII file format that you will need. EDLIN is awkward for large files, and we recommend its use only as a last resort.

Your editor must create standard ASCII files. We assume that you have a suitable editor at hand. If you have doubts about its ability to produce ASCII files, test your editor with the following steps.

Text Editor Test

Load your text editor. Get into its edit mode and make a new file named TEXT.TXT.

Write a paragraph of text and copy it to get a few screens full.

Save the file and exit to DOS. Then test it:

`C:\>CD \`*`directory`*	*Directory* is the name of your text editor's directory.
`C:\IA-ACAD>TYPE TEXT.TXT`	All the text you entered scrolls by if your editor produced a standard ASCII file.
`C:\IA-ACAD>DEL TEXT.TXT`	

Your text editor is okay if you saw text identical to what you typed in your editor, with no extra åÇäÆ characters or control codes. If you got any garbage, particularly at the top or bottom of the file, then your text editor is not suitable, or is not configured correctly for use as a development editor.

When you have determined that your text editor can create and edit ASCII (text-only) files, you will be ready to customize your system's configuration files.

Configuring Your DOS Boot Files

When your system boots, the CPU runs through a self-test, then reads two hidden files from the root directory of your boot drive. With MS-DOS, these files are called IO.SYS and MSDOS.SYS. Then, the system looks for two startup files — CONFIG.SYS and AUTOEXEC.BAT — in your root directory.

CONFIG.SYS contains entries that load system-level device drivers such as memory managers, RAM drives, and disk caches. You can also load device drivers for peripherals such as a mouse in CONFIG.SYS. In addition, CONFIG.SYS should contain entries that set the number of files that a program can have open at one time, and that specify the number of disk buffers to be created by the system.

AUTOEXEC.BAT contains entries that set your system prompt, set your path and other system variables, and run batch files or other programs to execute automatically during startup.

Tip: Keep your AUTOEXEC.BAT and CONFIG.SYS files as uncluttered as possible. Keep your path down to the absolute minimum to avoid possible conflicts, and only install device drivers that are necessary in CONFIG.SYS. You may be able to load a .COM device driver from the DOS command line or a batch file, rather than a .SYS device driver in CONFIG.SYS.

Tailoring Your CONFIG.SYS File

CONFIG.SYS is read automatically by the system at boot, and must be located in the root directory of the boot disk. To list the contents of your CONFIG.SYS file, type the following commands from the DOS system prompt.

Examining CONFIG.SYS

`C:\IA-ACAD>CD \`	Change to the root directory.
`C:\>TYPE CONFIG.SYS`	Displays the contents of CONFIG.SYS.

The typical CONFIG.SYS file contains:

`BUFFERS=32`	A number from 20 to 48 is adequate.
`FILES=24`	(AutoCAD 386 requires `FILES=40`.)
`BREAK=ON`	Allows <^C> and <BREAK> to interrupt a program whenever possible.
`SHELL=C:\COMMAND.COM /P /E:256`	/E:256 is for DOS 3.2 or later. Use E:16 for DOS 3.0 or 3.1.

You can edit or create a CONFIG.SYS file in your root directory using your tested ASCII text editor. Use the discussion below to help you in any modifications. Note that if you installed AutoCAD 386 or Release 11, INSTALL may have modified your CONFIG.SYS for you.

The BUFFERS line allocates RAM to hold your recently used data. If a program frequently accesses recently used data, buffers reduce disk accesses and increase speed. Each two-buffer increment uses 1K of base (conventional) DOS memory. You may have to use a smaller number if AutoCAD runs short of memory.

The FILES line tells DOS the maximum number of files your applications expect to have open at one time. FILES uses very little memory; a large value helps with AutoCAD and AutoLISP. For Release 11, use FILES=40.

The SHELL line defines the command processor to be used by DOS. By default, the system command interpreter is COMMAND.COM. Setting SHELL in CONFIG.SYS allows you to specify the amount of RAM to store environment variable settings and other information in. AutoCAD and AutoLISP use several of these. You will need at least 256 bytes. If you receive the error message, "Out of environment space," you may need to try a higher number. Increase the number for DOS 3.2 or later by 16 (bytes), reboot, and try the operation that caused the error again. Repeat the process if needed until the error message disappears. For DOS versions before 3.2, increase the number by 1 each time.

AUTOEXEC.BAT File

AUTOEXEC.BAT is a batch file like any other, with one important exception: it is automatically executed every time the system is booted. Like CONFIG.SYS, it must be in the root directory.

The AUTOEXEC.BAT file is the place to install your TSR (terminate and stay resident) programs like Prokey, Sidekick, and Superkey. It also is the place to install the other setup commands, ADI drivers with a .COM or .EXE extension, and DOS environment settings that you need to complete an application environment. Examine your AUTOEXEC.BAT file. We recommend that it include the following lines.

Examining the AUTOEXEC.BAT file

Be sure you are in the root C:\ directory.

`C:\>TYPE AUTOEXEC.BAT`   Examine it.

The following are DOS environment modifiers.

```
PROMPT=$P$G
PATH C:\;C:\DOS
```

Other information may follow. Your path may include other directories. It is not necessary to place your AutoCAD directory on your path if you use a batch file to start AutoCAD that explicitly invokes ACAD.EXE.

Edit your AUTOEXEC.BAT file. If you do not have one, create one.

Edit or create your AUTOEXEC.BAT in your root directory, using your tested ASCII text editor. Use the discussion below to help you with any modifications. Your

AUTOCAD.BAT file may also contain settings shown in the startup batch file later in this chapter.

PROMPT PG is extremely valuable. It causes the DOS prompt to display your current directory path so you don't get lost.

PATH is essential for automatic directory access to programs and DOS commands. The C:\ root and C:\DOS paths are essential to our recommended setup. If your DOS files are in a different directory, substitute the directory.

Use whatever is relevant to your setup. It is more than likely that your path contains additional directories. The CONFIG.SYS and AUTOEXEC.BAT changes do not take effect until you reboot your computer. To perform a warm reboot of your system, press <CTRL-ALT-DEL>.

Using Microsoft Windows With AutoCAD

If you are running the AutoCAD 386 version of Release 11 and also running other programs that use DOS extenders like Microsoft Windows, you may have a conflict between the memory manager used by the other program and AutoCAD. For example, Microsoft Windows uses the memory manager HIMEM.SYS. If HIMEM.SYS is loaded in your system and you run AutoCAD, AutoCAD will run very slowly. To avoid that, you can use multiple CONFIG.SYS and AUTOEXEC.BAT files.

Using Multiple CONFIG.SYS and AUTOEXEC.BAT Files

Only one file at a time can have the name CONFIG.SYS or AUTOEXEC.BAT. Create a file called ACAD.SYS that contains your CONFIG.SYS command lines for AutoCAD. Create a second file called WIN.SYS that contains your CONFIG.SYS command lines for Windows. Then create two batch files called GOWIN.BAT and GOACAD.BAT with the following lines:

GOWIN.BAT File
```
COPY C:\WIN.SYS C:\CONFIG.SYS
@ECHO    REBOOT System to run Windows.
```

GOACAD.BAT File
```
COPY C:\ACAD.SYS C:\CONFIG.SYS
@ECHO    REBOOT System to run AutoCAD.
```

Note: With versions prior to DOS 3.3, substitute REM for @ECHO.

When you want to run AutoCAD, type GOACAD and press <RETURN>. The proper file will be copied to CONFIG.SYS. Then, press <CTRL-ALT-DEL> to reboot your computer using the new CONFIG.SYS file. Do the same for running Windows, except type GOWIN instead.

The PGP File

You can run other programs, utilities, or operating system commands without ending AutoCAD. A few predefined *external commands* are included with AutoCAD to do this. They are defined in a file, ACAD.PGP. PGP stands for ProGram Parameter file.

AutoCAD's standard SHELL features are set in the ACAD.PGP file, giving direct access to DOS commands. This access can be general purpose access or predefined access to jump out and run a specific DOS command or program. If you followed the installation procedure earlier in this appendix, the ACAD.PGP file should be in your ACAD directory.

In addition to giving you access to external DOS commands and other applications, ACAD.PGP also contains abbreviated aliases for AutoCAD commands. For example, instead of typing REDRAW, you can simply type R, because R has been defined as an alias for REDRAW.

You can use the DOS MORE command to list the contents of the standard ACAD.PGP file. We've added one line to run Microsoft Word.

Listing the PGP File

```
C:\>CD ACAD                        Change to the book's directory.
C:\ACAD>MORE<ACAD.PGP              Displays the contents of
                                   ACAD.PGP a page at a time.
; acad.pgp - External Command and Command Alias definitions
; External Command format:
;   <Command name>,[<DOS request>],<Memory reserve>,[*]<Prompt>,<Return code>
; Examples of External Commands for DOS
CATALOG,DIR /W,      33000, File specification: ,0
DEL,DEL,             33000, File to delete: ,0
DIR,DIR,             33000, File specification: ,0
EDIT,EDLIN,          42000, File to edit: ,0
SH,,                 33000, *OS Command: ,0
SHELL,,             127000, *OS Command: ,0
TYPE,TYPE,           33000, File to list: ,0
WORD,E:\WORD\WORD,400000,File to edit: ,4
```

Listing the PGP File—continued

```
; Command alias format:
;   <Alias>,*<Full command name>
; Sample aliases for AutoCAD Commands
; These examples reflect the most frequently used commands.
; Each alias uses a small amount of memory, so don't go
; overboard on systems with tight memory.
- - MORE - -
```
Press <RETURN> or the space bar to display the next page.

The last DOS entry in the example above will load Microsoft Word from drive E:. To execute it in AutoCAD, you would type WORD and press <RETURN>. The optional prompt, File to edit:, would appear on the screen, pausing to allow you to enter a filename. The program would be allocated 400K of memory.

Any command in the ACAD.PGP file can be invoked within AutoCAD just like the standard AutoCAD commands. Command entries in ACAD.PGP have the following five fields:

```
Keyword,Command,Memory,Prompt,Return Code
```

The *keyword* is the command's alias — the name you type in AutoCAD to invoke it. It can be any word you like. The *command* entry is the actual command invoked when you type the keyword. It should be exactly the same as what you type at the operating system prompt to execute the command or program. It can include blanks. *Memory* specifies the amount of memory to be allocated to the command when it executes. The memory value is ignored by all versions except 640K DOS AutoCAD, but must still be present. *Prompt* is an optional prompt that can appear after you invoke the command. The *return code* specifies the screen to which AutoCAD returns when the external command has been completed. A return code of 0 returns to the text screen, a 4 returns to the previous text or graphics screen, and the 1 and 2 codes control DXB importations.

Customize your ACAD.PGP file by adding additional DOS commands, utilities, or programs that you would like to access from AutoCAD.

You should add a SHELL command for the text editor you plan to use with AutoCAD. If you use an existing SHELL command to change the ACAD.PGP file, you have to exit and reload your drawing before the changes take effect.

AutoCAD Command Aliases

In addition to DOS SHELL commands, you can also specify alias names for any AutoCAD command. Typically, the alias will be a one- or two-letter mnemonic that you can type instead of a full command. To see the current list of AutoCAD command aliases, list the next page of the ACAD.PGP file.

Listing Command Aliases in ACAD.PGP

- - MORE - -   Press <RETURN> or the space bar
                                                         to display the next page.

The second page of ACAD.PGP should now be on your screen. The following is a partial list of aliases in the standard ACAD.PGP.

```
A,      *ARC
C,      *CIRCLE
CP,     *COPY
DV,     *DVIEW
E,      *ERASE
L,      *LINE
LA,     *LAYER
M,      *MOVE
MS,     *MSPACE
P,      *PAN
PS,     *PSPACE
PL,     *PLINE
R,      *REDRAW
Z,      *ZOOM
;for scripts that may use the old 3DLINE command 3DLINE, #LINE
;easy access to _PKSER (serial number) system variable SERIAL, *_PKSER
; These are the local aliases for AutoCAD AME commands.
; Comment out any you don't want or add your own
- - More - -
```

Press <^C> to cancel and return to the DOS prompt.

The ACAD.PGP file contains aliases for a number of AutoCAD commands, but not for all of them. Unless your system has lots of memory (over 4Mb), you should only define those you are apt to use, because each alias uses a small amount of memory.

To add a command alias, first make a backup of ACAD.PGP with another filename, then use your text editor to edit the file. Simply enter the alias followed by a comma and the command to be referenced by that alias. The AutoCAD command must be prefixed with an asterisk, as shown in the file above. The IA DISK includes an IA6ACAD.PGP file with aliases for every command — you can rename and edit it to remove those aliases you don't need.

Using a Startup Batch File

AutoCAD lets you preset several of its startup settings. These control its memory usage and support file search order. We create the book's simple IA.BAT startup batch file in Chapter 1. It simply changes directories and starts AutoCAD. A startup batch file can also set memory allocations and file search order. The following is an example of a more sophisticated startup batch file. You can create a file like this for each of your jobs or applications, each with a unique name.

The STARTUP.BAT file assumes your AutoCAD path is ACAD. If not, substitute your own path.

An Example STARTUP.BAT File

```
SET ACAD:\ACAD\SUPPORT;C:\ACAD\SAMPLE;C:\ACAD\ADS
SET ACADCFG=C:\ACAD
```
Version and hardware-dependent memory settings go here.
AutoLISP memory management statements go here.
```
C:
CD \IA-ACAD
\ACAD\ACAD %1 %2
```
AutoLISP memory release statements go here.
```
CD\
SET ACAD=
SET ACADCFG=
```
Memory release statements go here.

SET ACAD= Tells AutoCAD what directories to look in if it doesn't find a needed support file in the current directory. This includes shape files, slide files, and other support files. (In Release 10, it can set only one directory name.)

SET ACADCFG= Tells AutoCAD where to look for configuration files. Create several configuration directories and corresponding startup batch files if you need to support more than one environment or if you need to support more than one device, like different plotters.

Note: If you have AutoCAD 386, no memory settings are necessary for AutoCAD or AutoLISP except to keep AutoCAD from using memory that you may want to reserve for another program.

Version and Hardware-Dependent Memory Settings — The startup file can also include settings for control of extended memory (SET ACADXMEM=), expanded memory (SET ACADLIMEM=), and extended AutoLISP memory allocation (SET

LISPXMEM=). If you are using the 640K DOS or DOS 286 version of AutoCAD and you have more than 2Mb of free extended or expanded memory, you may find that limiting its use may improve performance. Memory which is in use before you load AutoCAD, memory which you exclude from AutoCAD's use, and memory assigned to extended AutoLISP is *not* free. AutoCAD must use normal memory to implement extended or expanded memory. Too much extended or expanded memory starves the 640K DOS and DOS 286 versions of AutoCAD for normal I/O page space and free RAM, and can actually reduce performance.

AutoLISP Memory Management Statements — If you will be using regular AutoLISP, you can include statements to modify AutoLISP's memory usage. These would be SET statements for LISPSTACK and LISPHEAP. The default values should work well for you, but if you receive the error message, "Out of node space," you may need to enlarge the AutoLISP heap. If you have extended memory and use Release 10 extended AutoLISP, you need to insert a line to execute EXTLISP.EXE instead of setting LISPSTACK or LISPHEAP.

C: Ensures that you are on the right drive. Substitute another letter if your hard drive containing AutoCAD isn't drive C:.

CD \IA-ACAD Changes to the working directory. In this case, IA-ACAD, but yours can change to any working directory.

\ACAD\ACAD %1 %2 executes ACAD. If ACAD is on your path, you could use ACAD alone here, but specifying the directory avoids having DOS search the path. The %1 and %2 are replaceable parameters for which you can enter a drawing name (%1) and script name (%2) when you run the STARTUP.BAT batch file. For example, to run a script with the name MYSCRIPT on a drawing MYDWG, you would enter STARTUP MYDWG MYSCRIPT and the batch file would execute this line as \ACAD\ACAD MYDWG MYSCRIPT. AutoCAD would then execute MYSCRIPT at the main menu with MYDW as the default drawing.

AutoLISP Memory Release Statements — If you load EXTLISP.EXE, put a line here to execute REMLISP.EXE to release memory for other programs.

CD Returns you to the root directory.

SET ACADCFG= and **SET ACAD=** clear their settings, so they won't conflict with any other AutoCAD configurations that you might use.

Memory Release Statements — Finally, if you made any other memory settings, insert lines here to clear them as well.

Tip: Use SET *variable=* to clear any settings that you make in a startup batch file, like IA.BAT. If you do not clear your settings, your other AutoCAD applications will find the settings and be directed to the wrong configuration and support files.

Common Problems Encountered When Running AutoCAD

Here are some common problems encountered in setting up and running AutoCAD.

Common Problems With CONFIG.SYS

If your CONFIG.SYS settings do not run smoothly, your only indication may be that some things don't work. If you get the error message:

```
Bad or missing FILENAME
```

DOS can't find the file as it is specified. Check your spelling, and provide a full path.

```
Unrecognized command in CONFIG.SYS
```

means that you made a syntax error, or your version of DOS doesn't support the configuration command. Check your spelling.

Watch closely when you boot your system. These error messages flash by very quickly. If you suspect an error, temporarily rename your AUTOEXEC.BAT so that the system stops after loading CONFIG.SYS. You also can try to send the screen messages to the printer by pressing <CTRL-PRINTSCREEN> as soon as DOS starts reading the CONFIG.SYS file. Another <CTRL-PRINTSCREEN> turns the printer echo off.

Problems With ADI Drivers

If you have a problem with a device that uses an ADI driver, suspect the driver first and contact your dealer or the manufacturer for help.

Common Problems With AUTOEXEC.BAT

Errors in AUTOEXEC.BAT are harder to troubleshoot. There are many causes. Often, the system just doesn't behave as you think it should. Here are some troubleshooting tips:

- Isolate errors by temporarily editing your AUTOEXEC.BAT. You can disable a line with a leading colon, for example:

  ```
  : NOW DOS WILL IGNORE THIS LINE!
  ```

- Many AUTOEXEC.BAT files have echo to the screen turned off by the command ECHO OFF or @ECHO OFF. Disable echo off to see what they are doing. Put a leading colon on the line.

- Echo to the printer. Press <CTRL-PRINTSCREEN> while booting to see what is happening.

- Make sure the prompt, path, and other environment settings precede any TSR (memory resident) programs in the file.

- Check your path for completeness and syntax. Unsophisticated programs that require support or overlay files in addition to their .EXE or .COM files may not work, even if they are in the path. Directories do not need to be in the path unless you want to execute files in them from other directories.

- APPEND (DOS 3.3 or later) works like PATH to let programs find their support and overlay files in other directories. It uses about 5K of RAM. All files in an appended directory are recognized by programs as if they were in the current directory. If you use APPEND, use it *cautiously*. If you modify an appended file, the modified file will be written to the current directory, *not* the appended directory. Loading an AutoCAD .MNU file from an appended directory creates an .MNX file in the current directory. AutoCAD searches an appended directory before completing its normal directory search pattern, so appended support files will get loaded instead of those in the current directory.

- SET environment errors are often obscure. Type SET <RETURN> to see your current environment settings. If a setting is truncated or missing, you probably are out of environment space. Fix it in your CONFIG.SYS file. Do not use extraneous spaces in a SET statement.

- If your AUTOEXEC.BAT file doesn't seem to complete its execution, you may have tried to execute another .BAT file from your AUTOEXEC.BAT file. If you nest execution of .BAT files, the second one will take over and the first will not complete. There are two ways to nest .BAT files. With DOS 3.0 to 3.2, use:

  ```
  COMMAND /C NAME
  ```

  where NAME is the name of the nested .BAT file. With DOS 3.3 or later, use:

  ```
  CALL NAME
  ```

- If you are fighting for memory, insert temporary lines in the AUTOEXEC.BAT to check your available memory. Once you determine what uses how much, you can decide what to sacrifice. Use:

  ```
  CHKDSK
  PAUSE
  ```

  at appropriate points to display the remaining memory. Reboot to see the effect. Remove the lines when you are done.

- Run CHKDSK /F at the DOS prompt on a regular basis. It will verify your hard disk file structure and free up "lost clusters" found. Lost clusters are sometimes created when programs crash. Answer N when it asks if you want to convert the clusters to files. Do not run CHKDSK /F from the SHELL command while in AutoCAD.

- If you have unusual occurrences or lockups, and you use TSRs, suspect the TSRs as your problem source. Cause and effect may be hard to pin down. Disable TSRs one at a time in your AUTOEXEC file. Reboot and test.

Losing Screen or Digitizer Configuration

Sometimes your digitizer configuration or screen gets disturbed when you are drawing. This can happen when you use memory resident (TSR) programs or use AutoCAD's SHELL command to access other programs from AutoCAD. Rather than end your drawing, you can start a PLOT command, then <^C> to cancel as soon as the plot prompt screen appears. This resets all devices and redraws the screen. (It also clears Undo and reloads the menu.)

Using AutoCAD With a RAM Disk

Running AutoCAD from a RAM disk can be even more efficient than using extended/expanded memory for I/O page space. If you want to run AutoCAD from a RAM disk, there are three things that you want to consider putting on it. In order of importance, they are: AutoCAD's program files, temporary files, and the drawing itself.

Finding Support Files

When you ask AutoCAD to find a support file such as a menu file, it searches in a particular order. A typical search order is:

```
"STUFF.mnu": Can't open file
  in C:\PROJECT\ (current directory)          First the current directory.
  or c:\DWGS\                                  Then the current drawings
                                               directory
  or C:\SUPFILES\                              Then the directory designated
                                               by SET ACAD=.
  or D:\                                       Then the .OVL directory found
                                               on the PATH, if any.
  or C:\ACAD\                                  Last the program directory,
                                               home of ACAD.EXE.

Enter another menu file name (or RETURN for none):
```

If you keep AutoCAD's search order in mind, it will help you avoid errors in finding the wrong support files. A common cause of finding the wrong support files is the environment variable ACAD setting in a startup batch file. Make sure to clear your settings. Remember that appended directories are always searched first.

Current Directory Errors

If you use SHELL to change directories from within AutoCAD, you may get strange results. New drawings will not default to the changed current directory, yet SAVE defaults to save files in the changed current directory. Subsequent attempts to load support files, such as .MNX files, can crash AutoCAD.

If you must change directories on SHELL excursions, automate it with a batch file that also changes back to the original directory.

SHELL Errors

Here are some common errors encountered in using SHELL:

```
SHELL error swapping to disk
```

is usually caused by insufficient disk space. Remember that the temporary files used by AutoCAD can easily use up a megabyte of disk space.

```
SHELL error: insufficient memory for command
```

May be caused by an ill-behaved program executed during a previous SHELL, or before entering AutoCAD. Some ill-behaved programs leave a dirty environment behind that causes AutoCAD to erroneously believe insufficient memory exists.

```
Unable to load XYZABC: insufficient memory
Program too big to fit in memory
```

If SHELL got this far, these are correct messages. You need to modify your ACAD.PGP to allocate more memory space.

```
SHELL error in EXEC function (insufficient memory)
```

Can be caused by the default (24000 byte) SHELL memory allocation being too small to load DOS. Exactly how much memory you need to allocate depends on your versions of DOS and AutoCAD, and on what you have in your CONFIG.SYS file. Recall that DOS 3.2 and later DOS versions must have at least 25000 bytes allocated in the ACAD.PGP. Use 30000 to give a little cushion.

Common AutoLISP Errors

The *AutoLISP Programmer's Reference* has a complete listing of error messages. The following list gives a few hints of where and how to look for some other causes.

```
error: invalid dotted pair
error: misplaced dot
```

Look for a missing or an extra quotation mark above the apparent error location.

Look for " imbedded in a string where it should be \".

Look for strings that exceed 132 characters. STRCAT two strings if you need to.

n> or prompts such as **3>**

Look for the same quotation mark error as shown in the dot errors example, or look for a missing closing parenthesis.

If the error occurs while you are loading a .LSP file, look in the file.

```
Unknown command
```

May be caused by AutoLISP, if you have a command expression containing " ". The " " tries to repeat the last command entered at the ACAD prompt, not the last command sent to ACAD via the COMMAND function.

Miscellaneous Problems

If you run under a multi-tasking environment like Software Carousel or DESQview, you may get an error claiming a file should be in a directory it never was in. For example, you may get:

```
Can't find overlay file D:\ACAD\ACAD.OVL
Retry, Abort?
```

Or any other .OVL or ACAD.EXE. Don't type an A until you give up. Try an R to retry. If that doesn't work, copy the file to the directory listed in the error message. Flip partitions. You may need to press another R during the flip. Copy the file, flip back, and try R again.

```
Expanded memory disabled
```

When you start ACAD from DOS, this error message can be caused by a previously crashed AutoCAD. Sometimes a crashed AutoCAD does not fully clear its claim on expanded memory. This causes the program to think none is available. Reboot to clear it.

Tracing and Curing Errors

You are your best source of error diagnosis. When problems occur, log them so you can recognize patterns to cure them. Here are some tips and techniques:

- Use screen capture programs to document the text screen.
- Dump the screen to the printer.
- Write down what you did in as much detail as possible, as far back as you can remember.
- Dump a copy of AutoCAD's status screen to the printer.
- Dump a copy of the screen of the DOS command SET to check settings.

Avoidance is the best cure.

Clearing Up File Problems After a System Crash

When your system goes down unexpectedly in the middle of an AutoCAD session, you may end up with extraneous files on disk, or with files locked and inaccessible.

First run CHKDSK /F at the DOS prompt to restore any disk space occupied by abandoned sessions. Do not run CHKDSK /F from SHELL.

Removing Extraneous Swap Files

When AutoCAD 386 terminates abnormally, you may find files on your hard drive with names that are hexadecimal numbers, such as 092A314F.SWR, or 103B272D (no extension). Typically these files will have a file size of either 0K, 100K, or of nearly 400K. Normally, AutoCAD erases these files whenever you exit the program. But if the system locks up for some reason, the files will remain on your disk until you erase them.

Use the DOS DEL or ERASE commands to erase these files. You can erase all files having an extension of .SWR by entering:

```
DEL *.SWR
```

If you have a number of these files without extensions, they will probably begin with the same one or two digits. For example, if they all begin with 0, you can delete them all by entering:

```
DEL 0*.
```

However, be aware that this will delete every file in the current directory that begins with 0 and has no extension. If you have other files in the current directory that do not have extensions and you wish to keep them, you will have to erase the swap files one by one or with a wildcard combination common to them all.

Unlocking Locked Files

If you have file locking enabled and your AutoCAD session terminates abnormally, the drawing file you were editing will still be locked. If you try to edit it again, you will be unable to do so.

To unlock a locked file, first verify that the file is not actually in use by someone else on your network. If not, enter the [File Utilities] menu by selecting option 6 from AutoCAD's main menu. Then, select option 6, Unlock file, and specify the name of the file to unlock, including its file extension. AutoCAD will then unlock the file.

Recovering Corrupted Drawings

If you receive an error message beginning with words like EREAD or SCANDR when trying to load a drawing, the file may be corrupted. If the drawing was made with Release 11, AutoCAD itself may be able to salvage some or all of it. Drawings created with prior releases will have to be recovered with a third-party utility or be redrawn.

Main menu option 9 will try to recover as much of your drawing as possible. You can process multiple drawings by using the same wildcard conventions available within AutoCAD and by entering several names separated by commas. It will perform an automatic audit of the file and present you with the results in the drawing editor. Any warning messages AutoCAD displays are also written to a log file with the same name as the recovered drawing except the extension, which will be .ADT.

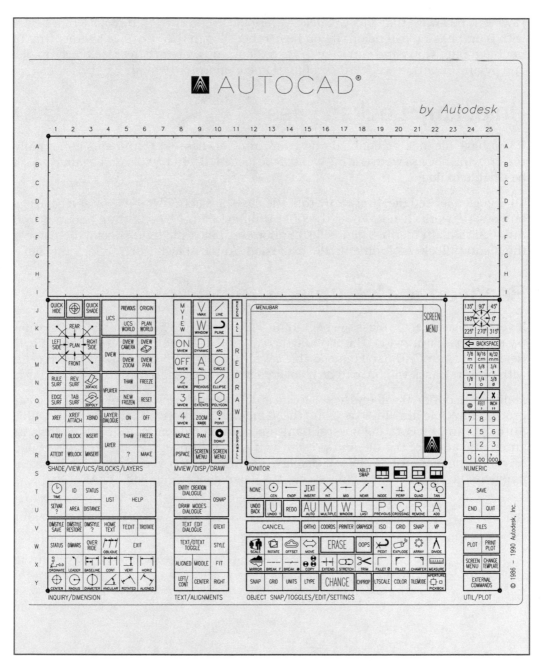

Figure C.1:
An AutoCAD standard tablet menu.

The AutoCAD Tablet Menu and System Variables

AutoCAD's Standard Tablet Menu

AutoCAD Release 11 comes with a standard tablet menu and includes a plastic template for an 11" x 11" digitizer tablet. To use the standard AutoCAD tablet menu, you affix the AutoCAD standard plastic template to your digitizer, and use the AutoCAD TABLET command to let the program know where the tablet "boxes" are located.

The TABLET.DWG Drawing

AutoCAD also comes with a drawing file named TABLET.DWG. This is a drawing file like any other AutoCAD drawing file. You can view it on the screen, edit it, and plot it. You also can use this drawing to create a custom template drawing for your digitizer.

Once you know how to edit drawings and customize the tablet menu, you can make your own tablet drawing, supporting the menu with your own tablet menu programs. If you customize your tablet menu, we suggest you first make a copy of TABLET.DWG, call it MYTABLET.DWG, and make your changes to the copy, not the original.

Configuring Your Tablet Menu

We assume that you are using an 11" x 11" digitizer that has been set up according to AutoCAD's *Installation and Performance Guide.* We also assume that you have already configured your system (Appendix B), and have loaded AutoCAD.

If you are using the AutoCAD template, place it on your digitizer. If you are using the plotted TABLET drawing, trim the drawing, leaving about a 1/2-inch border, and tape it to your digitizer. Since every tablet is different and since every user trims and tapes differently, you have to configure the tablet to let AutoCAD know exactly where the tablet commands are located on the surface of the tablet.

You use the TABLET command from inside the drawing editor to configure the tablet. AutoCAD provides a series of tablet pick points on the drawing (or template) as a guide to loading each of the four menu areas prompted by the TABLET command. These are donut points on the menu.

The standard menu is divided into four menu areas by columns and rows. Look at figure C.1. The columns are numbered 1 to 25 across the top. The rows are lettered A to Y on the left. Menu area 1 is the top rectangular area. The first "donut" pick point is near A and 1 in the top left corner. Menu area 1 has 25 columns and 9 rows of menu "boxes."

To configure the tablet, you pick three points for each menu area, and enter the number of columns and rows. Use figure C.2 as a guide for picking points.

Configuring the AutoCAD Tablet Menu

Begin a NEW drawing named TEST.

The drawing screen appears with the screen menu.

```
Command: TABLET
Option (ON/OFF/CAL/CFG): CFG
Enter the number of tablet menus desired (0-4) <0>: 4
```

Digitize the upper left corner of menu area 1:	Pick point.
Digitize the lower left corner of menu area 1:	Pick point.
Digitize the lower right corner of menu area 1:	Pick point.
Enter the number of columns for menu area 1: **25**	
Enter the number of rows for menu area 1: **9**	
Digitize the upper left corner of menu area 2:	Pick point.
Digitize the lower left corner of menu area 2:	Pick point.
Digitize the lower right corner of menu area 2:	Pick point.
Enter the number of columns for menu area 2: **11**	
Enter the number of rows for menu area 2: **9**	
Digitize the upper left corner of menu area 3:	Pick point.
Digitize the lower left corner of menu area 3:	Pick point.

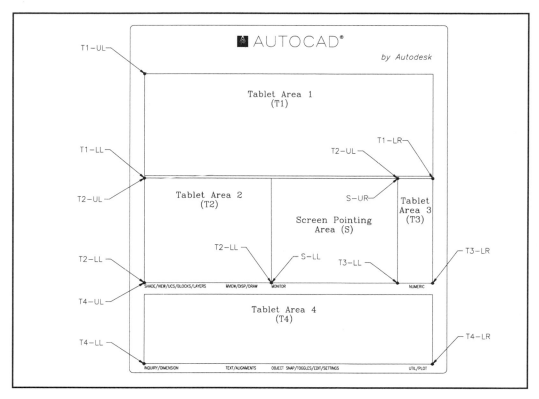

Figure C.2:
Configuring the AutoCAD standard tablet menu.

Configuring the AutoCAD Tablet Menu—continued

```
Enter the number of columns for menu area 3: 9          Yes, that is 9.
Enter the number of rows for menu area 3: 13

Digitize the upper left corner of menu area 4:          Pick point.
Digitize the lower left corner of menu area 4:          Pick point.
Digitize the lower right corner of menu area 4:         Pick point.
Enter the number of columns for menu area 4: 25
Enter the number of rows for menu area 4: 7

Do you want to respecify the screen pointing area (Y) <RETURN>

Digitize lower left corner of screen pointing area:     Pick point.
Digitize upper right corner of screen pointing area:    Pick point.
```

Try picking a few commands from the tablet and drawing in the screen pointing area to test the configuration.

```
Command: QUIT                                           Quit the TEST drawing.
```

The standard AutoCAD tablet menu is configured for your digitizer and the configuration parameters are stored on your disk in a file.

Swapping Tablet Menu Areas

Release 11 adds a new capability to the digitizer menu — swapping menu areas. Swapping a menu area changes its function from the default to a different, predefined menu. To swap a particular menu area, select one of the four corresponding tablet swap icons located on the digitizer overlay below the monitor area. The following is a description of the default and alternate menus for each swap icon.

- **Menu Area 1** — Top menu area.

    Default — AME and AutoShade menus.

    Swap — Replaces AME and AutoShade menus with a blank menu area that can be used for personal applications and menu items.

- **Menu Area 2** — Left menu area.

    Default — Display commands are transparent, and VPOINT and DVIEW refer to the WCS.

    Swap — Display commands cancel a command in progress, and VPOINT and DVIEW refer to the current UCS.

- **Menu Area 3** — Right menu area.

    Default — American units.

    Swap — Metric units.

- **Menu Area 4** — Lower menu area.

    Default — Osnap picks are temporary.

    Swap — Changes osnap picks to running osnap picks.

When you swap a menu area, the corresponding asterisk in the screen menu below [AutoCAD] will change to a number to indicate which menu has been switched. Selecting [AutoCAD] resets all menu areas to their defaults.

For more information on tablet swapping and customization, see *MAXIMIZING AutoCAD, Volume I* from New Riders Publishing.

AutoCAD System Variables

This appendix contains a table of AutoCAD system variables. Use it to find AutoCAD's environment settings and their values. Table C.1 presents all the variable settings available through AutoCAD's SETVAR command or AutoLISP's SETVAR and GETVAR functions. The system variable name and the default AutoCAD proto-type drawing (ACAD.DWG) settings are shown. A brief description is given for each variable, and the meaning is given for each code flag. All values are saved with the drawing unless noted with <CFG> for ConFiGuration file, or <NS> for Not Saved. Variables marked <RO> are read only, meaning you can't type their names or use SETVAR or the (setvar) function to change them. Variable names shown in bold are not in Release 10.

Table C1:
AutoCAD System Variables

VARIABLE NAME	DEFAULT SETTING	DEFAULT MEANING	COMMAND NAME	VARIABLE DESCRIPTION
ACADPREFIX	"C:\ACAD\"			AutoCAD directory path **<NS>**, **<RO>**
ACADVER	"11"			AutoCAD release version **<RO>**
AFLAGS	0		ATTDEF	Sum of: Invisible=1 Constant=2 Verify=4 Preset=8
ANGBASE	0	EAST	UNITS	Direction of angle 0
ANGDIR	0	CCW	UNITS	Clockwise=1 Counter clockwise=0
APERTURE	10	10	APERTURE	Half of aperture height in pixels **<CFG>**
AREA	0.0000		AREA,LIST	Last computed area **<NS>**, **<RO>**
ATTDIA	0		PROMPTS	Insert uses: DDATTE dialogue box=1 Attribute prompts=0
ATTMODE	1	ON	ATTDISP	Attribute display Normal=1 ON=2 OFF=0
ATTREQ	1	PROMPTS		Insert uses: Prompts=1 Defaults=0
AUNITS	0	DEC. DEG.	UNITS	Angular units Dec=0 Deg=1 Grad=2 Rad=3 Survey=4
AUPREC	0	0	UNITS	Angular units decimal places
AXISMODE	0	OFF	AXIS	Axis ON=1 Axis OFF=0
AXISUNIT	0.0000,0.0000		AXIS	Axis X,Y Increment
BACKZ	0.0000		DVIEW	Back clipping plane offset - See VIEWMODE **<RO>**
BLIPMODE	1	ON	BLIPMODE	Blips=1 No Blips=0
CDATE	19881202.144648898		TIME	Date.Time **<NS>**, **<RO>**
CECOLOR	"BYLAYER"		COLOR	Current entity color **<RO>**
CELTYPE	"BYLAYER"		LINETYPE	Current entity linetype **<RO>**
CHAMFERA	0.0000		CHAMFER	Chamfer distance for A
CHAMFERB	0.0000		CHAMFER	Chamfer distance for B
CLAYER	"0"		LAYER	Current layer **<RO>**
CMDECHO	1	ECHO	SETVAR	Command echo in AutoLISP Echo=1 No Echo=0 **<NS>**
COORDS	0	OFF	[^D] [F6]	Update display Picks=0 ON=1 Dist>Angle=2
CVPORT	1		VPORTS	Identification number of the current viewport
DATE	2447498.61620926		TIME	Julian time **<NS>**, **<RO>**
DIASTAT	1	OK	DD?????	Dialog box exit code 0=cancel 1=OK **<RO>**

Table C1—continued

VARIABLE NAME	DEFAULT SETTING	DEFAULT MEANING	COMMAND NAME	VARIABLE DESCRIPTION
DIMALT	0	OFF	DIMALT	Use alternate units ON=1 OFF=0
DIMALTD	2	0.00	DIMALTD	Decimal precision of alternate units
DIMALTF	25.4000		DIMALTF	Scale factor for alternate units
DIMAPOST	""	NONE	DIMAPOST	Suffix for alternate dimensions **<RO>**
DIMASO	1	ON	DIMASO	Associative=1 Line,Arrow,Text=0
DIMASZ	0.1800		DIMASZ	Arrow Size=Value (also controls text fit)
DIMBLK	""	NONE	DIMBLK	Block name to draw instead of arrow or tick **<RO>**
DIMBLK1	""	NONE	DIMBLK1	Block name for 1st end, see DIMSAH **<RO>**
DIMBLK2	""	NONE	DIMBLK2	Block name for 2nd end, see DIMSAH **<RO>**
DIMCEN	0.0900	MARK	DIMCEN	Center mark size=Value Add center lines=Negative
DIMCLRD	0	COLOR	DIMCLRD	Dimension line, arrow, and dim line leader color
DIMCLRE	0	COLOR	DIMCLRE	Dimension extension line color
DIMCLRT	0	COLOR	DIMCLRT	Dimension text color
DIMDLE	0.0000	NONE	DIMDLE	Dimension line extension=Value
DIMDLI	0.3800		DIMDLI	Increment between continuing dimension lines
DIMEXE	0.1800		DIMEXE	Extension distance for extension lines=Value
DIMEXO	0.0625		DIMEXO	Offset distance for extension lines=Value
DIMGAP	0.0900		DIMGAP	Gap between text and dimension line
DIMLFAC	1.0000	NORMAL	DIMLFAC	Overall linear distance factor=Value
DIMLIM	0	OFF	DIMLIM	Add tolerance limits ON=1 OFF=0
DIMPOST	""	NONE	DIMPOST	User defined dimension suffix (eg: "mm") **<RO>**
DIMRND	0.0000	EXACT	DIMRND	Rounding value for linear dimensions
DIMSAH	0	OFF	DIMSAH	Allow separate DIMBLKS ON=1 OFF=0
DIMSCALE	1.0000		DIMSCALE	Overall dimensioning scale factor=Value
DIMSE1	0	OFF	DIMSE1	Suppress extension line 1 Omit=1 Draw=0
DIMSE2	0	OFF	DIMSE2	Suppress extension line 2 Omit=1 Draw=0
DIMSHO	0	OFF	DIMSHO	Show associative dimension while dragging
DIMSOXD	0	OFF	DIMSOXD	Suppress dim. lines outside extension lines Omit=1 Draw=0
DIMSTYLE	*UNNAMED		Dim: SAVE	Current dimension style **<RO>**

Table C1—continued

VARIABLE NAME	DEFAULT SETTING	DEFAULT MEANING	COMMAND NAME	VARIABLE DESCRIPTION
DIMTAD	0	OFF	DIMTAD	Text above dim. line ON=1 OFF(in line)=0
DIMTIH	1	ON	DIMTIH	Text inside horizontal ON=1 OFF(aligned)=0
DIMTIX	0	OFF	DIMTIX	Force text inside extension lines ON=1 OFF=0
DIMTM	0.0000	NONE	DIMTM	Minus tolerance=Value
DIMTOFL	0	OFF	DIMTOFL	Draw dim. line even if text outside ext. lines
DIMTOH	1	ON	DIMTOH	Text outside horizontal ON=1 OFF(aligned)=0
DIMTOL	0	OFF	DIMTOL	Append tolerance ON=1 OFF=2
DIMTP	0.0000	NONE	DIMTP	Plus tolerance=Value
DIMTSZ	0.0000	ARROWS	DIMTSZ	Tick size=Value Draw arrows=0
DIMTVP	0.0000		DIMTVP	Text vertical position
DIMTXT	0.1800		DIMTXT	Text size=Value
DIMZIN	0		DIMZIN	Controls leading zero (see AutoCAD manual)
DISTANCE	0.0000		DIST	Last computed distance **<NS>,<RO>**
DRAGMODE	2	AUTO	DRAGMODE	OFF=0 Enabled=1 Auto=2
DRAGP1	10		SETVAR	Drag regen rate **<CFG>**
DRAGP2	25		SETVAR	Drag input rate **<CFG>**
DWGNAME	"TEST"			Current drawing name **<RO>**
DWGPREFIX	"C:\IA-ACAD\"			Directory path of current drawing **<NS>,<RO>**
ELEVATION	0.0000		ELEV	Current default elevation
ERRNO	0	NONE	SETVAR	Error number generated by AutoLISP and ADS apps. (See AutoLISP or ADS Programmer's Reference Manual)
EXPERT	0	NORMAL	SETVAR	Suppresses "Are you sure" prompts (See AutoCAD Reference Manual)
EXTMAX	-1.0000E+20,-1.0000E+20			Upper right drawing extents X,Y **<RO>**
EXTMIN	1.0000E+20,1.0000E+20			Lower left drawing extents X,Y **<RO>**
FILEDIA	1	ON	SETVAR	Enables/disables dialogue box for filenames **<CFG>**
FILLETRAD	0.0000		FILLET	Current fillet radius
FILLMODE	1		FILL	Fill ON=1 Fill OFF=0
FLATLAND	0		SETVAR	Temporary 3D compatibility setting (Rel. 10 only) Act like Release 9=1 R10=0
FRONTZ	0.0000		DVIEW	Front clipping plane offset - See VIEWMODE **<RO>**
GRIDMODE	0	OFF	GRID	Grid ON=1 Grid OFF=0
GRIDUNIT	0.0000,0.0000		GRID	X,Y grid increment

Table C1—continued

VARIABLE NAME	DEFAULT SETTING	DEFAULT MEANING	COMMAND NAME	VARIABLE DESCRIPTION
HANDLES	0		HANDLES	Entity handles Enabled=1 Disabled=0 **<RO>**
HIGHLIGHT	1		SETVAR	Highlight selection ON=1 OFF=0 **<NS>**
INSBASE	0.0000,0.0000		BASE	Insert base point of current drawing X,Y
LASTANGLE	0		ARC	Last angle of the last arc **<NS>, <RO>**
LASTPOINT	0.0000,0.0000,0.0000			Last @ pickpoint X,Y,Z **<NS>**
LASTPT3D	0.0000,0.0000,0.0000			Last @ pickpoint X,Y,Z (Rel. 10 only) **<NS>**
LENSLENGTH	50.0000		DVIEW	Length of lens in perspective in millimeters **<RO>**
LIMCHECK	0	OFF	LIMITS	Limits error check ON=1 OFF=0
LIMMAX	12.0000,9.0000		LIMITS	Upper right X,Y limit
LIMMIN	0.0000,0.0000		LIMITS	Lower left X,Y limit
LTSCALE	1.0000		LTSCALE	Current linetype scale
LUNITS	2	DEC.	UNITS	Linear units: Scientific=1 Dec=2 Eng=3 Arch=4 Frac=5
LUPREC	4	0.0000	UNITS	Unit precision decimal places or denominator
MAXACTVP	16		SETVAR	Max. no. of viewports to regen **<NS>, <RO>**
MAXSORT	200		SETVAR	Max. no. symbol/filenames sorted by commands **<CFG>**
MENUECHO	0	NORMAL	SETVAR	Normal=0 Suppress echo of menu items=1 No prompts=2 No input or prompts=3 **<NS>**
MENUNAME	"ACAD"		MENU	Current menu name **<RO>**
MIRRTEXT	1	YES	SETVAR	Retain text direction=0 Reflect text=1
ORTHOMODE	0	OFF	[^O] [F8]	Ortho ON=1 Ortho OFF=0
OSMODE	0	NONE	OSNAP	Sum of: Endp=1 Mid=2 Cen=4 Node=8 Quad=16 Int=32 Ins=64 Perp=128 Tan=256 Near=512 Quick=1024
PDMODE	0	POINT	SETVAR	Controls style of points drawn
PDSIZE	0.0000	POINT	SETVAR	Controls size of points
PERIMETER	0.0000		AREA,LIST	Last computed perimeter **<NS>, <RO>**
PFACEVMAX	4		SETVAR	Maximum number of vertexes per face **<NS>, <RO>**
PICKBOX	3		SETVAR	Half the pick box size in pixels **<CFG>**
PLATFORM	VARIES	VARIES		A string such as "DOS", "386 DOS Extender", "Sun 4/SPARCstation", "OS/2", "Apple Macintosh", etc.
POPUPS	1			AUI Support=1 No Support=0 **<NS>, <RO>**

Table C1—continued

VARIABLE NAME	DEFAULT SETTING	DEFAULT MEANING	COMMAND NAME	VARIABLE DESCRIPTION
QTEXTMODE	0	OFF	QTEXT	Qtext ON=1 Qtext OFF=0
REGENMODE	1	ON	REGENAUTO	Regenauto ON=1 Regenauto OFF=0
SCREENSIZE	570.0000,410.0000			Current size of viewport in pixels, X and Y **<RO>**
SHADEDGE	3		SETVAR	Controls display of edges and faces by SHADE command
SHADEDIF	70		SETVAR	Ratio of ambient light to diffuse light
SKETCHINC	0.1000		SKETCH	Recording increment for sketch
SKPOLY	0	LINE	SETVAR	Polylines=1 Sketch with Line=0
SNAPANG	0		SNAP	Angle of SNAP/GRID rotation
SNAPBASE	0.0000,0.0000		SNAP	X,Y base point of SNAP/GRID rotation
SNAPISOPAIR	0	LEFT	SNAP [^E]	Isoplane Left=0 Top=1 Right=2
SNAPMODE	0	OFF	SNAP [^B] [F9]	Snap ON=1 Snap OFF=0
SNAPSTYL	0	STD	SNAP	Isometric=1 Snap standard=0
SNAPUNIT	1.0000,1.0000		SNAP	Snap X,Y increment
SPLFRAME	0		SETVAR	Display spline frame ON=1 OFF=0
SPLINESEGS	8		SETVAR	Number of line segments in each spline segment
SPLINETYPE	6	CUBIC	SETVAR	PEDIT spline generates: Quadratic B-Spline=5 Cubic B-Spline=6
SURFTAB1	6		SETVAR	Rulesurf and tabsurf tabulations, also revsurf and edgesurf M density
SURFTAB2	6		SETVAR	Revsurf and edgesurf N density
SURFTYPE	6	CUBIC	SETVAR	Pedit smooth surface generates: Quadratic B-Spline=5 Cubic B-Spline=6 Bezier=8
SURFU	6		SETVAR	M direction surface density
SURFV	6		SETVAR	N direction surface density
TARGET	0.0000,0.0000,0.0000		DVIEW	UCS coords of current viewport target point **<RO>**
TDCREATE	2447498.61620031		TIME	Creation time (Julian) **<RO>**
TDINDWG	0.00436285		TIME	Total editing time **<RO>**
TDUPDATE	2447498.61620031		TIME	Time of last save or update **<RO>**
TDUSRTIMER	0.00436667		TIME	User set elapsed time **<RO>**
TEMPPREFIX	""			Directory location of AutoCAD's temporary files, defaults to drawing directory **<NS>**, **<RO>**
TEXTEVAL	0	TEXT	SETVAR	Evaluate leading "(" and "!" in text input as: Text=0 AutoLISP=1 **<NS>**
TEXTSIZE	0.2000		TEXT	Current text height
TEXTSTYLE	"STANDARD"		TEXT,STYLE	Current text style **<RO>**
THICKNESS	0.0000		SETVAR	Current 3D extrusion thickness
TILEMODE	1	ON	TILEMODE	Enables/disables paper space and viewport entities
TRACEWID	0.0500		TRACE	Current width of traces

Table C1—continued

VARIABLE NAME	DEFAULT SETTING	DEFAULT MEANING	COMMAND NAME	VARIABLE DESCRIPTION
UCSFOLLOW	0		SETVAR	Automatic plan view in new UCS-1 Off=0
UCSICON	1		UCSICON	Sum of: Off=0 On=1 Origin=2
UCSNAME	""		UCS	Name of current UCS Unnamed="" **\<RO>**
UCSORG	0.0000,0.0000,0.0000		UCS	WCS origin of current UCS **\<RO>**
UCSXDIR	1.0000,0.0000,0.0000		UCS	X direction of current UCS **\<RO>**
UCSYDIR	0.0000,1.0000,0.0000		UCS	Y direction of current UCS **\<RO>**
UNITMODE	0		SETVAR	0=Display units standard 1=display in input mode
USERI1 - 5	0		SETVAR	User integer variables USERI1 to USERI5
USERR1 - 5	0.0000		SETVAR	User real variables USERR1 to USERR5
VIEWCTR	6.2518,4.5000		ZOOM,PAN,VIEW	X,Y center point of current view **\<RO>**
VIEWDIR	0.0000,0.0000,1.0000		DVIEW	Camera point offset from target in WCS **\<RO>**
VIEWMODE	0		DVIEW,UCS	Perspective and clipping settings (See AutoCAD Reference Manual) **\<RO>**
VIEWSIZE	9.0000		ZOOM,PAN,VIEW	Height of current view **\<RO>**
VIEWTWIST	0		DVIEW	View twist angle **\<RO>**
VPOINTX	0.0000		VPOINT	X coordinate of VPOINT (Rel. 10 only) **\<RO>**
VPOINTY	0.0000		VPOINT	Y coordinate of VPOINT (Rel. 10 only) **\<RO>**
VSMAX	12.5036,9.0000,0.0000		ZOOM,PAN,VIEW	Upper right of virtual screen X,Y **\<NS>**, **\<RO>**
VSMIN	0.0000,0.0000,0.0000		ZOOM,PAN,VIEW	Lower left of virtual screen X,Y **\<NS>**, **\<RO>**
WORLDUCS	1		UCS	UCS equals WCS=1 UCS not equal to WCS=0 **\<RO>**
WORLDVIEW	1		DVIEW,UCS	DVIEW and VPOINT coordinate input: WCS=1 UCS=0

\<NS> Not Saved   **\<CFG>** Configuration File   **\<RO>** Read Only

INDEX

B

E

I

K

Z

AUTOCAD PULL-DOWN MENUS

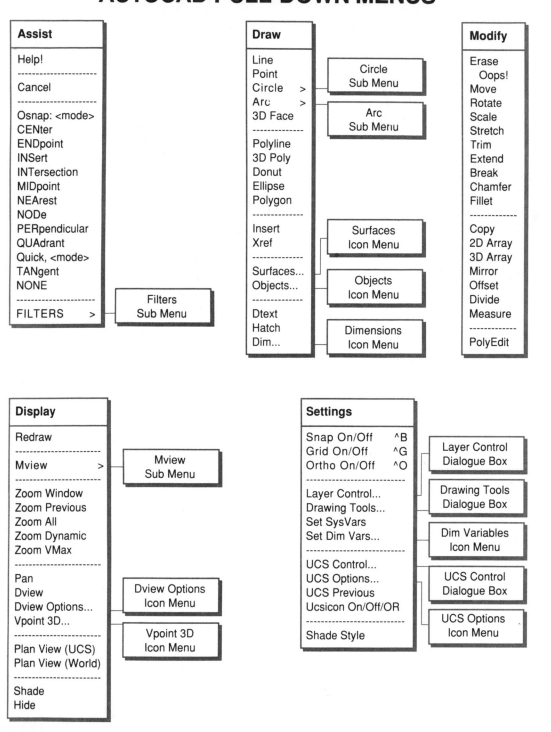

Assist

Help!

Cancel

Osnap: <mode>
CENter
ENDpoint
INSert
INTersection
MIDpoint
NEArest
NODe
PERpendicular
QUAdrant
Quick, <mode>
TANgent
NONE

FILTERS   >

Filters
Sub Menu

Draw

Line
Point
Circle   >
Arc   >
3D Face

Polyline
3D Poly
Donut
Ellipse
Polygon

Insert
Xref

Surfaces...
Objects...

Dtext
Hatch
Dim...

Circle
Sub Menu

Arc
Sub Menu

Surfaces
Icon Menu

Objects
Icon Menu

Dimensions
Icon Menu

Modify

Erase
    Oops!
Move
Rotate
Scale
Stretch
Trim
Extend
Break
Chamfer
Fillet

Copy
2D Array
3D Array
Mirror
Offset
Divide
Measure

PolyEdit

Display

Redraw

Mview   >

Zoom Window
Zoom Previous
Zoom All
Zoom Dynamic
Zoom VMax

Pan
Dview
Dview Options...
Vpoint 3D...

Plan View (UCS)
Plan View (World)

Shade
Hide

Mview
Sub Menu

Dview Options
Icon Menu

Vpoint 3D
Icon Menu

Settings

Snap On/Off   ^B
Grid On/Off   ^G
Ortho On/Off   ^O

Layer Control...
Drawing Tools...
Set SysVars
Set Dim Vars...

UCS Control...
UCS Options...
UCS Previous
Ucsicon On/Off/OR

Shade Style

Layer Control
Dialogue Box

Drawing Tools
Dialogue Box

Dim Variables
Icon Menu

UCS Control
Dialogue Box

UCS Options
Icon Menu